Beginning XML
4th Edition

Beginning XML
4th Edition

David Hunter,
Jeff Rafter,
Joe Fawcett,
Eric van der Vlist,
Danny Ayers,
Jon Duckett,
Andrew Watt, and
Linda McKinnon

Wiley Publishing, Inc.

Beginning XML, 4th Edition

Published by
Wiley Publishing, Inc.
10475 Crosspoint Boulevard
Indianapolis, IN 46256
www.wiley.com

Published simultaneously in Canada

ISBN: 978-0-470-11487-2

Manufactured in the United States of America

10 9 8 7 6 5 4

Library of Congress Cataloging-in-Publication Data:

Beginning XML / David Hunter ... [et al.]. -- 4th ed.
   p. cm.
  ISBN 978-0-470-11487-2 (paper/website)
  1. XML (Document markup language) I. Hunter, David, 1974 May 7-
  QA76.76.H94B439 2007

  006.7'4--dc22

                  2007006580

I would like to thank God, for continuing to give me opportunities to do what I love; my church family, for giving me more support than I deserve; and Andrea, for giving me more support than anyone deserves.
I would also like to thank the editors, for their constant help.
Their dedication to the quality of this book was a major factor in its success.
—David

To Ali and Jude, for their loving patience.
—Jeff

To my two brothers, Peter and Stephen, who have both helped me in my life and career in their own ways, many thanks.
—Joe

To my wife, Catherine, and children, Deborah, David, Samuel, and Sarah, for their patience and support while I am busy writing books.
—Eric

To my late grandmother, Mona Cartledge, who once gave me a Commodore Pet.
—Danny

About the Authors

David Hunter is a Senior Technical Consultant for CGI, a full-service IT and business process services partner. Providing technical leadership and guidance for solving his clients' business problems, he is a jack-of-all-trades and master of some. With a career that has included design, development, support, training, writing, and other roles, he has had extensive experience building scalable, reliable, enterprise-class applications. David loves to peek under the hood at any new technology that comes his way, and when one catches his fancy, he really gets his hands dirty. He loves nothing more than sharing these technologies with others.

Jeff Rafter is an independent consultant based in Redlands, California. His focus is on emerging technology and web standards, including XML and validation. He currently works with Baobab Health Partnership with a focus on improving world health.

Joe Fawcett (`http://joe.fawcett.name`) started programming in the 1970s and worked briefly in IT when leaving full-time education. He then pursued a more checkered career before returning to software development in 1994. In 2003 he was awarded the title of Microsoft Most Valuable Professional in XML for community contributions and technical expertise; he has subsequently been re-awarded every year since. Joe currently works in London and is head of software development for FTC Kaplan Ltd., a leading international provider of accountancy and business training.

Eric van der Vlist is an independent consultant and trainer. His domains of expertise include web development and XML technologies. He is the creator and main editor of XMLfr.org, the main site dedicated to XML technologies in French, the lead author of *Professional Web 2.0 Programming*, the author of the O'Reilly animal books *XML Schema* and *RELAX NG* and a member or the ISO DSDL (`http://dsdl.org`) working group focused on XML schema languages. He is based in Paris and can be reached at `vdv@dyomedea.com`, or meet him at one of the many conferences where he presents his projects.

Danny Ayers is a freelance developer and consultant specializing in cutting-edge web technologies. His blog (`http://dannyayers.com`) tends to feature material relating to the Semantic Web and/or cat photos.

Linda McKinnon has more than 10 years of experience as a successful trainer and network engineer, assisting both private and public enterprises in network architecture design, implementation, system administration, and RFP procurement. She is a renowned mentor and has published numerous Linux study guides for Wiley Press and Gearhead Press.

Credits

Senior Acquisitions Editor
Jim Minatel

Development Editors
Sara Shlaer
Lisa Thibault

Technical Editor
Phred Menyhert

Production Editor
William A. Barton

Copy Editor
Luann Rouff

Editorial Manager
Mary Beth Wakefield

Production Manager
Tim Tate

Vice President and Executive Group Publisher
Richard Swadley

Vice President and Executive Publisher
Joseph B. Wikert

Graphics and Production Specialists
Brooke Graczyk
Denny Hager
Joyce Haughey
Jennifer Mayberry
Barbara Moore
Alicia B. South

Quality Control Technician
John Greenough

Project Coordinator
Lynsey Osborn

Media Development Specialists
Angie Denny
Kit Malone
Kate Jenkins
Steve Kudirkan

Proofreading
Aptara

Indexing
Broccoli Information Management

Anniversary Logo Design
Richard Pacifico

Acknowledgments

This book would not have been possible without the work of the many developers dedicated to improving the Web through standards. We would also like to thank the countless contributors to mailing lists, IRC channels, forums, and friends that have helped us through the difficult corners of the specifications and technologies presented in this book.

Thanks to Nicholas C. Zakas for his ideas and assistance in implementing the AutoSuggest Control. Many thanks to Phillip Pearson, who runs TopicExchange.com. He provided much-needed technical support that otherwise would have meant rewriting most of Chapter 14. We would also like to thank Jim Ley and Doug Schepers for their assistance on the case study and Chapter 19. Special thanks to our lead editor, Sara Shlaer, for her gentle and not so gentle persuasive powers and attention to detail; to editor Lisa Thibault, for her thoughtful assistance; and to Phred Menyhert, for a rigorous technical edit. Many thanks to our acquisitions editor, Jim Minatel, who has shepherded this book through many incarnations.

Contents

Contents

Part II: Validation   93

Contents

Part III: Processing

Contents

Contents

Contents

Contents

Contents

Contents

Introduction

Welcome to Beginning XML, Fourth Edition, the book I wish I'd had when I was first learning the language!

When we wrote the first edition of this book, XML was a relatively new language but already gaining ground fast and becoming more and more widely used in a vast range of applications. By the time we started the second edition, XML had already proven itself to be more than a passing fad, and was in fact being used throughout the industry for an incredibly wide range of uses. As we began the third edition, it was clear that XML was a mature technology, but more important, it became evident that the XML landscape was dividing into several areas of expertise. In this edition, we needed to categorize the increasing number of specifications surrounding XML, which either use XML or provide functionality in addition to the XML core specification.

So what is XML? It's a markup language, used to describe the structure of data in meaningful ways. Anywhere that data is input/output, stored, or transmitted from one place to another, is a potential fit for XML's capabilities. Perhaps the most well-known applications are web-related (especially with the latest developments in handheld web access—for which some of the technology is XML-based). However, there are many other non-web-based applications for which XML is useful—for example, as a replacement for (or to complement) traditional databases, or for the transfer of financial information between businesses. News organizations, along with individuals, have also been using XML to distribute syndicated news stories and blog entries.

This book aims to teach you all you need to know about XML—what it is, how it works, what technologies surround it, and how it can best be used in a variety of situations, from simple data transfer to using XML in your web pages. It answers the fundamental questions:

❑ What is XML?

❑ How do you use XML?

❑ How does it work?

❑ What can you use it *for*, anyway?

Who Is This Book For?

This book is for people who know that it would be a pretty good idea to learn XML but aren't 100 percent sure why. You've heard the hype but haven't seen enough substance to figure out what XML is and what it can do. You may be using development tools that try to hide the XML behind user interfaces and scripts, but you want to know what is really happening behind the scenes. You may already be somehow involved in web development and probably even know the basics of HTML, although neither of these qualifications is absolutely necessary for this book.

What you don't need is knowledge of markup languages in general. This book assumes that you're new to the concept of markup languages, and we have structured it in a way that should make sense to the beginner and yet quickly bring you to XML expert status.

The word "Beginning" in the title refers to the style of the book, rather than the reader's experience level. There are two types of beginner for whom this book is ideal:

❏ Programmers who are already familiar with some web programming or data exchange techniques. Programmers in this category will already understand some of the concepts discussed here, but you will learn how you can incorporate XML technologies to enhance those solutions you currently develop.

❏ Those working in a programming environment but with no substantial knowledge or experience of web development or data exchange applications. In addition to learning how XML technologies can be applied to such applications, you will be introduced to some new concepts to help you understand how such systems work.

How This Book Is Organized

We've arranged the subjects covered in this book to take you from novice to expert in as logical a manner as we could. In this Fourth Edition, we have structured the book in sections that are based on various areas of XML expertise. Unless you are already using XML, you should start by reading the introduction to XML in Part I. From there, you can quickly jump into specific areas of expertise, or, if you prefer, you can read through the book in order. Keep in mind that there is quite a lot of overlap in XML, and that some of the sections make use of techniques described elsewhere in the book.

❏ We begin by explaining what exactly XML is and why the industry felt that a language like this was needed.

❏ After covering the *why*, the next logical step is the *how*, so we show you how to create well-formed XML.

❏ Once you understand the whys and hows of XML, you'll go on to some more advanced things you can do when creating your XML documents, to make them not only well formed, but valid. (And you'll learn what "valid" really means.)

❏ After you're comfortable with XML and have seen it in action, we unleash the programmer within and look at an XML-based programming language that you can use to transform XML documents from one format to another.

❏ Eventually, you will need to store and retrieve XML information from databases. At this point, you will learn not only the state of the art for XML and databases, but also how to query XML information using an SQL-like syntax called XQuery.

❏ XML wouldn't really be useful unless you could write programs to read the data in XML documents and create new XML documents, so we'll get back to programming and look at a couple of ways that you can do that.

❏ Understanding how to program and use XML within your own business is one thing, but sending that information to a business partner or publishing it to the Internet is another. You'll learn about technologies that use XML that enable you to send messages across the Internet, publish information, and discover services that provide information.

❏ Since you have all of this data in XML format, it would be great if you could easily display it to people, and it turns out you can. We'll show you an XML version of HTML called XHTML. You'll also look at a technology you may already be using in conjunction with HTML documents called CSS. CSS enables you to add visual styles to your XML documents. In addition, you'll learn how to design stunning graphics and make interactive forms using XML.

❏ Finally, we end with a case study, which should help to give you ideas about how XML can be used in real-life situations, and which could be used in your own applications.

What's Covered in This Book

This book builds on the strengths of the earlier editions, and provides new material to reflect the changes in the XML landscape—notably XQuery, RSS and Atom, and AJAX. Updates have been made to reflect the most recent versions of specifications and best practices throughout the book. In addition to the many changes, each chapter has a set of exercise questions to test your understanding of the material. Possible solutions to these questions appear in Appendix A.

Part I: Introduction

The introduction is where most readers should begin. The first three chapters introduce some of the goals of XML as well as the specific rules for constructing XML. Once you have read this part you should be able to read and create your own XML documents.

Chapter 1: What Is XML?

Here we cover some basic concepts, introducing the fact that XML is a markup language (a bit like HTML) whereby you can define your own elements, tags, and attributes (known as a *vocabulary*). You'll see that tags have no presentation meaning—they're just a way to describe the structure of the data.

Chapter 2: Well-Formed XML

In addition to explaining what well-formed XML is, we offer a look at the rules that exist (the XML 1.0 and 1.1 Recommendations) for naming and structuring elements—you need to comply with these rules in order to produce well-formed XML.

Chapter 3: XML Namespaces

Because tags can be made up, you need to avoid name conflicts when sharing documents. Namespaces provide a way to uniquely identify a group of tags, using a URI. This chapter explains how to use namespaces.

Part II: Validation

In addition to the well-formedness rules you learn in Part I, you will most likely want to learn how to create and use different XML vocabularies. This Part introduces you to DTDs, XML Schemas, and RELAX NG: three languages that define custom XML vocabularies. We also show you how to utilize these definitions to validate your XML documents.

Chapter 4: Document Type Definitions

You can specify how an XML document should be structured, and even provide default values, using Document Type Definitions (DTDs). If XML conforms to the associated DTD, it is known as *valid* XML. This chapter covers the basics of using DTDs.

Chapter 5: XML Schemas

XML Schemas, like DTDs, enable you to define how a document should be structured. In addition to defining document structure, they enable you to specify the individual datatypes of attribute values and element content. They are a more powerful alternative to DTDs.

Chapter 6: RELAX NG

RELAX NG is a third technology used to define the structure of documents. In addition to a new syntax and new features, it takes the best from XML Schemas and DTDs, and is therefore very simple and very powerful. RELAX NG has two syntaxes; both the full syntax and compact syntax are discussed.

Part III: Processing

In addition to defining and creating XML documents, you need to know how to work with documents to extract information and convert it to other formats. In fact, easily extracting information and converting it to other formats is what makes XML so powerful.

Chapter 7: XPath

The XPath language is used to locate sections and data in the XML document, and it's important in many other XML technologies.

Chapter 8: XSLT

XML can be transformed into other XML documents, HTML, and other formats using XSLT stylesheets, which are introduced in this chapter.

Part IV: Databases

Creating and processing XML documents is good, but eventually you will want to store those documents. This section describes strategies for storing and retrieving XML documents and document fragments from different databases.

Chapter 9: XQuery, the XML Query Language

Very often, you will need to retrieve information from within a database. XQuery, which is built on XPath and XPath2, enables you to do this in an elegant way.

Chapter 10: XML and Databases

XML is perfect for structuring data, and some traditional databases are beginning to offer support for XML. This chapter discusses these, and provides a general overview of how XML can be used in an n-tier architecture. In addition, new databases based on XML are introduced.

Part V: Programming

At some point in your XML career, you will need to work with an XML document from within a custom application. The two most popular methodologies, the Document Object Model (DOM) and the Simple API for XML (SAX), are explained in this part.

Chapter 11: The Document Object Model (DOM)

Programmers can use a variety of programming languages to manipulate XML using the Document Object Model's objects, interfaces, methods, and properties, which are described in this chapter.

Chapter 12: Simple API for XML (SAX)

An alternative to the DOM for programmatically manipulating XML data is to use the Simple API for XML (SAX) as an interface. This chapter shows how to use SAX and utilizes examples from the Java SAX API.

Part VI: Communication

Sending and receiving data from one computer to another is often difficult, but several technologies have been created to make communication with XML much easier. In this part we discuss RSS and content syndication, as well as web services and SOAP. This edition includes a new chapter on Ajax techniques.

Chapter 13: RSS, Atom, and Content Syndication

RSS is an actively evolving technology that is used to publish syndicated news stories and website summaries on the Internet. This chapter not only discusses how to use the different versions of RSS and Atom, it also covers the future direction of the technology. In addition, we demonstrate how to create a simple newsreader application that works with any of the currently published versions.

Chapter 14: Web Services

Web services enable you to perform cross-computer communications. This chapter describes web services and introduces you to using remote procedure calls in XML (using XML-RPC and REST), as well as giving you a brief look at major topics such as SOAP. Finally, it breaks down the assortment of specifications designed to work in conjunction with web services.

Chapter 15: SOAP and WSDL

Fundamental to XML web services, the Simple Object Access Protocol (SOAP) is one of the most popular specifications for allowing cross-computer communications. Using SOAP, you can package up XML documents and send them across the Internet to be processed. This chapter explains SOAP and the Web Services Description Language (WSDL) that is used to publish your service.

Chapter 16: Ajax

Ajax enables you to utilize JavaScript with web services and SOAP, or REST communications. Additionally, Ajax patterns can be used within web pages to communicate with the web server without refreshing. This chapter is new to the Fourth Edition.

Part VII: Display

Several XML technologies are devoted to displaying the data stored inside of an XML document. Some of these technologies are web-based, and some are designed for applications and mobile devices. In this part we discuss the primary display strategies and formats used today.

Chapter 17: Cascading Style Sheets (CSS)

Website designers have long been using Cascading Style Sheets (CSS) with their HTML to easily make changes to a website's presentation without having to touch the underlying HTML documents. This power is also available for XML, enabling you to display XML documents right in the browser. Or, if you need a bit more flexibility with your presentation, you can use XSLT to transform your XML to HTML or XHTML and then use CSS to style these documents.

Chapter 18: XHTML

XHTML is a new version of HTML that follows the rules of XML. In this chapter we discuss the differences between HTML and XHTML, and show you how XHTML can help make your sites available to a wider variety of browsers, from legacy browsers to the latest browsers on mobile phones.

Chapter 19: Scalable Vector Graphics (SVG)

Do you want to produce a custom graphic using XML? SVG enables you to describe a graphic using XML-based vector commands. In this chapter we teach you the basics of SVG and then dive into a more complex SVG-based application that can be published to the Internet.

Chapter 20: XForms

XForms are XML-based forms that can be used to design desktop applications, paper-based forms, and of course XHTML-based forms. In this chapter we demonstrate both the basics and some of the more interesting uses of XForms.

Part VIII: Case Study

Throughout the book you'll gain an understanding of how XML is used in web, business-to-business (B2B), data storage, and many other applications. The case study covers an example application and shows how the theory can be put into practice in real-life situations. The case study is new to this edition.

Chapter 21: Case Study: Payment Calculator

This case study explores some of the possibilities and strategies for using XML in your website. It includes an example that demonstrates a loan payment calculator by creating a web page using XHTML and CSS, communicating with a local web service using AJAX, utilizing an XML Schema to build data structures in .NET, and ultimately using the Document Object Model to display the results in SVG. An online version of this case study on the book's website covers the same material using Ruby on Rails instead of .NET.

Appendixes

Appendix A provides answers to the exercise questions that appear throughout the book. The remaining appendixes provide reference material that you may find useful as you begin to apply the knowledge gained throughout the book in your own applications.

The appendixes consist of the following:

- ❑ Appendix A: Exercise Solutions
- ❑ Appendix B: XPath Reference
- ❑ Appendix C: XSLT Reference
- ❑ Appendix D: The XML Document Object Model
- ❑ Appendix E: XML Schema Element and Attribute Reference
- ❑ Appendix F: XML Schema Datatypes Reference
- ❑ Appendix G: SAX 2.0.2 Reference

Appendixes A, B, and C are included within the book; Appendixes D–G are available on the book's website.

What You Need to Use This Book

Because XML is a text-based technology, all you really need to create XML documents is Notepad or an equivalent text editor. However, to truly appreciate some of these samples in action, you might want to have a current Internet browser that can natively read XML documents, and even provide error messages if something is wrong. In any case, screenshots are provided throughout the book so that you can see what things should look like. Additionally, note the following:

- ❑ If you do have Internet Explorer, you also have an implementation of the DOM, which you may find useful in the chapters on that subject.
- ❑ Some of the examples and the case studies require access to a web server, such as Microsoft's IIS (or PWS) or Apache.
- ❑ Throughout the book, other (freely available) XML tools are used, and we give instructions for obtaining these.

Within the validation section of the book we provide instructions on how to use Codeplot (http://codeplot.com). Codeplot is an online collaborative code editor with support for a wide assortment of XML technologies. Because many validation tools require programming experience or large downloads, the examples in this section instead use Codeplot. Codeplot can also be used to check the well-formedness of your XML documents, to transform XML documents using XSLT, and to assist you in coding XHTML, CSS, and SVG. The editor is free and was built using many of the techniques described in this book.

Programming Languages

We have tried to demonstrate the ubiquity of XML throughout the book. Some of the examples are specific to Windows, but most of the examples include information on working with other platforms, such as Linux. Many of the samples were rewritten in this edition to enable you to use any operating system or web browser.

Additionally, we have attempted to show the use of XML in a variety of programming languages, including Java, JavaScript, PHP, Python, Visual Basic, ASP, C#, and Ruby on Rails. Therefore, while there is a good chance that you will see an example written in your favorite programming language, there is also a good chance you will encounter an example in a language you have never used. Whenever a new language is introduced, we include information on downloading and installing the necessary tools to use it. Because our focus is XML, regardless of which programming language is used in an example, the core XML concept is explained in detail.

Conventions

To help you get the most from the text and keep track of what's happening, we've used several conventions throughout the book.

Try It Out

The Try It Out is an exercise you should work through, following the text in the book.

1. They usually consist of a set of steps.
2. Each step has a number.
3. Follow the steps with your copy of the database.

How It Works

After each Try It Out, the code is explained in detail.

> **Boxes like this one hold important, not-to-be forgotten information that is directly relevant to the surrounding text.**

Tips, hints, tricks, and asides to the current discussion are offset and placed in italics like this.

As for styles in the text:

- ❑   We *highlight* new terms and important words when we introduce them.
- ❑   We show filenames, URLs, and code within the text like so: `persistence.properties`.
- ❑   We present code in two different ways:

```
In code examples we highlight new and important code with a gray background.
```

```
The gray highlighting is not used for code that's less important in the present
context, or has been shown before.
```

Source Code

As you work through the examples in this book, you may choose either to type in all the code manually or to use the source code files that accompany the book. All of the source code used in this book is available for download at www.wrox.com. Once at the site, simply locate the book's title (either by using the Search box or by using one of the title lists) and click the Download Code link on the book's detail page to obtain all the source code for the book.

> *Because many books have similar titles, you may find it easiest to search by ISBN; this book's ISBN is SB 978-0-470-11487-2*

Once you download the code, just decompress it with your favorite compression tool. Alternately, you can go to the main Wrox code download page at www.wrox.com/dynamic/books/download.aspx to see the code available for this book and all other Wrox books.

Errata

We make every effort to ensure that there are no errors in the text or in the code. However, no one is perfect, and mistakes do occur. If you find an error in one of our books, such as a spelling mistake or a faulty piece of code, we would be very grateful for your feedback. By sending in errata you may save another reader hours of frustration, and at the same time you will be helping us provide even higher quality information.

To find the errata page for this book, go to www.wrox.com and locate the title using the Search box or one of the title lists. Then, on the book details page, click the Book Errata link. On this page you can view all errata that has been submitted for this book and posted by Wrox editors. A complete book list, including links to each book's errata, is also available at www.wrox.com/misc-pages/booklist.shtml.

If you don't spot "your" error on the Book Errata page, go to www.wrox.com/contact/techsupport.shtml and complete the form there to send us the error you have found. We'll check the information and, if appropriate, post a message to the book's errata page and fix the problem in subsequent editions of the book.

p2p.wrox.com

For author and peer discussion, join the P2P forums at p2p.wrox.com. The forums are a web-based system for you to post messages relating to Wrox books and related technologies and interact with other readers and technology users. The forums offer a subscription feature to e-mail you topics of interest of your choosing when new posts are made to the forums. Wrox authors, editors, other industry experts, and your fellow readers are present on these forums.

At http://p2p.wrox.com you will find a number of different forums that will help you not only as you read this book, but also as you develop your own applications. To join the forums, just follow these steps:

1. Go to p2p.wrox.com and click the Register link.
2. Read the terms of use and click Agree.

3. Complete the required information to join as well as any optional information you wish to provide and click Submit.

4. You will receive an e-mail with information describing how to verify your account and complete the joining process.

You can read messages in the forums without joining P2P, but in order to post your own messages, you must join.

Once you join, you can post new messages and respond to messages other users post. You can read messages at any time on the Web. If you would like to have new messages from a particular forum e-mailed to you, click the Subscribe to this Forum icon by the forum name in the forum listing.

For more information about how to use the Wrox P2P, be sure to read the P2P FAQs for answers to questions about how the forum software works as well as many common questions specific to P2P and Wrox books. To read the FAQs, click the FAQ link on any P2P page.

Part I
Introduction

What Is XML?

XML (Extensible Markup Language) is a buzzword you will see everywhere on the Internet, but it's also a rapidly maturing technology with powerful real-world applications, particularly for the management, display, and organization of data. Together with its many related technologies, which are covered in later chapters, XML is an essential technology for anyone working with data, whether publicly on the web or privately within your own organization. This chapter introduces you to some XML basics and begins to show you why learning about it is so important.

This chapter covers the following:

❑   The two major categories of computer file types — binary files and text files — and the advantages and disadvantages of each

❑   The history behind XML, including other markup languages such as SGML and HTML

❑   How XML documents are structured as hierarchies of information

❑   A brief introduction to some of the other technologies surrounding XML, which you will work with throughout the book

❑   A quick look at some areas where XML is useful

While there are some short examples of XML in this chapter, you aren't expected to understand what's going on just yet. The idea is simply to introduce the important concepts behind the language so that throughout the book you can see not only how to use XML, but also why it works the way it does.

Of Data, Files, and Text

XML is a technology concerned with the description and structuring of *data*, so before you can really delve into the concepts behind XML, you need to understand how computers store and access data. For our purposes, computers understand two kinds of data files: binary files and text files.

Binary Files

A *binary file*, at its simplest, is just a stream of *bits* (1s and 0s). It's up to the application that created a binary file to understand what all of the bits mean. That's why binary files can only be read and produced by certain computer programs, which have been specifically written to understand them.

For instance, when a document is created with Microsoft Word, the program creates a binary file with an extension of "doc," in its own proprietary format. The programmers who wrote Word decided to insert certain binary codes into the document to denote bold text, codes to denote page breaks, and other codes for all of the information that needs to go into a "doc" file. When you open a document in Word, it interprets those codes and displays the properly formatted text or prints it to the printer.

The codes inserted into the document are *meta data*, or information about information. Examples could be "this word should be in bold," "that paragraph should be centered," and so on. This meta data is really what differentiates one file type from another; the different types of files use different kinds of meta data. For example, a word processing document has different meta data than a spreadsheet document, because they are describing different things. Not so obviously, documents from different word processing applications, such as Microsoft Word and WordPerfect, also have different meta data, because the applications were written differently (see Figure 1-1).

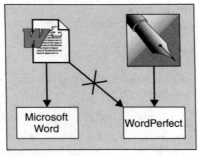

Figure 1-1

You can't assume that a document created with one word processor will be readable by another, because the companies who write word processors all have their own proprietary formats for their data files. Word documents open in Microsoft Word, and WordPerfect documents open in WordPerfect.

Luckily, most word processors come with translators or import utilities, which can translate documents from other word processors into formats that can be understood natively. If I have Microsoft Word installed on my computer and someone gives me a WordPerfect document, I might be able to import it into Word so that I can read the document. Of course, many of us have seen the garbage that sometimes occurs as a result of this translation; sometimes applications are not as good as we'd like them to be at converting the information.

Binary file formats are advantageous because it is easy for computers to understand these binary codes — meaning that they can be processed much faster than nonbinary formats — and they are very efficient for storing this meta data. There is also a disadvantage, as you've seen, in that binary files are proprietary. You might not be able to open binary files created by one application in another application, or even in the same application running on another platform.

Text Files

Like binary files, *text files* are also streams of bits. However, in a text file these bits are grouped together in standardized ways, so that they always form numbers. These numbers are then further mapped to characters. For example, a text file might contain the following bits:

```
1100001
```

This group of bits would be translated as the number 97, which could then be further translated into the letter a.

> *This example makes a number of assumptions. A better description of how numbers are represented in text files is given in the "Encoding" section in Chapter 2.*

Because of these standards, text files can be read by many applications, and can even be read by humans, using a simple text editor. If I create a text document, anyone in the world can read it (as long as they understand English, of course) in any text editor they wish. Some issues still exist, such as the fact that different operating systems treat line-ending characters differently, but it is much easier to share information when it's contained in a text file than when the information is in a binary format.

Figure 1-2 shows some of the applications on my machine that are capable of opening text files. Some of these programs only allow me to *view* the text, while others will let me *edit* it as well.

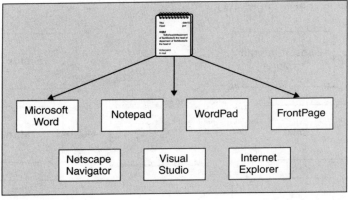

Figure 1-2

In its early days, the Internet was almost completely text-based, which enabled people to communicate with relative ease. This contributed to the explosive rate at which the Internet was adopted, and to the ubiquity of applications such as e-mail, the World Wide Web, newsgroups, and so on.

The disadvantage of text files is that adding other information—our meta data, in other words—is more difficult and bulky. For example, most word processors enable you to save documents in text form, but if you do, you can't mark a section of text as bold or insert a binary picture file. You will simply get the words with none of the formatting.

A Brief History of Markup

You can see that there are advantages to binary file formats (easy to understand by a computer, compact, the ability to add meta data), as well as advantages to text files (universally interchangeable). Wouldn't it be ideal if there were a format that combined the universality of text files with the efficiency and rich information storage capabilities of binary files?

This idea of a universal data format is not new. In fact, for as long as computers have been around, programmers have been trying to find ways to exchange information between different computer programs. An early attempt to combine a universally interchangeable data format with rich information storage capabilities was *Standard Generalized Markup Language (SGML)*. SGML is a text-based language that can be used to mark up data — that is, add meta data — in a way that is *self-describing*. (You'll see in a moment what self-describing means.)

SGML was designed to be a standard way of marking up data for any purpose, and took off mostly in large document management systems. When it comes to huge amounts of complex data, a lot of considerations must be taken into account, so SGML is a very complicated language. However, with that complexity comes power.

A very well-known language based on the SGML work is the *HyperText Markup Language (HTML)*. HTML uses many of SGML's concepts to provide a universal markup language for the display of information, and the linking of different pieces of information. The idea was that any HTML document (or web page) would be presentable in any application that was capable of understanding HTML (termed a *web browser*). A number of examples are given in Figure 1-3.

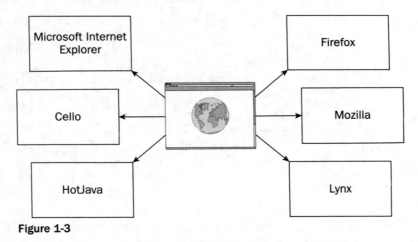

Figure 1-3

Not only would that browser be able to display the document, but if the page contained links (termed *hyperlinks*) to other documents, the browser would also be able to seamlessly retrieve them as well.

Furthermore, because HTML is text-based, anyone can create an HTML page using a simple text editor, or any number of web page editors, some of which are shown in Figure 1-4.

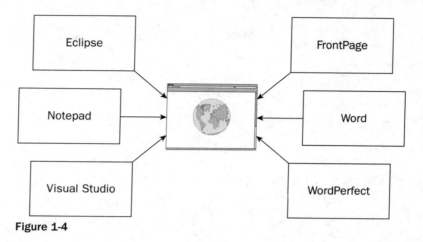

Figure 1-4

Even many word processors, such as WordPerfect and Word, allow you to save documents as HTML. Think about the ramifications of Figures 1-3 and 1-4: Any HTML editor, including a simple text editor, can create an HTML file, and that HTML file can then be viewed in any web browser on the Internet!

So What Is XML?

Unfortunately, SGML is such a complicated language that it's not well suited for data interchange over the web. In addition, although HTML has been incredibly successful, it's limited in scope: It is only intended for displaying documents in a browser. The tags it makes available do not provide any information about the content they encompass, only instructions about how to display that content. This means that you could create an HTML document that displays information about a person, but that's about all you could do with the document. You couldn't write a program to figure out from that document which piece of information relates to the person's first name, for example, because HTML doesn't have any facilities to describe this kind of specialized information. In fact, HTML wouldn't even know that the document was about a person at all. Extensible Markup Language (XML) was created to address these issues.

> Note that despite the acronym, it's spelled "Extensible," not "eXtensible." Mixing these up is a common mistake.

XML is a subset of SGML, with the same goals (markup of any type of data), but with as much of the complexity eliminated as possible. XML was designed to be fully compatible with SGML, meaning any document that follows XML's syntax rules is by definition also following SGML's syntax rules, and can therefore be read by existing SGML tools. It doesn't go both ways, however, so an SGML document is not necessarily an XML document.

It is important to realize that XML is not really a "language" at all, but a standard for creating languages that meet the XML criteria (we go into these rules for creating XML documents in Chapter 2). In other words, XML describes a syntax that you use to create your own languages. For example, suppose you have data about a name, and you want to be able to share that information with others as well as use that information in a computer program. Instead of just creating a text file like this:

```
John Doe
```

or an HTML file like this

```
<html>
<head><title>Name</title></head>
<body>
<p>John Doe</p>
</body>
</html>
```

you might create an XML file like the following:

```
<name>
   <first>John</first>
   <last>Doe</last>
</name>
```

Even from this simple example, you can see why markup languages such as SGML and XML are called "self-describing." Looking at the data, you can easily tell that this is information about a <name>, and you can see that there is data called <first> and more data called <last>. You can give the tags any names you like, but if you're going to use XML, you might as well use it right and give things *meaningful* names.

You can also see that the XML version of this information is much larger than the plain-text version. Using XML to mark up data adds to its size, sometimes enormously, but achieving small file sizes isn't one of the goals of XML; it's only about making it easier to write software that accesses the information, by giving structure to the data.

> **This larger file size should not deter you from using XML. The advantages of easier-to-write code far outweigh the disadvantages of larger bandwidth issues.**

If bandwidth is a critical issue for your applications, you can always compress your XML documents before sending them across the network — compressing text files yields very good results.

If you're running Internet Explorer 5 or later, you can view the preceding XML in your browser, as shown in the following Try It Out. (You can also use other web browsers, such as Firefox, to display the XML examples in this chapter. All of the screenshots shown, however, are of Internet Explorer 6.)

Try It Out   Opening an XML File in Internet Explorer

1.   Open Notepad and type in the following XML:

```
<name>
   <first>John</first>
   <last>Doe</last>
</name>
```

2. Save the document to your hard drive as name.xml. If you're using Windows XP, be sure to change the Save as Type drop-down option to All Files. (Otherwise, Notepad will save the document with a .txt extension, causing your file to be named name.xml.txt.) You might also want to change the Encoding drop-down to Unicode, as shown in Figure 1-5. (Find more information on encodings in Chapter 2.)

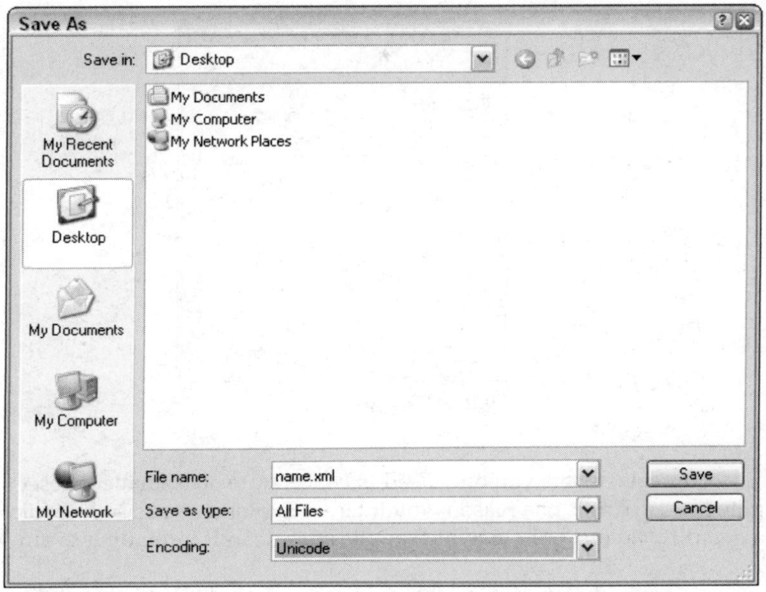

Figure 1-5

3. You can then open the file in Internet Explorer (for example, by double-clicking on the file in Windows Explorer), where it will look something like Figure 1-6.

Figure 1-6

How It Works

Although your XML file has no information concerning display, the browser formats it nicely for you, with your information in bold and your markup displayed in different colors. In addition, <name> is collapsible, like your file folders in Windows Explorer. Try clicking on the minus sign (–) next to <name> in the browser window. It should then look like Figure 1-7.

Figure 1-7

For large XML documents, where you only need to concentrate on a smaller subset of the data, this feature can be quite handy. This is one reason why Internet Explorer can be so helpful when authoring XML: It has a default *stylesheet* built in, which applies this default formatting to any XML document.

> *XML styling is accomplished through another document dedicated to the task, called a* stylesheet. *In a stylesheet, the designer specifies rules that determine the presentation of the data. The same stylesheet can then be used with multiple documents to create a similar appearance among them. A variety of languages can be used to create stylesheets. Chapter 8 explains a transformation stylesheet language called Extensible Stylesheet Language Transformations (XSLT), and Chapter 17 looks at a stylesheet language called Cascading Style Sheets (CSS).*

As you'll see in later chapters, you can also create your own stylesheets for displaying XML documents. This way, the same data that your applications use can also be viewed in a browser. In effect, by combining XML data with stylesheets, you can separate your data from your presentation. That makes it easier to use the data for multiple purposes (as opposed to HTML, which doesn't provide any separation of data from presentation — in HTML, *everything* is presentation).

What Does XML Buy Us?

I can hear what some of you are thinking. Why go to the trouble of creating an XML document? Wouldn't it be easier to just make up some rules for a file about names, such as "The first name starts at the beginning of the file, and the last name comes after the first space?" That way, your application could still read the data, but the file size would be much smaller.

As a partial answer, suppose that we want to add a middle name to our example:

```
John Fitzgerald Doe
```

Okay, no problem. We'll just modify our rules to say that everything after the first space and up to the second space is the middle name, and everything after the second space is the last name. However, if there is no second space, we have to assume that there is no middle name, and the first rule still applies. We're still fine, unless a person happens to have a name like the following:

```
John Fitzgerald Johansen Doe
```

Whoops! There are two middle names in there. The rules get more complex. While a human might be able to tell immediately that the two middle words compose the middle name, it is more difficult to program this logic into a computer program. We won't even discuss "John Fitzgerald Johansen Doe the 3rd"!

Unfortunately, when it comes to problems like this, many software developers simply define more restrictive rules, instead of dealing with the complexities of the data. In this example, a software developer might decide that a person can only have *one* middle name, and the application won't accept anything more than that.

> *This is pretty realistic, I might add. My full name is David John Bartlett Hunter, but because of the way in which many computer systems are set up, a lot of the bills I receive are simply addressed to David John Hunter or David J. Hunter. Maybe I can find some legal ground to stop paying my bills, but in the meantime, my vanity takes a blow every time I open my mail.*

This example is probably not all that hard to solve, but it highlights one of the major focuses behind XML. Programmers have been structuring their data in an infinite variety of ways, and every new way of structuring data brings a new methodology for pulling out the information we need. With those new methodologies comes a lot of experimentation and testing to get it just right. If the data changes, the methodologies also have to change, and testing and tweaking has to begin again. XML offers a standardized way to get the information we need, no matter how we structure it.

In addition, remember how trivial this example is. The more complex the data you have to work with, the more complex the logic you'll need to do that work. You'll appreciate XML the most in larger applications.

XML Parsers

If we just follow the rules specified by XML, we can be sure that getting at our information will be easy. This is because there are programs called *parsers* that can read XML syntax and extract the information for us. We can use these parsers within our own programs, meaning our applications will never have to look at the XML directly; a large part of the workload will be done for us.

> *Parsers are also available for parsing SGML documents, but they are much more complex than XML parsers. Because XML is a subset of SGML, it's easier to write an XML parser than an SGML parser.*

In the past, before these parsers were around, a lot of work would have gone into the many rules we were looking at (such as the rule that the middle name starts after the first space, and so on), but with our data in XML format, we can just give an XML parser a file like this:

```
<name>
  <first>John</first>
  <middle>Fitzgerald Johansen</middle>
  <last>Doe</last>
</name>
```

The parser can tell us that there is a piece of data called `<middle>`, and that the information stored there is `Fitzgerald Johansen`. The parser writer didn't have to know any rules about where the first name ends and where the middle name begins, because the parser simply uses the `<middle>` and `</middle>` tags to determine where the data begins and ends. The parser didn't have to know anything about my application at all, nor about the types of XML documents the application works with. The same parser could be used in my application, or in a completely different application. The language my XML is written in doesn't matter to the parser either; XML written in English, Chinese, Hebrew, or any other language could all be read by the same parser, even if the person who wrote it didn't understand any of these languages.

> **Just as any HTML document can be displayed by any web browser, any XML document can be read by any XML parser, regardless of what application was used to create it, or even what platform it was created on. This goes a long way toward making your data universally accessible.**

There's another added benefit here: If I had previously written a program to deal with the first XML format, which had only a first and last name, that application could also accept the new XML format, without me having to change the code. Because the parser takes care of the work of getting data out of the document for us, you can add to your XML format without breaking existing code, and new applications can take advantage of the new information if they wish. If we were using our previous text-only format, any time we changed the data at all, every application using that data would have to be modified, retested, and redeployed.

As long as an existing application were simply looking for information called "first" and information called "last," it would continue to work, even if we added to the document. Of course, if we *subtracted* information from our `<name>` example, or changed the names we used for the data, we would still have to modify our applications to deal with the changes.

Because it's so flexible, XML is targeted to be the basis for defining data exchange languages, especially for communication over the Internet. The language facilitates working with data within applications, such as an application that needs to access the previously listed `<name>` information, but it also facilitates sharing information with others. We can pass our `<name>` information around the Internet and, even without our particular program, the data can still be read. People can pull the file up in a regular text editor and look at the raw XML if they like, or open it in a viewer such as Internet Explorer.

Why "Extensible?"

Because we have full control over the creation of our XML document, we can shape the data in any way we wish, so that it makes sense for our particular application. If we don't need the flexibility of our `<name>` example, and don't need to know which part of the "name" is the "first name," and which is the "last name," we could decide to describe a person's name in XML like this:

```
<designation>John Fitzgerald Johansen Doe</designation>
```

If we want to create data in a way that only one particular computer program will ever use, we can do so; and if we decide that we want to share our data with other programs, or even other companies across the Internet, XML gives us the flexibility to do that as well. We are free to structure the same data in different ways that suit the requirements of an application or category of applications.

This is where the extensible *in Extensible Markup Language comes from: Anyone is free to mark up data in any way using the language, even if others are doing it in completely different ways.*

HTML, on the other hand, is not extensible, because you can't add to the language; you have to use the tags that are part of the HTML specification. For example, web browsers can understand the following:

```
<p>This is a paragraph.</p>
```

The `<p>` tag is a predefined HTML tag. However, web browsers can't understand the following:

```
<paragraph>This is a paragraph.</paragraph>
```

The `<paragraph>` tag is not a predefined HTML tag.

The benefits of XML become even more apparent when people use the same format to do common things, because this allows us to interchange information much more easily. There have already been numerous projects to produce industry-standard vocabularies to describe various types of data. For example, *Scalable Vector Graphics (SVG)* is an XML vocabulary for describing two-dimensional graphics (we'll look at SVG in Chapter 19); *MathML* is an XML vocabulary for describing mathematics as a basis for machine-to-machine communication; *Chemical Markup Language (CML)* is an XML vocabulary for the management of chemical information. The list goes on and on. Of course, you could write your own XML vocabularies to describe this type of information if you so wished, but if you use a common format, there is a better chance that you will be able to produce software that is immediately compatible with other software. Better yet, you can reuse code already written to work with these formats.

Because XML is so easy to read and write in your programs, it is also easy to convert between different vocabularies when required. For example, if you want to represent mathematical equations in your particular application in a certain way, but MathML doesn't quite suit your needs, you can create your own vocabulary. If you want to export your data for use by other applications, you might convert the data in your vocabulary to MathML for the other applications to read. In fact, Chapter 8 covers a technology called *XSLT*, which was created for transforming XML documents from one format to another, and which could potentially make these kinds of transformations very simple.

HTML and XML: Apples and Red Delicious Apples

What HTML does for display, XML is designed to do for data exchange. Sometimes XML isn't up to a certain task, just as HTML is sometimes not up to the task of displaying certain information. How many of us have Adobe Acrobat readers installed on our machines for those documents on the web that HTML just can't display properly? When it comes to display, HTML does a good job most of the time, and those who work with XML believe that, most of the time, XML will do a good job of communicating information. Just as HTML authors sometimes sacrifice precise layout and presentation for the sake of making their information accessible to all web browsers, XML developers sacrifice the small file sizes of proprietary formats for the flexibility of universal data access.

Of course, a fundamental difference exists between HTML and XML: HTML is designed for a *specific* application, to convey information to humans (usually visually, through a web browser), whereas XML has no specific application; it is designed for whatever use you need it for.

This is an important concept. Because HTML has its specific application, it also has a finite set of specific markup constructs (`<p>`, `<ul>`, `<h2>`, and so on), which are used to create a correct HTML document. In theory, we can be confident that any web browser will understand an HTML document because all it has to do is understand this finite set of tags. In practice, of course, I'm sure you've come across web pages that displayed properly in one web browser and not in another, but this is usually a result of nonstandard HTML tags, which were created by browser vendors instead of being part of the HTML specification itself.

On the other hand, if you create an XML document, you can be sure that any XML parser will be able to retrieve information from that document, even though you can't guarantee that any application will be able to understand *what that information means*. That is, just because a parser can tell you that there is a piece of data called `<middle>` and that the information contained therein is `Fitzgerald Johansen`, it doesn't mean that there is any software in the world that knows what a `<middle>` is, what it is used for, or what it means.

In other words, you can create XML documents to describe any information you want, but before XML can be considered useful, applications must be written that understand it. Furthermore, in addition to the capabilities provided by the base XML specification, there are a number of related technologies, some of which are covered in later chapters. These technologies provide more capabilities for us, making XML even more powerful than we've seen so far.

> *Some of these technologies exist only in draft form, so exactly how powerful these tools will be, or in what ways they'll be powerful, is yet to be seen. Other technologies, however, have been in use for a number of years, and are already proving useful in real-world applications.*

Hierarchies of Information

The syntactical constructs that make up XML are discussed in the next chapter, but first it might be useful to examine how data is structured in an XML document.

When it comes to large, or even moderate, amounts of information, it's usually better to group it into related subtopics, rather than to have all of the information presented in one large blob. For example, this chapter is divided into subtopics, and further subdivided into paragraphs. Similarly, a tax form is divided into subsections, across multiple pages. This makes the information easier to comprehend, as well as making it more accessible.

Software developers have been using this paradigm for years, using a structure called an *object model*. In an object model, all of the information being modeled is divided into various objects, and the objects themselves are then grouped into a hierarchy.

Hierarchies in HTML

For example, when working with Dynamic HTML (DHTML), an object model is available for working with HTML documents, called the *Document Object Model (DOM)*. This enables us to write code in an HTML document, such as the following JavaScript:

```
alert(document.title);
```

Here we are using the `alert()` function to pop up a message box indicating the title of an HTML document. That's achieved by accessing an object called `document`, which contains all of the information needed about the HTML document. The `document` object includes a property called `title`, which returns the title of the current HTML document.

The information that the object provides appears in the form of properties, *and the functionality available appears in the form of* methods.

Hierarchies in XML

XML also groups information in hierarchies. The items in our documents relate to each other in parent/child and sibling/sibling relationships.

> These "items" are called *elements*. **Chapter 2 provides a more precise definition of what exactly an element is. For now, just think of them as the individual pieces of information in the data.**

Consider our `<name>` example, shown hierarchically in Figure 1-8.

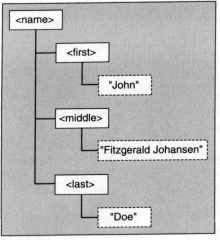

Figure 1-8

`<name>` is a parent of `<first>`. `<first>`, `<middle>`, and `<last>` are all siblings to each other (they are all children of `<name>`). Note also that the text is a child of the element. For example, the text `John` is a child of `<first>`.

This structure is also called a *tree,* and any parts of the tree that contain children are called *branches,* while parts that have no children are called *leaves.*

These are fairly loose terms, rather than formal definitions, which simply facilitate discussing the tree-like structure of XML documents. You might have seen the term "twig" in use, although it is much less common than "branch" or "leaf."

Because the <name> element has only other elements for children, and not text, it is said to have *element content*. Conversely, because <first>, <middle>, and <last> have only text as children, they are said to have *simple content*.

Elements can contain both text and other elements, in which case they are said to have *mixed content*, as shown in the following example:

```
<doc>
   <parent>this is some <em>text</em> in my element</parent>
</doc>
```

Here, <parent> has three children:

❑   A text child containing the text this is some

❑   An <em> child

❑   Another text child containing the text in my element

The structure is shown in Figure 1-9.

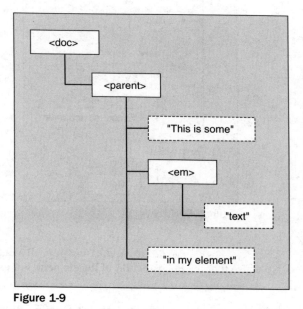

Figure 1-9

Relationships can also be defined by making the family tree analogy work a little bit harder: <doc> is an *ancestor* of <em>; <em> is a *descendant* of <doc>.

Once you understand the hierarchical relationships between your items (and the text they contain), you'll have a better understanding of the nature of XML. You'll also be better prepared to work with some of the other technologies surrounding XML, which make extensive use of this paradigm.

Chapter 11 gives you an opportunity to work with the document object model (DOM) mentioned earlier, which enables you to programmatically access the information in an XML document using this tree structure.

What's a Document Type?

XML's beauty comes from its ability to create a document to describe any information we want. It's completely flexible in terms of how we structure our data, but eventually we're going to want to settle on a particular design for our information, and specify "to adhere to our XML format, structure the data like this."

For example, when we created our <name> XML above, we created *structured data*. Not only did we include all of the information about a name, but our hierarchy also contains implicit information about how some pieces of data relate to other pieces (our <name> contains a <first>, for example).

More important, we also created a specific set of elements, which is called a *vocabulary*. That is, we defined a number of XML elements that all work together to form a name: <name>, <first>, <middle>, and <last>.

But wait; it's even more than that! The most important thing we created was a *document type*. We created a specific type of document, which must be structured in a specific way, to describe a specific type of information. Although we haven't explicitly defined them yet, there are certain rules to which the elements in our vocabulary must adhere in order for our <name> document to conform to our document type. For example:

- ❑ The top-most element must be the <name> element.
- ❑ The <first>, <middle>, and <last> elements must be children of that element.
- ❑ The <first>, <middle>, and <last> elements must be in that order.
- ❑ There must be information in the <first> element and in the <last> element, but there doesn't have to be any information in the <middle> element.

Unfortunately, there is nothing in our XML document itself which indicates what these rules are; we would have to write any applications that use this data to know the rules, and make sure that they're obeyed. In later chapters, you'll see different syntaxes that you can use to formally define an XML document type. Some XML parsers know how to read these syntaxes, and can use them to determine whether your XML document really adheres to the rules in the document type or not. This is good, because the more work the parser does, the less work your application has to do!

However, all of the syntaxes used to define document types so far are lacking; they can provide some type checking, but not enough for many applications. Furthermore, they can't express the human meaning of terms in a vocabulary. For this reason, when creating XML document types, human-readable documentation should also be provided. For our <name> example, if we want others to be able to use the same format to describe names in their XML, we should provide them with documentation to describe how it works.

17

In real life, this human-readable documentation is often used in conjunction with one or more of the syntaxes available. Ironically, the self-describing nature of XML can sometimes make this human-readable documentation even more important. Often, because the data is already labeled within the document structure, it is assumed that people working with the data will be able to infer its meaning, which can be dangerous if the inferences are incorrect, or even just different from the original author's intent.

No, Really — What's a Document Type?

Well, okay, maybe I was a little bit hasty in labeling our `<name>` example a "document type." The truth is that others who work with XML may call it something different.

One of the problems people encounter when they communicate is that they sometimes use different terms to describe the same thing, or, even worse, use the same term to describe different things. For example, I might call the thing that I drive a car, whereas someone else might call it an auto, and someone else again might call it a G-class vehicle. Furthermore, when I say car I *usually* mean a vehicle that has four wheels, is made for transporting passengers, and is smaller than a truck. (Notice how fuzzy this definition is, and that it depends further on the definition of a truck.) When someone else uses the word car, or if I use the word car in certain circumstances, it may instead just mean a land-based motorized vehicle, as opposed to a boat or a plane.

The same thing is true in XML. When you're using XML to create document types, you don't really have to think (or care) about the fact that you're creating document types; you just design your XML in a way that makes sense for your application, and then use it. If you ever did think about exactly what you were creating, you might have called it something other than a document type.

> We picked the terms "document type" and "vocabulary" for this book because they do a good job of describing what we need to describe, but they are not universal terms used throughout the XML community. Regardless of the terms you use, the concepts are very important.

Origin of the XML Standards

One of the reasons why HTML and XML are so successful is that they're *standards*. That means anyone can follow the specification and the solutions they develop will be able to interoperate. So who creates these standards?

What Is the World Wide Web Consortium?

The *World Wide Web Consortium (W3C)* was started in 1994, according to its website (`www.w3.org`), "to lead the World Wide Web to its full potential by developing common protocols that promote its evolution and ensure its interoperability." Recognizing this need for standards, the W3C produces *Recommendations*, or *specifications*, that describe the basic building blocks of the web. They call them "recommendations" instead of "standards" because it is up to others to follow the recommendations to provide the interoperability.

Their most famous contribution to the web is the HTML Recommendation; when web browser producers claims that their product follows version 3.2 or 4.01 of the HTML Recommendation, they're talking about the recommendation developed under the authority of the W3C.

Recommendations from the W3C are so widely implemented because the creation of these standards is a somewhat open process: Any company or individual can join the W3C's membership, and membership allows these companies or individuals to take part in the standards process. This means that web browsers such as Mozilla Firefox and Microsoft Internet Explorer are more likely to implement the same version of the HTML Recommendation, because developers of both applications were involved in the evolution of that recommendation.

Because of the interoperability goals of XML, the W3C is a good place to develop standards around the technology. Most of the technologies covered in this book are based on standards from the W3C: the XML 1.0 Recommendation, the XSLT Recommendation, the XPath Recommendation, and so on.

Components of XML

Structuring information is a pretty broad topic, and it would be futile to try to define a specification to cover it fully. For this reason, a number of interrelated specifications and recommendations all work together to form the XML family of technologies, with each specification covering different aspects of communicating information. Here are some of the more important ones:

❑ *XML 1.0* is the base recommendation upon which the XML family is built. It describes the syntax that XML documents have to follow, the rules that XML parsers have to follow, and anything else you need to know to read or write an XML document. It also defines document type definitions (DTDs), although they sometimes are treated as a separate technology.

❑ Because we can make up our own structures and element names for our documents, *DTDs* and *schemas* provide ways to define our document types. We can check to ensure that other documents adhere to these templates, and other developers can produce compatible documents. DTDs and schemas are discussed in Chapters 4 and 5, respectively.

❑ *Namespaces* provide a means to distinguish one XML vocabulary from another, which enables us to create richer documents by combining multiple vocabularies into one document type. Namespaces are discussed in detail in Chapter 3.

❑ *XPath* describes a querying language for addressing parts of an XML document. This enables applications to ask for a specific piece of an XML document, instead of having to always deal with one large chunk of information. For example, XPath could be used to get "all the last names" from a document. We discuss XPath in Chapter 7.

❑ As mentioned earlier, sometimes we may want to display our XML documents. For simpler cases, we can use *Cascading Style Sheets (CSS)* to define the presentation of our documents. For more complex cases, we can use *Extensible Stylesheet Language (XSL)*; this consists of *XSLT*, which can transform our documents from one type to another, and *formatting objects*, which deal with display. XSLT is covered in Chapter 8, and CSS is covered in Chapter 17.

❑ Although the syntax for HTML and the syntax for XML look very similar, they are actually not the same — XML's syntax is much more rigid than that of HTML. This means that an XML parser cannot necessarily read an HTML document. This is one of the reasons why *XHTML* was created — an XML version of HTML. XHTML is very similar to HTML, so HTML developers will have no problem working with XHTML, but the syntax used is more rigid and is readable by XML parsers (since XHTML *is* XML). XHTML is discussed in Chapter 18.

❑ The *XQuery* Recommendation is designed to provide a means of querying data directly from XML documents on the web. It is discussed in Chapter 9.

❑ To provide a means for more traditional applications to interface with XML documents, there is a document object model (DOM), discussed in Chapter 11. An alternative way for programmers to interface with XML documents from their code is to use the Simple API for XML (SAX), which is the subject of Chapter 12.

❑ In addition to the specifications and recommendations for the various XML technologies, some specifications also exist for specific XML document types:

❑ The *RDF Site Summary (RSS)* specification is used by websites that want to syndicate news stories (or similar content that can be treated similarly to news stories), for use by other websites or applications. RSS is discussed in Chapter 13.

❑ The *Scalable Vector Graphics (SVG)* specification is used to describe two-dimensional graphics, and is discussed in Chapter 19.

Where XML Can Be Used, and What You Can Use It For

XML can be used anywhere. It is platform- and language-independent, which means it doesn't matter that one computer may be using, for example, a Visual Basic application on a Microsoft operating system, and another computer might be a UNIX machine running Java code. Anytime one computer program needs to communicate with another program, XML is a potential fit for the exchange format. The following are just a few examples, and such applications are discussed in more detail throughout the book.

Reducing Server Load

Web-based applications can use XML to reduce the load on the web servers by keeping all information on the client for as long as possible, and then sending the information to those servers in one big XML document.

For example, a consulting company may write a timesheet application whereby employees can enter how much time they've spent on different tasks; the time entered would be used to bill their clients appropriately. Although employees would often have more than one task to fill, the application could cache all of that data in the browser until the user was finished, meaning that the browser wouldn't have to send or receive any data from the web server. Then, when the user is completely finished, an XML document could be sent to the server, with all of the user's data.

Website Content

It was mentioned earlier that there are technologies — such as CSS and XSLT — that can be used to transform XML from one format to another, or to "style" XML for viewing in a browser. This allows for some very powerful applications of your data.

For example, the W3C uses XML to publish its recommendations. These XML documents can then be transformed into HTML for display (by XSLT), or transformed into a number of other presentation formats. Because all of the presentation formats come from the same XML data file, this solution is faster and less error-prone than having someone re-enter the data in different formats.

Some websites also use XML entirely for their content, where traditionally HTML would have been used. This XML can then be transformed into HTML via XSLT, or displayed directly in browsers via CSS. In fact, the web servers can even determine dynamically what kind of browser is retrieving the information, and then decide what to do — for example, transform the XML into HTML for older browsers, and just send the XML straight to the client for newer browsers, reducing the load on the server.

As an author, I could also use this concept for my writing. After writing a chapter for a book I'm working on, saving it as XML could give me a lot of flexibility:

❑ I could use a technology such as CSS to make the chapter available on my website.

❑ I could use a technology such as XSLT to create a "stripped down" version of the chapter if I wanted to publish the content in a magazine article. For example, I might ignore certain aspects of the chapter in the magazine article that I would want to show up in the book. To give myself the most flexibility, I would probably alter the markup in the content in such a way that I could indicate to myself where it should appear: book, magazine article, web, or all of the above.

❑ I could even transform the XML to a different XML format, which could be understood by a word processor, so that I could further edit it. Most modern word processors — such as Microsoft Word and OpenOffice.org Writer — understand XML formats.

In fact, this can be generalized to *any* content. If your data is in XML, you can use it for any purpose. Presentation on the web is just one possibility.

Distributed Computing

XML can also be used as a means for sending data for distributed computing, where objects on one computer call objects on another computer to do work. There have been numerous standards for distributed computing, such as DCOM, CORBA, and RMI/IIOP, but as Chapters 14 and 15 show, using XML and HTTP with technologies like web services and/or SOAP enables this to occur even through a firewall, which would normally block such calls, providing greater opportunities for distributed computing.

e-Commerce

e-commerce is another one of those buzzwords that you hear everywhere now. Companies are discovering that by communicating via the Internet, instead of by more traditional methods (such as faxing, human-to-human communication, and so on), they can streamline their processes, decreasing costs and increasing response times. Whenever one company needs to send data to another, XML is the perfect format for the exchange.

When the companies involved in the exchange have some kind of ongoing relationship, this is known as *business-to-business* (B2B) e-commerce. *Business-to-consumer* (B2C) transactions also take place — a system you may have used if you bought this book on the Internet. Both types of e-commerce have their potential uses for XML.

XML is also a good fit for many other applications. After reading this book, you should be able to decide when XML will work in your applications and when it won't.

Summary

This chapter provided an overview of what XML is and why it's so useful. You've seen the advantages of text and binary files, and the way that XML combines the advantages of both, while eliminating most of the disadvantages. You have also seen the flexibility you can enjoy in creating data in any format you wish.

Because XML is a subset of a proven technology, SGML, there are many years of experience behind the standard. In addition, because other technologies are built around XML, you can create applications that are as complex or simple as your situation warrants.

Much of the power that we get from XML comes from the standard way in which documents must be written. Chapter 2 takes a closer look at the rules for creating well-formed XML.

Exercise Questions

Suggested solutions to these questions can be found in Appendix A.

Question 1

Modify the <name> XML document you've been working with to include the person's title (e.g., Mr., Ms., Dr., and so on).

Question 2

The <name> example we've been using so far has been in English, but XML is language-agnostic, so you can create XML documents in any language you wish. Therefore, create a new French document type to represent a name. You can use the following table for the names of the XML elements.

English	French
name	identité
first	prénom
last	nom
middle	deuxième-prénom

Well-Formed XML

Chapter 1 discussed some of the reasons why XML makes sense for communicating data, so now it's time to get your hands dirty and learn how to create your own XML documents. This chapter covers all you need to know to create *well-formed* XML. Well-formed XML is XML that meets certain syntactical rules outlined in the XML 1.0 recommendation.

This chapter includes the following:

- ❑ How to create XML elements using start-tags and end-tags
- ❑ How to further describe elements with attributes
- ❑ How to declare your document as being XML
- ❑ How to send instructions to applications that are processing the XML document
- ❑ Which characters aren't allowed in XML — and how to use them in your documents anyway!

Because the syntax rules for XML and HTML are so similar, and because you may already be familiar with HTML, we'll be making comparisons between the two languages in this chapter. However, if you don't have any knowledge of HTML, you shouldn't find it hard to follow along.

If you have Microsoft Internet Explorer 5 or later, you may find it useful to save some of the examples in this chapter on your hard drive and view the results in the browser. If you don't have IE5 or later, some of the examples include screenshots to show what the results look like. One nice advantage of doing this is that the browser will indicate whether you make a syntax mistake. I do this quite often, to ensure I haven't mistyped anything.

The examples given in this chapter are also available for download from the Wrox website, at www.wrox.com; just find the entry for this title and click the Download Code link. If you wish to save yourself some typing, you can download the code from there, but typing these examples manually — and occasionally making mistakes! — will help you to learn and understand things better.

Parsing XML

The main reason for creating all these rules about writing well-formed XML documents is so that you can create a computer program to read in the data, and easily tell markup from information.

> According to the XML recommendation (www.w3.org/TR/REC-xml#sec-intro), "A software module called an XML processor is used to read XML documents and provide access to their content and structure. It is assumed that an XML processor is doing its work on behalf of another module, called the application."

An XML processor is more commonly called a *parser*, as it simply parses XML and provides the application with any information it needs. That is, it reads through the characters in the document, determines which characters are part of the document's markup and which are part of the document's data, and does all of the other processing of an XML document that happens before an application can make use of it. Several XML parsers are available, many of them free. Some of the better-known ones include the following:

❑ **Microsoft Internet Explorer Parser** — Microsoft's XML parser, MSXML, first shipped with Internet Explorer 4, and implemented an early draft of the XML recommendation. With the release of IE5, the XML implementation was upgraded to reflect the XML version 1 recommendation. The latest version of the parser is available for download from Microsoft's MSDN site, at http://msdn.microsoft.com, and it comes built-in with the Internet Explorer browser.

❑ **Apache Xerces** — The Apache Software Foundation's Xerces subproject of the Apache XML Project (http://xml.apache.org/) has resulted in XML parsers in Java and C++, plus a Perl wrapper for the C++ parser. These tools are free, and the distribution of the code is controlled by the GNU Public License (GPL).

❑ **Expat** — Expat is an XML 1.0 parser toolkit written in C. You can find more information at http://expat.sourceforge.net. It is free for both private and commercial use.

Tags and Text and Elements, Oh My!

It's time to stop calling things just "items" and "text"; we need some names for the pieces that make up an XML document. To get cracking, let's break down the simple name.xml document we created in Chapter 1:

```
<name>
   <first>John</first>
   <middle>Fitzgerald Johansen</middle>
   <last>Doe</last>
</name>
```

The text starting with a < character and ending with a > character is an XML *tag*. The information in our document (our data) is contained within the various tags that constitute the markup of the document. This makes it easy to distinguish the *information* in the document from the *markup*.

As you can see, the tags are paired, so that any opening tag (for example, <name>) must have a closing tag (</name>). In XML parlance, these are called *start-tags* and *end-tags*. The end-tags are the same as the start-tags except that they have a / right after the opening < character.

In this regard, XML tags work the same as start-tags and end-tags in HTML. For example, you would mark a section of HTML to appear bold like this:

```
<b>This is bold.</b>
```

As you can see, there is a `<b>` start-tag, and a `</b>` end-tag, just like we use for XML.

All of the information from the beginning of a start-tag to the end of an end-tag, and including everything in between, is called an *element*. For example:

- ❑ `<first>` is a start-tag
- ❑ `</first>` is an end-tag
- ❑ `<first>John</first>` is an element

The text between the start-tag and end-tag of an element is called the *element content*. The content between tags will often just be data (as opposed to other elements). In this case, the element content is referred to as *parsed character data*, which is almost always referred to using its acronym, *PCDATA*, or with a more general term such as "text content" or even "text node."

> *Whenever you come across a strange-looking term like PCDATA, it's usually a good bet the term is inherited from SGML. Because XML is a subset of SGML, there are a lot of these inherited terms.*

The whole document, starting at `<name>` and ending at `</name>`, is also an element, which happens to include other elements (and, in this case, because it contains the entire XML document, the element is called the *root element*, which we'll talk about later).

If you wish, you can include a space before the closing > of a tag. For example, you could create markup like the following, with a space between the first `<first` and the closing tag:

```
<first >John</first>
```

or the following, with a space between both `<first` and `</first` and their closing tags:

```
<first >John</first >
```

or even

```
<first
>John</first>
```

Later you'll see where this might come in handy. You cannot, however, put a space after the opening < character in a tag, or the / character in an end-tag; the XML parser expects your element's name to come right after that < or / character. Therefore, the following is not proper XML syntax:

```
< first >John< /first >
```

Neither is this:

```
< first >John< / first >
```

To put this newfound knowledge into action, the following Try It Out shows you how to create an example that contains more information than just a name.

Try It Out   Creating a Distribution Process

The examples in this chapter refer to a fictional company, Serna Inc., which has developed a new portable music device. Serna provides a subscription service called sernaDirect that works with the devices so that the subscribers can regularly update the musical selection on their devices by downloading songs from Serna. Because Serna Inc. wishes to focus on developing its product line and building the subscription service, it has contracted another company, Ferna Distribution, to handle distribution of the products to customers. The distribution process works like this:

1. The customer calls a Ferna Distribution customer service representative (CSR) or visits the Ferna website to place an order. The customer can also change or cancel an order.

2. The order is captured into Ferna Distribution's back-end systems, and once a day a file is sent to Serna Inc., with all of the day's orders (including canceled and updated orders).

3. Once Serna Inc., has received a file, its systems are updated with the new, canceled, and updated orders. Based on this, the music for the sernaDirect subscription service can be sent to the appropriate subscribers (based on the ID of their device).

This process is illustrated in Figure 2-1.

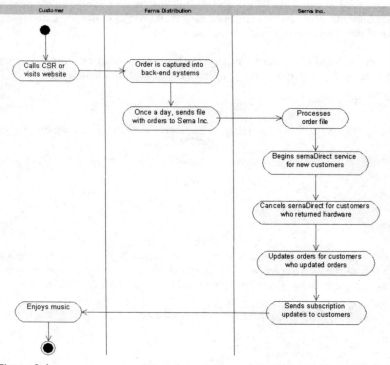

Figure 2-1

For this Try It Out, you're concerned with the file that Ferna Distribution sends to Serna each day, with the new, canceled, and updated orders. This is exactly the place where XML shines, and you'll use XML to create the daily file to Serna Inc., but before you break out Notepad and start typing, you need to know what information you're capturing.

In Chapter 1, you learned that XML is hierarchical in nature; information is structured like a tree, with parent-child relationships. This means that the order information has to be arranged in a tree structure as well:

1. Because this XML layout will contain information about orders, you need to capture information such as the customer's name and address, the type of hardware that has been purchased, information about the subscription to sernaDirect, and so on.

   Figure 2-2 shows the hierarchy you'll be creating.

   Notice that for the sake of brevity, we haven't included all of the layers of information. For example, the address will be further broken down for the address information, and the credit card element will contain child elements for the credit card information.

   Some of these elements, such as `<Date>`, will only appear once; others, such as `<Product>` or `<Order>`, might appear multiple times in the document. In addition, some will have PCDATA only, while some will include their information as child elements instead. For example, the `<Date>` element will contain PCDATA (no child elements) only: the date the order was placed. Conversely, the `<Address>` element won't contain any PCDATA of its own, but will contain child elements that further break down the information, such as `<State>` and `<City>`.

2. With this in mind, it's time to start entering XML. If you have Internet Explorer 5 or later installed on your machine, type the following into Notepad and save it to your hard drive as `order.xml`:

```
<Orders>
  <Order>
    <Type>N</Type>
    <Date>Jan 1, 2004, 14:29</Date>
    <Customer>
      <SernaDirect>
        <SubscriptionType>B</SubscriptionType>
        <SubscriptionLength>12</SubscriptionLength>
      </SernaDirect>
      <Address>
        <Address1>123 Somewhere Ave.</Address1>
        <Address2></Address2>
        <City>Some Town</City>
        <State>TA</State>
        <Zip>000000000</Zip>
      </Address>
      <CreditCard>
        <Number>4111111111111111</Number>
        <CardHolderName>John Q Public</CardHolderName>
        <Expiry>11/09</Expiry>
      </CreditCard>
      <Phone>5555555555</Phone>
      <Name>John Public</Name>
      <Email>jpublic@someprovider.com</Email>
```

```
      </Customer>
      <ID>0000000001</ID>
      <Number>x582n9</Number>
      <Products>
        <Product>
          <Model>X9</Model>
          <Price>129.95</Price>
          <ID>x9000059</ID>
        </Product>
      </Products>
    </Order>
    <Order>
      <Type>N</Type>
      <Date>Jan 1, 2004, 16:00</Date>
      <Customer>
        <SernaDirect>
          <SubscriptionType>D</SubscriptionType>
          <SubscriptionLength>12</SubscriptionLength>
        </SernaDirect>
<Address>
          <Address1>89 Subscriber's Street</Address1>
          <Address2>Box 882</Address2>
          <City>Smallville</City>
          <State>XQ</State>
          <Zip>000000000</Zip>
        </Address>
        <CreditCard>
          <Number>4512451245124512</Number>
          <CardHolderName>Helen P Someperson</CardHolderName>
          <Expiry>01/08</Expiry>
        </CreditCard>
        <Phone>5554443333</Phone>
        <Name>Helen Someperson</Name>
        <Email>helens@isp.net</Email>
      </Customer>
      <ID>0000000002</ID>
      <Number>a98f78d</Number>
      <Products>
        <Product>
          <Model>Y9</Model>
          <Price>229.95</Price>
          <ID>y9000065</ID>
        </Product>
      </Products>
    </Order>
  </Orders>
```

For the sake of brevity, we'll only enter two orders.

3. Open the file in IE. (Navigate to the file in Explorer and double-click on it, or open the browser and enter the path in the URL bar.) If you're running on Windows XP Service Pack 2 or later, Internet Explorer will pop up a security warning just below the address bar because it doesn't like opening XML files from the local file system. You can ignore this warning, or click the information bar and tell Internet Explorer to allow the blocked content. If you have typed in the tags exactly as shown, the order.xml file will look something like what is shown in Figure 2-3.

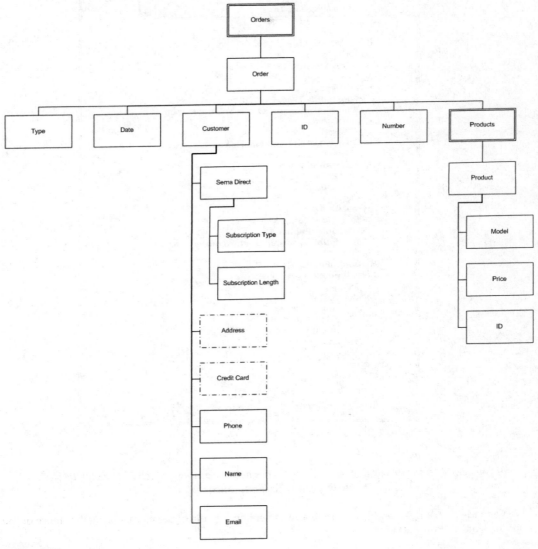

Figure 2-2

Figure 2-3

If you get IE's security warning, you'll have to click on the warning and tell IE to allow the blocked content before you'll be able to use this expand/collapse functionality.

We've made use of IE's handy collapse feature to collapse some of the elements, so that more of the document would fit on the screen.

How It Works

In this example, you created a hierarchy of information about a series of orders that have been placed through Ferna Distribution, so you name the root element accordingly: <Orders>.

Each <Order> element has children for the type of order, the date the order was placed, and the ID and number of the order (these types of systems often have multiple IDs attached to an order, as there are multiple systems dealing with it, so we added two separate numbers for realism — the `<ID>` and `<Number>` elements). There are also child elements for handling information about the customer and the products purchased by that customer.

You may have noticed that the browser changed `<Address2></Address2>` in our first order to `<Address2/>` when it displayed the information. We'll talk about this shorthand syntax a little later, but don't worry: This is called a *self-closing tag* and it's perfectly legal.

Rules for Elements

Obviously, if you could just create elements in any old way you wanted, you wouldn't be any further along than the text file examples from the previous chapter. There must be some rules for elements, which are fundamental to the understanding of XML.

> **XML documents must adhere to certain rules to be well formed.**

Here's a brief list of the rules, before getting into the details:

- ❑ Every start-tag must have a matching end-tag, or be a self-closing tag.
- ❑ Tags can't overlap; elements must be properly nested.
- ❑ XML documents can have only one root element.
- ❑ Element names must obey XML naming conventions.
- ❑ XML is case sensitive.
- ❑ XML will keep whitespace in your PCDATA.

It is these rules that make XML such a universal format for interchanging data. As long as your XML documents follow all of the rules in the XML specification, any available XML parser will be able to read the information they contain.

Every Start-Tag Must Have an End-Tag

One of the problems with parsing HTML documents is that not every element requires a start-tag and an end-tag. Take the following example:

```
<html>
<body>
<p>Here is some text in an HTML paragraph.
<br>
Here is some more text in the same paragraph.
<P>And here is some text in another HTML paragraph.</p>
</body>
</html>
```

Notice that the first `<p>` tag has no closing `</p>` tag. This is allowed in HTML, because most web browsers can figure out where the end of the paragraph should be. (In fact, years ago, this type of practice was even encouraged in some circles to reduce file size.) In this case, when the browser comes across the second <P> tag, it knows to end the first paragraph and begin a new paragraph. Then there's the <br> tag (line break), which by definition has no closing tag.

In addition, notice that the second, uppercase <P> start-tag is matched by a </p> end-tag, in lowercase. This is not a problem for HTML browsers, because HTML is not case sensitive; but as you'll soon see, this would cause a problem for an XML parser.

The problem is that this makes HTML parsers harder to write. Developers must add code to take into account all of these factors, which often makes the parsers larger and much harder to debug. What's more, the way in which files are parsed is not standardized — different browsers do it differently, leading to incompatibilities (perhaps not in this simple example, but when it comes to HTML tables, browser inconsistencies are a nightmare, and badly created HTML markup makes things much worse!).

For now, just remember that in XML the end-tag is required, and its name has to exactly match the start-tag's name.

Elements Must Be Properly Nested

Because XML is strictly hierarchical, you must be careful to close the child elements before you close their parents. (This is called *properly nesting* your tags.) Take a look at another HTML example to demonstrate this:

```
<p>Some <strong>formatted <em>text</strong>, but</em> no grammar no good!</p>
```

This would produce the output shown in Figure 2-4 on a web browser.

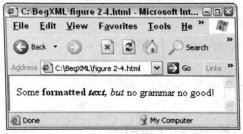

Figure 2-4

As you can see in Figure 2-4, the <strong> tags cover the text formatted text, while the <em> tags cover the text text, but. Therefore, the word text has both types of markup.

Is <em> a child of <strong>, or is <strong> a child of <em>? Or are they both siblings, and children of <p>? According to our stricter XML rules, the answer is none of the above. As written, the HTML code can't be arranged as a proper hierarchy, and therefore could not be well-formed XML.

> *Actually, in later versions of the HTML specification, the HTML example here isn't really proper HTML either; according to the HTML 4 specification, tags should not overlap like this, but web browsers will do their best to render the content anyway.*

If ever you're in doubt as to whether your XML tags are overlapping, try to rearrange them visually to be hierarchical. If the tree makes sense, then you're okay. Otherwise, you'll have to rework your markup.

For example, you could get the same effect as above with the following:

```
<p>Some <strong>formatted <em>text</em></strong><em>, but</em> no grammar no
good!</p>
```

The preceding example can be properly formatted in a tree like this:

```
<p>
  Some
  <strong>
    formatted
    <em>
      text
    </em>
  </strong>
  <em>
    , but
  </em>
  no grammar no good!
</p>
```

This example now makes it clear which elements are parents of which other elements, and to what element each piece of text belongs, which makes it properly nested. Not only is this a better way to write HTML, but it also makes the example well formed to an XML parser.

An XML Document Can Have Only One Root Element

In our <name> document from Chapter 1, the <name> element is called the *root element*. This is the top-level element in the document, and all the other elements are its children, or descendants. An XML document must have one and only one root element: In fact, it must have a root element even if it has no content.

For example, the following XML is not well formed, because it has two root elements:

```
<name>John</name>
<name>Jane</name>
```

To make this well formed, you would need to add a top-level element, like this:

```
<names>
    <name>John</name>
    <name>Jane</name>
</names>
```

Even the following is a well-formed document, because it includes one—and only one—root element:

```
<name></name>
```

While it may seem a bit of an inconvenience, it turns out that it's incredibly easy to follow this rule. If you have a document structure with multiple rootlike elements, simply create a higher-level element to contain them.

Elements Must Obey XML Naming Conventions

If you're going to be creating elements you're going to have to give them names, and XML is very generous in the names you're allowed to use. For example, there aren't any reserved words to avoid in XML, as there are in most programming languages, so you have a lot of flexibility in this regard.

However, you do need to follow some rules:

- ❑ Names can start with letters (including non-Latin characters) or the underscore (_) character, but not numbers or other punctuation characters.

- ❑ After the first character, numbers, hyphens, and periods are allowed.

- ❑ Names can't contain spaces.

- ❑ Names can't contain the colon (:) character. Strictly speaking, this character *is* allowed, but the XML specification says that it's "reserved." You should avoid using it in your documents, unless you are working with namespaces (which we'll be looking at in the next chapter).

- ❑ Names can't start with the letters xml, in uppercase, lowercase, or mixed — you can't start a name with xml, XML, XmL, or any other combination.

  Unfortunately, the XML parser shipped with Internet Explorer doesn't enforce this rule. However, even if you are using IE's XML parser, you should never name elements starting with the characters xml, *because your documents would not be considered well formed by other parsers.*

- ❑ There can't be a space after the opening < character; the name of the element must come immediately after it. However, there can be space before the closing > character, if you desire.

Here are some examples of valid names:

```
<first.name>
<résumé>
```

Following are some examples of invalid names:

```
<xml-tag>
```

which starts with xml,

```
<123>
```

which starts with a number,

```
<fun=xml>
```

because the equals sign (=) sign is illegal, and

```
<my tag>
```

which contains a space.

> Remember these rules for element names — they also apply to naming other things in XML.

Case Sensitivity

Another important point to keep in mind is that the tags in XML are *case sensitive*. (This is a big difference from HTML, which is case insensitive.) This means that `<first>` is different from `<FIRST>`, which is different from `<First>`.

This sometimes seems odd to English-speaking users of XML, as English words can easily be converted to uppercase or lowercase with no loss of meaning. In many other languages, the concept of case either is not applicable (e.g., the German "ß") or is extremely important (and the answer may differ depending on the context). Putting intelligent rules into the XML specification for converting between uppercase and lowercase (sometimes called case folding) would probably have doubled or tripled its size, and only benefited certain sections of the population. Luckily, it doesn't take long to get used to having case-sensitive names.

Our previous `<P></p>` HTML example would not work in XML. Because XML is case sensitive, an XML parser would not be able to match the `</p>` end-tag with any start-tags, and neither would it be able to match the `<P>` start-tag with any end-tags.

> Warning! Because XML is case sensitive, you could legally create an XML document that has both `<first>` and `<First>` elements, which have different meanings, but this is a bad idea and will cause nothing but confusion! You should always try to give your elements distinct names, for your sanity, and for the sanity of those who use your code.

To help combat these kinds of problems, it's a good idea to pick a naming style and stick to it. Some examples of common styles are as follows:

- ❑   `<first_name>`
- ❑   `<firstName>`
- ❑   `<first-name>`
- ❑   `<FirstName>`

Which style you choose isn't important; what is important is that you stick to it. A naming convention only helps when it's used consistently. For this book, we usually use the `<FirstName>` convention.

Whitespace in PCDATA

There is a special category of characters called *whitespace* that includes things such as the space character, new lines (what you get when you press the Enter key), and tabs. Whitespace is used to separate words, as well as to make text more readable.

Those familiar with HTML are probably quite aware of the practice of *whitespace stripping*. In HTML, any whitespace considered insignificant is stripped out of the document when it is processed. For example, take the following HTML:

```
<p>This is a paragraph.     It has a whole bunch
   of space.</p>
```

As far as HTML is concerned, anything more than a single space between the words in a `<P>` is insignificant, so all of the spaces between the first period and the word `It` would be stripped, except for one. In addition, the line feed after the word `bunch` and the spaces before `of` would be stripped down to one space. As a result, the previous HTML would be rendered in a browser as shown in Figure 2-5.

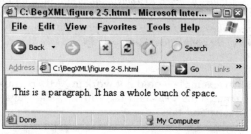

Figure 2-5

In order to get results to appear spaced as in the HTML code, you'd have to add special HTML markup to the source, like the following:

```
<p>This is a paragraph.     It has a whole
bunch<br>  of space.</p>
```

Here, ` ` signifies that we should insert a space (nbsp stands for *nonbreaking space*), and the `<br>` tag specifies that there should be a line feed. This would format the output as it appears in Figure 2-6.

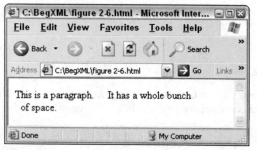

Figure 2-6

Alternatively, if you wanted to have the text displayed *exactly* as it appears in the source file, you could use the `<pre>` tag. This specifically tells the HTML parser not to strip the whitespace, but to display the text exactly as it appears in the HTML document, so you could write the following and get the desired results:

```
<pre>This is a paragraph.    It has a whole bunch
   of space.</pre>
```

This would produce output like that shown in Figure 2-7.

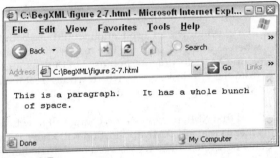

Figure 2-7

However, in most web browsers, the `<pre>` tag also has the added effect that the text is rendered in a fixed-width font, like the Courier font used for code in this book (which is why Figure 2-7 looks slightly different from Figure 2-6).

Whitespace stripping is very advantageous for a language like HTML, which is primarily a means for displaying information. It allows the source for an HTML document to be formatted in a readable way for the person writing the HTML, while displaying it formatted in a readable, and possibly quite different, way for the user who views the document in a browser.

In XML, however, no whitespace stripping takes place for PCDATA. This means that for the XML tag

```
<Tag>This is a paragraph.    It has a whole bunch
   of space.</Tag>
```

the PCDATA is

```
This is a paragraph.    It has a whole bunch
   of space.
```

Just like the second HTML example, none of the whitespace has been stripped out. As far as whitespace stripping goes, all XML elements are treated just as they are for the HTML `<pre>` tag. This makes the rules much easier to understand for XML than they are for HTML.

> **In XML, the whitespace stays.**

Unfortunately, if you view the preceding XML example in Internet Explorer, the whitespace will be stripped out — or will seem to be. This is because IE is not actually showing you the XML directly; it uses a technology called XSL to transform the XML to HTML, and it displays the HTML. Then, because IE is an HTML browser, it strips out the whitespace from that HTML!

End-of-Line Whitespace

There is one form of whitespace stripping that XML does perform on PCDATA, which is the handling of *newline* characters. The problem is that two characters are used for new lines — the *linefeed* character and the *carriage return* character — and Windows, UNIX, and Macintosh computers all use these characters differently.

For example, to get a new line in Windows, an application would use both the line feed and the carriage return character together, whereas on UNIX only the line feed would be used. This could prove to be very troublesome when creating XML documents, because UNIX machines would treat the new lines in a document differently from the Windows boxes, which would treat them differently from the Macintosh boxes, and our XML interoperability would be lost.

For this reason, it was decided that XML parsers would change all new lines to a single linefeed character before processing. This means that any XML application will know, no matter which operating system it's running under, that a new line will be represented by a single linefeed character. This makes data exchange among multiple computers running different operating systems that much easier, as programmers don't have to deal with the (sometimes annoying) end-of-line logic.

Whitespace in Markup

As well as the whitespace in your data, there could also be whitespace within an XML document that's not actually part of the data, as shown here:

```
<Tag>
  <AnotherTag>This is some XML</AnotherTag>
</Tag>
```

While any whitespace contained within `<AnotherTag>`'s PCDATA is part of the data, there is also a newline after `<Tag>`, and some spaces before `<AnotherTag>`. These spaces could be there just to make the document easier to read, while not actually being part of its data. This "readability" whitespace is called *extraneous whitespace*.

While an XML parser must pass all whitespace through to the application, it can also indicate to the application which whitespace is not actually part of an element's PCDATA but is just extraneous whitespace.

How does the parser decide whether this is extraneous whitespace or not? That depends on what kind of data you specify `<Tag>` should contain. If `<Tag>` can only contain other elements (and no PCDATA), then the whitespace will be considered extraneous. However, if `<Tag>` is allowed to contain PCDATA or mixed content, then the whitespace will be considered to be part of that PCDATA, so it will be retained.

Unfortunately, from this document alone an XML parser would have no way to tell whether `<Tag>` is supposed to contain PCDATA or not, which means that it has to assume none of the whitespace is extraneous. You'll see how to get the parser to recognize this as extraneous whitespace in Chapter 5, when we discuss content models.

In many cases, your applications won't care whether the space is there or not; the application will simply ask the parser for the data contained in the <AnotherTag> element, and won't bother to query for any PCDATA in the <Tag> element.

Attributes

In addition to tags and elements, XML documents can also include *attributes*. Attributes are simple name/value pairs associated with an element. They are attached to the start-tag, but not to the end-tag, as shown in the following code:

```
<name nickname="Shiny John">
    <first>John</first>
    <middle>Fitzgerald Johansen</middle>
    <last>Doe</last>
</name>
```

Attributes must have values — even if that value is just an empty string (such as "") — and those values must be in quotes. The following example, which is part of a common HTML tag, is not legal in XML:

```
<input checked>
```

Nor is the following legal:

```
<input checked=true>
```

Either single quotes or double quotes are fine, but they have to match. For example, to make this into well-formed XML, you can use

```
<input checked='true'>
```

or

```
<input checked="true">
```

but you can't use

```
<input checked="true'>
```

Because either single or double quotes are allowed, it's easy to include quote characters in your attribute values, such as "John's nickname" or 'I said "hi" to him'. You just have to be careful not to accidentally close your attribute, like 'John's nickname'; if an XML parser sees an attribute value like this, it will think you're closing the value at the second single quote, and will raise an error when it sees the "s" that follows right after it.

The same rules apply to naming attributes as apply to naming elements: Names are case sensitive, can't start with xml, and so on. In addition, you can't have more than one attribute with the same name on an element. For example, if you create an XML document like the following line of code, then you will get the IE5 error shown in Figure 2-8:

```
<bad att="1" att="2"></bad>
```

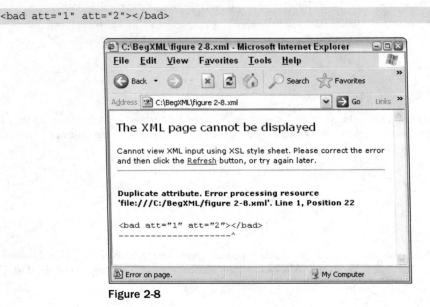

Figure 2-8

You should also be aware that the XML parser will "normalize" the data in an attribute before it passes it on to the application. In other words, it does a bit of pre-processing of the text. The most important thing done by the parser is to strip out newline characters and replace them with a single space. For example, you can write XML markup like this, with a newline in the attribute value:

```
<test myAttr='some data
goes
here'>some other data</test>
```

However, when the XML parser passes the data from the myAttr attribute back to an application, it will simply pass the data as

```
some data goes here
```

Finally, the order in which attributes are included on an element is not considered relevant. In other words, if an XML parser encounters an element like

```
<name first="John" middle="Fitzgerald Johansen" last="Doe"></name>
```

it doesn't necessarily have to give us the attributes in that order, but can do so in any order it wishes. Therefore, if information in an XML document must appear in a certain order, you should put that information into elements, rather than attributes — parsers always report elements in the order in which they appear in the document.

Try It Out   **Adding Attributes to Our Orders**

In the previous Try It Out, you entered a lot of information about the various orders captured through-out the day. However, notice that the `<Orders>` element can contain multiple `<Order>` elements, and the `<Products>` element can contain multiple `<Product>` elements. Often, programmers find it handy to include an attribute on these types of "container" elements to indicate how many items are in the list. You could get the same value by counting the child elements, but it's sometimes useful to have this as a separate piece of information, for a sanity check. In addition, both `<Order>` and `<Product>` have child elements for ID — this is often the type of information that's captured in an attribute, instead of a child element.

1.   Open your `order.xml` file created earlier, and resave it to your hard drive as `order2.xml`.

2.   With your newfound attributes knowledge, add `count` attributes to `<Orders>` and `<Products>`, and change any `<ID>` elements to an ID attribute on the parent instead. The result should look like the following (the changed lines are highlighted):

```
<Orders Count="2">
<Order ID="0000000001">
    <Type>N</Type>
    <Date>Jan 1, 2004, 14:29</Date>
    <Customer>
      <SernaDirect>
        <SubscriptionType>B</SubscriptionType>
        <SubscriptionLength>12</SubscriptionLength>
      </SernaDirect>
      <Address>
        <Address1>123 Somewhere Ave.</Address1>
        <Address2></Address2>
        <City>Some Town</City>
        <State>TA</State>
        <Zip>000000000</Zip>
      </Address>
      <CreditCard>
        <Number>4111111111111111</Number>
        <CardHolderName>John Q Public</CardHolderName>
        <Expiry>11/09</Expiry>
      </CreditCard>
      <Phone>5555555555</Phone>
      <Name>John Public</Name>
      <Email>jpublic@someprovider.com</Email>
    </Customer>
    <Number>x582n9</Number>
    <Products Count="1">
      <Product>
        <Model>X9</Model>
        <Price>129.95</Price>
        <ID>x9000059</ID>
      </Product>
```

```
        </Products>
      </Order>
      <Order ID="0000000002">
        <Type>N</Type>
        <Date>Jan 1, 2004, 16:00</Date>
        <Customer>
          <SernaDirect>
            <SubscriptionType>D</SubscriptionType>
            <SubscriptionLength>12</SubscriptionLength>
          </SernaDirect>
          <Address>
            <Address1>89 Subscriber's Street</Address1>
            <Address2>Box 882</Address2>
            <City>Smallville</City>
            <State>XQ</State>
            <Zip>000000000</Zip>
          </Address>
          <CreditCard>
            <Number>4512451245124512</Number>
            <CardHolderName>Helen P Someperson</CardHolderName>
            <Expiry>01/08</Expiry>
          </CreditCard>
          <Phone>5554443333</Phone>
          <Name>Helen Someperson</Name>
          <Email>helens@isp.net</Email>
        </Customer>
        <Number>a98f78d</Number>
        <Products Count="1">
          <Product>
            <Model>Y9</Model>
            <Price>229.95</Price>
            <ID>y9000065</ID>
          </Product>
        </Products>
      </Order>
    </Orders>
```

3. Save the file and view it in IE. It will look something like Figure 2-9.

How It Works

Using attributes, you added some extra information about the number of items contained in any "lists." Again, this is information that could easily be inferred from the content of the document, but if a list showed that it was supposed to have two elements and only one was in the document, then you'd know that you had a problem.

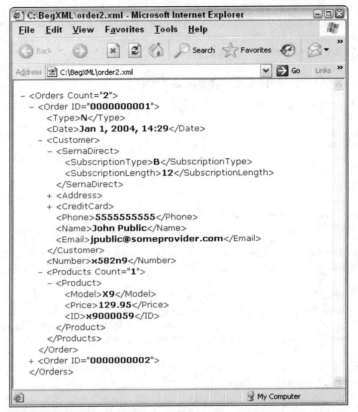

Figure 2-9

When to Use Attributes

There have been many debates in the XML community about whether attributes are really necessary, and, if so, where they should be used. The following subsections address some of the main points in that debate.

Using Attributes to Separate Different Types of Information

In the previous example, the number of `<Order>` elements under `<Orders>` isn't really part of the data you're sending, so it may make sense to make that information an attribute. This logically separates the data most applications will need from the data that most applications won't need.

In reality, there is no such thing as *pure* meta data — all information is data to *some* application. Consider HTML; you could break the information in HTML into two types of data: the data to be shown to a human and the data to be used by the web browser to format the human-readable data. From one standpoint, the data used to format the data would be meta data, but to the browser or the person writing the HTML, the meta data *is* the data. Therefore, attributes make sense when you're separating one type of information from another.

What Attributes Offer That Elements Don't

Can't elements do anything attributes can do? In other words, on the face of it, there's really no difference between

```
<name nickname='Shiny John'></name>
```

and

```
<name>
   <nickname>Shiny John</nickname>
</name>
```

In both cases, we have a child of the `<name>` element, named "nickname," with the content "Shiny John." Why bother to pollute the language with two ways of doing the same thing?

The main reason why XML was invented was because SGML could do some great things but it was too massively difficult to use without a full-fledged SGML expert on hand, so one driving concept behind XML is a kinder, gentler, simpler SGML. For this reason, many people don't like attributes, because attributes add a complexity to the language that they feel is unnecessary.

Conversely, some people find attributes easier to use — for example, they don't require nesting and you don't have to worry about crossed tags.

Why Use Elements If Attributes Use So Much Less Space?

Wouldn't it save bandwidth to use attributes instead? For example, if you were to rewrite the `<name>` document to use only attributes, it might look like the following, which takes up much less space than our earlier code using elements:

```
<name nickname='Shiny John' first='John'
  middle='Fitzgerald Johansen' last='Doe'></name>
```

However, in systems where size is really an issue, it turns out that simple compression techniques would work much better than trying to optimize the XML. Moreover, because of the way compression works, you end up with files of almost the same size regardless of whether attributes or elements are used. Besides, when you try to optimize XML this way, you lose many of the benefits XML offers, such as readability and descriptive tag names.

Elements Can Be More Complex Than Attributes

When you use attributes, you are limited to simple text as a value. However, when you use elements, your content can be as simple or as complex as you need. That is, when your data is in an element, you have room for expansion, by adding other child elements to further break down the information.

Similarly, if line endings will be important in your data, you will have to put the data into an element, rather than an attribute, because these line endings are stripped out of attribute values.

Sometimes Elements Can Get in the Way

Imagine a case where you have a `<note>` element, which contains annotations about the text in your XML document. Sometimes the note will be informational, and sometimes a warning. You could include the type of note using an element such as the following:

```
<note>
  <type>Information</type>
  This is a note.
</note>
```

or

```
<note><Information>This is a note.</Information></note>
```

However, it would probably be much less intrusive to include the information in an attribute, as shown here:

```
<note type="Information">This is a note.</note>
```

Attributes Are Unordered

As noted earlier, the order of attributes is considered irrelevant. Hence, sometimes you may need to use elements, rather than attributes, for information that must appear in the document in a certain order.

Visual Preferences

Many people have different opinions as to whether attributes or child elements "look better." The answer comes down to a matter of personal preference and style.

In fact, much of the attributes versus elements debate hinges on personal preference. Many, but not all, of the arguments boil down to "I like the one better than the other," but because XML has both elements and attributes, and neither one is going to go away, you're free to use both. Choose whichever works best for your application, whichever looks better to you, or whichever you're most comfortable with.

Comments

Using *comments,* you can insert into an XML document text that isn't really part of the document, but rather is intended for people who are reading the XML markup itself.

Anyone who has used a programming language will be familiar with the idea of comments: You want to be able to annotate your code (or your XML), so that those coming after you will be able to figure out what you were doing. (And remember: The one who comes after you may be you! Code you wrote six months ago might be as foreign to you as code someone else wrote.)

Of course, comments may not be as relevant to XML as they are to programming languages; after all, this is just data, and it's self-describing to boot. Still, you never know when they're going to come in handy, and there are cases where comments can be very useful, even in data.

Comments start with the string <!--and end with the string -->, as shown here:

```
<name nickname='Shiny John'>
  <first>John</first>
<!--John lost his middle name in a fire-->
  <middle></middle>
  <last>Doe</last>
</name>
```

Note a couple of points about comments. First, you can't have a comment inside a tag, so the following is illegal:

```
<middle></middle> <!--John lost his middle name in a fire--> >
```

Second, you can't use the double-dash string (--) inside a comment, so the following is also illegal:

```
<!--John lost his middle name -- in a fire-->
```

The XML specification states that an XML parser doesn't need to pass these comments on to the application, meaning that you should never count on being able to use the information inside a comment from your application. Comments are only there for the benefit of someone reading your XML markup.

> **HTML programmers have often used the trick of inserting scripting code in comments, to protect users with older browsers that didn't support the <script> tag. That kind of trick can't be used in XML, as comments won't necessarily be available to the application. Therefore, if you have data that you need to get at later from your applications, put it in an element or an attribute!**

Try It Out   Some Comments on Our Orders

The type of distribution system we're working with can be very complicated. In this example, you'll add some comments to your order XML to clarify how and why you've structured some of the data the way you have:

1. Open your order2.xml file, make the following changes, and save the modified XML file as order3.xml:

```
<Orders Count="2">
  <Order ID="0000000001">
    <Type>N</Type>
    <!--Indicates the type of order: N(ew), C(ancel), or U(pdate)-->
    <Date>Jan 1, 2004, 14:29</Date>
    <!--we're only capturing order date, but often systems will capture
    a separate shipment date as well-->
    <Customer>
```

```xml
    <SernaDirect>
      <SubscriptionType>B</SubscriptionType>
      <!--Type of subscription: B(asic) or D(eluxe)-->
      <SubscriptionLength>12</SubscriptionLength>
      <!--length of subscription in months-->
    </SernaDirect>
    <Address>
    <!--systems often require separate Home, Billing, and Delivery
    addresses, but for the sake of simplicity we're only capturing one-->
      <Address1>123 Somewhere Ave.</Address1>
      <Address2></Address2>
      <City>Some Town</City>
      <State>TA</State>
      <Zip>000000000</Zip>
    </Address>
    <CreditCard>
      <Number>4111111111111111</Number>
      <CardHolderName>John Q Public</CardHolderName>
      <Expiry>11/09</Expiry>
    </CreditCard>
    <Phone>5555555555</Phone>
    <!--systems often require separate home and business #'s, but we're
    only capturing the one-->
    <Name>John Public</Name>
    <Email>jpublic@someprovider.com</Email>
  </Customer>
  <Number>x582n9</Number>
  <!--in this type of distributed system, there are often multiple
  ID's/numbers associated with an order, because of the multiple
  back-end systems involved-->
  <Products Count="1">
   <Product>
      <Model>X9</Model>
      <Price>129.95</Price>
      <ID>x9000059</ID>
   </Product>
  </Products>
</Order>
<Order ID="0000000002">
  <Type>N</Type>
  <Date>Jan 1, 2004, 16:00</Date>
  <Customer>
    <SernaDirect>
      <SubscriptionType>D</SubscriptionType>
      <SubscriptionLength>12</SubscriptionLength>
    </SernaDirect>
    <Address>
      <Address1>89 Subscriber's Street</Address1>
      <Address2>Box 882</Address2>
      <City>Smallville</City>
      <State>XQ</State>
      <Zip>000000000</Zip>
    </Address>
    <CreditCard>
```

```
          <Number>4512451245124512</Number>
          <CardHolderName>Helen P Someperson</CardHolderName>
          <Expiry>01/08</Expiry>
        </CreditCard>
        <Phone>5554443333</Phone>
        <Name>Helen Someperson</Name>
        <Email>helens@isp.net</Email>
      </Customer>
      <Number>a98f78d</Number>
      <Products Count="1">
        <Product>
          <Model>Y9</Model>
          <Price>229.95</Price>
          <ID>y9000065</ID>
        </Product>
      </Products>
    </Order>
  </Orders>
```

2. Figure 2-10 shows the new document in IE.

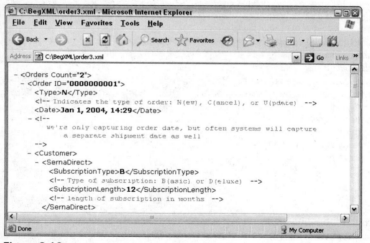

Figure 2-10

How It Works

With the new comments, anyone who reads the source for your XML document will be able to learn a bit more about how to create their own order file. This particular XML document might be used as a sample document that can be sent to new distributors as they begin working with Serna Inc.

In this example, the XML parser included with IE *does* pass comments up to the application, so the browser has displayed your comments; but remember that for all intents and purposes, this information is only available to people reading the source file. The information in comments *may or may not* be passed up to your application, depending on which parser you're using. You can't count on it, unless you specifically choose a parser that does pass them through.

If a developer uses this XML document as a sample and forgets to delete the comments before sending it to Serna it won't matter. They'll be in the document, but they won't actually be part of the document's data, so they won't do any harm.

Empty Elements

Sometimes an element has no PCDATA. Recall our earlier example in which the `<middle>` element contained no name:

```
<name nickname='Shiny John'>
  <first>John</first>
  <!--John lost his middle name in a fire-->
  <middle></middle>
  <last>Doe</last>
</name>
```

In this case, you also have the option of writing this element using the special *empty element* syntax (this syntax is also called a *self-closing tag*):

```
<middle/>
```

This is the one case where a start-tag doesn't need a separate end-tag, because they are combined into this one tag. In all other cases, you must have both tags.

Recall from our discussion of elements that the only place you can have a space within the tag is before the closing >. This rule is slightly different when it comes to empty elements. The / and > characters always have to be together, so you can create an empty element like this

```
<middle />
```

or this

```
<middle/>
```

but not like this

```
<middle/ >
```

or this

```
<middle / >
```

Empty elements really don't buy you anything—except that they take less typing—so you can use them or not at your discretion. Keep in mind, however, that as far as XML is concerned, `<middle></middle>` is *exactly* the same as `<middle/>`; for this reason, XML parsers will sometimes change your XML from one form to the other. You should never count on your empty elements being in one form or the other, but since they're syntactically exactly the same, it doesn't matter. (This is why Internet Explorer felt free to change our earlier `<Address2></Address2>` syntax to just `<Address2/>`.)

Interestingly, the XML community doesn't seem to mind the empty element syntax, even though it doesn't add anything to the language. This is especially interesting considering the passionate debates that have taken place regarding whether attributes are really necessary.

One place where empty elements are very often used is for elements that have no (or optional) PCDATA, but instead have all of their data contained in attributes. For example, if we rewrote our `<name>` example without child elements, instead of a start-tag and end-tag we would probably use an empty element, like this:

```
<name first="John" middle="Fitzgerald Johansen" last="Doe"/>
```

Or, for readability, XML authors will often write the XML like this:

```
<name first="John"
      middle="Fitzgerald Johansen"
      last="Doe"
      />
```

Another common example is the case where just the element name is enough; for instance, the HTML `<br>` tag would be converted to an XML empty element, such as the XHTML `<br/>` tag. (XHTML is the latest XML-compliant version of HTML and is discussed in Chapter 18.)

XML Declarations

It is often very handy to be able to identify a document as being of a certain type. On computers running Windows, giving a file an extension of `.xml` identifies the file as an XML file to Windows, but on other operating systems this will not work. In addition, you might want the flexibility of creating XML files with other extensions.

XML provides the *XML declaration* to label documents as being XML, along with giving the parsers a few other pieces of information. You don't need to have an XML declaration — a parser can usually tell a document is XML without it — but it's considered good practice to include it. A typical XML declaration looks like this:

```
<?xml version='1.0' encoding='UTF-16' standalone='yes'?>
<name nickname='Shiny John'>
  <first>John</first>
  <!--John lost his middle name in a fire-->
  <middle/>
  <last>Doe</last>
</name>
```

Note the following about the XML declaration:

❑   The XML declaration starts with the characters `<?xml` and ends with the characters `?>`.

❑   If you include a declaration, you must include the `version`, but the `encoding` and `standalone` attributes are optional.

❑   The `version`, `encoding`, and `standalone` attributes must be in that order.

❑ The version should be 1.0 or 1.1, as outlined below.

❑ The XML declaration must be right at the beginning of the file. That is, the first character in the file should be that <; no line breaks or spaces. Some parsers are more forgiving about this than others.

For example, an XML declaration can be as full as the previous one or as simple as the following:

```
<?xml version='1.0'?>
```

The next two sections describe more fully the encoding and standalone attributes of the XML declaration.

Version

The version attribute specifies which version of the XML specification the document adheres to. There are two versions of the XML specification, 1.0 and 1.1, so when you're using this attribute, it must be set to either 1.0 or 1.1:

```
<?xml version="1.0"?>
```

or

```
<?xml version="1.1"?>
```

If a browser comes across a document with a version it doesn't recognize, it will simply reject the document and stop processing it.

These versions of the XML specification are virtually the same, except regarding how certain Unicode characters are treated for the purpose of naming elements, and how end-of-line characters are treated on certain mainframe systems.

The Unicode *character code is discussed in the next section.*

At the time this edition of the book was printed, the 1.1 version of XML was very new, and most parsers didn't yet support it. Therefore, unless you're working with some Unicode data that just won't work under the 1.0 specification, you should always specify 1.0 for the version.

If you really need the changes in the XML 1.1 specification, make sure that your XML parser supports it. In addition, if you'll be exchanging XML documents with others, then you need to make sure that their XML parsers support XML 1.1 too, or you'll have interoperability issues.

Encoding

It should come as no surprise that text is stored in computers using numbers, since 1s and 0s are all that computers really understand. A *character code* is a one-to-one mapping between a set of characters and the corresponding numbers to represent those characters. *Character encoding* is the method used to represent the numbers in a character code digitally (in other words, how many bytes should be used for each number, and so on).

One character code that you might have come across is the *American Standard Code for Information Interchange (ASCII)*. In ASCII, for example, the lowercase character "a" is represented by the number 97, and the uppercase character "A" is represented by the number 65.

There are 7-bit and 8-bit ASCII encoding schemes. 7-bit ASCII uses 7 bits for each character, which limits it to 128 different values, while 8-bit ASCII uses one full byte (8 bits) for each character, which limits it to 256 different values. 7-bit ASCII is a much more universal standard for text, while there are a number of 8-bit ASCII character codes — which were created to add additional characters not covered by ASCII — such as ISO-8859-1. Each 8-bit ASCII encoding scheme might have slightly different sets of characters represented, and those characters might map to different numbers. However, the first 128 characters are always the same as the 7-bit ASCII character code.

ASCII can easily handle all of the characters needed for English, which is why it was the predominant character encoding used on personal computers in the English-speaking world for many years. Of course, there are many more than 256 characters in all of the world's languages, so obviously ASCII (or any other 8-bit encoding limited to 256 characters) can only handle a small subset of these. This is why Unicode was invented.

When it comes to the ASCII character set, the question of encoding is very simple: Characters each require exactly one byte of storage. For 7-bit ASCII, the eighth bit in the byte is not used.

Unicode

Unicode is a character code designed from the ground up with internationalization in mind, aiming to include enough possible characters to cover all of the characters in any human language. There are two major character encodings for Unicode: *UTF-16* and *UTF-8*. UTF-16 takes the easy way, simply using two bytes for every character (2 bytes = 16 bits = 65,356 possible values).

UTF-8 is more clever: It uses one byte for the characters covered by 7-bit ASCII and then uses some tricks so that any other characters may be represented by two or more bytes. This means that 7-bit ASCII text can actually be considered a subset of UTF-8, and processed as such. For text written in English, for which most or all of the characters would fit into the ASCII 7-bit character encoding, UTF-8 will result in smaller file sizes (because each character requires only one byte), but for text in other languages, UTF-16 can be smaller (because UTF-8 can require three or more bytes for some characters, whereas UTF-16 would only require two).

Because of the work done with Unicode to make it international, the XML specification states that all XML processors must use Unicode internally. Unfortunately, very few of the documents in the world are encoded in Unicode. Most are encoded in ISO-8859-1, or Windows-1252, or EBCDIC (used very commonly in mainframe computers), or one of a large number of other character codes. (Many of these character codes, such as ISO-8859-1 and Windows-1252, are actually 8-bit ASCII character codes. They are not, however, subsets of UTF-8 in the same way that "pure" 7-bit ASCII is.)

Specifying a Character Encoding for XML

This is where the `encoding` attribute in an XML declaration comes in. It allows you to specify to the XML parser what character encoding your text is in. The XML parser can then read the document in the proper encoding and translate it into Unicode characters internally. If no encoding is specified, UTF-8 or UTF-16 is assumed (parsers must support at least UTF-8 and UTF-16). If no encoding is specified and the document is not UTF-8 or UTF-16, the parser raises an error.

That said, sometimes an XML processor is allowed to ignore the encoding specified in the XML declaration. If the document is being sent via a network protocol such as HTTP, protocol-specific headers may specify a different encoding than the one specified in the document. In such a case, the HTTP header would take precedence over the encoding specified in the XML declaration. However, if there are no external sources for the encoding, and the encoding specified is different from the actual encoding of the document, an error results.

If you're running Windows XP, Notepad gives you the option of saving your text files in Unicode, in which case you can omit the `encoding` attribute in your XML declarations (see Figure 2-11).

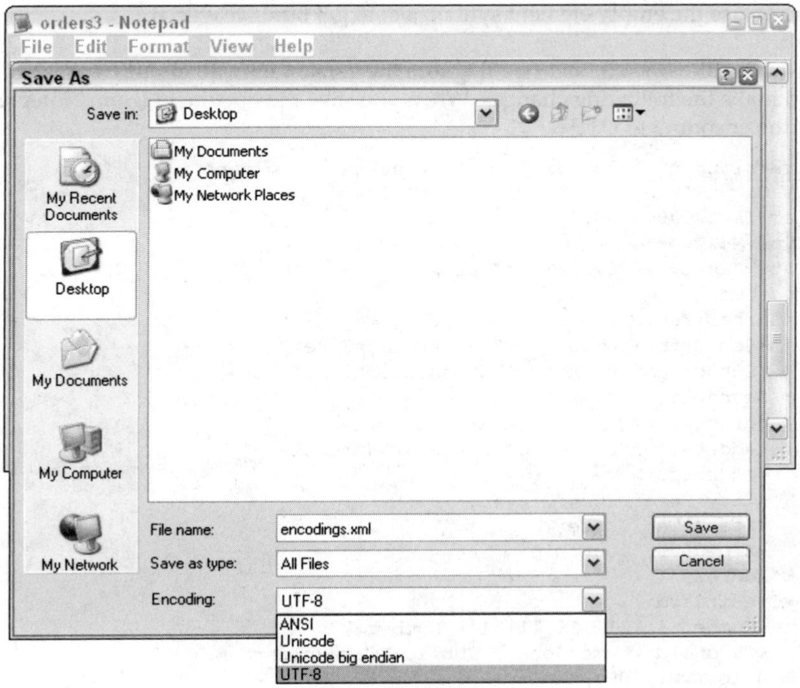

Figure 2-11

In this case, your best bet is to save the document using the UTF-8 encoding and specify it as such in the XML declaration.

Standalone

If the `standalone` attribute is included in the XML declaration, it must be set to either `yes` or `no`:

- ❑ yes specifies that the document exists entirely on its own, without depending on any other files.
- ❑ no indicates that the document may depend on an external DTD (DTDs are covered in Chapter 4).

This little attribute actually has its own name: the *Standalone Document Declaration*, or *SDD*. The XML Recommendation doesn't actually require a parser to do anything with the SDD. It is considered more of a hint to the parser than anything else.

It's time to take a look at how the XML declaration works in practice.

Try It Out   Declaring Our Orders to the World

In this example, you declare your XML document so that any parsers can immediately determine what it is. In addition, while you're at it, you should take care of any elements that don't have any content, and change them to use the empty element syntax, just to get familiar with it.

1.   Open the file `order2.xml` (we'll ignore the version with all of our comments, to reduce clutter), and make the following changes. When you save the document (from Notepad) make sure you set the encoding to UTF-8.

```xml
<?xml version="1.0" encoding="UTF-8" standalone="yes"?>
<Orders Count="2">
  <Order ID="0000000001">
    <Type>N</Type>
    <Date>Jan 1, 2004, 14:29</Date>
    <Customer>
      <SernaDirect>
        <SubscriptionType>B</SubscriptionType>
        <SubscriptionLength>12</SubscriptionLength>
      </SernaDirect>
      <Address>
        <Address1>123 Somewhere Ave.</Address1>
        <Address2/>
        <City>Some Town</City>
        <State>TA</State>
        <Zip>000000000</Zip>
      </Address>
      <CreditCard>
        <Number>4111111111111111</Number>
        <CardHolderName>John Q Public</CardHolderName>
        <Expiry>11/09</Expiry>
      </CreditCard>
      <Phone>5555555555</Phone>
      <Name>John Public</Name>
      <Email>jpublic@someprovider.com</Email>
    </Customer>
    <Number>x582n9</Number>
    <Products Count="1">
      <Product>
        <Model>X9</Model>
        <Price>129.95</Price>
        <ID>x9000059</ID>
      </Product>
    </Products>
  </Order>
  <Order ID="0000000002">
    <Type>N</Type>
    <Date>Jan 1, 2004, 16:00</Date>
    <Customer>
```

```
      <SernaDirect>
        <SubscriptionType>D</SubscriptionType>
        <SubscriptionLength>12</SubscriptionLength>
      </SernaDirect>
      <Address>
        <Address1>89 Subscriber's Street</Address1>
        <Address2>Box 882</Address2>
        <City>Smallville</City>
        <State>XQ</State>
        <Zip>000000000</Zip>
      </Address>
      <CreditCard>
        <Number>4512451245124512</Number>
        <CardHolderName>Helen P Someperson</CardHolderName>
        <Expiry>01/08</Expiry>
      </CreditCard>
      <Phone>5554443333</Phone>
      <Name>Helen Someperson</Name>
      <Email>helens@isp.net</Email>
    </Customer>
    <Number>a98f78d</Number>
    <Products Count="1">
      <Product>
        <Model>Y9</Model>
        <Price>229.95</Price>
        <ID>y9000065</ID>
      </Product>
    </Products>
  </Order>
</Orders>
```

2. Save the file as `order4.xml` and view it in IE, shown in Figure 2-12.

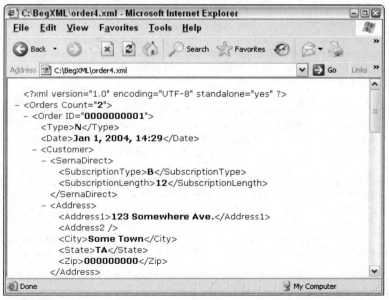

Figure 2-12

How It Works

With your new XML declaration, any XML parser can tell right away that it is indeed dealing with an XML document, and that the document is claiming to conform to version 1.0 of the XML Recommendation.

Furthermore, the document indicates that it is encoded using UTF-8 character encoding. In addition, because the Standalone Document Declaration declares that this is a standalone document, the parser knows that this one file is all that it needs to fully process the information.

Finally, because the address for the first order has no information in the <Address2> element, the syntax has been changed to the empty element syntax. Remember, though, that to the parser <Address2/> is exactly the same as <Address2></Address2>, which is why this part of your document looks the same in the browser as it did in the earlier screenshots.

Processing Instructions

Although it isn't all that common, sometimes you need to embed application-specific instructions into your information to affect how it will be processed. XML provides a mechanism to allow this, called *processing instructions* or *PIs*. These PIs enable you to enter instructions into your XML that are not part of the data of the document, but which are passed up to the application, as shown in the following code:

```
<?xml version='1.0'?>
<name nickname='Shiny John'>
  <first>John</first>
  <!--John lost his middle name in a fire-->
  <middle/>
  <?nameprocessor PRINT nickname?>
  <last>Doe</last>
</name>
```

There aren't really a lot of rules regarding PIs. They're basically just a <? followed by the name of the application that is supposed to receive the PI (the *PITarget*). The rest, up until the ending ?>, is whatever you want the instruction to be. The PITarget is bound by the same naming rules as elements and attributes, so in this example the PITarget is nameprocessor, and the actual text of the PI (the instructions) is PRINT nickname.

PIs are pretty rare, and are often frowned upon in the XML community, especially when used frivolously. Nonetheless, if you have a valid reason to use them, then go for it. For example, PIs can be an excellent place to put the kind of information (such as scripting code) that in HTML is put in comments. While you can't assume that comments will be passed on to the application, PIs always are.

This may leave you wondering whether the XML declaration is a processing instruction. At first glance, you might think that the XML declaration is a PI that starts with xml. It uses the same <? ?> notation, and provides instructions to the parser (but not the application). Is it a PI?

Actually, no: The XML declaration isn't a PI, but in most cases it really doesn't make any difference whether it is or not. The only places where you'll get into trouble are the following:

❑ **Trying to get the text of the XML declaration from an XML parser** — Some parsers erroneously treat the XML declaration as a PI and will pass it on as if it were, but most will not. In most cases, your application will never need the information in the XML declaration; that information is only for the parser. (Even the character encoding shouldn't matter to your application, because by the time the parser passes on the text, it will be Unicode, regardless of what encoding was originally used in the document.) One notable exception might be an application that wants to display an XML document to a user, in the way that we're using Internet Explorer to display the documents in this book.

❑ **Including an XML declaration somewhere other than at the beginning of an XML document** — Although you can put a PI anywhere you want, an XML declaration must appear at the beginning of a file.

Try It Out   **An Order to Be Processed**

Just to see what it looks like, try adding a processing instruction to your order XML:

1. Make the following changes to `order4.xml`, and save the new file as `order5.xml`:

```
<?xml version="1.0"?>
<Orders Count="2">
  <Order ID="0000000001">
    <?SernaProcessor ManualIntervention reason:Insufficient Funds?>
    <Type>N</Type>
    <Date>Jan 1, 2004, 14:29</Date>
    <Customer>
      <SernaDirect>
        <SubscriptionType>B</SubscriptionType>
        <SubscriptionLength>12</SubscriptionLength>
      </SernaDirect>
      <Address>
        <Address1>123 Somewhere Ave.</Address1>
        <Address2/>
        <City>Some Town</City>
        <State>TA</State>
        <Zip>000000000</Zip>
      </Address>
      <CreditCard>
        <Number>4111111111111111</Number>
        <CardHolderName>John Q Public</CardHolderName>
        <Expiry>11/09</Expiry>
      </CreditCard>
      <Phone>5555555555</Phone>
      <Name>John Public</Name>
      <Email>jpublic@someprovider.com</Email>
    </Customer>
    <Number>x582n9</Number>
    <Products Count="1">
      <Product>
        <Model>X9</Model>
        <Price>129.95</Price>
        <ID>x9000059</ID>
      </Product>
```

```
      </Products>
    </Order>
    <Order ID="0000000002">
      <Type>N</Type>
      <Date>Jan 1, 2004, 16:00</Date>
      <Customer>
        <SernaDirect>
          <SubscriptionType>D</SubscriptionType>
          <SubscriptionLength>12</SubscriptionLength>
        </SernaDirect>
        <Address>
          <Address1>89 Subscriber's Street</Address1>
          <Address2>Box 882</Address2>
          <City>Smallville</City>
          <State>XQ</State>
          <Zip>000000000</Zip>
        </Address>
        <CreditCard>
          <Number>4512451245124512</Number>
          <CardHolderName>Helen P Someperson</CardHolderName>
          <Expiry>01/08</Expiry>
        </CreditCard>
        <Phone>5554443333</Phone>
        <Name>Helen Someperson</Name>
        <Email>helens@isp.net</Email>
      </Customer>
      <Number>a98f78d</Number>
      <Products Count="1">
        <Product>
          <Model>Y9</Model>
          <Price>229.95</Price>
          <ID>y9000065</ID>
        </Product>
      </Products>
    </Order>
  </Orders>
```

2. In IE, the result looks like Figure 2-13.

How It Works

For this example, you are targeting a *fictional* application called SernaProcessor, and giving it the instruction ManualIntervention reason:Insufficient Funds. The instruction has no meaning in the context of the XML itself, only to the SernaProcessor application, so it's up to the SernaProcessor to do something meaningful with it.

In addition, because your document is UTF-8 (which the parser can infer), and because the SDD isn't doing too much, you shortened the XML declaration to the shorter syntax.

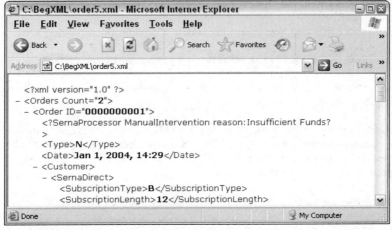

Figure 2-13

Illegal PCDATA Characters

There are some reserved characters that you can't include in your PCDATA because they are used in XML syntax: the < and & characters:

```
<!--This is not well-formed XML!-->
<comparison>6 is < 7 & 7 > 6</comparison>
```

Viewing the preceding XML in Internet Explorer results in the error shown in Figure 2-14.

Figure 2-14

Even if the parser had gotten past this, the same error would have occurred at the & character.

This error may seem confusing, but it could be worse. Consider the following XML:

```
<blah>Some <text in an element</blah>
```

In this case, an error would still be raised, but the error message would read "Missing equals sign between attribute and attribute value."

The reason for this strange error message is that the XML parser comes across the < character and expects a tag name. In the first document it found a space, which is not allowed, and in the second example it thought that text was the tag name, but then assumed that in was an attribute and expected to find an equals sign for the attribute's value.

All of this means that you can't put raw < or & characters into PCDATA. (Why & characters can't be included will become evident when the syntax for escaping characters is covered in the next section.) There are two ways you can get around this: *escaping characters*, or enclosing text in a *CDATA section*.

Escaping Characters

To escape the < or & characters, you simply replace any < character with < and any & character with &. (In addition, you can also escape the > character with >. It isn't necessary, but it does make things more consistent, as you need to escape all of the < characters.) The previous XML example could be made well formed by doing the following:

```
<comparison>6 is &lt; 7 &amp; 7 &gt; 6 </comparison>
```

This displays properly in the browser, as shown in Figure 2-15.

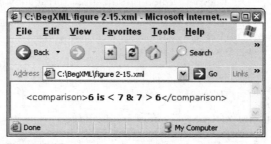

Figure 2-15

Notice that IE's XML parser is showing the un-escaped characters when it displays the document; in other words, it replaces the <, &, and > strings with <, &, and > characters. This is because the content of the <comparison> element really *is* 6 is < 7 & 7 > 6 — we had to escape the < and & characters so as not to confuse the parser, but once the parser has read in the markup, it knows the real content of the PCDATA.

< and & are known as *entity references*. The following entities are defined in XML:

❑   & — the & character

❑   < — the < character

❑   > — the > character

❑   ' — the ' character

❑   " — the " character

Other characters can also be escaped by using *character references*. These are strings such as &#nnn;, where nnn would be replaced by the Unicode number of the character you want to insert. (Or &#x nnn; with an x preceding the number, where nnn is a hexadecimal representation of the Unicode character you want to insert. All of the characters in the Unicode specification are specified using hexadecimal, so allowing the hexadecimal numbers in XML means that XML authors don't have to convert back and forth between hexadecimal and decimal.)

Escaping characters in this way can be quite handy if you are authoring documents in XML that use characters your XML editor doesn't understand, or can't output, because the characters escaped are *always* Unicode characters, regardless of the encoding being used for the document. As an example, you could include the copyright symbol ((c)) in an XML document by inserting © or ©.

CDATA Sections

If you have a lot of < and & characters that need escaping, you may find that your document quickly becomes very ugly and unreadable with all of those entity references. Luckily, there are also *CDATA sections*. Recall that CDATA is another inherited term from SGML; it stands for character data. Using CDATA sections, you can tell the XML parser not to parse the text, but to let it all go by until it gets to the end of the section. CDATA sections look like this:

```
<comparison><![CDATA[6 is < 7 & 7 > 6]]></comparison>
```

Everything starting after the <![CDATA[and ending at the]]> is ignored by the parser, and passed through to the application as is.

Unfortunately, the CDATA syntax introduces another complexity to XML markup: The character sequence]]> is not allowed, either in a CDATA section or out. If you really needed to have those three characters together, you'd have to use this:

```
]]&gt;
```

In these trivial cases, CDATA sections may look more confusing than the escaping did, but in other cases it can turn out to be more readable. For example, consider the following example, which uses a CDATA section to keep an XML parser from parsing a section of JavaScript:

```
<script language='JavaScript'><![CDATA[
function myFunc()
{
    if(0 < 1 && 1 < 2)
        alert("Hello");
}
]]></script>
```

Figure 2-16 shows how this displays in IE5 or later browsers.

Figure 2-16

Notice the vertical line at the left-hand side of the CDATA section. This indicates that although the CDATA section is indented for readability, the actual data itself starts at that vertical line. You can visually see exactly what whitespace is included in the CDATA section.

If you're familiar with JavaScript, you'll probably find the `if` statement much easier to read than the following:

```
if(0 &lt; 1 &amp;&amp; 1 &lt; 2)
```

Try It Out   Talking about HTML in XML

Suppose you want to create XML documentation to describe some of the various HTML tags in existence. You might develop a simple document type such as the following:

```
<HTML-Doc>
  <tag>
    <tag-name></tag-name>
    <description></description>
    <example></example>
  </tag>
</HTML-Doc>
```

In this case, you know that your `<example>` element will need to include HTML syntax, meaning that a lot of < characters are included. This makes `<example>` the perfect place to use a CDATA section, so that you don't have to search through all of your HTML code looking for illegal characters. This way you can include text like `<html>` and have the parser simply treat that as six characters, rather than as a tag. To demonstrate, let's document a couple of HTML tags:

1. Create a new file (or just open Notepad) and type this code:

```
<HTML-Doc>
  <tag>
    <tag-name>p</tag-name>
    <description>Paragraph</description>
    <example><![CDATA[
<p>Paragraphs can contain <em>other</em> tags.</p>
]]></example>
  </tag>
  <tag>
    <tag-name>html</tag-name>
    <description>HTML root element</description>
    <example><![CDATA[
<html>
<head><title>Sample HTML</title></head>
<body>
<p>Stuff goes here</p>
</body>/html>
]]></example>
  </tag>
  <!--more tags to follow...-->
</HTML-Doc>
```

2. Save this document as `html-doc.xml` and view it in IE5 or later (see Figure 2-17).

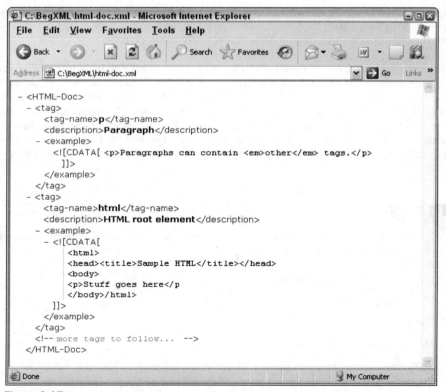

Figure 2-17

How It Works

Because of your CDATA sections, you can put whatever you want into the `<example>` elements, and not have to worry about the text being mixed up with the actual XML markup of the document. This means that even though there are typos in the second `<example>` element (the `</p` is missing the `>` and `/html>` is missing a `<`), your XML is not affected.

Errors in XML

In addition to specifying how a parser should get the information from an XML document, the XML Recommendation also specifies how a parser should deal with errors in XML. Two types of errors are defined: *errors* and *fatal errors*.

❑ An error is simply a violation of the rules in the recommendation, where the results are undefined; the XML processor is allowed to recover from the error and continue processing.

❑ Fatal errors are more serious: According to the recommendation, a parser is *not allowed to continue as normal* when it encounters a fatal error. (It may, however, keep processing the XML document to search for further errors.) This is called *draconian error handling*. Any error that causes an XML document to cease being well formed is a fatal error.

The reason for this drastic handling of non-well–formed XML is simple: It would be hard for parser writers to try to handle "well-formedness" errors, and it is extremely simple to make XML well formed. (Web browsers don't force documents to be as strict as XML does, but this is one of the reasons why web browsers are so incompatible; they must deal with *all* the errors they may encounter, and try to figure out what the person who wrote the document was really trying to code.)

Draconian error handling doesn't just benefit the parser writers; it also benefits us when we're creating XML documents. If you write an XML document that doesn't properly follow XML's syntax, you can find your mistake right away and fix it. Conversely, if the XML parser tried to recover from these errors, it might misinterpret what you were trying to do, but you wouldn't know about it because no error would be raised. In this case, bugs in your software would be much harder to track down, instead of being caught right at the beginning when you were creating your data. Even worse, if you sent your XML document to someone else, his or her parser might interpret the mistake differently.

Summary

This chapter has provided you with the basic syntax for writing well-formed XML documents. Highlighted in the chapter were the following:

❑ Elements and empty elements

❑ How to deal with whitespace in XML

❑ Attributes

❑ How to include comments

❑ XML declarations and encodings

❑   Processing instructions

❑   Entity references, character references, and CDATA sections

You've also learned why the strict rules of XML grammar actually benefit you in the long run, as they force you to catch your errors sooner rather than later, and how some of the rules for authoring HTML are different from the rules for authoring well-formed XML.

In the next chapter you'll learn about a very important part of XML: namespaces.

Exercise Questions

Suggested solutions to these questions can be found in Appendix A.

Question 1

For the addresses in our Order XML, we used a common format of "Address Line 1, Address Line 2, City, State, and Zip Code." Other applications need to be stricter with their addresses, and have separate elements for street number, street name, and so on. Rewrite the last version of the Order XML using the following information, instead of the Address Line 1/Address Line 2 format:

❑   Street number

❑   Street name

❑   Apt. number

❑   City

❑   State

❑   Zip code

❑   Additional Information

Question 2

Sometimes the syntax used by XML can be a little troublesome to figure out. The following XML document contains a few syntactical errors, preventing it from being well formed. Correct them so that the document can be read by IE.

Hint: When I'm trying to correct a file like this, I often open it in the browser and fix errors as the browser reports them to me. Be warned—some of the errors are a bit more difficult to figure out than others.

```
<?xml version="1"?>
<document>
  <--There are a couple of problems with this document.-->
  <Information>This document
  contains some < bold>information</bold>. Once
  it's corrected, it can be read by a parser.</Information>
</Document>
```

XML Namespaces

You have seen why XML provides some benefits over binary formats and can now create well-formed XML documents. At some point, however, your applications will become more complex, and you will need to combine elements from various document types into one XML document.

Unfortunately, two document types often have elements with the same name, but with different meanings and semantics. This chapter introduces *XML namespaces*, the means by which you can differentiate elements and attributes of different XML document types from each other when combining them into other documents, or even when processing multiple documents simultaneously.

In this chapter, you will learn the following:

- ❑ Why you need namespaces
- ❑ What namespaces are, conceptually, and how they solve the problem of naming clashes
- ❑ The syntax for using namespaces in XML documents
- ❑ What is a URI, a URL, and a URN

Why We Need Namespaces

Because of the nature of XML, it is possible for any company or individual to create XML document types that describe the world in their own terms. If your company feels that an <order> should contain a certain set of information, while another company feels that it should contain a different set of information, both companies can go ahead and create different document types to describe that information. Both companies can even use the name <order> for entirely different uses if desired.

However, if everyone is creating personalized XML vocabularies, you'll soon run into a problem: Only so many words are available in human languages, and a lot of them are going to be snapped up by people defining document types. How can you define a <title> element to be used to denote the title in a person's name (such as Dr. or Mrs.) when XHTML already has a `<title>` element used to describe the title of an HTML document? How can you then further distinguish those two `<title>` elements from the title of a book?

If all of these documents were to be kept separate, this still would not be a problem. If you saw a `<title>` element in an XHTML document, you'd know what kind of title it referred to, and if you saw one in your own proprietary XML document type, you'd know what that meant too. Unfortunately, life isn't always that simple, and eventually you'll need to combine various XML elements from different document types into one XML document. For example, you might create an XML document type containing information about a person, including that person's title, but also containing the person's résumé, in XHTML form. Such a document may look similar to this:

```
<?xml version="1.0"?>
<person>
  <name>
    <title>Sir</title>
    <first>John</first>
    <middle>Fitzgerald Johansen</middle>
    <last>Doe</last>
  </name>
  <position>Vice President of Marketing</position>
  <résumé>
    <html>
    <head><title>Resume of John Doe</title></head>
    <body>
      <h1>John Doe</h1>
      <p>John's a great guy, you know?</p>
    </body>
    </html>
  </résumé>
</person>
```

If you want to type this XML into Notepad and view the results in IE, remember to save the document using an appropriate encoding, such as Unicode or UTF-8. The "é" characters in the `<résumé>` element are not part of the basic ASCII character set, so they'll cause problems for the XML parser when it tries to read the document if it doesn't have an appropriate character set to work with. However, if the document is saved as one of the Unicode encodings, then the parser won't have any problems with it.

To an XML parser, there isn't any difference between the two `<title>` elements in this document. If you do a simple search of the document to find John Doe's title by looking for `<title>` elements, you might accidentally get `Resume of John Doe` instead of "`Sir`". Even in your application, you can't know which elements are XHTML elements and which aren't without knowing in advance the structure of the document. That is, you'd have to know that there is a `<résumé>` element, which is a direct child of `<person>`, and that all of the descendents of `<résumé>` are a separate type of element from the others in your document. If your structure ever changed, all of your assumptions would be lost. In the preceding document it looks like anything inside the `<résumé>` element is XHTML, but in other documents it might not be so obvious, and to an XML parser it isn't obvious at all.

Using Prefixes

The best way to solve this problem is for every element in a document to have a completely distinct name. For example, you might come up with a naming convention whereby every element for your proprietary XML document type gets your own prefix, and every XHTML element gets another prefix.

You could rewrite the previous XML document to something like this:

```
<?xml version="1.0"?>
<pers:person>
  <pers:name>
    <pers:title>Sir</pers:title>
    <pers:first>John</pers:first>
    <pers:middle>Fitzgerald Johansen</pers:middle>
    <pers:last>Doe</pers:last>
  </pers:name>
  <pers:position>Vice President of Marketing</pers:position>
  <pers:résumé>
    <xhtml:html>
    <xhtml:head><xhtml:title>Resume of John Doe</xhtml:title></xhtml:head>
    <xhtml:body>
    <xhtml:h1>John Doe</xhtml:h1>
    <xhtml:p>John's a great guy, you know?</xhtml:p>
    </xhtml:body>
    </xhtml:html>
  </pers:résumé>
</pers:person>
```

This is just an example to illustrate the theory: If you try to view this document in Internet Explorer, IE will give you an error about an "undeclared namespace." You'll see why as we investigate the namespace syntax in more detail.

This is a bit uglier, but at least you — and your XML parser — can immediately tell what kind of title you're talking about: a `<pers:title>` or an `<xhtml:title>`. Doing a search for `<pers:title>` will always return `Sir`. You can always immediately tell which elements are XHTML elements, without having to know in advance the structure of your document.

The drawback to doing this is that you're no longer using proper XHTML elements. Browsers that are able to display XHTML understand the `<p>` element, but they don't understand the `<xhtml:p>` element, so if you wrote an application to read this XML document and it wanted to display the XHTML portions in a browser, it would have to rename all of the elements first, to get rid of the `xhtml` prefix.

By separating these elements using a prefix, you have effectively created two kinds of elements in your document: `pers` types of elements and `xhtml` types of elements. Any elements with the `pers` prefix belong to the same "category" as each other, just as any elements with the `xhtml` prefix belong to another "category." These "categories" are called *namespaces*.

These two namespaces are illustrated in Figure 3-1.

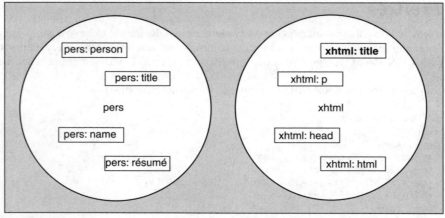

Figure 3-1

Note that namespaces are concerned with a *vocabulary*, not a *document type*. That is, the namespace distinguishes which names are in the namespace, but not what they mean or how they fit together. It is simply a "bag of names."

> **A namespace is a purely abstract entity; it's nothing more than a group of names that belong with each other conceptually.**

The concept of namespaces also exists in certain programming languages, such as Java, where the same problem exists. How can you name your Java variables whatever you want and not have those names conflict with names already defined by others, or even by the Java library itself? The answer is that Java code is broken up into packages, whereby the names within a package must be unique, but the same name can be used in any package.

For example, one class defined in Java is named `java.applet.Applet`. *The actual name of the class is just* `Applet`; `java.applet` *is the package that contains that class. This means that you can create your own package, and in that package you can define a class of your own, named Applet. You can even use* `java.applet.Applet` *from within your package, as long as you specify the package in which it resides, so that Java always knows which "Applet" you're referring to.*

Why Doesn't XML Just Use These Prefixes?

Unfortunately, there is a drawback to the prefix approach to namespaces used in the previous XML: Who will monitor the prefixes? The whole reason for using them is to distinguish names from different document types, but if it is going to work, then the prefixes themselves also have to be unique. If one company chose the prefix `pers` and another company also chose that same prefix, the original problem still exists.

In fact, this prefix administration would have to work a lot like it works now for domain names on the Internet. A company or individual would go to the "prefix administrators" with the prefix they would like to use. If that prefix weren't already being used, they could use it; otherwise, they would have to pick another one.

To solve this problem, you could take advantage of the already unambiguous Internet domain names in existence and specify that *URIs* must be used for the prefix names.

> **A URI (Uniform Resource Identifier) is a string of characters that identifies a resource. It can be in one of two flavors: URL (Uniform Resource Locator) or URN (Universal Resource Name). The differences between URLs and URNs are discussed later in this chapter.**

For example, because I'm writing this book for Wiley, which owns the domain name `www.wiley.com`, I could incorporate that into the prefix. Perhaps the document might end up looking like this:

```
<?xml version="1.0"?>
<{http://www.wiley.com/pers}person>
  <{http://www.wiley.com/pers}name>
  <{http://www.wiley.com/pers}title>
    Sir
  </{http://www.wiley.com/pers}title>
<!--etc...-->
```

Voila! We have solved our problem of uniqueness. Because Wiley owns the `www.wiley.com` domain name, I know that nobody else will be using that `http://www.wiley.com/pers` prefix in their XML documents, and if I want to create any additional document types, I can just keep using our domain name, and add the new namespace name to the end, such as `http://www.wiley.com/other-namespace`.

If you visit `http://www.wiley.com/pers`, you'll notice that there is no document at that location. The Wiley website will give you an error message instead. Does this mean that our namespace is broken? Actually, not at all. The URL we're using is simply used as a name, for the namespace; the XML parser won't try to pull back any resources from that location, or use it for any purpose other than naming the namespaces in the document. We'll talk about this more in a bit, but for now you can remember the following:

> **Even though it looks like a URL, a namespace name is only used as a name, not a location.**

It's important to note that we need more than just the `www.wiley.com` part of the URI; we need the whole thing. Otherwise, there would be a further problem: Different people could have control of different sections on that domain, and they might all want to create namespaces. For example, the company's HR department could be in charge of `http://www.wiley.com/hr` and might need to create a name space for `names` (of employees), and the sales department could be in charge of `http://www.wiley.com/sales`, and also need to create a namespace for `names` (of customers). As long as we're using the

whole URI, we're fine — we can create both namespaces (in this case, `http://www.wiley`
`.com/hr/names` and `http://www.wiley.com/sales/names`, respectively). We also need the protocol
(`http`) in there because there could be yet another department — for example, `ftp://www.wiley`
`.com/hr` and `ftp://www.wiley.com/sales`.

The only drawback to this solution is that our XML is no longer well formed. Our names can now
include a myriad of characters that are allowed in URIs but not in XML names: / characters, for example. In addition, for the sake of this example, we used { } characters to separate the URL from the name,
neither of which is allowed in an XML element or attribute name.

What we really need to solve all of our namespace-related problems is a way to create three-part names
in XML: One part would be the name we are giving this element, the second part would be a URI associated with the name, for the element's namespace, and the third part would be an arbitrarily chosen prefix that *refers* to a URI, which specifies the namespace to which this element belongs. In fact, this is what
XML namespaces provide.

How XML Namespaces Work

The XML Namespaces Recommendation introduces a standard syntax for declaring namespaces and
identifying the namespace for a given element or attribute in an XML document.

> *The XML namespaces specification is located at* `http://www.w3.org/TR/REC-xml-names/`.

To use XML namespaces in your documents, elements are given *qualified names*. (In most W3C specifications, *qualified name* is abbreviated to *QName*.) These qualified names consist of two parts: the *local part*,
which is the same as the names we have been giving elements all along, and the *namespace prefix*, which
specifies to which namespace this name belongs.

For example, to declare a namespace called `http://www.wiley.com/pers` and associate a `<person>`
element with that namespace, you would do something like the following:

```
<pers:person xmlns:pers="http://www.wiley.com/pers"/>
```

The key is the `xmlns:pers` attribute (`xmlns` stands for XML Namespace). Here you are declaring the
`pers` namespace prefix and the URI of the namespace that it represents (`http://www.wiley.com/`
`pers`). We can then use the namespace prefix with our elements, as in `pers:person`. As opposed to our
previous prefixed version, the prefix itself (`pers`) doesn't have any meaning — its only purpose is to
point to the namespace name. For this reason, we could replace our prefix (`pers`) with any other prefix,
and this document would have exactly the same meaning. (The prefix does, however, have to follow the
same naming conventions as element names.)

This prefix can be used for any descendants of the `<pers:person>` element, to denote that they also
belong to the `http://www.wiley.com/pers` namespace, as shown in the following example:

```
<pers:person xmlns:pers="http://www.wiley.com/pers">
  <pers:name>
    <pers:title>Sir</pers:title>
  </pers:name>
</pers:person>
```

Notice that the prefix is needed on both the start-tags and end-tags of the elements. They are no longer simply being identified by their names, but by their QNames.

Only elements that are specifically prefixed are part of a namespace. For example, consider this document:

```
<pers:person xmlns:pers="http://www.wiley.com/pers">
  <first/>
</pers:person>
```

The `<first>` element is not part of the same namespace as the `<person>` element because it doesn't have a namespace prefix. In fact, in this case, the `<first>` element is not in a namespace at all.

> *By now you have probably realized why colons in element names are so strongly discouraged in the XML 1.0 specification (and in this book). If you were to use a name that happened to have a colon in it with a namespace-aware XML parser, the parser would get confused, thinking that you were specifying a namespace prefix.*

Internally, when this document is parsed, the parser simply replaces any namespace prefixes with the namespace itself, creating a name much like the names we used earlier in the chapter. That is, internally a parser might consider `<pers:person>` to be similar to `<{http://www.wiley.com/pers\person>`. For this reason, the `{http://www.wiley.com/pers\person}` notation is often used in namespace discussions to talk about *fully qualified names*. Just remember that this is only for the benefit of easily discussing namespace issues; it is not valid XML syntax.

Try It Out   Adding XML Namespaces to Your Document

In this example, you see what the document would look like with proper XML namespaces. Luckily, there is already a namespace defined for XHTML, which is `http://www.w3.org/1999/xhtml`. You can use this namespace for the HTML you're embedding in your document.

1.   Open Notepad and type in the following XML:

```
<?xml version="1.0"?>
<pers:person xmlns:pers="http://www.wiley.com/pers"
             xmlns:html="http://www.w3.org/1999/xhtml">
  <pers:name>
    <pers:title>Sir</pers:title>
    <pers:first>John</pers:first>
    <pers:middle>Fitzgerald Johansen</pers:middle>
    <pers:last>Doe</pers:last>
  </pers:name>
  <pers:position>Vice President of Marketing</pers:position>
  <pers:résumé>
  <html:html>
    <html:head><html:title>Resume of John Doe</html:title></html:head>
    <html:body>
    <html:h1>John Doe</html:h1>
    <html:p>John's a great guy, you know?</html:p>
    </html:body>
  </html:html>
  </pers:résumé>
</pers:person>
```

2. Save this document to your hard drive as `namespace.xml`.

3. Open `namespace.xml` in IE. You should get the normal color-coded view of your XML document, similar to what is shown in Figure 3-2. (If you don't, go back and make sure you haven't made any mistakes!)

How It Works

You now have a document with elements from two separate namespaces, which you defined in the highlighted code; and any namespace-aware XML parser will be able to tell them apart. (The fact that the file opens fine in Internet Explorer indicates that the parser bundled with this browser understands namespaces properly; if it didn't, the document might raise errors instead.) The two namespaces now look more like Figure 3-3.

The `xmlns` attributes specify the namespace prefixes you are using to point to your two namespaces:

```
<pers:person xmlns:pers="http://www.wiley.com/pers"
             xmlns:html="http://www.w3.org/1999/xhtml">
```

That is, you declare the `pers` prefix, which is used to specify elements that belong to the "pers" namespace, and the `html` prefix, which is used to specify elements that belong to the XHTML namespace. However, remember that the prefixes themselves mean nothing to the XML parser; they are replaced with the URI internally. You could have used `pers` or `myprefix` or `blah` or any other legal string of characters for the prefix; it's only the URI to which they point that the parser cares about—although using descriptive prefixes is good practice!

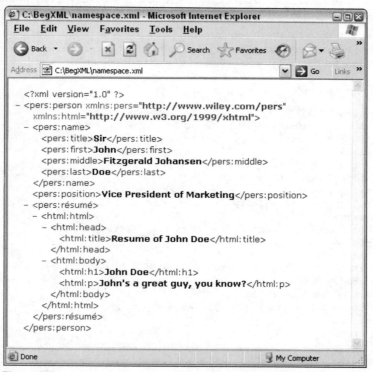

Figure 3-2

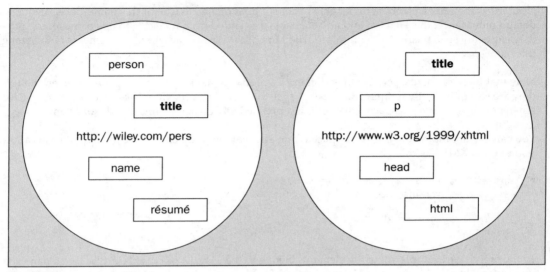

Figure 3-3

Because you have a way of identifying which namespace each element belongs to, you don't have to give them special, unique names. You have two vocabularies, each containing a `<title>` element, and you can mix both of these `<title>` elements in the same document. If you ever need a person's title, you can easily find any {`http://www.wiley.com/pers\title`} elements you need and ignore the {`http://www.w3 .org/1999/xhtml`}\title elements.

However, even though your `<title>` element is prefixed with a namespace prefix, the name of the element is still `<title>`. It's just that you have now declared what namespace that `<title>` belongs to so that it won't be confused with other `<title>` elements that belong to other namespaces.

Default Namespaces

Although the previous document solves all of our namespace-related problems, it's just a little bit ugly. You have to give every element in the document a prefix to specify the namespace to which it belongs, which makes the document look very similar to the first prefixed version. Luckily, you have the option to create *default namespaces*.

> A default namespace is just like a regular namespace except that you don't have to specify a prefix for all of the elements that use it.

Using default namespaces, our document might look more like this:

```
<person xmlns="http://www.wiley.com/pers">
  <name>
    <title>Sir</title>
  </name>
</person>
```

Notice that the `xmlns` attribute no longer specifies a prefix name to use for this namespace. As this is a default namespace, this element and any elements descended from it belong to this namespace, unless they explicitly specify another namespace. Therefore, the `<name>` and `<title>` elements both belong to this namespace.

Note that these elements, because they don't use a prefix, are no longer called QNames, even though they are still universally unique. Many people use the generic term *universal name*, or *UName*, to describe any name that's in a namespace, whether it is a prefixed QName or a name in a default namespace.

You can declare more than one namespace for an element, but only one can be the default. This allows you to write XML like this:

```
<person xmlns="http://www.wiley.com/pers"
        xmlns:xhtml="http://www.w3.org/1999/xhtml">
  <name/>
  <xhtml:p>This is XHTML</xhtml:p>
</person>
```

In the preceding example, all of the elements belong to the `http://www.wiley.com/pers` namespace, except for the `<p>` element, which is part of the XHTML namespace. (You declared the namespaces and their prefixes, if applicable, in the root element so that all elements in the document can use these prefixes.) However, you can't write XML like this:

```
<person xmlns="http://www.wiley.com/pers"
        xmlns="http://www.w3.org/1999/xhtml">
```

This tries to declare two default namespaces. In this case, the XML parser wouldn't be able to figure out to what namespace the `<person>` element belongs (not to mention that this is a duplicate attribute, which, as you saw in Chapter 2, is not allowed in XML).

Try It Out   Default Namespaces in Action

In this Try It Out you rewrite your previous document, but use a default namespace to make it cleaner:

1. Make the following changes to `namespace.xml` and save it as `namespace2.xml`:

```
<?xml version="1.0"?>
<person xmlns="http://www.wiley.com/pers"
        xmlns:html="http://www.w3.org/1999/xhtml">
  <name>
    <title>Sir</title>
    <first>John</first>
    <middle>Fitzgerald Johansen</middle>
    <last>Doe</last>

  </name>
    <position>Vice President of Marketing</position>
    <résumé>
      <html:html>
        <html:head><html:title>Resume of John Doe</html:title></html:head>
```

```
    <html:body>
    <html:h1>John Doe</html:h1>
    <html:p>John's a great guy, you know?</html:p>
    </html:body>
  </html:html>
 </résumé>
</person>
```

2.   When you view the file in Explorer, it should look like Figure 3-4.

How It Works

In the <person> start-tag, the first xmlns attribute doesn't specify a prefix to associate with this namespace, so this becomes the default namespace for the element, along with any of its descendents, which is why you don't need any namespace prefixes in many of the elements, such as <name>, <title>, and so on.

However, because the XHTML elements are in a different namespace, you do need to specify the prefix for them, such as the following:

```
<html:head><html:title>Resume of John Doe</html:title></html:head>
```

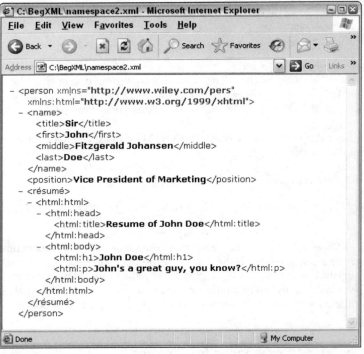

Figure 3-4

Declaring Namespaces on Descendants

So far, when we have had multiple namespaces in a document, we've been declaring them all in the root element, so that the prefixes are available throughout the document. For example, in the previous Try It Out, we declared a default namespace, as well as a namespace prefix for our HTML elements, all on the `<person>` element.

This means that when you have a default namespace mixed with other namespaces, you would create a document like this:

```
<person xmlns="http://www.wiley.com/pers"
        xmlns:xhtml="http://www.w3.org/1999/xhtml">
  <name/>
  <xhtml:p>This is XHTML</xhtml:p>
</person>
```

However, you don't *have* to declare all of your namespace prefixes on the root element; in fact, a namespace prefix can be declared on any element in the document. You could also have written the previous XML like this:

```
<person xmlns="http://www.wiley.com/pers">
  <name/>
  <xhtml:p xmlns:xhtml="http://www.w3.org/1999/xhtml">
  This is XHTML</xhtml:p>
</person>
```

In some cases this might make your documents more readable because you're declaring the namespaces closer to where they'll actually be used. The downside to writing documents like this is that the `xhtml` prefix is available only on the `<p>` element and its descendants; you couldn't use it on your `<name>` element, for example, or any other element that wasn't a descendant of `<p>`.

You can take things even further and declare the XHTML namespace to be the *default* namespace for the `<p>` element and its descendents, like this:

```
<person xmlns="http://www.wiley.com/pers">
  <name/>
  <p xmlns="http://www.w3.org/1999/xhtml">This is XHTML</p>
</person>
```

Although `http://www.wiley.com/pers` is the default namespace for the document as a whole, `http://www.w3.org/1999/xhtml` is the default namespace for the `<p>` element, and any of its descendants. In other words, the `http://www.w3.org/1999/xhtml` namespace overrides the `http://www.wiley.com/pers` namespace, so that it doesn't apply to the `<p>` element. Again, in some cases this can make your documents more readable because you are declaring the namespaces closer to where they are used.

Try It Out   Default Namespaces for Children

In the interest of readability, in this example you will write the XML from the previous Try It Out again, to declare the default namespace for the `<html>` tag and its descendants:

1. Make the highlighted changes to `namespace2.xml`:

```
<?xml version="1.0"?>
<person xmlns="http://www.wiley.com/pers">
  <name>
    <title>Sir</title>
    <first>John</first>
    <middle>Fitzgerald Johansen</middle>
    <last>Doe</last>
  </name>
  <position>Vice President of Marketing</position>
  <résumé>
    <html xmlns="http://www.w3.org/1999/xhtml">
      <head><title>Resume of John Doe</title></head>
      <body>
      <h1>John Doe</h1>
      <p>John's a great guy, you know?</p>
      </body>
    </html>
  </résumé>
</person>
```

2. Save this as `namespace3.xml`. This looks a lot tidier than the previous version and represents the same thing.

3. View the file in Explorer. Your screen should look like the one shown in Figure 3-5.

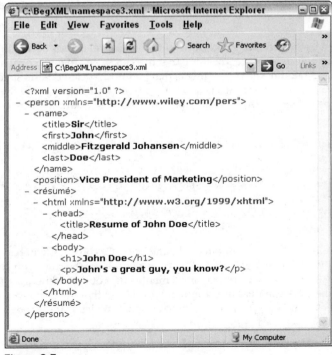

Figure 3-5

How It Works

Because you have completely eliminated the prefixes from your document, the element names become "cleaner." The document is no longer cluttered with the `pers:` and `html:` prefixes everywhere, which can make it easier to read for a human reader.

Canceling Default Namespaces

Sometimes you might be working with XML documents in which not all of the elements belong to a namespace. For example, you might be creating XML documents to describe employees in your organization, and those documents might include occasional XHTML comments about the employees, such as in the following short fragment:

```
<employee>
  <name>Jane Doe</name>
  <notes>
    <p xmlns="http://www.w3.org/1999/xhtml">I've worked
    with <name>Jane Doe</name> for over a <em>year</em>
    now.</p>
  </notes>
</employee>
```

In this case, you have decided that anywhere the employee's name is included in the document it should be in a `<name>` element, in case the employee changes his or her name in the future, such as if Jane Doe gets married and becomes Jane Smith. (In this case, changing the document would then be a matter of looking for all `<name>` elements that aren't in a namespace and changing the values.) In addition, because these XML documents will be used only by your own application, you don't have to create a namespace for it.

However, as shown in the preceding code, one of the `<name>` elements occurs under the `<p>` element, which declares a default namespace, meaning that the `<name>` element also falls under that namespace. Therefore, if you searched for `<name>` elements that had no associated namespace, you wouldn't pick this one up. The way to get around this is to use the `xmlns` attribute to *cancel* the default namespace by setting the value to an empty string, as shown in the following example:

```
<employee>
  <name>Jane Doe</name>
  <notes>
    <p xmlns="http://www.w3.org/1999/xhtml">I've worked
    with <name xmlns="">Jane Doe</name> for over a <em>year</em>
    now.</p>
  </notes>
</employee>
```

Now the second `<name>` element is not in any namespace. Of course, if you had a namespace specifically for your `<employee>` document, this would become a non-issue, because you could just use the methods you've already learned to declare that an element is part of that namespace (using a namespace prefix or a default namespace). In this case, you're not declaring that the element is part of a namespace — you're trying to declare that it's *not* part of any namespace, which is the opposite of what you've been doing so far.

Normally, if you're doing this type of processing of XML, and looking for elements or attributes in a specific namespace, you would be using some type of XML-aware tool: a SAX parser, a DOM implementation, or some type of XPath-related tool. You'll take a look at all of these technologies — and more! — in later chapters of the book.

Typically, if you're going to be working with XML documents that mix and match elements from different namespaces, you would create namespaces for *all* of the elements. You wouldn't usually use elements that aren't in a namespace in the same document with UNames. However, if you ever need to, the flexibility exists.

Do Different Notations Make Any Difference?

You've now seen three different ways to combine elements from different namespaces. You can fully qualify every name, like this:

```
<pers:person xmlns:pers="http://www.wiley.com/pers"
             xmlns:xhtml="http://www.w3.org/1999/xhtml">
  <pers:name/>
  <xhtml:p>This is XHTML</xhtml:p>
</pers:person>
```

Alternatively, you can use one namespace as the default, and just qualify any names from other namespaces, like this:

```
<person xmlns="http://www.wiley.com/pers"
        xmlns:xhtml="http://www.w3.org/1999/xhtml">
  <name/>
  <xhtml:p>This is XHTML</xhtml:p>
</person>
```

You can also just use defaults everywhere, like this:

```
<person xmlns="http://www.wiley.com/pers">
  <name/>
  <p xmlns="http://www.w3.org/1999/xhtml">This is XHTML</p>
</person>
```

This raises the question whether these three fragments of XML really mean exactly the same thing.

From the pure namespaces point of view, yes — these documents mean exactly the same thing. All three documents have the same three elements; and in each instance, each element still belongs to the same namespace as it does in the other two instances.

From the point of view of most applications, these fragments also mean the same thing. When you're doing work with an XML document, you usually only care about what elements you're dealing with; you don't care whether the element's namespace was declared using a default declaration or an explicit prefix, any more than you care whether an element with no data was written as a start-tag and end-tag pair or as an empty element.

However, some applications actually do differentiate between the preceding three examples, such as an application that reads in XML and displays the source code to a user. As you may have noticed if you used IE5 or later to view the XML from the previous Try It Out exercises, each one is displayed differently. Take a look at each of the three preceding code examples in Figures 3-6, 3-7, and 3-8, respectively.

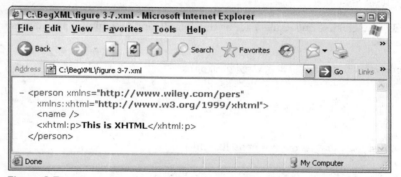

Figure 3-6

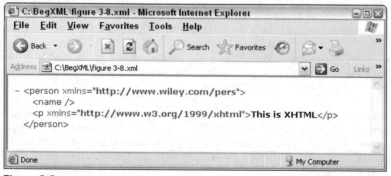

Figure 3-7

Figure 3-8

As you can see, the browser displays the documents exactly as they were written, so if you declare your namespaces using defaults, the browser displays them using defaults; if you declare them with prefixes, the browser displays them with prefixes.

The two dominant technologies to programmatically get information out of XML documents, the Document Object Model (DOM) and Simple API for XML (SAX), covered in Chapters 11 and 12, respectively, provide methods that enable you to get not only the namespace URI for a QName, but also the prefix, for those applications that need it. This means that not only can you find the fully qualified namespace names for these elements; you can also see *how* the XML author wrote those names. In real life, however, you hardly ever need the namespace prefix, unless you are writing applications to display the XML as entered to a user. Internet Explorer's default XSL stylesheet can differentiate between the preceding cases because it pulls this information from the DOM implementation shipped with the browser.

Namespaces and Attributes

So far, all of our discussions have been centered on elements, and we've been pretty much ignoring attributes. Do namespaces work the same for attributes as they do for elements?

The answer is no, they don't. In fact, attributes usually don't have namespaces the way elements do. They are just "associated" with the elements to which they belong. Consider the following fragment:

```
<person xmlns="http://www.wiley.com/pers">
  <name id="25">
    <title>Sir</title>
  </name>
</person>
```

You know that the `<person>`, `<name>`, and `<title>` elements all belong to the same namespace, which is declared in the `<person>` start-tag. The `id` attribute, however, is not part of this namespace; it's simply associated with the `<name>` element, which itself is part of that default namespace. You could use a notation like the following to identify it for discussion:

```
"{http://www.wiley.com/pers}\name:id"
```

That is, the `id` attribute is attached to the `<name>` element, which is in the `http://www.wiley.com/pers` namespace.

However, if you used prefixes, you *could* specify that `id` is in a namespace like so:

```
<a:person xmlns:a="http://www.wiley.com/pers">
  <a:name a:id="25">
    <a:title>Sir</a:title>
  </a:name>
</a:person>
```

There is now an attribute called `id`, in the `http://www.wiley.com/pers` namespace, attached to the `<name>` element, which is *also* in the `http://www.wiley.com/pers` namespace.

Unfortunately, the namespaces specification contains a bit of a gray area concerning attributes. For example, consider the following two fragments:

```
<a:name id="25">
<a:name a:id="25">
```

Are these two fragments identical or different? Well, actually, programmers can make up their own minds whether an application should treat these two cases as the same or different. (In XSLT, for example, the two cases would be considered to be different.) For this reason, if you need ensure that an application specifically recognizes an attribute as being part of a namespace, instead of just being attached to an element, you should design the application such that the attributes include a prefix. This also means that you would have to declare a prefix for your namespace, even if you're using default namespaces for your elements. On the other hand, most applications treat the two situations identically.

Consider the case in which you want to perform some processing on every attribute in the `http://www .wiley.com/pers` namespace. If an application considers both of the preceding cases to be the same, then in both cases the `id` attribute is processed. Conversely, if the application doesn't consider both of the preceding fragments to be the same, then you get only the second `id` attribute because it is specifically declared to be in the namespace you're looking for, whereas the first one isn't.

Is this purely theoretical? In most cases, yes. Applications don't usually look for attributes on their own; they look for particular elements, and then process the attributes on those elements.

However, attributes from a particular namespace can also be attached to elements from a different namespace. Attributes that are specifically declared to be in a namespace are called *global attributes*. A common example of a global attribute is the XHTML `class` attribute, which might be used on any XML element, XHTML or not. This would make things easier when using *Cascading Style Sheets (CSS)* to display an XML document.

Try It Out   **Adding Attributes**

To see this in action, you will add an `id` attribute to your `<name>` element and add a `style` attribute to the HTML paragraph portion of your résumé:

1.   Change `namespace2.xml` to the following, and save it as `namespace4.xml`:

```
<?xml version="1.0"?>
<person xmlns="http://www.wiley.com/pers">
  <name id="1">
    <title>Sir</title>
    <first>John</first>
    <middle>Fitzgerald Johansen</middle>
    <last>Doe</last>
  </name>
  <position>Vice President of Marketing</position>
  <résumé>
    <html:html xmlns:html="http://www.w3.org/1999/xhtml">
    <html:head><html:title>Resume of John Doe</html:title></html:head>
    <html:body>
    <html:h1>John Doe</html:h1>
    <html:p html:style="FONT-FAMILY: Arial">
```

```
      John's a great guy, you know?
    </html:p>
    </html:body>
    </html:html>
  </résumé>
</person>
```

Because you want the `style` attribute to be specifically in the XHTML namespace, you have gone back to using prefixes on your XHTML elements instead of a default namespace. Another alternative would be to declare the XHTML namespace twice: once as the default, for `<html>` and all of its descendents, and once with a prefix, which could be attached to the `style` attribute.

2. Open the document in IE to view the results. It should look like Figure 3-9.

How It Works

The `id` attribute that you added is associated with the `<name>` element, but it doesn't actually have a namespace.

Similarly, the `style` attribute is associated with the `<p>` element, but in this case the attribute is specifically in the XHTML namespace.

```
<?xml version="1.0" ?>
- <person xmlns="http://www.wiley.com/pers">
 - <name id="1">
    <title>Sir</title>
    <first>John</first>
    <middle>Fitzgerald Johansen</middle>
    <last>Doe</last>
  </name>
  <position>Vice President of Marketing</position>
 - <résumé>
  - <html:html xmlns:html="http://www.w3.org/1999/xhtml">
   - <html:head>
      <html:title>Resume of John Doe</html:title>
    </html:head>
   - <html:body>
      <html:h1>John Doe</html:h1>
      <html:p html:style="FONT-FAMILY: Arial">John's a
       great guy, you know?</html:p>
    </html:body>
   </html:html>
  </résumé>
</person>
```

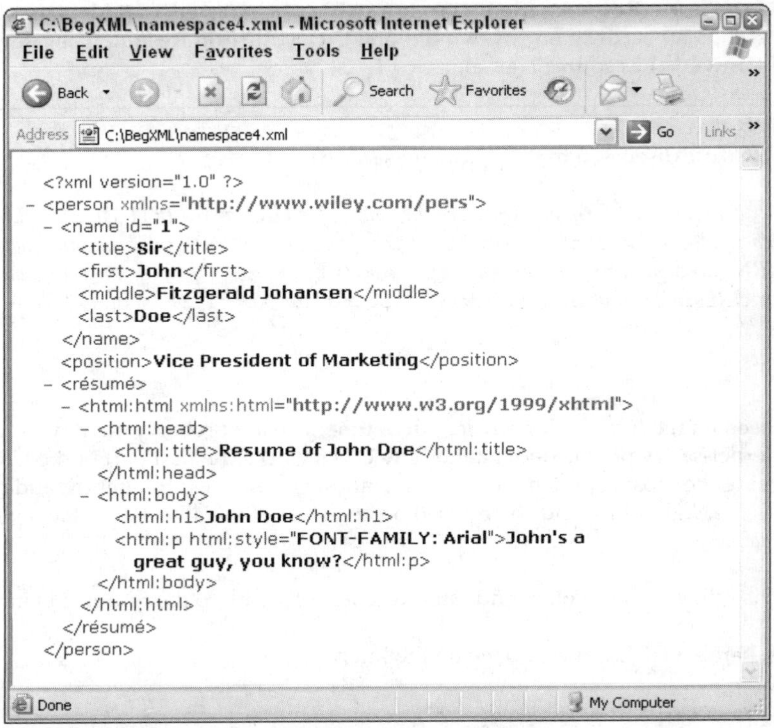

Figure 3-9

Again, applications may or may not treat both of these the same and consider them to be in the same namespace as the elements to which they are attached. All applications will treat the `style` attribute as being in the XHTML namespace, because you have specifically said so, but some will think `id` is in the same namespace as `<name>`, and some won't.

Understanding URIs

We have mentioned that namespaces are specified using URIs, and most of the examples shown so far have been URLs. To really understand namespaces, we have to look at this concept a little further.

Because so much of the work done on the Internet somehow involves finding and retrieving *resources*, much thought has been put into this process. What is a resource? Well, simply put, a resource is anything that has *identity*. It could be a tangible item, such as a `.gif` file or a book, or it could be a conceptual item, like the current state of the traffic in Toronto. It could be an item that is retrievable over the Internet, such as an HTML document, or an item that is not retrievable over the Internet, such as the person who wrote that HTML document.

Recall our earlier definition of a URI:

> **A URI (Uniform Resource Identifier) is a string of characters that identifies a resource. It can occur in one of two flavors: URL (Uniform Resource Locator), or URN (Universal Resource Name).**

URLs and URNs are discussed in the following sections.

There is a document that formally describes the syntax for URIs at the IETF (Internet Engineering Task Force) website, located at `http://www.ietf.org/rfc/rfc2396.txt` *; one that describes the syntax for URNs, located at* `http://www.ietf.org/rfc/rfc2141.txt` *; and one that describes the syntax for URLs, located at* `http://www.ietf.org/rfc/rfc1738.txt`.

URLs

If you have been on the Internet for any length of time, you are probably already familiar with URLs, and most Internet-savvy people understand how URLs work. The first part of the URL specifies the *protocol*, `http` being the most common, with `mailto` and `ftp` also used frequently, and others (such as `gopher`, `news`, `telnet`, `file`, and so on) used on occasion. (Officially, the protocol part of the URL is called a *scheme*.)

The protocol is followed by a colon, and after the colon is a path to the resource being identified.

For example, here's a URL to a web page on the Internet:

```
http://www.google.com/intl/en/about.html
```

This URL contains information that can be used to retrieve a file named `about.html` from a server on the Internet named `www.google.ca`. It specifies that the file is in the `/intl/en` directory (or virtual directory) and that the file should be retrieved via the HTTP protocol.

You can also create a URL to an e-mail account, like so:

```
mailto:someone@somewhere.com
```

Of course, there is a limitation on the resources that can be retrieved via URLs: Obviously, they must be resources of a type that is retrievable from a computer! (The resource identified in the `mailto:` URL is a bit of an exception, as it isn't actually *retrieved*; instead, a mail client is usually triggered, and a new e-mail is created to the given address.)

URNs

URNs are not as commonly seen as URLs. In fact, most people, even those who have been using the Internet their whole lives, have never seen a URN. They exist to provide a persistent, location-independent name for a resource.

For example, a person's name is similar to a URN, because the person has the same name, no matter where they are. Even after a person dies, the name still refers to the person who used to have it when they were alive. A name is different from a URN, though, because more than one person can have the same name, whereas URNs are designed to be unique across time and space.

A URN looks something like this:

```
urn:foo:a123,456
```

First is the string `urn`, uppercase or lowercase, and a colon. After the first colon is the *Namespace Identifier*, or *NID* (`foo` in this case), followed by another colon. Last is the *Namespace Specific String*, or *NSS* (`a123,456`, for example). As you can see from the terminology, URNs were designed with namespaces already in mind. (Not necessarily XML namespaces, but namespaces in general.)

The NID portion of the URN declares what type of URN this is. For example, to create URNs for Canadian citizens, we might declare an NID of `Canadian-Citizen`.

The NSS portion of the URN is the part that must be unique and persistent. In Canada, all citizens are assigned unique Social Insurance Numbers, so a URN for a Canadian citizen with a Social Insurance Number of 000-000-000 might look like this:

```
urn:Canadian-Citizen:000-000-000
```

Why Use URLs for Namespaces, Not URNs?

The XML namespace specification states that namespaces are identified with URIs, which leaves the possibility of using either URLs or URNs. It seems that URNs are better suited for naming namespaces than URLs — after all, a namespace is a *conceptual* resource, not one that can be retrieved via the Internet. Why then are most namespaces named using URLs instead?

Some people find it easier to create unique namespace names using URLs, as they are already guaranteed to be unique. If Wiley owns the `www.wiley.com` domain name, they can incorporate them into their namespace names and know that they will be unique.

Of course, this is still by convention; nothing stops someone at another company — say, Malicious Names, Inc., — from stealing Wiley's domain name and maliciously using it as the name for a namespace. However, if everyone follows the convention, we can be sure that there won't be *accidental* collisions, which is good enough for our purposes. You could still construct a URN like `urn:WileyHR:name`, but many people feel that things are just simpler if you use URLs.

There can also be side benefits of using URLs as namespace names. If you wanted to, you could put a document at the end of the URL that describes the elements in that namespace. For example, we have been using `http://www.wiley.com/pers` as a fictional namespace. If Wiley wanted to make the `pers` namespace public, for use in public document types, they could put a document at that location that describes the various XML elements and attributes in that namespace.

But regardless of what people are doing, the possibility of using a URN as a namespace identifier still exists, so if you have a system of URNs that you feel is unique, it is perfectly legal. URNs provide no benefits over URLs, except for the conceptual idea that they're a closer fit to what namespace names are trying to do — that is, *name* something, not *point to* something.

What Do Namespace URIs Really Mean?

Now that you know how to use namespaces to keep your element names unique, what exactly do those namespace URIs mean? In other words, what does `http://www.wiley.com/pers` really represent?

The answer, according to the XML namespaces specification, is that it doesn't mean anything. The URI is simply used to give the namespace a name, but it doesn't mean anything on its own, just as the words *John Doe* don't mean anything on their own — they are just used to identify a particular person. As you saw earlier, the namespace name, although it looks like a URL, is just a name; the XML parser will never try to go to the URL you've used and try to retrieve anything.

Many people feel that this isn't enough for XML. In addition to keeping element names distinct, they would also like to give those elements meaning — that is, not just distinguish `<my:element>` from `<your:element>`, but also define what `<my:element>` means. What is it used for? What are the legal values for it? If we could create some kind of "schema" that would define our document type, the namespace URI might be the logical place to declare this document as adhering to that schema.

The XML Namespaces specification (`http://www.w3.org/TR/REC-xml-names/`) states "it is not a goal that [the namespace URI] be directly useable for retrieval of a schema (if any exists)." (A *schema* is a document that formally describes an XML document type. Several languages are available for creating schemas, such as *DTDs* and the *XML Schema* language from the W3C, which are covered in Chapters 4 and 5.) In other words, as we've been saying, the URI is just a name or identifier; it doesn't have any inherent meaning. However, it is not strictly forbidden for it to have a meaning. For this reason, someone creating an application could legally decide that the URI used in a namespace actually does indicate some type of documentation, whether that is a prose document describing this particular document type or a technical schema document of some sort. Nonetheless, in this case, the URI still wouldn't mean anything to the *XML parser*; it would be up to the higher-level application to read the URI and do something with it.

In other words, if I'm writing an application that will process a particular kind of XML file, using namespaces, and I want to put something at the end of the URL that I'm using for my namespace name, I'm free to do that. I just have to remember that the XML parser won't care. It will give me the information from my XML document, including what namespace each element belongs to, but it would be up to my application to then go to that URL and retrieve something from it.

As an example of where this might be useful, consider a corporate information processing system whereby users enter information to be stored in XML format. If different namespaces are defined for different types of documents, and those namespaces are named with URLs, then you could put a help file at the end of each URL. If users are viewing a particular type of XML document in the special application you have written for them, all they have to do is press *F1* to get help and find out about this particular type of document. All your application has to do is open a web browser and point it to the URL that defines the namespace.

You may also have noticed in the namespace for XHTML that the W3C decided to include the date of the recommendation in the string (`http://www.w3.org/1999/xhtml`). This means that documents using this namespace are also implicitly stating what version of the XHTML Recommendation they're adhering to; if/when the W3C comes out with a new XHTML Recommendation, they can change the URL, to distinguish the new XHTML namespace from the old one.

That's true only if the W3C wants to distinguish the two versions of XHTML that way. Because a namespace is just a name, they could just as easily decide that they want to continue using the same string, `http://www.w3.org/1999/xhtml`, *for the namespace, even if the new XHTML Recommendation is published after 1999.*

RDDL

Therefore, in addition to providing human-readable documentation for your namespace, the options of providing schemas also exist. However, there are a number of these languages available (a few of which are covered in this book). How do we decide what to put at the end of a URL we use for a namespace name? Do we put human-readable documentation that describes the namespace? Or do we put a document in one of these machine-readable formats? One answer is to use the *Resource Directory Description Language*, or *RDDL* (the RDDL specification can be found at `http://www.openhealth.org/RDDL/`).

RDDL was created to combine the benefits of human-readable documentation with the benefits of providing machine-readable documentation for an XML namespace. An RDDL document is actually an XHTML document, which makes it human-readable. However, because XHTML is XML, other machine-readable resources can be included in the document, using a technology called *XLink* to link the various documents together. In this way, human-readable documentation can be provided on an XML namespace, while at the same time providing links to as many other resources as needed, such as machine-readable documents on the namespace, executable code, and so on.

When to Use Namespaces

By this point, this chapter has covered everything that you need to know about namespaces from a technical standpoint. You know what they mean, how to use them, and how to combine them. Sit back for a while now, put your feet up, and let's talk philosophy. When should you create a new namespace, and when should you add new elements to an existing one?

In the course of this chapter, we have created the `http://www.wiley.com/pers` namespace for use in our documents. We decided to use one namespace, to cover all of the elements that are used to create an XML document about a person. We could have instead split our namespace up, and created separate namespaces for each element, or we could have created one namespace for the overall document and another for the résumé. Why did we choose to do it this way?

Remember that a namespace is just a "bag of names" — that is, it's a group of element names that belong together, and that are distinct from element names in other namespaces. The key is the phrase *belong together*. You might think of the elements in a namespace as being the vocabulary for a language, the same way that English words are in the English vocabulary. Any words that belong to that language would go in that namespace, and words from other languages would go into other namespaces. It's up to you to decide which elements belong in the same vocabulary, and which ones should go in different vocabularies.

The W3C went through this process when creating XHTML, the HTML language "redone" in XML. The problem is that XHTML is based on HTML 4, which has three flavors: *frameset* (which includes support for HTML frames), *strict* (which is designed for clean structural markup, free from all layout tags), and *transitional* (which allows formatting markup for older browsers, such as a `bgcolor` attribute on the `<body>` tag). Some HTML elements, such as `<p>`, appear in all three flavors, while others, such as `<frameset>`, may only appear in certain flavors.

This led the W3C, in the initial specifications for XHTML, to indicate that three different namespaces would be used, one for each flavor. However, the web community strongly disagreed with this approach. Most people consider HTML (or XHTML) to be one language — even though there may be more than one "flavor" or "dialect" of that language — so they argued that XHTML should have only one namespace associated with it. In the end, the W3C decided to go with the one-namespace approach (the namespace they chose is `http://www.w3.org/1999/xhtml`, which is why we've been using it for our XHTML examples).

Summary

This chapter introduced the concept of namespaces, along with their implementation in XML. Highlights of this chapter include the following:

- ❑ What benefit namespaces can potentially give you in your documents
- ❑ How to declare and use namespaces
- ❑ How to effectively use a URI as the name of a namespace

The idea behind namespaces may not seem all that relevant, unless you're combining elements from various vocabularies into one XML document. You may be thinking, "If I'm just going to create XML documents to describe my data, why mess around with all of this namespace stuff?" However, when you remember that you will be using other XML vocabularies, such as XSLT, to transform your documents, or XHTML to display your data, namespaces become much more relevant. Learning the concepts behind namespaces will help you combine your documents with these other document types, in addition to any further document types you may create yourself.

Exercise Questions

Suggested solutions to these questions can be found in Appendix A.

Question 1

In this chapter you saw the following XML document, in which you had to cancel the default namespace:

```
<employee>
  <name>Jane Doe</name>
   <notes>
       <p xmlns="http://www.w3.org/1999/xhtml">I've worked
       with <name xmlns="">Jane Doe</name> for over a <em>year</em>
      now.</p>
   </notes>
</employee>
```

Assuming that this document is for Wiley's HR department, create a namespace for employees, and use it in this document. Be sure to keep the XHTML elements in their namespace.

Question 2

Imagine that Wiley has been going through the employee records and realized that they don't have a good, unique way to identify each employee. Create a global `id` attribute that can be attached to any XML element in the employee namespace you created earlier.

Put this attribute into effect by modifying the XML you created in Question 1, and mark the Jane Doe employee as employee number x125.

Question 3

Create a new XML file for an employee named Alfred Neuman, with employee number x393. In the notes for Alfred, mention that he has worked closely with Jane Doe, being sure to use the `<name>` element to refer to her.

Part II
Validation

4

Document Type Definitions

As you've seen in the first few chapters, the rules for XML are straightforward. It doesn't take much to create well-formed XML documents to describe any information that you want. When you create XML documents, you can categorize them into groups of similar document types based on the elements and attributes they contain. You learned that the elements and attributes that make up a document type are known as the document's *vocabulary*. In Chapter 3, you learned how to use multiple vocabularies within a single document using namespaces. By this time, you may be wondering how to define your own types of documents and check whether certain documents follow the rules of your vocabulary.

Suppose you are developing an application that uses the <name> sample from Chapter 1. In the <name> sample, you created a simple XML document that allowed you to enter the first, middle, and last name of a person. In the sample, you used the name *John Fitzgerald Johansen Doe*. Now suppose that users of your application input information that does not match the vocabulary you developed. How could you verify that the content within the XML document is valid? You could write some code within your web application to check whether each of the elements is correct and in the correct order, but what if you want to modify the type of documents you can accept? You would have to update your application code, possibly in many places. This isn't much of an improvement from the text documents discussed in Chapter 1.

The need to validate documents against a vocabulary is common in markup languages. In fact, it is so common that the creators of XML included a method for checking validity in the XML Recommendation. An XML document is *valid* if its content matches its definition of allowable elements, attributes, and other document pieces. By using special *Document Type Definitions*, or *DTDs*, you can check the content of a document type with special parsers. The XML Recommendation separates parsers into two categories: validating and nonvalidating. Validating parsers, according to the recommendation, must implement validity checking using DTDs. Using a validating parser, you can remove the content-checking code from the application and depend on the parser to verify the content of the XML document against the DTD.

Although you will learn everything you need to know about DTDs in this chapter, you might like to see the XML Recommendation and its discussion of DTDs for yourself. If so, you can look it up at `http://www.w3.org/TR/REC-xml#dt-doctype`.

In this chapter, you will learn how to do the following:

- ❑ Create DTDs
- ❑ Validate an XML document against a DTD
- ❑ Use DTDs to create XML documents from multiple files

Running the Samples

You've already learned about some of the benefits of DTDs, but it will probably help if you look at an example DTD before moving on. To see how a DTD works, you will create one for the `<name>` example from Chapter 1.

Preparing the Ground

You need a program that can validate an XML document against a DTD. Throughout this chapter and the next two, the examples utilize the Codeplot editor at `http://codeplot.com`. The Codeplot editor enables you to create XML documents, DTDs, and other files in a virtual folder. It also enables you to check a document's well-formedness and validity. Simply sign up on the Codeplot home page and you can begin creating XML documents and DTDs. Of course, you can also use a text editor or XML-specific editor to work through the examples. If you do so, simply use the built-in functionality of the tool you choose, or use a validating parser to check the validity of your documents.

How do you use a validating parser? This chapter only covers building and verifying DTD documents. Apart from using a specialized editor to work with your documents, you can write a program that validates your XML documents against a DTD. For more information on utilizing parsers in your own programs, see Chapters 11 and 12.

After you sign up you are ready to validate an XML documents against a DTD—all you need now is a DTD.

Try It Out   **What's in a Name?**

In this example, you embed a DTD that defines the `<name>` vocabulary directly within an XML document. Later, you will see how separating the definition from the XML document can be useful in distributed environments.

1.   Open the Codeplot website, click the Create link to create a new document, and name it `name2.xml`. Type in the following document, making sure you include the spaces as shown. You may notice that this file looks like the `name.xml` sample from Chapter 1; much of the content is the same:

```
<?xml version="1.0"?>
<!DOCTYPE name [
  <!ELEMENT name (first, middle, last)>
  <!ELEMENT first (#PCDATA)>
  <!ELEMENT middle (#PCDATA)>
  <!ELEMENT last (#PCDATA)>
]>
<name>
  <first>John</first>
  <middle>Fitzgerald Johansen</middle>
  <last>Doe</last>
</name>
```

2. Click Save to save the file.

3. You are ready to validate the document. Simply click the Validate button. You should see the output shown in Figure 4-1.

4. If the output suggests that the validation completed but that there was an error in the document, correct the error (the parser reports the line number and column number of the error) and try again. When editing XML manually, it is common to make errors when you first begin. Soon you will be able to see an error and correct it preemptively.

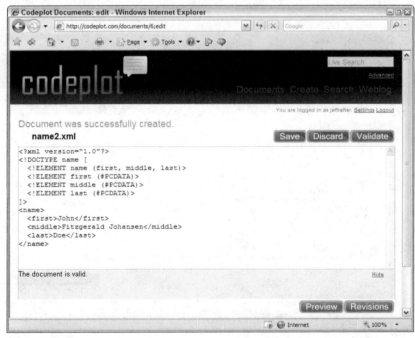

Figure 4-1

5. Create a new document called `name3.xml` by clicking the Create link again. Change the name of the `<first>` element to `<given>` within the `name2.xml` document:

```xml
<?xml version="1.0"?>
<!DOCTYPE name [
  <!ELEMENT name (first, middle, last)>
  <!ELEMENT first (#PCDATA)>
  <!ELEMENT middle (#PCDATA)>
  <!ELEMENT last (#PCDATA)>
]>
<name>
   <given>John</given>
   <middle>Fitzgerald Johansen</middle>
   <last>Doe</last>
</name>
```

6. Save the file and try validating again. This time the program should indicate errors, as shown in Figure 4-2.

The program reported that the element `<given>` was undeclared and that the content of the XML document didn't match what was specified in the DTD.

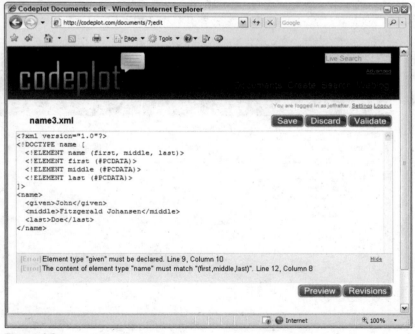

Figure 4-2

How It Works

This Try It Out used the DTD to check whether the content within the XML document matched the vocabulary. Internally, parsers handle these checks in different ways. At the most basic level, the parser reads the DTD declarations and stores them in memory. Then, as it reads the document, it validates each element that it encounters against the matching declaration. If it finds an element or attribute that does not appear within the declarations or appears in the wrong position, or if it finds a declaration that has no matching XML content, it raises a validity error.

Let's break the DTD down into smaller pieces so that you can get a preview of what you will learn later:

```
<?xml version="1.0"?>
```

As you have seen in all of the XML documents, you begin with the XML declaration. Again, this is optional, but it is highly recommended that you include it to avoid XML version conflicts later.

```
<!DOCTYPE name [
```

Immediately following the XML header is the *Document Type Declaration*, commonly referred to as the DOCTYPE. This informs the parser that a DTD is associated with this XML document. When using a DTD, the Document Type Declaration must appear at the start of the document (preceded only by the XML header) — it is not permitted anywhere else within the document. The DOCTYPE declaration has an exclamation mark (!) at the start of the element name. The XML Recommendation indicates that *declaration elements* must begin with an exclamation mark. Declaration elements may appear only as part of the DTD. They may not appear within the main XML content.

> At this point, you may have noticed that the syntax for DTDs is very different from the rules for basic XML documents. DTDs were originally used with the Standard Generalized Markup Language (SGML). To maintain compatibility with SGML, the designers of XML decided to keep the declaration language similar. In fact, the DTD syntax in XML is a simpler form of its SGML counterpart, so you need to learn many new syntax rules in order to construct DTDs.

In the previous example, you created a relatively simple DOCTYPE declaration; later you will look at some more advanced DOCTYPE declaration features. Directly following the DOCTYPE declaration is the body of the DTD. This is where you declare elements, attributes, entities, and notations.

```
<!ELEMENT name (first, middle, last)>
<!ELEMENT first (#PCDATA)>
<!ELEMENT middle (#PCDATA)>
<!ELEMENT last (#PCDATA)>
```

In the preceding DTD, you have declared several elements that make up the vocabulary of the <name> document. Like the DOCTYPE declaration, the element declarations must start with an exclamation mark.

```
]>
```

Finally, the declaration section of the DTD is closed using a closing bracket and a closing angle bracket. This effectively ended the definition, and the XML document immediately follows.

> *Now that you have seen a DTD and a validating parser in action, you may feel ready to create DTDs for all of your XML documents. Remember, however, that validation uses more processing power, even for a small document, so in many circumstances you may not want to use a DTD. For example, when using XML documents that are created by your company, or that are machine-generated (not hand-typed), you can be relatively sure that they follow the rules of your vocabulary. In such cases, checking validity may be unnecessary. In fact, it may negatively affect your overall application performance.*

The Document Type Declaration

The Document Type Declaration, or DOCTYPE, informs the parser that your document should conform to a DTD. It also indicates where the parser can find the rest of the definition. In the first example, the DOCTYPE was simple:

```
<!DOCTYPE name [ ]>
```

The Document Type Declaration always begins in the same way, with <!DOCTYPE, and there must be some whitespace following the word DOCTYPE, just as there is after element names. In addition, whitespace is not allowed to appear in between DOCTYPE and the opening "<!".

After the whitespace, the name of the XML document's root element must appear. It must appear *exactly* as it will in the document, including any namespace prefix. Because the document's root element is <name>, the word name follows the opening <!DOCTYPE in the declaration.

> *Remember that XML is case sensitive. Therefore, anytime you see a name in XML, it is case sensitive. When the recommendation says the name must appear exactly as it will in the document, this includes character case. You will see this throughout the DTD; any reference to XML names implies case sensitivity.*

Following the name of the root element, you have several options for specifying the rest of the Document Type Declaration. In the <name> example, the element declarations appeared between the [and] of the DTD. When declarations appear between the [and], as in the sample, they are called *internal subset declarations*. It is also possible to have some or all of your declarations in a separate document. DTD declarations that appear in external documents are *external subset declarations*. You can refer to an external DTD in one of the following two ways:

❑   System identifiers

❑   Public identifiers

System Identifiers

A *system identifier* allows you to specify the location of an external file containing DTD declarations. It is comprised of two parts: the keyword SYSTEM and a URI reference pointing to the document's location. A URI can be a file on your local hard drive, a file on your intranet or network, or even a file available on the Internet:

```
<!DOCTYPE name SYSTEM "name.dtd" [...]>
```

You must type the word SYSTEM after the name of the root element in your declaration. Following the SYSTEM keyword is the URI reference to the location of the file, in quotation marks. The following examples use system identifiers:

```
<!DOCTYPE name SYSTEM "file:///c:/name.dtd" [ ]>
```

```
<!DOCTYPE name SYSTEM "http://wiley.com/hr/name.dtd" [ ]>
```

```
<!DOCTYPE name SYSTEM "name.dtd">
```

Notice that the last example has no [and] characters. This is perfectly normal. Specifying an internal subset is optional. An XML document might conform to a DTD that uses only an internal subset, only an external subset, or both. If you do specify an internal subset, it appears between the [and], immediately following the system identifier.

You will see how to use an external DTD in the next Try It Out, but before you do, let's look at public identifiers.

Public Identifiers

Public identifiers provide a second mechanism to locate DTD resources:

```
<!DOCTYPE name PUBLIC "-//Beginning XML//DTD Name Example//EN">
```

Much like the system identifier, the public identifier begins with a keyword PUBLIC, followed by a specialized identifier. However, instead of a reference to a file, public identifiers are used to identify an entry in a catalog. According to the XML specification, public identifiers can follow any format; however, a commonly used format is called *Formal Public Identifiers*, or *FPIs*.

> *The syntax for an FPI is defined in the document ISO 9070. ISO 9070 also defines the process for registration and recording of formal public identifiers. The International Organization for Standardization, or ISO, is a group that designs government-approved standards. You can learn more about the ISO by going to its website at* http://www.iso.ch/.

The syntax for FPIs matches the following basic structure:

```
-//Owner//Class Description//Language//Version
```

At the most basic level, public identifiers function similarly to namespace names, but public identifiers cannot be used to combine two different vocabularies in the same document. This makes namespaces much more powerful than public identifiers.

Following the identifier string, you may include an optional system identifier as well. This enables the processor to find a copy of the document if it cannot resolve the public identifier (most processors cannot resolve public identifiers). When including the optional system identifier, the SYSTEM keyword shown earlier isn't required. A valid document type declaration that uses a public identifier might look like the following:

```
<!DOCTYPE name PUBLIC "-//Beginning XML//DTD Name Example//EN" "name.dtd">
```

The preceding declaration assumes you are defining a document type for a document whose root element is <name>. The definition has the following public identifier:

```
-//Beginning XML//DTD Name Example//EN
```

In case this cannot be resolved, there is an URI to a file called name.dtd. In the preceding example, no internal subset is included.

> So far, you've learned about catalogs and registered and unregistered public identifiers, but are these concepts commonly used in XML development? Yes. In fact, many web browsers, when identifying the versions of an XHTML document, use the public identifier mechanism. For example, many XHTML web pages will use the public identifier -//W3C//DTD XHTML 1.0 Strict//EN to identify the DTD associated with the document. When the web browser reads the file, it may use a built-in DTD that corresponds to the public identifier instead of downloading a copy from the Web. This enables web browsers to cache the DTD locally, reducing processing time. When you are developing your applications, you can use the same strategy. Using public identifiers simply gives you a way to identify a vocabulary, just as namespaces do.

Now that you have learned how to use public and system identifiers, let's try to create an external DTD file and associate it with the XML document. Remember that you can have an internal subset, an external subset, or both. When using an internal subset, the DTD declarations will appear within the XML document. When using an external subset, the DTD declarations will appear in a separate file.

Try It Out   The External DTD

By using an external DTD, you can easily share your vocabulary with others in your company, or even your own industry. Likewise, you can use vocabularies that others have already developed, by referring to external files they have created. This exercise reconfigures the <name> example so that the DTD is defined separately from the XML document:

1. Create a new document to form the external DTD. In Codeplot, click the Create link and name the document name4.dtd. In the editor, type in the following:

```
<!ELEMENT name (first, middle, last)>
<!ELEMENT first (#PCDATA)>
<!ELEMENT middle (#PCDATA)>
<!ELEMENT last (#PCDATA)>
```

2. Click Save to save the document.

3. Create another new document called name4.xml. This document will be similar to the name3.xml document from the last example:

```
<?xml version="1.0"?>
<!DOCTYPE name PUBLIC "-//Beginning XML//DTD Name Example//EN" "name4.dtd">
<name>
```

```
    <first>John</first>
    <middle>Fitzgerald Johansen</middle>
    <last>Doe</last>
</name>
```

4. If you copied and pasted the contents of the document from the `name3.xml` document, make sure you have also changed the element `<given>` back to `<first>` after the last Try It Out. Save the `name4.xml` document.

5. You are ready to validate the document again. Click the Validate button.

You should see the output shown in Figure 4-3, which indicates that the validation was successful.

If you received any errors, check whether you have typed everything correctly and try again.

How It Works

In this Try It Out, you used an external DTD to check the XML content. As you may have guessed, the syntax for the DTD changed very little. The main difference between the internal DTD and external DTD was the absence of a DOCTYPE declaration within the external DTD. The DOCTYPE declaration is always located within the main XML document. In addition, within the `name4.xml` document, there was no internal subset. Instead, you used a public identifier and system identifier to indicate which DTD the validation program should use.

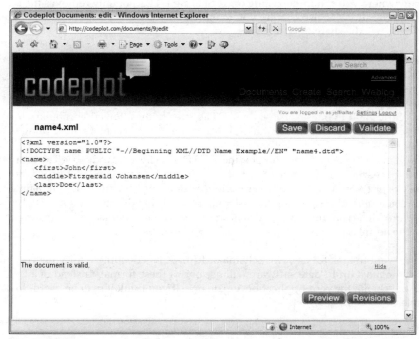

Figure 4-3

In this case, the validation program had no way to resolve public identifiers. The processor instead used the optional URI reference that you included to find the correct DTD for validation. In this example, the XML parser had to find the file `name4.dtd`. Because this is a relative URL reference (it does not contain a website address or drive letter), the parser began looking in the current directory — where the XML document it was parsing was located. The XML Recommendation does not specify how parsers should handle relative URL references, but most XML parsers will treat the path of the XML document as the base path, just as this example did. Be sure to check your XML parser's documentation before you use relative URL references.

Using external DTDs can be very beneficial in many situations. For example, because the DTD appears in a single separate document, it is easier to make changes. If the same DTD is repeated in each XML file, upgrading can be much more difficult. Later in the chapter, you will look at XML documents and DTDs that consist of many files using entities. You must remember, however, that looking up the DTD file takes extra processing time. In addition, if the DTD file is located on the Internet, you have to wait for it to download. Often, it is better to keep a local copy of the DTD for validation purposes. If you are maintaining a local copy, you should check for changes to the DTD at the original location.

Sharing Vocabularies

In reality, most DTDs will be much more complex than the first example, so it is often better to share vocabularies and use DTDs that are widely accepted. Before you start creating your own DTDs, it is good to know where you can find existing ones. Sharing DTDs not only removes the burden of having to create the declarations, it also enables you to more easily integrate with other companies and XML developers who use the shared vocabularies.

Many individuals and industries have developed DTDs that are de facto standards. Scientists use the Chemical Markup Language (CML) DTD to validate documents they share. In the mortgage industry, many businesses use the Mortgage Industry Standards Maintenance Organization's (MISMO) DTD when exchanging information. XHTML, the XML version of HTML 4.01, maintains three DTDs: Transitional, Strict, and Frameset. These three DTDs specify the allowed vocabulary for XHTML. Using these, browser developers can ensure that XHTML content is valid before attempting to display it.

You can check many places when trying to find a DTD for a specific industry. The first place to look, of course, is your favorite search engine. Most often, this will turn up good results. Another great place to check is the Cover Pages. *Cover Pages* is a priceless resource of XML information maintained by Robin Cover; it can be found at `http://xml.coverpages.org/`. In addition, you might also want to check the Dublin Core Metadata Initiative, which is an online resource dedicated to creating interoperable standards. The address is `http://www.dublincore.org`.

You may also want to look for an XML Schema or RELAX NG document for your vocabulary. In fact, it is likely that the most up-to-date software will use one of these formats instead of a DTD. If you can't find a DTD or schema for your application, create one. If you think it may be useful to others in your industry, release it on the Internet.

Anatomy of a DTD

Now that you have seen a DTD, let's look at each of the DTD declarations in more detail. Generally, DTDs consist of three basic parts:

- ❏ Element declarations
- ❏ Attribute declarations
- ❏ Entity declarations

The current name example needs to be expanded to explore the more complex aspects of DTDs. In this section, you will create an XML vocabulary for listing contacts — all of your friends and family. Note, however, that there are many existing vocabularies for contacts on the Internet. Using a simplified format will enable you to quickly create your own vocabulary.

Element Declarations

The beginning of this chapter demonstrated element declarations in use, but you have not yet looked at an element declaration in detail. When using a DTD to define the content of an XML document, you must declare each element that appears within the document. As you will soon see, DTDs can also include declarations for *optional elements*, elements that may or may not appear in the XML document.

```
<!ELEMENT name (first, middle, last)>
```

Element declarations consist of three basic parts:

- ❏ The ELEMENT declaration
- ❏ The element name
- ❏ The element content model

As you have seen with the DOCTYPE declaration, the ELEMENT declaration is used to indicate to the parser that you are about to define an element. Much like the DOCTYPE declaration, the ELEMENT declaration begins with an exclamation mark. The declaration can appear only within the context of the DTD.

Following the ELEMENT keyword is the name of the element that you are defining. Just as you saw in the DOCTYPE, the element name must appear exactly as it will within the XML document, including any namespace prefix.

> *The fact that you must specify the namespace prefix within DTDs is a major limitation. Essentially this means that users are not able to choose their own namespace prefix but must use the prefix defined within the DTD. This limitation exists because the W3C completed the XML Recommendation before finalizing how namespaces would work. As you will see in the next two chapters, XML Schemas and RELAX NG documents are not limited in this way.*

The content model of the element appears after the element name. An element's *content model* defines the allowable content within the element. An element may contain element children, text, a combination of children and text, or the element may be empty. This is essentially the crux of the DTD, where the entire document's structure is defined. As far as the XML Recommendation is concerned, four kinds of content models exist:

- ❑ Element
- ❑ Mixed
- ❑ Empty
- ❑ Any

Let's look at each of these content models in more detail.

Element Content

Many elements in XML contain other elements. In fact, this is one of the primary reasons for creating XML. When defining a content model with element content, you simply include the allowable elements within parentheses. For example, if you had a `<contact>` element that was allowed to contain only a `<name>` element, the declaration would read as follows:

```
<!ELEMENT contact (name)>
```

In the contact list, however, the `<contact>` element needs to include more than just the name. For now, you will include as its children a `<name>`, `<location>`, `<phone>`, `<knows>`, and `<description>` element:

```
<!ELEMENT contact (name, location, phone, knows, description)>
```

Each element that you specify within this element's content model must also have its own definition within the DTD. Therefore, in the preceding example, you would include ELEMENT declarations for the `<name>`, `<location>`, `<phone>`, `<knows>`, and `<description>` elements to complete the DTD.

Even when an element is used in multiple content models, you should only declare it once. In fact, the XML Recommendation does not allow you to declare two elements with the same name inside a DTD.

The processor needs this information so that it knows how to handle each element when it is encountered. You may put the ELEMENT declarations in any order you like. As you may have guessed, the element name in the content model must appear exactly as it will in the document, including a namespace prefix, if any.

Of course, even in this small example at the start of the chapter the element had more than one child. This will often be the case. There are two fundamental ways of specifying the element children:

- ❑ Sequences
- ❑ Choices

Sequences

Often the elements within these documents must appear in a distinct order. If this is the case, you define the content model using a *sequence*. When specifying a sequence of elements, you simply list the element names separated by commas. Again, this will be within the parentheses that immediately follow the name of the element you are declaring. All of the examples that had more than one element have used a sequence when declaring the content model:

```
<!ELEMENT name (first, middle, last)>
```

In the preceding example, the declaration indicates that the `<name>` element must have exactly three children: `<first>`, `<middle>`, and `<last>` and that they must appear in this order. Likewise, the `<contact>` element must have exactly five children in the order specified:

```
<!ELEMENT contact (name, location, phone, knows, description)>
```

If your XML document were missing one of the elements within the sequence, or if your document contained more elements, the parser would raise an error. If all of the specified elements were included within the XML document but appeared in another order such as `<last>`, `<middle>`, `<first>`, the processor would raise an error.

Note that in an element-only content model (as you have here), whitespace doesn't matter. Therefore, using the preceding declaration, the allowable content for the `<name>` element might appear as follows:

```
<name>
  <first>John</first>
  <middle>Fitzgerald Johansen</middle>
  <last>Doe</last>
</name>
```

Because the whitespace within the element's content doesn't matter, you could also have the content appear as shown here:

```
<name><first>John</first><middle>Fitzgerald
Johansen</middle><last>Doe</last></name>
```

The spacing of the elements in an element-only content model is only for readability. It has no significance to the validation program.

Choices

Although you have used sequences throughout this chapter, in many circumstances a sequence doesn't allow you to model the element content. Suppose you needed to allow one element or another, but not both. Obviously, you would need a choice mechanism of some sort. Consider the `<location>` element, which specifies where each contact lives:

```
<!ELEMENT location (address)>
```

Instead of requiring one element, you could require a choice between two elements:

```
<!ELEMENT location (address | GPS)>
```

This declaration would allow the `<location>` element to contain one `<address>` or one `<GPS>` element. If the `<location>` element were empty, or if it contained more than one of these elements, the parser would raise an error.

Constructing a choice content model is very similar to constructing a sequence content model. Instead of separating the elements by commas, however, you must use the vertical bar (|) character. The vertical bar functions as an exclusive OR. An exclusive OR allows one and only one element of the possible options.

Combining Sequences and Choices Using Groups

Many XML documents need to leverage much more complex rules, beyond simple sequences and choices. Suppose you wanted to declare <latitude> and <longitude> elements within the <location> content model instead of the single <GPS> element.

When creating the <location> declaration, you would need to specify that the content can include either an <address> element *or* the <latitude> and <longitude> sequence of elements, but not both. The XML Recommendation allows you to mix sequences and choices. Knowing this, you can declare the model as follows:

```
<!ELEMENT location (address | (latitude, longitude))>
```

As in the earlier examples, you have enclosed the entire content model within parentheses. In this example, however, you have a second set of parentheses within the content model. It is good to think of this as a content model within a content model. The inner content model, in the preceding example, is a sequence specifying the elements <latitude> and <longitude>. The XML Recommendation allows content models within content models within content models, and so on, infinitely.

The processor handles each inner content model much like a simple mathematical equation. Because the processor handles each model individually, it can treat each model as a separate entity. This enables you to use models in sequences and choices. In the preceding example, you had a choice between an element and a sequence content model. You could easily create a sequence of sequences, or a sequence of choices, or a choice of sequences — almost any combination you can think of.

Mixed Content

The XML Recommendation specifies that any element with text in its content is a *mixed content model* element. Within mixed content models, text can appear by itself or it can be interspersed between elements.

> *In everyday usage, people refer to elements that can contain only text as* text-only elements *or* text-only content.

The rules for mixed content models are similar to the element content model rules that you learned in the last section. You have already seen some examples of the simplest mixed content model — text only:

```
<!ELEMENT first (#PCDATA)>
```

The preceding declaration specifies the keyword #PCDATA within the parentheses of the content model. You may remember from Chapter 2 that PCDATA is an abbreviation for Parsed Character DATA. This keyword simply indicates that the character data within the content model should be parsed by the parser. An example element that adheres to this declaration might look like the following:

```
<first>John</first>
```

Mixed content models can also contain elements interspersed within the text. Suppose you wanted to include a description of each contact in your XML document. You could create a new <description> element that enables you to specify where line breaks should occur, and indicate when the text should be emphasized (italic) or strong (bold):

```
<description>Jeff is a developer and author for Beginning XML <em>4th
edition</em>.<br/>Jeff <strong>loves</strong> XML!</description>
```

In this sample, you have a <description> element. Within the <description> element, you have interspersed the text with elements such as the <em> (indicating italic text) and the <strong> (indicating a bold section of text) and the <br> element (indicating a line break).

If you are familiar with HTML or XHTML you may recognize the <em>, <strong>, and <br> elements. HTML frequently uses mixed content models to specify parts of the document.

There is only one way to declare a mixed content model within DTDs. In the mixed content model, you must use the choice mechanism when adding elements. This means that each element within the content model must be separated by the vertical bar (|) character:

```
<!ELEMENT description (#PCDATA | em | strong | br)*>
```

The preceding sample declares the new <description> element. Notice that you use the choice mechanism to describe the content model; a vertical bar separates each element. You cannot use commas to separate the choices.

When including elements in the mixed content model, the #PCDATA keyword must always appear first in the list of choices. This allows validating parsers to immediately recognize that it is processing a mixed content model, rather than an element content model. Unlike with element-only content models, you cannot have inner content models in a mixed declaration.

You should also notice the * outside of the parentheses of the content model. When you are including elements within the mixed content model, you are required to include the * at the end of the content model, which tells the parser to repeat the content model. The * character is known as a *cardinality indicator*. You will learn more about cardinality indicators later in this chapter.

Because you are using a repeated choice mechanism (the * cardinality indicator), you have no control over the order or number of elements within the mixed content. You can have an unlimited number of <strong> elements, an unlimited number of <em> elements, and any amount of text. All of this can appear in any order within the <description> element. This simple text validation is considered a major limitation of DTDs. In the next chapter, you will learn how XML Schema has improved validation of mixed content models.

In summary, every time you declare elements within a mixed content model, they must follow four rules:

- ❏ They must use the choice mechanism (the vertical bar | character) to separate elements.
- ❏ The #PCDATA keyword must appear first in the list of elements.
- ❏ There must be no inner content models.
- ❏ If there are child elements, the * cardinality indicator *must* appear at the end of the model.

Empty Content

Recall from Chapter 2 that some elements may or may not have content:

```
<middle></middle>
<middle/>
```

In Chapter 2, the `<middle>` element sometimes had content and sometimes was empty. Some elements within your XML documents might *never* need to contain content. In fact, in many cases it wouldn't make sense for an element to contain text or elements. Using the `<br/>` element you can insert a line break into the `<description>` elements. It would not make much sense to include text within the `<br/>` element. Moreover, no elements would logically fit into a `<br/>` tag. This is a perfect candidate for an empty content model.

To define an element with an empty content model, simply include the word EMPTY following the element name in the declaration:

```
<!ELEMENT br EMPTY>
```

Remember that this requires the element to be empty within the XML document. Using the EMPTY keyword, you shouldn't declare elements that *may* contain content. For example, the `<middle>` element may or may not contain other elements. As you will see, even though an element is not declared with an empty content model, it may still be empty. Because the `<middle>` element may contain elements, you have to declare the element by using a mixed content model, rather than the EMPTY keyword.

Any Content

Finally, you can declare an element using the ANY keyword. The ANY keyword allows you to be even less restrictive about the content model. If you wanted, you could declare the `<description>` element using the ANY keyword:

```
<!ELEMENT description ANY>
```

In the preceding example, the ANY keyword indicates that any elements declared within the DTD can be used within the content of the `<description>` element and that they can be used in any order any number of times. The ANY keyword does not allow you to include elements that are not declared within the DTD. In addition to elements, any character data can appear within the `<description>` element.

Because DTDs are used to restrict content, the ANY keyword is not very popular, as it does very little to restrict the allowed content of the element you are declaring.

Try It Out   "Making Contact"

You are likely ready to build a much more complex DTD with all of this newfound knowledge — you are also probably eager to see the more complete contacts example. In this Try It Out, you start with the basics and add more features in following examples:

1. Open Codeplot or another text editor and create a new document called `contacts1.xml`. Input the following XML document:

```
<?xml version="1.0"?>
<!DOCTYPE contacts PUBLIC "-//Beginning XML//DTD Contact Example//EN"
"contacts1.dtd">
<contacts>
  <contact>
    <name>
      <first>Jeff</first>
      <middle>Craig</middle>
      <last>Rafter</last>
    </name>
    <location>
      <latitude>34.031892</latitude>
      <longitude>-117.207642</longitude>
    </location>
    <phone>001-909-555-1212</phone>
    <knows>David Hunter, Danny Ayers</knows>
    <description>Jeff is a developer and author for Beginning XML <em>4th
edition</em>.<br/>Jeff <strong>loves</strong> XML!</description>
  </contact>
</contacts>
```

2. Save the document.

Notice that you have added a document type declaration that refers to an external system file called `contacts1.dtd`. In addition, the root element in this document and the element name within the `DOCTYPE` declaration are the same.

3. Create a new document called `contacts1.dtd`. This file will be where you define your DTD.

Because you have a sample XML document, you can base most of your declarations on the text that you have. You were probably taught that when programming, you should plan and design first, and then implement. Building a DTD based on an existing sample, however, is by far the easiest method available. When designing a DTD, it is much easier to create a sample and let the document evolve before the vocabulary is set in stone. Of course, you must remember that some elements might not appear in your sample (such as some elements in choice content models).

4. In the XML document, `<contacts>` is the root element. This is the easiest place to start, so begin by declaring it in the DTD:

```
<!ELEMENT contacts ()>
```

5. You haven't specified a content model. Looking at the sample document, you can see that the `<contacts>` element contains a `<contact>` element. There is only one child element, so this content model should be easy to define:

```
<!ELEMENT contacts (contact)>
```

Allowing for only one contact as you have done is a little clumsy, but you'll improve this content model a little later in the chapter.

6. Of course, because you have specified a `contact` element in the content model, you know that you must declare it in the DTD:

```
<!ELEMENT contact (name, location, phone, knows, description)>
```

7. Again, you need to declare each element that is used within the content model. Declare the `<name>` element and each of its children:

```
<!ELEMENT name (first, middle, last)>
<!ELEMENT first (#PCDATA)>
<!ELEMENT middle (#PCDATA)>
<!ELEMENT last (#PCDATA)>
```

The `<first>`, `<middle>`, and `<last>` elements represent each part of the contact's name. They are all text-only elements, so you have declared that they can contain only #PCDATA. Remember that this qualifies as a mixed content model even though there are no element children.

8. The contacts list won't be very useful if you don't include information about where to find the contact or how to call them, so you should include an element to describe their location and their phone number. You can use a complex content model for the `<location>` element, as shown earlier in the chapter:

```
<!ELEMENT location (address | (latitude, longitude))>
```

This declaration allows each location to include either an address or the latitude and longitude coordinates. Even though you didn't include the `<latitude>` or `<longitude>` elements in the `<location>` element in the sample, you should still include them in the content model declaration so that they can be used in other documents.

9. The `<address>`, `<latitude>`, and `<longitude>` elements are text-only elements:

```
<!ELEMENT address (#PCDATA)>
<!ELEMENT latitude (#PCDATA)>
<!ELEMENT longitude (#PCDATA)>
```

10. The `<phone>` element must also be declared in your DTD and will be text-only:

```
<!ELEMENT phone (#PCDATA)>
```

11. There is a `<knows>` element in the sample document. For now, you can declare it as text-only:

```
<!ELEMENT knows (#PCDATA)>
```

12. You can use a truly mixed content model for the description. This enables your XML document to contain a mix of text and elements but still allows the DTD to be restrictive about which child elements can be used:

```
<!ELEMENT description (#PCDATA | em | strong | br)*>
```

13. Finally, you must include declarations for the `<em>`, `<strong>`, and `<br>` elements:

```
<!ELEMENT em (#PCDATA)>
<!ELEMENT strong (#PCDATA)>
<!ELEMENT br EMPTY>
```

At this point you have completed the DTD. All of the children that were listed in content models now have their own element declarations. The final DTD should look like the following:

```
<!ELEMENT contacts (contact)>
<!ELEMENT contact (name, location, phone, knows, description)>

<!ELEMENT name (first, middle, last)>
```

```
<!ELEMENT first (#PCDATA)>
<!ELEMENT middle (#PCDATA)>
<!ELEMENT last (#PCDATA)>

<!ELEMENT location (address | (latitude, longitude))>
<!ELEMENT address (#PCDATA)>
<!ELEMENT latitude (#PCDATA)>
<!ELEMENT longitude (#PCDATA)>

<!ELEMENT phone (#PCDATA)>
<!ELEMENT knows (#PCDATA)>

<!ELEMENT description (#PCDATA | em | strong | br)*>
<!ELEMENT em (#PCDATA)>
<!ELEMENT strong (#PCDATA)>
<!ELEMENT br EMPTY>
```

14. Save the file.

15. You are ready to validate the document again. Open the `contacts1.xml` document again and click Validate. If you typed everything correctly, you should see the results shown in Figure 4-4. If you received any errors, confirm that you input the documents correctly and click Validate again.

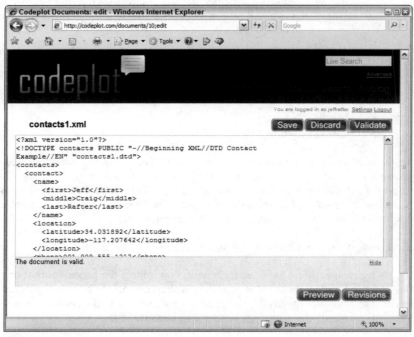

Figure 4-4

How It Works

Just as you saw with the original <name> example, the validator processed your XML document, checking that each element it encountered was declared in the DTD. The DTD for your contacts list was much more complex than the original example. It used all choice and sequence content models, text-only content models, and mixed content models. You even declared an empty element.

Unfortunately, the contacts DTD is severely limited. It only allows one contact. How can you fix the problem? You can't yet. You need a way to tell the processor that the (contact) sequence may appear many times or not at all. You must learn how to tell the processor how many times the elements will appear.

Cardinality

An element's *cardinality* defines how many times it will appear within a content model. Each element within a content model can have an indicator following the element name that tells the parser how many times it will appear. DTDs allow four indicators for cardinality, as shown in the following table:

Indicator	Description
[none]	As you have seen in all of the content models thus far, when no cardinality indicator is used, it indicates that the element must appear once and only once. This is the default behavior for elements used in content models.
?	Indicates that the element may appear either once or not at all
+	Indicates that the element may appear one or more times
*	Indicates that the element may appear zero or more times

Let's look at these indicators in action.

In many cultures it is common to have several first names. Let's examine what you want to accomplish in that case. You know that every contact you create will have at least one first name. You also know that each contact might have more than one first name. You don't know how many first names each contact will have. You need to use a cardinality indicator specifying that the <first> element can appear one or more times within the <name> element. The + indicator does just that:

```
<!ELEMENT name (first+, middle?, last)>
```

By including a + when specifying the first element, you inform the processor that one or more first names can be included within the content model. It is also common to have no middle name. To allow for this, you can use a ? when specifying the middle element within the content model. This indicates that the <name> may or may not contain a <middle> element.

If you were to validate the document again, the parser would not raise validity errors if there were multiple <first> elements and the <middle> element was missing. With this new declaration, all of the following <name> elements are allowable:

```
<name>
   <first>John</first>
   <last>Doe</last>
</name>
```

```
<name>
   <first>John</first>
   <first>Fitzgerald</first>
   <last>Doe</last>
</name>
```

```
<name>
   <first>John</first>
   <first>Fitzgerald</first>
   <first>Simon</first>
   <middle>Johansen</middle>
   <last>Doe</last>
</name>
```

```
<name>
   <first>John</first>
   <middle>Johansen</middle>
   <last>Doe</last>
</name>
```

In each of the preceding cases, you can see that the `<middle>` element may or may not appear. In addition, the `<first>` element may appear one or several times. Remember that because you didn't explicitly use a cardinality indicator for the `<last>` element, it must appear once and only once. In addition, even though you have used cardinality indicators, when elements do appear, they must be in the order that you defined within your sequence.

> Remember that the cardinality indicator affects only the content model where it appears. Even though you specify that the `<middle>` element within the `<name>` content model can appear once or not at all, this does not affect the declaration of the `<middle>` element, or any other use of the `<middle>` element in the DTD.

Perhaps the largest deficiency remaining in the contacts DTD is that you can only have one contact. Currently your DTD allows only one `<contact>` element to appear as a child of the `<contacts>` root element. This won't let you get very far in documenting all of your friends and family. You need to indicate that the element can appear zero, one, or many times. Fortunately, the * cardinality indicator does just that. You could improve the DTD by changing the earlier `<contacts>` declaration:

```
<!ELEMENT contacts (contact*)>
```

Though it is unlikely that you would ever have an empty contacts list, it is possible. Therefore, utilizing the * cardinality indicator gives you the flexibility you need. This solves the problem completely, as it represents the desired content model perfectly. Before you go back to the example, though, let's look at some other ways you could spruce up your contacts DTD.

It might also be helpful to support multiple addresses for each contact. To enable this, you could modify the <location> declaration:

```
<!ELEMENT location (address* | (latitude, longitude))>
```

By using the * cardinality indicator for address, you specify that the <location> element may contain zero or more <address> elements *or* a single instance of <latitude> and <longitude> elements.

Adding the * to address allows for multiple addresses, but what if a contact has multiple GPS locations instead? Luckily, the XML Recommendation allows you to apply cardinality indicators to content models as well. Remember that the content model is everything that appears within parentheses, and content models can contain inner content models. Therefore, you can change the <location> declaration again:

```
<!ELEMENT location (address* | (latitude, longitude)*)>
```

The * indicator is functioning exactly as it did earlier. This time, however, you are indicating that the entire sequence (latitude, longitude) may appear zero or more times. Remember that this is still part of a choice. The new declaration indicates that each location may contain zero or more <address> elements *or* it may contain zero or more sequences of <latitude> and <longitude> elements. It could not contain both <address> elements and <latitude> and <longitude> elements. Moreover, the <location> element could never contain a <latitude> element without the subsequent <longitude> element. This might be good enough but it would be nice to have some more options, such as changing the order and allowing for both addresses and latitude/longitude pairs.

```
<!ELEMENT location (address | (latitude, longitude))*>
```

In this example, the * is outside of the parentheses. This indicates that you want the entire content model to appear zero or more times. In this case, the entire content model consists of a choice between addresses or the sequence of latitude and longitude. Repeating a choice means that you can choose one option the first time and another the second. For example, the following <location> element would be valid:

```
<location>
    <address>Redlands, CA, USA</address>
    <latitude>34.031892</latitude>
    <longitude>-117.207642</longitude>
    <latitude>-13.955059</latitude>
    <longitude>33.800125</longitude>
</location>
```

In the first example, you have an <address> element followed by two sets of <latitude> and <longitude> elements. From the validator's perspective, you chose the <address> element, then you chose the <latitude> and <longitude> sequence, and finally you chose another <latitude> and <longitude> element. These choices could repeat infinitely. You could even choose to have the <latitude> and <longitude> before you chose to have an <address> element:

```
<location>
    <address>Redlands, CA, USA</address>
    <latitude>34.031892</latitude>
    <longitude>-117.207642</longitude>
</location>
```

You could choose to have an `<address>` element in between two `<latitude>` and `<longitude>` sequences:

```
<location>
  <latitude>34.031892</latitude>
  <longitude>-117.207642</longitude>
  <address>Redlands, CA, USA</address>
  <latitude>-13.955059</latitude>
  <longitude>33.800125</longitude>
</location>
```

By placing the * outside of the parentheses, you have constructed an extremely flexible content model for the `<location>` element, which should satisfy all of the possible contacts you encounter.

Try It Out   "Making Contact" — Part 2

Now that you have learned how to correct and improve the DTD, let's get down to business and integrate the changes you have read about so far:

1. Create a new document called `contacts2.dtd`. To make this easier, copy the content from the file `contacts1.dtd` and modify the highlighted sections:

```
<!ELEMENT contacts (contact*)>
<!ELEMENT contact (name, location, phone, knows, description)>

<!ELEMENT name (first+, middle?, last)>
<!ELEMENT first (#PCDATA)>
<!ELEMENT middle (#PCDATA)>
<!ELEMENT last (#PCDATA)>

<!ELEMENT location (address | (latitude, longitude))*>
<!ELEMENT address (#PCDATA)>
<!ELEMENT latitude (#PCDATA)>
<!ELEMENT longitude (#PCDATA)>

<!ELEMENT phone (#PCDATA)>
<!ELEMENT knows (#PCDATA)>

<!ELEMENT description (#PCDATA | em | strong | br)*>
<!ELEMENT em (#PCDATA)>
<!ELEMENT strong (#PCDATA)>
<!ELEMENT br EMPTY>
```

2. Save the file.

3. Of course, now that you have created a new DTD file, you need to update your XML document to refer to it. Create a new document called `contacts2.xml`. Again, you can copy the contents of `contacts1.xml` and modify the DOCTYPE declaration so that it refers to the new DTD. You will also change the `<middle>` element for the first contact to a `<first>` element and add an `<address>`. In order to see the flexibility in the DTD, you can add two more contacts:

```
<?xml version="1.0"?>
<!DOCTYPE contacts PUBLIC "-//Beginning XML//DTD Contact Example//EN"
"contacts2.dtd">
```

```
<contacts>
  <contact>
    <name>
      <first>Jeff</first>
      <first>Craig</first>
      <last>Rafter</last>
    </name>
    <location>
      <address>Redlands, CA, USA</address>
      <latitude>34.031892</latitude>
      <longitude>-117.207642</longitude>
    </location>
    <phone>001-909-555-1212</phone>
    <knows>David Hunter, Danny Ayers</knows>
    <description>Jeff is a developer and author for Beginning XML <em>4th
edition</em>.<br/>Jeff <strong>loves</strong> XML!</description>
  </contact>
  <contact>
    <name>
      <first>David</first>
      <last>Hunter</last>
    </name>
    <location>
      <address>Address is not known</address>
    </location>
    <phone>416 555 1212</phone>
    <knows>Jeff Rafter, Danny Ayers</knows>
    <description>Senior Technical Consultant for CGI.</description>
  </contact>
  <contact>
    <name>
      <first>Daniel</first>
      <middle>John</middle>
      <last>Ayers</last>
    </name>
    <location>
      <latitude>43.847156</latitude>
      <longitude>10.50808</longitude>
      <address>Mozzanella, 7 Castiglione di Garfagnana, 55033 Lucca Italy</address>
    </location>
    <phone>+39-0555-11-22-33-</phone>
    <knows>Jeff Rafter, David Hunter</knows>
    <description>A Semantic Web developer and technical author specializing in
cutting-edge technologies.</description>
  </contact>
</contacts>
```

4. Save the file.

5. You are ready to validate the document again. Click the Validate button.

Your output should show a complete validation without errors, as shown in Figure 4-5. If you received any errors this time, check whether you have typed everything correctly and try again.

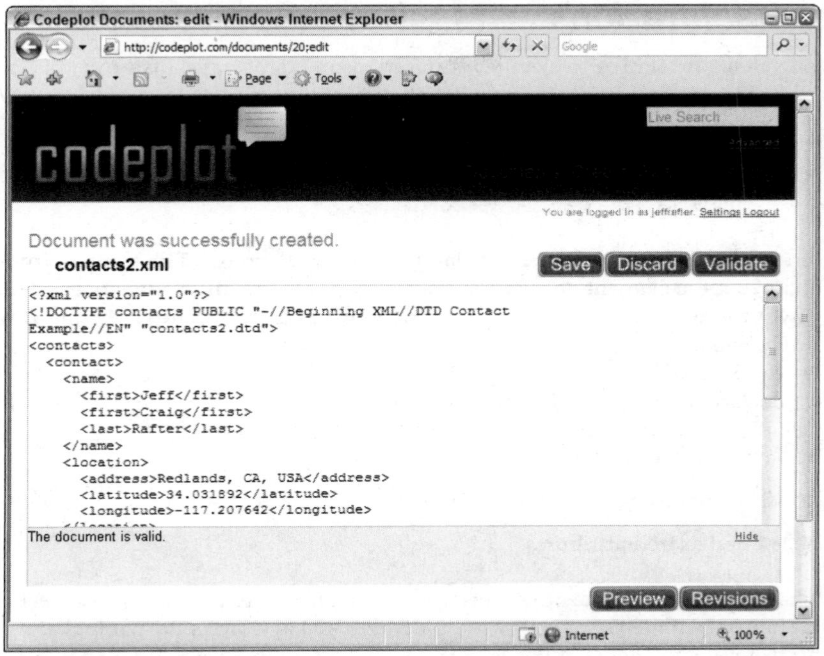

Figure 4-5

How It Works

This Try It Out implements much of what you learned throughout this section. To sum it up, you set out to design a DTD that could be used to describe a complete list of contacts. You used an assortment of complex content models so that your DTD would reflect various XML documents. Of course, when you first began designing your DTD, you didn't include many options (in fact, there were some severe limitations). After you had the basic structure designed, you modified the DTD to correct some problems and add some features. The design strategy is very common among XML developers.

> Some XML designers have taken this design strategy a step further. Instead of relying only on an example XML document, they use complex Unified Modeling Language (UML) diagrams or other types of visual aid. As shown in the next chapter, new syntaxes have evolved based on this strategy of using an example document to describe the vocabulary. For instance, Examplotron uses a syntax in which the example essentially is the declaration. More information on Examplotron can be found at http://examplotron.org/.

Now that you have a firm grasp on how to declare elements within the DTD, let's turn our attention to attributes.

Attribute Declarations

Attribute declarations are similar to element declarations in many ways. Instead of declaring allowable content models for elements, you declare a list of allowable attributes for each element. These lists are called ATTLIST *declarations*:

```
<!ELEMENT contacts (contact*)>
<!ATTLIST contacts source CDATA #IMPLIED>
```

The preceding example has the element declaration for your <contacts> element from the contacts list example. Following the element declaration is an ATTLIST declaration, which declares the allowable attributes of your <contacts> element. This particular ATTLIST declares only one attribute, source, for the <contacts> element.

An ATTLIST declaration consists of three basic parts:

❑ The ATTLIST keyword

❑ The associated element's name

❑ The list of declared attributes

Just as you have seen in all of the other declarations, the ATTLIST begins with an exclamation mark to indicate that it is part of the DTD. Following the ATTLIST keyword is the name of the associated element. In this example, the name of the associated element is contacts. By specifying this, you indicate that you are building a list of attributes only for a <contacts> element.

Following the ATTLIST name, you declare each attribute in the list. An ATTLIST declaration can include any number of attributes. Each attribute in the list consists of three parts:

❑ The attribute name

❑ The attribute type

❑ The attribute value declaration

Let's look at each section of the source attribute declaration:

```
source CDATA #IMPLIED
```

In the preceding declaration, the name of the attribute is source. The example declares that this source attribute can contain character data by using the CDATA keyword — this is the attribute's type. Lastly, the declaration indicates that the attribute has no default value, and that this attribute does not need to appear within the element using the #IMPLIED keyword. This third part of the attribute declaration is known as the *value declaration*; it controls how the XML parser handles the attribute's value. You will look at value declaration options in more detail a little later in this chapter.

Attribute Names

You learned in Chapter 2 that attribute names are very similar to element names. You must follow the basic XML naming rules when declaring an attribute. In addition to the basic naming rules, you must also ensure that you don't have duplicate names within the attribute list. Remember, duplicate attribute names are not allowed within a single element. To declare an attribute name, simply type the name exactly as it will appear in the XML document, including any namespace prefix.

> As far as DTDs are concerned, namespace declarations, such as `xmlns:contacts=` `"http://wiley.com/contacts"`, are also treated as attributes. Although the Namespace Recommendation insists that `xmlns` statements are declarations and not attributes, DTDs must declare them in an `ATTLIST` declaration if they are used. Again, this is because the W3C finalized the syntax for DTDs before the Namespace Recommendation was completed.

Attribute Types

When declaring attributes, you can specify how the processor should handle the character data that appears in the value. So far, you haven't seen anything like this in DTDs. Within the element declarations, you could specify that an element contained text, but you couldn't specify how the processor should treat the text value. To solve this problem, several new features are available for attribute declaration.

Let's look at the different attribute types:

Type	Description
CDATA	Indicates that the attribute value is character data. Notice that this is slightly different from the PCDATA keyword in ELEMENT declarations. Unlike PCDATA, within CDATA, the parser can ignore certain reserved characters.
ID	Indicates that the attribute value uniquely identifies the containing element
IDREF	Indicates that the attribute value is a reference, by ID, to a uniquely identifiable element
IDREFS	Indicates that the attribute value is a whitespace-separated list of IDREF values
ENTITY	Indicates that the attribute value is a reference to an external unparsed entity (you will learn more about entities later). The unparsed entity might be an image file or some other external resource such as an MP3 or some other binary file.
ENTITIES	Indicates that the attribute value is a whitespace-separated list of ENTITY values
NMTOKEN	Indicates that the attribute value is a name token. An NMTOKEN is a string of character data consisting of standard name characters.
NMTOKENS	Indicates that the attribute value is a whitespace-separated list of NMTOKEN values
Enumerated List	Apart from using the default types, you can also declare an enumerated list of possible values for the attribute.

As you saw in the previous example, the attribute type immediately follows the attribute name. Let's look at each of these types in more detail.

CDATA

CDATA is the default attribute type. It specifies that the attribute value is character data. A processor won't do any additional type checking on a CDATA attribute because it is the most basic of the data types. Of course, the XML well-formedness rules still apply, but as long as the content is well formed, a validating parser will accept any text as CDATA.

ID, IDREF, and IDREFS

Attributes of type ID can be used to uniquely identify an element within an XML document. Once you have uniquely identified the element, you can later use an IDREF to refer to that element. Identifying elements is paramount in many XML technologies, as covered in Chapter 7, "XPath," and Chapter 8, "XSLT." Many of you may have already seen an ID mechanism in action. Within HTML, many elements can be identified with an ID attribute. Often JavaScript code accesses elements by their ID.

Remember several rules when using ID attributes:

❑ The value of an ID attribute must follow the rules for XML names.

❑ The value of an ID attribute must be unique within the entire XML document.

❑ Only one attribute of type ID may be declared per element.

❑ The attribute value declaration for an ID attribute must be #IMPLIED or #REQUIRED.

Suppose you added an ID attribute to the <contact> element:

```
<!ATTLIST contact person ID #REQUIRED>
```

In the document you could add the unique ID:

```
<contact person="Jeff_Rafter">
```

Is the value for the person attribute valid? You have declared it as an ID attribute. The first thing to notice about your ID value is the underscore (_) between "Jeff" and "Rafter". Remember that XML names cannot have spaces. If you simply used the contact name (with spaces in between each part of the name), it would be an invalid ID. Replacing each space in the value with an underscore makes the value legal.

> *Using the contact name as the basis for the* person *attribute helps ensure that each one is different. Remember that any attribute value of type* ID *must be unique — it must even be different from the* ID *attributes in different elements.*

You haven't declared more than one ID attribute type in a single element. When you declared the kind attribute, you chose to include the #REQUIRED keyword.

When you declare IDREF attributes the rules are similar:

- ❑ The value of an IDREF attribute must follow the rules for XML names.

- ❑ The value of an IDREF attribute must match the value of some ID within the XML document.

Often you need to refer to a list of elements. For example, within the <knows> element, you may want to refer to multiple contacts. You could use an IDREFS attribute store with a list of whitespace-separated IDREF values that refer to the person ID attributes defined for each of your contacts:

```
<knows contacts="David_Hunter Danny_Ayers"/>
```

ENTITY and ENTITIES

Attributes can also include references to unparsed entities. An *unparsed entity* is an entity reference to an external file that the processor cannot parse. For example, external images are unparsed entities; instead of actually including the image inside the document, you use special attributes to refer to the external resource. In XML you can declare *reusable* references inside your DTD using an ENTITY declaration. You haven't seen ENTITY declarations yet, which are covered in more detail later in this chapter.

For now, let's cover the rules for ENTITY attribute types. In ENTITY attributes, you must refer to an ENTITY that has been declared somewhere in the DTD. In addition, because you are referring to an ENTITY, the value must follow the rules for XML names. Consider the following attribute declaration:

```
<!ATTLIST contact portrait ENTITY #IMPLIED>
```

After declaring a portrait attribute, you can then refer to an ENTITY within your XML document:

```
<contact portrait="PictureOfJeffRafter">
```

The image attribute refers to an ENTITY that is named PictureOfJeffRafter. This assumes that you have declared the ENTITY somewhere in your DTD. In addition, notice that the value follows the rules for XML names: It begins with a letter and contains valid name characters.

The ENTITIES attribute type is simply a whitespace-separated list of ENTITY values. Therefore, you could declare the following:

```
<!ATTLIST contact pictures ENTITIES #IMPLIED>
```

A valid use of the preceding declaration might look like the following:

```
<contact pictures="PictureOfJeffRafter-Small
    PictureOfJeffRafter-Large">
```

The ENTITY names are still valid (recall that it is legal to use a dash in an XML name) and they are separated by whitespace. In fact, a linefeed and several spaces appear between the two values. This is legal — the XML processor doesn't care *how much* whitespace separates two values. The processor considers any number of spaces, tabs, linefeeds, and carriage return characters as whitespace.

NMTOKEN and NMTOKENS

You will often need to have attributes that refer to a concept or single word. This might be an element name, an entity name, an attribute name, or some other concept. In fact, the value that an NMTOKEN attribute uses doesn't even have to be declared. The NMTOKEN type enables you to create an attribute value that, as long as the value follows the rules for an XML name, the processor will treat as valid.

Suppose you added a `tag` attribute to the `<contact>` element that allowed you to specify an interesting keyword for the contact:

```
<!ATTLIST contact tag NMTOKEN #IMPLIED>
```

The following value would be allowable:

```
<contact tag="author">
```

When you learned the rules for XML names, you learned that names are not allowed to begin with a numerical digit. NMTOKEN values are not required to adhere to this rule. An NMTOKEN value may begin with any name character, including numbers.

As shown with other attribute types, the NMTOKENS type is simply a whitespace-separated list of NMTOKEN values. You could declare the `tag` attribute to allow multiple habitat values as follows:

```
<!ATTLIST contact tags NMTOKENS #IMPLIED>
```

The following value would be allowable:

```
<contact tags="author programmer poetry">
```

You haven't declared any of these values within the DTD; they simply follow the rules for NMTOKEN values.

Enumerated Attribute Types

Clearly, the ability to check types within attribute values is indispensable. Suppose you want to allow only a certain set of values in the attribute. You could use the existing types to restrict your attribute value, but it might not give you enough control. Suppose you want to add a `kind` attribute to the `<phone>` element. You could use this attribute to specify what kind of phone number is represented in each element. You might expect to see the values Home, Work, Cell, and Fax. All of these values are character data, so you could use the CDATA type. Of course, if you did this, someone could input the value 42, because it is character data. This isn't what you want at all. Instead, you could use the NMTOKEN attribute type because all of your choices are valid NMTOKEN values. Of course, this would also allow values like Blog. You need to limit the values that are allowed for the attribute with even greater control.

An *enumerated list* allows you to do just that. When you declare your attribute, you can specify a list of allowable values. Again, the whitespace within the declaration does not matter. You can use as much or as little whitespace before and after each enumerated value as you want. Each value must be a valid XML name (although it can start with any name character, including numeric digits). Therefore, the value itself cannot contain spaces. Let's see what a declaration for the `kind` attribute would look like using an enumerated list:

```
<!ATTLIST phone kind (Home | Work | Cell | Fax) #IMPLIED>
```

Here, all the possible values are listed within parentheses. Each value is separated by the vertical bar character (|). This declaration indicates that the value of the kind attribute must match one (and only one) of the listed values. Each item in the list must be a valid NMTOKEN value. Remember that the NMTOKEN type functions much like an XML name, but NMTOKEN values can begin with numerical digits.

Some *valid* uses of the new kind attribute would include

```
<phone kind="Cell">
```

or

```
<phone kind="Home">
```

Some *invalid* values would include

```
<phone kind="Dad's Phone">
```

or

```
<phone kind="HOME">
```

The first value is invalid because it attempts to use a value that is not in the list. In fact, it isn't even a valid NMTOKEN. The second value is not valid because although Home appears in the list of allowed values, HOME does not. Remember that because XML is case sensitive, the values in your list will be case sensitive as well.

Attribute Value Declarations

Within each attribute declaration you must specify how the value will appear in the document. Often, you will want to provide a default value for the attribute declaration. At times, you might simply require that the attribute be specified in the document. At other times, you might require that the value of the attribute be fixed at a given value. Each attribute can be declared with these properties.

The XML Recommendation allows you to specify that the attribute

❏   Has a default value

❏   Has a fixed value

❏   Is required

❏   Is implied (or *is optional*)

Default Values

Sometimes you need to provide a value for an attribute even if it hasn't been included in the XML document. By specifying a *default value* for the attribute, you can be sure that it is included in the final output. As the document is being processed, a validating parser automatically inserts the attribute with the default value if the attribute has been omitted. If the attribute has a default value but a value has also been included in the document, the parser uses the attribute included in the document, rather than the default. Remember that only validating parsers make use of the information within the DTD, so the default value is used only by a validating parser. The ability to specify default values for attributes is one of the most valuable features within DTDs.

Specifying a default attribute is easy; simply include the value in quotation marks after the attribute type:

```
<!ATTLIST phone kind (Home | Work | Cell | Fax) "Home">
```

Here, the `kind` attribute declaration has been modified so that it uses a default value. The default value is `Home`. When a validating parser is reading the `<phone>` element, if the `kind` attribute has been omitted, the parser will automatically insert the attribute `kind` with the value `Home`. If the parser encounters a `kind` attribute within the `<phone>` element, it will use the value that has been specified within the document.

When specifying a default value for your attribute declarations, you must ensure that the value you specify follows the rules for the attribute type you have declared. For example, if your attribute type is `NMTOKEN`, then your default value must be a valid `NMTOKEN`. If your attribute type is `CDATA`, then your default value can be any well-formed XML character data.

You are not permitted to specify a default value for attributes of type `ID`. This might seem strange at first, but it actually makes a good deal of sense. If a validating parser inserted the default value into more than one element, the `ID` would no longer be unique throughout the document. Remember that an `ID` value must be unique — if two elements have an `ID` attribute with the same value, the document is not valid.

Fixed Values

In some circumstances, an attribute's value must always be fixed. When an attribute's value can never change, you use the `#FIXED` keyword followed by the fixed value. *Fixed values* operate much like default values. As the parser is validating the file, if the fixed attribute is encountered, then the parser checks whether the fixed value and attribute value match. If they do not match, the parser raises a validity error. If the parser does not encounter the attribute within the element, it inserts the attribute with the fixed value.

A common use of fixed attributes is specifying version numbers. Often, DTD authors fix the version number for a specific DTD:

```
<!ATTLIST contacts version CDATA #FIXED "1.0">
```

As with default values, when specifying values in fixed attribute declarations, you must ensure that the value you specify follows the rules for the attribute type you have declared. As shown with default value declarations, you cannot specify a fixed value for an attribute of type `ID`.

Required Values

When you specify that an attribute is *required*, it must be included within the XML document. A document often must have the attribute to function properly; at other times, it is simply a matter of exercising control over the document content. Suppose you require the `kind` attribute:

```
<!ATTLIST phone kind (Home | Work | Cell | Fax) #REQUIRED>
```

In the preceding example, the declaration indicates that the `kind` attribute must appear within every `<phone>` element in the document. If the parser encounters a `<phone>` element without a `kind` attribute as it is processing the document, it raises an error.

To declare that an attribute is required, simply add the keyword `#REQUIRED` immediately after the attribute type. When declaring that an attribute is required, you are not permitted to specify a default value.

Implied Values

In most cases the attribute you are declaring won't be required and often won't even have a default or fixed value. In these circumstances, the attribute might or might not occur within the element. These attributes are called *implied attributes,* because sometimes no explicit value is available. When the attributes do occur within the element, a validating parser simply checks whether the value specified within the XML document follows the rules for the declared attribute type. If the value does not follow the rules, the parser raises a validity error.

When declaring an attribute, you must always specify a value declaration. If the attribute you are declaring has no default value, has no fixed value, and is not required, then you must declare that the attribute is *implied.* You can declare that an attribute is implied by simply adding the keyword `#IMPLIED` after the attribute's type declaration:

```
<!ATTLIST knows contacts IDREFS #IMPLIED>
```

Specifying Multiple Attributes

So far, the `ATTLIST` declarations in our examples have been limited. In each of the preceding examples, there is only a single attribute. This is fine, but many elements need more than one attribute. No problem — the `ATTLIST` declaration allows you to declare more than one attribute, as shown in the following example:

```
<!ATTLIST contacts version CDATA #FIXED "1.0"
                source CDATA #IMPLIED>
```

In the preceding `ATTLIST` declaration for the `<contacts>` element, there is both a `version` and a `source` attribute. The `version` attribute is a fixed character data attribute; the `source` attribute is also a character data attribute but is optional. When declaring multiple attributes, as in this example, simply use whitespace to separate the two declarations. This example includes a linefeed, and the attribute declarations have been aligned with some extra spaces. This type of formatting is common when declaring multiple attributes. In addition to being able to declare more than one attribute within an `ATTLIST` declaration, you are also permitted to declare more than one `ATTLIST` for each `ELEMENT` declaration:

```
<!ATTLIST contacts version CDATA #FIXED "1.0">
<!ATTLIST contacts source CDATA #IMPLIED>
```

Either style for declaring multiple attributes is legal.

Now that you have seen some common attribute declarations, let's revisit the contact list example and add some improvements. As you can now declare attributes, you will add a version attribute, a source attribute, a person attribute, and a kind attribute, and you will modify the <knows> element to use the IDREF mechanism built into DTDs:

1.   Create a new document called contacts3.xml. Begin by copying the contacts2.xml content. Modify the DOCTYPE declaration, add the new attributes, and then save the file:

```
<?xml version="1.0"?>
<!DOCTYPE contacts PUBLIC "-//Beginning XML//DTD Contact Example//EN"
"contacts3.dtd">
<contacts source="Beginning XML 4E" version="1.0">
  <contact person="Jeff_Rafter" tags="author xml poetry">
    <name>
      <first>Jeff</first>
      <first>Craig</first>
      <last>Rafter</last>
    </name>
    <location>
      <address>Redlands, CA, USA</address>
      <latitude>34.031892</latitude>
      <longitude>-117.207642</longitude>
    </location>
    <phone kind="Home">001-909-555-1212</phone>
    <knows contacts="David_Hunter Danny_Ayers"/>
    <description>Jeff is a developer and author for Beginning XML <em>4th
edition</em>.<br/>Jeff <strong>loves</strong> XML!</description>
  </contact>
  <contact person="David_Hunter" tags="author consultant CGI">
    <name>
      <first>David</first>
      <last>Hunter</last>
    </name>
    <location>
      <address>Address is not known</address>
    </location>
    <phone kind="Work">416 555 1212</phone>
    <knows contacts="Jeff_Rafter Danny_Ayers"/>
    <description>Senior Technical Consultant for CGI.</description>
  </contact>
  <contact person="Danny_Ayers" tags="author semantics animals">
    <name>
      <first>Daniel</first>
      <middle>John</middle>
      <last>Ayers</last>
    </name>
    <location>
```

```
      <latitude>43.847156</latitude>
      <longitude>10.50808</longitude>
      <address>Mozzanella, 7 Castiglione di Garfagnana, 55033 Lucca Italy</address>
    </location>
    <phone>+39-0555-11-22-33-</phone>
    <knows contacts="Jeff_Rafter David_Hunter"/>
    <description>A Semantic Web developer and technical author specializing in
cutting-edge technologies.</description>
  </contact>
</contacts>
```

2. Now that you have modified the XML document, you must declare these new attributes within the DTD. Create a new file named `contacts3.dtd`. Again, you can base this document on `contacts2.dtd`. Make the following modifications and save the file:

```
<!ELEMENT contacts (contact*)>
<!ATTLIST contacts version CDATA #FIXED "1.0">
<!ATTLIST contacts source CDATA #IMPLIED>

<!ELEMENT contact (name, location, phone, knows, description)>
<!ATTLIST contact person ID #REQUIRED>
<!ATTLIST contact tags NMTOKENS #IMPLIED>

<!ELEMENT name (first+, middle?, last)>
<!ELEMENT first (#PCDATA)>
<!ELEMENT middle (#PCDATA)>
<!ELEMENT last (#PCDATA)>

<!ELEMENT location (address | (latitude, longitude))*>
<!ELEMENT address (#PCDATA)>
<!ELEMENT latitude (#PCDATA)>
<!ELEMENT longitude (#PCDATA)>

<!ELEMENT phone (#PCDATA)>
<!ATTLIST phone kind (Home | Work | Cell | Fax) "Home">

<!ELEMENT knows EMPTY>
<!ATTLIST knows contacts IDREFS #IMPLIED>

<!ELEMENT description (#PCDATA | em | strong | br)*>
<!ELEMENT em (#PCDATA)>
<!ELEMENT strong (#PCDATA)>
<!ELEMENT br EMPTY>
```

3. You are ready to validate your document again. Open `contacts3.xml` and click the Validate button.

Your output should show a complete validation without errors, as shown in Figure 4-6. If you received any errors this time, check whether you have typed everything correctly and try again.

Figure 4-6

How It Works

In this Try It Out example, you added several ATTLIST declarations to your DTD. You added the attributes version and source to your <contacts> element. The version attribute could be used to indicate to an application what version of the DTD this contact list matches. Using the source attribute, you can provide a friendly description of who provided the information. If you had omitted the version attribute the XML parser would have inserted it for you because you declared that it had a fixed value of 1.0.

You also added attributes to identify the contact uniquely in the document, and included some information keywords. The unique identifiers were created by simply using the contact's name and replacing all the whitespace with underscores (so that it was a valid XML name). The tags attribute included names that weren't declared anywhere in the DTD but which still followed the rules for the NMTOKEN attribute type.

You also added a kind attribute that provided a list of possible phone number entries for the contact. Because there were only four choices for the value of the kind attribute, you decided to use an enumerated list. You also set the default value to Home because many of the contacts you listed included home phone numbers and you didn't want to type it repeatedly. Note that there was no kind attribute on the phone number in the contact for Danny Ayers. Because the kind attribute was omitted, a processor, as it is parsing the document, will automatically insert the attribute with the default value. The description for David Hunter, however, needed to include the kind attribute because the phone number was not a home phone number, and the default value was Home. Notice too that even when an attribute is defaulted to a specific value in the DTD, it is still allowable to have that same value appear in the XML document. You can see this in the contact phone number of Jeff Rafter.

Finally, the `<knows>` element was modified, specifying that it would be EMPTY and contain a single IDREFS attribute. This allowed you to connect contacts together through the ID/IDREF mechanism built into DTDs. This can be a very powerful feature. Unfortunately, though, the names you refer to must be present within your contacts list. Therefore, you couldn't say that Jeff knows Andrew_Watt because there is no Andrew_Watt ID within the contacts list.

Entities

In Chapter 2, you learned that you could escape characters or use entity references to include special characters within the XML document. You learned that five *entities* built into XML enable you to include characters that have special meaning in XML documents. In addition to these built-in entities, you also learned that you can use character references to include characters that are difficult to type, such as the (c) character:

```
<contacts source="Beginning XML 4E&apos;s Contact List" version="1.0">
<description>Jeff is a developer &amp; author for Beginning XML <em>4th
edition</em> &#169; 2006 Wiley Publishing.<br/>Jeff <strong>loves</strong>
XML!</description>
```

In the first example, there is an `&apos;` entity reference within the attribute content. This allows you to include a ' character without the XML parser treating it as the end of the attribute value. In the second example, there is an `&#169;` character reference within the element content. This allows you to include the (c) character by specifying the character's Unicode value.

In fact, entities are not limited to simple character references within XML documents. Entities can be used throughout the XML document to refer to sections of replacement text, other XML markup, and even external files. You can separate entities into four primary types, each of which may be used within an XML document:

- ❑ Built-in entities
- ❑ Character entities
- ❑ General entities
- ❑ Parameter entities

Let's look at each of these in more detail.

In fact, technically, each part of an XML document is an entity. For example, the root element within an XML document is called the document entity, *the DTD is another entity, and so on. Of course, you cannot use these entities as you can use the four main entity type types, so their usefulness is limited.*

Built-in Entities

You have already seen that five entities can be used within an XML document by default:

- ❑ `&amp;` — The & character
- ❑ `&lt;` — The < character
- ❑ `&gt;` — The > character

❑   ' — The ' character

❑   " — The " character

These five entities are often called *built-in entities* because according to the XML Recommendation, all XML parsers must support their use by default. You are not required to create declarations for them in the DTD, and you will soon see that other kinds of entities must be declared first within the DTD, before they are used within the document.

References to Built-in Entities

To use an entity, you must include an entity reference within the document. An *entity reference*, as the name implies, refers to an entity that represents a character, some text, or even an external file. A reference to a built-in entity takes the following form:

```
&apos;
```

The reference begins with the ampersand (&) character. Immediately following the ampersand is the name of the entity, in this case apos. At the end of the reference is a semicolon (;). Whitespace is not allowed anywhere within the reference.

In general, you can use entity references anywhere you can use normal text within the XML document. For example, you can include entity references within element contents and attribute values. You can also use entity references within your DTD within default and fixed attribute value declarations, as well as entity declarations (as shown later). Although the built-in entities allow you to refer to markup characters, they cannot be used in place of XML markup. For example, the following is *legal*:

```
<description>Author &amp; programmer</description>
```

Here, the & built-in entity allows you to include an ampersand (&) in the content of the <description> element. This is allowed because it is within the element's text content. Conversely, the following would be *illegal*:

```
<contacts version=&quot;1.0&quot;>
```

In this example, the " entity is used in place of actual quotation marks. As an XML parser processes the element, it would encounter the & after the = and immediately raise a well-formedness error. The XML within the document is first checked for well-formedness errors; only then are entity references resolved. Many XML parsers will check the well-formedness of a specific section of an XML document and then begin replacing entities within that section. This can be very useful in large documents. Consult your XML parser's documentation for more information. In addition, note that you cannot use entities within the names of elements or attributes.

Character Entities

Character entities, much like the five built-in entities, are not declared within the DTD. Instead, they can be used in the document within element and attribute content without any declaration. References to character entities are often used for characters that are difficult to type, or for non-ASCII characters.

References to Character Entities

Again, to use a character entity within your document, you must include an entity reference. The syntax for character entity references is very similar to syntaxes for the five built-in entities:

```
&#169;
```

As you can see from the example, the primary difference in character entity references is that there is no entity name. The reference begins with the ampersand (&) character, but instead of an entity name, there is a hash mark (#) followed by a number, in this case 169, which is the Unicode value for the (c) character. At the end of the reference is a semicolon (;). As shown in the references to built-in entities, whitespace is not allowed anywhere within the character entity reference.

You can also refer to a character entity by using the hexadecimal Unicode value for the character:

```
&#x00A9;
```

Here, the hexadecimal value 00A9 is used in place of the decimal value 169. When the value you are specifying is hexadecimal, you must include a lowercase x before the value, so that the XML parser knows how it should handle the reference. In fact, it is much more common to use the hexadecimal form because the Unicode specification lists characters using hexadecimal values.

> *The best place to find the hexadecimal values for characters is in the Unicode technical reports found at* http://www.unicode.org/charts. *For example, the character o that you used in your document can be found in the document* http://www.unicode.org/charts/PDF/U0080.pdf.

Just as you saw with built-in entity references, character entity references can be used anywhere you can use normal text, such as element content and attribute values. You can also use them within your DTD. Like the built-in entities, you cannot use character entities in place of actual XML markup or as part of the names of elements or attributes.

> **Does this mean that by using character references you can include any Unicode character in your XML document? Not exactly. Actually, you are permitted to include only those characters that are specified within the XML Recommendation, which was based on Unicode 3.0. As the Unicode specification has evolved, the need to use more characters in XML has also grown. In XML version 1.1 you can use any Unicode character that has not been explicitly forbidden, including characters from the more recent Unicode 5.0. This is why it is important that you include the XML version in the header at the start of your documents — to ensure that they are backwardly compatible. The current list of allowable XML 1.0 characters can be found in the XML Recommendation at** http://www.w3.org/TR/REC-xml/#NT-Char **and** http://www.w3.org/TR/REC-xml/#CharClasses. **If an XML parser encounters a character (or character entity reference) that is not allowed, the parser should immediately raise a fatal error. Illegal characters are considered well-formedness errors.**

General Entities

General entities function very similarly to the five built-in entities, but general entities must be declared within the DTD before they can be used within the XML document. Most commonly, XML developers use general entities to create reusable sections of *replacement text*. Instead of representing only a single character, general entities can represent characters, paragraphs, and even entire documents. This section describes many uses of general entities.

You can declare general entities within the DTD in two ways. You can specify the value of the entity directly in the declaration or you can refer to an external file. Let's begin by looking at an *internal entity declaration*:

```
<!ENTITY source-text "Beginning XML 4E&apos;s Contact List">
```

Just as you have seen with the earlier ELEMENT and ATTLIST declarations, the ENTITY declaration begins with an exclamation mark. Following the ENTITY keyword is the name of the entity, in this case source-text. You can use this name when referring to the entity elsewhere in the XML document. The name must follow the rules for XML names, just as you have seen throughout this chapter. After the entity name in the preceding declaration is a line of *replacement text*. Whenever an XML parser encounters a reference to this entity, it substitutes the replacement text at the point of the reference. This example is an internal entity declaration because the replacement text appears directly within the declaration in the DTD.

In the preceding example, the replacement text value is `The source of this contact list is Beginning XML 4E`. General entity values are not limited to simple characters or text values, however. Within a general entity, the replacement text can consist of any well-formed XML content. The only exception to this rule is that you are not required to have one root element within the replacement text. For example, the following are *legal* general entity values:

```
<!ENTITY address-unknown "The address for this location is &quot;Unknown&quot;">
<!ENTITY empty-gps "<latitude></latitude><longitude></longitude>">
```

Notice that entity references are included within the replacement text. Entity references can be used within your DTDs in place of normal text (default attribute values and entity replacement text values). In addition, notice that values might or might not have a root element, or might have no elements at all. Although you can include entity references within replacement text, an entity is not permitted to contain a reference to itself, either directly or indirectly. The following declaration is *not legal*:

```
<!ENTITY address-unknown "The address for this location is &address-unknown;">
```

This entity contains a reference to itself within its replacement text. When an entity refers to itself, it is known as a *recursive entity reference*. The replacement text for an entity must be well-formed:

```
<!ENTITY address-start "<address>">
<!ENTITY address-end "</address>">
```

These two examples are not legal because they are not well formed. In the first declaration, the start of an `<address>` element is specified but no closing tag is included. The second declaration contains only the closing tag of an `<address>` element. You are not permitted to begin an element in one entity and end it in another — each entity must be well formed on its own.

Because there are no limits on the length of replacement text, your DTD can quickly become cluttered by sections of replacement text, making it more difficult to read. You might want to store your replacement text in an external file instead of including it within the DTD. This can be very useful when you have a large section of replacement text. When declaring your entities, instead of declaring the replacement text internally you can refer to external files. When the replacement text for an entity is stored externally, the entity is declared using an *external entity declaration*. For example, you could declare your entities as

```
<!ENTITY jeff-description SYSTEM "jeff.txt">
```

or

```
<!ENTITY jeff-description PUBLIC
   "-//Beginning XML//Jeff Description//EN" "jeff.txt">
```

Just as you saw with the Document Type Declaration, when referring to external files, you can use a system identifier or a public identifier. When you use a public identifier, you can also include an optional URI reference, as this example does. Each of these declarations refers to an external file named `jeff.txt`. As an XML parser is processing the DTD, if it encounters an external entity declaration, then it *might* open the external file and parse it. If the XML parser is a validating parser, then it *must* open the external file, parse it, and be able to use the content when it is referenced. If the XML parser is not a validating parser, then it might or might not attempt to parse the external file.

The XML Recommendation makes the distinction between validating and nonvalidating parsers primarily to make it easier to create XML parsers that conform to the XML specification. Many XML parsers don't include the capability to validate a document against a DTD because of the additional processing or programming time it requires. Many of these same parsers have the capability to use external entities, however, because of the added functionality. If you are using a nonvalidating parser, check the documentation to see whether it can parse external entities.

Remember that just as you saw with the internal entity declaration, the replacement text must be well-formed XML (with the exception of requiring a single root element). When the parser encounters a well-formedness error within the external file, it raises an error and discontinues parsing.

References to General Entities

Now that you know how to declare entities within your DTD, let's look at how to refer to them within the document:

```
&jeff-description;
```

This entity reference looks very similar to the built-in entity references you learned about earlier. Again, the reference begins with the ampersand (&) character. Immediately following the ampersand is the name of the entity to which you are referring, in this case `jeff-description`. At the end of the reference is a semicolon (;). Whitespace is not allowed anywhere within the reference, but hyphens (-) and underscores (_) are. You can refer to any general entity that you have declared within your DTD, as the preceding example did. When the parser encounters the reference, it includes the replacement text declared within the DTD or the external file to which the entity declaration refers.

Now that you have seen the basics of how to declare and refer to general entities, let's look at an example that uses them.

"Making Contact" — Part 4

In this example, you'll rework the contacts example so that each of your contact descriptions can be stored in external files. For this exercise, you create text files for the descriptions. If you are using an XML editor, save the files in the same folder as the XML document.

1. Begin by creating an external file for David Hunter. Create a new document called `david.txt` and type in the following:

```
Senior Technical Consultant for CGI.
```

2. Create a description file for Jeff Rafter. Instead of using plain text, you'll mix in some XML elements. Create a new document called `jeff.txt` and type in the following:

```
Jeff is a developer &amp; author for Beginning XML <em>4th edition</em> &#169; 2006
Wiley Publishing.<br/>Jeff <strong>loves</strong> XML!
```

3. Create a description file for Danny Ayers. This time, you'll create a complete XML file, including the `<description>` element. Create a file called `danny.xml` and type in the following:

```
<description>A Semantic Web developer and technical author specializing in cutting-
edge technologies.</description>
```

4. Declare the new entities within your DTD. Create a new document called `contacts4.dtd`. Copy the contents of `contacts3.dtd`, add the following declarations to the end of the file, and save the file:

```
<!ENTITY source-text "The source of this contacts list is Beginning XML 4E">
<!ENTITY address-unknown "The address for this location is &quot;Unknown&quot;">
<!ENTITY empty-gps "<latitude></latitude><longitude></longitude>">

<!ENTITY jeff-description PUBLIC
   "-//Beginning XML//Jeff Description//EN" "jeff.txt">

<!ENTITY david-description PUBLIC
   "-//Beginning XML//David Description//EN" "david.txt">

<!ENTITY danny-description PUBLIC
   "-//Beginning XML//Danny Description//EN" "danny.xml">
```

Notice the new general entities that can be used when the address or GPS information, as in David's contact, is not known.

5. Create a new document called `contacts4.xml` based on `contacts3.xml` from the last example. You will use the references to the newly defined entities. You also need to change the DOC-TYPE declaration to refer to the new DTD. After you have completed these modifications, save the `contacts4.xml` file:

```
<?xml version="1.0"?>
<!DOCTYPE contacts PUBLIC "-//Beginning XML//DTD Contact Example//EN"
"contacts4.dtd">
<contacts source="&source-text;" version="1.0">
  <contact person="Jeff_Rafter" tags="author xml poetry">
    <name>
```

```
        <first>Jeff</first>
        <first>Craig</first>
        <last>Rafter</last>
      </name>
      <location>
        <address>Redlands, CA, USA</address>
        <latitude>34.031892</latitude>
        <longitude>-117.207642</longitude>
      </location>
      <phone kind="Home">001-909-555-1212</phone>
      <knows contacts="David_Hunter Danny_Ayers"/>
      <description>&jeff-description;</description>
    </contact>
    <contact person="David_Hunter" tags="author consultant CGI">
      <name>
        <first>David</first>
        <last>Hunter</last>
      </name>
      <location>
        <address>&address-unknown;</address>
        &empty-gps;
      </location>
      <phone kind="Work">416 555 1212</phone>
      <knows contacts="Jeff_Rafter Danny_Ayers"/>
      <description>&david-description;</description>
    </contact>
    <contact person="Danny_Ayers" tags="author semantics animals">
      <name>
        <first>Daniel</first>
        <middle>John</middle>
        <last>Ayers</last>
      </name>
      <location>
        <latitude>43.847156</latitude>
        <longitude>10.50808</longitude>
        <address>Mozzanella, 7 Castiglione di Garfagnana, 55033 Lucca Italy</address>
      </location>
      <phone>+39-0555-11-22-33-</phone>
      <knows contacts="Jeff_Rafter David_Hunter"/>
      &danny-description;
    </contact>
  </contacts>
```

6. You are ready to validate the document again. Open `contacts4.xml` and click the Validate button.

Your output should show a complete validation without errors. If you received any errors this time, confirm that you typed everything correctly and try again.

To prove that the text has been retrieved from the external files and inserted into the XML document, download the files and open `contacts4.xml` in Internet Explorer. Figure 4-7 shows a section of what you should see.

Figure 4-7

How It Works

In this Try It Out, you replaced the textual description of each contact with a general entity reference. As the XML parser processed the file, it encountered the entity declarations, read the system identifier, and attempted to retrieve the files. Once it retrieved the files, it parsed the content and stored a copy in memory so that it could replace any references to the entities in the document with the correct replacement text.

The `address-unknown` entity and each of the three descriptions were different, so you could experiment with some of the various features of entities. In the `address-unknown` entity, you created a simple text replacement. Within the replacement, you used references to the built-in `quot` entity.

Though the `david-description` entity was simply text, you created an external text file that you could refer to from the DTD. You used a public ID and a system ID to refer to the external file. The public ID was not used by the processor and, in fact, was not necessary. The simple text you used qualified as well-formed XML content even though there was no root element (in fact, there were no elements at all). The text was a valid replacement because the `<description>` element could legally contain simple text, or `#PCDATA`.

The `jeff-description` entity value was a mix of elements and text. Again, this qualified as well-formed XML content even though there was no root element. Additionally, the replacement text was valid because the `<strong>` element and the `<em>` element were declared within the DTD and allowable in the `<description>` element where the entity reference was used.

The `danny-description` entity value was an actual XML document. By itself, the document was well-formed XML content. Instead of using the entity reference inside of the `<description>` element, the reference completely replaced the `<description>` element. Looking at the `contacts4.xml` document in Internet Explorer (which processes the file before displaying it), you could see that the entire `danny-description` entity value was placed where you had the entity reference. Once all the entity references were replaced with their entity values by the processor, the document was still valid.

Note that you could also have used files stored on the Internet or HTML web pages. However, just as you saw with the local text files, the parser must parse each external document and check it for well-formedness. Most HTML files on the web are not well-formed XML; make sure that external files do not create a well-formedness error when parsed. Additionally, validating parsers will still check the external replacement values for validity. The ELEMENT declaration for the description element specifies that it contains #PCDATA or `<strong>` elements or `<em>` elements. If the XML parser encounters an `<html>` element within the `<description>` element, even as the result of an entity's replacement text, it raises a validity error because you haven't declared an `<html>` element within your DTD.

Earlier you learned that validation uses more processing power and that this might be a drawback to using DTDs. Likewise, using external entities can also decrease your application's performance. You might have noticed a significant performance decrease in the last example. Because external files must be opened and read, and often downloaded from the Internet, consider the pros and cons of using external entities before dividing your DTD into separate modules. You must also consider the trade-offs of performance and ease of maintenance. Splitting your XML and DTDs into separate modules can enable different departments or developers to focus on specific parts of the document.

Parameter Entities

Parameter entities, much like general entities, enable you to create reusable sections of replacement text. So far, you have seen that you can refer to entities within element and attribute content, within specific places inside the DTD, such as default attribute values, and within entity replacement text. Parameter entities, however, cannot be used in general content; you can refer to parameter entities only within the DTD. Unlike other kinds of entities, the replacement text within a parameter entity can be made up of DTD declarations or pieces of declarations.

Parameter entities can also be used to build DTDs from multiple files. This is often helpful when different groups work on DTDs. In addition, this enables you to reuse DTDs and portions of DTDs in your own XML documents. When XML documents or DTDs are divided into multiple files, they are said to be *modular*.

Parameter entity declarations are very similar to general entity declarations:

```
<!ENTITY % DefaultPhoneKind "Home">
```

This example contains a declaration for an internal parameter entity named `DefaultPhoneKind`. You know that this is a parameter entity because of the percent sign (%) before the name of the entity. This is the primary difference between the format of parameter entity declarations and general entity declarations. Notice the space between the ENTITY keyword and the percent sign, and between the percent sign and the name of the entity. This whitespace is required.

Like general entities, parameter entities can also refer to external files using a system or public identifier:

```
<!ENTITY % NameDeclarations SYSTEM "name4.dtd">
```

or

```
<!ENTITY % NameDeclarations
    PUBLIC "-//Beginning XML 4E//DTD External module//EN" "name4.dtd">
```

Instead of redeclaring the `<name>`, `<first>`, `<middle>`, and `<last>` elements in the DTD for the contacts list, you could refer to the `name4.dtd` from earlier in the chapter. Reusing existing declarations in your DTD through external parameter entities is a good way to modularize your vocabulary.

References to Parameter Entities

When referring to a parameter entity within a DTD, the syntax changes slightly. Instead of using an ampersand (`&`) you must use a percent sign (`%`), as shown in the following example:

```
%NameDeclarations;
```

The reference consists of a percent sign (`%`), followed by the entity name, followed by a semicolon (`;`). References to parameter entities are permitted only within the DTD. Suppose you wanted to make use of the `DefaultPhoneKind` parameter entity within the `ATTLIST` declaration for the phone element. You could change the declaration as follows:

```
<!ENTITY % DefaultPhoneKind "&#34;Home&#34;">
<!ATTLIST phone kind (Home | Work | Cell | Fax) %DefaultPhoneKind;>
```

In this example, the parameter entity called `DefaultPhoneKind` is used in place of the attribute value declaration. Parameter entity references can be used in place of DTD declarations or parts of DTD declarations. Unfortunately, you can't use the built-in entity `&quot;` because general entities and built-in entities that appear in parameter entity values are not expanded as they are elsewhere. Therefore, you instead use character entities for the quotation marks. The following is perfectly legal:

```
<!ATTLIST phone kind (Home | Work | Cell | Fax) "%DefaultPhoneKind;">
```

> In the previous example you referred to the parameter entity to build the ATTLIST declaration. In fact, this is permitted only because you are using an external DTD. Parameter entity references cannot be used within declarations inside of the internal subset.

Try It Out   "Making Contact" — Part 5

Let's take what you just learned and use it within your contacts DTD. This will enable you to parameterize the phone attribute declaration within your DTD.

1. Begin by making the appropriate modifications to the DTD file. Create a new document called `contacts5.dtd`. You can copy the content from `contacts4.dtd`, adding the new

`DefaultPhoneKind` parameter entity and modifying the `ATTLIST` declaration for the `<phone>` element. When you have made the changes, save the `contacts5.dtd` file:

```
<!ENTITY % DefaultPhoneKind '"Home"'>
<!ATTLIST phone kind (Home | Work | Cell | Fax) %DefaultPhoneKind;>
```

2. Change the XML file to refer to the new DTD. This is the only change you need to make within your XML document. Create a new document based on `contacts4.xml` from the last example. Change the Document Type Declaration to refer to your new DTD, and save the file as `contacts5.xml`:

```
<!DOCTYPE contacts PUBLIC "-//Beginning XML//DTD Contact Example//EN"
   "contacts5.dtd">
```

3. You are ready to validate the document again. Open `contacts5.xml` and click the Validate button.

Your output should show a complete validation without errors. If you received any errors this time, confirm that you have typed everything correctly and try again.

How It Works

In this last Try It Out, you were able to change `ATTLIST` declarations by using a parameter entity for the content model and a parameter entity for the attribute declarations. Just as you have seen throughout this section, parameter entities enable you to reuse DTD declarations or pieces of declarations. As the parser attempts to process the content model for the `<contact>` declaration, it encounters the parameter entity reference. It replaces the entity reference with the replacement text specified in the `ENTITY` declaration.

> *Actually, when a parser builds the replacement value for a parameter entity, it adds a single space character before and after the value you specify. This can create all kinds of confusion if you are not careful in defining your parameter entities. In fact, this is why you need to include the quotation marks as part of the parameter entity — so that there won't be extra spaces in the value.*

Note that the declaration of a parameter entity must occur in the DTD before any references to that entity.

Developing DTDs

Most of the DTDs you developed within this chapter were relatively simple. As you begin developing DTDs for your XML documents, you might find it difficult to present the DTDs in a linear order. Most of the declarations flowed in order, but often you won't be sure in what order your DTD declarations should occur. Don't worry; apart from entities that are used within the DTDs, declarations can appear in any order. It is common to keep associated declarations near one another. For example, in most DTDs, an `ATTLIST` declaration immediately follows the corresponding `ELEMENT` declaration.

As the flow of the DTDs becomes difficult to follow, it is important to document your declarations. You can use XML comments and processing instructions within a DTD, following rules similar to usage in XML content. Comments and processing instructions can appear in the internal or external subsets, but they cannot appear within markup declarations.

For example, the following is valid:

```
<!-- source : allows you to describe the source of the contacts list -->
<!ATTLIST contacts source CDATA #IMPLIED>
```

The following is not valid:

```
<!ATTLIST contacts
  <!-- source : allows you to describe the source of the contacts list -->
  source CDATA #IMPLIED>
```

When developing DTDs, it is not necessary to declare comments and processing instructions that are used within your XML document. In fact, there is no way to declare that they will be present at all.

As you have already seen, developing a DTD is easiest when you have an example XML document. What should you do if you have a very long example file with many elements? A good strategy is to divide the DTD into pieces, or modules. The best way to do this is by using external parameter entities. Instead of designing the whole DTD at once, try to create DTDs for subsections of your vocabulary and then use parameter entity references when testing. By dividing your DTD in this way, you can quickly identify and fix errors. Once you have your DTD working, you can combine the modules to increase performance.

DTD Limitations

This chapter has described some of the many benefits of using DTDs. They enable you to validate content without application-specific code, supply default values for attributes, and even create modular XML documents. Throughout your XML career, you will use existing DTDs and often design your own. Because of XML's strong SGML foundation, much of the early XML development focused on the markup of technical documents. Since that time, XML has been used in areas no one expected. While this was a great achievement for the XML community, it began to reveal some limitations of DTDs:

❑   Differences between DTD syntax and XML syntax

❑   Poor support for XML namespaces

❑   Poor data typing

❑   Limited content model descriptions

Before looking at these limitations in more detail, it is important to reiterate that even with their limitations, DTDs are a fundamental part of the XML Recommendation. DTDs will continue to be used in many diverse situations, even as other methods of describing documents emerge.

DTD Syntax

The syntax for expressing DTD declarations is different from the generic XML syntax you learned in the first few chapters. Why is the syntax so different? Early on, you learned that XML is based on SGML. Because many of the developers turning to XML used SGML, the creators of XML chose to adopt the DTD syntax that was originally developed for SGML.

This proved to be both a benefit and a limitation within XML. Initially, this made migration from SGML to XML easier. Many users had already developed DTDs for their SGML documents. Instead of having to completely redesign their vocabularies, they could reuse what they had already done, with minimal changes. As support for XML grew, new XML tools and standards were developed that enabled users to manipulate their XML data. Unfortunately, these tools were meant for generic XML, not for DTDs.

XML Namespaces

Whenever element or attribute names are declared within a DTD, the namespace prefix and colon must be included in the declaration. In addition to this limitation, DTDs must treat namespace declarations as attributes. This is because the XML Recommendation was completed before the syntax for XML namespaces was finalized. Forcing users to declare namespace prefixes in advance defeats the purpose of namespace prefixes altogether. Merging documents from multiple namespaces when the prefixes are predefined can be problematic and confusing.

Data Typing

As XML developers began using DTDs to model more complex data (such as databases and programming objects), the need for stronger datatypes emerged. The only available datatypes within DTDs are limited to use in attribute declarations, and even then the datatypes provide only a fraction of the needed functionality. No method exists for constraining the data within a text-only element to a specific type. For example, if you were modeling a database and wanted to specify that data within a specific element needed to be numeric, you couldn't do so using DTDs.

Limited Content Model Descriptions

In addition to needing more advanced datatypes, limitations in content model descriptions became apparent soon after the XML Recommendation was published. Developers wanted the capability to mimic object inheritance in their XML content models. Developers also found the cardinality operators limiting. For example, because DTDs lack strict control over the number of times an element occurs, it is difficult to require that a specific element can have more than one but less than ten occurrences.

Summary

By using DTDs, you can easily validate your XML documents against a defined vocabulary of elements and attributes. This reduces the amount of code needed within your application. An XML parser can be used to check whether the contents of an XML document are valid according to the declarations within a DTD. DTDs enable you to exercise much more control over your document content than simple well-formedness checks do.

In this chapter, you learned how to do the following:

❑ Validate a document against a DTD

❑ Create element declarations

❑ Create attribute declarations

❑   Create entity declarations

❑   Specify an XML document and DTD using external files

You also learned that DTDs have several limitations. The next two chapters illustrate how these limitations have been addressed in newer standards, such as XML Schemas and RELAX NG.

Exercise Questions

Suggested solutions to these questions can be found in Appendix A.

Question 1

Build a contact for yourself in the list based on the declarations in the contacts DTD. Once you have added the new contact, validate your document to ensure that it is correct.

Question 2

Add a `gender` attribute declaration for the `<contact>` elements. The attribute should allow two possible values: `male` and `female`. Make sure the attribute is required.

Question 3

Currently, each contact can have only one phone number. Modify the contact declaration so that each contact can have zero or more phone numbers. In addition, add declarations for `website` and `email` elements.

5

XML Schemas

In the last chapter, you learned that you can use Document Type Definitions (DTDs) to validate your XML documents. This avoids the need to write application-specific code to check whether your documents are valid. You also saw some of the limitations of DTDs. Since the inception of XML, several new formats have been developed that enable you to define the content of your vocabulary.

In 1999, the W3C began to develop XML Schemas in response to the growing need for a more advanced format for describing XML documents. Work had already begun previously on several efforts that were intended to better model the types of document being created by XML developers. The W3C's effort took the best of these early technologies and added more features. During development, several members of the W3C designed simpler schema languages with fewer features outside of the W3C. Perhaps the most important effort is RELAX NG, covered in depth in Chapter 6.

Today, XML Schemas are a mature technology used in a variety of XML applications. Apart from their use in validation, XML Schemas are used in XQuery, covered in Chapter 9. XML Schemas can also be used in conjunction with web services and SOAP, as shown in Chapters 14 and 15, respectively.

> A schema is any type of model document that defines the structure of something, such as database structures or documents. In this case, the *something* is an XML document. In fact, DTDs are a type of schema. Throughout this book, we have been using the term *vocabulary* where we could have used the word *schema*. So, what is an XML Schema? This is where it gets confusing. The term *XML Schema* is used to refer to the specific W3C XML Schema technology. W3C XML Schemas, much like DTDs, enable you to describe the structure of an XML document. When referring to W3C XML Schemas, the "S" in "Schema" should be capitalized. XML Schema definitions are also commonly referred to as XSDs.

This chapter covers the following:

- ❏ The benefits of XML Schemas
- ❏ How to create and use XML Schemas
- ❏ How to document your XML Schemas

Benefits of XML Schemas

At this point you have already invested time in learning DTDs. You know the syntax and can create complex, even modular, definitions for your vocabulary. Although XML Schemas are the next great thing, it is helpful to understand some of the benefits of XML Schemas before jumping in:

- ❏ XML Schemas are created using basic XML, while DTDs utilize a separate syntax.
- ❏ XML Schemas fully support the Namespace Recommendation.
- ❏ XML Schemas enable you to validate text element content based on built-in and user-defined datatypes.
- ❏ XML Schemas enable you to more easily create complex and reusable content models.
- ❏ XML Schemas enable the modeling of programming concepts such as object inheritance and type substitution.

Let's look at some of these benefits in more detail.

XML Schemas Use XML Syntax

In the last chapter, you spent most of your time learning the DTD syntax. The syntax, as you learned, adds a lot to the basic rules for XML well-formedness. When defining an XML Schema, the syntax is entirely in XML; although you still have to learn the rules regarding which elements and attributes are required in given declarations, you can use generic XML tools — even those that have no understanding of the rules specific to XML Schema documents. As you learn new XML technologies throughout this book, you will see how to apply them to any XML document. For example, Extensible Stylesheet Language Transformations (XSLT) can be used to work with XML Schemas, but cannot be used on DTDs. The next chapter describes RELAX NG, another schema language, which has two syntaxes.

XML Schema Namespace Support

Because XML Schemas were finalized after the Namespace Recommendation, the XML Schema specification was designed to support namespaces (for a refresher on namespaces, review Chapter 3). Unlike DTDs, which do not support the full functionality of namespaces, XML Schemas enable you to define vocabularies that utilize namespace declarations. More important, XML Schemas allow you to mix namespaces in XML documents with less rigidity. For example, when designing an XML Schema, it is not necessary to specify namespace prefixes as you must in DTDs. Instead, the XML Schema leaves this decision to the end-user.

XML Schema Data Types

When you were developing your DTDs, you could specify that an element had mixed content, element content, or empty content. Unfortunately, when your elements contained only text, you couldn't add any constraints on the format of the text. Attribute declarations gave you some control, but even then the types you could use in attribute declarations were very limited.

> XML Schemas divide datatypes into two broad categories: simple and complex. Elements that may contain attributes or other elements are declared using complex types. Attribute values and text content within elements are declared using simple types.

XML Schemas enable you to declare the type of textual data allowed within attributes and elements, using simple type declarations. For example, by utilizing these types you could specify that an element may contain only date values, only positive numbers, or numbers within a certain range. Many commonly used simple types are built into XML Schemas. This is, perhaps, the single most important feature within XML Schemas. By enabling you to specify the allowable type of data within an element or attribute, you can exercise more rigid control over documents. This enables you to easily create documents that are intended to represent databases, programming languages, and objects within programming languages. Simple types and complex types are shown later in this chapter.

XML Schema Content Models

To reuse a content model within a DTD, you had to utilize parameter entities. Using multiple parameter entities can lead to complex declarations within the DTD. XML Schemas provide several mechanisms for reusing content models. In addition to the simple models that you created in DTDs, XML Schema declarations can use object inheritance and content model inheritance. The advanced features of XML Schemas enable you to build content models upon content models, modifying the definition in each step.

Do We Still Need DTDs?

Wait a second. Why did you spend all of Chapter 4 learning about DTDs if we were just going to turn around and teach you a better way to validate documents? Don't worry — DTDs are extremely useful even with the advent of XML Schemas. Although XML Schemas provide better features for describing documents — as well as a more common syntax — they provide no ENTITY functionality. In many XML documents and applications, the ENTITY declaration is of paramount importance. On the merits of this feature alone, DTDs will live a long and happy life.

DTDs also have a special prominence because they are the only definition and validation mechanism embedded within the XML Recommendation. This enables DTDs to be embedded directly in the XML documents they are describing. All other syntaxes require a separate file. Parsers that support DTDs are trained to use the embedded declarations, while nonvalidating parsers can ignore the declarations. XML programming tools, such as the Document Object Model (DOM) and Simple API for XML (SAX) — covered in Chapters 11 and 12, respectively — have special features for DTD types.

Because DTDs inherit most of their behavior from Standard Generalized Markup Language (SGML), they are still widely used in legacy applications.

XML Schemas

As you progress through this chapter, you should begin to realize the benefits of XML Schemas. This chapter focuses on the basic parts of XML Schemas that are similar to DTDs and explains some of the datatype mechanisms.

Unfortunately, XML Schemas cannot be covered completely in one chapter. The advanced features of XML Schemas add significant confusion and complexity. Often these features are not supported correctly within different validators, and many experts recommend against their usage. This chapter covers the basic features — those that everyone agrees upon and recommends.

> *Although you will learn how to design and use XML Schemas in this chapter, you might like to see the XML Schema Recommendation for yourself. It is divided into three parts: an introduction to XML Schema concepts at* www.w3.org/TR/xmlschema-0/; *a document that defines all of the structures used in XML Schemas at* www.w3.org/TR/xmlschema-1/; *and a document that describes XML Schema datatypes at* www.w3.org/TR/xmlschema-2/.

The XML Schema Document

Most XML Schemas are stored within a separate XML document. In this respect, XML Schemas function very similarly to external DTDs; an XML document contains a reference to the XML Schema that defines its vocabulary. An XML document that adheres to a particular XML Schema vocabulary is called an XML Schema *instance* document.

> **As shown in the last chapter, validating a document against its vocabulary requires the use of a special parser. The XML Schema Recommendation calls these parsers** *schema validators.* **Not only do schema validators render a verdict on the document's schema validity, but many also provide type information to the application. This set of type information is called the** *Post Schema Validation Infoset (PSVI).* **The PSVI contains all of the information in the XML document and a basic summary of everything declared in the schema. For example, PSVI output is used by XQuery and XPath2.**

Running the Samples

You have learned some of the benefits of XML Schemas, but it helps if you see an entire XML Schema before you look at each part in detail. To illustrate how the XML Schema works, we will modify the name example from the previous chapter. Throughout this chapter, the examples assume you are using the Codeplot editor (http://codeplot.com). This is the same editor used in Chapter 4. In addition to being able to work with DTDs, Codeplot is capable of checking an XML Schema instance document against its XML Schema. If you need more information on using Codeplot, please refer to Chapter 4. You can also use a different XML editor that supports XML Schema validation if you prefer. Additionally, it is possible to create a program that validates your XML against an XML Schema using a validating parser library. More information on using parsers in your own programs is available in Chapters 11 and 12.

> At the time of this writing, support for XML Schemas is almost as widespread as support for DTDs. A list of XML Schema tools can be found on the XML Schema homepage at www.w3.org/XML/Schema#Tools.

Try It Out   What's in a Name?

This example creates an XML Schema that defines the name vocabulary. It shows how to refer to the XML Schema from the instance document:

1. Begin by creating the XML Schema. In Codeplot, create a new document and name it name5.xsd. Copy the following and save the file when you are finished:

```xml
<?xml version="1.0"?>
<schema xmlns="http://www.w3.org/2001/XMLSchema"
xmlns:target="http://www.example.com/name"
targetNamespace="http://www.example.com/name" elementFormDefault="qualified">
  <element name="name">
    <complexType>
      <sequence>
        <element name="first" type="string"/>
        <element name="middle" type="string"/>
        <element name="last" type="string"/>
      </sequence>
      <attribute name="title" type="string"/>
    </complexType>
  </element>
</schema>
```

2. Create the instance document. This document is very similar to the name4.xml example from the previous chapter. Instead of referring to a DTD, refer to the newly created XML Schema. Create a new document called name5.xml and copy the following; when you are finished, save the file:

```xml
<?xml version="1.0"?>
<name
  xmlns="http://www.example.com/name"
  xmlns:xsi="http://www.w3.org/2001/XMLSchema-instance"
  xsi:schemaLocation="http://www.example.com/name name5.xsd"
  title="Mr.">
  <first>John</first>
  <middle>Fitzgerald Johansen</middle>
  <last>Doe</last>
</name>
```

3. You are ready to validate your XML instance document against the XML Schema. Because you refer to your XML Schema within `name5.xml`, you don't need to select it within the validator. Simply click the Validate button in the Codeplot editor and observe the output results, shown in Figure 5-1. If the output suggests that the validation completed but there is an error in the document, correct the error and try again.

4. If you would like to see what happens when there is an error, then simply modify your `name5.xml` document and try validating again.

How It Works

This Try It Out created an XML Schema for the name vocabulary. Let's look at each part of the schema briefly, to get an idea of what to expect throughout the chapter.

You used the XML Schema to determine whether your instance document was schema valid. To connect the two documents, you included a reference to the XML Schema within your instance document. The internal process by which schema validators compare the document structure against the vocabulary varies greatly. At the most basic level, the schema validator reads the declarations within the XML Schema. As it is parsing the instance document, it validates each element that it encounters against the matching declaration. If it finds an element or attribute that does not appear within the declarations, or if it finds a declaration that has no matching XML content, then it raises a schema validity error.

```xml
<?xml version="1.0"?>
```

Figure 5-1

As shown in all of the XML documents, you begin with the XML declaration. Again, this is optional, but it is highly recommended that you include it to avoid XML version conflicts later:

```
<schema xmlns="http://www.w3.org/2001/XMLSchema" xmlns:target="http://www
.example.com/name" targetNamespace="http://www.example.com/name"
elementFormDefault="qualified">
```

The root element within your XML Schema is the `<schema>` element. Within the `<schema>` element, you have the namespace declaration. The namespace of the `<schema>` element is `http://www.w3 .org/2001/XMLSchema`. Within the `<schema>` element, you also include a `targetNamespace` attribute indicating that you are developing a vocabulary for the namespace `http://www.example.com/name`. Remember that this is just a unique name; the URL does not necessarily point to anything. You also declared a namespace that matches your `targetNamespace` with the prefix `target`. If you need to refer to any declarations within your XML Schema, you need this declaration, so you include it just in case. As with all namespace declarations, you are not required to use `target` as your prefix; you could choose any prefix you like.

You also included the attribute `elementFormDefault` with the value `qualified`. Essentially, this controls the way namespaces are used within your corresponding XML document. For now, it is best to get into the habit of adding this attribute with the value `qualified`, as it will simplify your instance documents. You will see what this means a little later in the chapter.

```
<element name="name">
```

Within the `<schema>` element is an `<element>` declaration. Within this `<element>` declaration, you specified that the name of the element is `name`. In this example, the content model is specified by including a `<complexType>` definition within the `<element>` declaration:

```
<complexType>
  <sequence>
    <element name="first" type="string"/>
    <element name="middle" type="string"/>
    <element name="last" type="string"/>
  </sequence>
  <attribute name="title" type="string"/>
</complexType>
```

Because the `<name>` element contains the elements `<first>`, `<middle>`, and `<last>`, it must be declared as a complex type. A `<complexType>` definition enables you to specify the allowable elements and their order as well as any attribute declarations.

Just as in your DTD, you must declare your content using a content model. In DTDs you could use sequences and choices when specifying your content model. In this example, you have indicated that you are using a sequence by including a `<sequence>` element. The `<sequence>` declaration contains three `<element>` declarations. Within these declarations, you have specified that their type is `string`. This indicates that the elements must adhere to the XML Schema simple type `string`, which allows any textual content.

In addition, within the `<complexType>` definition is an `<attribute>` declaration. This `<attribute>` declaration appears at the end of the `<complexType>` definition, after any content model information.

By declaring a `title` attribute, you can easily specify how you should address the individual described by your XML document. Because the title attribute is declared in the `<complexType>` declaration for the `<name>` element, the attribute is allowed to appear in the `<name>` element in the instance document.

Before we move on, take a quick look at the instance document:

```
<name
   xmlns="http://www.example.com/name"
   xmlns:xsi="http://www.w3.org/2001/XMLSchema-instance"
   xsi:schemaLocation="http://www.example.com/name name5.xsd"
   title="Mr.">
```

Within the root element of the instance document are two namespace declarations. The first indicates that the default namespace is `http://www.example.com/name`. This namespace matches the `targetNamespace` that you declared within your XML Schema. You also declare the namespace `http://www.w3.org/2001/XMLSchema-instance`. Several attributes from this namespace can be used within your instance document.

The instance document includes the attribute `schemaLocation`. This attribute tells the schema validator where to find the XML Schema document for validation. The `schemaLocation` attribute is declared within the namespace `http://www.w3.org/2001/XMLSchema-instance`, so the attribute has the prefix `xsi`. The value of the `schemaLocation` attribute is `http://www.example.com/name name5.xsd`. This is known as a namespace-location pair; it is the namespace of your XML document and the URL of the XML Schema that describes your namespace. This example used a very simple relative URL, `name5.xsd`. The XML Schema Recommendation allows you to declare several namespace-location pairs within a single `schemaLocation` attribute — simply separate the values with whitespace. This is useful when your XML document uses multiple namespaces.

The `schemaLocation` attribute is only a hint for the processor to use — the processor may not use the provided location at all. For example, the validator may have a local copy of the XML Schema that it uses instead of loading the file specified, to decrease processor usage. If your XML Schema has no `targetNamespace`, you cannot use a namespace-location pair. Instead, you must refer to the XML Schema using the `noNamespaceSchemaLocation` attribute within your instance document.

This has been an extremely brief overview of some difficult concepts in XML Schemas. Don't worry; this Try It Out is intended to give you an overall context for what you will be learning throughout the chapter. Each of these concepts is covered in much greater detail.

This chapter doesn't list all of the elements available with XML Schemas, but introduces the more common ones that you're likely to encounter. Furthermore, not all of the attributes are listed for some of the elements. For in-depth coverage of all of the XML Schema features and their use, see Professional XML Schemas *by Jon Duckett et al. (Wrox Press, 2001).*

<schema> Declarations

As you have already seen, the `<schema>` element is the root element within an XML Schema. The `<schema>` element enables you to declare namespace information as well as defaults for declarations throughout the document. You can also include a `version` attribute that helps to identify the XML Schema and the version of your vocabulary:

```
<schema targetNamespace="URI"
  attributeFormDefault="qualified or unqualified"
  elementFormDefault="qualified or unqualified"
  version="version number">
```

The XML Schema Namespace

In the first example, the namespace `http://www.w3.org/2001/XMLSchema` was declared within the `<schema>` element. This enables you to indicate that the `<schema>` element is part of the XML Schema vocabulary. Remember that because XML is case sensitive, namespaces are case sensitive. If the namespace does not match `http://www.w3.org/2001/XMLSchema`, the schema validator should reject the document. For example, you could use any of the following `<schema>`:

```
<schema xmlns="http://www.w3.org/2001/XMLSchema">
```

or

```
<xs:schema xmlns:xs="http://www.w3.org/2001/XMLSchema">
```

or

```
<xsd:schema xmlns:xsd="http://www.w3.org/2001/XMLSchema">
```

As shown in Chapter 3, the namespace prefix is insignificant — it is only a shortcut to the namespace declaration. You will usually see one of these three variations. The XML Schema Recommendation itself uses the prefix `xs`, and this is by far the most common usage. Using no prefix, as shown in the first of the preceding examples, is also very common. Because of its relative simplicity, this form is used in the examples throughout the chapter. Which prefix you use is a matter of personal preference.

Target Namespaces

The primary purpose of XML Schemas is to declare vocabularies. These vocabularies can be identified by a namespace that is specified in the `targetNamespace` attribute. Not all XML Schemas will have a `targetNamespace`. Many XML Schemas define vocabularies that are reused in another XML Schema, or vocabularies that are used in documents where the namespace is not necessary.

When declaring a `targetNamespace`, it is important to include a matching namespace declaration. You can choose any prefix you like, or you can use a default namespace declaration. The namespace declaration is used when you are referring to declarations within the XML Schema. You will see what this means in more detail later in the section "Referring to an Existing Global Element."

Some possible `targetNamespace` declarations include the following:

```
<schema xmlns="http://www.w3.org/2001/XMLSchema"
  targetNamespace="http://www.example.com/name"
  xmlns:target="http://www.example.com/name">
```

or

```
<xs:schema xmlns:xs="http://www.w3.org/2001/XMLSchema"
  targetNamespace="http://www.example.com/name"
  xmlns="http://www.example.com/name">
```

Notice that in the first declaration the `<schema>` element uses the default namespace. Because of this the target namespace `http://www.example.com/name` requires the use of a prefix. However, in the second declaration you see the exact opposite; the `<schema>` element requires the use of a prefix because the target namespace `http://www.example.com/name` is using a default namespace declaration. Again, user preference is the only difference.

Element and Attribute Qualification

Within the instance document, elements and attributes may be qualified or unqualified. An element or attribute is *qualified* if it has an associated namespace. For example, the following elements are qualified:

```
<name xmlns="http://www.example.com/name">
   <first>John</first>
   <middle>Fitzgerald</middle>
   <last>Doe</last>
</name>
```

Even though the elements in this example don't have namespace prefixes, they still have an associated namespace `http://www.example.com/name`, making them qualified *but not prefixed*. Each of the children elements is also qualified because of the default namespace declaration in the `<name>` element. Again, these elements have no prefixes.

It is also possible to qualify elements using namespace prefixes. In the following example, all of the elements are qualified *and* prefixed:

```
<n:name xmlns:n="http://www.example.com/name">
   <n:first>John</n:first>
   <n:middle>Fitzgerald</n:middle>
   <n:last>Doe</n:last>
</n:name>
```

Unqualified elements have no associated namespace:

```
<n:name xmlns:n="http://www.example.com/name">
   <first>John</first>
   <middle>Fitzgerald</middle>
   <last>Doe</last>
</n:name>
```

The `<name>` element is qualified, but the `<first>`, `<middle>`, and `<last>` elements are not. The `<first>`, `<middle>`, and `<last>` elements have no associated namespace declaration (default or otherwise); therefore, they are unqualified. This mix of qualified and unqualified elements may seem strange; nevertheless, it is the default behavior in XML Schemas.

Within the `<schema>` element you can modify the defaults specifying how elements should be qualified by including the following attributes:

❑   `elementFormDefault`

❑   `attributeFormDefault`

The `elementFormDefault` and `attributeFormDefault` attributes enable you to control the default qualification form for elements and attributes in the instance documents. The default value for both `elementFormDefault` and `attributeFormDefault` is `unqualified`.

Even though the value of the `elementFormDefault` attribute is `unqualified`, some elements must be qualified regardless. For example, global element declarations must always be qualified in instance documents (we will look at global and local declarations in detail in the next section). In the preceding example, this is exactly what we have done. We have qualified the `<name>` element with a namespace, but not the `<first>`, `<middle>`, and `<last>` elements.

Though the mix of qualified and unqualified elements may seem confusing, you may want to create a document that uses both qualified and unqualified elements. For example, XSLT and SOAP documents may contain both qualified and unqualified elements. However, most of your documents should qualify all of their elements. Otherwise, someone who is creating an XML document based on your vocabulary will need in-depth knowledge of your XML Schema to determine which elements should be qualified and which elements should be unqualified. Therefore, unless you have a very specific need to mix qualified and unqualified elements, always include the `elementFormDefault` attribute with the value `qualified`.

The default value for the `attributeFormDefault` is also `unqualified`. You should never have to change this value, as most attributes in XML documents are unqualified. Like global elements, globally declared attributes must be qualified in instance documents, so it is best not to declare attributes globally unless you want them to be qualified.

<element> Declarations

When declaring an element, you are actually performing two primary tasks: specifying the element name and defining the allowable content:

```
<element
   name="name of the element"
   type="global type"
   ref="global element declaration"
   form="qualified or unqualified"
   minOccurs="non negative number"
   maxOccurs="non negative number or 'unbounded'"
   default="default value"
   fixed="fixed value">
```

An element's allowable content is determined by its *type*. As you have already seen, element types are divided into simple types and complex types. XML Schemas allow you to specify an element's type in one of two ways:

❑   Creating a local type

❑   Using a global type

In addition to these two methods, you may also reuse existing element declarations instead of creating new ones. You do this by referring to a global element declaration. You do not need to specify a type in your reference; the type of the element is included in the global element declaration.

Global versus Local

Before you can understand these different methods for declaring elements, you must understand the difference between global and local declarations. XML Schema declarations can be divided into two broad categories: global declarations and local declarations.

❑   *Global declarations* are declarations that appear as direct children of the `<schema>` element. Global element declarations can be reused throughout the XML Schema.

❑   *Local declarations* do not have the `<schema>` element as their direct parent and can be used only in their specific context.

Let's look at the first example again:

```
<?xml version="1.0"?>
<schema xmlns="http://www.w3.org/2001/XMLSchema"
  xmlns:target="http://www.example.com/name"
  targetNamespace="http://www.example.com/name"
  elementFormDefault="qualified">
  <element name="name">
    <complexType>
      <sequence>
        <element name="first" type="string"/>
        <element name="middle" type="string"/>
        <element name="last" type="string"/>
      </sequence>
      <attribute name="title" type="string"/>
    </complexType>
  </element>
</schema>
```

This XML Schema has four element declarations. The first declaration, the`<name>` element, is a global declaration because it is a direct child of the `<schema>` element. The declarations for the `<first>`, `<middle>`, and `<last>` elements are considered local because the declarations are not direct children of the `<schema>` element. The declarations for the `<first>`, `<middle>`, and `<last>` elements are valid only within the `<sequence>` declaration — they cannot be reused elsewhere in the XML Schema.

Creating a Local Type

Of the two methods of element declaration, creating a local type should seem the most familiar. We used this model when we declared the `<name>` element in the example. To create a local type, you simply include the type declaration as a child of the element declaration:

```
<element name="name">
  <complexType>
    <sequence>
      <element name="first" type="string"/>
      <element name="middle" type="string"/>
      <element name="last" type="string"/>
    </sequence>
    <attribute name="title" type="string"/>
  </complexType>
</element>
```

or

```
<element name="name">
  <simpleType>
    <restriction base="string">
      <enumeration value="Home"/>
      <enumeration value="Work"/>
      <enumeration value="Cell"/>
      <enumeration value="Fax"/>
    </restriction>
  </simpleType>
</element>
```

These examples show that an element declaration may contain a `<complexType>` definition or a `<simpleType>` definition, but it cannot contain both at the same time.

Using a Global Type

Often, many of your elements will have the same content. Instead of declaring duplicate local types throughout your schema, you can create a global type. Within your element declarations, you can refer to a global type by name. In fact, you have already seen this:

```
<element name="first" type="string"/>
```

Here, the `type` attribute refers to the built-in datatype `string`. XML Schemas have many built-in datatypes, described later in the chapter. You can also create your own global declarations and refer to them. For example, suppose we had created a global type for the content of the `<name>` element:

```
<schema xmlns="http://www.w3.org/2001/XMLSchema"
  xmlns:target="http://www.example.com/name"
  targetNamespace="http://www.example.com/name"
  elementFormDefault="qualified">
  <complexType name="NameType">
    <sequence>
      <element name="first" type="string"/>
      <element name="middle" type="string"/>
      <element name="last" type="string"/>
    </sequence>
    <attribute name="title" type="string"/>
  </complexType>
  <element name="name" type="target:NameType"/>
</schema>
```

Even though the type is global, it is still part of the target namespace. Therefore, when referring to the type, you must include the target namespace prefix (if any). This example used the prefix `target` to refer to the target namespace, but it is equally correct to do the following:

```
<xs:schema xmlns:xs="http://www.w3.org/2001/XMLSchema"
  xmlns="http://www.example.com/name"
  targetNamespace="http://www.example.com/name"
  elementFormDefault="qualified">
  <xs:complexType name="NameType">
    <xs:sequence>
```

157

```
        <xs:element name="first" type="xs:string"/>
        <xs:element name="middle" type="xs:string"/>
        <xs:element name="last" type="xs:string"/>
      </xs:sequence>
      <xs:attribute name="title" type="xs:string"/>
    </xs:complexType>
    <xs:element name="name" type="NameType"/>
  </xs:schema>
```

Here the XML Schema namespace is declared using the prefix xs, and the target namespace has no prefix. Therefore, to refer to the global type NameType, you do not need to include any prefix.

Try It Out   **Creating Reusable Global Types**

Creating global types within an XML Schema is straightforward. In this example you convert the
<name> example to use a named global type, rather than a local type:

1. Begin by making the necessary changes to your XML Schema. In Codeplot, create a new docu-
    ment called name6.xsd. You can copy the content from name5.xsd and make the following
    changes:

```
<?xml version="1.0"?>
<schema xmlns="http://www.w3.org/2001/XMLSchema"
  xmlns:target="http://www.example.com/name"
  targetNamespace="http://www.example.com/name"
  elementFormDefault="qualified">
  <complexType name="NameType">
    <sequence>
      <element name="first" type="string"/>
      <element name="middle" type="string"/>
      <element name="last" type="string"/>
    </sequence>
    <attribute name="title" type="string"/>
  </complexType>
  <element name="name" type="target:NameType"/>
</schema>
```

2. Before you can validate your document, you must modify it so that it refers to your new XML
    Schema. Create a new document called name6.xml. Again, you can copy the content from
    name5.xml and change the xsi:schemaLocation attribute, as follows:

```
xsi:schemaLocation="http://www.example.com/name name6.xsd"
```

3. You are ready to validate your XML instance document against your XML Schema. Click the
    Validate button in the Codeplot editor. This should validate with no errors, as before.

How It Works

You had to make minor modifications to your schema in order to create a reusable complex type. First,
you moved the <complexType> definition from within your <element> declaration to your <schema>
element. Remember that a declaration is global if it is a direct child of the <schema> element. Once you
made the <complexType> definition global, you needed to add a name attribute so that you could refer
to it later. You named the <complexType> definition NameType so it would be easy to identify.

After you declared the `NameType` `<complexType>`, you modified your `<name>` element declaration to refer to it. You added a `type` attribute to your element declaration with the value `target:NameType`. Keep in mind that you have to include the namespace prefix `target` when referring to the type so the validator knows which namespace it should look in.

Referring to an Existing Global Element

As shown in the last example, referring to global types enables you to reuse content model definitions within your XML Schema. Often, you may want to reuse entire element declarations instead of just the type. To refer to a global element declaration, simply include a `ref` attribute and specify the name of the global element as the value:

```
<element ref="target:first"/>
```

Again, the name of the element must be qualified with the namespace. The preceding example is an element reference to a global element named `first` that was declared in the target namespace. Notice that when you refer to a global element declaration, you have no `type` attribute and no local type declaration. Your element declaration uses the type of the `<element>` declaration in the reference.

Try It Out   **Referring to Global Element Declarations**

This Try It Out modifies the last example to demonstrate how to create and refer to global element declarations:

1. Begin by making the necessary changes to the XML Schema. Create a new document called `name7.xsd`. You can copy the content from `name6.xsd` and make the following changes:

```
<?xml version="1.0"?>
<schema xmlns="http://www.w3.org/2001/XMLSchema"
  xmlns:target="http://www.example.com/name"
  targetNamespace="http://www.example.com/name"
  elementFormDefault="qualified">
<element name="first" type="string"/>
<element name="middle" type="string"/>
<element name="last" type="string"/>
<complexType name="NameType">
  <sequence>
    <element ref="target:first"/>
    <element ref="target:middle"/>
    <element ref="target:last"/>
  </sequence>
  <attribute name="title" type="string"/>
</complexType>
<element name="name" type="target:NameType"/>
</schema>
```

2. Before you can schema validate your XML document, you must modify it so that it refers to your new XML Schema. Create a new document called `name7.xml`. Copy the contents from `name6.xml` and change the `xsi:schemaLocation` attribute as follows:

```
xsi:schemaLocation="http://www.example.com/name name7.xsd"
```

3. You are ready to validate your XML instance document against your XML Schema. Open `name7.xml` and click Validate in the Codeplot editor. This should validate with no errors, just as you saw in the last Try It Out.

How It Works

This Try It Out utilized references to global element declarations within your content model. First you moved the declarations for the `<first>`, `<middle>`, and `<last>` elements from within your `<complexType>` definition to your `<schema>` element, making them global. After you created your global declarations, you inserted references to the elements within your `<complexType>`. In each reference, you prefixed the global element name with the prefix `target`.

At this point, it might help to examine what the schema validator is doing in more detail. As the schema validator processes your instance document, it first encounters the root element, in this case `<name>`. When it encounters the `<name>` element, it looks it up in the XML Schema. When attempting to find the declaration for the root element, the schema validator looks through only the global element declarations.

> In this case, you have four global element declarations: `<first>`, `<middle>`, `<last>`, and `<name>`. Any one of these could be used as the root element within an instance document; the example uses the `<name>` element as the instance document root element. Although the XML Schema Recommendation allows you to have multiple global `<element>` declarations, you are still limited to only one root element in your instance document.

Once the schema validator finds the matching declaration, it finds the associated type (in this case it is a global `<complexType>` definition `NameType`). It then validates the content of the `<name>` element within the instance against the content model defined in the associated type. When the schema validator encounters the `<element>` reference declarations, it imports the global `<element>` declarations into the `<complexType>` definition, as if they had been included directly.

Now that you have learned some of the basics of how elements are declared, let's look briefly at some of the features element declarations offer. Later in the chapter, you will look at complex type definitions and content models in more depth.

Naming Elements

Specifying a name in your element declaration is very straightforward. Simply include the `name` attribute and specify the desired name as the value. The name must follow the rules for XML names that you have already learned. In the last chapter, when creating names in DTDs, you had to include any namespace prefix in the element declaration. Because XML Schemas are namespace aware, this is unnecessary. Simply specify the name of the element; the schema validator can understand any prefix used within the instance document. The following are examples of *valid* element names:

```
<element name="first" type="string"/>
<element name="description" type="string"/>
```

The following are examples of *invalid* element names:

```
<element name="2ndElement" type="string"/>
<element name="target:middle" type="string"/>
```

The first of these examples is invalid because it begins with a number. XML names may *include* numerical digits, periods (.), hyphens (-), and underscores (_), but they must *begin* with a letter or an underscore (_). The second of these examples is invalid because it contains a colon (:). Since the inception of namespaces, the colon may be used only to indicate a namespace prefix. Recall that the prefix must not be included as part of the name in the element declaration.

Element Qualified Form

The `form` attribute allows you to override the default for element qualification. As shown earlier, if an element is qualified, then it must have an associated namespace when it is used in the instance document. You can specify whether the element must be qualified by setting the value of the `form` attribute to `qualified` or `unqualified`. If you do not include a `form` attribute, the schema validator uses the value of the `elementFormDefault` attribute declared in the `<schema>` element. Remember that elements declared globally must always be qualified, regardless of values in the `elementFormDefault` or `form` attributes.

Cardinality

In the last chapter you learned that when you are specifying elements in your content models, you can modify their cardinality. *Cardinality* represents the number of occurrences of a specific element within a content model. In XML Schemas, you can modify an element's cardinality by specifying the `minOccurs` and `maxOccurs` attributes within the element declaration.

> Note that the `minOccurs` and `maxOccurs` attributes are not permitted within global element declarations. Instead, use these attributes within the element references in your content models.

Within DTDs, you have very limited options when specifying cardinality. Using cardinality indicators, you can declare that an element would appear once and only once, once or not at all, one or more times, or zero or more times. This seems to cover the basics, but many times you need more control. XML Schemas do not have this limitation. Instead, you can specify the minimum and maximum separately.

Some possible uses of the `minOccurs` and `maxOccurs` attributes include the following:

```
<element name="first" type="string" minOccurs="2" maxOccurs="2"/>

<element ref="target:first" maxOccurs="10"/>

<element name="location" ""minOccurs="0" maxOccurs="unbounded"/>
```

The first of the preceding examples declares that the element `<first>` must appear within the instance document a minimum of two times and a maximum of two times. The second example declares our element using a reference to the global `<first>` declaration. Even though it is declared using the `ref` attribute, you are permitted to use the `minOccurs` and `maxOccurs` attributes to specify the element's cardinality. In this case, we have included a maxOccurs attribute with the value 10. We have not included a minOccurs attribute, so a schema validator would use the default value, 1. The final example specifies that <location> may or may not appear within our instance document because the minOccurs attribute has the value 0. It also indicates that it may appear an infinite number of times because the value of maxOccurs is unbounded.

The default value for the minOccurs attribute and the maxOccurs attribute is 1. This means that, by default, an element must appear only once. You can use the two attributes separately or in conjunction. The maxOccurs attribute allows you to enter the value unbounded, which indicates there is no limit to the number of occurrences. The only additional rule you must adhere to when specifying minOccurs and maxOccurs is that the value of maxOccurs must be greater than or equal to the value for minOccurs.

Default and Fixed Values

When designing the DTD for our contacts list in the last chapter, we made use of attribute default and fixed values. In XML Schemas, you can declare default and fixed values for elements as well as attributes. When declaring default values for elements, you can specify only a text value. You are not permitted to specify a default value for an element whose content model will contain other elements, unless the content model is mixed. By specifying a default value for your element, you ensure that the schema validator will treat the value as if it were included in the XML document — even if it is omitted.

To specify a default value, simply include the default attribute with the desired value. Suppose our <name> elements were being used to design the Doe family tree. We might want to make "Doe" the default for the last name element:

```
<element name="last" type="string" default="Doe"/>
```

This example declared that the element <last> has the default value "Doe", so when a schema validator encounters the <last> element in the instance document, it will insert the default value if there is no content. For example, if the schema validator encounters

```
<last></last>
```

or

```
<last/>
```

then it would treat the element as follows:

```
<last>Doe</last>
```

Note that if the element does not appear within the document or if the element already has content, then the default value is not used.

In the last chapter you learned that attributes may have fixed values. In XML Schemas, both elements and attributes may have fixed values. In some circumstances, you may want to ensure that an element's value does not change, such as an element whose value is used to indicate a version number. When an element's value can never change, simply include a fixed attribute with the fixed value. As the schema validator processes an element declared to have a fixed value, it checks whether the element's content and fixed attribute value match. If they do not match, then the validator raises a schema validity error. If the element is empty, then the parser inserts the fixed value.

To specify a fixed value, simply include the `fixed` attribute with the desired value:

```
<element name="version" type="string" fixed="1.0"/>
```

The preceding example specifies that the `<version>` element, if it appears, must contain the value `1.0`. The fixed value is a valid `string` value (the type of the `<version>` element is `string`). Therefore, the following elements would be *legal*:

```
<version>1.0</version>

<version></version>

<version/>
```

As the schema validator processes the file, it accepts elements with the value `1.0` or empty elements. When it encounters empty elements, it treats them as though the value `1.0` had been included. The following value is *not legal*:

```
<version>2.0</version>
```

When specifying fixed or default values in element declarations, you must ensure that the value you specify is allowable content for the type you have declared. For example, if you specify that an element has the type `positiveInteger`, you cannot use `Doe` as a default value because it is not a positive integer. Default and fixed values are not permitted to contain element content, so your element must have a simple type or a mixed content declaration. You are not permitted to use default and fixed values at the same time within a single element declaration.

Element Wildcards

You'll often want to include elements in your XML Schema without explicitly declaring which elements should be allowed. Suppose you want to specify that your element can contain any of the elements declared in your namespace, or any elements from another namespace. This is common when designing XML Schemas. Declarations that allow you to include any element from a namespace are called *element wildcards*.

To declare an element wildcard, use the `<any>` declaration:

```
<any
   minOccurs="non negative number"
   maxOccurs="non negative number or unbounded"
   namespace="allowable namespaces"
   processContents="lax or skip or strict">
```

The `<any>` declaration can appear only within a content model. You are not allowed to create global `<any>` declarations. When specifying an `<any>` declaration, you can specify the cardinality just as you would within an `<element>` declaration. By specifying the `minOccurs` or the `maxOccurs` attributes, you can control the number of wildcard occurrences allowed within your instance document.

The <any> declaration also enables you to control which namespace or namespaces the elements are allowed to come from. You do this by including the namespace attribute. The namespace attribute allows several values, shown in the following table:

Value	Description
##any	Allows elements from all namespaces to be included as part of the wildcard
##other	Allows elements from namespaces other than the targetNamespace to be included as part of the wildcard
##targetNamespace	Allows elements from only the targetNamespace to be included as part of the wildcard
##local	Allows any well-formed elements that are not qualified by a name space to be included as part of the wildcard
Whitespace-separated list of allowable namespace URIs	Allows elements from any listed namespaces to be included as part of the wildcard. Possible list values also include ##targetNamespace and ##local.

For example, suppose you wanted to allow any well-formed XML content from any namespace within the <name> element. Within the content model for your NameType complex type, you could include an element wildcard:

```
<complexType name="NameType">
  <sequence>
    <element ref="target:first"/>
    <element ref="target:middle"/>
    <element ref="target:last"/>
    <!-- allow any element from any namespace -->
    <any namespace="##any"
         processContents="lax"
         minOccurs="0"
         maxOccurs="unbounded"/>
  </sequence>
  <attribute name="title" type="string"/>
</complexType>
```

By setting the namespace attribute to ##any, you have specified that elements from all namespaces can be included as part of the wildcard. You have also included cardinality attributes to indicate the number of allowed wildcard elements. This case specifies any number of elements because the value of the minOccurs attribute is set to 0 and the value of maxOccurs is set to unbounded. Therefore, the content model must contain a <first>, <middle>, and <last> element in sequence, followed by any number of elements from any namespace.

When the schema validator is processing an element that contains a wildcard declaration, it validates the instance documents in one of three ways:

❑ If the value of the processContents attribute is set to skip, then the processor skips any wild-card elements in the instance document.

❑ If the value of `processContents` attribute is set to `lax`, then the processor attempts to validate the wildcard elements if it has access to a global XML Schema definition for them.

❑ If the value of the `processContents` attribute is set to `strict` (the default) or there is no `processContents` attribute, then the processor attempts to validate the wildcard elements. However, in contrast to using the `lax` setting, the schema validator raises a validity error if a global XML Schema definition for the wildcard elements cannot be found.

<complexType> Declarations

So far you have seen the basics of declaring elements. Each of the examples utilized a `<complexType>` definition. Let's look at type definitions in more detail. Elements that have element content are controlled by `<complexType>` definitions. Within `<complexType>` definitions, you can specify the allowable element content for the declaration:

```
<complexType
  mixed="true or false"
  name="Name of complexType">
```

All of the examples so far have used either a local or a global `<complexType>` to specify the content model for the `<name>` element declaration:

```
<element name="name">
  <complexType>
    <sequence>
      <element name="first" type="string"/>
      <element name="middle" type="string"/>
      <element name="last" type="string"/>
    </sequence>
    <attribute name="title" type="string"/>
  </complexType>
</element>
```

When we created a local declaration, we did not include a `name` attribute in our `<complexType>` definition. Local `<complexType>` definitions are *never* named; in fact, they are called *anonymous complex types*. As you have already seen, however, global `<complexType>` definitions are *always* named, so that they can be identified later.

Apart from the content models you have seen, `<complexType>` definitions can also be used to create mixed and empty content models. *Mixed* content models allow you to include both text and element content within a single content model. To create a mixed content model in XML Schemas, simply include the `mixed` attribute with the value `true` in your `<complexType>` definition:

```
<element name="description">
  <complexType mixed="true">
    <choice minOccurs="0" maxOccurs="unbounded">
      <element name="em" type="string"/>
      <element name="strong" type="string"/>
      <element name="br" type="string"/>
```

```
        </choice>
      </complexType>
</element>
```

The preceding example declared a `<description>` element, which can contain an infinite number of `<em>`, `<strong>`, and `<br>` elements. Because the complex type is declared as mixed, text can be interspersed throughout these elements. An allowable `<description>` element might look like the following:

```
<description>Jeff is a developer &amp; author for Beginning XML <em>4th
 edition</em> &#169; 2006 Wiley Publishing.<br/>Jeff <strong>loves</strong>
XML! </description>
```

In this `<description>` element, textual content is interspersed throughout the elements declared within the content model. As the schema validator is processing the preceding example, it ignores the textual content and entities and instead performs standard validation on the elements. The schema validator will not perform any validation on the text. Because the elements `<em>`, `<strong>`, and `<br>` may appear repeatedly, the example is valid.

To declare an empty content model in a `<complexType>` definition, you simply create the `<complexType>` definition without any `<element>` or content model declarations. Consider the following declarations:

```
<element name="knows">
  <complexType>
  </complexType>
</element>

<element name="knows">
  <complexType/>
</element>
```

Each of these declares an element named knows. In both cases, the `<complexType>` definition is empty, indicating that knows will not contain text or element children. When used in our instance document, `<knows>` must be empty. For example, the following elements would be valid:

```
<knows/>

<knows></knows>
```

Although you haven't looked at attribute declarations in XML Schemas, note that `<complexType>` definitions can also contain `<attribute>` declarations:

```
<element name="knows">
  <complexType>
    <attribute name="contacts" type="IDREFS"/>
  </complexType>
</element>
```

Even when you are declaring an empty element, attribute declarations may still appear within the `<complexType>`. You will examine this in more detail later in this chapter.

<group> *Declarations*

In addition to `<complexType>` definitions, XML Schemas also allow you to define reusable groups of elements. By creating a global `<group>` declaration, you can easily reuse and combine entire content models:

```
<group
  name="name of global group">
```

Just as you have seen with global `<complexType>` definitions, all global `<group>` declarations must be named. Simply specify the `name` attribute with the desired name. Again, the name that you specify must follow the rules for XML names and should not include a prefix. The basic structure of a global `<group>` declaration follows:

```
<group name="NameGroup">
 <!-- content model goes here -->
</group>
```

Try It Out   Using a Global Group

This example redesigns the schema so that you can create a reusable global `<group>` declaration:

1. Begin by making the necessary changes to our XML Schema. Create a new document called `name8.xsd`. Copy the contents from `name7.xsd` and make the following changes:

```
<?xml version="1.0"?>
<schema xmlns="http://www.w3.org/2001/XMLSchema"
  xmlns:target="http://www.example.com/name"
  targetNamespace="http://www.example.com/name"
  elementFormDefault="qualified">
 <group name="NameGroup">
    <sequence>
      <element name="first" type="string" minOccurs="1" maxOccurs="unbounded"/>
      <element name="middle" type="string" minOccurs="0" maxOccurs="1"/>
      <element name="last" type="string"/>
    </sequence>
  </group>
  <complexType name="NameType">
    <group ref="target:NameGroup"/>
    <attribute name="title" type="string"/>
  </complexType>
  <element name="name" type="target:NameType"/>
</schema>
```

2. Before you can schema validate your XML document, you must modify it so that it refers to your new XML Schema. Create a new document called `name8.xml`. Copy the contents from `name7.xml` and change the `xsi:schemaLocation` attribute as follows:.

```
xsi:schemaLocation="http://www.example.com/name name8.xsd"
```

3. You are ready to validate your XML instance document against the XML Schema. Open the `name8.xml` document and click Validate. This should validate with no errors, as shown in the last Try It Out.

How It Works

This Try It Out modified your XML Schema to use a global `<group>` declaration. Within the global `<group>` declaration named `NameGroup`, you declared the allowable elements for your content model. Instead of including element declarations in the `<complexType>` definition for your `<name>` element, you created a `<group>` reference declaration. When referring to the global `<group>` declaration, you included a `ref` attribute with the value `target:NameGroup`.

You also updated the `<element>` declarations to make use of the `minOccurs` and `maxOccurs` attributes. The values used in the `minOccurs` and `maxOccurs` attributes enabled you to mimic the various cardinality indicators used in the original DTD.

Notice that the `<attribute>` declaration still appeared within the `<complexType>` definition and not within the `<group>` declaration. This should give you some indication of the difference between a `<group>` and a `<complexType>` definition. A `<complexType>` declaration defines the allowable content for a specific element or type of element. A `<group>` declaration simply allows you to create a reusable content model that can replace other content model declarations in your XML Schema.

As the schema validator is processing the instance document, it processes the `<name>` element, similarly to the earlier examples. When it encounters the `<name>` element, it looks it up in the XML Schema. Once it finds the declaration, it finds the associated type (in this case it is a local `<complexType>` definition). When the schema validator encounters the `<group>` reference declaration, it treats the items within the group as if they had been included directly within the `<complexType>` definition. Even though the `<group>` declaration is global, the `<element>` declarations within the `<group>` are not.

Content Models

You have already seen that you can use `<complexType>` and `<group>` declarations to specify an element's allowable content. What you haven't seen is how to build more advanced content models. Luckily, XML Schemas provide greater flexibility than DTDs when specifying an element's content model. In XML Schemas you can specify an element's content model using the following:

- ❑ A `<sequence>` declaration
- ❑ A `<choice>` declaration
- ❑ A reference to a global `<group>` declaration
- ❑ An `<all>` declaration

By using these four primary declarations, you can specify the content model of your type in a variety of ways. Each of these declarations may contain the following:

- ❑ Inner content models
- ❑ Element declarations
- ❑ Element wildcards

\<sequence> Declarations

As shown with DTD content models, specifying your content model using a sequence of elements is very simple. In fact, the first example used a `<sequence>` declaration when defining the allowable children of the `<name>` element:

```
<sequence
  minOccurs="non negative number"
  maxOccurs="non negative number or unbounded">
```

The `<sequence>` declaration allows you to specify `minOccurs` and `maxOccurs` attributes that apply to the overall sequence. You can modify the cardinality (how many times this sequence of elements occurs) by changing the values of these attributes. The `minOccurs` and `maxOccurs` attributes function exactly as they did within the element declarations.

You have already seen that the `<sequence>` declaration may contain `<element>` declarations within it. In addition to `<element>` declarations, it may contain element wildcards or inner `<sequence>`, `<choice>`, or `<group>` references. You may have sequences within sequences within sequences, or you may have choices within sequences that are in turn within groups — almost any combination you can imagine.

A sample sequence might appear as follows:

```
<sequence>
  <element name="first" type="string" minOccurs="1" maxOccurs="unbounded"/>
  <element name="middle" type="string" minOccurs="0" maxOccurs="1"/>
  <element name="last" type="string"/>
</sequence>
```

By utilizing a `<sequence>` to specify your content model, you indicate that the elements must appear within your instance document in the *sequence*, or order, specified. For example, the following would be *legal*:

```
<first>John</first>
<middle>Fitzgerald Johansen</middle>
<last>Doe</last>
```

The following, however, would be *illegal*:

```
<last>Doe</last>
<middle>Fitzgerald</middle>
<first>John</first>
```

This example isn't allowable because the elements do not appear in the order specified within the `<sequence>`.

\<choice> Declarations

The basic structure of the `<choice>` declaration looks very much like the `<sequence>` declaration:

```
<choice
  minOccurs="non negative number"
  maxOccurs="non negative number or unbounded">
```

Again, you can specify `minOccurs` and `maxOccurs` attributes to modify the cardinality of a `<choice>` declaration. The `<choice>` declaration is also similar to its DTD counterpart. You can specify multiple child declarations within a `<choice>` declaration. In an instance document, however, only one of the declarations may be used. For example, suppose you declared the content model of the `<name>` element using a `<choice>` declaration:

```
<choice>
  <element name="first" type="string" minOccurs="1" maxOccurs="unbounded"/>
  <element name="middle" type="string" minOccurs="0" maxOccurs="1"/>
  <element name="last" type="string"/>
</choice>
```

If you declare your content model as shown in the preceding example, then within your instance document you could include only `<first>` elements, only a `<middle>` element, or only the `<last>` element. You could not include both a `<first>` and a `<last>` element within the instance. As shown in the `<sequence>` declaration, the `<choice>` declaration may contain `<element>` declarations, element wildcards, and inner `<sequence>`, `<choice>`, or `<group>` references.

`<group>` References

The `<group>` *reference* declaration allows you to refer to global element groups within your content model. You can define content models that can be grouped together and reused within other content models. Within a content model, the `<group>` reference declaration is used by creating a reference to one of these already declared groups:

```
<group
  ref="global group definition"
  minOccurs="non negative number"
  maxOccurs="non negative number or unbounded">
```

This can be done by including a `ref` attribute and specifying the name of the global `<group>` declaration:

```
<group name="NameGroup">
  <sequence>
    <element name="first" type="string" minOccurs="1" maxOccurs="unbounded"/>
    <element name="middle" type="string" minOccurs="0" maxOccurs="1"/>
    <element name="last" type="string"/>
  </sequence>
</group>
<element name="name">
  <complexType>
    <group ref="target:NameGroup"/>
    <attribute name="title" type="string"/>
  </complexType>
</element>
```

Here the group reference within the `<complexType>` definition has a `ref` attribute with the value `target:NameGroup`. This refers to the global group declaration named `NameGroup`. You must prefix the name with a namespace prefix — in this case, `target` — so that you can identify the namespace in which the `NameGroup` declaration appears.

Again, you can specify `minOccurs` and `maxOccurs` attributes to modify the cardinality of your `<group>` reference. However, the `<group>` reference may not contain element children. Instead, the global `<group>` declaration to which it refers contains the content model and element children that define the content model.

`<all>` Declarations

The `<all>` declaration enables you to declare that the elements within your content model may appear in any order:

```
<all
  minOccurs="0 or 1"
  maxOccurs="1">
```

To use the `<all>` mechanism, however, you must adhere to several rules:

❑ The `<all>` declaration must be the only content model declaration that appears as a child of a `<complexType>` definition.

❑ The `<all>` declaration may contain only `<element>` declarations as its children. It is not permitted to contain `<sequence>`, `<choice>`, or `<group>` declarations.

❑ The `<all>` declaration's children may appear once each in the instance document. This means that within the `<all>` declaration, the values for `minOccurs` for `maxOccurs` are limited to 0 or 1.

Even with the additional restrictions, the `<all>` declaration can be very useful. It is commonly used when the expected content is known, but not the order.

Why are there additional restrictions for the `<all>` declaration? These restrictions ensure that schema validators can easily understand and process instance documents. Without these restrictions, it would be very difficult to write software to validate XML Schemas that contained `<all>` declarations. Chapter 6 describes the interleave pattern, which was introduced in RELAX NG and has fewer limitations.

Suppose you declared the `<name>` content model using the `<all>` mechanism:

```
<element name="name">
  <complexType>
    <all>
      <element name="first" type="string"/>
      <element name="middle" type="string"/>
      <element name="last" type="string"/>
    </all>
    <attribute name="title" type="string"/>
  </complexType>
</element>
```

Notice that the `<all>` element is the only content model declaration within the `<complexType>` (`<attribute>` declarations do not count as content model declarations). In addition, note that the `<all>` declaration contains only `<element>` declarations as its children. Because the default value for `minOccurs` and `maxOccurs` is 1, each element can appear in the instance document once and only once.

By declaring the content model as shown in the preceding example, you can validate your element content but still allow your elements to appear in any order. The allowable content for a <name> element declared using an <all> declaration might include

```
<first>John</first>
<middle>Fitzgerald</middle>
<last>Doe</last>
```

or

```
<first>John</first>
<last>Doe</last>
<middle>Fitzgerald</middle>
```

As long as all of the elements you have specified appear, they can appear in any order. In the second example, the <middle> element was added last. Because the content model is declared using <all>, this is still allowable.

Try It Out   Making Contact

In order to use all of the XML Schema features that you have learned, it's time to turn to a more complex subject. This example creates an XML Schema for your contacts listing. Not only does this provide ample opportunity to use the functionality you have learned thus far, but it also enables you to compare a DTD and its XML Schema counterpart.

1. Begin by creating the XML Schema. In Codeplot, create a new document named contacts6 .xsd. Enter the following and when you are finished, save the file (the example is long, so you may want to download the code from www.wrox.com):

```xml
<?xml version="1.0"?>
<schema xmlns="http://www.w3.org/2001/XMLSchema"
  xmlns:contacts="http://www.example.com/contacts"
  targetNamespace="http://www.example.com/contacts"
  elementFormDefault="qualified">

<element name="contacts">
  <complexType>
    <sequence>
      <element name="contact" minOccurs="0" maxOccurs="unbounded">
        <complexType>
          <sequence>
            <element name="name" type="contacts:NameType"/>
            <element name="location" type="contacts:LocationType"/>
            <element name="phone" type="string"/>
            <element name="knows" type="contacts:KnowsType"/>
            <element name="description" type="contacts:DescriptionType"/>
          </sequence>
        </complexType>
      </element>
    </sequence>
  </complexType>
</element>

<complexType name="NameType">
```

```
        <group ref="contacts:NameGroup"/>
    </complexType>

    <group name="NameGroup">
        <sequence>
            <element name="first" type="string" minOccurs="1" maxOccurs="unbounded"/>
            <element name="middle" type="string" minOccurs="0" maxOccurs="1"/>
            <element name="last" type="string"/>
        </sequence>
    </group>

    <complexType name="LocationType">
        <choice minOccurs="0" maxOccurs="unbounded">
            <element name="address" type="string"/>
            <sequence>
                <element name="latitude" type="string"/>
                <element name="longitude" type="string"/>
            </sequence>
        </choice>
    </complexType>

    <complexType name="KnowsType">
    </complexType>

    <complexType name="DescriptionType" mixed="true">
        <choice minOccurs="0" maxOccurs="unbounded">
            <element name="em" type="string"/>
            <element name="strong" type="string"/>
            <element name="br" type="string"/>
        </choice>
    </complexType>
</schema>
```

2. Create the instance document. This document is very similar to the contacts sample from Chapter 4. Instead of referring to a DTD, you refer to your newly created XML Schema. To begin, you won't include any attributes; you will add them in later examples in this chapter. Create a new document called `contacts6.xml` and copy the following, saving the file when you are finished:

```
<?xml version="1.0"?>
<contacts
    xmlns="http://www.example.com/contacts"
    xmlns:xsi="http://www.w3.org/2001/XMLSchema-instance"
    xsi:schemaLocation="http://www.example.com/contacts contacts6.xsd">
    <contact>
        <name>
            <first>Jeff</first>
            <first>Craig</first>
            <last>Rafter</last>
        </name>
        <location>
            <address>Redlands, CA, USA</address>
```

```
      <latitude>34.031892</latitude>
      <longitude>-117.207642</longitude>
    </location>
    <phone>001-909-555-1212</phone>
    <knows/>
    <description>Jeff is a developer and author for Beginning XML <em>4th
    edition</em>.<br/>Jeff <strong>loves</strong> XML!</description>
  </contact>
  <contact>
    <name>
      <first>David</first>
      <last>Hunter</last>
    </name>
    <location>
      <address>Address is not known</address>
    </location>
    <phone>416 555 1212</phone>
    <knows/>
    <description>Senior Technical Consultant for CGI.</description>
  </contact>
  <contact>
    <name>
      <first>Daniel</first>
      <middle>John</middle>
      <last>Ayers</last>
    </name>
    <location>
      <latitude>43.847156</latitude>
      <longitude>10.50808</longitude>
      <address>Mozzanella, 7 Castiglione di Garfagnana, 55033 Lucca Italy</address>
    </location>
    <phone>+39-0555-11-22-33-</phone>
    <knows/>
    <description>A Semantic Web developer and technical author specializing
    in cutting-edge technologies.</description>
  </contact>
</contacts>
```

3. You are ready to validate your XML instance document against your XML Schema. Open `contacts6.xml` and click Validate in the Codeplot editor. This should validate with no warnings and no errors, as shown in the last Try It Out. If there is a validation error, then correct it and try validating again.

How It Works

Let's break down each section of the `<schema>` to figure out what is going on:

```
<schema xmlns="http://www.w3.org/2001/XMLSchema"
  xmlns:contacts="http://www.example.com/contacts"
  targetNamespace="http://www.example.com/contacts"
  elementFormDefault="qualified">
```

As shown in earlier examples, the XML Schema begins with the `<schema>` element. Again, you must specify the correct namespace for XML Schemas. You have also included a `targetNamespace` attribute to indicate the namespace for your vocabulary. You added a namespace declaration so that you can refer to items in your `targetNamespace` later. This time, instead of using the prefix *target* you used the prefix *contacts*. Finally, you included the attribute `elementFormDefault` with the value `qualified`:

```
<element name="contacts">
  <complexType>
    <sequence>
      <element name="contact" minOccurs="0" maxOccurs="unbounded">
        <complexType>
          <sequence>
            <element name="name" type="contacts:NameType"/>
            <element name="location" type="contacts:LocationType"/>
            <element name="phone" type="string"/>
            <element name="knows" type="contacts:KnowsType"/>
            <element name="description" type="contacts:DescriptionType"/>
          </sequence>
        </complexType>
      </element>
    </sequence>
  </complexType>
</element>
```

Next, you created a global `<element>` declaration for your `contacts` element. Recall that the `contacts` element must be declared globally because you are using it as your root element within your instance document. As your schema validator processes your instance document, it encounters the `contacts` element. The schema validator will then open your XML Schema document based on the `xsi:schemaLocation` attribute hint and find the global declaration for the `contacts` element.

You specified the type of your `contacts` element by declaring a local `<complexType>` within your `<element>` declaration. Within the `<complexType>` definition, you used a `<sequence>` content model containing only one element. Even if you only have one element inside of a complex type, you still need to declare it as part of a `<sequence>`. You specified that the `<contact>` element could occur an unbounded number of times or not occur at all.

You used another local `<complexType>` to define the content model for the `contact` element. It is possible to use local `<complexType>` declarations inside of other `<complexType>` declarations. In fact, you could define an entire schema in this manner. In general, it is better to use global type definitions whenever possible. Therefore, you referred to global `<complexType>` definitions for the `name`, `location`, `knows`, and `description` elements. You declared the `phone` element using the type `string`. By doing so, you specified that the instance document can only contain simple text and nothing else. You will need to change this later in the chapter when you learn about attributes.

```
<complexType name="NameType">
    <group ref="contacts:NameGroup"/>
</complexType>
```

The content model for the global `NameType` is defined using a reference to a `<group>`. To refer to the global `<group>` declaration, you needed to prefix the group name with the namespace prefix for your targetNamespace. In reality, you didn't need to use a global group to specify the content of the `<name>` element, but the name elements are fairly common, and global groups can be more easily combined and reused. Global complex types are more useful when using type-aware tools such as XPath2 and XQuery. When designing your own schemas it is really a matter of personal preference and which tools you plan on using with your XML Schemas.

```
<group name="NameGroup">
  <sequence>
    <element name="first" type="string" minOccurs="1" maxOccurs="unbounded"/>
    <element name="middle" type="string" minOccurs="0" maxOccurs="1"/>
    <element name="last" type="string"/>
  </sequence>
</group>
```

The `<group>` declaration for the NameGroup was very straightforward. It listed the allowable elements for the content model within a `<sequence>` declaration. This should look very similar to the `<name>` examples you have already seen.

```
<complexType name="LocationType">
  <choice minOccurs="0" maxOccurs="unbounded">
    <element name="address" type="string"/>
    <sequence>
      <element name="latitude" type="string"/>
      <element name="longitude" type="string"/>
    </sequence>
  </choice>
</complexType>
```

In the LocationType `<complexType>` definition you used a choice declaration to allow either the element address or the sequence of elements, including latitude and longitude. You specified that the choice may or may not appear and that it could appear an unbounded number of times.

The global declaration for KnowsType didn't contain any content model. Because of this, the `<knows>` element in the instance document must be empty:

```
<complexType name="KnowsType">
</complexType>
```

```
<complexType name="DescriptionType" mixed="true">
  <choice minOccurs="0" maxOccurs="unbounded">
    <element name="em" type="string"/>
    <element name="strong" type="string"/>
    <element name="br" type="string"/>
  </choice>
</complexType>
```

The DescriptionType `<complexType>` definition was a mixed declaration. To specify this, you added a mixed attribute with the value true. Within the mixed content model, to allow an unbounded number of `<em>`, `<strong>` and `<br>` elements to be interspersed within the text, you used a `<choice>` declaration. Again, minOccurs is sets to 0 and maxOccurs is set to unbounded so that the choice would be repeated.

```
</schema>
```

This completed the XML Schema for the contacts listing. You will continue to add features to this XML Schema throughout the rest of the chapter.

<attribute> Declarations

So far, you have spent most of this chapter learning how to create element declarations. Of course, this is only the very first step when creating an XML Schema. Within XML Schemas, attribute declarations are similar to element declarations. In the examples for the <name> element, you have already seen an attribute declaration for the title attribute. Attribute declarations have the following format:

```
<attribute
  name="name of the attribute"
  type="global type"
  ref="global attribute declaration"
  form="qualified or unqualified"
  use="optional or prohibited or required"
  default="default value"
  fixed="fixed value">
```

As shown with element declarations, there are two primary methods for declaring attributes:

❑   Creating a local type

❑   Using a global type

Unlike elements, which are divided into simple types and complex types, attribute declarations are restricted to simple types. Remember that complex types are used to define types that contain attributes or elements; simple types are used to restrict text-only content. Because an attribute can contain text only, you can use simple types only to define their allowable content.

You can also reuse attributes by referring to global attribute declarations. You do not need to specify a type in your attribute reference; the type of the attribute is included in the global attribute declaration.

Creating a Local Type

Creating a local type for an <attribute> declaration is similar to creating a local type for an <element> declaration. To create a local type, simply include the type declaration as a child of the <attribute> element:

```
<attribute name="title">
  <simpleType>
    <!-- type information -->
  </simpleType>
</element>
```

Notice that an attribute declaration may contain only a <simpleType> definition.

Using a Global Type

Just as you saw with the <element> declarations, many of the attributes have the same type of value. Instead of declaring duplicate local types throughout your schema, you can create a global

`<simpleType>` definition. Within your attribute declarations, you can refer to a global type by name. This type can be one of the built-in XML Schema datatypes:

```
<attribute name="title" type="string"/>
```

You can also create your own global declarations and refer to them. For example, suppose you created a global type for the content of the `kind` attribute:

```
<schema xmlns="http://www.w3.org/2001/XMLSchema"
  xmlns:contacts="http://www.example.com/contacts"
  targetNamespace="http://www.example.com/contacts"
  elementFormDefault="qualified">
  <simpleType name="KindType">
    <!-- type information -->
  </simpleType>
  <element name="phone">
    <complexType>
      <!-- content model information -->
      <attribute name="kind" type="contacts:KindType"/>
    </complexType>
  </element>
</schema>
```

When referring to the type, you must include the target namespace prefix (if any). In the preceding example, the prefix `contacts` is used to refer to the target namespace. However, the following is equally correct:

```
<xs:schema xmlns:xs="http://www.w3.org/2001/XMLSchema"
  xmlns="http://www.example.com/contacts"
  targetNamespace="http://www.example.com/contacts"
  elementFormDefault="qualified">
  <xs:simpleType name="KindType">
    <!-- type information -->
  </xs:simpleType>
  <xs:element name="phone">
    <xs:complexType>
      <!-- content model information -->
      <xs:attribute name="kind" type="KindType"/>
    </xs:complexType>
  </xs:element>
</xs:schema>
```

In this example, the XML Schema namespace is declared using the prefix `xs`, and the target namespace has no prefix. Therefore, to refer to the global type `KindType`, you do not need to include any prefix.

Referring to an Existing Global Attribute

Referring to global `<simpleType>` definitions enables you to reuse attribute types within your XML Schema. You'll often want to reuse entire attribute declarations, instead of just the type. XML Schemas enable you to reuse global attribute declarations within your `<complexType>` definition. To refer to a global attribute declaration, include a `ref` attribute in your declaration and specify the name of the global attribute as the value:

```
<attribute ref="contacts:kind"/>
```

Again, the name of the attribute must be qualified with the namespace. Notice that when you refer to a global attribute declaration, there is no `type` attribute and no local type declaration. The attribute uses the type of the `<attribute>` declaration to which you are referring.

Unfortunately, reusing global attribute declarations can create problems in your instance documents because of namespaces. Each attribute that you declare globally must be qualified by a namespace in your instance document. Because default namespace declarations do not apply to attributes, the only way to qualify them is by using a namespace prefix. This can make your instance documents complex and confusing. Instead of dealing with these issues, most XML Schema authors utilize global `<attributeGroup>` declarations when they need to reuse attributes. We will look at `<attributeGroup>` declarations a little later in this chapter.

Naming Attributes

As shown with element declarations, attribute names must follow the rules for XML names that you have already learned. In the last chapter, when creating names in DTDs, you learned that you have to include a namespace prefix if one is going to be used in the instance document. Because XML Schemas are namespace aware, this is unnecessary. Simply specify the name of the attribute; the schema validator can understand any prefix that is used within the instance document.

Attribute Qualified Form

The `form` attribute enables you to override the default for attribute qualification. Attribute qualification functions very similarly to element qualification. If an attribute is qualified, then it must have an associated namespace when it is used in the instance document. Remember that default namespaces don't apply to attributes in your instance document, so you can only qualify an attribute by using a namespace prefix.

You can specify whether the attribute must be qualified by setting the value of the `form` attribute to `qualified` or `unqualified`. If you don't include a `form` attribute, the schema validator uses the value of the `attributeFormDefault` attribute declared in the `<schema>` element. Any attribute declared globally must be qualified, regardless of the `form` and `attributeFormDefault` values.

> *Unlike elements, it is very common to have unqualified attributes within an instance document. Therefore, the* form *attribute is rarely used.*

Attribute Use

When declaring an attribute, you can specify that it is `required`, `optional`, or `prohibited` in the instance document. To control how an attribute is used, simply include the `use` attribute within the `<attribute>` declaration and specify the appropriate value. You cannot include a `use` attribute in a global `<attribute>` declaration.

By setting the value of the `use` attribute to `prohibited`, you can ensure that an attribute won't appear within your instance document. Developers commonly use `prohibited` attribute declarations in conjunction with attribute wildcards. Using this model, you can specify that you want to allow a large group of attributes and subsequently disallow specific attributes within the group.

If you specify that an attribute is `required`, then it must appear within the instance document. If the attribute is omitted, then the schema validator raises a validity error.

Most attributes are optional, so the default value for `use` is `optional`. By declaring that an attribute is `optional`, you indicate that it may or may not appear in the instance document. If you specify a default value for your attribute declaration, then the value of `use` cannot be `required` or `prohibited`.

Default and Fixed Values

You have already seen that XML Schemas allow you to declare default and fixed values for elements. You can declare default and fixed values for attributes in exactly the same way. To specify a default value, simply include the `default` attribute with the desired value:

```
<attribute name="kind" type="contacts:KindType" default="Home"/>
```

In the preceding declaration, the default value for the `kind` attribute is `Home`. If the schema validator finds that the `kind` attribute has been omitted, it inserts the attribute and sets the value to `Home`.

Fixed values operate much like default values. As the schema validator is processing the file, if it encounters a `fixed` attribute, then the parser checks whether the attribute value and `fixed` value match. If they do not match, the parser raises a schema validity error. If the attribute is omitted, then the parser inserts the attribute with the `fixed` value.

To specify a fixed value, simply include the `fixed` attribute with the desired value:

```
<attribute name="version" type="string" fixed="1.0"/>
```

When specifying fixed or default values, you must ensure that the value you specify is allowable content for the type declared for your attribute declaration. For example, if you specify that an attribute has the type `decimal`, then you cannot use `1.0 Beta` as a default value because it is not a decimal value. Moreover, you can't use default and fixed values at the same time within a single attribute declaration.

Attribute Wildcards

Earlier in the chapter, you learned about element wildcards—declarations that allow you to include any elements from a specific namespace or list of namespaces within your content model. You'll often want to declare similar behavior for attributes. Declarations that allow you to include any attribute from a namespace are called *attribute wildcards*.

To declare an attribute wildcard, use the `<anyAttribute>` declaration:

```
<anyAttribute
  namespace="allowable namespaces"
  processContents="lax or skip or strict">
```

The `<anyAttribute>` declaration can appear only within a `<complexType>` or `<attributeGroup>` declaration. You are not allowed to create global `<anyAttribute>` declarations. The `<anyAttribute>` declaration allows you to control which namespaces may be used, by including the `namespace` attribute. The `namespace` attribute allows several values:

Value	Description
`##any`	Allows attributes from all namespaces to be included as part of the wildcard
`##other`	Allows attributes from namespaces other than the `target-Namespace` to be included as part of the wildcard
`##targetNamespace`	Allows attributes from only the `targetNamespace` to be included as part of the wildcard
`##local`	Allows attributes that are not qualified by a namespace to be included as part of the wildcard
Whitespace-separated list of allowable namespace URIs	Allows attributes from any listed namespaces to be included as part of the wildcard. Possible list values also include `##targetNamespace` and `##local`.

Suppose you want to allow any unqualified attributes, as well as any attributes from the `http://www.w3.org/XML/1998/namespace` namespace. You can achieve this by including an attribute wildcard:

```
<complexType>
  <anyAttribute namespace="##local http://www.w3.org/XML/1998/namespace"
                processContents="lax"/>
</complexType>
```

Notice that the value of the `namespace` attribute is a whitespace-separated list with the values `##local` and `http://www.w3.org/XML/1998/ namespace`.

The namespace `http://www.w3.org/XML/1998/namespace` *contains the* `xml:lang` *and* `xml:space` *attributes. These attributes are commonly used to add information about the language or spacing of an XML document.*

When the schema validator processes an element that contains an attribute wildcard declaration, it validates the instance documents in one of three ways:

❑ If the value of the `processContents` attribute is set to `skip`, then the processor skips any wildcard attributes in the element.

❑ If the value of `processContents` attribute is set to `lax`, then the processor attempts to validate the wildcard attributes if it has access to an XML Schema that defines them.

❑ If the value of the `processContents` attribute is set to `strict` (the default) or there is no `processContents` attribute, then the processor attempts to validate the wildcard attributes. However, in contrast to using the `lax` setting, the schema validator raises a validity error if a global XML Schema definition for the wildcard elements cannot be found.

Try It Out — Making Contact — Adding Attributes

Now that you have seen all of the various options for attribute declarations, you can update your contacts schema. This example adds two attributes to your `<contacts>` root element:

1. Begin by making the necessary changes to your XML Schema. Create a new document called `contacts7.xsd`. You can copy the contents of the file `contacts6.xsd` and make the following changes. Because you need to change only the declaration for the `<contacts>` element, that is all we have shown. You add two attribute declarations after the content model. The rest of the XML Schema remains the same.

```
<element name="contacts">
  <complexType>
    <sequence>
      <element name="contact" minOccurs="0" maxOccurs="unbounded">
        <complexType>
          <sequence>
            <element name="name" type="contacts:NameType"/>
            <element name="location" type="contacts:LocationType"/>
            <element name="phone" type="string"/>
            <element name="knows" type="contacts:KnowsType"/>
            <element name="description" type="contacts:DescriptionType"/>
          </sequence>
        </complexType>
      </element>
    </sequence>
    <attribute name="version" type="string" fixed="1.0" />
    <attribute name="source" type="string"/>
  </complexType>
</element>
```

2. Before you can validate your instance document, you must modify it so that it refers to your new XML Schema. You also need to add attributes to your `<contacts>` element. Create a new document called `contacts7.xml`. As before, you can copy the contents of the file `contacts6.xml` and make the following changes to the `<contacts>` element — the rest of the file remains the same:

```
<contacts
  xmlns="http://www.example.com/contacts"
  xmlns:xsi="http://www.w3.org/2001/XMLSchema-instance"
  xsi:schemaLocation="http://www.example.com/contacts contacts7.xsd"
  source="Beginning XML 4E"
  version="1.0">
```

3. You are ready to validate your XML instance document against the XML Schema. Open `contacts7.xml` and click Validate in the Codeplot editor. This should validate with no warnings and no errors. If there is a validation error, then correct it and try validating again.

How It Works

This Try It Out added two attributes to the `<contacts>` element. You did this by adding the attribute declarations after the content model of the local `<complexType>` definition. Let's look at each of these attribute declarations in more detail. Your first attribute declaration defined the `version` attribute:

```
<attribute name="version" type="string" fixed="1.0"/>
```

This indicated that its value must be type `string` — meaning that any text value is allowed. In your DTD you used the type CDATA. No CDATA type exists for XML Schemas, so wherever you would have used CDATA, you should instead use string. When you declared the attribute, you included a fixed attribute with the value 1.0. This means that if the version attribute appears within your document, then it must have the value 1.0. If the version attribute is omitted, then the schema validator will insert the attribute with the value 1.0.

The second attribute declaration defined the source attribute:

```
<attribute name="source" type="string"/>
```

Again, you have indicated that the attribute value must be type string.

> Remember that within the instance document, attributes may appear in any order. In addition, no attribute may appear more than once in a single element.

<attributeGroup> Declarations

You have seen that by creating a global <group> declaration you can define reusable groups of elements. In addition to element groups, the XML Schema also allows you to define attribute groups:

```
<attributeGroup
    name="name of global attribute group">
```

Often, you will need to use the same set of attributes for many elements. In such cases, it is easier to create a global attribute group that can be reused in your <complexType> definitions. In DTDs, this was not possible without using parameter entities.

The <attributeGroup> declaration is very similar to the <group> declaration. Global <attributeGroup> declarations must be named. Simply specify the name attribute with the desired name. The name that you specify must follow the rules for XML names, and it should not include a prefix. The basic structure of a global <attributeGroup> declaration follows:

```
<attributeGroup name="ContactsAttributes">
    <!-- attribute declarations go here -->
</attributeGroup>
```

Instead of allowing content model declarations such as the <group> declarations shown earlier in the chapter, the <attributeGroup> declaration allows <attribute> declarations as children. It also allows attribute wildcards and references to global <attribute> and <attributeGroup> declarations.

Although <attributeGroup> declarations may include references to other global <attributeGroup> declarations as part of the content model, they may not recursively refer to themselves. For example, the following is an illegal <attributeGroup> declaration:

```
<attributeGroup name="AttGroup1">
    <attributeGroup ref="target:AttGroup1"/>
</attributeGroup >
```

This is illegal as well:

```
<attributeGroup name="AttGroup1">
  <attributeGroup ref="target:AttGroup2"/>
</attributeGroup >
<attributeGroup name="AttGroup2">
  <attributeGroup ref="target:AttGroup1"/>
</attributeGroup >
```

This second declaration is illegal because the declaration indirectly refers to itself.

To use an `<attributeGroup>`, simply include an `<attributeGroup>` reference within a `<complexType>` or global `<attributeGroup>` declaration. To specify which `<attributeGroup>` you are referring to, include the `ref` attribute with the name of the global `<attributeGroup>` as the value. As shown with other references, you need to specify the namespace when referring to the global declaration. To do this, include the namespace prefix in the value.

Try It Out   Making Contact — Using a Global Attribute Group

This Try It Out redesign the schema so that you can create a reusable global `<attributeGroup>` declaration. You add your new attribute declarations to an attribute group.

1. Begin by making the necessary changes to your XML Schema. Create a new file called `contacts8.xsd`. Copy the contents from the file `contacts7.xsd` and make the following changes:

```
<attributeGroup name="ContactAttributes">
  <attribute name="version" type="string" fixed="1.0" />
  <attribute name="source" type="string"/>
</attributeGroup>

<element name="contacts">
  <complexType>
    <sequence>
      <element name="contact" minOccurs="0" maxOccurs="unbounded">
        <complexType>
          <sequence>
            <element name="name" type="contacts:NameType"/>
            <element name="location" type="contacts:LocationType"/>
            <element name="phone" type="string"/>
            <element name="knows" type="contacts:KnowsType"/>
            <element name="description" type="contacts:DescriptionType"/>
          </sequence>
        </complexType>
      </element>
    </sequence>
    <attributeGroup ref="contacts:ContactAttributes"/>
  </complexType>
</element>
```

2. Before you can validate your XML document against your schema, you must modify it so that it refers to your new XML Schema. Create a new document called `contacts8.xml`. Copy the contents from the file `contacts7.xml` and change the `xsi:schemaLocation` attribute as follows:

```
xsi:schemaLocation="http://www.example.com/contacts contacts8.xsd"
```

3. You are ready to validate your XML instance document against your XML Schema. Open `contacts8.xml` and click Validate. This should validate with no warnings and no errors. If not, correct any errors and try validating again.

How It Works

This Try It Out has modified your XML Schema to use a global `<attributeGroup>` declaration. You created a global `<attributeGroup>` declaration named `ContactAttributes`. Within the declaration you included the declarations for the `source` and the `version` attributes. Within the `<complexType>` definition for the `<contacts>` element, you added an `<attributeGroup>` reference declaration. When referring to the global `<attributeGroup>` declaration, you included a `ref` attribute with the value `contacts:ContactAttributes`.

As the schema validator processes the instance document, it processes the `<contacts>` element, as shown in earlier examples. When it encounters the `<contacts>` element, it looks it up in the XML Schema. Once it finds the declaration, it finds the associated type (in this case it is a local `<complexType>` definition). When the schema validator encounters the `<attributeGroup>` reference declaration, it treats the `source` `<attribute>` declaration within the group as if it had been included directly within the `<complexType>` definition. It does this for each attribute declaration in the group.

The fixed declaration for the `source` attribute still applies even though you are using a group. Because the version of your contacts list is `1.0`, it matches the fixed value. You could have omitted the version attribute altogether. As the document is being processed, the schema validator adds the fixed value from the XML Schema if no value is specified in the XML document.

Creating Elements with Simple Content and Attributes

At this point you have learned two ways to specify the allowable content for an element. You learned how to construct complex element declarations, which can contain both elements and attributes using the `<complexType>` declaration. You also learned how to specify an `<element>` declaration's type using the `type` attribute and the value `string`. What if your element contains simple content *and* attributes? Unfortunately, this requires a little more work.

When declaring an element that has simple content, you start with a basic element declaration:

```
<element name="phone">
  <!-- Specify type here -->
</element>
```

Within the element declaration, you include a `<complexType>` declaration in which you specify that you want your element to have simple content. You do this by creating a `<complexType>` declaration that contains a `<simpleContent>` element. The `<simpleContent>` element indicates that the

`<complexType>` cannot contain child elements. It may contain attributes, but otherwise the content will be defined by a simple type:

```
<element name="phone">
  <complexType>
    <simpleContent>
      <!-- Specify type here -->
    </simpleContent>
  </complexType>
</element>
```

You also need to specify what kind of datatype should be used to validate your simple content. Within the `<simpleContent>` element, you can create an `<extension>` declaration. You must use an `<extension>` declaration because you will be extending an existing datatype by adding attribute declarations. Consider the following, for example:

```
<element name="phone">
  <complexType>
    <simpleContent>
      <extension base="string">
        <attribute name="kind" type="string" default="Home" />
      </extension>
    </simpleContent>
  </complexType>
</element>
```

In the `<extension>` declaration, you can add a `base` attribute whereby you specify the datatype `string` to use as the basis for your element's content. In the preceding example, the built-in `string` type is the base type, but you are not limited to using built-in datatypes. You can also refer to any global `<simpleType>` in your XML Schema.

After specifying the base type, you declared the attributes. As shown in the `<complexType>` declarations earlier in the chapter, you can include `<attribute>` and `<attributeGroup>` declarations inside the `<extension>` element.

Any of the following examples are allowable `<phone>` elements based on the previous declaration:

```
<phone kind="Home">001-909-555-1212</phone>
<phone>001-909-555-1212</phone>
<phone />
```

In the first of the preceding examples, the `<phone>` element contains a phone number string and a `kind` attribute. In the second example, the `kind` attribute is omitted. If a schema validator encountered this element, it would use the default value `Home` specified in the attribute declaration. The first two examples include a phone number string in the element content. In the final example, the `kind` attribute is omitted and the element doesn't include a phone number.

Datatypes

You have seen how to declare allowable elements and attributes using `<complexType>` definitions. At the start of the chapter, however, we promised that you would learn how to define the allowable content for text-only elements and attribute values. It's time that we made good on that promise.

The XML Schema Recommendation allows you to use the following:

❑ Built-in datatypes

❑ User-defined datatypes

Built-in Datatypes

The examples throughout this chapter have used the `string` type for our text-only content. The `string` type is a primitive datatype that allows any textual content. XML Schemas provide a number of built-in simple types that allow you to exercise greater control over textual content in your XML document. The following table lists all of the simple types built into XML Schemas:

Type	Description
string	Any character data
normalizedString	A whitespace-normalized string in which all spaces, tabs, carriage returns, and linefeed characters are converted to single spaces
token	A string that does not contain sequences of two or more spaces, tabs, carriage returns, or linefeed characters
byte	A numeric value from −128 to 127
unsignedByte	A numeric value from 0 to 255
base64Binary	Base64 encoded binary information
hexBinary	Hexadecimal encoded binary information
integer	A numeric value representing a whole number
positiveInteger	An integer whose value is greater than 0
negativeInteger	An integer whose value is less than 0
nonNegativeInteger	An integer whose value is 0 or greater
nonPositiveInteger	An integer whose value is less than or equal to 0
int	A numeric value from −2147483648 to 2147483647
unsignedInt	A numeric value from 0 to 4294967295
long	A numeric value from −9223372036854775808 to 9223372036854775807
unsignedLong	A numeric value from 0 to 18446744073709551615
short	A numeric value from −32768 to 32767
unsignedShort	A numeric value from 0 to 65535
decimal	A numeric value that may or may not include a fractional part

Table continued on following page

Type	Description
float	A numeric value that corresponds to the IEEE single-precision 32-bit floating-point type defined in the standard IEEE 754-1985. -0, INF, -INF, and NaN are also valid values.
double	A numeric value that corresponds to the IEEE double-precision 64-bit floating-point type defined in the standard IEEE 754-1985. -0, INF, -INF, and NaN are also valid values.
boolean	A logical value, including true, false, 0, and 1
time	An instant of time that occurs daily as defined in Section 5.3 of ISO 8601. For example, 15:45:00.000 is a valid time value.
dateTime	An instant of time, including both a date and a time value, as defined in Section 5.4 of ISO 8601. For example, 1998-07-12T16:30:00.000 is a valid dateTime value.
duration	A span of time as defined in Section 5.5.3.2 of ISO 8601. For example, P30D is a valid duration value indicating a duration of 30 days.
date	A date according to the Gregorian calendar as defined in Section 5.2.1 of ISO 8601. For example, 1995-05-25 is a valid date value.
gMonth	A month in the Gregorian calendar as defined in Section 3 of ISO 8601. For example, --07 is a valid gMonth value.
gYear	A year in the Gregorian calendar as defined in Section 5.2.1 of ISO 8601. For example, 1998 is a valid gYear value.
gYearMonth	A specific month and year in the Gregorian calendar as defined in Section 5.2.1 of ISO 8601. For example, 1998-07 is a valid gYearMonth value.
gDay	A recurring day of the month as defined in Section 3 of ISO 8601, such as the 12th day of the month. For example, ---12 is a valid gDay value.
gMonthDay	A recurring day of a specific month as defined in Section 3 of ISO 8601, such as the 12th day of July. For example, --07-12 is a valid gMonthDay value.
name	An XML name according to the Namespace Recommendation. XML names must begin with a letter or an underscore. Though this type can allow for ":" characters, it is best to avoid them for compatibility.
QName	A qualified XML name as defined in the Namespaces Recommendation. QNames may or may not contain a namespace prefix and colon.
NCName	A noncolonized XML name that does not include a namespace prefix or colon as defined in the Namespaces Recommendation

Type	Description
anyURI	A valid Uniform Resource Identifier (URI)
language	A language constant as defined in RFC 1766, such as en-US (RFC 1766 can be found at www.ietf.org/rfc/rfc1766.txt)

In addition to the types listed, the XML Schema Recommendation also allows the types defined within the XML Recommendation. These types include ID, IDREF, IDREFS, ENTITY, ENTITIES, NOTATION, NMTOKEN, and NMTOKENS. These types are covered in the last chapter.

Although we have used the string type throughout most of our examples, any of the preceding types can be used to restrict the allowable content within your elements and attributes. Suppose you want to modify the declarations of the <latitude> and <longitude> elements within your contacts XML Schema. By specifying a more restrictive type, you could ensure that users of your XML Schema enter valid values. You could modify your declarations as follows:

```
<element name="latitude" type="float"/>
<element name="longitude" type="float"/>
```

Now, instead of allowing any textual content, you require that users specify a floating-point number. For a more in-depth look at these types, see Appendix F or the XML Schema Recommendation at www.w3.org/TR/xmlschema-2/.

Try It Out — Making Contact — Built-in XML Schema Datatypes

This Try It Out modifies the contacts example so that you can take advantage of the built-in XML Schema datatypes. You will also include some additional attributes that utilize the built-in types:

1. Begin by making the necessary changes to your XML Schema. Create a new document called contacts9.xsd. Copy the contents from the file contacts8.xsd and make the following changes:

```
<?xml version="1.0"?>
<schema xmlns="http://www.w3.org/2001/XMLSchema"
  xmlns:contacts="http://www.example.com/contacts"
  targetNamespace="http://www.example.com/contacts"
  elementFormDefault="qualified">

  <attributeGroup name="ContactAttributes">
    <attribute name="version" type="decimal" fixed="1.0" />
    <attribute name="source" type="string"/>
  </attributeGroup>

  <element name="contacts">
    <complexType>
      <sequence>
        <element name="contact" minOccurs="0" maxOccurs="unbounded">
          <complexType>
            <sequence>
              <element name="name" type="contacts:NameType"/>
              <element name="location" type="contacts:LocationType"/>
```

```
                     <element name="phone" type="contacts:PhoneType"/>
                     <element name="knows" type="contacts:KnowsType"/>
                     <element name="description" type="contacts:DescriptionType"/>
                  </sequence>
                  <attribute name="tags" type="token"/>
                  <attribute name="person" type="ID"/>
               </complexType>
            </element>
         </sequence>
         <attributeGroup ref="contacts:ContactAttributes"/>
      </complexType>
   </element>

   <complexType name="NameType">
      <group ref="contacts:NameGroup"/>
      <attribute name="title" type="string"/>
   </complexType>

   <group name="NameGroup">
      <sequence>
         <element name="first" type="string" minOccurs="1" maxOccurs="unbounded"/>
         <element name="middle" type="string" minOccurs="0" maxOccurs="1"/>
         <element name="last" type="string"/>
      </sequence>
   </group>

   <complexType name="LocationType">
      <choice minOccurs="0" maxOccurs="unbounded">
         <element name="address" type="string"/>
         <sequence>
            <element name="latitude" type="float"/>
            <element name="longitude" type="float"/>
         </sequence>
      </choice>
   </complexType>

   <complexType name="PhoneType">
      <simpleContent>
         <extension base="string">
            <attribute name="kind" type="string" default="Home" />
         </extension>
      </simpleContent>
   </complexType>
   <complexType name="KnowsType">
      <attribute name="contacts" type="IDREFS"/>
   </complexType>

   <complexType name="DescriptionType" mixed="true">
      <choice minOccurs="0" maxOccurs="unbounded">
         <element name="em" type="string"/>
         <element name="strong" type="string"/>
         <element name="br" type="string"/>
      </choice>
   </complexType>

</schema>
```

2. Before you can schema validate your XML document, you must modify it so that it refers to your new XML Schema. You should also add some attributes. Create a new document called `contacts9.xml`. Copy the contents of the file `contacts8.xml` and change the `xsi:schemaLocation` attribute. Add the highlighted attributes:

```xml
<?xml version="1.0"?>
<contacts
  xmlns="http://www.example.com/contacts"
  xmlns:xsi="http://www.w3.org/2001/XMLSchema-instance"
  xsi:schemaLocation="http://www.example.com/contacts contacts9.xsd"
  source="Beginning XML 4E"
  version="1.0">
  <contact person="Jeff_Rafter" tags="author xml poetry">
    <name title="Mr.">
      <first>Jeff</first>
      <first>Craig</first>
      <last>Rafter</last>
    </name>
    <location>
      <address>Redlands, CA, USA</address>
      <latitude>34.031892</latitude>
      <longitude>-117.207642</longitude>
    </location>
    <phone kind="Home">001-909-555-1212</phone>
    <knows contacts="David_Hunter Danny_Ayers"/>
    <description>Jeff is a developer and author for Beginning XML <em>4th
edition</em>.<br/>Jeff <strong>loves</strong> XML!</description>
  </contact>
  <contact person="David_Hunter" tags="author consultant CGI">
    <name>
      <first>David</first>
      <last>Hunter</last>
    </name>
    <location>
      <address>Address is not known</address>
    </location>
    <phone kind="Work">416 555 1212</phone>
    <knows contacts="Jeff_Rafter Danny_Ayers"/>
    <description>Senior Technical Consultant for CGI.</description>
  </contact>
  <contact person="Danny_Ayers" tags="author semantics animals">
    <name>
      <first>Daniel</first>
      <middle>John</middle>
      <last>Ayers</last>
    </name>
    <location>
      <latitude>43.847156</latitude>
      <longitude>10.50808</longitude>
      <address>Mozzanella, 7 Castiglione di Garfagnana, 55033 Lucca Italy</address>
    </location>
    <phone>+39-0555-11-22-33-</phone>
    <knows contacts="Jeff_Rafter David_Hunter"/>
    <description>A Semantic Web developer and technical author specializing in
cutting-edge technologies.</description>
  </contact>
</contacts>
```

3. You are ready to validate your XML instance document against your XML Schema. Open
contacts9.xml and click Validate in the Codeplot editor. This should validate with no warnings and no errors, but if you do get a validation error, correct it and try validating again.

How It Works

As shown in the previous chapter, DTDs are not capable of advanced data typing. This Try It Out used some of the XML Schema built-in datatypes. These datatypes enable you to exercise more control over the textual content within your instance documents. Let's look at some of the types in a little more detail. You began by changing the type of your version attribute from string to decimal:

```
<attribute name="version" type="decimal" fixed="1.0" />
```

This is a perfect fit because your version number must always be a valid decimal number. (If you ever needed a complex version number such as 1.0.1, however, this datatype would be insufficient.) Next, you added a tags attribute to the <complexType> declaration for the contact element:

```
<attribute name="tags" type="token"/>
```

You specified that the type should be token, which allows you to use a whitespace-separated list as the value. You added a person attribute as well, specifying the type as ID:

```
<attribute name="person" type="ID"/>
```

To complement this attribute, you modified the KnowsType <complexType> declaration:

```
<complexType name="KnowsType">
  <attribute name="contacts" type="IDREFS"/>
</complexType>
```

Here you used the built-in types ID and IDREFS. Remember that these types were added to XML Schema for compatibility with DTDs and other XML tools. XML Schema actually allows you to build complex keys and key-references using its own built-in mechanism. Unfortunately, until recently these features were not widely supported, so it is usually better to use ID and IDREFS whenever possible. The phone <element> declaration was modified to refer to a new global type PhoneType:

```
<element name="phone" type="contacts:PhoneType"/>
```

And the PhoneType was added to the XML Schema:

```
<complexType name="PhoneType">
   <simpleContent>
     <extension base="string">
       <attribute name="kind" type="string" default="Home" />
     </extension>
   </simpleContent>
 </complexType>
```

The PhoneType <complexType> declaration allowed you to specify that the <phone> element could contain simple string content as well as a kind attribute.

Instead of using the built-in `string` type for the `latitude` and `longitude` `<element>` declarations, you modified these to use the built-in type `float`. The `float` type is similar to the `decimal` type in that it allows you to have decimal numbers, but it offers even more control and compatibility. Because the `float` type is based on existing standards, it is useful across various computer languages. For example, some XML applications such as XQuery and XPath2 can natively understand floating-point arithmetic.

As the schema validator processes the document, not only is it checking whether the element content models you have specified are correct, it is also checking whether the textual data you included in your elements and attributes is valid based on the type you specified.

User-Defined Datatypes

Although the XML Schema Recommendation includes a wealth of built-in datatypes, it doesn't include everything. As you are developing your XML Schemas, you will run into many elements and attribute values that require a type not defined in the XML Schema Recommendation. Consider the `kind` attribute for the `<phone>` element. Because you restricted its value to the `string` type, it still accepts unwanted values such as the following:

```
kind="Walkie-Talkie"
```

According to the declaration for the `kind` attribute, the value `Walkie-Talkie` is valid. What you need is to create a list of allowable values as you did in your DTD. No such built-in type exists within the XML Schema Recommendation, so you must create a new type using a `<simpleType>` definition.

<simpleType> Declarations

When designing your XML Schemas, you may need to design your own datatypes. You can create custom user-defined datatypes using the `<simpleType>` definition:

```
<simpleType
  name="name of the simpleType"
  final="#all or list or union or restriction">
```

When you declare a `<simpleType>`, you must always base your declaration on an existing datatype. The existing datatype may be a built-in XML Schema datatype, or it may be another custom datatype. Because you must derive every `<simpleType>` definition from another datatype, `<simpleType>` definitions are often called *derived types*. There are three primary derived types:

❑ Restriction types

❑ List types

❑ Union types

This section describes the basics of `<simpleType>` declarations and user-defined types. In addition, Appendix F covers datatypes in detail. If you are looking for an in-depth treatment of all of the features and options, see *Professional XML Schemas* by Jon Duckett et al. (Wrox Press, 2001).

<restriction> Declarations

The most common `<simpleType>` derivation is the restriction type. Restriction types are declared using the `<restriction>` declaration:

```
<restriction
  base="name of the simpleType you are deriving from">
```

A derived type declared using the `<restriction>` declaration is a subset of its base type. Facets control all simple types within XML Schemas. A *facet* is a single property or trait of a `<simpleType>`. For example, the built-in numeric type `nonNegativeInteger` was created by deriving from the built-in `Integer` type and setting the facet `minInclusive` to zero. This specifies that the minimum value allowed for the type is zero. By constraining the facets of existing types, you can create your own more restrictive types.

There are 12 constraining facets, described in the following table:

Facet	Description
minExclusive	Allows you to specify the minimum value for your type that excludes the value you specify
minInclusive	Allows you to specify the minimum value for your type that includes the value you specify
maxExclusive	Allows you to specify the maximum value for your type that excludes the value you specify
maxInclusive	Allows you to specify the maximum value for your type that includes the value you specify
totalDigits	Allows you to specify the total number of digits in a numeric type
fractionDigits	Allows you to specify the number of fractional digits in a numeric type (e.g., the number of digits to the right of the decimal point)
length	Allows you to specify the number of items in a list type or the number of characters in a string type
minLength	Allows you to specify the minimum number of items in a list type or the minimum number of characters in a string type
maxLength	Allows you to specify the maximum number of items in a list type or the maximum number of characters in a string type
enumeration	Allows you to specify an allowable value in an enumerated list
whiteSpace	Allows you to specify how whitespace should be treated within the type
pattern	Allows you to restrict string types using regular expressions

Not all types use every facet. In fact, most types can be constrained only by a couple of facets. For a complete list of what constraining facets can be used when restricting the built-in XML Schema types, see Appendix F.

Within a `<restriction>` declaration, you must specify the type you are restricting using the `base` attribute. The value of the `base` attribute is a reference to a global `<simpleType>` definition or built-in XML Schema datatype. As you have seen with all references in our XML Schema, the reference is a namespace-qualified value and, therefore, may need to be prefixed.

Suppose you want to create a restriction type that uses enumeration facets to restrict the allowable values for the `kind` attribute in your `<phone>` element:

```
<attribute name="kind">
  <simpleType>
    <restriction base="string">
      <enumeration value="Home"/>
      <enumeration value="Work"/>
      <enumeration value="Cell"/>
      <enumeration value="Fax"/>
    </restriction>
  </simpleType>
</attribute>
```

This declaration contains a `<restriction>` declaration with the base type `string`. Within the restriction are multiple enumeration facets to create a list of all of the allowable values for your type.

Try It Out   Making Contact — Creating a Restriction Simple Type

As shown in the section "User-Defined Datatypes" earlier in the chapter, the `kind` attribute should be more restrictive. Now that you know how to create your own `<simpleType>` definitions, in this Try It Out you create a `<restriction>` type for the `kind` attribute:

1. Begin by making the necessary changes to your XML Schema. Create a new document called `contacts10.xsd`. Copy the contents from the file `contacts9.xsd` and make the following changes. You need to modify only the `<attribute>` declaration for the `kind` attribute. The rest of the XML Schema remains the same:

```
<complexType name="PhoneType">
  <simpleContent>
    <extension base="string">
      <attribute name="kind" default="Home">
        <simpleType>
          <restriction base="string">
            <enumeration value="Home"/>
            <enumeration value="Work"/>
            <enumeration value="Cell"/>
            <enumeration value="Fax"/>
          </restriction>
        </simpleType>
      </attribute>
    </extension>
  </simpleContent>
</complexType>
```

2. Before you can schema validate your XML document, you must modify it so that it refers to your new XML Schema. Create a new document called `contacts10.xml`. Copy the contents of the file `contacts9.xml` and change the `xsi:schemaLocation` attribute as follows:

```
xsi:schemaLocation="http://www.example.com/contacts contacts10.xsd
```

3. You are ready to validate your XML instance document against your XML Schema. Open `contacts10.xml` and click Validate in the Codeplot editor. This should validate without warnings or errors. If you do get a validation error, correct it and try validating again.

How It Works

In this Try It Out, you modified the `kind` attribute declaration. You created a local `<simpleType>` definition that is a restriction derived from the built-in type `string`. This allowed you to limit which string values could be used within the `kind` attribute in your instance document. Each possible string was defined with a separate `<enumeration>` facet:

```
<attribute name="kind" default="Home">
  <simpleType>
    <restriction base="string">
      <enumeration value="Home"/>
      <enumeration value="Work"/>
      <enumeration value="Cell"/>
      <enumeration value="Fax"/>
    </restriction>
  </simpleType>
</attribute>
```

Because you changed your attribute's type to a local `<simpleType>`, you had to remove the original type by removing the `type` attribute.

`<list>` Declarations

You'll often need to create a list of items. Using a `<list>` declaration, you can base your list items on a specific `<simpleType>`:

```
<list
  itemType="name of simpleType used for validating items in the list">
```

When creating your `<list>` declaration, you could specify the type of items in your list by including the `itemType` attribute. The value of the `itemType` attribute should be a reference to a global `<simpleType>` definition or built-in XML Schema datatype. The reference is a namespace-qualified value, so it may need to be prefixed. The `<list>` declaration also allows you to specify your `itemType` by creating a local `<simpleType>` definition.

When choosing the `itemType`, remember that you are creating a whitespace-separated list, so your items cannot contain whitespace. Therefore, types that include whitespace cannot be used as `itemTypes`. A side effect of this limitation is that you cannot create a list whose `itemType` is itself a list.

Suppose you created a global `<simpleType>` called `ContactTagsType` whereby you enumerated all of the allowable tags for a contact:

```
<simpleType name="ContactTagsType">
  <restriction base="string">
    <enumeration value="author"/>
    <enumeration value="xml"/>
    <enumeration value="poetry"/>
    <enumeration value="consultant"/>
    <enumeration value="CGI"/>
    <enumeration value="semantics"/>
    <enumeration value="animals"/>
  </restriction>
</simpleType>
```

This simple type only allows for one of the enumerated values to be used. If you want to allow for multiple items, you could make a type called `ContactTagsListType`, which allows for a list of tags using the `<list>` declaration:

```
<simpleType name="ContactTagsListType">
  <list itemType="contacts:ContactTagsType"/>
</simpleType>
```

If you use this within your contacts XML Schema, it would allow you to specify multiple tags within your instance document but still require that they adhere to the enumerations you provide. Of course, you would probably want to expand your list of possible tags to include all kinds of values, but for now this ensures that each tag is validated.

`<union>` Declarations

Finally, when creating your derived types, you may need to combine two or more types. By declaring a `<union>`, you can validate the values in your instance document against multiple types at once:

```
<union
  memberTypes="whitespace separated list of types">
```

When creating a `<union>` declaration, you specify the types you are combining by including the `memberTypes` attribute. The value of the `memberTypes` attribute should be a whitespace-separated list of references to global `<simpleType>` definitions or built-in XML Schema datatypes. Again, these references are namespace-qualified values, so they may need to be prefixed. The `<union>` declaration also allows you to specify your `memberTypes` by creating local `<simpleType>` definitions.

Suppose that you wanted to allow the value `Unknown` in the `<latitude>` and `<longitude>` elements. To do this you could use a union of the built-in `float` type and a custom type that allows only the string `Unknown`, as shown in the following example:

```
<simpleType name="UnknownString">
  <restriction base="string">
    <enumeration value="Unknown"/>
  </restriction>
</simpleType>

<simpleType name="UnknownOrFloatType">
  <union memberTypes="float contacts:UnknownString"/>
</simpleType>
```

In this declaration, you have created the custom `UnknownString` type and a union of the two simple types `float` and `UnknownString`. Note that when you refer to the names of the `<simpleType>` definitions, you must make sure they are qualified with a namespace. In this case, the reference to `float` has no prefix because the default namespace for this document is the XML Schema namespace. The prefix `contacts` is used when referring to the type `UnknownString`, however, because it was declared in the target namespace. By referring to your newly created type, you can specify that your `<latitude>` and `<longitude>` elements must contain either `float` values or the string `Unknown`:

```
<element name="latitude" type="contacts:UnknownStringOrFloatType"/>
<element name="longitude" type="contacts:UnknownStringOrFloatType"/>
```

Some *valid* elements include the following:

```
<latitude>43.847156</latitude>
<longitude>Unknown</longitude>
```

Some *invalid* elements include these:

```
<latitude>unknown</latitude>
<longitude>43.847156 Unknown</longitude>
```

The first two elements both contain valid values. The third element is invalid because the value `unknown` is not listed in either of the unioned types — the values are case sensitive. The fourth element is invalid because the schema validator treats this as a single value. Although `Unknown` and `43.847156` are allowable by themselves, the value `43.847156 Unknown` is not listed in either of the unioned types.

Try It Out   Making Contact — More Simple Types

In this Try It Out, you add some new types to your contacts listing:

1. Begin by making the necessary changes to your XML Schema. Create a new document called `contacts11.xsd`. Copy the contents of the file `contacts10.xsd` and make the following changes (you first need to add the new `<simpleType>` declarations):

```
<simpleType name="ContactTagsType">
  <restriction base="string">
    <enumeration value="author"/>
    <enumeration value="xml"/>
    <enumeration value="poetry"/>
    <enumeration value="consultant"/>
    <enumeration value="CGI"/>
    <enumeration value="semantics"/>
    <enumeration value="animals"/>
  </restriction>
</simpleType>

<simpleType name="ContactTagsListType">
  <list itemType="contacts:ContactTagsType"/>
</simpleType>

<simpleType name="UnknownString">
  <restriction base="string">
```

```
      <enumeration value="Unknown"/>
    </restriction>
  </simpleType>

  <simpleType name="UnknownStringOrFloatType">
    <union memberTypes="float contacts:UnknownString"/>
  </simpleType>
```

2. Modify the `<latitude>` and `<longitude>` element declarations. The rest of the XML Schema remains the same:

```
    <element name="latitude" type="contacts:UnknownStringOrFloatType"/>
    <element name="longitude" type="contacts:UnknownStringOrFloatType"/>
```

3. Before you can schema validate your XML document, you must modify it so that it refers to your new XML Schema. Create a new document called `contacts11.xml`. Copy the contents of the file `contacts10.xml` and change the `xsi:schemaLocation` attribute as follows:

```
xsi:schemaLocation="http://www.example.com/contacts contacts11.xsd"
```

4. You should also update the latitude and longitude for David Hunter using the newly created Unknown string:

```
<contact person="David_Hunter" tags="author consultant CGI">
  <name>
    <first>David</first>
    <last>Hunter</last>
  </name>
  <location>
    <address>Address is not known</address>
    <latitude>Unknown</latitude>
    <longitude>Unknown</longitude>
  </location>
  <phone kind="Work">416 555 1212</phone>
  <knows contacts="Jeff_Rafter Danny_Ayers"/>
  <description>Senior Technical Consultant for CGI.</description>
</contact>
```

5. You are ready to validate your XML instance document against your XML Schema. Open `contacts11.xml` and click the `Validate` button in the Codeplot editor. This should validate with no warnings or errors. If you do get a validation error, then correct it and try validating again.

How It Works

This Try It Out added some more complex `<simpleType>` declarations to your schema. You first created a new type that enables you to control which tags can be used for each contact. Then you created two global `<simpleType>` declarations that enabled you to utilize floating-point numbers or use the string `"Unknown."` You then modified the `<latitude>` and `<longitude>` element declarations to use your new types.

Creating a Schema from Multiple Documents

So far, the XML Schemas in this chapter have used a single schema document to keep things simple. The XML Schema Recommendation introduces mechanisms for combining XML Schemas and reusing definitions. As mentioned in Chapter 4, reusing existing definitions is good practice — it saves you time when creating the documents and increases your document's interoperability.

The XML Schema Recommendation provides two primary declarations for use with multiple XML Schema documents:

❏ `<import>`

❏ `<include>`

<import> Declarations

The `<import>` declaration, as the name implies, allows you to import global declarations from other XML Schemas. The `<import>` declaration is used primarily for combining XML Schemas that have different `targetNamespaces`. By importing the declarations, the two XML Schemas can be used in conjunction within an instance document. Note that the `<import>` declaration allows you to *refer* to declarations only within other XML Schemas. The next section covers the `<include>` declaration, which *includes* the declarations directly into the XML Schema as if they had been declared. The `<include>` declaration can be used only for XML Schemas with the same `targetNamespace`:

```
<import
  namespace=""
  schemaLocation="">
```

The `<import>` declaration is always declared globally within an XML Schema (it must be a direct child of the `<schema>` element). This means that the `<import>` declaration applies to the entire XML Schema. When importing declarations from other namespaces, the schema validator attempts to look up the document based on the `schemaLocation` attribute specified within the corresponding `<import>` declaration. Of course, as shown earlier, the `schemaLocation` attribute serves only as a hint to the processor. The processor may elect to use another copy of the XML Schema. If the schema validator cannot locate the XML Schema for any reason, it may raise an error or proceed with lax validation.

To get a better idea of how this works, you need a sample XML Schema that uses the `<import>` declaration. Let's combine the examples that you have been working with throughout this chapter. Within the XML Schema for your contacts listing, you will import the declarations from your `<name>` vocabulary. You will use the imported `<name>` declarations in place of the existing declarations. Though it means you need to remove some declarations in this case, it is better to reuse XML Schemas whenever possible.

Try It Out   **Making Contact — Importing XML Schema Declarations**

This example modifies your contact listing to introduce an `<import>` declaration. You import the name vocabulary that you developed earlier in the chapter. You need to remove some existing declarations and modify your instance document to reflect the changes in your XML Schemas:

1. Begin by modifying your contacts vocabulary. You need to import the name vocabulary and use the imported types. Create a new document called `contacts12.xsd`. Copy the contents of the file `contacts11.xsd` and make the following changes:

```
<schema xmlns="http://www.w3.org/2001/XMLSchema"
  xmlns:contacts="http://www.example.com/contacts"
  xmlns:name="http://www.example.com/name"
  targetNamespace="http://www.example.com/contacts"
  elementFormDefault="qualified">

  <import namespace="http://www.example.com/name" schemaLocation="name8.xsd"/>
```

2. You also need to modify the declaration of the `<contact>` element to refer to the global `<name>` element declared in `name8.xsd`:

```
<element name="contacts">
  <complexType>
    <sequence>
      <element name="contact" minOccurs="0" maxOccurs="unbounded">
        <complexType>
          <sequence>
            <element ref="name:name"/>
            <element name="location" type="contacts:LocationType"/>
            <element name="phone" type="contacts:PhoneType"/>
            <element name="knows" type="contacts:KnowsType"/>
            <element name="description" type="contacts:DescriptionType"/>
          </sequence>
          <attribute name="person" type="ID"/>
          <attribute name="tags" type="token"/>
        </complexType>
      </element>
    </sequence>
    <attributeGroup ref="contacts:ContactAttributes"/>
  </complexType>
</element>
```

3. Remove the `NameType` `<complexType>` declaration and the `NameGroup` `<group>` declaration from your schema.

4. Now that you have modified your XML Schema document, you can create an instance document that reflects the changes. This document is very similar to the `contacts11.xml` document. Only the `<name>` elements will change. Create a new document called `contacts12.xml`. Copy the contents of the file `contacts11.xml` and make the following changes:

```
<?xml version="1.0"?>
<contacts
  xmlns="http://www.example.com/contacts"
  xmlns:name="http://www.example.com/name"
  xmlns:xsi="http://www.w3.org/2001/XMLSchema-instance"
  xsi:schemaLocation="http://www.example.com/contacts contacts12.xsd"
  source="Beginning XML 4E"
  version="1.0">
  <contact person="Jeff_Rafter" tags="author xml poetry">
```

```
      <name:name title="Mr.">
        <name:first>Jeff</name:first>
        <name:first>Craig</name:first>
        <name:last>Rafter</name:last>
      </name:name>
      <location>
        <address>Redlands, CA, USA</address>
        <latitude>34.031892</latitude>
        <longitude>-117.207642</longitude>
      </location>
      <phone kind="Home">001-909-555-1212</phone>
      <knows contacts="David_Hunter Danny_Ayers"/>
      <description>Jeff is a developer and author for Beginning XML <em>4th
    edition</em>.<br/>Jeff <strong>loves</strong> XML!</description>
     </contact>
     <contact person="David_Hunter" tags="author consultant CGI">
      <name:name>
        <name:first>David</name:first>
        <name:last>Hunter</name:last>
      </name:name>
      <location>
        <address>Address is not known</address>
        <latitude>Unknown</latitude>
        <longitude>Unknown</longitude>
      </location>
      <phone kind="Work">416 555 1212</phone>
      <knows contacts="Jeff_Rafter Danny_Ayers"/>
      <description>Senior Technical Consultant for CGI.</description>
     </contact>
     <contact person="Danny_Ayers" tags="author semantics animals">
      <name:name>
        <name:first>Daniel</name:first>
        <name:middle>John</name:middle>
        <name:last>Ayers</name:last>
      </name:name>
      <location>
        <latitude>43.847156</latitude>
        <longitude>10.50808</longitude>
        <address>Mozzanella, 7 Castiglione di Garfagnana, 55033 Lucca Italy</address>
      </location>
      <phone>+39-0555-11-22-33-</phone>
      <knows contacts="Jeff_Rafter David_Hunter"/>
      <description>A Semantic Web developer and technical author specializing in
    cutting-edge technologies.</description>
     </contact>
   </contacts>
```

5. You are ready to validate your XML instance document against your XML Schema. Open contacts12.xml and click Validate in the Codeplot editor. As before, this should validate with no warnings and no errors. If not, then correct any errors and try validating again.

How It Works

In this Try It Out, you imported one XML Schema into another. You used the `<import>` declaration because the two XML Schemas were designed for different `targetNamespaces`. Within your first XML Schema, you had already declared a single global element that could be used to describe names. In your second XML Schema, you were forced to do some more work:

```
<?xml version="1.0"?>
<schema xmlns="http://www.w3.org/2001/XMLSchema"
  xmlns:contacts="http://www.example.com/contacts"
  xmlns:name="http://www.example.com/name"
  targetNamespace="http://www.example.com/contacts"
  elementFormDefault="qualified">
```

The first addition you had to make was an XML namespace declaration in the root element. You added a namespace declaration for the namespace `http://www.example.com/name`. You needed to add this declaration so that you could refer to items declared within the namespace later in your XML Schema.

Next, you added an `<import>` declaration:

```
<import namespace="http://www.example.com/name"
  schemaLocation="name8.xsd"/>
```

This `<import>` declaration is straightforward. You are importing the declarations from the `http://www.example.com/name` namespace, which is located in the file `name8.xsd`. This declaration enables you to reuse the declarations from your `name8.xsd` XML Schema within your `contacts12.xsd` XML Schema. (If you are using another schema validator, you should check the documentation for special rules when referring to external files. For example, the Xerces parser handles relative URL references differently in older versions.)

Finally, you modified the `name` element declaration within your `<contact>` declaration:

```
<element ref="name:name" />
```

Notice that you use the namespace prefix declared within the root element when referring to the `name` element declaration from your `name8.xsd` file. Instead of using an element reference, you could have referred to the global type `NameType`.

Once you made these changes, you had to create a new, compliant instance document. The major difference (apart from the namespace declaration in the root element) was the modified content of your `<contact>` elements:

```
<contact person="Jeff_Rafter" tags="author xml poetry">
<name:name title="Mr.">
  <name:first>Jeff</name:first>
  <name:first>Craig</name:first>
  <name:last>Rafter</name:last>
</name:name>
<location>
  <address>Redlands, CA, USA</address>
  <latitude>34.031892</latitude>
```

```
        <longitude>-117.207642</longitude>
    </location>
    <phone kind="Home">001-909-555-1212</phone>
    <knows contacts="David_Hunter Danny_Ayers"/>
    <description>Jeff is a developer and author for Beginning XML <em>4th
  edition</em>.<br/>Jeff <strong>loves</strong> XML!</description>
    </contact>
```

This might seem a little more confusing than you would expect. Because you declared that the `elementFormDefault` of both XML Schemas was `qualified`, you are required to qualify all your elements with namespace prefixes (or a default namespace declaration).

In your instance document you were already using the default namespace to refer to elements from the namespace `http://www.example.com/contacts`. Therefore, you had to use a namespace prefix, in this case `name`, when referring to the elements from the namespace `http://www.example.com/name`. The `<first>`, `<middle>`, and `<last>` elements are all declared within the `http://www.example` `.com/name` namespace; therefore, you must qualify them with the `name` prefix you declared in the root element of your instance document.

The `title` attribute doesn't need to be qualified, because you didn't modify the `attribute` `FormDefault` within your XML Schemas—so it uses the default value `unqualified`.

<include> Declarations

The `<include>` declaration is very similar to the `<import>` declaration. Unlike the `<import>` declaration, however, the `<include>` declaration allows you to combine XML Schemas that are designed for the same `targetNamespace` (or no `targetNamespace`) much more effectively. When a schema validator encounters an `<include>` declaration, it treats the global declarations from the included XML Schema as if they had been declared in the XML Schema that contains the `<include>` declaration. This subtle distinction makes quite a difference when you are using many modules to define a single vocabulary.

```
<include
  schemaLocation="">
```

Notice that within the `<include>` declaration there is no `namespace` attribute. Again, unlike the `<import>` declaration, the `<include>` declaration can be used only on documents with the same `targetNamespace`, or no `targetNamespace`. Because of this, a `namespace` attribute would be redundant. Just as you saw before, the `schemaLocation` attribute allows you to specify the location of the XML Schema you are including. The `schemaLocation` value functions as a validator hint. If the schema validator cannot locate a copy of the XML Schema for any reason, then it may raise an error or proceed with lax validation.

To demonstrate the `<include>` declaration, you need an example that utilizes two XML Schema documents with the same `targetNamespace`. To do this, you can break your contacts XML Schema into two parts—moving the type declarations for the `ContactTagsType` to a new XML Schema that can be included in your main document.

Try It Out   Making Contact — Including XML Schema Declarations

This Try It Out divides your XML Schema into two parts and includes one in the other. This is known as dividing an XML Schema into *modules* — separate files that make up the overall XML Schema:

1. Create a new XML Schema called `contact_tags.xsd` that declares all of the allowable tags in your contact listing. To create the declarations, you can simply copy the declarations from `contacts12.xsd`:

```
<?xml version="1.0"?>
<schema xmlns="http://www.w3.org/2001/XMLSchema"
  xmlns:contacts="http://www.example.com/contacts"
  targetNamespace="http://www.example.com/contacts"
  elementFormDefault="qualified">
  <simpleType name="ContactTagsType">
    <restriction base="string">
      <enumeration value="author"/>
      <enumeration value="xml"/>
      <enumeration value="poetry"/>
      <enumeration value="consultant"/>
      <enumeration value="CGI"/>
      <enumeration value="semantics"/>
      <enumeration value="animals"/>
    </restriction>
  </simpleType>
</schema>
```

2. Now that you have created the `contact_tags.xsd` XML Schema, create a new document called `contacts13.xsd`. Copy the contents of the file `contacts12.xsd`. You need to insert an `<include>` declaration, and be sure to remove the `ContactTagsType` declaration:

```
<?xml version="1.0"?>
<schema xmlns="http://www.w3.org/2001/XMLSchema"
  xmlns:contacts="http://www.example.com/contacts"
  xmlns:name="http://www.example.com/name"
  targetNamespace="http://www.example.com/contacts"
  elementFormDefault="qualified">
```

```
  <include schemaLocation="contact_tags.xsd"/>
```

```
  <import namespace="http://www.example.com/name" schemaLocation="name8.xsd"/>
```

3. For clarity, insert a comment in your XML Schema where the `ContactTagsType` used to be:

```
  <!-- ContactTagsType moved to contact_tags.xsd -->
```

4. Before you can schema validate your instance document, you must modify it so that it refers to your new XML Schema. Create a new document called `contacts13.xml`. Copy the contents of the file `contacts12.xml` and change the `xsi:schemaLocation` attribute as follows:

```
xsi:schemaLocation="http://www.example.com/contacts contacts13.xsd"
```

5. You are ready to validate your XML instance document against your XML Schema. Open `contacts13.xml` and click Validate in the Codeplot editor. This should validate with no warnings or errors. If not, correct any errors and try validating again.

How It Works

Dividing complex XML Schemas into modules can be an excellent design technique. In this Try It Out, you divided your contacts vocabulary into two modules. You declared these modules in separate XML Schema documents, each with `http://www.example.com/contacts` as the `targetNamespace`. Because the two documents utilized the same `targetNamespace`, you simply used an `<include>` declaration to combine them.

```
<include schemaLocation="contact_tags.xsd" />
```

As the schema validator processes `contacts13.xsd`, it includes the declarations from `contact_tags.xsd` with the declarations for `contacts13.xsd` as if they had been declared in one document. Therefore, you were able to use all of the types as if they were declared within `contacts13.xsd`. Because you didn't introduce any namespace complexities, there was no need to change the instance document to support the new modular design.

> *What happens when the XML Schema you are including has no `targetNamespace`? Declarations within XML Schemas that have no `targetNamespace` are treated differently. These declarations are known as Chameleon components. Chameleon components take on the `targetNamespace` of the XML Schema that includes them. Therefore, even though they were declared with no `targetNamespace`, when they are included they take the `targetNamespace` of the XML Schema that is including them.*

Documenting XML Schemas

Throughout your programming career, and even in this book, you have heard that documenting your code is one of the best habits you can develop. The XML Schema Recommendation provides several mechanisms for documenting your code:

❑ Comments

❑ Attributes from other namespaces

❑ Annotations

Comments

In Chapter 2, you learned that XML allows you to introduce comments in your XML documents. Because the XML Schema is an XML document, you can freely intersperse XML comments throughout the declarations, as long as you follow the rules for XML well-formedness:

```
<!-- This complexType allows you to describe a person's name broken down
    by first, middle and last parts of the name. You can also specify a
    greeting by including the title attribute. -->
<complexType name="NameType">
    <!-- The NameGroup is a global group defined in this XML Schema. -->
    <group ref="target:NameGroup"/>
    <attribute name="title" type="string"/>
</complexType>
```

The preceding XML Schema fragment includes two comments. The first comment simply introduces the complex type and when it should be used. If someone were reading this XML Schema, this would surely give the user some guidance when creating his or her instance documents. The second comment informs the user that the referenced group is declared in this XML Schema.

While these comments are useful for someone reading this XML Schema, many processors will not report XML comments. Therefore, the document must be read by a human for the comments to be useful in all cases.

Attributes from Other Namespaces

The XML Schema Recommendation provides a second mechanism for documenting your XML Schemas. All of the elements defined within the XML Schema vocabulary allow you to include any attribute from another namespace. You can use the alternative attributes to introduce descriptive data that is included with your element.

Suppose you declared an attribute for comments within the namespace `http://www.example.com/documentation`. You could use this attribute throughout your XML Schema to include comments that are embedded within your elements:

```
<?xml version="1.0"?>
<schema xmlns="http://www.w3.org/2001/XMLSchema"
  xmlns:target="http://www.example.com/name"
  xmlns:doc="http://www.w3.org/documentation"
  targetNamespace="http://www.example.com/name"
  elementFormDefault="qualified">
 <group name="NameGroup">
    <sequence>
      <element name="first" type="string" minOccurs="1" maxOccurs="unbounded"/>
      <element name="middle" type="string" minOccurs="0" maxOccurs="1"/>
      <element name="last" type="string"/>
    </sequence>
  </group>
  <complexType name="NameType" doc:comments="This complexType allows you to
    describe a person's name broken down by first, middle and last parts of the
    name. You can also specify a greeting by including the title attribute.">
    <group ref="target:NameGroup" doc:comments="The NameGroup is a global
      group defined in this XML Schema."/>
    <attribute name="title" type="string"/>
  </complexType>
  <element name="name" type="target:NameType"/>
</schema>
```

In this example, there is a namespace declaration for a fictitious vocabulary for documentation. Suppose that your fictitious namespace contained a declaration for the `comments` attribute. Throughout the XML Schema document, you could include descriptions of the items you were declaring by including the `comments` attribute from the documentation vocabulary.

As a schema validator processes the document, it ignores all of the `comments` attributes because they are declared in another namespace. The attributes can still be used to pass information on to other applications. In addition, the comments provide extra information for those reading your XML Schema.

Annotations

The primary documenting features introduced in the XML Schema Recommendation are called *annotations*. Annotations enable you to provide documentation information, as well as additional application information:

```
<annotation
    id="unique identifier">
```

The <annotation> declaration can appear as a child of most XML Schema declarations. The <annotation> declaration allows you to add two forms of information to your declarations:

❑ Application information

❑ Documentation information

Each <annotation> declaration may contain the elements <appinfo> and <documentation>. These elements may contain *any* XML content from *any* namespace. Each of these elements may also contain a source attribute. The source attribute is used to refer to an external file that may be used for application information or documentation information. Typically, <appinfo> declarations are used to pass information such as example files, associated images, or additional information for validation. Annotations usually include <documentation> declarations to describe the features, or uses, of a particular declaration within the XML Schema.

Consider the following example:

```
<?xml version="1.0"?>
<schema xmlns="http://www.w3.org/2001/XMLSchema"
    xmlns:target="http://www.example.com/name"
    xmlns:doc="http://www.w3.org/documentation"
    targetNamespace="http://www.example.com/name"
    elementFormDefault="qualified">
    <annotation>
        <appinfo source="name8.xml"/>
        <documentation xmlns:html="http://www.w3.org/1999/xhtml">
            <html:p>
                The name vocabulary was created for a Chapter 2 sample. We have
                upgraded it to an <html:strong>XML Schema</html:strong>. The
                appinfo of this <html:pre>&lt;annotation&gt;</html:pre> element
                points to a sample XML file. The sample should be used <html:em>
                only as an example</html:em>.
            </html:p>
        </documentation>
    </annotation>

    <group name="NameGroup">
        <sequence>
            <element name="first" type="string" minOccurs="1" maxOccurs="unbounded"/>
            <element name="middle" type="string" minOccurs="0" maxOccurs="1"/>
            <element name="last" type="string"/>
        </sequence>
    </group>
    <complexType name="NameType" doc:comments="This complexType allows you to
```

```
    describe a person's name broken down by first, middle and last parts of the
    name. You can also specify a greeting by including the title attribute.">
    <group ref="target:NameGroup" doc:comments="The NameGroup is a global group
defined in this XML Schema."/>
    <attribute name="title" type="string"/>
  </complexType>
  <element name="name" type="target:NameType">
    <annotation>
      <documentation source="name.html"/>
    </annotation>
  </element>
</schema>
```

This example XML Schema contains two `<annotation>` declarations. The first `<annotation>` declaration is contained within the `<schema>` element. It is used to add information that is applicable to the entire XML Schema document.

Within the first `<annotation>` declaration are both the `<appinfo>` and `<documentation>` elements. We didn't include any content within our `<appinfo>` element. Instead, we included a `source` attribute that pointed to an example XML instance document. Of course, schema validators must be programmed to utilize the `<appinfo>` declaration. Many programs define different behavior for the `<appinfo>` declaration. Often, the `<appinfo>` declaration contains additional validation information, such as other schema languages.

> *Schematron is another language for defining your vocabulary. Schematron definitions, because they offer additional features, are often embedded directly within the `<appinfo>` declaration. Several processors that can use Schematron in conjunction with XML Schemas have been written. The Topologi Schematron Validator that we have been using throughout our examples is written specifically for this purpose. It is covered in detail within* Professional XML Schemas *by Jon Duckett et al. (Wrox Press, 2001).*

The `<documentation>` declaration within our first annotation contains an HTML fragment that could be used when generating a user's manual for our XML Schema. Our second annotation included only a `<documentation>` declaration. Unlike the first `<documentation>` declaration, the second declaration was empty and instead used the `source` attribute to refer to an external file called `name.html`.

Summary

In this chapter, you learned how to create XML Schemas that can be used to schema validate your XML documents. You again started with the simple `name` examples and then progressed to the more complex `contact` examples. Highlights of this chapter included the following:

- ❑ The advantages of XML Schemas over Document Type Definitions
- ❑ How to associate an XML Schema with an XML document
- ❑ How to declare element and attribute types
- ❑ How to declare groups and attribute groups
- ❑ How to specify allowable XML content using simple types and complex types

❏ How to create an XML Schema using multiple documents and namespaces

❏ How to document your XML Schema

While we have not discussed all of the options available within XML Schemas, we have established a foundation upon which you can build many XML Schemas.

> *Now that you understand the basics of XML Schemas, you are ready to create your own vocabularies. Even with the basics, however, you have many styles and options when designing your XML Schemas. Roger Costello, with the help of many volunteers, has created an XML Schemas Best Practices document that gives advice on what the best choice or style is for many different situations. See* `www.xfront.com/BestPracticesHomepage.html`.

Exercise Questions

Suggested solutions to these questions can be found in Appendix A.

Question 1

Add a `gender` attribute declaration for the `<contact>` elements. The attribute should allow two possible values: *male* and *female*. Make sure the attribute is required.

Question 2

Currently, each contact can have only one phone number. Modify the contact declaration so that each contact can have zero or more phone numbers, and add declarations for `website` and `email` elements.

Question 3

Modify the `<description>` declaration to include an element wildcard. Within the wildcard, specify that the description element can accept any elements from the namespace `http://www.w3.org/1999/xhtml`. Set the `processContents` attribute to `lax`.

6

RELAX NG

RELAX NG is a very powerful, yet easy to understand schema technology that can be used to validate XML instance documents. Like W3C XML Schemas, covered in the previous chapter, RELAX NG is grammar-based. It is possible for many XML instance documents to be valid according to a single RELAX NG schema document. Alternatively, it is possible for a single XML instance document to be valid with respect to multiple RELAX NG schema documents.

Here are some of the key features of RELAX NG:

- ❑ It's simple and easy to learn.
- ❑ It uses pattern-based grammar with a strong mathematical foundation.
- ❑ It has two different syntaxes: XML syntax and compact syntax.
- ❑ It supports XML Schema datatypes.
- ❑ It supports user-defined datatypes.
- ❑ It supports XML namespaces.
- ❑ It's highly composable.
- ❑ Elements and attributes are treated the same.

RELAX NG is a normalized grammar based on James Clark's Tree Regular Expression for XML (TREX), and Makoto Murata's Regular Language description for XML (RELAX). Because RELAX NG was created after DTDs and XML Schemas, the authors were able to address many of the problems in the earlier schema languages. They were able to remove the complexity associated with W3C XML Schemas while embracing some of its features. Additionally, the authors based RELAX NG on strong mathematical models. Having such models simplifies validator development and enables schema authors to make mathematical assertions about their schemas. XML Schema is the most widely supported validation technology, but RELAX NG is considered to be the simplest technology, and it is often favored when support is available. RELAX NG takes a different approach to validating XML documents, when compared to XML Schemas. RELAX NG schemas are based on patterns, whereas XML Schemas are based on types. In fact, the power of RELAX NG centers on its use of patterns. RELAX NG schemas can use pattern composition and named patterns to create reusable sections of schema documents.

Though RELAX NG does not have the type hierarchy of XML Schemas and does not support type inheritance, datatyping is supported. RELAX NG supports the datatypes provided by the W3C XML Schema Part II, Datatypes Recommendation. For example, RELAX NG schemas have full use of XML Schema datatypes, such as `xs:int`, `xs:double`, and `xs:decimal`, as well as the XML Schema facets previously discussed. In fact, RELAX NG was designed with pluggable datatypes in mind. That is, users can invent their own type system, and RELAX NG schemas can be built using user-defined types, instead of, or in addition to, using the XML Schema datatypes.

In this chapter, you will learn the following:

- RELAX NG syntaxes
- RELAX NG patterns, which are the building blocks of RELAX NG schemas
- Composing and combining patterns into higher-level components for reuse, as well as full schema grammars
- The remaining features of RELAX NG, including namespaces, name-classes, datatyping, and common design patterns

XML and Compact Syntaxes

In the last chapter, you learned that XML Schemas use an XML syntax. Because the syntax is entirely in XML, you can use generic XML tools — even those that have no understanding of the rules specific to XML Schema documents. RELAX NG also uses XML syntax, enabling you to work with schemas using eXtensible Stylesheet Language Transformations (XSLT) or other XML tools.

As shown in the last chapter, XML Schemas can be very long. In some cases, the DTDs for your documents were much simpler to read than the corresponding XML Schemas. Because of this, RELAX NG allows you to construct schemas using a compact syntax. The RELAX NG compact (RNC) syntax is, well, compact, and tailored for users who are creating and modifying RELAX NG schemas.

Most RELAX NG validators today need the XML syntax in order to validate the document, but some are becoming available that can validate directly using documents written in the compact syntax.

> Trang is a Java program that can convert the compact syntax to the XML syntax and back. Trang can also convert RELAX NG schemas into DTDs or XML Schemas. Because the compact syntax of RELAX NG is easier for humans to read and write, you'll use that syntax in this book to describe RELAX NG. Every compact syntax schema shown can be converted to the XML syntax using Trang. Trang can be downloaded from `http://thaiopensource.com/relaxng/trang.html`.

Running the Samples

Because the examples use the compact syntax, you need an editor and validator that support the compact syntax. A full list of RELAX NG tools can be found on the RELAX NG website at www
.relaxng.org. As in the previous two chapters, you can use any validator or editor you like. The

examples use the Codeplot editor (http://codeplot.com). In addition to XML Schemas and DTDs, the Codeplot editor supports both the RELAX NG XML syntax and the compact syntax. It also enables you to specify which RELAX NG schemas should be used for validation by allowing you to add validation resources to your XML document.

RELAX NG Patterns

RELAX NG schemas are made up of patterns. Within a RELAX NG schema, you can describe patterns of XML elements and attributes, including sequences and choices. As you will see, patterns of simple data enumerations can also be described. Patterns can be *nested*, enabling the schema author to describe the entire XML structure from top to bottom starting from a single top-level pattern. This section covers patterns that are common to all RELAX NG schemas. In the next section, you'll see how patterns can be given names and be reused.

Element, Attribute, and Text Patterns

You can use many different kinds of patterns, and patterns can be combined in various ways. The most basic patterns in RELAX NG are the element, attribute and text patterns:

Pattern Name	Pattern
element pattern	element name {pattern}
attribute pattern	attribute name {pattern}
text pattern	text

Note that patterns are *recursive* in nature. That is, the element and attribute patterns are defined by placing another pattern inside the curly braces ({) and (}). This recursive ability is very powerful, although it takes some getting used to.

The patterns listed here show three RELAX NG (compact syntax) keywords: element, attribute, and text. The element and attribute patterns are followed by a name. For now, you can think of this as simply being the element or attribute name. In fact, though, it is a name class. Name classes are a nice feature of RELAX NG described later in this chapter.

Try It Out   **What's in a Name?**

Let's take a look at a simple XML instance document and work our way into a RELAX NG schema. We'll continue to use the name vocabulary from Chapters 4 and 5 so that you can quickly compare RELAX NG schemas with XML Schemas and DTDs.

1.   Begin by creating the XML document. In the Codeplot editor, create a new document called name9.xml. Copy the following and when you are finished save the file:

```
<?xml version="1.0"?>
<name title="Mr.">
   <first>John</first>
   <middle>Fitzgerald Johansen</middle>
   <last>Doe</last>
</name>
```

Notice that there is no reference to a RELAX NG document in the XML. Unlike DTD or XML Schema, RELAX NG does not define a technique for an XML instance document to reference the schema document. It is up to the user (via editing tools, command-line arguments, or processing code) to select the schema at runtime. A conscious decision was made by the RELAX NG committee to not provide such a mechanism. One reason is security issues. In addition, it is entirely possible that a particular instance document may need to be validated against different schemas, at different times, for different reasons.

2. Create the RELAX NG schema. As mentioned previously, these examples use the compact syntax. In the Codeplot editor, create a new document called `name9.rnc`. Copy the following; when you are finished, save the file:

```
element name {
  attribute title { text },
  element first { text },
  element middle { text },
  element last { text }
}
```

3. You are ready to validate the XML instance document against the RELAX NG schema. Codeplot allows you to add `name9.rnc` as a validation resource to `name9.xml`. Simply open `name9.xml` and click the Resources button. You will see the resource listing for `name9.xml`. Click New to add a new resource. You can give the resource a title such as "RELAX NG." Choose the RELAX NG Compact Syntax option as the resource kind and Validation for the purpose. The path of the resource is `name9.rnc` (see Figure 6-1).

4. When you have entered the resource information, click Save. In the resource listing, click the Document button to return to `name9.xml`. Click Validate to validate the XML document using the associated `name9.rnc` resource (see Figure 6-2).

The validation should have completed with no errors and with `name9.rnc` read. If the output suggests that the validation completed but there was an error in the document, correct the error and try again.

5. To see what happens when an error occurs, simply modify your `name9.xml` document and try validating again.

Figure 6-1

Figure 6-2

How It Works

In this Try It Out, you created a RELAX NG schema for your name vocabulary. Note that it is not XML syntax; it is a compact syntax. This small snippet is a complete RELAX NG schema. A `name` element must contain a `title` attribute, and must have one `first` element, followed by one `middle` element, and one `last` element. The `first`, `middle`, and `last` elements can contain text.

Unlike in earlier examples, you had to specify which schema to use for validation in the editor instead of the in XML document. Once selected, the validator began reading the XML document and checking its contents against specified schema. In this schema, there isn't any real difference between how you declare the `title` attribute and the other elements. In general, RELAX NG treats patterns equally.

Elements and Attributes

Although RELAX NG treats elements and attributes as equals, there are a few differences between element and attribute patterns. One difference is that the order of the attribute patterns does not matter. As in XML, attributes can appear in any order. This means that the following RNC schema, with the `title` attribute at the end, is identical to the previous example:

```
element name {
  element first { text },
  element middle { text },
  element last { text },
  attribute title { text }
}
```

However, if you switched the `first` and `last` element patterns, the schema would be different because element order is significant in a sequence.

Another difference is that the elements and attributes may contain different patterns. For example, an element pattern may contain text patterns, attribute patterns, or other element patterns. An attribute pattern cannot contain other attributes and cannot contain elements.

The concept of "similar syntax" for elements and attributes is very nice in that you don't need to carry around the "heavier syntax" used in XML Schemas. Namely, in RNC, there is no need to specify `<simpleType>` declarations or `<complexType>` declarations, `<group>` declarations versus `<attributeGroup>` declarations, or any other special-case syntax needed in XML Schemas or DTDs for declaring attributes versus elements.

Cardinality

Within RELAX NG, you can control how many times a pattern must occur, or the pattern's *cardinality*. By specifying a pattern's cardinality, you can make it optional, required, or repeatable. If not specified, then the cardinality of a pattern is 1. In the previous example, because no cardinality indicator is specified, one `first` element, one `middle` element, and one `last` element are expected to occur.

Cardinality Indicator	Meaning
?	Pattern may or may not appear
+	Pattern can appear one or more times
*	Pattern can appear zero or more times
No indicator (default)	Pattern must occur once and only once

Refer to Chapter 4 on DTDs for more discussion of cardinality.

Again, attribute and element patterns are treated similarly. Because you didn't specify a cardinality indicator for your `title` attribute pattern, the default was applied. That meant that the `title` attribute had to appear in your instance document. If you wanted it to be optional you could use the `?` indicator:

```
element name {
   element first { text },
   element middle { text },
   element last { text },
   attribute title { text }?
}
```

Attributes can be optional, but they cannot appear more than once on an individual element. Therefore, you would not find cardinality indicators of one or more + or zero or more * on attribute patterns.

Connector Patterns and Grouping

The previous two chapters described how to build complex content models using XML Schemas and DTDs. RELAX NG uses *connector patterns* to build content models. RELAX NG has three connector patterns: sequence, choice, and interleave.

Pattern Name	Pattern
sequence pattern	pattern, pattern
choice pattern	pattern | pattern
interleave pattern	pattern & pattern
group pattern	(pattern)

As shown with other patterns in this chapter, these patterns are recursive, so although only two items are shown in each example, the sequence, choice, and interleave patterns can repeat indefinitely.

Sequences and Choices

Elements, attributes, or other patterns can be combined with *sequence* or *choice connectors*. Therefore, you can have multiple patterns connected:

```
element date { element year{text}, element month{text}, element day{text} }
```

In the preceding example, the comma connector represents sequence, so the order of the elements in the instance document must be `<year>` first, then `<month>`, and then `<day>`, as shown in the following:

```
<date>
   <year>1959</year>
   <month>08</month>
   <day>14</day>
</date>
```

Note that as a result of the way the connector patterns are described, you cannot combine sequence and choice in the same group. That is, you are allowed to have a sequence in a group, like this:

```
element a{text} , element b{text} , element c{text}
```

Or, you can have a choice used in a group:

```
element a{text} | element b{text} | element c{text}
```

However, you cannot have a mixture of choice and sequence:

```
element a{text} , element b{text} | element c{text}
```

This last example tries to mix sequence and choice in a single group, which is not allowed. If you want to use more than one kind of connector, you must group your content model using the parentheses in the group pattern. The following example shows how sequence and choice could be used together to describe a content model:

```
element a { text } , ( element b { text } | element c { text } )
```

As long as the same connector is used inside the parentheses, all is well. You can also nest parentheses to any level, as in the following:

```
(element a {text}, (element b{text} | (element c {text} , element d {text} ) ) )
```

Remember also that grouping patterns supports cardinality, allowing you to add `*`, `?` and `+` symbols to the pattern as follows:

```
(element a{text}, (element b{text} | (element c{text},element d{text} ) * ) ? ) +
```

Moreover, because RELAX NG is based on patterns and tree automata, you can specify more complex and flexible validation concepts in RELAX NG compared to XML Schemas. For example, in RELAX NG, you can specify that an element `<payment>` has element `<amount>` and attribute `currency`, or put in another way: element `<credit>` and attribute `card`. The complete schema for this combination would be as follows:

```
element payment {
   ( attribute currency { text }, element cash { text } )   |
   ( attribute cardtype { text }, element creditcard { text } )
}
```

Here is one XML instance document that would be *valid* using the previous schema (combining `currency` and `cash` is OK):

```
<payment currency="USD">
  <cash>5.75</cash>
</payment>
```

Here is another (combining `cardtype` and `creditcard` is OK):

```
<payment cardtype="Visa">
  <creditcard>4111 1111 1111 1111</creditcard>
</payment>
```

However, the following XML instance would be *invalid*, because element `cardtype` is combined with attribute `cash`:

```
<payment cardtype="MasterCard">
  <cash>5.75</cash>
</payment>
```

Interleave

The third connector pattern available is the *interleave* pattern, which is quite powerful. As you've seen, the sequence connector requires that elements be ordered. The choice connector allows a choice between, say, two or more elements or other patterns. At a high level, interleave allows child elements (or other patterns) to occur in any order. For example, suppose you had to create an element that contained a person's name and phone number, as in the following XML instance:

```
<person>
  <name>Julie Gaven</name>
  <phone>555-1234</phone>
</person>
```

You could use the sequence connector if you wanted to force `<name>` to come before `<phone>`, but suppose that you really don't care about the order of the child elements `<name>` and `<phone>`. Instead, you want to require that both `<name>` and `<phone>` are present. The choice connector would not work in this case because you require both to be there; it's not an either/or situation. Hence, the interleave connector (`&`) is used, as shown in the following:

```
element person { element name { text } & element phone { text } }
```

The most common use of the interleave connector is to allow single-element patterns to occur in any order. However, because two patterns can appear on either side of the interleave connector, and not just a single-element pattern, you could make other types of content models possible. For example, suppose you had three elements — `<a/>`, `<b/>`, and `<c/>` — that had to occur in that order underneath a parent element. In addition, suppose you wanted to allow another element (say, an `<id/>` element) to be included anywhere underneath that parent element, but you didn't care where it occurred. The following would be a valid instance:

```
<root>
    <a/>
    <id>54643</id>
    <b/>
    <c/>
</root>
```

You can use two separate patterns, connected via the interleave connector, as follows:

```
element root {
  element id { text } &
  ( element a { text }, element b { text}, element c { text } )
}
```

Here, the sequence: a, b, c is *interleaved* with id. You could add one or more cardinality indicators (+) to id to allow multiple id elements to be interleaved with the a, b, c sequence.

Enumerated Values

In the name vocabulary, you had an title attribute that allowed you to enter the formal title for the person you were describing. In the example, you used the value Mr. In the schema you used the text pattern, which allows any string. Like XML Schema validation (and even DTD validation), RELAX NG allows a list of enumerated values to be defined in the schema. This list of values can be used to verify that the instance documents do not contain abnormal values.

If you wanted to specify enumerated values in a RELAX NG, you would use the enumeration pattern that appears as follows:

Pattern Name	Pattern
Enumeration Pattern	*datatype value*

The datatype value is a quoted string value that can use single or double quotes. When multiple values are permitted, you can use the choice connector (|) to separate the values. With the addition of this new pattern, you can modify the earlier schema:

```
element name {
  attribute title { "Mr." | "Mrs." | "Ms." | "Miss" | "Sir" | "Rev" | "Dr." }?,
  element first { text },
  element middle { text },
  element last { text }
}
```

The following document would be valid:

```
<?xml version="1.0"?>
<name title="Mr.">
    <first>Joe</first>
    <middle></middle>
    <last>Hughes</last>
</name>
```

However, this document would not be valid:

```
<?xml version="1.0"?>
<name title="">
    <first>Maria</first>
    <middle></middle>
    <last>Knapik</last>
</name>
```

It isn't valid because you left the `title` attribute empty, which wasn't one of your enumerated options.

Instead of using the RNC keyword `text`, you used a choice of literal values. Validating against enumerated values is a very common and useful technique. Enumerated value validation is also possible for use in element content. For example, if you only wanted to allow people with first names of Joe or Maria, you could define your `first` element this way:

```
element first { 'Joe' | 'Maria' }
```

As shown later, RELAX NG supports *datatype validation*, such as validating against numeric values, date, time, or even regular expressions.

Co-Occurrence Constraints

Because RELAX NG is built on patterns and allows flexible pattern combinations, you can construct schemas that support what are called *co-occurrence constraints*. Co-occurrence constraints allow you to change the way an element or attribute is validated based on the content of another element or attribute. Co-occurrence constraints are not legal in XML Schemas or DTDs.

Here is a sample XML instance to illustrate this concept:

```
<transportation>
  <vehicle type="Automobile" >
    <make>Ford</make>
  </vehicle>
  <vehicle type="Trolley">
    <fare>2.50</fare>
    <tax>1.00</tax>
  </vehicle>
</transportation>
```

The content allowed for the `<vehicle>` element depends on the *value* of the `type` attribute. If the value `Automobile` is found, a `<make>` element is allowed; if the value `Trolley` is found, then `<fare>` and `<tax>` must be present. Here is the RNC schema:

```
element transportation {
  element vehicle {
    (attribute type { 'Automobile' }, element make { text } ) |
    (attribute type { 'Trolley' }, element fare { text }, element tax { text } )
  }*
}
```

Mixed Content Pattern

DTD and XML Schema syntax both contain special constructs to handle mixed content. *Mixed content* allows you to mix text and other child elements freely when declaring the content model of a particular element. In RELAX NG, the mixed pattern handles mixed content:

Pattern Name	Pattern
mixed pattern	`mixed {`*pattern*`}`

Consider the `<description>` element from the previous two chapters. You wanted to allow the `<em>` element, `<strong>` element, and `<br>` element to be interspersed within the textual description:

```
<description>Jeff is a developer and author for Beginning XML <em>4th
  edition</em>.<br/>Jeff <strong>loves</strong> XML!</description>
```

As you can see, text is scattered in and around the `<em>` and `<strong>` child elements. The following RNC schema handles the previous document:

```
element description {
  mixed { element em { text } | element strong { text } | element br { empty } }*
}
```

By using the `mixed` keyword and a repeated choice (using the | and * symbols), the previous schema allows zero or more occurrences of `<em>` , `<strong>`, and `<br>` to be used as children of the `<description>` element, mixed in with text. This is a common design pattern for mixed content models. Note that DTD and XML Schemas are limited to this particular use of mixed content, but RELAX NG is not. You can use other patterns with mixed content, as any pattern can go inside the two curly braces of the mixed pattern. For example, you could have a mixed pattern for descriptions that require one `<em>` tag, followed by an optional `<strong>` tag, followed by zero or more `<br>` tags, and in that order. The RNC Schema for this new content model would be as follows:

```
element description {
  mixed { element em { text }, element strong { text }?, element br { empty }* }
}
```

Note that in the new content model, the `<br>` tag can occur multiple times, but `<em>` and `<strong>` cannot.

The Empty Pattern

XML has the concept of an *empty* element — that is, an element that contains no content, no child elements, and no text content. Empty elements *may* contain attributes, however. To provide for empty elements, RELAX NG has an *empty pattern*:

Pattern Name	Pattern
empty pattern	`empty`

If fact, the empty pattern was used in the previous example. We declared an element pattern for the element <br>, which has no attributes or child elements. That is, the <br> element is completely empty. The XML for the <br> element looked like this:

```
<br/>
```

Here is the schema:

```
element br { empty }
```

In your contacts vocabulary, the <knows> element was empty but it allowed a contacts attribute to be present. For example:

```
<knows contacts="David_Hunter Danny_Ayers"/>
```

The schema would be as follows:

```
element knows { attribute contacts { text },  empty }
```

Just as you saw in earlier examples, the order of attribute patterns is not important. The following would also be correct:

```
element knows { empty, attribute contacts { text } }
```

Try It Out　　**Making Contact**

This example creates a RELAX NG compact syntax schema for the example XML document used in the last two chapters: the contacts listing. Because the examples are long, you may want to download the content from the book's website at www.wrox.com.

1. Begin by creating the XML instance document. Modify the example from the last chapter to remove some of the XML Schema–specific items. Open Codeplot and create a new document called contacts14.xml. Copy the following and when you are finished, save the file:

```
<?xml version="1.0"?>
<contacts source="Beginning XML 4E" version="1.0">
  <contact person="Jeff_Rafter" tags="author xml poetry">
    <name title="Mr.">
      <first>Jeff</first>
      <first>Craig</first>
      <last>Rafter</last>
    </name>
    <location>
      <address>Redlands, CA, USA</address>
      <latitude>34.031892</latitude>
      <longitude>-117.207642</longitude>
    </location>
    <phone kind="Home">001-909-555-1212</phone>
    <knows contacts="David_Hunter Danny_Ayers"/>
    <description>Jeff is a developer and author for Beginning
      XML <em>4th edition</em>.<br/>Jeff <strong>loves</strong>
      XML!</description>
```

```
    </contact>
    <contact person="David_Hunter" tags="author consultant CGI">
      <name>
        <first>David</first>
        <last>Hunter</last>
      </name>
      <location>
        <address>Address is not known</address>
        <latitude>Unknown</latitude>
        <longitude>Unknown</longitude>
      </location>
      <phone kind="Work">416 555 1212</phone>
      <knows contacts="Jeff_Rafter Danny_Ayers"/>
      <description>Senior Technical Consultant for CGI.</description>
    </contact>
    <contact person="Danny_Ayers" tags="author semantics animals">
      <name>
        <first>Daniel</first>
        <middle>John</middle>
        <last>Ayers</last>
      </name>
      <location>
        <latitude>43.847156</latitude>
        <longitude>10.50808</longitude>
        <address>Mozzanella, 7 Castiglione di Garfagnana, 55033 Lucca
          Italy</address>
      </location>
      <phone>+39-0555-11-22-33-</phone>
      <knows contacts="Jeff_Rafter David_Hunter"/>
      <description>A Semantic Web developer and technical author specializing
        in cutting-edge technologies.</description>
    </contact>
  </contacts>
```

2. Create the RNC schema document. Using only the basic patterns you have already learned, you will build a schema that can validate the document. Create a new document in Codeplot, name the document contacts14.rnc, copy the following, and when you are finished save the file:

```
element contacts {
  attribute version { "1.0" },
  attribute source { text }?,
  element contact {
    attribute person { text }?,
    attribute tags { text }?,
    element name {
      attribute title { "Mr." | "Mrs." | "Ms." | "Miss" | "Sir" | "Rev" | "Dr." }?,
      element first { text }+,
      element middle { text }?,
      element last { text }
    },
    element location {
      ( element address { text } |
      ( element latitude { text }, element longitude { text } ) )*
    },
```

```
    element phone { attribute kind {"Home" | "Work" | "Cell" | "Fax"}?, text },
    element knows {
      attribute contacts { text },
      empty
    },
    element description {
      mixed {
        element em { text } | element strong { text } | element br { empty }
      }*
    }
  }*
}
```

3. You are ready to validate the XML instance document against the RELAX NG schema. Within Codeplot, open `contacts14.xml` and click the Resources button. You will see the resource listing for `contacts14.xml`. Click New to add a new resource. You can give the resource a title such as "RELAX NG." Choose the RELAX NG Compact Syntax option as the resource kind, and Validation for the purpose. The path of the resource is `contacts14.rnc`. Save the resource and return to the document. Click the Validate button. The Codeplot editor should indicate that the schema loaded and that there were no validation errors (see Figure 6-3).

Figure 6-3

How It Works

In this Try It Out example, you created an XML instance document for the contacts vocabulary you used in the previous two chapters, and then you created an RNC schema. The contacts XML has a root element, called `<contacts>`, which contains only one child element and two attributes, so you begin the schema this way:

```
element contacts {
   attribute version { "1.0" },
   attribute source { text }?,
   element contact {
   }*
}
```

The `<contact>` element also had two attributes and five children elements:

```
element contact {
   attribute person { text }?,
   attribute tags { text }?,
   element name {
   },
   element location {
   },
   element phone {
   },
   element knows {
   },
   element description {
   }
}*
```

Finally, you filled in each of the element patterns with the appropriate content models. The name element pattern looked very similar to the earlier examples. You simply added some cardinality indicators to allow for multiple first names and an optional middle name, and enumerated the choices for the title attribute:

```
element name {
   attribute title { "Mr." | "Mrs." | "Ms." | "Miss" | "Sir" | "Rev" | "Dr." }?,
   element first { text }+,
   element middle { text }?,
   element last { text }
}
```

The location pattern was a little more complex:

```
element location {
   ( element address { text } |
   ( element latitude { text }, element longitude { text } ) )*
}
```

Here you wanted to allow for a repeating choice between an `<address>` element and a `<latitude>` element followed by a `<longitude>` element. To do this, you created a group for all of the contents and a subgroup for the latitude and longitude patterns. Recall that this is required because you can't mix sequences and choices in a single group.

The remaining patterns, `phone`, `knows`, and `description`, used the patterns shown earlier in the chapter. These included the `empty` pattern and the `mixed` pattern. When the validator began to read your document, it built an in-memory tree and began attempting to match the patterns you declared against the document.

Combining and Reusing Patterns and Grammars

This section describes building patterns and entire grammars for reuse. You'll see how to break down patterns so that they can be reused and recombined in various ways. In addition, you'll take a look at breaking down the RELAX NG grammars into multiple physical files and learn how to redefine included patterns.

Named Patterns

All the RNC schemas shown thus far have been valid and complete RNC schemas. It is perfectly legal to create RNC schemas with one top-level, or *root*, element and add nested patterns, to any level, as needed. However, instead of creating one huge nested pattern, RELAX NG also allows you to construct complex schemas out of smaller pieces called *named pattern definitions*, which appear as follows:

Pattern Name	Pattern
named pattern definition	*Pattern Name = pattern*

Breaking one large pattern into multiple pieces (or named pattern definitions) makes it easier to manage complex schemas, and enables reuse. It can also make your schema smaller, more flexible, and easier to understand. For example, it is possible to create a named pattern definition for elements:

```
FirstNameDef = element first { text }
```

You can also create named pattern definitions for group patterns:

```
locationContents = element address { text } |
                 ( element latitude { text }, element longitude { text } )
```

Recursive and re-entrant patterns are allowed. A pattern reference can reference the current pattern name, either directly (recursive) or indirectly (re-entrant).

You can create a named pattern definition for any pattern you can create in RELAX NG. In the previous example, `FirstNameDef` and `locationContents` are named pattern identifiers. You can choose almost any name you like. The names do not have to start with an uppercase letter or follow any specific format. If you use one of the RNC keywords as your pattern name, however, you must precede it with a \, as in `\text = element textElement { text }`.

Once you have defined a named pattern definition, you can reference it from *inside* other patterns:

```
element location = { locationContents* }
```

Pattern reuse could not be any easier! You can simply use the named pattern identifier anywhere a pattern is allowed. The `locationContents` on the right-hand side of the equals sign (=) references the original `locationContents` definition defined earlier. Again, recall that `locationContents` and `FirstNameDef` are named pattern names; they are not element or attribute names.

Try It Out   Utilizing Named Patterns

This example revises the RELAX NG compact syntax schema from the previous examples. You convert most of the patterns within your schema to named pattern definitions. You don't need to modify your XML instance document for this example.

1. Create a new document in Codeplot called `contacts15.rnc`. The order in which you list the schema definitions is your choice, but for this example begin by declaring the `start` pattern:

```
start = contacts
```

This `start` pattern name is special in that it uses RNC's `start` keyword, which calls out the root element of the XML instance.

2. Create the named pattern definition for `contacts`:

```
contacts = element contacts { contactsContent }
contactsContent = (
  version,
  source?,
  contact*
)
version = attribute version { "1.0" }
source = attribute source { text }
```

Splitting every declaration to a separate named pattern as this example does isn't required but it makes your schema much more versatile. Here, there are separate named pattern definitions for the `contacts` element declaration and its content model. There are two named patterns for the `version` and `source` attributes. Within the `contactsContent` pattern, there are references to the attributes and the `contact` element pattern. Notice that the cardinality indicator for zero or more (*) has been added to the reference. This is perfectly legal.

3. Divide the `contact` pattern definition into separate parts, just as you did with the `contacts` pattern. Again, this is not necessary; it only makes the schema more readable and reusable:

```
contact = element contact { contactContents }
contactContents = (
  person?,
  tags?,
  name,
  location,
  phone,
  knows,
  description
)
person = attribute person { text }
tags = attribute tags { text }
```

4. Define each of the patterns you referenced in your `contactElements` declaration. When you declare the `name` pattern, you will continue to split the declaration and content model into separate patterns. The only difference here is the `title` attribute declaration. Move all the enumerated choices to a separate named pattern definition called `titles`:

```
name = element name { nameContents }
nameContents = (
  title?,
  first+,
  middle?,
  last
)
titles = ("Mr." | "Mrs." | "Ms." | "Miss" | "Sir" | "Rev" | "Dr.")
title = attribute title { titles }
first = element first { text }
middle = element middle { text }
last = element last { text }
```

Remember that any pattern can be used as part of a named pattern definition. This includes enumeration groups.

5. Declare the rest of the patterns in your schema using the same practices:

```
location = element location { locationContents* }
locationContents = (
  address | ( latitude, longitude )
)
address = element address { text }
latitude = element latitude { text }
longitude = element longitude { text }

phone = element phone { phoneContents }
phoneContents = (
  kind?,
  text
)
kinds = ("Home" | "Work" | "Cell" | "Fax")
kind = attribute kind { kinds }

knows = element knows { knowsContents }
knowsContents = (
  attribute contacts { text },
  empty
)

description = element description {
  mixed { descriptionContents }*
}
descriptionContents = ( em | strong | br )
em = element em { text }
strong = element strong { text }
br = element br { empty }
```

Notice that in the `knowsContents` declaration, the `contacts` attribute declaration is embedded (you don't create a separate named pattern definition). Again, this is completely legal. You can choose to use named patterns for any number of declarations in your schema.

6. You are ready to validate the XML instance document against the RELAX NG schema. Within Codeplot, open `contacts14.xml` and click the Resources button. You will see the resource listing for `contacts14.xml`. Modify your existing RELAX NG resource to point to the new `contacts15.rnc`. Save the resource and return to the document. Click the Validate button.

How It Works

In this Try It Out example, you modified the contacts RELAX NG schema so that it made use of named pattern definitions. Named patterns are quite useful and important for schema designers, making RELAX NG schemas easy to create, maintain, understand, and reuse. It is common to create named patterns for reusable components, or groups of attributes and/or elements. It's completely up to you how you want to expand your patterns into one or more pattern definitions, by employing the group pattern discussed earlier.

One additional feature about pattern names is very important to understand. RNC grammar syntax was designed so that you don't have to worry about name collisions between pattern names and element (or attribute) names. For that reason, many RNC schema designers use the same name for both the element (or attribute) and the pattern that defines that element. Why bother creating new unique names when you don't need to? It really depends on how you want to break down the reuse of your patterns and how much granularity and flexibility you need when combining and redefining multiple named patterns.

Combining Named Pattern Definitions

Up until this point, you have been using the = assign method for your named patterns. That is, you assign a name to a pattern using the equals sign. This technique works fine as long as your pattern names are unique. Creating two named patterns with the same name, however, is illegal. For example, the following schema is invalid:

```
start = name
name = element name {  attribute title { text }? }
name = element name {
  element first { text }+,
  element middle { text }?,
  element last { text }
}
```

This has defined the `name` pattern twice, making the schema invalid, as you can't have two identically named patterns (`name` in this case) that use the = assignment method. RELAX NG allows two identically named patterns, but you must choose another technique when combining the named patterns. Two combinations are possible: choice or interleave:

Pattern Name	Pattern
named pattern choice	`Pattern Name |= pattern`
named pattern interleave	`Pattern Name &= pattern`

Using additional assign methods, RELAX NG gives you complete control over how identically named patterns combine. For example, you can make the previous schema valid by using the interleave assignment method (&=):

```
start = name
name &= element name {  attribute title { text }? }
name &= element name {
  element first { text }+,
  element middle { text }?,
  element last { text }
}
```

This basically says that element <name> may contain the sequence of elements <first>, <middle>, and <last>, and that the title attribute can be interleaved anywhere within the pattern. If you used the choice assignment method (|=), you would declare that the <name> element may contain the sequence of elements <first>, <middle>, and <last>, *or* the title attribute, which is not what you wanted.

When combining patterns of elements, using the choice operator is common. Interleave is often used when combining patterns of attributes because ordering does not matter. You can also place the various assignment method symbols on the special start pattern. This enables you to combine multiple grammars that have different root elements.

You are not allowed to mix |= and &= on identically named patterns, but the following is legal:

```
start = name
name = element name {  attribute title { text }? }
name &= element name {
  element first { text }+,
  element middle { text }?,
  element last { text }
}
```

This used = on the first name definition, and &= on the second. This has the same meaning as if they both used &=.

> While using identically named patterns in a single schema file is rare, it is common for one schema file to include another, and in this case you might have to pay extra attention to the assignment method you employ on your named patterns. For example, in the previous schema, the first name pattern may come from schema1.rnc. The start pattern and second name pattern shown here may be found in schema2.rnc, which includes schema1.rnc.

Schema Modularization Using the include Directive

RELAX NG is extremely flexible when it comes to schema modularization. You are free to break down large schema files into smaller, reusable chunks. You can then combine these smaller files in various ways to develop your complete vocabulary. Schema files can include other schema files and at various levels. For example, instead of redeclaring the <name> element in the contacts vocabulary, you could simply include it. Consider the following file called name10.rnc:

```
name = element name { nameContents }
nameContents = (
  title?,
  first+,
  middle?,
  last
)
titles = ("Mr." | "Mrs." | "Ms." | "Miss" | "Sir" | "Rev" | "Dr.")
title = attribute title { titles }
first = element first { text }
middle = element middle { text }
last = element last { text }
```

Suppose you wanted to include this in your contacts vocabulary. You could simply remove the existing name patterns and add an `include` directive:

```
include "name10.rnc"
```

The `include` directive enables you to merge multiple physical schemas into one. A filename or URL may be specified. Some validators require the use of an absolute URL instead of a relative URL, as shown here. When you merge two or more schemas using the `include` directive, the named patterns in these schemas are combined into one schema. The assignment method discussed earlier becomes more important when identically named patterns are in the included schemas.

Recursive includes are not allowed. It is up to you to ensure that a single schema is only included once, either directly or indirectly.

Redefining Included Named Patterns

When multiple grammars are merged into one, all of the named patterns are combined. When you merge grammars like this, the *including* grammar has the ability to redefine one or more of the named patterns in the included grammar(s). For example, let's say you wanted to create an alternate version of the name vocabulary, replacing the `<first>` element with `<given>`, the `<last>` element with `<family>`, and completely removing the `<middle>` element.

Using the same `name10.rnc` file shown previously, you could modify the `include` statement to redefine the `name` pattern as it is included. The old `include` pattern was simply as follows:

```
include "name10.rnc"
```

You could insert a redefinition:

```
include "name10.rnc" {
  nameContents = (
    title?,
    element given { text }+,
    element family { text }
  )
}
```

The curly braces that follow the include directive contain a list of named patterns that replace the originals found in the name10.rnc file. You do not need to worry about the assignment method on the redefined patterns. There is no combination of patterns taking place; it is a total replacement. You can also replace the start pattern, if one exists, in the included grammar.

This granular redefining capability was only possible because the original name schema was created using separate named patterns for each piece of the name vocabulary. By using named patterns, you can enable other schemas to use your vocabulary and redefine patterns as needed.

Note that the contacts *schema could have replaced the* name *pattern with any RELAX NG pattern. For example, it was not required that the replacement had to be one element for another or one content model for another. Remember that you are replacing patterns, not elements. You could have replaced the* name *pattern with an attribute pattern, or a pattern with three attributes, or a pattern with a choice of two elements and an attribute — omitting the* <name> *element altogether.*

Removing Patterns with the notAllowed Pattern

Sometimes, instead of combining included named pattern definitions, you want to remove them completely. This is especially useful when one schema includes another and there are name collisions. To specify that an included named pattern isn't allowed, RELAX NG has a notAllowed pattern.

For example, suppose the name vocabulary had declared a start pattern:

```
start = name
name = element name { nameContents }
nameContents = (
  title?,
  first+,
  middle?,
  last
)
titles = ("Mr." | "Mrs." | "Ms." | "Miss" | "Sir" | "Rev" | "Dr.")
title = attribute title { titles }
first = element first { text }
middle = element middle { text }
last = element last { text }
```

Within your contacts vocabulary, you also defined a start pattern:

```
start = contacts
```

Clearly, you don't want to combine the two patterns, and having two patterns with the same name is not valid, so you need to use the notAllowed pattern in your include statement:

```
include "name10.rnc" {
  start = notAllowed
}
start |= contacts
```

Notice that you also had to modify your start pattern to use a named pattern choice (| =). Essentially, you are removing the included pattern using the notAllowed declaration and then combining that with the new definition in the contacts vocabulary. Effectively, this is the same as declaring the start pattern as follows:

```
start = notAllowed | contacts
```

This makes contacts the only reasonable choice for your start pattern — achieving what you set out to accomplish. Of course, removing named patterns using notAllowed is not limited to the start pattern. You can use the notAllowed declaration to remove any included named pattern.

Extensions and Restrictions

In the previous chapter on XML Schemas, you saw how XML Schemas support object-oriented inheritance features as a means for schema reuse. Using simple and complex types, XML Schemas can be extended and/or restricted. RELAX NG is quite a bit different from XML Schemas in this regard because it doesn't have the concept of types and is instead based on patterns. While RELAX NG does not support inheritance, this does not mean that reuse and extensibility are impossible.

RELAX NG makes it easy to reference other named patterns within definitions. Combining various named patterns is called *composition*. As you saw earlier, using many named pattern definitions allows for much more flexibility than one large pattern. By splitting the name vocabulary into more named pattern definitions, it is easier to extend or restrict.

When including the name10.rnc schema in another schema, you can redefine any of these named patterns to extend or restrict your definitions. Suppose you wanted to add a <generation> element after the <last> element in your schema. You could do this in a number of ways. You could redefine the nameContents pattern itself, or you could use the nameContents pattern to create a new extended pattern and then modify the name pattern to refer to the extension:

```
include "name.rnc" {
  name = element name { nameContentsExt }
}
nameContentsExt = (nameContents, generation?)
generation = element generation { text }
```

Here, the name pattern uses the new extended content model, nameContentsExt. In the extended content model, you can use composition to join the original nameContents pattern and the new generation named pattern definition. By following this practice in your RELAX NG schema, you can create much more versatile grammars.

As shown with extensions, using named pattern definitions simplifies restrictions. Suppose that you wanted to modify allowable enumerations for the title attribute to include only male titles:

```
include "name.rnc" {
  title = attribute title { maleTitles }
}
maleTitles = titles - ("Mrs." | "Ms." | "Miss")
```

Again, restricting and extending schemas is much easier in RELAX NG than it is using XML Schemas.

Nested Grammars

Oftentimes, you want to reuse names when working with various vocabularies. In these cases, you may not want to redefine or combine the various named patterns; you simply want to keep them separate. In order to do this, you need to keep the grammars separate using the RELAX NG `grammar` pattern. Suppose you wanted to add a `title` attribute to the `<contacts>` element in the `contacts` vocabulary. The title of a contacts listing might be "Business Contacts" or "Family and Friends."

```
version = attribute version { "1.0" }
source = attribute source { text }
title = attribute title { text }
contacts = element contacts {
  version,
  source?,
  title?,
  contact*
}
```

Clearly, the `title` attribute for the `<contacts>` element would be different from the `title` attribute that already exists for the `<name>` element. When including the name vocabulary in the contacts vocabulary, you would see an error because of the name collision. To fix the error, you could change the pattern names so that they were different, or you could use a nested grammar:

```
name = grammar {
  include "name10.rnc"
}
```

Here, the `include` directive is inside of a `grammar` declaration. When you have *nested grammars*, you have a nested set of named pattern declarations. The named patterns in the outer grammar (`contacts`, `contactsContent`, `title`, etc.) do not combine with the named patterns (`start`, `name`, `nameContents`, `title`, etc.) in the nested grammar. This means that you don't have to be concerned about how the two `title` patterns will combine. The `title` attribute in the included vocabulary and the `title` attribute in the contacts vocabulary won't collide.

Nested grammars aren't limited to `include` directives, though. They can be used within standalone schemas as well. For example, you could have just as easily declared all of the name vocabulary patterns inside of the `grammar` directive instead of using an `include` directive:

```
name = grammar {
  start = name
  name = element name { nameContents }
  nameContents = (
    title?,
    first+,
    middle?,
    last
  )
  titles = ("Mr." | "Mrs." | "Ms." | "Miss" | "Sir" | "Rev" | "Dr.")
  title = attribute title { titles }
  first = element first { text }
  middle = element middle { text }
  last = element last { text }
}
```

It is possible to allow patterns in nested grammars to refer to named patterns in their *parent grammar* by using the `parent` pattern. For example, if you wanted to add a `source` attribute to the `<name>` element, you could simply reuse the `source` pattern in your contacts vocabulary, as shown here:

```
name = grammar {
  start = name
  name = element name { nameContents }
  nameContents = (
    title?,
    parent source?,
    first+,
    middle?,
    last
  )
  titles = ("Mr." | "Mrs." | "Ms." | "Miss" | "Sir" | "Rev" | "Dr.")
  title = attribute title { titles }
  first = element first { text }
  middle = element middle { text }
  last = element last { text }
}
```

Here, you have referred to the named pattern definition for the `source` attribute just as you had before. The only difference is the addition of the `parent` directive, indicating to the RELAX NG validator that it should look in the parent grammar for the definition.

Additional RELAX NG Features

Let's now look at some additional RELAX NG features. These include namespaces, name-classes and wildcards, datatypes, list patterns, comments, and divisions.

Namespaces

XML allows instance documents to contain elements and attributes that belong to one or more namespaces. In Chapter 5, the contacts listing was part of the namespace `http://www.example .com/contacts`. In RELAX NG, you can do the same thing by adding a default namespace declaration to the schema:

```
default namespace = "http://www.example.com/contacts"
```

This specifies that any unprefixed element names (for example, `contacts`, `contact`, `name`) belong to the namespace `http://www.example.com/contacts`. Because none of the element names in your schema are prefixed, the default namespace declaration applies to all of them.

There are many differences in the way XML Schemas and RELAX NG handle namespaces. RELAX NG doesn't have the concept of a single `targetNamespace`. In RELAX NG, one schema document can describe many elements and attributes from many different namespaces.

Suppose you wanted to declare that the `<em>`, `<strong>`, and `<br>` elements that are part of the `<description>` actually belonged to the XHTML namespace. You could do this very easily by adding another namespace declaration after the default namespace declaration:

```
namespace xhtml = "http://www.w3.org/1999/xhtml"
```

Declare the element patterns using the newly declared prefix:

```
description = element description {
  mixed { descriptionContents }*
}
descriptionContents = ( em | strong | br )
em = element xhtml:em { text }
strong = element xhtml:strong { text }
br = element xhtml:br { empty }
```

Here, you have declared a namespace and prefix and then used that prefix in the element declarations. Note that element or attribute names can be assigned namespaces, but not pattern names.

It is not necessary for the schema document to use the same prefix strings as the instance document. Prefixes defined in your schema (xhtml in this case) are only used to reference items inside the schema. XML instances are not required to use the same prefix. For example, inside the instance document you could have the following:

```
<contacts:description xmlns:html="http://www.w3.org/1999/xhtml">Jeff is a developer
and author for Beginning XML <html:em>4th edition</html:em>.<html:br/>Jeff
<html:strong>loves</html:strong> XML!</contacts:description>
```

Here, the prefix contacts is used for the contacts namespace http://www.example.com/contacts, and the prefix html is used instead of xhtml to refer to the elements from the namespace http://www .w3.org/1999/xhtml.

> Refer to Chapter 3, "XML Namespaces," as there are many ways to construct this document, using different combinations of default namespace declarations and prefixes.

You can add as many namespace declarations as you want to your schema, enabling a single schema to support as many namespaces as you wish. Alternatively, you may elect to have a different default namespace for each schema document you create, and then combine the schemas via the include directive, producing a final logical schema that allows multiple namespaces. Either way, RELAX NG makes using namespaces quite easy and flexible.

Name-Classes

RELAX NG uses *name-classes* to describe the legal names that you can use for elements and attributes. Throughout the chapter, element and attribute names have been fairly basic. Now let's look at the features of element and attribute name declarations. Here are the element and attribute patterns shown at the beginning of this chapter:

Pattern Name	Pattern
element pattern	element *name* {*pattern*}
attribute pattern	attribute *name* {*pattern*}

The name part in each of these patterns is actually a name-class declaration. RELAX NG has four kinds of name-classes you can use when establishing a name for your element and attribute patterns:

❑   Basic names (including namespaces)

❑   Name-class choices and groups

❑   Namespaces with wildcard

❑   AnyName

Name-classes are available for both element and attribute patterns; however, the examples that follow use only element patterns.

Basic Names (Including Namespaces)

The first kind of name-class, Name, includes simple element and attribute names — with or without namespace prefixes. Every schema example presented so far in this chapter used this kind of name-class. Here is an element that uses the Name name-class, without a prefix:

```
element first { text }
```

This example includes a prefix:

```
element xhtml:em { text }
```

Most of the element (and attribute) patterns you develop for your RELAX NG schemas will use this kind of name-class.

Name-Class Choices and Groups

This second form of name-class allows you to provide a choice of names to use for your elements and attributes. Here is an example using a choice:

```
first = element first | given { text }
```

Modifying your schema this way would allow you to do either of the following:

```
<name>
  <first>Tom</first>
  <last>Gaven</last>
</name>
```

or:

```
<name>
  <given>Tom</given>
  <last>Gaven</last>
</name>
```

Optionally, you can add parentheses around the choice list:

```
first = element ( first | given ) { text }
```

Of course, you can add names with namespaces to the list of names, assuming you had the appropriate namespace declarations, as in the following:

```
descriptionContents = element ( xhtml:em | xhtml:strong | xhtml:br ) { text }
```

Keep in mind that this is a choice between which names to use for the element. This differs from the earlier choice patterns you saw whereby you could choose between various content model patterns. Using this choice feature of name-classes can make your schemas easier to read, but it only works if all the element names in the list have the same content model. In this case, you needed to use text for all of the elements; you couldn't use empty for the xhtml:br element. In general, when any of the element names listed require different content models, you need to create separate element patterns for each one.

Namespaces with Wildcards

This third name-class feature allows you to use wildcards for the names of elements (or attributes), which are attached to a particular namespace. For example, the <description> element allowed for the elements <em>, <strong>, and <br> from the XHTML namespace. Each of these elements was declared within your schema. Using a wildcard, you could instead allow for any element from the XHTML namespace regardless of whether or not it was declared:

```
description = element description {
  mixed { anyXHTML }*
}
anyXHTML = element xhtml:* { text }
```

The last line in this schema declares anyXHTML a pattern that matches any child element, containing text, as long as that child element is from the http://www.w3.org/1999/xhtml namespace. Notice that you do not have to add additional named patterns to describe the <em> or <strong> elements, or any other elements that might suddenly appear under <description>.

In addition to using namespace wildcards, you can optionally add *name exceptions*, which allow you to remove one or more names from the wildcard. For example, suppose you wanted to allow any XHTML element except <xhtml:script>. You use a minus sign to designate which names are disallowed. Here is the syntax:

```
anyXHTML = element xhtml:* - xhtml:script { text }
```

You could disallow both <xhtml:script> and <xhtml:object> with this syntax as follows:

```
anyXHTML = element xhtml:* - ( xhtml:script | xhtml:object ) { text }
```

You can also use the choice and group pattern from the previous section to allow for content from several namespaces at once. If you declared the namespace prefix for SVG, for example, you could do the following:

```
anyXHTMLorSVG = element (xhtml:* | svg:*) { text }
```

While namespace wildcards are a nice feature, you may have noticed one severe limitation with these schemas: All the xhtml elements — <em>, <strong>, <br>, and so on — must have text content. This is a big limitation! What if you wanted to really open up the content model to allow any XHTML element with any element (or attribute) content? You will see how to accomplish that using the last name-class feature, AnyName.

Using AnyName

The `AnyName` name-class feature opens up many different kinds of patterns involving wildcards. The `*` symbol for the name-class enables this feature, as the following illustrates:

```
description = element description {
  mixed { anyElementWithText }*
}
anyElementWithText = element * { text }
```

The last line allows any element, from any namespace, as long as it has text content. This might include elements from the XHTML namespace, the SVG namespace, or some unknown namespace the user decides to use.

Using the `AnyName` name-class pattern, and mixing in some pattern recursion, you can finally get rid of the text content limitation. The following pattern allows any element, with any child elements, to any depth:

```
anyElement = element * { anyElement | text }*
```

This single pattern can be used to validate any XML document, as long as there are no attributes. It states that each element may contain zero or more patterns of text or `anyElement` children (which could therefore contain zero or more recursive element or text patterns, and so on). If you want to add any attributes to the mix, then you can use the following pattern:

```
anyElement = element * { anyAttribute | anyElement | text }*
anyAttribute = attribute * { text }
```

This pattern can be compressed into the following:

```
any = element * { attribute * {text} | any | text }*
```

Unlike XML Schemas, `any`, `anyElement`, *and* `anyAttribute` *are not RELAX NG keywords; feel free to use any identifier you wish.*

The `AnyName` name-class also allows exceptions. You can disallow certain names from the `AnyName` wildcard, as shown earlier. You can also combine the four different name-class features to create flexible patterns. Following are some example patterns that employ exceptions.

Any element from any namespace, except elements with the local name of `script`:

```
anyExample1 = element * - *:script { text }
```

Any element from any namespace, except elements with the local names `script` or `object`:

```
anyExample2 = element * - (*:script | *:object ) { text }
```

Any element from any namespace, except elements with the local name `script` from the `xhtml` namespace:

```
anyExample3 = element * - xhtml:script { text }
```

Any element from any namespace, except any element from the `xhtml` namespace:

```
anyExample4 = element * - xhtml:*  { text }
```

Any element from any namespace, except elements from the null namespace:

```
namespace local = ""
anyExample5 = element * - local:* { text }
```

Finally, any element from the `xhtml` namespace or any element from any namespace with the local name `link`, except elements with local name `script` or elements from the `contacts` namespace:

```
anyExample6 = element (xhtml:* | *:link ) - (*:script | contacts:* ) { text }
```

All the samples here are shown with text content, but you can open up the content models as needed.

Datatypes

RELAX NG supports datatype validation through external datatypes. RELAX NG has a mechanism defined by which users can add custom datatype library systems. Of course, to use a datatype library, you need to have a RELAX NG validator that implements that library system. Most available RELAX NG validators ship with support for the XML Schema datatypes, including XML Schema *facets*. The datatype prefix xsd is used to reference the XML Schema datatypes, and is predefined in RELAX NG. All the RELAX NG validators listed at the end of the chapter support the XML Schema datatypes.

For example, here is a complete schema that uses the XML Schema `integer` datatype:

```
start = number
number = element number { xsd:integer }
```

This schema would validate the following instance document:

```
<number>1234</number>
```

The following would not be valid because the data is not of type `integer`:

```
<number>John Fitzgerald Johansen Doe</number>
```

You can also create custom XML Schema datatypes using the XML Schema facets. Suppose that you wanted to restrict the content of the <phone> element to a specific regular expression. You could do the following:

```
phone = element phone { phoneContents }
phoneContents = (
   kind?,
   PhonePattern
)
PhonePattern = (UsPhonePattern | IntlPhonePattern)
UsPhonePattern = xsd:string { pattern="\d{3}-\d{3}-\d{3}-\d{4}" }
IntlPhonePattern = xsd:string { pattern="\+\d{2}-\d{4}-\d{2}-\d{2}-\d{2}-" }
kinds = ("Home" | "Work" | "Cell" | "Fax")
kind = attribute kind { kinds }
```

Here you have created three new types: PhonePattern, UsPhonePattern, and IntlPhonePattern. Within the phoneContents declaration you have specified that you want to use the PhonePattern type to validate the content. You are free to use any XML Schema facets except for whitespace and enumeration.

If you are employing a custom user-defined datatype library, then your schema would use the datatypes declaration:

```
datatypes color = "http://www.example.com/colors"
start = house
house = element house { color:beige }
```

Again, in this case, you would need to rely on a RELAX NG validator that understands the datatypes URI, as well as the beige type.

Let's revisit the contacts schema, where you can see datatypes and facets in use. In the earlier schema, many elements were defined using RELAX NG's text patterns, as in the following:

```
first = element first { text }
```

Let's modify the schema to use the same datatypes from the last chapter:

```
namespace xhtml = "http://www.w3.org/1999/xhtml"
start = contacts

version = attribute version { xsd:decimal }
source = attribute source { text }
title = attribute title { text }
contacts = element contacts {
  version,
  source?,
  title?,
  contact*
}

contact = element contact { contactContents }
contactContents = (
  person?,
  tags?,
  name,
  location,
  phone,
  knows,
  description
)
person = attribute person { xsd:ID }
tags = attribute tags { xsd:token }

name = grammar {
  start = name
  name = element name { nameContents }
  nameContents = (
    title?,
```

```
      first+,
      middle?,
      last
    )
    titles = ("Mr." | "Mrs." | "Ms." | "Miss" | "Sir" | "Rev" | "Dr.")
    title = attribute title { titles }
    first = element first { text }
    middle = element middle { text }
    last = element last { text }
}

location = element location { locationContents* }
locationContents = (
  address | ( latitude, longitude )
)
address = element address { text }
unknownString = xsd:string { pattern="Unknown" }
unknownStringOrFloat = (xsd:float | unknownString)
latitude = element latitude { unknownStringOrFloat }
longitude = element longitude { unknownStringOrFloat }

phone = element phone { phoneContents }
phoneContents = (
  kind?,
  PhonePattern
)
PhonePattern = (UsPhonePattern | IntlPhonePattern)
UsPhonePattern = xsd:string {
  pattern="(\d{3}-\d{3}-\d{3}-\d{4})|(\d{3}\s\d{3}\s\d{4})" }
IntlPhonePattern = xsd:string { pattern="\+\d{2}-\d{4}-\d{2}-\d{2}-\d{2}-" }
kinds = ("Home" | "Work" | "Cell" | "Fax")
kind = attribute kind { kinds }

knows = element knows { knowsContents }
knowsContents = (
  attribute contacts { xsd:IDREFS },
  empty
)

description = element description {
  mixed { anyXHTML }*
}
anyXHTML = element * { text }
```

In this schema, you employ the new PhonePattern type as well as the xsd:decimal and xsd:float types.

List Patterns

List patterns enable you to validate a whitespace-separated list of tokens. As shown in the last chapter, you can make a whitespace-separated list of almost any datatype. For example, you could build a new datatype for your contact tags attribute:

```
tagNames = (
  "author" |
  "xml" |
  "poetry" |
  "consultant" |
  "CGI" |
  "semantics" |
  "animals"
)
tagList = list { tagNames }
tags = attribute tags { tagNames }
```

You created the `tagList` datatype by using the `list` keyword and placing the datatype for your list in brackets, ({ and }). In the XML instance, the individual items must be separated by whitespace:

```
<contact person="Jeff_Rafter" tags="author xml poetry">
```

You aren't limited to enumeration datatypes; you can use any datatype or combination of datatypes as the basis of your list.

Comments and Divisions

You can add comments to your schemas, and you can break an individual schema into parts (called *divisions*). The following schema was divided into three divisions: one for includes, one for header information, and one for detail information. Comments start with a # symbol and continue to the end of the line. Here is an example of using both comments and divisions:

```
div {
    # top-level includes
    include "extensions.rnc"
}

div {
   # header-level patterns
   start = root
   root = element root { header, detail  }
   header = element header { text }
}

div {
   # detail-level patterns
   detail = element detail { text }
}
```

You can quickly create subgroups to help organize your schema. Keep in mind, however, that divisions are different from nested grammars. They do not create separate scopes for named pattern definitions. This organization technique is very helpful when using the XML syntax, as it simplifies the processing of groups of declarations using tools such as XSLT. Adding comments throughout your schema is always a best practice, as it can greatly improve its readability.

Useful Resources

Here is a list of some RELAX NG–related URLs that you might find helpful:

- ❑ Main specifications — `www.relaxng.org`
- ❑ Validating parsers/processors
    - ❑ Jing — `www.thaiopensource.com/relaxng/jing.html`
    - ❑ Trang — `http://thaiopensource.com/relaxng/trang.html`
    - ❑ MSV — `wwws.sun.com/software/xml/developers/multischema`
    - ❑ Topologi — `www.topologi.com`
    - ❑ RNV — `www.davidashen.net/rnv.html`
- ❑ Editors
    - ❑ Xmlde — `www.xmldistilled.com`
    - ❑ Topologi — `www.topologi.com/products/tme/index.html`
    - ❑ Oxygen — `www.oxygenxml.com`
    - ❑ Nxml mode for GNU Emacs — `www.thaiopensource.com/download`
    - ❑ Codeplot Online Collaborative Editor — `http://codeplot.com`

Summary

In this chapter, you learned how to create RELAX NG compact schemas that can be used to validate XML instance documents. You've learned the basic RELAX NG patterns, including element, attribute, and enumerations, as well as pattern grouping and connectors (sequence, choice, and interleave). Then you found out how to create named patterns for reuse and how to modularize schemas into multiple files using the `include` directive. Next, you learned how to use nested grammars to avoid named pattern collisions, as well as how to create RNC schemas with extensibility in mind. Lastly, you learned how to use namespaces and name-classes in RNC schemas, and how to employ datatype validation, lists, comments, and divisions.

While this chapter doesn't cover every single option available with RELAX NG schemas, it certainly covered the vast majority of features. It is hoped that you have as much fun as we do using this fabulous technology!

Exercise Questions

Suggested solutions to these questions can be found in Appendix A.

Question 1

Break the contacts15.rnc schema file into two schemas. In contacts-main.rnc, place the main schema elements. In contacts-names.rnc, place the name pattern definitions. At the top level, place an include directive in contacts-main.rnc to include contacts-names.rnc.

Question 2

Add a wildcard extension to the descriptionContents pattern so that the users can extend the contacts schema by adding any elements they desire to the <description>.

Part III

Processing

7

XPath

When writing code to process XML, you often want to select specific parts of an XML document to process in a particular way. For example, you might want to select some invoices that fit a date range of interest. Similarly, you may want to specifically exclude some part(s) of an XML document from processing. For example, if you make basic human resources data available on your corporate intranet, you probably want to be sure not to display confidential information such as salary for an employee. To achieve those basic needs, it is essential to have an understanding of a technology that allows you to select a part or parts of an XML document to process. The XML Path Language, XPath, is designed to allow the developer to select specific parts of an XML document.

The latest incarnation of XPath to be given candidate recommendation status by the W3C is version 2.0. The specification can be viewed at `www.w3.org/TR/xpath20/`. Because the version is still not a recommendation and only appeared in June 2006, and is vastly larger than version 1.0, there are still only a few processors supporting it. The current champion is Saxon, which provides a Java and a .NET version and is available in free or paid for versions, the latter implementing some of the more advanced, and optional, features. You can read how to install and configure Saxon in Chapter 8, which is devoted to XSLT. XPath was designed specifically for use with Extensible Stylesheet Language Transformations (XSLT), and with XML Pointer (XPointer), which is not discussed in detail in this book. More recently, XForms 1.0 makes use of XPath 1.0, too. The use of XForms, which includes XPath expressions that bind a form control to the instance data of an XForms document, is discussed in Chapter 20. XPath is also used in XQuery, covered in Chapter 9, and most XML DOM parsers support using it to locate nodes (for more on the XML DOM, see Chapter 11).

This chapter concentrates on version 1.0 features but also notes where things have changed. Later in the chapter we will look at some of the newer functions and syntax of version 2.0.

> XPointer was intended for use with the XML Link Language, XLink. XLink, which became a W3C recommendation in 2001, has seen limited adoption to date. As a result, XPointer is currently also not widely used. Therefore, XPath in this chapter is described primarily in the context of how it is used with XSLT, and the code examples in the chapter use XSLT. To run XSLT code using the Saxon XSLT processor, see the information provided in Chapter 8.

This chapter covers the following:

- ❏ Ways of looking at an XML document, including the XPath data model
- ❏ How to visualize XPath and how the component parts of XPath syntax fit together to enable you to navigate around the XPath data model
- ❏ The XPath axes — the "directions" that are available to navigate around the XPath data model
- ❏ XPath 1.0 functions
- ❏ XPath 2.0 new functions and features

To understand what XPath is and how it is used, we will first consider ways in which an XML document can be represented.

Ways of Looking at an XML Document

In the early chapters of this book you saw how an XML document can be written as a nested structure of start-tags and end-tags, possibly together with processing instructions, comments, attributes, namespace declarations, and text content of elements. An XML document written in that way is simply a sequence of Unicode characters. When XML is expressed in that way, it is said to be *serialized*.

However, although serialized XML is convenient for the human reader, a serialized document is not the only way an XML document can be represented. It is often more useful to model the logical structure of an XML document in a way that describes the logical components that make up the XML document and exposes those components for programmatic manipulation. For example, consider the following XML markup:

```
<Paragraph>Some text.</Paragraph>
```

You probably think of it logically as a Paragraph element with some text content, rather than as a left-angled bracket followed by an uppercase P, and so on. Similarly, to process XML, you need some formal model of the logical content of the document.

The W3C has developed three specifications — XPath, the XML Document Object Model (DOM), and the XML Information Set — each of which represents a logical model of an XML document in similar but distinct ways.

This chapter focuses on the XPath 1.0 data model because it underlies how XPath is used. Representing an XML document using the XML DOM is discussed briefly here and in more detail in Chapter 11. A fourth way in which an XML document can be represented, the XML Information Set, often abbreviated as the XML infoset, is also described briefly.

Modeling XML Documents

In a serialized XML document, you write start-tags and end-tags, and, except in XML documents of trivial length, there is a nested structure of elements, such as in the following simple document:

```
<?xml version="1.0" encoding="UTF-8"?>
<!-- This is a comment. -->
<Book>
<Chapter>Some content</Chapter>
<Appendix>Some appendix content.</Appendix>
</Book>
```

By now, you should be familiar with such XML documents and how to write well-formed XML. How are these documents represented in the XPath data model and other models? Three ways to model XML documents are as follows:

❑ **The XPath data model** — The XPath data model represents most parts of a serialized XML document as a tree of nodes. Most, but not all, parts of an XML document are represented as nodes in the XPath data model. A root node represents the document itself. An element node represents each element in an XML document. Each attribute is represented by an attribute node and similarly for comments and processing instructions. A text node represents an element's text content. In-scope namespaces are represented by namespace nodes. We will look in more detail at each type of node in a moment.

A few parts of an XML document are not represented in the XPath data model. An XML declaration, if present, is not represented in any way in the XPath data model, nor is a document type declaration (DOCTYPE declaration) represented. In addition, while comments and processing instructions can be represented by comment nodes and processing instruction nodes, any comments and processing instructions contained in the document type declaration are not represented in the XPath data model.

❑ **The Document Object Model** — Like the XPath data model, the Document Object Model represents an XML document as a hierarchical tree of nodes. The types of nodes used in the DOM are different from those used in XPath. The nodes used in the DOM and writing code to manipulate the DOM are described in Chapter 11.

❑ **The XML Information Set** — The XML Information Set (infoset) represents an XML document as a hierarchical tree but uses a different approach from both the XPath model and the DOM. The XML Information Set recommendation is located at `http://www.w3.org/TR/xml-infoset/`. It is currently in its second edition.

The infoset represents an XML document as a tree of *information items*. Each information item is similar in concept to a node in the XPath model. Each information item has *properties,* which store values describing one of the item's characteristics. Many of the W3's specifications refer to the infoset, as it represents a very pure version of the information held in an XML document. It is also a platform and programming language infoset. When two documents need to be compared as XML, rather than just as text files, the infoset is commonly used. This overcomes the difficulties of a standard text comparison, such as whether attributes are quoted with single or double quote marks or their order in an element. Both of these aspects can vary in a document without its infoset changing.

Visualizing XPath

XPath can be a very abstract and confusing topic. One way of visualizing XPath that newcomers to XPath often find helpful is to think of XPath as street directions around the hierarchical tree of nodes that make up the XPath data model.

In real life, you can give street directions in two ways: relative to a fixed point or relative to the current position. In XPath, you can write absolute XPath expressions, which always start from a standard point, the root node. Alternatively, you can write relative XPath expressions, which vary depending on where you start. In XPath, the starting point is called the *context*.

> All legal XPath code can be called an expression. *An XPath expression that returns a node-set is called a* location path.

When giving street directions, you have four basic directions: north, south, east, and west. In XPath, there are 13 directions (see the "XPath 1.0 Axes" section later in this chapter for a discussion of these directions). In XPath, a direction is called an *axis*. Just as you might give someone street directions such as "Starting from the square, head east for one block and it's the first building on the right with a red door," in XPath, you might write something like this:

```
/Book/Chapter[@number=2]
```

If we were to express that XPath expression in English, we might say, "Starting from the root node, take the `child` axis and look for element nodes called `Book`; then, for each of those `Book` element nodes, look for element nodes called `Chapter`, also using the child axis; then select only those `Chapter` elements that have a `number` attribute whose value is 2." We can refer to a `child` axis when it isn't actually mentioned because the `child` axis, being the most commonly used, is the default axis in XPath. The part of the expression in square brackets is a *predicate*, which acts to filter nodes selected by the earlier part of the expression. Axes, predicates, and other XPath constructs are explored in more detail later.

A relative location path could be written as follows:

```
Chapter[@number=2]
```

This could be expressed in English as, "Starting from where you are currently located, take the `child` axis, select `Chapter` element nodes, and then filter those nodes to retain only `Chapter` element nodes that possess a `number` attribute whose value is 2." You will likely immediately realize that the result you get depends on your starting position (the XPath context), so it's important to understand just what *context* means in XPath.

Understanding Context

In XPath, the context indicates the location of the node where a processor is currently situated, so to speak. That node is called the *context node*. However, the context consists of more than just the context node. It also includes a context position and a context size. Consider the following XML document, `book.xml`:

```
<Book>
 <Chapter number="1">This is the first chapter</Chapter>
 <Chapter number="2">This is the second chapter</Chapter>
 <Chapter number="3">This is the third chapter</Chapter>
 <Chapter number="4">This is the fourth chapter</Chapter>
 <Chapter number="5">This is the fifth chapter</Chapter>
</Book>
```

Suppose the context node is the node that represents the `Chapter` element node for the second chapter. We can use the `position()` and `last()` functions, described in more detail later in this chapter, to show the position of the context node and the context size, as demonstrated in the following example.

The examples in this chapter rely on XSLT, as XPath does not exist in isolation, but always acts as a helper for another technology such as XSLT or XQuery. For a fuller explanation see Chapter 8, but the basics are explained here. An XSLT file consists of a number of templates that match specific nodes in the XML being processed. The standard way to select the nodes that are matched is by specifying them using an apply-templates *instruction. There are also built-in rules that start the process.*

The following XSLT (context-information.xslt) contains two templates. The first matches the root node and will be called automatically; the second matches any <Chapter> element and is called by the <xsl:apply-templates> instruction within the first template:

```
<xsl:stylesheet
 version="1.0"
 xmlns:xsl="http://www.w3.org/1999/XSL/Transform" >

<xsl:template match="/">
 <html>
  <head>
   <title>This shows the context position and context size.</title>
  </head>
  <body>
   <h3>Context position and context size demo.</h3>
   <xsl:apply-templates select="/Book/Chapter" />
  </body>
 </html>
</xsl:template>

<xsl:template match="Chapter">
 <xsl:if test="position()=2">
 <p>When the context node is the second <b>Chapter</b> element node then</p>
 <p>the context position is <xsl:value-of select="position()" /></p>
 <p>and the context size is <xsl:value-of select="last()" />.</p>
 <p>The text the <b> Chapter</b> element node contains is
'<xsl:value-of select="." />'.</p>
 </xsl:if>
</xsl:template>

</xsl:stylesheet>
```

To run the transform you need to install the Saxon processor, described in Chapter 8, and run the following at the command prompt. (Alternatively, follow the documentation for your chosen processor.) The command-line syntax for the .NET version is as follows:

```
Transform.exe -o book.html book.xml context-information.xslt
```

Use the following syntax if you are working with Java:

```
java -jar saxon8.jar -o book.html book.xml context-information.xslt
```

This assumes both context-information.xslt and book.xml are in the current directory.

The simple HTML document created by the stylesheet is shown in Figure 7-1.

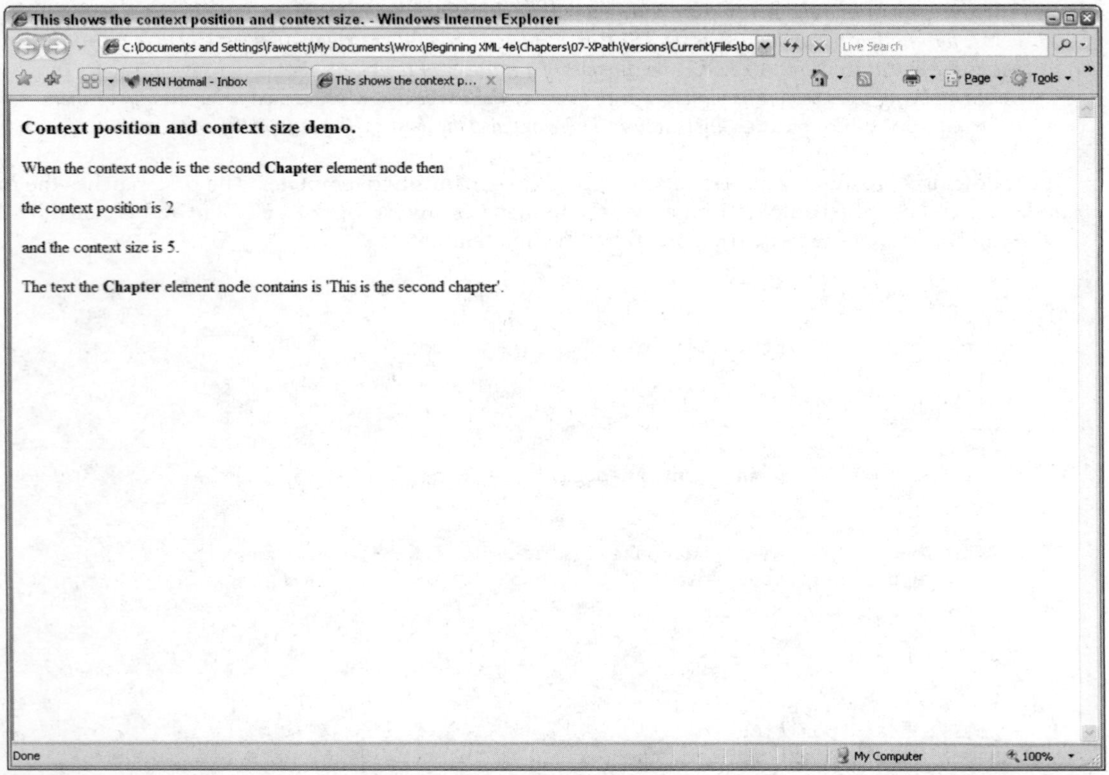

Figure 7-1

The file book.xml *and the XSLT examples are included in the code download. The instructions to install Saxon and run transformations are described more fully in Chapter 8, "XSLT."*

In the second template, the one matching Chapter elements, notice that in the value of the select attribute of the xsl:value-of element you see the position() function and the last() function. As shown in Figure 7-1, the context position is 2 and the context size is 5. This is because we selected five Chapter elements with our XPath. Had the XPath been more explicit, such as /Book/Chapter[2], then the context size and position would both have equaled 1.

What Is a Node?

A node is a representation in the XPath data model of a logical part of an XML document.

In XPath 1.0 there are seven types of nodes:

❑   Root node

❑   Element node

- ❑ Attribute node
- ❑ Text node
- ❑ Namespace node
- ❑ Comment node
- ❑ Processing Instruction node

Each node type is described in more detail in the following sections.

Root Node

The root node represents the document itself, independent of any content. The root node is the apex of the hierarchy of nodes that represents an XML document; it has no name and cannot be seen when the document is serialized. The element node (described next), which represents the document element, is a child of the root node. A root node can only have one child element — that is, the document element. The root node may also have child nodes, which are processing instruction nodes or comment nodes that correspond to any processing instructions or comments in the prolog of the serialized XML document.

> *It is vital to understand the difference between a node and an element, and especially important to differentiate between the root node and the document's root element. All the different items in an XML document are nodes; these can be elements, attributes, comments or any of the other types mentioned earlier. The root node is not visible in the document's serialized form and just serves as a starting point when navigating the document. The root element, however, is the first element in the document and is a child of the root node.*

The XML declaration and the document type declaration are not children of the root node. Neither of those features of a serialized XML document is represented in the XPath data model.

The root node's text value is the concatenation of the values of all descendant text nodes of the root node, in document order. Examine the following XML document:

```
<MixedContent>
Mary had a <Emphasis>little</Emphasis> lamb.
</MixedContent>
```

The text value of this document is `Mary had a little lamb.`

The root node does not have a name.

Element Node

Each element in an XML document is represented as an element node in the XPath data model.

Element nodes have a name that consists of the namespace URI of the element and the local part of its name. For developers it is easier to work with a qualified name, also called a *QName*, which is a namespace prefix followed by a colon character followed by the local part of the element type name:

```
prefix:localpart
```

255

The string value of an element node is the concatenation of the values of all its descendant text nodes, in document order.

An element node may possess an attribute that is defined to be of type ID. For an attribute to be defined this way, the XML document must have an associated Document Type Definition (DTD), either embedded into the XML or linked to it. The following XML, `book-with-ID-node.xml`, shows how an attribute can be specified to have a type of ID:

```
<!DOCTYPE Book [
  <!ELEMENT Book (Chapter+)>
  <!ELEMENT Chapter (#PCDATA)>
  <!ATTLIST Chapter number ID #REQUIRED>
]>
<Book>
 <Chapter number="c1">This is the first chapter</Chapter>
 <Chapter number="c2">This is the second chapter</Chapter>
 <Chapter number="c3">This is the third chapter</Chapter>
 <Chapter number="c4">This is the fourth chapter</Chapter>
 <Chapter number="c5">This is the fifth chapter</Chapter>
</Book>
```

In the preceding example, a DTD states that the document element is Book, which can contain one or more Chapter elements. The Chapter elements have text content — #PCDATA in DTD parlance — and possess a number attribute of type ID. Note how the attribute's name is number; it is not necessary for the attribute to be called ID, nor is it sufficient to call it ID for the id() function to work. IDs cannot begin with a digit, so the prefix c has been added. The following XSLT fragment shows the XPath to select the entire Chapter element whose number attribute equals c2:

<xsl:copy-of select="id('c2')"/>

Because of the difficulties associated with internal DTDs, including lack of good toolsets to create and maintain them, the id() function is not often encountered. In XSLT the key() function is used instead because it can retrieve nodes based on a much wider range of criteria and without the need for any supplementary information such as a DTD.

Attribute Node

Each attribute in an XML document is represented in the XPath model as an attribute node. The element node with which the attribute node is associated is said to be the parent node of the attribute node.

Attribute nodes have a name and a value. In XPath the attributes are not children of their parent element, which can lead to confusion. In practical terms, this means they are always accessed via the attribute axis, not the default child one.

Text Node

Text content of an element node is represented in the XPath data model as a text node. The string value of a text node is its character data. A text node does not have a name.

Namespace Node

Although a specific node can only belong to one namespace, any number of in-scope namespaces can be in effect for the node. In-scope namespaces are those for which there exists a valid prefix to URI mapping or where a URI is associated with an empty prefix, the default namespace.

All in-scope namespaces of an element node are represented as namespace nodes. XPath takes an extravagant approach to namespace nodes. Each element node has its own namespace node for all in-scope namespaces. For example, consider the XPath model of the following code:

```
<library:Book xmlns:library="http://www.XMML.com/booknamespace">
 <chapter:Chapter xmlns:chapter="http://www.XMML.com/chapter" number="1">
Some text content.</chapter:Chapter>
 <chapter:Chapter xmlns:chapter="http://www.XMML.com/chapter" number="2">
Some different text content.</chapter:Chapter>
</library:Book>
```

The Book element node has a namespace node associated with the namespace URI http://www.XMML.com/booknamespace mapped to the library prefix. Each of the Chapter element nodes also has its own namespace node associated with the same namespace URI, http://www.XMML.com/booknamespace. In addition, they have a namespace node associated with the http://www.XMML.com/chapter URI and bound to the chapter prefix. This simple document has five separate namespace nodes associated with the two namespace URIs declared in it. In complex documents, large numbers of namespace nodes can be associated with a single URI, and some elements deep in the hierarchy can have several namespace nodes.

The name() function returns the namespace prefix associated with the namespace node. The self::node() expression (which can be abbreviated to a period character) returns the namespace URI of the namespace node.

Comment Node

A comment node represents a comment in the XML document. Comments in the document type declaration are not represented in the XPath data model.

Processing Instruction Node

A processing instruction node in the XPath model represents a processing instruction in the corresponding XML document. Processing instructions in the document type declaration are not represented in the XPath data model.

The name of a processing instruction node is its target (turn to Chapter 2 for more on processing instructions). The string value of a processing instruction node is its content, excluding the target.

XPath 1.0 Types

XPath 1.0 has four expression types:

❑   Boolean

❑   node-set

❑   number

❑   string

These are greatly expanded in version 2.0, which is addressed later in the chapter.

Booleans

In an XPath 1.0 expression, a Boolean value is written as one of the values `true()` or `false()`. You may wonder why XPath doesn't simply use the values `true` and `false`. It is possible that an XML developer might choose to have a structure like this:

```
<true>
... some content
</true>
```

`true` is a legal XML name and therefore can be used to name an element. There are no reserved words in the XPath language, so the functions `true()` and `false()` are used instead, whereas in other languages constants such as `TRUE` and `FALSE` might be available. That way there is no ambiguity between selecting nodes and choosing a Boolean value.

Node-Sets

A node-set is a set of XPath nodes. Technically, an XPath 1.0 node-set is unordered. However, when used in XSLT, which is currently XPath's main use, processing of a node-set is always in the document order of the nodes for forward axes and in reverse document order for reverse axes. XPath axes are discussed later. Most axes, including the `child` axis, are forward axes.

Consider what document order means by examining the following simple document:

```
<PurchaseOrder>
 <Date>2005-01-01</Date>
 <To>XMML.com</To>
 <ShippingAddress>
  <Street>123 Any Street</Street>
  <City>Anytown</City>
  <State>AZ</State>
 </ShippingAddress>
 <ZipCode>12345</ZipCode>
</PurchaseOrder>
```

The `PurchaseOrder` element is first in document order. Document order among the children of the `PurchaseOrder` element is then `Date`, `To`, `ShippingAddress`, and `ZipCode`. All the child nodes of `ShippingAddress` appear earlier in document order than the `ZipCode` element.

Numbers

In XPath 1.0, numbers are floating-point numbers (more varieties are available in version 2.0). There is no way to directly represent an integer in XPath, although numeric functions will typically return a whole number — for example, from the `count()` function, which counts the number of nodes in a node-set.

Strings

A string value in XPath is a sequence of Unicode characters. Generally, like XML, XPath is not limited to ASCII characters but uses the much more extensive Unicode character set (turn to Chapter 2 for more on Unicode).

XPath 1.0 has no type corresponding to a date. All dates are treated in XPath as strings. Therefore, for example, manipulating strings that represent dates to extract the month from a date depends on knowing exactly how the string is written, and on using various XPath string manipulation functions.

So far, we have talked about XPath in a pretty abstract way. How is XPath written?

Abbreviated and Unabbreviated Syntax

XPath syntax is not written in XML, one reason being that we often use an XPath expression as the value of an attribute. For example, if you wanted to select the value of a `Section` element node, you might write the following:

```
<xsl:value-of select="/Book/Chapter/Section" />
```

If XPath were written using XML, there would be problems in achieving well-formedness. For example, you couldn't use left or right-angled brackets inside the `select` attribute. The syntax used in XPath is similar to the path syntax used for UNIX and Linux directories. The `xsl:value-of` element, by the way, is an XSLT element, which is described in Chapter 8.

The most common tasks you will perform using XPath, the selection of elements and attributes, can be written using an abbreviated syntax, as shown in the previous example. The unabbreviated syntax with the same meaning is written as follows:

```
<xsl:value-of select="/child::Book/child::Chapter/child::Section" />
```

To select an attribute using unabbreviated syntax, you can write the following:

```
attribute::attributename
```

Or, in the abbreviated form, simply write the following:

```
@attributename
```

So the XPath

```
/Book/Chapter/@number
```

would select the number attribute on a `<Chapter>` element that was a child of the document element, `<Book>`.

When using XPath, use the abbreviated syntax where possible. For the two most common tasks — selecting element nodes and attribute nodes using the `child` and `attribute` axes — your paths will be more concise and legible.

XPath 1.0 Axes

XPath 1.0 has a total of 13 axes, which are used to navigate the node tree of the XPath data model. XSLT supports all of these axes but for performance reasons, some XQuery processors, particularly those associated with relational databases, do not support them all. They ignore those that traverse backward through the document, the reverse axes, as well as some of the other less frequently used ones.

In the following list, notice that the first letter of the name of an axis is always lowercase. Because XPath, like XML, is case sensitive, using an uppercase initial letter for the name of an axis will cause unexpected results.

- ❏ child axis
- ❏ attribute axis
- ❏ ancestor axis
- ❏ ancestor-or-self axis
- ❏ descendant axis
- ❏ descendant-or-self axis
- ❏ following axis
- ❏ following-sibling axis
- ❏ namespace axis (not used in XQuery, and deprecated in XPath 2.0)
- ❏ parent axis
- ❏ preceding axis
- ❏ preceding-sibling axis
- ❏ self axis

The following sections look more closely at each axis in turn. You'll examine the `child` and `attribute` axes first because these are the axes you will use most often.

Child Axis

The `child` axis is the default axis in XPath. The `child` axis selects nodes that are immediate child nodes of the context node. Thus, consider a structure like this in an XML document:

```
<Invoice>
<Date>2004-01-02</Date>
<Item quantity="4">QD123</Item>
<Item quantity="5">AC345</Item>
</Invoice>
```

If the context node is the `Invoice` element node, the location path

```
child::Item
```

or, in abbreviated syntax

```
Item
```

will return a node-set containing both Item element nodes, which are child nodes of the Invoice element.

To select both the Date element node and Item element node, which are child nodes of the Invoice element node (which is also the context node), you can write the following:

```
child::*
```

Or, in abbreviated syntax, use the following:

```
*
```

The * indicates any name, and the only nodes in the child axis that have names are element nodes.

If you want to select all child nodes, including comment nodes, processing instruction nodes, and text nodes, you can write the following:

```
child::node()
```

Or, in abbreviated syntax, use the following:

```
node()
```

If you want to specifically select text node children of a context node, you can write the following:

```
child::text()
```

Or, in abbreviated syntax, use the following:

```
text()
```

Because it is the default axis, it is not necessary to express the child axis when using abbreviated syntax. Thus, the location paths

```
/child::Book/child::Chapter/child::Section
```

and

```
/Book/Chapter/Section
```

both mean the same thing. Starting at the root node, there are three location steps, each of which uses the child axis. In the first example, which uses the unabbreviated syntax, the child axis is expressed explicitly. In the second example, the child axis is not explicitly expressed.

At the end of the following section, the Try It Out example demonstrates the use of the child axis and the attribute axis.

attribute Axis

The `attribute` axis is used to select the attribute nodes associated with an element node. If the context node is an element node, the location paths

```
attribute::*
```

or

```
@*
```

will each return all the attribute nodes associated with that element node.

Alternatively, if you want to select a specific attribute node named `security`, you write either

```
attribute::security
```

or

```
@security
```

Remember that the @ character is an abbreviation for the `attribute` axis.

If the context node is not an element node, the `attribute` axis returns an empty node-set.

The following example shows the use of the `child` and `attribute` axes in a simple XSLT stylesheet. If you have no experience with XSLT, you may need to take a look at Chapter 8 for basic information.

Try It Out   Using Child and Attribute Axes

In this example you will use both the `child` and `attribute` axes. First take a look at using XPath in XSLT to create a very simple HTML web page. The source XML document, `PersonData.xml`, is shown here:

```xml
<?xml version='1.0'?>
<PersonData>
<Name DOB="1920/11/25">
 <FirstName>Jack</FirstName>
 <LastName>Slack</LastName>
</Name>
</PersonData>
```

The XSLT stylesheet, `PersonData.xslt`, is shown here:

```xml
<?xml version='1.0'?>
<xsl:stylesheet xmlns:xsl="http://www.w3.org/1999/XSL/Transform" version="1.0"
>

<xsl:template match="/">
 <html>
```

```
  <head>
    <title>Information about <xsl:value-of select="/PersonData/Name/FirstName"/>
    <xsl:text> </xsl:text>
    <xsl:value-of select="/PersonData/Name/LastName" />
    </title>
  </head>
<body>
<p><xsl:value-of select="/PersonData/Name/FirstName" /><xsl:text>
</xsl:text>
<xsl:value-of select="/PersonData/Name/LastName" /> was born on
<xsl:value-of select="/PersonData/Name/@DOB" /></p>
</body>
</html>

</xsl:template>

</xsl:stylesheet>
```

The following instructions assume that you have installed the Saxon XSLT processor, as described in Chapter 8:

1. Open a command window.

2. Navigate to the directory in which the files `PersonData.xml` and `PersonData.xslt` are located.

3. Enter the following command at the command line:

```
java -jar saxon8.jar -o PersonData.html PersonData.xml PersonData.xslt
```

   If you are using the .NET version, enter this:

```
transform.exe -o PersonData.html PersonData.xml PersonData.xslt
```

   If everything has worked correctly, you should see no error messages, although you may see a warning that you are running a version 1.0 stylesheet with a version 2.0 processor. If you see error messages from Saxon, review how you installed Saxon in light of the instructions in Chapter 8.

4. Double-click `PersonData.html`, and you should see a very simple web page with the following code:

```
<html>
  <head>
    <meta http-equiv="Content-Type" content="text/html; charset=UTF-8">
    <title>Information about Jack Slack</title>

  </head>
  <body>
    <p>Jack Slack was born on 1920/11/25</p>
  </body>
</html>
```

How It Works

First, look at how the content of the title element is created. The XSLT xsl:value-of element, shown in the following snippet, uses the child axis three times to select the value of the FirstName element:

```
<xsl:value-of select="/PersonData/Name/FirstName"/>
```

The location path is an absolute location path, which uses abbreviated syntax, so from the root node the PersonData element in the child axis is selected. Then, with the PersonData element node as context node, the Name element is selected. Finally, with the Name element node as context node, the FirstName element node is selected. The xsl:value-of element does what it says — it selects the value of the node specified, which in this case is the FirstName element node. Here, the value is the string value of the element's textual content.

Similarly, the following code retrieves the person's last name, also using the child axis three times:

```
<xsl:value-of select="/PersonData/Name/LastName" />
```

The date of birth displayed in the web page is retrieved using both the child axis and the attribute axis as follows:

```
<xsl:value-of select="/PersonData/Name/@DOB" />
```

The context node is the root node. First the child axis is used, and the PersonData element node is selected. In the next location step, the child axis is again used and the Name element node is selected. Finally, the attribute axis is used and the DOB attribute node is selected. This selects the value of the DOB attribute node.

ancestor Axis

The ancestor axis selects the parent node of the context node, the parent of that node, its parent, and so on until the root node of the document is selected. If the context node is the root node, the ancestor axis returns an empty node-set.

If you had an XML document such as

```
<Book>
 <Chapter number="1">
  <Section>This is the first section.</Section>
  <Section>This is the second section.</Section>
 </Chapter>
 <Chapter number="2">
  <!-- and so on -->
 </Chapter>
</Book>
```

and the context node were the element node corresponding to the second Section element node in Chapter 1, then the location path

```
ancestor::*
```

would return the Chapter element node, which has a number attribute node with a value of 1, the Book element node, and the root node.

Note that there is no way to express the ancestor *axis using abbreviated syntax.*

ancestor-or-self Axis

The ancestor-or-self axis includes all nodes in the ancestor axis plus the context node (which is in the self axis).

Using the document in the ancestor axis section and the same context node, the location path

```
ancestor::Section
```

returns an empty node-set because no ancestor element node is named Section, but the location path

```
ancestor-or-self::Section
```

would return the Section element node, which is the context node.

descendant Axis

The descendant axis selects the child nodes of the context node, the child nodes of those child nodes, and so on.

Consider the following XML document:

```
<Invoices>
 <Invoice>
  <Date>2004-01-01</Date>
  <Item>KDH987</Item>
  <Item>DSE355</Item>
 </Invoice>
<Invoice>
  <Date>2004-01-01</Date>
  <Item>RAH198</Item>
  <Item>DJE385</Item>
 </Invoice>
</Invoices>
```

If the Invoices element node were the context node, the location path

```
descendant::*
```

would select both the Invoice element nodes, both the Date element nodes, and all the Item element nodes. Location paths that use the descendant axis can be expressed only in unabbreviated syntax.

Examine the following, which uses the descendant axis with an absolute location path:

```
/descendant::Item
```

All the Item element nodes in the document that contain the context node would be selected.

Only elements can have child elements, so using descendant on any other type, such as attributes or text nodes, will return an empty node-set.

descendant-or-self Axis

The descendant-or-self axis includes all the nodes in the descendant axis plus the context node (which is contained in the self axis). The abbreviated form for the descendant-or-self axis is //.

This enables you to find nodes irrespective of their position. For example, if you want all the Chapter elements but are unsure of the XML hierarchy, or perhaps Chapter elements can be nested, then the XPath //Chapter will retrieve them all. However, this flexibility comes at a price, as the processor needs to do an extensive recursive search of the document tree. Contrary to many examples shown, you should only use this form of XPath when the exact path is unknown.

following Axis

The following axis contains all nodes that come after the context node in document order, but excludes all descendant nodes and any attribute nodes and namespace nodes associated with the context node.

It's probably easiest to demonstrate the use of the following axis using an example. (We will use the same XML document, Employees.xml, to demonstrate the use of the following-sibling axis, the preceding axis, and the preceding-sibling axis a little later in this section.)

Here is the source XML document, Employees.xml:

```xml
<Employees>
 <Person>
  <FirstName>Lara</FirstName>
  <LastName>Farmer</LastName>
  <DateOfBirth>1944-12-12</DateOfBirth>
 </Person>
 <Person>
  <FirstName>Patrick</FirstName>
  <LastName>Stepfoot</LastName>
  <DateOfBirth>1955-11-11</DateOfBirth>
 </Person>
 <Person>
  <FirstName>Angela</FirstName>
  <LastName>Paris</LastName>
  <DateOfBirth>1980-10-10</DateOfBirth>
 </Person>
</Employees>
```

Here is the XSLT stylesheet (Employees.xslt) that shows the element nodes in the following axis:

```xml
<xsl:stylesheet  version="1.0" xmlns:xsl="http://www.w3.org/1999/XSL/Transform" >

<xsl:template match="/">
 <html>
  <head>
```

```
    <title>This demonstrates the following axis.</title>
  </head>

  <body>
   <h3>Following axis demo.</h3>
   <xsl:apply-templates select="/Employees/Person[1]/FirstName" />
  </body>
 </html>
</xsl:template>

<xsl:template match="FirstName">
 <xsl:for-each select="following::*">
  <p><xsl:value-of select="name(.)" /> which contains the text
"<xsl:value-of select="." />".</p>
 </xsl:for-each>
</xsl:template>
</xsl:stylesheet>
```

Notice the use of the `following` axis in the `xsl:for-each` element toward the end of the XSLT:

```
<xsl:for-each select="following::*" />
```

The element nodes in the `following` axis are shown in Figure 7-2. Alongside each element node is its text content. Notice that for the `Person` elements all the text content of its child elements is shown.

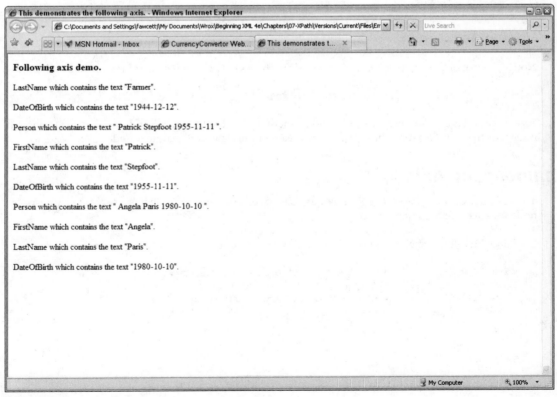

Figure 7-2

following-sibling Axis

The `following-sibling` axis includes any nodes in the `following` axis that share their parent node with the context node. Again, a demo may help you grasp the concept. We will use the same XML document, `Employees.xml`, used in the example for the `following` axis together with this XSLT stylesheet (`Employees2.xslt`):

```
<xsl:stylesheet  version="1.0" xmlns:xsl="http://www.w3.org/1999/XSL/Transform" >

<xsl:template match="/">
 <html>
  <head>
   <title>This demonstrates the following-sibling axis.</title>
  </head>
  <body>
   <h3>Following-sibling axis demo.</h3>
   <xsl:apply-templates select="/Employees/Person[1]/FirstName" />
  </body>
 </html>
</xsl:template>

<xsl:template match="FirstName">
 <xsl:for-each select="following-sibling::*">
  <p><xsl:value-of select="name(.)" /> which contains the text
"<xsl:value-of select="." />".</p>
 </xsl:for-each>
</xsl:template>

</xsl:stylesheet>
```

Notice the use of the `following-sibling` axis in the `xsl:for-each` element toward the end of the code:

```
<xsl:for-each select="following-sibling::*">
```

As shown in Figure 7-3, there are only two element nodes, the `LastName` and `DateOfBirth` element nodes for the same person whose `FirstName` element node was the context node.

namespace Axis

The `namespace` axis is used to select namespace nodes. An element node has a separate namespace node for each in-scope namespace.

Examine the following XML source document (`xmmlBook.xml`):

```
<xmml:Book xmlns:xmml="http://www.XMML.com/namespaces">
 <xmml:Chapter number="1">Some text.</xmml:Chapter>
 <xmml:Chapter number="2">Some more text.</xmml:Chapter>
</xmml:Book>
```

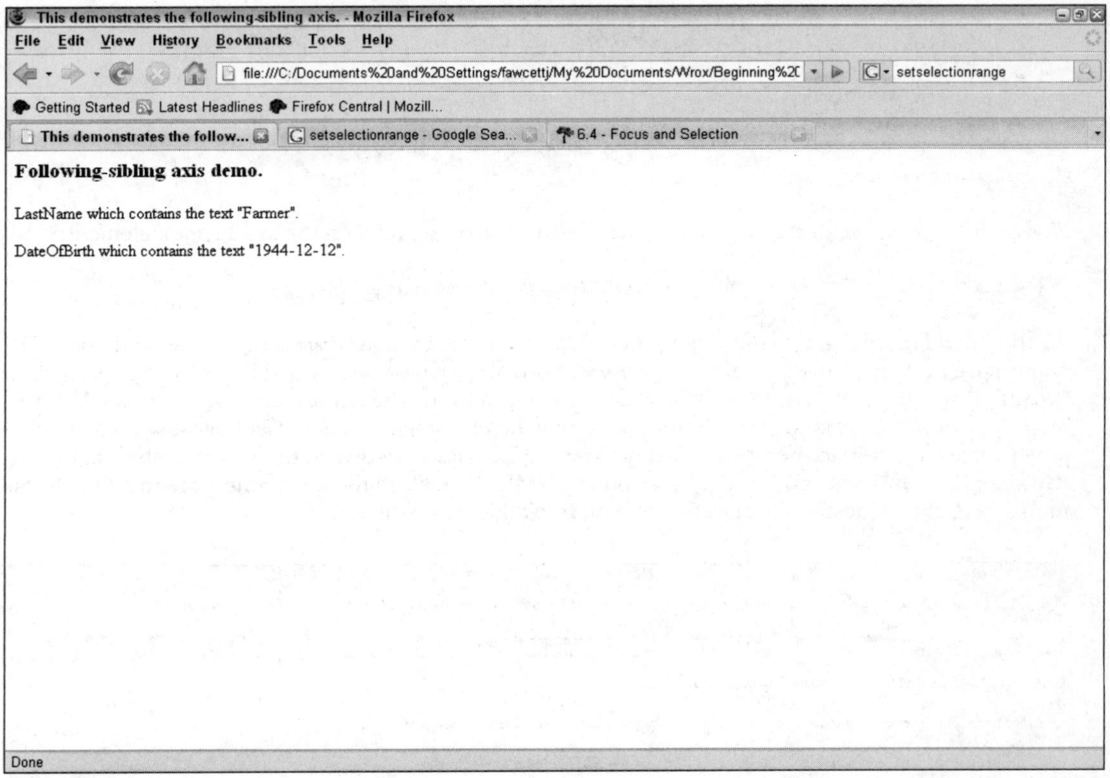

Figure 7-3

You can apply the following stylesheet (xmmlBook.xslt) to show the namespace nodes that exist on the xmml:Book element node:

```
<xsl:stylesheet  version="1.0" xmlns:xsl="http://www.w3.org/1999/XSL/Transform"
xmlns:xmml="http://www.XMML.com/namespaces" >

<xsl:template match="/">
 <html>
  <head>
   <title>This shows namespace nodes.</title>
  </head>
  <body>
   <h3>Namespace nodes of the xmml:Book element.</h3>
   <xsl:apply-templates select="/xmml:Book" />
  </body>
 </html>
</xsl:template>

<xsl:template match="xmml:Book">

 <xsl:for-each select="namespace::node()">
```

```
 <p><xsl:value-of select="position()" />. The namespace prefix
<b><xsl:value-of select="name(.)" /></b> has the namespace URI <b><xsl:value-of
select="." /></b>. </p>
 </xsl:for-each>
</xsl:template>

</xsl:stylesheet>
```

Notice the namespace declaration using the xmml namespace prefix on the xmml:Book element:

```
<xmml:Book xmlns:xmml="http://www.XMML.com/namespaces">
```

As shown in Figure 7-4, two namespace nodes are associated with the xmml:Book element node. The namespace node with the URI of http://www.XMML.com/namespaces will likely not be a surprise, because it was explicitly declared in a namespace declaration. The namespace node with the URI of http://www.w3.org/XML/1998/namespace may be unexpected. It is present because all XML element nodes have a namespace node with that namespace URI associated with them. Remember that you can use xml:lang and xml:space attributes on any XML element, so the xml namespace must be declared; in this case, the namespace declaration is built into all XML processors.

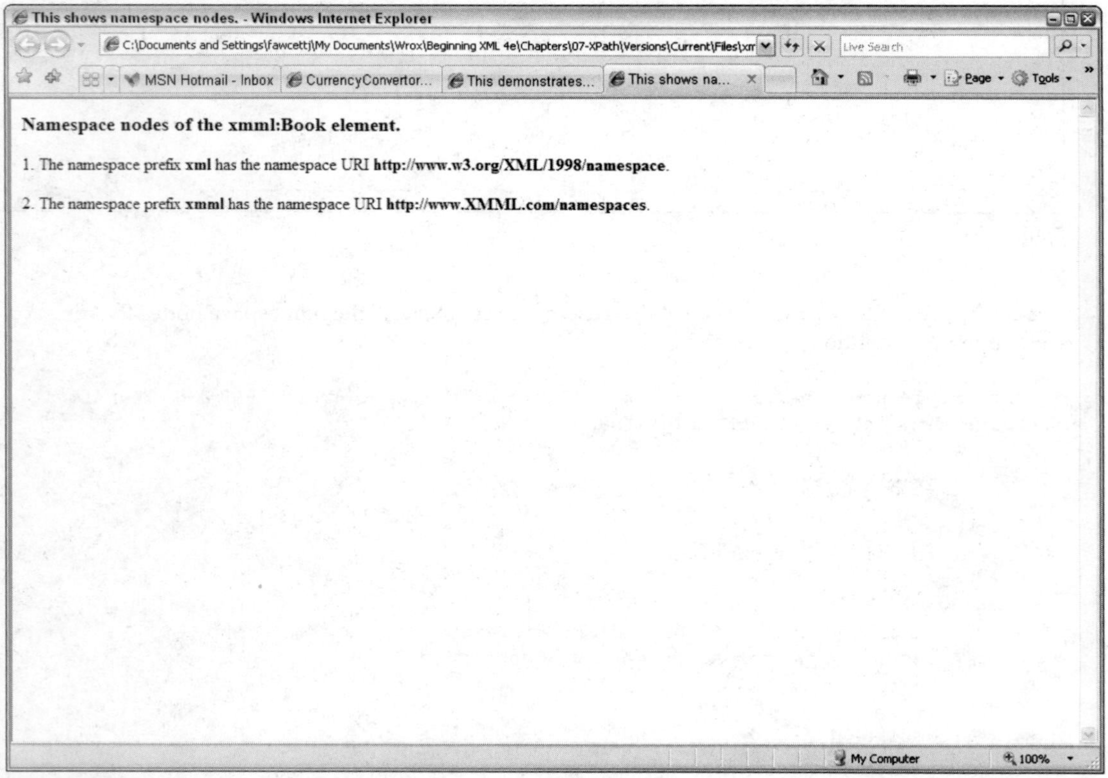

Figure 7-4

parent Axis

The `parent` axis is used to select the parent node of the context node. Examine the following document:

```
<Parts>
 <Part number="ABC123" />
 <Part number="DEF234" />
</Parts>
```

If the context node were a `Part` element node, then the following location path selects the parent node, which is the `Parts` element node:

```
parent::node()
```

Following is an abbreviated syntax for the `parent` axis:

```
..
```

This is probably familiar to you from encountering the same usage in directory paths on your hard disk.

If, however, the context node were the `Parts` element node, the same location path would select the root node of the document. In XPath 1.0, one way of testing whether the node you are dealing with is the root node is to see if the parent node is null. The root node is the only node without a parent.

preceding Axis

The `preceding` axis contains all nodes that come before the context node in document order, excluding nodes in the `ancestor` axis and attribute and namespace nodes.

To demonstrate the `preceding` axis, we will again use `Employees.xml` as the source XML document. The stylesheet (`Employees3.xslt`) is shown here:

```
<xsl:stylesheet  version="1.0" xmlns:xsl="http://www.w3.org/1999/XSL/Transform" >

<xsl:template match="/">
 <html>
  <head>
   <title>This demonstrates the preceding axis.</title>
  </head>
  <body>
   <h3>Preceding axis demo.</h3>
   <xsl:apply-templates select="/Employees/Person[3]/DateOfBirth" />
  </body>
 </html>
</xsl:template>

<xsl:template match="DateOfBirth">
 <xsl:for-each select="preceding::*">
```

```
   <p><xsl:value-of select="name(.)" /> which contains the text
   "<xsl:value-of select="." />".</p>
  </xsl:for-each>
 </xsl:template>

 </xsl:stylesheet>
```

Notice the use of the `preceding` axis in the `xsl:for-each` element:

```
<xsl:for-each select="preceding::*">
```

Figure 7-5 shows the element nodes in the `preceding` axis, with their contained text. The HTML output file (`Employees3.html`) is included in the code download for this book.

preceding-sibling Axis

The `preceding-sibling` axis includes those nodes that are in the `preceding` axis and that also share a parent node with the context node.

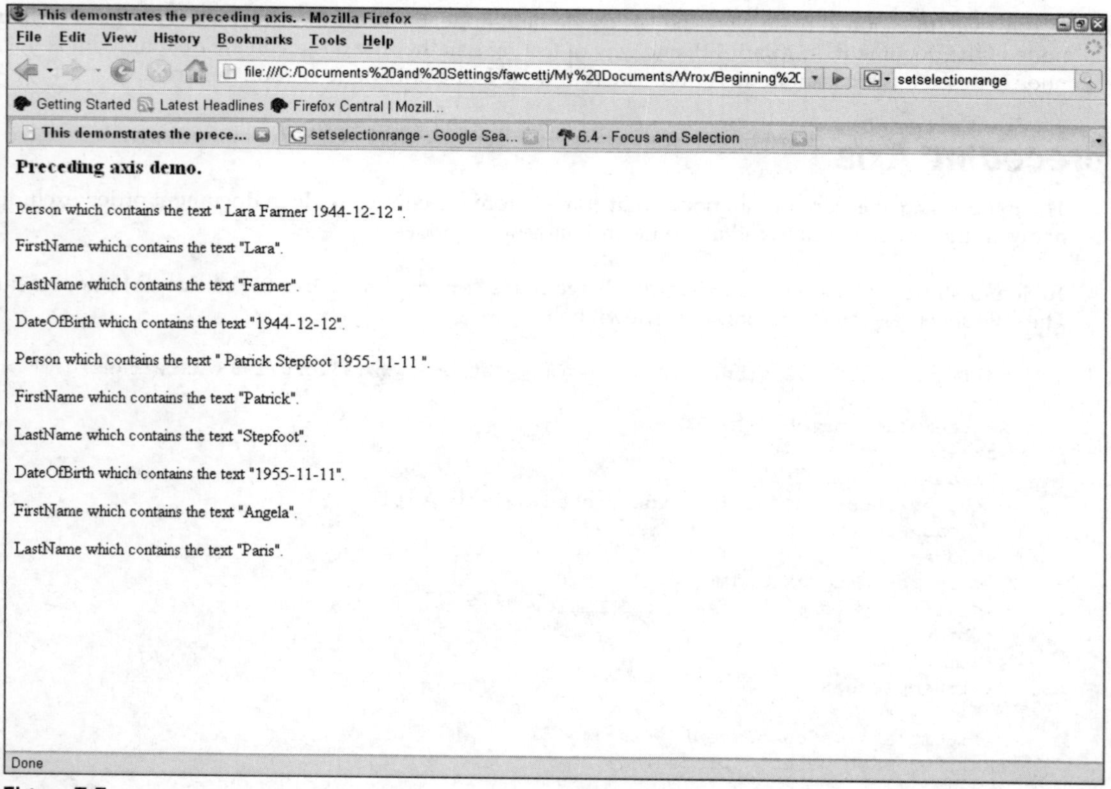

Figure 7-5

The following stylesheet (`Employees4.xslt`) displays the preceding siblings of the `DateOfBirth` element node of the third person in the source XML document:

```
<xsl:stylesheet  version="1.0" xmlns:xsl="http://www.w3.org/1999/XSL/Transform" >

<xsl:template match="/">
 <html>
  <head>
   <title>This demonstrates the preceding-sibling axis.</title>
  </head>
  <body>
   <h3>Preceding axis demo.</h3>
   <xsl:apply-templates select="/Employees/Person[3]/DateOfBirth" />
  </body>
 </html>
</xsl:template>

<xsl:template match="DateOfBirth">
 <xsl:for-each select="preceding-sibling::*">
  <p><xsl:value-of select="name(.)" /> which contains the text
"<xsl:value-of select="." />".</p>
 </xsl:for-each>
</xsl:template>

</xsl:stylesheet>
```

Figure 7-6 shows the element nodes in the `preceding-sibling` axis, with their text content.

self Axis

The `self` axis selects the context node. The unabbreviated syntax for the `self` axis is as follows:

```
self::node()
```

The abbreviated syntax for the context node is the period character. Thus, if you wanted to select the value of the context node using the `xsl:value-of` element, you would write the following:

```
<xsl:value-of select="." />
```

The unabbreviated syntax is as follows:

```
<xsl:value-of select="self::node()" />
```

XPath allows you to filter nodes selected from an axis using predicates. Predicates frequently use XPath functions, so next we'll look at the functions available in XPath 1.0 and at how predicates can be used to filter node-sets.

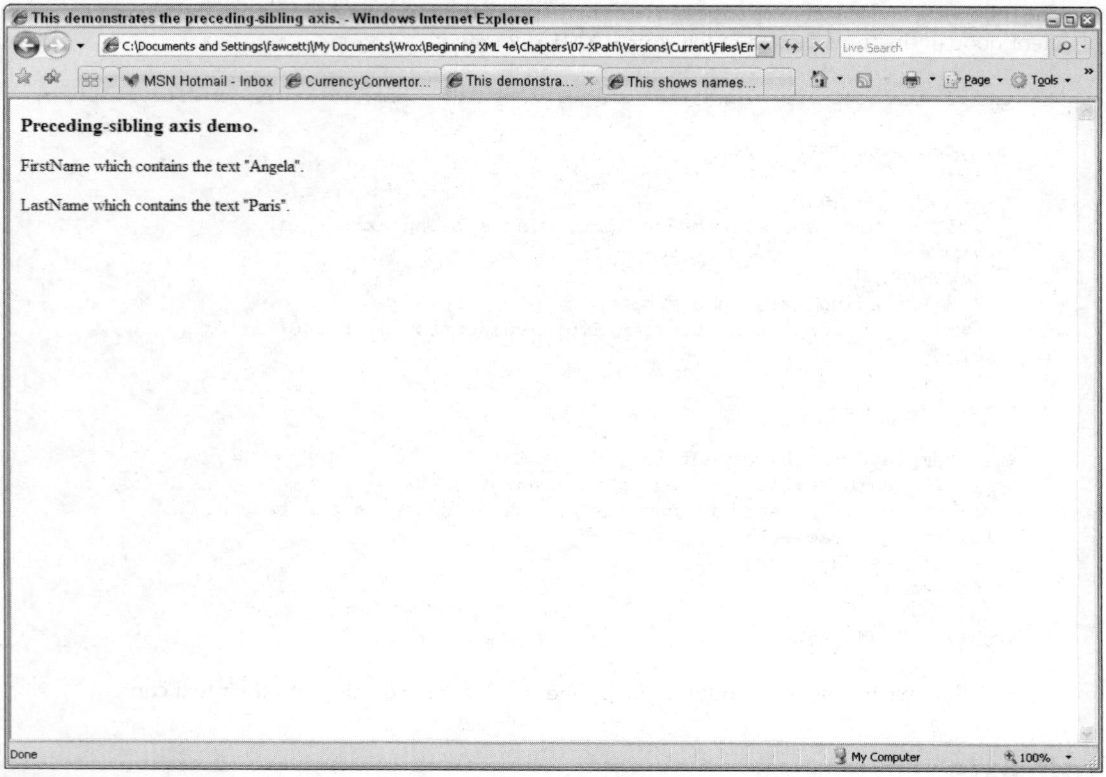

Figure 7-6

XPath 1.0 Functions

The XPath 1.0 specification defines a core function library. The functions making up the function library are listed here; some are used in XSLT examples in Chapter 8.

Boolean Functions

The XPath 1.0 Boolean functions are as follows:

❑   `boolean()` — Takes an object as its argument and returns a Boolean value. If the argument is a number, true is returned if the number is not zero or NaN. If the argument is a node-set, true is returned if the node-set is not empty. If the argument is a string, true is returned if the string is not empty.

❑   `false()` — Takes no argument and returns the Boolean value false

❑   `lang()` — Takes a string argument. Returns true if the language of the context node is the language indicated by the string argument or one of its sublanguages.

❏ `not()` — Takes a Boolean expression as its argument, returning true if the argument evaluates to false, and false if the argument evaluates to true

❏ `true()` — Has no argument and returns the Boolean value true

Node-Set Functions

The XPath 1.0 functions are as follows:

❏ `count()` — Takes a node-set argument and returns a value equal to the number of nodes in the node-set

❏ `id()` — Takes a string as its argument and returns a node-set containing any node that has an attribute of type ID equal to the function's argument

❏ `last()` — Returns a value equal to the context size

❏ `local-name()` — Takes zero or one node-sets as its argument and returns the local part of the element name if it exists; if no argument node-set exists, it returns the local part of the name of the context node. For example, the element `<library:Book xmlns:library=http://www .XMML.com/booknamespace/>` `local-name()` would return `Book`.

❏ `name()` — Takes zero or one node-set arguments and returns the name of the node in prefix:localpart format. For example, for the element `library:Book` shown above, `name()` would return `library:Book`.

❏ `namespace-uri()` — Takes zero or one node-sets as its argument and returns the namespace URI of the argument node-set; if there is no argument, the namespace URI of the context node is returned. For example, for the element `library:Book` in the last two examples, `namespace-uri()` would return `http://www.XMML.com/booknamespace`.

❏ `position()` — Returns a value equal to the context position

Numeric Functions

The number functions of XPath 1.0 are as follows:

❏ `ceiling()` — Takes a number as its argument and returns the smallest integer greater than this

❏ `floor()` — Takes a number as its argument and returns the largest integer that is lower than this

❏ `number()` — Takes a string, Boolean or node-set as its argument and returns a number. If there is a string argument and it contains characters that constitute a number, that number is returned; otherwise, NaN is returned. If the argument is the Boolean true, 1 is returned. If the argument is the Boolean false, 0 is returned. If the argument is a node-set, it is as if the `string()` function is applied to the node-set, and then the `number()` function is applied to the string value that results.

❏ `round()` — Takes a number as its argument and returns the integer that is closest to the number argument. The method of rounding is not specified, which may cause problems if a particular algorithm — for example, banker's rounding — is needed.

❑ sum() — Takes a node-set as its argument and returns the sum of the value of each individual node after converting the values to a numeric type if possible. Be careful when using sum(). If some of the values cannot be converted, then they will end up as NaN, *not a number*, and the sum itself will then be NaN.

String Functions

The string functions of XPath 1.0 are as follows:

❑ concat() — Takes two or more string arguments and returns the concatenation of those strings

❑ contains() — Takes two string arguments and returns a Boolean value that is true if the first string argument contains the second string argument

❑ normalize-space() — Takes a single string argument. Adjacent whitespace characters are replaced by single-space characters, and leading and trailing spaces are stripped.

❑ starts-with() — Takes two string arguments and returns a Boolean value that is true if the first argument string starts with the second argument string

❑ string() — Takes a Boolean, node-set, or number as its argument and returns a string value

❑ string-length() — Takes a single string argument and returns a number that indicates the length of the string

❑ substring() — Can take two or three arguments. When it takes two arguments, the first is a string (of which you select a substring) and the second is a number. It then returns a string beginning at the character of the first argument as indicated by the number argument and continuing to the end of the string. If a third argument is present, it indicates the character at which the returned string ends.

❑ substring-after() — Takes two string arguments and returns the part of the first string that occurs after the first occurrence of the second string argument in the first string argument

❑ substring-before() — Takes two string arguments and returns the part of the first string that occurs before the first occurrence of the second string

❑ translate() — Takes three string arguments and coverts each of the characters in the first argument that appear in the second to the corresponding characters in the third. A common use of the translate function is to turn text into all uppercase characters for a case-insensitive comparison. The following transform, LowerToUpper.xslt, shows how to use the translate() function:

```
<?xml version="1.0" encoding="utf-8"?>
<xsl:stylesheet version="1.0"
    xmlns:xsl="http://www.w3.org/1999/XSL/Transform">

<xsl:template match="/">
    <html>
    <body>
      <xsl:apply-templates select="//text()[normalize-space(.)]"/>
    </body>
    </html>
</xsl:template>
```

```
    <xsl:template match="text()">
      <xsl:variable name="upper"
        select="'ABCDEFGHIJKLMNOPQRSTUVWXYZ'"/>
      <xsl:variable name="lower"
        select="'abcdefghijklmnopqrstuvwxyz'"/>
      The input
      <span style="background-color: #c0c0c0; border: 1px solid #000000">
        <xsl:value-of select="."/></span>
        was translated to
        <span style="background-color: #ffd700; border: 1px solid #000000">
      <xsl:value-of select="translate(., $lower, $upper)"/>
          <br/>
    </span>
    </xsl:template>
</xsl:stylesheet>
```

If you run this transform against any XML that includes some text nodes — for example,
`Employees.xml` — you'll see output similar to what is shown in Figure 7-7.

Figure 7-7

All text nodes that do not consist entirely of whitespace are selected using the XPath `//text()[normalize-space(.)]`. Each character in the variable `$lower`, if found in the selected text node, is converted to the corresponding character in the variable `$upper`.

This sort of conversion can also be used to strip unwanted characters by not specifying a replacement character in the third argument. For example, use the following code to remove all the vowels from some text held in the variable `$text`:

> <xsl:value-of select="translate($text, 'aeiou', '')"/>

Be aware that the lower–to-uppercase translation only works when all relevant characters are supplied in the second and third parameters. The preceding example will not alter characters such as the é found in languages such as French. If you want to perform this sort of translation in XPath 2.0, you can use the `upper-case()` *and* `lower-case()` *functions.*

Predicates

Predicates are used to filter node-sets selected using an axis and location step. A predicate is optional in each location step of an XPath expression, and there can be more than one predicate in any one location step.

For example, if you had a document with various security levels assigned in a `security` attribute on a `Section` element, you could use predicates to decide which sections to display:

```
//Section[@security="confidential"]
```

This would select `Section` element nodes that possessed a `security` attribute whose value was the string `confidential`.

If the `Section` element also had a `version` attribute that identified draft or final sections, you could choose public, final sections using two predicates, like this:

```
//Section[@security="public"][@version="final"]
```

Each predicate selects only from nodes that are already selected.

Now that you have looked at each of the parts of XPath expressions, let's put the pieces together so you have a solid appreciation of what is and is not allowed in an XPath expression.

Structure of XPath Expressions

Most complex XPath expressions select node-sets — therefore, those expressions are also location paths.

A location path is made up of location steps. Depending on the context node and the complexity of the document, location paths can have many location steps.

Each location step is potentially made up of three parts:

- ❏ An axis
- ❏ A node test
- ❏ An optional predicate

Examine the following location path:

```
child::Paragraph[position()=2]
```

The axis is `child`, the node test is `Paragraph`, and the predicate (one predicate appears in this example) is `[position()=2]`.

An axis is present in every location path. However, when the `child` axis is used in abbreviated syntax, the axis is not actually expressed in the surface syntax of the location path.

The node test is used to specify what type of node in the axis should be selected. For example, to select all `child` element nodes of `Book` element nodes that are `Chapter` element nodes, you could write the following:

```
/Book/Chapter
```

This location path has two location steps. The initial / character indicates that the context node is the root node. The next location step, `Book`, selects all `Book` element nodes in the `child` axis. The second / character is a separator between location steps. The second location step is `Chapter`, which selects `Chapter` element nodes in the `child` axis. The same location path would be written in unabbreviated syntax like this:

```
/child::Book/child::Chapter
```

You may find that this syntax shows the parts of the location path more clearly.

The first location step starts at the root node and selects all `Book` element nodes that are children of the root node. If the document element is a `Book` element, a single `Book` element node is present in the node-set selected by the first location step (with any other document element, the node-set is empty and processing of the location path stops, with an empty node-set returned). Starting at that node, the next location step then looks for `Chapter` element nodes that are child element nodes of the `Book` element node returned by the first location step.

Suppose the location path had another location step, as shown here:

```
/child::Book/child::Chapter/child::Section
```

In that case, after finding all the `Chapter` element nodes that are selected by the second location step, any `Section` element nodes of each of the selected `Chapter` element nodes are chosen in turn.

Suppose the location path is modified to include a predicate, as shown here:

```
/child::Book/child::Chapter[position()=3]/child::Section
```

In this case, only the Chapter element node in the third position in document order would be selected by the second location step. Processing of all other Chapter element nodes would stop and those nodes would not be included in the returned node-set. For the Chapter element node in third position, all its Section element node children would be selected.

The only type of node in the child axis that has a name is the element node, but other nodes, such as comment nodes and text nodes, can also be present in the child axis. To select all nodes in the child axis that are child nodes of the Book element node, you would write the following:

```
/Book/node()
```

This location path would select all nodes in the child axis that are child nodes of Book element nodes, which are children of the root node.

Predicates are optional. Suppose you have a more complex structure that included Chapter elements, Section elements, and Paragraph elements, and you want to select the third paragraph in the second section in the first chapter. You could use a location path like this:

```
/Book/Chapter[1]/Section[2]/Paragraph[3]
```

The second, third, and fourth location steps each include a predicate. The same location path could be written in unabbreviated syntax, like this:

```
/child::Book/child::Chapter[position()=1]/child::Section[position()=2]/
child::Paragraph[position()=3]
```

Notice how a numeric expression can be used directly in a predicate, where it is short for position() = expression.

Predicates can also be multiple for any location step. Suppose you want to select the third paragraph in the second section in the first chapter only if the first Chapter element has a security attribute whose value is public. You could write the following:

```
/Book/Chapter[1][@security="public"]/Section[2]/Paragraph[3]
```

Or, using unabbreviated syntax, you could write this:

```
/child::Book/child::Chapter[position()=1][attribute::security="public"]/
child::Section[position()=2]/child::Paragraph[position()=3]
```

Notice that the second location step has two predicates, [1][@security="public"]. Both predicates must be satisfied before a Chapter element node can be selected. The order of predicates can also influence the node-set returned.

Be careful when using predicates such as [@security="public"] as the values of XSLT attributes, such as the select attribute of the xsl:value-of element. Make sure you use different paired quotes or apostrophes for the value inside the predicate than those used to delimit the attribute value. You could write the following:

```
<xsl:value-of select="/Book/Chapter[@security='public']" />
```

Alternatively, you could write this:

```
<xsl:value-of select='/Book/Chapter[@security="public"]' />
```

In other words, if you use paired quotes to delimit the value of the `select` attribute, use paired apostrophes inside the predicate; if you use paired apostrophes to delimit the attribute value, use paired quotes inside the predicate.

Before you move on to Chapter 8 and look at how XPath is used with XSLT, take a look at the new features and syntax in XPath version 2.0.

XPath 2.0

The latest version of the XPath 2.0 specification is located at `http://www.w3.org/tr/xpath20/`. *Functions for XPath 2.0 are specified in a separate document located at* `http://www.w3.org/TR/xpath-functions/`. *At the time of writing, further general information on XPath 2.0 can be found at* `http://www.w3.org/XML/Query`. *Currently, the XPath link from* `http://www.w3.org/` *describes only XPath 1.0.*

XPath 2.0 is a much more powerful language than XPath 1.0 and is significantly more complex. Unlike the XPath 1.0 specification, which is described in a single document, the XPath 2.0 specification is described in several supporting documents in addition to the XPath 2.0 specification itself.

XPath 2.0 is a syntactic subset of the XML Query Language (XQuery), which is described in Chapter 9, so reading Chapter 9 will give you a good overview of XPath 2.0 too.

Revised XPath Data Model

The data model underlying XPath 2.0 is significantly different from the XPath 1.0 model. Some highlights of differences are described here and in the following sections.

XPath 2.0 can be described as an expression language for processing sequences. A *sequence* is a generalization of the XPath 1.0 concept of a node-set to also include atomic values. Every XPath 2.0 expression returns a sequence. Unlike an XPath 1.0 node-set, an XPath 2.0 sequence is ordered. In XPath 1.0, a node-set is not allowed to contain duplicates. By contrast, an XPath 2.0 sequence may contain duplicates.

The XPath 2.0 data model is described at `www.w3.org/TR/xpath-datamodel/`.

W3C XML Schema Data Types

In XPath 1.0, a node has a rather primitive type system, which really doesn't intrude much into the developer's consciousness. In XPath 2.0, typing of nodes becomes much more formal and complex. Typing of nodes and items in XPath 2.0 uses the W3C XML Schema. (The W3C XML Schema is described in Chapter 5.)

XPath 2.0 adds the W3C XML Schema data types for date-time values. Because many XML documents, such as invoices and purchase orders, include date-time data, the ability to automatically validate values in XPath 2.0 is a potentially significant advantage, compared to the absence of date-time types in XPath 1.0.

Additional XPath 2.0 Functions

XPath 2.0 shares its function library with XQuery 1.0. Many more functions are provided in XPath 2.0 than were specified in XPath 1.0. In fact, XPath 2.0 contains so many functions that a separate specification describes them.

> *The document specifying XPath 2.0 functions is located at* http://www.w3.org/TR/ xpath-functions.

XPath 2.0 Features

The main feature improvements over XPath 1.0 are listed here and described in the following sections:

❑   Better string handling

❑   Better date and time handling

❑   The ability to create new sequences

❑   Conditional logic

❑   Ability to call user-defined functions

❑   More node tests

Better String Handling

Among other functions, XPath 2.0 adds a tokenize() function to split strings, and a matches() function to test strings against regular expressions.

The tokenize() function takes a string and returns a sequence created by splitting the string on the regular expression supplied as the second argument. For example, the XPath

> tokenize("I love Wrox books", "\s+")

returns the sequence of strings representing each separate word in the sentence. The regular expression \s+ means one or more whitespace characters. An optional third argument can be used to modify the tokenization.

The matches() function also uses a regular expression but returns a Boolean depending on whether the string matches the expression. For example, to verify that a particular variable, $phone, was composed entirely of digits, you could use the following XPath:

> matches($phone, "^\d+$")

The expression ^\d+$ tests that the input contains at least one digit and no other character.

The new version also offers a slew of functions such as normalize-unicode(), which enables input to be converted to a standardized form.

Better Date and Time Handling

There was no real support for dates and times in XPath 1.0. Version 2.0 has many functions designed to compare, create, and manipulate dates and times.

The `current-date()`, `current-DateTime()`, and `current-time()` functions do exactly what they say: they return the current date, date and time, or just time, in a standard ISO 8601 format. The one thing to be aware of is that if used twice in the same XSLT, the functions will return identical results, so you cannot attempt to time operations.

Functions such as `day-from-date()` and `hour-from-time()` extract parts of a full date or time, respectively.

Also available are functions that work on durations, rather than specific date-times. These all have sensible names such as `years-from-yearMonthDuration()`.

The time functions also support different time zones, so it is possible to convert and compare dates and times from different points on the planet.

Creating New Sequences

A powerful way of creating new sequences and dealing with current ones is available using the new `for` operator. As an example, if you want to construct a sequence of square numbers, you can use the following XPath:

for $i in 1 to 10 return $i * $i

This gives results in the sequence 1, 4, 9 . . . 100.

You can also write expressions such as the following:

sum(for $item in order/item return $item/@price * $item/@quantity)

This would return the total order value assuming a structure such as this:

```
<order>
  <item sku="abc123" value="10.00" quantity="3"/>
  <item sku="abc456" value="20.00" quantity="2"/>
  <item sku="abc789" value="30.00" quantity="1"/>
</order>
```

This sort of calculation can be very laborious in XPath 1.0.

Conditional Logic

XPath 2.0 supports an if/else construct:

<xsl:value-of select=

"if ($total > 1000) then $total * 0.9 else $total * 0.95"/>

This reduces `$total` by 10 percent if it's over 1,000; otherwise, by only 5 percent.

Ability to Call User-Defined Functions

Version 2.0 has the ability to call user-defined functions. Suppose you have a routine that calculates a customer's order total, which involves some complex logic. You can encapsulate it into a function such as `get-order-total()` that accepts the order ID. You can then use this function as you would a built-in one such as `string-length`:

```
<xsl:value-of select="get-order-total(order/@orderId)"/>
```

How do you define a function? Here's the catch: You can't in XPath. You can, however, in applications that support XPath such as XSLT and XQuery. As such, a fuller discussion of this topic is left to Chapters 8 and 9 in which those subjects are covered in more detail.

More Node Tests

In XPath 2.0 you can select nodes based on their type, a capability lacking in version 1.0. For example, you can select all elements in a document using `//element()`. You can also search for all nodes that are of type `xs:token` with `//element(*, xs:token)`. There is a similar syntax for attributes as well.

`XPath2.0.xslt` shows a number of the new features and can be run against any XML input document. You can see the results of the following code in Figure 7-8:

```
<xsl:stylesheet version="2.0"
    xmlns:xsl="http://www.w3.org/1999/XSL/Transform">

<xsl:template match="/">
    <html>
    <body>
    <h3>String handling</h3>
    <xsl:variable name="sentence" select="'I love Wrox books'"/>
    The sentence: '<xsl:value-of select="$sentence"/>' has
<xsl:value-of select="count(tokenize($sentence, '\s+'))"/> words.<br/>
    Case-sensitive match against 'wrox':
<xsl:value-of select="matches($sentence, 'wrox')"/><br/>
    Case-insensitive match against 'wrox':
<xsl:value-of select="matches($sentence, 'wrox', 'i')"/>
    <h3>Date and Time</h3>
    The current date is: <xsl:value-of select="current-date()"/><br/>
    The current time is: <xsl:value-of select="current-time()"/><br/>
    The day of the month is:
<xsl:value-of select="day-from-date(current-date())"/><br/>
    <h3>Creating sequences</h3>
    Showing <b>string-join()</b> and a <b>for</b> expression:
    <xsl:value-of select=
"string-join((for $i in 1 to 10 return string($i * $i)), ' => ')"/><br/>
    <h3>Node tests</h3>
    The 17th element in this document that is under the xsl:template is:<br/>
    <textarea rows="10" cols="60">
    <xsl:copy-of select="document('')/*/xsl:template//element()[18]"/>
    </textarea><br/>
    </body>
    </html>
</xsl:template></xsl:stylesheet>
```

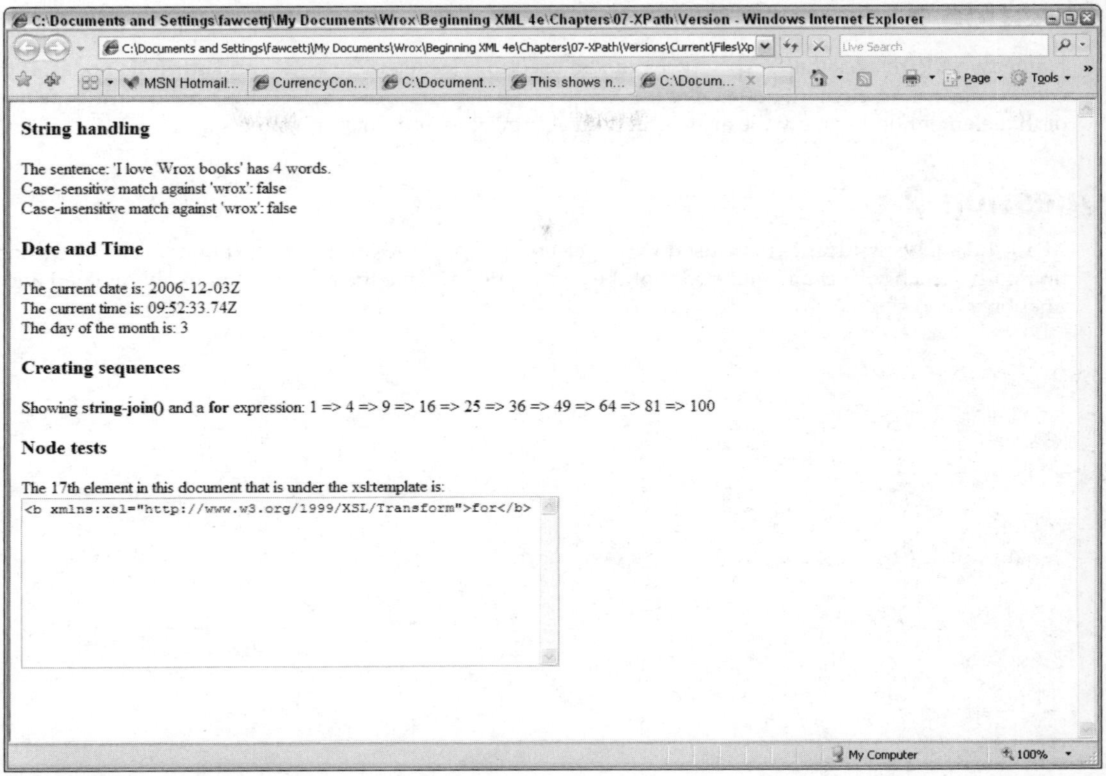

Figure 7-8

Because the XSLT doesn't need a source XML file, you can run it against itself. The command line for .NET would be as follows:

```
transform -o XPath2.0.html XPath2.0.xslt XPath2.0.xslt
```

Summary

This chapter covered the XML Path Language, XPath. You were introduced to the concept of the XPath model and the important concept of context was discussed. The XPath axes and the functions in the XPath function library were also described.

Exercise Questions

Suggested solutions to these questions can be found in Appendix A.

Question 1

Name two XPath axes that, respectively, can be used to select element nodes and attribute nodes. If the context node is an element node, give the XPath location path, which selects the number attribute node of that element node. Show the answer in both abbreviated and unabbreviated syntax.

Question 2

XPath 1.0 allows wildcards to be used when selecting child nodes of the context node. What is the location path, which selects all child nodes of the context node? Give the answer in both abbreviated and unabbreviated syntax.

XSLT

XSLT, Extensible Stylesheet Language Transformations, is a very important XML application in many XML workflows. In many business situations, data is either stored as XML or can be made available from a database as XML. XSLT is important because, typically, the way in which XML is stored needs to be changed before it is used. Wherever the data comes from, the XML might need to be presented to end-users or be shared with business partners in a format that is convenient for them. XSLT plays a key role in converting XML to its presentation formats and restructuring XML to fit the structures useful to business partners.

This chapter covers the following:

❑   How XSLT can be used to convert XML for presentation or restructure XML for business-to-business data interchange

❑   How XSLT differs from conventional procedural languages

❑   An XSLT transformation is described in terms of a source document and a result document. However, under the hood, the transformation taking place is a source tree (which uses the XPath data model) to a result tree (which also uses the XPath data model).

❑   How the elements that make up an XSLT stylesheet are used. For example, you look at how to use the `xsl:value-of` element to retrieve values from the source tree being transformed. In addition, you look at the `xsl:copy` and `xsl:copy-of` elements, which, respectively, shallow copy and deep copy nodes from the source tree.

❑   How to use XSLT variables and parameters

❑   The new features of XSLT 2.0 and how they make transformations easier

XSLT 2.0 reached W3C Recommendation status as of January 23, 2007.

What Is XSLT?

XSLT is a declarative programming language, written in XML, for converting XML to some other output. Often the output is XML or HTML, but in principle, XSLT can produce arbitrary output from any given XML source document. For example, an XML document can be restructured to conform to a business partner's schema, or a selection from an XML document can be made to correspond to specified criteria, such as selecting invoices from a specified period.

In XSLT 1.0 the source had to be XML. In version 2.0 this restriction does not apply and you can transform other formats, such as CSV files, where the data is separated by commas and carriage returns, into different structures.

Alternatively, XML data can be transformed so that the data is part of an HTML document, XHTML document, WML (Wireless Markup Language) page, or other presentation format. Just as it is efficient to store relational data once to avoid data inconsistencies, having one XML data source that can then be converted to multiple presentation formats results in an efficient and effective workflow when multiple formats, which may themselves be evolving, need to be produced.

XSLT uses XPath, to which you were introduced in Chapter 7, to select the parts of the source XML document that are used in the result document. All the XPath 1.0 functions are available to an XSLT processor, and XSLT 1.0 has a few functions of its own.

XSLT is a declarative language. Often, newcomers to XSLT find it difficult to adapt from the mindset that they use while programming in procedural languages such as Java or JavaScript. Therefore, you will take the first code examples slowly to help you understand the difference between a declarative language and a procedural one.

Restructuring XML

One of the major uses of XSLT is to restructure XML for use by another user — for example, a business partner. In a common scenario, two companies need to exchange XML documents electronically but for historical reasons have differences in the structures of basic documents such as invoices and purchase orders.

XSLT can copy selected parts of the source XML unchanged into the result document or can create new elements or attributes in the result document. The names of elements and attributes can be changed. Elements or attributes present in the source document can be selectively omitted from the result document. By combining these options, any arbitrary change can typically be achieved between the source document and the result document.

Presenting XML Content

XML is often presented as HTML or XHTML on the desktop, as well as various other options on mobile devices. XSLT is often used to transform select parts of the XML document for display. For example, you might create a linked set of HTML pages, each of which contains data from a specified time period. Using XSLT, appropriate data for each HTML page can be selected from the same XML document.

How an XSLT Processor Works

Before you start writing code, it is helpful to understand how, in general terms, an XSLT processor works. At its simplest, you can look at an XSLT processor as a piece of software that accepts an XML document (the *source document*), applies an XSLT stylesheet to it, and produces another document called the *result document,* which can be XML, HTML, or plain text.

If you have read Chapter 7 on XPath, then you will likely already be able to guess that this isn't the whole story. A slightly more detailed description of an XSLT processor is that it accepts a source document and creates an in-memory tree representation of that source document, according to the XPath data model, called the *source tree.* The XSLT processor processes the source tree according to the *templates* contained in the XSLT stylesheet. A *result tree* is created. The creation of a result tree from a source tree is called *transformation.* After the result tree is created, a process called *serialization* takes place, which creates a familiar, serialized XML (or other) document from the result tree.

Strictly speaking, an XSLT processor is responsible only for the transformation of the source tree to one or, in the case of XSLT 2.0, multiple result trees. However, most XSLT processor software also contains an XML parser that creates the source tree and a serializer component that serializes the result tree.

Running the Examples

The first examples used in this chapter are standard XSLT 1.0 code; toward the end of the chapter some version 2.0 transformations are shown. To run the version 1.0 transformations, virtually any processor will do. For version 2.0 you are limited, as many vendors are waiting for the final W3C recommendation. The main contender at the moment is the Saxon processor written by Wrox author Michael Kay. Details for installing this are provided later in the chapter.

> Information on the Java 2 and C++ versions of the Xalan XSLT processor are available at `http://xml.apache.org/`. Information on the MSXML software, which comprises a COM version called Microsoft XML Core Services as well as .NET, is available at `http://msdn.microsoft.com/xml/`. Useful support information on MSXML is available at `http://www.netcrucible.com/`.

In this chapter, step-by-step instructions are supplied for using the Saxon XSLT processor.

Introducing the Saxon XSLT Processor

All the examples in this chapter use the Saxon XSLT processor, which is written by Michael Kay, editor of the XSLT 2.0 specification. It has two versions, a free one called Saxon-B, for *basic*, and a commercial version named Saxon-SA, for *schema aware*. The examples in this book all use the free version. The differences are explained in the discussion of XSLT 2.0 later in the chapter. General information on the latest version of Saxon is located at `http://saxon.sourceforge.net/`. The version used when writing this chapter is Saxon 8.8, which incorporates both XSLT 1.0 and XSLT 2.0 functionality. If you want to explore only XSLT 1.0 functionality, you can use Saxon 6.5.5.

> *At the time of writing, the Saxon processor is being updated on an ongoing basis to add more complete XPath 2.0 and XSLT 2.0 functionality. Therefore, it is likely that the latest version when you read this will be a version other than 8.8 or 6.5.5. Take time to read the descriptions of the available versions at the Saxon web page to ensure that you choose a version that supports XSLT 1.0 (all versions currently do) and that is stable (from time to time quasi-experimental versions are released).*

Installing the Saxon XSLT Processor

Saxon now comes with installs for Java and .NET. The installation of the Java version is covered first.

Installing the Java Version

To run the Saxon XSLT processor, you need a Java Virtual Machine (JVM) installed. To check whether you have a JVM correctly installed, open a command window and type the following:

```
java -version
```

If Java is installed, then you will see a message similar to the following:

```
java version "1.5.1"
Java (TM)2 Runtime Environment, Standard Edition (build 1.5.1-b65)
Java HotSpot (TM) Client VM (build 1.5.1-b65, mixed mode)
```

If Java is not installed, you need to obtain a suitable version of Java and install it.

You can obtain a JVM by installing either a Java Runtime Environment (JRE) or a Java Software Development Kit (SDK). If you don't already have a JVM installed, then information on the current version of Java (you need J2SE, Java 2 Standard Edition, version 1.4 or higher, to run Saxon 7.8) is available at http://java.sun.com. Look for a link to additional information on J2SE.

Assuming that you have downloaded a Java 2 version 1.5 SDK, launch the installer and follow the onscreen installation instructions to install it. After you have completed the installation, open a command prompt window. At the command prompt, type

```
java -version
```

and press Enter. If a JVM has been successfully installed, then a message similar to the one shown earlier will be displayed.

You also need to install the selected version of Saxon to an appropriate directory. Launch the Saxon zip file that you downloaded and extract the files to the desired directory using a tool such as WinZip. In order to run saxon8.jar from any directory, you need to add the file, providing its full path, to your CLASSPATH environment variable.

To create or edit the CLASSPATH environment variable on Windows XP, click Start, select Control Panel, and select the System option. On the System Properties window, select the Advanced tab and click the Environment Variables button near the bottom. The Environment Variables window opens.

In the System Variables section look at the existing environment variables to see if CLASSPATH or classpath (it isn't case sensitive) is already present. If it is, then click the Edit button; the Edit System Variable window opens. Edit the Variable Value text box to reflect the location where you installed Saxon and the version that you chose to install. Once you are sure that you correctly typed the location, click OK.

If there is no CLASSPATH variable in the System Variables section, then look at the User Variables section to determine whether it's there. Assuming that it isn't, click the New button in the System Variables section. The New System Variable window opens. Enter CLASSPATH (either case) in the Variable Name text box and enter the location of Saxon in the Variable Value text box. Figure 8-1 shows the Edit System Variable window with the CLASSPATH variable added. Click OK.

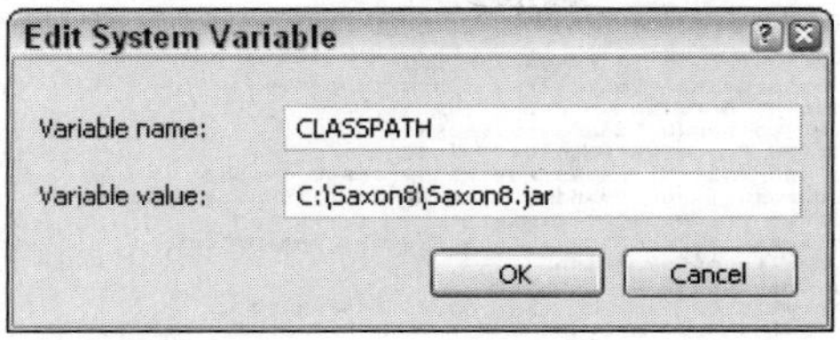

Figure 8-1

If you have a command prompt window open, you need to restart it so that the changes you made to the environment variables are applied to it.

Now you can test whether the installation of Saxon is working correctly. Navigate to the directory in which you intend to install your XML source files and your XSLT stylesheets. For the purposes of this chapter, they are installed on my machine at c:\BXML\Ch08. At the command prompt, type the following:

```
java -jar saxon8.jar
```

If everything is working correctly, you will see the default Saxon error message, which includes information about how to use the command-line switches (shown in Figure 8-2), indicating that you haven't entered a full command to make Saxon carry out a transformation. At the moment, you don't need to do anything more, because the display of that error message is an indication that Saxon is installed correctly.

Installing the .NET Version

The .NET version is simpler to set up once you have the .NET Framework 1.1 installed. You can download the framework from www.microsoft.com/downloads/details .aspx?FamilyID=262d25e3-f589-4842-8157-034d1e7cf3a3&displaylang=en. Alternatively, go to www.microsoft.com/downloads/ and search for *.NET framework redistributable*. Most Windows XP machines will have the .NET Framework 1.1 installed already.

Unzip the install package, saxonb8-8n.zip, for version 8.8, into a folder such as C:\program files\Saxon\. That's it. You can optionally install the libraries to the global assemble cache (GAC) if you want to use them in other applications without recopying them each time by running install-gac .cmd. You may need to modify the first line if you do not have a default installation of the .NET SDK. You can then run the examples by using Transform.exe, found in the bin directory.

The final step that will help is to add the bin folder to the Path environment variable. See the instructions for the Java install regarding how to change environment variables in Windows. You are almost ready to run your first XSLT example, but first let's look briefly at how procedural and declarative programming languages differ.

Figure 8-2

Procedural versus Declarative Programming

Many newcomers to XSLT find it tough to adjust to the difference in approach when using XSLT compared to using procedural programming languages. The following brief sections highlight the differences between the two approaches.

Procedural Programming

When using a procedural programming language such as JavaScript, you tell the computer what you want to do step by step. You might define a function, and then define each thing that the computer is supposed to do, assigning a variable, iterating through a loop, and so on. The mental picture of what the function is supposed to achieve exists only in your mind.

Declarative Programming

The procedural programming approach differs from declarative programming in that you tell the computer what you want to achieve. XSLT resembles SQL in that respect. For example, in SQL you tell the relational database management system (RDBMS) to SELECT certain columns, but you don't expect to tell it *how* to retrieve the desired data. XSLT is similar. You specify what the XSLT processor is to create each time it comes across a particular *pattern* in the source tree.

To specify what the XSLT processor is to do, you frequently use the xsl:template element with a match attribute that contains the relevant pattern.

For example, if you wanted to create certain output for every Chapter element in a source XML document you would have code like this:

```
<xsl:template match="Chapter">
 <!-- The content of the <xsl:template> element defines what is to be added -->
 <!-- to the result tree. -->
</xsl:template>
```

Notice how the pattern Chapter appears as the value of the match attribute of the xsl:template element.

XSLT is also a functional language. A *functional language* is one that relies entirely on functions that accept and return data and does not rely on maintaining state to carry out its tasks. You will see some of the effects of this later in the chapter, especially when dealing with variables.

Let's move on and create a simple XSLT stylesheet and see how it works.

Foundational XSLT Elements

In this section, you create an example that makes a simple HTML web page from the XML source document shown here. Refer to the People.xml file:

```
<People>
  <Person>
   <Name>Winston Churchill</Name>
   <Description>Winston Churchill was a mid 20th century British politician who
became famous as Prime Minister during the Second World War.</Description>
  </Person>
  <Person>
   <Name>Indira Gandhi</Name>
   <Description>Indira Gandhi was India's first female prime minister and was
assassinated in 1984.</Description>
  </Person>
  <Person>
   <Name>John F. Kennedy</Name>
   <Description>JFK, as he was affectionately known, was a United States president
who was assassinated in Dallas, Texas.</Description>
  </Person> </People>
```

As you can see from the file, People.xml contains brief information about three famous twentieth-century politicians.

The following stylesheet, People.xslt, creates a simple HTML web page, People.html, which contains the name and description information about the politicians:

```
<xsl:stylesheet
  xmlns:xsl="http://www.w3.org/1999/XSL/Transform"
  version="1.0" >

<xsl:template match="/">
 <html>
  <head>
   <title>Information about
<xsl:value-of select="count(/People/Person)" /> people.</title>
  </head>
  <body>
  <h3>Information about
<xsl:value-of select="count(/People/Person)" /> people.</h3>
  <br />
   <xsl:apply-templates select="/People/Person" />
  </body>
 </html>
</xsl:template>

<xsl:template match="Person">
 <h3><xsl:value-of select="Name" /></h3>
 <p><xsl:value-of select="Description" /></p>

<br />
</xsl:template>

</xsl:stylesheet>
```

The HTML page created by the transformation is shown in Figure 8-3.

The HTML code produced by the listing, with whitespace tidied for display, is shown in the following block (People.html):

```
<html>
   <head>
      <meta http-equiv="Content-Type" content="text/html; charset=UTF-8">
      <title>Information about 3 people.</title>
   </head>
   <body>
      <h3>Information about 3 people.</h3><br><h3>Winston Churchill</h3>
      <p>Winston Churchill was a mid 20th Century British politician who became
famous as Prime Minister during the Second World War.</p><br><h3>Indira Gandhi</h3>
      <p>Indira Gandhi was India's first female prime minister and was assassinated
in 1984.</p><br><h3>John F. Kennedy</h3>
      <p>JFK, as he was affectionately known, was a United States President who was
assassinated in Dallas, Texas.</p><br></body>

</html>
```

Next you will analyze the stylesheet People.xslt while you look at the XSLT elements that were used in it.

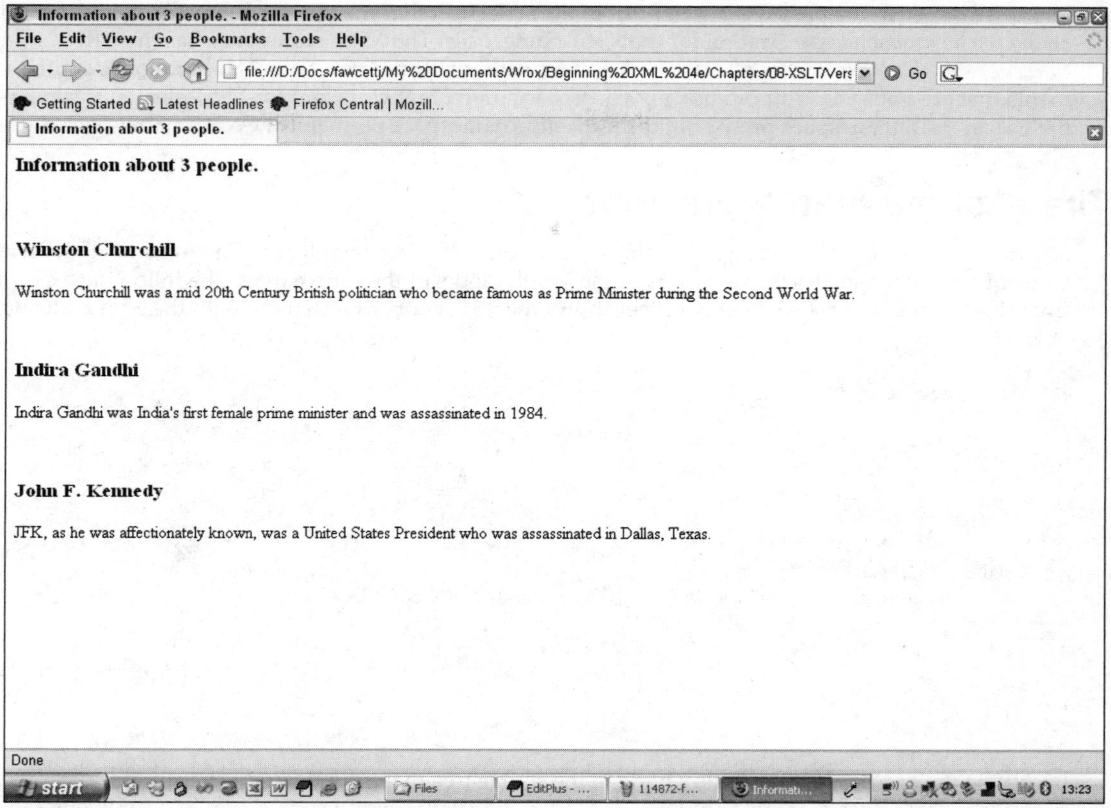

Figure 8-3

The <xsl:stylesheet> Element

Every full XSLT stylesheet has, as its document element, either an xsl:stylesheet element or an xsl:transform element.

For very simple XSLT stylesheets it is possible to omit the xsl:stylesheet element and have, for example, an HTML document that includes elements from the XSLT namespace scattered inside it, similar to Active Server Pages (ASP) or JavaServer Page (JSP) code. Because these simplified XSLT stylesheets are very limited in what they can do, they aren't discussed further here.

> *The <xsl:stylesheet> element is semantically identical to the <xsl:transform> element. You can use the elements interchangeably in your XSLT stylesheets. Most XSLT stylesheets that you are likely to see use the <xsl:stylesheet> element, so that element is used in this chapter.*

The start-tag of the xsl:stylesheet element has a mandatory version attribute. Most stylesheets in existence are version 1.0, although as version 2.0 processors become more common this will change. You can see this in the following excerpt from the People.xslt example stylesheet:

```
<xsl:stylesheet xmlns:xsl="http://www.w3.org/1999/XSL/Transform" version="1.0" >
```

You can also see in the preceding excerpt from the stylesheet that the `xsl:stylesheet` element must also have a namespace declaration for the XSLT namespace. The XSLT namespace has the URI `http://www.w3.org/1999/XSL/Transform`. Any other URI in a namespace declaration identifies elements that are not XSLT. You can use any namespace prefix that you want for XSLT elements; some people use an `xslt` namespace prefix, but the indicative namespace prefix for the XSLT namespace is `xsl`.

The <xsl:template> Element

An XSLT processor looks in a stylesheet for an `xsl:template` element that has a `match` attribute with value of `/` (which matches the root node of the XPath model of the source tree). The following excerpt from the `People.xslt` example stylesheet shows the `xsl:template` element with the `match` attribute of `/`:

```
<xsl:template match="/">
 <html>
  <head>
   <title>Information about
<xsl:value-of select="count(/People/Person)" /> people.</title>
  </head>
  <body>
  <h3>Information about
<xsl:value-of select="count(/People/Person)" /> people.</h3>
   <br />
   <xsl:apply-templates select="/People/Person" />
  </body>
 </html>
</xsl:template>
```

Each time the XSLT processor finds a node in the source tree that is a root node, the structure corresponding to the content of this template is added to the result tree. Of course, you have only one root node in an XPath model, so the nodes are added only once to the result tree.

Many of the elements in the template that match the root node are likely to be familiar to you as HTML/XHTML elements. These elements are added to the result tree literally, and so are called *literal result elements*. However, the template also contains several elements from the XSLT namespace. Those elements are called *instructions*.

A frequently used instruction is the `xsl:apply-templates` element.

The <xsl:apply-templates> Element

In the `People.xslt` stylesheet, there is one `xsl:apply-templates` element inside the template that matches the root node:

```
<xsl:apply-templates select="/People/Person" />
```

The `xsl:apply-templates` element causes the XSLT processor to look for matching nodes in the source tree. In this case, the nodes to be looked for are specified by the XPath location path `/People/Person`, which specifies `Person` element nodes that are child nodes of a `People` element node, which is, in turn, a child node of the root node. In the source document, `People.xml`, there are three `Person` elements (as is shown by the highlighted code lines in the following excerpt):

```
<People>
  <Person>
   <Name>Winston Churchill</Name>
   <Description>Winston Churchill was a mid 20th Century British politician who
 became famous as Prime Minister during the Second World War.</Description>
  </Person>
  <Person>
   <Name>Indira Gandhi</Name>
   <Description>Indira Gandhi was India's first female prime minister and was
 assassinated in 1984.</Description>
  </Person>
  <Person>
   <Name>John F. Kennedy</Name>
   <Description>JFK, as he was affectionately known, was a United States President
 who was assassinated in Dallas, Texas.</Description>
  </Person>
</People>
```

The XSLT processor then looks for a template that matches such a `Person` element node. The example stylesheet, `People.xslt`, has such a template, as follows:

```
<xsl:template match="Person">
 <h3><xsl:value-of select="Name" /></h3>
 <p><xsl:value-of select="Description" /></p>
 <br />

</xsl:template>
```

The preceding template has an `xsl:template` element with a `match` attribute that matches the XPath pattern `Person`, so it provides a match for the value of the `select` attribute of the `xsl:apply- templates` element. Each time the XSLT processor finds a `Person` element node that corresponds to the location path `/People/Person`, the content of this template is processed and content is added to the result tree. Because three such nodes exist, the content specified by the template is added to the result tree three times.

The content of the template consists partly of literal result elements that are HTML/XHTML elements and partly of elements in the XSLT namespace — specifically, the `xsl:value-of` element.

Getting Information from the Source Tree

When you are writing a stylesheet, it is often important to be able to use literal result elements, but typically, you will often also want to use information contained in the source tree. XSLT provides a number of ways to use information from the source tree. A frequently used XSLT instruction to achieve that is the `xsl:value-of` element.

The <xsl:value-of> Element

The `xsl:value-of` element, as its name implies, provides the value of a part of the source tree that represents the source XML document. The `xsl:value-of` element has a mandatory `select` attribute, whose value is an XPath location path.

In the template that matched the root node, you used the xsl:value-of element to provide the content of the title and h3 elements:

```
<html>
 <head>

   <title>Information about <xsl:value-of select="count(/People/Person)" />
people.</title>

 </head>
 <body>

   <h3>Information about <xsl:value-of select="count(/People/Person)" />
people.</h3>
```

The value of the select attribute uses the XPath count() function. The argument to the count() function is itself an XPath location path, /People/Person. That location path again matches each Person element node in the source tree, which has a People element node as its parent, which, in turn, has the root node as its parent. As you saw a short time ago, there are three such Person elements in the source document and therefore three corresponding Person element nodes in the source tree. Not surprisingly, the count() function counts how many such nodes are there and the XSLT processor replaces the xsl:value-of XSLT instruction with the literal value 3. For example, in the title element,

```
<title>Information about <xsl:value-of select="count(/People/Person)" />
people.</title>
```

in the stylesheet is replaced by

```
<title>Information about 3 people.</title>
```

in the result document.

Similarly, in the template that matches a Person element node (like the following one from the sample stylesheet),

```
<xsl:template match="Person">
 <h3><xsl:value-of select="Name" /></h3>
 <p><xsl:value-of select="Description" /></p>
 <br />
</xsl:template>
```

the xsl:value-of elements are replaced in the result document by text corresponding, respectively, to the Name element node and the Description element node that are child nodes of the Person element node that matches the value of the match attribute of the xsl:template element.

To clarify further, the value of the select attribute is the relative location path Name, which matches a Name element node that is a child node of the context node. When the template that matches the pattern Person is instantiated, the context node is defined by the select attribute of the xsl:apply-templates element, as indicated in the following excerpt from the sample stylesheet:

```
<xsl:apply-templates select="/People/Person" />
```

Therefore, the relative location path Name in

```
<h3><xsl:value-of select="Name" /></h3>
```

could be written as the following absolute location path:

```
/People/Person/Name
```

That path matches any of the three Name element nodes in the source tree, but by using the relative location path, you ensure that only the value of the Name element node that is the child of the present Person element node is added to the result tree.

The xsl:value-of element is the simplest XSLT element that extracts information from the source tree. It simply selects the value of a node-set, which might be only a single node, specified by the location path that is the value of the select attribute of the xsl:value-of element. If there is more than one node in the node-set, then the xsl:value-of element uses the value of the first node in document order only, not the values of all nodes. The xsl:value-of element is particularly useful when producing output for presentation, as in the example just shown, but it can also be used when XML is being restructured.

The next two elements discussed, the xsl:copy and xsl:copy-of elements, are useful primarily when XML is being restructured.

The <xsl:copy> Element

The xsl:copy element copies a node to the result tree, but it doesn't copy any descendant nodes; nor, if the context node is an element node, does it cause any attribute nodes to be copied. This can be useful when, for example, you want to use an element but change the structure of its content or add or remove attributes from it.

Try It Out   Using the xsl:copy Element

Let's look at how the xsl:copy element can be used. We'll first demonstrate how you can convert an element-based structure to one in which child elements in the source document are expressed in the result document as attributes.

The source XML, Persons.xml, is shown here:

```
<Persons>
 <Person>
  <FirstName>Jill</FirstName>
  <LastName>Harper</LastName>
 </Person>
 <Person>
  <FirstName>Claire</FirstName>
  <LastName>Vogue</LastName>
 </Person>
 <Person>
  <FirstName>Paul</FirstName>
  <LastName>Cathedral</LastName>
 </Person>
</Persons>
```

Notice that the first and last names are held as child elements of the Person element.

Suppose you want to restructure this so that the Person element has a FirstName attribute and a LastName attribute instead of the child elements shown previously. The stylesheet, Persons.xslt, can restructure the XML to achieve that:

```
<xsl:stylesheet
  xmlns:xsl="http://www.w3.org/1999/XSL/Transform"
  version="1.0" >

<xsl:template match="/">
 <Persons>
  <xsl:apply-templates select="/Persons/Person" />
 </Persons>
</xsl:template>

<xsl:template match="Person">
 <xsl:copy>
  <xsl:attribute name="FirstName"><xsl:value-of select="FirstName"/>
</xsl:attribute>
  <xsl:attribute name="LastName"><xsl:value-of select="LastName"/>
</xsl:attribute>
 </xsl:copy>
</xsl:template>

</xsl:stylesheet>
```

1. Navigate to the directory in which Persons.xml and Persons.xslt are stored.

2. To carry out the transformation, type the following at the command line if you are using the Java version:

```
java -jar saxon8.jar -o PersonsOut.xml Persons.xml Persons.xslt
```

Or type the following when using .NET:

```
transform.exe -o PersonsOut.xml Persons.xml Persons.xslt
```

How It Works

As before, there is a template that matches the root node of the source document. Instead of creating HTML/XHTML literal result elements as you did in the first example, you add a Persons literal result element. The xsl:apply-templates element is used with the absolute location path /Persons/Person. There is a template that has a match attribute with value of Person, which matches the value of the select attribute of the xsl:apply-templates element. Therefore, for each Person node in the source document, that template specifies how it is processed.

Notice first how the xsl:copy element is used inside the template:

```
<xsl:template match="Person">
 <xsl:copy>
  <xsl:attribute name="FirstName"><xsl:value-of select="FirstName"/>
</xsl:attribute>
```

```
    <xsl:attribute name="LastName"><xsl:value-of select="LastName"/>
  </xsl:attribute>
   </xsl:copy>
  </xsl:template>
```

The `xsl:copy` element is used when the context node is a `Person` element node. Therefore, a node that is the same as the context node is added to the result tree. In other words, a `Person` element node is added to the result tree, but its child nodes — the `FirstName` element node and the `LastName` element node — are not copied.

If you serialized the result document at this point, when only the `xsl:copy` element has been processed, then it would look like this:

```
<Persons>
 <Person />
 <Person />
 <Person />
</Person>
```

However, the template uses the `xsl:attribute` element to add a new attribute to the `Person` element node in the result tree. The `name` attribute of the `xsl:attribute` element specifies that the name of the new attributes are called `FirstName` and `LastName`:

```
<xsl:template match="Person">
 <xsl:copy>
   <xsl:attribute name="FirstName"><xsl:value-of select="FirstName"/>
 </xsl:attribute>
   <xsl:attribute name="LastName"><xsl:value-of select="LastName"/>
 </xsl:attribute>
  </xsl:copy>
</xsl:template>
```

The `xsl:value-of` element is used to specify the value of the newly created attributes. For the `FirstName` attribute, the value is the value of the `FirstName` element in the source document. For the `LastName` attribute, the value selected is the value of the `LastName` element in the source document. Figure 8-4 shows the result document displayed in Internet Explorer.

The result document, `PersonsOut.xml`, tidied for on-page presentation, is shown here:

```
<?xml version="1.0" encoding="UTF-8"?>
<Persons>
 <Person FirstName="Jill" LastName="Harper"/>
 <Person FirstName="Claire" LastName="Vogue"/>
 <Person FirstName="Paul" LastName="Cathedral"/>
</Persons>
```

Notice that the `Person` elements are now empty elements and that each `Person` element now has a `FirstName` attribute and a `LastName` attribute.

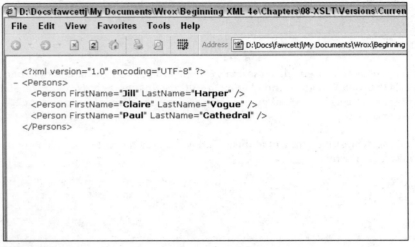

Figure 8-4

Try It Out   Adding Child Elements

Sometimes you need to do the opposite when restructuring an element. You can reverse the process, again using the xsl:copy element. Using PersonsOut.xml as the source document, remove the FirstName and LastName attributes and add new FirstName and LastName child elements to the Person element. The stylesheet Persons2.xslt is shown here:

```
<xsl:stylesheet  xmlns:xsl="http://www.w3.org/1999/XSL/Transform" version="1.0" >
<xsl:template match="/">
 <Persons>
  <xsl:apply-templates select="/Persons/Person" />
 </Persons>
</xsl:template>
<xsl:template match="Person">
 <xsl:copy>
  <xsl:element name="FirstName"><xsl:value-of select="@FirstName"/>
</xsl:element>
  <xsl:element name="LastName"><xsl:value-of select="@LastName"/>
</xsl:element>
 </xsl:copy>
</xsl:template>

</xsl:stylesheet>
```

1. Navigate to the directory containing the PersonsOut.xml and Persons2.xslt files.

2. To run the transformation, type the following at the command line:

```
java -jar saxon8.jar -o PersonsBack.xml PersonsOut.xml Persons2.xslt
```

or

```
transform.exe -o PersonsBack.xml PersonsOut.xml Persons2.xslt
```

In subsequent examples, only the Java style command line will be shown; for .NET, substitute `transform.exe` *for* `java -jar saxon8.jar`.

3. Open `PersonsBack.xml` in your favorite editor to see the structure created using the `Persons2.xslt` stylesheet.

How It Works

The stylesheet `Persons2.xslt` differs from the previous stylesheet, `Persons.xslt`, only in the content of the template that matches the `Person` element node:

```
<xsl:template match="Person">
 <xsl:copy>
   <xsl:element name="FirstName"><xsl:value-of select="@FirstName"/>
</xsl:element>
   <xsl:element name="LastName"><xsl:value-of select="@LastName"/>
</xsl:element>
 </xsl:copy>
</xsl:template>
```

The `xsl:copy` element, as before, adds a `Person` element node to the result tree. Each `xsl:element` element adds a child element node to the `Person` element node. The name of the new element node is specified in the `name` attribute of the `xsl:element` element. The value of the new element is specified using the `xsl:value-of` element:

```
<xsl:value-of select="@FirstName" />
```

The location path in the `select` attribute specifies that the value of the newly created `FirstName` element node is the value of the `FirstName` attribute in the source tree.

The preceding examples give you an idea of how to use the `xsl:copy` element. However, sometimes you will want to copy an entire structure from the source XML document to the result document. In that case, the `xsl:copy-of` element comes into play.

The *<xsl:copy-of>* Element

The `xsl:copy-of` element causes a deep copy to take place. In other words, a node, together with all its attribute nodes and descendant nodes, is copied to the result tree.

Suppose you receive a purchase order (`PurchaseOrder.xml` shown here) as a source document:

```
<PurchaseOrder>
 <From>Example.org</From>
 <To>XMML.com</To>
 <Address>
  <Street>234 Any Street</Street>
  <City>Any Town</City>
  <State>MO</State>
  <ZipCode>98765</ZipCode>
 </Address>
 <!-- Other purchase order information would go here. -->
</PurchaseOrder>
```

The stylesheet, `PurchaseOrder.xslt`, to create an Invoice, `Invoice.xml`, from the purchase order is shown here:

```
<xsl:stylesheet xmlns:xsl="http://www.w3.org/1999/XSL/Transform" version="1.0" >

<xsl:template match="/">
 <Invoice>

  <xsl:apply-templates select="/PurchaseOrder/To" />
  <xsl:apply-templates select = "/PurchaseOrder/From" />
  <xsl:apply-templates select="/PurchaseOrder/Address" />
  <xsl:comment>The rest of the Invoice would go here.</xsl:comment>
 </Invoice>
</xsl:template>

<xsl:template match="To">
 <xsl:element name="From"><xsl:value-of select="." /></xsl:element>
</xsl:template>

<xsl:template match="From">
 <xsl:element name="To"><xsl:value-of select="." /></xsl:element>
</xsl:template>

<xsl:template match="Address">
 <xsl:copy-of select="." />
</xsl:template>

</xsl:stylesheet>
```

To run the transformation, enter the following at the command line:

```
java -jar saxon8.jar -o Invoice.xml PurchaseOrder.xml PurchaseOrder.xslt
```

Now let's walk through what the stylesheet does. The template that matches the root node creates an `Invoice` element as a literal result element. Then three `xsl:apply-templates` element are used to create the content of the `Invoice` element:

```
<xsl:template match="/">
 <Invoice>
  <xsl:apply-templates select="PurchaseOrder/To" />
  <xsl:apply-templates select="PurchaseOrder/From" />
  <xsl:apply-templates select="PurchaseOrder/Address" />
  <xsl:comment>The rest of the Invoice would go here.</xsl:comment>
 </Invoice>
</xsl:template>
```

The first `xsl:apply-templates` element selects `To` element nodes in the source tree and matches this template:

```
<xsl:template match="To">
 <xsl:element name="From"><xsl:value-of select="." /></xsl:element>
</xsl:template>
```

A new element node, From, is created using the value of the To element node in the source tree. Remember that the value of the select attribute of xsl:value-of,

```
<xsl:value-of select="." />
```

is the abbreviated syntax for the context node, which is the To element node.

Similarly, the second xsl:apply-templates element matches From element nodes:

```
<xsl:template match="From">
 <xsl:element name="To"><xsl:value-of select="." /></xsl:element>
</xsl:template>
```

A new element, To, is created in the result tree and given the value of the From element node in the source tree.

The result of those two templates simply switches the From and To parties, which you would expect to be switched between a purchase order and an invoice.

The Address element in the source document can be used unchanged in the invoice:

```
<Address>
 <Street>234 Any Street</Street>
 <City>Any Town</City>
 <State>MO</State>
 <ZipCode>98765</ZipCode>
</Address>
```

Therefore, the third xsl:apply-templates element in the stylesheet selects the location path /PurchaseOrder/Address, and the following template matches:

```
<xsl:template match="Address">
 <xsl:copy-of select="." />
</xsl:template>
```

The xsl:copy-of element copies the Address element node from the source tree to the result tree, together with all its descendant nodes (and attribute nodes, if it had any).

The result document, Invoice.xml, is shown here:

```
<?xml version="1.0" encoding="UTF-8"?>
<Invoice>
 <From>XMML.com</From>
 <To>Example.org</To>
 <Address>
  <Street>234 Any Street</Street>
  <City>Any Town</City>
  <State>MO</State>
  <ZipCode>98765</ZipCode>
 </Address><!--The rest of the Invoice would go here.-->
</Invoice>
```

Influencing the Output with the <xsl:output> Element

XSLT can be used to produce XML, HTML, or text output. The developer makes a choice among these options by using the method attribute of the xsl:output element.

XML output is the default, and it is not necessary to specify XML as an output method. If you want to do it explicitly, then the following code is used:

```
<xsl:output method="xml" />
```

The value of the method attribute is case sensitive and must be all lowercase.

HTML output is specified like this:

```
<xsl:output method="html" />
```

Text output is specified like this:

```
<xsl:output method="text" />
```

In XSLT 1.0, there is no way to specify XHTML output although this has been added to version 2.0. For true XHTML, you should use the xml designation.

Sometimes the processor will guess that you want HTML rather than XML. This normally happens when the first literal result element is html, so in this case there is no need to specify the method as html. The basic difference between HTML output and XML is that many HTML elements — img or br, for example — are empty of content but have no closing tag. These violate the well-formedness of XML. Another difference is that of standalone attributes such as the SELECTED marker found on a select element's option. The text method of output has no restrictions on its format and is normally used to create any non-markup files.

Conditional Processing

So far you have seen pretty simple XSLT stylesheets that carry out a transformation in only one way each time a template is instantiated. At times, you will want to apply conditions when processing. The xsl:if and xsl:choose elements allow conditional processing in XSLT.

The <xsl:if> Element

The xsl:if element tests whether a Boolean condition is true or false. If it is true, then the content of the xsl:if element is instantiated. If it is false, then nothing specified inside the xsl:if element is added to the result tree.

Suppose you want to test whether the age data for some historical or fictional characters corresponded to an imposed upper realistic age limit of 110 years. The source document, Characters.xml, is shown here:

```
<Characters>
 <Character age="99">Julius Caesar</Character>
 <Character age="23">Anne Boleyn</Character>
 <Character age="41">George Washington</Character>
 <Character age="45">Martin Luther</Character>
 <Character age="800">Methuselah</Character>
 <Character age="119">Moses</Character>
 <Character age="50">Asterix the Gaul</Character>
</Characters>
```

A quick glance at a short document like this reveals that two characters have unusually high ages. When you have thousands or tens of thousands of `Character` elements, it is more appropriate to automate the checks.

The stylesheet `Characters.xslt` uses the `xsl:if` element to add to the result tree only when the value of the `age` attribute exceeds the specified upper age limit of 110:

```
<xsl:stylesheet  xmlns:xsl="http://www.w3.org/1999/XSL/Transform" version="1.0" >

<xsl:template match="/">
 <html>
  <head>
   <title>Age check on Characters.</title>
  </head>
  <body>
  <h3>The recorded age is unusually high. Please check original data.</h3>
  <xsl:apply-templates select="/Characters/Character" />
  </body>
 </html>
</xsl:template>
<xsl:template match="Character">
 <xsl:if test="@age &gt; 110 " >
 <p><b><xsl:value-of select="." /></b> is older than expected.
 Please check if this character's age, <b><xsl:value-of select="@age" /></b>
 , is correct.</p>
 </xsl:if>
</xsl:template>

</xsl:stylesheet>
```

The `xsl:apply-templates` element in the template that matches the root node selects `Character` element nodes for which the following template matches:

```
<xsl:template match="Character">
 <xsl:if test="@age &gt; 110 " >
 <p><b><xsl:value-of select="." /></b> is older than expected. Please check if
 this character's age, <b><xsl:value-of select="@age" /></b>, is correct.</p>
 </xsl:if>
</xsl:template>
```

Notice that the `xsl:if` element is a child element of the `xsl:template` element. Therefore, if the `test` attribute of the `xsl:if` element returns the Boolean value `false`, then nothing is output from the template for that `Character` element.

307

The output from the transformation is shown in Figure 8-5.

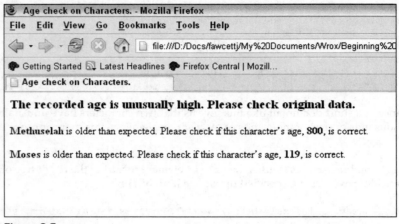

Figure 8-5

As you can see in Figure 8-5, only those characters whose age exceeds 110 are displayed in the web page created by the transformation.

While the `xsl:if` element either outputs something or outputs nothing, the `xsl:choose` element is intended to allow alternate output options.

The <xsl:choose> Element

Suppose that you want to indicate whether the age of a character is suspicious or acceptable. Using the same XML source document used in the previous section, `Characters.xml`, you can use the following stylesheet, `CharactersChoose.xslt`, to indicate an assessment for each character:

```
<xsl:stylesheet
 xmlns:xsl="http://www.w3.org/1999/XSL/Transform"
 version="1.0" >

<xsl:template match="/">
 <html>
  <head>
   <title>Age check on all Characters.</title>
  </head>
  <body>
  <h3>The following is the assessment of the age data.</h3>
  <xsl:apply-templates select="/Characters/Character" />
  </body>
 </html>
</xsl:template>

<xsl:template match="Character">
 <xsl:choose>
```

```
    <xsl:when test="@age &gt; 110 " >
     <p><b><xsl:value-of select="." /></b> - too high. Please check if this
     character's age, <b><xsl:value-of select="@age" /></b>, is correct.</p>
    </xsl:when>
    <xsl:otherwise>
     <p><b><xsl:value-of select="." /></b> - ok</p>.
    </xsl:otherwise>

   </xsl:choose>
  </xsl:template>

 </xsl:stylesheet>
```

To run the transformation, enter the following at the command line:

```
java -jar saxon8.jar -o AgeAssessed.html Characters.xml CharactersChoose.xslt
```

The key part of this transformation is in the template that matches `Character` element nodes:

```
<xsl:template match="Character">
 <xsl:choose>
  <xsl:when test="@age &gt; 110 " >
   <p><b><xsl:value-of select="." /></b> - too high. Please check if this
   character's age, <b><xsl:value-of select="@age" /></b>, is correct.</p>
  </xsl:when>
  <xsl:otherwise>
   <p><b><xsl:value-of select="." /></b> - ok</p>.
  </xsl:otherwise>
 </xsl:choose>
</xsl:template>
```

Notice how the `xsl:choose` element is nested immediately inside the `xsl:template` element. Therefore, output from that template is entirely controlled by the `xsl:choose` element.

Nested inside the `xsl:choose` element are an `xsl:when` element and an `xsl:otherwise` element. On the `xsl:when` element is a `test` attribute whose value is a Boolean value. If the value of the `test` attribute is the Boolean value `true`, then the content of the `xsl:when` element is output. If the value of the `test` attribute of the `xsl:when` attribute is `false`, then none of the content of the `xsl:when` element is output; the content of the `xsl:otherwise` element is output instead.

The HTML output, `AgeAssessed.html`, tidied for on-page display, is shown here:

```
<html>
 <head>
  <meta http-equiv="Content-Type" content="text/html; charset=UTF-8">
   <title>Age check on all Characters.</title>
 </head>
 <body>
  <h3>The following is the assessment of the age data.</h3>
  <p><b>Julius Caesar</b> - ok</p>
  <p><b>Anne Boleyn</b> - ok</p>
  <p><b>George Washington</b> - ok</p>
  <p><b>Martin Luther</b> - ok</p>
```

```
      <p><b>Methuselah</b> - too high. Please check if this character's age,
      <b>800</b>, is correct.</p>
      <p><b>Moses</b> - too high. Please check if this character's age, <b>119
      </b>, is correct.</p>
      <p><b>Asterix the Gaul</b> - ok</p>
    </body>
  </html>
```

Output is created for every `Character` element node in the source tree. If the value of the `age` attribute is greater than 110, then a message asking the user to check that character's age is output, as indicated by the content of the `xsl:when` element. Otherwise, an *ok* message is output, as specified in the `xsl:otherwise` element.

The resulting web page is shown in Figure 8-6.

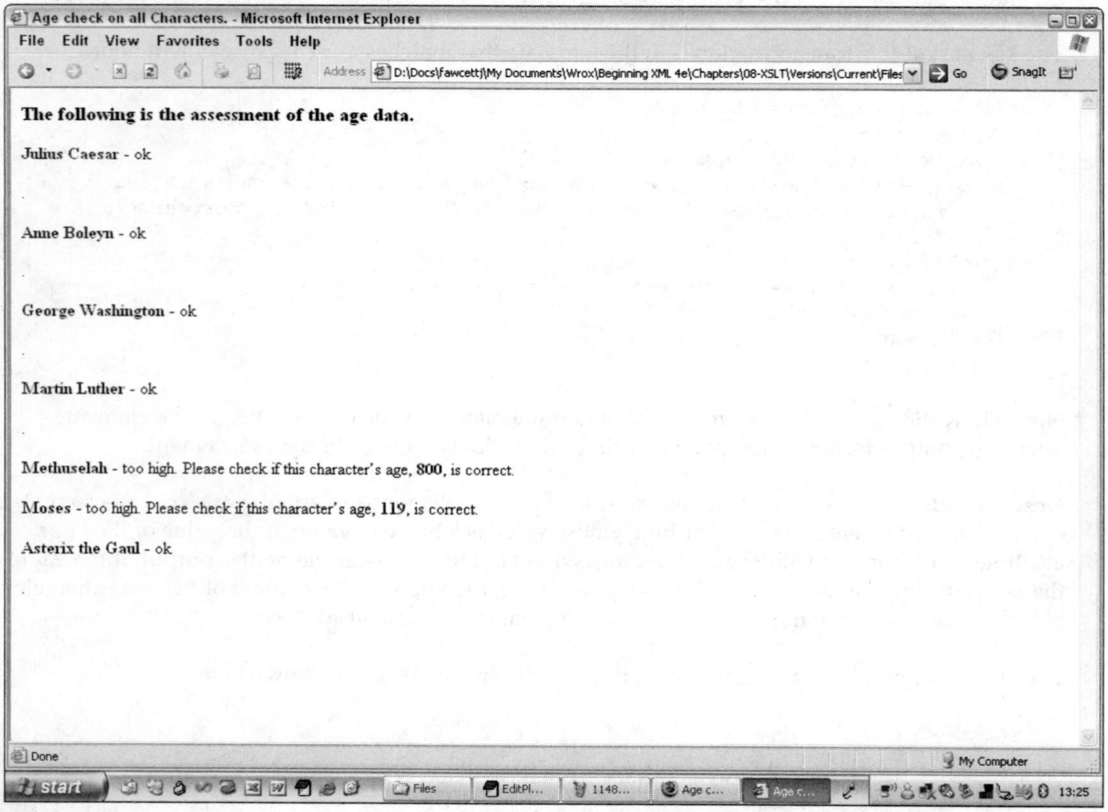

Figure 8-6

In the preceding example, the `xsl:choose` element had only one `xsl:when` element. However, it can have an arbitrary number of `xsl:when` elements as its children, each with a Boolean test specified in the `test` attribute. The content of the first `xsl:when` element that has a `test` attribute evaluating to the Boolean value `true` is output. All other `xsl:when` elements generate no output, and the `xsl:otherwise` is ignored. However, if none of the xsl:when elements has a test attribute that evaluates to the Boolean value true, then the content of the xsl:otherwise element, if one is present, is output.

Having looked at how you can make choices between processing options, let's move on to examine how you can process several nodes, with each being processed in the same way.

The <xsl:for-each> Element

The xsl:for-each element allows all nodes in a node-set to be processed according to the XSLT instructions nested inside the xsl:for-each element. For example, consider a source document, Objects.xml, that shows some characteristics of an object:

```
<?xml version="1.0"?>
<Objects>
 <Object name="Car">
  <Characteristic>Hard</Characteristic>
  <Characteristic>Shiny</Characteristic>
  <Characteristic>Has 4 wheels</Characteristic>
  <Characteristic>Internal Combustion Engine</Characteristic>
 </Object>
</Objects>
```

The xsl:for-each element can be used to iterate across this node-set and create some specified output for each node in the node-set. You could, for example, use the xsl:for-each element to create an HTML list item, a li element, for each characteristic of an object. The following code, object.xslt, shows a stylesheet that does this:

```
<?xml version="1.0"?>
<xsl:stylesheet xmlns:xsl="http://www.w3.org/1999/XSL/Transform" version="1.0"
 >

<xsl:template match="/">
 <html>
  <head>
   <title>Object Characteristics</title>
  </head>
  <body>
  <h3>Characteristics of <xsl:value-of select="Objects/Object/@name" /></h3>
  <xsl:apply-templates select="/Objects/Object" />
  </body>
 </html>
</xsl:template>

<xsl:template match="Object">
 <ul>
 <xsl:for-each select="Characteristic">
  <li><xsl:value-of select="." /></li>
 </xsl:for-each>
 </ul>
</xsl:template>

</xsl:stylesheet>
```

The interesting part of this stylesheet is the template that matches `Object` element nodes:

```
<xsl:template match="Object">
<ul>
<xsl:for-each select="Characteristic">
 <li><xsl:value-of select="." /></li>
</xsl:for-each>
</ul>
</xsl:template>
```

Inside the template, the start-tags and end-tags of an unordered list are specified using literal result elements. Between those tags you use the `xsl:for-each` element to create a list item for each `Characteristic` element node child of the context node, which is an `Object` element node.

Remember that XSLT is declarative, not procedural. `xsl:for-each` does not loop through the elements as you might loop through a collection or an array in other languages. In theory, the nodes can be processed in any order — with a multi-processor machine processing one per processor simultaneously, for example. This is why you cannot break out of a `for-each` as you can in, say, Java.

So far the order of the elements in the output document has matched that of the input document. However, you may need to output data in an order that differs from the order in the source document. The `xsl:sort` element provides the functionality to sort XML data during a transformation.

The `<xsl:sort>` Element

The `xsl:sort` element is used to specify sort order for node-sets. The `xsl:sort` element can be used together with the `xsl:apply-templates` element and the `xsl:for-each` element. The following example shows both usages.

Suppose you have a larger group of objects that you want to describe in an HTML web page. The source XML, `Objects2.xml`, is shown in the following code:

```
<?xml version="1.0"?>
<Objects>
 <Object name="Car">
  <Characteristic>Hard</Characteristic>
  <Characteristic>Shiny</Characteristic>
  <Characteristic>Has 4 wheels</Characteristic>
  <Characteristic>Internal Combustion Engine</Characteristic>
 </Object>
 <Object name="Orange">
  <Characteristic>Fruit</Characteristic>
  <Characteristic>Juicy</Characteristic>
  <Characteristic>Dimpled skin</Characteristic>
  <Characteristic>Citrus</Characteristic>
 </Object>
 <Object name="Giraffe">
  <Characteristic>Tall</Characteristic>
  <Characteristic>Four legs</Characteristic>
  <Characteristic>Big spots</Characteristic>
```

```
    <Characteristic>Mammal</Characteristic>
  </Object>
  <Object name="Prawn Cracker">
  <Characteristic>Crisp</Characteristic>
  <Characteristic>Savoury</Characteristic>
  <Characteristic>Off white</Characteristic>
  <Characteristic>Edible</Characteristic>
  </Object>
</Objects>
```

Now suppose you want to sort the data before displaying it. The objects are to be sorted in ascending alphabetical order, and the characteristics are to be sorted in descending alphabetical order. The stylesheet, `Objects.xslt`, creates an HTML file with those sort orders applied:

```
<?xml version="1.0"?>
<xsl:stylesheet

 xmlns:xsl="http://www.w3.org/1999/XSL/Transform" version="1.0"
 >

<xsl:template match="/">
 <html>
  <head>
   <title>Object Characteristics</title>
  </head>
  <body>
  <xsl:apply-templates select="/Objects/Object" >
   <xsl:sort select="@name" />
  </xsl:apply-templates>
  </body>
 </html>
</xsl:template>

<xsl:template match="Object">
  <h3>Characteristics of <xsl:value-of select="@name" /></h3>
 <ul>
 <xsl:for-each select="Characteristic">
 <xsl:sort select="." order="descending" />
  <li><xsl:value-of select="." /></li>
 </xsl:for-each>
 </ul>
</xsl:template>

</xsl:stylesheet>
```

First, look at the use of `xsl:sort` in association with the `xsl:apply-templates` element:

```
<xsl:apply-templates select="/Objects/Object" >
 <xsl:sort select="@name" />
</xsl:apply-templates>
```

As normal, you use the `select` attribute of the `xsl:apply-templates` element to specify a node-set. Unlike earlier examples, the `xsl:apply-templates` element is not an empty element; instead, it has an xsl:sort element nested inside it. The value of the select attribute of the xsl:sort element specifies the value by which the node-set is to be sorted. In this case, the value of the select attribute is a relative location path, @name, which specifies the name attribute node whose parent is an Object element node.

The default sort order is ascending so you don't need to specify that to produce the desired sort order for objects. However, when you want to sort the Characteristic element nodes, the desired sort order is descending, so that needs to be specified using the order attribute on the xsl:sort element:

```
<xsl:template match="Object">
  <h3>Characteristics of <xsl:value-of select="@name" /></h3>
  <ul>
  <xsl:for-each select="Characteristic">
  <xsl:sort select="." order="descending" />
  <li><xsl:value-of select="." /></li>
  </xsl:for-each>
  </ul>
</xsl:template>
```

Notice how the unordered list is created in the preceding template. The start- and end-tags of the ul element come outside the xsl:for-each element. The xsl:sort element is nested inside the xsl:for-each element, coming immediately after its start-tag. The node-set selected by the xsl:for-each element are Characteristic element nodes. It is the value of those nodes that you want to sort by, so you use the period character as the value of the select attribute of the xsl:sort element. Remember that the period character selects the context node itself, being an abbreviation for the location path self::node(). To sort the characteristics in descending order, you specify the value of the order attribute of the xsl:sort element as descending.

xsl:sort elements can be repeated so that if you wish to sort by one value and then another this is also possible. For example, if you want to process a number of Person elements that have a FirstName and a LastName element and have them sorted by LastName and then FirstName, the following xsl:apply-templates would be needed:

```
<xsl:apply-templates select="Person">
  <xsl:sort select="LastName"/>
  <xsl:sort select="FirstName"/>
</xsl:apply-templates>
```

Both these sorts were alphabetical, as the processor could tell from the Characteristic's type. If you want to sort numerically, you need to add the attribute data-type to the xsl:sort element and specify number as its value. If you wish to specify alphabetical sorting, specify text.

XSLT Modes

You have learned how you can select, for example, element nodes in the source tree and produce output corresponding to their content. So far in the examples that you have seen, a node in the source tree has been processed once or not at all. Sometimes, however, you will need to use a node in the source tree more than once. A classic situation is using a chapter title in the source document at the top of its own page and using the same information in a table of contents for the document.

The XSLT solution to this need to process certain nodes more than once is the *mode*. An XSLT mode is expressed using a mode attribute on an xsl:apply-templates element, like this:

```
<xsl:apply-templates select="/Book/Chapter" mode="TOC" />
```

Suppose the stylesheet had two templates, one with the start-tag

```
<xsl:template match="Chapter" >
```

and the other with the start-tag

```
<xsl:template match="Chapter" mode="TOC" >
```

Both templates match as far as the value of the match attribute is concerned. However, if the xsl:apply-templates element has a mode attribute, a template is instantiated only if it has both a matching value in the match attribute and in the mode attribute of the xsl:template element.

We can see this in operation to solve the example problem of processing chapter titles so that they are both used in a table of contents and displayed as the title of the chapter when the chapter is displayed. The content of a very abbreviated version of this book, BegXML.xml, is stored as XML and is shown here:

```
<?xml version="1.0"?>
<Book>
<Authors>
 <Author>David Hunter</Author>
 <Author>Danny Ayers</Author>
 <Author>Jeff Rafter</Author>
 <Author>John Duckett</Author>
 <Author>Eric van der Vlist</Author>
 <Author>Andrew Watt</Author>
 <Author>Joe Fawcett</Author>
</Authors>
<Year>2007</Year><Chapters>

<Chapter number="1" title="What is XML?">
XML is a markup language, derived from SGML.</Chapter>
<Chapter number="2" title="Well-formed XML">
To be well-formed an XML document  must satisfy several rules about its
structure.</Chapter>
<Chapter number="3" title="Namespaces">
To help unambiguously identify the names of elements and attributes the
notion of an XML namespace is used.</Chapter>
<Chapter number="4" title="DTD">
A document type definition, DTD, is a way to  specify the permitted
structure of an XML document.</Chapter>
<Chapter number="5" title="Schemas">
W3C XML Schema and Relax NG are two schema languages to specify the
structure of XML documents.</Chapter>
</Chapters>
</Book>
```

The aim is to create an HTML document with a table of contents and the chapter text, as shown in Figure 8-7.

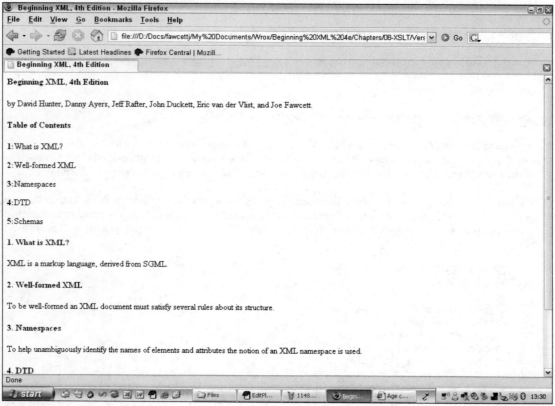

Figure 8-7

The stylesheet, `BegXML.xslt`, to create the HTML web page is shown here:

```
<?xml version="1.0"?>
<xsl:stylesheet xmlns:xsl="http://www.w3.org/1999/XSL/Transform" version="1.0"
 >

<xsl:template match="/">
 <html>
  <head>
   <title><xsl:value-of select="/Book/Title" /></title>
  </head>
  <body>
  <h3><xsl:value-of select="/Book/Title" /></h3>
  <p>by <xsl:apply-templates select="/Book/Authors/Author" />
  </p>
  <h3>Table of Contents</h3>
```

```
   <xsl:apply-templates select="/Book/Chapters/Chapter" mode="TOC" />
   <xsl:apply-templates select="/Book/Chapters/Chapter" mode="fulltext" />
   </body>
 </html>
</xsl:template>

<xsl:template match="Author">
<xsl:value-of select="." />
<xsl:if test="position() != last()"><xsl:text>, </xsl:text></xsl:if>
<xsl:if test="position() = last()-1"><xsl:text>and </xsl:text></xsl:if>
<xsl:if test="position() = last()"><xsl:text>.</xsl:text></xsl:if>
</xsl:template>

<xsl:template match="Chapter" mode="TOC">
 <p><b><xsl:value-of select="@number" />:</b> <xsl:value-of select="@title" />
</p>
</xsl:template>

<xsl:template match="Chapter" mode="fulltext">
<h3><xsl:value-of select="@number" />. <xsl:value-of select="@title" /></h3>
<p><xsl:value-of select="." /></p>
</xsl:template>

</xsl:stylesheet>
```

Note several differences from stylesheets that you have already seen. The template that matches the root node has three `xsl:apply-templates` elements in it:

```
<xsl:template match="/">
 <html>
  <head>
   <title><xsl:value-of select="/Book/Title" /></title>
  </head>
  <body>
  <h3><xsl:value-of select="/Book/Title" /></h3>
  <p>by <xsl:apply-templates select="/Book/Authors/Author" />
  </p>
  <h3>Table of Contents</h3>
  <xsl:apply-templates select="/Book/Chapters/Chapter" mode="TOC" />
  <xsl:apply-templates select="/Book/Chapters/Chapter" mode="fulltext" />
  </body>
 </html>
</xsl:template>
```

The first `xsl:apply-templates` element matches this template:

```
<xsl:template match="Author">
<xsl:value-of select="." />
<xsl:if test="position() != last()"><xsl:text>, </xsl:text></xsl:if>
<xsl:if test="position() = last()-1"><xsl:text>and </xsl:text></xsl:if>
<xsl:if test="position() = last()"><xsl:text>.</xsl:text></xsl:if>
</xsl:template>
```

The xsl:value-of element simply outputs an author's name, but punctuation is controlled using the xsl:if element and the XPath position() function and last() function. The first xsl:if element causes a comma followed by a space character to be output. This is done when the position of the Author element node is not last in document order among the Author element nodes in the node-set selected by the first of the three xsl:apply-templates elements in the template matching the root node.

The second xsl:if element produces output only if the Author element node is the second last Author element node in the node-set. The third xsl:if element produces a period character only when the Author element node is the last one.

Taken together, all this produces a correctly punctuated author list:

```
<p>by David Hunter, Danny Ayers, Jeff Rafter, John Duckett,
 Eric van der Vlist, and Joe Fawcett.</p>
```

The xsl:text element was used in each of the xsl:if elements. It is not needed here, and you could have obtained the same output without using it. However, the xsl:text element is essential if you want to output whitespace literally — either a space character or a newline character, for example. To output a space character, you could write the following:

```
<xsl:text> </xsl:text>
```

To output a newline character, you could write the following:

```
<xsl:text>
</xsl:text>
```

The second and third xsl:apply-templates from the BegXML.xslt stylesheet demonstrate the use of modes:

```
<xsl:apply-templates select="/Book/Chapters/Chapter" mode="TOC" />
<xsl:apply-templates select="/Book/Chapters/Chapter" mode="fulltext" />
```

The first xsl:apply-templates element matches this template, as shown in the following:

```
<xsl:template match="Chapter" mode="TOC">
 <p><b><xsl:value-of select="@number" />:</b> <xsl:value-of
 select= "@title" /></p>
</xsl:template>
```

Notice that the value of the select attribute of the xsl:apply-templates element matches the value of the match attribute of the xsl:template element, and at the same time the values of the two mode attributes are the same.

The content added to the result tree is straightforward using the xsl:value-of element that you have seen several times before. Importantly, using a mode attribute on both the xsl:apply-templates and xsl:template element leaves you free to process the Chapter nodes a second time, using another xsl:apply-templates element:

```
<xsl:apply-templates select="/Book/Chapters/Chapter" mode="fulltext" />
```

The preceding `xsl:apply-templates` element matches the following template:

```
<xsl:template match="Chapter" mode="fulltext">
<h3><xsl:value-of select="@number" />. <xsl:value-of select="@title" /></h3>
<p><xsl:value-of select="." /></p>
</xsl:template>
```

Note that the `match` attribute of the `xsl:template` element matches the `select` attribute of the `xsl:apply-templates` element, and the two `mode` attributes also match.

The HTML document, `BegXML.html`, that the stylesheet produces is shown here after tidying for on-page presentation:

```
<html>
   <head>
      <meta http-equiv="Content-Type" content="text/html; charset=UTF-8">
      <title>Beginning XML, 4th Edition</title>
   </head>
   <body>
      <h3>Beginning XML, 4th Edition</h3>
      <p>by David Hunter, Danny Ayers, Jeff Rafter, John Duckett,
         Eric van der Vlist, and Joe Fawcett.</p>
      <h3>Table of Contents</h3>
      <p><b>1:</b>What Is XML?
      </p>
      <p><b>2:</b>Well-Formed XML
      </p>
      <p><b>3:</b>Namespaces
      </p>
      <p><b>4:</b>DTD
      </p>
      <p><b>5:</b>Schemas
      </p>
      <h3>1. What Is XML?</h3>
      <p>XML is a markup language, derived  from SGML.</p>
      <h3>2. Well-formed XML</h3>
      <p>To be well-formed an XML document
         must satisfy several rules about its structure.</p>
      <h3>3. Namespaces</h3>
      <p>To help unambiguously identify the
      names of elements and attributes,
 the notion of an XML namespace is used.</p>
      <h3>4. DTD</h3>
      <p>A document type definition, DTD, is a way to
      specify the permitted structure of an XML document.</p>
      <h3>5. Schemas</h3>
      <p>W3C XML Schema and Relax NG are two schema
      languages to specify the structure of XML documents.</p>
   </body>
</html>
```

As you have seen, modes allow multiple processing of nodes in the source tree for different purposes.

XSLT Variables and Parameters

XSLT allows variables and parameters to be specified by the `xsl:variable` and `xsl:parameter` elements, respectively. Both variables and parameters are referenced using `$VariableName` or `$ParameterName` syntax.

> *Variables in XSLT can be confusing because they resemble constants in other languages; once their value is set it cannot be altered. This means that expressions common in other languages, such as `$VariableName = $VariableName + 1`, are illegal in XSLT. If you find yourself needing such constructs you will have to rethink the approach to fit with a functional language.*

Suppose you want to be able to enter the name of a person and find his or her age. A source document, `Ages.xml`, is shown here:

```
<?xml version="1.0"?>
<Ages>
 <Person name="Peter" age="21" />
 <Person name="Angela" age="12" />
 <Person name="Augustus" age="92" />
 <Person name="George" age="44" />
 <Person name="Hannah" age="30" />
</Ages>
```

Next, you show the stylesheet. Note the `xsl:param` element as a child element of the `xsl:stylesheet` element:

```
<?xml version="1.0"?>
<xsl:stylesheet xmlns:xsl="http://www.w3.org/1999/XSL/Transform" version="1.0"
 >
<xsl:param name="person" />

<xsl:template match="/">
 <html>
  <head>
   <title>Finding an age using an XSLT parameter</title>
  </head>
  <body>
   <xsl:apply-templates select="/Ages/Person[@name=$person]" />
  </body>
 </html>

</xsl:template>

<xsl:template match="Person">
<p>The age of <xsl:value-of select="$person" /> is <xsl:value-of
 select="@age"/> </p>
</xsl:template>

</xsl:stylesheet>
```

To pass in a parameter from the command line, use syntax like this:

```
java -jar saxon8.jar -o Ages.html Ages.xml Ages.xslt person="Peter"
```

This passes in `Peter` as the value of the `person` parameter. If you pass in the name `Hannah` to the stylesheet, the HTML output is as follows:

```
<html>
 <head>
  <meta http-equiv="Content-Type" content="text/html; charset=UTF-8">
  <title>Finding an age using an XSLT parameter</title>
 </head>
 <body>
  <p>The age of Hannah is 30</p>
 </body>
</html>
```

The `person` parameter is used twice in the stylesheet. First, it is used in a predicate in the value of the `select` attribute of the `xsl:apply-templates` element:

```
<xsl:apply-templates select="/Ages/Person[@name=$person]" />
```

Later, it is used inside the matching template to display the value of the `person` parameter using the `xsl:value-of` element:

```
<xsl:template match="Person">
<p>The age of <xsl:value-of select="$person" /> is <xsl:value-of
   select="@age"/></p>
</xsl:template>
```

XSLT variables behave in the same way as parameters but with one difference: Parameters can be passed into a transformation from outside. Variables are defined inside an XSLT stylesheet. There are two ways to specify an XSLT variable: the first way uses the `select` attribute of the `xsl:variable` element, as shown in the following:

```
<xsl:variable name=" variableName" select=" someExpression" />
```

The second way to specify an XSLT variable is to supply content between the start-tag and the end-tag of the `xsl:variable` element, as shown in the following:

```
<xsl:variable name=" variableName">
  <!-- Some content goes here which can define the value of the variable. -->
</xsl:variable>
```

Don't forget to enclose the contents of `param` or `variable` in quotes if you are using the `select` attribute and you want a string value. For example, if you have

<xsl:param name="searchLetter" select="'A'" />

then the param `$searchLetter` will be set to A unless set externally before the transform. If you omit the inner pair of single quotes, then it will default to the node set of all A elements under the context node.

The variable can then be employed by using the `$ variableName` notation at an appropriate place in the stylesheet.

Finally, as noted previously, a *global variable,* one residing as a child of the `xsl:stylesheet` element, can be set programmatically before the transform runs. The specification doesn't indicate how this must be done, so each processor has a slightly different technique. You need to look at the documentation for the particular transformer you are using.

Named Templates and the `<xsl:call-template>` Element

The `xsl:apply-templates` element that you have seen in use several times in this chapter allows addressing of selected parts of the source tree of nodes. However, at times you may want to use a template in a manner similar to using a function in, for example, JavaScript. *Named templates* in XSLT enable you to do this.

Named templates are identified, not surprisingly, by a `name` attribute on an `xsl:template` element:

```
<xsl:template name=" TemplateName">
<!-- The template content goes here. -->
</xsl:template>
```

Named templates are called using the `xsl:call-template` element.

The simplest use of `xsl:call-template` is when no parameter is passed to the named template:

```
<xsl:call-template name=" TemplateName" />
```

When you want to pass one or more parameters to a named template, you can do so using the `xsl:with-param` element, like this:

```
<xsl:call-template name=" TemplateName" >
 <xsl:with-param name=" ParameterName" />
 <!-- More <xsl:with-param> elements can go here. -->
</xsl:call-template>
```

The `xsl:with-param` element can optionally have a `select` attribute whose value is an expression, which can specify how the value to be passed is selected.

When a parameter is passed to a named template, the template is written like this:

```
<xsl:template name=" TemplateName">
 <xsl:with-param name=" ParameterName" />
 <!-- Rest of template goes here. -->
</xsl:template>
```

The content of a template called using `xsl:call-template` can use any of the XSLT elements described in this chapter.

XSLT Functions

All of the XPath 1.0 functions described in Chapter 7 are available to an XSLT processor. In addition to those functions, XSLT 1.0 provides a limited number of additional functions to provide functionality specifically relevant to XSLT, several of which are listed here:

❑ The document() function enables access to documents other than the document that contains the context node. This allows the use of multiple documents as source XML documents.

❑ The key() function can be used with the xsl:key element to provide an indexing mechanism for XML source documents.

❑ The format-number() function can be used with the xsl:decimal-format element to provide fine control of how numeric values are displayed in a result document.

❑ The generate-id() function allows the generation of ID attribute nodes in the result tree.

XSLT 2.0

XSLT 2.0 was a long time coming but finally made it as a W3C Recommendation in January 2007.

The latest version of the XSLT 2.0 specification is located at www.w3.org/tr/xslt20/.

As well as harnessing the more powerful XPath 2.0, a number of other improvements make XSLT 2.0 a much more powerful tool:

❑ **New data model** — The data model for XSLT 2.0 is the same data model that is used for XPath 2.0 and for the XML Query Language, XQuery. XQuery is described in Chapter 9.

❑ **W3C XML Schema datatypes** — W3C XML Schema datatypes replace the datatypes used in XPath 1.0 and in XSLT 1.0.

❑ **New elements** — Several new elements are added in XSLT 2.0, including elements that help with grouping tasks, which are difficult to accomplish in XSLT 1.0.

❑ **Non-XML input** — XSLT 2.0 enables you to transform textual data that is not well-formed XML.

❑ **Improved string handling** — As well as using XPath's regular expression functions, XSLT 2.0 has its own instructions that help with text parsing, The main addition is xsl:analyze-string.

❑ **Multiple outputs** — XSLT 2.0 allows more than one document to be output.

❑ **New functions** — XSLT 2.0 uses the additional functions that form part of XPath 2.0 as well as adding some of its own. This provides a much bigger function library than is standardly available in XSLT 1.0. You can also define your own custom functions.

Along with these new features are a number of rules that apply when a version 1.0 transform is carried out by a version 2.0 processor. Some elements, notably xsl:value-of, produce quite different results under version 2.0, so you need to be careful in specifying the version of the transformation and knowing which processor will apply it.

Another improvement is the abandonment of the result tree fragment. This means that variables created like this:

```
<xsl:variable name="newNodes">
  <newElement>
    <xsl:copy-of select="//person"/>
  </newElement>
</xsl:variable>
```

are directly usable as nodes without needing the node-set extension function that many processors were forced to implement.

The following sections looks at how these new features help with some common transformation requirements.

Grouping in Version 2.0

Grouping elements — for example, creating a list of contacts based on country of origin — was no mean feat in XSLT 1.0. A popular technique was *Muenchian grouping*, details of which can be found at `www.jenitennison.com/xslt/grouping/muenchian.xml`, but this technique was tricky to explain and difficult to write.

XSLT 2.0 solves this problem by having an `xsl:for-each-group` instruction allied to new functions such as `current-grouping-key()` and `current-group()`.

`xsl:for-each-group` has a variety of options, allowing you to group on specific values or by position, where there is some sort of header element, and where nodes needing grouping are adjacent in the document.

The following example uses a section of my address book, `contacts.xml`, to illustrate how the new grouping features work:

```
<Contacts>
  <Contact>
    <FirstName>Bruce</FirstName>
    <LastName>Willis</LastName>
    <Country>USA</Country>
  </Contact>
  <Contact>
    <FirstName>Stephen</FirstName>
    <LastName>Fry</LastName>
    <Country>UK</Country>
  </Contact>
  <Contact>
    <FirstName>Anne</FirstName>
    <LastName>Hathaway</LastName>
    <Country>USA</Country>
  </Contact>
  <Contact>
    <FirstName>Etienne</FirstName>
    <LastName>Pradier</LastName>
```

```
      <Country>France</Country>
    </Contact>
    <Contact>
      <FirstName>Bill</FirstName>
      <LastName>Gates</LastName>
      <Country>USA</Country>
    </Contact>
    <Contact>
      <FirstName>Kiera</FirstName>
      <LastName>Knightley</LastName>
      <Country>UK</Country>
    </Contact>
</Contacts>
```

The requirement is to produce a list of all contacts grouped by Country. You also want them listed alphabetically, by LastName and then FirstName. The transform, groupedContacts.xslt, produces the output shown in Figure 8-8.

```
<?xml version="1.0" encoding="utf-8"?>
<xsl:stylesheet version="2.0"
     xmlns:xsl="http://www.w3.org/1999/XSL/Transform">

  <xsl:template match="/">
    <html>
      <body>
        <h3>Contacts by Country</h3>
        <xsl:for-each-group select="Contacts/Contact" group-by="Country">
          <xsl:sort select="current-grouping-key()"/>
          <p>Contacts who live in:
            <b>
              <xsl:value-of select="current-grouping-key()"/>
            </b>
            <ul>
              <xsl:apply-templates select="current-group()">
                <xsl:sort select="LastName"/>
              </xsl:apply-templates>
            </ul>
          </p>
        </xsl:for-each-group>
      </body>
    </html>
  </xsl:template>

  <xsl:template match="Contact">
    <li>
      <xsl:value-of select="LastName"/>, <xsl:value-of select="FirstName"/>
    </li>
  </xsl:template>
</xsl:stylesheet>
```

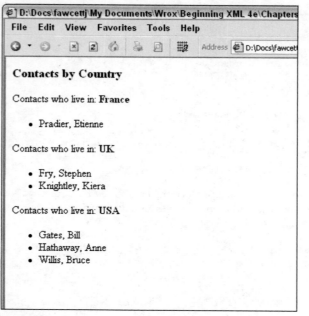

Figure 8-8

Aside from the standard HTML elements, this transformation has one notable section, the `xsl:for-each-group` instruction:

```
<xsl:for-each-group select="Contacts/Contact" group-by="Country">
  <!--more code here -->
</xsl:for-each-group>
```

The `select` attribute is used to choose the nodes that need grouping—in this case the `Contact` elements lying under the `Contacts` document element. The `group-by` attribute states how to group and the expression is relative to the nodes chosen to group—in this case the `Country` element, which is a child of `Contact`.

You want to sort by `Country`, so the next instruction is `xsl:sort`:

```
<xsl:for-each-group select="Contacts/Contact" group-by="Country">
  <xsl:sort select="current-grouping-key()"/>
  <!--more code here -->
</xsl:for-each-group>
```

The item to sort on is specified by the `select` attribute as normal, but a new function, `current-grouping-key()`, is used to obtain the specific `Country` element that the current group is based on.

The next stage is to ouput the group's heading:

```
<xsl:for-each-group select="Contacts/Contact" group-by="Country">
  <xsl:sort select="current-grouping-key()"/>
  <p>Contacts who live in:
    <b>
      <xsl:value-of select="current-grouping-key()"/>
    </b>
  <!--more code here -->
  </p>
</xsl:for-each-group>
```

The current group name is shown, again using the `current-grouping-key()` function.

Finally, the actual nodes in each group are selected; these will be matched by the `Contact` template and output as individual list items:

```
<xsl:for-each-group select="Contacts/Contact" group-by="Country">
  <xsl:sort select="current-grouping-key()"/>
    <p>Contacts who live in:
      <b>
        <xsl:value-of select="current-grouping-key()"/>
      </b>
      <ul>
        <xsl:apply-templates select="current-group()">
          <xsl:sort select="LastName"/>
        </xsl:apply-templates>
      </ul>
    </p>
</xsl:for-each-group>
```

The individual groups are sorted by an `xsl:sort` instruction with `LastName` chosen as the sort item.

Non-XML Input and String Handling

XSLT 2.0 allows non-XML to be used in a transformation. Although the principal input must be XML, secondary documents can be accessed via the new `unparsed-text()` function, which accepts a URL that can be a local file or a document accessed via HTTP. To illustrate the use of this function, let's take a look at another new instruction, `xsl:analyze-string`.

`xsl:analyze-string` breaks down a string based on a regular expression. It then passes those parts that match the expression to an `xsl:matching-substring` instruction, and those that don't to an `xsl:non-matching-substring` element.

For example, suppose you have a variable named `historicalDates` that contains a mixture of years and text:

Some famous years in history were 1066—the Battle of Hastings in England,

1776—the signing of the Declaration of Independence in America, and 1789—the

Storming of the Bastille in France.

To extract the actual years into an HTML list, use the following XSLT:

```
<ul>
  <xsl:analyze-string select="$historicalDates" regex="\d+">
    <xsl:matching-substring>
      <li><xsl:value-of select="."/></li>
    </xsl:matching-substring>
  </xsl:analyze-string>
</ul>
```

The regular expression \d+ matches a string of at least one digit. Each match is processed by the xsl:matching-substring instruction, where the actual match can be accessed via the context node.

You can also use the xsl:non-matching-substring instruction, where it's easier to match the characters you don't need and process those remaining. If necessary, both the xsl:matching-substring and xsl:non-matching-substring instructions can be used.

Try It Out   Reading and Using Non-XML Input

For an example of combining the unparsed-text() function and xsl:analyze-string instruction, start with a traditional INI file, config.ini:

```
name = joe
server = Socrates
role = admin
initial screen = accounts
```

Now suppose your requirement is to turn this into a more modern XML representation:

```
<config>
   <item name="name">joe</item>
   <item name="server">Socrates</item>
   <item name="role">admin</item>
   <item name="initial screen">accounts</item>
</config>
```

The following XSLT, createConfig.xslt, shows how it's done:

```
<?xml version="1.0" encoding="utf-8"?>
<xsl:stylesheet version="2.0"
    xmlns:xsl="http://www.w3.org/1999/XSL/Transform"
    xmlns:xs="http://www.w3.org/2001/XMLSchema">

  <xsl:param name="sourceUri" as="xs:string"/>

  <xsl:template name="main">
    <xsl:variable name="iniFile" select="unparsed-text($sourceUri)"/>
    <config>
    <xsl:analyze-string select="$iniFile" regex="\n">
      <xsl:non-matching-substring>
        <item>
          <xsl:for-each select="tokenize(., '\s+=\s+')">
```

```
            <xsl:choose>
              <xsl:when test="position() = 1">
                <xsl:attribute name="name">
                  <xsl:value-of select="."/>
                </xsl:attribute>
              </xsl:when>
              <xsl:otherwise>
                <xsl:value-of select="."/>
              </xsl:otherwise>
            </xsl:choose>
          </xsl:for-each>
        </item>
      </xsl:non-matching-substring>
    </xsl:analyze-string>
  </config>
  </xsl:template>
</xsl:stylesheet>
```

To test the transformation, use the following command line:

```
java –jar saxon8.jar  -o config.xml -it main createConfig.xslt sourceUri=config.ini
```

The stylesheet has no XML input, so the –it switch instructs processing to begin at a template named main. The xsl:param named sourceUri is also set to the name of the INI file.

How It Works

The template named main first uses the unparsed-text() function to read the INI file and store the text in a variable named iniFile:

```
<xsl:template name="main">
  <xsl:variable name="iniFile" select="unparsed-text($sourceUri)"/>
```

Then the document element config is created and xsl:analyze-string is used with a newline character as the regular expression:

```
<xsl:template name="main">
  <xsl:variable name="iniFile" select="unparsed-text($sourceUri)"/>
  <config>
  <xsl:analyze-string select="$iniFile" regex="\n">
```

The xsl:non-matching-substring instruction processes the name-value pairs and begins by creating an item element:

```
<xsl:template name="main">
  <xsl:variable name="iniFile" select="unparsed-text($sourceUri)"/>
  <config>
  <xsl:analyze-string select="$iniFile" regex="\n">
    <xsl:non-matching-substring>
      <item>
        <xsl:for-each select="tokenize(., '\s+=\s+')">
```

It then splits the name value based on a regular expression that looks for a number of spaces surrounding an equals sign:

```xslt
<xsl:template name="main">
  <xsl:variable name="iniFile" select="unparsed-text($sourceUri)"/>
  <config>
  <xsl:analyze-string select="$iniFile" regex="\n">
    <xsl:non-matching-substring>
      <item>
        <xsl:for-each select="tokenize(., '\s*=\s*')">
          <xsl:choose>
            <xsl:when test="position() = 1">
              <xsl:attribute name="name">
                <xsl:value-of select="."/>
              </xsl:attribute>
            </xsl:when>
            <xsl:otherwise>
              <xsl:value-of select="."/>
            </xsl:otherwise>
          </xsl:choose>
        </xsl:for-each>
      </item>
    </xsl:non-matching-substring>
```

The `xsl:choose` instruction uses the first node, the name, to create an attribute, and the second, the value, to create a text node.

Multiple Outputs

One of the most common questions in XSLT forums asks how to produce more than one document as output. In version 1.0, the only way was through extensions or scripting within the transformation. XSLT 2.0 introduces the `xsl:result-document` element, which enables any number of documents to be produced. As an example, suppose you wanted to group contacts as in the previous example, but this time each country's contacts should be output to a separate file and the main result will give an overall report.

The XSLT used is `separatedContacts.xslt`:

```xslt
<?xml version="1.0" encoding="utf-8"?>
<xsl:stylesheet version="2.0"
    xmlns:xsl="http://www.w3.org/1999/XSL/Transform">

  <xsl:template match="/">
    <html>
      <body>
        <h3>Contacts by Country</h3>
```

```
        <xsl:for-each-group select="Contacts/Contact" group-by="Country">
          <xsl:sort select="current-grouping-key()"/>
          <p>Number of contacts who live in:
            <b>
              <xsl:value-of select="current-grouping-key()"/>
            </b> is
            <xsl:value-of select="count(current-group())"/>
          </p>
          <xsl:result-document href="{current-grouping-key()}.xml">
            <Contacts>
              <xsl:copy-of select="current-group()"/>
            </Contacts>
          </xsl:result-document>
        </xsl:for-each-group>
      </body>
    </html>
  </xsl:template>
</xsl:stylesheet>
```

If you run this transform with the line

```
java -jar saxon8.jar -o ContactsReport.html Contacts.xml separatedContacts.xslt
```

you end up with three files named `France.xml`, `UK.xml`, and `USA.xml`. `USA.xml` looks like this:

```
<?xml version="1.0" encoding="UTF-8"?>
<Contacts>
  <Contact>
    <FirstName>Bruce</FirstName>
    <LastName>Willis</LastName>
    <Country>USA</Country>
  </Contact>
  <Contact>
    <FirstName>Anne</FirstName>
    <LastName>Hathaway</LastName>
    <Country>USA</Country>
  </Contact>
  <Contact>
    <FirstName>Bill</FirstName>
    <LastName>Gates</LastName>
    <Country>USA</Country>
  </Contact>
</Contacts>
```

You'll also get the main result document, `ContactsReport.html`, as shown in Figure 8-9.

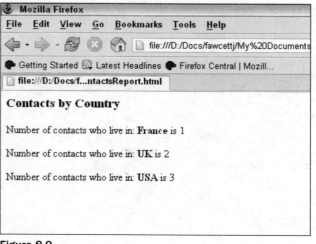

Figure 8-9

The main difference between this and the groupedContacts.xslt is the use of xsl:result-document:

```
<xsl:result-document href="{current-grouping-key()}.xml">
  <!--more code here -->
</xsl:result-document>
```

When the xsl:result-document is encountered, a new document node is constructed and eventually output to a file specified using the href attribute. In this example, the current-grouping-key() function is used to give each file a different name based on the location.

Using curly braces, {}, around an expression in an attribute is known as an Attribute Value Template. *You can use this technique on certain attributes to insert the result of an XPath expression where normally a fixed string would be expected.*

Within the result document, a document element, Contacts, is created' and then all of the current-group is copied in its entirety using the xsl:copy-of instruction:

```
<xsl:result-document href="{current-grouping-key()}.xml">
  <Contacts>
    <xsl:copy-of select="current-group()"/>
  </Contacts>
</xsl:result-document>
```

User-Defined Functions

XPath 2.0 adds the capability to call user-defined functions but has no way of actually defining them. It is up to the host—XSLT or XQuery, for example—to do this. XSLT 2.0 uses a new instruction, xsl:function, to define them.

Suppose you have a simple `orders.xml` document as follows:

```
<Orders CustomerId="abc123">
  <Order OrderId="ord1" OrderDate="2006-09-01">
    <Items>
      <Item ItemId="a1" Quantity="1" ItemPrice="2.00"></Item>
      <Item ItemId="b2" Quantity="1" ItemPrice="3.00"></Item>
      <Item ItemId="c3" Quantity="2" ItemPrice="1.50"></Item>
    </Items>
  </Order>
  <Order OrderId="ord2" OrderDate="2006-10-30">
    <Items>
      <Item ItemId="a1" Quantity="2" ItemPrice="2.00"></Item>
      <Item ItemId="d4" Quantity="2" ItemPrice="1.00"></Item>
      <Item ItemId="e5" Quantity="1" ItemPrice="3.50"></Item>
      <Item ItemId="h8" Quantity="1" ItemPrice="5.00"></Item>
    </Items>
  </Order>
  <Order OrderId="ord3" OrderDate="2006-11-19">
    <Items>
      <Item ItemId="e5" Quantity="3" ItemPrice="3.50"></Item>
      <Item ItemId="f6" Quantity="1" ItemPrice="4.00"></Item>
    </Items>
  </Order>
</Orders>
```

You want to show a summary of all the orders with their dates and totals. You can use some standard XSLT combined with a function that accepts an `Items` node and return the order total. The function is defined so:

```
<xsl:function name="udf:get-order-total" as="xs:double">
  <xsl:param name="items"/>
  <xsl:value-of
select="sum(for $item in $items/Item return $item/@Quantity * $item/@ItemPrice)"/>
</xsl:function>
```

The `name` of the function must be a qualified name; the `udf` prefix shown above is mapped to a URI in the `xsl:stylesheet` element. The return type of the function is specified by the `as` attribute. The function has one parameter, which is referenced as `$items`.

The function then uses one of the new constructs in XPath 2.0, a `for` expression. This states that for each `Item` element, the program will return the `Quantity` multiplied by the `ItemPrice` and return the `sum` of all these values. The full stylesheet, `orderSummary.xslt`, is shown here:

```
<?xml version="1.0" encoding="utf-8"?>
<xsl:stylesheet version="2.0"
    xmlns:xsl="http://www.w3.org/1999/XSL/Transform"
    xmlns:xs="http://www.w3.org/2001/XMLSchema"
    xmlns:udf="http://wrox.com/XSLT/functions">

  <xsl:template match="/">
    <html>
      <body>
```

```
            <h3>Order Summary for Customer
              <xsl:value-of select="Orders/@CustomerId"/>
            </h3>
            <table>
              <thead>
                <tr>
                  <th>Order ID</th>
                  <th>Order Date</th>
                  <th>Order Total</th>
                </tr>
              </thead>
              <tbody>
                <xsl:apply-templates select="Orders/Order">
                  <xsl:sort data-type="number"
                        select="translate(@OrderDate, '-', '')" />
                </xsl:apply-templates>
              </tbody>
            </table>
          </body>
        </html>
      </xsl:template>

      <xsl:template match="Order">
        <tr>
          <td>
            <xsl:value-of select="@OrderId"/>
          </td>
          <td>
            <xsl:value-of select="@OrderDate"/>
          </td>
          <td>
            <xsl:value-of select="udf:get-order-total(Items)"/>
          </td>
        </tr>
      </xsl:template>

      <xsl:function name="udf:get-order-total" as="xs:double">
        <xsl:param name="items"/>
        <xsl:value-of
    select="sum(for $item in $items/Item return $item/@Quantity * $item/@ItemPrice)"/>
      </xsl:function>
    </xsl:stylesheet>
```

xsl:value-of changes

The way xsl:value-of works has changed dramatically in version 2.0. In version 1.0, when a sequence of nodes is used as the select, only the first, converted to a string, was output. In version 2.0, all the nodes are output, separated by a space. Imagine you have the following nodes:

```
<persons>
  <person>Joe</person>
  <person>Peter</person>
  <person>Stephen</person>
</persons>
```

The instruction, assuming the context node is `persons`:

```
<xsl:value-of select="person"/>
```

in version 1.0 produces

```
Joe
```

with the first node converted to a string. In version 2.0, the output would be as follows:

```
Joe Peter Stephen
```

If you want to use a different separator — a comma, for instance — use the following syntax:

```
<xsl:value-of select="person" separator=","/>
```

If you want the same behavior as version 1.0, use a predicate:

```
<xsl:value-of select="person[1]"/>
```

There are many other new features and functions in XSLT 2.0. For a full reference see Michael Kay's *XSLT 2.0*, Third Edition (Wrox, 2004).

Summary

In this chapter, you learned that XML documents can be restructured for data interchange or transformed for presentation using XSLT. An XSLT transformation changes a source tree into a result tree. You saw how an XSLT stylesheet is created and how elements are available to retrieve values from a source tree, copy nodes from the source tree to the result tree, carry out conditional processing, iterate over nodes, and sort nodes. Finally, you learned how the new features in version 2.0 make transforming easier and allow the use of non-XML formats as input.

Exercise Questions

Suggested solutions to these questions can be found in Appendix A.

Question 1

If you need to process a node in the source tree more than once but in different ways each time, what technique does XSLT provide to achieve this?

Question 2

What are the two XSLT elements that provide conditional processing? Describe how the functionality provided by these two elements differs.

Part IV
Databases

XQuery, the XML Query Language

Large amounts of information are now being stored as XML or can be made available as XML from relational and other databases with XML functionality. As the volume of XML-based information increases, the need for a query language to efficiently query and make use of that XML data is obvious. At the time of writing, the W3C, the World Wide Web Consortium, is developing an XML query language called *XQuery*. This chapter introduces you to using XQuery and walks you through several working examples using XQuery's features.

XQuery is likely to become as important in the XML world as SQL has become in the relational database world. In the near future, any self-respecting developer who uses XML will be expected to have at least a basic understanding of XQuery and the skill to use it to carry out frequently used queries. Those who work routinely with large volumes of XML data will be expected to have significant expertise in using XQuery as they create programmatic solutions to XML data-handling business issues.

In this chapter you will learn the following:

❑ Why XQuery was created to complement languages such as SQL and XSLT

❑ How to get started with XQuery using the XQuery tools that are already available

❑ How to query an XML document using XQuery and how to create new elements in the result using element constructors

❑ About the XQuery data model and how to use the different types of expression in XQuery, including the important FLWOR (`for`, `let`, `where`, `order by`, `return`) expressions

❑ How to use some XQuery functions

❑ What further developments are likely in future versions of XQuery, including full-text searching and update functionality

At the time of writing, the specification of XQuery is not yet finalized at the W3C. However, much of the XQuery language is now stable and at the Proposed Recommendation stage. General XQuery information is located at `http://www.w3.org/XML/Query`, including links to each of the several XQuery specification documents.

Why XQuery?

First, let's briefly look at a few of the factors that led to the creation of XQuery at the W3C.

Historical Factors

The expansion in storage of data as XML and the different approaches to storing that XML data — in conventional relational databases that are XML-enabled, in native XML databases, and so on — meant that the ways to access XML data could potentially splinter, with no single language being accepted as *the* XML query language. This would mean that an important advantage of XML, that it can be processed using standard tools, would potentially be lost. The realization that several vendors and experts were working on the development of XML query languages resulted in an effort at the W3C to create a single, standard XML query language, which is now called *XQuery*.

When relational databases became a standard technology for enterprise and desktop databases, the advantages of having a common language for retrieving, inserting, deleting, or updating data in a relational data store were recognized and applied when the Structured Query Language (SQL) was created. Due, perhaps, to intercompany rivalry and the timescale of the development of the SQL standard compared to commercial need, significant differences in how individual relational products implemented SQL developed and still exist. Similar processes to develop distinct XML-targeted query languages were underway but have, in the end, been brought together to support the development of XQuery at the W3C.

Despite these efforts at cooperation, XQuery may still be at risk of suffering partial splintering into proprietary approaches, in part because XQuery 1.0 won't have all the necessary functionality that is needed in an XML query language for an enterprise data-handling system. XQuery 1.0 will be able to query XML data, but will have no functionality to delete, update, or insert XML data. The XQuery Working Group is, of course, well aware of those additional needs but took a pragmatic decision that it is better to get the most commonly used part of an XML query language — the capacity to retrieve data — finished as a W3C Recommendation in a reasonable time frame, rather than attempt to do everything in XQuery 1.0 but risk substantial slippage of the timeline for doing so. The data model used by XQuery has been designed with the future needs for deleting, updating, and inserting in mind, so it is hoped that once development of the XQuery 1.0 specification is complete, users of XQuery shouldn't have to wait too long for an update with the additional functionality just mentioned.

Technical Factors

Storing the huge volumes of business data that are around today in lengthy sequences of Unicode characters as serialized XML documents is probably a very inefficient way to store that data, and retrieval would be difficult, too. Therefore, under the hood, the data that can be made available as XML is likely to be stored in some binary format, whether in an enterprise relational database management system or in a native XML database.

Databases that can store or emit XML data are discussed in Chapter 10.

XQuery is designed primarily around a data model that has the property of being able to be serialized as XML. Therefore, when developing a query language for XML, significant effort was focused on defining a data model appropriate for use in large data stores.

XML data, like any other data stored in large quantity and that typically is at least partially confidential, requires many of the features already available in relational database management systems. For example, indexing of XML data is needed to enable speedy retrieval. Security capabilities are also essential in any real-life scenario.

Current Status

At the time of writing, the XQuery specifications are at Proposal Recommendation status at the W3C. This means that it is unlikely any major changes will be made to the final version; its status offers one final chance for any bugs to be spotted. The *Update* specifications, however, which include insert, update, and delete functionality, are at a *Working Draft* stage. This means that a lot could change before the standard settles down.

Developing XQuery, XSLT 2.0, and XPath 2.0

Work on XSLT 1.0 and on the predecessor prototypes for XQuery started as separate processes. The background of XSLT, and of XPath, is in document processing. The historical background of XQuery is in querying databases. Of course, XML can express both documents and data, a notion often expressed by referring to document-centric XML and data-centric XML. When the various efforts started, the extent of the potential for common ground in querying document-centric XML and data-centric XML was very likely not fully appreciated.

In the XSLT 1.0 specification, it was specifically stated that XSLT was not intended as a general-purpose transformation language. Therefore, several potentially useful features were not included in XSLT 1.0, and XSLT was targeted primarily at producing result documents for human consumption. It was reasonable that the XSLT processing should attempt to produce some output, rather than fail completely if a source document wasn't structured quite as expected. Because at that time it was often assumed that XSLT processing would be carried out on the client side, it was rightly assumed that it would be inappropriate to deliver some error message to an end-user who had no control over the stylesheet producing the error.

Because of the refusal to attempt a general-purpose transformation language, some potentially useful functionality such as strong math support and text manipulation did not feature in XSLT 1.0. Developers of XSLT might also plausibly have been assumed to be working with XML, using XML tools, and so would be comfortable using a language expressed in XML. Therefore, a language expressed in XML made a lot of sense.

The background to the need for XQuery differed significantly. XQuery was intended for retrieval of data from large collections of XML documents, in contrast to the common scenario in which XSLT is used to process a single source XML document or a small number of XML documents. Unlike source documents to be processed by XSLT, the XML to be processed by XQuery would be unlikely to be held in memory at one time; single documents or collections of documents would be simply too large to allow a Document

Object Model (DOM) tree to be constructed in memory. The large size of XML documents to be queried increased the importance of optimizing queries, including indexing of the XML to be queried. Potential users of XQuery would likely come from a database background where they would expect document structure to be defined by a schema, in contrast to the relatively permissive approach accepted when using XSLT to process document-centric XML. Error handling would appropriately be rigorous in the context of a large data store and so error handling is much stricter in XQuery than it was in XSLT 1.0.

As you can probably appreciate, despite the differences highlighted, there is considerable overlap in what the two initially separate communities wanted to do with XML using XSLT and XQuery, respectively. Both XSLT and XQuery have XML as input, create a result that takes nodes from the source XML tree(s), and combine and filter the source, often adding arbitrary literal content (supplied either statically or dynamically) to the result. Both XSLT and XQuery provide a library of functions (much more extensive in XSLT 2.0 than XSLT 1.0) and allow the creation of user-defined functions. Both languages allow nested iteration — using the xsl:for-each element in XSLT and the FLWOR expression (described later in this chapter) in XQuery. Both XSLT and XQuery take a similar approach to variables, in that the value of variables may not be changed once the variable is created, a characteristic that many newcomers to XSLT find surprising. Both XSLT and XQuery are declarative functional languages without a full assignment statement, although XQuery does have a limited assignmentlike let clause available.

Given a different history, it is quite possible that only one XML query language, rather than two, would have been developed at the W3C. Even had that been the case, sufficient flexibility to accommodate the differing emphases described previously would likely have been necessary.

Using XSLT and XQuery

XSLT is probably used most for converting XML documents to HTML (and to a lesser extent XHTML) for display. XSLT is also used to create other XML-based presentation formats such as Scalable Vector Graphics (SVG), which is described in Chapter 19. The final part of XSLT is in the conversion of one XML document structure to another XML document structure in business-to-business (B2B) transactions. It seems likely that the latter usage will continue to increase significantly. XSLT 2.0 also adds the capability to transform non-XML formats, so as version 2.0 becomes more established this facility will lead to even further uptake.

XQuery, on the other hand, will likely be used more in querying databases, a task that can be accomplished using XSLT (at least where the data is exposed as XML) but may most appropriately be carried out using XQuery. The practical needs associated with using XQuery mean that it is likely to be used either in an enterprise-level database management system or programmatically using C#, Java, or a similar programming language. The absence of XML syntax in XQuery makes it easier to use XQuery with other programming languages. An alternative XML-based syntax for XQuery, named XQueryX, is under development and has reached *Proposed Recommendation* status, but it is very verbose and initial uptake looks likely to be slow.

Comparing XSLT, XPath, and XQuery

XSLT is written using XML syntax. By contrast, XQuery uses a non-XML syntax. The fact that XSLT stylesheets are written in XML means that XSLT stylesheets can be generated by or modified by XML tools, including other XSLT stylesheets. Such use of XSLT isn't uncommon in large-scale programs. XQuery cannot be sculpted using such tools because it uses a non-XML syntax.

Both XSLT and XQuery can be used to add nodes to a result tree and they both require XPath as a means to select nodes to process. The roles of the two languages can be broadly summarized as follows: XPath selects nodes from a source tree (which models an XML document), and XSLT causes nodes to be added to a result tree. Similarly, much of XQuery depends on its XPath 2.0 subset.

There are some similarities between the two approaches. In XSLT the value of some attributes is an *attribute value template*, which is an expression enclosed in paired curly brackets. This resembles the syntax used in XQuery for expressions. For example, the code

```
<a href="{@URL}">Click for further information</a>
```

can be written in both XSLT and XQuery. The paired curly brackets are used in XSLT to indicate an attribute value template. In XQuery, paired curly brackets enclose an XQuery expression. In XQuery it is possible to nest expressions, which, given the XML syntax limitations of XSLT, is not possible in XSLT.

XPath 1.0 has been adapted in version 2.0 to form a subset of XQuery 1.0. The use of XPath 2.0 to select nodes in XQuery is not surprising because XQuery needs to carry out similar retrieval of specified XML data. You will see in a moment that you can use XPath expressions in XQuery to retrieve nodes. In XQuery the retrieved nodes (and, if present, the values that are also allowed) are called a *sequence*, rather than the XPath 1.0 term, *node-set*.

XQuery Tools

Despite the fact that XQuery is still relatively new, a large number of software companies and independent developers have developed partial or more complete implementations of XQuery. The proliferation of XQuery tools indicates that many software vendors see XQuery as an important XML standard with significant commercial potential.

On an ongoing basis, the W3C updates a web page where links to XQuery implementations and other sources of useful XQuery information are included. Visit www.w3.org/XML/Query and follow the link to Products to explore XQuery implementations.

> *Because, at the time of writing, XQuery has not been finalized, none of the prototype XQuery tools can yet be finalized. Tools are being updated on different schedules, with some prototypes now being visibly outdated (at least in publicly available versions) compared to the most recent XQuery draft specification documents.*

The examples in this chapter use the Saxon XQuery engine, which is a free and very up-to-date implementation of XQuery. The creator of Saxon, Michael Kay, is a member of the working groups that are creating XQuery, XPath 2.0, and XSLT 2.0. Therefore, Saxon is typically among the most up-to-date implementations, with the latest release normally passing all the W3C's test cases.

Saxon

If you chose to download Saxon version 8.8 in Chapter 8, then you are well placed to process XQuery queries. If not, then to use Saxon to process XQuery queries, visit http://saxon.sourceforge.net/ again and look for the currently available versions of Saxon that support XQuery. Versions after Saxon 7.6 have some XQuery support. At the time of writing, Saxon 8.8 is the latest version and has full XQuery functionality.

If necessary, first install the Saxon processor, following the instructions given in Chapter 8. To test whether Saxon XQuery functionality is present, type the following at the command line:

```
java net.sf.saxon.Query -?
```

If you are using the .NET version, enter this:

```
Query -?
```

If everything is working correctly, then you should see a screen detailing various options, as shown in Figure 9-1.

Figure 9-1

Remember that Java is case sensitive; accidentally typing an incorrect uppercase or lowercase character on the command line will likely lead to an error message when `java.exe` *runs.*

If you used Saxon in Chapter 8 to carry out XSLT transformations, you will notice that the command-line syntax to access Saxon's XQuery functionality is significantly different from the syntax used when using XSLT.

Saxon comes with extensive help files. Typically, installation of Saxon creates a `doc` directory, which includes several HTML help files. Look for a file labeled `using-xquery.html`, or something similar, and check the latest information about which parts of XQuery are supported.

Several other online XQuery demos are available, and several other products or prototypes support XQuery. Some are mentioned in the following sections.

X-Hive.com Online

You can find a very user-friendly XQuery demonstration online at `www.x-hive.com/xquery/`. An example query and its result are shown in Figure 9-2. You can use one of the pre-built queries that were used in the XQuery use cases document or edit them to test your increasing understanding of XQuery; the results, or, if you get things wrong, lengthy Java error messages, are displayed in the right panel. If you get the syntax hopelessly wrong as you try to adapt existing queries, then you can restore a query with correct syntax simply by reselecting it from a drop-down list.

Figure 9-2

At the time of this book's writing, the X-Hive online demo had not been updated for some time and bases its syntax on the April 2005 Working Draft, rather than the newer specifications. Therefore, some minor differences exist between it and the latest XQuery draft. Nonetheless, it offers a very nice interactive interface to explore the creation of XQuery queries.

X-Hive Database

The X-Hive database that underpins the X-Hive.com database also supports XQuery. Further information is located at `www.x-hive.com`.

Tamino Database

You can find an online demo of XQuery using Software AG's Tamino database located at `http://tamino.demozone.softwareag.com/demoXQuery/XQueryDemo/index.jsp`. Tamino was one of the first commercial products to support XQuery and is used in many successful XML applications.

Microsoft SQL Server 2005

Microsoft's enterprise relational database management system, SQL Server, includes XQuery support starting in version 2005. It supports a useful working subset of the whole specification and adds extensions for updates and deletes in advance of the W3C finalizing its recommendation. There are examples of XQuery specific to SQL Server 2005 in Chapter 10. You can find more details about SQL Server 2005 and plans for the next version, code-named Katmai, at `www.microsoft.com/sql/`.

Oracle

Oracle is also working on XQuery support for its database products. You can find more information on XQuery and a downloadable demo available for the Oracle database at `www.oracle.com/technology/tech/xml/xquery/index.html`. If the preceding URL is not available when you are reading this chapter, then visit `http://otn.oracle.com/` and insert XQuery in the Search text box to find the current information about XQuery in Oracle.

> *The implementations mentioned in the preceding sections are only a few of many. Visit* `www.w3.org/XML/Query` *to check for further implementations and for links to current information about them.*

Let's now move on to run some simple XQuery examples so that you begin to have a feel for what XQuery queries look like.

Some XQuery Examples

Saxon can run XQuery queries from Java or .NET applications, but for the purposes of this chapter we will run queries from the command line. One difference between the Saxon syntax for XSLT processing and for XQuery processing is that the location of the XML document to be queried is not specified on the command line. Rather, it is specified using one of XQuery's input functions.

Input Functions

At the time of writing, the XQuery input functions are the `doc()` function and the `collection()` function, and both are implemented in Saxon 8.8.

The doc() Function

The doc() function is used to specify the XML document that you want to query. To demonstrate basic XQuery functionality, you will query the following simple XML document, SimpleBooks.xml. It is used here and later in the chapter as a source XML document:

```
<?xml version="1.0"?>
<Books>
  <Book>Beginning XML, 4th Edition</Book>
  <Book>Beginning XML Databases</Book>
  <Book>Professional Web 2.0 Programming</Book>
</Books>
```

For convenience, we will specify XQuery queries in documents with a .xquery suffix, but you can use another suffix if you prefer. Using Saxon from the command line, you simply specify the filename that contains the XQuery query.

The first query you will run is contained in the file SimpleBooks.xquery, and contains the following single line of code:

```
doc("SimpleBooks.xml")/Books/Book
```

The query consists of the doc() function, whose single string argument specifies that the XML document SimpleBooks.xml is to be used as the source document for the query. The remaining part of the query should remind you of XPath location paths that you were introduced to in Chapter 7, because that is exactly what they are. Recall that XPath 2.0 is a subset of XQuery. The expression /Books/Book is an XQuery expression that could also be an XPath 2.0 expression — the syntax and semantics are the same in both XQuery and XPath 2.0. This means that you can apply your understanding of XPath, gained in Chapter 7, to some parts of XQuery syntax.

The expression is evaluated from left to right. The initial / character indicates that evaluation starts at the document node of SimpleBooks.xml, that a Books element node (there can be only one element node child of the document node in a well-formed XML document) that is a child node of the document node is selected, and then using that node as context, its Book child element node(s) are selected.

The XQuery doc() function is similar to the XSLT document() function. The doc() function returns a single document. The document() function processes a sequence of URIs, enabling multiple XML documents to be processed.

To have Saxon run the query and display the output to the command window, enter

```
java net.sf.saxon.Query SimpleBooks.xquery
```

or, if using the .NET version, enter

```
Query SimpleBooks.xquery
```

at the command line.

From this point on, only the Java version will be shown for command-line execution.

The filename SimpleBooks.xquery is supplied to the Saxon XQuery processor. The output of the query is shown in Figure 9-3.

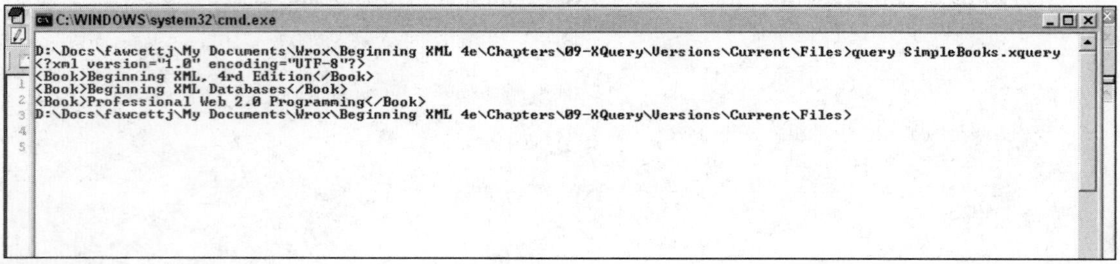

Figure 9-3

Notice that an XML declaration is output to the command window, followed by three Book elements and their text content. That behavior occurs because all XQuery queries return a *sequence* of *items*. Each Book element node selected by the XPath expression /Books/Book is in the sequence returned by the query. Notice how the result is only a document fragment; it's not a full XML document because it lacks a root element.

The collection() Function

The collection() function is used to process several XML documents at one time. The collection() function takes as its argument a string that is an xsd:anyURI value. The collection() function can be used to access a collection of nodes in a database or to process all files in a specified folder.

Because you are primarily using individual XML documents as the target of queries in this chapter, you will focus on the use of the doc() function.

Retrieving Nodes

As you have seen, in XQuery you can retrieve nodes in a fairly straightforward way using XPath expressions. However, XQuery 1.0 has a few limitations when compared to XPath. All XQuery processors lack the XPath namespace axis. In addition, some XQuery processors lack support for the following XPath axes:

❑ ancestor

❑ ancestor-or-self

❑ following

❑ following-sibling

❑ preceding

❑ preceding-sibling

XQuery implementations that support the preceding axes are said to support the *full-axis feature*, but even those XQuery processors are not "full" in a certain sense, because the namespace axis is not supported.

Those that do not support the full-axis feature are still following the recommendations and support the other axes, and, optionally, some of the axes on the preceding list.

The decision in XQuery, at least as currently drafted, to drop these axes seems to have arisen from a difference in view between those familiar with XPath and those who think more in terms of relational databases. In any case, unless later drafts reverse the situation, it will be necessary to accept the absence of the axes mentioned in some XQuery processors and code accordingly.

Try It Out   Retrieving Nodes

This exercise carries out some queries using a source XML document adapted from the W3C's use case sample data. It is shown here and contained in the file `BibAdapted.xml`.

1. The following data will be used as the source XML in several example queries:

```xml
<?xml version="1.0"?>
<bib>
 <book year="1988">
  <title>The C Programming Language</title>
  <author><last>Kernighan</last><first>Brian</first></author>
  <author><last>Ritchie</last><first>Dennis</first></author>
  <publisher>Prentice Hall</publisher>
  <price> 44.20</price>
 </book>

 <book year="2004">
  <title>XSLT 2.0 Programmer's Reference</title>
  <author><last>Kay</last><first>Michael</first></author>
  <publisher>Wrox Press</publisher>
  <price>39.99</price>
 </book>

 <book year="2006">
  <title>Professional Web 2.0 Programming</title>
  <author><last>van der Vlist</last><first>Eric</first></author>
  <author><last>Ayers</last><first>Danny</first></author>
  <author><last>Bruchez</last><first>Eric</first></author>
  <author><last>Vernet</last><first>Alessandro</first></author>
  <author><last>Fawcett</last><first>Joe</first></author>
  <publisher>Wrox Press</publisher>
  <price>39.99</price>
 </book>

 <book year="2002">
  <title>The Economics of Technology and Content for Digital TV</title>
  <editor>
   <last>Gerbarg</last><first>Darcy</first>
   <affiliation>CITI</affiliation>
  </editor>
  <publisher>Kluwer Academic Publishers</publisher>
  <price>129.95</price>
 </book>

<book year="2004">
  <title>Beginning XML, 4th Edition</title>
```

```
<author><last>Hunter</last><first>David</first></author>
<author><last>Watt</last><first>Andrew</first></author>
<author><last>Rafter</last><first>Jeff</first></author>
<author><last>Cagle</last><first></first>Kurt</author>
<author><last>Duckett</last><first>John</first></author>
<author><last>Fawcett</last><first>Joe</first></author>

<publisher>Wrox Press</publisher>
<price>TBA</price>
</book>

</bib>
```

As you can see, the document element is a `bib` element, inside of which are nested several `book` elements, each of which has some basic data such as year of publication and authors or editors.

2. Select all book elements in `BibAdapted.xml` using the following query, which is contained in the file `BibQuery1.xquery`:

```
doc("BibAdapted.xml")/bib/book
```

3. Send the result of the query to an output file `BibQuery1Out.xml` by typing the following at the command line:

```
java net.sf.saxon.Query -o BibQuery1Out.xml BibQuery1.xquery
```

Notice that the name of the output file is specified by the `-o` switch followed by the output filename, before the name of the file that contains the XQuery query. Part of that result document is shown here in `BibQuery1Out.xml` (trimmed to reduce page length, only two of the five `book` elements are shown):

```
<?xml version="1.0" encoding="UTF-8"?>
<book year="1988">
   <title>The C Programming Language</title>
   <author>
       <last>Kernighan</last>
       <first>Brian</first>
   </author>
   <author>
       <last>Ritchie</last>
       <first>Dennis</first>
   </author>
   <publisher>Prentice Hall</publisher>
   <price> 44.20</price>
</book>

<!-- other books removed -->

<book year="2004">
   <title>Beginning XML, 4th Edition</title>
   <author>
       <last>Ayers</last>
       <first>Danny</first>
   </author>
   <author>
       <last>Watt</last>
```

```
    <first>Andrew</first>
  </author>
<author>
    <last>Rafter</last>
    <first>Jeff</first>
  </author>
<author>
    <last>van der Vlist</last>
    <first/>Eric</author>
<author>
    <last>Duckett</last>
    <first>John</first>
  </author>
<author>
    <last>Fawcett</last>
    <first>Joe</first>
  </author>
<publisher>Wrox Press</publisher>
<price>TBA</price>

</book>
```

How It Works

One important thing to observe here is that XQuery can output a document that is not well-formed XML. Notice there is no single document element in `BibQuery1Out.xml`.

This contrasts with XSLT, which (assuming you use the `xml` output method) will not let you create a stylesheet to output markup that is not well formed. In XQuery the responsibility of producing well-formed XML lies very much with the creator of the query.

Creating a well-formed result in this case is straightforward. You simply add an element constructor to the query and ensure that the XQuery expression is nested inside it. Let's introduce element constructors and look at how they are used.

Element Constructors

In XSLT, new elements can be added to the result document using *literal result elements*. In XQuery you can similarly create new XML elements by including literal start-tags and end-tags in appropriate places in the XQuery query.

A very simple example of using an element constructor is the following query, which is contained in the file `SimpleBooks2.xquery`:

```
<Books>
{doc("SimpleBooks.xml")/Books/Book}
</Books>
```

The element constructor has a literal start-tag for a `Books` element, followed by the expression shown earlier that retrieves `Book` element nodes from the file `SimpleBooks.xml`. Then, after all the selected `Book` element nodes have been found, it adds a literal end-tag for the `Books` element.

To display the output to the command window, you can enter the following at the command line:

```
java net.sf.saxon.Query -o SimpleBooks2Out.xml SimpleBooks2.xquery
```

The output file, SimpleBooks2Out.xml, is shown here:

```
<?xml version="1.0" encoding="UTF-8"?>
<Books>
    <Book>Beginning XML, 4rd Edition</Book>
    <Book>Beginning XML Databases</Book>
    <Book>Professional Web 2.0 Programming</Book></Books>
```

Notice that in the preceding query the XQuery expression doc("SimpleBooks.xml")/Books/Book is contained inside paired curly brackets. If you omit the paired curly brackets, then the XPath expression is treated as text. The XPath expression is displayed literally. The output document when you make that error is SimpleBooks2WRONGOut.xml, shown here:

```
<?xml version="1.0" encoding="UTF-8"?>
<Books>
doc("SimpleBooks.xml")/Books/Book&#xD;
</Books>
```

You can create well-formed XML from the BibAdapted.xml file using the following query:

```
<myNewBib>{
doc("BibAdapted.xml")/bib/book}</myNewBib>
```

This appears in the code downloads as BibQuery2.xquery. The query creates the start-tag for a new element named myNewBib, uses an XQuery expression similar to those you have used before to select all the book elements, and then outputs the end-tag of the newly created myNewBib element.

The output document, BibQuery2Out.xml (trimmed for presentation) is shown here:

```
<?xml version="1.0" encoding="UTF-8"?>
 <?xml version="1.0" encoding="UTF-8"?>
<myNewBib>
    <book year="1988">
        <title>The C Programming Language</title>
        <author>
            <last>Kernighan</last>
            <first>Brian</first>
        </author>
        <author>
            <last>Ritchie</last>
            <first>Dennis</first>
        </author>
        <publisher>Prentice Hall</publisher>
        <price> 44.20</price>
    </book>

    <!-- other books removed -->

    <book year="2004">
```

```
      <title>Beginning XML, 4th Edition</title>
      <author>
          <last>Ayers</last>
          <first>Danny</first>
      </author>
      <author>
          <last>Watt</last>
          <first>Andrew</first>
      </author>
      <author>
          <last>Rafter</last>
          <first>Jeff</first>
      </author>
      <author>
          <last>van der Vlist</last>
          <first/>Eric</author>
      <author>
          <last>Duckett</last>
          <first>John</first>
      </author>
      <author>
          <last>Fawcett</last>
          <first>Joe</first>
      </author>
      <publisher>Wrox Press</publisher>
      <price>TBA</price>
    </book>
  </myNewBib>
```

Up to this point, you have used simple XPath expressions to output content based only on the structure of the source XML. In practice, you will want to manipulate or filter that XML in various ways. One option is simply to filter using an XPath *predicate*.

> *A predicate in XPath filters a sequence by limiting its elements to those where the predicate is true. The predicate is placed between square brackets. For example:*

```
//Chapter[@status = 'approved']
```

> *selects only those* Chapter *elements that have their* status *attribute set to* approved.

You can use XPath predicates in an XQuery query, as in the following code:

```
<myNewBib>{
doc("BibAdapted.xml")/bib/book[@year > 2005]
}</myNewBib>
```

This is contained in the file BibQuery3.xquery. The predicate [@year >2005] tests whether the value of the year attribute of a book element in BibAdapted.xml is greater than 2005; if it is, then that book element is selected and, together with its content, output.

That query filters out all but one book in BibAdapted.xml, and the output it produces, in BibQuery3Out.xml, is shown here:

```xml
<?xml version="1.0" encoding="UTF-8"?>
<myNewBib>
    <book year="2006">
        <title>Professional Web 2.0 Programming</title>
        <author>
            <last>van der Vlist</last>
            <first>Eric</first>
        </author>
        <author>
            <last>Ayers</last>
            <first>Danny</first>
        </author>
        <author>
            <last>Fawcett</last>
            <first>Joe</first>
        </author>
        <author>
            <last>Vernet</last>
            <first>Alessandro</first>
        </author>
        <publisher>Wrox Press</publisher>
        <price>39.99</price>
    </book>
    <book year="2007">
        <title>Beginning XML, 4th Edition</title>
        <author>
            <last>Ayers</last>
            <first>Danny</first>
        </author>
        <author>
            <last>Watt</last>
            <first>Andrew</first>
        </author>
        <author>
            <last>Rafter</last>
            <first>Jeff</first>
        </author>
        <author>
            <last>van der Vlist</last>
            <first/>Eric</author>
        <author>
            <last>Duckett</last>
            <first>John</first>
        </author>
        <author>
            <last>Fawcett</last>
            <first>Joe</first>
        </author>
        <publisher>Wrox Press</publisher>
        <price>TBA</price>
    </book>

</myNewBib>
```

As you can see, even a very simple answer like this can take up quite a bit of space. Whitespace in XML documents has always been a bone of contention between the data-centric developers and the document-centric ones. In general, those who use XML as a way of passing data like to ignore insignificant whitespace such as newlines between the end-tag of one element and the start-tag of the next. Those who use XML to mark up documents like to preserve all whitespace, so XQuery allows control of whitespace in the *prolog* of an XQuery query, described next.

The XQuery Prolog

The *prolog* of an XQuery document is used to provide the XQuery processor with pieces of information that might be necessary for correct processing of a query. The prolog is written before the main part of an XQuery query.

Strictly speaking, the version declaration and module declaration come before the prolog proper, but most developers are likely to treat them as effectively part of the prolog. The important thing to remember is the following order:

1. The *version declaration*, if present, must always come first.
2. Next is the *module declaration* (if there is one).
3. Then comes the rest of the prolog.

The XQuery Version Declaration

You might want to first specify the version of XQuery being used. It is optional, but if it is present, then it must come first. At the time of writing, that requirement is rather superfluous because only a single version — version 1.0 — exists, but after a version of XQuery with update and other functionality is added, other XQuery versions are likely to be available.

To specify that the query is XQuery 1.0, use the following code:

```
xquery version "1.0";
```

Notice the `xquery` keyword (all lowercase), followed by `version`, and then the version number as a string contained in paired quotes or paired apostrophes. The declaration is completed by a semicolon character. Unlike XML, there is no = character between `version` and the version number. If you are used to writing XML code, that's an easy mistake to make.

XQuery Modules

XQuery queries may consist of one or more modules. The examples in this chapter consist of a single module, but reuse of XQuery code is likely to be common in the construction of complex queries.

The prolog of an XQuery module contains the following declaration:

```
module namespace WROX = "http://www.wrox.com/XQuery/Books";
```

The `module` declaration identifies the module as a library module. In the preceding declaration, the namespace prefix `WROX` is associated with the Uniform Resource Identifier (URI) `http://www.wrox.com/XQuery/Books`. An XQuery module declaration is similar to an XML namespace declaration in that a namespace prefix is associated with a namespace URI. In a library module, as in standalone XQuery documents, the version declaration, if present, comes first, and then the module declaration precedes the rest of the prolog.

XQuery Prolog Continued

Having looked at the version declaration and module declaration, the remaining prolog items can be examined. These can be written in any convenient order.

The base-uri Declaration

URIs can be relative or absolute. Relative URIs are resolved in relation to a base URI. The `base-uri` is declared in XQuery using the `base-uri` declaration, similar to the following:

```
declare base-uri "http://someRelevantURI.com";
```

This means that if you specify a file location as `myFile.xml` — for example, as an argument to a `doc()` function such as `doc("myFile.xml")` — the XQuery processor will try to retrieve it from `http://someRelevantURI.com/myFile.xml`.

The namespace Declaration

Also included in the prolog are the relevant namespace declarations. For example, in an XQuery that is creating output that includes elements that are namespace qualified, it is necessary to declare the namespace to which those elements belong. Like an XML namespace declaration, an XQuery namespace declaration associates a namespace prefix with a namespace URI. If you intended to use XQuery to create an XSLT stylesheet, you might include a namespace declaration like this:

```
declare namespace xsl = "http://www.w3.org/1999/XSL/Transform"
```

Later, in the body of the query, you might see the following:

```
<xsl:stylesheet version = "1.0" xmlns:xsl="http://www.w3.org/1999/XSL/Transform">
```

This indicates the start of an XSLT 1.0 stylesheet.

Default namespace Declarations

Any default namespace declarations are also included in the prolog. For convenience, you may want to write element or function names without a namespace prefix. This is done using the default namespace declarations.

To declare a default namespace for elements, use the following syntax:

```
declare default element namespace "http://someRelevantURI.com"
```

To declare a default namespace for functions, use this syntax:

```
declare default function namespace "http://someRelevantURI.com"
```

Schema Imports

You may want to have access to element, attribute, or type definitions from a particular schema; this too is expressed in the prolog. This schema can be imported using the following syntax:

```
import schema namespace xhtml = "http://www.w3.org/1999/xhtml"
```

This imports the schema for an XHTML document. If you want to specify a URL at which the schema is located, you can use a schema import of the following type:

```
import schema namespace xhtml = "http://www.w3.org/1999/xhtml"
at "http://ActualSchemaLocation.com/xhtml.xsd"
```

This specifies a URL from which the schema can be accessed.

Variable Declarations

You may want to declare XQuery variables. If so, that too is done in the prolog. To declare a variable $seven and specify that its value is the integer 7, you can use the following syntax:

```
declare variable $seven as xs:integer :=7;
```

You could also omit the type; if you do this the processor will try to infer the type from the expression used to initialize it (in the preceding example, 7):

```
declare variable $seven :=7;
```

You can also declare a variable that will be set externally by the processor before the XQuery runs:

```
declare variable $seven as xs:integer external;
```

The xs prefix is automatically bound to the XML Schema namespace of http://www.w3.org/2001/XMLSchema.

How an external variable is set depends on the XQuery implementation. It might be from a command-line parameter, as is the case for Saxon, by reading an external file or using an environment variable.

Validation Declaration

You may also want to specify in the prolog how validation is to be carried out. Permitted values are lax, skip, or strict. To specify strict validation, you can write a validation declaration like this:

```
declare validation strict;
```

The boundary-space Declaration

One of the prolog's declarations indicates whether to strip or preserve whitespace, as shown in the following query, BibQuery4.xquery:

```
xquery version "1.0";
declare boundary-space strip;
(: The above line is the XQuery way to strip whitespace :)
```

```
<myNewBib>{
doc("BibAdapted.xml")/bib/book[@year>2002]
}</myNewBib>
```

Whitespace in XQuery is handled a little differently from whitespace in XML. In XQuery the concept of *boundary whitespace* indicates whitespace that occurs at the boundaries of elements (before the start-tag or after the end-tag) or expressions. Such boundary whitespace can be useful in laying out complex queries neatly. If you want to strip extraneous boundary whitespace, you can use the construct shown in the second line of the preceding code.

Also shown here is the XQuery way of writing comments, which is discussed a bit later in the chapter.

At the time of this writing, Saxon seems to ignore the declaration to strip boundary whitespace using the syntax just shown. If you want to explicitly specify that boundary whitespace be preserved, use the following construct:

```
declare boundary-space preserve;
```

You saw earlier how to use element constructors to add XML elements literally to the output of a query. Now take a look at how to create computed constructors.

Computed Constructors

In earlier examples you saw how literal start-tags and end-tags can be used to construct elements in the result of a query. Another syntax allows elements and attributes to be constructed at runtime.

Now you'll create a simple library using element and attribute constructors. For clarity, you will use string literals to provide the values of the created attributes and elements. Of course, you can substitute any arbitrary XQuery expression in place of the string literals to achieve similar but more complex things. The query, Library.xquery, is shown here:

```
element library{
 element book {
  attribute year {2007},
  element title {
   "Beginning XML, 4thEdition"
   }
  },
 element book {
  attribute year {2006},
  element title {
   "Beginning XML Databases"
   }
  },
 element book {
  attribute year {2006},
  element title {
   "Professional Web 2.0 Programming"
   }
 }

}
```

The `library` element, which is the document element of the output XML document, is created using the following construct:

```
element library {
  ...
}
```

All attributes and descendants are created inside that construct.

When creating a single child element of the `library` element, the `book` element, a similar syntax is followed:

```
element book {
  attribute year {2004},
  element title {
   "Beginning XML,4th Edition"
   }
  }
```

Any attributes that belong to the `book` element are specified first, using a comma as the separator between attribute specifications. Then any child elements of the `book` element are added in the order in which they are to be included in the output document.

If you have a sequence of elements to be constructed, then a comma is added after the relevant closing curly bracket.

The output document, `LibraryOut.xml`, is shown here:

```
<?xml version="1.0" encoding="UTF-8"?>
<library>
   <book year="2007">
      <title>Beginning XML, 4th Edition</title>
   </book>
   <book year="2006">
      <title>Beginning Beginning XML Databases</title>
   </book>
   <book year="2006">
      <title>Professional Web 2.0 Programming</title>
   </book></library>
```

When creating queries of this type, once you get beyond fairly simple queries, such as the preceding one, it is very easy to make mistakes by failing to correctly pair up curly braces or omitting the crucial comma that separates attributes and child elements. If you make such basic mistakes in long queries, you will most likely receive several error messages—due, for example, to omitting a single comma fairly early in the query. The best way to avoid such errors is to create the elements and attributes from the outside in, pairing up curly brackets as you add an element or attribute.

Syntax

The following two sections briefly introduce a couple of aspects of XQuery syntax of which you need to be aware when writing XQuery code.

XQuery Comments

In XQuery, comments are written using scowling and smiley faces to start and end the comment, respectively:

```
(: After the scowl, we smile when the comment ends. :)
```

This notation is used only to define comments inside the query. Unlike HTML comments, for example, it is permissible to nest XQuery comments, which can be useful when using comments to comment out suspect code when debugging by hand.

No syntax to create a "to end of line" comment, equivalent to the // notation in JavaScript, for example, exists in XQuery.

Delimiting Strings

Strings in XQuery are delimited by paired double quotes or by paired apostrophes, as shown in the example that created elements and supplied their content as string literals. For example, a Paragraph element with text content can be written in either of the two following ways:

```
element Paragraph {
"Some content contained in paired double quotes"
}
```

or

```
element Paragraph {
 'Some content contained in paired apostrophes.'
}
```

The XQuery Data Model

The XQuery data model is significantly different from the XPath 1.0 data model to which you were introduced in Chapter 7, but it also has similarities to the XPath 1.0 data model.

Shared Data Model with XPath 2.0 and XSLT 2.0

The XQuery data model and XPath 2.0 and XSLT 2.0 data models are the same, so once you have learned the data model for one of these technologies, you know the foundations of the other two. Chapter 8 mentioned that XSLT transformations use a source tree as input to a transformation. Similarly, all XQuery queries use an instance of the XQuery data model as input, and another instance of the data model as output. Each of those instances of the data model is represented as a treelike hierarchy broadly similar to an XSLT source tree.

Many parts of an XML document can be represented by nodes in the XQuery data model. Let's move on to look briefly at each of the nodes available in XQuery.

Node Kinds

Node kinds in XQuery are similar to the types of node available in XPath 1.0. The one notable change is that the root node of XPath 1.0 is replaced by the document node in XQuery 1.0. The XQuery 1.0 node kinds are document, element, attribute, namespace, text, comment, and processing instruction. Each node represents the corresponding part of an XML document indicated by its name. Every XQuery node has identity that distinguishes it from all other nodes, including nodes with the same name and content.

Sequences of Node-Sets

In XQuery, the XPath 1.0 node-set is replaced by a sequence. A *sequence* can contain nodes or atomic values or a mixture of nodes and atomic values. The term *item* is the collective term in XQuery for nodes and atomic values. An atomic value corresponds to a W3C XML Schema `simple-Type`.

Sequences are written inside paired parentheses, and items are separated by commas. Sequences cannot be nested, so the sequence

```
(1,2, (3, 4, 5), 6)
```

is equivalent to writing

```
(1, 2, 3, 4, 5, 6)
```

Document Order

In XQuery, all nodes created when parsing an XML document are in an order called *document order*. Attributes associated with an element are considered to occur after the element in document order and before any child elements. The actual order of the attributes is considered irrelevant by the XML Infoset so you cannot rely on position to select an attribute, nor can you guarantee ordering in the output.

Comparing Items and Nodes

The XQuery data model generalizes the idea of a node-set that was present in XPath 1.0. In XQuery, the result of an expression is a sequence. A sequence can include nodes (just like XPath 1.0) but can also include atomic values.

Types in XQuery

In XQuery, the W3C XML Schema type system is used. Chapter 5 introduced W3C XML Schema types.

Axes in XQuery

As mentioned earlier in the chapter, XQuery processors do not support the XPath `namespace` axis. Only XQuery processors that support the full-axis feature support processing of the `ancestor`, `ancestor-or-self`, `following`, `following-sibling`, `preceding` or `preceding-sibling` axes. All XQuery processors support the `child`, `parent`, `descendant`, or `descendant-or-self` axes.

XQuery Expressions

As mentioned earlier, XQuery expressions include XPath expressions, which tend to principally focus on path expressions. However, XQuery adds a rich feature set on top of the XPath functionality. The FLWOR expression adds significant power to queries that cannot be expressed by traditional XPath path expressions.

FLWOR Expressions

The FLWOR expression is a pivotal part of XQuery's power. It owes much to the SELECT statement in SQL. A FLWOR expression binds variables to sequences of values in the for and let clauses and then uses those variables in the construction of the output of the query. Because binding is an essential part of a FLWOR expression, every FLWOR expression must have either a for clause or a let clause, and many FLWOR expressions have both.

The first four components of FLWOR can be expressed in XSLT using, respectively, the xsl:for-each, xsl:variable, xsl:if, and xsl:sort elements to produce similar results. Therefore, many XQuery FLOWR expressions can be expressed in XSLT with very similar semantics.

If you make the error of using the wrong case for any of the keywords for, let, where, order by, and return, you can expect to get some very puzzling error messages from the Saxon XQuery processor, perhaps mentioning odd characters beyond the end of the query. For example, if you use uppercase FOR instead of the correct lowercase for, then among the error messages you are likely to get is an indication that a variable is undeclared, as any variable declared in the for statement in which you mistakenly used uppercase FOR is not recognized as having been declared. If you see mention of an undeclared variable, then it is worth checking the case of either for or let in your query, as for clauses bind multiple variables and let clauses bind single variables; a case error would lead to the relevant variable or variables not being bound. However, other XQuery processors, or indeed later versions of Saxon, may give more informative error messages.

for Expressions

One version of the for expression is the for ... in expression, as shown in ForIn.xquery:

```
<items>
{for $i in (1,2,3,4) return <item>{$i}</item>}
</items>
```

If you run the preceding query from the command line, you receive the following output in file ForInOut.xml:

```
<?xml version="1.0" encoding="UTF-8"?>
<items>
  <item>1</item>
  <item>2</item>
  <item>3</item>
  <item>4</item>
</items>
```

The query contains an element constructor that is a literal start-tag of the enclosing items element in the output document. The for statement binds the items in the sequence (1, 2, 3, 4) to the variable $i.

Because the in keyword is used in the for statement, each individual item in the sequence is, in turn, considered to be represented by $i, in much the same way you could use an XPath expression to return a sequence of nodes (in XPath 1.0 a node-set of nodes).

The return statement specifies that for each item in $i an item start-tag is created, an expression $i is evaluated and inserted as text, and a literal end-tag for the item element is added. After all possible values for the $i variable have been processed, the end-tag for the items element is added.

It doesn't matter whether items are values or nodes because both values and nodes are *items*, as the following example demonstrates. The source XML is Products.xml, shown here:

```
<?xml version="1.0"?>
<Products>
 <Product>Widget</Product>
 <Product>Gadget</Product>
 <Product>Knife</Product>
 <Product>Spoon</Product>
</Products>
```

The query, ForIn2.xquery, is shown here:

```
<items>
{for $i in (1,2, doc("Products.xml")/Products/Product/text(), 3, 4) return
<item>{$i}</item>}
</items>
```

Notice that between the first pair of items in the sequence in the for statement and the last pair of items in the sequence an XPath expression doc("Products.xml")/Products/Product/text() has been inserted. For each value in $i, whether it is a value or a text node selected by the XPath expression, the value of $i is inserted between the start-tag and end-tag of an item element.

The output document, ForIn2Out.xml, is shown here:

```
<?xml version="1.0" encoding="UTF-8"?>
<items>
    <item>1</item>
    <item>2</item>
    <item>Widget</item>
    <item>Gadget</item>
    <item>Knife</item>
    <item>Spoon</item>
    <item>3</item>
    <item>4</item>
</items>
```

Items supplied as literal values in the sequence in the for statement of the query and items selected by the XPath expression are treated the same.

The for statement also has a for ... in ... to option that can be used with integers. In other words, instead of writing

```
for $i in (1,2,3,4,5)
```

you can write

```
for $i in 1 to 5
```

Therefore, if you run ForIn3.xquery, as here:

```
<items>
{for $i in 1 to 5 return <item>{$i}</item>}
</items>
```

you produce the output in ForIn3Out.xml, shown here:

```
<?xml version="1.0" encoding="UTF-8"?>
<items>
    <item>1</item>
    <item>2</item>
    <item>3</item>
    <item>4</item>
    <item>5</item>
</items>
```

You can use this structure in combination with other literal values, as here in ForIn4.xquery:

```
<items>
{for $i in (1 to 5, 7, 8)
return <item>{$i}</item>}
</items>
```

The second line of the preceding example is a convenient shorthand for the following:

```
{for $i in (1, 2, 3, 4, 5, 7, 8)
```

The output is in the code download in the file ForIn4Out.xml. An item element is created that contains a value contained in the input sequence.

It is also possible to nest for statements, as shown here in ForNested.xquery:

```
<items>
{for $i in (1 to 5, 7, 8) return
 <group>{ for $a in (1 to ($i - 2)) return<item>{$a}</item>}
 </group>
 }
</items>
```

The output, ForNestedOut.xml, is shown here:

```
<?xml version="1.0" encoding="UTF-8"?>
<items>
    <group/>
    <group/>
    <group>
        <item>1</item>
    </group>
```

```
      <group>
         <item>1</item>
         <item>2</item>
      </group>
      <group>
         <item>1</item>
         <item>2</item>
         <item>3</item>

      </group>
      <group>
         <item>1</item>
         <item>2</item>
         <item>3</item>
         <item>4</item>
         <item>5</item>
      </group>
      <group>
         <item>1</item>
         <item>2</item>
         <item>3</item>
         <item>4</item>
         <item>5</item>
         <item>6</item>
      </group>
   </items>
```

The variable $i is specified in the outer for statement and is equivalent to the sequence (1, 2, 3, 4, 5, 7, 8). For each value of $i, a group element is created.

The content of each group element is defined by the nested for expression:

```
{ for $a in (1 to ($i - 2))
return<item>{$a}</item>}
```

When $i is 1 or 2, no item elements are added to the corresponding group elements because the value $i - 2 is less than 1.

When $i is 3, then a single item element is generated because

```
for $a in (1 to ($i - 2))
```

is equivalent to

```
for $a in 1 to 1
```

Therefore, one item element is output. As $i becomes larger, additional item elements are nested in subsequent group elements.

Filtering with the where Clause

Often, you will want to filter the output of a FLWOR statement using a where clause. The where clause is used in for expressions to filter what is returned in the result. For example, suppose you wanted to find any books in `BibAdapted.xml` that were published by Wrox Press. The query shown here, `Publisher.xquery`, can do that:

```
<books>{
for $book in doc("BibAdapted.xml")/bib/book
            where $book/publisher = "Wrox Press" return

 element book {
  attribute year {$book/@year},
  element title {$book/title/text()}
  }
 }
</books>
```

A `books` element is created literally, and its content is defined using a FLWOR expression. The where clause selects only books for which the `publisher` element has the value `Wrox Press`. The content of such books, of which there are three in the example, is specified using the expression

```
element book { attribute year {$book/@year}, element title {$book/title/text()}
 }
```

which constructs a `book` element and uses XPath expressions to assign a value to its `year` attribute and its title `child` element.

The output is shown in `PublisherOut.xml`:

```
<?xml version="1.0" encoding="UTF-8"?>
<books>
   <book year="2004">
      <title>XSLT 2.0 Programmer's Reference</title>
   </book>
   <book year="2006">
      <title>Professional Web 2.0 Programming</title>
   </book>
   <book year="2007">
      <title>Beginning XML, 4th Edition</title>
   </book>
</books>
```

Sorting Using the order by Clause

The `order by` clause allows the sorting of the output in a specified order. The following query, `OrderByTitle.xquery`, shows how the `order by` clause is used:

```
<books>{
  for $book in doc("BibAdapted.xml")/bib/book
  let $t := $book/title/text() order by $t return
  <book><title>{$t}</title></book>
  }
</books>
```

The `order by` clause

```
order by $t
```

specifies that the output is to be ordered by the value of the text content of the title element of book elements in the source XML document. In other words, the output is sorted alphabetically by title, as demonstrated in the output of the query OrderByTitleOut.xml shown here:

```
<?xml version="1.0" encoding="UTF-8"?>
<books>
   <book>
      <title>Beginning XML, 4th Edition</title>
   </book>
   <book>
      <title>Professional Web 2.0 Programming</title>
   </book>
   <book>
      <title>The C Programming Language</title>
   </book>
   <book>
      <title>The Economics of Technology and Content for Digital TV</title>
   </book>
   <book>
      <title>XSLT 2.0 Programmer's Reference</title>
   </book>
</books>
```

If you wanted the order in reverse alphabetical order, you could write the order by clause as follows:

```
order by $t descending
```

Conditional Expressions

The FLWOR expression enables you to iterate over a sequence of items. However, sometimes you need to process nodes only in certain circumstances using XQuery's support for conditional processing.

Conditional expressions in XQuery use the if keyword.

Try It Out   Using Conditional Expressions

In this example, you produce a query on BibAdapted.xml that outputs a book's title and a count of its authors only if the number of authors exceeds two.

Enter the following query, MultiAuthor.xquery:

```
<MultiAuthor>
{for $book in doc("BibAdapted.xml")/bib/book
return  if (count($book/author) gt 2)
   then <book>
        <title>{$book/title/text()}</title>
        <NumberOfAuthors>{count($book/author)}</NumberOfAuthors>
        </book>
   else ()
}
</MultiAuthor>
```

You should see the following output (`MultiAuthorOut.xml`):

```
<?xml version="1.0" encoding="UTF-8"?>
<MultiAuthor>
    <book>
        <title>Professional Web 2.0 Programming</title>
        <NumberOfAuthors>4</NumberOfAuthors>
    </book>
    <book>
        <title>Beginning XML, 4th Edition</title>
        <NumberOfAuthors>6</NumberOfAuthors>
    </book></MultiAuthor>
```

How It Works

The query uses a `for` statement to associate the variable `$book` with each book element in `BibAdapted.xml`. All of the `return` statement is governed by the conditional statement

```
if (count($book/author) gt 2)
```

`gt` *is a new comparison operator used to compare values. In this example, the older comparator, >, would also have worked. The value comparison operators are covered in Chapter 7.*

The `count()` function counts how many `author` elements are child elements of `$book`. For example, if the number of `author` elements that are child elements of `$book` exceeds two, then the `then` clause specifies the corresponding output:

```
then <book>
    <title>{$book/title/text()}</title>
    <NumberOfAuthors>{count($book/author)}</NumberOfAuthors>
    </book>
```

Conversely, if the number of author elements does not exceed two, then the `else` clause, which is mandatory, comes into play:

```
else ()
```

In this case, producing the empty sequence is signified by `()`.

XQuery Functions

XQuery provides a huge range of functions to allow an extensive set of tools to manipulate and filter data. You just saw a simple use of the `count()` function to count the number of `author` element nodes in an example describing conditional processing. This section describes a couple of commonly used functions.

A full description of the XQuery functions is contained in a lengthy, separate W3C document located at `www.w3.org/tr/xpath-functions`. *The URL describes the functions common to XPath 2.0 (hence the final part of the URL) and XQuery 1.0.*

The concat() Function

The concat() function is used to concatenate strings. The following shows a simple example. The source XML, Parts.xml, contains two strings that we want to join together:

```
<?xml version="1.0"?>
<Parts>
 <Part>To be or not to be,</Part>
 <Part>that is the question!</Part>
</Parts>
```

The query, ASaying.xquery, is shown here:

```
<ASaying>{
for $a in doc("Parts.xml")/Parts/Part[1]
  for $b in doc("Parts.xml")/Parts/Part[2]
  return  concat($a, " ", $b)
}</ASaying>
```

Notice that you declare two variables, $a and $b, using XPath path expressions to select relevant parts of the source XML document. In the return statement, the concat() function is used to concatenate the strings while interspersing a space between the two; and the output, ASayingOut.xml, is shown here:

```
<?xml version="1.0" encoding="UTF-8"?>
<ASaying>To be or not to be, that is the question!</ASaying>
```

The concat() function is unusual in that it can take any number of arguments. It is not possible to define your own functions this way; it's only possible with the built-in functions.

The count() Function

Let's use the count() function to calculate the number of Book elements that are present in SimpleBooks.xml, shown earlier in the chapter. The query is contained in the file Count.xquery, whose content is shown here:

```
<library count="{count(doc("SimpleBooks.xml")/Books/Book)}">
 { for $b in doc("SimpleBooks.xml")/Books/Book return <book>{$b/text()}</book>
 }
</library>
```

To run the query, type the following at the command line:

```
java net.sf.saxon.Query -o CountOut.xml Count.xquery
```

Notice that the count() function is used inside the value of the count attribute of the element library, which is created literally. The expression used to create the value of the count attribute, count(doc('SimpleBooks.xml')/Books/Book), uses the count() function with the argument doc('SimpleBooks.xml')/Books/Book. That expression selects all the Book elements in SimpleBook.xml and returns them in a sequence. At the risk of stating the obvious, there are three Book element nodes in the sequence. The count() function then counts those nodes and returns the value 3 in the count attribute.

The query uses two nested expressions to create the content of the `library` element. The `for` statement is used to iterate over `Book` element nodes. The result of the query is shown in `CountOut.xml`, which is displayed here:

```xml
<?xml version="1.0" encoding="UTF-8"?>
<library count="3">
    <book>Beginning XML, 4rd Edition</book>
    <book>Beginning XML Databases</book>
    <book>Professional Web 2.0 Programming</book></library>
```

Using Parameters with XQuery

External parameters may be passed to an XQuery query. In XQuery, a *parameter* is considered to be a variable that is declared as external.

To pass a string `"Hello World!"` to an XQuery, `ParameterExample.xquery`, and display the output on the console, use the following syntax at the command line:

```
java net.sf.saxon.Query ParameterExample.xquery input="Hello, World!"
```

The query is shown here:

```
declare variable $input as xs:string external;
<output>
 {$input}
</output>
```

Notice the variable declaration specifies that the variable `$input` is external and of type `xs:string`. In the absence of a namespace declaration to the contrary, the namespace prefix `xs` is treated as the namespace prefix for the W3C XML Schema namespace.

In this simple example, you simply use an element constructor to create an `output` element and specify that the element's content is an XQuery expression `$input`. The output is shown in Figure 9-4.

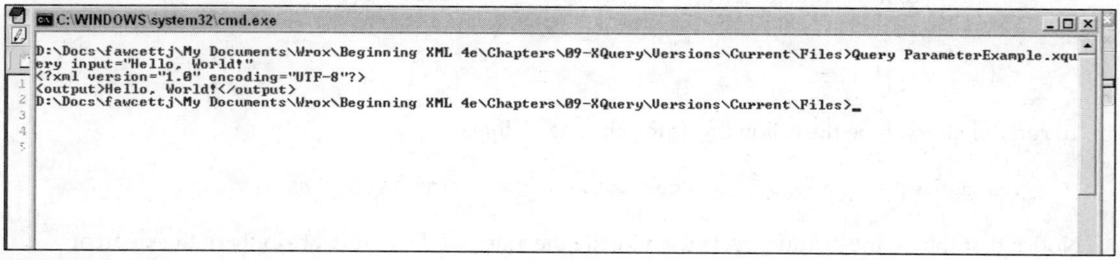

```
C:\WINDOWS\system32\cmd.exe                                                          _|□|x|

D:\Docs\fawcettj\My Documents\Wrox\Beginning XML 4e\Chapters\09-XQuery\Versions\Current\Files>Query ParameterExample.xqu
ery input="Hello, World!"
<?xml version="1.0" encoding="UTF-8"?>
<output>Hello, World!</output>
D:\Docs\fawcettj\My Documents\Wrox\Beginning XML 4e\Chapters\09-XQuery\Versions\Current\Files>_
```

Figure 9-4

User-Defined Functions

Although XPath 2.0 enables you to call custom functions, there is no inherent way to define these functions. That is left to the technology using XPath, be it XSLT, XQuery, or some other host.

XQuery uses a straightforward way of declaring these functions in the XQuery prolog. A simple declaration is shown here:

```
declare namespace math = "http://wrox.com/namespaces/xquery/math";
declare function math:add($op1 as xs:integer, $op2 as xs:integer) as xs:integer
{
    $op1 + $op2
};
```

After declaring a suitable namespace URI and prefix for the function, it is declared using a syntax similar to most modern languages. There is a parameter list with each argument's name preceded by a dollar sign, and the return type is either one of the built-in schema types or a type from a user-defined schema. The curly braces then hold the function body, which follows the normal XQuery rules of evaluation. `SimpleFunction.xquery` shows how to use this function in a simple scenario:

```
declare namespace math = "http://wrox.com/namespaces/xquery/math";
declare function math:add($op1 as xs:integer, $op2 as xs:integer) as xs:integer
{
    $op1 + $op2
};
declare variable $op1 as xs:integer := 1;
declare variable $op2 as xs:integer := 2;
<add>
    <op1>{$op1}</op1>
    <op2>{$op2}</op2>
    <result>{math:add($op1, $op2)}</result>
</add>
```

Here is a more useful function that calculates the factorial of a number, something not available in the standard library:

The factorial of a number, written as $x!$, is the product of that number with all smaller integers greater than one. So $4! = 4 \times 3 \times 2 = 24$.

```
declare namespace math = "http://wrox.com/namespaces/xquery/math";
declare variable $n as xs:integer external;
declare function math:factorial($integer as xs:integer) as xs:double
{
    if ($integer gt 1) then $integer * math:factorial($integer - 1) else 1
};
```

This time a *recursive function* is used. If the input to the function is greater than 1, the function returns the input multiplied by the factorial of the input less 1. Once the input reaches 1, the function unwinds and the final result is returned. Recursion is common in functional languages because alternative techniques, such as an iterative loop, cannot work without altering the value of variables. This is not allowed in functional languages.

The function can be tested using `FactorialFunction.xquery`:

```
declare namespace math = "http://wrox.com/namespaces/xquery/math";
declare variable $n as xs:integer external;
declare function math:factorial($integer as xs:integer) as xs:double
{
  if ($integer gt 1) then $integer * math:factorial($integer - 1) else 1
};
concat($n, "! = ", math:factorial($n))
```

You can test this query by using the following from the command line:

```
java net.sf.saxon.Query FactorialFunction.xquery n=5
```

Looking Ahead

As mentioned earlier in the chapter, it is likely that the XQuery specification will be finalized shortly after this book is published. However, almost everyone who has taken an interest in XQuery during its development recognizes that XQuery 1.0 is only a step toward a full-featured XQuery language. Two important aspects of the future of XQuery are mentioned here.

Update Functionality

Any XML data store that relies on XQuery as its primary query language must, like XML, be able to insert, delete, and update arbitrary parts of XML content. XQuery 1.0 has no such functionality, but the W3C Working Group has made it clear that such functionality is very much in its plans for XQuery after version 1.0. At the time of writing, the main URL for update features is www.w3.org/TR/xqupdate/. You can also find some use cases that demonstrate the need for the functionality at www.w3.org/TR/xqupdateusecases/.

Full-Text Search

Currently, the W3C has issued a working draft concerned with text searching within XML documents. The draft is available at www.w3.org/TR/xquery-full-text/. You can also find use cases at www.w3.org/TR/xqupdateusecases/.

Summary

In this chapter, you learned about some foundational aspects of the upcoming XML query language, XQuery. XQuery is based on XPath 2.0 and has a number of similarities to XSLT 2.0, which is also under development at the W3C. The XQuery prolog defines a number of components that determine how an XQuery will be processed. XQuery uses XPath path expressions for simple data retrieval but adds the very flexible and powerful FLWOR expressions to add a new dimension to querying XML data.

Exercise Questions

Suggested solutions to these questions can be found in Appendix A.

Question 1

What notation is used in an XQuery expression to indicate that its content is created dynamically?

Question 2

What are the component parts of a FLWOR expression, and what does each do?

10

XML and Databases

The volume of XML used by businesses is increasing as enterprises send increasing numbers of messages as XML. Many websites use XML as a data store, which is transformed into HTML or XHTML for online display. The diversity of sources of XML data is increasing, too. For example, a new generation of forms products and technologies, such as Microsoft's InfoPath and W3C XForms, is also beginning to supply XML data directly to data stores such as Microsoft Access or SQL Server from forms filled in by a variety of information workers.

To monitor business activity, you need to be able to store or exchange possibly huge amounts of data as XML and to recognize the benefits of XML's flexibility to reflect the structure of business data and to process or interchange it further. In addition, XML is being used increasingly for business-critical data, some of which is particularly confidential and needs to be secured from unauthorized eyes. This raises many issues that need to be considered when storing XML in a production setting. It isn't enough that data is available as XML; other issues such as security and scalability enter the picture, too.

In Chapter 9 you looked at XQuery, the XML query language under development at the W3C. This chapter covers broader issues that relate to the use of XML with databases. These issues are illustrated with examples that use XML with a native XML database and two different XML-enabled SQL databases.

This chapter includes the following:

- ❑ Use cases for XML-enabled database systems
- ❑ How to perform foundational tasks using eXist, an Open Source native XML database
- ❑ How to use some of the XML functionality in Microsoft SQL Server and MySQL, two major relational databases with XML functionalities

The Need for Efficient XML Data Stores

Efficiency is an important criterion when considering how to store data as XML. If XML is stored as text documents, how can it be processed efficiently? When data is measured in gigabytes, creating an in-memory Document Object Model (DOM) becomes impractical in many situations and alternative approaches must be explored.

When volumes of XML data grow, the efficiency of searching becomes important. Whatever method is used to actually store the XML, the addition of indexes to speed up searching that XML becomes increasingly necessary. Efficiency of data retrieval is important in many practical settings. For example, when XML data is used in web-based user interaction or in XML web services, performance is of great importance if the user is to feel that the system is sufficiently responsive.

If data is stored as something other than XML, the issue of how fast, for example, data held in relational form can be transformed into XML comes into play. Can an individual database product supply data as XML fast enough for users or other business processes to use, without imposing unacceptable delays?

Issues of reliability also come into play. You may have designed an XML database that works well — at least, it works well when it's working — but if it doesn't stay online almost 100 percent of the time when it is needed and has evident dips in performance in certain circumstances, then that database may simply be unacceptable in a production setting.

The Increasing Amount of XML

I began using XML in early 1999 and first wrote about using it about a year later. At first XML was seen as a pretty specialized, abstract topic that I suspect many people failed to see as relevant. I remember thinking when I first used XML that it could be an important technology. While I expected XML use to grow enormously, I had no idea just how much and how fast it would grow. XML's growth in nine years has been astonishing.

Of course, XML has its limitations. I see XML as the paper clip of business communication. It helps bring the organization where it wasn't possible or wasn't easy before, and it's going to continue growing as its value in connecting all sorts of data becomes clearer to business users.

One of the underlying factors that support the increasing use of XML is that XML has enormous flexibility in representing data. It can represent data structures that are difficult or inefficient to represent as relational data. In some settings, native XML databases that handle XML that a relational database might not easily handle may carve out a niche. But the situation is fluid and fuzzy. You will find no universally accepted definition of a native XML database. Perhaps the most practical definition of a *native XML database* is a database designed primarily or only to handle XML data.

People who come from a relational database background tend to refer to relational data as *structured data*, overlooking the reality that many other types of data are also structured, but structured in a different, more complex, or more variable way. Used here, the term *structured data* refers primarily to relational data, although it is also relevant to keep in mind that relational data is, in a real sense, simply structured data.

The terms *semi-structured data* and *loosely structured data* have no clear boundaries. *Semi-structured data* is a term used often by relational database folks to refer to nonrelational data, very often XML data. *Loosely structured data* typically refers to document-centric XML. XML documents, such as XHTML web pages or DocBook documents, can vary enormously in structure. They are, of course, still structured and, assuming they are correctly written, correspond to a schema. A big difference between a relational mindset and an XHTML or DocBook document is that there is much more flexibility in the XHTML document and much more variation allowed than what is allowed in a relational database.

Whether you view relational data as inflexibly and simply structured data or simply as "structured data" (as if there were no other kind) is as much a matter of philosophy or perspective as anything else. Similarly, whether you view XML documents as loosely structured data (the relational viewpoint) or as richly structured, flexibly structured data is again a matter of perspective.

Comparing XML-Based Data and Relational Data

Before we move on to examine approaches to using XML in modern databases, this section briefly compares the structure of relational data and XML. If you don't appreciate these simple differences, much of what follows may be hard for you to understand.

In a relational database, data is stored in tables that consist of rows and columns. In a column, data of a particular kind is stored for all records in the table. Each record in the table is represented as a row. The order of rows in a relational table does not indicate any ordering of the data. This contrasts with XML, where document order is intrinsically present and affects, for example, the data that is returned by an XPath function such as position().

Only the simplest relational data can be stored in a single table, and a typical relational database will have multiple tables with complex logical relationships between the tables. Data in different tables is associated with the use of *keys*. For example, a CustomerID field (or column) may exist in a Customers table. Identification of orders for that customer is likely to be facilitated by the existence of a corresponding value in the CustomerID column of an Orders table.

Relationships between data can be one-to-one (think of son to father), one-to-many (think of son to parents or customer to orders), or many-to-many (think of products to orders — one product can appear in many orders, and one order can contain many products). Each of these types of relationships can be represented by storing data in two or more relational tables.

Relational databases, as typically structured, have no hierarchy as such, unlike XML documents, which are intrinsically hierarchical, as exemplified in the XPath data model, the Document Object Model, and the XML Infoset.

XML data is intrinsically ordered, as in this simple example:

```
<Orders>
 <Order Customer="Acme Industries" Date="2003-12-11" Value="1234.56" Currency="US
Dollars" />
 <Order Customer="Fiction Fabricators" Date="2004-02-11" Value="4300.12"
Currency="US Dollars" />
<Order Customer="Aspiring Assemblers" Date="2005-07-11" Value="10000.00"
Currency="US Dollars" />
 </Orders>
```

XML's intrinsic hierarchy is a condition imposed by the criteria that define a well-formed XML document. Storing even simple data like this in a relational table would lose the ordering of orders. Whether that matters or not depends on whether you need to assemble the data in XML at a later date to recapture the original structure.

Approaches to Storing XML

The need to store XML doesn't occur in a vacuum. Huge amounts of data had already been stored for years before XML was invented, much of it in conventional relational database management systems.

Storing XML on File Systems

Even though this chapter is about XML and databases, keep in mind that most XML documents are stored on file systems. The very notion of an XML "document" suggests storage on disk just like you store any other kind of "document" on your desktop. Many applications never go beyond this first step and continue to store XML documents on file systems. In fact, the main reason why XML databases have been so slow to take off is likely because storing XML documents on file systems works so well.

Storing XML documents on file systems is not only simple and natural because the term "XML document" suggests doing so, but also because the hierarchical organization of a file system is very similar to the hierarchical organization of a file document. There is a strong parallel between the syntax of file URLs or Unix paths and the simplest XPath expressions, and it's very natural to access the "/bat/baz" node from the "/foo/bar.xml" document! Before moving on to "real" XML databases, it is worth looking at the limitations of storing XML documents on file systems.

Document Size

Keeping your XML documents on disk makes sense when you need to read or serve static documents with a reasonably small size on the Web. File systems can now efficiently support gigabytes; and as long as you know the path to any XML document, you can retrieve that document efficiently. The important factor to consider here is the granularity of the information you need to retrieve. If you always need to retrieve a full document, this system works fine, but if you need to retrieve small pieces from big documents through DOM or XPath, you will incur a huge overhead because you have to read the full document before you can extract the small part in which you're interested.

In addition, don't forget that you'll need to parse these documents each time you want to access them through DOM or XPath. Of course, this only applies if you need to perform this kind of access. If you only need to serve the documents without modification or transformation on the Web, it is beneficial to get them "ready to serve" in XML.

Updates

Another issue you have if you store XML documents on disk are updates. If you are manually managing a collection of XML documents alone on your desktop or web server, updates may not be an issue, but as soon as you want to enable multiple users to update these documents, or, even worse, if you're writing a transactional application, you need to take extra care to perform these updates. One way to do so is to store your documents on a WebDAV repository that will take care of locking and concurrent accesses for you. A path to explore if you're interested in this approach is to use a version control system such as Subversion (http://subversion.tigris.org/). Subversion can act as a WebDAV repository and offers all the features of a version control system, including a full history of any modifications to your documents. This is a very important feature for some applications, and one that isn't natively supported by the database systems shown in this chapter.

Whatever solution you find for supporting document updates, consider again the granularity of the information. If most of your updates apply to small pieces of big documents, you'll have significant overhead because you need to replace the full document by the updated version. In transactional applications, this also means that the whole document will be locked when you update one of its nodes, which can have serious performance consequences.

Indexes

The last issue you may encounter if you store your documents on disk are queries. For example, if you needed to find all the documents written by a specific author in a big collection of documents, you would need to implement some kind of indexing mechanism. If you have few predefined fields to index, you can use the directory structure as an index: To index authors, you have directories per author. If you also need to index per date, you can add symbolic links to create virtual directories per date, but if you increase the number of these fields or you want to support full-text search, you need to find something else.

If you're using a version control system as advised in the previous section, you can take advantage of the features of this system. For instance, with Subversion, you can easily get a list of documents for a specific version, committed by a specific user, modified between two dates, and so on. Furthermore, Subversion lets you add your own user-defined properties, which you can also store and query. This is handy, for example, when you need to store the name of the author of a document and it is different from the user who performs an update, or when the date of a text is different from the commit date. As a little icing on the cake, Subversion commands have an option to format their results in XML, meaning you can format them with XSLT to be presented in a web page.

If you're mostly interested in full-text search, you can use a search engine such as Lucene (`http://lucene.apache.org/`). Lucene comes with an API that enables you to define which elements need to be indexed and how they must be treated. It supports large collections efficiently and provides features that will be immediately familiar to your users because they are similar to those used in their favorite search engines on the Web.

Even if you were convinced in Chapter 9 that XQuery is what you need, you can find XQuery implementations that run on top of collections of XML documents stored on disk. This is the case with XQEngine (`http://xqengine.sourceforge.net/`).

Building Your Own

Although most issues can be worked around, keeping XML documents on disk with write access and indexes is a "build your own" kind of solution and exposes you to a fair amount of integration work. By contrast, XML databases give you a much more packaged approach. Of course, packaged means that trade-offs will have been made for you, and you may find XML databases weaker than the solution that you would have built yourself. This is the case for version control features: You won't find in XML databases the features you find in a version control system and for full-text search. Most XML databases do not match search engine features. On the other hand, you can save a lot of time by using a stable XML database instead of adding a bunch of software on top of your file system storage to implement features that are natively available in these databases.

Using XML With Conventional Databases

Relational databases are one of the most popular ways to store data. They are mature, very well fitted to store structured data, store a huge amount of legacy data, and are well understood by a large number of developers. These reasons make them good candidates to use together with XML, and you have different options to do so.

Producing XML from Relational Databases

Large numbers of HTML and XHTML websites are created, directly or indirectly, from relational data. Widely used combinations are PHP with the MySQL database or ASP or ASP.NET with SQL Server or Microsoft Access. Data is stored conventionally as relational tables, and the programmer writes code to create HTML or XHTML, sometimes using XML as an intermediate stage. XHTML is an XML application language. Creating XHTML web pages from relational data demonstrates one way in which relational data can be used to produce a presentation-oriented form of XML. That common activity demonstrates that it is possible to map relational data to hierarchical XML structures and return those hierarchical structures to a user.

For example, when using PHP to query data from a couple of tables in MySQL to present it to a user of a web page, it is unlikely that the developer will want to present the data only in tables similar to the structures in the database. More likely, the developer will convert the non-ordered, nonhierarchical structure of relational data into something with at least some order and hierarchy, since that fits well into HTML and XHTML web pages, which are themselves hierarchical.

If individual programmers have figured out ways to convert relational data to XML, then it is not surprising that vendors of database products have also recognized the opportunity to get into a growing XML market that the ability to export XML from a relational data store would bring. In fact, many relational databases allow XML to be returned to the user from data held in relational tables.

Moving XML to Relational Databases

Similarly, many relational database management systems now have the capability to accept XML data from a user, convert it into a relational form, and then store that latter data in relational tables. Depending on whether any meta data about ordering is captured in the process of shredding XML into parts that a relational database can handle, it may be possible to reconstitute the original XML document. (*Shredding* refers to processing XML and inserting its contents into standard database tables.) In many situations such precise reconstitution is not needed.

The ability to shred and put back together bits of data to mimic XML functionality is fine, not least because it works for many situations, but this task is tedious to apply by hand and can be automated. Enter data binding.

Data Binding

Data binding frameworks acknowledge the fact that several representations of the same data need to co-exist in applications, automating the mapping between those representations. The representations that are most often supported by data binding frameworks are XML, SQL databases, and objects.

Data binding frameworks that can directly map XML and SQL databases include ADO.NET (http://msdn.microsoft.com/data/ref/adonet/) in Microsoft's world and Castor (http://www.castor.org/) in the Java open-source community. They act as the "glue" between XML and relational databases that is so tedious to develop by hand. They are very flexible, can be configured in a number of ways, and are good solutions if you need to expose as XML the content of existing databases.

In addition to such a direct data binding between XML and relational databases, you may encounter more complex scenarios, such as those in which a relational database is used as a persistence layer for objects, which in turn generate XML or XHTML documents. In these scenarios the persistence layer is nothing more than a data binding framework used to map the relational database and the objects.

Depending on the situation, the XML or XHTML is generated manually, through templates, or through another data binding library.

Sound complex? This is not necessarily the case, and Ruby on Rails, a shining star praised for its simplicity among Web 2.0 frameworks, is following this approach!

If you are attracted by more integrated approaches, native XML databases are what you're looking for.

Native XML Databases

What is a native XML database? You won't find one single, universally agreed upon definition, but a simple and reasonably helpful definition is that a native XML database is designed to store XML. If it also stores data structures other than XML, however, then does it stop being a native XML database?

A native XML database might choose to implement XML using a model like the XML Infoset, the XML DOM, XPath, or Simple API for XML (SAX) events. It is also likely to capture aspects of an XML document, such as document order.

Relational database technology is now pretty mature, having a sound theoretical basis and a couple of decades of practical experience in widely used products. By contrast, native XML databases are recent introductions; they don't have the same kind of theoretical underpinning as relational databases do, and they are evolving and are likely to continue to evolve for some years to come.

Whatever the underlying storage mechanism, a native XML database product also maps an XML document to the storage model. The mapping differs substantially, perhaps, from the detail of the shredding of an XML document into a relational database.

Native XML databases often store XML documents in collections, and queries can be made across a collection. Depending on the product, a collection may be defined by a schema or may contain documents of differing structure. The latter approach is likely to be greeted with horror by anyone used to the predictability of a relational model.

At the time of writing, many native XML databases use XQuery as the query language, even though it is not yet a W3C Recommendation. However, few of them support the W3C XML Schema features of XQuery.

Updates to native XML databases currently lack standardization. The lack of insert, delete, and update functionality in XQuery 1.0 means that nonstandard update mechanisms are likely to persist in the native XML database world for some time.

In practice, the boundary between native XML databases and XML-enabled relational databases is becoming progressively blurred. For example, Microsoft's SQL Server, Oracle, Sybase Adaptive Server Enterprise, and IBM's DB2 9 have the ability to store a new xml datatype without discarding their traditional strengths as relational database management systems.

For many practical purposes it won't matter whether you are using a native XML database or an XML-enabled relational database product. As user or developer, you send XML into both types and you get XML back, so why worry about what is under the hood? Usually you don't need to. Making a choice between an XML-enabled relational database versus a native XML database is similar to making any other software decision. Clearly define your needs and then find the best fit for those functional needs depending on price, supported operating system(s), and a host of other criteria.

The rest of this chapter looks at three very different database products as examples of native XML databases and XML-enabled database management systems:

❑   eXist is the most mature open-source XML database, written in Java.

❑   SQL Server is a Microsoft enterprise-capable relational database management system with some XML functionality.

❑   MySQL is the open-source database most widely used to power websites. Its XML capabilities are still well behind those of its commercial competitors but this chapter will give you the first look at what they are in the 5.1.2 beta version.

Using Native XML Databases

As mentioned earlier, native XML databases vary in their approach. Individual databases in the native XML database category vary significantly in their capabilities. This chapter uses eXist to explore how one native XML database works.

Obtaining and Installing eXist

Before doing anything with eXist, visit its website at http://exist-db.org/. From there, you'll find links to download the latest version. The download is available in different flavors; for an easy standalone installation, choose the latest version of the "Installer based on IzPack" (at the time of this writing, this version is eXist-1.1.1-newcore.jar). eXist is written in Java, so before you install the downloaded jar file, ensure that you have a recent version of Java installed. Currently, a JDK version 1.4.2 or later was required.

> *If you are not sure which version of Java is installed on your computer, type **java -version** in a DOS or Unix terminal.*

Once you have your download ready and have the right version of Java installed, you should be able to install eXist by clicking on the jar file on any properly configured workstation. If that's not the case, open a terminal and type **java -jar eXist-<version>.jar**. A fancy graphical installer will pop up and guide you through the installation, which is very straightforward.

When that's done, you have a ready-to-run native XML database that can be used in three different modes:

❑   You can use eXist as a Java library to embed a database server in your own Java application.

❑   You can run it as a standalone database server as you would run a SQL database server.

❑   You can run it embedded in a web server and get the features of both a standalone database and a web interface to access the database.

After the installation, eXist can be used in the last two modes using a different set of scripts that you can find in its bin subdirectory:

❑   server (.sh or .bat depending on your platform) is used to run eXist as a standalone database server.

❑   `startup` (.sh or .bat) is used to start eXist embedded in a web server, and `shutdown` (.sh or .bat) is used to stop this web server. This is the mode that you will use for the exercises in this chapter because it is the one that includes most features.

To check that the installation is correct, launch `startup.sh` or `startup.bat` in a terminal. You should get a series of warnings and information, concluding with (if everything is okay) the following two lines:

```
20 Nov 2006 16:47:55,485 [main] INFO  (SocketListener.java [start]:204) - Started
SocketListener on 0.0.0.0:8080
20 Nov 2006 16:47:55,485 [main] INFO  (HttpServer.java [start]:690) - Started
org.mortbay.jetty.Server@858bf1
```

These lines mean that jetty (the Java web server that comes with this eXist download) is ready to accept connections on port 8080.

By default, the web server listens to port 8080. This means that it will fail to start if another service is already bound to this port on your computer. If that's the case, either stop this service before you start eXist or change eXist's configuration to listen to another port. You can find instructions to do so on eXist's website.

The last step to check that everything runs smoothly is to open you favorite web browser to `http://localhost:8080/exist/` and confirm that eXist's home page, shown in Figure 10-1, opens.

Figure 10-1

Interacting with eXist

Congratulations, you have your first native XML database up and running! Now it's time to find out how you can interact with it. You will soon see that eXist is so open you have many options for doing so.

Using the Web Interface

The first of these options is to use the web interface at `http://localhost:8080/exist/`. Scroll down this web page to the section "Administration," on the left side. Click Admin to go to `http://local host:8080/exist/admin/admin.xql`, where you need to log in as user "admin" with an empty password until you have set up a more secure password.

Once you're logged in, you have access to the commands from the left-side menu. Feel free to explore by yourself how you can manage users and set up the example that eXist suggests you install.

When you are ready to continue this quick tour of eXist, click Browsing Collection (see Figure 10-2). (XML documents are organized in *collections*, a collection being equivalent to a directory on a file system. They are really the same concept. You can think of an eXist database as a black box that packages the features you lack when you store XML documents on disk, while retaining the same paradigm of a hierarchical structure of collections, or directories.)

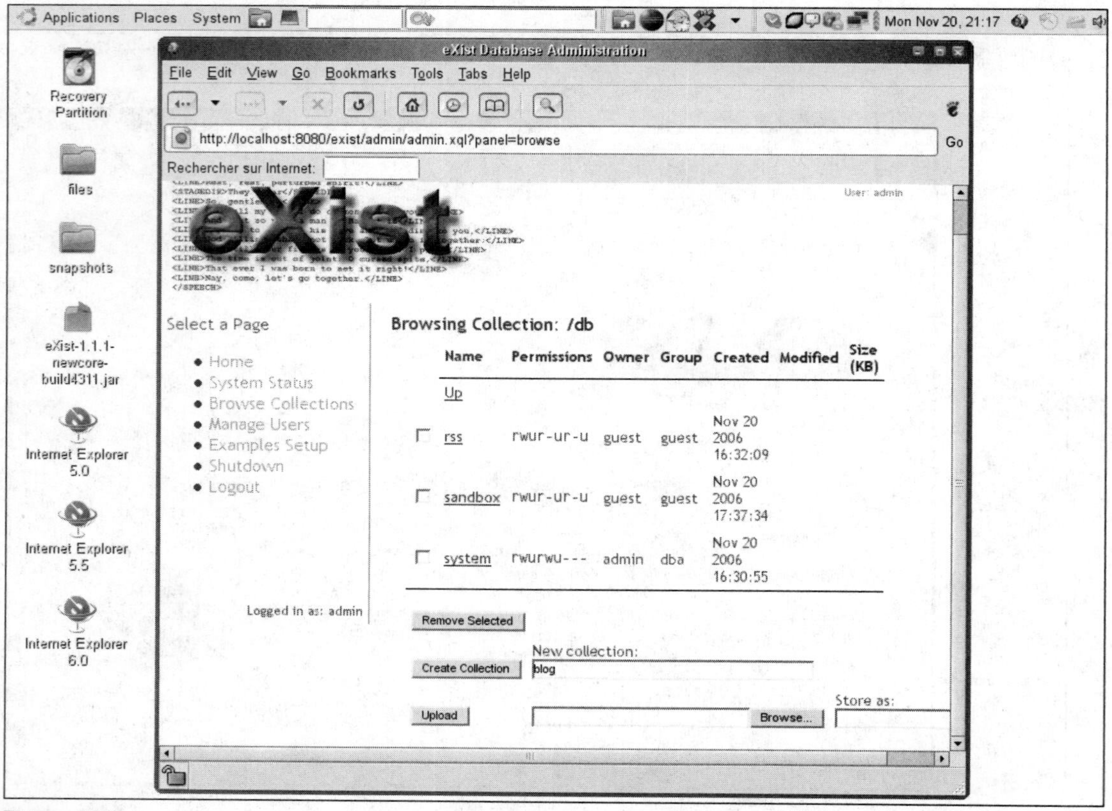

Figure 10-2

A brand-new eXist installation has a number of existing collections, but you will create a new one named `blog` using the Create Collection button. Once this collection is created, follow the link to browse it. This new collection is empty. Using the Upload button, upload the documents `blogitem1.xml` and `blogitem2.xml`, which you can download from the code samples for this chapter on the Wrox site. These documents are sample blog entries such as the following (`blogitem1.xml`):

```xml
<?xml version="1.0"?>
<item id="1">
  <title>Working on Beginning XML</title>
  <description>
    <p>
      <a href="http://www.wrox.com/WileyCDA/WroxTitle/productCd-0764570773.html">
        <img
   src="http://media.wiley.com/product_data/coverImage/73/07645707/0764570773.jpg"
          align="left"/>
      </a> I am currently working on the next edition of <a
        href="http://www.wrox.com/WileyCDA/WroxTitle/productCd-0764570773.html">
        WROX's excellent "Beginning XML".</a>
    </p>
    <p>It's the first time I am working on editing a book that I haven't written
and I must say that I like it even better than I had expected when I
        accepted WROX's offer.</p>
    <p>I knew that the book was solid and that I would be working with a team of
        very professional authors, but what I hadn't anticipated is how fun it
        can be to create a new version out of existing material. You have a lot
        of room to reorganize what you are editing and when the material is good,
        it's like creating your own stuff, except that 80% of the hard work is
        already done!</p>
  </description>
  <category>English</category>
  <category>XML</category>
  <category>Books/Livres</category>
  <pubDate>2006-11-13T17:32:01+01:00</pubDate>
  <comment-count>0</comment-count>
</item>
```

After you have uploaded these documents, you can display them by clicking on their links. Now that you have documents in the `/db/blog` collection, you can query these documents, still using the Web interface. To do so, click on the Home link to go back to the home page and follow the link to the XQuery sandbox, which you can reach at `http://localhost:8080/exist/sandbox/sandbox.xql`.

It's time to remember what you learned of XPath in Chapter 7 and XQuery in Chapter 9: The big text area expects a query written in XPath or XQuery! If you start with something simple such as `/item[@id='1']` and press Send, you'll get all the documents from all the collections that have an `item` root element with an `id` attribute equal to 1. If you've followed the instructions that led to this point, you should get only the content of the first blog entry.

Of course, you can write more complex queries. For example, if you want to determine the titles, IDs, and links of blog entries with a link on the Wrox site, you can write the following (`xquery1.xq`), as shown in Figure 10-3:

```
for $item in /item
  where .//a[contains(@href, 'wrox.com')]
  return <match>
     <id>{string($item/@id)}</id>
     {$item/title}
     {$item//a[contains(@href, 'wrox.com')]}
  </match>
```

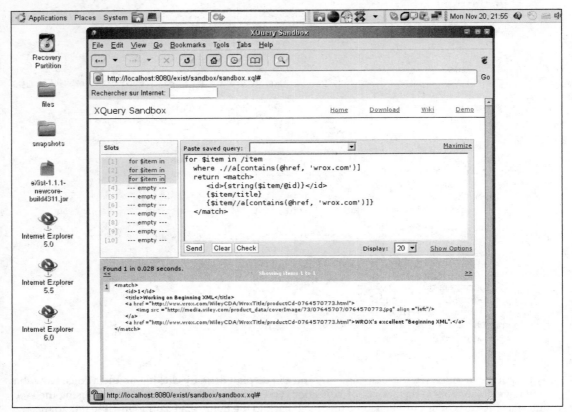

Figure 10-3

Feel free to try as many queries as you like, and then move on to discover the eXist client.

Using the eXist Client

The eXist client is a standalone graphical tool that can perform the same kind of operations as the web interface. To start it, just click on the script `client.sh` or `client.bat`, depending on your environment. You should get a login screen. If you have set up a password for the admin user, enter that password. Before you click the OK button, note the URL entry field. By default, this field has the value `xmldb: exist://localhost:8080/exist/xmlrpc`. We won't cover details about the different components of this URL, but note the `localhost:8080` piece: It means that this client tool uses HTTP to connect to the eXist database and that you can administer eXist databases on other machines.

The next screen enables you to browse the collections or your database. If you click "blog," you again find your two blog entries; and if you click one of them, you get a window in which you can edit it. Back at the main window, the button with binoculars opens the Query dialog, where you can try again your XPath and XQuery expertise. Note the Trace tab in the Results window at the bottom: You find there the execution path of your queries, which may contain useful information to debug or optimize them. Figure 10-4 shows the previous query run in the eXist client.

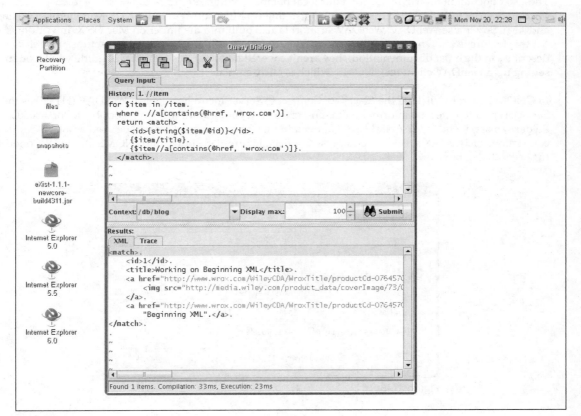

Figure 10-4

There is much more to explore with this client, which you can also use to save and restore collections or full databases. Once you're done with it, read on to see how eXist can be used as a WebDAV server.

Using WebDAV

WebDAV stands for Web-based Distributed Authoring and Versioning. It designates a set of IETF RFCs that define how HTTP can be used to not only read resources, but also to write them. WebDAV is widely and natively implemented in most common operating systems and tools, and eXist's ability to expose its collections as WebDAV repositories can greatly facilitate the way you import and export documents.

The IETF (Internet Engineering Task Force) is the standardization organization that publishes most of the protocol-oriented Internet specifications, including HTTP. Its specifications are called RFCs (Requests For Comments); and despite this name, they are de facto standards.

As a first contact with WebDAV, try to point your Web browser to `http://localhost:8080/exist/webdav/db/`. You need to again enter the login and password of your database admin. Then you will see a page where you can browse the collections and content of your database. Without browser extensions, you have read-only access; you need to set up your WebDAV client to gain write access and see the eXist database as a repository.

The eXist documentation available on your local database at `http://localhost:8080/exist/webdav.xml` includes detailed instructions for setting up Microsoft Windows, KDE Konqueror, oXygen, and XML Spy to use WebDAV. WebDAV support is also built into the finder on Mac OS X. In Windows XP, this feature is known as *web folders* and is fairly easy to configure. Because these setups are well described in the eXist documentation, they aren't covered here, but this section will guide you through setting up a WebDAV client on GNOME, which is fairly similar.

In GNOME, start by clicking the Places ➪ Connect to Server menu item. Select WebDAV (HTTP) as the Service type and enter the information that matches your configuration: Server=localhost, Port=8080, Folder=/exist/webdav/db/, and User Name=admin. Choose a name that will be used as a label for this connection, such as "eXist (local)" and press Connect. Figure 10-5 shows the GNOME WebDAV Connect to Server dialog box.

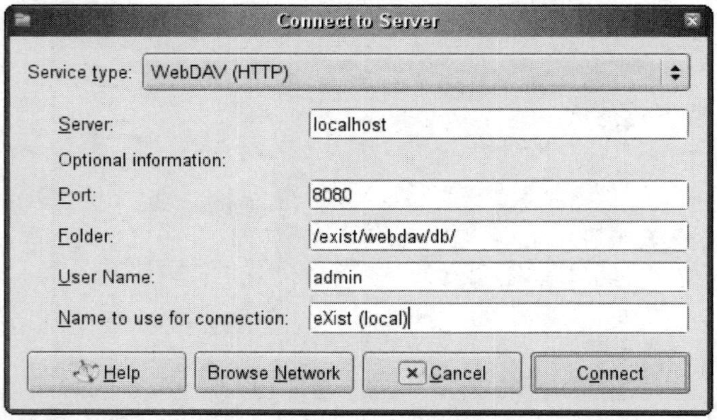

Figure 10-5

Your WebDAV client is configured. To use it, select this new connection in the Places menu. You will be prompted for the password associated with the admin user, and Nautilus (Nautilus is the name of the default GNOME file manager) will open with a window to browse the content of your eXist database, exactly as if it were a filesystem.

At this point, on whatever environment, you should be able to access the resources in your eXist database using your favorite file manager. This means that not only can you open the documents that you find there, you can also edit them, move resources between eXist and your local file system, create new collections, delete existing ones, and so on. Figure 10-6 shows the GNOME default file manager, Nautilus, browsing the eXist database exposed as a WebDav repository.

If you've kept your eXist client or web browser open on the administration interface or XQuery sandbox, you can confirm that the updates applied through WebDAV are immediately visible in the database, or vice versa: The modifications applied directly on the database are visible as soon as you refresh your file manager.

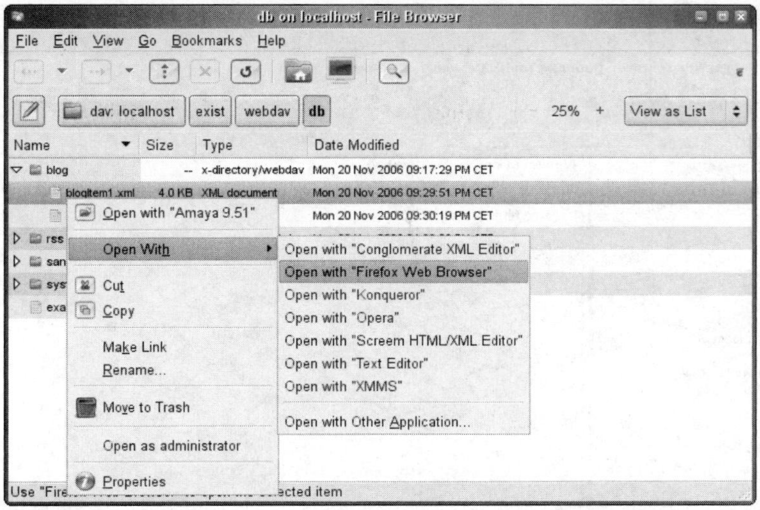

Figure 10-6

The only feature that you lack using the WebDAV interface is the capability to execute queries, but you will see next that you can regain this feature if you use an XML IDE.

Using an XML IDE

Your favorite XML IDE can probably access your eXist database through WebDAV. If it is interfaced with eXist, you can also execute queries from the IDE itself. This is the case with oXygen 8.0, available as a 30-day evaluation license from their site at http://www.oxygenxml.com/.

To configure the connection to your eXist database, select the database perspective using either its icon on the toolbar or the Perspective menu. Then, click the Configure Database Sources button situated at the upper-right corner of the Database Explorer window. This opens the database preferences window. Create a new data source with type eXist and add the exist.jar, xmldb.jar, and xmlrpc-1.2-patched.jar libraries (located in your eXist installation). The easiest way to search these version-dependent libraries is to search for them in the directories embedded in your eXist installation directory. Save this data source and create a connection using it with the eXist connection parameters. Save this connection and the database preferences and you're all set.

The Database Explorer should show the newly created connection, and you can now browse and update the eXist database as you would browse and open documents on your local file system.

So far, all that you've done could be done through Web DAV. To execute a query, create a new document through the File New icon or menu item. Choose a type XQuery for this document and type your query. When you're done, click the Apply Transformation Scenario button on the toolbar or select this action though the Document ⇨ XML Document ⇨ Apply Transformation Scenario menu item. Because no scenario is attached to this document yet, this opens the Configure Transformation Scenario dialog. The default scenario uses the Saxon XQuery engine. To use the eXist XQuery engine, create a new scenario and select your eXist database connection as the Transformer. Save this scenario and click Transform Now to run the query. Figure 10-7 shows the same query run in oXygen.

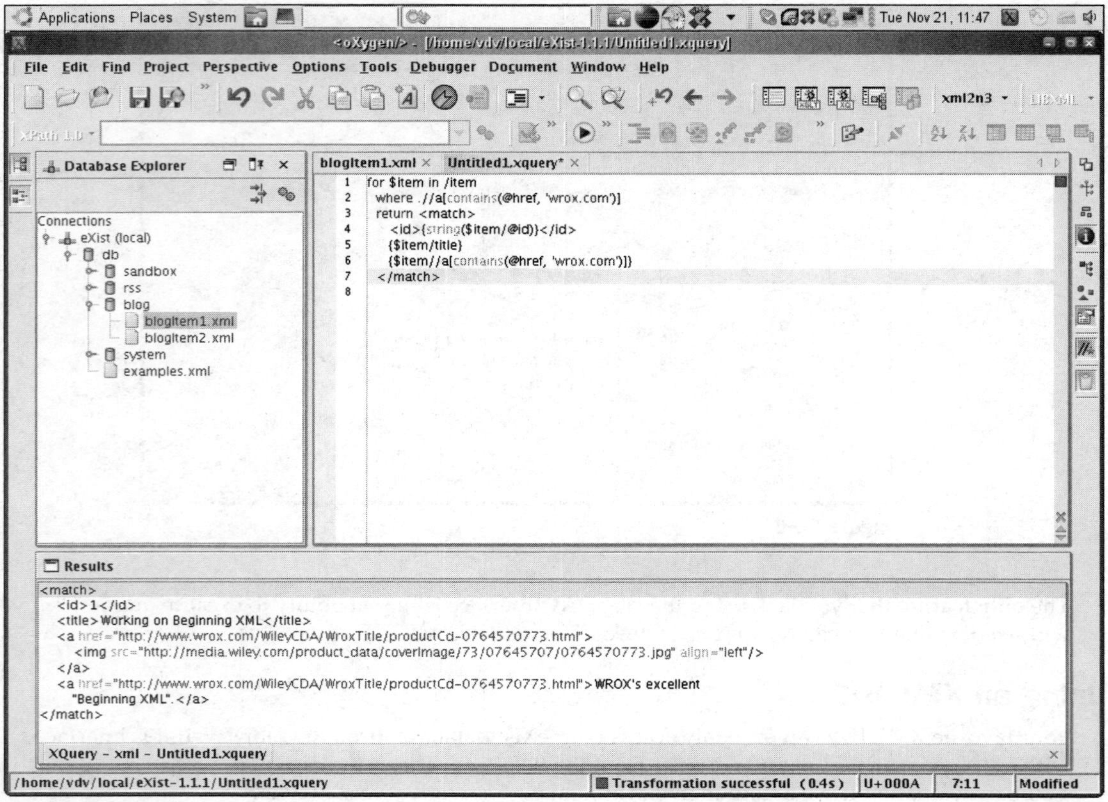

Figure 10-7

Now that this scenario is attached to your query document, you can update the query and click the Apply Transformation Scenario button to run it without needing to go through this configuration again.

All the methods you've seen provide handy user interfaces, but you still need to see how web applications can access your database.

Using the REST Interface

What better way to interface your database with a web application could there be than using HTTP as it was meant to be used? This is the purpose of the REST interface. As a first contact, you can point your browser to `http://localhost:8080/exist/rest/`. Doing so will show you the content of your database root exposed as an XML document. This XML format is less user friendly than browsing the content of your collections through the admin web interface or even through browsing the WebDAV repository, but far more easy to process in an application!

The full content of the database is available through this interface. For instance, `http://localhost:8080/exist/rest/db/blog/` shows the content of the blog collection, and `http://localhost:8080/exist/rest/db/blog/blogItem1.xml` gets you the first blog item. This becomes more interesting when you start playing with query strings. The REST interface accepts a number of parameters, including a `_query` parameter that you can use to send XPath or XQuery simple queries straight away!

For instance, if you want to get all the links from all the documents in the collection /db/blog, you can query http://localhost:8080/exist/rest/db/blog/?_query=//a. In the current version (eXist-1.1.1-newcore) of eXist, the media type for these queries is improperly configured as text/html, and your browser will try to display it as if it were HTML, as shown in Figure 10-8.

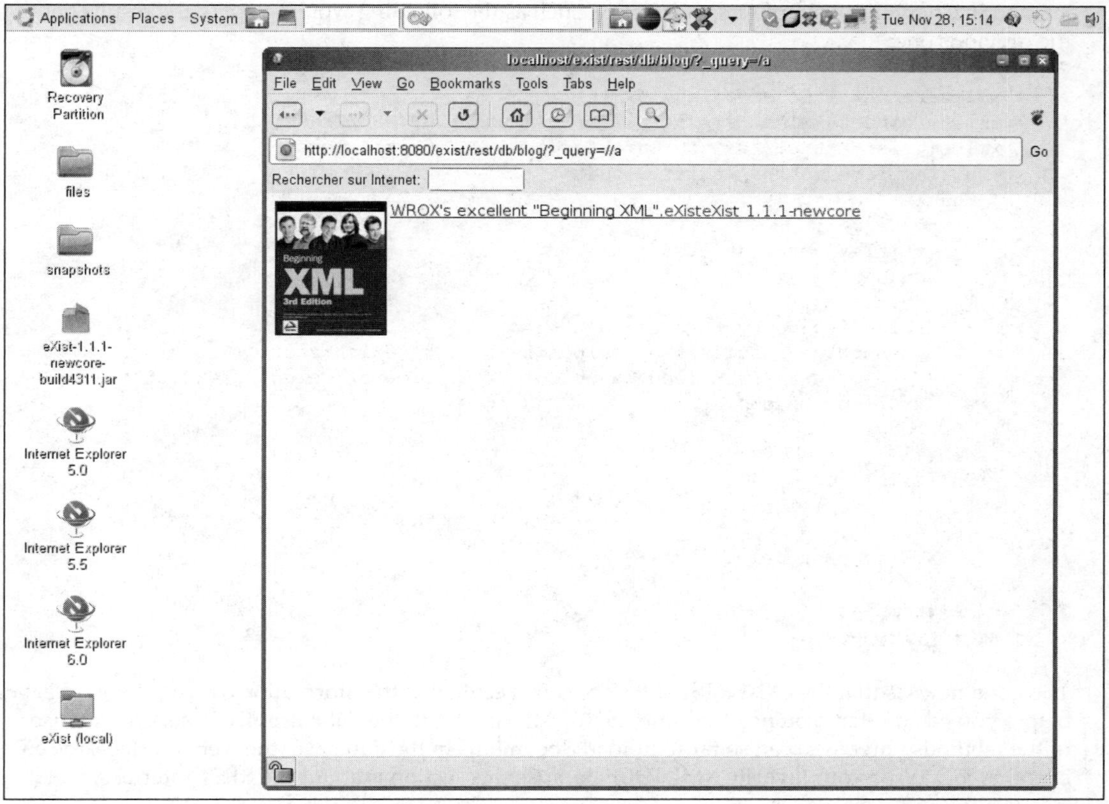

Figure 10-8

This can be confusing, but if you look at the source that is returned, you will see an XML document such as this one:

```
<exist:result xmlns:exist="http://exist.sourceforge.net/NS/exist"
  exist:hits="4" exist:start="1" exist:count="4">
  <a href="http://www.wrox.com/WileyCDA/WroxTitle/productCd-0764570773.html">
    <img

src="http://media.wiley.com/product_data/coverImage/73/07645707/0764570773.jpg"
      align="left"/>
  </a>
  <a href="http://www.wrox.com/WileyCDA/WroxTitle/productCd-0764570773.html">
    WROX's excellent"Beginning XML".</a>
  <a href="http://exist-db.org/">eXist</a>
<a href="http://prdownloads.sourceforge.net/exist/eXist-1.1.1-newcore-
```

```
   build4311.jar">
    eXist 1.1.1-newcore</a>
   </exist:result>
```

This XML deserves a XSLT transformation to be presented as HTML; and if you remember what you learned in Chapter 8, a simple transformation such as the following would display the results better than the previous one:

```
<?xml version="1.0" encoding="UTF-8"?>
<xsl:stylesheet xmlns:xsl="http://www.w3.org/1999/XSL/Transform"
  xmlns:exist="http://exist.sourceforge.net/NS/exist" version="1.0">
  <xsl:template match="/exist:result">
    <html>
      <head>
        <title>Query results</title>
      </head>
      <body>
        <h1>eXist query results</h1>
        <p>Showing results <xsl:value-of select="@exist:start"/> to <xsl:value-of
            select="@exist:end"/> out of <xsl:value-of select="@exist:hits"/>:</p>
        <xsl:apply-templates/>
      </body>
    </html>
  </xsl:template>
  <xsl:template match="*">
    <p>
      <xsl:copy-of select="."/>
    </p>
  </xsl:template>
</xsl:stylesheet>
```

The good news is that the eXist REST interface can execute this transformation for you if you like, but before you can do that, you need to store the transformation in the database. To do so, you can use any of the methods you have seen so far to upload documents in the database (the web interface, the eXist client, WebDAV, or your favorite XML IDE). Because this section is about the REST interface, you can also use this interface.

Storing documents with the REST interface uses an HTTP PUT request; unfortunately, you can't do that with your web browser. To send an HTTP PUT request, you need to either do a bit of programming (all the programming languages have libraries available to support this) or use a utility such as curl (http://curl.haxx.se/).

This program has a lot of different command-line options. If you have curl installed on your machine, to store the document rest-query-results.xsl at location http://localhost:8080/exist/rest/ db/xslt/, just type the following command in a Unix or DOS window:

```
curl -T rest-query-results.xsl http://localhost:8080/exist/rest/db/xslt/
```

This command simply sends this document through an HTTP PUT. The eXist REST interface also supports HTTP DELETE requests, and you can also delete this document. To do so, use the -X option, which enables you to define the HTTP method that you want to use and write:

```
curl -X DELETE localhost:8080/exist/rest/db/xslt/rest-query-results.xsl
```

Of course, if you have run the previous command, you need to upload the transformation again before you can use it! Now that your stylesheet is stored in the database, to use it you just add a `_xsl` parameter, specifying its location. The URL to paste or type in your browser is then `http://localhost:8080/exist/rest/db/blog/?_query=//a&_xsl=/db/xslt/rest-query-results.xsl`. The result is shown in Figure 10-9.

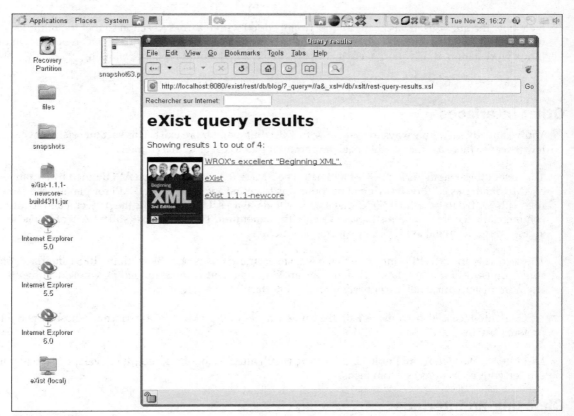

Figure 10-9

You have seen how to use HTTP GET, PUT, and DELETE methods. If you are familiar with HTTP, you may be wondering whether the REST interface supports the HTTP POST method. Yes, this method is used to send requests that are too big to be easily pasted in the query string of a HTTP GET request. These queries have to be wrapped into an XML document, the structure of which is defined in the eXist documentation. For instance, the query shown previously would become the following:

```
<?xml version="1.0" encoding="UTF-8"?>
<query xmlns="http://exist.sourceforge.net/NS/exist">
  <text>
    <![CDATA[
  for $item in /item
  where .//a[contains(@href, 'wrox.com')]
  return <match>
    <id>{string($item/@id)}</id>
```

```
        {$item/title}
        {$item//a[contains(@href, 'wrox.com')]}
    </match>
  ]]>
    </text>
</query>
```

Note how the query itself has been cautiously embedded within a CDATA section so that it qualifies as well-formed XML. To send this query using the REST interface, you can use curl and a -d option. On my Linux workstation, if this query were in linksToWrox.xml, I would type the following:

```
curl -d @linksToWrox.xml http://localhost:8080/exist/rest/db/
```

Other Interfaces

You've already seen four ways to interact with eXist, but many more exist. This section briefly covers a few (because there are many other cool, important topics to cover in this chapter).

The first of these methods is the XML:DB API. The XML:DB API is a common API defined by a number of XML databases editors. Its original purpose was to define a vendor-neutral API for playing the same role with XML databases that JDBC plays with SQL databases. Unfortunately, the project failed to attract commercial vendors and seems to have lost all its momentum. The XML:DB is still an API of choice to access your eXist database if you are developing in Java.

The second is an XML-RPC interface that covers everything that is possible with the REST interface, plus some bonuses — for example, you can update an XML fragment without uploading whole documents and administer your database entirely with this interface.

A SOAP interface is also available with the same features of the XML-RPC interface for those of you who prefer SOAP over XML-RPC.

Last but not least, an Atom Publishing Protocol (APP) interface has been recently developed so that you can see your collections as Atom feeds.

Choosing an Interface

With so many options, how do you decide which one you should be using? Ask yourself whether it really matters. You can think of your eXist database as a black box that encapsulates your XML documents. These documents are located in collections that are similar to file directories. The black box acts like a filesystem with XQuery capabilities and provides a number of different interfaces to access the same set of documents in different ways. Whatever interface is used, the effect is the same. You can choose, case by case, the interface that is most convenient for the task you have to do.

If you need a filesystem-like type of access to your documents, WebDAV is a sure choice. If all you have is a browser, the web interface is what you need. If your XML IDE supports eXist, that makes your life easier. If you're using a tool that is a good Web citizen and can use the different HTTP requests such as XForms, which you'll see in Chapter 20, you can plug the REST interface directly. If you're developing in Java, have a look at the XML:DB API. If you want to integrate your database with Atom tools, the APP interface is designed for you, and if you're a web services fan, you will choose either the XML-RPC or the SOAP interface.

The richness of this set of interfaces means that your documents will never be locked in the database and can remain accessible in any environment.

XML in Commercial RDBMSs

The practical reality is that huge volumes of data are currently stored in relational database management systems (RDBMSs). Moving that data to native XML storage, even if it were desirable and possible, would be a huge logistical task. For reasons similar to the continuing existence of the COBOL language in many enterprises, the task will never be carried out. Relational data works well for many practical business purposes, and many business processes depend critically on at least some of that relational data, so it would be folly to risk breaking something that works by moving all relational data to XML.

However, there is also an opposite pressure: the desire to use data derived from those traditional relational data stores in modern XML-based business processes, either within an enterprise or between enterprises. The question then becomes *how can additional XML-relevant functionality be added to existing relational databases?*

The vendors of major enterprise relational database management systems such IBM's DB2, Oracle, and Microsoft's SQL Server have taken different approaches. This section looks briefly at the XML functionality in SQL Server 2000, which can be considered a first-generation XML-enabled relational database management system. We also look in more depth at SQL Server 2005, which has added many more features, including XQuery and schema-based typing. Finally, we glance at some of the features being touted for the next version, currently known as Katmai.

> **SQL Server is available free as an edition known as SQL Express. You can download the database and tools from** `http://msdn.microsoft.com/vstudio/express/sql/`. **You are advised to download the version with advanced services, as well as Books Online and the sample databases to test the code in this chapter. Once everything is installed, you can open the manager, SSMS, by selecting Start ⇨ All programs ⇨ Microsoft SQL Server 2005 ⇨ SQL Server Management Studio Express.**

XML Functionality in SQL Server 2000

SQL Server 2000 was the first version of SQL Server to have any XML functionality. Microsoft describes SQL Server 2000 as an XML-enabled database. When you are introduced a little later to the XML functionality in SQL Server 2005, you will see that, in comparison, SQL Server 2000 is a partly XML-enabled database. The functionality in SQL Server 2000 that makes it an XML-enabled database includes the following:

- ❑ Support for XDR schemas (later upgraded to XSD schemas)
- ❑ HTTP access to SQL Server 2000
- ❑ SQLXML functionality (added in SQLXML 1.0)
- ❑ A SOAP component (added in SQLXML 3.0)
- ❑ Retrieval of XML using the SELECT statement and FOR XML clause
- ❑ Writing XML using the OPENXML rowset provider
- ❑ Retrieval of XML data using XPath 1.0

> SQL keywords are not case sensitive. Many people who code in SQL use uppercase for SQL keywords, but that is a convention only.

Most of these features are also available in SQL Server 2005, although some of the ways of accessing XML data in SQL Server 2000, particularly via HTTP, are now considered to be risky from a security standpoint or are too reliant on other applications such as IIS, and have been superseded by more secure ones in the newer version. SQL Server 2005 also includes its own web server.

XML Functionality in SQL Server 2005, the version followed SQL Server 2000, adds a raft of new features, including many centered on XML. It also has the capability to use .NET code to create stored procedures as well as enhanced T-SQL and built-in support for web services.

The basic XML features, such as returning records as XML instead of as tabular data, are backwardly compatible with SQL Server 2000, although there are now more options to provide precisely the data format needed. The examples that follow were all run on SQL Server 2005, but also indicate which ones will work on the previous version.

Returning Data as XML Using FOR XML

FOR XML allows most standard SQL queries to return data as XML, rather than as a recordset.

Several options are available to control the format of the XML, element names, whether data is output as elements or attributes, and how child records are nested. Consider the following query, which uses the AdventureWorks catalog included as a sample with the downloads recommended previously:

```
SELECT [PurchaseOrderID]
    , [Status]
    , [EmployeeID]
    , [VendorID]
    , [ShipMethodID]
    , [OrderDate]
    , [ShipDate]
    , [SubTotal]
    , [TaxAmt]
    , [Freight]
    , [TotalDue]
FROM [AdventureWorks].[Purchasing].[PurchaseOrderHeader]
WHERE [TotalDue] > 300000
```

This query selects the listed columns from the PurchaseOrderHeader table and limits the results returned to only those whose total exceeds $300,000.

The results resemble the output shown in Figure 10-10.

To convert this query to produce XML, add the phrase FOR XML followed by the type of XML query you want. There are four options, RAW, AUTO, EXPLICIT, and PATH, the last one new to SQL Server 2005.

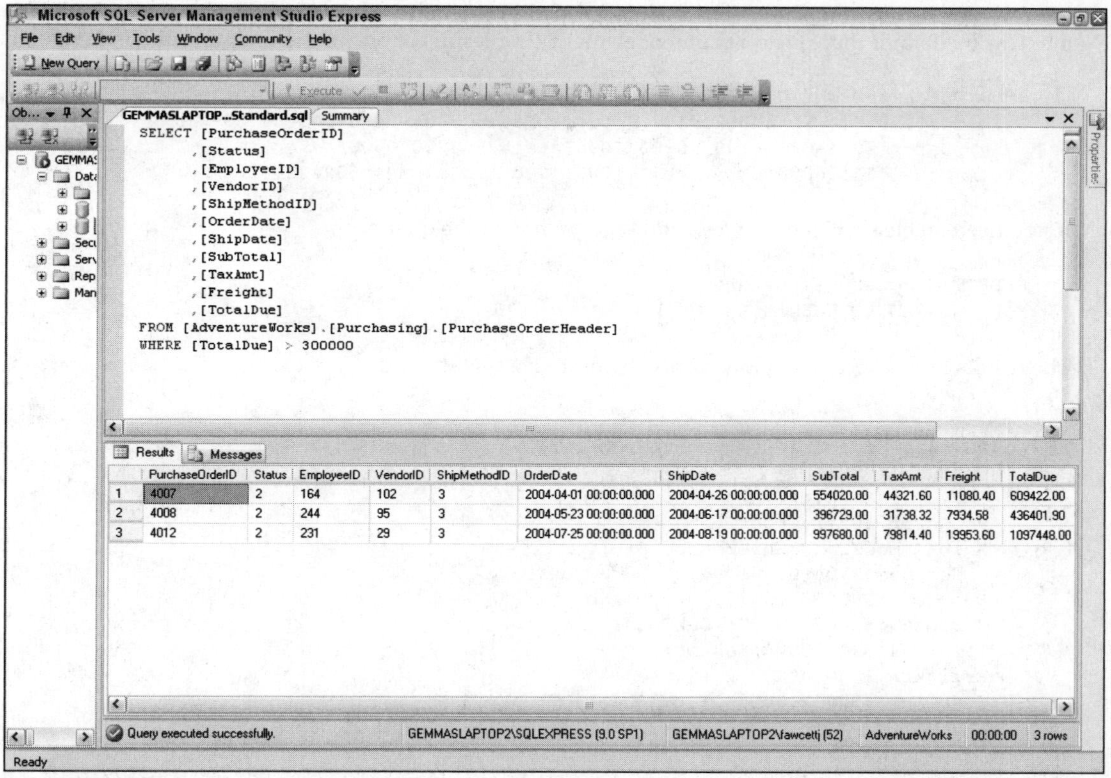

Figure 10-10

Using FOR XML RAW

To execute a query using the RAW option, use the following syntax:

```
SELECT [PurchaseOrderID]
      , [Status]
      , [EmployeeID]
      , [VendorID]
      , [ShipMethodID]
      , [OrderDate]
      , [ShipDate]
      , [SubTotal]
      , [TaxAmt]
      , [Freight]
      , [TotalDue]
  FROM [AdventureWorks].[Purchasing].[PurchaseOrderHeader]
  WHERE [TotalDue] > 300000
FOR XML RAW
```

FOR XML RAW returns the data as attributes wrapped in a generic <row> element. The XML is only a fragment, as by default there is no document element. The results of one of the rows are shown here:

```
<row PurchaseOrderID="4007" Status="2" EmployeeID="164"
  VendorID="102" ShipMethodID="3" OrderDate="2004-04-01T00:00:00"
  ShipDate="2004-04-26T00:00:00" SubTotal="554020.0000"
  TaxAmt="44321.6000" Freight="11080.4000" TotalDue="609422.0000" />
```

If you need an element-centric view, add , ELEMENTS to the query:

```
SELECT -- query as before
FOR XML RAW, ELEMENTS
```

The results now appear as follows (only the first <row> is shown):

```
<row>
  <PurchaseOrderID>4007</PurchaseOrderID>
  <Status>2</Status>
  <EmployeeID>164</EmployeeID>
  <VendorID>102</VendorID>
  <ShipMethodID>3</ShipMethodID>
  <OrderDate>2004-04-01T00:00:00</OrderDate>
  <ShipDate>2004-04-26T00:00:00</ShipDate>
  <SubTotal>554020.0000</SubTotal>
  <TaxAmt>44321.6000</TaxAmt>
  <Freight>11080.4000</Freight>
  <TotalDue>609422.0000</TotalDue>
</row>
```

Note two things you are likely to want to change when using FOR XML RAW. First, you may want to change the name of the default row element. Second, you may want to turn the fragment into a document by having an all-containing document element.

To change the name of the row element, specify your preferred name in parentheses after the RAW key word, as in FOR XML RAW('Order'). To specify the document element, add the keyword ROOT followed by the name in parentheses:

```
SELECT -- query as before
FOR XML RAW('Order'), ROOT('Orders') , ELEMENTS
```

The output of this query is shown in Figure 10-11.

A common problem when interfacing with data held in a relational database from object-oriented languages such as C# or Java is handling nulls. This also occurs when returning data as XML. The traditional approach in XML is to omit from the output an element or attribute whose value is null. For example, if a shipped order appears as

```
<Order>
  <PurchaseOrderID>4007</PurchaseOrderID>
  <Status>2</Status>
  <EmployeeID>164</EmployeeID>
  <VendorID>102</VendorID>
  <ShipMethodID>3</ShipMethodID>
```

```
    <OrderDate>2004-04-01T00:00:00</OrderDate>
    <ShipDate>2004-04-26T00:00:00</ShipDate>
    <SubTotal>554020.0000</SubTotal>
    <TaxAmt>44321.6000</TaxAmt>
    <Freight>11080.4000</Freight>
    <TotalDue>609422.0000</TotalDue>
    <OrderQty>5000</OrderQty>
    <ProductID>849</ProductID>
    <UnitPrice>24.7500</UnitPrice>
  </Order>
```

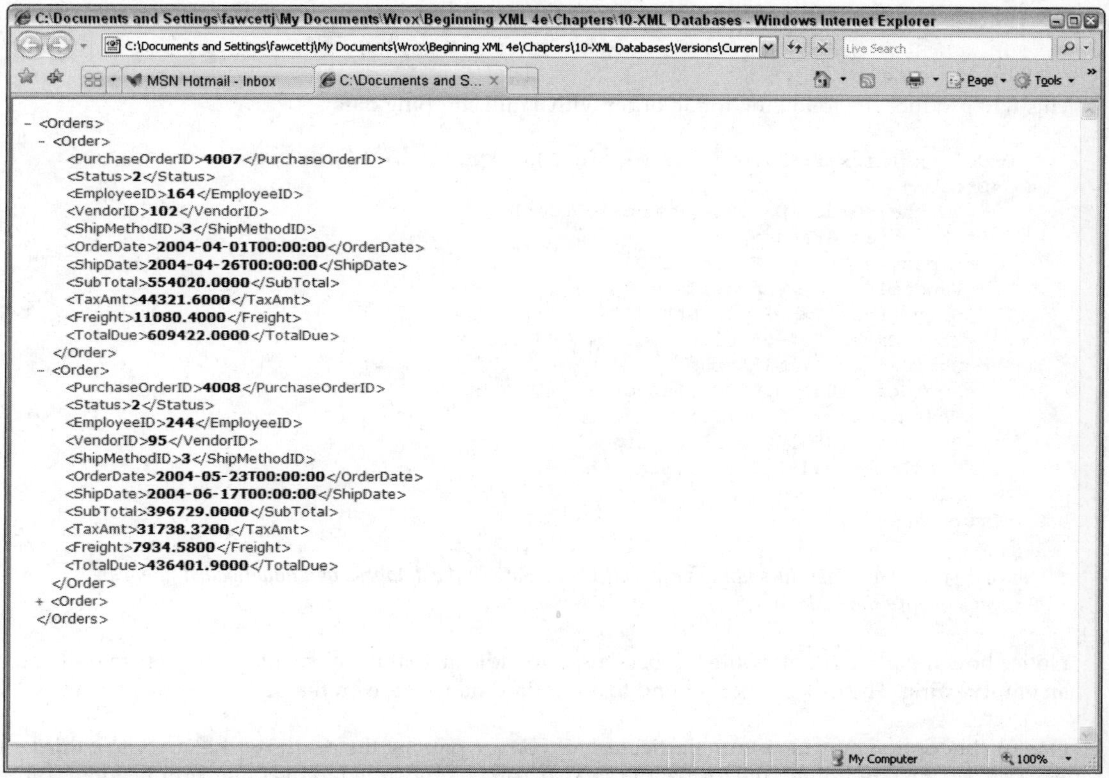

Figure 10-11

the following would show that the shipped date was NULL:

```
<Order>
  <PurchaseOrderID>4007</PurchaseOrderID>
  <Status>2</Status>
  <EmployeeID>164</EmployeeID>
  <VendorID>102</VendorID>
  <ShipMethodID>3</ShipMethodID>
  <OrderDate>2004-04-01T00:00:00</OrderDate>
  <SubTotal>554020.0000</SubTotal>
  <TaxAmt>44321.6000</TaxAmt>
```

```
        <Freight>11080.4000</Freight>
        <TotalDue>609422.0000</TotalDue>
    </Order>
```

This is not always convenient to process. Sometimes it is easier to have an empty element as a representation of a null:

```
        <ShipDate/>
```

To request that format, add XSINIL after the ELEMENTS keyword:

```
SELECT -- query as before
FOR XML RAW('Order'), ROOT('Orders'), ELEMENTS XSINIL
```

This will produce the following for an order with a null shipping date:

```
<Orders xmlns:xsi="http://www.w3.org/2001/XMLSchema-instance">
  <Order>
    <PurchaseOrderID>4007</PurchaseOrderID>
    <Status>2</Status>
    <EmployeeID>164</EmployeeID>
    <VendorID>102</VendorID>
    <ShipMethodID>3</ShipMethodID>
    <OrderDate>2004-04-01T00:00:00</OrderDate>
    <ShipDate xsi:nil="true" />
    <SubTotal>554020.0000</SubTotal>
    <TaxAmt>44321.6000</TaxAmt>
    <Freight>11080.4000</Freight>
    <TotalDue>609422.0000</TotalDue>
  </Order>
</Orders>
```

If that particular order does not have a NULL ship date in the database you downloaded, you can always modify the table first.

Notice how the xsi:nil attribute has been used to indicate that the element's contents are null and not an empty string. The xsi prefix is bound to a standard namespace on the Orders element.

One further option may be useful, particularly if you are passing the results of the query to a third party: An XML schema describing the format of the XML can be prepended to the data. Simply add a comma followed by XMLSCHEMA to the existing query:

```
FOR XML RAW('Order'), ROOT('Orders'), ELEMENTS XSINIL, XMLSCHEMA
```

The results will be identical to the previous output, but a schema such as the following will be shown:

```
<Orders xmlns:xsi="http://www.w3.org/2001/XMLSchema-instance">
  <xsd:schema targetNamespace="urn:schemas-microsoft-com:sql:SqlRowSet1"
        xmlns:xsd=http://www.w3.org/2001/XMLSchema
        xmlns:sqltypes=http://schemas.microsoft.com/sqlserver/2004/sqltypes
        elementFormDefault="qualified">
    <xsd:import namespace=http://schemas.microsoft.com/sqlserver/2004/sqltypes
        schemaLocation=
            "http://schemas.microsoft.com/sqlserver/2004/sqltypes/sqltypes.xsd"/>
    <xsd:element name="Order">
      <xsd:complexType>
        <xsd:sequence>
          <xsd:element name="PurchaseOrderID" type="sqltypes:int" nillable="1" />
          <xsd:element name="Status" type="sqltypes:tinyint" nillable="1" />
          <xsd:element name="EmployeeID" type="sqltypes:int" nillable="1" />
          <xsd:element name="VendorID" type="sqltypes:int" nillable="1" />
          <xsd:element name="ShipMethodID" type="sqltypes:int" nillable="1" />
          <xsd:element name="OrderDate" type="sqltypes:datetime" nillable="1" />
          <xsd:element name="ShipDate" type="sqltypes:datetime" nillable="1" />
          <xsd:element name="SubTotal" type="sqltypes:money" nillable="1" />
          <xsd:element name="TaxAmt" type="sqltypes:money" nillable="1" />
          <xsd:element name="Freight" type="sqltypes:money" nillable="1" />
          <xsd:element name="TotalDue" type="sqltypes:money" nillable="1" />
        </xsd:sequence>
      </xsd:complexType>
    </xsd:element>
  </xsd:schema>
  <!-- rest of order data as before -->
</Orders>
```

Using *FOR XML AUTO*

Although using FOR XML RAW gives you quite a bit of flexibility, it falters when your query produces nested data, such as all orders with their individual line items. Instead of a hierarchical XML document, you will still get one element containing all the order data and the item data for each line item ordered. This is difficult to process, wasteful of resources, and fails to capitalize on one of XML's strengths: its ability to clearly represent nested data. To overcome some of the problems with this, you can use FOR XML AUTO, as demonstrated in the following Try It Out.

Try It Out   **Using FOR XML AUTO**

1. To try FOR XML AUTO, simply replace the RAW keyword with AUTO in the basic query introduced in the preceding section:

```
SELECT [PurchaseOrderID]
      ,[Status]
      ,[EmployeeID]
      ,[VendorID]
      ,[ShipMethodID]
      ,[OrderDate]
      ,[ShipDate]
      ,[SubTotal]
```

```
         , [TaxAmt]
         , [Freight]
         , [TotalDue]
FROM [AdventureWorks] . [Purchasing] . [PurchaseOrderHeader]
WHERE [TotalDue] > 300000
FOR XML AUTO
```

You won't see much difference in the results of this query compared to the RAW version other than the fact that the name of the element holding the data is derived from the table name rather than being a generic row element:

```
<AdventureWorks.Purchasing.PurchaseOrderHeader
   PurchaseOrderID="4007" Status="2" EmployeeID="164" VendorID="102"
   ShipMethodID="3" OrderDate="2004-04-01T00:00:00" ShipDate="2004-04-26T00:00:00"
   SubTotal="554020.0000" TaxAmt="44321.6000" Freight="11080.4000"
   TotalDue="609422.0000" />
```

Again the result is a fragment with no all-enclosing document element.

2. The real difference becomes apparent when a query extracting data from two linked tables is executed. The following SQL shows all the previous orders along with their individual line items:

```
SELECT [PurchaseOrderHeader] . [PurchaseOrderID]
     , [PurchaseOrderHeader] . [Status]
     , [PurchaseOrderHeader] . [EmployeeID]
     , [PurchaseOrderHeader] . [VendorID]
     , [PurchaseOrderHeader] . [ShipMethodID]
     , [PurchaseOrderHeader] . [OrderDate]
     , [PurchaseOrderHeader] . [ShipDate]
     , [PurchaseOrderHeader] . [SubTotal]
     , [PurchaseOrderHeader] . [TaxAmt]
     , [PurchaseOrderHeader] . [Freight]
     , [PurchaseOrderHeader] . [TotalDue]
     , [PurchaseOrderDetail] . [OrderQty]
     , [PurchaseOrderDetail] . [ProductID]
     , [PurchaseOrderDetail] . [UnitPrice]
FROM [Purchasing] . [PurchaseOrderHeader] PurchaseOrderHeader
     INNER JOIN  Purchasing.PurchaseOrderDetail PurchaseOrderDetail
     ON PurchaseOrderHeader. [PurchaseOrderID] =
                          PurchaseOrderDetail. [PurchaseOrderID]
WHERE [PurchaseOrderHeader] . [TotalDue] > 300000
```

Here the tables have been joined on the PurchaseOrderId field and the tables have been aliased. The results of this query are shown in Figure 10-12.

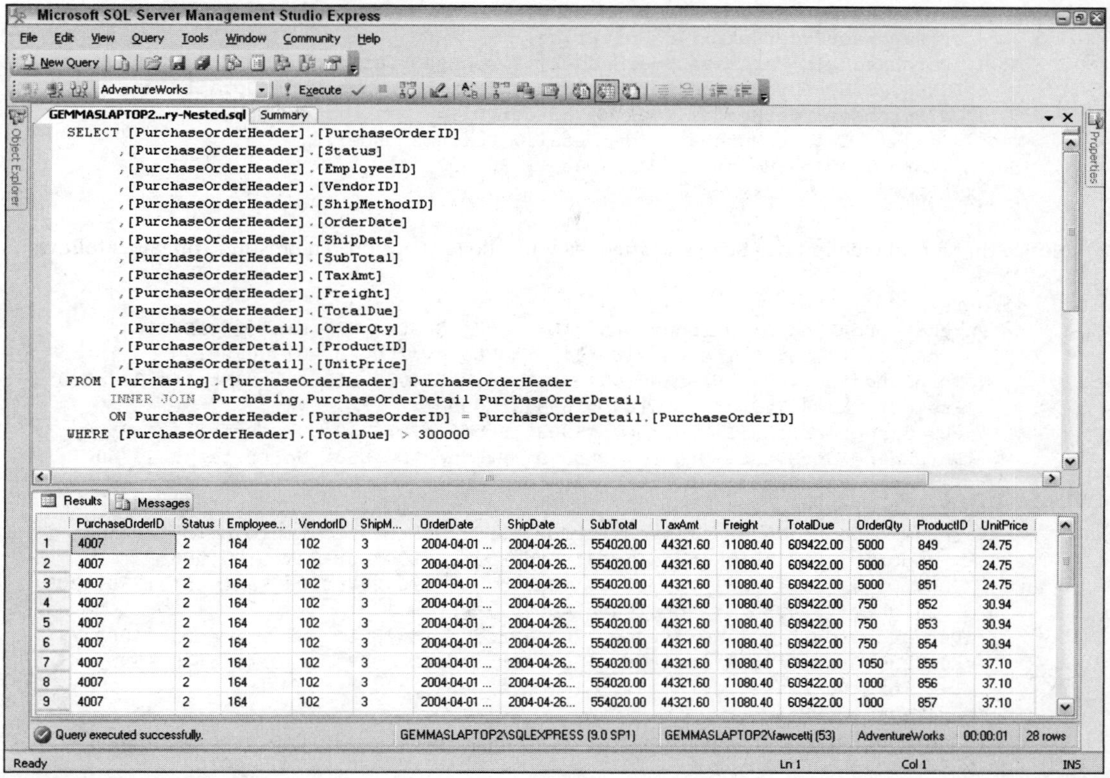

Figure 10-12

How It Works

Although the actual line item data, the last three columns in the result set, belong to the individual orders, this isn't readily apparent and each order header has to be repeated for these individual items. The actual nesting of the data is lost somewhat by the tabular representation of the results.

If this is query is modified to use FOR XML AUTO, the hierarchy is immediately obvious:

```
SELECT [PurchaseOrderHeader].[PurchaseOrderID]
     , [PurchaseOrderHeader].[Status]
     , [PurchaseOrderHeader].[EmployeeID]
     , [PurchaseOrderHeader].[VendorID]
     , [PurchaseOrderHeader].[ShipMethodID]
     , [PurchaseOrderHeader].[OrderDate]
     , [PurchaseOrderHeader].[ShipDate]
     , [PurchaseOrderHeader].[SubTotal]
     , [PurchaseOrderHeader].[TaxAmt]
     , [PurchaseOrderHeader].[Freight]
     , [PurchaseOrderHeader].[TotalDue]
     , [PurchaseOrderDetail].[OrderQty]
```

```
      ,[PurchaseOrderDetail].[ProductID]
      ,[PurchaseOrderDetail].[UnitPrice]
FROM [Purchasing].[PurchaseOrderHeader] PurchaseOrderHeader
      INNER JOIN  Purchasing.PurchaseOrderDetail PurchaseOrderDetail
      ON PurchaseOrderHeader.[PurchaseOrderID] =
                      PurchaseOrderDetail.[PurchaseOrderID]
WHERE [PurchaseOrderHeader].[TotalDue] > 300000
FOR XML AUTO, ROOT('Orders')
```

Notice that a root element has been specified, as with the RAW option. The results appear as follows:

```
<Orders>
  <PurchaseOrderHeader PurchaseOrderID="4007" Status="2" EmployeeID="164"
      VendorID="102" ShipMethodID="3" OrderDate="2004-04-01T00:00:00"
      ShipDate="2004-04-26T00:00:00" SubTotal="554020.0000" TaxAmt="44321.6000"
      Freight="11080.4000" TotalDue="609422.0000">
    <PurchaseOrderDetail OrderQty="5000" ProductID="849" UnitPrice="24.7500" />
    <PurchaseOrderDetail OrderQty="5000" ProductID="850" UnitPrice="24.7500" />
    <!-- more PurchaseOrderDetail elements -->
  </PurchaseOrderHeader>
  <PurchaseOrderHeader PurchaseOrderID="4008" Status="2" EmployeeID="244"
      VendorID="95" ShipMethodID="3" OrderDate="2004-05-23T00:00:00"
      ShipDate="2004-06-17T00:00:00" SubTotal="396729.0000" TaxAmt="31738.3200"
      Freight="7934.5800" TotalDue="436401.9000">
    <PurchaseOrderDetail OrderQty="700" ProductID="858" UnitPrice="9.1500" />
    <PurchaseOrderDetail OrderQty="700" ProductID="859" UnitPrice="9.1500" />
    <!-- more PurchaseOrderDetail elements -->
  </PurchaseOrderHeader>
  <PurchaseOrderHeader PurchaseOrderID="4012" Status="2" EmployeeID="231"
      VendorID="29" ShipMethodID="3" OrderDate="2004-07-25T00:00:00"
      ShipDate="2004-08-19T00:00:00" SubTotal="997680.0000" TaxAmt="79814.4000"
      Freight="19953.6000" TotalDue="1097448.0000">
    <PurchaseOrderDetail OrderQty="6000" ProductID="881" UnitPrice="41.5700" />
    <PurchaseOrderDetail OrderQty="6000" ProductID="882" UnitPrice="41.5700" />
    <!-- more PurchaseOrderDetail elements -->
  </PurchaseOrderHeader>
</Orders>
```

The other options available to FOR XML RAW, such as ELEMENTS, XSINIL, and XMLSCHEMA, are also available to FOR XML AUTO.

Also available are several less commonly used features, such as those to return binary data and to use GROUP BY in XML queries. These are covered at length in the SQL SERVER 2005 Books Online (BOL) available for download from www.microsoft.com/technet/prodtechnol/sql/2005/downloads/books.mspx.

Despite the different options available to both the RAW and the AUTO versions of FOR XML, you will likely encounter cases where neither alternative produces the output needed. The most common scenario is when you need a combination of both elements and attributes, rather than one or the other. Two options are available for this purpose, FOR XML EXPLICIT and FOR XML PATH, the latter being a new feature of SQL Server 2005.

Using FOR XML EXPLICIT

The EXPLICIT option enables almost unlimited control over the resulting XML format, but this comes at a price. The syntax is difficult to grasp, and because the mechanism used to construct the resulting XML is based on a forward-only XML writer, the results must be grouped and ordered in a very specific way. Unless you are stuck with SQL Server 2000, the advice from Microsoft and other experts is to use the PATH option instead. If you do need to use EXPLICIT, the full details are available in the SQL Server BOL.

Using FOR XML PATH

The PATH option makes building nested XML with combinations of elements and attributes relatively simple. Take the very first query results example, in which orders over $300,000 were retrieved and returned as attribute-centric XML using the AUTO option:

```
<Orders>
  <PurchaseOrderHeader PurchaseOrderID="4007" Status="2" EmployeeID="164"
      VendorID="102" ShipMethodID="3" OrderDate="2004-04-01T00:00:00"
      ShipDate="2004-04-26T00:00:00" SubTotal="554020.0000" TaxAmt="44321.6000"
      Freight="11080.4000" TotalDue="609422.0000" />
  <PurchaseOrderHeader PurchaseOrderID="4008" Status="2" EmployeeID="244"
      VendorID="95" ShipMethodID="3" OrderDate="2004-05-23T00:00:00"
      ShipDate="2004-06-17T00:00:00" SubTotal="396729.0000" TaxAmt="31738.3200"
      Freight="7934.5800" TotalDue="436401.9000" />
  <PurchaseOrderHeader PurchaseOrderID="4012" Status="2" EmployeeID="231"
      VendorID="29" ShipMethodID="3" OrderDate="2004-07-25T00:00:00"
      ShipDate="2004-08-19T00:00:00" SubTotal="997680.0000" TaxAmt="79814.4000"
      Freight="19953.6000" TotalDue="1097448.0000" />
</Orders>
```

What if a different layout were needed, one where the PurchaseOrderID, EmployeedID, and status were attributes but the other data appeared as elements? The PATH option uses aliases of the columns to specify how the XML is structured. The syntax is similar to XPath, covered in Chapter 7, hence the PATH keyword.

The PATH query for the order data as a mix of attributes and elements would be as follows:

```
SELECT [PurchaseOrderID] [@PurchaseOrderID]
      ,[Status] [@Status]
      ,[EmployeeID] [@EmployeeID]
      ,[VendorID]
      ,[ShipMethodID]
      ,[OrderDate]
      ,[ShipDate]
      ,[SubTotal]
      ,[TaxAmt]
      ,[Freight]
      ,[TotalDue]
FROM [AdventureWorks].[Purchasing].[PurchaseOrderHeader] PurchaseOrderHeader
WHERE [TotalDue] > 300000
FOR XML PATH('Order'), ROOT('Orders')
```

Notice how data that needs to be returned as attributes is aliased to a column name beginning with @. Unaliased columns are returned as elements. The results of this query would resemble this XML:

```
<Orders>
  <Order PurchaseOrderID="4007" Status="2" EmployeeID="164">
    <Vendor>102</Vendor>
    <ShipMethodID>3</ShipMethodID>
    <OrderDate>2004-04-01T00:00:00</OrderDate>
    <ShipDate>2004-04-26T00:00:00</ShipDate>
    <SubTotal>554020.0000</SubTotal>
    <TaxAmt>44321.6000</TaxAmt>
    <Freight>11080.4000</Freight>
    <TotalDue>609422.0000</TotalDue>
  </Order>
  <!-- more Order elements here -->
</Orders>
```

The PATH option also provides control over nesting. The usual way to do this, rather than use a SQL JOIN as shown previously, is to use a subquery. The following snippet shows the order header as attributes, with the order details as nested elements:

```
SELECT [PurchaseOrderHeader].[PurchaseOrderID] [@PurchaseOrderID]
      ,[PurchaseOrderHeader].[Status] [@Status]
      ,[PurchaseOrderHeader].[EmployeeID] [@EmployeeID]
      ,[PurchaseOrderHeader].[VendorID] [@VendorID]
      ,[PurchaseOrderHeader].[ShipMethodID] [@ShipMethodID]
      ,[PurchaseOrderHeader].[OrderDate] [@OrderDate]
      ,[PurchaseOrderHeader].[ShipDate] [@ShipDate]
      ,[PurchaseOrderHeader].[SubTotal] [@SubTotal]
      ,[PurchaseOrderHeader].[TaxAmt] [@TaxAmt]
      ,[PurchaseOrderHeader].[Freight] [@Freight]
      ,[PurchaseOrderHeader].[TotalDue] [@TotalDue]
      ,(
          SELECT [PurchaseOrderDetail].[OrderQty]
                ,[PurchaseOrderDetail].[ProductID]
                ,[PurchaseOrderDetail].[UnitPrice]
          FROM [Purchasing].[PurchaseOrderDetail] PurchaseOrderDetail
          WHERE PurchaseOrderHeader.[PurchaseOrderID] =
                              PurchaseOrderDetail.[PurchaseOrderID]
          ORDER BY PurchaseOrderDetail.[PurchaseOrderID]
          FOR XML PATH('OrderDetail'), TYPE
      )
FROM [Purchasing].[PurchaseOrderHeader] PurchaseOrderHeader
WHERE [PurchaseOrderHeader].[TotalDue] > 300000
FOR XML PATH('Order'), ROOT('Orders')
```

The main part of the query, without the inner SELECT, is much the same as before except all the output columns are specified as attributes, as shown by the alias name beginning with the @ symbol.

```
SELECT [PurchaseOrderHeader].[PurchaseOrderID] [@PurchaseOrderID]
      ,[PurchaseOrderHeader].[Status] [@Status]
      ,[PurchaseOrderHeader].[EmployeeID] [@EmployeeID]
      ,[PurchaseOrderHeader].[VendorID] [@VendorID]
      ,[PurchaseOrderHeader].[ShipMethodID] [@ShipMethodID]
```

```
    ,[PurchaseOrderHeader].[OrderDate] [@OrderDate]
    ,[PurchaseOrderHeader].[ShipDate] [@ShipDate]
    ,[PurchaseOrderHeader].[SubTotal] [@SubTotal]
    ,[PurchaseOrderHeader].[TaxAmt] [@TaxAmt]
    ,[PurchaseOrderHeader].[Freight] [@Freight]
    ,[PurchaseOrderHeader].[TotalDue] [@TotalDue]
    ,(
            -- Inner query here
    )
FROM [Purchasing].[PurchaseOrderHeader] PurchaseOrderHeader
WHERE [PurchaseOrderHeader].[TotalDue] > 300000
FOR XML PATH('Order'), ROOT('Orders')
```

The inner query returns the order detail relating to the customer specified in the outer query. This is accomplished by equating the `PurchaseOrderDetail.PurchaseOrderId` field in the outer query to the `PurchaseOrderDetail.PurchaseOrderID` in the nested query. (In pure SQL terms, this is known as a *correlated subquery*.)

```
SELECT [PurchaseOrderDetail].[OrderQty]
            ,[PurchaseOrderDetail].[ProductID]
            ,[PurchaseOrderDetail].[UnitPrice]
        FROM [Purchasing].[PurchaseOrderDetail] PurchaseOrderDetail
        WHERE PurchaseOrderHeader.[PurchaseOrderID] =
                PurchaseOrderDetail.[PurchaseOrderID]
        ORDER BY PurchaseOrderDetail.[PurchaseOrderID]
        FOR XML PATH('OrderDetail'), TYPE
```

Note the TYPE option at the end of the subquery. This is new to SQL Server 2005 and specifies that the resulting data should be converted to the XML datatype (this is covered more fully later in the chapter). This option ensures that the data is inserted as XML, rather than a string. The actual output from the query appears as follows:

```
<Orders>
  <Order PurchaseOrderID="4007" Status="2" EmployeeID="164" VendorID="102"
        ShipMethodID="3" OrderDate="2004-04-01T00:00:00"
        ShipDate="2004-04-26T00:00:00" SubTotal="554020.0000"
        TaxAmt="44321.6000" Freight="11080.4000" TotalDue="609422.0000">
    <OrderDetail>
      <OrderQty>5000</OrderQty>
      <ProductID>849</ProductID>
      <UnitPrice>24.7500</UnitPrice>
    </OrderDetail>
    <OrderDetail>
      <OrderQty>5000</OrderQty>
      <ProductID>850</ProductID>
      <UnitPrice>24.7500</UnitPrice>
    </OrderDetail>
    <OrderDetail>
      <OrderQty>5000</OrderQty>
      <ProductID>851</ProductID>
      <UnitPrice>24.7500</UnitPrice>
    </OrderDetail>
    <!-- more OrderDetails elements -->
```

```
    </Order>
    <Order PurchaseOrderID="4008" Status="2" EmployeeID="244" VendorID="95"
           ShipMethodID="3" OrderDate="2004-05-23T00:00:00"
           ShipDate="2004-06-17T00:00:00" SubTotal="396729.0000"
           TaxAmt="31738.3200" Freight="7934.5800" TotalDue="436401.9000">
      <OrderDetail>
        <OrderQty>700</OrderQty>
        <ProductID>858</ProductID>
        <UnitPrice>9.1500</UnitPrice>
      </OrderDetail>
      <!-- more OrderDetails elements -->
    </Order>
    <Order PurchaseOrderID="4012" Status="2" EmployeeID="231" VendorID="29"
           ShipMethodID="3" OrderDate="2004-07-25T00:00:00"
           ShipDate="2004-08-19T00:00:00" SubTotal="997680.0000"
           TaxAmt="79814.4000" Freight="19953.6000" TotalDue="1097448.0000">
      <OrderDetail>
        <OrderQty>6000</OrderQty>
        <ProductID>881</ProductID>
        <UnitPrice>41.5700</UnitPrice>
      </OrderDetail>
      <!-- more OrderDetails elements -->
    </Order>
</Orders>
```

As no aliasing was applied to the inner query, the columns are represented by XML elements.

If you remove the , TYPE from the inner query, the order details are inserted as escaped XML because they are treated as text data, not markup.

Plenty of other options are available. The final example shows how to group data within elements. The two dates associated with the order are grouped under a Dates element, and an OrderDetails element is used to hold the individual line items:

```
SELECT [PurchaseOrderHeader].[PurchaseOrderID] [@PurchaseOrderID]
      ,[PurchaseOrderHeader].[Status] [@Status]
      ,[PurchaseOrderHeader].[EmployeeID] [@EmployeeID]
      ,[PurchaseOrderHeader].[VendorID] [@VendorID]
      ,[PurchaseOrderHeader].[ShipMethodID] [@ShipMethodID]
      ,[PurchaseOrderHeader].[SubTotal] [@SubTotal]
      ,[PurchaseOrderHeader].[TaxAmt] [@TaxAmt]
      ,[PurchaseOrderHeader].[Freight] [@Freight]
      ,[PurchaseOrderHeader].[TotalDue] [@TotalDue]
      ,[PurchaseOrderHeader].[OrderDate] [Dates/Order]
      ,[PurchaseOrderHeader].[ShipDate] [Dates/Ship]
      , (
          SELECT [PurchaseOrderDetail].[OrderQty]
                ,[PurchaseOrderDetail].[ProductID]
                ,[PurchaseOrderDetail].[UnitPrice]
          FROM [Purchasing].[PurchaseOrderDetail] PurchaseOrderDetail
          WHERE PurchaseOrderHeader.[PurchaseOrderID] =
                PurchaseOrderDetail.[PurchaseOrderID]
          ORDER BY PurchaseOrderDetail.[PurchaseOrderID]
```

```
           FOR XML PATH('OrderDetail'), TYPE
         ) [OrderDetails]
FROM [Purchasing].[PurchaseOrderHeader] PurchaseOrderHeader
WHERE [PurchaseOrderHeader].[TotalDue] > 300000
FOR XML PATH('Order'), ROOT('Orders')
```

In the preceding code, the key change is to the OrderDate and ShipDate in the outer SELECT. The columns are aliased to Date/Order and Dates/Ship so SQL Server creates a new element, Dates, to hold these two values. There is also an alias on the entire subquery, OrderDetails, that causes all of its results to be grouped under one element. The resulting XML looks like this:

```
<Orders>
  <Order PurchaseOrderID="4007" Status="2" EmployeeID="164" VendorID="102"
ShipMethodID="3" SubTotal="554020.0000" TaxAmt="44321.6000" Freight="11080.4000"
TotalDue="609422.0000">
    <Dates>
      <Order>2004-04-01T00:00:00</Order>
      <Ship>2004-04-26T00:00:00</Ship>
    </Dates>
    <OrderDetails>
      <OrderDetail>
        <OrderQty>5000</OrderQty>
        <ProductID>849</ProductID>
        <UnitPrice>24.7500</UnitPrice>
      </OrderDetail>
      <OrderDetail>
        <OrderQty>5000</OrderQty>
        <ProductID>850</ProductID>
        <UnitPrice>24.7500</UnitPrice>
      </OrderDetail>
      <OrderDetail>
        <OrderQty>5000</OrderQty>
        <ProductID>851</ProductID>
        <UnitPrice>24.7500</UnitPrice>
      </OrderDetail>
      <!-- More OrderDetail elements -->
    </OrderDetails>
  </Order>
  <!-- More Order elements here -->
</Orders>
```

There are dozens more options for PATH queries, including how to produce comments, how to create text content, and how to add namespace declarations. For a full discussion, refer to Books Online.

This section dealt with producing XML given a relational source. The next topic, OPENXML, deals with the opposite challenge — how to parse XML and insert it into related tables.

Using OPENXML

There are three basic stages to processing XML and inserting its contents into standard database tables, also called *shredding*.

The first stage, analogous to loading a DOMDocument, uses a special stored procedure named `sp_xml_prepareDocument` to provide a pointer that is used by other methods to access the XML. The basic syntax is as follows:

```
DECLARE @XmlData NVARCHAR(MAX)
DECLARE @XmlPointer INT
SET @XmlData = '<root><element>One</element><element>Two</element></root>'
EXEC sp_xml_preparedocument @XmlPointer OUTPUT, @XmlData
```

`NVARCHAR(MAX)` *is a new variable type in SQL Server 2005 that is designed to replace other large text types such as* `NTEXT`. *When using SQL Server 2000, you can use* `NVARCHAR(4000)` *in the examples instead.*

In the background, SQL Server parses the text as XML and stores details of the document in an internal table. The variable `@XmlPointer` is used to retrieve this data.

The next stage is to actually process the XML. The `OPENXML` keyword is used to present the XML as a table. This is followed by a schema specifying which attributes and element data to return:

```
SELECT *
FROM OPENXML (@XmlPointer, '/root/element', 2)
     WITH (newName NVARCHAR(100) '.')
```

The first argument to `OPENXML` is the pointer to the parsed XML document. The second argument is the XPath to the nodes that will be used in each row of the output; in this case, each element is used to form an output row. The third argument specifies the mapping, attribute-centric or element-centric one: 1 is for attributes, 2 is for elements.

The `WITH` clause maps data from each element to the output. The first item is the column name, the second is the SQL datatype, and the third is the XPath to the data. The result will be a table with one column, as shown in Figure 10-13.

As an alternative to specifying the mapping using a `WITH` *clause, you can specify what is known as an edge table. Full details are provided in Books Online.*

The final stage of using `OPENXML` is to delete the XML document from SQL Server's internal table. If this is not done, then eventually the server runs out of memory and you won't be able to create any more XML documents. The deletion is done via the stored procedure `sp_xml_removedocument`:

```
EXEC sp_xml_removedocument @XmlPointer
```

One big advantage of `OPENXML` is that it enables you to construct stored procedures that accept arguments in the form of an array. This is virtually impossible using standard SQL. As a real-world example, imagine you have an e-commerce application that uses a traditional shopping basket. After customers finalize their choices, you need to pass the basket details to a stored procedure, maybe to calculate shipping or for other processing. Because the basket can hold a variable number of items, it is difficult to design the stored procedure. Using an XML string, life becomes much easier.

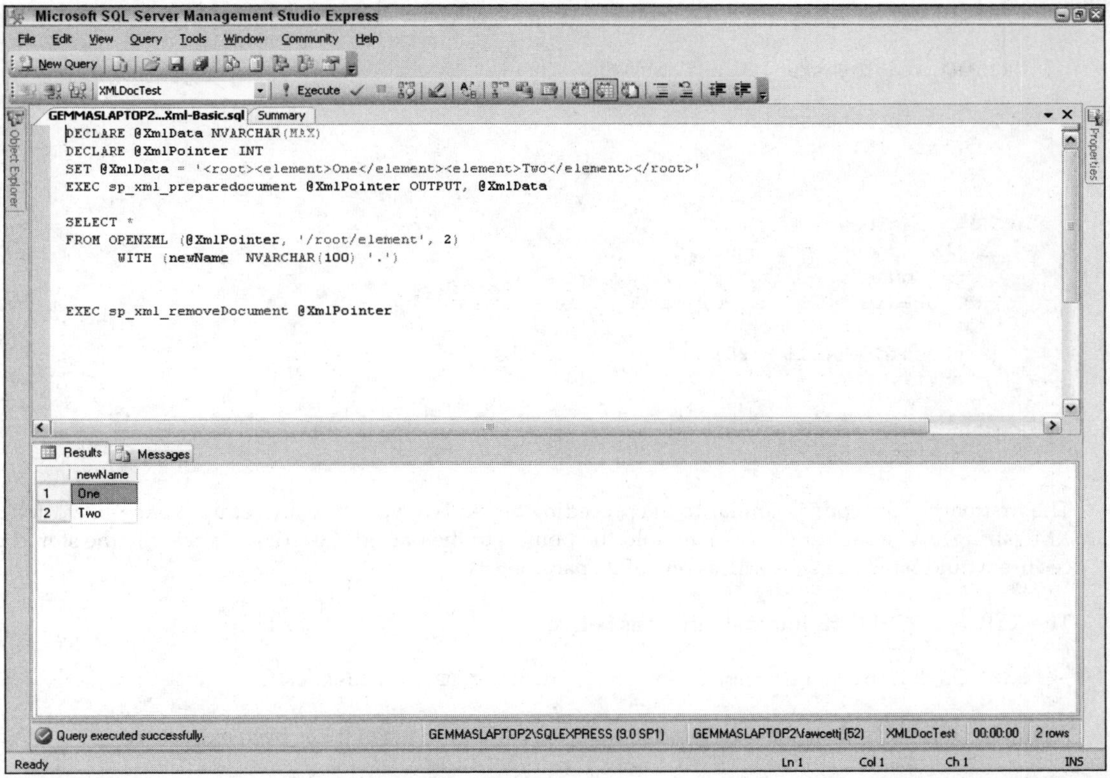

Figure 10-13

First, you need to decide on a format for the basket. Imagine each item is represented by an item element that has two attributes, the item's ID and the quantity requested:

```
<basket customerId="12345">
  <item productId="a123" quantity="1"/>
  <item productId="b456" quantity="3"/>
  <item productId="c789" quantity="2"/>
</basket>
```

The following SQL script will convert this into a table, ready for further processing or permanent storage:

```
DECLARE @BasketXml NVARCHAR(MAX)
DECLARE @BasketPointer INT
SET @BasketXml = '<basket customerId="12345">
                    <item productId="a123" quantity="1"/>
                    <item productId="b456" quantity="3"/>
                    <item productId="c789" quantity="2"/>
                  </basket>'
```

```
EXEC sp_xml_preparedocument @BasketPointer OUTPUT, @BasketXml

DECLARE @BasicBasket TABLE
(
  ProductId NVARCHAR(20),
  Quantity INT
)

INSERT @BasicBasket
  SELECT productId ProductId,
         quantity Quantity
  FROM OPENXML (@BasketPointer, '/basket/item', 1)
  WITH
  (productId NVARCHAR(20),
   quantity INT)

EXEC sp_xml_removedocument @BasketPointer
SELECT * FROM @BasicBasket
```

The first part of the code is similar to the preceding block. Two variables are set up: @BasketXml for the XML string, and @BasketPointer to hold the pointer to the parsed XML data. In real life the stored procedure would have @BasketXml as one of its parameters.

The XML is parsed to its internal format as before:

```
EXEC sp_xml_prepareDocument @BasketPointer OUTPUT, @BasketXml
```

A simple table variable is then declared to hold the XML data when it has been extracted:

```
DECLARE @BasicBasket TABLE
(
  ProductId NVARCHAR(20),
  Quantity INT
)
```

Then comes the crucial OPENXML statement:

```
SELECT productId ProductId,
       quantity Quantity
FROM OPENXML (@BasketPointer, '/basket/item', 1)
WITH
(productId NVARCHAR(20),
 quantity INT)
```

In this example, the third parameter to OPENXML is 1, specifying attribute mapping. The WITH clause specifies the two resulting columns as NVARCHAR(20) and INT, and there is no need for the third argument, as attributes are the default.

Finally, the XML pointer is released and the results displayed, as shown in Figure 10-14.

The next section deals with the most revolutionary addition to SQL Server 2005: the XML datatype.

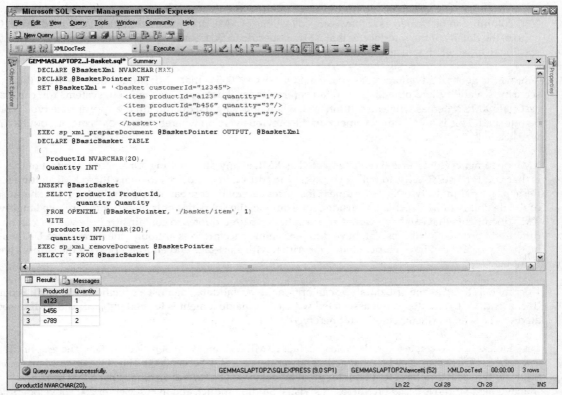

Figure 10-14

The xml Datatype

SQL Server 2005 adds a new `xml` datatype, which means that XML documents can be stored in a SQL Server 2005 database without — as was the only option in SQL Server 2000 — being shredded into parts and stored in multiple relational tables that conform with the relational data model or stored simply as a sequence of characters, which loses the logical content of the XML document. XML data stored as the `xml` datatype can, in effect, be treated as if it were still an XML document. In reality, the `xml` datatype is stored in a proprietary binary format under the hood, but as far as the developer is concerned, it is accessible as XML, with its logical structure intact.

> *There are one or two differences between the data stored by SQL Server and the original document, and it is not possible to round-trip between the two and get an identical copy, although the XML Infoset is preserved (see Chapter 7 for details).*

This is a significant improvement over SQL Server 2000, where XML documents were either shredded using `OpenXML` as described earlier or saved as a text format that could be retrieved only as a series of characters. Queries on the latter documents could not necessarily rely on well-formedness or validity of the text cum XML that was being retrieved, and all XML-specific processing needed to take place outside the database, often in the middle tier of a three-tier application.

The existence of the xml datatype means that XML documents stored, for example, in an SQL Server 2005 column, can be treated as if they were collections of XML documents sitting on your hard drive. Of course, the details of the interface to that XML is specific to SQL Server 2005, just as there were aspects specific to eXist when you accessed XML stored in it.

Among the general advantages of storage in SQL Server 2005 is that XML storage benefits from the security, scalability, and other aspects of an enterprise-level database management system. You can also associate XML schemas with the column and, when querying the document, the appropriate type will be returned. This is a vast improvement on the previous version whereby much CASTing or CONVERTing was needed.

XML documents stored in 2005 can be treated as XML in any other setting. One practical effect of that is that you can use XQuery, to which you were introduced in Chapter 9, to query these XML columns. Perhaps surprisingly, two XML document instances cannot be compared in this release, in part because of the flexibility of XML syntax. Consider, for example, the subtleties of trying to compare two lengthy XML documents that can have paired apostrophes or paired quotes to contain attribute values, can have differently ordered attributes, can have different namespace prefixes although the namespace URI may be the same, and can have empty elements written with start-tags and end-tags or with the empty element tag.

Documents stored as the XML datatype can optionally be validated against a specified W3C XML Schema document. XML data that is not associated with a schema document is termed *untyped*, and XML associated with a schema documented is termed *typed*.

Let's look at how to create a simple table to contain XML documents in SQL Server 2005. The graphical interface in SQL Server 2005 has changed significantly from SQL Server 2000. The SQL Server Management Studio is the main graphical tool for manipulating database objects and writing SQL code. The SQL Management Studio is based on Microsoft's Visual Studio product, and in SQL Server 2005 developers can create solutions and projects in ways that are likely to be familiar to them if they are users of Visual Studio.

Try It Out   Creating XML Documents in SQL Server

1. After following the installation instructions on the download page, http://msdn.microsoft.com/vstudio/express/sql/, open the Management Studio and connect to the instance of SQL Server that is of interest.

2. In the Object Explorer, expand the nodes so that User Databases is shown. Right-click and select the New Database option. A dialog box opens into which you insert the name of the database — XMLDocTest for this example. Before clicking OK, make sure that the Full Text Indexing option is checked.

3. Create a table called Docs using the following SQL:

```
CREATE TABLE dbo.Docs (
 DocID INTEGER IDENTITY PRIMARY KEY,
 XMLDoc XML
 )
```

The column XMLDoc is of type xml. Because this is an SQL statement, the datatype is not case sensitive. Now you have an empty table.

4. For the purposes of this example, you will add simple XML documents with the following structure:

```
<Person>
 <FirstName></FirstName>
 <LastName></LastName>
</Person>
```

5. Insert XML documents using the SQL INSERT statement, as follows, which shows insertion of a single XML document:

```
INSERT Docs
VALUES ('<Person><FirstName>Joe</FirstName>
<LastName>Fawcett</LastName></Person>'
)
```

6. After modifying the values of the FirstName and LastName elements and adding a few documents to the XMLDoc column, confirm that retrieval works correctly using the following SQL statement:

```
SELECT XMLDoc FROM Docs
```

The result of that SQL Query is shown in Figure 10-15.

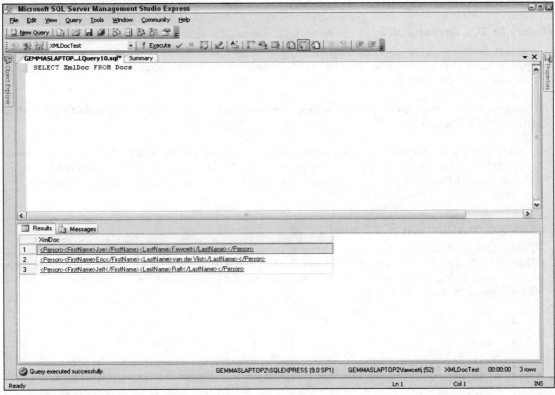

Figure 10-15

The values contained in the XMLDoc column are displayed in the lower pane of the figure. A little later, you will create some simple XQuery queries.

How It Works

The first step created a table, Docs, which had one of the columns, XmlDoc, defined as the new XML type. The next stage used a traditional INSERT query to add some text to this column. Because the column was defined as XML, the data was converted from text to an XML document. The document can be retrieved by using a traditional SELECT query.

As an alternative to retrieving the whole XML document, you can also select only parts of it (this is shown later in the chapter).

XML documents in SQL Server 2005 can be indexed for more efficient retrieval, and optionally a full-text index can be created. To create a full-text index on a document, use a command like the following:

```
--If no catalog exists so far
CREATE FULLTEXT CATALOG ft ON DEFAULT
CREATE FULLTEXT INDEX ON dbo.Docs(XmlDoc) KEY INDEX <primary key name>Doc)
```

The xml datatype allows the following methods to be used: query(), value(), exist(), modify(), and nodes().

XQuery in SQL Server 2005

The xml datatype can be queried using the XQuery language, introduced in Chapter 9. In SQL Server 2005, XQuery expressions are embedded inside Transact-SQL. Transact-SQL is the flavor of the SQL language used in SQL Server.

Standard XQuery is covered in detail in Chapter 9, so the following sections concentrate on the additions offered by SQL Server.

Microsoft has learned from its past mistakes and has chosen to separate the nonstandard update functionality from the standardized XQuery. This way, it can add the capability to insert, delete, and replace, when these become part of XQuery, without breaking past code. It will then deprecate the nonstandard extensions and eventually phase them out.

Extensions to XQuery in SQL Server 2005

The W3C XQuery specification is limited in that it can only query an XML (or XML-enabled) data source. There is no facility in XQuery 1.0 to carry out deletions, to insert new data, or (combining those actions) to modify data. In SQL Server 2005, the XML Data Modification Language (DML) adds three keywords to the functionality available in XQuery 1.0:

❑   delete

❑   insert

❑   replace value of

Note that although SQL itself is not case sensitive, the preceding commands are; if you use DELETE instead of delete, you will receive a cryptic error message.

Try It Out   **Deleting with XML DML**

For this exercise, let's first look at using the `delete` keyword. The following code shows an example of how it can be used:

```
DECLARE @myDoc XML
SET @myDoc = '<Person><FirstName>Joe</FirstName>
 <LastName>Fawcett</LastName></Person>
 '
SELECT @myDoc
SET @myDoc.modify(' delete /Person/*[2]
')
SELECT @myDoc
```

If you have access to SQL Server 2005, follow these steps:

1.   Open the SQL Server Studio.

2.   Connect to the default instance.

3.   From the menu, select New SQL Server Query.

4.   Enter the preceding code.

5.   Press F5 to run the SQL code. If you have typed in the code correctly, the original document should be displayed, with the modified document displayed below it. In the modified document, the `LastName` element has been removed.

6.   Adjust the width of the columns to display the full XML.

How It Works

The first line of the code declares a variable `myDoc` and specifies the datatype as `xml`. The `SET` statement

```
SET @myDoc = '<Person><FirstName>Joe</FirstName>
 <LastName>Fawcett</LastName></Person>
 ')
```

specifies a value for the `myDoc` variable. It's a familiar `Person` element with `FirstName` and `LastName` child elements and corresponding text content.

The `SELECT` statement following the `SET` statement causes the value of `myDoc` to be displayed. Next, the `modify` function is used to modify the value of the `xml` datatype:

```
SET @myDoc.modify('
 delete /Person/*[2]
')
```

The Data Modification Language statement inside the `modify` function is, like XQuery, case sensitive. The `delete` keyword is used to specify which part of the XML document is to be deleted. In this case, the XPath expression `/Person/*[2]` specifies that the second child element of the `Person` element is to be deleted, which is the `LastName` element.

The final `SELECT` statement shows the value of `myDoc` after the deletion has taken place. Figure 10-16 shows the results of both `SELECT` statements.

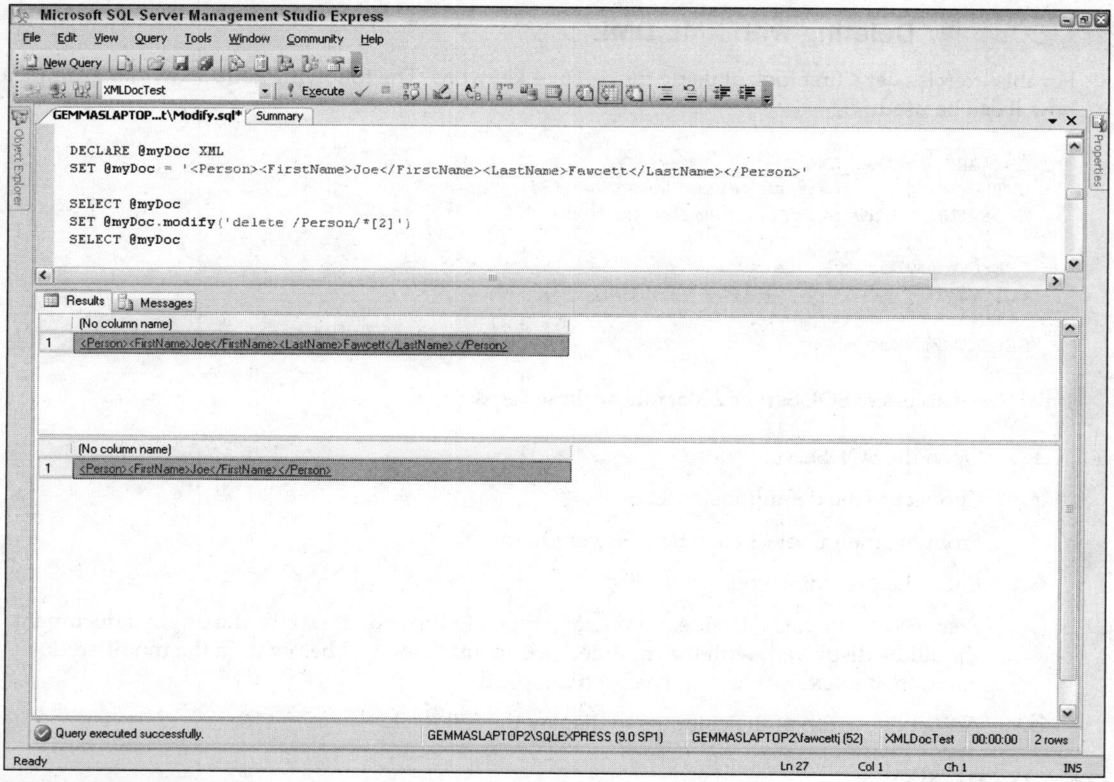

Figure 10-16

Try It Out   Inserting with XML DML

This example uses the `insert` keyword. The Transact-SQL code is shown here:

```
DECLARE @myDoc XML
SET @myDoc = '<Person><LastName>Fawcett</LastName></Person>'
SELECT @myDoc
SET @myDoc.modify(' insert <FirstName>Joe</FirstName> as first into /Person[1]
')
SELECT @myDoc
```

1.   Open the SQL Server Studio.

2.   Connect to the default instance.

3.   From the Start page, select New SQL Server Query.

4. Enter the preceding code.

5. Press F5 to run the SQL code. If you have typed in the code correctly, the original document should be displayed, with the modified document displayed below it. The modified document has a new FirstName element.

6. Adjust the width of the columns to display the full XML.

How It Works

In the first line you declare a variable myDoc and specify it has the datatype xml. In the code

```
SET @myDoc = '<Person><LastName>Fawcett</LastName></Person>'
```

you set the value of the myDoc variable and specify a Person element that contains only a LastName element, which contains the text Fawcett.

The modify function is used to contain the XQuery extension that you want to use. The insert keyword specifies that the modification is an insert operation. The XML to be inserted follows the insert keyword. Notice that it is not enclosed by apostrophes or quotes. The clause as first specifies that the inserted XML is to be inserted first, and the into clause uses an XPath expression, /Person, to specify that the FirstName element and its content is to be added as a child element to the Person element. Given the as first clause, you know that the FirstName element is to be the first child of the Person element.

As alternatives to into, you could also use after or before. Whereas into adds children to a parent node, after or before add siblings. The preceding query could be rewritten as follows:

```
DECLARE @myDoc XML
SET @myDoc = '<Person><LastName>Fawcett</LastName></Person>'
SELECT @myDoc
SET @myDoc.modify(' insert <FirstName>Joe</FirstName>
 before (/Person/LastName)[1]')
SELECT @myDoc
```

When you run the Transact-SQL, the first SELECT statement causes the original XML to be displayed, and the second SELECT statement causes the XML to be displayed after the insert operation has completed. The results are shown in Figure 10-17.

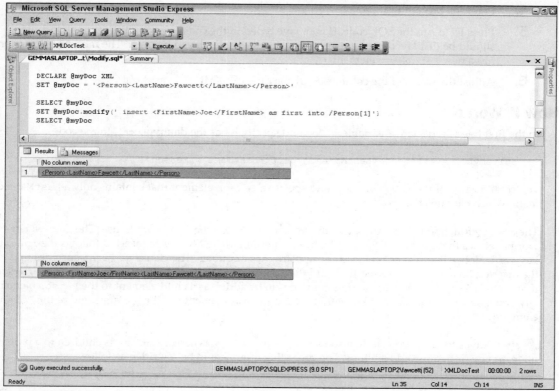

Figure 10-17

Updating with XML DML

The final example using the Data Modification Language updates the content of an XML variable so that the value of the FirstName element is changed from Joe to Gillian. The code is shown here:

```
DECLARE @myDoc XML
SET @myDoc = '<Person><FirstName>Joe</FirstName>
 <LastName>Fawcett</LastName></Person>'
SELECT @myDoc
SET @myDoc.modify(' replace value of (/Person/FirstName/text())[1] with "Gillian"
 ')
SELECT @myDoc
```

1. Open the SQL Server Studio.
2. Connect to the default instance.
3. From the Start page, select New SQL Server Query.
4. Enter the preceding code.

5. Press F5 to run the SQL code. If you have typed in the code correctly, the original document should be displayed, with the modified document displayed below it. The document now has Gillian instead of Joe for the FirstName element's contents.

6. Adjust the width of the columns to display the full XML.

How It Works

Notice the modify function:

```
SET @myDoc.modify('
  replace value of (/Person/FirstName/text())[1]
  with "Gillian"
  ')
```

The replace value of keyword indicates an update, and an XPath expression indicates which part of the XML the update is to be applied to. In this case it is the text node that is the child of the FirstName element — in other words, the value of the FirstName element — specified by the XPath expression /Person/FirstName/text().

The results of the two SELECT statements are shown in Figure 10-18.

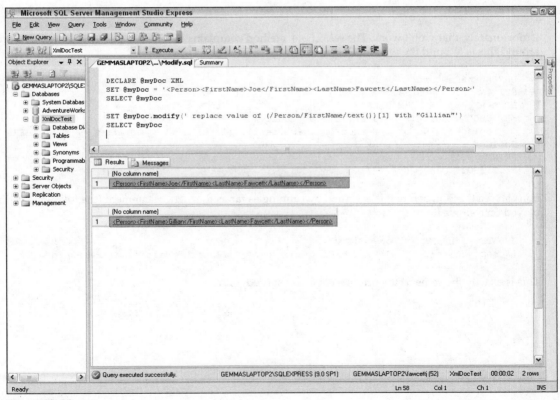

Figure 10-18

One of the main problems with using the `modify()` method is that it expects a hard-coded string as its argument. It is therefore difficult to make dynamic queries that are needed in the real world — for example, queries in which the new XML is brought in from another table. There are two ways around this. First, you can construct the query as a string and execute it dynamically using EXEC. Alternatively, you can use the built-in functions `sql:column` and `sql:function`. An example of each of these techniques follows.

For these examples you can use the `Docs` table created earlier. First, here's a reminder of what a static update looks like:

```
UPDATE Docs
SET XmlDoc.modify
(' replace value of (/Person/LastName/text())[1] with "Salt"')
WHERE DocId = 1
```

Now suppose you want to replace the hard-coded value `Salt` with a variable. You might first try this:

```
DECLARE @NewName NVARCHAR(100)
SET @NewName = N'Salt'
UPDATE Docs
SET XmlDoc.modify(' replace value of (/Person/LastName/text())[1] with "' +
@NewName + '"')
WHERE DocId = 1
```

Unfortunately, that won't work. The `modify()` method complains that it needs a string literal. One way around this is to build the whole SQL statement dynamically:

```
DECLARE @NewName NVARCHAR(100)
SET @NewName = N'Salt'
DECLARE @SQL NVARCHAR(MAX)
SET @SQL = 'UPDATE Docs SET XmlDoc.modify(
'' replace value of (/Person/LastName/text())[1] with "' + @NewName + '"'') WHERE
DocId = 1'
PRINT(@SQL)
EXEC(@SQL)
```

You can see the SQL before it is executed by running as far as the PRINT statement (the following is displayed on a single line):

```
UPDATE Docs SET XmlDoc.modify
(' replace value of (/Person/LastName/text())[1] with "Salt"') WHERE DocId = 1
```

This is exactly the same as the original code you started with.

The recommended way, however, is to use the built-in functions `sql:column` or `sql:variable`. `sql:column` is used when the new data is being retrieved from a table, so here `sql:variable` is needed:

```
DECLARE @NewName NVARCHAR(100)
SET @NewName = N'Salt'
UPDATE Docs
SET XmlDoc.modify
(' replace value of (/Person/LastName/text())[1] with sql:variable("@NewName")')
WHERE DocId = 1
```

The basic syntax is the name of the variable enclosed in double quotes as an argument to `sql:variable()`.

The query() Method

The `query()` method enables you to construct XQuery statements in SQL Server 2005. The syntax follows the XQuery syntax discussed in Chapter 9, and all the queries in that chapter can be run against a suitable XML data column.

The following query uses the `query()` method to output the names of each person in a newly constructed `Name` element, with the value of the `LastName` element followed by a comma and then the value of the `FirstName` element. The code is shown here:

```
SELECT XMLDoc.query
('for $p in /Person return
 <Name>{$p/LastName/text()}, {$p/FirstName/text()}</Name>')
FROM Docs
```

The first line indicates that a selection is being made using the `query()` method applied to the `XMLDoc` column (which, of course, is of datatype `xml`).

The `for` clause specifies that the variable `$p` is bound to the `Person` element node.

The `return` clause specifies that a `Name` element is to be constructed using an element constructor. The first part of the content of each `Name` element is created by evaluating the XQuery expression `$p/LastName/text()`, which, of course, is the text content of the `LastName` element. A literal comma is output, and then the XQuery expression `$p/FirstName/text()` is evaluated.

Figure 10-19 shows the output when the SELECT statement containing the XQuery query is run.

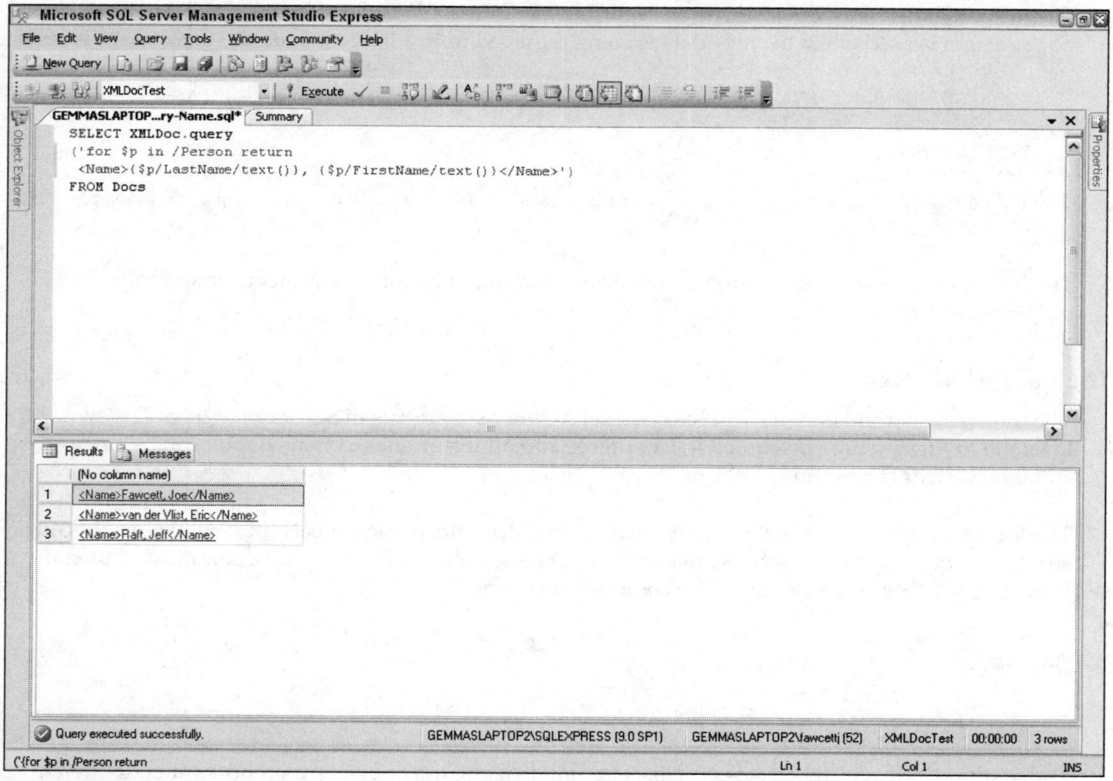

Figure 10-19

W3C XML Schema in SQL Server 2005

It was mentioned earlier that the new xml datatype is now a first-class datatype in SQL Server 2005. This datatype can be used to store untyped and typed XML data, so it shouldn't be surprising that, just as relational data is specified by a schema, the new xml datatype can be associated with a W3C XML Schema document to specify its structure. The XDR schema language that was used in SQL Server 2000 has been replaced by W3C XML Schema in SQL Server 2005.

Let's look at how you can specify a schema for data of type xml. The first task is to create a schema collection together with its first XML Schema. You need to give the collection a name — in this example EmployeesSchemaCollection — and the W3C XML Schema document itself needs to be delimited with single quote marks. For example, if you wanted to create a very simple schema for a document that could contain a Person element and child elements named FirstName and LastName, you could do so using the following syntax:

```
CREATE XML SCHEMA COLLECTION EmployeesSchemaCollection AS
'<xsd:schema xmlns:xsd="http://www.w3.org/2001/XMLSchema"
targetNamespace="http://wiley.com/namespaces/Person"
xmlns="http://wiley.com/namespaces/Person">
```

```
  <xsd:element name="Person">
   <xsd:complexType>
    <xsd:sequence>
     <xsd:element name="FirstName" />
     <xsd:element name="LastName" />
    </xsd:sequence>
   </xsd:complexType>
  </xsd:element>
 </xsd:schema>'
```

If you want to drop the XML Schema collection, you need to issue a DROP XMLSCHEMA statement:

```
DROP XML SCHEMA COLLECTION EmployeesSchemaCollection
```

Once you have a collection you can add new schemas using the following syntax:

```
ALTER XML SCHEMA COLLECTION EmployeesSchemaCollection ADD
'<xsd:schema>
  <!--new schema inserted here -->
</xsd:schema>'
```

Untyped and typed xml data can be used in an SQL Server column, variable, or parameter. If you want to create a Docs table and associate it with a W3C XML Schema document, you can do so using code like the following:

```
CREATE TABLE [dbo].[Docs](
  [DocID] [int] IDENTITY(1,1) PRIMARY KEY,
  [XMLDoc] [xml] (EmployeesSchemaCollection))
```

The advantage of applying a schema collection is twofold. First, it acts as a validation check; XML not conforming to one of the schemas in the collection will be rejected in the same way that a column declared as an INT will not accept random textual data. Second, queries against the XML will return typed data as specified by the schema, rather than generic text.

For optimization, XML Schemas are shredded and stored internally in a proprietary format. Most of the schema can be reconstructed as an XML document from this proprietary format using the xml_schema_ namespace intrinsic function. Therefore, if you had imported the schema shown earlier, you could retrieve it using the following code:

```
SELECT xml_schema_namespace(N'dbo', N'EmployeesSchemaCollection')
```

Remember, too, that there can be multiple ways of writing a functionally equivalent W3C XML Schema document — for example, using references, named types, or anonymous types. SQL Server will not respect such differences when reconstituting a schema document.

In addition, parts of the schema that are primarily documentation — for example, annotations and comments — are not stored in SQL Server's proprietary format. Therefore, to ensure precise recovery of an original W3C XML Schema document, it is necessary to store the serialized XML Schema document separately. One possibility is to store it in a column of type xml or varchar(max) in a separate table.

Web Service Support

SQL Server 2000 provided various means of accessing XML data over HTTP based on the underlying relational tables in a catalog. Much of this is still available to some degree in SQL Server 2005, but it has been superseded somewhat by the native support for web services. Unfortunately, this extra power comes at a price; the newer functionality is more difficult to set up and relies on a number of different components working together in order to use even a basic service.

The stages involved are fully documented in SQL Server Books Online under the heading "Using Native XML Web Services."

The main advantages of using the native functionality are listed here:

- ❑ **Greater availability** — Any client capable of issuing HTTP requests and parsing XML can take advantage of the new services.

- ❑ **Standards compliant** — The SOAP standard is now well defined and in use all over the Web. Rather than need special ways to access the data, the client will not even know that it is SQL Server operating in the background.

- ❑ **Built-in web server** — There is no need for a separate instance of IIS to be running.

- ❑ **Better security** — SQL Server has a relatively easy to use security model that allows suitable authentication and authorization for any services offered.

- ❑ **Reuse of existing monitoring tools** — Numerous tools are already available that can be used to monitor and tweak performance of the services while they are running on the server.

XML in Open Source RDBMS

The driving factors to add XML support within open-source RDBMSs are the same as those of their commercial competitors, but open-source RDBMSs appear to lag well behind in this area. The reasons are diverse. Open-source projects are often less prone than commercial companies to "get big fast" and absorb all their surroundings. They are also more used to collaborating with other projects. It is also possible that they are less influenced by the trendy buzzword to adopt "XML anywhere." In addition, they often have fewer financial resources for their development.

Of the three major open-source relational databases, two (PostgreSQL and Ingres) have close to no XML support; and the third, MySQL, is introducing its first XML features in version 5.1, which is in beta as this chapter is being written.

Installing MySQL

MySQL can be downloaded from `http://dev.mysql.com/downloads/`. Follow the links to Community Server and choose version 5.1 (or later if available). Stable versions of MySQL are also available from the packaging systems of various Linux distributions, but currently that is not an option, because the features shown here are currently only available in MySQL version 5.1, which is still beta.

The download page includes a sources download and a number of binary downloads for the most common platforms, including Windows, many Linux distributions, and Mac OS X. Choose the option that is the best match for your platform and follow the instructions for that platform.

For this chapter, you need to install the server and the client programs. If you are a Debian or Ubuntu user, then select the "Linux x86 generic RPM (dynamically linked) downloads," convert the .rpm packages into .deb packages using the Debian alien package and `alien` command, and install it like any other package using the Debian `dpkg -i` command.

If you like fancy user interfaces, you can also download and install MySQL GUI tools. These tools are also available from the main MySQL download page in version 5.0. They are not fully compatible with version 5.1 of the server, but most of their features work well; and those that fail seem to fail without doing any harm. (Because they are not available in their own version 5.1, you can simply use those that come with your favorite Linux distribution if you are using one.)

If you were installing a MySQL database for anything else than test purposes, it is recommended that you set up proper users and passwords to protect your database. For the tests covered in this chapter, just leave the default configuration to make your life slightly simpler during this first encounter with MySQL. Of course, if you want to keep this setup afterward, add proper passwords.

Adding Information in MySQL

To interact with MySQL you can use a GUI tool, but if you really want to understand what's going on behind the scene, the mysql command-line utility is your best friend. Open a Unix or DOS terminal and type **mysql -u root**. If everything is OK, you should see the mysql prompt:

```
vdv@grosbill:~/beginning-xml/0764570773/ch 10 $ mysql -u root
Welcome to the MySQL monitor.  Commands end with ; or \g.
Your MySQL connection id is 14
Server version: 5.1.12-beta-log MySQL Community Server (GPL)

Type 'help;' or '\h' for help. Type '\c' to clear the buffer.

mysql>
```

If you created a password for the root user when you installed MySQL, you need to provide a –p option.

The following Try It Out exercise creates a new database and adds information.

Try It Out   **Creating and Populating a MySQL Database**

Before you can add information in MySQL you must create a database. A database acts as a container in which you group information related to a project. Note that unlike the collections you've seen in eXist, there is only one level of databases in a MySQL server.

1.   To create a database named myBlog with UTF-8 as a character set, type the following:

```
mysql> create database myBlog DEFAULT CHARACTER SET 'utf8';
Query OK, 1 row affected (0.00 sec)

mysql>
```

2. Move into the newly created database by typing the following:

```
mysql> use myBlog;
Database changed
mysql>
```

A big difference between a native XML database such as eXist and a relational database is that a relational database is highly structured. In all the tests you've done with eXist, you have stored documents without defining any schema or DTD. The database learned the structure of your documents when you loaded them, without needing any prior definition. This isn't possible with a relational database. In a relational database, information is stored in tables with rows and columns. These tables are similar to spreadsheet tables, except that the name and type of the columns needs to be defined before you can use them.

3. Create one of these tables to hold the information needed for the exercises in this chapter. This table will be named *entries* and, for the sake of simplicity, it will have only two columns:

❑ A column named `id` that will be used as a primary key when you want to retrieve a specific blog entry

❑ A column named `content` to hold the blog entry in XML

Of course, this is a very minimal schema. You might want to add more columns to this table to simplify and optimize specific queries.

To create this table, type the following:

```
mysql> create table entries (
    -> id int PRIMARY KEY,
    -> content LONGTEXT
    -> );

Query OK, 0 rows affected (0.27 sec)

mysql>
```

Note that you don't have to type the -> at the beginning of the second and subsequent lines of the `create table` SQL instruction; these are just prompts sent by the mysql command-line utility.

4. The database is now ready to accept your blog entries. In a real-world application, these entries would be added by a nice web application, but this chapter will continue to use the mysql command-line utility to add them. In SQL, adding information is done through an `insert` statement. Enter a couple of your own blog entries following this pattern:

```
mysql> insert into entries values (
    -> 1,
    -> '<?contentxml version="1.0"?>
    '> <item id="1">
    '>  <title>Working on Beginning XML</title>
    '>  <description>
    '>   <p>
    '>    <a href="http://www.wrox.com/WileyCDA/WroxTitle/productCd-
0764570773.html">
    '>     <img

src="http://media.wiley.com/product_data/coverImage/73/07645707/0764570773.jpg"
```

```
'>      align="left"/>
'>    </a> I am currently working on the next edition of <a
'>    href="http://www.wrox.com/WileyCDA/WroxTitle/productCd-0764570773.html">
'>    WROX\'s excellent "Beginning XML".</a>
'>    </p>
'>    <p>It\'s the first time I am working on editing a book that I haven\'t
'>        written and I must say that I like it even better than I had
'>        expected when I accepted WROX\'s offer.</p>
'>    <p>I knew that the book was solid and that I would be working with a team
'>      of very professional authors, but what I hadn\'t anticipated is how
'>      fun it can be to create a new version out of existing material.
'>      You have a lot of room to reorganize what you are editing and when the
'>        material is good, it\'s like creating your own stuff, except that
'>        80% of the hard work is already done!</p>
'>    </description>
'>    <category>English</category>
'>    <category>XML</category>
'>    <category>Books/Livres</category>
'>    <pubDate>2006-11-13T17:32:01+01:00</pubDate>
'>    <comment-count>0</comment-count>
'> </item>
'> ');
Query OK, 1 row affected (0.34 sec)

mysql>
```

Note that the XML document that you're including is embedded in a SQL string delimited by single quotes. Any single quotes within your XML document must be escaped to fit in that string, and the SQL way to escape is by backslashing as follows: \ '.

If you are feeling lazy, you can copy these statements from the `mysql.sql` file on the book's website; it contains all the SQL statements used in this section plus some cleanup statements to ensure that you can run the whole document as a batch multiple times with consistent results.

How It Works

In this Try It Out, you have created a database that serves as the container where information is stored, and a table that defines the structure of your data. Then you entered data in this structure.

Now that your database is ready for further use, you can try out mysql-admin, the graphical user interface that comes with MySQL for its administration. After you start it, connect to the database server. If you haven't changed it, the hostname should be localhost, and the username root and the password are left empty. Among other features, mysql-admin enables you to display and even update the table definitions, as shown in Figure 10-20.

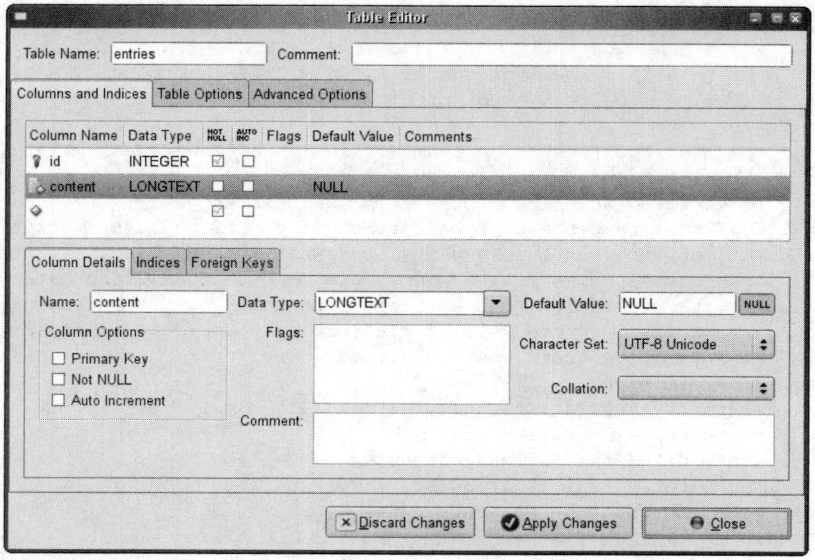

Figure 10-20

Querying MySQL

Now that you have your first two blog entries, what can you do with them? Of course, MySQL is a SQL database, so you can use all the power of SQL to query the content of your database. To show all the entries, just type the following:

```
select * from entries;
```

The result is too verbose to print in a book, but if you want something more concise, you can select only the first characters of each entry:

```
mysql> select id, substring(content, 1, 80) from entries;
+----+--------------------------------------------------------------------------------+
| id | substring(content, 1, 80)                                                      |
+----+--------------------------------------------------------------------------------+
|  1 | <?xml version="1.0"?>
<item id="1">
  <title>Working on Beginning XML</title>
   |
|  2 | <?xml version="1.0"?>
<item id="2">
  <title>eXist: getting better with each rel |
+----+--------------------------------------------------------------------------------+
2 rows in set (0.00 sec)

mysql>
```

Or, if you just want the number of entries:

```
mysql> select count(*) from entries;
+----------+
| count(*) |
+----------+
|        2 |
+----------+
1 row in set (0.00 sec)

mysql>
```

Fine, but all that is pure SQL and could be done with any SQL database without XML support. How could you, for instance, display the content of the title element?

The XML support in MySQL 5.1 comes from two XML functions documented at http://dev.mysql .com/doc/refman/5.1/en/xml-functions.html. These are ExtractValue and UpdateXML. The following Try It Out shows you how to use ExtractValues to query data.

Try It Out   Using ExtractValue to Extract Title Data

1. The first function, ExtractValue, evaluates the result of an XPath expression over an XML fragment passed as a string. Note that only a fairly restricted subset of XPath is currently implemented, which severely limits your ability to query XML fragments, but this is still enough to extract the title from content columns:

```
mysql> select id, ExtractValue(content, '/item/title') as title FROM entries;
+----+-------------------------------------+
| id | title                               |
+----+-------------------------------------+
|  1 | Working on Beginning XML            |
|  2 | eXist: getting better with each release |
+----+-------------------------------------+
2 rows in set (0.03 sec)

mysql>
```

This function can be used wherever you want in SQL statement.

2. To retrieve the ID of the blog entry with a specific title, use the following:

```
mysql> select id from entries where ExtractValue(content, '/item/title') =
    ->    'eXist: getting better with each release';
+----+
| id |
+----+
|  2 |
+----+
1 row in set (0.00 sec)

mysql>
```

How It Works

The behavior of ExtractValue is often somewhat counterintuitive if you are familiar with XPath. For instance, if you try to apply the same technique to fetch the description of your blog entries, you'll get the following:

```
mysql> select id, ExtractValue(content, '/item/description') as title FROM entries;
+----+-----------------------+
| id | title                 |
+----+-----------------------+
|  1 |

|  2 |


|
+----+-----------------------+
2 rows in set (0.00 sec)

mysql>
```

If you are used to the XPath behavior that translates elements into strings by concatenating the text nodes from all their descendants, you might assume that ExtractValue would do the same, but that's not the case: ExtractValue only concatenates the text nodes directly embedded in elements. In our case, the only text nodes that are direct children from description elements are whitespaces, which explains the preceding output.

To get the default XPath behavior, you need to explicitly state that you want the text nodes at any level:

```
mysql> select id, ExtractValue(content, '/item/description//text()')
    ->    as description FROM entries;
+----+------------------------- .../... -+
| id | description                                                            |
+----+------------------------- .../... -+
|  1 |


        I am currently working on the next edition of WROX's excellent
        "Beginning XML".
.
.
.

2 rows in set (0.00 sec)

mysql>
```

(This listing has been edited for conciseness.)

How would you select entries that contain images? In XPath, you would use `//img` directly in a test, and this would be considered true if and only if there is at least one `img` element somewhere in the document. If you're familiar with XPath, you might be tempted to write something like this:

```
mysql> select id, ExtractValue(content, '/item/title') as title
    ->    from entries
    ->    where ExtractValue(content, '//img') != '';
Empty set (0.00 sec)

mysql>
```

This doesn't work because `img` elements are empty: They don't have any child text node and `ExtractValue` converts them into empty strings. To make that query work, you need to select a node that will have a value (such as `//img/@src`) or count the number of `img` elements and test that the result is greater than zero:

```
mysql> select id, ExtractValue(content, '/item/title') as title from entries
    ->    where ExtractValue(content, '//img/@src') != '';
+----+-------------------------+
| id | title                   |
+----+-------------------------+
|  1 | Working on Beginning XML |
+----+-------------------------+
1 row in set (0.00 sec)

mysql> select id, ExtractValue(content, '/item/title') as title from entries
    ->    where ExtractValue(content, 'count(//img)') > 0;
+----+-------------------------+
| id | title                   |
+----+-------------------------+
|  1 | Working on Beginning XML |
+----+-------------------------+
1 row in set (0.00 sec)

mysql>
```

You'll hit another limitation pretty soon if you use this function: Most of the string functions of XPath are not implemented. For instance, if you want to find entries with links to URIs from the Wrox site, you might be tempted to write something such as the following:

```
select id, ExtractValue(content, '/item/title') as title
  from entries
  where ExtractValue(content,
    'count(//a[starts-with(@href,"http://www.wrox.com")])') >0;
```

Unfortunately, the `starts-with` function is not implemented; you need to use SQL to do what you can't do with XPath:

```
mysql> select id, ExtractValue(content, '/item/title') as title
    ->    from entries where ExtractValue(content, '//a/@href')
    ->    like '%http://www.wrox.com%';
```

```
+----+------------------------+
| id | title                  |
+----+------------------------+
|  1 | Working on Beginning XML |
+----+------------------------+
1 row in set (0.01 sec)

mysql>
```

If you are not a command-line aficionado, you will be happy to learn that you can execute these commands using mysql-query-browser, the second GUI tool that can be installed from the MySQL website, shown in Figure 10-21.

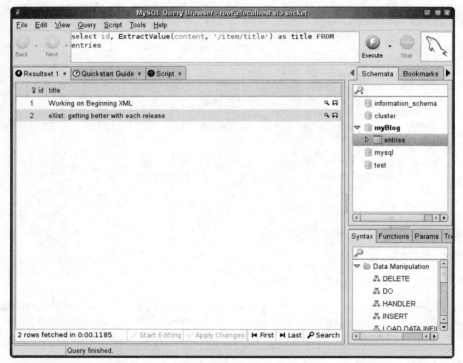

Figure 10-21

This tool not only enables you to run all the queries that you've seen, it also provides a feature that enables you to edit the table values in a table view similar to a spreadsheet and even field by field, which is most convenient for editing the XML documents you've stored in the database. Figure 10-22 illustrates the editing feature.

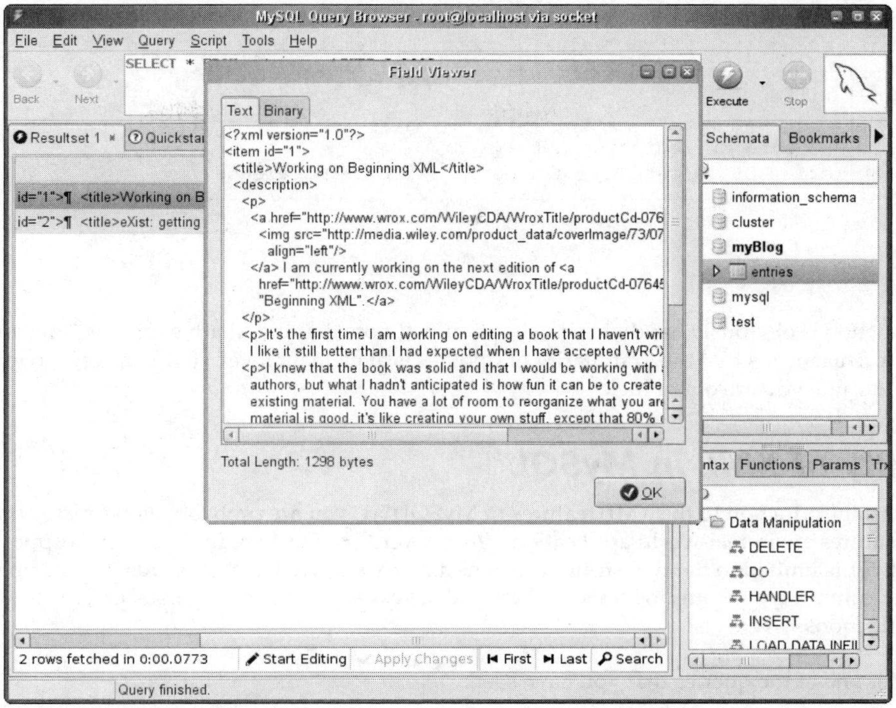

Figure 10-22

Updating XML in MySQL

The second XML function introduced by MySQL 5.1 is called `UpdateXML`. Like any SQL function, `UpdateXML` doesn't perform database updates, but it is handy when you use it in update statements.

`UpdateXML` takes three parameters. The first is a string containing an XML document. The second is an XPath expression that points to an element, and the third is an XML fragment. `UpdateXML` takes the XML document, replaces the element pointed to the XPath expression by the XML fragment passed as the third parameter, and returns the result of this operation as a string.

To change the title of the second blog entry, for example, use the following:

```
mysql> update entries
    ->    set content = UpdateXml(content,
    ->      '/item/title',
    ->      '<title>eXist DB is getting much better with each release</title>')
    ->    where id=2;
Query OK, 1 row affected (0.00 sec)
Rows matched: 1  Changed: 1  Warnings: 0
```

```
mysql>
mysql> select id, ExtractValue(content, '/item/title') as title FROM entries;
+----+--------------------------------------------------+
| id | title                                            |
+----+--------------------------------------------------+
|  1 | Working on Beginning XML                         |
|  2 | eXist DB is getting much better with each release |
+----+--------------------------------------------------+
2 rows in set (0.01 sec)

mysql>
```

This function is obviously handy in this situation, but note that the XPath expression must point to an element. This means that the granularity of updates is at element level, so if you want to update an attribute value you are out of luck.

Usability of XML in MySQL

After this introduction to the XML features of MySQL 5.1, you are probably wondering how usable these features are in real-world applications. To answer this question, first note that support of XML in MySQL 5.1 is limited to the two string functions already shown. In other words, there's no such thing as an XML column type. Your documents are stored as text and need to be parsed each time you use one of these functions.

Consider one of the queries that you have seen:

```
select id from entries where ExtractValue(content, '/item/title') =  'eXist:
getting better with each release'.
```

To process this query, the database engine needs to read the full content of all the blog entries, parse this content, and apply the XPath expression that extracts the title. That's fine with our couple of blog entries, but probably not something you want to do if you are designing a Technorati clone able to store millions of blog entries.

To optimize the design of the sample database that you created, you would probably extract the information that is most commonly used in user queries and move it into table columns. In this example, obvious candidates for that would be the title, the categories, and the publication date. Having this data available as columns enables direct access for the engine; and if you need further optimization, that gives you the opportunity to create indexes using these columns.

The other consideration to keep in mind is the mismatch between the current implementation and the XPath usages. You saw an example of that when you had to explicitly specify that you wanted to concatenate text nodes from all the descendants. If you use these functions, then you will see more examples. This mismatch is likely to be reduced in future releases, and this is something to watch carefully because it could lead to incompatible changes.

With these restrictions in mind, if you are both a MySQL and XML user, you will find these first XML features most welcome and there is no reason to ignore them. They don't turn MySQL into a native XML database yet, but they are a step in the right direction!

Client-Side XML Support

The features that you have seen so far are all server-side features implemented by the database engine. You don't need anything to support XML client side, and it is very easy using any programming language to convert SQL query results into XML. However, you might find it disappointing to leave this chapter without at least a peek at an XML feature that can be handy when you use the mysql command-line utility.

To see it in action, leave your mysql session and type the mysql command, adding a --xml option:

```
vdv@grosbill:~/beginning-xml/0764570773/ch 10 $ mysql -u root --xml myBlog
Reading table information for completion of table and column names
You can turn off this feature to get a quicker startup with -A

Welcome to the MySQL monitor.  Commands end with ; or \g.
Your MySQL connection id is 31
Server version: 5.1.12-beta-log MySQL Community Server (GPL)

Type 'help;' or '\h' for help. Type '\c' to clear the buffer.

mysql>
```

This option has switched the XML mode on, and the query results will now be output as XML:

```
mysql> select id, ExtractValue(content, '/item/title') as title FROM entries;
<?xml version="1.0"?>

<resultset
  statement="select id, ExtractValue(content, '/item/title') as title FROM
entries;">
  <row>
      <field name="id">1</field>
      <field name="title">Working on Beginning XML</field>
  </row>

  <row>
      <field name="id">2</field>
      <field name="title">eXist DB is getting much better with each
release</field>
  </row>
</resultset>
2 rows in set (0.02 sec)

mysql>
```

Of course, that's not very readable or useful as such, but it's a useful feature when you use mysql in shell or DOS scripts: You get your results as XML documents on which you can run XML tools such as XSLT transformations. If you need a truly simple way to turn out a query result in XHTML, this is definitely something that you'll find useful.

Choosing a Database to Store XML

At the end of the day, knowing a little of the theory behind XML and databases isn't the direction from which most businesses will approach storage of XML. Businesses are likely to have large amounts of existing data in conventional relational database management systems and want to leverage the skills and knowledge that their database administrators and other employees have of such RDBMS. For that reason, much of the enterprise attention on XML and databases is likely to be focused on adding XML support to existing RDBMS such as IBM's DB2, Oracle, Sybase, MySQL, or Microsoft's SQL Server. Of course, as XML functionality is added to such products, it is unclear whether they remain an RDBMS or become some other hybrid entity. For most businesses, that will be academic. They want a database that works, that is secure, that scales as business volume grows, that is easy to manage, and so on.

On the other hand, for some business uses, a custom application that uses a native XML database such as eXist may be an appropriate approach.

Looking Ahead

At present there is no standard update technique for native XML databases, and there is unlikely to be one until a version of XQuery after version 1.0 is released. In an ideal world we would have a standard update language, in the sense that XQuery is pretty tightly standardized across different commercial database products. That tight standardization of the query aspect of XQuery contrasts with the significant impact of proprietary aspects of implementing SQL in many relational database management systems. SQL Server 2005 provides one proprietary solution to fill this gap in the specification. In time it is likely that the W3C will produce a standard data modification language, either as part of a later version of XQuery or to complement it. Meanwhile, users of native XML databases and enterprise XML-enabled relational database management systems will have to decide which proprietary data modification language they prefer.

Summary

In this chapter you learned about the increasing business need to store or expose data as XML. The characteristics of a viable XML-enabled database were discussed, and three different examples of XML-enabled databases were shown. First, eXist, a native XML database, was examined. Microsoft's SQL Server 2000 was then explored, together with a preliminary look at the upcoming SQL Server 2005, to see how additional XML functionality is being added to one commercial enterprise-grade relational database management system. Finally, you looked at the latest release of the popular open-source MySQL relational database, the first version to include XML features.

Exercise Questions

Suggested solutions to these questions can be found in Appendix A.

Question 1

List some reasons why adding XML functionality to a relational database management system may be preferable to using a native XML database.

Question 2

What methods are available in SQL Server 2005 to manipulate data in a database column that is of type `xml`?

Question 3

Write a SQL query to get the ID and title of blog items from the XML category of the MySQL database. Would you expect this query to scale if your blog grows and includes many blog entries? What would you do to increase performance in that case?

Part V
Programming

The XML Document Object Model (DOM)

This chapter explores the XML Document Object Model, often called the *XML DOM* or simply the *DOM*, and how it can be manipulated in various ways. The XML DOM is primarily used by programmers as a way to manipulate the content of an XML document. The XML DOM is useful for tasks as diverse as manipulating data from an RSS feed to animating part of an SVG graphic.

> *Although many XML programmers refer to the XML DOM simply as the DOM, the term DOM can also be used to refer to the HTML Document Object Model, the XML Document Object Model, or both. In this chapter the focus is on the XML DOM.*

This chapter covers the following:

❏ The purpose of the XML Document Object Model

❏ How the DOM specification was developed at the W3C

❏ Important XML DOM interfaces and objects, such as the `Node` and `Document` interfaces

❏ How to add and delete elements and attributes from a DOM and manipulate a DOM tree in other ways

❏ How the XML DOM is used "under the covers" in Microsoft InfoPath 2003

Purpose of the XML DOM

The XML DOM provides an interface for programmers to create XML documents; to navigate them; and to add, modify, or delete parts of those XML documents while they are held in memory. There are a number of ways that an in-memory representation can be created:

❏ One of the possibilities is to read a file from disk. This is a common technique now when dealing with configuration files; user options held in an XML format are easier to deal with than traditional techniques such as INI files or registry settings.

❑   A second option is to convert a string representation embedded in the source code. This is popular for examples but not often used in real-life scenarios because of the difficulty in changing the XML when needed.

❑   A third method is to accept a stream piped from another source such as a response from a web service or a database stored procedure.

These three techniques all come under the category of XML parsing. *Parsing* means taking a stream of characters and producing an internal representation conforming to a predetermined structure. However the source was received, the result is an in-memory model of the XML, known as the XML DOM. Parsing also means that entities are not represented in the XML DOM, because any entities referenced in the XML would be expanded by an XML parser before the DOM tree was constructed. For example, in the XML DOM the predefined entity `&amp;` would be represented by the single character `&`. This raises corresponding issues when serializing an XML DOM. The character `&` in a DOM node would need to be expanded to `&amp;` to avoid constructing an XML document that was not well formed.

Some other features of the input are lost after parsing, such as the XML declaration and its specified encoding, as well as details such as whether attributes were quoted with single or double quote marks. In general the DOM deals with an idealized version of the XML known as the *XML Information Set* (or *Infoset*). This means two differently constructed documents, once parsed, can yield the same Infoset. Full details of this concept can be found at `www.w3.org/TR/xml-infoset/`.

Serialization *is the process of storing an object's state to a permanent form, such as a file or a database, or converting it to a form that can be transmitted between machines.* Deserialization *is the opposite process of generating an object based on its stored form.*

In XML the object is the DOM Document, which exists as a tree of nodes. When serialized it is represented using angular bracket notation (although other notations have been proposed to reduce the size of the serialized form). Figure 11-1 shows two different forms of the same document for comparison.

There is a fourth possibility when producing an XML DOM that does not need an input stream of any sort. The DOM can be created directly in memory using the appropriate DOM methods such as `createElement()` and `appendChild()`. An example of this is shown later in the chapter.

The DOM provides a logical view of the in-memory structure that represents an XML document. Like the XPath document model introduced in Chapter 7, the XML DOM represents an XML document in a way that is equivalent to a hierarchical treelike structure consisting of *nodes*. A DOM implementation isn't obliged to create a tree as long as it appears to a developer to be equivalent to an in-memory tree.

The XML document itself is represented as a `Document` node. Like the root node in XPath 1.0, a DOM `Document` node is always situated at the apex of a tree. However, the `Document` node differs significantly from an XPath root node in its characteristics, and its descendant nodes are also significantly different representations of parts of an XML document compared to XPath 1.0 nodes.

An XML document might typically be parsed by an XML parser, which checks for well-formedness and, optionally, validity of the document. The XML DOM may then be constructed as an in-memory representation of the XML document. However, this doesn't happen in a vacuum. Typically, the XML DOM will be associated with some other application. In many of the examples later in this chapter, for the sake of illustrating principles relating to the XML DOM, that other application will be a web browser, but the options are almost limitless given XML's increased use in all types of business processes. Later in this chapter you will look briefly at how the XML DOM is used in an enterprise XML forms product from Microsoft called *InfoPath 2003*.

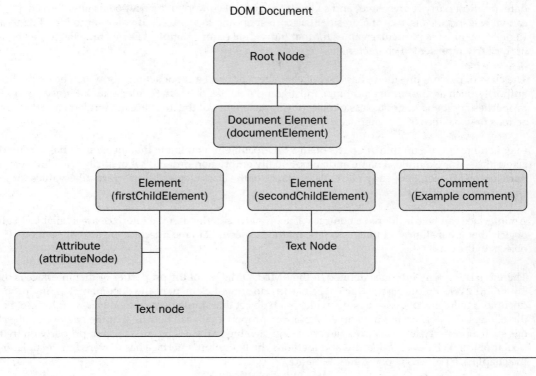

DOM Document

Serialized verson

```
<documentElement>
<firstChildElement attributeNode="attributeValue">Text Node</firstChildElement>
<secondChildElement>Text Node</secondChildElement>
<!-- Example comment -->
</documentElement>
```

Figure 11-1

In the MSXML component, which is used by Internet Explorer and can be harnessed programmatically, the XML parser, a DOM implementation, and several other XML technologies are implemented in one component. In Mozilla-based browsers, the XML parser is separate from other components such as the XSLT processor, and it cannot be accessed outside of the browser.

Interfaces and Objects

Interfaces and objects are often discussed as if the two terms were pretty much interchangeable, but that is not really the case. An interface is a more abstract concept than an object.

Outside the programming world you might, loosely speaking, have a class of person characterized by success in an electoral process and residence at 1600 Pennsylvania Avenue. Very probably you would guess that the class of person you are talking about is a president of the United States. Apart from electoral information, a president would have assorted other properties such as name, inauguration date, political party represented, and so on. If the general concept of a president is an interface, you can view a specific *instance* of a president as corresponding to an object. If you refer to John Fitzgerald Kennedy, you have particular values for that individual—for example, "Democratic Party" as the value of the party represented characteristic.

The class of person, president, has a set of characteristics and a set of actions for which he or she has authority, such as appointing a cabinet and signing Acts of Congress. Similarly, an interface describes the properties and behavior of a class of objects. Characteristics of the interface are termed *properties*, and actions or capacities of the interface are termed *methods*.

In general terms, if you think of parts of an XML document, you know that an element has certain characteristics—for example, a name and an optionally empty non-ordered set of attributes. However, any particular XML element—any particular instance of the class element—has particular values for the characteristics of that class.

An interface can be considered a contract. The properties defined in the interface are available on all objects that are instances of that class. The methods specified in the interface are also present on all objects in the class.

There is a `Document` interface defined in the XML DOM. One of the properties of that interface is the `documentElement` property, which specifies the document element of the document. For any particular document there is a `Document` node, which is an object that implements the `Document` interface. Because the `Document` interface has a `documentElement` property, you can be sure that the `Document` object also has such a property, and you can query or assign a value to the `documentElement` property on that particular object. Whatever properties and methods the `Document` interface has (covered in detail later in the chapter), a `Document` object has the same.

Because an object is an instance of an interface and has all the characteristics (properties and methods) of that interface, it is very easy to slip from describing an interface to describing an instance of it—an object. It isn't easy in natural writing to be technically wholly consistent in separating interfaces from objects, a difficulty that the creators of the DOM also seem to have found because, arguably, what they created was a Document Interface Model, rather than a Document Object Model.

The Document Object Model at the W3C

The official specifications of the XML DOM have been developed by the World Wide Web Consortium (W3C). The various editions of the DOM specification have been referred to as *levels*. The first DOM specification was finalized as the Document Object Model Level 1 Recommendation in October 1998. DOM Level 1 provided an approach both to the DOM for HTML and for XML. This chapter focuses only on those aspects of DOM Level 1 that apply to XML. The HTML interfaces are not described.

> *The main page for the DOM specification is* www.w3.org/DOM/. *As noted earlier, this chapter deals with the XML side of the DOM.*

The XML DOM, like XPath 1.0, is a *logical* model of an XML document. An implementer of the XML DOM is free to implement the DOM in any way that presents the interface to the developer as if it, logically, corresponded to a hierarchical treelike structure. The DOM Level 1 specification also left the technique and syntax to achieve creation of a `Document` node up to the creators of DOM implementations. Similarly, serialization of an XML DOM was not defined in the Level 1 recommendation.

The XML DOM Level 1 provides an interface for developers to use to manipulate XML documents. Equally, the DOM can be presented as an interface to proprietary structures that themselves allow manipulation of structures representing XML, thereby providing a common means across programs to manipulate models of XML. The big advantage of the XML DOM is that as far as users are concerned, they appear to have a standard interface to allow manipulation of XML.

Having a shared interface potentially improves a programmer's productivity, because familiarity with only one common interface is needed. Of course, in practice, that hasn't always been delivered, in part because the DOM Level 1 specification provided no common interface to create a representation of XML documents. Therefore, that basic functionality had to be essentially proprietary.

The DOM also failed to provide a universal interface in the sense that it is not ideal or suitable for larger XML documents. The DOM, although useful for relatively small-scale XML programming, becomes impractical for handling very large XML documents, because the DOM requires a single tree (or equivalent structure) to be created in memory. For very large XML documents, the Simple API for XML (SAX), described in Chapter 12, or .NET's XmlReader, provide an approach that scales better than the XML DOM. In practice, therefore, many XML developers need to be familiar with both the XML DOM as well as at least one of these alternatives.

DOM Level 1 did not include a way to create an XML document. Nor did it include a specification of XML events. DOM Level 1 specified language bindings—how different languages would represent the methods and properties—for Java and ECMAScript. For example, in Java you can retrieve the document that a node belongs to by using using the `getOwnerDocument()` method on the node. In ECMAScript you use the `ownerDocument` property.

> *ECMAScript is a standard ratified by ECMA, the European Computer Manufacturers Association. It is commonly known as JavaScript when used in most browsers other than IE, where it is called JScript.*

DOM Level 2 added some new functionality, which resulted in the XML DOM specification being split into several modules. The Core module had few changes from DOM Level 1, including such things as support for namespaced elements. For example, a node included new properties such as `namespaceURI`, `localName`, and `prefix`.

> *The DOM Level 2 specification documents and their location can be found at* `www.w3.org/TR/DOM-Level-2-Core/`.

In 2004 DOM Level 3 was finalized. This introduced, among other things, standards for URI handling, namespace resolution, and how the DOM maps to the XML Infoset. The Core level documentation can be found at `www.w3.org/TR/DOM-Level-3-Core/`.

XML DOM Implementations

A DOM implementation provides all interfaces described in a particular level of the DOM specification. However, an implementer is free to provide additional interfaces. For example, in DOM Level 1 it was essential that implementers provided some additional interfaces because DOM Level 1 provided no standard mechanism for creating an XML DOM `Document` object.

Similarly, implementers may use the XML DOM for specialized purposes that benefit from specialized functionality. The Adobe SVG Viewer, which is a widely used SVG viewer at the time of writing, provides several additional properties and methods for manipulation of objects in the SVG DOM in addition to those required to comply with the XML DOM specifications. See Chapter 19 for more information on SVG.

Two Ways to View DOM Nodes

The XML DOM provides two ways in which you can look at DOM nodes:

❑ One way of looking at a DOM tree is as a hierarchy of Node objects, some of which expose specialized interfaces. Viewed in this way, all XML DOM objects are Node objects. This way of viewing an XML DOM is particularly useful when you identify properties and methods that are common to all DOM nodes.

❑ The alternative way to view a DOM tree is to view the root of the tree as a Document node (or object) whose descendant nodes are objects of different specialized types. For example, the child nodes of the Document object may be a DocumentType object (which represents a DOCTYPE declaration), an Element object (which represents the document element of the document), and zero or more ProcessingInstruction objects and Comment objects (which represent any processing instructions and comments in the prolog of the XML document). If you recall the permitted structure of an XML document and, specifically, its prolog, the allowed objects should be fairly self-explanatory. Remember that an XML declaration is not, strictly speaking, a processing instruction; therefore, it is not represented as a ProcessingInstruction node in the XML DOM. As an example of a commonly used ProcessingInstruction, the following line can be added to an XML document so that when it is opened in a browser, the XSL transformation, example.xslt, is applied to the document:

```
<?xml-stylesheet type="text/xsl" href="example.xslt"?>
```

The XML declaration, however, sits at the beginning of an XML file and is most commonly used to state the encoding for the contents:

```
<?xml version="1.0" encoding="ISO-8859-1"?>
```

The difference between the prolog and the XML declaration is that the prolog consists of both an XML declaration and a DTD, both of which are optional.

The second viewpoint tends to be more intuitive when trying to visualize the effect that the code has or is intended to have on nodes within the DOM, so the text mostly uses that approach in the descriptions of the DOM that follow.

Overview of the XML DOM

This section briefly describes the objects or interfaces that make up the XML DOM so you can get the general picture of how an XML document is represented. Each of the node types is briefly mentioned here, but several of the node types are discussed in more detail and demonstrated in example code later in the chapter.

As the following allowed node types are described, you may find it helpful to consider how those node types correspond to parts of serialized XML documents.

As mentioned earlier, the root of the DOM hierarchy is always a Document node if an XML document is being represented. The child nodes of the Document node are the DocumentType node, Element node, ProcessingInstruction nodes, and Comment nodes. The DocumentType, Comment, and ProcessingInstruction node types may not have child nodes.

If the DOM tree represents a fragment of an XML document — for example, snipped from an existing DOM tree or newly created — then the root of the hierarchy is a DocumentFragment node. Given the circumstances in which it is used, it is not surprising that the child nodes of a DocumentFragment node need not conform to XML's well-formedness rules, although once the nodes in the document fragment have been added to a full XML DOM tree, the equivalent of well-formedness rules apply again. The most common child nodes of the DocumentFragment node are likely to be Element nodes but other allowed child node types are Comment, ProcessingInstruction, Text, CDATASection, and EntityReference.

Element nodes represent the document element of an XML document and all other elements in the document. The permitted child node types of an Element node are Element, Comment, ProcessingInstruction, Text, CDATASection, and EntityReference. Notice that the permitted child nodes of the Element node are the same as the allowed child nodes of the DocumentFragment node.

Attributes in an XML document are represented by the Attr node type. An Attr node is associated with an Element node but is not considered to be a child node of the Element node. In the DOM an Attr node is not a child node of the Element node and therefore is not considered part of the DOM tree, despite the Attr node implementing the Node interface. Thus, the parentNode, previousSibling, and nextSibling attributes of the Attr node have a Null value. The text content of an attribute is represented in a Text node.

> The DOM representation of attributes differs significantly from the representation of attributes in the XPath data model, described in Chapter 7. In XPath an attribute node is not considered to be a child of the element node with which it is associated, but seemingly paradoxically, in the XPath model the element node is considered to be the parent node of the attribute node.

Most of the code you write to manipulate the XML DOM is likely to include the Document, Element, Attr, and Text node types.

The CDATASection and the Notation node types correspond to the similarly named structures in an XML document. The Entity node type represents a parsed or unparsed entity in an XML document. An Entity node may have child nodes of the following node types: Element, Comment, ProcessingInstruction, Text, CDATASection, and EntityReference.

An EntityReference node may have the following child node types: Element, Comment, ProcessingInstruction, Text, CDATASection, and EntityReference.

In the examples in this chapter you won't look further at the use of CDATASection, Entity, and EntityReference node types. To explore those node types further, see the DOM Core specification at www.w3.org/TR/DOM-Level-3-Core/.

Now that you have an overview of the node types that make up an XML DOM document or document fragment, let's move on to the tools you need to run the examples.

Tools to Run the Examples

All the examples in this chapter run in a browser, as this provides the easiest way to both process easily changeable script examples and display the output in a user-friendly fashion. Originally, only Internet Explorer (IE) could process XML, but now all the Mozilla-based browsers such as Firefox have this capability, as well as others such as Safari. You need IE 5.5 or later, Firefox 1.2 or later, or Netscape 7 or later.

This chapter refers to either Microsoft's or Mozilla's implementation, the latter covering all the other browsers mentioned above.

Browser Differences

The Microsoft and Mozilla implementations of XML share the DOM interface discussed earlier, but they are implemented internally in two very different ways. The former is a COM class, sometimes known as an *ActiveX component*, that can be used by any COM-aware language, such as VB6, C#, or Microsoft's version of JavaScript, called *JScript*, for instance. The class can be used within IE or by other applications. Mozilla's version is built in to the browser in the same way that the `alert()` method is. The advantage of this is that you don't run into the problems that can arise when users disable ActiveX. The disadvantage is that it's not reusable outside the browser environment.

Because they share the same interface, the methods and properties between browsers are substantially the same, although initial setup and configuration varies somewhat. In general, Microsoft's implementation is easier to work with and has a number of extra features designed to speed up development. Fortunately, Mozilla's classes can be extended to also implement extra features, a capability not present in Microsoft's COM.

Try It Out   Navigating to the Document Element

In this first example, you learn how to create a simple in-memory DOM by loading an XML string; you then access the document element, which, as you may remember, is the first element in the document and contains all the other content — apart, possibly, from any comments and processing instructions.

The following page, `DocumentElement-IE.html`, uses Microsoft's XML classes to load and view the data:

```
<html>
<head>
<title>Document Element - IE</title>
<script type="text/javascript">

function getDom()
{
  var oDom = null;
  try
  {
    oDom = new ActiveXObject("Msxml2.DomDocument.3.0");
  }
  catch (e)
  {
    alert("This code needs msxml version 3 installed to operate.");
```

```
    }
    return oDom;
}

function getXml()
{
    return document.getElementById("txtXml").value;
}

function showParseError(err)
{
    var sMessage = "Error parsing input.\n"
                 + "Reason: " + err.reason
                 + "\nSource: " + err.srcText;
    alert(sMessage);
}

function showResults(text)
{
    var oResults = document.getElementById("txtResults");
    oResults.value += text + "\n";
}

function showProperties()
{
    var oDom = getDom();
    if (!oDom) return;
    var bLoaded = oDom.loadXML(getXml());
    if (!bLoaded)
    {
        showParseError(oDom.parseError);
        return;
    }
    showResults("The document element is: " + oDom.documentElement.nodeName);
}
</script>

</head>
<body>
<textarea cols="40" rows="20" id="txtXml"><root><data>
<item value="1">This is some text.</item></data></root></textarea>
<textarea cols="40" rows="20" id="txtResults"></textarea>
<br>
<input type="button" value="Show XML Properties" onclick="showProperties();">
  
<input type="button" value="Clear Results"
 onclick="document.getElementById('txtResults').value = '';">
</body>
</html>
```

The page displays some XML in the left-hand side. Upon clicking the button, it displays some data in the right-hand area. If the XML is not well formed, an error message shows; otherwise, the result is similar to what is shown in Figure 11-2.

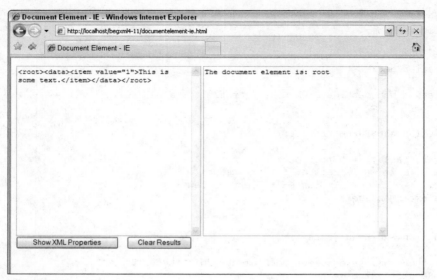

Figure 11-2

How It Works

The following HTML `input` element creates a simple button that has an `onclick` attribute:

```
<input type="button" value="Show XML Properties" onclick="showProperties();">
```

Clicking the button calls the `showProperties()` function; this relies on a number of helper functions, the first of which is `getDom()`:

```
function getDom()
{
  var oDom = null;
  try
  {
    oDom = new ActiveXObject("Msxml2.DomDocument.3.0");
  }
  catch (e)
  {
    alert("This code needs msxml version 3 installed to operate.");
  }
  return oDom;
}
```

`getDom()` begins by declaring a variable, `oDom`, to hold the XML parser object. It attempts to assign a COM object specified by the progID of `Msxml2.DomDocument.3.0`, which is Microsoft's implementation of the standard DOM document.

Microsoft has released a number of XML libraries with different progIDs. The latest one is version 6.0, although you should only rely on 3.0 being available. Never use the older progID of Microsoft .XmlDom, *as this sometimes produces a pre-standards version that can lead to poor performance and unexpected results.*

The code is surrounded in a try/catch block, and if the object is not created, either because it is not installed or the user has increased the level of security settings, then an alert is given. If oDom is found to be null, then the showProperties() returns the following:

```
function showProperties()
{
  var oDom = getDom();
  if (!oDom) return;
  var bLoaded = oDom.loadXML(getXml());
//more code
}
```

showProperties() then attempts to load the string returned from getXml() into the parser. This function simply obtains a reference to the textarea using its ID and returns its value:

```
function getXml()
{
  return document.getElementById("txtXml").value;
}
```

The XML parser uses its loadXML() method, which accepts a string and returns a Boolean, which is true if the load succeeded or false if it failed. A failure usually results from XML that was not well formed:

```
function showProperties()
{
  var oDom = getDom();
  if (!oDom) return;
  var bLoaded = oDom.loadXML(getXml());
  if (!bLoaded)
  {
    showParseError(oDom.parseError);
    return;
  }
//more code
}
```

The bLoaded variable is tested and if it is found to be false, the document's parseError object is passed to showParseError(), where the reason and source are displayed:

```
function showParseError(err)
{
  var sMessage = "Error parsing input.\n"
              + "Reason: " + err.reason
              + "\nSource: " + err.srcText;
  alert(sMessage);
}
```

The final piece of code displays the name of the document element using the `documentElement` property of the DOM object and the `nodeName` property of the document element itself:

```
function showProperties()
{
  var oDom = getDom();
  if (!oDom) return;
  var bLoaded = oDom.loadXML(getXml());
  if (!bLoaded)
  {
    showParseError(oDom.parseError);
    return;
  }
  showResults("The document element is: " + oDom.documentElement.nodeName);
}
```

The `nodeName` property exists for all nodes, but not all nodes return something useful. It is most commonly used for elements and attributes.

If you change the text in the left-hand area — for example, by removing the final *t* in the closing `</root>` element to leave `</roo>`, — and click the button again, you will get an error stating that the end-tag *roo* does not match the start-tag *root*, and listing the offending text.

Now that you've seen how the basics work in IE, you will rewrite the example to use the Mozilla classes (in the following code of `DocumentElement-Mozilla.html`). As you will see, the core interface is the same, but parts that are not specified in the standard, such as how the basic DOM document is created and how errors are handled, vary somewhat.

The HTML code remains the same; only the script is different:

```
<html>
<head>
<title>Document Element - Mozilla</title>
<script type="text/javascript">

function getDomFromXml(xml)
{
  var oDom = null;
  try
  {
    var oParser = new DOMParser();
    oDom = oParser.parseFromString(xml, "text/xml");
  }
  catch (e)
  {
    alert("This code needs DOMparser available to operate.");
  }
  return oDom;
}

function getXml()
{
```

```
      return document.getElementById("txtXml").value;
}

function removeEntities(text)
{
  var oDiv = document.createElement("div");
  oDiv.innerHTML = text;
  return oDiv.firstChild.nodeValue;;
}

function showParseError(dom)
{
  var oSerializer = new XMLSerializer();
  var sXml = oSerializer.serializeToString(dom, "text/xml");
  var oRE = />([\s\S]*?)Location:([\s\S]*?)Line Number (\d+), Column
(\d+):<sourcetext>([\s\S]*?)(?:\-*\^)/;
  oRE.test(sXml);
  var sMessage = "Error parsing input.\n"
                 + "Reason: " + removeEntities(RegExp.$1)
                 + "\nSource: " + removeEntities(RegExp.$5);
  alert(sMessage);
}

function showResults(text)
{
  var oResults = document.getElementById("txtResults");
  oResults.value += text + "\n";
}

function showProperties()
{
  var oDom = getDomFromXml(getXml());
  if (!oDom) return;
  var sName = oDom.documentElement.nodeName;
  if (sName == "parsererror")
  {
    showParseError(oDom);
    return;
  }
  showResults("The document element is: " + sName);
}
</script>
</head>
<body>
<textarea cols="40" rows="20" id="txtXml">
<root><data><item value="1">This is some text.</item></data></root></textarea>
<textarea cols="40" rows="20" id="txtResults"></textarea>
<br>
<input type="button" value="Show XML Properties" onclick="showProperties();">
  
<input type="button" value="Clear Results"
onclick="document.getElementById('txtResults').value = '';">
</body>
</html>
```

The first major change is creating a DOM document from the XML in the text area. showProperties() begins by passing the XML to getDomFromXml():

```
function showProperties()
{
  var oDom = getDomFromXml(getXml());
```

getDomFromXml accepts the XML string and creates a DOMParser:

```
function getDomFromXml(xml)
{
  var oDom = null;
  try
  {
    var oParser = new DOMParser();
//more code
}
```

DOMParser is a built-in Mozilla class that has a number of methods to build a DOM document, the most frequently used being parseFromString():

```
function getDomFromXml(xml)
{
  var oDom = null;
  try
  {
    var oParser = new DOMParser();
    oDom = oParser.parseFromString(xml, "text/xml");
//more code
}
```

parseFromString() takes the actual string as the first argument, and the MIME type of the document as the second. If text/xml is provided as the MIME type, an XML DOM document is returned:

```
function getDomFromXml(xml)
{
  var oDom = null;
  try
  {
    var oParser = new DOMParser();
    oDom = oParser.parseFromString(xml, "text/xml");
  }
  catch (e)
  {
    alert("This code needs DOMparser available to operate.");
  }
  return oDom;
}
```

As with Internet Explorer, the code is wrapped in a try/catch block and an alert is displayed if the relevant classes are not available. Otherwise, a loaded DOM document is returned.

The DOMParser uses a different technique from Microsoft's DomDocument to report errors. Instead of a Boolean value indicating success or failure, the DOMParser itself holds a special XML document containing the error details. This document has a document element named parsererror and you can test for that name by checking for that name:

```
function showProperties()
{
  var oDom = getDomFromXml(getXml());
  if (!oDom) return;
  var sName = oDom.documentElement.nodeName;
  if (sName == "parsererror")
  {
    showParseError(oDom);
    return;
  }
  showResults("The document element is: " + sName);
}
```

If the name does equal parsererror, the showParseError() function displays this to the user. This is more complicated than Microsoft's version because the details need to be extracted from the text in the error message:function showParseError(dom)

```
{
  var oSerializer = new XMLSerializer();
  var sXml = oSerializer.serializeToString(dom, "text/xml");
  var oRE = />([\s\S]*?)Location:([\s\S]*?)Line Number (\d+), Column
(\d+):<sourcetext>([\s\S]*?)(?:\-*\^)/;
  oRE.test(sXml);
  var sMessage = "Error parsing input.\n"
            + "Reason: " + removeEntities(RegExp.$1)
            + "\nSource: " + removeEntities(RegExp.$5);
  alert(sMessage);
}
```

First, another class is instantiated, XMLSerializer. Then the serializeToString() method is called; again, the second argument specifies the MIME type of text/xml. Next, a regular expression is constructed to parse the individual sections from the string, and a helper method named removeEntities() converts such entities as < into the more readable <.

Figure 11-3 shows an error report in Mozilla.

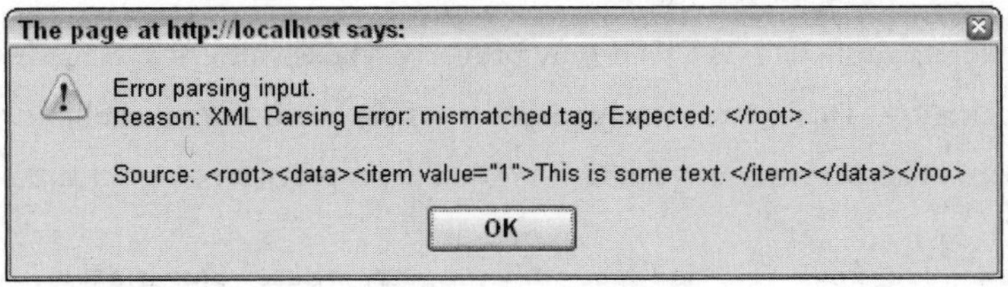

The page at http://localhost says:

⚠ Error parsing input.
Reason: XML Parsing Error: mismatched tag. Expected: </root>.

Source: <root><data><item value="1">This is some text.</item></data></roo>

OK

Figure 11-3

As you can see, the Mozilla version is more long-winded, and in real life you would not want to write two sets of pages to cope with both models. To overcome this problem, a number of cross-browser libraries are available that use browser sniffing to determine which classes are available and return objects that share a common set of methods. The library used for the following examples is zXml, written by Nicholas C. Zakas and available from www.nczonline.net/downloads/.

The Node Object

It was mentioned earlier that one way to view nodes in an XML DOM is as specializations of the Node object. One very good reason for viewing an XML DOM in that way is that the Node object has properties and methods that are also available on all other types of XML DOM nodes shown in this chapter. XML DOM programming consists of retrieving and setting some of these properties, either directly or using the methods defined in an interface to manipulate the object that instantiates that interface or related objects. The following sections describe the properties and methods that are available to a developer, whatever type of DOM node is being used.

Properties of the Node Object

The Node object in DOM Level 2 has 14 properties:

❑   attributes — This is a read-only property whose value is a NamedNodeMap object.

❑   childNodes — This is a read-only property whose value is a NodeList object.

❑   firstChild — This is a read-only property whose value is a Node object.

❑   lastChild — This is a read-only property whose value is a Node object.

❑   localName — This is a read-only property that is a String.

❑   namespaceURI — This is a read-only property whose value is a String.

❑   nextSibling — This is a read-only property whose value is a Node object.

❑   nodeName — This is the name of the node, if it has one, and its value is a String type.

❑   nodeType — This is a read-only property that is of type number. The number value of the nodeType property maps to the names of the node types mentioned earlier.

❑   nodeValue — This property is of type String. When the property is being set or retrieved, a DOMException can be raised.

❑   ownerDocument — This is a read-only property whose value is a Document object.

❑   parentNode — This is a read-only property whose value is a Node object.

❑   prefix — This property is a String. When the property is being set, a DOMException can be raised.

❑   previousSibling — This is a read-only property whose value is a Node object.

These properties enable the developer to learn a great deal about the node itself and the XML DOM surrounding the currently selected node. Depending on the particular node object, there may not be a retrievable useful value for some properties made available by the Node interface. For example, a

`Document` object does not have a parent node, and a `Comment` node has no attributes or child nodes. For `Element` nodes, it is frequently of interest to know what child nodes it has, so the `childNodes` property is of significance for that node type.

You can retrieve several pieces of information about the node using the `Node` object's properties. You can retrieve its name in the `nodeName` property. If the name of the node is namespace-qualified, you can retrieve the local part of its qualified name in the `localName` property, its namespace prefix in the `prefix` property, and the namespace URI in the `namespaceURI` property. If the node is an `Element` node and has attributes, then they are retrieved from the `attributes` property. Of course, if the node has a value, the `nodeValue` property gives you the necessary information.

> *A Uniform Resource Identifier (URI) is a string of characters that uniquely identifies a resource. It normally follows the same pattern as a Uniform Resource Locator (URL),e.g.,* `http://www.w3.org/1999/XSL/Transform`*, for example, but this is just to avoid clashes with other URIs. There is no guarantee that a file can be accessed by typing a URI into a browser.*

A common mistake when coming across the XML DOM for the first time is assuming that the `nodeValue` of an element is the text it contains — for example, to believe the `nodeValue` of the `<root>` element in `<root>Text here</root>` is `Text here`. In fact, an element's `nodeValue` is null. According to the specification, only text nodes and attributes have a non-null `nodeValue`.

In addition to accessing information about the current node itself, you can find out useful information about that node's surroundings in the DOM. For example, you can obtain a list of the child nodes of the currently selected node using the `childNodes` property. Within that list of child nodes, you can specify the first node using the `firstChild` property, and the last child using the `lastChild` property. You can get information about its parent node using the `parentNode` property, and about its adjacent sibling nodes using the `nextSibling` property. In a broader context, the `ownerDocument` property indicates the document to which the node belongs.

Try It Out   Exploring Child Nodes

This example uses the techniques you have already seen to navigate around a simple XML document:

1. Create the following file and save it as `NodeProperties.html`:

```
<html>
<head>
<title>Node Properties</title>
<script type="text/javascript" src="zXml.src.js"></script>
<script type="text/javascript">

function getXml()
{
  return document.getElementById("txtXml").value;
}

function showResults(text)
{
  var oResults = document.getElementById("txtResults");
  oResults.value += text + "\n";
```

```
    }

    function showProperties()
    {
      var oDom = zXmlDom.createDocument();
      oDom.loadXML(getXml());
      var oDocumentElement = oDom.documentElement;
      showResults("With respect to the document element - ");
      showResults("First child node has name: " +
      oDocumentElement.firstChild.nodeName);
      showResults("First child node has text content of: " +
      oDocumentElement.firstChild.firstChild.nodeValue);
      showResults("Last child node has name: " + oDocumentElement.lastChild.nodeName);
      showResults("Last child node has text content of: " +
      oDocumentElement.lastChild.firstChild.nodeValue);
      showResults("There are " + oDocumentElement.childNodes.length + " child nodes.");
    }
    </script>
    </head>
    <body>
    <textarea cols="40" rows="20" id="txtXml">
    <Book><Chapter>This is Chapter 1.</Chapter>
    <Chapter>This is Chapter 2.</Chapter>
    <Chapter>This is Chapter 3.</Chapter></Book>
    </textarea>
    <textarea cols="40" rows="20" id="txtResults"></textarea>
    <br>
    <input type="button" value="Show XML Properties" onclick="showProperties();">
      
    <input type="button" value="Clear Results"
    onclick="document.getElementById('txtResults').value = '';">
    </body>
    </html>
```

In the actual file, the XML in the `textarea` *should all be on one line.*

2. Navigate to this file in IE or a Mozilla-based browser such as Firefox and click the Show Properties button. Information about the left `textarea` nodes is shown in the right-hand pane.

How It Works

The main change is using the cross-browser library, which is referenced by adding a second script block at the head of the page:

```
<script type="text/javascript" src="zXml.src.js"></script>
```

For production, you can use the more compact `zXml.js` but when debugging, it's easier to see what's going on with `zXml.src.js`, as this has formatting and is commented. The rest of the code is similar to that shown earlier. The XML in `txtXml` is loaded into the DOM document created as follows:

```
var oDom = zXmlDom.createDocument();
```

The document element is then stored in a variable to avoid having to retrieve it multiple times:

```
var oDocumentElement = oDom.documentElement;
```

Next, various properties such as `firstChild`, `lastChild`, and `childNodes` are used and displayed to the user:

```
showResults("With respect to the document element - ");
showResults("First child node has name: " +
oDocumentElement.firstChild.nodeName);
showResults("First child node has text content of: " +
oDocumentElement.firstChild.firstChild.nodeValue);
showResults("Last child node has name: " + oDocumentElement.lastChild.nodeName);
showResults("Last child node has text content of: " +
oDocumentElement.lastChild.firstChild.nodeValue);
showResults("There are " + oDocumentElement.childNodes.length + " child nodes.");
```

Notice that when the content of a node is needed the `nodeValue` of the `firstChild` is shown. This is because elements don't have a `nodeValue` but text nodes do. The `firstChild` in `lastChild` `.firstChild`, therefore, refers to the text node of the `<chapter>` element.

> *If you fail to put all the XML on one line, you may get some odd-looking results from this page in Mozilla but not in IE. This is because they treat whitespace such as carriage returns and newlines differently. Microsoft contravenes the standard by stripping insignificant whitespace during parsing. You can change this by setting the DOM document's `preserveWhitespace` property to true before loading the document. There is more on this subject later in the chapter.*

In addition to the preceding properties, Microsoft's parser also supports two nonstandard ones: `text`, which gives a concatenation of all the elements' text nodes, and `xml`, which gives the actual markup. In the preceding example, `oDocumentElement.xml` would return all of the initial XML as a string. Although they are not standard, they can be extremely useful, especially when debugging, and they are supported by the zXml library.

Methods of the Node Object

The `Node` object has many methods. The common ones are listed here and include some that you will use frequently in XML DOM programming. In the list that follows, the names of method arguments will, in working programs, be replaced by variables that you define in your script or other code:

❑ `appendChild(newChild)` — This method returns a `Node` object. The `newChild` argument is a `Node` object. This method can raise a `DOMException` object.

❑ `cloneNode(deep)` — This method returns a `Node` object. The `deep` argument is a `Boolean` value. If true, then all nodes underneath this node are also copied; otherwise, only the node itself.

❑ `hasAttributes()` — This method returns a `Boolean` value. It has no arguments.

❑ `hasChildNodes()` — This method returns a `Boolean` value. It has no arguments.

❑ `insertBefore(newChild, refChild)` — This method returns a `Node` object. The `newChild` and `refChild` arguments are each `Node` objects. This method can raise a `DOMException` object.

- ❏ isSupported(feature, version) — This method returns a Boolean value. The feature and version arguments are each String values.

- ❏ normalize() — This method has no return value and takes no arguments.

- ❏ removeChild(oldChild) — This method returns a Node object. The oldChild argument is a Node object. This method can raise a DOMException object.

- ❏ replaceChild(newChild, oldChild) — This method returns a Node object. The newChild and oldChild arguments are each Node objects. This method can raise a DOMException object.

The names of most of the methods of the Node object are self-explanatory. The insertBefore() method, for example, allows a new child node to be inserted before a specified existing child node. The appendChild() method allows a new child node to be added. The removeChild() method allows a specified node to be removed from the XML DOM tree. The cloneNode() method allows a node to be copied.

Just as the properties of the Node object tell us a lot about the node and its DOM environment, so the methods of the Node object allow the developer to manipulate the XML DOM tree by adding and removing nodes and so on. Later in the chapter you will use these properties and methods of the Node object as well as the more specialized properties and methods of more specialized types of node.

Before you look at examples using the methods of the Node object, let's first look at how to load an existing XML document.

Loading an XML Document

A common scenario is loading a document from a stream such as a file, rather than a string of XML. In Microsoft's parser, the load() method is called and passed a URL. This can be a local file, if security requirements are met, or a file accessed via a web server. In a standard web browser, only files hosted on the same domain as the original document can be read. As an alternative to using Msxml2.DomDocument, you can also use Msxml2.XmlHttpRequest to retrieve XML and other files via HTTP. There are many examples of this in Chapter 16, "Ajax."

Mozilla also offers two options: using the DOMParser.parseFromStream() method or using the XMLHttpRequest class. Again, you can find many examples of this in Chapter 16, so the examples here concentrate on using the XML node's methods after the document has been loaded.

Try It Out   Deleting a Node

A common task in DOM programming is deleting an existing node. The following example deletes the first child node of the document element:

1.   Create the following file and save it as DeleteNode.html:

```
<html>
<head>
<title>Delete Node</title>
<script type="text/javascript" src="zXml.src.js"></script>
```

```
<script type="text/javascript">


function showResults(text)
{
  var oResults = document.getElementById("txtResults");
  oResults.value += text + "\n";
}

function showXml(xml)
{
  var oInput = document.getElementById("txtXml");
  oInput.value = xml;
}

function deleteNode()
{
  var oReq = zXmlHttp.createRequest();
  oReq.open("GET", "book.xml", false);
  oReq.send(null);
  var oDom = oReq.responseXML;
  showXml(oDom.xml);
  var oNodeToDelete = oDom.documentElement.firstChild;
  oNodeToDelete.parentNode.removeChild(oNodeToDelete);
  showResults(oDom.xml);
}
</script>
</head>
<body>
<textarea cols="40" rows="20" id="txtXml">
</textarea>
<textarea cols="40" rows="20" id="txtResults"></textarea>
<br>
<input type="button" value="Delete Node" onclick="deleteNode();">
  
<input type="button" value="Clear Results"
onclick="document.getElementById('txtResults').value = '';">
</body>
</html>
```

2. This example loads a file, rather than an XML string, so you also need to create book.xml in the same folder as DeleteNode.html:

```
<Book><Chapter>This is Chapter 1.</Chapter>
<Chapter>This is Chapter 2.</Chapter>
<Chapter>This is Chapter 3.</Chapter></Book>
```

3. DeleteNode.html needs to be served via HTTP because Mozilla browsers, and IE in some configurations, won't allow files to be loaded from a local disk without special security settings. You need to create a virtual folder to store the files and navigate via the HTTP protocol.

Chapter 16 contains detailed instructions on creating a virtual folder.

4. Click the Delete Node button. The original XML is shown on the left; the resulting XML, with the deleted node, is shown on the right.

How It Works

The HTML is mostly the same as before. When the Delete Node button is clicked, `deleteNode()` begins by creating an XML HTTP request:

```
function deleteNode()
{
  var oReq = zXmlHttp.createRequest();
//more code
}
```

The request class is covered extensively in Chapter 16, but essentially it can connect via HTTP and retrieve content using the same underlying techniques as a browser:

```
function deleteNode()
{
  var oReq = zXmlHttp.createRequest();
  oReq.open("GET", "book.xml", false);
  oReq.send(null);
//more code
}
```

The request then initiates a GET request to the host server and asks for `book.xml`. The third parameter, set to `false` in this example, indicates that the code should wait after the `send()` call until the request is completed before processing the next statement. The `send()` method then fires the request; no data is needed with this example, so `null` is passed as its only argument:

```
function deleteNode()
{
  var oReq = zXmlHttp.createRequest();
  oReq.open("GET", "book.xml", false);
  oReq.send(null);
  var oDom = oReq.responseXML;
  showXml(oDom.xml);
//more code
}
```

When an XML document is asked for, the `responseXML` property contains a DOM document representing the response. The XML is shown in the left hand `textarea`.

To delete a node, you first obtain a reference to it using the `documentElement` and its `firstChild` property:

```
function deleteNode()
{
  var oReq = zXmlHttp.createRequest();
  oReq.open("GET", "book.xml", false);
  oReq.send(null);
  var oDom = oReq.responseXML;
  showXml(oDom.xml);
  var oNodeToDelete = oDom.documentElement.firstChild;
  oNodeToDelete.parentNode.removeChild(oNodeToDelete);
  showResults(oDom.xml);
}
```

The next line uses the parentNode property to access the node's parent. This is because the removeChild() method can only be called from the immediate parent of the node to be deleted. The removeChild() method is called and passed the reference of the targeted node. Finally, the resulting DOM document is displayed in the right-hand textarea.

It may seem strange to use the properties of a node to remove it from the tree, but the code's order of execution means that the reference to the parentNode is obtained before the deletion is attempted.

The result of running the code is shown in Figure 11-4.

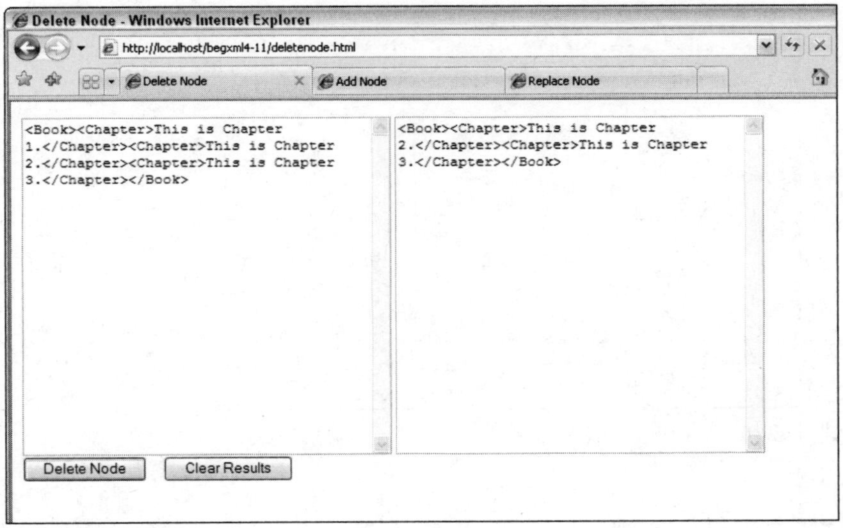

Figure 11-4

The next example shows another common task: adding a new node.

Try It Out   Adding New Nodes

The HTML for this example is the same as the previous Try It Out; the only difference is that the deleteNode() method has been replaced with addNode():

1.   Create a new file with the following code and name it AddNode.html:

```
function addNode()
{
  var oReq = zXmlHttp.createRequest();
  oReq.open("GET", "book.xml", false);
  oReq.send(null);
  var oDom = oReq.responseXML;
  showXml(oDom.xml);
  var oNewElement = oDom.createElement("Chapter");
  var oNewText = oDom.createTextNode("This is Chapter 4.");
  oNewElement.appendChild(oNewText);
```

```
    oDom.documentElement.appendChild(oNewElement);
    showResults(oDom.xml);
}
```

The result is shown in Figure 11-5.

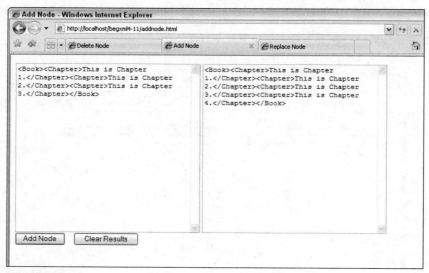

Figure 11-5

How It Works

The code starts as before by retrieving book.xml and displaying it in the left-hand area:

```
function addNode()
{
  var oReq = zXmlHttp.createRequest();
  oReq.open("GET", "book.xml", false);
  oReq.send(null);
  var oDom = oReq.responseXML;
  showXml(oDom.xml);
  var oNewElement = oDom.createElement("Chapter");
  var oNewText = oDom.createTextNode("This is Chapter 4.");
  //more code
}
```

The code then uses createElement() and createTextNode to create two new nodes; these are stored in oNewElement and oNewText, respectively:

```
function addNode()
{
  var oReq = zXmlHttp.createRequest();
```

```
    oReq.open("GET", "book.xml", false);
    oReq.send(null);
    var oDom = oReq.responseXML;
    showXml(oDom.xml);
    var oNewElement = oDom.createElement("Chapter");
    var oNewText = oDom.createTextNode("This is Chapter 4.");
    oNewElement.appendChild(oNewText);
    //more code
}
```

The new text node is appended to the new element, and the code finishes by appending the element to the document element's existing child nodes:

```
function addNode()
{
    var oReq = zXmlHttp.createRequest();
    oReq.open("GET", "book.xml", false);
    oReq.send(null);
    var oDom = oReq.responseXML;
    showXml(oDom.xml);
    var oNewElement = oDom.createElement("Chapter");
    var oNewText = oDom.createTextNode("This is Chapter 4.");
    oNewElement.appendChild(oNewText);
    oDom.documentElement.appendChild(oNewElement);
    showResults(oDom.xml);
}
```

The last method is `replaceChild()`. The `replace()` method is similar to `addNode()` but it needs a reference to the element that will be replaced. In this example, you choose the `lastChild` of the document element:

```
function replace ()
{
    var oReq = zXmlHttp.createRequest();
    oReq.open("GET", "book.xml", false);
    oReq.send(null);
    var oDom = oReq.responseXML;
    showXml(oDom.xml);
    var oNewElement = oDom.createElement("Chapter");
    var oNewText = oDom.createTextNode("This is a different Chapter 3.");
    oNewElement.appendChild(oNewText);
    var oOldElement = oDom.documentElement.lastChild;
    //more code
    showResults(oDom.xml);
}
```

Then the `replaceChild()` method is called:

```
    oDom.documentElement.replaceChild(oNewElement, oOldElement);
```

The result is shown in Figure 11-6.

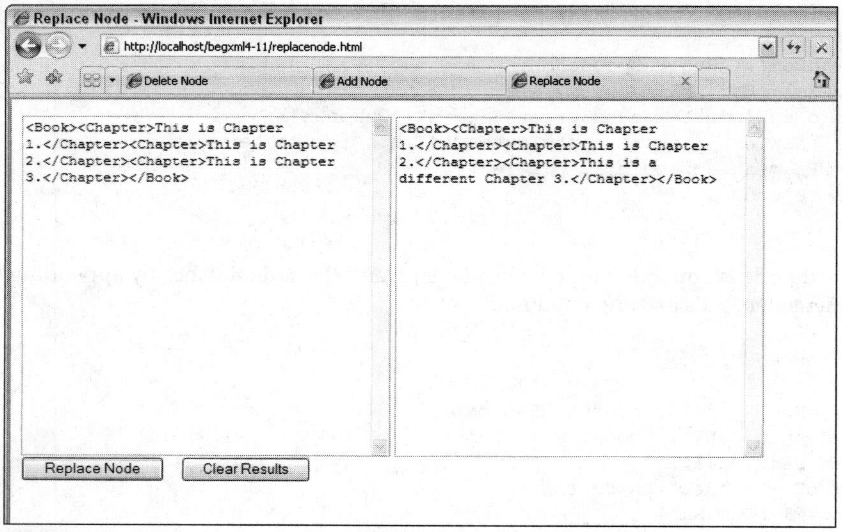

Figure 11-6

The Effect of Text Nodes

A common technique is to iterate through the child nodes of a specified Element node and retrieve or set information of some type. However, the issue of whitespace (or in XML DOM terms, Text nodes) becomes important if you don't want unwelcome surprises.

The following HTML page, TextNodes.html, loads three different versions of the same document, depending on the drop-down list, and displays information about the document element's child nodes:

```
<html>
<head>
<title>Text Nodes</title>
<script type="text/javascript" src="zXml.src.js"></script>
<script type="text/javascript">


function showResults(text)
{
  var oResults = document.getElementById("txtResults");
  oResults.value += text + "\n";
}

function showXml(xml)
{
  var oInput = document.getElementById("txtXml");
  oInput.value = xml;
}

function displayNodes()
```

```
{
  var oReq = zXmlHttp.createRequest();
  var oLst = document.getElementById("lstFiles");
  var sFile = oLst.options[oLst.selectedIndex].value;
  oReq.open("GET", sFile, false);
  oReq.send(null);
  var oDom = oReq.responseXML;
  showXml(oDom.xml);
  var colChildNodes = oDom.documentElement.childNodes;
  for (var i = 0; i < colChildNodes.length; i++)
  {
    var oChild = colChildNodes[i];
    var sDetail = "Child (" + i + ") has name: " + oChild.nodeName;
    showResults(sDetail);
  }
}
</script>
</head>
<body>
<textarea cols="40" rows="20" id="txtXml">
</textarea>
<textarea cols="40" rows="20" id="txtResults"></textarea>
<br>
<select id="lstFiles">
  <option value="book.xml">One line file</option>
  <option value="book-indented.xml">Indented file without xml:space</option>
  <option value="book-xml-space.xml">Indented file with xml:space</option>
</select><br>
<input type="button" value="Display Nodes" onclick="displayNodes();">
  
<input type="button" value="Clear Results"
onclick="document.getElementById('txtResults').value = '';">
</body>
</html>
```

The three document files are subtly different. book.xml and book-indented.xml are the same but book.xml is written on one line with no indentation. Book-indented.xml looks as follows:

```
<Book>
  <Chapter>This is Chapter 1.</Chapter>
  <Chapter>This is Chapter 2.</Chapter>
  <Chapter>This is Chapter 3.</Chapter>
</Book>
```

The third file, book-xml-space.xml, is also indented but has the xml:space attribute added to the document element:

```
<Book xml:space="preserve">
  <Chapter>This is Chapter 1.</Chapter>
  <Chapter>This is Chapter 2.</Chapter>
  <Chapter>This is Chapter 3.</Chapter>
</Book>
```

Running this page in IE can produce different results from Mozilla, noticeably for `book-indented.xml`. The difference in the output is most noticeable for the indented files shown in Figures 11-7 and 11-8; note how the `xml:space` attribute changes how MSXML sees the file by choosing "Indented file with xml:space" in the drop-down menu.

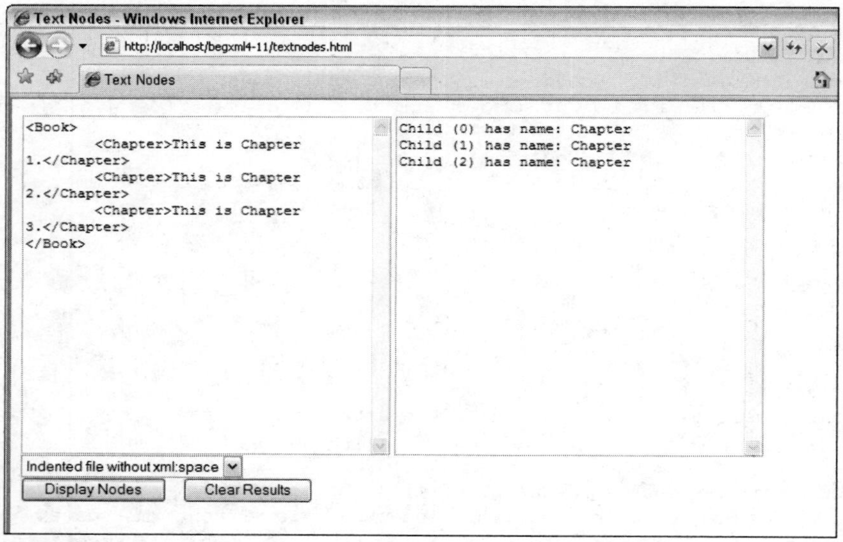

Figure 11-7

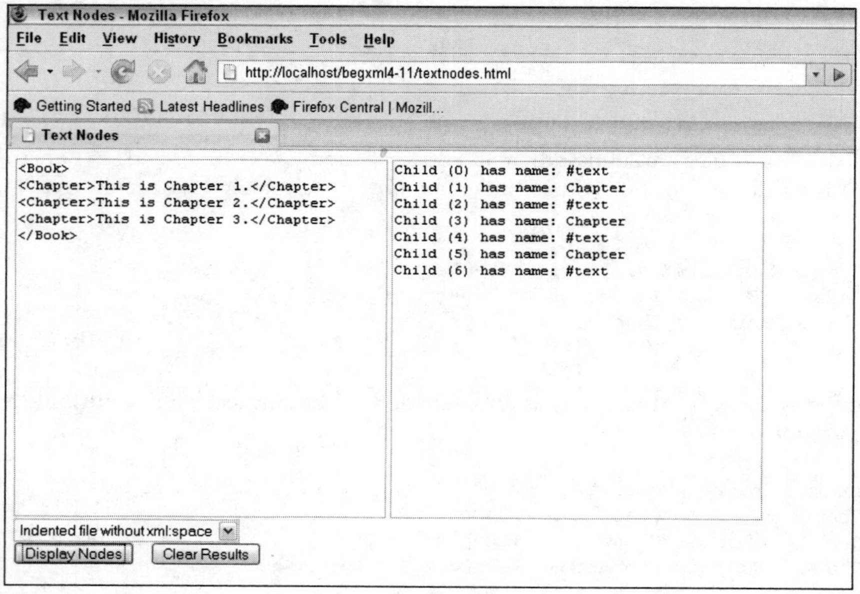

Figure 11-8

The difference is explained by the way the two parsers handle whitespace such as carriage returns and linefeeds. In Microsoft's parser, these are removed when they appear between elements, which is contrary to the specification. In Mozilla they are not. To avoid this problem, you have two possible solutions: If you have control over the source, then add xml:space="preserve" to the document element, as is the case in the third version:

```
<Book xml:space="preserve">
    <Chapter>This is Chapter 1.</Chapter>
    <Chapter>This is Chapter 2.</Chapter>
    <Chapter>This is Chapter 3.</Chapter>
</Book>
```

The results will then appear the same for both browsers.

If you don't have access to the source and are loading using the load() or loadXML() methods, your other option is to set the preserveWhitespace property of the DOM document to true before loading:

```
var oDom = new ActiveXObject("Msxml2.DomDocument.3.0");
oDom.preserveWhitespace = true;
oDom.load("book-indented.xml");
```

If neither solution helps, then the best course of action is to access nodes in a different manner, such as selectNodes(), which uses XPath (see Chapter 7).

The NamedNodeMap Object

Earlier in the chapter you learned about the attributes property of the Node object and that its value was a NamedNodeMap object. A *named node map* is an unordered set of objects. As you probably recall, the attributes of an XML element are unordered, so you can't use ordered constructs such as lists to refer to attributes.

When the Node object is an Element node, then the attributes property holds information about all the attributes of the element that the Element node represents.

The NamedNodeMap object has a single property, the length property, which is a Number value. The value of the length property indicates how many nodes are in the named node map.

The NamedNodeMap object has seven methods:

❑ getNamedItem(name) — This method returns a Node object. The name argument is a String value.

❑ getNamedItemNS(namespaceURI, localName) — This method returns a Node object. The namespaceURI and localName arguments are String values.

❑ item(index) — This method returns a Node object. The index argument is a Number value.

❑ removeNamedItem(name) — This method returns a Node object. The name argument is a String value. This method can raise a DOMException object if the item doesn't exist.

❑ removeNamedItemNS(namespaceURI, localName) — This method returns a Node object. The namespaceURI and localName arguments are String values. This method can raise a DOMException object if the item does not exist.

❑ setNamedItem(node) — This method returns a Node object. The node argument is a new Node. This method can raise a DOMException object if the new node belongs to a different document.

❑ setNamedItemNS(node) — This is the same as setNamedItem except it handles namespaced nodes.

The preceding list is based on the W3C recommendations, and not all implementations follow the standard precisely. For example, IE raises an error if you use setNamedItem to add an attribute to an element when the attribute originated from a different document, whereas Firefox allows it.

A NamedNodeMap object is used to retrieve the attributes of an element, and typically you use a name corresponding to the attribute's name. For example, the getNamedItem() method has a name as its argument.

Notice, too, that there are separate pairs of methods for getting and setting nodes in the named node map depending on whether or not the Node objects in the named node map are in a namespace. When the nodes are not in a namespace, the getNamedItem(), removeNamedItem(), and setNamedItem() methods are used. For nodes in a namespace, the getNamedItemNS(), removeNamedItemNS(), and setNamedItemNS() methods are used.

The *NS versions of the methods are designed to handle nodes in a namespace and were introduced after the original methods; they are not supported by Microsoft's parser. You have to use XPath to access namespaced nodes if necessary.

Try It Out   Adding and Removing Attributes

This example uses book3.xml, which has a similar structure to the other XML files but also has attributes describing the chapter number and the author's initials:

1. Create the following file and save it as book3.xml (you can download the files for the example from the book's website):

```xml
<Book xml:space="preserve">
<Chapter number="1" author="JJF">This is Chapter 1.</Chapter>
<Chapter number="2" author="EVL">This is Chapter 2.</Chapter>
<Chapter number="3" author="DA">This is Chapter 3.</Chapter>
</Book>
```

2. Create the following file and name it NamedNodeMap.html. This file is similar to the other examples but has three new methods to add, remove, and modify attributes:

```html
<html>
<head>
<title>NamedNodeMap</title>
<script type="text/javascript" src="zXml.src.js"></script>
<script type="text/javascript">
var oDom = null;

function showResults(text)
{
  var oResults = document.getElementById("txtResults");
  oResults.value += text + "\n";
}

function showXml(xml)
```

```
{
  var oInput = document.getElementById("txtXml");
  oInput.value = xml;
}

function init()
{
  var oReq = zXmlHttp.createRequest();
  oReq.open("GET", "book3.xml", false);
  oReq.send(null);
  oDom = oReq.responseXML;
  showXml(oDom.xml);
}

function add()
{
  var oNewAtt = oDom.createAttribute("new");
  oNewAtt.nodeValue = "I'm new!";
  var oTargetElement = oDom.documentElement.getElementsByTagName("Chapter")[0];
  oTargetElement.attributes.setNamedItem(oNewAtt);
  showXml(oDom.xml);
  showResults("New attribute added to first Chapter element.");
}

function remove()
{
  var oTargetElement = oDom.documentElement.getElementsByTagName("Chapter")[1];
  oTargetElement.attributes.removeNamedItem("number");
  showXml(oDom.xml);
  showResults("Attribute 'number' removed from second Chapter element.");
}

function modify()
{
  var oTargetElement = oDom.documentElement.getElementsByTagName("Chapter")[2];
  var oTargetAttribute = oTargetElement.attributes.getNamedItem("author");
  oTargetAttribute.nodeValue = "JJF";
  showXml(oDom.xml);
  showResults("Attribute 'author' from third Chapter element modified.");
}

</script>
</head>
<body onload="init();">
<textarea cols="40" rows="20" id="txtXml">
</textarea>
<textarea cols="40" rows="20" id="txtResults"></textarea>
<br>
<input type="button" value="Add Attribute" onclick="add();">
  
<input type="button" value="Remove Attribute" onclick="remove();">
  
<input type="button" value="Modify Attribute" onclick="modify();">
  
<input type="button" value="Clear Results"
```

```
onclick="document.getElementById('txtResults').value = '';">
</body>
</html>
```

3. As the buttons are clicked, the action is described in the right-hand pane and the resulting XML is shown in the left. The results are shown in Figure 11-9.

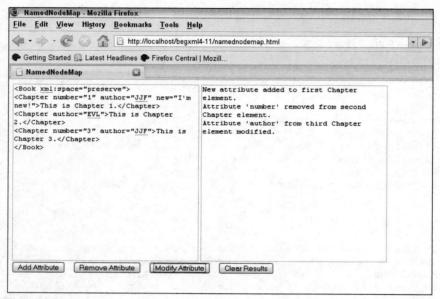

Figure 11-9

How It Works

The HTML begins in a similar fashion to the previous scripts by loading the DOM document. It does this in the init() method, which is called when the body's onload event fires:

```
function init()
{
  var oReq = zXmlHttp.createRequest();
  oReq.open("GET", "book3.xml", false);
  oReq.send(null);
  oDom = oReq.responseXML;
  showXml(oDom.xml);
}
```

The oDom variable is global so it can be accessed later in other functions. Also shown are three methods: add(), remove() and modify():

```
function add()
{
  var oNewAtt = oDom.createAttribute("new");
  oNewAtt.nodeValue = "I'm new!";
```

```
      var oTargetElement = oDom.documentElement.getElementsByTagName("Chapter")[0];
      oTargetElement.attributes.setNamedItem(oNewAtt);
      showXml(oDom.xml);
      showResults("New attribute added to first Chapter element.");
}
```

add() first creates a new attribute using the DOM document's createAttribute() method, which takes the name of the attribute as its sole argument.

The nodeValue is set and the element to add it to is retrieved using getElementsByTagName(). This accepts an element name and returns a NodeList. The first item in the list is used as the target element.

Then the attributes' setNamedItem() method is used and passed the new attribute. The other two methods are very similar; remove() simply uses removeNamedItem():

```
      function remove()
      {
        var oTargetElement = oDom.documentElement.getElementsByTagName("Chapter")[1];
        oTargetElement.attributes.removeNamedItem("number");
        showXml(oDom.xml);
        showResults("Attribute 'number' removed from second Chapter element.");
      }
```

Finally, modify() retrieves a particular attribute using getNamedItem() and changes its nodeValue:

```
      function modify()
      {
        var oTargetElement = oDom.documentElement.getElementsByTagName("Chapter")[2];
        var oTargetAttribute = oTargetElement.attributes.getNamedItem("author");
        oTargetAttribute.nodeValue = "JJF";
        showXml(oDom.xml);
        showResults("Attribute 'author' from third Chapter element modified.");
      }
```

As you can see from the results in the browser, the NamedNodeMap is "live" in the sense that changes to the attributes are reflected immediately in the underlying document, although you still need to refresh the details in the left-hand text area to see the changes.

The NodeList Object

When looking at the childNodes property of the Node object, you learned that the childNodes property has a value that is a NodeList. The NodeList object can be used to process all child nodes of a specified node.

The NodeList object has one property, the length property, which is a read-only property of type Number. The length property indicates how many nodes are present in the list of nodes. Knowing that can be useful when, for example, creating a for loop to process all child nodes of a particular node.

The NodeList object has one method, the item() method. The item() method takes a single argument, which is a Number value, and returns a Node object. The code item(3) returns the *fourth* child node, because the first child node is returned by item(0). The item() method was used in an earlier example.

The DOMException Object

In almost any programming situation something can go wrong. For example, you might type some syntax incorrectly, get a property or method name wrong, forget that a property is read-only and try to change it, or simply try to do something that isn't allowed. In programming of the XML DOM, when an error occurs, an exception is said to be thrown. The exception is then caught by an exception handler.

Try It Out   Creating a DOMException

Let's create a simple example to deliberately cause a DOMException object to be raised. The following code is contained in DOMException.html:

```html
<html>
<head>
<title>DomException</title>
<script type="text/javascript" src="zXml.src.js"></script>
<script type="text/javascript">
var oDom = null;
oDom = zXmlDom.createDocument();

function showResults(text)
{
  var oResults = document.getElementById("txtResults");
  oResults.value += text + "\n";
}

function showXml(xml)
{
  var oInput = document.getElementById("txtXml");
  oInput.value = xml;
}

function tryAddElement(elementName)
{
  var oNewElement = oDom.createElement(elementName);
  var sMessage = "";
  try
  {
    oDom.appendChild(oNewElement);
    sMessage = "Element '" + elementName + "' added.";
    showXml(oDom.xml);
  }
  catch (e)
  {
    sMessage = "Element '" + elementName + "' not added because '"
          + e.message + "'.";
  }
  showResults(sMessage);
}

</script>
</head>
<body>
```

```
<textarea cols="50" rows="20" id="txtXml">
</textarea>
<textarea cols="50" rows="20" id="txtResults"></textarea>
<br>
<input type="button" value="Add Element"
onclick="tryAddElement(document.getElementById('txtElement').value);">
  <input type="text" id="txtElement" value="element">  
<input type="button" value="Clear Results" onclick=
  "document.getElementById('txtResults').value = '';">
</body>
</html>
```

If you click the Add Element button once a new element is added, but the second time an exception is raised. The error messages vary slightly between IE and Firefox. IE complains that *Only one top level element is allowed in an XML document* (shown in Figure 11-10), whereas Firefox has a more generic *Node cannot be inserted at the specified point in the hierarchy.*

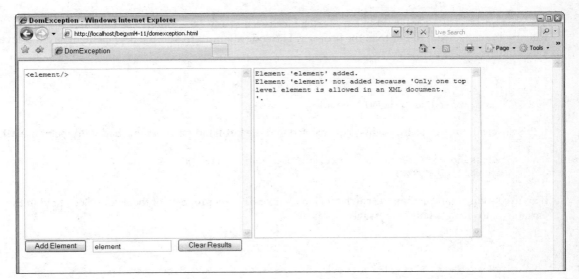

Figure 11-10

How It Works

The basic structure of the page follows the pattern of others in this chapter: The XML is shown on the left and the messages appear on the right.

The function that creates the new element, and possibly causes an exception to be thrown, is tryAddElement():

```
function tryAddElement(elementName)
{
  var oNewElement = oDom.createElement(elementName);
  var sMessage = "";
  try
```

```
  {
    oDom.appendChild(oNewElement);
    sMessage = "Element '" + elementName + "' added.";
    showXml(oDom.xml);
  }
  catch (e)
  {
    sMessage = "Element '" + elementName + "' not added because '"
        + e.message + "'.";
  }
  showResults(sMessage);
}
```

The function accepts the name of the new element and uses the `createElement()` method to create a new element:

```
var oNewElement = oDom.createElement(elementName);
```

The next bit of code is contained in a try/catch block so that any exceptions raised are handled gracefully by the code itself, rather than the browser. The code attempts to add the new element as a top-level element by using `appendChild()`:

```
try
{
  oDom.appendChild(oNewElement);
```

If this succeeds, a success message is constructed and the left-hand pane is refreshed with the new XML:

```
sMessage = "Element '" + elementName + "' added.";
showXml(oDom.xml);
```

If an exception is raised, then the catch block uses the `message` property of the error object, held in the variable `e`, to create a failure message:

```
catch (e)
{
  sMessage = "Element '" + elementName + "' not added because '"
      + e.message + "'.";
}
```

Finally, the relevant message is shown in the right-hand text area:

```
  showResults(sMessage);
}
```

The Document Interface

The `Document` interface has featured in several examples earlier in this chapter, which is inevitable because all XML DOMs have a `Document` object. The `Document` interface has three properties:

❑ documentElement — This read-only property returns an Element object.

❑ doctype — This read-only property is a DocumentType object, corresponding to a DOCTYPE declaration, if present, in the XML document.

❑ implementation — This read-only property is a DOMImplementation object.

As shown in earlier examples, the documentElement property is very useful for getting a handle on the document element of the XML. From there, you can navigate around the XML DOM.

The Document interface has 14 methods:

❑ createAttribute(name) — This method returns an Attr object. The name argument is a String value. This method can raise a DOMException object if the name contains an invalid character, such as <.

❑ createAttributeNS(namespaceURI, qualifiedName) — This method returns an Attr object. The namespaceURI and qualifiedName arguments are String values. This method can raise a DOMException object if the name contains an invalid character.

❑ createCDATASection(data) — This method returns a CDATASection object. The data argument is a String value.

❑ createComment(data) — This method returns a Comment object. The data argument is a String value.

❑ createDocumentFragment() — This method takes no argument and returns a DocumentFragment object.

❑ createElement(tagName) — This method returns an Element object. The tagName argument is a String value. This method can raise a DOMException object if the name contains an invalid character.

❑ createElementNS(namespaceURI, qualifiedName) — This method returns an Element object. The namespaceURI and qualifiedName arguments are String values. This method can raise a DOMException object if the name contains an invalid character.

❑ createEntityReference(name) — This method returns an EntityReference object. The name argument is a String value. This method can raise a DOMException object if the name contains an invalid character.

❑ createProcessingInstruction(target, data) — This method returns a ProcessingInstruction object. The target and data arguments are each of type String. This method can raise a DOMException object if the target contains an invalid character.

❑ createTextNode(data) — This method returns a Text object. The data argument is a String value.

❑ getElementById(elementId) — This method returns an Element object. The elementId argument is a String value.

❑ getElementsByTagName(tagname) — This method returns a NodeList object. The tagname argument is a String value.

❑ getElementsByTagNameNS(namespaceURI, localName) — This method returns a NodeList object. The namespaceURI and localName arguments are String values.

❏ importNode(importedNode, deep) — This method returns a Node object. The importedNode argument is a Node object. The deep argument is a Boolean value. This method can raise a DOMException object for some of the nodes — for example, when trying to import an element from an XML 1.1 document, which allows most Unicode characters in element names, into an XML 1.0 version, which only allows a much smaller set.

As noted earlier, the *NS versions of the methods are designed for working with namespaced elements and are not available in MSXML.

You have already seen many of these methods in action throughout the chapter; they are pivotal to the process of adding new nodes to a document. Earlier examples showed how the createElement(), createTextNode(), and createAttribute() methods of the Document object can be used to create new nodes of the specified type, which can later be appended to or inserted into the XML DOM at the desired place. The createElement() and createAttribute() methods take an argument of type String, but you need to make sure that the string is also a legal XML name.

When you are creating new Element and Attr nodes that are in a namespace — for example, when manipulating SVG — then you must use the createElementNS() and createAttributeNS() methods to achieve the correct results.

You will likely use the createCDATASection(), createComment(), and createProcessing Instruction() methods less often, but they are there if you need to add the corresponding components to an XML document.

The getElementsByTagName() method is useful to retrieve all elements that are not in a namespace and have a particular element name. For example, to retrieve all Chapter nodes in a DOM you would use code like the following:

```
oDom.getElementsByTagName("Chapter");
```

You would then have a NodeList object containing all such Chapter nodes for further processing.

If you are retrieving Element nodes that are in a namespace — for example, SVG — then you need to use the getElementsByTagNameNS() method. Remember that namespace URIs must match character for character if you are to successfully retrieve the intended node(s).

If you are manipulating XML documents that had ID attributes, then you can use the getElementById() method to retrieve a specific Element node.

A full listing of the DOM Level 2 interfaces is available in Appendix B, but it is hoped that having worked through the examples, you now feel you have the knowledge to manipulate the XML DOM — for example, to add and remove nodes and to alter their value.

As indicated earlier, the XML DOM is typically embedded in an application, and represents at least part of the way in which XML is used in an application. To briefly illustrate this, the next section introduces InfoPath 2007 and discusses how the XML DOM is used in it.

How the XML DOM Is Used in InfoPath 2007

InfoPath 2007 is an enterprise XML-based forms tool from Microsoft that is designed to produce XML data from forms without requiring the end-user to have any understanding or awareness of XML. At the heart of InfoPath 2007 are several XML technologies, including the Microsoft implementation of the XML DOM in MSXML 6.

A free trial of InfoPath is available as part of Office 2007. Go to `http://office.microsoft.com/en-us/infopath/default.aspx` and click "Download a free trial."

The data of an InfoPath form is held as XML in a DOM. As far as the InfoPath developer is concerned, this is exposed as a "data source" that reflects the node hierarchy in the XML DOM but without requiring, for simple forms at least, the developer to have an understanding of how the XML DOM works. The data source for an InfoPath form is shown in Figure 11-11.

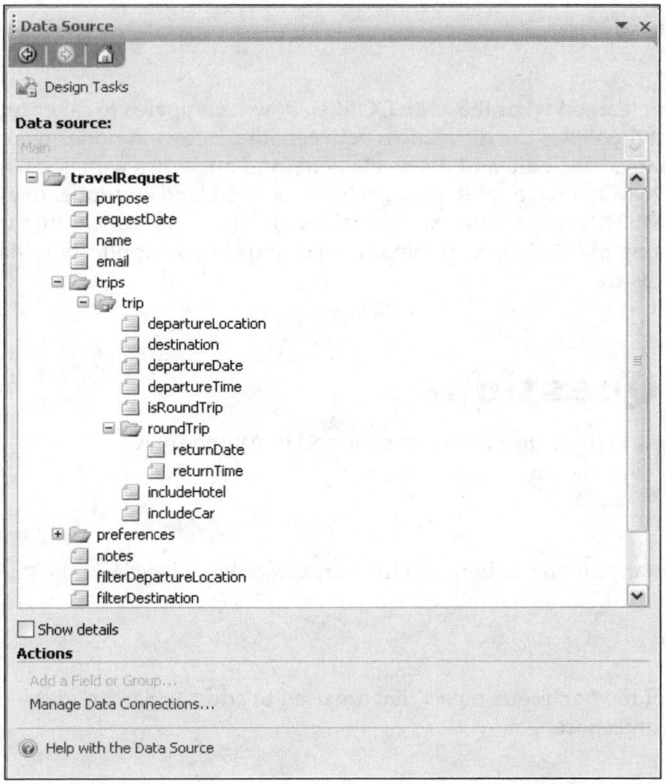

Figure 11-11

The simplest InfoPath forms use a single XML DOM to hold the data returned from a query or data that is to be submitted to a relational database or XML web service. However, many forms have multiple XML DOMs in a single InfoPath solution. The values available in, for example, drop-down list form controls are secondary XML DOMs and can be retrieved from XML documents or from relational data sources.

> As mentioned earlier, many DOM implementations have proprietary extensions. Manipulation of the InfoPath XML DOM depends on proprietary Microsoft methods that allow XPath strings to be used as arguments to those methods. The W3C is working on proposals to incorporate these or similar methods into the DOM to facilitate interoperability of XPath and DOM, but those are not finalized yet.

The use of the XML DOM in InfoPath serves to illustrate how the DOM can be used as part of a larger application, whether custom coded or, with InfoPath 2007, a commercial application with XML DOM under the covers.

Summary

In this chapter, you learned what the XML DOM is, how it compares to other representations, and a little about its history at the W3C. The differences between interfaces and nodes were discussed, and many of the methods used to create, edit, and delete elements and attributes were shown. Several of the most commonly used DOM interfaces and objects were described, and a number of examples were demonstrated using the MSXML parser and the equivalent Mozilla classes, including what happens when an error in manipulating the DOM occurs. Finally, an example of an application that uses the DOM extensively, InfoPath, was shown.

Exercise Questions

Suggested solutions to these questions can be found in Appendix A.

Question 1

Describe an important difference between the NamedNodeMap object and the NodeList object.

Question 2

List the methods of the Document object that are used to add Element nodes — first, in no namespace, and second, in a namespace.

12

Simple API for XML (SAX)

In the last chapter, you learned about the Document Object Model (DOM) and how it can be used to work with your XML documents. The DOM is great when you work with relatively small documents that can easily fit into memory, but what do you do when you need to read an XML file that is several megabytes or even several gigabytes large? Loading this kind of data into memory can be very slow, and in many cases not possible. Luckily, you have another way to get the data out of an XML document: SAX.

This chapter covers the following:

❑   What is SAX?

❑   Where to download SAX and how to set it up

❑   How and when to use the primary SAX interfaces

> **Because SAX is an application programming interface (API), you need to learn some in-depth programming concepts within this chapter. As in the last chapter, you will learn it step by step, but you need to have some programming experience under your belt. In order to work through the many examples, this chapter explains how to download and install the Java Development Kit (JDK). If you do not plan to program applications for XML, but rather plan to use XML for its design- and document-driven nature, you may want to skip this chapter.**

What Is SAX and Why Was It Invented?

The *Simple API for XML*, or *SAX*, was developed to provide a standardized way to parse XML and enable more efficient analysis of large XML documents. The problem with the DOM is that before you can use it to traverse a document it has to build up a massive in-memory map of the document. This takes up space and — more important — time. If you're trying to extract a small amount of information from the document, this can be extremely inefficient.

Parsing an XML document using SAX is similar to watching a train pass by. It is very easy to catalog certain events of the train's passing. For example, you might observe the start of the train (the engine) and the end of the train (the caboose). You also might note the start of each car and the end of each car. Ideally, you would note the contents and characteristics of each car: color, length, engineer, baggage, passengers, and so on. Using this method, you could survey every part of the train.

SAX treats XML documents in much the same way. As the XML parser parses the documents, it reports a stream of events back to the application — events for the start of the document, the end of the document, the start and end of each element, the character contents of each element, and so on.

Unfortunately, receiving the events emitted by a SAX parser is like watching a runaway train. Once it is started, the parser cannot be interrupted so you can go back and look at an earlier part of the document. Unlike DOM, which gives you access to the entire document at once, SAX stores little or nothing from event to event. Although this seems like a major limitation, it is this very characteristic that gives SAX its speed and power.

> **Is it possible to pause the stream of events from a SAX parser and come back to it later? Because SAX parsers "push" the data back to the application, they are generally referred to as *push processors*. The DOM model, which allows the application to retrieve the information when ready, is more generally a *pull process*. Some SAX parsers have emerged that allow you to pull the events when you're ready. These parsers work by enabling you to pause and resume the parsing process. Although it still does not allow you to go backward, it adds greater flexibility in the design of applications.**

A Brief History of SAX

The extraordinary thing about SAX is that it isn't owned by anyone. It doesn't belong to any consortium, standards body, company, or individual. In other words, it doesn't survive because some organization or government says that you must use it to comply with their standards, or because a specific company supporting it is dominant in the marketplace. It survives because it's simple and it works.

SAX arose out of discussions on the XML-DEV mailing list now hosted by OASIS. You can read the archives at `http://lists.xml.org/archives/xml-dev/`. The mailing list was aimed at resolving incompatibilities between different XML parsers (this was back in the infancy of XML in late 1997). David Megginson took on the job of coordinating the process of specifying a new API with the group. On May 11, 1998, the SAX 1.0 specification was completed. A whole series of SAX 1.0–compliant parsers then began to emerge, both from large corporations, such as IBM and Sun, and from enterprising individuals, such as James Clark. All of these parsers were freely available for public download.

Eventually, a number of shortcomings in the specification became apparent, and David Megginson and his colleagues got back to work, finally producing the SAX 2.0 specification on May 5, 2000. The improvements centered on added support for namespaces and tighter adherence to the XML specification. Since that time, several enhancements were made to expose additional information in the XML document, but the core of SAX was very stable. On April 27, 2004, these changes were finalized and released as version 2.0.2.

SAX is specified as a set of Java interfaces, which initially meant that if you were going to do any serious work with it, you were looking at doing some Java programming, using JDK 1.1 or later. Now, however, a wide variety of languages have their own version of SAX, some of which you will learn about later in the chapter. In deference to the SAX tradition, however, the examples in this chapter are written in Java.

Where to Get SAX

All the latest information about SAX can be found at `www.saxproject.org`. It remains a public domain open-source project hosted by SourceForge. To download SAX you can go to the home page and browse for the latest version, or you can go directly to the SourceForge project page at `http://sourceforge .net/projects/sax`.

The distribution contains all of the Java interfaces, the extension interfaces, some helper files, and the documentation. Not included is a SAX parser. To actually use SAX, you need to download one of the many XML parsers that have been developed to work with SAX.

The following table shows some popular Java SAX parsers:

Parser	Driver Class Name	Description
Xerces2-J	`org.apache.xerces .parsers.SAXParser`	The Xerces2 parser, used throughout this chapter, is maintained by the Apache group. It is available at `http://xml.apache.org/xerces2-j`. The original Xerces Java Toolkit also contains a SAX2-compatible parser.
AElfred2	`gnu.xml.aelfred2 .XmlReader`	The AElfred2 parser is highly conformant, as it was written and modified by the creators of SAX. It is available as part of the GNU JAXP project at `www.gnu.org/software/classpathx/jaxp/`.
Crimson	`org.apache.crimson .parser.XMLReaderImpl`	The Crimson parser was originally part of the Crimson project at `http://xml.apache.org/ crimson/`. It is now included as part of Sun's Java API for XML Parsing, available at `http://java .sun.com/xml`.
Oracle	`oracle.xml.parser .v2.SAXParser`	Oracle maintains a SAX parser as part of its XML Toolkit. It can be downloaded from the Oracle Technology Network at `http://otn.oracle .com/tech/xml/index.html`.
XP	`com.jclark.xml.sax .SAX2Driver`	XP is an XML 1.0 parser written by James Clark. A SAX2 driver was created for use with the latest versions of SAX. More information can be found at `www.xmlmind.com/_xpforjaxp/docs/index .html` or the original `www.jclark.com/xml/xp/ index.html`.

Setting Up SAX

Before trying it out, you need to get hold of some software:

❑   Download the SAX libraries. You can do this by going to www.saxproject.org, and downloading the latest version. Currently, that is sax2r3.zip (final).

❑   For the parser, you're going to use the latest Java version of Apache Xerces, available from
http://xml.apache.org/xerces2-j.

❑   You also need the Java Development Kit, release 1.1 or later. If you don't already have it
installed, your best bet is to download the latest edition of the Sun Java 2 Platform, Standard
Edition from http://java.sun.com/javase/downloads/index.jsp. However, this is a
pretty large download, so if you have limited bandwidth, JDK 1.1 is quite acceptable and is still
available from http://java.sun.com/products/archive/index.html, although even this
is still a large download, so you might want to get this ready well in advance.

You can store the Xerces2-J and SAX libraries wherever you like. For the examples in this chapter, you
need the sax2.jar from the SAX distribution and the xercesImpl.jar from the Xerces2-J distribution.
You could add references to these in your CLASSPATH environment variable, or simply include references to them in the command-line calls.

Receiving SAX Events

You may be wondering how you're going to be receiving these events. Remember the discussion on
interfaces in the last chapter? If not, it might be a good time to take a look again to refresh your memory.
You will write a Java class that *implements* one of the SAX interfaces, which means your class will have
all of the same functions as the interface.

In Java, you specify that a class implements an interface by declaring it like this:

```
public class MyClass implements ContentHandler
```

MyClass is the name of the new class, and ContentHandler is the name of the interface. Actually, this is
the most important interface in SAX, as it is the one that defines the callback methods for content-related
events (that is, events about elements, attributes, and their contents). What you're doing here is creating
a class that contains methods that a SAX-aware parser knows about.

The ContentHandler interface contains a whole series of methods, most of which in the normal course
of events you don't really want to be bothered with. Unfortunately, when you implement an interface,
you have to provide implementations of *all* the methods defined in that interface. However, SAX provides you with a default, empty implementation of them, called DefaultHandler, so rather than *implement* ContentHandler, you can instead *extend* DefaultHandler, like this:

```
public class MyClass extends DefaultHandler
```

You can then choose which methods you want to provide your own implementations, to trap
specific events. This is called *overriding* the methods. If you leave things as they are, the base class
(DefaultHandler in this case) provides its own implementation of them for use by MyClass. For

example, there's a method in the `ContentHandler` interface called `startDocument`. Whenever another piece of code invokes the `startDocument` method of `MyClass`'s implementation of `ContentHandler`, the method invoked is actually `DefaultHandler.startDocument`. This is because `DefaultHandler` is providing a default implementation of `startDocument`. This is called *inheriting an implementation*.

If you provide your own implementations of the methods by overriding the inherited methods, then your methods are used instead. The method invoked would now be `MyClass.startDocument`. This might do something totally different from `DefaultHandler`'s implementation.

Actually, `DefaultHandler` is a very hard-working class because it also provides default implementations of the three other core SAX interfaces: `ErrorHandler`, `DTDHandler`, and `EntityResolver`. You'll come across them in a little while, but for the time being you'll focus on `ContentHandler`.

ContentHandler Interface

The `ContentHandler` interface, as the name implies, is designed to control the reporting of events for the content of the document. This includes information about the text, attributes, processing instructions, elements, and even the document itself. Here is a quick summary of methods that a `ContentHandler` must implement:

Event	Description
startDocument	Event to notify the application that the parser has read the start of the document
endDocument	Event to notify the application that the parser has read the end of the document
startElement	Event to notify the application that the parser has read an element start-tag
endElement	Event to notify the application that the parser has read an element end-tag. Note that this event will be fired immediately after the `startElement` event for empty elements where the end-tag is implicit.
characters	Event to notify the application that the parser has read a block of characters. Multiple `characters` events may be fired for a single section of text.
ignorableWhitespace	Event to notify the application that the parser has read a block of whitespace that can probably be ignored, such as formatting and spacing of elements. Multiple `ignorableWhitespace` events may be fired for a single section of whitespace.
skippedEntity	Event to notify the application that the parser has skipped an external entity
processingInstruction	Event to notify the application that the parser has read a processing instruction

Table continued on following page

Event	Description
startPrefixMapping	Event to notify the application that the parser has read an XML namespace declaration, and that a new namespace prefix is in scope
endPrefixMapping	Event to notify the application that a namespace prefix mapping is no longer in scope
setDocumentLocator	Event that allows the parser to pass a Locator object to the application

You will learn about each of these events in more detail. Let's try a small example to see how it works.

Try It Out   The Start of Something Big

1. Begin by creating a sample XML document that you can use throughout this chapter — the examples will continue to use the train analogy used at the beginning of the chapter:

```xml
<?xml version="1.0"?>
<train>
  <car type="Engine">
    <color>Black</color>
    <weight>512 tons</weight>
    <length>60 feet</length>
    <occupants>3</occupants>
  </car>
  <car type="Baggage">
    <color>Green</color>
    <weight>80 tons</weight>
    <length>40 feet</length>
    <occupants>0</occupants>
  </car>
  <car type="Passenger">
    <color>Green and Yellow</color>
    <weight>40 tons</weight>
    <length>60 feet</length>
    <occupants>23</occupants>
  </car>
  <car type="Caboose">
    <color>Red</color>
    <weight>90 tons</weight>
    <length>30 feet</length>
    <occupants>4</occupants>
  </car>
</train>
```

It may not be a very long train, but it has a caboose, so it's complete. A better example of SAX's power, however, would be much larger. Save this file as Train.xml in a directory that you can use for your project.

2. Create a Java class that does the work of starting the parser and handling the events. You begin the class by telling the compiler that you will be using the SAX library by importing several packages:

```
import javax.xml.parsers.SAXParserFactory;
import javax.xml.parsers.SAXParser;
import org.xml.sax.*;
import org.xml.sax.helpers.*;
```

3. You can now begin your class, called `TrainReader`:

```
public class TrainReader extends DefaultHandler
{

  public static void main(String[] args)
    throws Exception
  {
    System.out.println("("Running train reader...");...");
    TrainReader readerObj = new TrainReader();
    readerObj.read(args[0]);
  }
```

The `main` method declaration is standard Java: This is the piece of code that is executed when you start the class. It prints out a message, creates a new instance of the class that it resides in, and invokes a method called `read()`.

The `void` part of the declaration, incidentally, means that the method doesn't return a value to its caller, and the `throws Exception` part means that if anything happens that it can't cope with, it passes the exception back so the caller can deal with it. You'll see more exception declarations later.

```
public void read(String fileName)
  throws Exception
{
  XMLReader reader =
    XMLReaderFactory.createXMLReader("org.apache.xerces.parsers.SAXParser");
  reader.setContentHandler(this);
  reader.parse(fileName);
}
```

The first line of this method creates an `XMLReader` object using a factory helper object. This is the only place in the code where you explicitly indicate that the Xerces parser is used. You could substitute the qualified name of another parser here if you happened to have one installed.

4. Now you can start working with the events themselves, which is why you are writing the class. You start with the simplest of events, the start of the document:

```
public void startDocument()
  throws SAXException
{
  System.out.println("Start of the train");
}
```

5. Now you can create a function to catch the event that is executed when the parser reaches the end of the XML document:

```
public void endDocument()
  throws SAXException
{
  System.out.println("End of the train");
}
```

6. Finally, you can add the closing of the class:

```
}
```

Save this as file `TrainReader.java` in the same folder that you saved `Train.xml`. In these examples, it is assumed that you are compiling and executing your Java classes from a command prompt (or a terminal window if you are working in Linux). If you are on Windows, you can find a shortcut to open a command prompt by selecting Start ➪ Accessories. You may already be using a Java Integrated Development Environment (Java IDE), which is fine as long as you have access to view the console output.

At the command prompt, change to the directory where you have saved `TrainReader.java` and compile:

```
javac TrainReader.java
```

If you receive an error such as

```
'javac' is not recognized as an internal or external command, operable program or
batch file.
```

then it is likely that you have not added your Java bin folder to your PATH environment variable. Check your setup and try again. If you receive another error compiling, confirm that you typed the code correctly and try again.

If you have added the SAX and Xerces packages to your CLASSPATH environment variable, you can run your `TrainReader` program:

```
java TrainReader Train.xml
```

If you did not want to modify your CLASSPATH variable, you could simply copy the `xercesImpl.jar` file and `sax2r2.jar` file into your project directory and type the following:

```
java -cp .;sax2.jar;xercesImpl.jar TrainReader Train.xml
```

> The Sun JDK on Linux uses the colon (:) instead of the semicolon (;) to separate CLASSPATH **components.**

You should see the following:

```
Running train reader...
Start of the train
End of the train
```

Though this may not seem like groundbreaking output, the code behind your `TrainReader` class is the basis of any SAX project. From here you can quickly expand your code to examine any part of any XML document, regardless of size.

If you see an error, confirm that you typed in `Train.xml` *correctly and try again. Possible errors are covered in more detail later in the chapter.*

How It Works

Before moving on to another example, let's break down some important parts of the `TrainReader` class. In the `main()` function you created an `XMLReader` object by sending a registered parser name to a factory function:

```
XMLReader reader = XMLReaderFactory.createXMLReader("org.apache.xerces
.parsers.SAXParser");
```

Before you parsed, you indicated to the `XMLReader` that your class should receive events about the content of the XML document:

```
reader.setContentHandler(this);
```

Then you started the parsing, passing the name of the file you wanted to parse:

```
reader.parse(fileName);
```

At that point, the SAX parser took over. As it parsed the document, it called the event handlers that were registered. Therefore, when the parser encountered the start of the document, it reported a `startDocument` event to the registered `ContentHandler`, your `TrainReader` class. It did this by executing the `startDocument` function:

```
public void startDocument()
  throws SAXException
{
  System.out.println("Start of the train");
}
```

Finally, when it reached the end of the document, it called the similar `endDocument` function:

```
public void endDocument()
    throws SAXException
  {
    System.out.println("End of the train");
  }
```

Handling Element Events

Now that you have learned the basics of handling events using the `ContentHandler` interface, let's look at how to handle element events, beginning with the `startElement` function:

```
public void startElement(String uri, String localName, String qName,
  Attributes atts) throws SAXException
```

The first three parameters help to identify the element that the parser encountered — they enable you to identify the element based on its namespace name and local name, or by its qualified name. If you remember the discussion of namespaces from Chapter 3, this behavior enables you to uniquely identify similar elements in different vocabularies.

For example, if the parser encountered

```
<myPrefix:myElement xmlns:myPrefix="http://example.com">
```

then it would fire an event for the start of the element with the following values:

Parameter	Value
uri	http://example.com
localName	myElement
qName	myPrefix:myElement

As you can see, the uri parameter represents the namespace URI associated with the element. The localName parameter contains part of the element name after the ":". The qName parameter is the qualified name — or the local name and the namespace prefix. If there is no prefix for the element name (for example, if there is no namespace or a default namespace), then the localName and qName should be the same.

> Though most SAX parsers report identical strings for the localName and qName parameters when there is no prefix, some do not. By default, some parsers may report an empty string for the qName parameter if the element has a namespace. Therefore, it is recommended that you first check the uri parameter for null. If the uri parameter is not null, then use the combination of the uri and the localName instead of the qName parameter. You may be wondering why this is preferred. Remember that any prefix can be used to refer to a namespace, and this may change from document to document. Using the namespace URI directly is more reliable.

The startElement event also provides a fourth parameter — the attributes. The Attributes interface enables you to easily look up the attributes and their values at the start of each element. The default Attributes interface provides you with the following functions:

Method	Description
getLength	Determines the number of attributes available in the Attributes interface
getIndex	Retrieves the index of a specific attribute in the list. The getIndex function enables you to look up the index by using the attribute's qualified name or by using both the local name and namespace URI.

Method	Description
getLocalName	Retrieves a specific attribute's local name by sending the index in the list
getQName	Retrieves a specific attribute's qualified name by sending the index in the list
getURI	Retrieves a specific attribute's namespace URI by sending the index in the list
getType	Retrieves a specific attribute's type by sending the index in the list, by using the attribute's qualified name or by using both the local name and namespace URI. If there is no Document Type Definition (DTD), this function will always return CDATA.
getValue	Retrieves a specific attribute's value by sending the index in the list, by using the attribute's qualified name, or by using both the local name and namespace URI

As shown with elements, you can access the attributes through their qualified names or through the local names and namespace URIs. Note that namespace declarations (the xmlns declarations you learned about in Chapter 3) are not reported as attributes by default.

In the latest version of SAX, some parsers expose extended behavior through an interface called Attributes2, which enables you to check whether an attribute was declared in a DTD, whether the attribute value appeared in the XML document, or whether it appeared because of a DTD or XML Schema attribute default declaration. Extension interfaces are covered a little later in the chapter.

Let's look at an example of working with elements and attributes.

Try It Out   Element and Attribute Events

In this example, you simply try to report the type of each train car as your SAX parser fires the appropriate events. You use the same XML document, Train.xml, from the first example and modify the Java program a little.

1. Begin by opening TrainReader.java and adding the following function just after the endDocument function:

```java
public void startElement(String uri, String localName, String qName,
  Attributes atts) throws SAXException
{
  if ("car".equals(localName)) {
    if (atts != null) {
      System.out.println("Car: " + atts.getValue("type"));
    }
  }
}
```

2. Save this as file TrainReader.java in the same folder that you saved Train.xml. At the command prompt, change to the directory where you have saved TrainReader.java and compile:

```
javac TrainReader.java
```

3. Once you have compiled the class, you can run the program:

```
java TrainReader Train.xml
```

You should see the following:

```
Running train reader...
Start of the train
Car: Engine
Car: Baggage
Car: Passenger
Car: Caboose
End of the train
```

How It Works

The core of this Try It Out is exactly the same as the first example. The only thing you did differently was create an event handler for the start of each element:

```
if ("car".equals(localName)) {
```

The first thing you did in the handler was check the element's local name. Because you are using Xerces, you know that the localName and qName parameters are always reliable and always the same for documents without namespaces. Still, in this example, you used the localName parameter to get in the habit of doing so when it is unknown whether the parser supports the qName parameter. When the element's local name was car, the attributes were processed:

```
if (atts != null) {
   System.out.println("Car: " + atts.getValue("type"));
}
```

The first step was to check whether the passed in Attributes interface was not null. According to the SAX specification, it should never be null. However, some early parsers did not follow this constraint. Next, you printed out the value of the type attribute. Note that if the type attribute is not found in the Attributes list, then the getValue function returns null. In a more complete application, where the source XML documents vary, it would be a good idea to check for this case.

Handling Character Content

In addition to working with elements and the attribute events, SAX makes it easy to work with the character content in the document. Working with the characters event is very similar to the events you have already seen:

```
public void characters(char[] ch, int start, int len)
   throws SAXException
```

Notice that the characters are delivered as a buffer, rather than a string. This enables parser designers to more easily reuse internal buffers, which can effectively reduce the number of memory allocations and increase overall performance. Passing in the start position and length to copy from the buffer can also help to increase performance. Luckily, it is very easy to create strings in Java with these parameters.

Unfortunately, working with the `characters` function is not quite as straightforward as it might seem. The parser writer is not obligated to deliver all the character data between two tags as a single block of text. It may report the text using multiple `characters` callbacks. (When you think about it, this is actually quite reasonable — after all, the string might turn out to be extremely long, which could result in a very clumsy parser implementation.) From an application point of view, this just means that you may need to build up your string over a number of `characters` events.

Try It Out   Adding Colorful Characters

Though you are sticking with the trains, you add quite a bit in this Try It Out, which should output the color of each car and its car type:

1. For starters, add some private variables to your class:

```java
import javax.xml.parsers.SAXParserFactory;
import javax.xml.parsers.SAXParser;
import org.xml.sax.*;
import org.xml.sax.helpers.*;

public class TrainReader extends DefaultHandler
{
  private boolean isColor;
  private String trainCarType = "";
  private StringBuffer trainCarColor = new StringBuffer();
  public static void main(String[ ] args)
    throws Exception
  {
    System.out.println("Running train reader...");
    TrainReader readerObj = new TrainReader();
    readerObj.read(args[0]);
  }

  public void read(String fileName)
    throws Exception
  {
    XMLReader reader =
      XMLReaderFactory.createXMLReader("org.apache.xerces.parsers.SAXParser");
    reader.setContentHandler(this);
    reader.parse(fileName);
  }

  public void startDocument()
    throws SAXException
  {
    System.out.println("Start of the train");
  }

  public void endDocument()
    throws SAXException
  {
    System.out.println("End of the train");
  }
```

2. Modify the `startElement` function to record some of the data before the parser continues. Just because the SAX parser doesn't remember data from event to event doesn't mean your application can't. Set the `isColor` flag to indicate whether the parser has started parsing a color element, and record the car type instead of just outputting it immediately, as in the last example:

```java
public void startElement(String uri, String localName, String qName,
  Attributes atts) throws SAXException
{
  if ("car".equals(localName)) {
    if (atts != null) {
      trainCarType = atts.getValue("type");
    }
  }

  if ("color".equals(localName)) {
    trainCarColor.setLength(0);
    isColor = true;
  } else {
    isColor = false;
  }
}
```

Notice that you are again working with the `localName` parameter instead of the `qName` parameter. If `localName` is `color`, then set your flag to `true`; otherwise, set it to `false`. Be sure to reset the `trainCarColor` `StringBuffer` to be empty at the start of each new `color` element.

3. You can now add your `characters` event handler:

```java
public void characters(char[] ch, int start, int len)
  throws SAXException
{
  if (isColor)
  {
    trainCarColor.append(ch, start, len);
  }
}
```

Remember that the parser may report the characters for an element in multiple chunks (even when the character data is very small), so you need to collect all the `characters` events into a single `StringBuffer`, appending the data with each new call. In addition, make sure you are appending the data only from `color` elements by checking the `isColor` flag you set in the `startElement` event.

4. Finally, add an event handler to catch the end of the color element:

```java
public void endElement(String uri, String localName, String qName)
  throws SAXException
{
  if (isColor) {
    System.out.println("The color of the " + trainCarType + " car is " +
      trainCarColor.toString());
    isColor = false;
  }
}
```

Here you can output a message including the `StringBuffer` that you built up in the `characters` event. You should also set the `isColor` flag back to `false` so that you don't collect unneeded character data in the `characters` event.

Again, save this as file `TrainReader.java` in the same folder that you saved `Train.xml` and compile the class:

```
javac TrainReader.java
```

Once you have compiled the class, you can run the program:

```
java TrainReader Train.xml
```

You should see the following:

```
Running train reader...
Start of the train
The color of the Engine car is Black
The color of the Baggage car is Green
The color of the Passenger car is Green and Yellow
The color of the Caboose car is Red
End of the train
```

How It Works

The examples are now beginning to hint at the power, and difficulty, of SAX. As you can see, retrieving the data from the SAX model is fairly simple. However, the complexity of the application grows very quickly when you need to associate and store data between event callbacks.

As shown throughout the chapter, the process began very simply. As the SAX parser began parsing the document, it called the `startDocument` function. Then, for each new element, it called the `startElement` function. When the parser encountered a `car` element and fired the event, you stored the `type` attribute for later use:

```
trainCarType = atts.getValue("type");
```

Until the parser encountered another `car` element, the `trainCarType` variable remained unchanged. When the parser encountered the start of a `color` element, you set a flag to alert the application to append any character data to the `trainCarColor` `StringBuffer`:

```
if (isColor)
{
  trainCarColor.append(ch, start, len);
}
```

Instead of outputting the train car's color immediately, you wait until the `endElement` event to ensure that you have collected all of the character content in the color element. For example, if the parser had fired the following events:

```
Start of element: color
Character data: Green and
Character data: Yellow
End of element: color
```

and you simply assigned the `trainCarColor` instead of appending the data each time, then you would overwrite Green and with Yellow during the second `characters` event.

When to Ignore ignorableWhitespace

The `ignorableWhitespace` event is very similar to the `characters` event. In fact, the parameter lists for the two functions are identical:

```
public void ignorableWhitespace(char[ ] ch, int start, int len)
    throws SAXException
```

Not only are the parameters identical, but the functionality is very similar. Parsers may call the `ignorableWhitespace` function multiple times within a single element.

Why have the `ignorableWhitespace` event? Whitespace, such as spaces, tabs, and linefeeds, which are used to make an XML document more readable, are often not important to the application, even though they are part of the XML content. For example, the linefeed and the spaces between the end of the color element and the start of the `weight` element have no meaning, whereas the space between 512 and tons within the `weight` element is very meaningful:

```
<car type="Engine">
 <color>Black</color>
 <weight>512 tons</weight>
 <length>60 feet</length>
 <occupants>3</occupants>
</car>
```

The only way a SAX parser can know that whitespace is ignorable is when an element is declared, as in a DTD, to not contain PCDATA (remember PCDATA is short for "parsed" character data). Therefore, only validating parsers can report this event. If the parser has no knowledge of the DTD, then it must assume that all character data, including whitespace, is important, and it must report it in the `characters` event.

Skipped Entities

The `skippedEntity` event, much like the `ignorableWhitespace` event, alerts the application that the SAX parser has encountered information it believes the application can or must skip. In the case of the `skippedEntity` event, the SAX parser has not expanded an entity reference it encountered in the XML document. An entity might be "skipped" for several reasons:

❑   The entity is a reference to an external resource that cannot be parsed or cannot be found.

❑   The entity is an external general entity and the `http://xml.org/sax/features/external-general-entities` feature is set to false.

❑   The entity is an external parameter entity and the `http://xml.org/sax/features/external-parameter-entities` feature is set to false.

You learn about the `external-general-entities` and `external-parameter-entities` features later in this chapter. The `skippedEntity` event is declared as follows:

```
public void skippedEntity(String name)
    throws SAXException
```

The name parameter is the name of the entity that was skipped. It begins with % in the case of a parameter entity. SAX considers the external DTD subset an entity, so if the name parameter is [dtd], then it means the external DTD subset was not processed. For more information on DTDs, refer to Chapter 4.

Handling Special Commands with Processing Instructions

Processing instructions, as you may remember from Chapter 2, allows XML document authors to pass specific instructions to applications. SAX allows you to receive these special instructions in your application through the processingInstruction event:

```
public void processingInstruction(String target, String data) throws SAXException
```

Consider the following processing instruction:

```
<?instructionForTrainPrograms blowWhistle?>
```

Here the target would be instructionForTrainPrograms and the data would be blowWhistle. Using the processingInstruction event, adding special functionality to your application becomes relatively easy. In reality, though, processing instructions are seldom used. In fact, many people argued against the inclusion of processing instructions in the XML specification. With that said, processing instructions are legal and intended for use within applications.

You probably don't need to be reminded at this point that the XML declaration at the start of an XML document is *not* really a processing instruction, and as such it shouldn't result in a processing Instruction event. If it does, then you should switch to another parser quickly.

Namespace Prefixes

When working with the element events, you saw that it is best to use the namespace URI and local name instead of the prefix, but what if you want keep track of the prefixes used for each namespace? SAX processors will fire a startPrefixMapping event and endPrefixMapping event for any namespace declaration:

```
public void startPrefixMapping(String prefix, String uri)
   throws SAXException

public void endPrefixMapping(String prefix) throws SAXException
```

The prefix parameter is the namespace prefix that is being declared. In the case of a default namespace declaration, the prefix should be an empty string. The uri parameter is the namespace URI being declared, so for the namespace declaration

```
xmlns:example="http://example.com"
```

the prefix parameter would be "example" and the uri parameter would be "http://example.com." A startPrefixMapping event occurs immediately before the startElement event for the element where a namespace declaration appears. Likewise, an endPrefixMapping event will occur immediately after the corresponding endElement event. Keep in mind that the xml prefix is built in, so a SAX parser will not fire startPrefixMapping and endPrefixMapping events when an attribute or declaration with the xml prefix is encountered.

Stopping the Process in Exceptional Circumstances

In Chapters 4, 5, and 6, you learned how to validate documents against a DTD, XML Schema, or RELAX NG schema. What should you do if you have a rule that is so complex that it cannot be expressed in one of these languages? The designers of SAX considered this problem. As you may have noticed, all the event functions used so far have declared that they may throw a SAXException. This allows you to create a new SAXException when you want to stop the processing.

Let's try another example.

Try It Out   Pulling the Brakes

This example makes a small modification to the last example, adding a new rule to require that the caboose be Red. After all, nobody likes a train with a caboose that isn't red.

1.   The only change that you make is in the endElement function: Check the trainCarType for Caboose and then check the color:

```
public void endElement(String uri, String localName, String qName)
  throws SAXException
{
  if (isColor) {
    System.out.println("The color of the " + trainCarType + " car is " +
      trainCarColor.toString());
    isColor = false;
    if (("Caboose".equals(trainCarType)) &&
        (!"Red".equals(trainCarColor.toString())))
      throw new SAXException("The caboose is not red!");
  }
}
```

This is all you need to do to stop the parsing process. Save this as file TrainReader.java in the same folder that you saved Train.xml and compile the class:

```
javac TrainReader.java
```

Once you have compiled the class, you can run the program:

```
java TrainReader Train.xml
```

You should see the following:

```
Running train reader...
Start of the train
The color of the Engine car is Black
The color of the Baggage car is Green
The color of the Passenger car is Green and Yellow
The color of the Caboose car is Red
End of the train
```

Of course, the caboose is red, so you don't receive an error. Now change the color of the caboose in Train.xml and save the file as Train2.xml:

```
<car type="Caboose">
  <color>Green</color>
  <weight>90 tons</weight>
```

```
<length>30 feet</length>
<occupants>4</occupants>
</car>
```

Try running the TrainReader again:

```
java TrainReader Train2.xml
```

You should now see the following:

```
Running train reader...
Start of the train
The color of the Engine car is Black
The color of the Baggage car is Green
The color of the Passenger car is Green and Yellow
The color of the Caboose car is Green
Exception in thread "main" org.xml.sax.SAXException: The caboose is not red!
        at TrainReader.endElement(TrainReader.java:76)
        at org.apache.xerces.parsers.AbstractSAXParser.endElement(Unknown Source)
        at org.apache.xerces.impl.XMLNSDocumentScannerImpl.scanEndElement
        (Unknown Source)
        at org.apache.xerces.impl.XMLDocumentFragmentScannerImpl$
        FragmentContentDispatcher.dispatch(Unknown Source)
        at org.apache.xerces.impl.XMLDocumentFragmentScannerImpl.scanDocument
        (Unknown Source)
        at org.apache.xerces.parsers.XML11Configuration.parse(Unknown Source)
        at org.apache.xerces.parsers.XML11Configuration.parse(Unknown Source)
        at org.apache.xerces.parsers.XMLParser.parse(Unknown Source)
        at org.apache.xerces.parsers.AbstractSAXParser.parse(Unknown Source)
        at TrainReader.read(TrainReader.java:25)
        at TrainReader.main(TrainReader.java:16)
```

Notice that when the exception is raised it stops the whole application. This is because the exception isn't handled anywhere. Let's add that to the application now.

2. Add a try/catch block around the call to the parse function where you start reading the document:

```
public void read(String fileName)
  throws Exception
{
  XMLReader reader =
    XMLReaderFactory.createXMLReader("org.apache.xerces.parsers.SAXParser");
  reader.setContentHandler(this);
  try
  {
    reader.parse(fileName);
  }
  catch (SAXException e)
  {
    System.out.println("Parsing stopped : " + e.getMessage());
  }
}
```

Once this is complete, you can again compile TrainReader.java:

```
javac TrainReader.java
```

After compiling the class, you can run the program:

```
java TrainReader Train2.xml
```

You should see the following:

```
Running train reader...
Start of the train
The color of the Engine car is Black
The color of the Baggage car is Green
The color of the Passenger car is Green and Yellow
The color of the Caboose car is Green
Parsing stopped : The caboose is not red!
```

How It Works

Taking advantage of the exception mechanism built into SAX enables you to quickly stop the parsing process if you deem it necessary. This means that you can add additional validation for more complex constraints that cannot be modeled using DTDs or XML Schemas. In the example, you used the exception mechanism to ensure that the caboose was red, but this same concept can be used to model any type of business rules needed in your application, including complex calculations or specialized lookups.

Once the exception was thrown, you didn't receive any more SAX events, even though the parser had not completed parsing the document. Many SAX parsers are designed to fire an endDocument event even when there is an exception or error in the document. This design provides applications with a guaranteed time to do any miscellaneous cleanup such as releasing memory. Currently, however, the Xerces parser, the Crimson parser, and the Oracle parser do not fire the endDocument event if an error or exception is encountered. Therefore, it is safest to assume that the endDocument function will not be called, which means you should always have a try...finally block surrounding calls to the parse function if you need to ensure that certain actions are taken even when there is an exception.

Providing the Location of the Error

Although you have provided an error message for the problem XML document, you haven't given the author of the XML document very much information for fixing the error. It would be helpful to provide the line number and the column position of the error, which SAX enables you to pass along in the message.

The only event callback you haven't used from the ContentHandler so far in this chapter is setDocumentLocator. The setDocumentLocator callback allows the parser to pass the application a Locator interface. Using this interface you can easily determine the line number and column position at any time within your application. The methods of the Locator object are shown in the following table:

Method	Description
getLineNumber	Retrieves the line number for the current event
getColumnNumber	Retrieves the column number for the current event (the SAX specification assumes that the column number is based on right-to-left reading modes)
getSystemId	Retrieves the system identifier of the document for the current event. Because XML documents may be composed of multiple external entities, this may change throughout the parsing process.

Method	Description
getPublicId	Retrieves the public identifier of the document for the current event. Because XML documents may be composed of multiple external entities, this may change throughout the parsing process.

The latest version of SAX has also introduced an extended version of the Locator interface, called Locator2. The Locator2 interface enables you to retrieve the XML version and encoding declaration. You will learn about the extension interfaces later in the chapter.

The setDocumentLocator callback, if it is called, occurs before any other event callbacks. It may not be called at all, or it may be passed a null locator object, so always check for null before using the locator. All the parsers listed in the beginning of the chapter except XP provide locator information that can be used throughout the parsing process.

Try It Out   Which Stop Is This?

Let's add some information to that exception you created using the document locator. If the parser provides a locator, you display the document name, the line number, and the column position when the exception is thrown:

1. To start, add a private variable to hold on to the locator object when it is passed in the callback. Call this trainLocator:

```
private boolean isColor;
private String trainCarType = "";
private StringBuffer trainCarColor = new StringBuffer();
private Locator trainLocator = null;
```

2. Add the handler for the setDocumentLocator event:

```
public void setDocumentLocator(Locator locator)
{
  trainLocator = locator;
}
```

Notice that this function does not declare that a SAXException can be thrown. Until the startDocument event has been fired, error information is unreliable.

3. Finally, modify the exception message in the endElement event handler:

```
public void endElement(String uri, String localName, String qName)
  throws SAXException
{
  if (isColor) {
    System.out.println("The color of the " + trainCarType + " car is " +
      trainCarColor.toString());
    isColor = false;
    if (("Caboose".equals(trainCarType)) &&
        (!"Red".equals(trainCarColor.toString()))) {
      if (trainLocator != null)
```

```
            throw new SAXException("The caboose is not red at line " +
              trainLocator.getLineNumber() + ", column " +
              trainLocator.getColumnNumber() );
          else
            throw new SAXException("The caboose is not red!");
      }
    }
  }
```

Again, you must ensure that the locator is not null before you can use it. Let's compile `TrainReader.java`:

```
javac TrainReader.java
```

Once you have compiled the class, you can run the program:

```
java TrainReader Train2.xml
```

You should see the following:

```
Running train reader...
Start of the train
The color of the Engine car is Black
The color of the Baggage car is Green
The color of the Passenger car is Green and Yellow
The color of the Caboose car is Green
Parsing stopped : The caboose is not red at line 22, column 25
```

How It Works

By handling the `setDocumentLocator` event, you were able to access the `Locator` object supplied by the XML parser. This allowed you to easily notify the user where the error occurred in the XML document. In a small document, such as the sample that you are working with, the benefit may not be very obvious. In a multi-gigabyte document, however, this information would be invaluable.

The information provided by the `Locator` is not always absolute. Some parsers are better than others at determining the location in the document. For the most part, the line number is accurate. The reported column position can vary wildly between parsers, however, so it is probably best to use the `Locator` information in situations where the exact position is not critical.

ErrorHandler Interface

You still aren't finished with errors. What if you want to do your own handling of parser errors? It probably won't come as a great surprise to find out that you implement some methods of an interface. However, these new methods aren't part of `ContentHandler`; they're part of another interface altogether, called `ErrorHandler`. As it happens, the `DefaultHandler` class provides you with a rudimentary implementation of this interface as well, although it doesn't actually do anything apart from throw a `SAXException` to print out a trace of the call stack, like the one in the earlier example.

Event	Description
warning	Allows the parser to notify the application of a warning it has encountered in the parsing process. Though the XML Recommendation provides many possible warning conditions, very few SAX parsers actually produce warnings.
error	Allows the parser to notify the application that it has encountered an error. Even though the parser has encountered an error, parsing can continue. Validation errors should be reported through this event.
fatalError	Allows the parser to notify the application that it has encountered a fatal error and cannot continue parsing. Well-formedness errors should be reported through this event.

To receive error events, you must call `setErrorHandler` and pass a reference to the `TrainReader` object. This is the exact analog of the call to `setContentHandler` that you used to tell the parser where to send the content-related events.

Try It Out   **To Err Is Human, To Handle Errors Is Divine**

This example extends the `TrainReader` class so that you can catch parser errors and report their location. In addition to overriding some of `DefaultHandler`'s implementation of `ContentHandler`, you override some of its implementation of `ErrorHandler`. You also upgrade the sample by creating a DTD for the `Train` vocabulary and validating the XML document. This enables you to see how the `ErrorHandler` works with different kinds of errors.

1. Begin by modifying the sample XML document. Add an internal DTD so that you can validate the document:

```
<?xml version="1.0"?>
<!DOCTYPE train [
  <!ELEMENT train (car*)>
  <!ELEMENT car (color, weight, length, occupants)>
  <!ATTLIST car type CDATA #IMPLIED>
  <!ELEMENT color (#PCDATA)>
  <!ELEMENT weight (#PCDATA)>
  <!ELEMENT length (#PCDATA)>
  <!ELEMENT occupants (#PCDATA)>
]>
```

Save this file as `Train3.xml` in the directory that you are using for your project.

2. Modify the `TrainReader` class. First, add a call to `setErrorHandler` and set the validation feature to `true` to turn on validation:

```
public void read(String fileName)
  throws Exception
{
  XMLReader reader =
    XMLReaderFactory.createXMLReader("org.apache.xerces.parsers.SAXParser");
  reader.setContentHandler(this);
```

```
      reader.setErrorHandler(this);
      try
      {
        reader.setFeature("http://xml.org/sax/features/validation", true);
      }
      catch (SAXException e)
      {
        System.err.println("Cannot activate validation");
      }
      try
      {
        reader.parse(fileName);
      }
      catch (SAXException e)
      {
        System.out.println("Parsing stopped : " + e.getMessage());
      }
    }
```

Notice that you set the validation feature within a try/catch block. You will learn more about features and properties later in the chapter.

3. Next add the error-handling functions to the TrainReader class. These will override the minimal implementations provided by DefaultHandler:

```
public void warning (SAXParseException exception)
  throws SAXException {
  System.err.println("[Warning] " +
    exception.getMessage() + " at line " +
    exception.getLineNumber() + ", column " +
    exception.getColumnNumber() );
}

public void error (SAXParseException exception)
  throws SAXException {
  System.err.println("[Error] " +
    exception.getMessage() + " at line " +
    exception.getLineNumber() + ", column " +
    exception.getColumnNumber() );
}

public void fatalError (SAXParseException exception)
  throws SAXException {
  System.err.println("[Fatal Error] " +
    exception.getMessage() + " at line " +
    exception.getLineNumber() + ", column " +
    exception.getColumnNumber() );
  throw exception;
}
```

All you're doing here is printing out the location of the error, taken from the incoming SAXParseException object, and then — in the case of fatalError — rethrowing the error back to the parser. In most parsers, rethrowing the exception is unnecessary, but it ensures that regardless of the parser chosen, parsing will stop when a fatal error is encountered. It's worth noting that if the parser doesn't support `Locator`, then it's not going to provide you with anything meaningful in these methods on `SAXParseException`.

Let's compile `TrainReader.java`:

```
javac TrainReader.java
```

Once you have compiled the class, you can run the program:

```
java TrainReader Train3.xml
```

You should see the following:

```
Running train reader...
Start of the train
The color of the Engine car is Black
The color of the Baggage car is Green
The color of the Passenger car is Green and Yellow
The color of the Caboose car is Green
Parsing stopped : The caboose is not red at line 31, column 25
```

You have the same output you had in the last example. Obviously, you didn't change the color of the caboose back to `Red`. Note that the exception thrown by the application wasn't passed through any of the new error-handling methods. When you create an exception to stop parsing, it is immediate.

4. Now insert a couple of errors into the XML document so that you can see the new error functions in action. First, rename the `occupants` element for the `Engine` to be a `conductors` element. Then, delete the ">" on the closing `car` tag. Finally, change the caboose color to `Red`:

```xml
<?xml version="1.0"?>
<!DOCTYPE train [
  <!ELEMENT train (car*)>
  <!ELEMENT car (color, weight, length, occupants)>
  <!ATTLIST car type CDATA #IMPLIED>
  <!ELEMENT color (#PCDATA)>
  <!ELEMENT weight (#PCDATA)>
  <!ELEMENT length (#PCDATA)>
  <!ELEMENT occupants (#PCDATA)>
]>
<train>
  <car type="Engine">
    <color>Black</color>
    <weight>512 tons</weight>
    <length>60 feet</length>
    <conductors>3</conductors>
  </car
  <car type="Baggage">
    <color>Green</color>
    <weight>80 tons</weight>
    <length>40 feet</length>
    <occupants>0</occupants>
  </car>
  <car type="Passenger">
    <color>Green and Yellow</color>
```

```
        <weight>40 tons</weight>
        <length>60 feet</length>
        <occupants>23</occupants>
    </car>
    <car type="Caboose">
        <color>Red</color>
        <weight>90 tons</weight>
        <length>30 feet</length>
        <occupants>4</occupants>
    </car>
</train>
```

Save this file as `Train4.xml` and run the program:

```
java TrainReader Train4.xml
```

You should see the following:

```
Running train reader...
Start of the train
The color of the Engine car is Black
[Error] Element type "conductors" must be declared. at line 16, column 17
[Fatal Error] The end-tag for element type "car" must end with a '>' delimiter. at
line 18, column 3
Parsing stopped : The end-tag for element type "car" must end with a '>' delimiter.
```

How It Works

By handling the errors reported by the parser, you are able to provide useful error messages to the application, and ultimately the user. The three levels of errors enable you to either report the information even when parsing can continue or stop parsing for all errors and warnings. Let's look at the output in more detail:

```
Running train reader...
Start of the train
The color of the Engine car is Black
```

The process begins as it has in every other example, firing off events normally. Then the parser encountered the first error, the `conductors` element that you added:

```
[Error] Element type "conductors" must be declared. at line 16, column 17
```

The Xerces parser raised an error when it encountered the `conductors` element because it was not declared in the DTD provided with your document. Some parsers will also raise an error about the missing `occupants` element. The error that was raised was only a validation error, which meant that parsing could continue because the document could still be well formed even if it was not valid. The parsing, and events, continued until it reached the well-formedness error you introduced:

```
[Fatal Error] The end-tag for element type "car" must end with a '>' delimiter. at
line 18, column 3
```

Once the parser encounters a well-formedness error, it cannot continue trying to parse the document according to the XML specification. After outputting the message, the application threw the exception that was then caught by the exception handler around the call to the `parse` function:

```
Parsing stopped : The end-tag for element type "car" must end with a '>' delimiter.
```

Again, a message about the error was output. Of course, with your newly added error-handling code, the message was redundant.

DTDHandler Interface

Now that you have added a DTD to your document you may want to receive some events about the declarations. The logical place to turn is the DTDHandler interface. Unfortunately, the DTDHandler interface provides you with very little information about the DTD itself. In fact, it allows you to see the declarations only for notations and unparsed entities.

Event	Description
notationDecl	Allows the parser to notify the application that it has read a notation declaration
unparsedEntityDecl	Allows the parser to notify the application that it has read an unparsed entity declaration

When parsing documents that make use of notations and unparsed entities to refer to external files—such as image references in XHTML or embedded references to non-XML documents—the application must have access to the declarations of these items in the DTD. This is why the creators of SAX made them available through the DTDHandler, one of the default interfaces associated with an XMLReader.

The declarations of elements, attributes, and internal entities, however, are not required for general XML processing. These declarations are more useful for XML editors and validators. Therefore, the events for these declarations were made available in one of the extension interfaces, DeclHandler. You'll look at the extension interfaces in more detail later in the chapter.

Using the DTDHandler interface is very similar to using the ContentHandler and ErrorHandler interfaces. The DefaultHandler class you used as the base class of the TrainReader also implements the DTDHandler interface, so working with the events is simply a matter of overriding the default behavior, just as you did with the ErrorHandler and ContentHandler events. To tell the XMLReader to send the DTDHandler events to your application, you can simply call the setDTDHandler function, as shown in the following:

```
reader.setDTDHandler(this);
```

> You may be wondering if there is an interface for receiving XML Schema events. Surprisingly, there isn't. In fact, no events are fired for XML Schema declarations either. The creators of SAX wanted to ensure that all the information outlined in the XML recommendation was available through the interfaces. Remember that DTDs are part of the XML Recommendation, but XML Schemas are defined in their own, separate recommendation.

EntityResolver Interface

The `EntityResolver` interface enables you to control how a SAX parser behaves when it attempts to resolve external entity references within the DTD, so much like the `DTDHandler`, it is frequently not used. However, when an XML document utilizes external entity references, it is highly recommended that you provide an `EntityResolver`.

The `EntityResolver` interface defines only one function:

Event	Description
resolveEntity	Allows the application to handle the resolution of entity lookups for the parser

As shown with the other default interfaces, the `EntityResolver` interface is implemented by the `DefaultHandler` class. Therefore, to handle the event callback, you simply override the `resolveEntity` function in the `TrainReader` class and make a call to the `setEntityResolver` function:

```
reader.setEntityResolver(this);
```

Consider the following entity declaration:

```
<!ENTITY train PUBLIC "-//TRAINS//freight cars xml 1.0//EN"
    "http://example.com/freighttrain.xml">
```

In this case, `resolveEntity` function would be passed `-//TRAINS//freight cars xml 1.0//EN` as the public identifier, and `http://example.com/freighttrain.xml` as the system identifier. The `DefaultHandler` class's implementation of the `resolveEntity` function returns a null `InputSource` by default. When handling the `resolveEntity` event, however, your application can take any number of actions. It could create an `InputSource` based on the system identifier, or it could create an `InputSource` based on a stream returned from a database, hash table, or catalog lookup that used the public identifier as the key. It could also simply return `null`. These options and many more enable an application to control how the processor opens and connects to external resources.

Features and Properties

As shown earlier in this chapter, some of the behavior of SAX parsers is controlled through setting features and properties. For example, to activate validation, you needed to set the `http://xml.org/sax/features/validation` feature to `true`. In fact, all features in SAX are controlled this way, by setting a flag to `true` or `false`. The feature and property names in SAX are full URIs so that they can have unique names — much like namespace names.

Working with Features

To change a feature's value in SAX, you simply call the `setFeature` function of the XMLReader:

```
public void setFeature(String name, boolean value)
    throws SAXNotRecognizedException, SAXNotSupportedException
```

When doing this, however, it is important to remember that parsers may not support, or even recognize, every feature. If a SAX parser does not recognize the name of the feature, then the setFeature function will raise a SAXNotRecognizedException. If it recognizes the feature name but does not support a feature (or does not support changing the value of a feature at a certain time), then the setFeature function will raise a SAXNotSupportedException. For example, if a SAX parser does not support validation, then it will raise a SAXNotSupportedException when you attempt to change the value to true.

The getFeature function allows you to check the value of any feature:

```
public boolean getFeature(String name)
    throws SAXNotRecognizedException, SAXNotSupportedException
```

Like the setFeature function, the getFeature function may raise exceptions if it does not recognize the name of the feature or does not support checking the value at certain times (such as before, during, or after the parse function has been called). Therefore, place all of your calls to the setFeature and getFeature functions within a try/catch block to handle any exceptions.

All SAX parsers should recognize, but may not support, the following features:

Feature	Default	Description
http://xml.org/sax/features/validation	*Unspecified*	Controls whether the parser will validate the document as it parses. In addition to controlling validation, it also affects certain parser behaviors. For example, if the feature is set to true, all external entities must be read.
http://xml.org/sax/features/namespaces	true	In the latest version of SAX, this feature should always be true, meaning that namespace URI and prefix values will be sent to the element and attribute functions when available.
http://xml.org/sax/features/namespace-prefixes	false	In the latest version of SAX, this feature should always be false. It means that names with colons will be treated as prefixes and local names. When this flag is set to true, raw XML names are sent to the application.
http://xml.org/sax/features/xmlns-uris	false	Allows you to control whether xmlns declarations are reported as having the namespace URI http://www.w3.org/2000/xmlns/. By default, SAX conforms to the original namespaces in the XML Recommendation and will not report this URI. The 1.1 Recommendation and an erratum to the 1.0 edition modified this behavior. This setting is only used when xmlns declarations are reported as attributes.

Table continued on following page

Feature	Default	Description
`http://xml.org/sax/features/resolve-dtd-uris`	true	Controls whether the SAX parser will "absolutize" system IDs relative to the base URI before reporting them. Parsers will use the Locator's `systemID` as the base URI. This feature does not apply to `EntityResolver.resolveEntity`, nor does it apply to `LexicalHandler.startDTD`.
`http://xml.org/sax/features/external-general-entities`	*Unspecified*	Controls whether external general entities should be processed. When the validation feature is set to true, this feature is always true.
`http://xml.org/sax/features/external-parameter-entities`	*Unspecified*	Controls whether external parameter entities should be processed. When the validation feature is set to true, this feature will always be true.
`http://xml.org/sax/features/lexical-handler/parameter-entities`	*Unspecified*	Controls the reporting of the start and end of parameter entity inclusions in the `LexicalHandler`
`http://xml.org/sax/features/is-standalone`	*None*	Allows you to determine whether the standalone flag was set in the XML declaration. This feature can be accessed only after the `startDocument` event has completed. This feature is read-only and returns true only if the standalone flag in the XML declaration has a value of yes.
`http://xml.org/sax/features/use-attributes2`	*Unspecified*	Check this read-only feature to determine whether the `Attributes` interface passed to the `startElement` event supports the `Attributes2` extensions. The `Attributes2` extensions enable you to examine additional information about the declaration of the attribute in the DTD. For more information on the `Attributes2` interface, see Appendix G on this book's website. Because this feature was introduced in a later version of SAX, some SAX parsers will not recognize it.
`http://xml.org/sax/features/use-locator2`	*Unspecified*	Check this read-only feature to determine whether the `Locator` interface passed to the `setDocumentLocator` event supports the `Locator2` extensions. The `Locator2` extensions enable to you determine the XML version and encoding declared in an entity's XML declaration. For more information on the `Locator2` interface, see Appendix G on this book's website. Because this feature was introduced in a later version of SAX, some SAX parsers will not recognize it.

Feature	Default	Description
`http://xml.org/sax/features/use-entity-resolver2`	`true` (if recognized)	Set this feature to true (the default) if the `EntityResolver` interface passed to the `setEntityResolver` function supports the `EntityResolver2` extensions. If it does not support the extensions, then set this feature to false. The `EntityResolver2` extensions allow you to receive callbacks for the resolution of entities and the external subset of the DTD. For more information on the `EntityResolver2` interface, see Appendix G on this book's website. Because this feature was introduced in a later version of SAX, some SAX parsers will not recognize it.
`http://xml.org/sax/features/string-interning`	*Unspecified*	Allows you to determine whether the strings reported in event callbacks were interned using the Java function `String.intern`. This allows for fast comparison of strings.
`http://xml.org/sax/features/unicode-normalization-checking`	`false`	Controls whether the parser reports Unicode normalization errors as described in Section 2.13 and Appendix B of the XML 1.1 Recommendation. Because these errors are not fatal, if encountered they are reported using the `ErrorHandler.error` callback.
`http://xml.org/sax/features/xml-1.1`	*Unspecified*	Read-only feature that returns `true` if the parser supports XML 1.1 and XML 1.0. If the parser does not support XML 1.1, then this feature will be `false`.

Working with Properties

Working 4with properties is very similar to working with features. Instead of `boolean` flags, however, properties may be any kind of object. The property mechanism is most often used to connect helper objects to an `XMLReader`. For example, SAX comes with an extension set of interfaces called `DeclHandler` and `LexicalHandler` that allow you to receive additional events about the XML document. Because these interfaces are considered extensions, the only way to register these event handlers with the `XMLReader` is through the `setProperty` function:

```
public void setProperty(String name, Object value)
   throws SAXNotRecognizedException, SAXNotSupportedException

public Object getProperty(String name)
   throws SAXNotRecognizedException, SAXNotSupportedException
```

As you saw with the `setFeature` and `getFeature` functions, all calls to `setProperty` and `getProperty` should be safely placed in `try/catch` blocks, as they may raise exceptions. Some of the default property names include the following:

Property Name	Description
`http://xml.org/sax/properties/declaration-handler`	Specifies the `DeclHandler` object registered to receive events for declarations within the DTD
`http://xml.org/sax/properties/lexical-handler`	Specifies the `LexicalHandler` object registered to receive lexical events, such as comments, CDATA sections, and entity references
`http://xml.org/sax/properties/document-xml-version`	Read-only property that describes the actual version of the XML Document, such as `1.0` or `1.1`. This property can only be accessed during the parse and after the `startDocument` callback has been completed.

Extension Interfaces

The two primary extension interfaces are `DeclHandler` and `LexicalHandler`. Using these interfaces, you can receive events for each DTD declaration and specific items such as comments, CDATA sections, and entity references as they are expanded. It is not required by the XML specification that these items be passed to the application by an XML processor. All the same, the information can be very useful at times, so the creators of SAX wanted to ensure that they could be accessed.

The `DeclHandler` interface declares the following events:

Event	Description
`attributeDecl`	Allows the parser to notify the application that it has read an attribute declaration
`elementDecl`	Allows the parser to notify the application that it has read an element declaration
`externalEntityDecl`	Allows the parser to notify the application that it has read an external entity declaration
`internalEntityDecl`	Allows the parser to notify the application that it has read an internal entity declaration

The `LexicalHandler` interface declares the following events:

Event	Description
comment	Allows the parser to notify the document that it has read a comment. The entire comment is passed back to the application in one event call; it is not buffered as it may be in the `characters` and `ignorableWhitespace` events.
startCDATA	Allows the parser to notify the document that it has encountered a CDATA section start marker. The character data within the CDATA section is always passed to the application through the `characters` event.
endCDATA	Allows the parser to notify the document that it has encountered a CDATA section end marker
startDTD	Allows the parser to notify the document that it has begun reading a DTD
endDTD	Allows the parser to notify the document that it has finished reading a DTD
startEntity	Allows the parser to notify the document that it has started reading or expanding an entity
endEntity	Allows the parser to notify the document that it has finished reading or expanding an entity

Because these are extension interfaces, they must be registered with the `XMLReader` using the property mechanism, as you just learned. For example, to register a class as a handler or `LexicalHandler` events, you might do the following:

```
reader.setProperty("http://xml.org/sax/properties/lexical-handler", lexHandler);
```

Note that the `DefaultHandler` class, which you used as the basis of the `TrainReader` class, does not implement any of the extension interfaces. In the latest version of SAX, however, an extension class was added called `DefaultHandler2`. This class not only implements the core interfaces, but the extension interfaces as well. Therefore, if you want to receive the `LexicalHandler` and `DeclHandler` events, it is probably a good idea to descend from `DefaultHandler2` instead of the `DefaultHandler` class.

Good SAX and Bad SAX

Now that you're thoroughly familiar with SAX, this is a good point at which to review both what SAX is good at and what it isn't so good at, so you can decide when to use it and when to use another approach, such as the DOM.

As you've seen, SAX is great for analyzing and extracting content from XML documents. Let's look at what makes it so good:

❑　It's simple: You need to implement only three or perhaps four interfaces to get going.

❑　It doesn't load the whole document into memory, so it doesn't take up vast amounts of space. Of course, if your application is using SAX to build up its own in-memory image of the document, it's likely to end up taking a similar amount of space as the DOM would have (unless your in-memory image is a lot more efficient than the DOM!).

❑ The parser itself typically has a smaller footprint than that of its DOM cousin. In fact, DOM implementations are often built on top of SAX.

❑ It's quick, because it doesn't need to read in the whole document before you start work on it.

❑ It's great at filtering data, enabling you to concentrate on the subset that you're interested in.

Why not use it for everything? Here are a few drawbacks:

❑ You get the data in the order that SAX gives it to you. You have absolutely no control over the order in which the parser searches. As shown in the Try It Out sections, this means that you may need to build up the data that you need over several event invocations. This can be a problem if you're doing particularly complex searches.

❑ SAX programming requires fairly intricate state keeping, which is prone to errors. Even in our simple examples we needed to maintain information between various events. In larger applications, keeping this kind of information can become very difficult.

❑ If you're interested in analyzing an entire document, DOM is much better, because you can traverse your way around the DOM in whichever direction you want, as many times as you want.

Consumers, Producers, and Filters

Throughout this chapter, you have learned the basics of SAX. You created an application that receives, or *consumes*, SAX events. Although this is the most common usage of SAX, you can use it in other ways. In addition to consuming events from an XMLReader, it is possible to write classes that *produce* SAX events. For example, you might want to write a class that reads a comma-delimited file and fires SAX events, similar to an XMLReader. You would then have a single application that could receive events from either an XML document or a comma-delimited file.

Instead of producing or consuming events, you may want to simply *filter* events as they pass from XMLReader to the event handler. A SAX filter acts as a middleman between the parser and the application. Filters can insert, remove, or even modify events before passing them on to the application. Using the earlier train analogy, you could say that a filter is very similar to a tunnel through which the train passes. While in the tunnel, the train might be painted, or new cars might be added or removed.

In fact, many filters already exist for SAX, which enable you to do anything from specialized validation to document transformation. Many filters can be chained together, creating a SAX *pipeline*. Included in SAX is an XMLFilter interface that is intended for standardizing how filters are created.

Considering the many ways to use SAX enables you to create more complex and more powerful applications.

Other Languages

Because the SAX model works so well for processing XML documents, the Java interfaces have been translated to many programming languages and environments. Currently, the most widely accepted are as follows:

Language	Available Interfaces
C++	Xerces-C++, the counterpart to the Xerces-J toolkit you are using from Apache, defines a set of C and C++ bindings available at `http://xml.apache.org/xerces-c`.
	Microsoft Core XML Services (formerly MSXML) provides C++ and COM interfaces (including ActiveX wrappers) available at `http://msdn.microsoft.com/xml`.
	Arabica toolkit provides C++ bindings that make more extensive use of C++ language features, available at `http://www.jezuk.co.uk/cgi-bin/view/Arabica`.
Perl	SAX bindings for Perl can be found at `http://perl-xml.sourceforge.net/libxml-perl/`.
Python	Python 2.0 includes support for SAX processing in its markup toolkit as part of the default distribution available at `http://www.python.org/`.
Pascal	SAX for Pascal bindings can be found at `http://saxforpascal.sourceforge.net/`.
Visual Basic	MSXML, the Microsoft XML Toolkit, provides Visual Basic interfaces available at `http://msdn.microsoft.com/library/en-us/xmlsdk/html/ac6be45a-177e-4b80-a918-dc73e357f7bb.asp`.
.NET	The `System.Xml` classes distributed with .NET provide psuedo-SAX implementations usable in various .NET languages. The interfaces are "pull-based" and are not exact correlations. To use SAX interfaces in .NET, visit the SAX for .NET project at `http://saxdotnet.sourceforge.net`.
Curl	Curl is a web content management system with its own SAX bindings, available at `http://www.curl.com/`.

In general, these versions of SAX have retained the spirit of the original Java interfaces while making good use of their own individual language features.

Summary

SAX is an excellent API for analyzing and extracting information from large XML documents without incurring the time and space overhead associated with the DOM. In this chapter, you learned how to use SAX to catch events passed by a parser, by implementing a known SAX interface, ContentHandler. You used this to extract some simple information from an XML document.

You also looked at error handling, and learned how to implement sophisticated intelligent parsing, reporting errors as you did so. In addition, you looked at how to supplement the error-handling mechanisms in the parser by using the Locator object. Finally, you read about the strengths and weaknesses of SAX.

Now that you are well versed in the APIs used to work with XML in applications, you can look more closely at how XML can be used to communicate between multiple applications.

Exercise Questions

Suggested solutions to these questions can be found in Appendix A.

Question 1

Calculate the weight, length, and total number of occupants on the entire train. Once the document has been parsed, print out the result of the calculations.

Question 2

Print out a list of all elements declared in the DTD. To do this, descend the `TrainReader` class from `DefaultHandler2` instead of `DefaultHandler`. Register the `TrainReader` class with the parser so that you can receive `DeclHandler` events. (Hint: You need to use a property.)

Part VI

Communication

RSS, Atom, and Content Syndication

One of the interesting characteristics of the Web is the way that certain ideas seem to arise spontaneously, without any centralized direction. Content syndication technologies definitely fall into this category, and they have emerged as a direct consequence of the linked structure of the Web and general standardization regarding the use of XML.

This chapter focuses on a number of aspects of content syndication, including the RSS and Atom formats and their role in such areas as blogs, news services, and the like. There is no doubt these technologies will play a major role in the next logical leap in the connectedness of the Web, so it's useful to understand them not just from an XML-format standpoint but also in terms of how they are shaping the future Internet.

This chapter covers the following:

❑   Concepts and technologies of content syndication and meta data

❑   A brief look at the history of RSS, Atom, and related languages

❑   What the feed languages have in common and how they differ

❑   How to implement a simple newsreader/aggregator using Python

❑   Examples of XSLT used to generate and display newsfeeds

There is a lot more to RSS, Atom, and content syndication than can be covered in a single chapter, so the aim here is to give you a good grounding in the basic ideas, and then provide a taste of how XML tools such as SAX and XSLT can be used in this rapidly expanding field.

Syndication and Meta Data

Turn on your TV and you'll see spontaneous snapshots of the current state of the TV "space," one channel at a time. Information is transmitted to the box in front of you, mostly appearing in the form of shows. Some shows are instantly familiar to you (the ill-fated man in a red shirt jumping in front of the Klingon phaser — you'd think these guys would learn!), and some may require a little bit of time to figure out what's going on. If you're lucky, you'll jump to a commercial break and see the transitional title, but some programming remains mystifying no matter how long you watch.

One of the largest circulated magazines on the planet is *TV Guide*. Although it has some editorial content, people typically do not buy the magazine for that content. They are interested in the listings — what channel transmits what show at what time. *TV Guide* listings provide a certain amount of information for each such show beyond this, such as abstracts describing the show itself, the stars, a family rating, and a key number used by automated video recorders to set them to record the show automatically.

The deployment of resources on a network (whether television or computer) is called *syndication*. The TV guide provides descriptions of the shows, information about information. Stepping down into the less human-friendly computer world, we have something very similar, *meta data*, which is data about data. The essence of RSS and related formats is found where these two ideas join: syndication and meta data.

A *syndication feed* is simply an XML file comprised of meta data elements and in most cases some content as well. There are several distinct standard formats — notably, RSS 1.0, RSS 2.0, and Atom. As XML formats, these (and various other RSS x.x dialects) are largely incompatible, having different document structures and element definitions, though they each share a common basic model of a syndication feed. There is the feed itself, which has characteristics such as a title and publication date. The feed carries a series of discrete blocks of data, known as *items* or *entries*, each of which also has a set of individual characteristics, again such as title and date. These items are little chunks of information, which either describe a resource on the Web (a link is provided) or are a self-contained unit, carrying content along with them.

Syndication Systems

Like most other Web systems, *syndication systems* are generally based around the client-server model. At one end you have a web server delivering data using the Hypertext Transfer Protocol (HTTP), and at the other end is a client application receiving it. On the Web, the server uses a piece of software such as Apache or IIS, and the client uses a browser such as Internet Explorer (IE) or Mozilla Firefox. HTML-oriented web systems tend to have a clear distinction between the roles and location of the applications: the server is usually part of a remote system, and the client appears on the user's desktop. HTML data is primarily intended for immediate rendering and display for users to read on their home computer.

However, syndication material is intended for machine-readability first, and there is at least one extra stage of processing before the content appears on the user's screen. *Machine-readability* means that it is possible to pass around and process the data relatively easily, allowing a huge amount of versatility in systems. The net result is that applications that produce material for syndication purposes can appear either server-side or client-side (desktop), as can applications that consume this material.

Perhaps the key to understanding the differences between syndication and typical web pages is the aspect of time. A syndicated resource (an item in a feed) is generally only available for a short period of time at a given point in the network, at which stage it disappears from the feed, although an archived version of the information is likely archived on the publisher's site.

The different kinds of syndication software components can roughly be split into four categories: server-producer, client-consumer, client-producer, and server-consumer. In practice, software products may combine these different pieces of functionality, but it helps to look at these parts in isolation.

The following sections provide an overview of each, with the more familiar systems first.

Server-Producer

A *server-side producer* of syndication material is in essence no different from that used to publish regular HTML web pages. At minimum, this would be a static XML file in one of the syndication formats placed on a web server. More usefully the XML data will be produced from some kind of content management system. The stereotypical content management systems in this context are weblog (blog) tools. The main page of the (HTML) website features a series of diarylike entries, with the most recent entry appearing first. Behind the scenes is some kind of database containing the entry material, and the system presents this in reverse chronological order on a nicely formatted web page. In parallel with the HTML-generating subsystems of the application are syndication feed format (RSS and/or Atom) producing subsystems. These two subsystems are likely to be very similar, as the results usually only differ in format. Many blogging systems include a common templating system to produce either HTML or syndication format XML.

Client-Consumer

Although it is possible to view certain kinds of syndicated feeds in a web browser, one of the major benefits of syndication comes into play with so-called newsreaders or aggregator tools. The reader application enables users to subscribe to a large number of different feeds and present the material from these feeds in an integrated fashion. There are two common styles of feed-reader user interface:

❑ *Single pane* styles present items from the feeds in sequence, as they might appear on a weblog.

❑ *Multipane* styles are often modeled on e-mail applications, and present a selectable list of feeds in one panel and the content of the selected feed in another.

The techniques used to process and display this material vary considerably. Many pass the data directly to display, whereas others incorporate searching and filtering, usually with data storage behind the scenes; and occasionally Semantic Web technologies are used to provide integration with other kinds of data.

Several newsreaders (for example, Radio and AmphetaDesk) use a small web server running on the client machine to render content in a standard browser. There are also wide variations in the sophistication of these tools. Some provide presentation of each feed as a whole; others do it item-by-item by date, through user-defined categories or any combination of these and other alternatives. You will see the code for a very simple aggregator later in this chapter.

Client-Producer

OK, you know that the server-producer puts content on a web server, and the client-consumer processes and displays this content, but where does the content come from in the first place? Again, blogging tools are the stereotype. Suppose an author of a weblog uses a tool to compose posts containing his thoughts for the day and cat photos. Clicking a button submits this data to a content management system that will typically load the content into its database for subsequent display, as in the preceding server-producer. The client-producer category covers desktop blogging clients such as BlogEd, ecto, and Microsoft Windows Live Writer, which run as conventional applications. It seems likely that many existing desktop authoring tools will soon incorporate post-to-blog facilities (there are already plug-ins for MS Word and OpenOffice). When the user clicks Submit (or similar), the material will be sent over the Web to the content management system. However, the four categories presented here break down a little at this point, as many blogging tools provide authoring tools from the web server as well, with users being presented a web form in which to enter their content.

A technical issue should be mentioned at this point. When it comes to communications, the server-producer and client-consumer systems generally operate in exactly the same way as HTML-oriented web servers and clients using the HTTP protocol directly. The feed material is delivered in one of the syndication formats: RSS or Atom.

However, when it comes to posting material to a management system, other strategies are commonly used. In particular, developers of the Blogger blogging service designed a specification for transmitting blog material from the author's client to the online service. Although the specification was only intended as a prototype, the "Blogger API" became the de facto standard for posting to blogging and similar content management systems. The Blogger API defines a small set of XML-RPC (Remote Procedure Calling) elements to encode the material and pass it to the server. There were certain limitations of this specification, which led to the MetaWeblog API from UserLand, which extends the elements in a way that makes it possible to send all the most common pieces of data that might be required. There was a partial recognition in the MetaWeblog API that a degree of redundancy existed in the specifications. The data that is passed from an authoring tool is essentially the same in structure and content as the material passed from the server to newsreaders, so the MetaWeblog API uses some of the vocabulary of RSS 2.0 to describe the structural elements.

Since the XML-RPC blogging APIs came out, there has been a growing realization in the developer community that not only is there redundancy at the level of naming parts of the messages being passed around, but also in the fundamental techniques used to pass them around. To transfer syndicated material from a server to a client, the client sends an HTTP GET message to the server, and the server responds with a bunch of RSS/Atom-formatted data. On the other hand, when transferring material from the client to the server, the blogging APIs wrap the content in XML-RPC messages and use a HTTP POST to send that. The question is, why use XML-RPC format when there is already a perfectly good RSS or Atom format? Recent developments have led to a gradual shift from XML-RPC to the passing of XML data directly over HTTP, and more use of the less familiar HTTP verbs, such as PUT (to replace an XML document on the web) and DELETE (to remove a resource). Leading the field in this direction is the Atom Publication Protocol (http://bitworking.org/projects/atom/), a specification from the Atom Working Group that at the time of writing is approaching finalization.

Server-Consumer

The notion of a server-consumer component covers several different kinds of functionality. First, there's the functionality needed to receive material sent from a client-producer, blog posts, and the like. This in itself isn't particularly interesting; typically it's really just a refactoring of authoring directly on the server through HTML forms.

Second, it's possible to take material from other syndication servers and either render them directly, acting as an online equivalent of the desktop newsreader, or process the aggregated data further. This approach is increasingly common, and online newsreaders such as Bloglines are very popular. The fact that feed data is suitable for subsequent processing and integration means it offers considerable potential for the future. Various online services such as PubSub and Tailrank use syndicated data to provide enhanced search capabilities, and enable you to register a search query and then subscribe to a feed of the results, which are extracted from millions of feeds.

TechMeme (www.techmeme.com/) is an example of a (moderately) smarter aggregator, in that it uses heuristics (rules of thumb) on the data found on blogs to determine the most significant stories, treating an incoming link as a sign of importance for an entry (it isn't altogether clear whether TechMeme uses

RSS/Atom feeds or the HTML representation of blogs, but conceptually it doesn't matter). These are all fairly centralized, mass-appeal services, but there's also been a lot of development in the open-source world of tools that can offer similar services for special-interest groups, organizations, or even individuals. It's relatively straightforward to set up your own "Planet" aggregations of topic-specific feeds by downloading and installing the Planet (`www.planetplanet.org/`) or Chumpalogica (`www.hackdiary.com/projects/chumpologica/`) online aggregation applications. The Planet Venus aggregator (`http://intertwingly.net/code/venus/docs/`), an offshoot of Planet, includes various pieces of additional functionality, such as a personalized "meme-tracker" similar to TechMeme. An example of how such systems can be customized is Planète Web Sémantique (`http://planete.websemantique.org/`). This site uses Planet Venus to aggregate French language posts on the topic of the Semantic Web. Because many of the bloggers on its subscription list also regularly post on other topics and in English, such material is filtered out (actually hidden by JavaScript).

It's worth noting that the distinction between server-consumer as the recipient of a single author's blog posts and server-consumer as an online information aggregator is likely to blur as HTTP + syndication format client-producer systems become more widespread. The *Atom Publishing Protocol* offers a simple means of posting material to a site and is effectively a mirror image of Atom for feed subscription, so interconnectivity is bound to accelerate when people start integrating support into their systems. But that's looking ahead; to get a handle on how syndication works and its practical problems, it's useful to look how we arrived at the present situation.

The Origin of RSS Species

Where and when did these systems and the formats they use originate? The meta-data side of RSS can be said to have begun in the mid-1990s, with the development of the *Meta Content Framework (MCF)* at Apple, essentially a table of contents for a website. The notion of building a syndication network for the Internet came about in large part from the idea of a *push* model for publication. In this model, information such as news alerts would be pushed to the client from the server, describing a set of "channels" and their associated web content, including when this content was to be published and when it would expire. By doing this, the thinking went, large concerns could *push* their content specifically through these channels, establishing the traditional media concept of brand-naming channels and turning the Internet into something with properties more similar to a television set than the document server that had characterized the Web up to that point. Modern syndication is usually based around a *pull* approach, in which the client gets the data from servers. Because this happens automatically, the net effect simulates push, in that data is being broadcast from the server. However, the client and server are very loosely coupled compared with true push, and significantly it's the client that manages subscriptions.

Microsoft's Content Definition Format

Specifically XML syndication formats really began around 1997 when Microsoft entered the fray with the *Content Definition Format (CDF)*. This was specifically targeted to be a comprehensive syndication format that would appeal to traditional broadcasters, and the roster of companies that provided content initially read like a who's who of the entertainment industry. The CDF format, and Active Channel, the Windows-based component within Internet Explorer that supported it, was oriented toward a true syndication model, with the publishers being the big names. The Channel bar would periodically download content based upon the syndication schedule within the CDF format, caching the content that would then be available immediately upon demand.

The CDF model of a feed and its items is essentially the same model in use today in all syndication formats, and it contains features that found their way into RSS and have stayed there ever since — channel, item, title, and so on. Internet Explorer only lost support for CDF with IE 7 (though it gained a whole RSS platform).

The Great Push Revolution that was supposed to herald a complete reshaping of the Web more or less failed to materialize. A big part of the reason may have been that although push technology makes a great deal of sense to marketers — you deliver your message to your customers rather than have your customers come to you — it held far less value to the recipients of such push technology.

UserLand and Scripting News

The content management company UserLand played a prominent role in the history of XML syndication, a notable move being their introduction of the *Scripting News* format in late 1997. This followed experiments by the company with Apple's MCF and Microsoft's CDF.

Netscape and RSS 0.9

MCF moved to Netscape with its lead developer, R. V. Guha, and subsequently Netscape submitted its XML version of MCF to the W3C (not long after Microsoft's submission of CDF), but Netscape's real entrance to the syndication arena came with its introduction of the *RDF Site Summary (RSS) 0.9* language in early 1999. This format used the fledgling *Resource Description Framework (RDF)* language, and RSS defined a simple structure for collecting linked information and publishing it in a customized part of its browser section. RDF evolved from MCF and various other sources, and played an important role in the internal workings of the Netscape Navigator browser (as it still does in its descendants, Mozilla and Firefox). The syntax of RSS 0.9 appeared very much like that of the Scripting News and CDF formats, yet its RDF base made a significant conceptual difference.

Simply RDF

The Resource Description Framework, RDF is, not surprisingly, all about describing resources, and is described in a suite of six specifications from the W3C. Although very simple in principle, RDF takes a lot of material to describe in full because of its theoretical grounding in logic and various practical requirements. It's at the heart of the W3C's *Semantic Web initiative*, which is based on a vision of how the existing Web can be improved with the help of meta data and a little logic. Anyone working with syndication feeds or interested in the future of the Web should at least read the RDF Primer (www.w3.org/TR/rdf-primer/) or the (rather friendlier) tutorials at rdfabout.com. The interchange format for RDF is known as *RDF/XML*, which forms the basis of RSS 0.9 and 1.0. An example of the XML syntax of RSS 0.9 will be shown in just a moment, but you need a little more information to be able to interpret it correctly — there's more to it than meets the eye.

The key to RDF is the concept of a resource. A *resource* is usually something that can be identified on the Web. Many resources have a *universal identifier (URI)*, which in the case of web pages will be the same as their address (URL). Pretty much anything else (people, places, and concepts) can be identified in this way by assigning URIs. Descriptions are made in RDF using *statements*, which have the following three parts:

❑ The thing being described

❑ The characteristic of interest

❑ The value of that characteristic

For example, the thing being described might be a book — say, *A Christmas Carol*; the characteristic of interest (property) could be the author; and the value would be the name of the author, Charles Dickens. In RDF jargon, these three parts are the *subject*, *predicate*, and *object*, and together they form a *triple*. This grouping roughly corresponds to the English sentence structure of subject, verb, and object. Each triple corresponds to a single statement. The subject is a resource, the predicate is a special kind of resource used to denote a property, and the object can either be another resource or literal text. As resources, the predicates are identified using URIs, and the same predicates are often reused — when we ask who the author of a book is, we are asking the same question regardless of the book we are talking about or whoever happens to be the author. However, a lot of the time it isn't convenient or even possible to give everything we want to talk about a URI (what is the URI of *A Christmas Carol*?), and in these circumstances RDF uses a stand-in for the URI called a *blank node*. So you can say in effect resourceX has author Charles Dickens, and resourceX has the title *A Christmas Carol*. Those two properties in combination make it pretty unambiguous which resource is under discussion.

Now that you know the core concepts of RDF, take look at the RSS 0.9 shown in the following:

```xml
<?xml version="1.0"?>
<rdf:RDF
    xmlns:rdf="http://www.w3.org/1999/02/22-rdf-syntax-ns#"
    xmlns="http://my.netscape.com/rdf/simple/0.9/">

    <channel>
        <title>The Metaphorical Web</title>
        <link>http://www.metaphoricalweb.com</link>
        <description>Kurt Cagle's Metaphorical Web site, filled with information
        on XML, XSLT, SVG and other things X-related.</description>
    </channel>
    <item>
        <title>The Metaphorical Web #23: The  of Things to Come</title>
        <link>http://www.metaphoricalweb.com/?method=showPage&amp;
        src=metaphorica123.xml
        </link>
        <description>Resolutions and Reflections on the State of Tech in
        2004</description>
    </item>

    <item>
        <title>SVG 1.2: Into the interface</title>
        <link>http://www.metaphoricalweb.com/?
        method=showPage&amp;src=svg12.xml</link>
            <description>A look at the recently announced SVG 1.2
        specification.</description>
    </item>

</rdf:RDF>
```

It has a root <rdf:RDF> element, and a couple of namespaces are declared, but it certainly isn't obvious how it has anything to do with the triple things. Take a look again at the first two lines inside the outer element:

```xml
...
<channel>
    <title>The Metaphorical Web</title>
...
```

What this is saying in the RDF interpretation is that there is a resource of the *type* channel, which has a property called title and whose value is The Metaphorical Web. *Type* here refers to an RDF term that expresses class membership — another way of saying the resource in question is a member of the class channel. The channel resource isn't associated with a URI, so it's a blank node. Through the standard XML namespaces interpretation, both channel and title are qualified with the namespace http://my.netscape.com/rdf/simple/0.9/, which means both these terms are unambiguously associated with URIs. Expressed as triples (giving the blank node the temporary identifier id0), the preceding two lines become the following:

```
subject: id0
predicate: http://www.w3.org/1999/02/22-rdf-syntax-ns#type
object: http://my.netscape.com/rdf/simple/0.9/channel

subject: id0
predicate: http://my.netscape.com/rdf/simple/0.9/title
object: "The Metaphorical Web"
```

It's no coincidence that the RSS 0.9 RDF/XML syntax look similar to the plain XML CDF material. It's conveying much the same kind of information, except in a form that can be interpreted by a computer as globally unambiguous logical statements. Another important point about the use of RDF/XML is that this is no longer merely about the language of syndication. Different vocabularies, each having its own namespace, can be defined using RDF Schema and used together in the same document. Alongside the channels, items, and titles, it's also possible to use terms defined elsewhere. The item might actually be a *book*, with the *author* Charles Dickens. The RDF model allows such terms to be incorporated and interpreted in exactly the same way as the core RSS vocabulary. This is a major boon for extensibility.

Referring back to the full example, you can see that the structure is divided into a channel and multiple items. The *human* meaning of a channel is a little ambiguous — you could associate it with an organizational entity (CNN, Netscape, Microsoft, etc.) or with a specific website. The *link* associated with the channel can consequently point to the main web page of that organization's website, or to a specific RSS-oriented channel page that pulls the appropriate relevant meta data. The channel's *description* provides the abstract or rationale for this particular channel, telling the receiver a little more about itself.

Each of the item elements in turn has a similar structure, describing a title, a link, and an abstract description. The original 0.9 specification included a few other primary fields, including links to icons and posting dates, but these were very much secondary to what amounted to a collection of editorial links.

The RSS 0.9 specification proved to be fairly robust, and though it's very rare nowadays it can be seen as a baseline RSS specification. It is also the immediate precursor of the RSS 1.0 format. It's rather confusing, but the RSS 0.91–0.94 and RSS 2.0 specifications are very different from RSS 0.9 and 1.0. The growth of syndication has been marred by political battles over the best approach to take — in a nutshell, the conflict centers around whether it is more important for the format to be easily read by humans or machines.

Netscape, UserLand, and RSS 0.9x

Netscape backed away from its original RDF-oriented approach to RSS, and influenced by UserLand's Scripting News and the way people were actually using the format, toward the end of 1999 Netscape dropped the RDF approach in RSS 0.91. Along with RDF, out went namespaces and in came a DTD and a new name: *Rich Site Summary*. Not long after this Netscape dropped RSS altogether. It was picked up by UserLand, and further minor changes were made (the DTD was discarded and a *different* version of

RSS 0.91 was released). The format was effectively promoted by UserLand, which also introduced some of the first software applications dedicated to blogging and syndication. The following is a typical example of RSS 0.91:

```
<rss version="0.91">
  <channel>
    <title>The Metaphorical Web</title>
    <link>http://www.metaphoricalweb.com/</link>
    <description>Kurt Cagle's Metaphorical Web site, filled with
        information on XML, XSLT, SVG and other things X-related.
    </description>
    <language>en-us</language>
    <item>
      <title>The Metaphorical Web #23: The  of Things to Come</title>
      <link>http://www.metaphoricalweb.com/metaphorical23.xml
</link>
      <description>Resolutions and Reflections on the State of Tech
        in 2004
      </description>
    </item>
    <item>
      <title>SVG 1.2: Into the interface</title>
      <link>http://www.metaphoricalweb.com/svg12.xml</link>
      <description>A look at the recently announced
        SVG 1.2 specification.
      </description>
    </item>
  </channel>
</rss>
```

On the surface the syntax is fairly similar to the 0.90 version, and if you ignore the removal of the rdf:RDF element and namespaces, the biggest difference is that the channel is now a container of various items, rather than a sibling.

RSS 0.91's greatest strength was that it was simple. As a straightforward XML format, its main weakness was that it was rather poorly specified with several ambiguous element definitions, and the lack of namespace support meant that its use with other XML languages was severely impaired. One advantage "vanilla" XML has over RDF/XML is that simple DTDs can be used for validation, but the DTD Netscape provided with their version 0.91 was removed when the spec was adopted by UserLand.

Still, a fair proportion of syndicated feeds are to this day RSS 0.91, and this UserLand style of RSS evolved through versions 0.92, 0.93, and (briefly) 0.94 before becoming RSS 2.0, which you will look at later in the chapter; but first we return to RDF.

RSS-DEV and RSS 1.0

Around the same time UserLand was working on the RSS 0.91 line, an informal mailing list sprang up, *RSS-DEV*, with a general consensus that the RDF-based approach of RSS 0.9 (and Netscape's original planned future direction for RSS) was the best; and the result was the RSS 1.0 specification, published in December 2000. Unfortunately, the RSS-DEV proposal clashed head-on with the RDF/namespace-free 0.91 approach followed by UserLand. Agreement wasn't forthcoming on a way forward, and as a result RSS forked. One thread carried the banner of simplicity, the other of interoperability. This is the source of considerable confusion to newcomers to RSS, as both forms are designed for the same primary purpose, yet differ considerably in their construction. The rebranding of UserLand's RSS as *Really Simple Syndication* helps a little in contrast to RSS-DEV's RDF Site Summary.

RSS-DEV reintroduced the RDF basis, taking advantage of the modularity offered by that language, and made it possible to reuse terms from the library community's Dublin Core Metadata Initiative standard (`http://dublincore.org`) and add "modules" (RDF vocabularies) for content and syndication-specific terms. This is what RSS 1.0 looks like:

```xml
<?xml version="1.0" encoding="iso-8859-1"?>
<rdf:RDF xmlns:rdf="http://www.w3.org/1999/02/22-rdf-syntax-ns#"
            xmlns:dc="http://purl.org/dc/elements/1.1/"
            xmlns:sy="http://purl.org/rss/1.0/modules/syndication/"
            xmlns="http://purl.org/rss/1.0/">

  <channel rdf:about="http://journal.dajobe.org/journal/index.rdf">
    <title>Dave Beckett - Journalblog</title>
    <link>http://journal.dajobe.org/journal/</link>
    <description>Semantic web and free software hacking.</description>
    <language>en</language>
    <dc:date>2004-04-16T08:22:58+00:00</dc:date>
    <sy:updatePeriod>hourly</sy:updatePeriod>
    <sy:updateFrequency>1</sy:updateFrequency>

    <items>
      <rdf:Seq>
        <rdf:li
    rdf:resource="http://journal.dajobe.org/journal/2004_03.html#001678" />
        <rdf:li
    rdf:resource="http://journal.dajobe.org/journal/2004_03.html#001677" />
      </rdf:Seq>
    </items>
  </channel>

  <item rdf:about="http://journal.dajobe.org/journal/archives/
    2004_03.html#001678">
    <title>MySQL lifts restrictive licensing terms</title>
    <description> MySQL lifts restrictive licensing terms (Silicon.com)
      by Stephen Shankland. Reports the adding of a Free and Open Source
    Software...</description>
    <link>http://journal.dajobe.org/journal/archives/2004_03.html#001678</link>
    <dc:subject>comment</dc:subject>
    <dc:creator>dajobe</dc:creator>
    <dc:date>2004-03-16T20:56:39+00:00</dc:date>
  </item>

  <item rdf:about="http://journal.dajobe.org/journal/archives/
    2004_03.html#001677">
  <title>The trouble with Rover is revealed</title>
    <description> The trouble with Rover is revealed by Ron Wilson, EE Times
      on how the Spirit Mars rover got stuck...</description>
    <link>http://journal.dajobe.org/journal/archives/2004_03.html#001677</link>
    <dc:subject>link</dc:subject>
```

```
      <dc:creator>dajobe</dc:creator>
      <dc:date>2004-03-08T18:06:35+00:00</dc:date>
    </item>

  </rdf:RDF>
```

To a human with a text editor, this format appears considerably more complex than RSS 0.91. It restores the role of RDF as the namespace that provides descriptive content, and a valid RSS 1.0 document is also a valid RDF document (and not coincidentally a valid XML document). To a computer (for example, either a namespace-aware XML parser or an RDF tool), it contains the same kind of information as "simple" RSS expressed in a less ambiguous and more interoperable form.

Like RSS 0.9, the XML has an outer <rdf:RDF> element (which incidentally is no longer a requirement of RDF/XML in general). After the namespace declarations is a channel block, which first describes the channel feed itself and then lists the individual items found in the feed. The channel resource is identified with a URI, which makes the information portable. There's no doubt what the title, description, and so on refer to. Title, link, description, and language are all defined in the core RSS 1.0 specification. XML namespaces (with the RDF interpretation) are employed to provide properties defined in the Dublin Core (dc:date) and Syndication (sy:updatePeriod, sy:updateFrequency) modules.

The channel has an items property, which has the rdf:Seq type. The RSS 1.0 specification describes this as a sequence used to contain all the items and to denote item order for rendering and reconstruction. After this statement, the items contained in the feed are listed, each identified with a URI, so the channel block describes this feed, specifying which items it contains.

The items themselves are listed separately: Each is identified by a URI, and the channel block associates these resources with the channel, so there's no need for XML element nesting to group them together. Each item has its own set of properties, a title, and a description, as shown in the preceding RSS formats, along with a link that is defined as the item's URL. Usually, this is the same as the URI specified by the item's own rdf:about attribute. Again, terms from Dublin Core are used for the subject, creator (author), and date. This makes it much better suited for broad-scale syndication, as Dublin Core has become the de facto standard for dealing with document-descriptive content.

Looking again from an RDF perspective, note that the object of the statements that list the item URIs become the subject of the statements that describe the items themselves. In most XML languages this kind of connection is made through element nesting, and it's clear that tree structures can be built this way. However, using identifiers for the points of interest (the resource URIs) in RDF also makes it possible for any resource to be related to any other resource, allowing arbitrary node and arc graph structures. Loops and self-references can occur. This versatility is an important feature of RDF, and is very similar to the arbitrary hyperlinking of the Web. The downside is that there isn't any elegant way to represent graph structures in a tree-oriented syntax like XML, which is a major reason why RDF/XML syntax can be hard on the eye.

UserLand and RSS 2.0

After a period of simmering unrest in the syndication world, and several 0.x releases in the Simple Syndication thread, each making minor modifications, in 2002 UserLand released an RSS 2.0 specification. This followed the RSS 0.91 side of the fork, and the syntax is completely incompatible with RSS 1.0. Most of the changes from RSS 0.91 are relatively minor, although two are significant: the introduction of the <guid> element and (limited) namespace support. You can see in the following code example how similar the syntax appears to the earlier "simple" version. Small differences prevent true backward compatibility, but in practice this is unlikely to be a problem, as a high degree of flexibility is needed for a tool to support *any* version of RSS!

The `<guid>` element is defined as being an optional globally unique identifier for each item. The specification doesn't prescribe what this should be, other than a string. In practice, people tend to use URIs, which are the global identifiers of the Web. This makes sense because if the `isPermalink` attribute has a value of `true`, then the `<guid>` contains the URL of an archived (usually HTML) version of the item. Here is the example:

```
<rss version="2.0">
 <channel>
        <title>inessential.com</title>
        <link>http://inessential.com/</link>
        <description>Brent Simmons' weblog.</description>
        <language>en-us</language>
        <managingEditor>Brent Simmons (brent@ranchero.com)</managingEditor>
        <webMaster>Brent Simmons (brent@ranchero.com)</webMaster>
        <pubDate>Thu, 15 Apr 2004 19:56:13 GMT</pubDate>
        <lastBuildDate>Thu, 15 Apr 2004 19:56:13 GMT</lastBuildDate>
        <item>
            <title>Bowie</title>
            <link>http://inessential.com/?comments=1&amp;postid=2836</link>
            <description>Sheila and I saw David Bowie at the Key Arena last
            night. He was great, the band rocked&amp;mdash;and Sheila and I
            both have &amp;ldquo;All the Young Dudes&amp;rdquo; stuck in
            our head.\&lt;br /\&gt;\&lt;br /\&gt;</description>

<guid isPermaLink="true">http://inessential.com/?comments=1\&amp;
postid=2836</guid>
            <pubDate>Thu, 15 Apr 2004 19:56:13 GMT</pubDate>
            </item>
        <item>
            <title>Socializing at WWDC</title>
            <link>http://inessential.com/?comments=1\&amp;postid=2835</link>
            <description>Buzz Andersen proposes a \&lt;a href=\&quot;
            http://www.scifihifi.com/weblog/wwdc2004/Socializing-
            at-WWDC.html\&quot;\&gt;weblogger get-together at WWDC\&lt;/a\&gt;.
            Good thinking. Count me in.</description>
            <guid isPermaLink="true">http://inessential.com/?
            comments=1\&amp;
            postid=2835</guid>
            <pubDate>Fri, 02 Apr 2004 00:53:57 GMT</pubDate>
            </item>
        </channel>
    </rss>
```

XML namespace support in RSS 2.0 is limited in the sense that although material from other namespaces can be included within an RSS 2.0 feed, the format doesn't have a namespace of its own, which precludes the use of RSS 2.0 elements in other XML languages.

The principle differences between the 1.0 and 2.0 versions ultimately come back to whether or not RDF is used as the foundation. RDF offers versatility; RSS 2.0 offers simplicity. Unlike RSS 1.0, RSS 2.0 lacks a general framework (such as RDF) into which extensions can be placed. You can more or less add whatever you like to RSS 2.0, but you have to rely completely on tool developers to support those extensions. Anything goes, and there's no guarantee that one person's extension will be compatible with another (for example, Yahoo! Media RSS and Apple's iTunes RSS extensions have virtually nothing in common). However, such issues only started arising in the few years — RSS's success has been largely due to the core functionality of publishing newslike information in a lightweight fashion.

This is by no means the end of the story. One particular aspect of extensibility probably caused the greatest upheaval since RSS 2.0. The original syndication specifications were metadata-oriented and pointed to content elsewhere on the Web. The `<description>` element was intended to describe that remote resource. However, with the growth in blogging and newsreader tools, a demand for *content* within feeds grew. RSS 1.0 responded with the addition of the Content module. In the RSS 2.0 thread the response manifested itself as a shift in the semantics of the `<description>` element. It no longer describes some other piece of content; it *contains* that content.

Other significant changes with RSS 2.0, of a political nature, followed. The RSS 2.0 specification was frozen and has in effect been declared the last in the line of Really Simple Syndication formats. The specification was placed in the repository of the Berkman Center for Internet and Society at Harvard Law School, under the Creative Commons license, with the explicit caveat that the document is considered normative and *final*. The move to Berkman was welcomed, though doubts have been expressed about the wisdom of freezing the specification at this point.

The demand for content in feeds highlighted a significant problem with the RSS 2.0 specification: It says that the `<description>` element may contain HTML, and that's all it says. There is no way for applications to distinguish HTML from plain text, so how do you tell what content is markup and what content is just talking about markup? The spec was now frozen, so developers started to work around the problem using namespace-qualified extensions, such as `xhtml:body`, to insert well-defined markup. Soon after this, there was controversy over the use of extensions with RSS 2.0 — specifically, the use of the Dublin Core element to express information that could appear in core elements. Where previously there had been criticism of "simple" RSS from the RSS-DEV camp, dissent was now appearing among supporters of the "simple" standard. This led to another open community initiative being launched in the summer of 2003, with the aim of fixing the problems of RSS 2.0 and unifying the syndication world (including the RSS 1.0 developers). Accepting the roadmap for RSS presented in the RSS 2.0 specification meant the name RSS couldn't be used, and after lengthy discussion the new project got a name: *Atom*.

Atom

As you've no doubt gathered, historically the RSS space has been something of a mess. Not only did the "format wars" make choices difficult for developers, but the highly fluid and decentralized nature of blog space itself contributes to uncertainty as well. Nonetheless, being optimistic, Atom does offer an opportunity for the two main syndication camps to unite. Unlike RSS 1.0 and 2.0, it has been developed as a true open community project, through the auspices of a widely respected standards organization, the Internet Engineering Task Force (IETF). The Atom Publishing Format and Protocol (atompub) working group is open to anyone interested in participating, and with the IETF process being based on consensus, broad community input counts.

The initial aim for Atom was to fix the problems of RSS, and it was realized early on that any sane solution would not only look at the format, but also take into account the protocols used in authoring, editing, and publication. Hence, this was included in atompub's charter. The first deliverable of the group, the Atom Syndication Format (RFC 4287, `www.ietf.org/rfc/rfc4287.txt`) was published in

December 2005. It seems likely that the other specification covered by the charter, the Atom Publishing Protocol, will be finalized early in 2007 (the latest working draft is available from `http://bitworking.org/projects/atom/`).

> During its development, an experimental version of the format (Atom 0.3) was published and soon gained support in many of the leading blogging and syndication tool creators. This version was only a trial, however; the only official version of Atom is the one described by RFC 4287.

The Atom format is structurally and conceptually very much like its RSS predecessors, and its practical design lies somewhere between the RSS 1.0 and 2.0 versions. Though the syntax isn't RDF/XML, full namespace support is included, and work is under way to provide a mapping to the RDF model (see `http://atomowl.org`). Most of the elements are direct descendants of those found in RSS, although considerable work has given it robust support for inline content, using a new `<content>` element.

Atom mostly includes all the features that have ever been seen in feed formats, along with a few new ones. Most of the elements are self-explanatory, although the naming of parts differs from RSS, so an Atom feed corresponds to an RSS channel, an Atom `entry` corresponds to an RSS `item`, and so on:

```
<feed xmlns="http://www.w3.org/2005/Atom">
   <link rel="self" href="http://example.org/blog/index.atom"/>
   <id>http://example.org/blog/index.atom</id>
   <icon>../favicon.ico</icon>
   <title>An Atom Sampler</title>
   <subtitle>No Splitting</subtitle>
   <author>
      <name>Ernie Rutherford </name>
      <email>ernie@example.org</email>
      <uri>.</uri>
   </author>
   <updated>2006-10-25T03:38:08-04:00</updated>
   <link href="."/>
   <entry>
      <id>tag:example.org,2004:2417</id>
      <link href="2006/10/23/moonshine"/>
      <title>Moonshine</title>
      <content type="text">
         Anyone who expects a source of power from the transformation of the atom
is talking moonshine.
      </content>
      <published>2006-10-23T15:33:00-04:00</published>
      <updated>2006-10-23T15:47:31-04:00</updated>
   </entry>
   <entry>
      <id>>tag:example.org,2004:2416</id>
      <link href="2006/10/21/think"/>
      <title type="html">&lt;strong&gt;Think!&lt;/strong&gt;</title>
      <content type="xhtml">
         <div xmlns="http://www.w3.org/1999/xhtml">
            <p>We haven't got the money, so we've got to think!</p>
```

```
            </div>
        </content>
        <updated>2006-10-21T06:02:39-04:00</updated>
    </entry>
</feed>
```

The first real enhancement is the `<id>` element, which roughly corresponds to the `<guid>` of RSS 2.0 and the `rdf:about` attribute found in RSS 1.0 to identify entities. Rather than leave it to chance that this will be a unique string, the specification makes this a URI, which by definition is unique (to be more precise, it's defined as an *Internationalized Resource Identifier (URI)* — for typical usage there's no difference). Note the use of a `tag:` scheme URI in the example, these are not retrievable like http: scheme URIs. In effect, the identifiers (URIs) and locators (URLs) of entities within the format have been separated. This was a slightly controversial move, as many would argue that the two should be interchangeable. Time will tell whether this is a good idea or not. It is acceptable to use an `http:` URI in the `<id>` element, though in practice it's probably better to follow the spirit of the Atom specification. Whereas the `<id>` element identifies, the `<link>` element locates. The Atom `<link>` element is modeled on its namesake in HTML, to provide a link and information about related resources.

Whereas the `<id>` makes it considerably easier and more reliable to determine whether two entries are the same, the `<content>` element offers a significant enhancement in the description of the material being published. It's designed to allow virtually anything that can be passed over XML. In the first entry in the preceding example, the `<entry>` element has the attribute `type="text"`. This explicitly states that the material within the element should not be treated as markup (and must not contain any child elements). The common case of HTML content is taken care of by making the attribute `type="html"`. Again, there should be no child elements, and any HTML in the content should be escaped according to XML rules, so it would be `&lt;h1&gt;` (or one of the equivalent alternatives), rather than `<h1>`. However, although HTML content may be common, it's not the most useful. Atom is an XML format, and namespaces make it possible for it to carry data in other XML formats, which can be addressed using standard XML tools. The third kind of content support built in to Atom is `type="xhtml"`. To use XHTML in Atom, it has to be wrapped in a (namespace-qualified) `<div>` element. The `<div>` itself should be ignored by any rendering or processing tool that consumes the feed; it's only there for demarcation purposes.

Additionally, it's possible to include other kinds of content by specifying the `type` attribute as the media type. For XML-based formats this is straightforward; for example, the Description of a Project format (`http://usefulinc.com/doap`) uses RDF, which has a media type of `"application/rdf+xml"`, and the DOAP vocabulary has the namespace `"http://usefulinc.com/ns/doap#"`. For example, a project description payload in Atom would look something like this:

```
<content type="application/rdf+xml">
    <doap:Project xmlns:doap="http://usefulinc.com/ns/doap#">
    <doap:name>My Blogging Tool</doap:name>
...
    </doap:Project>
</content>
```

Of course, not all data is found in XML formats. Text-based formats (i.e., those with a type that begins `"text/"`), can be included as content directly as long as only legal XML characters are used and the usual escaping is applied to reserved characters. Other data formats can be represented in Atom using Base 64 encoding. This is a mapping from arbitrary sequences of binary data into a 65-character subset of US-ASCII.

Working with News Feeds

Over the course of the twentieth century, newspapers evolved into news organizations with the advent of each new medium. Initially, most newspapers operated independently, and coverage of anything beyond local information was usually handled by dedicated reporters in major cities. However, for most newspapers, such reporters are typically very costly to maintain. Consequently, these news organizations pool their resources together to create syndicates, feeding certain articles (and columns) to the syndicates, who would then license them out to other publishers. These news syndicates, or services, specialize in certain areas. Associated Press (AP) and United Press International (UPI) handle syndication within the United States, while Reuters evolved as a source for European news, especially financial news. Similarly, comic strips are usually handled by separate syndicates (such as King Features Syndicate).

These news services act as *aggregators:* They aggregate news from a wide variety of different sources and publish the result as a unified whole, the newspaper. One advantage of this approach is that it is possible to bundle related content together, regardless of the initial source. For instance, a sports-dedicated publication may pull together all articles on baseball, football, and basketball, but the feed wouldn't include finance articles unless they were sports-related. In essence, such a syndication service provides a perspective or viewpoint on the data made available — it creates an *editorial* judgment that all of the articles in the bundle will target a particular type of user. Content published through RSS or Atom feeds is often topic-specific, either at the feed level (a particular blogger might always write about XML) or at the level of individual entries.

This has made RSS news feeds ideal for creating highly targeted bundles of related content. For instance, it's possible for a website that promotes XML technology to generate an RSS feed about articles that deal with XML in some fashion. Some of these may be in-house articles, and some may be press releases, articles, or white papers from other locations on the Web. By combining them, the website is able to act in the role of an aggregator.

Newsreaders

The web makes it possible to do a similar kind of targeted syndication, except for an audience of one. The tools are available so that anyone can set up their own personal "newspaper", with content selected from the millions of feeds published on the web.

These aggregators are usually known as *newsreaders*, applications that enable you to both add and otherwise manage RSS feeds into a single "newspaper" of articles. Popular online newsreaders include Bloglines (http://bloglines.com) and Google Reader (www.google.com/reader). A large number of desktop applications are available, often free, such as RSS Bandit (www.rssbandit.org/) and BottomFeeder (www.cincomsmalltalk.com/BottomFeeder/). Both the Firefox and IE 7 browsers have RSS/Atom newsreading capability built in. Although public awareness of feed reading is still minimal, the technology is becoming ubiquitous and many Web users are reading material that has passed through RSS/Atom syndication without realizing it.

Data Quality

Whenever we work with material on the Web, keep in mind that not all data purporting to be XML actually *is* XML. It's relatively common to find RSS feeds that are not well formed. One of the most common failings is that the characters in the XML document aren't from the declared encoding (UTF-8, ISO-8859-1, or something similar). Another likely corruption is that characters within the textual content of the feed are incorrectly escaped. A stray < instead of a < is enough to trip up a standard XML processor. Unfortunately, many of the popular blogging tools make it extremely easy to produce an ill-formed feed, a factor not really taken into account by the "simple" philosophy of syndication.

There was considerable discussion by the Atom developers on this issue, and responses ranged from the creation of an "ultra-liberal" parser that does its best to read *anything*, to the suggestion that aggregation tools simply reject ill-formed feeds to discourage their production. The approach that found the most support in the Atom working group was (as you might expect) a compromise — the parser should attempt to display the data as intended, but notify end-users that the feed contained errors and encourage users to notify the feed producer. Current newsreaders tend very much toward the liberal.

> *There is a simple way of checking the quality of RSS and Atom feeds — the Feed Validator at* `http://`
> `feedvalidator.org` *(or the W3C's installation at* `http://validator.w3.org/feed/`*). You*
> *can use it online or download it. It's backed by a huge array of test cases, providing reliable results and*
> *explanations of any errors or warnings.*

A Simple Aggregator

The application described here is a simple newsreader that aggregates news items from several channels. It is provided with a list of feed addresses in a text file, and when run will present the most recent five items from those feeds. To keep things simple, the reader has only a command-line user interface and won't remember what it has read from the feeds previously.

Modeling Feeds

The programmer has many options for dealing with XML data, and the choice of approach often depends on the complexity of the data structures. In many circumstances the data can be read directly into a DOM model and processed from there, but there is a complication with syndicated material — the source data can be in one of three completely different syntaxes: RSS 1.0, RSS 2.0 (and its predecessors), and Atom. Because the application is only a simple newsreader, the sophistication offered by the RDF model behind RSS 1.0 isn't needed, but a simple model is implicit in news feeds: A feed comprises a number of items, and each of those items has a set of properties. Therefore, at the heart of the aggregator presented here is an object-oriented version of that model. A feed is represented by a `Feed` object, and items are represented by `Item` objects. Each `Item` object has member variables to represent the various properties of that item. To keep things simple, the code here only uses three properties of each item in the feeds: title, date, and content. The item itself and these three properties can be mapped to an XML element in each of the three main syntaxes, as shown in the following table:

Model	RSS 1.0	RSS x.x	Atom
Item	`rss:item`	`item`	`atom:entry`
Title	`dc:title`	`title`	`atom:title`
Date	`dc:date`	`pubDate`	`atom:updated`
Content	`dc:description,` `content:encoded`	`description, xhtml:body`	`atom:content`

The namespaces of the elements are identified by their usual prefixes as follows (note that the "simple" RSS dialects don't have a namespace):

❑ rss is RSS 1.0 (http://purl.org/rss/1.0/)

❑ dc is Dublin Core (http://purl.org/dc/elements/1.1/)

❑ xhtml is XHTML (www.w3.org/1999/xhtml)

❑ content is the content module for RSS 1.0 (http://purl.org/rss/1.0/modules/content/)

❑ atom is, you guessed it, Atom (www.w3.org/2005/Atom)

The correspondence between the different syntaxes is only approximate. Each version has its own definitions, and although they don't coincide exactly, they are close enough in practice to be used in a basic newsreader.

Syntax Isn't Model

Though there's a reasonable alignment between the different elements listed in the preceding table, this doesn't hold for the overall structure of the different syndication syntaxes. In particular, both plain XML RSS and Atom use element nesting to associate the items with the feed. If you look back at the sample of RSS 1.0, it's clear that something different is going on. RSS 1.0 uses the interpretation of RDF in XML to indicate that the channel resource has a property called items, which points to a Seq (sequence) of item instances. The item instances in the Seq are identified with URIs, as are the individual item entries themselves, which enables an RDF processor to know that the same resources are being referred to. In short, the structural interpretation is completely different.

> All of this sounds very complicated, but it is still essentially the same subject-predicate-object triple structure discussed earlier, with the object of one triple (channel-items-Seq) appearing as the subject in others (Seq-li-resource).

Two pieces of information implicit in the XML structure of simple RSS are made explicit in RSS 1.0. In addition to the association between the feed and its component items, there is also the order of the items. The use of a Seq in RSS 1.0 and the document order of the XML elements in the RSS x.x dialects provide an ordering, though there isn't any common agreement on what this ordering signifies. Atom explicitly states that the order of entries shouldn't be considered significant.

To keep the code simple in the aggregator presented here, two assumptions are made about the material represented in the various syntaxes:

❑ The items in the file obtained from a particular location are all part of the same conceptual feed. This may seem obvious; in fact, it has to be the case in plain XML RSS, which can only have one root <rss> element, but in RDF/XML (on which RSS 1.0 is based), it is possible to represent practically anything in an individual file. In practice, though, it's a relatively safe assumption.

❑ The second assumption is that in a news-reading application, the end-user won't be interested in the order of the items in the feed (element or Seq order), but the dates on which the items were published.

The first assumption means there is no need to check where in the document structure individual items appear, and the second means there is no need to interpret the Seq or remember the element order. There is little or no cost to these assumptions in practice, yet it enables considerable code simplification. All that is needed is to recognize when an element corresponding to an item (rss:item, item or atom:entry) occurs within a feed and to start recording its properties. In all the syntaxes the main properties are provided in child elements of the item element, so only a very simple structure has to be managed.

What you have here are different syntaxes, but a part of the structure is common to all three despite differences in element naming. An object model can be constructed from a simple one-to-one mapping from each set of elements. On encountering a particular element in the XML, a corresponding action needs to be carried out on the objects. An XML programming tool is ideally suited to this situation: SAX.

SAX to the Rescue!

As shown in Chapter 12, SAX works by responding to method calls generated when various different entities with the XML document are encountered. The entities of interest for this simple application are the following:

❑   The elements correspond to items

❑   The elements corresponding to the properties of the items and the values of those properties

Three SAX methods can provide all the relevant information: startElement, characters, and endElement. The first of these signals which element has been encountered, providing its name and namespace (if it has one). It's easy enough to tell if that element corresponds to an item. From the previous table, we know its name will either be item or entry. Similarly, each of the three kinds of properties elements can be identified. The data sent to characters is the text content of the elements, which are the values of the properties. A call to the endElement method signals that the element's closing tag has been encountered, so the program can deal with whatever is inside it.

Again using the previous table, we can derive the following simple rules that determine the nature of the elements encountered:

❑   rss:item | item | atom:entry = item

❑   dc:title | title | atom:title = title

❑   dc:date | pubDate | atom:updated = date

❑   dc:description | content:encoded |description | xhtml:body | atom:content = content

If startElement has been called, any subsequent calls matching the last three elements will pass on the values of that particular property of that element, until the endElement method is called. There may be calls to the property elements outside of an item block, and we can reasonably assume that those properties apply to the feed as a whole. This makes it straightforward to extract the title of the feed.

You may notice that the element names are pretty well separated between each meaning — there is little likelihood of the title data being purposefully published in an element called <date>, for example. This makes coding these rules somewhat easier, although in general it is good practice to make it possible to get at the namespace of elements to avoid naming clashes.

Program Flow

When the main application is run, the list of feeds is picked up from the text file. Each of the addresses in turn is passed to an XML parser. The aggregator then reads the data found on the Web at that address. In more sophisticated aggregators, you will find a considerable amount of code devoted to the reading of data over HTTP in a way that both respects the feed publisher and makes the system as efficient as possible, but the parsers in PyXML are capable of reading data directly from a web address. Therefore, to keep things simple, that's what's shown in Figure 13-1.

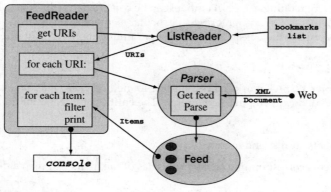

Figure 13-1

Implementation

The aggregator is written in Python, a language that has reasonably sophisticated XML support (PyXML), and everything we need to run it is available as a free download from www.python.org. If you're not familiar with Python, don't worry — it's a very simple language, and the code is largely self-explanatory. All you really need to know is that it uses indentation to separate functional blocks, rather than braces {}. In addition, the # character means that the rest of the line is a comment.

> *It would be very straightforward to port the code given here to any other languages with good XML support, such as Java or C#.*

The code is contained in the following four files:

❑   feed_reader.py controls the operation.

❑   feed.py models the feed and items.

❑   feed_handler.py constructs objects from the content of the feed.

❑   list_reader.py reads a list of feed addresses.

Address List Reader: ListReader

We also need the addresses of the feeds we'd like to aggregate. At its simplest, this can be a text file containing the URIs:

```
http://www.25hoursaday.com/weblog/SyndicationService.asmx/GetRss
http://dig.csail.mit.edu/breadcrumbs/blog/feed/4
http://www.markbaker.ca/blog/feed/atom/
```

An aggregator should be able to deal with all the major formats. Here we have a selection: The first feed is in RSS 2.0 format, the second is RSS 1.0, and the third is Atom. A text list is the simplest format in which the URIs can be supplied. For convenience, a little string manipulation makes it possible to use IE or Netscape/Mozilla bookmarks file to supply the list of URIs. The addresses of the syndication feeds should be added to a regular bookmark folder in the browser. With IE it's possible to export a single bookmark folder to use as the URI list, but with Netscape/Mozilla all the bookmarks are exported in one go. The following code is set up to read the links only in the first folder in such a bookmark file.

The `list_reader.py` source file contains a single class, `ListReader`, with a single method, `get_uris`:

```python
import re

class ListReader:
    """ Reads URIs from file """

    def get_uris(self, filename):
        """ Returns a list of the URIs contained in the named file """
        file = open(filename, 'r')
        text = file.read()
        file.close()

        # get the first block of a Netscape file
        text = text.split('</DL>')[0]

        # get the uris
        pattern = 'http://\S*\w'
        return re.findall(pattern,text)
```

Try It Out   **Reading a List of URIs**

The purpose here is just to confirm that our Python installation is working correctly. If you're not familiar with Python, then this also demonstrates how useful command-line interaction with the interpreter can be. Before starting, you need to download and install Python (it's available from `http://python.org`).

Python comes in a complete package as a free download, available for most platforms — as its enthusiasts say, batteries are included. Installation is very straightforward, and a Windows installer is included. The standard package provides the Python interpreter, which may be run interactively or from a command line or even a web server. There's also a basic Integrated Development Environment tool called IDLE and plenty of documentation.

Once Python is installed (you may have to add it to your system PATH; see the documentation for details), you can try out the following:

1. Open a text editor, type in the previous listing, and save it as `list_reader.py`.

2. Open a new text editor window and type in the following three URIs:

```
http://www.25hoursaday.com/weblog/SyndicationService.asmx/GetRss
http://dig.csail.mit.edu/breadcrumbs/blog/feed/4
http://www.markbaker.ca/blog/feed/atom/
```

3. Save this as `feeds.txt` in the same folder as `list_reader.py`.

4. Open a common prompt and **cd** to the folder containing these files.

5. Type in the command **python** and press Enter. You should see something like this:

```
D:\rss-samples\test>python
Python 2.3.3 (#51, Dec 18 2003, 20:22:39) [MSC v.1200 32 bit (Intel)] on win32
Type "help", "copyright", "credits" or "license" for more information.
>>
```

You are now in the Python interpreter.

6. Type in the following lines and press Enter after each line (the interpreter will display the >>> prompt):

```
>>> from list_reader import ListReader
>>> reader = ListReader()
>>> print reader.get_uris("feeds.txt")
```

After the last line, the interpreter should respond with the following:

```
['http://www.25hoursaday.com/weblog/SyndicationService.asmx/GetRss',
 'http://dig.csail.mit.edu/breadcrumbs/blog/feed/4',
 'http://www.markbaker.ca/blog/feed/atom']
>>>
```

How It Works

The first line you gave the interpreter was as follows:

```
from list_reader import ListReader
```

This makes the class `ListReader` in the package `list_reader` available to the interpreter (the package is contained in the file `list_reader.py`). The line

```
reader = ListReader()
```

creates a new instance of the `ListReader` class and assigns it to the variable reader. The next line you asked to be interpreted was as follows:

```
print reader.get_uris("feeds.txt")
```

This calls the `get_uris` method of the reader object, passing it a string, which corresponds to the file-name of interest. The `print` method was used to display the object (on the command line) returned by the `get_uris` method. The object returned was displayed as follows:

```
['http://www.25hoursaday.com/weblog/SyndicationService.asmx/GetRss',
 'http://dig.csail.mit.edu/breadcrumbs/blog/feed/4',
 'http://www.markbaker.ca/blog/feed/atom']
```

This is the syntax for a standard Python list, here containing three items, which are the three URIs extracted from `feeds.txt`.

For an explanation of how `list_reader.py` worked internally, here's the source again:

```python
import re

class ListReader:
    """ Reads URIs from file """

    def get_uris(self, filename):
        """ Returns a list of the URIs contained in the named file """
        file = open(filename, 'r')
        text = file.read()
        file.close()

        # get the first block of a Netscape file
        text = text.split('</DL>')[0]

        # get the uris
        pattern = 'http://\S*\w'
        return re.findall(pattern,text)
```

The `get_uris` method is called with a single parameter. This is the name of the file containing the list of URIs (the `self` parameter is an artifact of Python's approach to methods and functions, and refers to the `method` object). The file opens as read-only (`r`), and its contents are read into a string called `text` and then closed. To trim a Netscape bookmark file, the built-in `split` string method divides the string into a list, with everything before the first occurrence of the `</DL>` tag going into the first part of the list, which is accessed with the index `[0]`. The `text` variable will then contain this trimmed block or the whole of the text if there aren't any `</DL>` tags in the file. A regular expression finds all the occurrences within the string of the characters `http://` followed by any number of nonwhitespace characters (signified by `\S*`) and terminated by an alphanumeric character. It's crude, but it works well enough for text and bookmark files. The URIs are returned from this method as another list.

Application Controller: FeedReader

The list of URIs is the starting point for the main control block of the program, which is the `FeedReader` class contained in `feed_reader.py`. If you refer to Figure 13-1, you should be able to see how the functional parts of the application are tied together. Here are the first few lines of `feed_reader.py`, which acts as the overall controller of the application:

```python
import urllib2
import xml.sax
import list_reader
```

```
import feed_handler
import feed

feedlist_filename = 'feeds.txt'
def main():
    """ Runs the application """
    FeedReader().read(feedlist_filename)
```

The code starts with the library imports. `urllib2` and `xml.sax` are only used here to provide error messages if something goes wrong with HTTP reading or parsing. `list_reader` is the previous URI list reader code (in `list_reader.py`), `feed_handler` contains the custom SAX handler (which you'll see shortly), and `feed` contains the class that models the feeds.

The name of the file containing the URI list is given as a constant. You can either save your list with this filename or change it here. Because Python is an interpreted language, any change takes effect the next time you run the program. The `main()` function runs the application by creating a new instance of the `FeedReader` class and telling it to read the named file. When the new instance of `FeedReader` is created, the `init` method is automatically called, which is used here to initialize a list, which will contain all the items obtained from the feeds:

```
class FeedReader:
    """ Controls the reading of feeds """
    def __init__(self):
        """ Initializes the list of items """
        self.all_items = []
```

The `read` method looks after the primary operations of the aggregator and begins by obtaining a parser from a local helper method, `create_parser`, and then getting the list of URIs contained in the supplied file, as shown in the following:

```
def read(self, feedlist_filename):
    """ Reads each of the feeds listed in the file """
    parser = self.create_parser()

    feed_uris = self.get_feed_uris(feedlist_filename)
```

The next block of code selects each URI in turn and does what is necessary to get the items out of that feed, which is to create a SAX handler and attach it to the parser to be called as the parser reads through the feed's XML. The magic of the SAX handler code will appear shortly, but reading data from the Web and parsing it is a risky business, so the single command that initiates these actions, `parser.parse(uri)`, is wrapped in a `try...except` block to catch any errors. Once the reading and parsing occur, the `feed_handler` instance will contain a `feed` object, which in turn contains the items found in the feed (you will see the source to these classes in a moment). To indicate the success of the reading/parsing, the number of items contained in the feed is then printed. The items are available as a list of `handler.feed.items`, the length of this list (`len`) is the number of items, and the standard `str` function is used to convert this number to a string for printing to the console:

```
for uri in feed_uris:
        print 'Reading '+uri,
        handler = feed_handler.FeedHandler()
```

```
                parser.setContentHandler(handler)
                try:
                    parser.parse(uri)
                    print ' : ' + str(len(handler.feed.items)) + ' items'
                    self.all_items.extend(handler.feed.items)

                except xml.sax.SAXParseException:
                    print '\n XML error reading feed : '+uri
                    parser = self.create_parser()
                except urllib2.HTTPError:
                    print '\n HTTP error reading feed : '+uri
                    parser = self.create_parser()
            self.print_items()
```

If an error occurs while either reading from the Web or parsing, a corresponding exception is raised, and a simple error message is printed to the console. The parser is likely to have been trashed by the error, so a new instance is created. Whether or not the reading/parsing was successful, the program now loops back and starts work on the next URI on the list. Once all the URIs have been read, a helper method (shown in an upcoming code example), `print_items`, is called to show the required items on the console. The following methods in `FeedReader` are all helpers used by the `read` method in the previous listing.

The `get_feed_uris` method creates an instance of the `ListReader` class shown earlier, and its `get_uris` method returns a list of the URIs found in the file:

```
def get_feed_uris(self, filename):
    """ Use the list reader to obtain feed addresses """
    lr = list_reader.ListReader()
    return lr.get_uris(filename)
```

The `create_parser` method makes standard calls to Python's SAX library to create a fully namespace-aware parser as follows:

```
def create_parser(self):
    """ Creates a namespace-aware SAX parser """
    parser = xml.sax.make_parser()
    parser.setFeature(xml.sax.handler.feature_namespaces, 1)
    parser.setFeature(xml.sax.handler.feature_namespace_prefixes, 1)
    return parser
```

The next method is used in the item sorting process, using the built-in `cmp` function to compare two values—in this case, the date properties of two items. Given the two values x and y, the return value is a number less than zero if x < y, zero if x = y, and greater than zero if x > y. The date properties are represented as the number of seconds since a preset date (usually January 1, 1970), so a newer item here will actually have a larger numeric date value. Here is the code that does the comparison:

```
def newer_than(self, itemA, itemB):
    """ Compares the two items """
    return cmp(itemB.date, itemA.date)
```

The `get_newest_items` method uses the `sort` method built into Python lists to reorganize the contents of the `all_items` list. The comparison used in the sort is the `newer_than` method from earlier, and a Python "slice" (`[:5]`) is used to obtain the last five items in the list. Putting this together, we have the following:

```
def get_newest_items(self):
        """ Sorts items using the newer_than comparison """
        self.all_items.sort(self.newer_than)
        return self.all_items[:5]
```

Note that the slice is a very convenient piece of Python syntax and selects a range of items in a `sequence` *object. For example,* `z = my_list[x:y]` *would copy the contents of* `my_list` *from index* `x` *to index* `y` *into list* `z`.

The `print_items` method applies the sorting and slicing previously mentioned and then prints the resultant five items to the console, as illustrated in the following code:

```
def print_items(self):
        """ Prints the filtered items to console """
        print '\n*** Newest 5 Items ***\n'
        for item in self.get_newest_items():
            print item
```

The final part of `feed_reader.py` is a Python idiom used to call the initial `main()` function when this file is executed:

```
if __name__ == '__main__':
    """ Program entry point """
    main()
```

Model: Feed and Item

The preceding `FeedReader` class uses a SAX handler to create representations of feeds and their items. Before looking at the handler code, here is the `feed.py` file, which contains the code that defines those representations. It contains two classes, `Feed` and `Item`. The plain XML RSS dialects generally use the older RFC 2822 date format used in e-mails, whereas RSS 1.0 and Atom use a specific version of the ISO 8601 format used in many XML systems, known as W3CDTF. As mentioned earlier, the dates are represented within the application as the number of seconds since a specific date, so libraries that include methods for conversion of the e-mail and ISO 8601 formats to this number are included in the imports. The significance of `BAD_TIME_HANDICAP` is explained next, but first take a look at the `feed.py` file:

```
import email.Utils
import xml.utils.iso8601
import time

BAD_TIME_HANDICAP = 43200
```

The `Feed` class in the following listing is initialized with a list called `items` to hold individual items found in a feed, and a string called `title` to hold the title of the feed (with the title initialized to an empty string):

```
class Feed:
    """ Simple model of a syndication feed data file """
    def __init__(self):
""" Initialize storage """
        self.items = []
        self.title = "
```

Although items are free-standing entities in a sense, they are initially derived from a specific feed, which is reflected in the code by having the Item instances created by the Feed class. The create_item method creates an Item object and then passes the title of the feed to the Item object's source property. Once initialized in this way, the Item is added to the list of items maintained by the Feed object:

```
def create_item(self):
    """ Returns a new Item object """
    item = Item()
    item.source = self.title
    self.items.append(item)
    return item
```

To make testing easier, the Feed object overrides the standard Python __str__ method to provide a useful string representation of itself. All the method here does is run through each of the items in its list and adds the string representation of them to a combined string:

```
def __str__(self):
    """ Custom 'toString()' method to pretty-print """
    string ="
    for item in self.items:
        string.append(item.__str__())
    return string
```

The item class essentially wraps four properties that will be extracted from the XML: title, content, source (the title of the feed it came from), and date. Each of these is maintained as an instance variable, the values of the first three being initialized to an empty string. It's common to encounter date values in feeds that aren't well formatted, so it's possible to initialize the date value to the current time (given by time.time()). The only problem with this approach is that any items with bad date values appear newer than all the others. As a little hack to prevent this without excluding the items altogether, a handicap value is subtracted from the current time. At the start, the constant BAD_TIME_HANDICAP was set to 43,200, represented here in seconds, which corresponds to 12 hours, so any item with a bad date is considered 12 hours old, as shown here:

```
class Item:
    """ Simple model of a single item within a syndication feed """
    def __init__(self):
        """ Initialize properties to defaults """
        self.title = "
        self.content = "
        self.source = "
        self.date = time.time() - BAD_TIME_HANDICAP # seconds from the Epoch
```

The next two methods make up the setter for the value of the date. The first, set_rfc2822_time, uses methods from the e-mail utility library to convert a string (like Sat, 10 Apr 2004 21:13:28 PDT) to the number of seconds since 01/01/1970 (1081656808). Similarly, the set_w3cdtf_time method converts an ISO 8601-compliant string (for example, 2004-04-10T21:13:28-00:00) into seconds. If either conversion fails, then an error message is printed, and the value of date remains at its initial (handicapped) value, as illustrated in the following:

```
def set_rfc2822_time(self, old_date):
    """ Set email-format time """
    try:
        temp = email.Utils.parsedate_tz(old_date)
        self.date = email.Utils.mktime_tz(temp)
    except ValueError:
        print "Bad date : \%s" \% (old_date)

def set_w3cdtf_time(self, new_date):
    """ Set web-format time """
    try:
        self.date = xml.utils.iso8601.parse(new_date)
    except ValueError:
        print "Bad date : \%s" \% (new_date)
```

The get_formatted_date method uses the e-mail library again to convert the number of seconds into a human-friendly form — for example, Sat, 10 Apr 2004 23:13:28 +0200), as follows:

```
def get_formatted_date(self):
    """ Returns human-readable date string """
    return email.Utils.formatdate(self.date, True)
    # RFC 822 date, adjusted to local time
```

Like the Feed class, Item also has a custom __str__ method to provide a nice representation of the object. This is simply the title of the feed it came from and the title of the item itself, followed by the content of the item and finally the date, as shown in the following:

```
def __str__(self):
    """ Custom 'toString()' method to pretty-print """
    return (self.source + ' : '
        + self.title +'\n'
        + self.content + '\n'
        + self.get_formatted_date() + '\n')
```

That's how feeds and items are represented, and you will soon see the tastiest part of the code, the SAX handler that builds Feed and Item objects based on what appears in the feed XML document. This file (feed_handler.py) contains a single class, FeedHandler, which is a subclass of xlm.sax .ContentHandler. An instance of this class is passed to the parser every time a feed document is to be read; and as the parser encounters appropriate entities in the feed, three specific methods are automatically called: startElementNS, characters, and endElementNS. The namespace-enhanced versions of these methods are used because the elements in feeds can come from different namespaces.

XML Markup Handler: FeedHandler

As discussed earlier, there isn't much structure to deal with — just the feed and contained items, but there is a complication not mentioned earlier. The title and content elements of items may contain markup. This shouldn't happen with RSS 1.0; the value of content:encoded is enclosed in a CDATA section or the individual characters escaped as needed. However, the parent RDF/XML specification does describe XML Literals, and material found in the wild often varies wildly from the spec. In any case, the rich content model of Atom is designed to allow XML, and the RSS 2.0 specification is unclear on the issue, so markup should be expected. If the markup is, for example, HTML 3.2 and isn't escaped, then the whole document won't be well formed and by definition won't be XML — a different kettle of fish. However, if the markup is well-formed XML (for example, XHTML), then there will be a call to the SAX start and end element methods for each element within the content.

The code has an instance variable state to keep track of where the parser is within an XML document's structure. This variable can take the value of one of the three constants. If its value is IN_ITEM, then the parser is reading somewhere inside an element that corresponds to an item. If its value is IN_CONTENT, then the parser is somewhere inside an element that contains the body content of the item. If neither of these is the case, then the variable will have the value IN_NONE.

The code itself begins with imports from several libraries, including the SAX material you might have expected as well as the regular expression library re and codecs, which contain tools that are used for cleaning up the content data. The constant TRIM_LENGTH determines the maximum amount of content text to include for each item. For demonstration purposes and to save paper, this is set to a very low 100 characters. This constant is followed by the three alternative state constants, as shown in the following:

```
import xml.sax
import xml.sax.saxutils
import feed
import re
import codecs

# Maximum length of item content
TRIM_LENGTH = 100

# Parser state
IN_NONE = 0
IN_ITEM = 1
IN_CONTENT = 2
```

The content is stripped of markup, and a regular expression is provided to match any XML-like tag (for example, <this>). However, if the content is HTML, then it's desirable to retain a little of the original formatting, so another regular expression is used to recognize <br> and <p> tags, which are replaced with newline characters, as shown in the following:

```
# Regular expressions for cleaning data
TAG_PATTERN = re.compile("<(.rt \n)+?>")
NEWLINE_PATTERN = re.compile("(<br.*>)rt(<p.*>)")
```

The FeedHandler class itself begins by creating a new instance of the Feed class to hold whatever data is extracted from the feed being parsed. The state variable begins with a value of IN_NONE, and an instance variable text is initialized to the empty string. The text variable is used to accumulate text encountered between the element tags, as shown here:

```
# Subclass from ContentHandler in order to gain default behaviors
class FeedHandler(xml.sax.ContentHandler):
    """ Extracts data from feeds, in response to SAX events """
def __init__(self):
```

```
        "Initialize feed object, interpreter state and content"
        self.feed = feed.Feed()
        self.state = IN_NONE
        self.text = "
        return
```

The next method, `startElementNS`, is called by the parser whenever an opening element tag is encountered and receives values for the element name — the prefix-qualified name of the element along with an object containing the element's attributes. The name variable actually contains two values (it's a Python tuple): the namespace of the element and its local name. These values are extracted into the separate `namespace`, `localname` strings. If the feed being read were RSS 1.0, then a `<title>` element would cause the method to be called with the values name = (`'http://purl.org/rss/1.0/'`, `'title'`), qname = `'title'`. (If the element uses a namespace prefix, like `<dc:title>`, then the qname string includes that prefix, such as `dc:title` in this case.) In this simple application the attributes aren't used, but SAX makes them available as an `NSAttributes` object.

A *tuple* is an ordered set of values. A pair of geographic coordinates is one example, an RDF triple another. In Python, a tuple can be expressed as a comma-separated list of values, usually surrounded in parentheses — for example, (1, 2, 3, "go"). In general, the values within tuples don't have to be of the same type. It's common to talk of *n*-tuples, where *n* is the number of values — the example here is a 4-tuple.

The `startElementNS` method determines whether the parser is inside content, by checking whether the state is `IN_CONTENT`. If this isn't the case, then the content accumulator `text` is emptied by setting it to an empty string. If the name of the element is one of those that corresponds to an item in the simple model (`item` or `entry`), then a new item is created, and the state changes to reflect the parser's position within an item block. The last check here tests whether the parser is already inside an item block, and if it is, whether the element is one that corresponds to the content. The actual string comparison is done by a separate method to keep the code tidy, as there are several alternatives. If the element name matches, then the state is switched into `IN_CONTENT`, as shown in the following:

```
def startElementNS(self, name, qname, attributes):
        "Identifies nature of element in feed (called by SAX parser)"
        (namespace, localname) = name

        if self.state != IN_CONTENT:
            self.text = " # new element, not in content

        if localname == 'item' or localname == "entry": # RSS or Atom
            self.current_item = self.feed.create_item()
            self.state = IN_ITEM
            return

        if self.state == IN_ITEM:
            if self.is_content_element(localname):
            self.state = IN_CONTENT
        return
```

The `characters` method merely adds any text encountered within the elements to the `text` accumulator:

```
def characters(self, text):
        "Accumulates text (called by SAX parser)"
        self.text = self.text + text
```

The `endElementNS` method is called when the parser encounters a closing tag, such as `</this>`. It receives the values of the element name and qname, and once again the `name` tuple is split into its component `namespace`, `localname` parts. What follows are a lot of statements, which are conditional based on the name of the element and/or the current state (which corresponds to the parser's position in the XML). This essentially carries out the matching rules between the different kinds of elements that may be encountered in RSS 1.0, 2.0, or Atom, and the `Item` properties in the application's representation. You may want to refer to the table of near equivalents shown earlier and the examples of feed data to see why the choices are made where they are. Here is the `endElementNS` method:

```
def endElementNS(self, name, qname):
        "Collects element content, switches state as appropriate
        (called by SAX parser)"
        (namespace, localname) = name
```

OK, first choice — has the parser come to the end of an item? If so, revert to the `IN_NONE` state:

```
if localname == 'item' or localname == 'entry': # end of item
        self.state = IN_NONE
        return
```

Next, are we in content? If so, is the tag the parser just encountered one of those classed as the end of content? If both answers are yes, then the content accumulated from characters in `text` is cleaned up and passed to the current item object. As it's the end of content, the state also needs shifting back down to `IN_ITEM`. Regardless of the answer to the second question, if the first answer is yes, then you're done here, as shown in the following:

```
if self.state == IN_CONTENT:
        if self.is_content_element(localname): # end of content
            self.current_item.content = self.cleanup_text(self.text)
            self.state = IN_ITEM
        return
```

Now that the content is out of the way with its possible nested elements, the rest of the text that makes it this far represents the simple content of an element. You can clean it up, as outlined in the following:

```
# cleanup text - we probably want it
        text = self.cleanup_text(self.text)
```

At this point, if the parser isn't within an item block and the element name is `title`, then what you have here is the title of the feed. Pass it on as follows:

```
if self.state != IN_ITEM: # feed title
        if localname == "title":
            self.feed.title = self.text
        return
```

The parser must now be within an item block thanks to the last choice, so if there's a `title` element here, then it must refer to the item. Pass that on too:

```
if localname == "title":
        self.current_item.title = text
        return
```

Now we get to the tricky issue of dates. If the parser finds an RSS 1.0 date (`dc:date`) or an Atom date (`atom:updated`), then it will be in ISO 8601 format, so we need to pass it to the item through the appropriate converter:

```
if localname == "date" or localname == "updated":
        self.current_item.set_w3cdtf_time(text)
        return
```

RSS 2.0 and most of its relatives use a `pubDate` element in RFC 2822 e-mail format, so pass that through the appropriate converter as shown here:

```
if localname == "pubDate":
        self.current_item.set_rfc2822_time(text)
        return
```

Handler Helpers

The rest of `feed_handler.py` is devoted to helper methods. The first, `is_content_element`, checks the alternatives to determine whether the local name of the element corresponds to that of an item:

```
def is_content_element(self, localname):
        "Checks if element may contain item/entry content"
        return (localname == "description" or # most RSS x.x
            localname == "encoded" or # RSS 1.0 content:encoded
            localname == "body" or # RSS 2.0 xhtml:body
            localname == "content") # Atom
```

The next three methods are related to tidying up text nodes (which may include escaped markup) found within the content. Cleaning up the text begins by stripping whitespace from each end. This is more important than it might seem, because depending on the layout of the feed data there may be a host of newlines and tabs to make the feed look nice but which only get in the way of the content. These unnecessary newlines should be replaced by a single space.

Next, a utility method, `unescape`, in the SAX library is used to unescape characters such as <this> to <this>. This is followed by a class to another helper method, `process_tags`, to do a little more stripping. If this application used a browser to view the content, then this step wouldn't be needed (or even desirable), but markup displayed to console just looks bad, and <a href="..."> hyperlinks <a> won't work.

The next piece of cleaning is a little controversial. The content delivered in feed can be Unicode, with characters from any international character set, but most consoles are ill prepared to display such material. The standard string encode method is used to flatten everything down to plain old ASCII. This is rather drastic, and there may well be characters that don't fit in this small character set. The second value determines what should happen in this case—possible values are `strict` (default), `ignore`, or `replace`. The `replace` alternative swaps the character for a question mark, hardly improving legibility.

The `strict` option throws an error whenever a character won't fit, and it's not really appropriate here either. The third option, `ignore`, simply leaves out any characters that can't be correctly represented in the chosen ASCII encoding. The following code shows the sequence of method calls used to make the text more presentable:

```
def cleanup_text(self, text):
    "Strips material that won't look good in plain text"
    text = text.strip()
    text = text.replace('\n', ' ')
    text = xml.sax.saxutils.unescape(text)
    text = self.process_tags(text)
    text = text.encode('ascii','ignore')
    text = self.trim(text)
    return text
```

The `process_tags` method (called from `cleanup_text`) uses regular expressions to first replace any `<br>` or `<p>` tags in the content with `newline` characters, and then to replace any remaining tags with a single space character:

```
def process_tags(self, string):
    """ Turns <br/> into \n then removes all <tags> """
    re.sub(NEWLINE_PATTERN, '\n', string)
    return re.sub(TAG_PATTERN, ' ', string)
```

The cleaning done by the last method in the `FeedHandler` class is really a matter of taste. The amount of text found in each post varies greatly between different sources. You may not want to read whole essays through your newsreader, so the `trim` method cuts the string length down to a preset size determined by the `TRIM_LENGTH` constant. However, just counting characters and chopping results in some words being cut in half, so this method looks for the first space character in the text after the `TRIM_LENGTH` index and cuts there. If there aren't any spaces in between that index and the end of the text, then the method chops anyway. Other strategies are possible, such as looking for paragraph breaks and cutting there. Although it's fairly crude, the result is quite effective. The code that does the trimming is as follows:

```
def trim(self, text):
    "Trim string length neatly"
    end_space = text.find(' ', TRIM_LENGTH)
    if end_space != -1:
        text = text[:end_space] + " ..."
    else:
        text = text[:TRIM_LENGTH] # hard cut
    return text
```

That's it, the whole of the aggregator application. There isn't a lot of code, largely thanks to libraries taking care of the details.

Try It Out   Running the Aggregator

To run the code, you need to have Python installed (see the note with the Reading a List of URIs Try it Out earlier in the chapter) and be connected to the Internet:

1. Download and install the latest version of the PyXML package, which is a small download (`http://pyxml.sourceforge.net/`) and a simple install.

PyXML is a very popular Python XML library that implements the standard SAX and DOM APIs, although it isn't currently being maintained. If you are using Python 2.5 or later you may need to download PyXML as source and build it locally, or tweak the code to use a different XML library such as the comprehensive (and significantly larger) 4Suite, from `http://4suite.org`*.*

2. Open a command prompt window, and **cd** to the folder containing the source files.

3. Type the following:

```
python feed_reader.py
```

An alternative way to run the code is to use IDLE, a very simple IDE with a syntax-coloring editor and various debugging aids. Start IDLE by double-clicking its icon and then using its File menu, opening the `feed_reader.py` *file in a new window. Pressing the F5 key when the code is in the editor window runs the application.*

Whichever way you run the application, you should see something like this:

```
python feed_reader.py
Reading http://www.25hoursaday.com/weblog/SyndicationService.asmx/GetRss  :
14 items
Reading http://dig.csail.mit.edu/breadcrumbs/blog/feed/4  :
9 items
Reading http://www.markbaker.ca/blog/feed/atom  :
10 items

*** Newest 5 Items ***

Web Things, by Mark Baker : links for 2006-10-28
Sam goes to WSO2
Sam considering WSO2.  See my comment.
(tags: webservices  rest ...
Mark Baker
Sat, 28 Oct 2006 07:24:46 +0200

timbl's blog : Reinventing HTML
 Making standards is hard work.  Its hard because it involves listening to
other people and figuring ...

Fri, 27 Oct 2006 23:14:10 +0200

Web Things, by Mark Baker : links for 2006-10-27
                        Tom Palaima: The evil that men do lives after
them     &#8220;Evil doesn&#8217;t come like ...
Mark Baker
Fri, 27 Oct 2006 07:24:45 +0200

Dare Obasanjo aka Carnage4Life : Jubilee Thoughts: Adding Podcasts to iTunes
or WMP Playlists
 what about the Aggregator Vendors?  I'm reminded that there is ...

Thu, 26 Oct 2006 16:11:14 +0200

Web Things, by Mark Baker : links for 2006-10-26
Apollo - the Adobe Web browser
```

```
&#8220;We spent a considerable amount of time researching ...
Mark Baker
Thu, 26 Oct 2006 07:25:44 +0200
```

How It Works

You've already seen the details of how this works, but here are the main points:

- ❏ A list of feed addresses is loaded from a text file.

- ❏ Each of the addresses is visited in turn, and the data is passed to a SAX handler.

- ❏ The handler creates objects corresponding to the feed and items within the feed.

- ❏ The individual items from all feeds are combined into a single list and sorted.

- ❏ The items are printed in the command window.

Extending the Aggregator

Obviously, a thousand and one things could be done to improve this application, but whatever enhancement is made to the processing or user interface, you are still dependent on the material pumped out to feeds. XML is defined by its acronym as *extensible*, which means that elements outside of the core language can be included with the aid of XML namespaces. According to the underlying XML namespaces specification, producers can potentially put material from other namespaces pretty much where they like, but this isn't as simple as it sounds because consumers have to know what to do with them. So far, two approaches have been taken to extensibility in syndication.

RSS 2.0 leaves the specification of extensions entirely up to developers. This sounds desirable but has significant drawbacks because there nothing within the specification indicates how an element from an extension relates to other elements in a feed. One drawback is that each extension appears like a completely custom application, needing all-new code at both the producer and consumer ends. Another drawback is that without full cooperation between developers, there's no way of guaranteeing that the two extensions will work together.

The RSS 1.0 approach is to fall back on RDF, specifically the structural interpretation of RDF/XML. The structure in which elements and attributes appear within an RDF/XML document gives an unambiguous interpretation according to the RDF model, irrespective of the namespaces. You can tell that certain elements/attributes correspond to resources, and that others correspond to relationships between those resources. The advantage here is that much of the lower-level code for dealing with feed data can be reused across extensions, as the basic interpretation will be the same. It also means that independently developed extensions for RSS 1.0 are automatically compatible with each other.

Atom takes a compromise approach to extensions, through the specification of two constructs: Simple Extension Elements and Structured Extension Elements. The *Structured Extension Element* provides something similar to the extensibility of RSS 2.0 in that a block of XML that is in a foreign (i.e., not-Atom) namespace relies on the definition of the extension for interpretation (or to be ignored). Unlike RSS 2.0, there are some restrictions on where such a block of markup may appear in the feed, but otherwise it's open-ended. The *Simple Extension Element* provides something similar to the extensibility of RSS 1.0 in that it is interpreted as a property of its enclosing element, as shown here:

```
<feed xmlns="http://www.w3.org/2005/Atom"
      xmlns:im="http://example.org/im/">
  ...
```

```
        <author>
          <name>John Smith</name>
          <im:nickname>smiffy</im:nickname>
        </author>
...
</feed>
```

The Simple Extension Element, `<im:nickname>` here, must be in a foreign namespace. The namespace (`http://example.org/im/` with prefix `im:`) is given in this example on the root `<feed>` element, although following XML conventions it could be specified in any of the ancestor elements of the extension element, or even on the extension element itself. A Simple Extension Element can't have any child nodes, except for a mandatory text node that provides the value of the property, so this example indicates that the author has a property called `im:nickname` with the value `"smiffy"`.

To give you an idea of how you might incorporate support for extensions in the tools you build, here is a simple practical example for the demo application. As mentioned at the start of this chapter, a growing class of tools takes material from one feed (or site) and quotes it directly in another feed (or site). Of particular relevance here are online aggregators, such as the "Planet" sites: Planet Gnome, Planet Debian, Planet RDF, and so on. These are webloglike sites, the posts of which come directly from the syndication feeds of existing blogs or news sites. They each have syndication feeds of their own. You may want to take a moment to look at Planet RDF: The human-readable site is at `http://planetrdf.com`, and it has an RSS 1.0 feed at `http://planetrdf.com/index.rdf`. The main page contains a list of the source feeds from which the system aggregates. The RSS is very much like regular feeds, except the developers behind it played nice and included a reference back to the original site from which the material came. This appears in the feed as a per-item element from the Dublin Core vocabulary, as shown in the following:

```
...
<dc:source>Lost Boy by Leigh Dodds</dc:source>
...
```

The text inside this element is the title of the feed from which the item was extracted. It's pretty easy to capture this in the aggregator described here. To include the material from this element in the aggregated display, two things are needed: a way to extract the data from the feed and a suitable place to put it in the display.

Like the other elements the application uses, the local name of the element is enough to recognize it. It is certainly possible to have a naming clash on "source," though unlikely. This element is used to describe an item, and the code already has a way to handle this kind of information. Additionally, the code picks out the immediate source of the item (the title of the feed from whence it came) and uses this in the title line of the displayed results. All that is needed is another conditional, inserted at the appropriate point, and the source information can be added to the title line of the results.

Try It Out   Extending Aggregator Element Handling

This is a very simple example, but it demonstrates how straightforward it can be to make aggregator behavior more interesting:

1. Open the file `feed_handler.py` in a text editor.

2. At the end of the `endElementNS` method, insert the following code:

```
...
      if localname == "pubDate":
          self.current_item.set_rfc2822_time(text)
          return

  if localname == "source":

          self.current_item.source = '('+self.current_item.source+') '+text
          return

      def is_content_element(self, localname):
          "Checks if element may contain item/entry content"
...
```

3. Open `feeds.txt` in the editor and add the following feed URI:

```
http://www.25hoursaday.com/weblog/SyndicationService.asmx/GetRss
http://dig.csail.mit.edu/breadcrumbs/blog/feed/4
http://www.markbaker.ca/blog/feed/atom/
http://planetrdf.com/index.rdf
```

4. Run the application again (see the previous Try It Out).

How It Works

Among the items that the aggregator shows you, you should see something like this:

```
(Planet RDF) Tim Berners-Lee : Reinventing HTML
    Making standards is hard work. Its hard because it involves listening
to other people and figuring ...
Tim Berners-Lee
Fri, 27 Oct 2006 23:14:10 +0200
```

The name of the aggregated feed from which the item has been extracted is in parentheses (Planet RDF), followed by the title of the original feed from which it came.

Transforming RSS with XSLT

Because syndicated feeds are usually XML, you can process them using XSLT directly (turn to Chapter 8 for more on XSLT). There are three common situations in which you might want to do this:

❑ Generating a feed from existing data

❑ Processing feed data for display

❑ Pre-processing feed data for other purposes

The first situation assumes you have some XML available for transformation, although because this could be XHTML from cleaned-up HTML, it isn't a major assumption. The other two situations are similar to each other, taking syndication feed XML as input. The difference is that the desired output of the second is likely to be something suitable for immediate rendering, whereas the third situation translates data into a format appropriate for subsequent processing.

Generating a Feed from Existing Data

One additional application worth mentioning is that an XSLT transformation can be used to generate other feed formats when only one is available. If your blogging software only produces RSS 1.0, then a standard transformation can provide your site with feeds for Atom and RSS 2.0. A web search will provide you with several examples (names like `rss2rdf.xsl` are popular!).

Be warned that the different formats may carry different amounts of information. For example, in RSS 2.0 most elements are optional, in Atom most elements are mandatory, virtually anything can appear in RSS 1.0, and there isn't one-to-one correspondence of many elements. Therefore, a conversion from one to the other may be lossy or may demand that you artificially create values for elements. For demonstration purposes, the examples here only use RSS 2.0, a particularly undemanding specification for the publisher.

The following XSLT transformation will generate RSS from an XHTML document (`xhtml2rss.xsl`):

```xsl
<xsl:stylesheet version="1.0"
    xmlns:xsl="http://www.w3.org/1999/XSL/Transform"
    xmlns:xhtml="http://www.w3.org/1999/xhtml">

<xsl:output method="xml" indent="yes"/>

<xsl:template match="/xhtml:html">
  <rss version="2.0">
    <channel>
    <description>This will not change</description>
    <link>http://example.org</link>
    <xsl:apply-templates />
    </channel>
  </rss>
</xsl:template>

<xsl:template match="xhtml:title">
  <title>
    <xsl:value-of select="." />
  </title>
</xsl:template>

<xsl:template match="xhtml:body/xhtml:h1">
  <item>
    <title>
      <xsl:value-of select="." />
    </title>
    <description>
      <xsl:value-of select="following-sibling::xhtml:p" />
    </description>
  </item>
</xsl:template>

<xsl:template match="text()" />

</xsl:stylesheet>
```

Try It Out   **Generating RSS from XHTML**

1. Open a text editor and type in the previous listing (or simply download it from the book's website).

2. Save the file as xhtml2rss.xsl.

3. Type the following into the text editor:

```
<?xml version="1.0" encoding="UTF-8"?>
<!DOCTYPE html PUBLIC "-//W3C//DTD XHTML 1.0 Strict//EN"
        "http://www.w3.org/TR/xhtml1/DTD/xhtml1-strict.dtd">
<html xmlns="http://www.w3.org/1999/xhtml">
    <head>
        <title>My Example Document</title>
    </head>
    <body>
 <h1>A first discussion point</h1>
        <p>Something related to the first point.</p>
 <h1>A second discussion point</h1>
        <p>Something related to the second point.</p>
    </body>
</html>
```

4. Save the preceding code as document.html in the same folder as xhtml2rss.xsl.

5. Use an XSLT processor to apply the transformation to the document.

Refer to Chapter 8 for details describing how to do this. A suitable processor is Saxon, available from http://saxon.sourceforge.net/.

The command line for Saxon with saxon8.jar and the data and XSLT file in the same folder is as follows:

```
java -jar saxon8.jar -o document.rss document.html xhtml2rss.xsl
```

6. Open the newly created document.rss in the text editor. You should see the following RSS 2.0 document:

```
<?xml version="1.0" encoding="UTF-8"?>
<rss version="2.0" xmlns:xhtml="http://www.w3.org/1999/xhtml">
   <channel>
      <description>This will not change</description>
      <link>http://example.org</link>
      <title>My Example Document</title>
      <item>
         <title>A first discussion point</title>
         <description>Something related to the first point.</description>
      </item>
      <item>
         <title>A second discussion point</title>
         <description>Something related to the second point.</description>
      </item>
   </channel>
</rss>
```

How It Works

The root element of the stylesheet declares the prefixes for the required namespaces, `xsl:` and `xhtml:`. The output element is set to deliver indented XML:

```
<xsl:stylesheet version="1.0"
    xmlns:xsl="http://www.w3.org/1999/XSL/Transform"
    xmlns:xhtml="http://www.w3.org/1999/xhtml">

<xsl:output method="xml" indent="yes"/>
```

The first template in the XSLT is designed to match the root `html` element of the XHTML document. In that document, the XHTML namespace is declared as the default, but in the stylesheet it's necessary to refer explicitly to the elements using the `xhtml:` prefix to avoid conflicts with the no-namespace RSS. The template looks like this:

```
<xsl:template match="/xhtml:html">
  <rss version="2.0">
    <channel>
    <description>This will not change</description>
    <link>http://example.org</link>
    <xsl:apply-templates />
    </channel>
  </rss>
</xsl:template>
```

This will output the `rss` and `channel` start-tags followed by preset `description` and `link` elements, and then it applies the rest of the templates to whatever is inside the root `xhtml:html` element. The template then closes the `channel` and `rss` elements.

The next template is set up to match any `xhtml:title` elements:

```
<xsl:template match="xhtml:title">
  <title>
    <xsl:value-of select="." />
  </title>
</xsl:template>
```

There is just one matching element in the XHTML document, which contains the text `My example document`. This is selected and placed in a `title` element. Note that the input element is in the XHTML namespace, and the output has no namespace, to correspond to the RSS 2.0 specification.

The next template is a little more complicated. The material in the source XHTML document is considered to correspond to an item of the form:

```
<h1>Item Title</h1>
      <p>Item Description</p>
```

To pick these blocks out, the stylesheet matches on `xhtml:h1` elements contained in an `xhtml:body`, as shown here:

```
<xsl:template match="xhtml:body/xhtml:h1">
  <item>
```

```
<title>
  <xsl:value-of select="." />
</title>
<description>
  <xsl:value-of select="following-sibling::xhtml:p" />
</description>
</item>
</xsl:template>
```

An outer no-namespace `<item>` element wraps everything produced in this template. It contains a `<title>` element, which is given the content of whatever's in the context node, which is the `xhtml:h1` element. Therefore, the header text is passed into the item's `title` element. Next, the content for the RSS `<description>` element is extracted by using the `following-sibling::xhtml:p` selector. This addresses the next `xhtml:p` element after the `xhtml:h1`.

The final template is needed to mop up any text not directly covered by the other elements, which would otherwise appear in the output:

```
<xsl:template match="text()" />
</xsl:stylesheet>
```

Note that the stylesheet presented here assumes the source document will be well-formed XHTML, with a heading/paragraph structure following that of the example. In practice, the XSLT must be modified to suit the document structure. If the original document isn't XHTML (HTML 3.2, for example), then a tool such as HTML Tidy (`http://tidy.sourceforge.net/`) can be used to convert it before applying the transformation.

If the authoring of the original XHTML is under your control, then you can take more control over the conversion process. You can add markers to the document to indicate which parts correspond to items, descriptions, and so on. This is the approach taken in the Atom microformat (`http://microformats.org/wiki/hatom`) — for example, `<div class="hentry">`. This enables an Atom feed to be generated from the XHTML and is likely to be convenient for CSS styling.

One final point: Although this general technique for generating a feed has a lot in common with *screen-scraping* techniques (which generally break when the page author makes a minor change to the layout), it's most useful when the authors of the original document *are* involved. The fact that the source document is XML greatly expands the possibilities. Research is ongoing into methods of embedding more general meta data in XHTML and other XML documents, with recent proposals available at the following sites:

❑   `http://microformats.org` (microformats)

❑   `www.w3.org/2004/01/rdxh/spec` (Gleaning Resource Descriptions from Dialects of Languages, or GRDDL)

Processing Feed Data for Display

What better way to follow a demonstration of XHTML-to-RSS conversion than an RSS-to-XHTML stylesheet? This isn't quite as perverse as it may sound — it's useful to be able to render your own feed for browser viewing, and this conversion offers a simple way to view other people's feeds. Though it is relatively straightforward to display material from someone else's syndication feed on your own site this way, it certainly isn't a good idea without obtaining permission first. Aside from copyright issues, every time your page is loaded it will call the remote site, adding to their bandwidth load. There are ways around this — basically, caching the data locally — but that's beyond the scope of this chapter.

Generating XHTML from RSS isn't very different from the other way around, as you can see in this listing (rss2xhtml.xsl):

```
<xsl:stylesheet version="1.0"
    xmlns:xsl="http://www.w3.org/1999/XSL/Transform"
    xmlns="http://www.w3.org/1999/xhtml">

<xsl:output method="html" indent="yes"/>
<xsl:template match="rss">
  <xsl:text disable-output-escaping="yes">
    \&lt;!DOCTYPE html PUBLIC "-//W3C//DTD XHTML 1.0 Strict//EN"
    "http://www.w3.org/TR/xhtml1/DTD/xhtml1-strict.dtd"\&gt;
  </xsl:text>
  <html>
    <xsl:apply-templates />
  </html>
</xsl:template>

<xsl:template match="channel">
  <head>
    <title>
      <xsl:value-of select="title" />
    </title>
  </head>
  <body>
    <xsl:apply-templates />
  </body>
</xsl:template>

<xsl:template match="item">
  <h1><xsl:value-of select="title" /></h1>
  <p><xsl:value-of select="description" /></p>
</xsl:template>

<xsl:template match="text()" />

</xsl:stylesheet>
```

Try It Out   Generating XHTML from an RSS Feed

1. Enter the previous listing into a text editor (or download it from the book's website).

2. Save it as rss2xhtml.xsl in the same folder as document.rss.

3. Apply the stylesheet to document.rss. The command line for Saxon with saxon7.jar and the data and XSLT file in the same folder is as follows:

```
java -jar saxon8.jar -o document.xml document.rss rss2xhtml.xsl
```

4. Open the newly created `document.xml` in the text editor. You should see the following XHTML document:

```
<!DOCTYPE html PUBLIC "-//W3C//DTD XHTML 1.0 Strict//EN"
 "http://www.w3.org/TR/xhtml1/DTD/xhtml1-strict.dtd">
<html xmlns="http://www.w3.org/1999/xhtml">
    <head>
        <title>My Example Document</title>
    </head>
    <body>
<h1>A first discussion point</h1>
        <p>Something related to the first point.</p>
        <h1>A second discussion point</h1>
        <p>Something related to the second point.</p>
    </body>
</html>
```

As you can see, it closely resembles the XHTML original (`document.html`) used to create the RSS data.

How It Works

As in the previous stylesheet, the namespaces in use are those of XSLT and XHTML. This time, however, the output method is `html`. The `xml` output method can be used to produce equally valid data, as XHTML is XML, but the syntax is a little tidier (this is likely to vary between XSLT processors):

```
<xsl:stylesheet version="1.0"
    xmlns:xsl="http://www.w3.org/1999/XSL/Transform"
    xmlns="http://www.w3.org/1999/xhtml">

<xsl:output method="html" indent="yes"/>
```

The first template here matches the root `<rss>` element of the RSS 2.0 document. The template puts in place an appropriate DOCTYPE declaration, which is wrapped in an `xsl:text` element with escaping disabled to allow the end `<...>` characters to appear in the output without breaking this XML's well-formedness. The root element of the XHTML document is put in position, and the other templates are applied to the rest of the feed data. Here is the first template:

```
<xsl:template match="rss">
    <xsl:text disable-output-escaping="yes">
    &lt;!DOCTYPE html PUBLIC "-//W3C//DTD XHTML 1.0 Strict//EN"
    "http://www.w3.org/TR/xhtml1/DTD/xhtml1-strict.dtd"&gt;
    </xsl:text>
    <html>
        <xsl:apply-templates />
    </html>
</xsl:template>
```

The next template matches the `<channel>` element. This actually corresponds to two separate sections in the desired XHTML: the head and the body. All that's needed in the head is the content of the `title` element, which appears as an immediate child of channel. The material that must appear in the body of the XHTML document is a little more complicated, so other templates are applied to sort that out. Here then is the `channel` template:

```
<xsl:template match="channel">
  <head>
    <title>
      <xsl:value-of select="title" />
    </title>
  </head>
  <body>
    <xsl:apply-templates />
  </body>
</xsl:template>
```

For each item element that appears in the feed, a pair of `<h1>` and `<p>` elements are created, corresponding to the RSS `<title>` and `<description>`. Here is the template, and you can see how the content is transferred from the RSS kinds of element to their XHTML mappings:

```
<xsl:template match="item">
  <h1><xsl:value-of select="title" /></h1>
  <p><xsl:value-of select="description" /></p>
</xsl:template>
```

Once more a utility template is included to mop up any stray text, before the closing `xsl:stylesheet` element closes this document:

```
<xsl:template match="text()" />

</xsl:stylesheet>
```

Browser Processing

A bonus feature of modern web browsers, such as Mozilla and IE, is that they have XSLT engines built in. This means it's possible to style a feed format document in the browser. All that's needed is an XML Processing Instruction that points toward the stylesheet. This is very straightforward, as shown here, modifying `document.rss`:

```
<?xml version="1.0"?>
<?xml-stylesheet type="text/xsl" href="rss2xhtml.xsl"?>
<rss version="2.0">
  <channel>
...
```

If you save this modified version as `document.xml` and open it with your browser, you'll see a rendering that's exactly the same as what you see with the XHTML version listed earlier.

Browsers aren't that smart at figuring out what kind of document they're being presented with, so when saved and loaded locally, the filename extension has to be something the browser recognizes. If you try to load a file `document.rss` into a browser, chances are good it will ask you where you want to save it.

When it comes to displaying XML (such as RSS and Atom) in a browser, the world's your oyster — you can generate XHTML using a stylesheet and the resulting document can be additionally styled using CSS. There's no real need for anyone to see raw XML in his or her browser. This is one reason the Atom group has created the `<info>` element, which can be used along with client-side styling to present an informative message about the feed alongside a human-readable rendering of the XML.

Pre-processing Feed Data

Another reason you might want to process feed data with XSLT would be to interface easily with existing systems. For example, if you wanted to store the feed items in a database, you could set up a transformation to extract the content from a feed and format it as SQL statements, as follows:

```
INSERT INTO feed-table
   VALUES (item-id, "This is the title", "This is the item description");
```

One particularly useful application of XSLT is to use *transformation* to "normalize" the data from the various formats into a common representation, which can then be passed on to subsequent processing. This is in effect the same technique used in the aggregator application just shown, except there the normalization is to the application's internal representation of a feed model.

A quick Web search should yield something suitable for most requirements like this, or at least something that you can modify to fit your specific needs. Two examples of existing work are Morten Frederiksen's anything-to-RSS 1.0 converter (`http://purl.org/net/syndication/subscribe/feed-rss1.0.xsl`) and Aaron Straup Cope's Atom-to-RSS 1.0 and 2.0 stylesheets (`www.aaronland.info/xsl/atom/0.3/`).

Reviewing the Different Formats

There are at least three different syndication formats for a feed consumer to deal with, and you may want to build different subsystems to deal with each individually. Even when XSLT is available this can be desirable, as no single feed model can really do justice to all the variations. How do you tell what format a feed is? Here are the addresses of some syndication feeds:

```
http://news.bbc.co.uk/rss/newsonline_world_edition/front_page/rss091.xml
http://blogs.it/0100198/rss.xml
http://purl.org/net/morten/blog/feed/rdf/
http://swordfish.rdfweb.org/people/libby/rdfweb/webwho.xrdf
http://icite.net/blog/?flavor=atom\&smm=y
```

You might suppose a rough rule of thumb is to examine the filename. It is, but this is pretty unreliable for *any* format on the Web. A marginally more reliable approach (and one that counts as good practice against the Web specifications) is to examine the MIME type of the data. A convenient way of doing this is to use the wget command-line application to download the files (this is a standard Unix utility; a Windows version is available from `http://unxutils.sourceforge.net/`).

In use, wget looks like this:

```
D:\rss-samples>wget http://blogs.it/0100198/rss.xml
-16:23:35-  http://blogs.it/0100198/rss.xml
         => 'rss.xml'
Resolving blogs.it... 213.92.76.66
Connecting to blogs.it[213.92.76.66]:80... connected.
```

```
HTTP request sent, awaiting response... 200 OK
Length: 87,810 [text/xml]

100%[======================================>] 87,810          7.51K/s     ETA 00:00

16:23:48 (7.91 KB/s) - 'rss.xml' saved [87810/87810]
```

It provides a lot of useful information: the IP address of the host called, the HTTP response (200 OK), the length of the file in bytes (87,810), and then the part of interest: [text/xml]. If you run wget with each of the previous addresses, you can see the MIME types are as follows:

```
[application/atom+xml ] http://news.bbc.co.uk/rss/
                   newsonline_world_edition/front_page/rss091.xml
 [text/xml] http://blogs.it/0100198/rss.xml
[application/rdf+xml] http://purl.org/net/morten/blog/feed/rdf/
[text/plain] http://swordfish.rdfweb.org/people/libby/rdfweb/webwho.xrdf
[application/atom+xml] http://icite.net/blog/?flavor=atom\&smm=y
```

In addition to the preceding MIME types, it's not uncommon to see application/rss+xml used, although that has no official standing.

Has that helped determine what formats these are? Hardly. The only reliable way to find out is to look inside the files and see what it says there, and even then it can be tricky, so run wget to get the previous files, and have a look inside with a text editor. Snipping off the XML prolog (and irrelevant namespaces), the data files begin like this (this one is from http://news.bbc.co.uk/rss/newsonline_world_ edition/front_page/rss091.xml):

```
<rss version="0.91">
   <channel>
   <title>BBC News  News Front Page  World Edition</title>
...
```

OK, that's clearly RSS, flagged by the root element. It even tells you that it's version 0.91. Here's another from http://blogs.it/0100198/rss.xml:

```
<rss version="2.0">
<channel>
   <title>Marc's Voice</title>
_
```

Again, a helpful root tells you it's RSS 2.0. Now here's one from http://purl.org/net/morten/ blog/feed/rdf/:

```
<rdf:RDF xmlns="
http://purl.org/rss/1.0/" xmlns:rdf="http://www.w3.org/1999/02/22-rdf-syntax-ns#">

<channel rdf:about="http://purl.org/net/morten/blog/rdf">
 <title>Binary Relations</title>
...
```

The `rdf:RDF` root suggests, and the `rss:channel` element confirms, this is RSS 1.0. However, the following from `http://swordfish.rdfweb.org/people/libby/rdfweb/webwho.xrdf` is less clear:

```
<rdf:RDF
    xmlns:rdf="http://www.w3.org/1999/02/22-rdf-syntax-ns#"
    xmlns:foaf="http://xmlns.com/foaf/0.1/">
...>

<rdf:Description rdf:about="">
  <foaf:maker>
    <foaf:Person>
      <foaf:name>Libby Miller</foaf:name>
...
```

The `rdf:RDF` root and a lot of namespaces could indicate that this is RSS 1.0 using a bunch of extension modules. You might have to go a long way through this file to be sure. The interchangeability of RDF vocabularies means that RSS 1.0 terms can crop up almost anywhere; whether or not you wish to count any document as a whole as a syndication feed is another matter. As it happens, there aren't any RSS elements in this particular file; it's a *FOAF* (Friend-of-a-Friend) Personal Profile Document. It's perfectly valid data; it's just simply not a syndication feed as such.

Now for a last example from `http://icite.net/blog/?flavor=atom &smm=y`:

```
<feed version="0.3"
    xmlns="http://purl.org/atom/ns#"
    xmlns:dc="http://purl.org/dc/elements/1.1/"
    xml:lang="en">

    <title>the iCite net development blog</title>
...
```

The `<feed>` gives this away from the start: this is Atom. The version is only 0.3, but chances are good it will make it to version 1.0 without changing that root element.

These examples were chosen because they are all *good* examples — that is to say, they conform to their individual specifications. In the wild, things might get messy, but at least the preceding checks give you a place to start.

Useful Resources

Here's a selection of some additional resources for further information on the topics discussed in this chapter. The following sites are good specifications resources:

❏ RSS 1.0: `http://purl.org/rss/1.0/spec`

❏ RSS 2.0: `http://blogs.law.harvard.edu/tech/rss`

❏ Atom: `www.ietf.org/rfc/rfc4287.txt`

❏ Atom Wiki: `www.intertwingly.net/wiki/pie/FrontPage`

❏ RDF: `www.w3.org/RDF/`

These sites offer tutorials:

- ❑ rdf:about: `www.rdfabout.com/`
- ❑ Atom Enabled: `www.atomenabled.org/`
- ❑ Syndication Best Practices: `www.ariadne.ac.uk/issue35/miller/`
- ❑ The Absolute Minimum Every Software Developer Absolutely, Positively Must Know About Unicode and Character Sets (No Excuses!), by Joel Spolsky: `www.joelonsoftware.com/articles/Unicode.html`

Some miscellaneous resources include the following:

- ❑ Feed Validator: `http://feedvalidator.org`
- ❑ RDF Validator: `www.w3.org/RDF/Validator/`
- ❑ Dave Beckett's RDF Resource Guide: `www.ilrt.bris.ac.uk/discovery/rdf/resources/`
- ❑ RSS-DEV Mailing List: `http://groups.yahoo.com/group/rss-dev/`

Summary

The beginning of this chapter showed how the current ideas of content syndication grew out of "push" technologies and early meta data efforts, the foundations laid by CDF and MCF followed by Netscape's RSS 0.9 and Scripting News format. It described how the components of syndication systems carry out different roles: server-producer, client-consumer, client-producer, and server-consumer. The chapter then covered the basic ideas behind the Resource Description Framework (RDF) on which RSS 1.0 is built, as well as the relatively straightforward syntax of RSS 2.0. This was followed by a discussion of Atom, an open language that hopes to get beyond political divisions that have been the bane of the RSS community and concentrate on advancing the technology.

After a brief discussion of some of the practical issues of syndication, you learned about an aggregator written in Python. It is hoped that you tried the application and undoubtedly thought of ways in which it can be extended. Most of the development around syndication has been from the grassroots, and it's a fertile area for new ideas. It really is worthwhile putting your ideas into practice.

The chapter then briefly covered some of the things that can be achieved by using XSLT with feed formats, such as generation of feed data from XHTML and rendering to a browser. The topic of RSS and content syndication is wide and deep, and a single chapter cannot do justice to it. However, you have learned the fundamental concepts, a small sample of the techniques that can be applied, and one or two of the problems developers face. You have also seen how XML is central to content syndication. You are now equipped to change the world — or at least a geeky corner of it.

Exercise Questions

Suggested solutions to these questions can be found in Appendix A.

Question 1

At the end of the description of the simple Python aggregator, it was demonstrated how relatively simple it is to extend the range of the elements covered, by adding support for dc:source. Your first challenge is to extend the application so that it also displays the author of a feed entry, if that information is available.

You should check the specs and some real-world feeds yourself, but the elements used for identifying the author of an item are usually one of the following: author, dc:creator, atom:name, or foaf:name. The author element appears in the "simple" RSS versions (0.9x, 2.0) and has no namespace. However, note a slight complication: There is also an element in RSS 2.0 called name, which is used for the name of the text object in a text input area (the text input area elements are rarely encountered in practice, but it does make for a more interesting exercise). Therefore, part of this exercise is to ensure that this element won't be mistaken for the name of the author.

Question 2

You saw toward the end of the chapter how the most common syndication formats show themselves, and earlier in the chapter you saw how it is possible to run an XSLT stylesheet over RSS feeds to produce an XHTML rendering. The exercise here is to apply the second technique to the first task. Try to write an XSLT transformation that indicates the format of the feed, together with its title.

14

Web Services

So far, we've covered what XML is and how to create well-formed and valid XML documents, and you've even seen a couple of programmatic interfaces into XML documents in the form of DOM and SAX. We also discussed the fact that XML isn't really a language on its own; it's a meta language, to be used in the creation of other languages.

This chapter takes a slightly different turn. Rather than discuss XML itself, it covers an application of XML: *web services* enable objects on one computer to call and make use of objects on other computers. In other words, web services are a means of performing distributed computing.

This chapter includes the following:

❑ What a remote procedure call (RPC) is, and what RPC protocols exist currently

❑ Why web services can provide more flexibility than previous RPC protocols

❑ How XML-RPC works

❑ Why most web services implementations should use HTTP as a transport protocol, and how HTTP works under the hood

❑ How the specifications that surround web services fit together

What Is an RPC?

It is often necessary to design *distributed systems*, whereby the code to run an application is spread across multiple computers. For example, to create a large transaction processing system, you might have a separate server for business logic objects, one for presentation logic objects, a database server, and so on, all of which need to talk to each other (see Figure 14-1).

In order for a model like this to work, code on one computer needs to call code on another computer. For example, the code in the web server might need a list of orders for display on a web page, in which case it would call code on the business objects server to provide that list of orders. That code in turn might need to talk to the database. When code on one computer calls code on another computer, this is called a *remote procedure call (RPC)*.

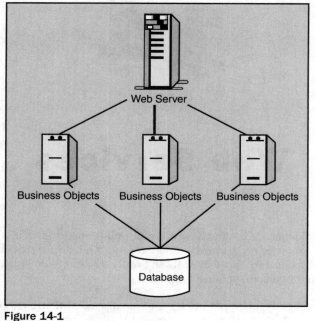

Figure 14-1

In order to make an RPC, you need to know the following things:

❑ Where does the code you want to call reside? If you want to execute a particular piece of code, you need to know where that code is!

❑ Does the code need any parameters? If so, what type? For example, if you want to call a remote procedure to add two numbers, then that procedure needs to know what numbers to add.

❑ Will the procedure return any data? If so, in what format? For example, a procedure to add two numbers would probably return a third number, which would be the result of the calculation.

In addition, you need to deal with networking issues, packaging any data for transport from computer to computer, and a number of other issues. For this reason, a number of RPC *protocols* have been developed.

> A protocol is a set of rules that enables different applications, or even different computers, to communicate. For example, TCP (Transmission Control Protocol) and IP (Internet Protocol) are protocols that enable computers on the Internet to talk to each other, because they specify rules regarding how data should be passed, how computers are addressed, and so on.

These protocols specify how to provide an address for the remote computer, how to package data to be sent to the remote procedures, how to retrieve a response, how to initiate the call, how to deal with errors, and all of the other details that need to be addressed to allow multiple computers to communicate with each other. (Such RPC protocols often piggyback on other protocols; for example, an RPC protocol might specify that TCP/IP must be used as its network transport.)

RPC Protocols

Several protocols exist for performing remote procedure calls, but the most common are *DCOM* (*Distributed Component Object Model*) and *IIOP* (*Internet Inter-ORB Protocol*), both of which are extensions of other technologies: COM and CORBA, respectively, and Java RMI. Each of these protocols provides the functionality needed to perform remote procedure calls, although each has its drawbacks. The following sections discuss these protocols and those drawbacks, without providing a lot of technical details.

DCOM

Microsoft developed a technology called the *Component Object Model*, or *COM* (see www.microsoft .com/com/default.asp), to help facilitate *component-based software*, software that can be broken down into smaller, separate components, which can then be shared across an application, or even across multiple applications. COM provides a standard way of writing objects so they can be discovered at runtime and used by any application running on the computer. In addition, COM objects are language independent. That means you can write a COM object in virtually any programming language—C, C++, Visual Basic, and so on—and that object can talk to any other COM object, even if it was written in a different language.

A good example of COM in action is Microsoft Office: Because much of Office's functionality is provided through COM objects, it is easy for one Office application to make use of another. For example, because Excel's functionality is exposed through COM objects, you might create a Word document that contains an embedded Excel spreadsheet.

However, this functionality is not limited to Office applications; you could also write your own application that makes use of Excel's functionality to perform complex calculations, or uses Word's spell-checking component. This enables you to write your applications faster, as you don't have to write the functionality for a spell-checking component or a complex math component yourself. By extension, you could also write your own shareable components for use in others' applications.

COM is a handy technology to use when creating reusable components, but it doesn't tackle the problem of distributed applications. In order for your application to make use of a COM object, that object must reside on the same computer as your application. For this reason, Microsoft developed a technology called *Distributed COM*, or *DCOM*. DCOM extends the COM programming model, enabling applications to call COM objects that reside on remote computers. To an application, calling a remote object from a server using DCOM is just as easy as calling a local object on the same PC using COM—as long as the necessary configuration has been done ahead of time.

Nonetheless, as handy as COM and DCOM are for writing component-based software and distributed applications, they have one major drawback: Both of these technologies are Microsoft-specific. The COM objects you write, or that you want to use, will only work on computers running Microsoft Windows; and even though you can call remote objects over DCOM, those objects also must be running on computers using Microsoft Windows.

> *DCOM implementations have been written for non-Microsoft operating systems, but they haven't been widely accepted. In practice, when someone wants to develop a distributed application on non-Microsoft platforms, they use one of the other RPC protocols.*

For some people, this may not be a problem. For example, if you are developing an application for your company and you have already standardized on Microsoft Windows for your employees, then using a Microsoft-specific technology might be fine. For others, however, this limitation means that DCOM is not an option.

IIOP

Prior even to Microsoft's work on COM, the *Object Management Group*, or *OMG* (see www.omg.org/) developed a technology to solve the same problems that COM and DCOM try to solve, but in a platform-neutral way. They called this technology the *Common Object Request Broker Architecture*, or *CORBA* (see www.corba.org/). As with COM, CORBA objects can be written in virtually any programming language, and any CORBA object can talk to any other, even if it was written in a different language. CORBA works similarly to COM, the main difference being who supplies the underlying architecture for the technology.

For COM objects, the underlying COM functionality is provided by the operating system (Windows), whereas with CORBA, an *Object Request Broker (ORB)* provides the underlying functionality (see Figure 14-2). In fact, the processes for instantiating COM and CORBA objects are similar.

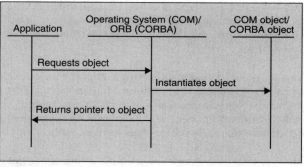

Figure 14-2

Although the concepts are the same, using an ORB instead of the operating system to provide the base object services offers one important advantage: It makes CORBA platform independent. Any vendor that creates an ORB can create versions for Windows, Unix, Linux, and so on.

Furthermore, the OMG created the *Internet Inter-ORB Protocol (IIOP)*, which enables communication between different ORBs. This means that you not only have platform independence, you also have ORB independence. You can combine ORBs from different vendors and have remote objects talking to each other over IIOP (as long as you avoid any vendor-specific extensions to IIOP).

Neither COM nor CORBA are easy to work with, which dramatically reduced their acceptance and take-up. Although COM classes are reasonably easy to use, and were the basis of thousands of applications including Microsoft Office, they are difficult to design and create. CORBA suffered similar problems, and these difficulties, as well as such scenarios as *DLL hell* in COM (mismatched incompatible versions of libraries of a machine) led to the design of other techniques.

Java RMI

Both DCOM and IIOP provide similar functionality: a language-independent way to call objects that reside on remote computers. IIOP goes a step further than DCOM, enabling components to run on different platforms. However, a language already exists that is specifically designed to enable you to "write once, run anywhere": Java.

Java provides the *Remote Method Invocation,* or *RMI,* system (see `http://java.sun.com/products/jdk/rmi/`) for distributed computing. Because Java objects can be run from any platform, the idea behind RMI is to just write everything in Java and then have those objects communicate with each other.

Although Java can be used to write CORBA objects that can be called over IIOP, or even to write COM objects using certain nonstandard Java language extensions, using RMI for distributed computing can provide a smaller learning curve because the programmer isn't required to learn about CORBA and IIOP. All of the objects involved use the same programming language, so any datatypes are simply the built-in Java datatypes, and Java exceptions can be used for error handling. Finally, Java RMI can do one thing DCOM and IIOP can't: It can transfer code with every call. That is, even when the remote computer you're calling doesn't have the code it needs, you can send it and still have the remote computer perform the processing.

The obvious drawback to Java RMI is that it ties the programmer to one programming language, Java, for all of the objects in the distributed system.

The New RPC Protocol: Web Services

With the Internet fast becoming the platform on which applications run, it's no surprise that a truly language- and platform-independent way of creating distributed applications has become the Holy Grail of software development. Currently, it looks as though that Holy Grail has made itself known in the form of *web services*.

> *The exact definition of a web service is one of those never-ending discussions. Some would describe even a simple request for a standard web page as an example. In this book, a web service is a service that accepts a request and returns data or carries out a processing task. The data returned is normally formatted in a machine-readable form, without a focus on the content and the presentation, as you would expect in a standard web page. Another distinction is that made between a service and an XML web service. The latter means that at least one aspect, the request or the response, consists of XML. In this chapter, web services means XML web services unless otherwise stated.*

Web services are a means for requesting information or carrying out a processing task over the Internet, but, as stated, they typically involve the encoding of both the request and the response in XML. Along with using standard Internet protocols for transport, this encoding makes messages universally available. That means that a Perl program running on Linux can call a .NET program running on Windows.NET, and nobody will be the wiser.

Of course, nothing's ever quite that simple, at least this early in the game. In order to make these web services available, there must be standards so that everyone knows what information can be requested, how to request it, and what form the response will take.

The following pages look at XML-RPC, a simple form of web services. The discussion is then extended to look at the more heavy-duty protocols and how they fit together. The next chapter takes a closer look at two of the most commonly used protocols: SOAP and WSDL.

There are two main designs for XML Web services; they differ in their approach to how the request is made. The first technique, known as XML-RPC, mimics how traditional function calls are made — with the name of the method and individual parameters wrapped in an XML format. The second version uses a *document* approach. This simply specifies that the service expects an XML document as its input, the format of which is predefined, usually by an XML Schema. The service then processes the document and carries out the necessary tasks.

XML-RPC

One of the easiest ways to see web services in action is to look at the XML-RPC protocol. Designed to be simple, it provides a means for calling a remote procedure by specifying the procedure to call and the parameters to pass. The client sends a command, encoded as XML, to the server, which performs the remote procedure call and returns a response, also encoded as XML.

The protocol is simple, but the process — sending an XML request over the Web and getting back an XML response — is the foundation of web services, so understanding how it works will help you understand more complex protocols such as SOAP.

The service examined here is the Internet Topic Exchange (`http://topicexchange.com/`), a set of "channels" that list postings on particular topics. For example, when Wiley Publishing publicizes new editions on its website, they can add an entry to the "books" channel.

Let's start by looking at the API we're going to be calling.

The Target API

The Internet Topic Exchange has only three available methods. The first is as follows:

```
struct topicExchange.getChannels()
```

This method does exactly what it says it does: It returns a list of existing channels. (Don't worry about the `struct` yet.) It doesn't have any parameters, so calling it is very simple.

Now take a look at the second method:

```
struct topicExchange.ping(string topicName, struct details)
```

This method is used to add a new entry to a particular topic, as defined by the `topicName`.

The third method has the following signature:

```
struct topicExchange.getChannelInfo(string topicName)
```

This method retrieves information on a specific channel. It accepts the name of the channel as a string and returns a struct with the relevant details, such as the topic's URL and a description of its contents. We'll look at actually making the request in a moment, but first let's look at how to construct an XML web services message.

A Simple Request

The simplest XML-RPC request is one that executes a method with no parameters. In this example, that would be the `topicExchange.getChannels()` method, shown in the following:

```
<methodCall>
    <methodName>topicExchange.getChannels</methodName>
</methodCall>
```

In this case, the process is straightforward; you simply call the `topicExchange.getChannels()` method, as specified in the `methodName` element. When you send this XML snippet to the service, the service returns an XML document that lists existing channels. We'll look at that response in a moment, but first let's look at a more complex request.

Passing Parameters

Typically, the method you want to call requires parameters, so XML-RPC includes a way to specify them within the XML request. For example, the `topicExchange.ping()` method requires a `string` and a `struct`. The string is easy to specify, as shown in the following:

```
<methodCall>
  <methodName>topicExchange.ping</methodName>
  <params>
    <param>
      <value><string>books</string></value>
    </param>
  </params>
</methodCall>
```

Here you specify a set of parameters using the `params` element, and then a single parameter using the `param` element. Within the `param` element you specify the first parameter, the channel name, noting that it is to be treated as a string. XML-RPC actually specifies seven types of scalar values: `<i4>` (or `<int>`, a 4-byte signed integer), `<boolean>` (0 for false, or 1 for true), `<string>`, `<double>`, `<dateTime.iso8601>` (a date/time value, such as 20040422T16:12:04), and `<base64>` (base64-encoded binary data). In some cases, the parameter is not a single scalar value, but a group of values, known as a `struct`.

Using a struct

A `struct` is a set of named values passed as you might pass an object. For example, the Internet Topic Exchange expects the information on the posting to which you're linking as a single `struct`:

```
<methodCall>
  <methodName>topicExchange.ping</methodName>
  <params>
    <param>
      <value><string>books</string></value>
    </param>
    <param>
      <value>

        <struct>
          <member>
            <name>blog_name</name>
            <value><string>Wiley Today</string></value>
```

```
            </member>
            <member>
              <name>title</name>
              <value><string>Latest Publications</string></value>
            </member>
            <member>
              <name>url</name>
              <value>
                <string>http://www.wiley.com/WileyCDA/Section/index.html </string>
              </value>
            </member>
            <member>
              <name>excerpt</name>
              <value><string>Wiley latest publications have something for everyone.
Beginning XML is proving to be this year's hottest selling item.
</string></value>
            </member>
          </struct>
```

```
        </value>
      </param>
    </params>
</methodCall>
```

In this case, the `details` parameter consists of a single value, but that value is a `struct`. The `struct` consists of four `members`, with each member having a `name` and a `value`. As before, the value is a scalar of one of the seven types, but that's not actually a requirement. A `struct` can have a `struct` as one or more of its members, as shown here in the response returned from the `getChannels()` method:

```
<methodResponse>
  <params>
    <param>
      <value>
        <struct>
          <member>
            <name>channels</name>
            <value>
              <struct>
```

```
                <member>
                  <name>books</name>
                  <value>
                    <struct>
                      <member>
                        <name>url</name>
                        <value>
                          <string>http://topicexchange.com/t/books/</string>
                        </value>
                      </member>
                    </struct>
                  </value>
                </member>
                <member>
```

```
                        <name>logic</name>
                        <value>
                          <struct>
                            <member>
                              <name>url</name>
                              <value>
                                <string>http://topicexchange.com/t/logic/</string>
                              </value>
                            </member>
                          </struct>
                        </value>
                      </member>
    <!-- more member elements -->
                    </struct>
                  </value>
                </member>
              </struct>
            </value>
          </param>
        </params>
      </methodResponse>
```

This response has been snipped for brevity's sake, but the structure is just as it would be for the dozens of other channels. That's it, as far as XML-RPC syntax is concerned. Now we just have to look at how to actually send a request.

The Network Transport

Generally, web services specifications allow you to use any network transport to send and receive messages. For example, you could use IBM MQSeries or Microsoft Message Queue (MSMQ) to send SOAP messages asynchronously over a queue, or even use SMTP to send SOAP messages via e-mail. However, the most common protocol used is probably HTTP. In fact, the XML-RPC specification requires it, so that is what we concentrate on in this chapter.

HTTP

Many readers may already be somewhat familiar with the HTTP protocol, as it is used every time you request a web page in your browser. Most web services implementations use HTTP as their underlying protocol, so take a look at how it works under the hood.

The *Hypertext Transfer Protocol (HTTP)* is a request/response protocol. This means that when you make an HTTP request, at its most basic, the following steps occur:

1. The client (in most cases, the browser) opens a connection to the HTTP server.

2. The client sends a request to the server.

3. The server performs some processing.

4. The server sends back a response.

5. The connection is closed.

An HTTP message contains two parts: a set of *headers*, followed by an optional *body*. The headers are simply text, with each header separated from the next by a new line character, while the body might be text or binary information. The body is separated from the headers by two newline characters.

For example, suppose you attempt to load an HTML page, located at `http://www.wiley.com/WileyCDA/Section/index.html` (Wiley's home page) into your browser, which in this case is Internet Explorer 7.0. The browser sends a request similar to the following to the `www.wrox.com` server:

```
GET /WileyCDA/Section/index.html  HTTP/1.1
Accept: */*
Accept-Language: en-us
Accept-Encoding: gzip, deflate
User-Agent: Mozilla/4.0 (compatible; MSIE 7.0; Win32)
Host: www.wiley.com
```

The first line of your request specifies the method to be performed by the HTTP server. HTTP defines a few types of requests, but this has specified GET, indicating to the server that you want the resource specified, which in this case is `/WileyCDA/Section/index.html`. (Another common method is POST, covered in a moment.) This line also specifies that you're using the HTTP/1.1 version of the protocol. There are several other headers there as well, which specify to the web server a few pieces of information about the browser, such as what types of information it can receive. Those are as follows:

❑ Accept tells the server what MIME types this browser accepts — in this case, `*/*`, meaning any MIME types.

❑ Accept-Language tells the server what language this browser is using. Servers can potentially use this information to customize the content returned. In this case, the browser is specifying that it is the United States (us) dialect of the English (en) language.

❑ Accept-Encoding specifies to the server whether the content can be encoded before being sent to the browser. In this case, the browser has specified that it can accept documents that are encoded using gzip or deflate. These technologies are used to compress the data, which is then decompressed on the client.

For a GET request, there is no body in the HTTP message. In response, the server sends something similar to the following:

```
HTTP/1.1 200 OK
Server: Microsoft-IIS/5.0
Date: Fri, 09 Mar 2007 15:30:52 GMT
Content-Type: text/html
Last-Modified: Thu, 06 Mar 2007 12:19:57 GMT
Content-Length: 98

<html>
<head><title>Hello world</title></head>
<body>
<p>Hello world</p>
</body>
</html>
```

Obviously, the real Wiley home page is a little more complicated than this. Again, there is a set of HTTP headers, this time followed by the body. In this case, some of the headers sent by the HTTP server were as follows:

❑ A status code, 200, indicating that the request was successful. The HTTP specification (ftp://ftp.isi.edu/in-notes/rfc2616.txt) defines a number of valid status codes that can be sent in an HTTP response, such as the famous (or infamous) 404 code, which means that the resource being requested could not be found.

❑ A Content-Type header, indicating what type of content is contained in the body of the message. A client application (such as a web browser) uses this header to decide what to do with the item; for example, if the content type were a .wav file, the browser might load an external sound program to play it or give the user the option of saving it to the hard drive instead.

❑ A Content-Length header, which indicates the length of the body of the message

The GET method is the most common HTTP method used in regular everyday surfing. The second most common is the POST method. When you do a POST, information is sent to the HTTP server in the body of the message. For example, when you fill out a form on a web page and click the Submit button, the web browser will usually POST that information to the web server, which processes it before sending back the results. Suppose you create an HTML page that includes a form like this:

```
<html>
<head>
<title>Test form</title>
</head>
<body>
<form action="acceptform.asp" method="POST">
  Enter your first name: <input name="txtFirstName" /><br />
  Enter your last name: <input name="txtLastName" /><br />
  <input type="submit" />
</form>
</body>
</html>
```

This form will POST any information to a page called acceptform.asp, in the same location as this HTML file, similar to the following:

```
POST /acceptform.asp HTTP/1.1
Accept: */*
Referer: http://www.wiley.com/myform.htm
Accept-Language: en-us
Content-Type: application/x-www-form-urlencoded
Accept-Encoding: gzip, deflate
User-Agent: Mozilla/4.0 (compatible; MSIE 7.0; Win32)
Host: www.wiley.com
Content-Length: 36

txtFirstName=Joe&txtLastName=Fawcett
```

Whereas the GET method provides for surfing the Internet, it's the POST method that allows for things like e-commerce, as information can be passed back and forth.

As you'll see later in the chapter, the GET *method can also send information by appending it to the* URL, *but in general* POST *is used wherever possible.*

Why HTTP for Web Services?

It was mentioned earlier that most web services implementations probably use HTTP as their transport. Here are a few reasons why:

❑ HTTP is already a widely implemented, and well understood, protocol.

❑ The request/response paradigm lends itself to RPC well.

❑ Most firewalls are already configured to work with HTTP.

❑ HTTP makes it easy to build in security by using Secure Sockets Layer (SSL).

Widely Implemented

One of the primary reasons for the explosive growth of the Internet was the availability of the World Wide Web, which runs over the HTTP protocol. There are millions of web servers in existence, serving up HTML and other content over HTTP, and many, many companies use HTTP for e-commerce.

HTTP is a relatively easy protocol to implement, which is one of the reasons why the Web works as smoothly as it does. If HTTP had been hard to implement, then a number of implementers would have probably gotten it wrong, meaning some web browsers wouldn't have worked with some web servers.

Using HTTP for web services implementations is therefore easier than other network protocols would have been. This is especially true because web services implementations can piggyback on existing web servers — in other words, use their HTTP implementation. This means you don't have to worry about the HTTP implementation at all.

Request/Response

Typically, when a client makes an RPC call, it needs to receive some kind of response. For example, if you make a call to the getChannels() method, then you need to get a list of channels back, or it wouldn't be a very useful procedure to call. In other instances, such as submitting a new entry to a topic, you may not need data returned from the RPC call, but you may still need confirmation that the procedure executed successfully. For example, an order to a back-end database may not require data to be returned, but you should know whether the submission failed or succeeded.

HTTP's request/response paradigm lends itself easily to this type of situation. For your "add entry" remote procedure, you must do the following:

1. Open a connection to the server providing the XML-RPC service.

2. Send the information on the entry to be added.

3. Process the addition.

4. Get back the result, including an error code if it didn't work, or a ping identifier if it did.

5. Close the connection.

In some cases, such as in the SOAP specification, messages are one-way instead of two-way. This means two separate messages must be sent: one from the client to the server with, say, numbers to add, and one from the server back to the client with the result of the calculation. In most cases, however, when a specification requires the use of two one-way messages, it also specifies that when a request/response protocol, such as HTTP, is used, these two messages can be combined in the request/response of the protocol.

Firewall-Ready

Most companies protect themselves from outside hackers by placing a *firewall* between their internal systems and the external Internet. Firewalls are designed to protect a network by blocking certain types of network traffic. Most firewalls allow HTTP traffic (the type of network traffic that would be generated by browsing the Web) but disallow other types of traffic.

These firewalls protect the company's data, but they make it more difficult to provide web-based services to the outside world. For example, consider a company selling goods over the Web. This web-based service would need certain information, such as which items are available in stock, which it would have to get from the company's internal systems. In order to provide this service, the company probably needs to create an environment such as the one shown in Figure 14-3.

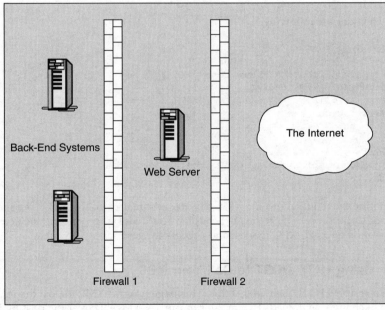

Figure 14-3

This is a very common configuration, in which the web server is placed between two firewalls. (This section, between the two firewalls, is often called a *demilitarized zone*, or *DMZ*.) Firewall 1 protects the company's internal systems and must be carefully configured to allow the proper communication between the web server and the internal systems, without letting any other traffic get through. Firewall 2 is configured to let traffic through between the web server and the Internet, but no other traffic.

This arrangement protects the company's internal systems, but because of the complexity added by these firewalls — especially for the communication between the web server and the back-end servers — it makes it a bit more difficult for the developers creating this web-based service. However, because firewalls are configured to let HTTP traffic go through, it's much easier to provide the necessary functionality if all of the communication between the web server and the other servers uses this protocol.

Security

Because there is already an existing security model for HTTP, the *Secure Sockets Layer (SSL)*, it is very easy to make transactions over HTTP secure. SSL encrypts traffic as it passes over the Web to protect it from prying eyes, so it's perfect for web transactions, such as credit card orders. In fact, SSL is so common that there are even hardware accelerators available to speed up SSL transactions.

Using HTTP for XML-RPC

Using HTTP for XML-RPC messages is very easy. You only need to do two things with the client:

❑   For the HTTP method, use POST.

❑   For the body of the message, include an XML document comprising the XML-RPC request.

For example, consider the following:

```
POST /RPC2 HTTP/1.1
Accept: */* Accept-Language: en-us
Content-Type: application/x-www-form-urlencoded
Accept-Encoding: gzip, deflate
User-Agent: Mozilla/4.0 (compatible; MSIE 5.5; Windows NT 5.0)
Host: www.wiley.com
Content-Length: 79

<methodCall>
    <methodName>topicExchange.getChannels</methodName>
</methodCall>
```

The headers define the request, and the XML-RPC request makes up the body. The server knows how to retrieve that body and process it. In the next chapter, you'll look at processing the actual request, but for now you'll just send an XML-RPC request and process the response.

Try It Out   Using HTTP POST to Call Your RPC

You can write a simple HTML page to test this. This page uses MSXML to post the information to the Internet Topic Exchange, so it needs IE 5 or later to run. (Next we'll cover the posting in other browsers.)

1.   Enter the following code (PostTester-IE.html in the code download). Note that the important code, the JavaScript, is highlighted in the following:

```
<html><head><title>POST Tester - IE</title>
  <script language="JavaScript">

  var xhHTTP;

  function doPost()
```

```
..{
    var xdDoc, sXML;

    sXML = "<methodCall>"
        + "<methodName>topicExchange.ping</methodName>"
        + "<params><param><value><string>test</string></value></param>"
        + "<param><value><struct>"
        + "<member><name>blog_name</name>"
        + "<value><string>" + pingForm.blog_name.value +
                            "</string></value></member>"
        + "<member><name>title</name>"
        + "<value><string>" + pingForm.title.value + "</string></value></member>"
        + "<member><name>url</name>"
        + "<value><string>" + pingForm.url.value + "</string></value></member>"
        + "<member><name>excerpt</name>"
        + "<value><string>" + pingForm.excerpt.value +
                            "</string></value></member>"
        + "</struct></value>"
        + "</param></params>"
        + "</methodCall>";
    xdDoc = new ActiveXObject("MSXML2.DOMDocument.3.0");
    xdDoc.async = false;
    xdDoc.loadXML(sXML);
    xhHTTP = new ActiveXObject("MSXML2.XMLHTTP.3.0");
    xhHTTP.onreadystatechange = handleReadyStateChange;
    xhHTTP.open("POST", "http://topicexchange.com/RPC2", true);
    xhHTTP.send(xdDoc);
}

function handleReadyStateChange()
{
    if (xhHTTP.readyState == 4)
    {
        var xdDoc = xhHTTP.responseXML;
        xdDoc.setProperty("SelectionLanguage", "XPath");
        var oErrorNode = xdDoc.selectSingleNode("//member[name='flError']/value");
        if(oErrorNode && oErrorNode.text == "1")
        {
            var oMessageNode = xdDoc.selectSingleNode("//member[name='message']/value")
            var msg = "Error:\n" + oMessageNode.text;
        }
        else
        {
            var oPingNode = xdDoc.selectSingleNode("//member[name='pingid']/value");
            var oTopicNode = xdDoc.selectSingleNode("//member[name='topicUrl']/value");
            var msg = "Success! Ping "
                    + oPingNode.text
                    + " successfully added to URL "
                    + oTopicNode.text;
        }
        alert(msg);
    }
}

</script>
```

```
    </head>
<body>
  <form name="pingForm" id="pingForm">
  <table width="100%">
    <tr><td>Blog name:</td>
        <td><input id="blog_name" name="blog_name" size="45"></td></tr>
    <tr><td>Post title:</td>
        <td><input id="title" name="title" size="45" ></td></tr>
    <tr><td>Post url:</td>
        <td><input id="url" name="url" size="45"></td></tr>
    <tr><td>Post excerpt:</td>
        <td><textarea rows="6" cols="34" id="excerpt"
             name="excerpt"></textarea></td></tr>
  </table>
  <input type="button" value="Send The Ping" id="btnPost" name="btnPost"
          onclick="doPost()">
  </form>
</body>
</html>
```

2. Save this as `posttester.html` and then open it in IE. Fill in the textboxes with sample information — the actual text doesn't matter, as this is a "test" channel — and click the Send the Ping button to perform the POST and get the results. Figure 14-4 shows a successful result.

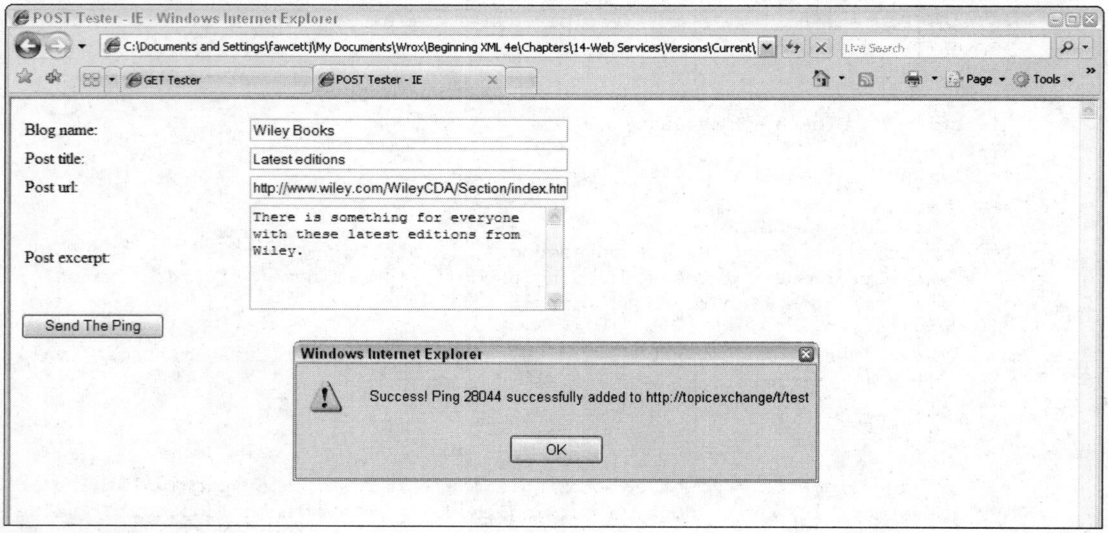

Figure 14-4

If you try sending a ping that already exists, you get the error message shown in Figure 14-5.

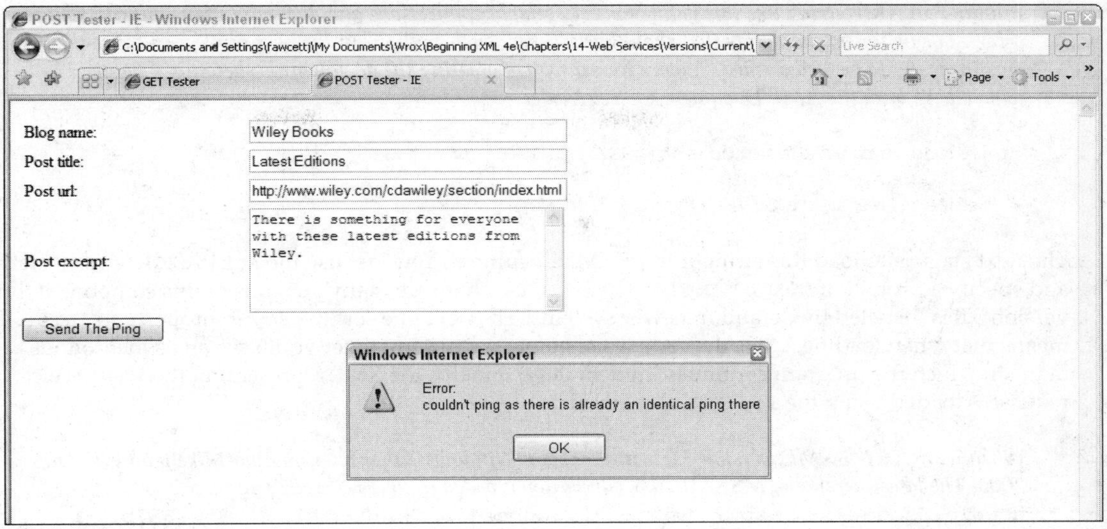

Figure 14-5

How It Works

A standard HTML form is used to provide the three textboxes and the text area needed for the post details. The variable xhHTTP is declared outside of the two functions so it is in scope and accessible to both of them. Instead of actually posting the data using a Submit button, a standard button calls the doPost() function:

```
function doPost()
..{
    var xdDoc, sXML;

    sXML = "<methodCall>"
        + "<methodName>topicExchange.ping</methodName>"
        + "<params><param><value><string>test</string></value></param>"
        + "<param><value><struct>"
        + "<member><name>blog_name</name>"
        + "<value><string>" + pingForm.blog_name.value +
"</string></value></member>"
        + "<member><name>title</name>"
        + "<value><string>" + pingForm.title.value + "</string></value></member>"
        + "<member><name>url</name>"
        + "<value><string>" + pingForm.url.value + "</string></value></member>"
        + "<member><name>excerpt</name>"
        + "<value><string>" + pingForm.excerpt.value +
"</string></value></member>"
        + "</struct></value>"
        + "</param></params>"
        + "</methodCall>";
```

The first part of the function builds a string in the required XML format and inserts the four values from the HTML form: the blog name, title, URL, and excerpt.

Building an XML string like this is fine for very simple applications and demonstrations but can lead to errors. For instance, characters that should be escaped, such as the & in the user input, can cause the document not to be well formed. A more robust way of creating the document is shown in Chapter 11, which deals with the XML Document Object Model.

```
xdDoc = new ActiveXObject("MSXML2.DOMDocument.3.0");
xdDoc.async = false;
xdDoc.loadXML(sXML);
```

The next stage is to load this string into an XML document. You first use the `ActiveXObject()` method and specify a prog id of `MSXML2.DOMDocument.3.0`. There are many versions of this component, but version 3.0 is installed by default in newer systems. The next line sets the `async` property to `false`. This means that when loading XML, the code waits before continuing (later you'll see an asynchronous call made in which the program continues immediately). Finally, the XML representing the Web service request is loaded using the `loadXML()` method.

When using IE MSXML, version 3.0 is available on Windows XP or later and most likely on Windows 2000. The latest version of MSXML, 6.0, can be downloaded from www.microsoft.com/ downloads/details.aspx?familyid=993c0bcf-3bcf-4009-be21-27e85e1857b1.

```
xhHTTP = new ActiveXObject("MSXML2.XMLHTTP.3.0");
xhHTTP.onreadystatechange = handleReadyStateChange;
xhHTTP.open("POST", "http://topicexchange.com/RPC2", true);
xhHTTP.send(xdDoc);
```

After the document is loaded, a second ActiveX object is created. The `MSXML2.XMLHTTP` class is named confusingly, for it is capable of making requests using any format, not just XML. Again, version 3.0 represents a compromise between performance and what is generally available.

The `onreadystatechange` property dictates what should happen when the state of the request changes. There are five stages in all, beginning with 0, uninitialized, and finishing with 4, completed; stage 4 is the stage that we are interested in. The property accepts a function pointer, the name of the function without any quote marks or parentheses.

The HTTP request is then initialized using the `open()` method. This takes three parameters: the method, usually GET or POST, the actual URL, and whether to perform an asynchronous request. In this case, the last option has been set to `true`. There are many advantages in making requests asynchronously, one being that the user can perform other tasks while the request completes. This capability forms the mainstay of Ajax programming (see Chapter 16 for more on Ajax).

After the `open()` method, the XML data is posted to the server using the `send()` method. Control now returns to the user until the `handleReadyState()` function is called:

```
function handleReadyStateChange()
{
  if (xhHTTP.readyState == 4)
  {
    var xdDoc = xhHTTP.responseXML;
    xdDoc.setProperty("SelectionLanguage", "XPath");
```

As mentioned earlier, the `handleReadyStateChanged()` function is called whenever the status of xhHTTP alters. You are only concerned when the response has been completed, as shown by a `readyState` equal to 4. When this happens, the XML document returned is stored in `xdDoc`. Then the `setProperty()` method is used to instruct `xdDoc` to use XPath as a selection language. (This step is necessary because when Microsoft originally released these libraries, XPath was not fully finished and XSLPattern, a similar but now obsolete syntax, was used instead for searches and selections.)

```
var oErrorNode = xdDoc.selectSingleNode("//member[name='flError']/value");
if(oErrorNode && oErrorNode.text == "1")
{
   var oMessageNode = xdDoc.selectSingleNode("//member[name='message']/value")
   var msg = "Error:\n" + oMessageNode.text;
}
```

The `selectSingleNode()` method first looks for a `<member>` element that has a child named `<name>`. If this has the value `flError`, then the `<value>` child is stored in `oErrorNode`. If this node's `text` value is one, then an error has occurred and a similar XPath is used to retrieve the actual error message:

```
      else
      {
         var oPingNode = xdDoc.selectSingleNode("//member[name='pingid']/value");
         var oTopicNode = xdDoc.selectSingleNode("//member[name='topicUrl']/value");
         var msg = "Success! Ping "
                 + oPingNode.text
                 + " successfully added to URL "
                 + oTopicNode.text;
      }
   alert(msg);
   }
}
```

If no error has occurred, then two nodes are selected providing the ID of the new post and the topic URL, which should match what was sent in the request. Finally, the error or success message is presented to the user. The information is posted to the server in a format similar to this:

```
POST /RPC2 HTTP/1.1
Accept:*/*
Accept-Language: en-us
Content-Type: application/x-www-form-urlencoded
Accept-Encoding: gzip, deflate
User-Agent: Mozilla/4.0 (compatible; MSIE 7.0; Win32)
Host: www.wiley.com
Content-Length: 591

<methodCall><methodName>topicExchange.ping</methodName><params><param><value>
<string>test</string></value></param><param><value><struct><member>
<name>blog_name</name><value><string>Wiley Books</string></value>
</member><member><name>title</name><value><string>Latest Editions</string>
</value></member><member><name>url</name><value><string>
 http://www.wiley.com/CDASection/index.html
</string></value></member><member><name>excerpt</name>
<value><string>  There is something for everyone with these latest editions from
Wiley.</string></value>
</member></struct></value></param></params></methodCall>
```

Meanwhile, the information is returned in a format like this:

```
HTTP/1.1 200 OK
Server: Microsoft-IIS/5.0
Date: Fri, 06 Jul 2001 17:48:34 GMT
Content-Length: 48
Content-Type: text/xml

<methodResponse>
  <params>
    <param>
      <value>
        <struct>
          <member>
            <name>topicUrl</name>
            <value><string>http://topicexchange.com/t/test/</string></value>
          </member>
          <member>
            <name>flError</name>
            <value><boolean>0</boolean></value>
          </member>
          <member>
            <name>editkey</name>
            <value><string>cqvq9v20805830945mv0a9w4850239185932850</string>
            </value>
          </member>
          <member>
            <name>errorCode</name>
            <value><int>0</int></value>
          </member>
          <member>
            <name>pingid</name>
            <value><string>28044</string></value>
          </member>
          <member>
            <name>message</name>
            <value><string>New ping added.</string></value>
          </member>
          <member>
            <name>topicName</name>
            <value><string>test</string></value>
          </member>
        </struct>
      </value>
    </param>
  </params>
</methodResponse>
```

So far we have created a system in which messages are passed back and forth, via HTTP POST, in which all of the data is encoded in XML. This is very handy, but only a very small part of the overall picture.

Posting with Firefox and Netscape

The preceding example works only with Internet Explorer on Windows. For browsers based on the Gecko engine, such as Firefox and Netscape, a different approach is needed. With these browsers, the ability to make an HTTP request is implemented within the browser, rather than as an external ActiveX component. To create the HttpRequest, use the following:

```
var xhHTTP = new XmlHttpRequest();
```

This has similar methods to the Microsoft class such as `open()` and `send()`. As it would be tedious to create two versions of code each time you wanted to develop a page using this functionality, a common approach is to abstract the interface by using a JavaScript library that automatically chooses which component to use. The library also adds a few methods to the XmlHttpRequest to make it similar to the Microsoft version.

> *One of the most popular cross-browser libraries was written by Nicholas C. Zakas, author of* Professional Ajax *(Wrox, 2006). The library is included in the code download for this book, but it can also be found, along with a number of other useful tools, at the author's website,* www.nczonline.net. *There are two versions: zxml.js for incorporation into your web page (compressed for speedy download), and zxml.src.js, which has the equivalent code but formatted and commented for instructive purposes.*

The basis of this library and many others is that the type of browser is detected and the appropriate object returned.

Try It Out   Posting with Firefox and Netscape

One of the chores handled by the library is getting the correct version of the XMLHttpRequest: the ActiveX one in IE versions earlier than 7.0 or the built-in object for Firefox and Netscape and IE 7.0. The basic code is shown here:

```
var zXml /*:Object*/ = {
    useActiveX: (typeof ActiveXObject != "undefined"),
    useDom: document.implementation && document.implementation.createDocument,
    useXmlHttp: (typeof XMLHttpRequest != "undefined")
};

zXml.ARR_XMLHTTP_VERS /*:Array*/ = ["MSXML2.XmlHttp.6.0","MSXML2.XmlHttp.3.0"];

zXml.ARR_DOM_VERS /*:Array*/ = ["MSXML2.DOMDocument.6.0","MSXML2.DOMDocument.3.0"];

/**
 * Static class for handling XMLHttp creation.
 * @class
 */
function zXmlHttp() {
}

/**
 * Creates an XMLHttp object.
 * @return An XMLHttp object.
 */
```

```
zXmlHttp.createRequest = function ()/*:XMLHttp*/ {

    //if it natively supports XMLHttpRequest object
    if (zXml.useXmlHttp) {
        return new XMLHttpRequest();
    } else if (zXml.useActiveX) { //IE < 7.0 = use ActiveX

        if (!zXml.XMLHTTP_VER) {
            for (var i=0; i < zXml.ARR_XMLHTTP_VERS.length; i++) {
                try {
                    new ActiveXObject(zXml.ARR_XMLHTTP_VERS[i]);
                    zXml.XMLHTTP_VER = zXml.ARR_XMLHTTP_VERS[i];
                    break;
                } catch (oError) {
                }
            }
        }

        if (zXml.XMLHTTP_VER) {
            return new ActiveXObject(zXml.XMLHTTP_VER);
        } else {
            throw new Error("Could not create XML HTTP Request.");
        }
    } else {
        throw new Error("Your browser doesn't support an XML HTTP Request.");
    }
};
```

The first step is determining whether to set the Microsoft `XmlHttp` class or the `XmlHttpRequest` built-in object:

```
var zXml /*:Object*/ = {
    useActiveX: (typeof ActiveXObject != "undefined"),
    useDom: document.implementation && document.implementation.createDocument,
    useXmlHttp: (typeof XMLHttpRequest != "undefined")
};
```

A variable named `zXml` is declared and three properties are added specifying whether to use ActiveX, the built-in DOM, and the built-in XmlHttpRequest.

There are many versions of the Microsoft XML-related classes, but the main choice is between version 6 and version 3, so the next step is to declare an array listing them:

```
zXml.ARR_XMLHTTP_VERS = ["MSXML2.XmlHttp.6.0", "MSXML2.XmlHttp.3.0"];
```

Later the code can loop through the array items and initialize the latest version available:

```
zXmlHttp.createRequest = function ()
{
    if (zXml.useXmlHttp) {
        return new XMLHttpRequest();
    }
```

The first part of the function simply returns the XmlHttpRequest object if it's available.

```
else if (zXml.useActiveX) {

        if (!zXml.XMLHTTP_VER) {
            for (var i=0; i < zXml.ARR_XMLHTTP_VERS.length; i++) {
                try {
                    new ActiveXObject(zXml.ARR_XMLHTTP_VERS[i]);
                    zXml.XMLHTTP_VER = zXml.ARR_XMLHTTP_VERS[i];
                    break;
                } catch (oError) {
                }
            }
        }
    }
```

The next part runs when a Microsoft browser is being used. If the code has run previously, then the latest version available is stored in zXml.XMLHTTP_VER. Otherwise, the code loops through the versions starting with the latest and if no error occurs, it returns a valid instance and stores the version used in zXml .XMLHTTP_VER. The rest of the function merely throws an error if no XML request can be created, either because the browser is too old or because the user's security settings forbid ActiveX.

The following code is the cross-browser version of PostTester-IE.html, PostTester-CrossBrowser .html. The <body> of the HTML is the same, only the script is different. Note the inclusion of the zXml.js library:

```
<script type="text/javascript" src="zXML.src.js"></script>
  <script type="text/javascript">

  var xhHTTP;

  function doPost()
  {
    var xdDoc, sXML;

    sXML = "<methodCall>"
        + "<methodName>topicExchange.ping</methodName>"
        + "<params><param><value><string>test</string></value></param>"
        + "<param><value><struct>"
        + "<member><name>blog_name</name>"
        + "<value><string>" + pingForm.blog_name.value +
"</string></value></member>"
        + "<member><name>title</name>"
        + "<value><string>" + pingForm.title.value + "</string></value></member>"
        + "<member><name>url</name>"
        + "<value><string>" + pingForm.url.value + "</string></value></member>"
        + "<member><name>excerpt</name>"
        + "<value><string>" + pingForm.excerpt.value +
"</string></value></member>"
        + "</struct></value>"
        + "</param></params>"
        + "</methodCall>";
    if (zXml.useXmlHttp && !zXml.useActiveX)
    {
      try
      {
```

```
          netscape.security.PrivilegeManager.enablePrivilege("UniversalBrowserRead");
        }
      catch (e)
      {
        alert("Permission UniversalBrowserRead denied.");
      }
    }
  xdDoc = zXmlDom.createDocument();
  xdDoc.loadXML(sXML);
  xhHTTP = zXmlHttp.createRequest();
  xhHTTP.onreadystatechange = handleReadyStateChange;
  xhHTTP.open("POST", "http://topicexchange.com/RPC2", true);
  xhHTTP.send(xdDoc);
}

function handleReadyStateChange()
{
  if (xhHTTP.readyState == 4)
  {
    if (zXml.useXmlHttp && !zXml.useActiveX)
    {
      try
      {
    netscape.security.PrivilegeManager.enablePrivilege("UniversalBrowserRead");
      }
      catch (e)
      {
        alert("Permission UniversalBrowserRead denied.");
      }
    }
    var xdDoc = xhHTTP.responseXML;
    var oErrorNode = zXPath.selectSingleNode(xdDoc.documentElement,
                        "//member[name='flError']/value");
    if (oErrorNode && oErrorNode.text == 1)
    {
      var oMessageNode = zXPath.selectSingleNode(xdDoc.documentElement,
                          "//member[name='message']/value")
      var msg = "Error:\n" + oMessageNode.text;
    }
    else
    {
      var oPingNode = zXPath.selectSingleNode(xdDoc.documentElement,
                        "//member[name='pingid']/value");
      var oTopicNode = zXPath.selectSingleNode(xdDoc.documentElement,
                        "//member[name='topicUrl']/value");
      var msg = "Success! Ping "
              + oPingNode.text
              + " successfully added to URL "
              + oTopicNode.text
    }
    alert(msg);
  }
}

</script>
```

How It Works

There are two main points of interest here. First is the use of `zXml`, `zXmlHttp`, and `zXPath` for creating the XML document and XML request, and for extracting information from the response. These are all designed to work with different browsers, and by ascertaining the browser type they can carry out their allotted task using the appropriate classes and methods.

Second is this piece of code:

```
if (zXml.useXmlHttp)
{
  try
  {
  netscape.security.PrivilegeManager.enablePrivilege("UniversalBrowserRead");
  }
  catch (e)
  {
    alert("Permission UniversalBrowserRead denied.");
  }
}
```

Although the Internet Explorer version of `PostTester-IE.html` can be opened from a local drive and run, the Mozilla version can't. The security restriction known as *cross-domain posting* forbids it. It also causes Internet Explorer to fail if run from a web server. Cross-domain posting means that the web service you are attempting to use resides on a domain other than the page from which the request is made.

Because this could be used by a maliciously designed page to send data nefariously to a third party, cross-domain posting is blocked by default. To allow it, the user must elevate the browser's permissions level. The preceding code produces a dialog box similar to the one shown in Figure 14-6.

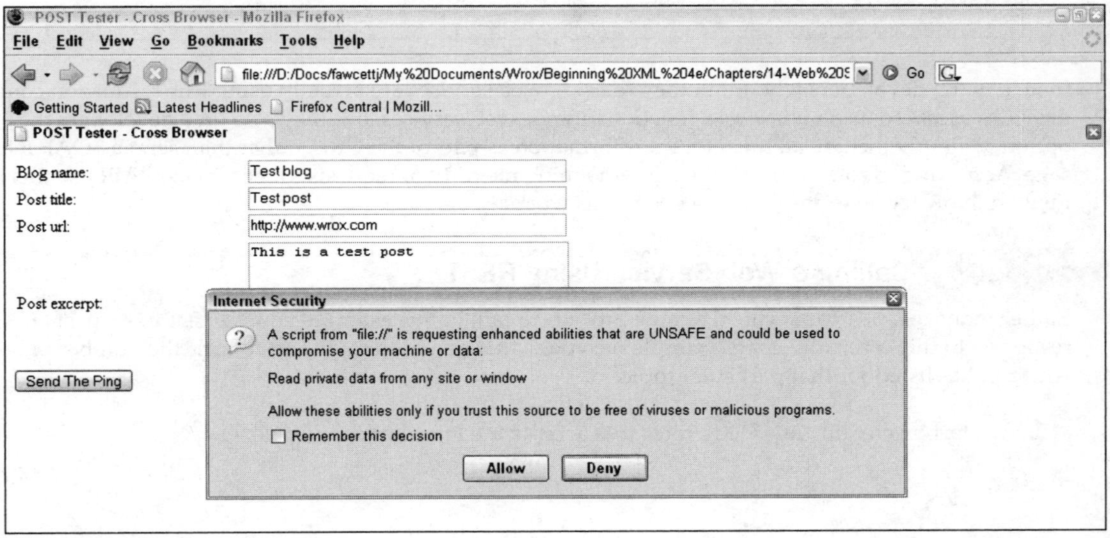

Figure 14-6

The user can choose to allow, forbid, or always allow the site the capability to cross-domain post. Obviously, this situation is not ideal. Chapter 16, which deals with Ajax, presents a better technique known as a *server-side proxy*, which circumvents this problem without inconveniencing the user.

Taking a REST

So far we've been working exclusively with the POST method. This section describes using web services with the GET method. In fact, it covers a web service that in some circles is not considered a web service at all. It was mentioned earlier in this chapter that technically, a "web service" is any information requested over the Web. For example, back in 1996, I built a Java applet that retrieved a calculation from a remote URL. At the time, there was no XML involved. The numbers involved in the calculation were simply included as part of the URL, and the response consisted of the result of the calculation.

That, in a nutshell, is REST. Short for *REpresentational State Transfer*, REST is not a specification, but rather an architecture, which asserts that all resources should be directly addressable by an URL. For example, the XML-RPC implementation would not be RESTful because you use a single URL for both the getChannels() and ping() methods; you can't tell the difference between requests just by the URL.

On the other hand, if you were to request an XML document from Amazon.com using the following URL, that would be an example of REST, because all of the necessary information is part of the URL:

```
http://xml.amazon.com/onca/xml3?t=thevanguardsc-20&dev-t=xxxxxxxxxxxxxx&Key
wordSearch=web+services&mode=books&type=lite&page=1&f=xml
```

> The xxxxxxxxxxxxxx in the preceding URL must be replaced with a valid user key, which can be obtained from https://aws-portal.amazon.com/gp/aws/developer/registration/index.html.

In fact, many developers who think they're using web services are actually using REST. Amazon.com provides access to its database and functionality via web services, but they also give developers the option to simply include all the relevant information as part of the URL, rather than send a SOAP message. According to some reports, the overwhelming majority of requests to the Amazon API use this method. Now try an example and see how this works.

Try It Out   Calling a Web Service Using REST

Rather than use POST to execute a remote procedure call, in this example you use GET to request an XML response. In this case, you create a simple web page that accepts a topic and returns the number of books Amazon has listed for that particular topic.

1. Start by creating an HTML form that accepts the information:

```
<html>
  <head>
      <title>GET Tester</title>
  </head>
  <body>
```

```
      <form name="searchForm" id="searchForm">
        <p>
          What topic would you like to research? <br />
          <input id="keyword" name="keyword" size="45">
        </p>
        <input type="button" value="Send The Request">
      </form>
    </body>
</html>
```

2. Add the JavaScript that adds the cross-browser library, takes the form information, and constructs a URL:

```
<html>
  <head>
      <title>GET Tester</title>

      <script type="text/javascript" src="zXML.js"></script>

      <script type="text/javascript">
      var keyword, xhHTTP;
      function doGet()
      {
          keyword = searchForm.keyword.value;
          sRequest = "http://xml.amazon.com/onca/xml3?t=webservices-20"
                  + "&dev-t=<Amazon key goes here>&KeywordSearch="
                  + keyword
                  + "&mode=books&type=lite&page=1&f=xml";  </head>
  <body>
    <form name="searchForm" id="searchForm">
      <p>
        What topic would you like to research? <br />
        <input id="keyword" name="keyword" size="45">
      </p>
      <input type="button" value="Send The Request" onclick="doGet()">
    </form>
  </body>
</html>
```

3. Send the request using the GET method and handle the result as shown in the earlier example in `PosterTester-CrossBrowser.html`. Again, Mozilla browsers need to be granted extra permissions for this script to work:

```
<html>
  <head>
      <title>GET Tester</title>
  <script language="JavaScript">
function doGet()
{
    var xdDoc, xhHTTP, sXML

    var keyword = searchForm.keyword.value;
    sRequest = "http://xml.amazon.com/onca/xml3?t=webservices-20"+
                "&dev-t=xxxxxxxxxxxxxxxxx&KeywordSearch="+keyword+
```

```
                         "&mode=books&type=lite&page=1&f=xml";

        if (zXml.useXmlHttp)
        {
          try
          {
            netscape.security.PrivilegeManager.enablePrivilege
                          ("UniversalBrowserRead");
          }
          catch (e)
          {
            alert("Permission UniversalBrowserRead denied.");
          }
        }
        xhHTTP = zXmlHttp.createRequest();
        xhHTTP.onreadystatechange = handleReadyStateChange;
        xhHTTP.open("GET", sRequest, true);
        xhHTTP.send(null);

    function handleReadyStateChange()
    {
      if (xhHTTP.readyState == 4)
      {
          if (zXml.useXmlHttp)
          {
            try
            {
              netscape.security.PrivilegeManager.enablePrivilege
                          ("UniversalBrowserRead");
            }
            catch (e)
            {
              alert("Permission UniversalBrowserRead denied.");
            }
          }
          var xdDoc = xhHTTP.responseXML;
          alert(xhHTTP.responseText);
          var oResultsNode = zXPath.selectSingleNode
                    (xdDoc.documentElement, "/ProductInfo/TotalResults");
          var iResults = oResultsNode.text;
          alert("Amazon lists " + iResults + " books on " + keyword + ".");
      }
    }}
    </script>
    </head>
    <body>
      <form name="searchForm" id="searchForm">
        <p>
          What topic would you like to research? <br />
          <input id="keyword" name="keyword" size="45">
        </p>
        <input type="button" value="Send The Request" onclick="doGet()">
      </form>
    </body>
</html>
```

4. Enter a topic and click the Send The Request button to see the results, shown in Figure 14-7.

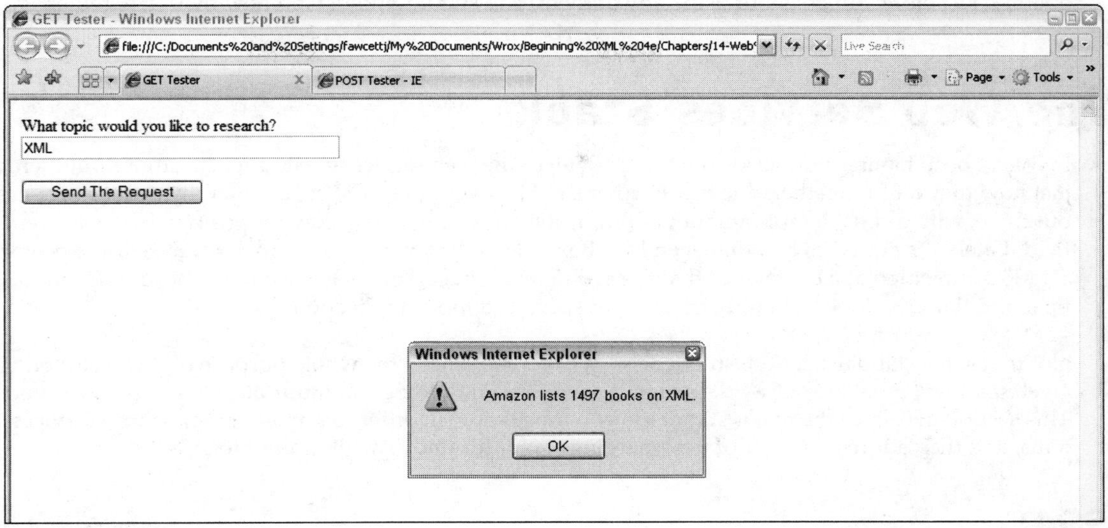

Figure 14-7

How It Works

Whereas in the first Try It Out you created an XML document to send to the remote web service, all you do here is construct the URL correctly. The URL consists of seven name/value pairs, such as `type=lite`, each separated by an ampersand (`&`). For example, the mode of the search is books. The browser actually pulls the keyword information from the web form and uses it to construct the URL.

In fact, you could construct virtually any request this way. For example, you might have posted to the TopicExchange without creating an XML-RPC message just by calling the URL:

```
http://topicexchange.com/t/books/?blog_name=Wiley+Books &title=Latest+Editions
&url=http://www.wiley.com/WileyCDA/section/index.html&excerpt=Our+latest+editions...
```

You don't do that, however, because it goes against the way the Web was designed. GET requests are only to be used for requests that have no "side effects." Otherwise, you're supposed to use POST. In other words, you can request the number of books Amazon carries using GET, but if you're going to actually place an order, use POST.

Once you've constructed the URL, you can send it to the server. This process is much the same as a POST request, but no body is sent with the request. The response is a pure XML document — to see it, add the command `alert(xdDoc.text)` to the script — from which you can pull a particular node or nodes.

So is REST a form of web services? Many (including those who first espoused REST) would disagree with me, but I say yes. True, you're not sending an XML request, but most of the time you are getting an XML response.

The moral of the story? Be careful when you say "web services." There are plenty of specifications to go around; make sure you know which one you're talking about. In fact, web-services-related standards abound, so before you go about using any of them, you should understand how they fit together.

The Web Services Stack

If you've been having trouble keeping track of all of the web services-related specifications out there and just how they all fit together, don't feel bad, it's not just you. In fact, there are literally dozens of specs out there, with a considerable amount of duplication as companies jockey for position in this nascent field. Lately it's gotten so bad that even Don Box, one of the creators of the major web services protocol, SOAP, commented at a conference that the proliferation in standards has led to a "cacophony" in the field and that developers should writer fewer specs and more applications.

Not that some standardization isn't necessary, of course. That's the whole purpose of the evolution of "web services" as an area of work — to find a way to standardize communications between systems. This section discusses the major standards you must know in order to implement most web services systems, and then addresses some of the emerging standards and how they all fit together.

SOAP

If you learn only one web-services-related protocol, *SOAP* is probably your best bet. Originally conceived as the Simple Object Access Protocol, SOAP has now been adapted for so many different uses that its acronym is no longer applicable.

SOAP is an XML-based language that provides a way for two different systems to exchange information relating to a remote procedure call or other operation. SOAP messages consist of a `Header`, which contains information about the request, and a `Body`, which contains the request itself. Both the `Header` and `Body` are contained within an `Envelope`.

SOAP calls are more robust than, say, XML-RPC calls, because you can use arbitrary XML. This enables you to structure the call in a way that's best for your application. For example, if your application ultimately needs an XML node such as

```
<totals>
  <dept id="2332">
    <gross>433229.03</gross>
    <net>23272.39</net>
  </dept>
  <dept id="4001">
    <gross>993882.98</gross>
    <net>388209.27</net>
  </dept>
</totals>
```

then rather than try to squeeze your data into an arbitrary format such as XML-RPC, you can create a SOAP message such as the following:

```
<?xml version="1.0" encoding="UTF-8"?>
<SOAP:Envelope xmlns:SOAP="http://www.w3.org/2003/05/soap-envelope">

  <SOAP:Header></SOAP:Header>
  <SOAP:Body>

    <totals xmlns="http://www.wiley.com/SOAP/accounting">
      <dept id="2332">
        <gross>433229.03</gross>
        <net>23272.39</net>
      </dept>
      <dept id="4001">
        <gross>993882.98</gross>
        <net>388209.27</net>
      </dept>
    </totals>

  </SOAP:Body>
</SOAP:Envelope>
```

SOAP also has the capability to take advantage of technologies such as XML-Signature for security. You can also use attachments with SOAP, so a request could conceivably return, say, a document or other information. In the next chapter, you'll create a complete SOAP server and client, and look at the syntax of a SOAP message.

Of course, this suggests another problem: How do you know what a SOAP request should look like, and what it will return as a result? As you'll see next, WSDL solves that problem.

WSDL

The *Web Services Description Language (WSDL)* is an XML-based language that provides a contract between a web service and the outside world. To understand this better, let's go back to our discussion of COM and CORBA. The reason why COM and CORBA objects can be so readily shared is that they have defined contracts with the outside world. This contract defines the methods an object provides, as well as the parameters to those methods and their return values. Interfaces for both COM and CORBA are written in variants of the *Interface Definition Language (IDL)*. Code can then be written to look at an object's interface to determine what functions are provided. In practice, this dynamic investigation of an object's interface often happens at design time, as a programmer is writing the code that calls another object. A programmer would find out what interface an object supports and then write code that properly calls that interface.

Web services have a similar contract with the outside world, except that the contract is written in WSDL instead of IDL. This WSDL document outlines what messages the SOAP server expects in order to provide services, as well as what messages it returns. Again, in practice, WSDL is likely used at design time. A programmer would use WSDL to figure out what procedures are available from the SOAP server and what format of XML is expected by that procedure, and then write the code to call it.

To take things a step further, programmers might never have to look at WSDL directly or even deal with the underlying SOAP protocol. Already available are several SOAP toolkits that can hide the complexities of SOAP. If you point one of these toolkits at a WSDL document, it can automatically generate code to make the SOAP call for you! At that point, working with SOAP is as easy as calling any other local

object on your machine. You can find many toolkits for developing SOAP applications at `www-128.ibm`
`.com/developerworks/views/webservices/downloads.jsp`. The next chapter looks at the syntax
for a WSDL document. After you've built it, how do you let others know that it's out there? Enter UDDI.

UDDI

The *Universal Discovery, Description, and Integration (UDDI)* protocol enables web services to be registered
so that they can be discovered by programmers and other web services. For example, if you're going to
create a web service that serves a particular function, such as providing up-to-the-minute traffic reports
by GPS coordinates, you can register that service with a UDDI registry. The global UDDI registry system
consists of several different servers that all mirror each other, so by registering your company with one,
you add it to all the others.

The advantage of registering with the UDDI registry is twofold. First, your company's contact information is available, so when another company wants to do business with you, it can use the *white pages*
type of lookup to get the necessary contact information. A company's listing not only includes the usual
name, phone number, and address type of information, but also information on the services available.
For example, it might include a link to a WSDL file describing the traffic reporting system.

The UDDI registry system also enables companies to find each other based on the types of web services
they offer. This is called a *green pages* type of listing. For example, you could use the green pages to find a
company that uses web services to take orders for widgets. Listings would also include information on
what the widget order request should look like and the structure of the order confirmation, or, at the
very least, a link to that information.

Many of the SOAP toolkits available, such as IBM's Web Services Toolkit, provide tools to work with
UDDI. UDDI seems to be another of those *seemed like a good idea at the time* specifications. Most real-
world developers naturally prefer to build their applications knowing that the web services they will
consume are available, and are unwilling to risk having to discover them dynamically. This is one of the
reasons why UDDI has never really taken off.

Surrounding Specifications

So far we've described a landscape in which you can use a UDDI registry to discover a web service for
which a WSDL file describes the SOAP messages used by the service. For all practical purposes, you
could stop right there, because you have all of the pieces that are absolutely necessary, but as you start
building your applications, you will discover that other issues need to be addressed.

For example, just because a web service is built using such specifications as SOAP and WSDL doesn't
mean that your client is going to flawlessly interact with it. Interoperability continues to be a challenge
between systems, from locating the appropriate resource to making sure types are correctly implemented. Numerous specifications have emerged in an attempt to choreograph the increasingly complex
dance between web service providers and consumers. Moreover, any activity that involves business
eventually needs security.

This section looks at some of the many specifications that have been working their way into the marketplace. Only time will tell which will survive and which will ultimately wither, but it helps to understand
what's out there and how it all fits together.

Interoperability

At the time of this writing, the big name in interoperability is the Web Services Interoperability Organization, or WS-I (www.ws-i.org). This industry group includes companies such as IBM, Microsoft, and Sun Microsystems, and the purpose of the organization is to define specific "profiles" for web services and provide testing tools so that companies can be certain that their implementations don't contain any hidden "gotchas." WS-I has released a Basic Profile as well as a number of use cases and sample implementations.

Some other interoperability-related specifications include the following:

❑ WS-Addressing (http://msdn.microsoft.com/ws/2003/03/ws-addressing/) provides a way to specify the "location" of a web service. Remember that we're not always talking about HTTP. WS-Addressing defines an XML document that indicates how to "find" a service, no matter how many firewalls, proxies, or other devices and gateways lie between you and that service.

❑ WS-Eventing (www.w3.org/Submission/WS-Eventing/) describes protocols that involve a publish/subscribe pattern, in which web services subscribe to or provide event notifications.

Details and descriptions of these and related services can also be found at http://msdn.microsoft .com/webservices/webservices/understanding/specs/default.aspx.

Coordination

For a while, it looked like the winner in coordination and choreography was going to be ebXML (www.ebxml.org), a web services version of Electronic Data Interchange (EDI), in which companies become "trading partners" and define their interactions individually. ebXML consists of a number of different modules specifying the ways in which businesses can define not only what information they're looking for and the form it should take, but the types of messages that should be sent from a multiple-step process. Although ebXML is very specific and seems to work well in the arena for which it was designed, it doesn't necessarily generalize well in order to cover web services outside the EDI realm.

As such, Business Process Execution Language for Web Services (BPEL4WS) (http://msdn2.microsoft .com/en-us/library/aa479359.aspx) has been proposed by a coalition of companies, including Microsoft and IBM. BPEL4WS defines a notation for specifying a business process ultimately implemented as web services. Business processes fall into two categories: *executable business processes* and *business protocols*. Executable business processes are actual actions performed in an interaction, whereas business protocols describe the effects (for example, orders placed) without specifying how they're actually accomplished. When BPEL4WS was introduced in 2002, it wasn't under the watchful eye of any standards body, which was a concern for many developers, so work is currently ongoing within the Web Services Business Process Execution Language (WS-BPEL) (www.oasis-open.org/committees/ tc_home.php?wg_abbrev=wsbpel) group at the OASIS standards body.

Not to be outdone, the World Wide Web Consortium has opened the WS-Choreography (www.w3.org/ 2002/ws/chor/) activity, which is developing a way for companies to describe their interactions with trading partners. In other words, they're not actually defining how data is exchanged, but rather the language to describe how data is exchanged. In fact, Choreography Definition Language is one of the group's deliverables.

In the meantime, Microsoft, IBM, and BEA are also proposing WS-Coordination (`www-106.ibm.com/developerworks/library/ws-coor/`), which is also intended to provide a way to describe these interactions. This specification involves the WS-AtomicTransaction specification for describing individual components of a transaction.

Security

Given its importance, perhaps it should come as no surprise that security is currently another hotly contested area. In addition to the basic specifications set out by the World Wide Web Consortium, such as XML Encryption (`www.w3.org/Encryption/2001/`) and XML Signature (`www.w3.org/Signature/`), the industry is currently working on standards for identity recognition, reliable messaging, and overall security policies.

Both the Liberty Alliance (`www.projectliberty.org`), which includes Sun Microsystems, and WS-Federation (Web Services Federation Language) (`www-106.ibm.com/developerworks/webservices/library/ws-fedworld/`), espoused by IBM and Microsoft, are trying to specify a means for creating a "federated identity." In other words, you should be able to sign on to one site with your username and password, smart card, fingerprint, or any other form of identification, and be recognized anywhere, even another site and another application.

Perhaps the most confusing competition is between WS Reliable Messaging (`www.oasis-open.org/committees/tc_home.php?wg_abbrev=wsrm`) and WS-ReliableMessaging (`www-106.ibm.com/developerworks/webservices/library/ws-rm/`). In essence, both specifications are trying to describe a protocol for reliably delivering messages between distributed applications within a particular tolerance, or Quality of Service. These specifications deal with message order, retransmission, and ensuring that both parties to a transaction are aware of whether a message has been successfully received.

Two other specifications to consider are WS-Security and WS-Policy:

❑ WS-Security (`www-106.ibm.com/developerworks/webservices/library/ws-secure/`) is designed to provide enhancements to SOAP that make it easier to control issues such as message integrity, message confidentiality, and authentication, no matter what security model or encryption method you use.

❑ WS-Policy (`www-106.ibm.com/developerworks/webservices/library/ws-polfram/`) is a specification meant to help people writing other specifications, and it provides a way to specify the "requirements, preferences, and capabilities" of a web service.

Summary

This chapter covered many aspects of web services, a group of XML-based protocols for performing remote procedure calls. You studied how web services can be used, and even put them into practice by creating an XML-RPC client using the Internet Explorer browser.

Because web services are based on easy-to-implement and standardized technologies such as XML and HTTP, they have the potential to become a universal tool. In fact, most of the hype surrounding web services concerns its interoperability. At least initially, companies providing web services software are concentrating on making their software as interoperable as possible with the software from other companies, instead of creating proprietary changes to the standards, but they're also creating a good number of new standards.

In general, web services are XML messages sent as the body of an HTTP POST request. The response is XML, which we can then analyze. We can also request a web services response via an HTTP GET request. For any level more complex than that, standards are still being shaken out.

The next chapter takes a deeper look at two of the most important web services specifications, SOAP and WSDL.

Exercise Questions

Suggested solutions to these questions can be found in Appendix A.

Question 1

Imagine you are trying to contact an XML-RPC-based web service to submit a classified ad for a lost dog. The required information includes your name, phone number, and the body of the ad. What might the XML request look like?

Question 2

You are trying to call a REST-based web service to check on the status of a service order. The service needs the following information:

```
cust_id: 3263827
order_id: THX1138
```

What might the request look like?

SOAP and WSDL

In the last chapter, you learned about web services and how they work toward enabling disparate systems to communicate. Of course, if everyone just chose their own formats in which to send messages back and forth, that wouldn't do much good in the interoperability area, so a standard format is a must. XML-RPC is good for remote procedure calls, but otherwise limited. SOAP overcomes that problem by enabling rich XML documents to be transferred easily between systems, even allowing for the possibility of attachments. Of course, this flexibility means that you need a way to describe your SOAP messages, and that's where Web Services Description Language (WSDL) comes in. WSDL provides a standard way to describe where and how to make requests to a SOAP-based service.

SOAP originally stood for Simple Object Access Protocol, but as most people found it anything but simple it is now officially a name rather than an acronym, so it doesn't stand for anything.

In this chapter you'll take it a step further by creating a simple web service using a method called REST (covered in the previous chapter). You'll expand your horizons by creating a SOAP service and accessing it via SOAP messages, describing it using WSDL so that other developers can make use of it if desired.

In this chapter you'll learn the following:

- ❑ Why SOAP can provide more flexibility than previous RPC protocols
- ❑ How to format SOAP messages
- ❑ When to use GET versus POST in an HTTP request
- ❑ What SOAP intermediaries are
- ❑ How to describe a service using WSDL
- ❑ The difference between SOAP styles

Laying the Groundwork

Any web services project requires planning, so before you jump into installing software and creating files, let's take a moment to look at what you're trying to accomplish. Ultimately, you want to send and receive SOAP messages, and describe them using WSDL. To do that, you need the following in place:

❑   **The client** — In the last chapter, you created an XML-RPC client in Internet Explorer. This chapter uses a lot of the same techniques to create a SOAP client.

❑   **The server** — You're going to create two kinds of SOAP services in this chapter, and they both use ASP.NET. Both use standard aspx pages, rather than .NET's specialized asmx page. There are two reasons for this. First, coding by hand ensures that you see how it works, and more important, you learn how to diagnose problems in real-life situations. Second, if you want to use these techniques in other languages, it's easier to port the code when it's not hidden by .NET's web service abstraction layer.

In order to run some of the examples in this chapter, you need Internet Information Services (IIS) version 5.0 or later with ASP.NET installed, or Visual Studio. The examples will work with Visual Studio Express Web Edition, which can be downloaded free from `http://msdn.microsoft.com/vstudio/express/`.

Running Examples in Windows 2003, XP, and 2000

The steps needed to install a web server on Windows depend on which operating system you're using. A version of IIS comes with Windows 2003, Windows XP Professional Edition, and Windows 2000. In most cases, it is installed by default, but if it's not, select Control Panel ⇨ Add/Remove Programs, and select Add/Remove Windows Components, under which you'll find the option to install Internet Information Services (IIS). Unfortunately, IIS doesn't come with Windows XP Home Edition, and neither IIS nor PWS can be installed on it.

You can also run the examples using the built-in web server that comes with Visual Studio. This has fewer options than IIS and is only suitable for development and testing, but it has the advantage that no extra install is needed and it makes the projects self-contained.

The New RPC Protocol: SOAP

According to the current SOAP specification, SOAP is "a lightweight protocol for exchange of information in a decentralized, distributed environment." In other words, it is a standard way to send information from one computer to another using XML to represent the information.

At the time of writing, you can find information on the current version of SOAP, SOAP 1.2, at `www.w3.org/2000/xp/Group/`.

In a nutshell, the SOAP recommendation defines a protocol whereby all information sent from computer to computer is marked up in XML, with the information transmitted via HTTP in most cases.

Technically, SOAP messages don't have to be sent via HTTP. Any networking protocol, such as SMTP or FTP, could be used, but for the reasons discussed in the last chapter, in practice HTTP is likely to remain the most common protocol used for SOAP for some time.

Let's look at some of the advantages of SOAP over other protocols such as DCOM or Java RMI:

DCOM and Java RMI are forerunners of SOAP and were both designed to solve the same problem: how to call methods of a class that resides on a remote machine and make the results available to the local machine. You can find a good tutorial about these techniques at `http://my.execpc.com/~gopalan/misc/compare.html`.

❑ **It's platform-, language-, and vendor-neutral** — Because SOAP is implemented using XML and (usually) HTTP, it is easy to process and send SOAP requests in any language, on any platform, without having to depend on tools from a particular vendor.

❑ **It's easy to implement** — SOAP was designed to be less complex than the other protocols. Even if it has moved away from that a bit in recent years, a SOAP server can still be implemented using nothing more than a web server and an ASP page or a CGI script.

❑ **It's firewall-safe** — Assuming that you use HTTP as your network protocol, you can pass SOAP messages across a firewall without having to perform extensive configuration.

In this chapter, you'll create part of a hypothetical music order service.

Try It Out   Creating an RPC Server in ASP.NET

Before you start creating SOAP messages, you need to look at the process of creating an RPC server that receives a request and sends back a response. This example begins with a fairly simple procedure to write: one that takes a unit price and quantity and returns the appropriate discount along with the total price.

To begin, you're going to create a simple ASP.NET page that accepts two numbers, evaluates them, and returns the results in XML. It won't be a fully-fledged SOAP service for reasons discussed later, but it contains a similar architecture. Later you'll convert it to a full SOAP XML service.

The example that follows uses Visual Studio. If you don't want to use this, just create the two files in a folder and make that folder a virtual directory in IIS.

Chapter 16 includes detailed instructions on how to set up a virtual folder.

1. Open Visual Studio and choose File ➪ New ➪ Web Site. Choose an ASP.NET website and call the folder `BasicOrderService`. Testing will be easier if you use IIS to host the site, rather than Visual Studio's own web server.

Rename `Default.aspx` to `GetTotal.aspx` and open it in the editor.

2. Remove all the content from the page except for the declaration at the top and add a new attribute, `ContentType`, with a value of `text/xml`. The page should now look like the following, although the code will all be on one line:

```
<%@ Page Language="C#" AutoEventWireup="true"
CodeFile="GetTotal.aspx.cs" Inherits="_Default"
ContentType="text/xml"%>
```

Save the page, right-click on it in the Solution Explorer, and choose Set as Start Up Page.

3. Right-click in the body of the page and choose View Code. You will see the code file `GetTotal.aspx.cs`. Replace the code with the following:

```
using System;
using System.Data;
using System.Configuration;
using System.Web;
using System.Web.Security;
using System.Web.UI;
using System.Web.UI.WebControls;
using System.Web.UI.WebControls.WebParts;
using System.Web.UI.HtmlControls;
using System.Xml;

public partial class _Default : System.Web.UI.Page
{
  protected void Page_Load(object sender, EventArgs e)
  {
    string clientXml = string.Empty;
    try
    {
      double unitPrice = Convert.ToDouble(Request.QueryString["unitPrice"]);
      int quantity = Convert.ToInt16(Request.QueryString["quantity"]);
      double discount = GetQuantityDiscount(quantity);
      double basicTotal = GetBasicTotal(unitPrice, quantity);
      double finalTotal = basicTotal * (1 - discount);
      clientXml = GetSuccessXml(finalTotal, discount * 100);
    }
    catch (Exception ex)
    {
      clientXml = GetErrorXml(ex);
    }
    XmlDocument doc = new XmlDocument();
    doc.LoadXml(clientXml);
    doc.Save(Response.OutputStream);
  }

  private double GetBasicTotal(double unitPrice, int quantity)
  {
    return unitPrice * quantity;
  }

  private double GetQuantityDiscount(int quantity)
  {
    if (quantity < 6) return 0;
    if (quantity < 11) return 0.05;
    if (quantity < 51) return 0.1;
    return 0.2;
  }
  private string GetSuccessXml(double totalPrice, double discount)
  {
    string clientXml = "<GetTotalResponse><Discount>{0}</Discount>"
                  + "<TotalPrice>{1}</TotalPrice></GetTotalResponse>";
```

```
        return string.Format(clientXml, Convert.ToString(discount),
                        Convert.ToString(totalPrice));
    }

    private string GetErrorXml(Exception ex)
    {
        string clientXml = "<Error><Reason>{0}</Reason></Error>";
        return string.Format(clientXml, ex.Message);
    }
}
```

The page is called with two values in the query string, `unitPrice` and `quantity`. The total price is calculated by multiplying the two values, and then a discount is applied. The discount depends on the quantity, and applies when the user requests more than five items. The results are returned in XML.

4. Test the page by right-clicking the project in the Solution Explorer and choosing View in Browser. When your browser appears it should show a listing of the project files and a URL similar to `http://localhost:1698/BasicOrderService/`. (The port may not show if you're using IIS.) Append the text `GetTotal.aspx?unitprice=8.5&quantity=6` to this and press Enter. You should see XML similar to that shown in Figure 15-1. If invalid values are entered, such as a quantity of x, then you should see the result shown in Figure 15-2.

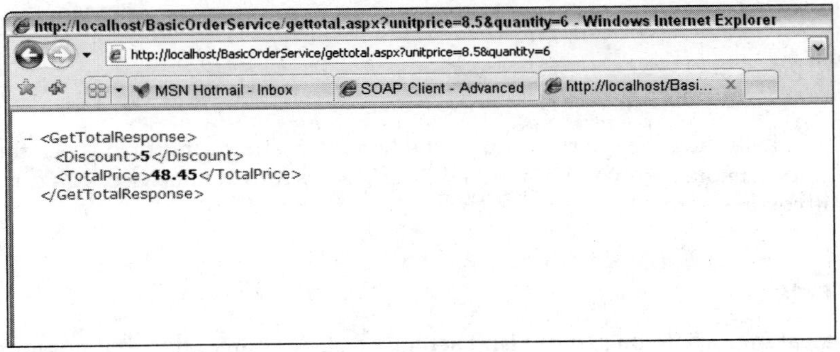

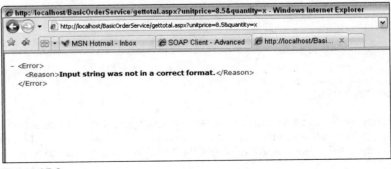

Figure 15-1

Figure 15-2

How It Works

This page pulls two values from the query string, converts them to numbers, and performs two actions. First, it requests a quantity discount using `GetQuantityDiscount()`, and then the page multiplies the two original numbers using `GetBasicTotal()`. Next, it returns the results as XML by loading a string of XML into an `XmlDocument` and saving to the `Response.OutputStream`. If either of the two values isn't numeric, meaning they can't be multiplied together, a different XML document is returned to the client, indicating a problem. This method of saving to the output stream is better than alternatives such as using `Response.Write`, as it preserves the character encoding that may be used in the document, whereas `Response.Write` always treats the content as `UTF-16`.

Note that this ASP.NET page isn't limited to being called from a browser. For example, you could load the XML directly and then retrieve the numbers from it, as in this VB.NET example:

```
Sub Main()
    Dim xdDoc As System.Xml.XmlDocument = new System.Xml.XmlDocument()

    xdDoc.Load
("http://localhost/BasicOrderService/gettotal.aspx?unitprice=8.5&quantity=6")

    If xdDoc.documentElement.name = "Error" Then
        MsgBox ("Unable to perform calculation")
    Else
        MsgBox
  (xdDoc.selectSingleNode("/*/TotalPrice").InnerText)
    End If
End Sub
```

You pass a URL, including the query string, to the `Load()` method, and then check the results. If the root element is named `Error`, then you know something went wrong. Otherwise, you can get the results using an XPath expression.

Just RESTing

Technically speaking, what you just did isn't actually a SOAP transaction, but not for the reasons you might think. The issue isn't that you sent a URL rather than a SOAP message in order to make the request; SOAP actually defines just such a transaction. The problem is that the response wasn't actually a SOAP message.

Take a look at the output:

```
<GetTotalResponse>
    <Discount>0.95</Discount>
    <TotalPrice>44.46</TotalPrice>
</GetTotalResponse>
```

This is a perfectly well-formed XML message, but it doesn't conform to the structure of a SOAP message. A SOAP message, as you'll see in the next section, consists of an `Envelope` element that contains a `Header` and `Body`. If this were a SOAP message, the XML you see here would have been contained in the SOAP `Body`.

Why go through all that? For one thing, this is still a perfectly valid way of creating a web service. Known as *REpresentational State Transfer* (REST), it's based on the idea that any piece of information on the World Wide Web should be addressable via a URL. In this case, that URL included a query string with parameter information.

REST is growing in popularity as people discover that it is, in many ways, much easier to use than SOAP. After all, you don't have to create an outgoing XML message, and you don't have to figure out how to POST it, as demonstrated in the previous chapter.

All of this begs the question: If REST is so much easier, why use SOAP at all? Aside from the fact that in some cases the request data is difficult or impossible to provide as a URL, the answer lies in the fundamental architecture of the Web. You submitted this request as a GET, which means that any parameters were part of the URL and not the body of the message. If you were to remain true to the way the Web is supposed to be constructed, GET requests are only for actions that have no "side effects," such as making changes to a database. That means you could use this method for getting information, but you couldn't use it for, say, placing an order, because the act of making that request changes something on the server.

When SOAP was still growing in popularity, some developers insisted that REST was better because it was simpler. SOAP 1.2 ends the controversy by adopting a somewhat RESTful stance, making it possible to use an HTTP GET request to send information and parameters and get a SOAP response. Before you see that in action, though, you should look at how SOAP itself works.

Basic SOAP Messages

As mentioned before, SOAP messages are basically XML documents, usually sent across HTTP. SOAP specifies the following:

❑   Rules regarding how the message should be sent. Although the SOAP specification says that any network protocol can be used, specific rules are included in the specification for HTTP, as that's the protocol most people use.

❑   The overall structure of the XML that is sent. This is called the *envelope*. Any information to be sent back and forth over SOAP is contained within this envelope, and is known as the *payload*.

❑   Rules regarding how data is represented in this XML. These are called the *encoding rules*.

When you send data to a SOAP server, the data must be represented in a particular way so that the server can understand it. The SOAP 1.2 specification outlines a simple XML document type, which is used for all SOAP messages. The basic structure of that document is as follows:

```
<soap:Envelope xmlns:soap="http://www.w3.org/2003/05/soap-envelope">
  <soap:Header>
    <head-ns:someHeaderElem xmlns:head-ns="some URI"
                            env:mustUnderstand="true{{vert}false"
                            env:relay="true{{vert}false"
                            env:role="some URI"/>
  </soap:Header>
  <soap:Body encodingStyle="http://www.w3.org/2003/05/soap-encoding">
    <some-ns:someElem xmlns:some-ns="some URI"/>
    <!-- OR -->
    <soap:Fault>
```

```
        <soap:Code>
          <soap:Value>Specified values</soap:Value>
          <soap:Subcode>
            <soap:Value>Specified values</soap:Value>
          </soap:Subcode>
        </soap:Code>
        <soap:Reason>
          <soap:Text xml:lang="en-US">English text</soap:Text>
          <v:Text xml:lang="fr">Texte francais</v:Text>
        </soap:Reason>
        <soap:Detail>
          <!-- Application specific information -->
        </soap:Detail>
      </soap:Fault>
    </soap:Body>
  </soap:Envelope>
```

Only three main elements are involved in a SOAP message itself (unless something goes wrong): `<Envelope>`, `<Header>`, and `<Body>`, and starting in version 1.2 of SOAP, a number of error-related elements. Of these elements, only `<Envelope>` and `<Body>` are mandatory; `<Header>` is optional, and `<Fault>` and its child elements are only required when an error occurs. In addition, all of the attributes (encodingStyle, mustUnderstand, and so on) are optional.

<Envelope>

Other than the fact that it resides in SOAP's envelope namespace, `www.w3.org/2003/05/soap-envelope`, the `<Envelope>` element doesn't really need any explanation. It simply provides the root element for the XML document and is usually used to include any namespace declarations. The next couple of sections talk about the other elements available, as well as the various attributes.

<Body>

The `<Body>` element contains the main body of the SOAP message. The actual RPC calls are made using direct children of the `<Body>` element (which are called *body blocks*). For example, consider the following:

```
<soap:Envelope xmlns:env="http://www.w3.org/2003/05/soap-envelope">
    <soap:Body>
        <o:AddToCart xmlns:o="http://www.wiley.com/soap/ordersystem">
            <o:CartId>THX1138</o:CartId>
            o:Item>ZIBKA</o:Item>
            <o:Quantity>3</o:Quantity>
            <o:TotalPrice>34.97</o:TotalPrice>
        </o:AddToCart>
    </soap:Body>
</soap:Envelope>
```

In this case, you're making one RPC call, to a procedure called AddToCart, in the `http://www.wiley.com/soap/ordersystem` namespace. (You can add multiple calls to a single message, if necessary.) The AddToCart procedure takes four parameters: CartId, Item, Quantity, and TotalPrice. Direct child elements of the `<soap:Body>` element must reside in a namespace other than the SOAP namespace. This namespace is what the SOAP server uses to uniquely identify this procedure so that it knows what code to run. When the procedure is done running, the server uses the HTTP response to send back a SOAP message. The `<soap:Body>` of that message might look similar to this:

```
<soap:Envelope xmlns:soap='http://www.w3.org/2003/05/soap-envelope'>

  <soap:Body>
    <o:AddToCartResponse xmlns:o='http://www.wiley.com/soap/ordersystem'>
      <o:CartId>THX1138</o:CartId>
      <o:Status>OK</o:Status>
      <o:Quantity>3</o:Quantity>
      <o:ItemId>ZIBKA</o:ItemId>
      </so:AddToCartResponse>
    </soap:Body>
</soap:Envelope>
```

The response is just another SOAP message, using an XML structure similar to the request, in that it has a `Body` in an `Envelope`, with the relevant information included as the payload.

Encoding Style

Usually, in the realm of XML, when you talk about encoding, you're talking about esoteric aspects of passing text around, but in the SOAP world, encoding is pretty straightforward. It simply refers to the way in which you represent the data. These examples use SOAP style encoding, which means you're using plain old elements and text, with maybe an attribute or two thrown in. You can let an application know that's what you're doing by adding the optional `encodingStyle` attribute, as shown here:

```
<soap:Envelope xmlns:soap='http://www.w3.org/2003/05/soap-envelope'>

  <soap:Body soap:encodingStyle="http://www.w3.org/2003/05/soap-encoding">
    <o:AddToCartResponse xmlns:o='http://www.wiley.com/soap/ordersystem'>
      <o:CartId>THX1138</o:CartId>
      <o:Status>OK</o:Status>
      <o:Quantity>3</o:Quantity>
      <o:ItemId>ZIBKA</o:ItemId>
    </o:AddToCartResponse>
  </soap:Body>

</soap:Envelope>
```

This distinguishes it from other encodings, such as RDF, shown in the following:

RDF stands for Resource Description Framework, a protocol used to represent information on the Web. It is a W3C Recommendation, and the full details are available at www.w3.org/RDF/.

```
<soap:Envelope xmlns: soap='http://www.w3.org/2003/05/soap-envelope'>
  <soap:Body>

    <rdf:RDF xmlns:rdf="http://www.w3.org/1999/02/22-rdf-syntax-ns{#"
          xmlns:o="http://www.wiley.com/soap/ordersystem'
       env:encodingStyle="http://www.w3.org/1999/02/22-rdf-syntax-ns{#">
      <o:AddToCartResponse
        rdf:About=
        "http://www.wiley.com/soap/ordersystem/addtocart.asp?cartid
         =THX1138">
        <o:CartId>THX1138</o:CartId>
        <o:Status>OK</o:Status>
```

```
        <o:qQuantity>3</o:Quantity>
        <o:ItemId>ZIBKA</o:ItemId>
    </o:AddToCartResponse>
```
```
    </rdf:RDF>
  </soap:Body>
```
```
</soap:Envelope>
```

The information is the same, but it's represented, or encoded, differently. You can also create your own encoding, but of course if your goal is interoperability, you need to use a standard encoding style. In the preceding example the `env:encodingStyle` is an attribute of the `rdf:RDF` element, but it could equally well have appeared on the `soap:Body`. In general, the attribute can appear anywhere and applies to all descendants of the one on which it appears as well as the element itself. This means that different parts of the same SOAP message can use different encodings if needed.

Try It Out   GETting a SOAP Message

The last Try It Out presented almost all of the benefits of SOAP. It works easily with a firewall, and all the information is passed over HTTP in XML, meaning you could implement your remote procedure using any language, on any platform, and you can call it from any language, on any platform. However, the solution is still a little proprietary. In order to make the procedure more universal, you need to go one step further and use a SOAP envelope for your XML.

This example still uses a `GET` request, but rather than return the raw XML, it is enclosed in a SOAP envelope, like so:

```
<soap:Envelope xmlns:soap="http://www.w3.org/2003/05/soap-envelope">
  < soap:Body>
<GetTotalResponse xmlns="http://www.wiley.com/soap/ordersystem">
    <Discount>10</Discount>
    <TotalPrice>243</TotalPrice>
  </GetTotalResponse>
  </ soap:Body>
</ soap:Envelope>
```

In this case, you'll also send the request and receive the response through an HTML form:

1. Create an HTML file in the text editor and save it as `soaptester.html` in a virtual folder. If you tried the last example, then just store the file in the same directory, `BasicOrderService`.

2. Add the following HTML to `SoapTester.html`:

```
<html>
  <head>
    <title>SOAP Client</title>
<!—script to go here -->
  </head>
  <body onload="init();">
    <h3>Soap Pricing Tool</h3>
    <form name="orderForm">
    <select  name="lstItems" style="width:350px" onchange="setPriceAndQuantity();">
      <option value="10.50" id="item1" selected>
```

```
Cool Britannia, by The Bonzo Dog Doo-Dah Band</option>
    <option value="12.95" id="item2">
Zibka Smiles, by The Polka Dot Zither Band</option>
    <option value="20.00" id="item3">
Dr Frankenstein's Disco Party, by Jonny Wakelin</option>
</select>
    <p>
        Unit price:<input type="text" name="txtUnitPrice" size="6" ReadOnly><br>
        Quantity: <input type="text" name="txtQuantity" size="2">
    </p>
    <input type="button" value="Get Price" onclick="doGet()"><br>
    Discount (%):<input type="text" name="txtDiscount" size="4" readonly><br>
    Total price:<input type="text" name="txtTotalPrice" size="6" readonly>
    </form>
</body>
```

The form has a drop-down box to pick an item; this sets the price in the first text box. The user then chooses the quantity and clicks the button. There are two read-only textboxes for the output: `txtDiscount` and `txtTotalPrice` (see Figure 15-3).

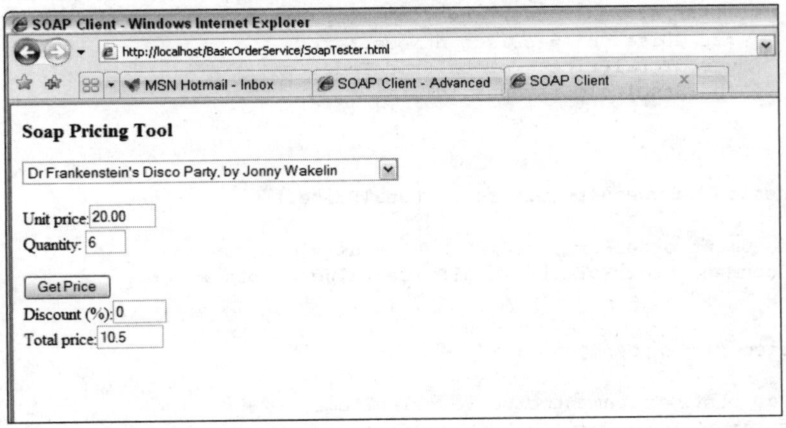

Figure 15-3

3. Add the script that's going to make the call to the SOAP server to the `soapclient.html` file:

```
<head>
    <title>SOAP Tester</title>
    <script type="text/javascript" src="zXML.src.js"></script>

    <script type="text/javascript">
    var xhHTTP;
    function doGet()
    {
        var dUnitPrice = document.orderForm.txtUnitPrice.value;
        var iQuantity = document.orderForm.txtQuantity.value;
        var sBaseUrl = "GetTotal2.aspx"
        var sQuery = "?unitprice=" + dUnitPrice + "&quantity=" + iQuantity;
        var sRequest = sBaseUrl + sQuery;
        xhHTTP = zXmlHttp.createRequest();
```

```
            xhHTTP.onreadystatechange = handleGetTotalResponse;
            xhHTTP.open("GET", sRequest, true);
            xhHTTP.send(null);
        }

      function handleGetTotalResponse()
      {
        if (xhHTTP.readyState == 4)
        {
            var xdDoc = xhHTTP.responseXML;
            alert(xdDoc.xml);
            var oNamespaceMapper = {ns: "http://www.wiley.com/soap/ordersystem"};
            if (xdDoc.documentElement.nodeName == "Error")
            {
              alert("ERROR!:\n" + xdDoc.documentElement.text);
              return;
            }
            var oDiscountNode = zXPath.selectSingleNode(xdDoc.documentElement,
                "/*/*/*/ns:Discount", oNamespaceMapper);
            var oTotalPriceNode = zXPath.selectSingleNode(xdDoc.documentElement,
                "/*/*/*/ns:TotalPrice", oNamespaceMapper);
            var dDiscount = oDiscountNode.text;
            var dTotalPrice = oTotalPriceNode.text;
            showResults(dDiscount, dTotalPrice);
        }
      }

      function showResults(discount, totalPrice)
      {
        document.orderForm.txtDiscount.value = discount;
        document.orderForm.txtTotalPrice.value = totalPrice;
      }

  function setPriceAndQuantity()
  {
      var oLst = document.orderForm.lstItems;
      document.orderForm.txtUnitPrice.value =
                           oLst.options[oLst.selectedIndex].value;
      document.orderForm.txtQuantity.value = 1;
  }

      function init()
  {
      setPriceAndQuantity();
  }

    </script>
</head>
```

There are two other functions. `setPriceAndQuantity()` populates `txtUnitPrice` with the price of the selected item and resets the quantity to 1. `init()` sets the initial values of these boxes when the page loads.

4. Create the ASPX page to serve the content. Save a copy of GetTotal.aspx and call it GetTotal2.aspx. Modify the content so that the CodeFile attribute points to GetTotal2.aspx.cs:

```
<%@ Page Language="C#" AutoEventWireup="true"CodeFile="GetTotal2.aspx.cs"
Inherits="_Default" ContentType="text/xml"%>
```

5. Copy the code file, GetTotal.aspx.cs, and name the new version GetTotal2.aspx.cs. Modify the GetSuccessXml to produce a SOAP-style message:

```
private string GetSuccessXml(double totalPrice, double discount)
{
    string clientXml =
"<soap:Envelope xmlns:soap=\"http://www.w3.org/2003/05/soap-envelope\"><soap:Body>"
                    + "<GetTotalResponse"
    + "xmlns=\"http://www.wiley.com/soap/ordersystem\"><Discount>{0}</Discount>"
    + "<TotalPrice>{1}</TotalPrice>"
    + "</GetTotalResponse></soap:Body></soap:Envelope>";
    return string.Format(clientXml, Convert.ToString(discount),
    Convert.ToString(totalPrice));
}
```

6. Before testing, ensure that the XML cross-browser library, zXML.src.js, is in the same folder as soaptester.html. Reload the soaptester.html page in the browser, change the quantity, and click the Get Price button. You should see an alert box with the returned SOAP message, shown in Figure 15-4. The results are extracted from the message and displayed in the bottom two textboxes, as shown in Figure 15-5.

Figure 15-4

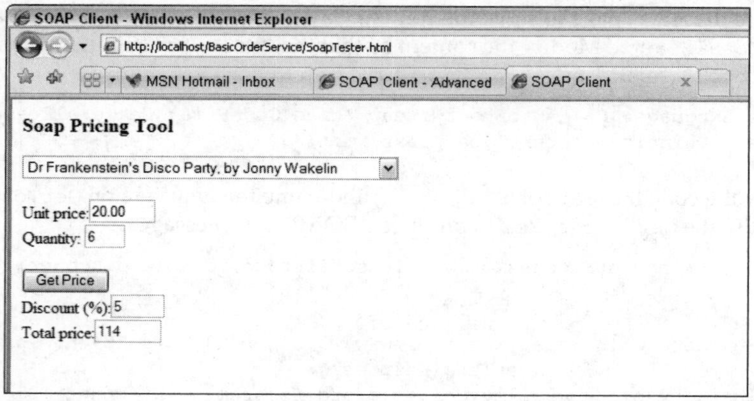

Figure 15-5

How It Works

This Try It Out illustrates a practical (if a bit contrived) example of working with a SOAP server. Using the browser, you created a simple SOAP client that retrieved information from the user interface (the quantity and unit price), sent a request to a SOAP server (the GET request), and displayed the results (the discount and extended price).

Because you created a client using the browser, you had to use a MIME type that the browser understands: text/xml. Under other circumstances, you'd want to use the actual SOAP MIME type, application/soap+xml. In other words, the ASP page would begin with the following:

```
Response.ContentType = "application/soap+xml"
```

This way, administrators can configure their firewalls to allow packets with this MIME type to pass through, even if they are blocking other types of content. Unfortunately, far too few clients understand this version so the less accurate text/xml is still more common.

Of course, you've only scratched the surface of what SOAP can do. Let's look at some detailed uses.

More Complex SOAP Interactions

Now that you know the basics of how SOAP works, it's time to delve a little more deeply. SOAP messages can consist of not just a Body, which contains the payload or data to be processed, but also a Header element containing information about the payload. The Header also gives you a good deal of control over how its information is processed.

This section also describes the structure of a SOAP Fault, and how to use SOAP in a POST operation, rather than a GET operation. First, take a look at the rest of the SOAP Envelope's structure.

<Header>

The <Header> element comes into play when you need to add additional information to your SOAP message. For example, suppose you created a system whereby orders can be placed into your database using SOAP messages, and you have defined a standard SOAP message format that anyone communicating with your system must use. You might use a SOAP header for authentication information, so that only authorized persons or systems can use your system. These elements, called *header blocks*, are specifically designed for *meta information*, or information about the information contained in the body.

When a <Header> element is used, it must be the first element child of the <Envelope> element. Functionally, the <Header> element works very much like the <Body> element; it's simply a placeholder for other elements in namespaces other than the SOAP envelope namespace, each of which is a SOAP message to be evaluated in conjunction with the main SOAP message(s) in the body. In general, however, it doesn't contain information to be processed.

The SOAP 1.2 Recommendation also defines optional attributes you can include on those header entries: mustUnderstand, role, and relay.

The mustUnderstand Attribute

The mustUnderstand attribute specifies whether it is absolutely necessary for the SOAP server to process a particular header block. A value of true indicates that the header entry is mandatory and the server must either process it or indicate an error. For example, consider the following:

```
<soap:Envelope xmlns:soap="http://www.w3.org/2003/05/soap-envelope">
  <soap:Header xmlns:some-ns="http://www.wiley.com/soap/headers/">

    <some-ns:authentication mustUnderstand="true">
      <UserID>User ID goes here...</UserID>
      <Password>Password goes here...</Password>
    </some-ns:authentication>

    <some-ns:log mustUnderstand="false">
      <additional-info>Info goes here...</additional-info>
    </some-ns:log>
    <some-ns:log>
      <additional-info>Info goes here...</additional-info>
    </some-ns:log>
  </soap:Header>
  <soap:Body xmlns:body-ns="http://www.wiley.com/soap/rpc">
    <body-ns:mainRPC>
      <additional-info/>
    </body-ns:mainRPC>
  </soap:Body>
</soap:Envelope>
```

This SOAP message contains three header entries: one for authentication and two for logging purposes.

For the <authentication> header entry, you specified a value of true for mustUnderstand. (In SOAP 1.1, you would have specified it as 1.) This means that the SOAP server must process the header block. If the SOAP server doesn't understand this header entry, it rejects the entire SOAP message — the server is not allowed to process the entries in the SOAP body. This forces the server to use proper authentication.

The second header entry specifies a value of false for mustUnderstand, which makes this header entry optional. This means that when the SOAP server doesn't understand this particular header entry, it can still go ahead and process the SOAP body anyway.

Finally, in the third header entry the `mustUnderstand` attribute was omitted. In this case, the header entry is optional, just as if you had specified the `mustUnderstand` attribute with a value of `false`.

The role Attribute

In some cases a SOAP message may pass through a number of applications on a number of computers before it arrives at its final destination. You might send a SOAP message to computer A, which might then send that message on to computer B. Computer A would be called a *SOAP intermediary*.

In these cases, using the `role` attribute you can specify that some SOAP headers must be processed by a specific intermediary. The value of the attribute is a URI, which uniquely identifies each intermediary. The SOAP specification also defines the following three roles:

❑   `http://www.w3.org/2003/05/soap-envelope/role/next` applies to the next intermediary in line, wherever it is.

❑   `http://www.w3.org/2003/05/soap-envelope/role/ultimateReceiver` only applies to the very last stop.

❑   `http://www.w3.org/2003/05/soap-envelope/role/none` effectively "turns off" the header block so that it is ignored at this stage of the process.

When an intermediary processes a header entry, it must remove that header from the message before passing it on. Conversely, the SOAP specification also says that a similar header entry can be inserted in its place, so you can process the SOAP header entry and then add another identical header block.

The relay Attribute

The SOAP specification also requires a SOAP intermediary to remove any headers it doesn't process, which presents a problem. What if you want to add a new feature and target it at any intermediary that might understand it? The solution is the `relay` attribute. By setting the `relay` attribute to `true`, you can instruct any intermediary that encounters it to either process it or leave it alone. (If the intermediary does process the header, the intermediary still must remove it.) The default value for the relay attribute is `false`.

<Fault>

Whenever computers are involved, things can go wrong, and there may be times when a SOAP server is unable to process a SOAP message, for whatever reason. Perhaps a resource needed to perform the operation isn't available, or invalid parameters were passed, or the server doesn't understand the SOAP request in the first place. In these cases, the server returns *fault codes* to the client to indicate errors.

Fault codes are sent using the same format as other SOAP messages. However, in this case, the `<Body>` element has only one child, a `<Fault>` element. Children of the `<Fault>` element contain details of the error. A SOAP message indicating a fault might look similar to this:

```
<soap:Envelope xmlns:soap="http://www.w3.org/2003/05/soap-envelope"
               xmlns:rpc="http://www.w3.org/2003/05/soap-rpc">
  <soap:Body>
   <soap:Fault>
     <soap:Code>
       <soap:Value>soap:Sender</soap:Value>
```

```
            <soap:Subcode>
               <soap:Value>rpc:BadArguments</soap:Value>
            </soap:Subcode>
         </soap:Code>
         <soap:Reason>
            <soap:Text xml:lang="en-US">Processing error</soap:Text>
            <soap:Text xml:lang="fr">Erreur de traitement </soap:Text>
      </soap:Reason>
         <soap:Detail>
            <o:orderFaultInfo xmlns:o="http://www.wiley.com/soap/ordersystem">
               <o:errorCode>WA872</o:errorCode>
               <o:message>Cart doesn't exist</o:message>
            </o:OrderFaultInfo>
         </soap:Detail>
      </soap:Fault>
   </soap:Body>
</soap:Envelope>
```

The <Code> element contains a <Value> consisting of a unique identifier that identifies this particular type of error. The SOAP specification defines five such identifiers, described in the following table:

Fault Code	Description
VersionMismatch	A SOAP message was received that specified a version of the SOAP protocol that this server doesn't understand. (This would happen, for example, if you sent a SOAP 1.2 message to a SOAP 1.1 server.)
MustUnderstand	The SOAP message contained a mandatory header that the SOAP server didn't understand.
Sender	The message was not properly formatted. That is, the client made a mistake when creating the SOAP message. This identifier also applies if the message itself is well formed, but doesn't contain the correct information. For example, if authentication information were missing, this identifier would apply.
Receiver	This indicates that the server had problems processing the message, even though the contents of the message were formatted properly. For example, perhaps a database was down.
DataEncodingUnknown	This indicates that the data in the SOAP message is organized, or encoded, in a way the server doesn't understand.

Keep in mind that the identifier is actually namespace-qualified, using the http://www.w3.org/2003/05/soap-envelope *namespace.*

You also have the option to add information in different languages, as shown in this example's <Text> elements, as well as application-specific information as part of the <Detail> element. Note that application-specific information in the <Detail> element must have its own namespace.

Try It Out   POSTing a SOAP message

The last two Try It Outs were devoted to simply getting information from the SOAP server. Because you weren't actually changing anything on the server, you could use the GET method and simply pass all of the information as part of the URL. (Remember that you're only supposed to use GET when there are no side effects from calling the URL.)

Now let's examine a situation where that isn't the case. In this Try It Out, you'll look at a SOAP procedure that adds an item to a hypothetical shopping cart. Because this is not an "idempotent" process — it causes side effects, in that it adds an item to the order — you'll have to submit the information via the POST method, which means creating a SOAP message within the client.

To call the AddToCart procedure, use this SOAP message (placeholders are shown in italics):

```
<soap:Envelope xmlns:soap="http://www.w3.org/2003/05/soap-envelope">
<soap:Body>
  <o:AddToCart xmlns:o="http://www.wiley.com/soap/ordersystem">
    <o:CartId>CARTID</o:CartId>
    <o:Item itemId="ITEMID">
      <o:Quantity>QUANTITY</o:Quantity>
      <o:TotalPrice>PRICE</o:TotalPrice>
    </o:Item>
  </o:AddToCart>
</soap:Body>
</soap:Envelope>   .
```

For the response, send the following XML back to the client:

```
<soap:Envelope xmlns:soap="http://www.w3.org/2003/05/soap-envelope">
  <soap:Body>
    <o:AddToCartResponse xmlns:o="http://www.wiley.com/soap/ordersystem">
      <o:CartId>CARTID</o:CartId>
      <o:Status>STATUS</o:Status>
      <o:Quantity>QUANTITY</o:Qntity>
      <o:ItemId>ITEMID</o:ItemId>
    </o:AddToCartResponse>
  </soap:Body>
</soap:Envelope>
```

You also need to handle the errors using a SOAP envelope. Use the following format for errors:

```
<soap:Envelope xmlns:soap="http://www.w3.org/2003/05/soap-envelope"
               xmlns:rpc="http://www.w3.org/2003/05/soap-rpc">
  <soap:Body>
   <soap:Fault>
     <soap:Code>
       <soap:Value>soap: FAULTCODE</soap:Value>
       <soap:Subcode>
         <soap:Value>SUBVALUE</soap:Value>
       </soap:Subcode>
     </soap:Code>
     <soap:Reason>
```

```
        <soap:Text>ERROR DESCRIPTION</soap:Text>
      </soap:Reason>
      <soap:Detail>
        <o:OrderFaultInfo xmlns:o="http://www.wiley.com/soap/ordersystem">
          <o:ErrorCode>APPLICATION-SPECIFIC ERROR CODE</o:ErrorCode>
          <o:Message>APPLICATION-SPECIFIC ERROR MESSAGE</o:Message>
        </o:OrderFaultInfo>
      </soap:Detail>
    </soap:Fault>
  </soap:Body>
</soap:Envelope>
```

1. Add a new web form to the example project named `AddToCart.aspx`. Similar to the previous aspx pages, it indicates that the returned content is XML. It also has a `ValidateRequest` attribute set to `false`; otherwise, the aspx handler rejects the request as malformed:

```
<%@ Page Language="C#" AutoEventWireup="true"
 CodeFile="AddToCart.aspx.cs" Inherits="AddToCart"
 ContentType="text/xml" ValidateRequest="false"%>
```

2. Go to `AddToCart.aspx.cs` to create the basic page that retrieves the submitted SOAP message and extracts the appropriate information. The first part of the page declares the namespaces of the libraries used in the service. These are the usual `System` and `System.Web`, as well as two for parsing and processing XML:

```
using System;
using System.Web;
using System.Xml;
using System.Xml.XPath;

public partial class AddToCart : System.Web.UI.Page
{
  protected void Page_Load(object sender, EventArgs e)
  {
    XmlDocument soapDoc = new XmlDocument();
    string responseXml = string.Empty;
    string cartId = string.Empty;
    int quantity = 0;
    string itemId = string.Empty;
    try
    {
      soapDoc.Load(Request.InputStream);
    }
```

3. After declaring an `XmlDocument` to hold the incoming SOAP request and some variables to hold the actual data, the request is loaded into the `XmlDocument` using its `InputStream` property. This is done in a `try/catch` block; if the `Load()` method fails, then a SOAP error is returned to the client:

```
    catch (Exception ex)
    {
      responseXml = GetFailureXml("Sender",
                                  "rpc:ProcedureNotPresent",
```

```
                              "Malformed request",
                              1,
                              "Unable to read SOAP request:" + ex.Message);
     }
```

The `GetFailureXml` *method is discussed later in the chapter.*

4. Now an `XmlNamespaceManager` is set up so that namespaced nodes can be retrieved:

```
XmlNamespaceManager nsm = new XmlNamespaceManager(soapDoc.NameTable);
nsm.AddNamespace("soap", "http://www.w3.org/2003/05/soap-envelope");
nsm.AddNamespace("o", "http://www.wiley.com/soap/ordersystem");
string xpath = "/soap:Envelope/soap:Body/o:AddToCart";
XmlNode procedureNode = soapDoc.SelectSingleNode(xpath, nsm);
XmlNode node = null;
```

Then the first node of interest, `AddToCart`, is retrieved using a standard XPath statement.

5. Check the node. If it's null, then the message isn't recognized and again an error is returned to the client:

```
XmlNode procedureNode = soapDoc.SelectSingleNode(xpath, nsm);
XmlNode node = null;
if (procedureNode == null)
{
    responseXml = GetFailureXml("Sender",
                          "rpc:ProcedureNotPresent",
                          "Unable to find AddToCart element",
                          2,
                          "Unable to find AddToCart element");
}
```

A similar approach is now taken with the other three nodes of interest, `CartId`, `ItemId`, and `Quantity`. If any of these are null, then an error is returned. If all three are located, then the data is processed by `SaveCart()`, which in this example does nothing but in real life would probably save to a database.

6. Finally, a SOAP response is generated and saved to the `Response.OutputStream`:

```
soapDoc.LoadXml(responseXml);
soapDoc.Save(Response.OutputStream);
```

7. The two methods that create the SOAP response, either the successful one or the SOAP fault, are very similar. They contain an XML template into which the appropriate variables are inserted. Here's the `GetSuccessXml()` method:

```
private string GetSuccessXml(string CartId, int Quantity, string ItemId)
{
    string responseXml = "<soap:Envelope
xmlns:soap=\"http://www.w3.org/2003/05/soap-envelope\">"
                        + "<soap:Body><o:AddToCartResponse "
                        + "xmlns:o=\"http://www.wiley.com/soap/ordersystem\">"
                        + "<o:CartId>{0}</o:CartId>"
                        + "<o:Status>OK</o:Status>"
                        + "<o:Quantity>{1}</o:Quantity>"
```

```
                        + "<o:ItemId>{2}</o:ItemId>"
                        + "</o:AddToCartResponse>"
                        + "</soap:Body></soap:Envelope>";
        return string.Format(responseXml, CartId, Quantity, ItemId);
    }
```

The `GetFailureXML()` method accepts a number of parameters detailing the conventional error message such as `rpc:BadArguments`, and a more user-friendly one such as `CartId not found`:

```
    private string GetFailureXml(string faultCode, string subValue, string reason,
int errorCode, string message)
    {
        string responseXml = "<soap:Envelope
xmlns:soap=\"http://www.w3.org/2003/05/soap-envelope\" "
                        + "xmlns:rpc=\"http://www.w3.org/2003/05/soap-rpc\">"
                        + "<soap:Body><soap:Fault><soap:Code>"
                        + "<soap:Value>soap:{0}</soap:Value>"
                        + "<soap:Subcode><soap:Value>{1}</soap:Value>"
                        + "</soap:Subcode></soap:Code><soap:Reason>"
                        + "<soap:Text>{2}</soap:Text></soap:Reason>"
                        + "<soap:Detail><o:OrderFaultInfo "
                        + "xmlns:o=\"http://www.wiley.com/soap/ordersystem\">"
                        + "<o:ErrorCode>{3}</o:ErrorCode>"
                        + "<o:Message>{4}</o:Message></o:OrderFaultInfo>"
                        + "</soap:Detail></soap:Fault></soap:Body></soap:Envelope>";
        return string.Format(responseXml, faultCode, subValue, reason, errorCode,
message);
    }
```

8. Now the client needs amending. Once the total price has been retrieved, the user can add the items to the cart. There are two changes to the HTML. First, the item's ID is stored against each `select` option so it can be sent with the SOAP request:

```
<select  name="lstItems" style="width:350px" onchange="setPriceAndQuantity();">
    <option value="10.50" id="item1" selected>
                    Cool Britannia, by The Bonzo Dog Doo-Dah Band</option>
    <option value="12.95" id="item2" >
                    Zibka Smiles, by The Polka Dot Zither Band</option>
    <option value="20.00" id="item3" >
                    Dr Frankenstein's Disco Party, by Jonny Wakelin</option>
</select>
```

9. The other addition is a new function to create the request, `doPost()`, and one to handle the return, `handleAddToCartResponse()`. Both work exactly as previously but create a POST request instead of a GET. The full listing of `SoapTester-Post.html` is shown here, and Figure 15-6 shows it in action:

```
<html>
  <head>
    <title>SOAP Tester - Advanced</title>
    <script type="text/javascript" src="zXML.src.js"></script>

    <script type="text/javascript">
```

```
    var xhHTTP;
    function doGet()
    {
        var dUnitPrice = document.orderForm.txtUnitPrice.value;
        var iQuantity = document.orderForm.txtQuantity.value;
        var sBaseUrl = "GetTotal2.aspx"
        var sQuery = "?unitprice=" + dUnitPrice + "&quantity=" + iQuantity;
        var sRequest = sBaseUrl + sQuery;
        xhHTTP = zXmlHttp.createRequest();
        xhHTTP.onreadystatechange = handleGetTotalResponse;
        xhHTTP.open("GET", sRequest, true);
        xhHTTP.send(null);
    }


    function handleGetTotalResponse()
    {
      if (xhHTTP.readyState == 4)
      {
          var xdDoc = xhHTTP.responseXML;
          alert(xdDoc.xml);
          var oNamespaceMapper =
{ns: "http://www.wiley.com/soap/ordersystem"};
          if (xdDoc.documentElement.nodeName == "Error")
          {
            alert("ERROR!:\n" + xdDoc.documentElement.text);
            return;
          }
          var oDiscountNode = zXPath.selectSingleNode(xdDoc.documentElement,
"/*/*/*/ns:Discount", oNamespaceMapper);
          var oTotalPriceNode = zXPath.selectSingleNode(xdDoc.documentElement,
"/*/*/*/ns:TotalPrice", oNamespaceMapper);
          var dDiscount = oDiscountNode.text;
          var dTotalPrice = oTotalPriceNode.text;
          showResults(dDiscount, dTotalPrice);
      }
    }
```

SoapTester-Post.html
```
  function doPost()
  {
    var oLst = document.orderForm.lstItems
    var sItemId = oLst.options[oLst.selectedIndex].id;
    var dTotalPrice = document.orderForm.txtTotalPrice.value;
    var sCartId = document.orderForm.cartId.value;
    var iQuantity = document.orderForm.txtQuantity.value;
    var sSoapRequest =
"<soap:Envelope xmlns:soap=\"http://www.w3.org/2003/05/soap-envelope\">"
+ "<soap:Body><o:AddToCart xmlns:o=\"http://www.wiley.com/soap/ordersystem\">"
            + "<o:CartId>" + sCartId + "</o:CartId>"
                        + "<o:Item ItemId=\"" + sItemId + "\">"
                        + "<o:Quantity>" + iQuantity + "</o:Quantity>"
            + "<o:TotalPrice>" + dTotalPrice + "</o:TotalPrice>"
                        + "</o:Item></o:AddToCart></soap:Body></soap:Envelope>";
    var sRequest = "AddToCart.aspx";
    xhHTTP = zXmlHttp.createRequest();
    xhHTTP.onreadystatechange = handleAddToCartResponse;
```

```
    xhHTTP.open("POST", sRequest, true);
    xhHTTP.send(sSoapRequest);
  }

  function handleAddToCartResponse()
    {
      if (xhHTTP.readyState == 4)
      {
          var xdDoc = xhHTTP.responseXML;
          alert(xdDoc.xml);
          var oNamespaceMapper =
{soap: "http://www.w3.org/2003/05/soap-envelope",
 o: "http://www.wiley.com/soap/ordersystem"};
      var sXPath = "/soap:Envelope/soap:Body/o:AddToCartResponse";
      var oResponseNode = zXPath.selectSingleNode(xdDoc.documentElement, sXPath,
 oNamespaceMapper);
      if (oResponseNode)
      {
        var sSuccessMessage = "Item added to cart.";
      alert(sSuccessMessage);
          }
      else
      {
      var sErrorMessage = "Error adding item to cart:\n";
      sXPath = "/soap:Envelope/soap:Body/soap:Fault/soap:Code/soap:Value/text()";
          var node = zXPath.selectSingleNode(xdDoc.documentElement, sXPath,
 oNamespaceMapper);
      sErrorMessage += "\nFault value: " + node.nodeValue;
      sXPath =
"/soap:Envelope/soap:Body/soap:Fault/soap:Code/soap:Subcode/soap:Value/text()";
          node = zXPath.selectSingleNode(xdDoc.documentElement, sXPath,
 oNamespaceMapper);
          sErrorMessage += "\nFault subvalue: " + node.nodeValue;
      sXPath = "/soap:Envelope/soap:Body/soap:Fault/soap:Reason/soap:Text/text()";
          node = zXPath.selectSingleNode(xdDoc.documentElement, sXPath,
 oNamespaceMapper);
          sErrorMessage += "\nFault text: " + node.nodeValue;
      sXPath =
"/soap:Envelope/soap:Body/soap:Fault/" +
 "soap:Detail/o:OrderFaultInfo/o:ErrorCode/text()";
          node = zXPath.selectSingleNode(xdDoc.documentElement, sXPath,
 oNamespaceMapper);
          sErrorMessage += "\nFault error code: " + node.nodeValue;
      sXPath =
"/soap:Envelope/soap:Body/soap:Fault/soap:Detail/o:OrderFaultInfo/o:Message/text()"
;
          node = zXPath.selectSingleNode(xdDoc.documentElement, sXPath,
 oNamespaceMapper);
          sErrorMessage += "\nFault message: " + node.nodeValue;
      alert(sErrorMessage);
      }
      }
    }

    function showResults(discount, totalPrice)
```

```
        {
          document.orderForm.txtDiscount.value = discount;
          document.orderForm.txtTotalPrice.value = totalPrice;
        }

     function setPriceAndQuantity()
     {
         var oLst =  document.orderForm.lstItems;
         document.orderForm.txtUnitPrice.value =
                     oLst.options[oLst.selectedIndex].value;
         document.orderForm.txtQuantity.value = 1;
     }

     function init()
     {
         setPriceAndQuantity();
     }

     </script>
  </head>
  <body onload="init();">
     <h3>Soap Pricing Tool</h3>
     <form name="orderForm">
     <select  name="lstItems" style="width:350px" onchange="setPriceAndQuantity();">
        <option value="10.50" id="item1" selected>
Cool Britannia, by The Bonzo Dog Doo-Dah Band</option>
        <option value="12.95" id="item2" >
Zibka Smiles, by The Polka Dot Zither Band</option>
        <option value="20.00" id="item3" >
Dr Frankenstein's Disco Party, by Jonny Wakelin</option>
     </select>
        <p>
           Unit price:<input type="text" name="txtUnitPrice" size="6" ReadOnly><br>
            Quantity: <input type="text" name="txtQuantity" size="2">
        </p>
        <input type="button" value="Get Price" onclick="doGet()"><br>
        Discount (%):<input type="text" name="txtDiscount" size="4" readonly><br>
        Total price:<input type="text" name="txtTotalPrice" size="6" readonly><br>
     <input type="text" readonly name="cartId" value="cart123"><br>
     <input type="button" value="Add to Cart" onclick="doPost();">
     </form>
  </body>
</html>
```

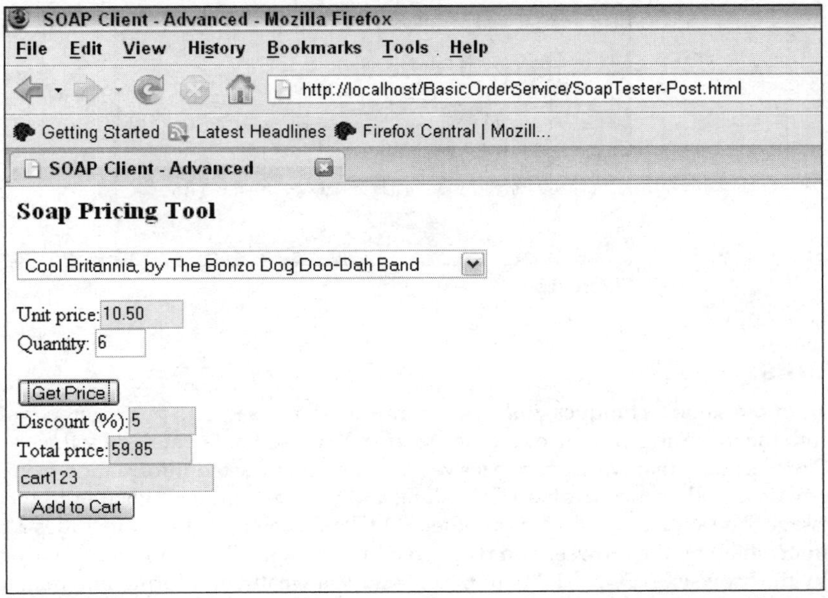

Figure 15-6

Figure 15-7 shows the raw XML response received after the Add to Cart button is clicked.

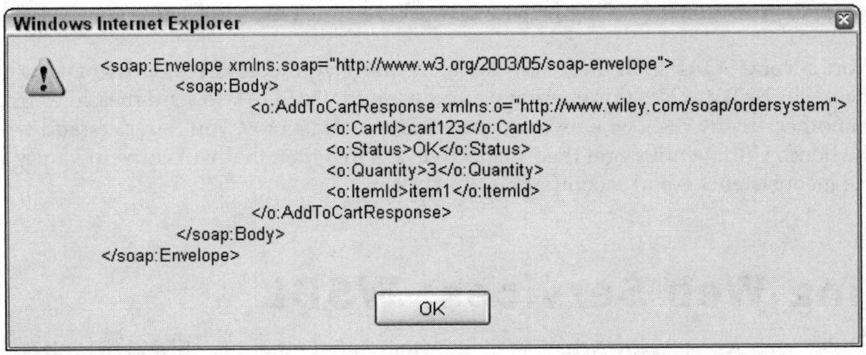

Figure 15-7

If an error occurs (and you can test this by modifying the SOAP template by changing the AddToCart element to AddToCar), then a SOAP fault is returned, as shown in Figure 15-8.

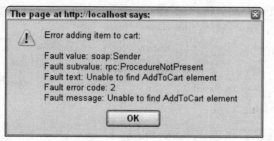

Figure 15-8

How It Works

Here you used the same techniques you used for raw XML messages to put together valid SOAP messages on both the incoming and the outgoing streams. You used data entered by the user on a form to create a SOAP message that was sent to a server. The server extracted information from that SOAP message using typical XML tactics, evaluated the data, and then determined whether to send a success or failure message. The success message is another SOAP message that simply includes a payload, which was then interpreted by the browser and displayed on the page. The failure message, or fault, was also analyzed by the browser. A SOAP 1.2 Fault can include a wealth of information, related to both SOAP and the application itself.

Yes, this seems like a lot of work for a very simple operation, but realize that you have created, from scratch, all of the plumbing necessary to create an entire SOAP service. Implementing a more difficult SOAP service, such as some type of order-processing system, would require the same level of plumbing, even though the functionality being provided would be much more difficult.

In addition, several SOAP toolkits are available, meaning you won't necessarily have to generate the SOAP messages by hand like this every time you want to use SOAP to send messages from one computer to another. In any case, whenever you use those toolkits now, you'll understand what's going on under the hood. Until vendors get their respective acts together, that will come in handy when the inevitable inconsistencies and incompatibilities appear.

Defining Web Services: WSDL

You've built a web service. Now what? Well, it is hoped that other people and organizations start using the service you've built. In order to do that, however, they need to know two things:

❑   How to call the service

❑   What to expect as a response from the service

Fortunately, there's an easy way to provide answers to both questions: Web Services Description Language (WSDL). WSDL provides a standardized way to describe a web service. That means you can create a WSDL file describing your service, make the file available, and then sit back as people use it.

Of course, a WSDL file isn't just for people. Recall the toolkits that take most of the work out of creating SOAP messages. They're built on the principle that they can automatically generate a client for your web service just by analyzing the WSDL file. In this way, WSDL helps to make web services truly platform- and language-independent.

How's that, you ask? It's simple. A WSDL file is written in XML, describing the data to be passed and the method for passing it, but it doesn't lean toward any particular language. That means a web services client generator can use the WSDL information to generate a client in any language. For example, a code generator for Java could create a client to access your ASP-based service, and the best part is that the client is pure Java. A developer writing an application around it doesn't have to know the details of the service, just the methods of the proxy class that actually accesses the service. The proxy sits between the client and the actual service, translating messages back and forth.

> *The latest version of WSDL, version 2.0, reached Candidate Recommendation in March 2006 but has had little impact so far. Most services still use the earlier version. The major differences between the two versions are highlighted when the various parts of the WSDL schema are discussed later in this chapter.*
>
> *You can read the specification for WSDL, WSDL 1.1, at* www.w3.org/TR/wsdl.

This chapter uses WSDL to describe a service that sends SOAP messages over HTTP, but in actuality WSDL is designed to be much more general. First, you define the data that will be sent, and then you define the way it will be sent. In this way, a single WSDL file can describe a service that's implemented as SOAP over HTTP as well as, say, SOAP over e-mail or even a completely different means.

This chapter sticks with SOAP over HTTP because that's by far the most common usage right now.

<definitions>

A WSDL file starts with a `<definitions>` element:

```xml
<?xml version="1.0"?>
<definitions name="temperature"
    targetNamespace="http://www.example.com/temperature"
    xmlns:typens="http://www.example.com/temperature"
    xmlns:xsd="http://www.w3.org/2000/10/XMLSchema"
    xmlns:soap="http://schemas.xmlsoap.org/wsdl/soap/"
    xmlns="http://schemas.xmlsoap.org/wsdl/">

</definitions>
```

The first task in a WSDL file is to define the information that will be sent to and from the service. A WSDL file builds the service up in levels. First, it defines the data to be sent and received, and then it uses that data to define messages.

<types>

Remember that there's no way to know for sure that the service will use SOAP, or even that the information will be XML, but WSDL enables you to define the *information set* — in other words, the information itself, regardless of how it's ultimately represented — using XML Schemas (discussed in Chapter 5). For example, consider a simple service that takes a postal code and date and returns an average temperature. The service would have two types of data to deal with, as shown in the following:

```
<types>
   <xsd:schema xmlns=""
         xmlns:xsd="http://www.w3.org/2000/10/XMLSchema"
         targetNamespace="http://www.example.com/temperature">
      <xsd:complexType name="temperatureRequestType">
         <xsd:sequence>
            <xsd:element name="where" type="xsd:string" />
            <xsd:element name="when" type="xsd:date"/>
         </xsd:sequence>
      </xsd:complexType>
      <xsd:complexType name="temperatureResponseType">
         <xsd:sequence>
            <xsd:element name="temperature" type="xsd:integer"/>
         </xsd:sequence>
      </xsd:complexType>
   </xsd:schema>
</types>
```

Just as in a normal schema document, you define two types: `temperatureRequestType` and `temperatureResponseType`. You can use them to define messages.

<messages>

When you define a message in a WSDL file, you're defining the content, rather than the representation. Sure, when you send SOAP messages, you are sending XML in a SOAP envelope, but that doesn't matter when you define the messages in the WSDL file. All you care about is what the message is, what it's called, and what kind of data it holds. Take the following example:

```
<message name="TemperatureRequestMsg">
   <part name="getTemperature" type="typens:temperatureRequestType"/>
</message>
<message name="TemperatureResponseMsg">
   <part name="temperatureResponse" type="typens:temperatureResponseType"/>
</message>
```

In the preceding code, you defined a message that consists of an element called `getTemperature` of the type `temperatureRequestType`. This translates into the following SOAP message:

```
<env:Envelope xmlns:env="http://www.w3.org/2003/05/soap-envelope">
   <env:Body>
      <getTemperature>
         <where>{{it{POSTAL} CODE}}</where>
         <when>{{it{DATE}}}</when>
      </getTemperature>
   </env:Body>
</env:Envelope>
```

Notice that the namespace for the payload is still missing. You take care of that later in the WSDL file. In WSDL 2.0, messages are described within the `types` element and rely on XML Schemas.

<portTypes>

portTypes contains a number of portType elements that describe the individual operation provided by the service. These operations come in two varieties, input and output, and are made up of the messages you defined earlier. Consider the following example:

```
<portType name="TemperatureServicePortType">
   <operation name="GetTemperature">
      <input message="typens:TemperatureRequestMsg"/>
      <output message="typens:TemperatureResponseMsg"/>
   </operation>
</portType>
```

This portType shows that you're dealing with a request-response pattern; the user sends an input message, the structure of which is defined as a TemperatureRequestMsg, and the service returns an output message in the form of a TemperatureResponseMsg.

One of the major improvements coming in WSDL 2.0 is the change of the <portTypes> element to the <interfaces> element. Although portType seems to make sense from a structural point of view — later, you'll reference it when you define an actual port — it really is more of an interface, as it defines the various operations you can carry out with the service. interfaces can also be extended using the extends attribute, which allows inheritance and greater reuse of already successful code.

Next, you have to define how those messages are sent.

<binding>

Up until now, this section actually hasn't described anything related to SOAP. You've defined messages and put them together into operations, but you haven't learned anything about the protocol you use to send them. The binding element sets up the first part of this process. In this case, you bind the operations to SOAP as follows:

```
<binding name="TemperatureBinding" type="typens:TemperatureServicePortType">
   <soap:binding style="rpc" transport="http://schemas.xmlsoap.org/soap/http"/>
   <operation name="GetTemperature">
      <soap:operation />
      <input>
         <soap:body use="encoded"
                    encodingStyle="http://www.w3.org/2003/05/soap-encoding"
                    namespace="http://www.example.com/temperature" />
      </input>
      <output>
         <soap:body use="encoded"
                    encodingStyle="http://www.w3.org/2003/05/soap-encoding"
                    namespace="http://www.example.com/temperature" />
      </output>
   </operation>
</binding>
```

Notice that the soap: namespace finally comes into play at this point. Let's take this one step at a time.

<soap:binding>

The `<soap:binding>` element specifies that you are, in fact, dealing with a SOAP message, but it does more than that. The `transport` attribute is easy; it simply specifies that you're sending the message via HTTP. The `style` attribute is a little more complex (but just a little).

Both this chapter and the previous one concentrate on using web services as another means of performing remote procedure calls, but that's not their only use. In fact, in many cases information is simply passed to the service, which acts upon the data, rather than the data determining what should be done.

The `style` attribute has two possible values: `rpc` and `document`. The `rpc` value is a message in which you simply have a method name and parameters. For example, in our message, the payload represents a call to the `getTemperature` method with the parameters `34652` and `2004-5-23`, as shown in the following:

```
<env:Envelope xmlns:env="http://www.w3.org/2003/05/soap-envelope">
   <env:Body>
<getTemperature>
      <where>34652</where>
      <when>2004-05-23</when>
   </getTemperature>
   </env:Body>
</env:Envelope>
```

The data is contained in an outer element (`getTemperature`), which is itself contained within the `<env:Body>` element.

When you use the `document` style, however, the situation is slightly different. In that case, the entire contents of the `<env:Body>` element are considered to be the data in question. For example, you might have created a SOAP message of the following:

```
<env:Envelope xmlns:env="http://www.w3.org/2003/05/soap-envelope">

   <env:Body>
      <where>34652</where>
      <when>2004-05-23</when>
   </env:Body>
</env:Envelope>
```

The document style also enables you to send more complex documents that might not fit into the RPC mold. Note that neither of these examples shows the namespaces for the payload. That is set in the `soap:body` element, which you'll learn about shortly.

<soap:operation>

If the `<soap:operation>` element looks out of place just sitting there with no attributes, that's because in many ways it is out of place. The SOAP 1.1 specification required all services to use a `SOAPAction` header defining the application that was supposed to execute it. This was an HTTP header, so you'd see something like this:

```
POST /soap.asp HTTP/1.1
```

```
Accept: image/gif, image/x-xbitmap, image/jpeg, image/pjpeg, */*
Accept-Language: en-us
Content-Type: application/x-www-form-urlencoded
Accept-Encoding: gzip, deflate
User-Agent: Mozilla/4.0 (compatible; MSIE 5.5; Windows NT 5.0)
Host: www.example.com
Content-Length: 242
SOAPAction: "http://www.example.org/soap/TemperatureService.asp"

<env:Envelope xmlns:env="http://www.w3.org/2003/05/soap-envelope">
  <env:Body>
    <getTemperature>
      <where>34652</where>
      <when>2004-05-23</when>
    </getTemperature>
  </env:Body>
</env:Envelope>
```

The SOAP 1.2 specification did away with the SOAPAction header, but it's still necessary to specify that this is a SOAP message — hence, the soap:operation element.

<soap:body>

The binding element references an operation, which, in this case, is already defined as having an input and an output message. Within the binding element, you define how those messages are to be presented using the soap:body element. For example, you specify the following:

```
<soap:body use="encoded"
           encodingStyle="http://www.w3.org/2003/05/soap-encoding"
           namespace="http://www.example.com/temperature" />
```

For the input message, you're specifying that it's a SOAP message. Like the style attribute, the use attribute has two possible values: literal and encoded. When the use is specified as literal, it means that the server is not to assume any particular meaning in the XML, but to take it as a whole. Normally, you use the literal use with the document style. If you specify the use as encoded, you have to specify the encodingStyle. In this case, you specify the SOAP style, but you could use other encodings, such as RDF or even an entirely new encoding style. Finally, you specify the namespace of the payload, so you wind up with a complete message as follows:

```
<env:Envelope xmlns:env="http://www.w3.org/2003/05/soap-envelope">
  <env:Body>
    <t:getTemperature xmlns:t="http://www.example.com/temperature">
      <t:where>34652</t:where>
      <t:when>2004-05-23</t:when>
    </t:getTemperature>
S   </env:Body>
</env:Envelope>
```

Now you just need to know where to send it.

<service>

The final step in creating a WSDL file is to specify the service that you're creating by putting all of these pieces together, as shown in the following:

```
<service name="TemperatureService">
    <port name="TemperaturePort" binding="typens:TemperatureBinding">
        <soap:address location="http://www.example.com/temp/getTemp.asp"/>
    </port>
</service>
```

When you create a service, you're specifying where and how to send the information. In fact, the port element shown here will likely be renamed to endpoint in WSDL 2.0 because that's what it is: the endpoint for the connection between the server and a client. First, you reference the binding you just created, and then you send it as a SOAP message to the address specified by the location attribute. That's it. Now let's try it out.

Try It Out   Specifying the Order Service via WSDL

In this Try It Out you'll create a WSDL file that describes the service you created earlier in the chapter:

1. Open a new text file and name it WileyShopping.wsdl.

2. Start by creating the overall structure for the file:

```
<?xml version="1.0"?>
<definitions name="WileyShopping"
    targetNamespace="http://www.wiley.com/soap/ordersystem"
    xmlns:typens="http://www.wiley.com/soap/ordersystem"
    xmlns:xsd="http://www.w3.org/2000/10/XMLSchema"
    xmlns:soap="http://schemas.xmlsoap.org/wsdl/soap/"
    xmlns:soapenc="http://schemas.xmlsoap.org/soap/encoding/"
    xmlns:wsdl="http://schemas.xmlsoap.org/wsdl/"
    xmlns="http://schemas.xmlsoap.org/wsdl/">
<!-- more WSDL will go here -->
</definitions>
```

3. Add types for the XML in the messages to be passed as children of the definitions element:

```
<types>
        <xsd:schema xmlns=""
            xmlns:xsd="http://www.w3.org/2000/10/XMLSchema"
            targetNamespace="http://www.wiley.com/soap/ordersystem">
                <xsd:complexType name="AddToCartType">
                    <xsd:sequence>
                        <xsd:element name="CartId" type="xsd:string" />
                        <xsd:element name="Item">
                            <xsd:complexType>
                                <xsd:sequence>
                                    <xsd:element name="Quantity"
                                                        type="xsd:string"/>
                                    <xsd:element name="TotalPrice"
                                                        type="xsd:string"/>
                                </xsd:sequence>
                                <xsd:attribute name="ItemId"
```

```
                                                         type="xsd:string" />
                        </xsd:complexType>
                    </xsd:element>
                </xsd:sequence>
            </xsd:complexType>
            <xsd:complexType name="AddToCartResponseType">
                <xsd:sequence>
                    <xsd:element name="CartId" type="xsd:string"/>
                    <xsd:element name="Status" type="xsd:string"/>
                    <xsd:element name="Quantity" type="xsd:string"/>
                    <xsd:element name="ItemId" type="xsd:string"/>
                </xsd:sequence>
            </xsd:complexType>
        </xsd:schema>
</types>
```

4. Define the messages to be sent to and from the service:

```
<message name="AddToCartRequestMsg">
   <part name="AddToCart" type="typens:AddToCartType"/>
</message>
<message name="AddToCartResponseMsg">
   <part name="AddToCartResponse" type="typens:AddToCartResponseType"/>
</message>
```

5. Now define the portType, or interface, that will use the messages:

```
<portType name="WileyPort">
   <operation name="AddToCart">
      <input message="typens:AddToCartRequestMsg"/>
      <output message="typens:AddToCartResponseMsg"/>
   </operation>
</portType>
```

6. Bind the portType to a particular protocol, in this case, SOAP:

```
<binding name="WileyBinding"
                        type="typens:WileyPort">
   <soap:binding style="rpc"
      transport="http://schemas.xmlsoap.org/soap/http"/>
   <operation name="AddToCart">
      <soap:operation />
         <input>
            <soap:body use="encoded"
                    namespace="http://www.wiley.com/soap/ordersystem"
                    encodingStyle="http://schemas.xmlsoap.org/soap/encoding/"/>
         </input>
         <output>
            <soap:body use="encoded"
                    namespace="http://www.wiley.com/soap/ordersystem"
                    encodingStyle="http://schemas.xmlsoap.org/soap/encoding/"/>
         </output>
   </operation>
</binding>
```

7. Finally, define the actual service by associating the binding with an endpoint. This results in the following final file:

```xml
<?xml version="1.0"?>
<definitions name="WileyShopping"
    targetNamespace="http://www.wiley.com/soap/ordersystem"
    xmlns:typens="http://www.wiley.com/soap/ordersystem"
    xmlns:xsd="http://www.w3.org/2000/10/XMLSchema"
    xmlns:soap="http://schemas.xmlsoap.org/wsdl/soap/"
    xmlns:soapenc="http://schemas.xmlsoap.org/soap/encoding/"
    xmlns:wsdl="http://schemas.xmlsoap.org/wsdl/"
    xmlns="http://schemas.xmlsoap.org/wsdl/">

<types>
        <xsd:schema xmlns=""
            xmlns:xsd="http://www.w3.org/2000/10/XMLSchema"
            targetNamespace="http://www.wiley.com/soap/ordersystem">
            <xsd:complexType name="AddToCartType">
                <xsd:sequence>
                    <xsd:element name="CartId" type="xsd:string" />
                    <xsd:element name="item">
                        <xsd:complexType>
                            <xsd:sequence>
                                <xsd:element name="Quantity"
                                                type="xsd:string"/>
                                <xsd:element name="TotalPrice"
                                                type="xsd:string"/>
                            </xsd:sequence>
                            <xsd:attribute name="ItemId"
                                                type="xsd:string" />
                        </xsd:complexType>
                    </xsd:element>
                </xsd:sequence>
            </xsd:complexType>
            <xsd:complexType name="addToCartResponseType">
                <xsd:sequence>
                    <xsd:element name="CartId" type="xsd:string"/>
                    <xsd:element name="Status" type="xsd:string"/>
                    <xsd:element name="Quantity" type="xsd:string"/>
                    <xsd:element name="ItemId" type="xsd:string"/>
                </xsd:sequence>
            </xsd:complexType>
        </xsd:schema>
</types>

<message name="AddToCartRequestMsg">
        <part name="AddToCart" type="typens:AddToCartType"/>
</message>
<message name="AddToCartResponseMsg">
        <part name="AddToCartResponse" type="typens:AddToCartResponseType"/>
</message>

<portType name="WileyPort">
        <operation name="AddToCart">
                <input message="typens:AddToCartRequestMsg"/>
                <output message="typens:AddToCartResponseMsg"/>
```

```
                </operation>
        </portType>
        <binding name="WileyBinding"
                                type="typens:WileyPort">
                <soap:binding style="rpc"
                        transport="http://schemas.xmlsoap.org/soap/http"/>
                <operation name="AddToCart">
                        <soap:operation/>
                        <input>
                                <soap:body use="encoded"
        namespace="http://www.wiley.com/soap/ordersystem"
        encodingStyle="http://schemas.xmlsoap.org/soap/encoding/"/>
                        </input>
                        <output>
                                <soap:body use="encoded"
        namespace="http://www.wiley.com/soap/ordersystem"
        encodingStyle="http://schemas.xmlsoap.org/soap/encoding/"/>
                        </output>
                </operation>
        </binding>
        <service name="WileyService">
                <port name="WileyPort" binding="typens:WileyBinding">
                        <soap:address
        location="http://localhost/BasicOrderService/AddToCart.aspx"/>
                </port>
        </service>
</definitions>
```

How It Works

Here you created a simple WSDL file describing the SOAP messages sent to and from the hypothetical Wiley Shopping Service. First, you created the datatypes for the messages to be sent. Next, you combined them into messages, created operations out of the messages, and finally bound them to a protocol and a service.

Other Bindings

It's important to understand that WSDL doesn't necessarily describe a SOAP service. Earlier in this chapter, you looked at a situation in which messages were passed by HTTP without the benefit of a SOAP wrapper. These REST messages can also be defined via WSDL by adding the HTTP binding.

The basic process is the same as it was for SOAP: Define the datatypes, group them into messages, create operations from the messages and portTypes from the operations, and then create a binding that ties them all in to a particular protocol, as shown in the following:

```
<?xml version="1.0"?>
<definitions name="WileyShopping"
    targetNamespace="http://www.wiley.com/soap/ordersystem"
    xmlns:typens="http://www.wiley.com/soap/ordersystem"
    xmlns:xsd="http://www.w3.org/2000/10/XMLSchema"
    xmlns:soap="http://schemas.xmlsoap.org/wsdl/soap/"
    xmlns:soapenc="http://schemas.xmlsoap.org/soap/encoding/"
```

```
        xmlns:wsdl="http://schemas.xmlsoap.org/wsdl/"

        xmlns:http="http://schemas.xmlsoap.org/wsdl/http/"
        xmlns:mime="http://schemas.xmlsoap.org/wsdl/mime/"
        xmlns="http://schemas.xmlsoap.org/wsdl/">

<types>
        <xsd:schema xmlns=""
            xmlns:xsd="http://www.w3.org/2000/10/XMLSchema"
            targetNamespace="http://www.wiley.com/soap/ordersystem">
                <xsd:complexType name="AddToCartType">
                        <xsd:sequence>
                                <xsd:element name="CartId" type="xsd:string" />
                                    <xsd:element name="ItemId" type="xsd:string"/>
                            <xsd:element name="Quantity" type="xsd:string"/>
                            <xsd:element name="TotalPrice" type="xsd:string"/>
                        </xsd:sequence>
                </xsd:complexType>
                <xsd:complexType name="AddToCartResponseType">
                <xsd:sequence>
                        <xsd:element name="CartId" type="xsd:string"/>
                        <xsd:element name="Status" type="xsd:string"/>
                        <xsd:element name="Quantity" type="xsd:string"/>
                    <xsd:element name="ItemId" type="xsd:string"/>
                </xsd:sequence>
        </xsd:complexType>

        <xsd:complexType name="GetTotalResponseType">
                <xsd:sequence>
                        <xsd:element name="Discount" type="xsd:string" />
                            <xsd:element name="TotalPrice"
type="xsd:string"/>
                </xsd:sequence>
        </xsd:complexType>
        </xsd:schema>
</types>
<message name="AddToCartRequestMsg">
        <part name="AddToCart" type="typens:AddToCartType"/>
</message>
<message name="AddToCartResponseMsg">
        <part name="AddToCartResponse" type="typens:AddToCartResponseType"/>
</message>


<message name="UpdateTotalsRequestMsg">
        <part name="Quantity" type="xsd:number"/>
        <part name="UnitPrice" type="xsd:number"/>
</message>
<message name="GetTotalResponseMsg">
        <part name="GetTotalResponse" type="typens:
         GetTotalResponseType"/>
</message>
<portType name="WileyPort">
        <operation name="AddToCart">
                <input message="typens:AddToCartRequestMsg"/>
                <output message="typens:AddToCartResponseMsg"/>
        </operation>
```

```
        </portType>
<portType name="WileyRESTPort">

        <operation name="GetTotal2.aspx">
                <input message="typens:UpdateTotalsRequestMsg"/>
                <output message="typens:UpdateTotalsResponseMsg"/>
        </operation>
</portType>

<binding name="WileyBinding"
                         type="typens:WileyPort">
        <soap:binding style="rpc"
                transport="http://schemas.xmlsoap.org/soap/http"/>
        <operation name="AddToCart">
                <soap:operation/>
                <input>
                        <soap:body use="encoded"
namespace="http://www.wiley.com/soap/ordersystem"
encodingStyle="http://schemas.xmlsoap.org/soap/encoding/"/>
                </input>
                <output>
                        <soap:body use="encoded"
namespace="http://www.wiley.com/soap/ordersystem"
encodingStyle="http://schemas.xmlsoap.org/soap/encoding/"/>
                </output>
        </operation>
</binding>
<binding name="WileyRESTBinding"
                         type="typens:WileyRESTPort">
        <http:binding verb="GET"/>
        <operation name="GetTotal2.aspx">
                <http:operation location="GetTotal.aspx"/>
                <input>
                        <http:urlEncoded/>
                </input>
                <output>
                        <mime:content type="text/xml"/>
                </output>
        </operation>
</binding>
<service name="WileyService">
        <port name="WileyPort" binding="typens:WileyBinding">
                <soap:address
location="http://localhost/BasicOrderService/GetTotal.aspx"/>
        </port>

        <port name="WileyRESTPort" binding="typens:WileyRESTBinding">
                <http:address location="http://localhost/BasicOrderService/"/>
        </port>

</service>
</definitions>
```

In this way, you can define a service that uses any protocol using WSDL.

In real life, WSDL is created by the SOAP tool you use. Occasionally, a tweak or two might be needed—for example, the port or binding sections may need amending when you switch from development to live. In ASP.NET, for instance, if you build a service using asmx pages, the WSDL is created automatically.

Summary

In this chapter, you looked at SOAP, an XML-based protocol for performing remote procedure calls and passing information between computers. You studied how this protocol is used and even put it into practice by creating a SOAP-based shopping cart system.

Because SOAP is based on easy-to-implement and standardized technologies, such as XML and HTTP, it has the potential to become a very universal protocol indeed. In fact, most of the hype surrounding SOAP concerns its interoperability. At least initially, companies providing SOAP software are concentrating on making their product as interoperable as possible with the software from other companies, instead of creating proprietary changes to the standard.

With the backing of companies such as Microsoft, IBM, DevelopMentor, Lotus, UserLand Software, Sun Microsystems, and Canon, SOAP is already a widely implemented technology. The web services built on top of SOAP also have huge potential for creating widely accessible functionality over the Web.

That said, SOAP is not the only game in town. You also looked at a simpler form of web service, REST, which is currently growing in popularity. The chapter also described Web Services Definition Language (WSDL), which is designed to enable you to provide other developers with all of the information they might need in order to access your service. WSDL can be used with any protocol but is particularly well suited to SOAP. You examined the various parts of a WSDL document and created one for the SOAP and REST services you built earlier in the chapter.

Exercise Questions

Suggested solutions to these questions can be found in Appendix A.

Question 1

Create a SOAP message that fulfills the following requirements:

1. It corresponds to an RPC called `getRadioOperators()`.
2. It passes the following information:
   - City and State or Postal Code
   - Radius
   - License Class
3. The server must receive and verify a call sign from the sender.

Question 2

Create a WSDL file that describes the document in Question 1.

Ajax

The term Ajax was first used in early 2005 by Jesse James Garrett as an acronym for Asynchronous JavaScript and XML. The term is a little misleading because (a) the technique is not always asynchronous; (b) XML is not necessarily used; and (c) if you're happy for your code to be Internet Explorer–specific, then you can replace JavaScript with VBScript.

The crux of Ajax, though, is making requests behind the scenes in a web application and incorporating any data returned in the page without reloading the entire HTML. The normal way that this is carried out is by using an *HTTP Request* controlled by client-side scripting. Data is passed in the request, often as XML, and a response, also commonly XML, is received. The information contained in this response is then incorporated in the page using dynamic HTML.

These techniques have made possible the kind of responsiveness and functionality that previously were only to be found in desktop applications. Two of the most famous Ajax uses both originate from Google. Google Suggest, `www.google.com/webhp?complete=1&hl=en`, enables a textbox to suggest suitable entries chosen from a drop-down list; and Gmail, `mail.google.com/mail/help/intl/en/about.html`, is a web e-mail client with almost as much functionality as a traditional desktop application such as Microsoft's Outlook Express.

This chapter first describes previous endeavors to improve the user experience before the Ajax technique was formalized. You will learn the differences between the two main browser camps, IE and Mozilla, and how this led to the use of a cross-browser library to simplify development. You will also see how background requests are passed using the XMLHttpRequest, and how the two main options for data formats, XML and JSON, compare. Two Ajax applications are examined in detail: a simple web service that validates credit card numbers and a more complex AutoSuggest textbox. The chapter finishes with an explanation of how the *same source origin policy* limits your use of third-party web services, and how to overcome this using a server-side proxy.

Early Attempts at Asynchronous Updates

Web developers often want their programs to be able to carry out background tasks while the user continues to view and use the current page. One of the ways of passing data to a server behind the scenes is to use the `Image` object. Suppose when users land on a page in your site you want to record from which page they got there. You can use the following JavaScript, assuming the `referrer` property has been populated:

```
var oImage = new Image();
var sRef = "ref=" + encodeURIComponent(document.referrer);
var sMe = "me=" + encodeURIComponent(location.href);
oImage.src = "myLoggingPage.aspx?" +sRef + "&" + sMe
```

Obviously, you need to set up a page named `myLoggingPage.aspx` to record the data. `encodeURIComponent` is used to escape any problematic characters.

This sort of approach is used by Google Analytics to produce tracking figures for sites but it has two drawbacks: the amount and structure of the data sent in a query string is limited, and, more important, there is no means to receive a response. These problems were initially solved in a number of ways, including the following:

❑   **Hidden frames or iframes** — Using this technique, which is still the only option on some older browsers, data was posted by manipulating the form elements in a hidden frame or iframe. The frame was then submitted programmatically. The resulting page could then be accessed and the returned data passed to the main content page. The main problems with this approach were that hidden frames can cause problems with some devices, and the structure of the data that could be passed was somewhat restricted. It was also necessary to hand-craft much of the code, with little reusability.

❑   **Java applets** — Java applets overcame some of the problems with hidden frames. They provided a more common interface and removed some of the drudge work. The problems with applets was that they needed to be installed on the client, which often meant an update to the Java Runtime, and differences between different implementations of the Java Virtual Machine (between Microsoft's and Sun's) meant that some applets worked only on one version.

One of the turning points that led to today's move to Ajax occurred in 1998 when Microsoft released Internet Explorer 5.0, and with it came support for XML. Included in the library was a class named `XmlHttp`, a strange choice because it could actual initiate any HTTP request; it wasn't confined to sending or receiving XML. This class had the ability, among other things, to make GET and POST requests and could return the results to the caller in a variety of formats, such as text, XML, or a byte stream. Slowly but surely developers of other browsers noticed how useful this was and began to incorporate similar functionality into their browsers. The main difference in how the functionality is implemented is that Microsoft's version is a COM, or ActiveX, library, whereas in other browsers it is a built-in component, part of the `window` object. Support for the capability to make background requests via `XmlHttp` classes now exists in all the Mozilla-based browsers such as Firefox and Netscape, as well as, to a lesser extent, Safari and Opera.

Microsoft versus Mozilla

As noted, Microsoft's library needs to be instantiated via the standard ActiveX extensions to JavaScript:

```
var oXmlHttp = new ActiveXObject("MSXML2.XmlHttp.3.0");
```

The program id, or string, that needs to be passed to the `ActiveXObject()` function consists of the library name, `MSXML2`, and the member name, along with the version. To date, Microsoft has released six versions of the class, but version 3.0 is installed by default on all modern machines.

Because ActiveX can be harnessed for malicious purposes, its use in browsers is controlled by the origin of the page hosting it and the security settings for that page's zone. For example, a page from your company's intranet, the *local intranet* zone, will allow freer use than a site from the *Internet* zone. Some features of the MSXML2 library are not normally available when the control is used on a web page — for example, saving an XML file to the local disk.

The Mozilla way of doing things is to incorporate the class into the browser object model. The following snippet shows how to create the object in a Mozilla browser:

```
var oXmlHttp = new XMLHttpRequest();
```

Both return a similar object, with Microsoft's having the edge on functionality. Fortunately, because of JavaScript's built-in extensibility, it is possible to add required features using standard scripting techniques.

Cross-Browser Solutions

When designing web pages, it would be tedious to have to write one version for Microsoft and another for other browsers when needing to use the `XmlHttp` functionality. To overcome this, several cross-browser libraries are available that detect which platform they are running on and return the correct version of the object. They also add in the missing features of the Mozilla version so that any subsequent script can ignore any differences in methods.

The client-side examples in this chapter use the library introduced in `zXml.js` *in Chapter 14.*

Once the capability to make background requests and receive a response became available in most browsers, people began to see the benefits of the techniques that would eventually be labeled *Ajax*. It was no longer necessary to request a complete HTML page every time a small portion of the page needed updating. A common example is address lookup; many sites where users need to supply an address now have the facility to automatically fill in address details when a zip code is entered. Rather than make a complete round-trip to the server and have to store and repopulate all the other fields on the page that the user had already completed, a mechanism that allows just the zip code to be sent to the server and the address returned means a better user experience, less bandwidth used, and simpler state management. Given the emerging popularity of XML at the same time, and the fact that only data — devoid of presentation — needs to be exchanged, it was natural this format was chosen as the medium. Examples of this sort of application existed some eight years before the term Ajax was coined.

The next several sections describe the principles behind how Ajax works and provide specific examples of each step.

Some of the examples that follow require a virtual web directory to be created. In IIS this is accomplished by opening the IIS manager, either by going to Start ⇨ Administrative Tools ⇨ Internet Information Services Manager or by selecting Start ⇨ Run and entering either `C:\WINDOWS\system32\Inetsrv6\iis6.msc` or `C:\WINDOWS\system32\Inetsrv\iis.msc`, depending on which version of the manager you are using, and clicking OK. Then create a new folder on your machine where the web files will be stored.

You then need to expand the tree view on the left to Default Web Site. Right-click and choose New ⇨ Virtual Directory as shown in Figure 16-1. Follow the wizard's instructions. You can accept the defaults, and just choose a friendly name for the folder and the actual location for the folder just created. When you're finished, right-click on the new folder in the IIS manager and choose Properties. From the Directory tab, click the Create button next to the Application textbox and set the permissions in the drop-down menu to Scripts only, as shown in Figure 16-2. Click OK to back out of the properties box.

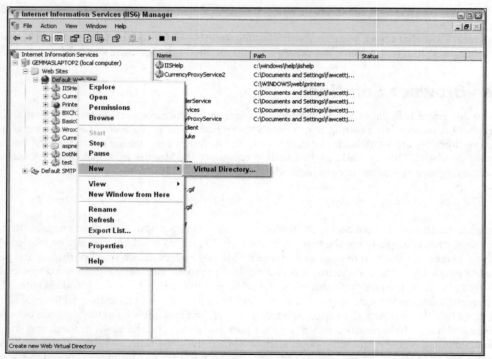

Figure 16-1

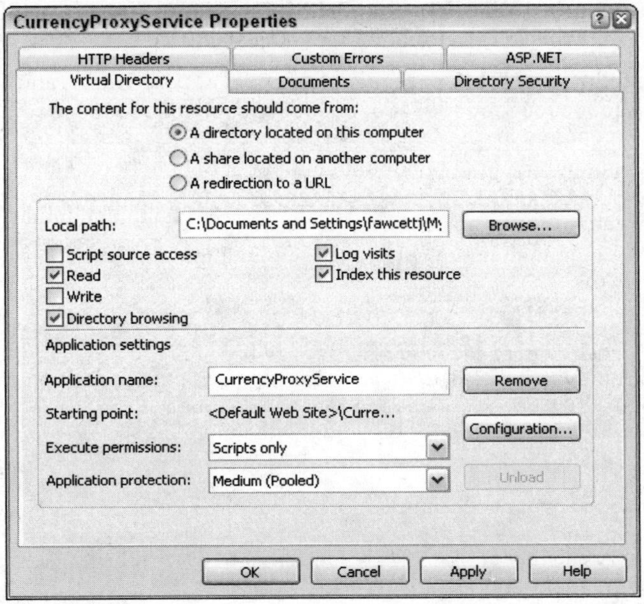

Figure 16-2

Basic Posting Techniques

The basic steps involved in making an HTTP request using XmlHttp are as follows:

1. Create an instance of the XmlHttp request class.

2. Specify a function to call to deal with the response.

3. Open a connection to the server specifying the URL and method, either GET or POST.

4. Send the request together with any data if necessary.

5. Process the returned data using the function specified in step 2.

Try It Out   **Making a Background Post**

This example demonstrates how these steps translate into JavaScript using the zXml cross-browser library.

1. Create a new folder on your machine named WroxServices and turn it into a new virtual directory, also called WroxServices.

2. Create a file named BasicRetrievalDemo.aspx, which is just a minimal web form with some hard-coded XML:

```
<%@ Page Language="C#" ContentType="text/xml"%>
<response>How to retrieve XML data</response>
```

(If you are not using ASP.NET — but PHP, for instance — create a similar file for your chosen language.) Save this in the virtual folder you just created.

3. Create the following HTML page, `BasicRetrievalDemo.html`, and save it to `WroxServices`:

```
<html>
<head>
<title>Basic Retrieval Demo</title>
<script type="text/javascript" src="zXML.src.js"></script>
<script type="text/javascript">
var oXmlHttp;

function fetchData()
{
  oXmlHttp = zXmlHttp.createRequest();
  oXmlHttp.onreadystatechange = handleReadyStateChange;
  oXmlHttp.open("POST", "BasicRetrievalDemo.aspx", true);
  oXmlHttp.send("<data/>");
}

function handleReadyStateChange()
{
  if (oXmlHttp.readyState == 4)
  {
    alert(oXmlHttp.responseText);
  }
}
</script>
</head>
<body onload="fetchData();">
</body>
</html>
```

4. Browse to `http://localhost/wroxservices/BasicRetrievalDemo.aspx`. You should see an alert box containing the raw XML from the aspx file.

How It Works

The page that returns the XML, `BasicRetrievalDemo.aspx`, has no processing attached to it; it may as well have been a regular XML file except that some web servers, including IIS, will not allow, by default, a `POST` request to be made to a static XML file.

The HTML is mainly JavaScript. First the cross-browser library is referenced using a standard script include:

```
<script type="text/javascript" src="zXML.src.js"></script>
```

In the examples in this chapter, `zXML.src.js` *is used because it is commented and indented to make debugging easier. In a production application, the more compact, but functionally equivalent,* `zXML.js` *would be a better choice.*

Within the next script block, a variable is created to hold the XMLHttpRequest:

```
var oXmlHttp;
```

There are two functions in the second script block, fetchData() and handleReadyStateChange(). The former is called when the page has loaded as instructed by the onload attribute in the body element. When fetchData() is called, it first creates an XMLHttpRequest and assigns it to the previously declared oXmlHttp variable:

```
oXmlHttp = zXmlHttp.createRequest();
```

For IE, the zXmlHttp class automatically returns the most suitable ActiveX version; for Mozilla, it returns an instance of XMLHttpRequest. If the browser supports neither, an error is thrown.

Next, it assigns a function, known as a *callback*, to onreadystatechange:

```
oXmlHttp.onreadystatechange = handleReadyStateChange;
```

The second function in the script, handleReadyStateChange(), is assigned to be called when the readystatechange event fires. Mozilla's XMLHttpRequest does not actually call this event, only Microsoft's version does, but the library adds the necessary code for this to work. Microsoft defines five states for the readyState starting with 0, uninitialized, and finishing with 4, which equates to completed. Until state 4 appears, the response is not ready to be processed. The zXml library fakes this behavior for Mozilla but only state 4, completed, can be relied on.

```
oXmlHttp.open("POST", "http://localhost/wroxservices/BasicRetrievalDemo.aspx", true);
```

The connection is opened, this time using POST, rather than GET. POST is normally used in three situations: when a large amount of data needs to be sent, when the structure is awkward to represent using name/value pairs, or when updates will be made by the server. GET is used in other circumstances, such as when data is requested but no updates are being made. The third parameter, true in this case, specifies whether to make an asynchronous connection or not. Normally, an asynchronous connection is preferred because it allows other scripts to execute and the user can continue to use the page while the request is being satisfied.

Most clients allow a maximum of two simultaneous connections to the same host. Although this behavior can be overridden, you need to build your applications based on this limit. This means that if you initiate three HTTP requests, the third one will be blocked until one of the other two completes.

An easy way to see this in action is to try to download three non-HTML files simultaneously from a site. The progress report on the third request will stay at 0% until one of the two earlier requests completes.

```
oXmlHttp.send("<data/>");
```

The data, if any, is sent to the server. The server processes the request and issues a response. When this happens, handleReadyStateChange is called:

```
function handleReadyStateChange()
{
  if (oXmlHttp.readyState == 4)
  {
    alert(oXmlHttp.responseXML.xml);
  }
}
```

The first step is to ensure that the `readyState` is 4, completed. If so, the response can be used. If XML has been returned, the XML document is accessed via the `responseXML` property. In this example, the actual XML is just alerted; in the real world you probably need to parse the XML and extract the data needed.

If you need to make another request to the same server, you must call the `open()` *method again. You can't just call* `send` *with different parameters.*

Transport and Processing on the Server

Now that you know how to send a request and deal with the response, consider how the server processes the request and what format the request and response should take. Original exponents of XmlHttp simply wrote pages that read the posted data, parsed it, and carried out whatever processing was necessary. The problem with this was that each page needed data in a different format and there was little interoperability between sites. As web services standardized, many came to use the SOAP model and so did many sites using Ajax; others stuck to using XML but in a variety of formats. Some, however, decided on a different approach to passing data. Among these is a technique called *JavaScript Object Notation (JSON)*. All these techniques are covered in this chapter.

JSON

JavaScript Object Notation is a popular alternative in Ajax to using XML for data representation. It seeks to address the following issues with using XML:

❑   XML can be very verbose; even small amounts of data carry quite a large overhead.

❑   You need an XML parser to consume it, and possibly other classes as well such as an XSL processor and a serializer.

❑   The syntax can be quite daunting and you must give a lot of thought to the serialization process.

JSON solves these problems by representing data as JavaScript literals. It does not need any XML classes to process it and is usually terser, which results in less traffic across the network. What are JavaScript literals? Most languages support literals of one sort or another. In C#, for instance, a string literal can be used to initialize a new string object:

```
string myString = "this is a string literal";
```

This is very similar to JavaScript, the difference being the use of `string` instead of `var`.

JavaScript also supports array literals. Instead of creating an array and populating it one element at a time, you can do it all in one statement:

```
var myArray = new Array();
myArray[0] = "One";
myArray[1] = "Two";
myArray[2] = "Three";

//Equivalent literal syntax
var myArray = ["One", "Two", "Three"];
```

Finally, it's also possible to have object literals:

```
var myObject = new Object();
myObject.name = "Joe";
myObject.age = 44;
myObject.lastUpdated = new Date();
//Equivalent literal syntax
var myObject = {name: "Joe", age: 44, lastUpdated: new Date()};
```

As an alternative, you can quote the member names.

The idea behind JSON is to transform data needed for the HTTP request to a literal. When the web service returns the data, also a literal, it is passed to JavaScript's `eval()` function, which converts the literal back into data that can be used by the web page. An example is shown later in the second version of the AutoSuggest control.

Although JSON has its advantages, it hasn't yet replaced XML as the method of data representation altogether, for the following reasons:

❑ For more complicated data structures, it can be difficult to turn the data into a literal. This is especially true when the data is a document, rather than individual members.

❑ The use of `eval()` can consume resources, sometimes even more so than an XML parser. Each time `eval()` is called, a new instance of the JavaScript engine is created; this is one reason why it's frowned upon to use it in standard web pages.

Several JSON libraries are available that simplify the task of converting data to literals and vice versa. A popular one is Douglas Crockford's, which you can find at `www.json.org/js.html`.

Our first example of a fully working Ajax component is the AutoSuggest drop-down, one of the first uses of Ajax seen by many people. From Google Labs, you can see it in Action at `www.google.com/webhp?complete=1&hl=en`.

Three examples are presented in this chapter. The first is a relatively simple one that verifies whether a given payment card number is valid. It uses a simple web service and a small amount of JavaScript. The second example is a fully functional AutoSuggest textbox that can be used when the number of options makes a traditional drop-down impractical. Because this control manipulates the user interface to a large extent, considerably more JavaScript is needed. The final example shows how third-party web services can be used by your own website.

Many thanks to Nicholas Zakas for his ideas and assistance in implementing the AutoSuggest control.

Payment Card Validator

The first example of a real-world Ajax application uses what is known as *Luhn's algorithm* to test whether a payment card number is valid. Most payment cards in use today follow a certain pattern that helps avoid fraud and ensures that if errors are made when entering or transmitting the number, then the payment request is rejected. You can read about how algorithm works, including some of its weak points, at `http://en.wikipedia.org/wiki/Luhn`.

The basic process is as follows:

1. Enter a card number into a standard web page textbox.

2. Click the Validate button.

3. The card number is normalized, to remove spaces, hyphens, and so on.

4. The number is passed to the verification web service.

5. The Web service tests the number and returns true or false.

6. The web page displays the result.

Try It Out   Validating a Payment Card Number

1. If you haven't done so already, create a new virtual directory called WroxServices.

2. Create a new file, CheckPaymentCard.aspx, with the following code and save it in WroxServices:

```
<%@ Page Language="C#" ContentType="text/xml"%>

<script runat="server">
  protected void Page_Load(object sender, EventArgs e)
  {
    string cardNumber = Request.QueryString["cn"];
    if (string.IsNullOrEmpty(cardNumber))
    {
      SendResponse(false);
    }
    SendResponse(PerformLuhnCheck(cardNumber));
  }

  private bool PerformLuhnCheck(string cardNumber)
  {
    int sum = 0;
    try
    {
      for (int i = cardNumber.Length - 1; i >= 0; i--)
      {
        int currentDigit = int.Parse(cardNumber[i].ToString());
        if (i % 2 == 0)
        {
          currentDigit *= 2;
          if (currentDigit > 9)
          {
            currentDigit -= 9;
          }
        }
        sum += currentDigit;
      }
      return sum % 10 == 0;
    }
    catch (Exception)
    {
```

```
        return false;
    }
  }

  private void SendResponse(bool succeeded)
  {
    string xml = "<boolean>{0}</boolean>";
    Response.Write(string.Format(xml, succeeded));
    Response.End();
  }
</script>
```

3. Create another file, `CheckPaymentCard.html`, and save it to the same folder:

```html
<html>
<head>
  <title>Check Payment Card Demo</title>
  <script type="text/javascript" src="zXML.src.js"></script>
  <script type="text/javascript">
    var oXmlHttp;

    function validateCardNumber(cardNumber)
    {
      oXmlHttp = zXmlHttp.createRequest();
      showOutput("");
      oXmlHttp.onreadystatechange = handleReadyStateChange;
      cardNumber = cardNumber.replace(/\D/g, "");
      document.getElementById("txtCardNumber").value = cardNumber;
      var sUrl = "CheckPaymentCard.aspx?cn=" + cardNumber;
      oXmlHttp.open("GET", sUrl, true);
      oXmlHttp.send(null);
    }

    function handleReadyStateChange()
    {
      if (oXmlHttp.readyState == 4)
      {
        var sXPath = "/*/text()";
        var oResultNode = zXPath.selectSingleNode
                       (oXmlHttp.responseXML.documentElement, sXPath);
        showOutput(oResultNode.nodeValue);
      }
    }

    function showOutput(cardValid)
    {
      var oOutput = document.getElementById("spnOutput");
      oOutput.innerHTML = cardValid;
    }
  </script>

</head>
<body>
Card Number:<input type="text"
```

```
                          maxlength="20"
                          id="txtCardNumber"
                          value="4111111111111111"> 
     <input
     onclick="validateCardNumber(document.getElementById('txtCardNumber').value);"
          type="button"
          value="Validate"><br>
          <div>Card valid: <span id="spnOutput"></span></div>
     </body>
     </html>
```

4. Navigate to http://localhost/wroxservices/CheckPaymentCard.html, and try a number such as 4111111111111111, as shown in Figure 16-3. This is a standard testing number and should validate, whereas changing the last digit to a zero should result in the validation failing.

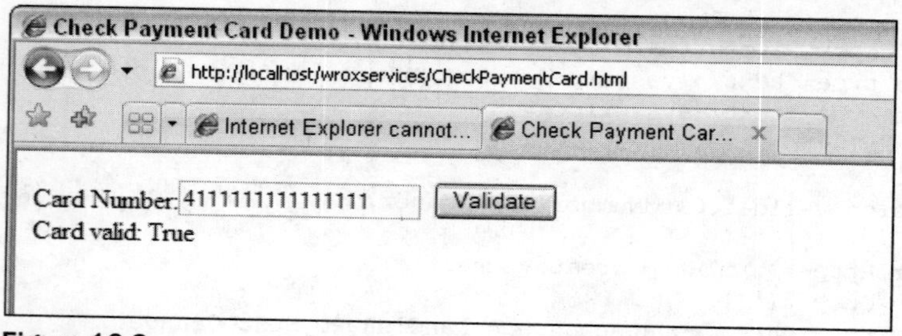

Figure 16-3

How It Works

The web service side of this process consists of three parts. The first extracts the target payment card number from the Request.QueryString if it exists. If not, the card number is treated as invalid:

```
protected void Page_Load(object sender, EventArgs e)
{
  string cardNumber = Request.QueryString["cn"];
  if (string.IsNullOrEmpty(cardNumber))
  {
    SendResponse(false);
  }
  SendResponse(PerformLuhnCheck(cardNumber));
}
```

If a card number is found, PerformLuhnCheck() is called. This basically starts from the far right of the string and sums the odd-numbered digits with twice the value of the even-numbered ones (full details can be found at the Wikipedia link given previously):

```
private bool PerformLuhnCheck(string cardNumber)
{
  int sum = 0;
  try
  {
    for (int i = cardNumber.Length - 1; i >= 0; i--)
    {
```

```
      int currentDigit = int.Parse(cardNumber[i].ToString());
      if (i % 2 == 0)
      {
        currentDigit *= 2;
        if (currentDigit > 9)
        {
          currentDigit -= 9;
        }
      }
      sum += currentDigit;
    }
    return sum % 10 == 0;
  }
  catch (Exception)
  {
    return false;
  }
}
```

If an error occurs at any stage, the card number is invalid; otherwise, the results of the check are output via SendResponse():

```
private void SendResponse(bool succeeded)
{
  string xml = "<boolean>{0}</boolean>";
  Response.Write(string.Format(xml, succeeded));
  Response.End();
}
```

SendResponse() uses a basic template, which is filled with the value True or False depending on the parameter succeeded.

The HTML page is very similar to BasicRetrievalDemo.html. A standard web page consists of a textbox and a button that, when clicked, pass the value of the textbox to a JavaScript function named validateCardNumber():

```
function validateCardNumber(cardNumber)
{
  oXmlHttp = zXmlHttp.createRequest();
  showOutput("");
  oXmlHttp.onreadystatechange = handleReadyStateChange;
  cardNumber = cardNumber.replace(/\D/g, "");
  document.getElementById("txtCardNumber").value = cardNumber;
  var sUrl = "CheckPaymentCard.aspx?cn=" + cardNumber;
  oXmlHttp.open("GET", sUrl, true);
  oXmlHttp.send(null);
}
```

validateCardNumber() assigns a new XMLHttpRequest to the previously declared variable oXmlHttp. It then assigns a callback, handleReadyStateChange(), that will process the returned XML. The line

```
cardNumber = cardNumber.replace(/\D/g, "");
```

uses a regular expression to remove any nondigits from the string, and then writes this back to the web form, before calling the web service.

`handleReadyStateChange()` introduces some new code to retrieve the necessary data from the returned XML. This code uses the `zXPath` class to locate the target node via XPath:

```
function handleReadyStateChange()
{
  if (oXmlHttp.readyState == 4)
  {
    var sXPath = "/*/text()";
    var oResultNode = zXPath.selectSingleNode
                        (oXmlHttp.responseXML.documentElement, sXPath);
    showOutput(oResultNode.nodeValue);
  }
}
```

The key step here is the XPath used, `/*/text()`; this means "fetch the text node of the document element." The next line retrieves the actual `nodeValue`, `True` or `False`, and passes this to `showOutput()` for display. This next example uses a combination of XML, XSLT, and JavaScript to implement the AutoSuggest functionality. A second version shows how it could be adapted to use JSON.

The AutoSuggest Box

If you visited the Google link mentioned earlier, you saw how the AutoSuggest box works. After entering characters into the main textbox, a list of matching suggestions appears underneath in the form of a list. The textbox itself also adds the first suggestion but with the added part selected so that it can easily be overtyped. You can also use the up and down arrow keys to choose one of the suggestions and then use the mouse or the Enter key to place it in the textbox. The AutoSuggest box is ideal for situations when a traditional drop-down would be cumbersome due to an excessive number of options.

The example here uses a list of world countries, which number nearly 200. This would be awkward to set up if the options could not be restricted somehow. Here's a list of the requirements and functionality:

❑ **Suggestions** — You need a way to restrict the list of countries to those starting with the characters already typed.

❑ **Show a suggestion** — As the user types, the textbox will be filled with a suggestion from the list. The part of the suggestion that wasn't actually entered by the user will be highlighted.

❑ **User control** — The options can be selected using the mouse or the keyboard, using the up and down arrows and the Enter key. The list can also be hidden by pressing the Esc key.

As this book is an XML primer, the first implementation uses XML for storing and transporting the data; a second version will see what changes need to be made to use JSON.

There are quite of number of parts to this example: the HTML, a substantial amount of JavaScript, CSS, and the web service to deliver the suggestions. The full listings are available in the code download for this book, but are not presented in the chapter.

The following files are used for this example:

- ❏ `zXml.src.js`: The standard XML library as used by the other examples in the chapter
- ❏ `AutoSuggest.js`: The basic JavaScript for the control
- ❏ `CountriesSuggestionProvider.js`: JavaScript specific to retrieving the countries data. There is also a second version, `CountriesSuggestionProvider2.js`, for the JSON example.
- ❏ `AutoSuggest.css`: A CSS stylesheet to control how the suggestions are displayed
- ❏ `AutoSuggestDemo.html`: An example of the control in action
- ❏ `GetCountries.aspx`: The entry point for the web service; there is also `GetCountries2.aspx` for the JSON version.
- ❏ `GetCountries.aspx.cs`: The code for the web service and a second version for the JSON version
- ❏ `Countries.xml`: The list of countries
- ❏ `Countries.xslt`: Retrieves a filtered list of countries from `Countries.xml` based on the letters provided. There is also a second version, `Countries2.xslt`, for JSON. The starting point for the whole control is a standard textbox:

```
<input type="text" name="txtSuggest" id="txtSuggest" autocomplete="off">
```

The `autocomplete` attribute set to `off` ensures that the usual browser feature of providing past entries as suggestions will not interfere with your own list.

Much of the look of a standard drop-down, as well as such features as highlighting the current suggestion, is achieved using CSS. The list of suggestions is held in a `div` that has a CSS class of `suggestions`:

```
div.suggestions
{
  position: absolute;
  background-color: #ffffff;
  border: 1px solid #000000;
  box-sizing: border-box;
  -moz-box-sizing: border-box;
}
```

The background color is set to `#ffffff` (white), and the border is set to `#000000` (black). The `-moz-box-sizing` setting is needed for some older browsers so that they follow the CSS standard. Later you'll learn how to position the `div` so that it sits underneath the textbox.

Class Design

There are two main classes: a `SuggestionProvider` and the actual `AutoSuggestControl` itself. The provider is responsible for retrieving the suggestions and passing them to the `AutoSuggestControl`. The `SuggestionProvider` only has one method, `fetchSuggestions()`, which is called by the `AutoSuggestControl` class when the user types a character into the textbox.

The `AutoSuggestControl` must be able to access both the provider and the textbox, so both of these are passed to the constructor:

```
function AutoSuggestControl(textbox, provider)
{
  this.textbox = textbox;
  this.provider = provider;
}
```

Showing a Suggestion

Showing a suggestion involves examining the user input and making one or more suggestions that match the input. For example, if the user types in the letter *L*, then the countries beginning with this letter would be displayed (see Figure 16-4).

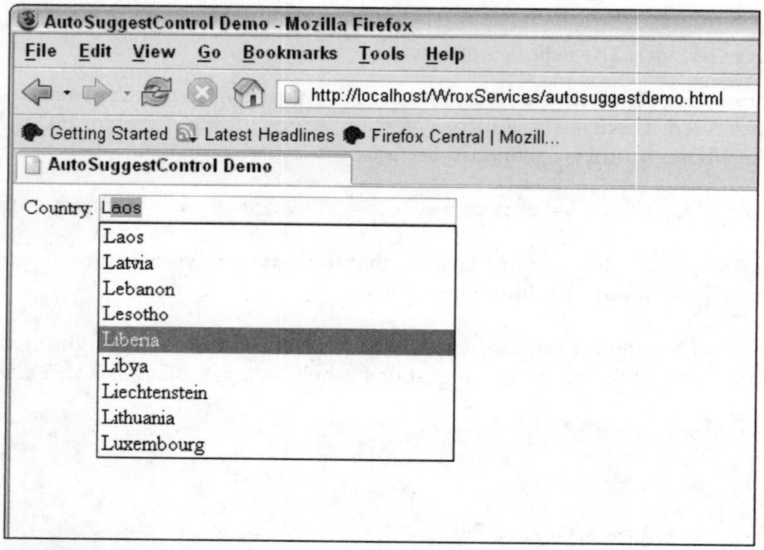

Figure 16-4

The first suggestion — in this example, Laos — would be shown in the textbox but only *aos* would be highlighted. If the user then entered the letter *e*, the countries Lebanon and Lesotho would be suggested, and, for example, Lebanon would appear in the textbox with *banon* highlighted.

To achieve this functionality, you need to be able to select a portion of the text. Originally browsers only had an all-or-nothing approach using the `select()` method. Nowadays, both Internet Explorer and Mozilla provide ways to select any contiguous portion of text. You probably won't be surprised to learn that they implement different ways of achieving this, although what is somewhat surprising is that for once IE actually follows the W3C standard, whereas Mozilla has a proprietary system. The code must therefore detect the browser's capabilities and apply the appropriate method.

In Internet Explorer the key to manipulating text lies with the `TextRange` class. Here is code to select all the characters in a textbox except the first two:

```
var oSuggest = document.getElementById("txtSuggest");
var oRange = oSuggest.createTextRange();
oRange.moveStart("character", 0);
oRange.moveEnd("character", 2 - oSuggest.value.length);
oRange.select();
oSuggest.focus();
```

After obtaining a reference to the textbox and storing it in oSuggest, a TextRange is created.

The actual text to be highlighted is obtained by specifying the starting and ending points using the moveStart() and moveEnd() methods. These accept a string indicating the units to use; instead of character you can also choose word, sentence, or textedit; the last of these indicates the start or end of the text. The second parameter indicates how many units to move, and must be negative if you want to move from the end toward the beginning.

The Mozilla version, albeit nonstandard, has the merit of simplicity; it just needs the start and end index of the characters to select:

```
var oSuggest = document.getElementById("txtSuggest");
oSuggest.setSelectionRange(2, oSuggest.value.length);
oSuggest.focus();
```

The setSelectionRange() method simply takes two integers specifying the zero-based index of the start and end points. Note that in both cases you need to apply the focus() method after specifying the selection. This ensures that the selection is highlighted and that it will be replaced by any additional characters typed by the user.

To add this functionality to the AutoSuggestControl, test which version is needed. The method itself is called selectTextRange:

```
AutoSuggestControl.prototype.selectTextRange = function(start, end)
{
  if (this.textbox.createTextRange)
  {
    var oRange = this.textbox.createTextRange();
    oRange.moveStart("character", start);
    oRange.moveEnd("character", end - this.textbox.value.length);
    oRange.select();
  }
  else if (this.textbox.setSelectionRange)
      {
          this.textbox.setSelectionRange(start, end);
      }
  this.textbox.focus();
}
```

The selectTextRange() method is used by the showFullSuggestion() method. This accepts one suggestion, inserts it into the textbox, and highlights only the characters not entered by the user:

```
AutoSuggestControl.prototype.showFullSuggestion = function (suggestion)
{
  if (this.textbox.createTextRange || this.textbox.setSelectionRange)
```

```
{
    var iCharCount = this.textbox.value.length;
    this.textbox.value = suggestion;
    this.selectTextRange(iCharCount, suggestion.length);
    }
}
```

The function first determines whether either the `createTextRange` or the `setSelectionRange` method is available. If neither is, then no suggestion is shown.

Implementing the suggest Method

When the coding is finished, the `suggest()` method accepts all the suggestions and displays them underneath the textbox. At this stage, it will just deal with the main suggestion. When we are dealing with an alphabetical list of countries, the main suggestion will be the first one.

```
AutoSuggestControl.prototype.suggest = function (suggestions, show)
{
    if (suggestions.length > 0)
    {
        this.showFullSuggestion(suggestions[0]);
    }
}
```

Notice a second parameter named `show`. The reason for this is explained later when the code for dealing with special keys, such as Backspace, is covered.

Handling Input and Control Keys

Three possibilities are of interest when the user presses a key. The first is when the user enters a character into the textbox; the second is when the user presses a control key such as the down arrow to highlight a suggestion; and the third case (when you don't want to interfere) is when the user is interacting with another control on the page. To handle the first two cases, you need to hook into the textbox's events. There are three contenders: `keydown`, `keypress`, and `keyup`. The first two don't do quite what we need, because they fire too early, before the text has actually changed. The `keyup` event is therefore what you'll use to respond to user input.

When the browser fires the `keyup` event, you can determine which key was pressed by using the `keyCode` property of the event object. Again, events are handled slightly differently in Internet Explorer than in Mozilla; the former has a global `event` object, whereas the latter passes an `Event` object to the handler.

At this stage you are only concerned with handling character input for the textbox and fetching suggestions based on the input; this means you can ignore other keys such as Home or Print Screen.

Key codes can be viewed at www.jpsoft.com/help/index.htm?keyscanexpl.htm.

The following code filters out the key codes to be ignored and only passes on the textbox's value when the character keys, the Backspace key, or the Delete key is released:

```
AutoSuggestControl.prototype.handleKeyUp = function (e)
{
  var iCode = e.keyCode;
  if (!(iCode < 8
      || (iCode > 8 && iCode < 32)
      || (iCode > 32 && iCode < 46)
      || (iCode > 111 && iCode < 124)))
  {
    this.provider.fetchSuggestions(this);
  }
}
```

Now you need to make sure that the textbox's own `keyup` event fires the preceding handling code:

```
AutoSuggestControl.prototype.init = function()
{
  var me = this;
  this.textbox.onkeyup = function (e)
  {
    me.handleKeyUp(e || window.event);
  }
}
```

A reference to `this` is stored in the variable `me`; this means you can access the instance of the control from elsewhere in code. The textbox's `onkeyup()` method is assigned an anonymous function, which passes the event object, taking into account the differences between Mozilla and Internet Explorer.

The `init()` method is called in the `AutoSuggestControl` constructor:

```
function AutoSuggestControl(textbox, provider)
{
  this.textbox = textbox;
  this.provider = provider;
  this.init();
}
```

Creating the Suggestions List

The actual div holding the suggestions will be created dynamically; the tricky part is aligning it underneath the main textbox. A reference to it is stored in an instance variable named `suggestionsBox`, which is initially null:

```
function AutoSuggestControl(textbox, provider)
{
  this.textbox = textbox;
  this.provider = provider;
  this.suggestionsBox = null;
}
```

A few methods are needed to deal with this div: You need to create it, hide it, and highlight the current selection. The method that hides the suggestions is shown here:

```
AutoSuggestControl.prototype.hideSuggestionsBox = function ()
{
  this.suggestionsBox.style.visibility = "hidden";
}
```

The method that creates the div is createSuggestionsBox():

```
AutoSuggestControl.prototype.createSuggestionsBox = function ()
{
  this.suggestionsBox = document.createElement("div")
  this.suggestionsBox.className = "suggestions";
  this.suggestionsBox.style.visibility = "hidden";
  this.suggestionsBox.style.width = this.textbox.offsetWidth;
  document.body.appendChild(this.suggestionsBox);
}
```

This method creates the div and assigns a CSS class of suggestions. It initially needs to be hidden, as no suggestions are available until the user types at least one letter; and its width matches that of the main textbox. The offsetWidth gives the actual width of the textbox after the page has rendered, rather than what might have initially been set via CSS.

The final method of the suggestions div is highlightSuggestion():

```
AutoSuggestControl.prototype.highlightSuggestion = function (suggestionElement)
{
  for (var i = 0; i < this.suggestionsBox.childNodes.length; i++)
  {
    var oElement = this.suggestionsBox.childNodes[i];
    if (oElement == suggestionElement)
    {
      oElement.className = "current";
    }
    else if (oElement.className == "current")
      {
        oElement.className = "";
      }
  }
}
```

highlightSuggestion() takes one parameter, a reference to the element representing the desired suggestion. It loops through all the div's children and compares each to the suggestion. If they match, the CSS class is set to current. If not, the current class is removed by setting className to an empty string.

To align the div accurately, you need to know where the textbox is. This position cannot be read directly; it must be calculated using the offsetTop and offsetLeft properties. These provide the position relative to an element's offsetParent, normally its parent; and by working back up the element tree until the body is reached, the absolute position can be reached. Two new helper methods are therefore added to the AutoSuggestControl:

```
AutoSuggestControl.prototype.getLeft = function ()
{
  var oElement = this.textbox;
```

```
    var iLeft = 0;

    while (oElement.tagName != "BODY")
    {
      iLeft += oElement.offsetLeft;
      oElement = oElement.offsetParent;
    }
    return iLeft;
}

AutoSuggestControl.prototype.getTop = function ()
{
    var oElement = this.textbox;
    var iTop = 0;

    while (oElement.tagName != "BODY")
    {
      iTop += oElement.offsetTop;
      oElement = oElement.offsetParent;
    }
    return iTop + this.textbox.offsetHeight;
}
```

Both these methods recurse through the DOM tree until they hit the body, adding the offset values as they go. The getTop() method also takes into account the height of the textbox in the final calculation. The methods then return the final measurement.

Handling Mouse Actions

Suggestions can be selected by using the mouse or the keyboard. The keyboard method is discussed later; for now, the three mouse actions needing attention are onmouseover, onmousedown, and onmouseup. onmouseover highlights the suggestion underneath the cursor, onmousedown places the suggestion under the cursor into the textbox, and onmouseup sets the focus on it.

First the code for onmouseover:

```
AutoSuggestControl.prototype.createSuggestionsBox = function ()
{
    this.suggestionsBox = document.createElement("div")
    this.suggestionsBox.className = "suggestions";
    this.suggestionsBox.style.visibility = "hidden";
    this.suggestionsBox.style.width = this.textbox.offsetWidth;
    document.body.appendChild(this.suggestionsBox);

    var me = this;
    this.suggestionsBox.onmouseover = function (e)
    {
      var oEvent = e || window.event;
      var oSuggestion = oEvent.target || oEvent.srcElement;
      me.highlightSuggestion(oSuggestion);
    }
    //Other handlers to follow

}
```

The interesting code here is that which tests for the different objects exposed by Mozilla and Internet Explorer. Once the chosen element is referenced, it is passed to `highlightSuggestion()`.

The code for `onmousedown` comes immediately afterward:

```
this.suggestionsBox.onmousedown = function (e)
{
  var oEvent = e || window.event;
  var oSuggestion = oEvent.target || oEvent.srcElement;
  me.textbox.value = oSuggestion.firstChild.nodeValue;
  me.hideSuggestionsBox();
}
```

After referencing the suggestion, you take its first child, a text node, and insert its `nodeValue`, the actual text, into the main textbox.

`onmouseup` simply focuses on the textbox itself:

```
this.suggestionsBox.onmouseup = function ()
{
  me.textbox.focus();
}
```

Adding the Suggestions

The next step is to create a process to add suggestions to the suggestions box. It will accept an array of strings representing the suggestions and create a new div for each one:

```
AutoSuggestControl.prototype.showSuggestions = function (suggestions)
{
  this.suggestionsBox.innerHTML = "";
  for (var i = 0; i < suggestions.length; i++)
  {
    var oDiv = document.createElement("div");
    oDiv.appendChild(document.createTextNode(suggestions[i]));
    this.suggestionsBox.appendChild(oDiv);
  }
  this.suggestionsBox.style.left = (this.getLeft() + "px");
  this.suggestionsBox.style.top = (this.getTop() + "px");
  this.suggestionsBox.style.visibility = "visible";
}
```

Here you create a new div for each suggestion and append a text node, with its value set to the suggested country.

Now revisit the `suggest()` method and make a small modification to allow for the fact that users may try to erase a character with the Backspace or Delete key:

```
AutoSuggestControl.prototype.suggest = function (suggestions, show)
{
  if (suggestions.length > 0)
  {
```

```
      if (show)
      {
        this.showFullSuggestion(suggestions[0]);
      }
      this.showSuggestions(suggestions);
    }
    else
    {
      this.hideSuggestionsBox();
    }
  }
```

The logic here is simple: If there are no suggestions, then you hide the box. If there are suggestions and the second parameter is `true`, you add the suggestion to the textbox and then show the alternative suggestions.

Next, you modify the `handleKeyUp()` function so that if the Backspace or Delete keys are used, then the `showFullSuggestion()` method is not called. Otherwise, the user's deleted text would keep reappearing. The Backspace key has a key code of 8; the Delete key is 46:

```
AutoSuggestControl.prototype.handleKeyUp = function (e)
{
  var iCode = e.keyCode;
  if (!(iCode < 8
      || (iCode > 8 && iCode < 32)
      || (iCode > 32 && iCode < 46)
      || (iCode > 111 && iCode < 124)))
  {
    if (iCode == 8 || iCode == 46)
    {
      this.provider.fetchSuggestions(this, false);
    }
    else
    {
      this.provider.fetchSuggestions(this, true);
    }
  }
}
```

Handling Keyboard Selection

Now you need code to enable users to run up and down the suggestion list with the arrow keys. Two new variables are needed: The first holds the index of the current suggestion, or -1 if no suggestion has been chosen; the second variable holds the actual text the user has entered so far:

```
function AutoSuggestControl(textbox, provider)
{
  this.textbox = textbox;
  this.provider = provider;
  this.suggestionsBox = null;
  this.currentSuggestionIndex = -1;
  this.actualText = textbox.value;
  this.init();
}
```

The function called when the user presses an arrow key is goToSuggestion():

```
AutoSuggestControl.prototype.goToSuggestion = function (offset)
{
  var colSuggestionNodes = this.suggestionsBox.childNodes;
  if (colSuggestionNodes.length > 0)
  {
    var oNode = null;
    if (offset > 0)
    {
      if (this.currentSuggestionIndex < colSuggestionNodes.length - 1)
      {
        oNode = colSuggestionNodes[++this.currentSuggestionIndex];
      }
    }
    else if (this.currentSuggestionIndex > 0)
        {
            oNode = colSuggestionNodes[--this.currentSuggestionIndex];
        }
    if (oNode)
    {
      this.highlightSuggestion(oNode);
      this.textbox.value = oNode.firstChild.nodeValue;
    }
  }
}
```

The goToSuggestion() method takes one argument: A positive integer moves one suggestion down the list, a negative one moves one up. First, the child nodes of the div are stored. The div's only children are the individual suggestions in their own divs, so if there are no child nodes, then the method does nothing. If the offset is positive and you aren't at the end of the list, a reference to the next div is stored in oNode. If the offset is negative and you aren't at the start, the previous div is assigned to oNode. If oNode is not null, then it is passed to highlightSuggestion() and the textbox value is updated.

It is also necessary to reset the currentSuggestionIndex when a suggestion is chosen, so add the following line to the suggest() method:

```
AutoSuggestControl.prototype.suggest = function (suggestions, show)
{
  this.currentSuggestionIndex = -1;
  if (suggestions.length > 0)
  {
    if (show)
    {
      this.showFullSuggestion(suggestions[0]);
    }
    this.showSuggestions(suggestions);
  }
  else
  {
    this.hideSuggestionsBox();
  }
}
```

The `actualText` variable needs to be updated in the key handling routine:

```
AutoSuggestControl.prototype.handleKeyUp = function (e)
{
    this.actualText = this.textbox.value;
    var iCode = e.keyCode;
    if (!(iCode < 8
        || (iCode > 8 && iCode < 32)
        || (iCode > 32 && iCode < 46)
        || (iCode > 111 && iCode < 124)))
    {
        if (iCode == 8 || iCode == 46)
        {
            this.provider.fetchSuggestions(this, false);
        }
        else
        {
            this.provider.fetchSuggestions(this, true);
        }
    }
}
```

Next is the code to trap the `keydown` event and call the appropriate method:

```
AutoSuggestControl.prototype.handleKeyDown = function (e)
{
    switch (e.keyCode)
    {
    case 38: //up arrow
        this.goToSuggestion(-1);
    break;
    case 40: //down arrow
        this.goToSuggestion(1);
    break;
    case 27: //escape key
        this.textbox.value = this.actualText;
        this.selectTextRange(this.actualText.length, 0);
    case 13: //enter key
        this.hideSuggestionsBox();
        e.returnValue = false;
        if (e.preventDefault) e.preventDefault();
    break;
    }
}
```

If an arrow key is pressed, then the `goToSelection()` method is called with the appropriate offset. If the Esc key is pressed, then the textbox is returned to the text the user typed and the selection changes to reflect this. The code then continues to the final `case`, which is also called when the Enter key is pressed. The suggestions box is hidden and `preventDefault()` is called if a Mozilla browser is being used. Setting the return value to `false` cancels any spurious events caused by these two keys.

You can now update the `init` function to hook the `handleKeyDown()` method:

```
AutoSuggestControl.prototype.init = function()
{
  var me = this;
  this.textbox.onkeyup = function (e)
  {
    me.handleKeyUp(e || window.event);
  }
  this.textbox.onkeydown = function (e)
  {
    me.handleKeyDown(e || window.event);
  }
}
```

The last addition to init() is adding an onblur handler to the textbox such that if the user clicks on a part of the document other than the suggestions box, then the hideSuggestionsBox() is called:

```
AutoSuggestControl.prototype.init = function()
{
  var me = this;
  this.textbox.onkeyup = function (e)
  {
    me.handleKeyUp(e || window.event);
  }
  this.textbox.onkeydown = function (e)
  {
    me.handleKeyDown(e || window.event);
  }
  this.textbox.onblur = function ()
  {
    me.hideSuggestionsBox();
  }
  this.createSuggestionsBox();
}
```

You also add a call to createSuggestionsBox() to the init() method.

Coping with Speed Typists

There is one more issue to consider: speed typists. If a user types quickly into the textbox, then too many requests are sent, and due to the asynchronous nature of the XmlHttp request, suggestions could be returned in the wrong order. To allow for this, add a delay before calling the fetchSuggestions() method. If the user types quickly and another request is waiting when a new one appears, the previous one is canceled. This functionality is easily achieved using setTimeout().

setTimeout() is a method of the window object, which returns a timeoutId that can be passed to clearTimeout() to cancel a pending request. First add the timeout value, in milliseconds, and an instance variable to store the timeoutId:

```
function AutoSuggestControl(textbox, provider)
{
  this.textbox = textbox;
  this.provider = provider;
  this.suggestionsBox = null;
```

```
        this.currentSuggestionIndex = -1;
        this.actualText = textbox.value;
        this.timeoutId = null;
        this.defaultTimeout = 200;
        this.init();
    }
```

Then change the handlers to use the setTimeout() method.

```
    AutoSuggestControl.prototype.handleKeyUp = function (e)
    {
        var me = this;
        clearTimeout(this.timeoutId);
        this.actualText = this.textbox.value;
        var iCode = e.keyCode;
        if (!(iCode < 8
            || (iCode > 8 && iCode < 32)
            || (iCode > 32 && iCode < 46)
            || (iCode > 111 && iCode < 124)))
        {
          if (iCode == 8 || iCode == 46)
          {
            this.timeoutId = setTimeout( function () {
                      me.provider.fetchSuggestions(me, false);}, this.defaultTimeout);
          }
          else
          {
            this.timeoutId = setTimeout( function () {
                      me.provider.fetchSuggestions(me, true);}, this.defaultTimeout);
          }
        }
    }
```

Store a reference to this in me to prevent it from going out of scope. Then wrap the calls to fetchSuggestions() in setTimeout().

The code is now finished! Now to implement the SuggestionProvider.

Implementing the SuggestionProvider

The SuggestionProvider is actually very straightforward. It uses a web service, to be implemented later, and simply forwards the text typed so far. When the web service returns the matching suggestions, it calls the suggest() method on the AutoSuggestControl.

The actual web service does the work of taking the user's text and finding any matching entries. You are going to write two services: a SOAP-based one and one that uses JSON.

The SuggestionProvider makes use of the zXml cross-browser library and starts with a constructor that creates a new XML HTTP request object. The constructor accepts the URL of the web service providing the suggestions:

```
function SuggestionProvider(serviceUrl)
{
  this.httpRequest = zXmlHttp.createRequest();
  this.serviceUrl = serviceUrl;
}
```

The fetchSuggestions() method needs a reference to the actual AutoSuggestControl so that it can extract the search text and call the suggest method once the results have been returned.

The only method to implement is fetchSuggestions(), and this begins by accessing the httpRequest declared above and checking whether it is currently in use. This would occur if a previous request had not completed. If a request is pending, it is canceled by calling abort():

```
SuggestionProvider.prototype.fetchSuggestions = function (autoSuggestControl, show)
{
  var request = this.httpRequest;
  if (request.readyState != 0)
  {
    request.abort();
  }
  var sQueryString = "?countryText=" +
                       encodeURIComponent(autoSuggestControl.actualText);
  var sUrl = this.serviceUrl + sQueryString;
```

The query string is built from the serviceUrl and the actualText public member of the AutoSuggestControl:

```
SuggestionProvider.prototype.fetchSuggestions = function (autoSuggestControl, show)
{
  var request = this.httpRequest;
  if (request.readyState != 0)
  {
    request.abort();
  }
  var sQueryString = "?countryText=" +
                       encodeURIComponent(autoSuggestControl.actualText);
  var sUrl = this.serviceUrl + sQueryString;
  request.onreadystatechange = function ()
  {
    if (request.readyState == 4)
    {
      var oResultsXml = request.responseXML;
      var oNamespaceMapper =
                        {wrox: "http://www.wrox.com/webservices/GetCountries"};
      var sXPath = "/*/*/*/wrox:countries/wrox:country";
      var colCountries = zXPath.selectNodes
                      (oResultsXml.documentElement, sXPath, oNamespaceMapper);
      var arrCountries = new Array();
      for (var i = 0; i < colCountries.length; i++)
      {
        arrCountries.push(colCountries[i].firstChild.nodeValue);
      }
      autoSuggestControl.suggest(arrCountries, show);
```

```
      }
    }
    request.open("GET", sUrl, true);
    request.send(null);
  }
```

The brunt of the work is done in the onreadystatechange handler. Here, the <country> elements are extracted, and then an array is created using the text node of the <country> element as its value. This array is then passed to the AutoSuggestControl.suggest() method.

See Chapter 15 for more details about using zXPath.

Implementing the Web Service

The web service is implemented as an aspx page. The reason for that, rather than using the built-in functionality of asmx, is twofold: First, this is a book devoted to XML, and several useful XML techniques in the service could not be shown using an asmx. Second, you are going to rewrite the service to use JSON, which will be easier if it is hand-coded.

The service consists of four files: GetCountries.aspx, GetCountries.aspx.cs, countries.xml, and countries.xslt.

GetCountries.aspx consists of just the following, which needs to be on one line:

```
<%@ Page Language="C#"
AutoEventWireup="true" CodeFile="GetCountries.aspx.cs"
Inherits="_Default" ContentType="text/xml"%>
```

The only unusual thing about this is the addition of the ContentType attribute, which specifies that the output MIME type should be text/xml.

The actual work is done by the code-beside file, GetCountries.aspx.cs:

```
using System;
using System.Data;
using System.Configuration;
using System.Web;
using System.Web.Security;
using System.Xml;
using System.Xml.Xsl;
using System.Web.Caching;

public partial class _Default : System.Web.UI.Page
{
  protected void Page_Load(object sender, EventArgs e)
  {
    XmlDocument countriesXml = new XmlDocument();
    if (Cache["countriesXml"] == null)
    {
      string xmlPath = Server.MapPath("countries.xml");
      countriesXml.Load(xmlPath);
      Cache.Insert("countriesXml", countriesXml, new CacheDependency(xmlPath));
```

```
      }
      else
      {
        countriesXml = (XmlDocument)Cache["countriesXml"];
      }
      XslCompiledTransform countriesXslt = new XslCompiledTransform();
      if (Cache["countriesXslt"] == null)
      {
        string xsltPath = Server.MapPath("countries.xslt");
        countriesXslt.Load(xsltPath);
        Cache.Insert("countriesXslt", countriesXslt, new CacheDependency(xsltPath));
      }
      else
      {
        countriesXslt = (XslCompiledTransform)Cache["countriesXslt"];
      }
      try
      {
        string countryText = Request.QueryString["countryText"];
        XsltArgumentList args = new XsltArgumentList();
        args.AddParam("countryText", "", countryText);
        countriesXslt.Transform(countriesXml, args, Response.OutputStream);
      }
      catch (Exception ex)
      {
        SendErrorXml(ex);
      }
    }

    private void SendErrorXml(Exception ex)
    {
      string errorXml = "<?xml version=\"1.0\" encoding=\"utf-8\"?>"
            + "<soap:Envelope xmlns:soap=\"http://www.w3.org/2003/05/soap-envelope\""
            + "xmlns:wrox=\"http://www.wrox.com/webservices/GetCountries\">"
            + "<soap:Body><wrox:GetCountriesResponse><wrox:countries/>"
            + "</wrox:GetCountriesResponse></soap:Body></soap:Envelope>";
      XmlDocument errorDoc = new XmlDocument();
      errorDoc.LoadXml(errorXml);
      errorDoc.Save(Response.OutputStream);
    }
}
```

After declaring a number of namespaces to allow easy access to the System.Xml classes and caching features, the Page_Load method starts by obtaining the countries.xml file:

```
public partial class _Default : System.Web.UI.Page
{
  protected void Page_Load(object sender, EventArgs e)
  {
    XmlDocument countriesXml = new XmlDocument();
    if (Cache["countriesXml"] == null)
    {
      string xmlPath = Server.MapPath("countries.xml");
```

```
      countriesXml.Load(xmlPath);
      Cache.Insert("countriesXml", countriesXml, new CacheDependency(xmlPath));
   }
   else
   {
      countriesXml = (XmlDocument)Cache["countriesXml"];
   }
```

It first checks to see whether the XmlDocument representing the countries has been stored in the cache. If not, such as when the page is called for the first time, then it is loaded and stored in the cache with a file dependency, which means it remains in the cache until either the machine needs to reclaim memory for a more important task or, and this is more likely, the file has been modified. This means that after the first access, countries.xml won't need to be read from disk unless you have added or removed a <country> element:

```
      XslCompiledTransform countriesXslt = new XslCompiledTransform();
      if (Cache["countriesXslt"] == null)
      {
         string xsltPath = Server.MapPath("countries.xslt");
         countriesXslt.Load(xsltPath);
         Cache.Insert("countriesXslt", countriesXslt, new CacheDependency(xsltPath));
      }
      else
      {
         countriesXslt = (XslCompiledTransform)Cache["countriesXslt"];
      }
```

A similar process happens with the XSLT transform, countries.xslt. It is fetched from cache if possible and loaded into an instance of XslCompiledTransform. This class is new to .NET 2.0 and provides better performance and other features:

```
      try
      {
         string countryText = Request.QueryString["countryText"];
         XsltArgumentList args = new XsltArgumentList();
         args.AddParam("countryText", "", countryText);
         countriesXslt.Transform(countriesXml, args, Response.OutputStream);
      }
      catch (Exception ex)
      {
         SendErrorXml(ex);
      }
```

The reason for the transformation is to retrieve only those countries from Countries.xml that match the initial characters entered by the user.

The final part of Page_Load retrieves the value of the query string and adds it as an argument to the transform. The actual transformation saves the result directly into the Response.OutputStream, a much better choice than using such methods as Response.Write().

Should an error occur, `SendErrorXml()` is called:

```
private void SendErrorXml(Exception ex)
{
  string errorXml = "<?xml version=\"1.0\" encoding=\"utf-8\"?>"
      + "<soap:Envelope xmlns:soap=\"http://www.w3.org/2003/05/soap-envelope\""
      + "xmlns:wrox=\"http://www.wrox.com/webservices/GetCountries\">"
      + "<soap:Body><wrox:GetCountriesResponse><wrox:countries/>"
      + "</wrox:GetCountriesResponse></soap:Body></soap:Envelope>";
  XmlDocument errorDoc = new XmlDocument();
  errorDoc.LoadXml(errorXml);
  errorDoc.Save(Response.OutputStream);
}
```

Not much can be done on an error, so you just return a SOAP document that looks like the following, with an empty `<countries>` element:

```
<?xml version="1.0" encoding="utf-8"?>
<soap:Envelope xmlns:soap="http://www.w3.org/2003/05/soap-envelope"
xmlns:wrox="http://www.wrox.com/webservices/GetCountries">
  <soap:Body>
    <wrox:GetCountriesResponse>
      <wrox:countries />
    </wrox:GetCountriesResponse>
  </soap:Body>
</soap:Envelope>
```

The `countries.xml` file is simple; it just has a number of `<country>` elements wrapped in `<countries>`:

```
<countries>
<country>Afghanistan</country>
<country>Albania</country>
<country>Algeria</country>
<!- More countries here -->
<country>Zambia</country>
<country>Zimbabwe</country>
</countries>
```

The last file needed is the XSL transform, `countries.xslt`. Begin by declaring the namespaces needed on the `<xsl:stylesheet>` element:

```
<xsl:stylesheet version="1.0"
    xmlns:xsl="http://www.w3.org/1999/XSL/Transform"
    xmlns:soap="http://www.w3.org/2003/05/soap-envelope"
    xmlns:wrox="http://www.wrox.com/webservices/GetCountries">

  <xsl:param name="countryText"/>
  <xsl:variable name="lower" select="'abcdefghijklmnopqrstuvwxyz'"/>
  <xsl:variable name="upper" select="'ABCDEFGHIJKLMNOPQRSTUVWXYZ'"/>

  <!-- templates go here -->
</xsl:stylesheet>
```

You also need to declare an `<xsl:Param>` to hold the search text, and two variables that will be used later to make the search case insensitive, using the following `Countries.xslt` file:

```
<xsl:stylesheet version="1.0"
    xmlns:xsl="http://www.w3.org/1999/XSL/Transform"
    xmlns:soap="http://www.w3.org/2003/05/soap-envelope"
    xmlns:wrox="http://www.wrox.com/webservices/GetCountries">

  <xsl:param name="countryText"/>
  <xsl:variable name="lower" select="'abcdefghijklmnopqrstuvwxyz'"/>
  <xsl:variable name="upper" select="'ABCDEFGHIJKLMNOPQRSTUVWXYZ'"/>

  <xsl:template match="/">
    <xsl:variable name="lowercaseSearch"
select="translate($countryText, $upper, $lower)"/>
    <soap:Envelope>
      <soap:Body>
        <wrox:GetCountriesResponse>
          <wrox:countries>
            <xsl:apply-templates select=
"countries/country[starts-with(translate(., $upper, $lower), $lowercaseSearch)]">
              <xsl:sort select="." data-type="text"/>
            </xsl:apply-templates>
          </wrox:countries>
        </wrox:GetCountriesResponse>
      </soap:Body>
    </soap:Envelope>
  </xsl:template>
</xsl:stylesheet>
```

The main template first translates the search into lowercase and stores the result in `lowercaseSearch`. It then creates the `<soap:Envelope>` and `<soap:Body>`. Next is the payload, the `<wrox:GetCountriesResponse>` and `<wrox:countries>` elements. Then the following XPath is used to select the countries:

```
countries/country[starts-with(translate(., $upper, $lower), $lowercaseSearch)
```

In English, this means select all the `<country>` elements with a `<countries>` parent where the string value of the element, when translated to lowercase, starts with the characters in the variable `lowercaseSearch`. Before the relevant `<country>` elements are processed by the final template, they are sorted alphabetically, so new counties can be added to `Countries.xml` at any position.

The elements selected by the preceding XPath are dealt with by the last template:

```
<xsl:template match="country">
  <wrox:country><xsl:value-of select="."/></wrox:country>
</xsl:template>
```

This simply recreates the `<country>` element but this time in the `wrox` namespace.

Now you can finally test your control! Create a virtual directory for your files named `WroxServices` and add the following, all of which are available in the code download for this book:

❑ GetCountries.aspx: the entry point for the web service

❑ GetCountries.aspx.cs: The actual web service code

❑ AutoSuggest.js: The JavaScript for the control

❑ CountriesSuggestionProvider.js: The code for the SuggestionProvider

❑ AutoSuggest.css: The CSS stylesheet for the suggestions box

❑ zXml.js: The cross-browser library

❑ Countries.xml: The XML holding the country list

❑ Countries.xslt: The XSL transformation to create the SOAP response

❑ AutoSuggestDemo.html: The test page, shown below

The file to test the control contains the textbox and one JavaScript method to connect the AutoSuggestControl, the textbox, and the SuggestionProvider:

```html
<html>
<head>
<title>AutoSuggestControl Demo</title>
<link rel="stylesheet" type="text/css" href="autosuggest.css">
<script type="text/javascript" src="zXml.src.js"></script>
<script type="text/javascript" src="AutoSuggest.js"></script>
<script type="text/javascript" src="CountriesSuggestionProvider.js"></script>
<script type="text/javascript">
  function init()
  {
    var oASC = new AutoSuggestControl(document.getElementById("txtSuggest"),
    new SuggestionProvider("http://localhost/WroxServices/GetCountries.aspx"));
  }

</script>
</head>

<body onload="init();">
  <form>
    Country: 
<input type="text" name="txtSuggest" id="txtSuggest" size="40" autocomplete="off">
  </form>
</body>
</html>
```

Now navigate to http://localhost/WroxServices/AutoSuggestDemo.html and start to type. You should see something like what is shown in Figure 16-4.

Next, you will modify the code to use JSON instead of XML.

Try It Out   Modifying the Control to Work with JSON

There are three main things to change to implement the AutoSuggestControl using JSON. The actual AutoSuggest.js stays the same; the changes are made to the SuggestionProvider and the web service itself:

1. Modify the `GetCountries.aspx` file by removing the `ContentType` attribute. You are no longer sending XML, but a simple string:

```
<%@ Page Language="C#" AutoEventWireup="true"
CodeFile="GetCountries2.aspx.cs" Inherits="_Default"%>
```

2. Save this file as `GetCountries2.aspx` after modifying the `CodeFile` value to be `GetCountries2.aspx.cs`.

3. Now modify `GetCountries.aspx.cs` as follows and save it as `GetCountries2.aspx.cs`:

```
using System;
using System.Data;
using System.Configuration;
using System.Web;
using System.Web.Security;
using System.Xml;
using System.Xml.Xsl;
using System.Web.Caching;

public partial class _Default : System.Web.UI.Page
{
  protected void Page_Load(object sender, EventArgs e)
  {
    XmlDocument countriesXml = new XmlDocument();
    if (Cache["countriesXml"] == null)
    {
      string xmlPath = Server.MapPath("countries.xml");
      countriesXml.Load(xmlPath);
      Cache.Insert("countriesXml", countriesXml, new CacheDependency(xmlPath));
    }
    else
    {
      countriesXml = (XmlDocument)Cache["countriesXml"];
    }
    XslCompiledTransform countriesXslt = new XslCompiledTransform();
    if (Cache["countries2Xslt"] == null)
    {
      string xsltPath = Server.MapPath("countries2.xslt");
      countriesXslt.Load(xsltPath);
      Cache.Insert("countries2Xslt", countriesXslt, new CacheDependency(xsltPath));
    }
    else
    {
      countriesXslt = (XslCompiledTransform)Cache["countries2Xslt"];
    }
    try
    {
      string countryText = Request.QueryString["countryText"];
      XsltArgumentList args = new XsltArgumentList();
      args.AddParam("countryText", "", countryText);
      countriesXslt.Transform(countriesXml, args, Response.OutputStream);
    }
    catch (Exception ex)
    {
```

```
        SendError(ex);
    }
}

    private void SendError(Exception ex)
    {
      string errorString = "[];";
      Response.Write(errorString);
    }
}
```

How It Works

The XSL transform now points to `countries2.xslt`, and the `SendXmlError()` has been changed to `SendError()`. It now returns the JavaScript literal for an empty array.

`Countries2.xslt` is somewhat smaller now:

```
<xsl:stylesheet version="1.0"
 xmlns:xsl="http://www.w3.org/1999/XSL/Transform">

  <xsl:output method="text"/>
  <xsl:param name="countryText"/>
  <xsl:variable name="lower" select="'abcdefghijklmnopqrstuvwxyz'"/>
  <xsl:variable name="upper" select="'ABCDEFGHIJKLMNOPQRSTUVWXYZ'"/>
  <xsl:template match="/">
    <xsl:variable name="lowercaseSearch"
    select="translate($countryText, $upper, $lower)"/>
    <xsl:text>[</xsl:text>
    <xsl:apply-templates select=
"countries/country[starts-with(translate(., $upper, $lower), $lowercaseSearch)]">
        <xsl:sort select="." data-type="text"/>
    </xsl:apply-templates>
    <xsl:text>];</xsl:text>
  </xsl:template>

  <xsl:template match="country">
    <xsl:text>"</xsl:text>
      <xsl:value-of select="."/>
    <xsl:text>"</xsl:text>
    <xsl:if test="position() != last()">, </xsl:if>
  </xsl:template>

</xsl:stylesheet>
```

The first changes are the removal of the namespace declarations needed for the SOAP version and the addition of an `<xsl:output>` element so that you can specify the output to be text, rather than XML or HTML.

The main template now has no need to create the `<soap:Envelope>` and `<soap:Body>`; it just adds brackets to form the literal array syntax.

The last template outputs the string value of each selected <country> element. If the element is not the last, then it appends a comma. The resulting output for the search text *Ch* looks something like this:

["Chad", "Chile", "China"];

The `CountriesSuggestionProvider2.js` is also simpler; only the `fetchSuggestions()` method has changed:

```
SuggestionProvider.prototype.fetchSuggestions =
function (autoSuggestControl, show)
{
  var request = this.httpRequest;
  if (request.readyState != 0)
  {
    request.abort();
  }
  var sQueryString =
"?countryText=" + encodeURIComponent(autoSuggestControl.actualText);
  var sUrl = this.serviceUrl + sQueryString;
  request.onreadystatechange = function ()
  {
    if (request.readyState == 4)
    {
      var sData = request.responseText;
      var arrCountries = eval((sData));
      autoSuggestControl.suggest(arrCountries, show);
    }
  }
  request.open("GET", sUrl, true);
  request.send(null);
}
```

Instead of accessing `responseXML`, you access `responseText` and use `eval()` to assign it to `arrCountries`. Notice the two pairs of parentheses around `sData`. One pair would be sufficient in this example but a second pair is advisable to ensure that any statements are fully evaluated.

Now navigate to `http://localhost/WroxServices/AutoSuggestDemo2.html`. You shouldn't see any change in behavior or functionality. Overall, developing with JSON is easier than with XML provided you are passing around data that is not too complex.

Server-Side Proxies

A perennial problem with using Ajax and web services in general is that with normal security settings, client-side code can only make requests and receive responses from services in the same domain as the page itself. Without this provision it would be impossible for users to determine whether to send confidential data using an HTML form. Currently, when a site uses SSL, therefore encrypting the data being sent, the browser shows a security symbol, normally a padlock on the status bar. If the site's certificate is outdated or the name doesn't match the server, then a warning dialog appears. If JavaScript could post data to a completely different site, with or without encryption, then this system breaks down.

Of course, one of the main ideas behind web services is reusability. It would be hopeless if you had to write, or at least incorporate, the code for each service your site needed and place it on your own server. The way around this is to use a *server-side proxy*. The proxy receives the data from the user and passes it to a service running on the same domain as the original page. The service does very little; it just passes the data on to the real service and relays the response back to the client.

Any restrictions on posting from the server are controlled by the site administrators, so there is no problem with client-side security settings. The next example involves creating a server-side proxy and describes how to utilize it, client-side, from a web page.

The Currency Converter Proxy

This example shows how to take advantage of a currency conversion service, one of several free services found at www.xmethods.net/ve2/index.po.

The basic signature of the service is as follows:

> float rate getRate(string countryFrom, string countryTo)

It accepts the ISO standard country abbreviation (as found in a URL) for two countries, and returns the conversion rate between their currencies. For example, calling getRate() with *us* and *uk* might return 0.57.

There are three steps to this example:

1. Create a web service with a reference to the currency conversion service.
2. Implement a method that accepts the two country strings, passes them to the service, and returns the result.
3. Create a client to take advantage of the service.

Creating the Web Service

Follow these steps to create the web service:

1. Open Visual Studio 2005 and choose New ⇨ Web Site from the File menu.
2. Pick an ASP.NET web service as the project and choose HTTP as the location.
3. Call the project CurrencyProxyService. The full URL is http://localhost/CurrencyProxyService. Click OK to create the project.
4. Right-click the project in Solution Explorer and choose Add Web Reference.
5. Enter the following URL, found on the webserviceX.NET website, into the URL box: http://www.webservicex.net/CurrencyConvertor.asmx. Click Go.
6. You should see the ConversionRate method listed. Rename the Web Reference Name to **webservicex** and click Add Reference, as shown in Figure 16-5.

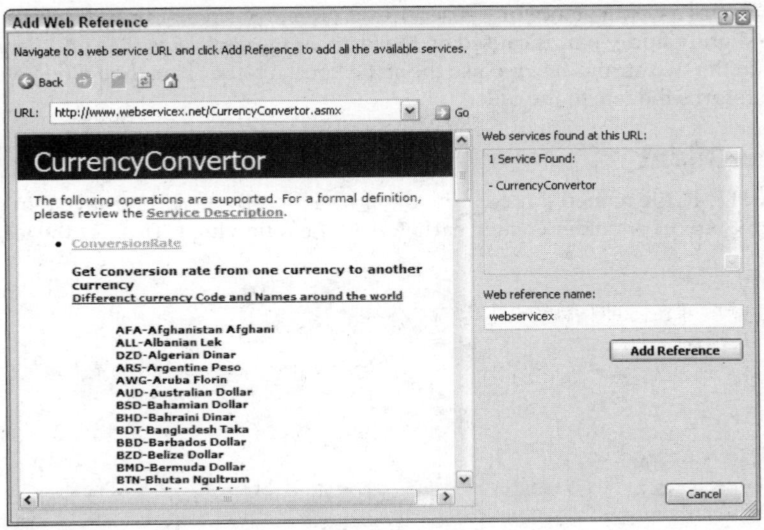

Figure 16-5

Implementing the GetRate() Method

Open `service.cs` in the `App_Code` folder file and modify it as shown:

```
using System;
using System.Web;
using System.Web.Services;
using System.Web.Services.Protocols;

[WebService(Namespace = "http://www.wrox.com/webservices/CurrencyProxyService")]
[WebServiceBinding(ConformsTo = WsiProfiles.BasicProfile1_1)]
public class Service : System.Web.Services.WebService
{
    [WebMethod(Description =
"Accepts two currency codes and returns the currency exchange rate as a double.")]
    public double GetRate(string currencyFrom, string currencyTo)
    {
      webservicex.CurrencyConvertor exchange = new webservicex.CurrencyConvertor();
      webservicex.Currency from =
(webservicex.Currency)Enum.Parse(typeof(webservicex.Currency), currencyFrom);
      webservicex.Currency to =
 (webservicex.Currency)Enum.Parse(typeof(webservicex.Currency), currencyTo);
      double rate = exchange.ConversionRate(from, to);
      return rate;
    }
}
```

As stated, the code is very short. Aside from the standard namespaces needed for the service, it has one method, GetRate().

The method creates a new instance of webservicex.CurrencyConvertor and calls its ConversionRate() method. The slightly fiddly part is caused by the fact that the service uses an enumeration for the currency codes, so the two strings need to use the static Enum.Parse() method along with a cast to convert them. It then returns the rate to the caller.

Creating the Client

Create a new HTML file named currencyProxyServiceDemo.html and save it in the CurrencyProxyService folder created earlier. Add the following HTML for the test form:

```
<html><head>
<title>Currency Service Proxy Demo</title>
<!-script to come -->

</head>

<body>
  Currency from: 
<input type="text" id="txtCurrencyFrom" value="USD" size="4"><br>
  Currency to: 
<input type="text" id="txtCurrencyTo" value="GBP" size="4"><br>
  Amount from: <input type="text" id="txtAmountFrom" value="1" size="10"><br>
  Amount to: <input type="text" id="txtAmountTo" size="10" readonly><br>
  <input type="button" value="Convert"
        onclick=
      "getRate(document.getElementById('txtCurrencyFrom').value,
        document.getElementById('txtCurrencyTo').value);">
</body>
</html>
```

Now add the following script:

```
<head>
<title>Currency Service Proxy Demo</title>
<script type="text/javascript" src="zXml.src.js"></script>

<script type="text/javascript">
var oHttpReq = null;
  function getRate(from, to)
  {
    var sServiceUrl = "Service.asmx/GetRate";
    var sQuery = "?currencyFrom=" + from + "&currencyyTo=" + to;
    var sUrl = sServiceUrl + sQuery;
    oHttpReq = zXmlHttp.createRequest();
    oHttpReq.onreadystatechange = handleReadyStateChange;
    oHttpReq.open("GET", sUrl, true);
    oHttpReq.send(null);
  }

  function handleReadyStateChange()
  {
    if (oHttpReq.readyState == 4)
    {
```

```
        if (oHttpReq.status == 200 && oHttpReq.responseXML)
        {
          showResults(oHttpReq.responseXML.documentElement.firstChild.nodeValue);
        }
        else
        {
          throw new Error("Unable to retrieve rate.");
        }
      }
    }

    function showResults(rate)
    {
      var dAmount = document.getElementById("txtAmountFrom").value;
      document.getElementById("txtAmountTo").value = dAmount * rate;
    }
</script>
</head>
```

This page uses the zXml library so that needs to be in the virtual folder. The first script block adds the zXml library so that this client works on both Internet Explorer and Mozilla browsers. When the user clicks the Convert button, the two values from txtCurrencyFrom and txtCurrencyTo are passed to the getRate() method:

```
function getRate(from, to)
{
  var sServiceUrl = "Service.asmx/GetRate";
  var sQuery = "?currencyFrom=" + from + "&currencyTo=" + to;
  var sUrl = sServiceUrl + sQuery;
  oHttpReq = zXmlHttp.createRequest();
  oHttpReq.onreadystatechange = handleReadyStateChange;
  oHttpReq.open("GET", sUrl, true);
  oHttpReq.send(null);
}
```

The method builds the full URL to your web service, including the query string, and opens a connection to the service. The handleReadyStateChange() function is assigned to be called to deal with the response:

```
function handleReadyStateChange()
{
  if (oHttpReq.readyState == 4)
  {
    if (oHttpReq.status == 200 && oHttpReq.responseXML)
    {
      showResults(oHttpReq.responseXML.documentElement.firstChild.nodeValue);
    }
    else
    {
      throw new Error("Unable to retrieve rate.");
    }
  }
}
```

When the `readyState` is equal to 4, the status is checked to see if it equals 200, which means the server received the request and responded correctly. A code of 404, for example, would mean that the resource could not be found. The response actually arriving looks like this:

```
<double xmlns="http://www.wrox.com/..... ">0.5263</double>
```

Therefore, to read the rate, simply take the value of the document element's first child.

There is one final step to take before testing the page. By default, ASP.NET allows only SOAP requests to a web service; GET and POST requests are forbidden. Because this service uses GET and passes the two currencies in the query string, a new section must added to the web.config file for the service. Add the following code to the `<system.web>` element:

```
<webServices>
  <protocols>
    <!-- <add name="HttpPost"/> -->
    <add name="HttpGet"/>
  </protocols>
</webServices>
```

Navigate to `http://localhost/CurrencyProxyService/currencyProxyServiceDemo.html` to see the whole page in action, as shown in Figure 16-6.

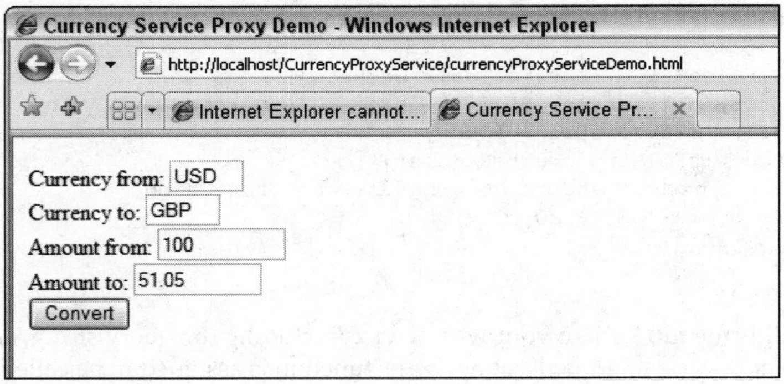

Figure 16-6

Summary

This chapter covered the origins of Ajax and how it evolved from a number of disparate techniques into the standard used today. You learned about the main forms of data representation, XML and JSON, and the differences in calling services with GET, POST and SOAP. The example developed an Ajax-enabled control, a textbox that provides suitable suggestions as the user types. It first used XML for the data communication and then was modified to use JSON. Finally, you learned how server-side proxies can relieve you of the security problems associated with using web services that are hosted on domains other than that of the calling page.

Exercise Questions

Suggested solutions to these questions can be found in Appendix A.

Question 1

Construct the equivalent JSON literal for this XML:

```
<person>
  <forename>Joe</forename>
  <surname>Fawcett</surname>
  <profession>Developer</profession>
  <children>
    <child>
      <forename>Persephone</forename>
      <sex>female</sex>
    </child>
    <child>
      <forename>Xavier</forename>
      <sex>male</sex>
    </child>
  </children>
</person>
```

Question 2

Why is it necessary to use a server-side proxy when calling a third-party web service?

Question 3

What is the maximum number of simultaneous connections allowed by most browsers to a single URL?

Part VII
Display

Cascading Style Sheets (CSS)

This chapter examines Cascading Style Sheets (CSS) as a means of styling XML documents for use on the Web. You may well have already used CSS with HTML or XHTML. Dealing with other XML document types, however, requires some different techniques, which are covered in this chapter.

You'll see XHTML in the next chapter, but for the time being you only need to know that XHTML documents can be styled like HTML documents. Styling XHTML and HTML documents is so similar that this chapter uses the term "(X)HTML" to represent "HTML or XHTML."

Even when you remove stylistic markup from an (X)HTML document, the browser still knows how to display elements, such as tables, lists of different levels of headings, and so on. In other XML vocabularies, you won't even have this most rudimentary help with layout. After all, a `<table>` element in your XML vocabulary might be used to describe a piece of wood with four legs. Considering that a browser won't know how any of the elements in your XML vocabulary need to be displayed, you have a lot more work to do when styling XML documents with CSS than (X)HTML documents.

If you know that your XML documents will be displayed on the Web, some of the points you learn in this chapter might even affect the way in which you write your vocabulary or schema. For example, by the end of the chapter, you will understand why CSS is much better suited to displaying element content than attribute values.

In this chapter you will learn the following:

❑   How CSS relies upon a box model for styling documents, whereby the content of each element inhabits a box

❑   How to use CSS to style (X)HTML documents, rather than relying on stylistic markup

❑   How to give your XML documents a visual structure so that they can look like (X)HTML documents with features such as tables, lists, links, and images, even though the browser does not know how to present any of the elements.

Before looking at CSS, however, it is important to reiterate the reasons why you need stylesheets.

This chapter uses Internet Explorer 6 and Firefox 1.5 or later, or other Gecko-based browsers such as Mozilla and Netscape 6 or later. Most features described and demonstrated here are available in recent versions of other browsers such as Opera and Safari.

Why Stylesheets?

(X)HTML documents contain the following three types of markup:

❑ **Structural markup** — Describes the structure of a document, the headings, paragraphs, line breaks, and lists, using elements such as `<h1>`, `<p>`, `<br>`, `<ul>`, and `<li>` elements

❑ **Semantic markup** — Indicates something about the document you are marking up — for example, the `<meta>` and `<title>` elements

❑ **Stylistic markup** — Indicates how the document should be presented on a browser, using elements such as `<font>` and `<s>`, and attributes such as `bgcolor`

There is an odd-one-out here: stylistic markup. The other two tell you something about the content of the document, whereas the stylistic markup just tells you how the document should be presented for one medium (the desktop PC browser), not about the document itself. While a `<font>` element might indicate in which typeface a designer wanted a line of a page to be shown, the `<font>` element doesn't indicate anything about the structure of the document in the same way a heading or paragraph element does — and the same designer might want a different font for the same text in a different medium. That's why this markup has been deprecated in HTML 4.01 and, as you'll see in the next chapter, in XHTML.

Because applications of XML are supposed to create self-describing documents, styling doesn't indicate anything about the content of the document and should not be included in most of your documents. Rather than use stylistic markup in your documents, you can use another language in a separate document to indicate how your documents should be rendered, and you can even have different stylesheets for different mediums — one each for PC browsers, browsers in set top boxes for TVs, printer-friendly versions of pages, and so on, all of which have different types of display (in particular, different resolutions).

Remember that most XML languages do not include markup that indicates how the document should be styled. Indeed, many XML languages are never styled because they are used to transfer data between applications.

This chapter addresses how you can use this separate language, CSS, to style XML documents. Some of the things shown in this chapter are only beginning to be supported in browsers, so the material presented here not only takes you to the limits of what is possible with CSS in browsers now, but also whets your appetite for what is likely to be possible in the near future.

The topics covered in this chapter include the following:

❑ How CSS works

❑ How to style XML documents with CSS

❑ Using CSS selectors to indicate the elements to which a CSS rule applies

❑ The box model that CSS is based upon

❑ Positioning schemes that enable CSS to control page layouts

❑ Laying out tabular XML data with CSS

❑ Linking between XML documents

❑ Adding images to XML documents

❑ Adding text to your documents from the stylesheet

❑ Using attribute values in documents

The first thing to do is make sure you are familiar with writing a basic CSS stylesheet and how the presentational or stylistic CSS rules are applied to a document.

Two versions of CSS have already been published as recommendations by the W3C: CSS1 and CSS2. CSS2 built upon the functionality of CSS1. It added so many features that it required a bit of cleaning, and a new clarified and simplified version has been published as CSS2.1. Both CSS1 and CSS2.1 are covered in this chapter under the general term CSS. A third version (CSS3) is currently under development by the W3C to add new features to CSS2.1.

Introducing CSS

CSS enables you to style a document by associating presentation rules with the elements that appear in the document you want to style; these rules indicate how the content of those elements should be rendered. Figure 17-1 shows an example of a CSS rule. Rather than use a <font> element to specify typefaces, this rule indicates that all <h1> elements should use the Arial typeface.

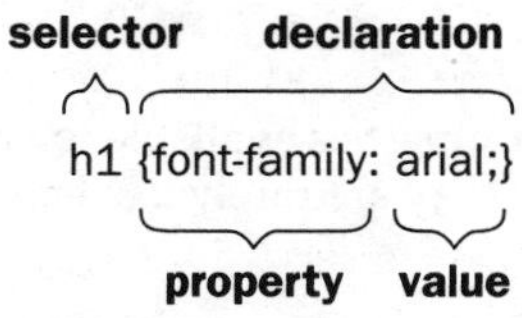

selector   declaration

h1 {font-family: arial;}

property   value

Figure 17-1

The rule is split into two parts:

❑ The *selector* indicates the element or elements to which the declaration applies (you can have a comma-separated list of several elements or more elaborate patterns to indicate complex conditions on elements).

❑ The *declaration* sets out how the elements should be styled. In this case, the content of the <h1> elements should be in the Arial typeface.

The declaration is also split into two parts, separated by a colon:

❑ A *property* of the selected element(s) that you want to affect; Figure 17-1 sets the font-family property.

❑ A *value* is a specification for this property; in this case, it is the arial typeface.

Although you do not need to add a semicolon at the end of a single declaration, a declaration can consist of several property-value pairs, and each property-value pair within a rule must be separated by a semicolon. Therefore, it is good practice to start adding them from the beginning in case you want to add another later, because if you forget to add the semicolon, any further property-value pairs will be ignored.

Following is an example of a CSS rule that applies to several elements (<h1>, <h2>, and <h3>), with each element's name separated by a comma. It also specifies several properties for these elements, with each rule separated by a semicolon. All the properties are kept inside the curly braces, as shown in the following:

```
h1, h2, h3 { color:#000000;
             background-color:#FFFFFF;
             font-family:arial, verdana, sans-serif;
             font-weight:bold; }
```

This should be fairly straightforward: The content of each heading element is written in a bold, black, Arial typeface (unless the computer does not have it, in which case it will look for Verdana, and then any sans-serif font), with a white background.

If you have done any XHTML work at all, this should be quite familiar to you. Rather than use the bgcolor attribute on an element, you use the background-color property in CSS. Rather than use a <font> element to describe the typeface you want to use, you add the font-family property to the rule for that element. Rather than use <b></b> tags, you use the font-weight property.

CSS Properties

The following table shows the main properties available to you from CSS1 and CSS2 (there are other properties in these specifications, but they are rarely used and are not supported yet by the major browsers):

Font	Border	Dimensions
font	border	height
font-family	border-bottom	line-height
font-size	border-bottom-color	max-height
font-style	border-bottom-style	max-width
font-variant	border-bottom-width	min-height
font-weight	border-color	min-width
Text	border-left	width

color	border-left-color	Positioning
direction	border-left-style	bottom
letter-spacing	border-left-width	clip
text-align	border-right	left
text-decoration	border-right-color	overflow
text-indent	border-right-style	right
text-transform	border-right-width	top
unicode-bidi	border-style	vertical-align
white-space	border-top	z-index
word-spacing	**border-top-color**	**Outlines**
Background	border-top-style	outline
background	border-top-width	outline-color
background-attachment	border-width	outline-style
background-color	Padding	outline-width
background-image	**padding**	**Margin**
background-position	padding-bottom	margin
background-repeat	padding-left	margin-bottom
Table	padding-right	margin-left
border-collapse	padding-top	margin-right
border-spacing caption-side	Generated Content	margin-top
empty-cells	**content**	**Classification**
table-layout	counter-increment	clear
List and Marker	counter-reset	cursor
list-style	quotes	display
list-style-image		float
list-style-position		position
list-style-type		visibility

Inheritance

There is a good reason why the word "cascading" appears at the beginning of the name for CSS. Many of the CSS properties can be inherited by child elements, so once you have declared a rule, that rule applies to all child elements of the element to which it was applied. For example, if you set up a rule on the `<body>` element in an XHTML document, then the rule will apply to all elements in the body of the document. If you indicate a `font-family` property for the `<body>` element, all of the text in the document should appear in that font. You can, however, override a rule by creating a more specific rule for certain child elements — for example, you might want all headings in a different font than the rest of the page.

Now revisit the CSS rule shown earlier in the chapter:

```
h1, h2, h3 { color:#000000;
             background-color:#FFFFFF;
             font-family:arial, verdana, sans-serif;
             font-weight:bold; }
```

Imagine that you now want the `<h3>` element to be italic as well. Just add the following rule:

```
h1, h2, h3 {color:#000000; background-color:#FFFFFF;
            font-family:arial, verdana, sans-serif;
            font-weight:bold; }
```

```
h3              {font-style:italic; }
```

This saves rewriting all the property-value pairs that the h3 element has in common with other heading elements. The more specific a rule within the stylesheet, the greater precedence it has in the cascade. For example, if you don't want the h3 element to be bold when it is immediately preceded by an h2 element, you could just add the following rule:

```
h2 + h3              {font-weight:normal; }
```

The selector h2 + h3 matches h3 elements only when they are immediately preceded by an h2 element. It is more specific than the h3 selector, which also defines a `font-weight` property, and would override it.

The order in which rules appear within the stylesheet matters only when a property is defined several times with the same `font-weight`. For instance, if you want none of the h3 elements to be bold, you can add the following rule in the same stylesheet after the common rule for h1, h2, and h3 elements:

```
h3              {font-weight:normal; }
```

When two rules have the same weight, the last rule wins, so `normal` overrides the `font-weight` property.

This is a great useful feature but it needs to be used with moderation! Overriding properties rapidly leads to stylesheets that are hard to read and error prone.

There is another reason CSS stylesheets have "cascading" in the title: You can use rules from several stylesheets by importing one into another or use several stylesheets with the same document. You might use multiple stylesheets if, for example, you wanted to include all the styles common to the whole site in one CSS document (such as company colors and fonts), and all the styles just for a subsection of the site in another (such as specific layout for a certain section of the site).

Try It Out   **Styling an XML Document with CSS**

The first type of XML document to style is a DocBook document. If you have never used DocBook, don't worry. This one is quite straightforward — a small extract of this chapter expressed as a DocBook article. There's nothing too adventurous in this first example — just some basic rules about how this document should be presented to get you into the swing of writing CSS.

> *Like TEI, DocBook is a schema that can be used to mark up complete books. While TEI aims to be very generic and could be used to mark up very different types of text, from the Bible to the latest Harry Potter, without forgetting the entire works of Shakespeare, DocBook was designed to mark up technical documentation, and has specific elements to represent things such as program listings and screen outputs. Among many other uses, the Linux Documentation Project has chosen DocBook as its source format, so if you are a Linux user, chances are good that you can find thousands of DocBook documents on your workstation!*

Download or edit and save the following document as `ch17_eg01.xml`:

```xml
<?xml version="1.0" encoding="UTF-8"?>
<?xml-stylesheet type="text/css" href="ch17_eg01.css"?>
<article>
  <title>Styling XML documents with CSS</title>
  <section>
    <title>Introduction</title>
    <para>This article addresses how we can use this separate language,
      CSS, to style XML documents. Some of the things we will see in this
      chapter are only starting to be supported in browsers, so the chapter
      will not only take you to the limits of what is possible with CSS in browsers
      now, but also whet your appetite for what will be possible in the near
      future.</para>
    <para>The topics covered in this article include:</para>
    <itemizedlist>
      <listitem>
        <para>How CSS works</para>
      </listitem>
      <listitem>
        <para>How to style XML documents with CSS</para>
      </listitem>
      <listitem>
        <para>Using CSS selectors to indicate which elements a
          CSS rule applies to</para>
      </listitem>
      <listitem>
        <para>The box model that CSS is based upon</para>
      </listitem>
    </itemizedlist>
  </section>
</article>
```

2. If you open this document with your preferred browser right now, you can see that it displays all the text together. That's because the CSS stylesheet doesn't exist yet and, even if that seems obvious to you, the browser has no clue that a `<title>` element is meant to be a title or that a `para` element is meant to be a paragraph. The following steps will express all this in CSS.

3. Using your favorite web or text editor, create a file called `ch17_eg01.css` for your stylesheet.

4. The first rules you should write indicate the settings for the whole document, so the first selector should indicate that you want to apply rules to the `<article>` element:

```
article {}
```

5. Having written the selector, you need to add the declarations indicating that the background of the document should be white and the text should be black—and while you're at it, specify a typeface. To do this, add the following to the rule:

```
article {
  color:#000000;
  background-color:#FFFFFF;
  font-family:arial, verdana, sans-serif;}
```

6. Indicate that the titles should be italicized, the `<title>` and `<para>` elements should be displayed as blocks, and the `listitem` elements should be considered . . . list items!

```
title {font-style:italic;}
title, para {display:block}
listitem {display:list-item; list-style: circle outside; margin-left: 2em}
```

7. Save the CSS file you have just written and open the XML document in a browser. You should end up with something that looks like Figure 17-2.

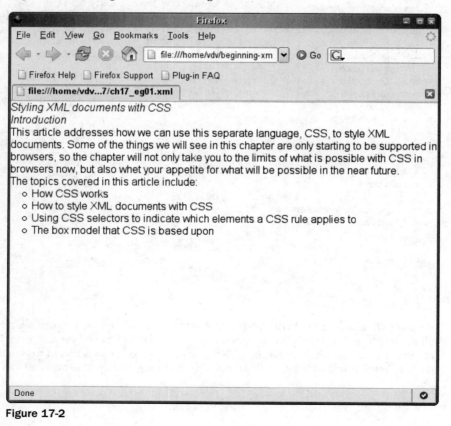

Figure 17-2

How It Works

First, the `<?xml-stylesheet?>` processing instruction in the source XML document indicates that a CSS stylesheet is available that can be applied to the document:

```
<?xml-stylesheet type="text/css" href="ch17_eg01.css"?>
```

Remember that there are two parts to a CSS rule: the selector, which indicates the element(s) to which the rule applies, and the declarations (which are made up of properties and their values). Looking at the first rule in the stylesheet, the selector applies to the `<article>` element; and because the rules cascade, the declarations for the `<article>` element also apply to all other child elements (unless a more specific rule overrides a given attribute).

```
article {
  color:#000000;
  background-color:#FFFFFF;
  font-family:arial, verdana, sans-serif;}
```

The first two rules, setting the `color` property to black and the `background-color` to white, are the same as the default values for these settings in most browsers. The third, `font-family`, indicates that the computer should try to render text in an Arial typeface. If it cannot find Arial, then it should look for Verdana; if it can't find Verdana, then it should use any sans-serif font.

The other three rules act on specific elements: All `<title>` elements should be italicized; all `<title>` and `<para>` elements must be displayed as blocks; and the `<listitem>` elements should be considered a list item:

```
title, para {display:block}
listitem {display:list-item; list-style: circle outside; margin-left: 2em}
```

It may seem obvious that a `<para>` element is a paragraph and needs to be displayed as a block or that a `<listitem>` element is a list item, but remember that this isn't (X)HTML and that the browser has no clue what these elements represent. This is quite different from what you may have experienced if you've been using CSS with (X)HTML. Browsers have a set of predefined rules to style (X)HTML, and your own CSS rules complement or overload these predefined rules, meaning if you neglect to define a rule — for example, that `<p>` elements need to be displayed as blocks — then the predefined rule applies and your document will look OK. With XML, if you neglect to state that the `<para>` elements must be displayed as blocks, then they will be displayed in line, without any linefeeds before or after them.

Attaching the Stylesheet to an XML Document

When you use CSS with (X)HTML, the CSS rules can be put inside a `<style>` element contained within the head of the document, rather than in a separate document. In other XML vocabularies, however, you *must* use a standalone stylesheet.

For non-(X)HTML XML vocabularies, you must use a processing instruction to link a stylesheet to a document instance, like the following:

```
<?xml-stylesheet type="text/css" href="ch17_eg13.css" ?>
```

The processing instruction requires the following attributes:

Attribute	Description
href	Indicates the location of the stylesheet — its value is a URL
type	Indicates the MIME type of the stylesheet, which is text/css for CSS stylesheets. If the user agent does not understand the type (perhaps it's a non-CSS-aware mobile phone), it will not need to download it.

The processing instruction can also take the following optional attributes:

Attribute	Description
Title	The name or title of the stylesheet
Media	Indicates which media the specified stylesheet has been written to work with. Values include screen (primarily for color computer screens), as well as aural, Braille, handheld, and tv.
Charset	Indicates the character set used
Alternate	Indicates whether the stylesheet is the preferred stylesheet. It can take the values yes or no; if not supplied, the default value is no. The idea is to provide multiple stylesheets for a single XML document, giving a hint to user agents so that they can choose one and leave it up to users if they want to select another one.

You can include as many stylesheets as you like by adding further processing instructions for each of the stylesheets you want to use with the document. You can also add processing instructions to include an XSLT stylesheet (see Chapter 8).

Selectors

As shown earlier, the selector is the portion of the CSS rule that indicates the elements to which the rule should apply.

In addition to providing the element name as a selector, you can use the following as selectors:

❑ **Universal selector** — An asterisk indicating a wildcard and matching all element types in the document:

```
*{}
```

❑ **Type selector** — Matches all of the elements specified in the comma-delimited list. The following would match all page, heading, and paragraph elements:

```
page, heading, paragraph {}
```

❏ **Child selector** — Matches an element that is a direct child of another. In this case, it matches `child` elements that are direct children of `parent` elements:

```
parent > child {}
```

❏ **Descendant selector** — Matches an element type that is a descendant of another specified element, at any level of nesting — not just a direct child. In this case, it matches `<a>` elements that are contained within a `<p>` element:

```
p a {}
```

❏ **Adjacent sibling selector** — Matches an element type that is the next sibling of another. Here it matches `<second>` elements that have the same parent as a `<first>` element and appear immediately after the `<first>` element (it would not match a `<second>` element that comes after another `<second>` element):

```
first + second
```

There are also a series of selectors called *attribute selectors*, covered later in the chapter in the section "Attribute Selectors."

You might have used the *class selector*, which matches the value of a `class` attribute, in (X)HTML documents, but it only works with these languages because the browser already knows the meaning of the `class` attribute for these vocabularies. Even if your XML contained a `class` attribute, the browser would not associate it with the class selector.

There is also an *ID selector*, which works like the `class` attribute but only works with attributes of ID type. Although the browser understands this for (X)HTML elements, for other XML vocabularies the browser needs to know that an attribute is of type ID. This requires a DTD or schema that specifies the attribute's type. Because the browser is not forced to validate with a DTD or schema, even if one is specified for the XML document, you cannot rely on it knowing when an attribute is of type ID.

Using CSS for Layout of XML Documents

You have already seen that even when your XML vocabulary has an element called `<p>` or `<b>`, the browser won't know you want its content to be displayed as a paragraph or in bold. Similarly, if you have an `<img>` element in your XML vocabulary, the browser won't know you want an image displayed; and if you had a `<ul>` element, the browser won't know it should add bullet points. Therefore, you need to address the following issues:

❏ How to create sophisticated layouts without the use of tables, as web designers often rely on tables to create layouts they require

❏ How to present tabular data in XML

❏ How to link between XML documents

❏ How to display bullet points

❏ How to display images in your documents

Furthermore, in order to evaluate whether it is best to use CSS or look at another technology, such as XSLT, to transform your documents into (X)HTML, you need to consider the following:

❑ The extent to which you can reorder the content so that elements are presented in a different sequence from the one in which they appear in the original XML document

❑ How you can add content that is not in the XML document, such as new headings that explain the content of the element. (After all, in the XML file, the element's name describes its content, but the element name is not viewed in the browser.)

❑ How you can display attribute content, because many XML files contain important data you may wish to view in attribute values

One of the great things about using CSS with (X)HTML is that you can begin to get results very quickly. You don't need to understand everything about how it works first: Attach styles to elements and off you go. When you work with XML, however, in particular when it comes to positioning and layout, it is important to understand how CSS renders a page. CSS operates on something known as the *box model*, so you need to learn how this works before looking at how it's implemented when laying out pages in this model.

Understanding the Box Model

When displaying a document, CSS treats each element in the document as a rectangular box. Each box is made up of four components: *content* surrounded by *padding*, a *border*, and *margins*.

The margins of each box are transparent, borders can have styles (for example, solid or dashed), and backgrounds apply to the area inside the border, which includes padding and content. The padding is the area between the border and the content (see Figure 17-3).

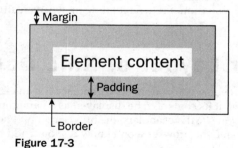

Figure 17-3

The default width for margins, borders, and padding is zero, but the width can be specified using CSS — in fact, different widths can be specified for each side of the box. For example, you might have a wider border on the top and more padding to the right.

If you specify a width and height for a box, you are actually setting the width and height of the content area, although some versions of Internet Explorer actually read width and height values as measuring the height and width of the content plus padding plus border.

Block and Inline Boxes

Each box can contain other boxes, corresponding to elements that are nested inside of it. There are two types of boxes in CSS: *block* and *inline*. In (X)HTML, block boxes are created by elements, such as `<p>`, `<div>`, or `<table>`, whereas inline boxes are created by tags such as `<b>`, `<em>`, and `<span>`, as well as content such as text and images. Block boxes deal with a block of content (each paragraph is treated as if it has a carriage return before and after its content), while the contents of inline boxes can flow together, without the carriage returns (such as a reference being italicized or an important statement being in bold text in the middle of a sentence).

> *Some elements in (X)HTML such as lists and tables have other types of boxes, but the browser treats them as a block or inline box when it comes to positioning, so we won't go into that here.*

When styling XML with CSS, the browser doesn't know which elements should be displayed as block and which as inline, so you need to specify this as a property of the element. To do this you use the `display` property, which takes a value of either `block` or `inline`. As you will see, how you lay out your document and the style of a parent box can affect these properties (for example, an absolutely positioned element is always treated as a block-level element even if it has a `display` property whose value is `inline`).

You can also set the `display` property to have a value of `none`, in which case the browser acts as if neither the element nor any of its children exist (even if those children have declared `display` values of `block` or `inline`).

Try It Out   Playing with the Box Model

To demonstrate the box model, a paragraph of text is all that is needed. This paragraph will be a block-level element and contain some inline elements:

1. Create a document called `ch17_eg02.xml`. Start your document with the XML processing instruction, and then add the processing instruction to attach a stylesheet called `ch17_eg02.css`, which is in the same folder:

```
<?xml version="1.0" encoding="UTF-8" ?>
<?xml-stylesheet type="text/css" href="ch17_eg02.css" ?>
```

2. Add the following fragment of XML:

```
<paragraph>This book is called <reference>Beginning XML</reference>, it will help
you to learn <keyword>XML</keyword>.</paragraph>
```

3. Open a blank document to create your CSS stylesheet, write selectors for each element of the fragment of XML, and put curly braces next to each element:

```
paragraph {}
reference {}
keyword {}
```

4. Specify whether each element should be block or inline with the `display` property (don't forget to add the semicolon at the end; you will be adding more declarations to the rule next):

```
paragraph {
    display:block;}
reference {
    display:inline;}
keyword {
    display:inline;}
```

5.   Finally, add other rules indicating how you want that box to be presented. Note the use of gray borders for each element so that you can see where the edges of the box are:

```
paragraph {
    display:block;
    padding:10px;
    border:solid; border-width:4px; border-color:#CCCCCC;}

reference {
    display:inline;
    font-style:italic;
    color:#CC3333;
    border:solid; border-width:2px; border-color:#CCCCCC;}

keyword {
    display:inline;
    font-weight:bold;
    color:#990000;
    border:solid; border-width:2px; border-color:#CCCCCC;}
```

The result should look something like what is shown in Figure 17-4.

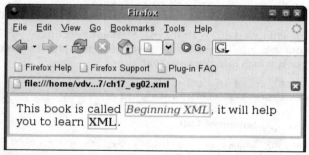

Figure 17-4

How It Works

In this example, the <paragraph> element is a block-level element that acts as the containing element for the inline <reference> and < keywords> elements.

Because the <paragraph> element is given a display property with a value of block, nothing appears to the left or right of it, as if there were a carriage return before or after the content of this element. Meanwhile, the <reference> and <keywords> elements are given a display property with a value of inline, which means they appear in the flow of the rest of the sentence, rather than in a block box standing on its own.

You will see later in the chapter how to get two block-level elements to be displayed next to each other, which, for example, you could use to create two columns of text.

In the same way that an element containing another element is called a containing element, *a box that contains another box, or several boxes, is known as a* containing box *or* containing block.

Anonymous Boxes

In order to simplify the way CSS positioning works, the direct children of a block box will be either all inline boxes or all block boxes, so when the children of an element, which is supposed to be displayed as a block-level element, are to be displayed as both block and inline, an *anonymous box* is created to make the inline element a block-level element.

To illustrate this, take the paragraph from the last example and put it inside a `<page>` element. You can also add an inline `<pageNumber>` element inside it at the same level as the `<paragraph>` element, as shown in the following example (this file is available with the downloadable code for this chapter and is called `ch17_eg03.xml`):

```
<?xml version="1.0" encoding="UTF-8" ?>
<?xml-stylesheet type="text/css" href="ch17_eg03.css" ?>
<page>
    <pageNumber>1</pageNumber>
    <paragraph>This book is called <reference>Beginning XML</reference>,
    it will help you to learn <keywords>XML</keywords>.</paragraph>
</page>
```

Now add the following styles to the stylesheet from the previous example and rename it `ch17_eg03.css`:

```
page {
    display:block;
    padding:10px;
    margin:10px;
    border-style:solid; border-width:4px; border-color:#000000;}

pageNumber {
    display:inline;
    font-style:italic;
    border-style:solid; border-width:4px; border-color:#CCCCCC;}
```

Here you can see that the `<page>` element has two direct children: the inline `<pageNumber>` element and the block-level `<paragraph>` element. Although the `<pageNumber>` element has its display property set to `inline`, it behaves like a block box because an anonymous block box is created around it. This is just an invisible container for the inline element so that it gets treated as a block box.

There is no need to set rules for anonymous boxes; rather, you make the element a block-level box in the first place (see Figure 17-5).

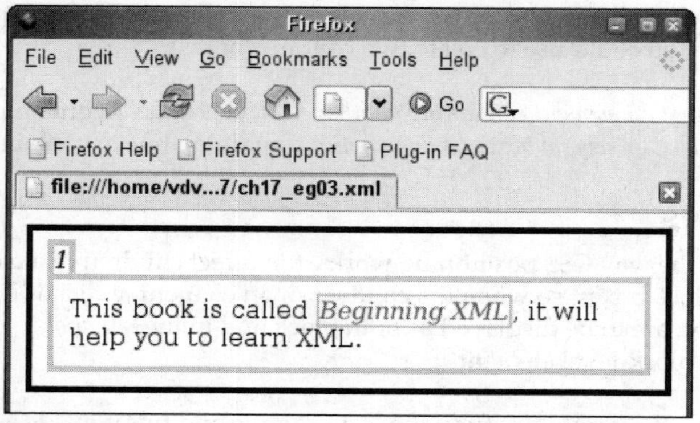

Figure 17-5

Positioning in CSS

We have already established that in order to lay out XML documents using CSS, you need to understand the box model. Knowing that the content of each element can be displayed as a box, the layout process becomes a matter of deciding which type of box you want an element to be in (inline or block) and where you want that box to appear on the page.

CSS 2 has three types of positioning: *normal flow*, *float positioning* (or *floated* for short), and *absolute positioning*. It is important to understand how you can use these to position the boxes corresponding to each element.

Normal Flow

Normal flow is the default type of positioning that you get without specifying any other type of positioning; block boxes flow from the top to the bottom of the page in the order they appear in the source document, starting at the top of their containing block, while inline boxes flow horizontally from left to right.

Try It Out   **Normal Flow**

To see normal flow working, simply add another paragraph to the XML of the simple example you have been using so far:

1. Add the following line to the XML in the previous example and save it as `ch17_eg04.xml`:

```
<?xml version="1.0" encoding="UTF-8" ?>
<?xml-stylesheet type="text/css" href="ch17_eg03.css" ?>
<page>
    <pageNumber>1</pageNumber>
    <paragraph>This book is called <reference>Beginning XML</reference>,
    it will help you to learn <keyword>XML</keyword>.</paragraph>
    <paragraph>The current chapter focuses on using CSS to display
    XML documents.</paragraph>
</page>
```

2. Open the new XML document in a browser. It should look something like Figure 17-6.

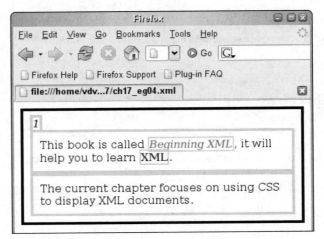

Figure 17-6

How It Works

The `<page>` and `<paragraph>` elements are block-level elements, and the `<pageNumber>` element is treated as a block-level element because it is put in an anonymous box. Each of these block-level items is treated as if it has a carriage return before and after it; the items appear to flow from top to bottom within the page.

The `<keyword>` and `<reference>` elements, meanwhile, flow within the normal text of the paragraph, left to right. Inline boxes are wrapped as needed, moving down to a new line when the available width is exceeded.

Vertical Margins Collapse in Normal Flow

Note also here that vertical margins of boxes collapse in the normal flow, so instead of adding the bottom margin of a block box to create the distance between their respective borders, only the larger of the two values is used. Horizontal margins, however, are never collapsed.

Relative Positioning

There is another type of positioning that falls under the banner of normal positioning: *relative positioning*. This renders the page just like normal flow but then offsets the box by a given amount. You indicate that a box should be relatively positioned by giving the `position` property a value of `relative`. Then you use the `left`, `right`, `top`, and `bottom` properties to specify the offset values.

One scenario in which this is particularly useful is when rendering subscript or superscript text. The following adds a `<footnoteNumber>` after the `<reference>` element in the example (`ch17_eg05.xml`):

```
<page>
    <pageNumber>1</pageNumber>
    <paragraph>This book is called <reference>Beginning XML</reference>
```

```
    <footnoteNumber>3</footnoteNumber>, it will help you to learn
    <keywords>XML</keywords>.</paragraph>
</page>
```

Here is the rule for the `<footnoteNumber>` element (`ch17_eg05.css`):

```
footnoteNumber {
    position:relative; top:3px;
    display:inline;
    font-size:9pt; font-weight:bold;
    color:#990000;
    border-style:solid; border-width:2px; border-color:#CCCCCC;}
```

Figure 17-7 shows how the `top` offset has been used to push the box down.

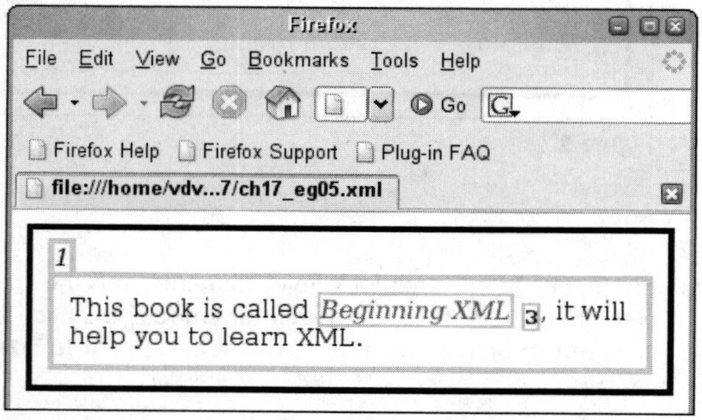

Figure 17-7

You should only specify a left or right offset and a top or bottom offset. If you specify both, one must be the absolute negative of the other (for example, `top:3px; bottom:-3px;`). If you have top and bottom or left and right, and they do not have absolute negative values of each other, the right or bottom offset is ignored.

Overlapping Relative Positioning

When you use relative positioning, some boxes may end up overlapping others. Because you are offsetting a box relative to normal flow, one box will end up on top of another if the offset is large enough. This may create an effect you are looking for, but be aware of the following pitfalls:

❑ Unless you set a background for a box (either a background color or image) it will, by default, be transparent, so when the overlapping of text occurs, you get an unreadable mess.

❑ The CSS specification does not specify which element should appear on top when relatively positioned elements overlap each other, so there can be differences between browsers.

To illustrate this possibility, the file `ch17_eg06.css` (for use with `ch17_eg06.xml`) contains a relatively positioned `<keywords>` element, and the background is set to white:

```
keywords {
    display:inline;
    position:relative; right:45px;
    background-color:#ffffff;
    color:#990000;
    font-weight:bold;
    border:solid; border-width:2px; border-color:#CCCCCC;}
```

Figure 17-8 shows the result.

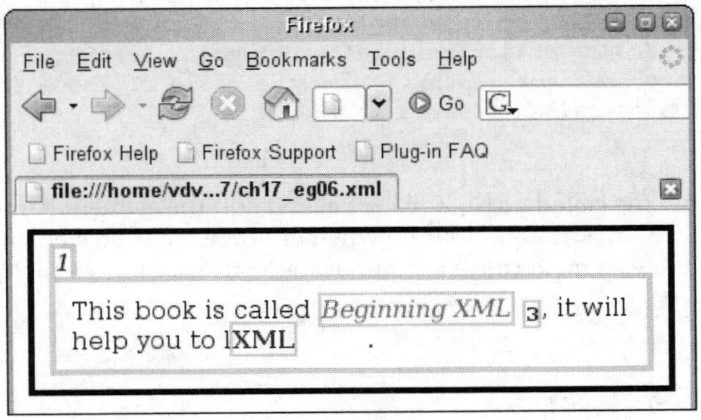

Figure 17-8

In IE and Firefox, the relatively positioned element appears at the front; in Opera the order in which the elements appear in the document determines which one appears on the top.

Float Positioning

The second type of positioning creates a box that *floats*, enabling other content to flow around it. A box that is floated is shifted as far to the left or right of the containing box as possible within that block's padding. (Its vertical margins, however, are not collapsed above or below it as block boxes in normal flow can; rather, it is aligned with the top of the containing box.)

To indicate that you want a box floated either to the left or the right of the containing box, you set the `float` property to have a value of either `left` or `right`. Even if these boxes are defined as inline boxes, they will be treated as block-level boxes.

Whenever you specify a `float` property, set a `width` property too — to indicate the width of the containing box that the floating box should occupy; otherwise, it will automatically take up 100 percent of the width of the containing box (leaving no space for things to flow around it, leaving it just like a plain block-level element).

Try It Out   **Creating a Floating Box**

1. Create a file called `ch17eg_07.xml`. Then add the XML declaration and a link to a stylesheet called `ch17_eg07.css`:

```
<?xml version="1.0" encoding="UTF-8" ?>
<?xml-stylesheet type="text/css" href="ch17_eg06.css" ?>
```

2. Add the following XML, which contains a < pullQuote> element you will float, to the file:

```
<review>
    <title>The Wrox Review</title>
    <pullQuote>If you want to learn XML, this is the book.</pullQuote>
    <paragraph>Extensible Markup Languages is a rapidly maturing technology
        with powerful real-world applications, particularly for the management,
        display, and transport of data. Together with its many related
        technologies, it has become the standard for data and document delivery
        on the web. <reference>Beginning XML</reference> is for any developer
        who is interested in learning to use <keyword>XML</keyword> in web,
        e-commerce, or data storage applications. Some knowledge of markup,
        scripting, and/or object oriented programming languages is
        advantageous, but not essential, as the basis of these techniques is
        explained as required.</paragraph>
</review>
```

3. Create another file called `ch17_eg07.css`, and add the element names in the XML document you just created. In addition, indicate whether you want each element to be a block-level element or an inline element (the exception is the <pullQuote> element, covered in a moment):

```
review {display:block;}
title {display:block;}
pullQuote {}
paragraph {display:block;}
keyword {display:inline;}
```

4. You want to make the <pullQuote> element float to the left of the paragraph, so add the `float` property with a value of `left` and a `width` property with a value of 20 percent. Remember that if you don't add the `width` property, the floated element will be displayed just like any other block-level element.

```
pullQuote {
    float:left;
    width:20%;}
```

5. Now add the rest of the rules indicating how the document should be styled. The title of the book should be in a black box with white text, and each box should have a border to illustrate where the edges of the box are, as shown here:

```
review {
    display:block;
    padding:10px;
    margin:10px;
    border-style:solid; border-width:4px; border-color:#000000;}
```

```
title {
    display:block;
    font-size:24px;
    padding:5px;
    color:#FFFFFF; background-color:#000000;}
```

```
pullQuote {
    float:left;
```

```
    width:20%;
    font-style:italic;
    padding:10px; margin:10px;
    border:solid; border-width:4px; border-color:#CCCCCC;}

paragraph {
    display:block;
    padding:10px;
    border:solid; border-width:4px; border-color:#CCCCCC;}

keyword {
    display:inline;
    font-weight:bold;
    color:#990000;
    border:solid; border-width:2px; border-color:#CCCCCC;}
```

6. Open the XML file in your browser. You should see something like what is shown in Figure 17-9.

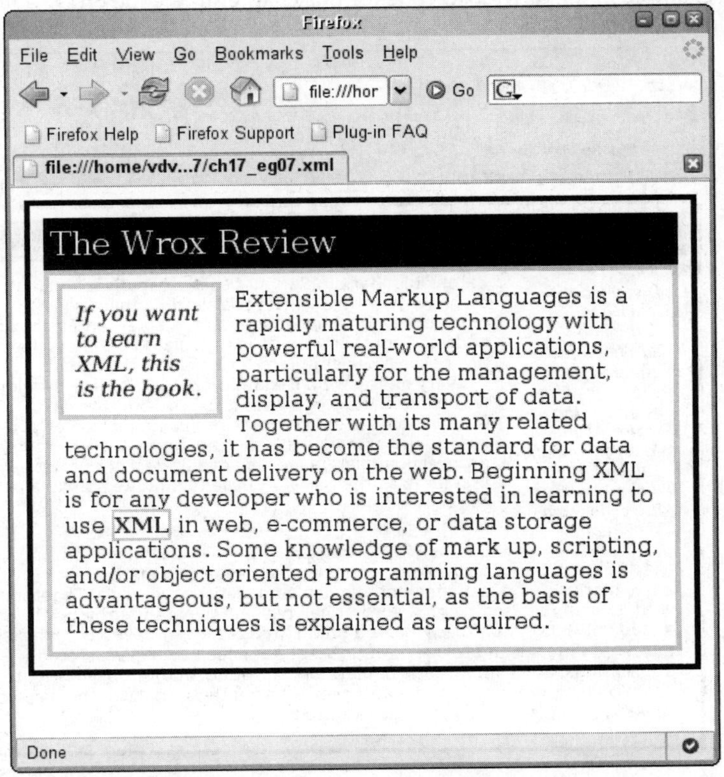

Figure 17-9

How It Works

The <pullQuote> element has been given a property of float, with a value of left, which indicates that the box should be floated to the left of the containing <review> element. Remember that the width property is vital when adding a float; otherwise, the whole content of the element would be treated like any block-level element and take up the full width of the containing box.

Note that regardless of whether the <pullQuote> element appears before or after the paragraph element, it is still in the same place. This has important implications for the ability to present the contents of an XML document in a sequence other than the one it follows in the XML source. A float can be used to bring the content of any element to the top of a document.

Overlapping Floated Boxes

Like relatively positioned boxes, floated boxes can cause overlap problems. A floated box can overlap block-level boxes that are in normal flow mode. Figure 17-10 shows what happens when you add another <paragraph> element and increase the length of the <pullQuote> so it is long enough to overlap (there is an example in the download code for this chapter in the file ch17_eg08.xml).

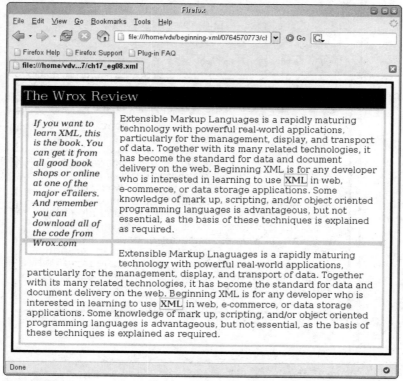

Figure 17-10

Using the Clear Property to Prevent an Overlap

If you don't want the content of an element to wrap around the content of a floated element, you can use the clear property. In the example just shown, you would use the clear property on the second paragraph element:

```
paragraph2 {clear:left;}
```

The value of the property can be any of the following:

Value	Description
Left	The left side of box must not be adjacent to an earlier floating box.
Right	The right side of box must not be adjacent to an earlier floating box.
Both	Neither the left nor right side of box may be adjacent to an earlier floating box.
None	The default setting; content is placed adjacent to the floated element on either side
Inherit	Inherits the parent element's property

You can see how clear works in Figure 17-11. (ch17_eg09.xml and ch17_eg09.css illustrate this in the code download.)

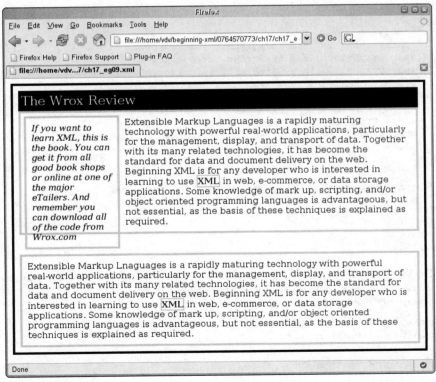

Figure 17-11

Absolute Positioning

The third method of positioning is *absolute positioning*. Absolutely positioned elements are completely removed from the normal flow. They are always treated as block-level elements and are positioned within their containing block using offset values for the left, top, right, and bottom properties. For example, you might want a <page> element to appear 10 pixels in from the left of the browser window and 20 pixels from the top of the window, with the <title> within the <page> element 10 pixels from the top of the <page> and 5 pixels in from the left.

You indicate that an element's content should be absolutely positioned using the position property with a value of absolute. Remember, however, that the content of the containing element will not float around the absolutely positioned box as it does with a floated box; rather, it will appear above or be placed on top of the containing box.

> *IE 6 doesn't correctly display offset values given for the* right *and* bottom *properties, although Firefox and other browsers handle them correctly. It's best to rely on the* left *and* top *properties.*

Try It Out	Using Absolute Positioning to Create Columns of Text

In this example, you will create a page with two columns of text. The XML file will contain a root element called <page> and have two child elements, <column1> and <column2>, each of which contains a paragraph of text. Here is the XML file called ch17_eg10.xml:

```
<?xml version="1.0" encoding="UTF-8" ?>
<?xml-stylesheet type="text/css" href="ch17_eg10.css" ?>
<page>
   <column1>
      <paragraph>This is a paragraph...</paragraph>
      <paragraph>This is a paragraph...</paragraph>
      <paragraph>This is a paragraph...</paragraph>
   </column1>
   <column2>
      <paragraph>This is a paragraph...</paragraph>
      <paragraph>This is a paragraph...</paragraph>
      <paragraph>This is a paragraph...</paragraph>
   </column2>
</page>
```

1. Start a stylesheet called ch17_eg10.css and add these elements to it:

```
page{}
column1{}
column2{}
paragraph{}
```

2. Decide which elements are to be absolutely positioned and which elements are block-level or inline. Remember that all absolutely positioned elements are treated as block-level elements, so you do not need to add a display property to them:

```
page{display:block;}
column1{position:absolute;}
column2{position:absolute;}
paragraph{display:block;}
```

3. Now you can decide where you want your absolutely positioned elements. The `<page>` element is the containing element, so `<column1>` can be the left-hand column, and `<column2>` can be the right-hand column.

You often need to specify the width or height of boxes when using absolute positioning; after all, you use offsets to position boxes, and if you do not set the widths of boxes, you might cause overlap. The columns should therefore be set to be 200 pixels wide, so you can position the second column 250 pixels in from its containing element as follows:

```
page {
   display:block;
   width:470px;
   height: 400px;}

column1 {
   position:absolute;
   left:10px; top:10px;
   width:200px;}

column2 {
   position:absolute;
   left:250px; top:10px;
   width:200px;}

paragraph {
   display:block;
   padding-bottom:10px;}
```

4. Add some padding and borders so you can see where the boxes' borders are:

```
page {
   display:block;
   width:470px;
   height: 400px;
   padding:10px;
   border-style:solid; border-width:2px; border-color:#000000;}

column1 {
   position:absolute;
   left:10px; top:10px;
   width:200px;
   padding:10px;
   border-style:solid; border-width:2px; border-color:#CCCCCC;}

column2 {
   position:absolute;
   left:250px; top:10px;
   width:200px;
   padding:10px;
   border-style:solid; border-width:2px; border-color:#CCCCCC;}

paragraph {
   display:block;
   padding-bottom:10px;}
```

5. Finally, open the XML page in your browser to see how it looks; you should end up with something like what is shown in Figure 17-12.

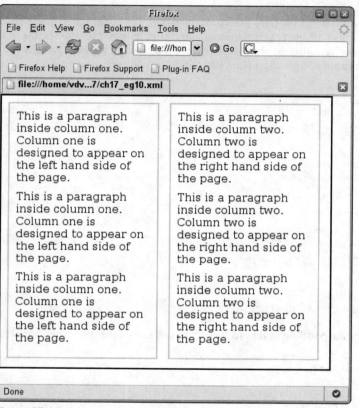

Figure 17-12

How It Works

This example created two columns of text by using absolute positioning to position the `<column1>` and `<column2>` elements. The `<column1>` element was positioned 10 pixels in from the left of the browser window and 10 pixels from the top. It was given a width of 200 pixels. Meanwhile, the `<column2>` element was positioned 250 pixels in from the left and 10 pixels from the top; it was also 200 pixels wide.

Because the width of these column elements were specified, it was possible to position them next to each other in the browser window using the top and left offsets. The content of these elements is then positioned using normal flow inside their respective containing blocks.

Fixed Positioning

Fixed positioning is a special subset of absolute positioning whereby the box does not move when users scroll down the page. To give a box fixed positioning, you add the position property with a value of fixed. To position the box, you use offsets just as you would with absolute positioning, although the box is positioned relative to the browser window, not its containing element.

Firefox and Opera support fixed positioning, but IE 6 and IE 7 do not.

Try It Out   **Fixed Positioning**

This exercise adds a new element to the last example. The new element is a heading for the page.

1.   Open the last example and add the following <heading> element just after the opening <page> tag. Call the file ch17_eg11.xml:

```
<page>
   <heading>This is a Heading</heading>
   <column1>
```

2.   Change the value for the href attribute on the <link> element to point to the new stylesheet, which is called ch17_eg11.css:

```
<?xml-stylesheet type="text/css" href="ch17_eg11.css" ?>
```

3.   Open the stylesheet ch17_eg10.css, add the following rule for the heading element, and then save it as ch17_eg11.css:

```
heading {
   position:fixed;
   width:100%; padding:20px;
   top:0px; left:0px;
   color:#FFFFFF; background-color:#666666;
   font-family:arial, verdana, sans-serif; font-size:22px; }
```

4.   Save the file and open it in the browser. If your browser supports fixed positioning, you should see something like what is shown in Figure 17-13.

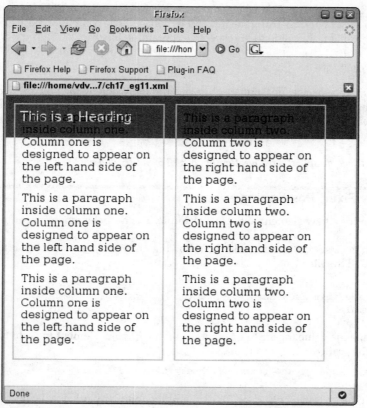

Figure 17-13

How It Works

As you can see in the stylesheet, the `<heading>` element has been given the `position` property with a value of `fixed` to ensure that the heading stays in the same place. The `width` property ensures that the heading spans the whole page, and the `top` and `left` offsets indicate that it should be positioned at the top left-hand corner of the browser window.

You might have noticed a bit of a problem here, however: The columns inside the page overlap the heading. Furthermore, if they did not overlap the heading, they would be masked by it. You need to do two things to address this issue. First, add an offset to the columns so that they appear below the `<heading>` element. Second, arrange the order of the elements so that the columns are not displayed above the heading when the user scrolls down the page.

Overlapping Absolutely Positioned Elements and Z-Index

Absolutely positioned elements have a tendency to overlap each other and nonpositioned elements. When this happens, the default behavior is to place the first elements underneath later ones. This is known as *stacking context*. You can, however, control which element appears on top using the `z-index` property. If you are familiar with graphic design packages, it is similar to using the "bring to top" and "send to back" features.

The value of the z-index property is a number, and the higher the number the nearer the top that element should be displayed.

Laying Out Tabular Data

When you look at laying out tabular data in XML, the problem is pretty obvious: You don't have the `<table>` element and related row and cell elements you had in (X)HTML.

If you knew how many rows and columns of data there were going to be, you could use absolute positioning to position each cell (but your stylesheet would only accommodate this number of columns and rows). Luckily, the display property can take a value of table, which helps us in this matter.

The display property takes the following values, which correspond with (X)HTML meanings for `<table>`, `<tr>`, `<td>` and `<caption>` elements, designed specifically for laying out tabular data:

Value of display	Description
display:table;	Indicates that an element's content represents a table
display:table-row;	Indicates that an element's content represents a table row
display:table-cell;	Indicates that an element's content represents a table cell
display:table-caption;	Indicates that an element's content represents a table caption

The CSS table properties do not work in IE 6 and IE 7, although they do work with Firefox, Safari, and Opera browsers.

Try It Out   **Using display to Display Tabular Data**

This example creates a tabular presentation of the following XML data. Although the element names in this example match the tabular content, they could equally be some other data structure:

```
<?xml version="1.0" encoding="UTF-8" ?>
<?xml-stylesheet type="text/css" href="ch17_eg12.css" ?> <page>
  <table>
    <tableRow>
      <tableCell1>One</tableCell1>
      <tableCell2>Two</tableCell2>
      <tableCell3>Three</tableCell3>
    </tableRow>
    <tableRow>
      <tableCell1>Four</tableCell1>
      <tableCell2>Five</tableCell2>
      <tableCell3>Six</tableCell3>
    </tableRow>
  </table>
</page>
```

1. Create a new stylesheet document called `ch17_eg12.css` and add element names and their appropriate display properties to each element like so:

```
page {display:block;}
table {display:table;}
tableRow {display:table-row;}
tableCell1, tableCell2, tablecell3 {display:table-cell;}
```

2. Add some padding and shading so you can see where each element begins and ends:

```
page {
  display:block;
  color:#000000; background-color:#EFEFEF;
  border-style:solid; border-width:2px; border-color:#000000; }

table {
  display:table;
  padding:20px;
  color:#000000; background-color:#CCCCCC;
  border-style:solid; border-width:2px; border-color:#000000; }

tableRow {display:table-row;}

tableCell1, tableCell2, tableCell3 {
  display:table-cell;
  padding:10px;
  color:#000000; background-color:#EFEFEF;
  border-style:solid; border-width:2px; border-color:#000000; }
```

3. Save the stylesheet and open the XML file in a browser. In Firefox, Safari, or Opera, you should end up with a result similar to what is shown in Figure 17-14.

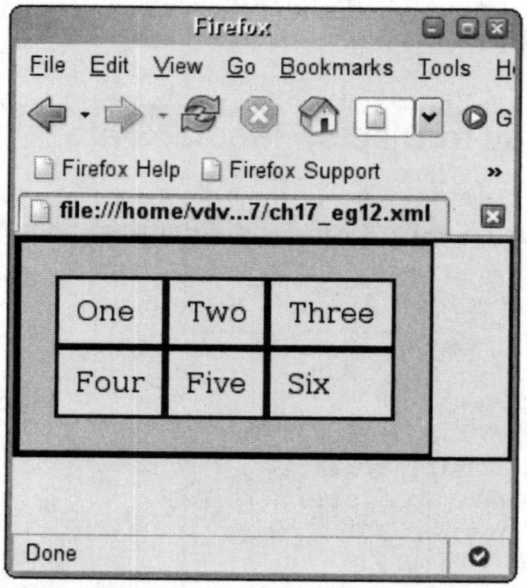

Figure 17-14

How It Works

Obviously, the key to this example are the special values for the `display` property that enable you to specify to the browser which elements indicate rows or cells of a table. Note, however, an issue that greatly limits this approach. The technique relies on the XML file having a structure like the one in the example XML. The element corresponding to the row must contain the elements corresponding to cells, so you need a repeating structure for this technique to work.

The cells could have the same name. They are different here to illustrate that they might have different names, as more real-life uses of XML are likely to follow this structure. However, you cannot miss an element in any row; it must be present even if its content is empty. Nor can you have any extra elements in any of the rows, or the table will not display properly. In short, your XML must have a strict structure if you are going to display it as a table. Having seen how to display tables, let's move onto another type of markup that you will miss from (X)HTML, namely links.

Links in XML Documents

In the XML 1.0 Recommendation, there is no equivalent of the <a> element to create hyperlinks, so if you are going to use CSS to display your XML documents, then you need a way of indicating which element should be a link.

While the XML Recommendation itself does not offer a way to create links in XML documents, another W3C recommendation, *XLink*, provides a mechanism for linking that goes far beyond what you are used to with HTML links. XLink is a powerful and complicated technology that provides users with advanced features, such as enabling authors to offer multiple destinations from a single link, and the ability to define links in separate link documents or databases, rather than the source files.

Firefox supports a limited subset of XLink, and it is enough to reproduce the functionality of the <a> and <img> tags in HTML. Opera and IE have yet to add any implementation of XLink (although Opera does have a proprietary extension to CSS to enable you to define a link).

> *A complete discussion of XLink is beyond the scope of this chapter, although you will look at the subset of it implemented by Firefox.*

XLink Support in Firefox

The limited support for XLink introduced in Firefox enables users to create links with the same functionality as those of HTML. You can embed an XLink into the document, and the document the link points to can replace the current document (just like a normal link in (X)HTML) or open the document in a new window (which is similar to using `target="_new"` on a link in (X)HTML). You can even open a link automatically when a page loads, which enables you to create pop-up windows when the page loads or replace the content of the current page that is loading.

Any element in an XML document can be a linking element. You simply add attributes from the XLink namespace to that element to indicate that the element should be treated as a link. The attributes are listed in the following table:

Attribute	Description
xlink:type	Indicates whether the link is a *simple* or *extended* link. Firefox only supports simple links, so you can give it a value of Simple. Simple links are just like those you are familiar with using in (X)HTML: They link from one document to another. The URL of the document you are linking to is given as a value of the href attribute.
xlink:href	Indicates the target of the link, just as it does in (X)HTML, and its value is a URI
xlink:title	Enables you to provide a title that describes what the user might find in the destination document for the link, and is similar to the title attribute on (X)HTML links
xlink:show	Indicates where the target document should appear. It can take the following values: new if the document should appear in a new window, replace if the document should replace the content of the window, or embed if the document should be inserted at the current point in the document.
xlink:actuate	Enables you to specify when the link should be activated. There are two possible values: onRequest to wait for the user to activate the link, or onLoad to activate the link when the page loads.

As you can see, the attributes are shown here with a namespace prefix of xlink: because attributes without prefixes are assumed to belong to the same namespace as the element that carries them. As these attributes belong to the XLink namespace, you add the following namespace declaration to the root element of your documents:

```
xmlns:xlink="http://www.w3.org/1999/xlink"
```

Try It Out   **Using XLink in Firefox**

In this example, you create a simple link that takes the user from one page to a new page. You need to pay special attention to the XML, as that is where the real work is being done with the XLink.

1. Create a file called ch17_eg13.xml and add the XML declaration and a stylesheet link to a stylesheet called ch17_eg13.css like so:

```
<?xml version="1.0" encoding="UTF-8" ?>
<?xml-stylesheet type="text/css" href="ch16_eg13.css" ?>
```

2. Add a root element called `<page>`. This element must contain the namespace declaration, like so:

```
<page xmlns:xlink="http://www.w3.org/1999/xlink">
```

3. Now there are a couple of paragraphs to explain the example. The interesting part is the `<link>` element, with the `xlink` attributes that actually create the link:

```
<paragraph>The following link uses XLink to replicate the functionality of HTML
hyperlinks between pages:</paragraph>

<paragraph><link xlink:type="simple"
   xlink:show="replace"
   xlink:actuate="onRequest"
   xlink:title="This link is like a link between pages in HTML"
   xlink:href="http://www.wrox.com">
    Click here</link>
   to be taken to a new page</paragraph>
```

4. Finish up the XML page with the closing root element's tag:

```
</page>
```

5. Create a simple stylesheet called `ch17_eg13.css` with the following rules. Note how the link is made blue and underlined to indicate that it is a link:

```
page {
   display:block;
   padding:10px;
   color:#000000; background-color:#FFFFFF;
   border-style:solid; border-width:2px; border-color:#000000;}
paragraph {
   display:block;
   font-family:arial, verdana, sans-serif; font-size:20px;
   padding:20px;
   color:#000000; background-color:#FFFFFF;}

link {
   display:inline;
   color:#0000FF;
   text-decoration:underline;}
```

6. Open the XML file in Firefox. You should see something like what is shown in Figure 17-15.

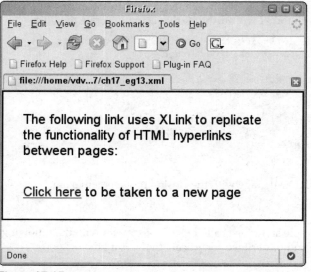

Figure 17-15

How It Works

The example works just like a link in an (X)HTML document, but if you view the source, you can see that it is still XML. The really interesting parts here are the XLink attributes, not the CSS.

The equivalent in (X)HTML would be the following:

```
<a href="http://www.wrox.com" title="This is the title of the link" >
```

In the case of XLink, not only do you have the `href` and `title` attributes; you also have a couple of new ones. First, you have to indicate whether it is a simple or complex link (although Netscape only supports simple links):

```
xlink:type="simple"
```

Then, you have the `actuate` attribute, to indicate when the link should be activated:

```
xlink:actuate="onRequest"
```

The `show` attribute indicates that you want the target of the link to replace this page:

```
xlink:show="replace"
xlink:title="This link is like a link between pages in HTML"
xlink:href="http://www.wrox.com">
```

Just like a links in (X)HTML, the content of the element used as a link is what the user can click. If there is no element content, then users have nothing to click, although this is not a problem if the `actuate` attribute has a value of `onLoad`.

Forcing Links Using the XHTML Namespace

There is an alternative to using XLink, which suffers from a lack of support in browsers. You can embed XHTML syntax into your XML documents using the XHTML namespace, so your browser picks up on the meaning of XHTML elements and renders them appropriately. This technique works fine on Opera, Firefox, and IEv6, but it doesn't work in IE 7.

To rework the example just shown using XHTML instead of XLink, you need to change the lines that are highlighted (this reworking of the previous example is called `ch17_eg14.xml`):

```
<page xmlns:xhtml="http://www.w3.org/1999/xhtml">
    <paragraph>The following link uses XHTML to replicate the functionality of HTML
     hyperlinks between pages:</paragraph>
    <paragraph>
    <xhtml:a href="http://www.wrox.com">Click here</xhtml:a>
    to be taken to a new page</paragraph>
</page>
```

While this works, it is not the ideal approach, because it forces you to use XHTML elements in a document that otherwise would not contain elements like these.

The HTML "namespace," `http://www.w3.org/TR/REC-html40`, *has also been used for this purpose but it is no longer supported by recent versions of Firefox. When you think about it, the notion of a namespace, which is purely XML, doesn't make a lot of sense for a markup language such as HTML, which isn't XML. However, dropping support of the HTML "namespace" is breaking the few applications that have been using this feature.*

Images in XML Documents

Having looked at using XLink to create links in your XML documents, you should have a good idea of how images can be included in XML documents — by giving the `xlink:show` attribute a value of `embed`, so that the image file is embedded in the document where the link appears. Unfortunately, however, neither IE, Firefox, nor Opera supports the embedding of images in documents using XLink.

You can see how this should work in theory in the following piece of code (`ch17_eg15.xml`); note how the `actuate` attribute needs a value of `onLoad` so that it loads with the rest of the page:

```
<link xlink:type="simple"
    xlink:show="embed"
    xlink:actuate="onLoad"
    xlink:title="An image inserted using XLink"
    xlink:href="wrox_logo.gif"></link>
```

You could also use a value of `replace` for the `show` attribute if you wanted an image to replace the whole document (which would work in Firefox).

One way around the lack of browser support for images in XML documents is through the use of the CSS `background-image` property. An element in the XML document can be associated with a CSS rule that uses the `background-image` property with a value of `url(file_name)`. This example contains an element called `<logo />` (`ch17_eg16.xml`):

```
<page>
  <logo />
  <paragraph>You should see an image above this paragraph, which was inserted
   into the page using the background-image property in a CSS style
   sheet.</paragraph>
</page>
```

The CSS rule associated with this element should look something like this (`ch17_eg16.css`):

```
logo {
  display:block;
  background-image:url(wrox_logo.gif);
  margin:5px;
  width:615px; height:25px;}
```

The benefit of this technique is that it works with IE 5+, Firefox, and Opera. The problem is that the source XML document must include a separate element for each image you want in the resulting document (until attribute selectors are better supported in browsers — you'll learn about attribute selectors later in the chapter). You must also have a rule in your CSS for each of these elements/images.

Using CSS to Add Content to Documents

Having seen how XSLT works in Chapter 8, you might wonder how you can add new text or images into your XML documents from the CSS file. In truth, the ways in which you can add to XML documents using CSS are very limited, although four pseudo-elements introduced in CSS2 offer some helpful results:

Pseudo-Element	Description
`:before`	Allows you to insert content before an element
`:after`	Allows you to insert content after an element
`:first_letter`	Allows you to add special styles to the first letter of the selector
`:first-line`	Allows you to add special styles to the first line of the text in a selector

The syntax for pseudo-elements is as follows:

```
selector:pseudo-element {property:value;}
```

For example, you could make the first letter of a paragraph larger than the rest by adding a rule like this:

```
paragraph:first-letter {font-size:42px;}
```

Making bulleted lists is another particularly helpful application of these pseudo-elements.

Try It Out   **Creating a Bulleted List Using the :before Pseudo-Element**

In this example you create a CSS that deals with different levels of bulleted lists. The XML document you will work with looks like this (`ch17_eg17.xml`):

```
<?xml version="1.0" encoding="UTF-8" ?>
<?xml-stylesheet type="text/css" href="ch17_eg17.css" ?>
<page>
  <paragraph>The effect of a bulleted list is created using CSS.</paragraph>

  <list>
    <bulletPoint>Item one</bulletPoint>
    <bulletPoint>Item two</bulletPoint>
    <bulletPoint>Item three</bulletPoint>
     <list>
        <bulletPoint>Item three point one</bulletPoint>
        <bulletPoint>Item three point two</bulletPoint>
     </list>
      <bulletPoint>Item four</bulletPoint>
  </list>

</page>
```

1. Add the element names and their `display` properties. Each element is a block-level element, including each bullet point, as each point should start on a new line:

```
page {display:block;}
paragraph {display:block;}
list {display:block;}
bulletPoint {display:block;}
```

2. Add another selector for the `<bulletPoint>` element, and use the `:before` pseudo-element with it so you can add a + sign to indicate your bullet point:

```
bulletPoint:before {content:"+ ";}
```

3. Finally, add some other styles, borders, fonts, colors, and padding, to make the page complete:

```
page {
  display:block;
  padding:10px;
  color:#000000; background-color:#FFFFFF;
  border-style:solid; border-width:2px; border-color:#000000;}
paragraph {
  display:block;
  font-family:arial, verdana, sans-serif; font-size:20px;
  padding:20px;
  color:#000000; background-color:#FFFFFF;}

list {
  display:block;
  padding-left:20px;}

bulletPoint {display:block;}
bulletPoint:before {content:"+ ";}
```

4. Save this file as `ch17_eg17.css` and take a look at it in a browser. The result should look something like what is shown in Figure 17-16.

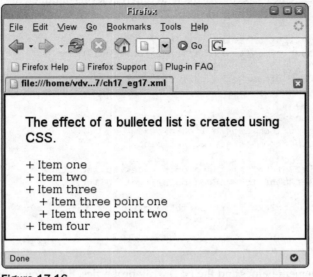

Figure 17-16

Note that this will not work in IE 6 or 7, which don't support generated content. With IE, you would need to stick to the `display:list` *property shown in the first example to implement bulleted lists.*

How It Works

This example illustrates the three steps that make a bulleted list work with an XML document. First, the containing element for the list needs to be displayed as a block-level element. In this case it is the `<list>` element:

```
list {display:block;}
```

Just as a `<ul>` or `<ol>` element in (X)HTML can contain another `<ul>` or `<ol>` element to create a nested list, you can do the same with this list element. The padding to the left of this block-level element makes it clear that it is a nested list:

```
list {
  display:block;
  padding-left:20px;}
```

Second, the `<bulletPoint>` element, which represents an item in the list, is specified as a block-level element. This makes each item appear on a new line using normal flow:

```
bulletPoint {display:block;}
```

Finally, using the :before pseudo-element adds the marker (or bullet point) before each item in the list. This inserts the + symbol before each item, as shown in the following:

```
bulletPoint:before {content:"+ ";}
```

CSS2 also introduced counters, which enable you to create numbered lists using this approach, although they are not yet supported by all the major browsers.

Attribute Content

You may well have noticed that throughout the chapter so far, the examples have only displayed and talked about displaying element content. To wrap up this topic, you need to understand how to use attributes in selectors and how to display attribute values.

Attribute Selectors

CSS2 introduced the capability to use attributes and their values in conjunction with element names as the selector for a CSS rule:

Selector	Matches
myElement[myAttribute]	An element called myElement carrying an attribute called myAttribute
myElement[myAttribute="myValue"]	An element called myElement carrying an attribute called myAttribute whose value is myValue
myElement[myAttribute~="myValue"]	An element called myElement carrying an attribute called myAttribute whose value is a list of space-separated words, one of which is exactly the same as myValue

Although none of these work in IE 6, they work fine in IE 7, Firefox, and Opera. When they do become supported, however, they will be powerful tools that enable you to apply a style to an element based on the presence of, or value of, an attribute.

Using Attribute Values in Documents

One of the biggest drawbacks of working with XML and CSS is that there is no simple method for displaying attribute values from your documents. You might have noticed that all of the examples so far have concentrated on element content, and the reason is because CSS is designed to style element content, not attribute values.

However, you can employ a trick that enables you to display values of attributes. The trick relies on the :before and :after pseudo-elements shown earlier in the chapter. Using these pseudo-elements, you can add attribute values before or after the element that carries that attribute — unfortunately, you cannot display an attribute value before or after any element other than the one that carries it.

729

The secret lies in a property called content, whose value can be set to attr(attributeName), where attributeName is the name of the attribute whose content you want to add before or after the element.

The drawback to this trick is that it only works in Firefox and Opera, not Internet Explorer.

Try It Out   Displaying Attribute Values

This example makes use of an earlier example, ch17_eg07.xml, adding an author attribute to the <title> element:

1. Open ch17_eg07.xml, change the stylesheet to point to ch17_eg18.css, and save the file as ch17_eg18.xml.

2. Add the following line and save the file:

```
<?xml version="1.0" encoding="UTF-8" ?>
<?xml-stylesheet type="text/css" href="ch17_eg18.css" ?>
<review>
    <title author="Tom Bishop">The Wrox Review</title>
    <pullQuote>If you want to learn XML, this is the book.</pullQuote>
    <paragraph>Extensible Markup Languages is a rapidly maturing technology
      with powerful real-world applications, particularly for the management,
      display, and transport of data. Together with its many related
      technologies, it has become the standard for data and document delivery
      on the web. <reference> Beginning XML</reference> is for any developer
      who is interested in learning to use <keyword>XML</keyword> in web,
      e-commerce, or data storage applications. Some knowledge of mark up,
      scripting, and/or object oriented programming languages is advantageous,
      but not essential, as the basis of these techniques is explained as
      required.</paragraph>
</review>
```

3. Open the stylesheet ch17_07.css and add the following rule:

```
title:after {
    display:block;
    font-size:14px;
    color:#efefef; font-weight:bold; font-style:italic;
    content:"Written by: " attr(author);}
```

4. Save this file as ch17_eg18.css.

5. Open ch17_eg18.xml in your browser. You should end up with a page something like the one shown in Figure 17-17.

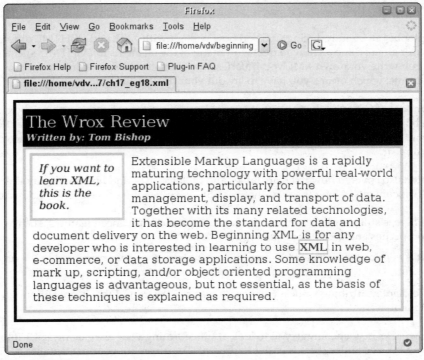

Figure 17-17

How It Works

This example not only takes an attribute value and displays it onscreen, but also writes some additional text beforehand. Recall the restriction that you can only write attribute values before or after the element that carries them. Therefore, this example used the :after pseudo-element to display the value of the <author> attribute after the <title> element. The pseudo-element is used in the selector, like so:

```
title:after {
```

The content property writes the attribute value to the screen as follows:

```
content:"Written by: " attr(author);}
```

As you can see, this example not only added the attribute value, but also some text saying Written by: so that the attribute value did not just appear out of the blue.

Summary

This chapter began by introducing CSS and how using it with XML and (X)HTML differs. As you saw, a web browser already knows how to deal with many of the elements in (X)HTML, such as `table`, `ul`, and `b`. When you write your own XML vocabularies, however, the browser won't know how to interpret any of the elements, which means you have to lay out your documents from scratch.

The box model of CSS puts the content of every element in either an inline or block box; and by positioning these boxes carefully, you can achieve complex layouts. You have seen that normal flow, relative positioning, float positioning, absolute positioning, and fixed positioning allow you to control where the elements appear.

The chapter also covered how to create tables and bulleted lists, and how to display links and images in your XML documents. Along the way, three of CSS's significant weaknesses were described:

❑   There is still very little support for some of the more advanced features, such as table layout properties and complex positioning.

❑   It is very difficult to reorder element content from the order presented in the original XML document.

❑   To display attribute values, you need to use a workaround that is not supported in Internet Explorer.

These drawbacks may encourage you to look at transforming your XML using XSLT into either XHTML or another XML vocabulary that is easier to present. Transforming your content into XHTML also gives you the advantage of being able to add images and links to your documents that would work in most browsers.

Alternatively, you may have the luxury of being able to write a vocabulary that will be easy to display using CSS now that you know where its strengths and weaknesses regarding presenting XML lie.

Exercise Questions

Suggested solutions to these questions can be found in Appendix A.

Question 1

The questions for this chapter focus on one example: a purchase order. Slowly build a more complex stylesheet beginning with the following XML file (`ch17_ex01.xml`):

```
<?xml version="1.0" encoding="UTF-8" ?>
<?xml-stylesheet type="text/css" href="ch17_ex01.css" ?>

<purchaseOrder orderID="x1129001">

<buyer>
   <companyName>Woodland Toys</companyName>
```

```
      <purchaserName>Tom Walter</purchaserName>
      <address>
        <address1>The Business Centre</address1>
        <address2>127 Main Road</address2>
        <town>Albury</town>
        <city>Seaforth</city>
        <state>BC</state>
        <zipCode>22001</zipCode>
      </address>
  </buyer>

  <orders>
      <item>
          <sku>126552</sku>

          <product>People Carrier</product>
          <description>Childs pedal operated car</description>
      </item>
      <item>
          <sku>122452</sku>
          <product>BubbleBaby</product>
          <description>Bean filled soft toy</description>
      </item>
      <item>
          <sku>129112</sku>
          <product>My First Drum Kit</product>
          <description>Childs plastic drum kit</description>
      </item>
  </orders>

  </purchaseOrder>
```

Create a rule to put the purchase order in a box, with a 1-pixel black border, 20 pixels of padding inside, and a 20-pixel margin to separate the box from the browser window.

Question 2

Create a rule that writes "Purchase Order Number" in a large, bold, Arial typeface as the heading (in case the user does not have Arial, you should add Verdana as a second option, and the default sans-serif font as the third option), and that collects the purchase order number from the `orderID` attribute.

Question 3

Add the buyer's details to the purchase order, with the company name in bold and each part of the address on a new line in a smaller Arial font (and if the user does not have Arial, specify Verdana or the default sans-serif font).

Question 4

Write out the items ordered in a table.

18

XHTML

When people say XHTML is the new HTML, it is not in the sense that fashion pundits might say brown is the new black; it is the W3C's replacement for HTML. Rather than create HTML 5, the W3C made XHTML, which is akin to Macromedia creating Flash MX instead of Flash 6, or Microsoft releasing Windows XP instead of Windows 2001. XHTML is actually the reformulation of HTML 4 written in XML, so you have a few new rules to learn, the first of which is that it shall be XML-compliant.

The good news is that the elements and attributes available to you in XHTML are almost identical to those in HTML 4 (after all, XHTML 1.0 is a version of HTML 4 written in XML), so you won't need to learn a new vocabulary in this chapter. There are, however, a few changes related to how construct documents, which is what you will learn in this chapter.

While XML is finding its way into many aspects of programming, data storage, and document authoring, it was primarily designed for use on the Web. It isn't surprising, therefore, that the W3C wanted to make these changes to HTML (the most widely used language on the Web) to make it an application of XML.

Why do you need to learn a new version of HTML? After all, existing browsers will continue to support HTML, as we know it, for the foreseeable future (and many sites on the Internet may never be upgraded). In fact, this chapter covers several reasons for upgrading old HTML pages, including the following:

- ❏ It can make your page size smaller and your code clearer to read.
- ❏ It can make your pages more accessible to readers with disabilities, including search engine crawlers!
- ❏ Your code can be used with all XML-aware processors (from authoring tools and validators to XSLT, DOM, and SAX processors).
- ❏ It addresses issues regarding creating web pages so that they can be viewed on all the new devices that can now access the Internet, from phones to fridges, without each type of device requiring its own different language.
- ❏ Some new browsers and devices are being written to only support XHTML.

As a reformulation of HTML 4 in XML, XHTML doesn't add new features to HTML. Code conciseness and accessibility can be achieved in HTML. However, the other points mentioned in the preceding list are specific to XML. Furthermore, XHTML is probably the most popular application of XML today; and if you are familiar with HTML, you will be writing XHTML pages in no time at all.

Covered in this chapter are two versions of XHTML: XHTML 1.0 and XHTML 1.1. The W3C is currently working on XHTML 2.0, which is a complete refactoring of XHTML (and HTML). XHTML 2.0 is still a work in progress and is briefly covered at the end of this chapter.

Before you even look at XHTML, however, you should be aware that in HTML 4.1 all stylistic markup (such as the `<font>` element and `bgcolor` attribute, which is used to indicate how a document should appear) was marked as *deprecated*, meaning it would be phased out in future versions of the specifications, so it is essential to address removal of the stylistic markup before starting on XHTML.

In this chapter, you will learn the following:

❑ How to keep style and content separate, and the benefits of doing so

❑ The different versions and document types of XHTML

❑ How to write XHTML 1.0 documents

❑ What modularized XHTML is and how it enables you to write pages for many different devices

This chapter assumes you have a basic knowledge of HTML. If you don't, plenty of free tutorials are available on the Web, including the following:

❑ www.w3.org/MarkUp/Guide/

❑ www.w3schools.com/html/html_intro.asp

❑ www.webreference.com/html/tutorials/

Separating Style from Content

All of the stylistic markup in HTML — markup such as the `<font>` element for indicating which typeface to use or the `bgcolor` attribute for indicating background colors — was deprecated in HTML 4.1, with the expressed purpose that document authors should stop using such markup to indicate how pages should be displayed. Anything that indicated how a document should be displayed, rather than being about the structure or content of the document, was marked for removal from future versions of the specification, with the exception of the `<style>` element and `style` attribute (both of which contain CSS rules or a link to a CSS style sheet). To understand why this markup was deprecated, you need to take a trip back in time.

The Web was originally created for transmitting scientific documents between researchers, to make the work more easily and widely available. Web page authors used markup to describe the structure of a document, identifying which parts of the document should be headings, paragraphs, bulleted or numbered lists, and tables. The browser would then use these tags to render the document correctly. The problem was that it all looked fairly boring.

As we all know, the rise of the Web was phenomenal. Very soon all kinds of people found new uses for it, and new users wanted far greater control over how their web pages looked. As a result, both the W3C and browser manufacturers introduced all kinds of markup that enabled web page authors to control how the pages appeared in browsers.

The problem with all this stylistic markup was that documents became much longer and more complicated. Whereas the first HTML documents only described the structure of a page, the addition of stylistic markup resulted in pages that were littered with markup that affected the presentation of the document. `<font>` tags were used to specify typefaces, sizes, and the color of text. Tables were used to specify the layout for a page, rather than to describe tabular data. Background colors and images were set for several types of elements.

> *Other stylistic markup that has been deprecated includes* `align`, `border`, `color`, `cellpadding`, `cellspacing`, `size`, `style`, `valign`, *and* `width` *attributes and the* `<s>`, `<strike>`, `<base-font>`, `<u>`, *and* `<center>` *elements. The rule of thumb is simple: If it merely indicates how the item should appear, then it has been deprecated.*

HTML markup no longer just described the structure and content of a document — its headings, paragraphs, lists, and so on — it also described how it should appear on a desktop PC web browser. Not only did this result in more complex documents, but a new problem emerged: The desktop PC was no longer the only device that accessed the Internet, and pages designed to work on a desktop PC would not work on all other devices.

Therefore, it was decided that all stylistic markup should be removed and put in a separate stylesheet, linked from the HTML document. The language for this is Cascading Style Sheets (CSS), which you may already be familiar with — if not, it is covered in detail in Chapter 17.

Separating style from content has several advantages over including style rules in the document:

❑ Pages are simpler because they do not contain tables to control presentation as well as markup.

❑ Pages are smaller because each page does not have to repeat the instructions for how the page should be styled; rather, the whole site (or several pages) can use the same stylesheet. Therefore, once the stylesheet has been downloaded, pages are quicker to load, and you do not have to send as much data from your server.

❑ If you (or your boss) want to make sitewide changes, such as changing the color of all pages, you can do so by just changing the stylesheet, rather than changing each page individually.

❑ It clearly separates the jobs of graphical designers, working on CSS style sheets, and content producers, who work on the XHTML. Working on different files makes it easier to work in parallel without tripping over each other's updates.

❑ The same HTML document can be used with different stylesheets for different purposes — for example, you could have one stylesheet for browsing onscreen and another for printing out information. This makes documents more reusable, rather than having to be recreated for different mediums.

❑ Markup just describes a document's structure and content (as it was originally intended).

❑ Web users with visual impairments can more effectively view pages, because they do not contain fixed sizes for fonts, making them easier to read and navigate. Furthermore, devices such as screen readers don't have to contend with markup that was incorrectly used — such as the use of tables to control layout.

The previous chapter covered CSS and you already know how to style XML documents. In this chapter, you'll see how CSS is applied to XHTML documents.

Learning XHTML 1.x

Having seen that XHTML is taking a step toward removing stylistic markup, instead of relying on stylesheets to control the presentation of documents, it's time to look at the other differences between HTML and XHTML. As already mentioned, the elements and attributes available to you in XHTML are virtually identical to those in other versions of HTML, so there is no need to learn a whole new vocabulary for XHTML documents. The key topics introduced in this section are as follows:

❑　The four document types of XHTML 1.0: Strict, Transitional, and Frameset, and XHTML 1.1, and when to use each one

❑　The basic changes to the elements are attributes of HTML to make them XML compliant.

❑　The advantages of having a stricter language

❑　How to validate your XHTML documents and why this is important. Also described are some pitfalls that you might come across when trying to validate XHTML documents.

First up are the four document types of XHTML 1.0 and XHTML 1.1. Each is different, but don't let that put you off. Though you may not have known it, there were three versions of HTML 4 too!

Document Type Definitions for XHTML

Like many other XML vocabularies, each version of XHTML has a Document Type Definition (DTD) that defines markup and the allowable structure of conforming documents (more recently these have also been made available in XML Schema). There are actually five main XHTML 1.x DTDs you can follow when writing XHTML pages:

❑　**XHTML 1.0 Transitional** — This DTD allows deprecated markup from HTML 4.1.

❑　**XHTML 1.0 Strict** — This DTD does not allow deprecated markup from HTML 4.1.

❑　**XHTML 1.0 Frameset** — Use this DTD when creating pages that use frames.

❑　**XHTML 1.1** — This DTD is derived from XHTML 1.0 Strict and is the latest stable version of XHTML.

❑　**XHTML Basic** — This is a stripped-down version of XHTML designed to be used in small devices. Among the notable features that have been dropped is scripting.

The idea of removing all stylistic markup may have sounded alarm bells for some of you. Without the stylistic markup we are used to, it is going to be very hard to create visually attractive pages. Even the latest browsers do not fully and perfectly support CSS2, which we are now supposed to use to style documents, never mind the older browsers that are still used to access your sites. Therefore, the *transitional* document type still allows you to use deprecated markup from HTML 4.

All of the element and attribute names, and allowable uses of them, are the same in transitional XHTML 1.0 as they are in HTML 4.01 — even the root element of the document is still <html> (rather than <xhtml>). However, you do need to consider some minor changes because you are writing a document conforming to the rules of XML, which are addressed in the following section.

The *strict* form of XHTML 1.0, as its name suggests, is stricter than transitional XHTML; it does not allow use of the deprecated markup — in particular, the deprecated styling markup (leaving only the <style> element and style attribute). This helps to fulfill one of the aims of XHTML: separating style from content. Nor should you use tables for layout purposes in strict XHTML 1.0, as this controls the presentation of the document, rather than its intended use of displaying tabular data.

The main differences between XHTML 1.1 and XHTML 1.0 Strict are that the lang attribute has been replaced by the xml:lang attribute, the name attribute has been replaced by the id attribute, and the Ruby collection of elements has been added to support ideographic scripts such as Japanese.

> *Ruby annotations are used by East Asian typography to provide phonetic transcriptions of characters that might be unfamiliar to readers. The Ruby collection of elements is a set of elements that associates such annotations to a text.*

As shown in the section "Modularized XHTML," the architecture of the XHTML 1.1 DTD is different from the architecture of its predecessors. This change was needed to enable the creation of variations over the XHTML DTDs, such as XHTML 1.1 and XHTML Basic, and compound documents mixing XHTML and other languages such as SVG or MathML.

As its name indicates, XHTML Basic is limited to the most basic features of XHTML, and its aim is to provide a set of features that can safely be used in any kind of environment, from small devices to desktop browsers.

The XHTML 1.0 *frameset* document enables you to create documents that utilize framesets to show multiple pages in a single window. This technique is still mainly used to create a navigation frame separated from the documents that are being shown.

Choosing between five different DTDs might seem daunting but it's simpler than it appears:

❑ If you are defining a frameset, you have to use XHTML 1.0 Frameset (note that the documents loaded in each of the frames can use any DTD).

❑ If you are translating HTML 4 documents into XHTML and want to minimize the number of changes, you can use XHTML 1.0 Transitional if you are using deprecated features or XHTML 1.0 Strict otherwise. Note that by minimizing the number of changes, you also minimize the benefits of using XHTML over HTML!

❑ If publishing on a wide range of devices is more important than achieving fancy presentations and animations, then you should use XHTML Basic.

❑ In other cases, which represent the vast majority of new projects, XHTML 1.1 is your best bet.

Basic Changes in Writing XHTML

Because you are now writing XML documents, you have to make some changes in the way you write HTML. Specifically, you need to do the following:

- ❑ Consider starting each document with the XML declaration.
- ❑ Include a DOCTYPE declaration.
- ❑ Only use lowercase characters for element and attribute names.
- ❑ Provide values for all attributes. These should be written inside double quotation marks.
- ❑ Make sure your document is well formed.
- ❑ Close empty elements with a forward slash after the tag name but before the closing angled bracket.
- ❑ Use id attributes instead of name attributes to uniquely identify fragments of documents.
- ❑ Specify the language in which the document is written. This should be specified using an ISO 639 language code (for example, en for English, us-en for US English, or fr for French).
- ❑ Specify the character encoding in which the document is saved (as you will see, this is particularly important if you use characters not included in the ASCII character set).

The following sections address each of these aspects in turn. You are not required to do *all* of these things, but it is advisable to develop good habits early.

XML Declaration

Because your XHTML documents are indeed XML documents, it is recommended that they start with the following XML declaration:

```
<?xml version="1.0" encoding=" ISO-8859-1" ?>
```

This should appear at the very beginning of the document, without even be a space before it. (We will come back to the encoding attribute at the end of this section when we look at specifying character encoding for a document.) This can cause a problem, however, because some older browsers have trouble with the XML declaration, resulting in one of the two following reactions:

- ❑ They will ignore it.
- ❑ They will display the declaration as if it were part of the text for the document.

The following browsers have problems with the XML declaration:

- ❑ Netscape Navigator 3.04 and earlier
- ❑ Internet Explorer 3.0 and earlier

If your documents need to be viewed by these ancient browser versions, you may choose to ignore the XML declaration.

DOCTYPE Declaration

Immediately following the XML declaration (or at the start of the document if the XML declaration is not present), you should put the *DOCTYPE declaration*, which indicates the kind of document you are writing. Because there are five XHTML 1.x document types (XHTML 1.0 Strict, Transitional, and Frameset, XHTML 1.1, and XHTML Basic), five options are possible for the DOCTYPE declaration:

❑ **Transitional documents** — For transitional XHTML 1.0 documents (which can include the deprecated markup from HTML 4.1 — in particular, the stylistic markup), use the following declaration:

```
<!DOCTYPE html PUBLIC "-//W3C//DTD XHTML 1.0 Transitional//EN"
    "http://www.w3.org/TR/xhtml1/DTD/xhtml1-transitional.dtd">
```

❑ **Strict documents** — For Strict XHTML 1.0 documents (with none of the markup deprecated in HTML 4.1 — in particular, the stylistic markup), use the following declaration:

```
<!DOCTYPE html PUBLIC "-//W3C//DTD XHTML 1.0 Strict//EN"
    "http://www.w3.org/TR/xhtml1/DTD/xhtml1-strict.dtd">
```

A strictly conforming XHTML document must contain the DOCTYPE declaration before the root element, although a Transitional or Frameset document may leave it out.

❑ **Frameset documents** — For Frameset XHTML 1.0 documents, use the following declaration:

```
<!DOCTYPE html PUBLIC "-//W3C//DTD XHTML 1.0 Frameset//EN"
    "http://www.w3.org/TR/xhtml1/DTD/xhtml1-frameset.dtd">
```

❑ **XHTML 1.1 documents** — For XHTML 1.1 documents, use the following declaration:

```
<!DOCTYPE html PUBLIC "-//W3C//DTD XHTML 1.1//EN"
    "http://www.w3.org/TR/xhtml11/DTD/xhtml11.dtd">
```

❑ **XHTML Basic documents** — For XHTML Basic documents, use the following declaration:

```
<!DOCTYPE html PUBLIC "-//W3C//DTD XHTML Basic 1.0//EN"
    "http://www.w3.org/TR/xhtml-basic/xhtml-basic10.dtd">
```

Case Sensitivity

XML is case sensitive, so it is hardly surprising to learn that XHTML is too. All element names and attributes in the XHTML vocabulary must be written in lowercase, as shown in the following example:

```
<body onclick="someFunction();">
```

Of course, the element content or value of an attribute does not have to be lowercase; you can write what you like between the opening and closing tags of an element and within the quotes of an attribute (except quotation marks, which would close the attribute).

The decision to make XML case sensitive was largely driven by internationalization efforts. Whereas you can easily convert English characters from uppercase to lowercase, some languages do not have such a direct mapping. There may be no equivalent in a different case, or it might depend upon the region. To enable the specification to use different languages, it was therefore decided to make XML case sensitive.

Attribute Values

Be aware of the following two points when writing XHTML attributes:

❑   All attributes must be enclosed in double quotation marks.

❑   A value must be given for each attribute.

Some versions of HTML allow you to write attributes without giving the value in quotes, as shown in the following example:

```
<TD align=center>
```

This is not allowed in XHTML documents. After all, your XHTML documents are XML documents, and putting attribute values in quotes is a basic requirement for a document to be well formed.

Furthermore, HTML also allowed some attributes to be written without a value. It was known as *attribute minimization*, and where a value was not given, a default would be used. For example, in an HTML form, when using the `<option>` element to create a drop-down list box, you could use the `selected` attribute without a value to indicate that this option should be shown when the page loads and act as the default value, as shown here:

```
<OPTION selected value="option1">
```

Even when the value is left blank, all attributes in XHTML must be given a value enclosed in double quotation marks, like this:

```
<option selected="selected" value="option1">
```

Note also that any trailing whitespace at the end of an attribute value would be stripped out of the document, and any line breaks or multiple spaces between words would be collapsed into one space, rather like most processors treat spaces in HTML.

Well-Formedness and Validity of Documents

As with all XML documents, all XHTML documents must be *well formed*. Recall from Chapter 2 the basic requirements for a well-formed document: A well-formed document is one that meets the syntactic rules of XML. With regard to this, you should look at the following:

❏ The unique root element — the `<html>` element

❏ Empty elements, because every start-tag must have a corresponding end-tag

❏ The correct nesting of elements

To be understood by an XHTML processor, such as a web browser, a document instance should also be able to be validated using the DTD specified in the `DOCTYPE` declaration. Validation is covered later in the chapter.

Unique Root HTML Element

In order to be well formed, an XML document must have a unique root element. In the case of XHTML documents, you might think that this would be `<xhtml>`, but it is not — the root element remains `<html>`.

This illustrated that XHTML really is the new version of HTML, not some alternative. It also means that older browsers will still display XHTML documents.

You can use a namespace on the root element to indicate the namespace to which the markup belongs. This is required in strictly conforming documents but is not necessary in transitional or frameset documents unless you are mixing different vocabularies within the same document (for example, using SVG inside an XHTML document).

Here is an example using namespace defaulting on the root element to indicate that the markup belongs to the XHTML 1.1 document type:

```
<!DOCTYPE html PUBLIC "-//W3C//DTD XHTML 1.1//EN"
    "http://www.w3.org/TR/xhtml11/DTD/xhtml11.dtd">
<html xmlns=" http://www.w3.org/1999/xhtml">
...
</html>
```

Empty Elements

An element that has no character content between its opening and closing tags is known as an *empty element*. In HTML, the `<img>` , `<hr>`, and `<br>` elements are examples of empty elements. As with all XML documents, you cannot just use an opening tag for empty elements; you must add a forward slash before the closing angled bracket of the tag. For example, the correct way of writing elements, such as `img` in XHTML, is as follows:

```
<img src="MyCompanyLogo.gif" alt="My Company Logo" />
```

Similarly, you would write hr and br elements as shown here:

```
<br />
<hr />
```

Note the space between the hr and the forward slash character, rather than writing <br/>. This is because some older browsers won't understand the tag unless this space is there and will ignore it. If you add the space before the closing slash, it will be displayed.

Correctly Nesting Elements

In XHTML all elements must nest correctly within each other. Most browsers would forgive the following HTML and show it onscreen:

```
<p>Here is some text in a paragraph. <em>And here is some emphasized text in a
paragraph.</p></em>
```

The preceding would not be allowed in XHTML, as it would not meet the requirements for the document to be considered well formed. Rather, it should be written like this:

```
<p>Here is some text in a paragraph. <em>And here is some emphasized text in a
paragraph.</em></p>
```

Names and IDs

In HTML the <a>, <applet>, <form>, <frame>, <iframe>, <img>, and <map> elements can carry the name attribute in order to identify a fragment of a document. One popular use of the name attribute is with anchor elements so links can be created that take you to a particular subsection of a page. For example, you might add the following to the top of your page so that you could create "back to top" links further down the page:

```
<a name="top"></a>
```

In XHTML the name attribute is replaced by another attribute, the id attribute. This is because fragment identifiers in XML must be of type ID, and each element can only have one attribute whose value is of type ID. Therefore, the id attribute in XHTML is of type ID, as shown in the following:

```
<a id="top"></a>
```

This can cause a problem if you want to create links to a specific part of a page or within a page, as older browsers still expect the name attribute to be used with a elements, including the following:

- ❑ Netscape Navigator 4.79 and earlier
- ❑ Internet Explorer 4.0 and earlier

For maximum browser compatibility when writing XHTML documents, you can therefore use Transitional XHTML 1.0 and include both the name and id attributes on the same element, although name has been deprecated in XHTML 1.0. Nowadays, the market share of these ancient browsers is so small that it is safe to ignore them, unless of course you are working for atypical populations in which such browsers represent a higher proportion.

Remember that because the id attribute is of XML ID type, its value must be unique within the document.

Specifying Language

It might seem perfectly obvious to you which language your web page is written in, but HTML 4 and XHTML 1.0 allow you to specify the language either for the whole documents or for the language used in specific elements. This is done using the `lang` attribute. Browsers can use this information to display the page using language-specific methods, such as the correct use of hyphenating characters, other applications could use it to check whether they can display or process the document, and screen readers would be able to read different languages in different voices if they needed to.

The value of the `lang` attribute should be an ISO 639 language code (for example, `en` for English, `fr` for French, `ja` for Japanese, and so on). You can find a full list of these language codes at `www.oasis-open.org/cover/iso639a.html`.

XHTML 1.1 replaces the `lang` attribute with the `xml:lang` attribute. Because `xml:lang` can be used in any XML document, it can also be used in XHTML 1.0 documents. Currently, there is very little support for either `lang` or `xml:lang`, but it is good practice to include the `xml:lang` attribute.

Character Encoding

A character encoding is a table that defines a numeric value for each character. You need these encodings because a computer does not store characters in the way you see them on the screen. As you learned in Chapter 2, XML processors, by default, are expected to understand at least two encodings: *UTF-8* and *UTF-16*. UTF-8 is a character encoding that supports the first 128 ASCII characters as well as additional characters from languages other than English that feature accents, as well as a wide range of other symbols. UTF-16 is even larger than UTF-8 and supports characters from many other languages such as Chinese and Japanese.

> *The key advantages of UTF-8 and UTF-16 are that programs written to support these character encodings can handle different languages without needing to be rewritten, and documents can easily be created that contain characters from several languages.*

By default, if you do not specify an encoding, XML documents are assumed to be written in UTF-8, but if the tool you are writing in uses a different encoding, then you can end up with characters that do not display properly.

In order to support characters from different languages, UTF-16 requires two or more bytes for each character, whereas ASCII and UTF-8 only require 1 byte for each character. This means that some text editors and browsers do not support UTF-16.

Remember that while you can often view XHTML documents in older browsers if they use the `text/html` mime type, these older processors do not contain XML processors and do not all support UTF-16 by default. Therefore, your documents written in UTF-16 may not display correctly.

> *You will also commonly see the character encoding set to `ISO-8859-1`, which is an ISO character encoding for the Latin alphabet for the U.K., North America, Western Europe, Latin America, The Caribbean, Canada, and Africa. Many document authoring programs, such as Macromedia Dreamweaver and Microsoft FrontPage, use this setting.*

How to Specify Character Encoding in XHTML

XHTML allows two ways to specify the character set your document uses (for the best chance of success, you should use both):

❑ The XML declaration

❑ The `meta` element

You have already seen the XML declaration at the beginning of most of the XML documents used in this book. Plenty of these examples have included the encoding attribute, like the following:

```
<?xml version="1.0" encoding="UTF-8">
```

Recall that some browsers either ignore the XML declaration or display the declaration as if it were part of the text for the document. Browsers that do this include Netscape Navigator 3.04 and earlier and Internet Explorer 3.0 and earlier. Conversely, if you omit this declaration, then the XML Recommendation requires your encoding to be either UTF-8 or UTF-16. XHTML documents using any other encoding, such as ISO-8859-1, are not well-formed XML if the XML declaration was omitted.

Even when the browser does not display the XML declaration as text, it does not necessarily mean that it understands it. Therefore, you should also declare your encoding in a `meta` element like so:

```
<meta http-equiv="Content-Type" content="text/html; charset=UTF-8" />
```

Using the `<meta>` tag with the `http-equiv` attribute set to `Content-Type` tells the browser what type of content the document contains. In the preceding example, the document type is set to `text/html`, and the encoding is specified as `UTF-8`.

The MIME type `text/html` actually means the browser will treat your page as if it were HTML. This is good news for older browsers, which can display it.

XHTML also introduced the MIME type `application/xhtml+xml`, which was supposed to be used on XHTML 1.0; however, note the following points if you are tempted to use it:

❑ Internet Explorer cannot handle this MIME type, so you need to serve it as `text/html` to most browsers.

❑ It must be valid XHTML, or Mozilla-based browsers will display an error.

❑ When using CSS selectors with XML documents, the selectors are case sensitive, so you must match the case of the selector to that of the element.

Some people avoid using the XML declaration in XHTML documents because it can be ignored by older browsers or treated as part of the text of the document.

When a document contains both the XML declaration and the `meta` element, the encoding value in the XML declaration takes precedence. Browsers that do not understand the XML declaration, however, still use the `meta` element.

Server-Side Content Types

If you are using a server-side technology — such as ASP, PHP, or JSP — to create XHTML documents, then the best way to specify an encoding is by using the HTTP header `Content-Type`. The implementations are specific to the server-side environment you choose (so you should refer to documentation for your chosen language), and it is not always an option, but where possible this is the most reliable way to specify the encoding.

If it is possible, the W3C recommends using the MIME type `application/xhtml+xml`. Unfortunately, this MIME type isn't supported by Internet Explorer and many web servers are configured to serve XHTML document with the MIME type `text/html`.

Summary of Changes Between Writing XHTML and HTML

You have already seen all the changes you need to know when writing XHTML, rather than HTML. If you are familiar with HTML, then writing XHTML documents should be a breeze! There are very few changes, and the elements and attributes remain the same (although you should avoid presentational markup where possible).

To summarize, when writing an XHTML 1.x document, you must be aware of the following:

- ❑ You can include the optional XML declaration.
- ❑ You should include a DOCTYPE declaration, indicating whether you are writing a document according to the XHTML 1.0 Transitional, Strict, or Frameset, XHTML 1.1, or XHTML Basic DTD.
- ❑ You must write all element and attribute names in lowercase.
- ❑ You must close all elements.
- ❑ All elements must nest correctly.
- ❑ Consider using `id` attributes instead of `name` attributes.
- ❑ Indicate the language your documents are written in using the `lang` or `xml:lang` attributes.
- ❑ Specify the character encoding the document is written in.

To demonstrate these simple changes, take a look at an example of an XHTML page.

Try It Out   Creating an XHTML 1.1 Document

In this example, you are going to create a strict XHTML 1.0 page that documents how to write lists in XHTML. It will look very similar to the type of HTML document that you're probably used to writing, but the example highlights the differences in writing XHTML.

1. Start your favorite web page editor, or text editor, and create a file called `eg01.html`.

2. Add the following XML declaration and encoding:

```
<?xml version="1.0" encoding="UTF-8" ?>
```

3. Add the DOCTYPE declaration, which indicates that the document is written according to the Strict XHTML 1.0 DTD:

```
<?xml version="1.0" encoding="UTF-8" ?>
<!DOCTYPE html PUBLIC "-//W3C//DTD XHTML 1.1//EN"
    "http://www.w3.org/TR/xhtml11/DTD/xhtml11.dtd">
```

4. Add the <html> element, and use namespace defaulting to indicate that it is part of the XHTML 1.0 namespace:

```
<?xml version="1.0" encoding="UTF-8" ?>
<!DOCTYPE html PUBLIC "-//W3C//DTD XHTML 1.1//EN"
    "http://www.w3.org/TR/xhtml11/DTD/xhtml11.dtd">
<html xmlns="http://www.w3.org/1999/xhtml" xml:lang="en">
</html>
```

5. Add the <head> element, with a <title> element, just as you would in any HTML document. In addition, add a meta element, to specify the content type of the document and the character encoding you are using. The document needs to work in IE 7 and older browsers, so stick with the text/html MIME type in the content attribute:

```
<head>
  <meta http-equiv="Content-Type" content="text/html; charset=UTF-8" />
  <title>Lists in XHTML</title>
</head>
```

6. Add the <body> elements and the following headings:

```
<body>
    <h1>Lists in XHTML</h1>
    <h2>Ordered Lists</h2>
    <h2>Unordered Lists</h2>
    <h2>Definition Lists</h2>
</body>
```

As you might use different levels of headings in a word processor, here is a main heading, with lower-level headings that mark the start of subsections. So far, the document is self-describing just as XML intends — the head, title, body, and different level headings all describe the content and structure of the document.

7. Add an unordered list that introduces the types of lists available in XHTML:

```
<ul>
  <li>Ordered List</li>
  <li>Unordered List</li>
  <li>Definition Lists</li>
</ul>
```

Note that you must close the line item element. HTML was more forgiving than this — if you omitted some closing tags, pages would still be displayed. XHTML, being an application of XML, is not so forgiving, so you must add the closing tags.

8. Ideally, you should link these list items to anchors inside each of the relevant headings:

```
<ul>
  <li><a href="#orderedList">Ordered List</a></li>
  <li><a href="#unorderedList">Unordered List</a></li>
```

```
    <li><a href="#definitionList">Definition Lists</a></li>
  </ul>

  <h2><a id="orderedList" />Ordered List</h2>
  <h2><a id="unorderedList" />Unordered List</h2>
  <h2><a id="definitionList" />Definition List</h2>
```

As with all attributes in XML, both the value of the `href` attribute on the link and the `id` attribute must be provided in double quotes.

9. You can now add the rest of the document, which contains paragraphs describing each type of bullet. It would also be good to add a back-to-top link to the bottom of the page (inside a `<div>` element, because it's an inline element and therefore shouldn't appear at block level). Here is the full page:

```
<?xml version="1.0" encoding="UTF-8"?>
<!DOCTYPE html PUBLIC "-//W3C//DTD XHTML 1.1//EN"
    "http://www.w3.org/TR/xhtml11/DTD/xhtml11.dtd">
<html xmlns="http://www.w3.org/1999/xhtml" xml:lang="en">

<head>
  <meta http-equiv="Content-Type" content="text/html; charset=UTF-8" />
  <title>Lists in XHTML</title>
</head>

<body>

  <h1><a id="lists">Lists in XHTML</a></h1>
  <p>Three types of list are available to us when writing an XHTML document.
    These are:</p>

  <ul>
    <li><a href="#orderedList">Ordered List</a></li>
    <li><a href="#unorderedList">Unordered List</a></li>
    <li><a href="#definitionList">Definition Lists</a></li>
  </ul>

  <h2><a id="orderedList">Ordered List</a></h2>
  <p>An ordered list allows you to create a list of items, each of which is
    preceeded by a number. The list is automatically numbered in ascending
    order.</p>
  <p>The list is started with a <code>nl</code> tag, which indicates the
    start of a numbered list. The <code>nl</code> element is the containing
    element, for the numbered list. Each list item is then placed inside a
    <code>li</code> element. </p>

  <h2><a id="unorderedList">Unordered List</a></h2>
  <p>An unordered list is a fancy name for a list of bullet points that are
    not preceeded by numbers. The containing element for the items in an
    unordered list is the <code>ul</code> element. Again each item in the
    list is put inside the <code>li</code> element.</p>

  <h2><a id="definitionList">Definition List</a></h2>
  <p>The least common type of list is a definition list, which tends to
    comprise of words and their definitions.</p>
```

```
    <p>The containing element for a definition list is <code>dl</code>
       element.Each term that has to be defined is contained inside a & gt;DT& lt;
       element, while the definition is contained in a & gt;DL& lt; element, like
       so.</p>
    <div><a href="#lists">Back to top</a></div>
  </body>
</html>
```

10. Save the file as `eg02.html` and open it in a browser (see Figure 18-1).

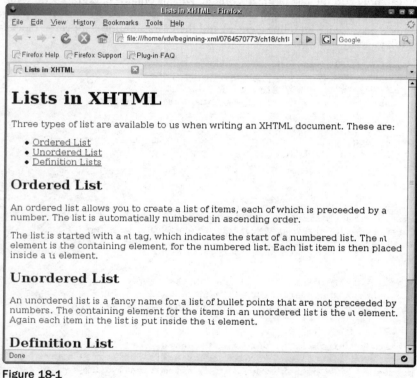

Figure 18-1

How It Works

Most of this document will be very familiar to you, so highlighted here are only the parts that are particularly noteworthy and different from HTML. The example began with the optional XML declaration, followed by a DOCTYPE declaration, which indicates which DTD the document obeys the rules of. In this case, it was the Strict XHTML DTD.

The root element was the `<html>` element, as with earlier HTML documents. However, it did carry a namespace to indicate that the markup belonged to the XHTML namespace. Both the `<meta>` element inside the head of the document and the XML declaration carried the `encoding` attributes to indicate the character encoding in which the document was written.

Every element must be closed properly. For example, the <meta> element was an example of an empty element; it had no content and therefore had a forward slash character before the closing angled bracket. Meanwhile, all other elements had an opening and closing element. All elements nested correctly to create a well-formed document, and all attribute values were given in quotes.

The bulleted list of topics covered was linked to the relevant headings using the id attribute, rather than the name attribute, to create destination anchors. The id attribute value must be of type ID, so it has to be unique within the document and must obey the rules of XML 1.0 names.

Finally, there is no stylistic markup (as suggested at the beginning of the chapter). In order to change the fonts, colors, and other presentational rules for this document, a link would be made to a CSS stylesheet using the <link> element. As you can see, this document doesn't differ greatly from an HTML document, but the rules for creating an XHTML document are stricter than those for creating HTML so you need to be clear about the few changes there are.

Styling XHTML Documents

Fortunately, everything you learned about CSS in the previous chapter applies to XHTML. That said, you should be aware of two differences between styling XHTML documents and styling other XML documents.

First, when you style an XML document, you must consider that the tools using your stylesheets have absolutely no prior clue how elements must be displayed. In the previous chapter, your stylesheets needed to be exhaustive, declaring which elements should be displayed as blocks, line items, tables, and so on. When using XHTML, the tools that display your documents already have a basic idea how elements need to be displayed. Browsers know perfectly well that a <p> element is a paragraph, a <table> element is a table, and a <li> element is a line item. This makes your life, as a CSS stylesheet author, easier because you just need to add rules for styles you want to specifically impose on browsers.

The second difference is the way in which stylesheets are attached to documents. In Chapter 17, you saw that stylesheets are attached to XML documents using <?xml-stylesheet?> processing instructions. Instead of using such a PI, XHTML follows the HTML way and uses <link> elements.

Try It Out   **Styling an XHTML 1.1 Document**

This example attaches a CSS stylesheet to the previous XHTML document to define the text and background colors and the preferred font families:

1. Edit your previous XHTML document and add the following <link> element in its <head>:

```
<link rel="stylesheet" type="text/css" href="ch18_eg02.css" />
```

2. Save the file as ch18_eg02.html.

3. Create a file named ch18_eg02.css with the following rules:

```
html {
   background-color:#232323;
}
body {
  border: 2em solid  #232323;
```

```
    padding: 1em;
    color:#464646;
    background-color:#FCFCFC;
    font-family:arial, verdana, sans-serif;}
h1, h2, h3 {
    color:#232323;}
```

4.   Open the XHTML document in a browser (see Figure 18-2).

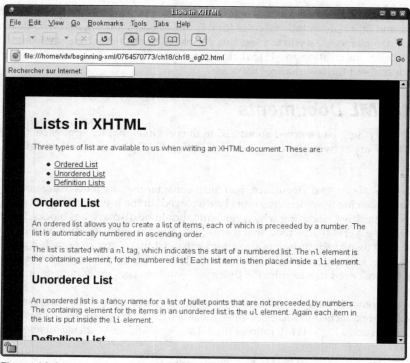

Figure 18-2

How It Works

Because you already know how CSS and XHTML work, this new example is just a matter of bringing these two technologies together. Compared with the examples shown in the previous chapter, note that although we have not defined that `<li>` are line items and that `<h1>` and `<h2>` are titles, `<li>` do display as line items, and `<h1>` and `<h2>` display as titles.

This example defined text colors that are variations of dark grays over a very light-gray background. The difference isn't obvious in print, but it conforms to many studies that have shown that dark texts over light backgrounds (also called "negative contrast") are usually more readable than light texts over dark backgrounds (called "positive contrasts"), and that high-level contrasts are aggressive and usually less readable than mid-level contrasts.

Stricter Documents Make Faster and Lighter Processors

As shown, there are new constraints on writing documents in XHTML (in particular, the strict document type). You can no longer omit closing `</li>` tags on your bullet points; line breaks and image tags must be written as empty elements; and the values of attributes must be given in quotes.

These extra requirements might seem like a hassle. After all, with HTML you can often get away with writing documents that contain all manner of mistakes and they still display correctly. Nonetheless, there is a very good reason for the strict approach, and you only need to download the latest version of one of the main browsers to see why.

Mainstream browsers tend to contain a lot of code that enables users to view HTML pages containing errors in the code — from tags that are not closed to elements that are not nested properly. While it may help people who are just learning to write pages to get them on the Internet, the cost is bigger browsers, which take longer to download.

When you consider the range of new devices that can connect to the Internet, it isn't reasonable to expect all of them to support megabytes of code just to allow some people to write pages incorrectly. Imagine if a mobile phone were expected to carry a program that weighs in at 52MB, which is the amount of hard disk space you need to run Netscape 7.1.

Other benefits from being strict with your code include the following:

- ❑ Pages can be displayed faster.
- ❑ Because the stricter rules make your XHTML documents conform to the rules of XML documents, you can use all kinds of XML tools with your XHTML documents, including DOM, SAX, and XSLT processors and authoring tools.
- ❑ As you shall see shortly in this chapter, you can use the same language, XHTML, on many different types of Internet-enabled devices.
- ❑ Pages are easier to access in JavaScript, which is especially important for Web 2.0 applications, which often heavily modify their pages in JavaScript. Simpler pages mean simpler scripts.

Therefore, for the sake of keeping what are good habits anyway, you get some real advantages as a developer (unless you want to learn new languages for each kind of device).

XHTML Tools

You don't need any fancy new tools to write XHTML documents; a plain-text editor such as Windows Notepad or Mac Simple Text suffices, providing it supports the character encoding in which you want to write. Many of the latest versions of document-authoring tools also support XHTML documents, such as Macromedia Dreamweaver and Microsoft FrontPage (but make sure you select the appropriate options in your program or it might continue to produce standard HTML code with some errors).

This is just the tip of the iceberg when it comes to tools you can use with your XHTML pages. Because XHTML documents are themselves XML documents, you can use any of the tools you have already met in this book to work with your XHTML pages:

❑ You can use any XML editor to write your XHTML pages, and though they may not be written specifically for XHTML, they will help you close tags, check well-formedness, and show allowable elements and attributes.

❑ You can use DOM- and SAX-aware processors to programmatically access your code.

❑ You can use XSLT to perform transformations on your XHTML. For example, you could use an XSLT stylesheet to transform a document conforming to the strict XHTML 1.0 DTD into one conforming to the transitional DTD so that it has better support for older browsers. This means you still have future-proofed strict XHTML documents and backwardly compatible versions generated from transformations.

❑ You can use any XML validation tools to validate your XHTML documents.

Validating your documents is a good practice to adopt, so that is addressed next.

Validating XHTML Documents

Although browsers are unlikely to validate your XHTML documents, and browsers on a desktop PC are likely to display your page even if it contains errors, it's a good idea to validate your documents manually when you have written them to ensure they do not contain any errors. While your desktop browser might show the XHTML page you created as you intended, validating a document is the best way to ensure you get the results you expect when the document is used with different applications (even if these are just browsers on other operating systems).

HTML browsers have been so forgiving of our errors that most people have developed at least one or two bad habits. Browsers tend to be much stricter when they read XHTML document, but as already mentioned, most XHTML documents are served with text/html MIME types, which switches this strictness off. Even if you think you stick rigidly to standards, you might be surprised. It is particularly useful to check your pages when you start to write XHTML. (After all, if you made a mistake, you wouldn't want to come back and change all your pages when your boss decides you have to perform XSLT transforms on each document next year).

To test how XHTML documents can be validated, first create a document with an error. You can use a previous example from this chapter, with the quotes removed from the attribute:

```
<li><a href=#orderedList>Ordered List</a></li>
```

Some authoring tools will validate your XHTML documents for you, or they will have interactive debugging features such as highlighting errors. For example, as shown in Figure 18-3, the oXygen XML IDE complains and displays an error as soon as you remove these quotes.

This is also the case with online XML IDEs such as http://codeplot.com, and several other options are available; because XHTML documents are themselves XML documents, you can use any validating XML processor to validate your XHTML documents. You already encountered some validating processors in this book; in particular, Chapter 4 looked at processors that validate documents against DTDs.

Probably the simplest way to check your XHTML documents is to use one of the free online XHTML validation services, such as the one provided by the W3C at http://validator.w3.org.

Figure 18-4 shows the error you receive from running the example with the missing quotes through the W3C validator.

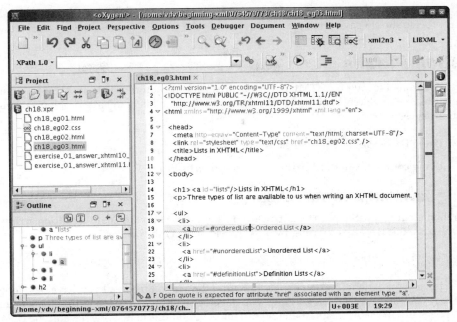

Figure 18-3

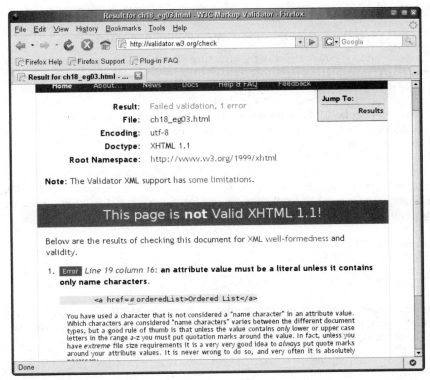

Figure 18-4

As shown in the figure, you are told where your errors are located so you can correct them. In the long run this process should save you time.

Validation Pitfalls

If you are seasoned in writing HTML pages or converting sites from HTML to XHTML, note the following scenarios you are likely to come across; otherwise, you are likely to have problems when you validate your pages:

❑ Using JavaScript in your pages

❑ Using content from third parties (such as advertising)

Including JavaScript in Your Page

Rather than include JavaScript in your pages, you should get into the habit of putting scripts in separate files, which are then referred to using the script element, as shown here:

```
<script type="text/javascript" src="scripts/formValidation.js"> </script>
```

This can have great benefits, as you are likely to find that in no time at all you have developed a script library that you can reuse, which will save you development time in the long run. It also means that if several pages use the same script, then you can make alterations to just one file and the changes will be replicated across the entire site. You won't have to manually alter each page.

If, however, you must include script in your page, then you must watch for the following things:

❑ XHTML processors can strip out anything in comment markers.

❑ The <, >, and & characters break the structure of an XHTML document unless they are placed in a CDATA section.

When writing JavaScript, you're probably in the habit of putting it inside comment marks so that older browsers that don't support JavaScript don't raise an error and can still display the page. With XHTML, however, both browsers and servers can strip out comments that they find in a document before displaying the data, which means JavaScript code would be lost.

To avoid having your script stripped out, place it within a CDATA section, as discussed in Chapter 2. This has the added advantage that you can use the <, >, and & characters without breaking the structure of the document. For example, the following code works with most older browsers (with the exception of Netscape Navigator 3 and earlier):

```
<script type="text/javascript"><![CDATA[
function validateEmail {...
... }
]]></script>
```

If your browser knows you're using XML, because you use the MIME type application/xhtml+xml (as opposed to using text/html, which browsers treat as if it were just HTML), you have the following additional issues to deal with:

❑ If you use `getElementsByTagName()` with the XML DOM, elements are returned in lowercase, whereas the HTML DOM returns them in uppercase.

❑ You cannot just use the `document.write()` method to write to the page; you have to create a new element in the document.

❑ To access contents of a document, you cannot use collections such as `document.form`; you have to use another method such as `getElementsByTagName()`.

Incorporating Content from Other People

There are many reasons why you might display content created by others within your web pages. For example, you might be syndicating some content from another content provider, or you might be showing advertisements from a third-party source.

This could be a problem because you might not be getting the latest version of XHTML. While you could ask for it in the correct format, this may not be possible with syndicated content, and it may hold you up when dealing with advertisers, thereby affecting advertising revenue. If you have to live with their versions, you have the following two options:

❑ Downgrade your version of XHTML to whatever the client is using. Although you might be happy to downgrade from Strict XHTML 1.0 to Transitional XHTML 1.0, you might be less willing to downgrade to HTML 3.2 if that is what your client uses.

❑ Use client-side JavaScript to include the information in the page. This ensures that your base page is a valid document, and that you can display your pages in both browsers that support the incorporated format and those that do not.

Having looked at some of these validation issues, it is hoped that you are confident with writing XHTML 1.x documents.

Mime Types Pitfalls

MIME types are important to your browser: It's by checking MIME types that the browser knows how it must handle documents. Depending on the MIME type, your browser decides whether it can manage the document by itself, through a plug-in or external application, or whether it should just offer to download and save it.

The W3C has registered the `application/xhtml+xml` MIME type for XHTML documents, which they recommend using to serve XHTML documents. This would be fine if IE supported this MIME type, but unfortunately it doesn't; even the most current version, Internet Explorer 7.0, offers no support for this MIME type, and offers to save documents served with it instead of displaying them.

The vast majority of XHTML documents are served with a `text/html` MIME type. This often makes no difference, but it can have some nasty side effects, as shown by the following XHTML document:

```
<?xml version="1.0" encoding="UTF-8"?>
<!DOCTYPE html PUBLIC "-//W3C//DTD XHTML 1.1//EN"
  "http://www.w3.org/TR/xhtml11/DTD/xhtml11.dtd">
<html xmlns="http://www.w3.org/1999/xhtml">
  <head>
```

```
         <title>Bitten by the text/html mime type</title>
         <script type="text/javascript">

           function init()  {
           // here, we still have a p[@id='bar'] element
           alert("bar's tag name is: " + document.getElementById("bar").tagName);
           document.getElementById("foo").innerHTML="This is division foo.";
           // but now, the p[@id='bar'] element has disappeared...
           alert("bar: " + document.getElementById("bar"));
           }

         </script>
     </head>
     <body onload="init()">
       <div id="foo" />
       <p id="bar" >This is paragraph "bar".</p>
     </body>
  </html>
```

This very simple XHTML document includes a division foo, which is initially empty, followed by a paragraph bar. A script replaces the empty content of division foo with some text. Two alerts have been added to display the tag name of the paragraph and the paragraph bar object after the replacement of the content of division foo.

If you serve this document with an application/xhtml+xml MIME type to a browser that supports this type, such as Firefox, the script works as expected:

❏   The first alert displays "bar's tag name is: p".

❏   The second alert displays "bar: [object HTMLParagraphElement]"

❏   After the second alert, the document shows two lines with "This is division foo." and "This is paragraph "bar"."

If you serve this same document with a text/html MIME type to the same browser or to Internet Explorer, you get a significantly different result:

❏   The first alert displays "bar's tag name is: P".

❏   The second alert displays "bar: null".

❏   After the second alert, the document shows only one line with "This is division foo.

What's happening? In Internet Explorer, even when the document is XHTML, it is read as HTML. As a result, the browser uses an HTML DOM instead of using an XHTML DOM. This is why the tag name is uppercase instead of lowercase, but that doesn't explain why the paragraph has disappeared. What's happening is that the HTML parser ignores trailing slashes in tags, and reads <div id="foo" /> as <div id="foo">. The rules of implicitly closing <div> tags in HTML being what they are, the <div> spans over the <p> element that follows, and the paragraph is now a child element of the division instead of being a following sibling. That's why you override the paragraph when you replace the content of the division by text!

The solution in this case is as follows:

❑ Take into account the difference of case folding between HTML and XHTML DOMs if you need to test tag names (or still better, convert tag names to lowercase to get portable scripts).

❑ Avoid writing `<div id="foo" />` and instead write `<div id="foo"></div>` or `<div id="foo"><!-- --></div>` (the latter has less risk of being converted back into `<div id="foo" />` by XML tools).

This is just an example of bugs that may creep into your scripts when you serve XHTML documents with `text/html` MIME types. Unfortunately, this kind of bug may be very difficult to debug.

Modularized XHTML

Having looked at XHTML 1.x and the changes you have to make when writing HTML as an application of XML, this section looks at the architecture of XHTML 1.1 DTDs, which takes a much larger step forward. Before XHTML 1.1 was produced, XHTML was split into a set of modules, and you do not need to look far in order to see why.

In the past few years, an increasing number of different devices can connect to the Internet, including mobile phones, PDAs, TVs, digital book readers, and refrigerators. Because of the inherent limitations (such as screen size) of some of these devices, not all of the HTML 4 specification is relevant to them. Furthermore, some of these devices don't have the power or memory to implement the full specification, so more compact languages have been developed specifically to support these new devices. Some examples include CHTML (Compact HTML), WML (Wireless Markup Language), and the HTML 4.0 Guidelines for Mobile Access.

The competing languages that have sprung up to support different devices share common features. Each language enables users to mark up the following types of information:

❑ Basic text, including headings, paragraphs, and lists

❑ Hyperlinks and links to related documents

❑ Basic forms

❑ Basic tables

❑ Images

❑ Meta information

The W3C understood that the various devices that can now access the Internet could no longer be served by one single language (HTML). Therefore, rather than have several competing languages for different devices, the W3C thought it would be much better if XHTML were split into *modules,* with each module covering some common functionality (such as basic text or hyperlinks). That way, these modules could be used as building blocks for the variations of XHTML developed for different devices.

Instead of reinventing the wheel, as CHTML and WML did, all languages could be built from these same basic building blocks. The new document types would be based on what is known as an *XHTML Host*

Language, which is then extended with other modules. For example, the XHTML 1.1 DTD contains 21 modules that cover the functionality of the XHTML 1.0 Strict DTD. We shall shortly cover XHTML Basic, designed as a host language for use on smaller devices, which uses just 11 modules.

> *When a new document type is being created and only part of a module's functionality is required, the whole module must be included in the language (it cannot just include part of a module). This makes it easier to learn a new language because the developer can specify which modules it uses, and the document author will know it supports all of the markup from that module, rather than having to check individual elements.*

The following table shows the full list of XHTML *abstract modules* in the first column (these are like the basic functionality of HTML split into related subsets). The second column contains the core modules required to be an application of XHTML. The third and fourth columns indicate which modules are used in the XHTML Basic DTD and the XHTML 1.1 DTD.

Module Name	Core Module	XHTML Basic DTD	XHTML 1.1 DTD
Structure	X	X	X
Text	X	X	X
Hypertext	X	X	X
List	X	X	X
Applet			
Object		X	X
Presentation			X
Edit			X
Bidirectional text			X
Frames	X		
IFrame			
Basic forms		X	
Forms			X
Basic tables		X	
Table			X
Image		X	X
Client-side image map			X
Server-side image map	X		X
Intrinsic events			X
Metainformation		X	X
Scripting			X

Module Name	Core Module	XHTML Basic DTD	XHTML 1.1 DTD
Stylesheet			X
Style attribute (deprecated)			X
Link		X	X
Target			
Base		X	X
Ruby annotation			X
Name identification			
Legacy			

Note that the legacy module supports elements that have been deprecated from earlier versions of HTML and XHTML, so it is helpful in writing code that supports older devices.

There is another benefit as well: Modularization makes it possible to create new document types that mix XHTML with other XML languages, such as SVG or MathML, resulting in what is known as a *hybrid document type*. Indeed, when new versions of XHTML come out, extensions to the language can take the form of new modules. This makes cross-browser development far easier, and you can finally say good-bye to deprecated features such as stylistic markup of HTML 4 that were allowed into XHTML 1.0.

Module Implementations

As you learned in Chapter 1, each document type has a DTD or XML Schema (or other schema) that defines the elements, attributes, and allowable structures of documents conforming to that type. A *module implementation* is a form of schema, such as a DTD or XML Schema, containing the element types, attribute-list declarations, and content model declarations that define the module. Having each module use a separate implementation makes it far easier to create markup languages using the modules, as opposed to fishing the appropriate parts from one large document.

While XHTML 1.1 was initially released with a DTD, the W3C later released an XML Schema version of the implementations.

XHTML 1.1

XHTML 1.1 uses a selection of the abstract modules defined by XHTML modularization, and the implementations of those modules, in a document type called XHTML 1.1. Therefore, XHTML 1.1 is an example of the modules combined into a specific document type. You saw the modules that XHTML 1.1 contains in the previous table.

The modules used offer the same functionality found in Strict XHTML 1.0. As already mentioned, the only changes you have to make are as follows:

1. The DOCTYPE declaration must precede the root element (which should carry the xmlns attribute). The public identifier, if present, should be represented as follows:

```
<!DOCTYPE html PUBLIC "-//W3C//DTD XHTML 1.1//EN"
    "http://www.w3.org/TR/xhtml11/DTD/xhtml11.dtd">
```

2. The lang attribute has been replaced by the xml:lang attribute.

3. The name attribute has been replaced by the id attribute.

4. The Ruby collection of elements has been added.

Ruby is a term for a run of small character annotations that are sometimes added to the characters of an ideographic script like Japanese to clarify the pronunciation (and/or the meaning) of those characters. In vertical text they are usually added in a very small font along the side of the ideogram, while in horizontal text they are used on the top.

5. The style attribute has been deprecated.

XHTML Basic

Another good example of the use of XHTML modularization is *XHTML Basic*, a document type in itself, which was designed for devices that don't support the full set of XHTML features, such as mobile phones, PDAs, car navigation systems, digital book readers, and smart watches.

Recall that the memory and power that would be required to implement the full HTML specification would be too high for some smaller devices. Therefore, rather than create a whole new language for these devices from scratch, XHTML Basic takes the four core modules of XHTML and extends them with additional modules. Here is a quick summary of the modules and elements available in XHTML Basic:

Module	Elements
Structure module*	body, head, html, title
Text module*	abbr, acronym, address, blockquote, br, cite, code, dfn, div, em, h1, h2, h3, h4, h5, h6, kbd, p, pre, q, samp, span, strong, var
Hypertext module*	a
List module*	dl, dt, dd, ol, ul, li
Basic forms module	form, input, label, select, option, textarea
Basic tables module	table, tr, td, th, caption
Image module	img
Object module	object, param
Meta-information module	meta
Link module	link
Base module	base

* = core module

XHTML Basic is not intended to be the one and only language that will ever be used on small devices. Rather, it is supposed to serve as a common base that can be extended. For example, it could be extended with the addition of the bi-directional text module, or one could create an event model to deal with behavior such as incoming call events (which would not apply to, say, televisions). It is this kind of subsetting and extending of XHTML that makes it a language that can serve as a strong basis for all kinds of future clients.

To finish this section, it is worthwhile to take a quick look at some of the markup and modules of XHTML that were not included in XHTML Basic, and why they were left out. You now know that HTML 4 contained features that not every device could support, and that several competing markup languages for mobile devices recreated common functionality. You also know that XHTML Basic serves as a base for further extensions of XHTML. Here is some of the markup that was left out, including some of the reasons why:

❑ The `<style>` element was left out because you can use the `<link>` element to link external stylesheets to a document, rather than use an internal stylesheet (if you don't know the difference between the two, you'll learn more in the next chapter). Therefore, browsers that support stylesheets can download them, but they are not required to support them in order to display information.

❑ `<script>` and `<noscript>` elements are not supported because small devices might not have the memory and CPU power to handle execution of scripts or programs. It was deemed that documents for these devices should be readable without requiring scripts.

❑ Event-handler attributes, which are used to invoke scripts, are not supported because events tend to be device-dependent. For example, a TV might have an `onChannelChange` event, while a phone might have an `incomingCall` event, neither of which applies to the other device. Ideally, it's better to use a generic event-handling mechanism than hardwire event names into the DTD.

❑ Whereas basic XHTML forms are supported, more complex form functions are not applicable to all small devices. For example, if a device does not have a local file system, then it won't be able to use the file and image input types in forms. This is why only the basic XHTML forms module is included.

❑ As with forms, only basic tables are supported. Tables can be difficult to display under the best circumstances on small devices, so features of the tables module won't apply to all small devices (for example, the nesting of tables is left out). It is recommended that users follow the Web Content Accessibility Guidelines 1.0 for creating accessible tables.

While XHTML Basic can be used as is, the intention is that it be used as a host language. These features could be added for a particular implementation that needs to support them. Adding markup from other languages results in a new document type that is an extension of XHTML Basic.

What's Next for XHTML

The W3C road map for XHTML is to build on the concept of modularization and create a framework in which different modules, and even document types, could be used. This would broaden the overall scope of the XHTML family to include applications such as SVG, MathML or SMIL, but XHTML itself would be stripped down from its frames, handled by a specific specification known as XFrames, and its forms implemented as XForms (XForms is the topic of the Chapter 20).

The next version of XHTML will be XHTML 2.0. XHTML 2.0 will be the first release to add new features since HTML 4 and the first major refactoring of HTML. The motivation behind this refactoring is that the W3C considers XHTML to have reached a point where new features shouldn't be added before XHTML is simplified and made more consistent. This motivation is so strong that XHTML 2.0 will not be backwardly compatible with previous versions.

In addition to elements that are removed from XHTML 2.0 because they belong to XFrames or XForms, the remaining presentational elements such as `<b>`, `<big>`, `<small>`, and `<tt>` are removed from XHTML 2.0, together with the `<acronym>` element, which is very close to the more generic `<abbr>` element. Other elements have been renamed, such as `<hr>` (horizontal rule), which is misleading when used in vertical text, and so has been renamed `<separator>`.

However, you miss the most spectacular changes between XHTML 1.1 and XHTML 2.0 if you focus on elements, as the most dramatic changes come from attributes! For one thing, XHTML 2.0 generalizes the usage of `src` and `href` attributes. In XHTML 1.1, these attributes were allowed only in a small set of elements. For instance, to make a link, you have to use an a element, and to include a picture you have to use a img element. With XHTML 2.0, this is no longer the case: Any element with a `src` attribute behaves like an object, and any element with a `href` attribute is considered a link.

XHTML 2.0 has been very strict regarding the number of new elements, which include `<section>` and `<summary>` elements and a new type of list, `<nl>`, for navigation lists. This doesn't mean that the W3C doesn't recognize that users need to express new concepts in XHTML. On the contrary, XHTML 2.0 has a new `role` attribute that can be used to express the role of any XHTML element. In the past, people have hijacked the `class` attribute to express all kinds of nonpresentational things (this is the main principal behind microformats), and the `role` attribute is meant to provide a cleaner way to do this kind of thing. You can learn everything about XHTML 2.0 at www.w3.org/TR/xhtml2/.

> The term "microformat" is used to designate a set of conventions that maps XHTML (or HTML) elements and attributes into a XML-like structure. For instance, the hCalendar microformat that describes calendar events uses an HTML element with a class event to define an event, and within this element identifies the summary though a class summary, the start date with a class dtstart, and so on. You can find more information on microformats at http://microformats.org/, and on hCalendar at http://microformats.org/wiki/hcalendar.

This is a very short introduction to XHTML 2.0 but it illustrates how ambitious this project is. As you might expect, such radical changes can create a strong reaction, and the WHATWG (http://whatwg.org/), an informal group of browser and web developers led by Mozilla, Apple, and Opera, is developing a counter proposal that would be more compatible with existing browsers and versions of XHTML. This proposal includes the following:

❑ Web Forms 2.0, an extension to HTML 4.01 forms, which is an alternative to XForms

❑ Web Applications 1.0, also known as HTML 5, which is an alternative to XHTML 2.0

Both proposals are backwardly compatible with HTML 4! The WHATWG argues that because most XHTML documents are served as text or HTML, this is proof that the XML foundation of XHTML isn't really important. The WHATWG believes that an HTML-based syntax is sufficient for Web 2.0 applications and will always be easier for web developers to write and understand. HTML 5 also adds a number of elements, such as `<article>`, `<header>`, `<footer>`, and `<section>`, to express various things that would be expressed using the `role` attribute in XHTML 2.0.

It is too early to say which proposal will succeed, and the answer might well depend on the attitude of Microsoft. Although the WHATWG includes most developers of alternative browsers, their cumulative market share is small, and Microsoft's decision to support XHTML 2.0, HTML 5, or neither of these is likely to determine whether the future resides in XHTML 2.0, HTML 5, or a status quo in which XHTML 1.1 would be a long-term best choice.

Summary

In this chapter you learned how HTML has been reformulated as an application of XML in XHTML 1.x. You were introduced to the five XHTML 1.x document types, and saw how converting HTML to an application of XML does not require learning much new, other than obeying rules that any well-formed XML document would, such as the following:

- The optional presence of an XML declaration
- A required DOCTYPE declaration
- Element and attribute names are case sensitive.
- All attributes must be given values, and the values must be given in double quotes.
- There must be a unique root <html> element.
- Empty elements must be written with the closing slash before the end of the tag, for example, <br />.
- Elements must be correctly nested.
- The name attribute is replaced by the id attribute, which is of XML ID type, for uniquely identifying a fragment (and its value must therefore be unique within the document).
- You can specify language and character encodings.

In return, you saw the following improvements:

- A stricter syntax, which makes it is possible to create processors that require less memory and power and is ideal for portable devices
- Pages that are simpler and will display quicker
- Pages are easier to animate in JavaScript and are thus more "Web 2.0 friendly."
- All tools that are XML-aware can be used when working with strict XHTML 1.0 documents, such as XSLT, DOM, and SAX. In particular, you can validate documents using any XML validation tool or one of the free online validation resources.

Some pitfalls to validating documents were also covered — in particular, handling JavaScript (which should be placed in external files or CDATA sections) and content from other sources (which can be imported using JavaScript).

Having looked at XHTML 1.x, you also saw how XHTML has been split into modules of related markup. These modules can be combined to create new document types for the wide range of new web-enabled devices that are coming onto the market. XHTML Basic is a rather minimal build of the modules designed for use on small devices, while XHTML 1.1 is an example of a larger build, avoiding the old presentation features, but offering a rich language for devices that have the required resources to support the larger language.

Finally, you had a brief glimpse of what the future of XHTML might look like, and saw that between two conflicting visions, XHTML 1.1 might be a good long-term choice.

Exercise Questions

Suggested solutions to these questions can be found in Appendix A.

Question 1

Take the following HTML 3.2 example and create a version in Strict XHTML 1.1 without any stylistic markup:

```
<HTML>
<HEAD>
    <TITLE>Exercise One</TITLE>
</HEAD>
<BODY bgcolor=white>

<A NAME="top"></A>
<H1 align=center>XHTML</H1>

<FONT face=arial size=2>
  XHTML 1.0 is the reformulation of HTML in XHTML. There are three XHTML 1.0
  document types:

  <UL>
    <LI>Transitional
    <LI>Strict
    <LI>Frameset
  </UL>

  XHTML has also been split into <b>modules</b>, from which document types
  such as XHTML 1.1 and XHTML Basic have been formed.
</FONT>

<A href="#top">Back to top</a>
</BODY>
</HTML>
```

Question 2

Take the same HTML 3.2 example, and create a second version that uses Transitional XHTML 1.0, can work in old browsers, and in which you could include legacy scripts and code. Once you have written your documents, validate them using the W3C validator at http://validator .w3.org/.

Scalable Vector Graphics (SVG)

This chapter describes Scalable Vector Graphics (SVG), an extremely versatile 2-D graphics format designed primarily for the Web. Its specification is defined and maintained by the World Wide Web Consortium (W3C), and it offers an open alternative to proprietary graphics systems.

Here you learn about the core concepts and some of the most commonly used features of SVG, along with corresponding practical code. The SVG specification is brimming with features — far too many to describe in a single chapter — but to come to grips with the language, you need to know how to write practical code and have a general idea of the kind of things SVG can do.

This chapter is divided into four sections:

❑ An overview of SVG, including the kind of things it's good for and what tools are available to you, the developer

❑ A hands-on section that demonstrates some of the basics of SVG in code examples

❑ A simple but complete browser-based SVG application constructed using XHTML and SVG, as well as a script manipulating the XML DOM

❑ A section-by-section summary of the contents of the SVG specification

The information in this chapter is quite densely packed, but once you start playing with SVG yourself, you will discover that not only is it easier to work with than it looks on the printed page, but it's also a lot of fun.

What Is SVG?

SVG is primarily a language for creating graphical documents. The language uses simple, intuitive terms such as *circle* and *line*, which makes it easy to learn. It's an XML language, which means it can be generated and processed using standard XML tools. SVG's use of XML's structural features makes it straightforward to construct complex diagrams based on simpler, modular parts. It has been designed with the Web in mind, and the documents can be viewed in browsers with the appropriate plug-in. In addition to offering animation and scripting capabilities, SVG also supports sophisticated graphic filtering, processing, and geometry, though none of these advanced features are necessary to get started creating useful images.

SVG has been used in Web environments, print environments, and even in Geographic Information Systems (GIS) and mapping applications. SVG isn't limited to the traditional Web; it is quickly becoming a dominant format on mobile phones and browsers. In fact, there are more mobile devices supporting SVG than desktop computers.

> Presently, the most current version of SVG is 1.1. The SVG specification is available at `www.w3.org/TR/SVG/`.

Scalable, Vector, Graphics

Rather than define images pixel by pixel as in bitmapped formats such as JPEG and GIF, SVG defines how images should be drawn using a series of statements. This approach has several advantages. First, SVG image files tend to be significantly smaller than their bitmap equivalents, a desirable characteristic on the Web. Second, parts of an image can be treated as separate objects and manipulated independently. This means complex diagrams can be built from simpler components, and dynamic effects (for example, animation) are relatively straightforward. Third, vector graphic images can easily be resized — this reflects the "scalable" part of the name — which is particularly useful on devices with small screens, such as mobile phones. Most viewers also enable you to *zoom* (enlarge and reduce) and *pan* (move side to side and up and down) the graphics.

On top of the versatility of vector graphics, SVG has an ace card — it is true XML. All the benefits described in this book about using XML apply to SVG. Tools such as XSLT (covered in Chapter 8), programming models such as DOM (covered in Chapter 11), interoperability, and internationalization — all of these are available for use in SVG thanks to its definition as XML. That's still not all, though. Not only can you draw graphics, you can also write applications — SVG has a powerful scripting facility built in.

Because the end product of SVG is visual, a lot of geometry and color theory is involved. Most of the theory is either trivial or makes intuitive sense, but some of the mathematics can seem daunting. Fortunately, several websites help out with this kind of theory, either specific to SVG or more general. For example, SVG uses complex coordinate spaces controlled through transformation matrices. More information on matrix mathematics can be found on Wikipedia at `http://en.wikipedia.org/wiki/Matrix_(mathematics)`.

Certain parts of SVG are difficult to describe with words alone. Fortunately, as a visual language it's straightforward to demonstrate these features. There isn't space in this chapter to cover SVG in great depth, but many resources and examples are available on the Web. The starting point is the W3C specification, which contains code for most things, but a search engine is likely to give you more complex, practical examples. As with XHTML (covered in Chapter 18), if you're not sure how something's been done, view the source code and find out. Additionally, a list of helpful SVG-related websites is provided at the end of this chapter.

Putting SVG to Work

The uses of SVG can loosely be divided into three categories:

❑ **Static graphics rendering** — The code is used to define a fixed image.

❑ **Self-contained applications** — The animation and scripting capabilities of SVG are used to provide dynamic, interactive graphics.

❑ **Server-based applications** — SVG provides the front end for bigger and more complex systems.

Static Graphics

In many situations traditional web graphics formats, such as GIF and JPEG, are unsuitable. For example, if you have a large and complex engineering drawing, then the size of the image file results in the file taking a long time to download; and once you have the image in your browser, it is very difficult to navigate around. Because they are *vector-based*, SVG diagrams can have much smaller file sizes, and the ability to zoom and pan means that navigation is straightforward.

Self-Contained Applications

Most SVG viewers support client-side scripting, and this combined with SVG's animation facilities makes it an extremely versatile tool for creating applications that run in the browser. Although several other systems are available for this purpose, such as Macromedia Flash and Java Applets, SVG is an open standard built on existing Web standards, such as XML, ECMAScript (JavaScript), and Cascading Style Sheets (CSS), whereas Flash is proprietary. SVG's focus on graphics makes it considerably easier to create visually appealing browser-based applications.

Additionally, SVG is designed to work with XHTML. It can be used within standard web applications and can be manipulated using Ajax and HTML Forms. Using forms to communicate with plug-ins such as Flash or Java Applets can create serious security implications. This type of application is much easier to build using SVG.

Server-Based Applications

SVG's web standards base means it's perfectly suited for constructing rich user interfaces to server-side systems. Where a graphic front end is needed for a system that handles a large amount of data or complex processing, SVG is a good solution. A typical example would be GIS, whereby the server can produce maps on-the-fly based on client requests. All the facilities available to client-side applications and static graphics are available to build browser-based clients that are as rich as the system demands. Because SVG is XML, it is relatively easy to generate from other XML data — generating charts for dynamically inclusion in reports is a typical example. The case study in Chapter 21 utilizes Ajax and HTML forms to build an SVG display of mortgage loan balances.

An SVG Toolkit

Thanks to the openness and versatility of SVG, it's practically impossible to recommend any single set of tools. To hand-build SVG files, you need some kind of editing tool; and to see the result, you need a viewer. The simplest of these would be a text editor and a SVG-enabled web browser, though considerably more sophisticated editors are available. If you want to build more dynamic systems or integrate with existing systems, then you need to consider what tools are available for the programming languages that you want to work with. Each of these jobs has a wide range of options; some of the better-known alternatives are listed in the following sections. The W3C maintains an official list of SVG implementations (www.svgi.org), although a Web search may turn up more up-to-date tools suited to your particular needs. Here are a few suggestions — most are free, and some are open source.

Viewers

The most popular way to view SVG files on a desktop computer is to use an SVG-enabled web browser such as Firefox, Opera, Konqueror, or Safari. Microsoft's Internet Explorer web browser, together with Adobe's plug-in (available from www.adobe.com/svg/), is another option. At the time of writing, the release version 3.0 is available for most platforms and languages, though support for it will be discontinued on January 1, 2008.

Batik, the Java toolkit for SVG, includes a cross-platform viewer called *Squiggle* (see http://xml .apache.org/batik). Squiggle is a good choice while you're developing with SVG because it provides more useful error messages than the browsers and plug-ins. In addition, work has also been done to ensure that Batik can be used as an applet.

Although support for SVG on Mozilla-based browsers (Netscape, Firefox, and others) is less than perfect, SVG has been declared one of the Mozilla project's priorities. Considerable work has already been done on native support for SVG in all of the major browsers except Internet Explorer. Additionally, SVG is used in a variety of products. For example, Adobe PDFs allow for embedded SVG (SVG is central to Adobe's Mars project for XML-based print formats). Several desktop environments also provide SVG-based theme and icon support.

Editors

Depending on what you want to do with SVG, a text editor is certainly adequate for simple hand-coding. To check your code, the W3C has produced an SVG Validator that can be used online or downloaded and run locally (http://jiggles.w3.org/svgvalidator).

Also from the W3C is Amaya, a combined web browser and editor with support for SVG and a lot more, available at www.w3.org/Amaya (the OpenGL version provides better SVG support).

A generic XML editor such as XMLSpy (www.xmlspy.com) or the online editor Codeplot (http:// codeplot.com) can make life easier by checking the validity of your data as you go along, and can advise which attributes are available for particular elements.

If you're interested in drawing, then Inkscape (www.inkscape.org/) is an open-source graphical editor, and the commercial SVGStudio (www.evolgrafix.de/htDocs/html/index.shtml) offers editing with animation support. Adobe Illustrator and GoLive are other commercial alternatives (www.adobe .com/svg). Qurvi (www.qurvi.com/), an online drawing application, enables you to create and save drawings and simple SVG applications without cost.

Programming Tools

If you're working with self-contained SVG applications, then pretty much any JavaScript editor can help, and many general-purpose text editors, such as the open-source jEdit (www.jedit.org), offer syntax highlighting along with other conveniences. Debugging SVG in Firefox is greatly simplified with the Firebug extension (www.joehewitt.com/software/firebug).

SVG-specific programming libraries are available for most languages. For instance, there's librsvg (`http://librsvg.sourceforge.net`) for Linux applications, several Perl modules at CPAN, and SVGDraw for Python (`www2.sfk.nl/svg`). There's a fairly new project for open-source SVG on .NET called SVG# (`www.sharpvectors.org//`). Probably the most sophisticated programmer's toolkit is Apache Batik (`http://xml.apache.org/batik/`), which provides just about everything you're likely to need for SVG work in Java.

The Dojo Toolkit (`http://dojotoolkit.org/`) is a JavaScript library that enables you to build cross-browser Ajax applications, and the library's SVG functionality degrades gracefully on older browsers. On Internet Explorer, the much older VML language is used for basic shapes and effects.

The list of tools that can generate SVG is actually very, very long thanks to its use of XML. Any tool that can create or modify XML can be applied to SVG. In particular, DOM (and similar) libraries for any language offer a straightforward way to dynamically generate SVG data. XSLT makes it possible to transform data from other XML formats into SVG for a graphic representation.

It's beyond the scope of this chapter to describe how to use SVG with other programming languages, but the material in the rest of this book related to using XML applies exactly the same when working with SVG as with any other XML language.

Getting Started

Getting started with SVG is very easy, as simple things really are simple. Most XML elements in the SVG format correspond to graphics elements, and most XML attributes correspond to attributes (or properties) of the elements. The names of elements and attributes are fairly self-explanatory: `<circle>` draws a circle, `<rect>` draws a rectangle, and so on. Here is a minimal example:

```
<?xml version="1.0"?>
<svg xmlns="http://www.w3.org/2000/svg">
  <rect x="100" y="10" width="100" height="100" fill="green" />
</svg>
```

The `<svg>` element clearly marks the boundaries of the SVG material, in this case the whole document. The namespace declaration is also needed to unambiguously identify the element and attribute names — SVG document fragments like this can be embedded in other XML documents, and without a namespace, clashes between element and attribute names might occur.

The `<rect>` element defines a rectangle, with its characteristics given as attributes. The x and y values are the coordinates of the top left-hand corner of the rectangle, measured across and down from the top left-hand corner of the viewing area. It is upside-down compared to Cartesian coordinates (used in maps and some graphs), but in most web browsers that top left-hand corner is the only fixed point. The width and height are both 100 units, resulting in a square. The `fill` attribute here says to color the inside of the shape green.

If you type this example into a text editor, save it, and open the resulting file in an SVG viewer (here using Batik Squiggle), you should see a green square, as shown in Figure 19-1 (minus the color, of course).

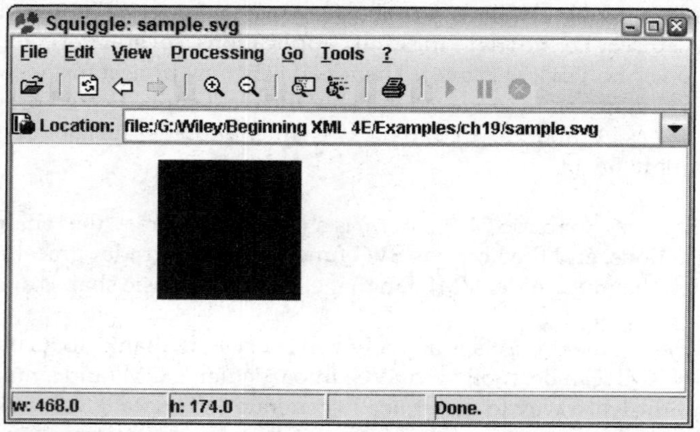

Figure 19-1

The preceding example included the SVG namespace (which is necessary in many viewers), but you can pass on more information to XML systems. Saying that the data is XML is a good start, and specifying a DOCTYPE enables a processor to determine whether the content is valid against a DTD. Here is the same fragment filled out to be a more complete XML document:

```
<?xml version="1.0"?>
<!DOCTYPE svg PUBLIC "-//W3C//DTD SVG 1.1//EN"
  "http://www.w3.org/Graphics/SVG/1.1/DTD/svg11.dtd">
<svg xmlns="http://www.w3.org/2000/svg" version="1.1">
    <rect x="100" y="10" width="100" height="100" fill="green" />
</svg>
```

The XML version specified here is 1.0. The newer SVG specifications, including SVG 1.2 and SVG Tiny 1.2, allow for XML 1.1 documents. In this example, the version of SVG is stated as 1.1, the latest W3C Recommendation. Most SVG viewers won't care very much about these niceties, but its good practice to include them. This is especially true if you are working on the Web, where there's no way of telling what tool might access your data.

Try It Out　　**Basic Shapes in SVG**

Using the handful of basic shapes available in SVG, you can build more complex images: rectangles (including ones with optional rounded corners), circles, ellipses, lines, polygons (enclosed areas), and polylines (line segments joined together):

1.　If you don't have Firefox, Opera, or another SVG-enabled browser, you need to obtain and install an SVG viewer. If you're using Internet Explorer, then the SVG viewer plug-in from Adobe is a good choice (www.adobe.com/svg/). You could also download Squiggle (http://xmlgraphics.apache.org/batik/svgviewer.html).

2.　Open a text editor and type in the following code:

```
<?xml version="1.0"?>
<!DOCTYPE svg PUBLIC "-//W3C//DTD SVG 1.1//EN"
    "http://www.w3.org/Graphics/SVG/1.1/DTD/svg11.dtd">
```

```
<svg xmlns="http://www.w3.org/2000/svg" version="1.1">

  <rect x="1" y="1" width="100" height="100"
        fill="none" stroke="blue" stroke-width="10" />

  <line x1="10" y1="10" x2="90" y2="90"
                    stroke="green" stroke-width="4"  />

  <circle cx="50" cy="50" r="30" fill="red" />
</svg>
```

3.   Save this document to your hard drive as shapes.svg.

4.   Open shapes.svg in your viewer. Double-clicking on the file in Windows Explorer should open the document and display the shapes, as shown in Figure 19-2. If the document is not displayed, you may need to allow the document to be opened in the plug-in by your browser. For example, Internet Explorer produces a security warning when you try to view local files. This doesn't happen for files on the Internet.

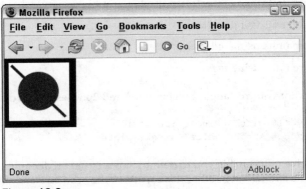

Figure 19-2

How It Works

The code starts with XML information, followed by SVG-specific material contained in the root <svg> element. The first child element is <rect>, which draws a rectangle. The x and y coordinates position this shape on the screen, just inside the top-left corner of the viewing area. This time the value of fill has been set to none, so the inside of this shape is the color of whatever's underneath. This <rect> element has two more attributes, stroke and stroke-width. The stroke draws the lines that define the shape, in this case the outline of the rectangle. The value of the stroke attribute determines the color of the outline; here it's blue. The stroke-width attribute indicates how thick the outline should be, in this case 10 units.

Next is a <line> element. Lines are *straight*, going from one point on screen to another. Those points are given as two sets of coordinates, the start point being (x1,y1) and the end point (x2,y2), so in the code the line starts at a point 10 units from the left-hand side of the viewing area (x1="10") and 10 units down from the top (y1="10"). The line runs to the point 90 units across (x2="90") and 90 units down from the top left-hand corner of the viewing area (y2="90"). A simple line doesn't enclose any space, so there is no fill attribute here, but a line can be stroked, and here the color is specified as green and the width of the line is specified as 4 units.

The third shape element is a `<circle>`. Circles are defined in SVG using the coordinates of their center point and their radius. The center point is expressed as the value of the cx and cy attributes, and the radius is set in the r attribute.

Views and Units

The examples thus far haven't specified what kind of unit to use for measurements. For example, when you wanted the rectangle to be 100 pixels wide, you used the attribute and value width="100". You assumed that value 100 meant 100 pixels. Actually, SVG allows for much greater control; you can use *relative units*, *absolute units*, or *percentages*. There are eight kinds of absolute units in SVG:

- ❑ em to measure units using *font height*
- ❑ ex to measure units using the height of the *"x" character*
- ❑ px to measure units using *pixels*
- ❑ pt to measure units using *points* (often used in graphic design and publishing)
- ❑ pc to measure units using *picas* (often used in graphic design and publishing)
- ❑ cm to measure units using *centimeters*
- ❑ mm to measure units using *millimeters*
- ❑ in to measure units using *inches*

For example, if you want your rectangle 2 inches wide and 2 inches high, you could use the following:

```
<rect x="1" y="1" width="2in" height="2in"
      fill="none" stroke="blue" stroke-width="10" />
```

Percentages and relative units enable you to define shapes based on document *views*. As you have seen, SVG documents can be embedded in other documents or they can be standalone XML files. In each of these cases, the root `<svg>` element is considered a view and can be customized using the width, height, and viewBox attributes. By default, though, the unit 1 in an SVG document is equal to 1px. Because you won't be using custom views in the examples, each of the units is treated as a pixel. Therefore, the value 100 in each of the examples should be rendered as 100 pixels.

The Painter's Model

In the previous example, the square outline defined by the `<rect>` element is clearly visible, as is the circle, but the middle section of the line has been obscured by the circle. This is a feature, not a bug! If you refer back to the source, inside the root `<svg>` element, there are three child elements at the same level: `<rect>`, `<line>`, and `<circle>`. The coordinates of these elements locate them in more or less the same area of the screen. The order in which the elements appear is significant; it is the order in which the visual objects are rendered. This is commonly referred to as the *painter's model*. The `<rect>` comes first, so a rectangle is painted on the "canvas." Next, the line is drawn on the canvas on top of whatever's already there. Finally, the circle is drawn on top of everything else.

If you rearrange the source data as follows so that the elements appear in the reverse order, then you can see the difference (see Figure 19-3):

```
<?xml version="1.0"?>
<!DOCTYPE svg PUBLIC "-//W3C//DTD SVG 1.1//EN"
    "http://www.w3.org/Graphics/SVG/1.1/DTD/svg11.dtd">
<svg xmlns="http://www.w3.org/2000/svg" version="1.1">
  <circle cx="50" cy="50" r="30" fill="red" />

  <line x1="10" y1="10" x2="90" y2="90"
        stroke="green" stroke-width="4"  />

  <rect x="1" y="1" width="100" height="100"
        fill="none" stroke="blue" stroke-width="10" />
</svg>
```

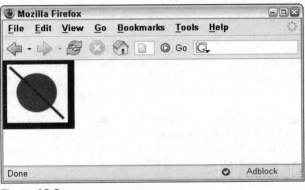

Figure 19-3

The circle is now painted first, followed by the line, and finally the rectangle. The line comes after the circle in the same location, so it's painted on top. Although the rectangle was painted last, you can still see the line and circle, as the `fill` attribute of `<rect>` is none. You are in effect looking through the square outline at the other objects.

Try It Out   Painter's Model

This Try It Out modifies the earlier SVG document to add a `<polygon>` and `<circle>` element. As shown in the last example, these basic shapes can be used to create more complex images.

1.   Open the example in your editor again and add the following:

```
<?xml version="1.0"?>
<!DOCTYPE svg PUBLIC "-//W3C//DTD SVG 1.1//EN"
    "http://www.w3.org/Graphics/SVG/1.1/DTD/svg11.dtd">
<svg xmlns="http://www.w3.org/2000/svg" version="1.1">

  <rect x="1" y="1" width="100" height="100"
        fill="none" stroke="blue" stroke-width="10" />

  <line x1="10" y1="10" x2="90" y2="90"
                  stroke="green" stroke-width="4"  />

  <polygon points="60,0 75,46 120,46 84,74
```

```
                         97,120 60,93 23,120 36,74
                         0,46 45,46"
               stroke="orange" fill="yellow" />

   <circle cx="50" cy="50" r="30" fill="red" />
 </svg>
```

2. Save this document to your hard drive as shapes2.svg.

3. Open shapes2.svg in your viewer.

You should now see the red circle on top of a yellow star, below which you can see the rectangle and line as before.

How It Works

The <polygon> is another of SVG's basic shapes. Unlike the other basic shapes, the <polygon> is described as a series of (absolute) points, and a straight line is drawn from point to point. The coordinates of the points are specified as (x,y) pairs in the points attribute of the polygon element. The <polygon> here defines the lines that make up the outline of a five-pointed star.

In the previous listing, the <polygon> (star) comes after the <rect> and <line> elements, so it is painted on top of them. The <circle> appears after the <polygon>, so it is painted on top. You may want to experiment with the order of the elements to confirm that the image appears as if each successive element were being painted on its predecessors.

Grouping

The <g> element enables you to group related elements using the hierarchical structure of XML. For example, if you wanted a circle and a line to behave as if they were a single element, you could wrap them in a <g> element like this:

```
<g stroke="green" stroke-width="4">
   <circle cx="50" cy="50" r="30" fill="red" />
   <line x1="10" y1="10" x2="90" y2="90" />
</g>
```

This is convenient if you want various elements to share the same properties — here the stroke and stroke-width attributes in the <g> element are applied to both the circle and the line. If either of these child elements had stroke or stroke-width attributes of its own, they would override the defaults inherited from the parent <g> element.

Transformations

The transform attribute enables modification of a shape or set of shapes defined in a group. Several simple expressions can be used in the transform attribute:

❑ translate displays the shapes shifted vertically or horizontally by specified distances.

❑ rotate rotates the shapes by a given angle around the origin or a specified point.

❑   scale makes the shapes larger or smaller by a specified ratio.

❑   skewX leans the shapes along the x-axis.

❑   skewY leans the shapes along the y-axis.

These operators can be used individually in attributes or in combination. For example, the following has the effect of drawing the rectangle starting from the point (101,101) and rotated by 45 degrees:

```
<rect x="1" y="1" width="100" height="100"
      fill="none" stroke="blue" stroke-width="10"
      transform="translate(100,100) rotate(45)"/>
```

Note that the order of the transforms makes a difference, so the transform value translate(100,100) rotate(45) is not the same as the transform value rotate(45) translate(100,100). You can also use the matrix operator to apply a transformation matrix to a shape or set of shapes, which shift and twist the shapes, though to use this successfully you need some knowledge of matrix arithmetic.

Unlike the x and y attributes, the transform attribute actually modifies the coordinate space of the element and its children elements, so it is common to use a transform attribute on a <g> element to move the entire group.

Paths

The basic shape elements are a convenient way of drawing common figures, but not the only way. Each of the shapes, and a whole lot more, can be created using a more fundamental drawing device, the *path*. An SVG <path> element describes the behavior of a virtual pen, which can be used to create practically any shape you like. The pen can be moved with or without drawing, and it can draw straight-line segments and curves. What the pen should draw is specified in an attribute of the path element named d, for data. As an example, you can duplicate the shapes drawn in the previous example using paths, starting with the following line:

```
<line x1="10" y1="10" x2="90" y2="90" stroke="green" stroke-width="4" />
```

This instructed the SVG renderer to paint a 4-pixel-wide green line between the points (10,10) and (90,90). This can be expressed as pen movements in a similar fashion as follows:

```
<path d="M 10,10 L 90,90" stroke="green" stroke-width="4" />
```

Inside the d attribute is the path *data*. The path data contains two commands: M 10,10 and L 90,90. The first command says to move (M) the virtual pen to the point (10,10), and the second says to paint a line *from the current point* to the absolute point (90,90). You aren't required to use absolute points, though. You can make a small change to the example and use relative points instead:

```
<path d="M 10,10 l 80,80" stroke="green" stroke-width="4" />
```

The difference is that the L is now lowercase, and the two values after it have each been reduced by 10. In an SVG viewer, the lines appear exactly the same. Path commands are case sensitive, which determines the meaning of the coordinates given. Uppercase letters (L, M, and so on) are used to signify that absolute coordinates should be used, and lowercase letters signify that relative coordinates should be used. In the first version, L 90,90 indicates the drawing of a line to the point (90,90) measured from the top left-hand corner (0, 0). In the second version, l 80,80 indicates drawing a line to the point (80,80) measured from the current point. Thanks to the initial movement of M 10,10 the current point is positioned 10 units down and 10 units to the right of the top left-hand corner of the screen, so the target point is that much closer. Relative to the point (10,10), the required target is 80 units to the right and 80 down.

In this example, you only have one move command followed by one line command — paths can be as long as you like, put together as a sequence of commands.

Here are the commands that can appear in paths. The specification uses shorthand names:

M	moveto	Moves to a new starting point
L	lineto	Draws a line from the current position to a new point
H	horizontal lineto	Draws a horizontal line from the current point to line up with a new point
V	vertical lineto	Draws a vertical line from the current point to line up with a new point
Z	closepath	Draws a straight line from the current point to current path's starting point
A	elliptical arc	Draws an elliptical arc from the current point to a new point. Other values in the data define the exact shape.
Q	quadratic Bézier curveto	Draws a quadratic Bézier curve from the current point to a new point. Other values in the data define the exact shape.
T	smooth quadratic Bézier curveto	Draws a quadratic Bézier curve from the current point to a new point. Values in a preceding curve's data define the exact shape.
C	curveto (cubic Bézier)	Draws a cubic Bézier curve from the current point to a new point. Other values in the data define the exact shape.
S	smooth curveto (cubic Bézier)	Draws a cubic Bézier curve from the current point to a new point. Values in a preceding curve's data define the exact shape.

Note that each of the commands can appear in uppercase (absolute coordinates) or lowercase (relative coordinates).

The first two you have already seen in the line example — M (moveto) changes the current point to a new location without drawing anything, and L (lineto) draws a straight line from the current point to the specified coordinates. The horizontal and vertical lineto commands H and V aren't followed by a pair of coordinates, just a single value (x for horizontal, y for vertical).

The z command, closepath, is used when you want to draw a closed shape, something that encloses an area. The command draws a straight line from the current point back to the initial starting point of the current subpath (for example, where the pen first touched the canvas in this particular part).

You can see how this works if you draw a rectangle using paths. The basic shape version looked like this:

```
<rect x="1" y="1" width="100" height="100"
   fill="none" stroke="blue" stroke-width="10" />
```

The top left-hand corner of the rectangle is specified, along with its dimensions. The path approach isn't anywhere near as easy to read (or, as shown later, to change with script):

```
<path d="M 1,1 L 1,100 L 100,100 L 100,1 z"
   fill="none" stroke="blue" stroke-width="10" />
```

The data starts with a command to move to the point $(1,1)$, which is followed by a line to the point $(1,100)$. Next is another line *from the current point* to the absolute position (100,100), followed by a line from there to $(100,1)$. Finally, a z command (note it's lowercase) closes the square, drawing a line from the current point $(100,1)$ back to the point where the pen last started drawing in this part of the path, which was $(1,1)$.

The remainder of the path commands (A, Q, T, C, and S) draw curves, based on different mathematical formulas. You don't actually need to know anything about the formula to use these commands to draw curves; the SVG Specification (Section 8.3) has examples of each kind. You can use the elliptical arc command to make a path version of the circle in the basic shape example.

Here again is the easy-to-read version:

```
<circle cx="50" cy="50" r="30" fill="red" />
```

The coordinates of the center of the circle are given along with its radius. There are several ways the circle could be drawn using a path, none of which are particularly straightforward. For example, you could use an elliptical arc command (A). The series of values that follow the elliptical arc command are listed in the specification as rx ry x-axis-rotation large-arc-flag sweep-flag x y:

```
<path d="M30,70.7 a30,30 1 1,1 1,1" fill="red" />
```

The first two values give the radius in the x and y directions; for a circle they're equal values. The arc is drawn from the current point to the point specified by the coordinates (x, y). Here we've used the relative version of the command (a), drawing the arc around the point (1,1), or 1 unit to the right and down of the origin. The other values provide further information about how the arc is to be drawn.

> **If the point (0,0) is used as the origin for an arc, the shape disappears altogether. This is because the rendering algorithm cannot determine directionality without a second reference point. By specifying the origin as (1,1), the algorithm can determine in which direction to arc.**

This section has only been using paths to paint very simple shapes. The <path> element is very useful when more complex drawings are needed. To show this in a very limited fashion, consider what you've seen so far: A virtual pen has drawn a line, another virtual pen has drawn a square, and a third virtual pen has drawn a circle. If you don't care about changing the pen's ink (the fill and stroke attributes), you can draw all three shapes in one path, as shown in the following code:

```
<path d="M1 1L1 100L100 100L100 1z M10 10180 80M30 70.7a30 30 1 1 1 1"
    stroke="pink" stroke-width="5" />
```

If you look at the data line carefully, you can see how each part has been taken from the three single <path> elements. The syntax here is a little different — there's no reason why the commas and spaces shouldn't have appeared as in the individual examples, but there are alternatives. Commas and/or whitespace can be used to separate the numbers in a path, as can the command letters themselves. This example uses the concise version without commas. The resulting image looks like Figure 19-4.

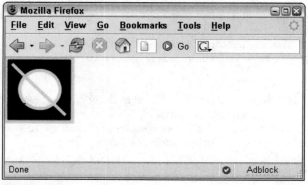

Figure 19-4

Paths are an extremely versatile way to draw shapes with SVG, but that versatility comes at a cost: It is considerably more difficult to write the code manually and make sense of existing code. In practice you probably won't want to write paths any more complex than the last example without the help of tools.

Images

Bitmap images such as GIFs, PNGs, and JPEGs can easily be incorporated into SVG documents using the <image> element. The following snippet draws a yellow rectangle with a green border, and places a picture of a flag on top of that:

```
<svg version="1.1"
    xmlns="http://www.w3.org/2000/svg"
    xmlns:xlink="http://www.w3.org/1999/xlink">

    <rect x="10" y="10" width="120" height="120"
        fill="yellow" stroke="green" stroke-width="4" />

    <image xlink:href="http://www.jpeg.org/images/flag_fr.jpg"
        type="image/jpeg" x="20" y="20" width="100" height="100" />

</svg>
```

The `<image>` element uses an attribute from the XLink namespace, so the namespace prefix `xlink` is declared in the root `<svg>` element. The MIME (Internet Media) type of the image is given as an attribute (`image/jpeg`) along with the required position and dimensions of the image (see Figure 19-5).

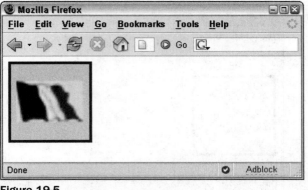

Figure 19-5

Note that the flag is distorted — the original image is actually smaller than the `width` and `height` values given in the `<image>` element, so the viewer stretches it to fit the specified values.

Text

The first thing to understand about text in SVG is that it is *real* text. Any kind of image can contain text, but try copying and pasting text from a JPEG image. In SVG, text is a first-class citizen. You can copy it from the rendered graphics and employ tools that can read the text from the source code or modify it in the DOM tree.

Support for text in SVG 1.1 is very sophisticated, yet lacking in one particular respect. The sophistication extends to using different character sets, styles, and orientations — virtually any written language can be rendered in SVG without much difficulty. You can even create your own font, defined as a set of graphical "glyphs" mapped to Unicode values for each character. Where SVG 1.1 falls short is in support for multi-line text. You can write series of lines of text easily enough, but a single block of text cannot be made to wrap to the next line as you might expect. Fortunately, this is a feature defined in the upcoming version of the SVG 1.2 specification.

In its basic form, as you are likely to want to use it most of the time, there's not a lot to learn about SVG text. Here is an example of some text that appears in a little frame, as in the image example:

```
<svg version="1.1" xmlns="http://www.w3.org/2000/svg">

    <rect x="10" y="10" width="120" height="120"
          fill="yellow" stroke="green" stroke-width="4" />

    <text x="15" y="70" font-size="20" fill="red">SVG is XML</text>

</svg>
```

The text is defined using a `<text>` element. The x and y attributes specify the point at which to start writing the text. In this simple example, this refers to the bottom left-hand side of the first character. The color of the text is specified by the `fill` attribute, and the size of the letters by the `font-size` attribute, which is defined by CSS2 (see Figure 19-6).

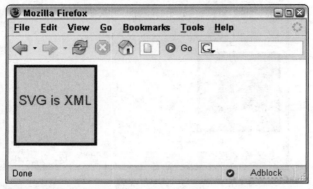

Figure 19-6

Virtually all the CSS2 properties can be applied to SVG: as inline style properties, as attributes, or by using stylesheets and classes. See Chapter 17 for more information about using CSS.

Comments, Annotation, and Metadata

A key benefit of SVG as XML is its machine readability. A computer can read and interpret the content of an SVG file beyond what's needed for the graphics display. Your SVG files may be read by software other than straightforward viewers — for example, robots building indexes for search engines. Even with viewers there are places to put information outside of the graphics display, such as the title bar of the viewer window, or in pop-up tooltips.

Three elements within SVG are available specifically for providing this kind of extra information: `<title>`, `<desc>`, and `<metadata>`. The first two of these are used in the following example:

```
<svg version="1.1" xmlns="http://www.w3.org/2000/svg">

  <!-- This is an XML comment -->

  <title>This is the title of the document</title>
  <desc>This is the description of the document</desc>

  <circle cx="60" cy="60" r="50" fill="red">
     <title>This is a circle</title>
     <desc>The color is red.</desc>
  </circle>

  <g>
     <title>This is a collection of squares</title>
     <desc>The squares are arranged in a grid.</desc>
```

```
            <rect x="45" y="45" width="10" height="10" />
            <rect x="65" y="45" width="10" height="10" />
            <rect x="45" y="65" width="10" height="10" />
            <rect x="65" y="65" width="10" height="10" />
        </g>
    </svg>
```

This example includes a regular XML comment. These should only be used to assist anyone reading the source code. Don't put anything too valuable in a comment. Next are `<title>` and `<desc>` elements as children of the root element. In this position, these are providing a title and a description of the document itself. You then have a `<circle>` element, which contains a `<title>` and a `<desc>`. Finally, there is a `<g>` element, which contains a `<title>`, `<desc>`, and four `<rect>` elements. The title and description in this case refer to this group of elements. Unlike the graphics elements, what the user agent (the software reading the document) does with the data in these elements is not mandated in the specification, although none of it is displayed directly as part of the graphics. As you might expect, this has led to some variation in what's been implemented in the viewers. Figure 19-7 shows the previous file in the viewer.

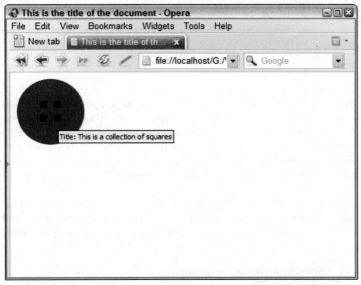

Figure 19-7

You can see that the document title ("This is the title of the document") is shown in the title bar. In some viewers, such as the Opera browser pictured, if the mouse pointer is over an element, or part of a group of elements, then a pop-up note showing the contents of the `<title>` and `<desc>` elements may be displayed.

The `<metadata>` element allows more complex machine-readable data to be included in the document. The W3C has been leading initiatives to make material on the Web more useful by adding as much machine-readable information as possible. There are others, but the leading metadata standard is the Resource Description Framework (http://w3.org/RDF), which makes it possible to say anything about virtually anything in a form that computers can use. The framework is really a data model, but the format used for interchange of this data is an XML language, RDF/XML. There has been considerable industry support for the W3C initiative; for example, all of Adobe's tools now embed RDF in their data files — JPEGS, PDF, and of course SVG. A good place to start finding out more about using SVG and RDF together is the "Co-depiction" site (http://rdfweb.org/2002/01/photo/), which is part of the FOAF (Friend-of-a-Friend) project (www.foafnaut.org/).

Remember that under most circumstances the contents of the <title>, <desc>, and <metadata> elements won't be visible as part of the SVG graphics, although some web browsers without a plug-in will display these as plain text.

> **Different Web users have different requirements, and many people can't use a browser in the regular fashion because of disabilities such as poor eyesight. Several features of SVG make it particularly good for communication in such circumstances, as discussed in the W3C note "Accessibility Features of SVG"** (www.w3.org/TR/SVG-access/). **For example, being able to zoom in on images makes SVG images more accessible to people with impaired vision. Providing text equivalents of images in** title **and** desc **elements also enables the information to be conveyed using text-to-speech screenreaders.**

Scripting

SVG has a scripting facility very similar to that of HTML. The language usually available is ECMAScript, which is the international standard version of JavaScript. It's beyond the scope of this book to provide an introduction to ECMAScript/JavaScript, but the examples used here are relatively self-explanatory. More information about the SVG object model used by the renderer and script engine can be found in the specification in Section 18. Because the SVG specification does not mandate scripting support, not all browsers provide it. Additionally, very few of the available browsers and plug-ins support all of the functions and properties defined in the specification.

The following code is in two parts. The first is an SVG graphic element that defines the triangle shape, and the second part is a piece of ECMAScript that responds to the mouse click and changes the triangle's color. If the code is opened in a viewer, you see a green triangle. Clicking the mouse on the triangle turns it red:

```
<?xml version="1.0" standalone="no"?>
<!DOCTYPE svg PUBLIC "-//W3C//DTD SVG 1.1//EN"
  "http://www.w3.org/Graphics/SVG/1.1/DTD/svg11.dtd">
<svg xmlns="http://www.w3.org/2000/svg" version="1.1">

  <polygon points="150,100, 50,100 100,29.3" fill="green"
         onclick="handleClick(evt)" />

  <script type="text/ecmascript">
    <![CDATA[

      function handleClick(evt) {
          var polygon = evt.target;
          polygon.setAttribute("fill", "red");
```

```
        }

    ]]>
  </script>
</svg>
```

The triangle is defined as a `<polygon>`. A triangle has three corners, so you have three sets of (x,y) coordinates. The `fill` attribute for the `<polygon>` is `green`, so it appears shaded in that color.

The `onclick` attribute is a special attribute that associates the element with an event and part of the script. In this example the event is a mouse click, and the part of the script is a user-defined function called `handleClick`. That function is passed an object (`evt`) that carries information relating to the mouse click event.

Scripts in SVG are included using a `<script>` element. As shown later in the chapter, it is possible to point to an external script file, but there isn't much code here, so it's included in the SVG document file itself.

The script listing is wrapped in a CDATA section, as there may be characters in the script (for example, <) that would break XML's well-formedness rule. Here the script is comprised of a single function, `handleClick`, which is called when the user clicks on the triangle.

The first statement of the function creates a new variable called `polygon` (the name isn't important) and sets this to the value of the `target` attribute of the `evt` object. The target is the object on which the event occurred, in this case the `<polygon>` element in the SVG part of the code. The next line uses a DOM method to set the `<polygon>` element's value to the `red` string. This has the effect of changing the value in memory of that part of the SVG to be equivalent to the following:

```
<polygon points="150,100, 50,100 100,29.3" fill="red"
         onclick="handleClick(evt)" />
```

Note that the actual source code doesn't change, only the in-memory representation, which is the DOM tree, but the result is the same: The triangle becomes red.

SVG on Your Website

Publishing SVG material on the Web is nearly as straightforward as publishing XHTML. Bear in mind that people who visit your site need an SVG-capable viewer, so it's a good to idea to have a link on one of your XHTML pages to one of the browsers or plug-ins.

Even if the visitor is using an SVG-capable browser, the browser may not realize that the material it's seeing is SVG. If you point your browser at one of your newly uploaded SVG masterpieces and all you see is XML code, don't be dismayed. There are two ways to give the browser a hint:

❑   Give the file an appropriate extension — .svg for regular SVG files and .svgz for gzip compressed files.

❑   Most important, ensure that the web server delivers the document with the right MIME type. At the time of writing, most web servers *don't*.

Depending on your setup, you may have to ask the server administrator to add the MIME type to the configuration for you. With most Apache-based services, it's possible to add the MIME type yourself. Simply create a file called .htaccess (note the initial dot) in the top-level directory, below which your SVG files appear, and enter the following text:

```
AddType image/svg+xml svg
AddType image/svg+xml svgz
AddEncoding gzip svgz
```

To check whether the material's being served correctly, you need a download tool such as *wget* (a GNU tool, Win32 ports are available), which will tell you what the MIME type is (for SVG it should be image/svg+xml).

Tangram: A Simple Application

To give you a taste of how an SVG application fits together, this section presents a little toy. Tangram is a jigsawlike Chinese puzzle based on seven flat geometric pieces, which can be arranged (without over-lap) to make various shapes, the simplest of which is a square. In the toy application shown in Figure 19-8, you begin with all the pieces in a square box and click a Scramble button to scatter them out of the box. The goal is to fit the pieces back into the box.

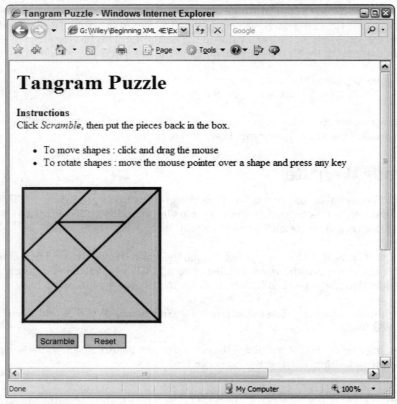

Figure 19-8

The application is composed of the following three files:

❏   `tangram.html` — An XHTML file that displays the puzzle and some instructions

❏   `tangram.svg` — An SVG file that defines the graphics, including control buttons

❏   `tangram.es` — An ECMAScript file that looks after movement of the pieces

XHTML Wrapper

SVG files can be viewed directly in capable browsers or they can form part of a regular XHTML page. The first file is standard XHTML, using the *Transitional* DOCTYPE. You will probably recognize most of its elements; they were all tags in legacy HTML, though the `<iframe>` element deserves some additional explanation:

```
<html xmlns="http://www.w3.org/1999/xhtml">
  <head>
    <title>Tangram Puzzle</title>
  </head>
  <body>
    <h1>Tangram Puzzle</h1>
    <p>
      <strong>Instructions</strong><br/>
      Click <em>Scramble</em>, then put the pieces back in the box.
    </p>
    <ul>
      <li>To move shapes : click and drag the mouse</li>
      <li>To rotate shapes : move the mouse over a shape and press any key</li>
    </ul>
    <iframe src="tangram.svg" width="750" height="550" frameborder="0">
    </iframe>
  </body>
</html>
```

The document begins with conventional XHTML material, and the body begins with a heading, a small paragraph of text (`<p>`) featuring some emphasis (`<em>` and `<strong>`), followed by an unnumbered list (`<ul>`) containing two items (`<li>`), which make up the instructions. After the instructions comes the interesting part — the `<iframe>` element that displays the SVG graphics in the XHTML page.

Historically, it's not been easy to display embedded objects and plug-ins in web pages in a consistent fashion, as different browsers supported different approaches. You could use the `<embed>` tag or an `<object>` tag, but at the time of writing, the code here works with all of the major browsers and plug-ins. By using an `<iframe>`, the browser can determine how to render the subframe. It may use a plug-in or its own internal rendering engine.

The data attribute contains a relative URI pointing to the SVG file (it's in the same directory as this XHTML file). The `width` and `height` attributes of the `<iframe>` element determine the size of the area into which the SVG graphics are drawn.

SVG Shapes

The SVG part of the application is relatively straightforward. Essentially, what you have is the box containing the puzzle pieces, with the pieces represented as polygons, and two labeled buttons. When the source code is stripped down to its elements, you can see the overall structure:

```
<svg>
    <script/>

    <title>Tangrams</title>
    <desc>An old Chinese puzzle</desc>

    <rect/> <!-- the pieces box -->

    <g> <!-- the pieces -->
        <polygon/>
        <polygon/>
        <polygon/>
        <polygon/>
        <polygon/>
        <polygon/>
        <polygon/>
    </g>

    <g><!-- "Scramble" button -->
        <rect/>
        <text>Scramble</text>
    </g>

    <g><!-- "Reset" button -->
        <rect/>
        <text>Reset</text>
    </g>
</svg>
```

In addition to the basic shapes and text, there is also a `<script>` element to link to an external ECMAScript file, which looks after mouse and keyboard interaction. A `<title>` element and `<desc>` element provide machine-readable annotation. The `<g>` elements are used to provide common attributes to their child elements and simplify events.

You need to be able to move the pieces around. Therefore, a mouse click-and-drag gesture is used, and you need listeners for various mouse events. To make the puzzle a little more interesting, you should also rotate the pieces to get them oriented properly. This is done by selecting a piece and then pressing any key. A piece is selected by simply moving the mouse cursor over it. When the mouse cursor is over a piece, it changes color to indicate it has been selected.

One other behavior to handle is responding to mouse clicks on the buttons. A click on the Scramble button scatters the pieces around, and a click on the Reset button returns them to their starting positions.

All this behavior has introduced a minor complication: The various elements have to respond to mouse and keyboard events. Therefore, hooks in the code call appropriate functions in the ECMAScript, though the keyboard event handling is set up in the script itself:

```
<?xml version="1.0" encoding="UTF-8"?>
<!DOCTYPE svg PUBLIC "-//W3C//DTD SVG 1.1//EN"
 "http://www.w3.org/Graphics/SVG/1.1/DTD/svg11.dtd">
<svg xmlns="http://www.w3.org/2000/svg"
 xmlns:xlink="http://www.w3.org/1999/xlink"
 version="1.1"
 width="750px"
 height="550px"
 viewBox="-10 -10 740 540"
 onload="init(evt)"
 onmouseup="mouseup(evt)"
 onmousemove="move(evt)"
 onmousedown="mousedown(evt)">
```

After the XML declaration and DOCTYPE declaration is the document's root <svg> element. As well as declaring the SVG namespace and version, this also has attributes to position and scale the graphics in a suitably sized area (the viewBox) within the initial viewport specified by the width and height attributes. Here, the viewBox data is used to shift all the graphics 10 pixels down and to the right to provide a margin. The onload attribute is one of several possible event attributes, and the effect here is that when the SVG document is loaded into the viewer, a user-defined (in the script) function called init is called and passed an object, evt, that models to the onload event.

All of the pieces in the document share the same behavior when responding to mouse events, so the event attributes (onmousemove and others) also appear in the root <svg> element. Each of these attributes contains a value corresponding to a function in the script. For instance, when the mouse cursor moves over any element in the document, the move method in the script is called. In the event, you check to ensure that you have an active <polygon> element selected. You could place the event attributes on each of the <polygon> elements instead of the root element, but then the events would only fire when the cursor was over the <polygon>. Because cursor movement in modern browsers is unpredictable, it is safer to place the event attributes on the root. You also add a background element for the whole document to ensure that events are caught.

```
<rect x="0" y="0" width="100%" height="100%" fill="white" opacity="0"/>
```

Here the opacity is set to 0; you don't want the background <rect> to be visible in the viewer, only to the event handler.

The next line links in the script, and like the element in the previous XHTML code, the type attribute gives the MIME type of the linked file so the viewer knows what to expect. Similarly, a relative link is made because the script file (tangram.es) will be in the same directory as this document. There then follows a title and description for this SVG document:

```
<script type="text/ecmascript" xlink:href="tangram.es"/>
<title>Tangrams</title>
<desc>An old Chinese puzzle</desc>
```

The main graphic elements start with the square container box. This rectangle is yellow and has a 5-pixel dark-blue outline, these characteristics being set in the elements' attributes, as shown in the following:

```
<rect x="0" y="0" width="200" height="200" fill="yellow"
  stroke="darkblue" stroke-width="5"/>
```

Next are the `<polygon>` elements, which paint the puzzle pieces. All these pieces share the same fill and outline (stroke) characteristics. Therefore, the `<polygon>` elements are grouped together in a `<g>` element, and those attributes appear with that element. The parent-child inheritance of the characteristics means that this is equivalent to adding the attributes to all the individual children. An attribute introduced here is `fill-opacity`. This can take a value from 0 (transparent) to 1 (opaque). Setting this at 0.8 gives the shapes an attractive translucency, rather like stained glass. To simplify the reference in the script, you give the `<g>` element an `id` attribute:

```
<g id="PolyGroup" fill="lightgreen" stroke="darkblue" stroke-width="3"
  fill-opacity="0.8" onmouseover="mouseover(evt)" onmouseout="mouseout(evt)">
```

Try It Out   Tangram Shapes

Let's see what this looks like in a browser just as static shapes. Remember that the code for the examples is available from the book's website at www.wrox.com.

1. Open a text editor and enter the previous code, starting from the following:

```
<?xml version="1.0" encoding="UTF-8"?>
<!DOCTYPE svg PUBLIC "-//W3C//DTD SVG 1.1//EN"
 "http://www.w3.org/Graphics/SVG/1.1/DTD/svg11.dtd">
<svg xmlns="http://www.w3.org/2000/svg"
  xmlns:xlink="http://www.w3.org/1999/xlink"
  version="1.1"
  width="750px"
  height="550px"
  viewBox="-10 -10 740 540"
  onload="init(evt)"
  onmouseup="mouseup(evt)"
  onmousemove="move(evt)"
  onmousedown="mousedown(evt)">
<rect x="0" y="0" width="100%" height="100%" fill="white" opacity="0"/>
<script type="text/ecmascript" xlink:href="tangram.es"/>
<title>Tangrams</title>
<desc>An old Chinese puzzle</desc>
<rect x="0" y="0" width="200" height="200" fill="yellow"
  stroke="darkblue" stroke-width="5"/>
<g id="PolyGroup" fill="lightgreen" stroke="darkblue" stroke-width="3"
  fill-opacity="0.8" onmouseover="mouseover(evt)" onmouseout="mouseout(evt)">
```

2. Add the following code:

```
<polygon points="0,0 0,100 100,0"
  transform="translate(0,0) rotate(0,0,0)"/>
<polygon points="100,0 50,50 150,50 200,0"
  transform="translate(0,0) rotate(0,0,0)"/>
<polygon points="50,50 0,100 50,150 100,100"
  transform="translate(0,0) rotate(0,0,0)"/>
<polygon points="50,50 100,100 150,50"
  transform="translate(0,0) rotate(0,0,0)"/>
<polygon points="200,0 100,100 200,200"
  transform="translate(0,0) rotate(0,0,0)"/>
<polygon points="0,100 0,200 50,150"
  transform="translate(0,0) rotate(0,0,0)"/>
```

```
      <polygon points="0,200, 200,200 100,100"
        transform="translate(0,0) rotate(0,0,0)"/>
    </g>
  </svg>
```

3. Save the file as `tangram.svg`.

4. Open the file in a browser or SVG viewer.

After an initial error message pop-up, you should see the Tangram pieces all neatly positioned in a box. Moving the mouse over the pieces should also produce error messages because calls are being made to a non-existent script.

> *If you're using IE and don't get an error message here, go into IE's Tools menu and select Internet Options. Click on the Advanced tab. Under Browsing, make sure the Disable Script Debugging and Display a Notification About Every Script Error options are not checked. Click OK. To view JavaScript errors in Firefox, open the JavaScript Console on the Tools menu.*

How It Works

The pieces themselves are defined as `<polygon>` elements, each having three (triangles) or four (quadri-laterals) pairs of coordinates. Each of the elements also has a `transform` attribute, containing a `translate` and `rotate` part. These attributes are used to hold the movement and rotation information of the pieces. The two values in the `translate` part indicate how far to shift the element across and down. The first value in the `rotate` part gives the rotation angle (in degrees), and the next two values are the x and y coordinates of the point around which the shape should be rotated. All these values are set to zero at first because there's no translation or rotation.

Try It Out   **Adding the Buttons**

Add the two control buttons, Scramble and Reset.

1. Open the file you just typed in, `tangram.svg`, in a text editor.

2. Delete the `</svg>` tag at the end and type in the following block of code:

```
  <g onclick="scramble()">
    <rect x="20" y="220" width="60" height="20"
      style="fill:coral;stroke:blue;stroke-width:2"/>
    <text x="50" y="220" transform="translate(0,14)" text-anchor="middle"
      style="fill:black;font-size:9pt;font-family:Arial">Scramble</text>
  </g>
  <g onclick="reset()">
    <rect x="90" y="220" width="60" height="20"
      style="fill:violet;stroke:blue;stroke-width:2"/>
    <text x="120" y="220" transform="translate(0,14)" text-anchor="middle"
      style="fill:black;font-size:9pt;font-family:Arial">Reset</text>
  </g>
</svg>
```

3. Save the file again as `tangram.svg`.

4. Open the file in your browser.

You should now see the buttons, but again you will be presented with an error message pop-up when the file is opened because of the incomplete script.

How It Works

Each button is drawn as a colored rectangle with a stroked outline and a text label positioned in the center of the rectangle. It's convenient to use the same vertical coordinates for both the rectangle and the text, making the small adjustment needed to center the text vertically with a simple `translate` transformation. For horizontal centering, the `text-anchor` attribute was added with the value `middle`. You also changed the horizontal position to be in the middle of the rectangle.

The behavior in response to mouse clicks is set up in `<g>` elements, as you want the same thing to happen whether the text or the rectangle is clicked. Clicking the first button calls the `scramble()` function in the script, and clicking the second button calls the `reset()` function. These functions haven't yet been defined, so for now the clicks produce error messages.

Tangram Script

The interactivity of the tangram puzzle is provided by the ECMAScript (JavaScript) in the file `tangram.es`. When the mouse is moved or clicked, the SVG DOM causes functions in the script to be called. Those functions in turn make changes to the DOM to carry out the required behavior — moving the puzzle pieces. For example, Figure 19-9 shows the visual result of clicking the Scramble button.

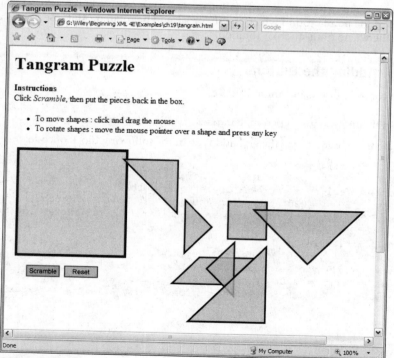

Figure 19-9

To give you an idea of how it all fits together before you look at the details of the source, here is an overview of the functions the script contains:

```
init(evt)
mousedown(evt)
mouseup(evt)
mouseover(evt)
mouseout(evt)
move(evt)

getTransformBlock(polygon, index)
getRotateAngle(polygon)
getCenter(polygon)

moveToFront(polygon)
rotatePolygon(evt)

scramble()
reset()
```

The first six functions are called in response to events generated from user interaction with the SVG document. The `init(evt)` function is called when the document is initially loaded into the viewer using the `onload` attribute in its top-level `<svg>` element. That function initializes the `svgDoc` variable and adds a new event. The rest of the functions here are called when particular mouse actions occur. For example, moving the mouse pointer over a puzzle piece causes the `mouseover(evt)` method to be called, and the `evt` object it receives contains a reference to that particular piece. These functions all have a hook in the SVG code in the form of event attributes pointing to these functions. The `mousedown(evt)` and `mouseup(evt)` functions are used to recognize the start and end of a click-and-drag gesture, which is used to move the pieces around. The actual movement is tracked by the `move(evt)` method. The `mouseover(evt)` and `mouseout(evt)` functions change the color of the piece the mouse pointer passes over.

The next functions are utilities to help in reading values from the SVG DOM. Each of the puzzle pieces (the `<polygon>` elements in the previous SVG) has a `transform` attribute as follows:

```
transform="translate(0,0) rotate(0,0,0)"
```

This attribute is a string with two distinct blocks: The first is a `translate` command and the second a `rotate` command. The `getTransformBlock(polygon, index)` function returns a string containing the whole of the command for the specified `<polygon>` element. If the index has value 0, then the `translate` block is returned; if it is 1, then the `rotate` block is returned. `getRotateAngle(polygon)` returns the angle specified in the `rotate` block.

The next two functions carry out operations on the pieces. `getCenter(polygon)` returns the coordinates of the center point of the specified polygon relative to the 0,0 point from which it is referenced. This is used to calculate the offsets needed to line up the center of the shapes to the mouse pointer when moving them around. If other puzzle pieces are lying on top of the piece selected, the `moveToFront(polygon)` function moves the selected piece to the top of the pile.

The last two functions look after operations when the Scramble or Reset buttons are clicked. The `scramble()` function scatters the pieces around by randomizing the transform values, and the `reset()` function returns all the pieces to their initial positions by setting all the transform values back to 0.

OK, now you might like to see the code itself. It begins by declaring the following three global variables illustrated in the following code:

❑ selectedPoly will be the individual <polygon> element corresponding to the piece the user has selected.

❑ track is true when a piece is being dragged around the screen, and false otherwise.

❑ svgDoc starts as null, but is assigned to the document in the init function.

```
var selectedPoly;
var track = false;
var svgDoc = null;
```

The init(evt) function is called when the SVG document is loaded into the viewer. It begins by getting a reference to the document itself from the event passed by the caller (the SVG DOM). To handle key presses, an event listener is added to the rootElement object, so whenever there's a key event, the rotatePolygon(evt) method is called. Attaching event listeners should only be done on the root element for compatibility, as shown in the following:

```
function init(evt) {
   svgDoc = evt.target.ownerDocument;
   svgDoc.rootElement.addEventListener("keydown", rotatePolygon, false);
}
```

When the mouse moves over an element, the mouseover(evt) method is called. The event object evt carries a reference to the element on which it was called, which may be a puzzle piece. The mouseover(evt) function should check whether a piece is already being dragged by checking the track variable. If the user is already dragging a piece, then you don't want to highlight another one. If no piece is currently being tracked, then you can check whether the DOM element under the cursor (the evt.target) is a puzzle piece by evaluating its name. If its name is polygon, set the selectedPoly variable reference to this element so that it can be moved or rotated later. In addition, set the fill attribute to orange, changing the color of the piece onscreen:

```
function mouseover(evt){
   if(!track){
      if(evt.target.nodeName == "polygon"){
         selectedPoly = evt.target;
         selectedPoly.setAttribute("fill", "orange");
      }
   }
}
```

When a mouse button is pressed, the mousedown method is called. If the selectedPoly variable has already been set by the mouseover(evt) method, the track variable can be set to true, as this action might mean the element is about to be dragged. The selected shape should also be moved in front of any other pieces:

```
function mousedown(){
   if(selectedPoly != null){
      track = true;
      selectedPoly = moveToFront(selectedPoly);
   }
}
```

When the mouse button is released, the `mouseup` function is called. All this function needs to do is reset the `track` variable to stop the dragging:

```
function mouseup(){
  track=false;
}
```

The `mouseout` function is called when the mouse pointer moves off a visual element, so it needs to reset the `fill` attribute and the color of the piece back to its original value of `lightgreen`. It can also clear the `selectedPoly` variable, which effectively deselects the piece:

```
function mouseout(){
  if(!track && selectedPoly != null){
    selectedPoly.setAttribute("fill", "lightgreen");
    selectedPoly=null;
  }
}
```

The `move(evt)` function begins by checking for an empty value in `selectedPoly`, or that the value of `track` specified not to drag the element. If either is the case, then the function returns without any further operations, except for resetting the `track` variable just to be sure. If the piece is to be moved, then a `center` object is created, which contains the x,y coordinates of the selected shape's current center point. The coordinates of the mouse pointer are then retrieved using the built-in event properties `clientX` and `clientY`. These have the corresponding values of the center variable subtracted from them to produce new values for the `translate` part of the shape's `transform` attribute. The value of the `transform` attribute is reconstructed from these new `translate` values and the existing rotate part, which is obtained using `getTransformBlock` with the index 1:

```
function move(evt){
  if(!track || selectedPoly == null){
    track = false;
    return;
  }
  var center = getCenter(selectedPoly);

  var x = evt.clientX-center.x;
  var y = evt.clientY-center.y;
  translateString = "translate("+x+","+y+")";

  selectedPoly.setAttribute("transform",
    translateString+" "+getTransformBlock(selectedPoly, 1));
}
```

The `getTransformBlock(poly, index)` function starts by getting the transform attribute from the supplied polygon. Here again is the form that attribute will take, with some arbitrary values:

```
transform="translate(11,23) rotate(90,100,100)"
```

The function returns either the `translate` or `rotate` part of a shape's `transform` attribute; and to get at this, the function employs a very useful piece of ECMAScript functionality: *regular expressions*. A complete discussion of regular expressions is beyond the scope of this chapter, but if you've not encountered them already, plenty of tutorials are on the Web. Here, the built-in `split` method is applied to the whole `transform` string. The `/\)/` argument is a regular expression that matches all single closing parentheses in the string. Returned from `split` is an array of strings, built from splitting the input string on whatever the regular expression matched. Applied to the previous `transform` string, `split(/\)/)[0]` would return the string `translate(11,23`, and `split(/\)/)[1]` would return `rotate(90,100,100`. Notice that the closing parenthesis has been removed in each of the previous strings. You need to add that back in the `return` statement:

```
function getTransformBlock(polygon, index){
  var transformString = polygon.getAttribute("transform");
  var transformPieces = transformString.split(/\)/);
  if (transformPieces.length > index)
    return transformPieces[index] + ")";
  return "";
}
```

The `getRotateAngle(polygon)` function can use the previous function to get the `rotate(90,100,100)` part, and then use another regular expression, `reg`, with the built-in `exec` function to extract the first number. The regular expression here matches any decimal number, such as 123 or 55.6, and the `exec` function applied to the `rotateString` returns the first matching value, which is the rotate angle. This value will be a string, so the built-in `parseFloat(string)` function is used to convert it into a floating-point number. Be careful to put this in a `try/catch` block, as shown in the following code:

```
function getRotateAngle(polygon){
  var rotateString = getTransformBlock(polygon, 1);
  var reg = /([0-9]+)(\.?)([0-9]*)/;
  try {
    return parseFloat(reg.exec(rotateString));
  } catch(e) {
    return 0;
  }
}
```

The `getCenter(polygon)` function is passed a polygon and returns an object containing a pair of values, the coordinates of the shape's center point relative to 0,0. This is calculated by taking the average of the x and y values of the polygon's corner points. The regular-expression-based `split` method is used again in the function. Here it is applied to the `points` attribute of the polygon, which looks something like `"0,200 200,200 100,100"`. Each pair of coordinates corresponds to one of the shape's corners. The pairs are separated by spaces, so you can separate each pair of numbers using `split(/ /)`. The length of the array this gives you is the same as the number of pairs of values. The function steps through each pair of values and applies the `split` method again, this time with a regular expression that matches commas. This gives an array containing two strings, which are converted into integers and then added to the running totals xSum and ySum. The `center` object is defined as having two properties, x and y, which are then given the calculated average values of x and y. The `center` object is then returned, as shown in the following:

```
function getCenter(polygon){
  var center = {
    x: 0,
    y: 0
  };
  try {
    var pointsString = polygon.getAttribute("points");
```

```
      var split = pointsString.split(/ /);
      var xSum = 0;
      var ySum = 0;
      var coords;
      for(var i=0;i<split.length;i++){
        coords = split[i].split(/,/);
        xSum = xSum + parseInt(coords[0]);
        ySum = ySum + parseInt(coords[1]);
      }
      center.x = xSum/split.length;
      center.y = ySum/split.length;
    } catch(e) {
    // do nothing
    }
    return center;
}
```

The `moveToFront(polygon)` function modifies the SVG DOM to move the specified polygon into the foreground, above any other objects onscreen. As shown earlier, SVG's painter's model means that graphic elements that appear earlier in the document are painted first. It follows that whichever shape appears last in the elements defining the puzzle pieces are painted last, or on top. Therefore, here the function does a little element juggling using standard XML DOM methods to make the specified polygon the last of the polygon's children. This is done by first cloning a copy of the polygon of interest and appending that to its parent node's (the <g> element) list of children. The original `polygon` element is then removed from the DOM tree, and its new clone returned, as shown in the following:

```
function moveToFront(polygon){
  var clone = polygon.cloneNode(true);
  polygon.parentNode.appendChild(clone);
  polygon.parentNode.removeChild(polygon);
  return clone;
}
```

The `rotatePolygon` function was attached to a keyboard listener in the `init()` function, and it is called when a key is pressed. The function receives an `evt` object from which further information could be extracted, such as which key was pressed. However, as there is only one action, this is ignored, and all key presses have the same result. First the current rotation angle (in degrees) is obtained using the `helper` function `getRotateAngle(polygon)` described previously. This has the value 22.5 added to it, which rotates the shape one-eighth of a circle clockwise. The `getCenter(polygon)` function is reused to provide the point around which the rotation should take place. A new string for the `transform` attribute is then built, consisting of the current translate block together with a revised rotate block, as shown in the following:

```
function rotatePolygon(evt){
  if (selectedPoly == null)
    return;
  var rotation = getRotateAngle(selectedPoly);
  rotation = rotation + 22.5;
  var center = getCenter(selectedPoly);
  var transformString = getTransformBlock(selectedPoly, 0)
    + " rotate(" + rotation + "," + center.x + "," + center.y + ")";
  selectedPoly.setAttribute("transform", transformString);
}
```

The last two methods are called when the Scramble or Reset buttons are clicked. The code to `scramble()` looks a lot more complex than it actually is. It starts by obtaining the set of `<polygon>` elements through the `childNodes` DOM property of the parent `polyGroup`, then steps through these, and randomizes the values contained in the transform attribute of each shape in turn. The individual child elements are accessed using the XML DOM method `item(x)`. Note that a check is made to ensure that the item in question actually is a `<polygon>` element, as text nodes corresponding to whitespace in the SVG also appear as children here. The random values are generated using the ECMAScript `Math.random` function and are scaled and offset as needed to make the shapes appear in a suitable part of the screen (to the right of the puzzle pieces' box). Again the attribute strings are built, and the value of the `transform` attribute in the DOM is set:

```
function scramble(){
  var polyGroup = svgDoc.getElementById("PolyGroup");
  var children = polyGroup.childNodes;

  var transformString;
  var randX;
  var randY;
  var randAngle;
  var center;

  for(var i=0;i<children.length;i++){
    if(children.item(i).nodeName == "polygon"){
      center = getCenter(children.item(i));
      randX = 200+Math.floor (200*Math.random());
      randY = Math.floor (200*Math.random());
      randAngle = Math.floor (8*Math.random()) * 45;

      transformString = "translate("+randX+","+randY+") ";
      transformString = transformString
        + "rotate(" + randAngle + "," + center.x + "," + center.y + ")";
      children.item(i).setAttribute("transform", transformString);
    }
  }
  track=false;
}
```

One of the most straightforward functions, `reset()`, steps through the shapes in exactly the same manner as `scramble()`, but this time it resets the values contained in the `transform` attribute back to 0, thus putting all the pieces back into their starting positions:

```
function reset(){
  var polyGroup = svgDoc.getElementById("PolyGroup");
  var children = polyGroup.childNodes;
  var transformString = "translate(0,0) rotate(0,0,0)";
  for(var i=0;i<children.length;i++){
    if(children.item(i).nodeName == "polygon"){
      children.item(i).setAttribute("transform", transformString);
    }
  }
  track=false;
}
```

Running the Tangram Application

1.   Open a new window in your text editor.

2.   Type in the code listed previously.

3.   Save the file as `tangram.es` in the same folder as `tangram.svg`.

4.   Open `tangram.svg` in your browser.

5.   Click the Scramble button.

6.   Try to place the pieces back into the box.

How It Works

The application works by manipulating the in-memory DOM model of the SVG. Mouse behavior causes functions in the script to be called. Moving the mouse over a shape leads to a call to `mouseover(evt)`, which changes the color of a shape by setting the shape's `fill` attribute. If the shape in the `evt.target` is a `<polygon>` element, it is saved as the value of `selectedPoly`.

Clicking on a piece automatically makes a call to `mousedown`, which in turn calls `moveToFront(poly-gon)`, which moves the `<polygon>` element corresponding to that shape below the others in the DOM tree, causing it to be painted last, on top of the others. Clicking the mouse button down on the shape also sets the `track` variable to `true`, indicating that this puzzle piece can be moved.

When a shape is clicked and dragged, the `move(evt)` function adjusts the `translate` part of the `<polygon>` element's `transform` attribute according to the mouse movements. An event listener notices when a key has been pressed and automatically calls `rotatePolygon(polygon)`, which adds 22.5 degrees to the `rotate` angle in the currently selected `<polygon>` element's transform attribute.

A mouse click on the Scramble button leads to a call to the `scramble()` function, which randomizes the values in each `<polygon>` element's `transform` attribute. Clinking the Reset button leads to a call to the `reset()` function, which zeros all the `transform` values.

Further Applications

This tangram code shows how the scripting facilities of SVG enables you to give your applications custom interactivity. There wasn't adequate space to cover it here, but if you imagine an application like this delivered from a web server, it's relatively straightforward to use HTTP methods to pass information back to the server. Simple hyperlinking can enable other SVG documents to be loaded in response to user interactions. Relatively complex standalone applications can be built using SVG with scripting, and relatively rich custom clients for web applications can be created in the same way.

Useful Resources

Here are some other helpful SVG resources:

❑   SVG.org community news and feeds: `http://svg.org/`

❑   SVG wiki: `http://wiki.svg.org/`

❑   SVG specifications and news at W3C: `www.w3.org/Graphics/SVG/`

- ❑ SVG developers mailing list: `http://groups.yahoo.com/group/svg-developers/`
- ❑ Accessibility features of SVG: `www.w3.org/TR/SVG-access/`
- ❑ Apache Batik SVG Toolkit: `http://xml.apache.org/batik/`
- ❑ Croczilla SVG samples: `www.croczilla.com/svg/samples/`
- ❑ Adobe SVG Zone (there is also a mailing list): `www.adobe.com/svg/`

Summary

This chapter has demonstrated that SVG is an extremely versatile drawing format. In addition, thanks to XML and scripting support, SVG is highly programmable. The chapter overview provided grounding in what SVG is and what it is good for. The introductory code section showed how you can use basic shapes and other core features of SVG, as well as how SVG fits into the web environment.

The Tangram application demonstrated that it is relatively straightforward to build a visually appealing, interactive application for the Web. It was pointed out that SVG is a far bigger topic than one chapter can do justice to, but it is hoped that the overview of the SVG specification offered a general idea of the kind of features that are available.

Finally, if you've played with the code a little, it has undoubtedly occurred to you that SVG can be a great deal of fun!

Exercise Questions

Suggested solutions to these questions can be found in Appendix A.

Question 1

Figure 19-10 shows a picture of a stylized windmill. Write the SVG code needed to draw it. You can use the Hint if necessary, but you if you like a challenge, try the exercise before looking at the Hint. Squared paper can help in working out the coordinates, and don't forget that the y-axis starts with zero at the top.

Figure 19-10

Hint: *There are several different ways of doing this with SVG, but here the body of the windmill was constructed from a (yellow)* <polygon> *element with a (yellow)* <circle> *element half-overlapping on top. The four (blue) vanes are* <polygon> *elements with three points. The shape in the middle of the vanes is a (blue)* <rect> *element, with a transform to rotate it 45 degrees. At the bottom of the windmill is a (green)* <line> *element.*

Question 2

Get a tangram puzzle application to start with the pieces organized into the stylized cat pictured in Figure 19-11. Everything else should stay the same — clicking Reset should still place all the pieces into the square box.

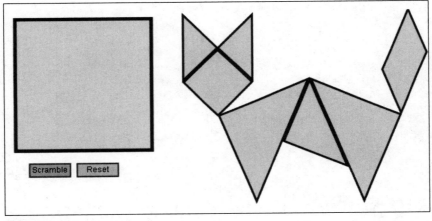

Figure 19-11

20

XForms

XForms is an XML-based forms technology specified by the World Wide Web Consortium (W3C). XForms' initial intent was to replace HTML forms, which are now at least a decade old. The power and flexibility of XForms goes well beyond this initial goal, and XForms is well suited to be used as a general-purpose tool for designing user interfaces for Web applications.

In several earlier chapters, you learned how to manipulate XML using technologies such as XPath, XSLT, XQuery, and the XML DOM, but you have yet to discover how to collect data to form part of an XML-based workflow. XForms is an important tool in the XML developer's toolbox, because XForms submits data from forms as well-formed XML documents.

Forms are an integral part of day-to-day business activity. Filling in paper forms or electronic forms is almost inescapable for anyone who is an information worker. As XML-based workflows become more prevalent in large enterprises and progressively trickle down into smaller businesses, the advantages of submitting XML data will become more widely appreciated.

XForms isn't the only XML-based forms tool, and although the main focus of this chapter is XForms, other proprietary solutions to XML-based forms are described briefly toward the end of the chapter.

This chapter covers the following:

❑   How XForms improves on existing HTML forms technology

❑   The state of the main XForms implementations

❑   How the XForms model is created, including a discussion and examples of using the `xforms:model`, `xforms:instance`, `xforms:submission`, and `xforms:bind` elements

❑   How the W3C XML Schema, XPath, and XML namespaces are used in XForms

❑   How to use XForms form controls

❑   Alternatives to XForms

How XForms Improves on HTML Forms

If you are going to work with XML on the server, the fact that XForms documents submit data as well-formed XML documents is a significant advantage. Thus, if you are using an XML-based workflow, the standard XML tools can be directly applied to the data being sent across the wire.

Another advantage is that XForms has a different way of associating form controls that are visible to the end-user with the underlying data that is collected. In HTML forms, a single HTML element defines the visual appearance of a form control, and accepts a value from the user. This inextricably ties together the form's appearance and the data collected, which becomes undesirable as the range of browser clients becomes wider. Defining a single data structure (which is to be submitted regardless of the type of client device) can have coding maintenance benefits. One has to be realistic about how far that principle can be taken. It is very easy to create forms for a desktop browser that would not be feasible to display on, say, a mobile phone because of its limited screen real estate.

XForms uses the W3C XML Schema for typing data. XForms processors can validate user-entered data and automatically identify invalid entries, often without any need for client-side scripting or a round-trip to the server. In addition, both client-side and server-side validation are possible using a single W3C XML Schema document, an approach that offers distinct advantages compared to, for example, validating data on the client side using JavaScript and on the server side with, say, Python or Perl. The client-side code and server-side code can both reference a single W3C XML Schema document, so the developer only has to make updates to the schema in a single place, avoiding the need for coding changes in two different languages to cope with evolving business needs.

XForms form controls incorporate labels, which increase accessibility. In addition, XForms form controls may include tooltips to improve usability by providing suggestions to help users understand what data is expected for each form control.

Assuming that these potential benefits are sufficient to tempt you into trying out XForms, read on to see what tools you need to get up and running.

XForms Tools

To create and test XForms documents effectively, you need two types of tools: one to create an XForms document, and an XForms viewer. Several XForms viewers are available, but much fewer XForms designers. Both types of tool are listed on the W3C XForms page at www.w3.org/MarkUp/Forms/#implementations. Note that the page is often not kept comprehensively updated, so it's prudent to follow links to check on the current status of the projects.

XForms viewers typically take one of the following forms:

❑ Native browser implementations (mainly Firefox)
❑ Browser plug-ins (typically for Internet Explorer)

❏ JavaScript implementations (still in progress)

❏ Client/server implementations

❏ As part of other applications

The lack of native XForms implementations in the major browsers is probably the main reason for the relatively slow adoption of this technology by web developers. The only major browser currently working on implementing XForms is Firefox. At the time of writing, this implementation, available as the XForms 0.7 extension, still lacks too many features to be used in real-world applications. It has made good progress but it can't run all the XForms examples in this chapter. Figure 20-1 shows a simple form displayed by Firefox using this implementation.

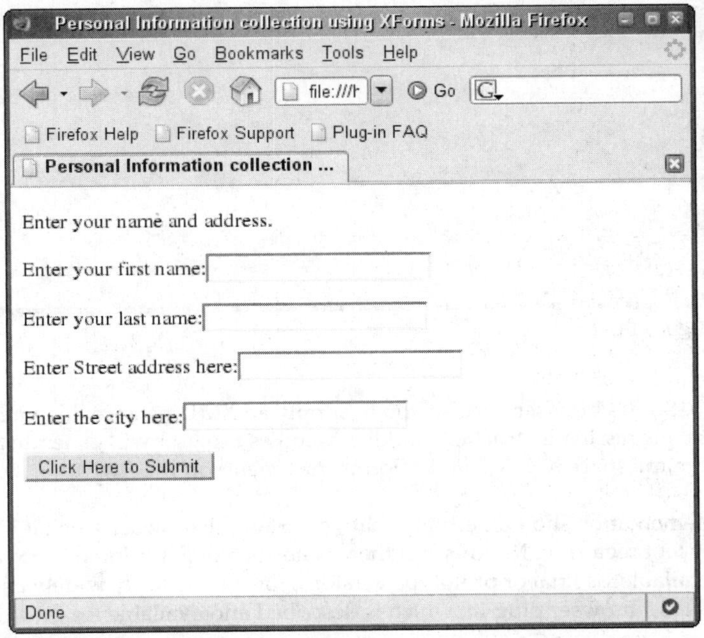

Figure 20-1

The X-Smiles browser (downloadable www.x-smiles.org) has been developed as a showcase for XML technologies on the Web. Supported XML formats include XForms, XSLT, XHTML, SVG, XSL-FO, and SMIL 2.0 Basic. Figure 20-2 shows the same form in X-Smiles.

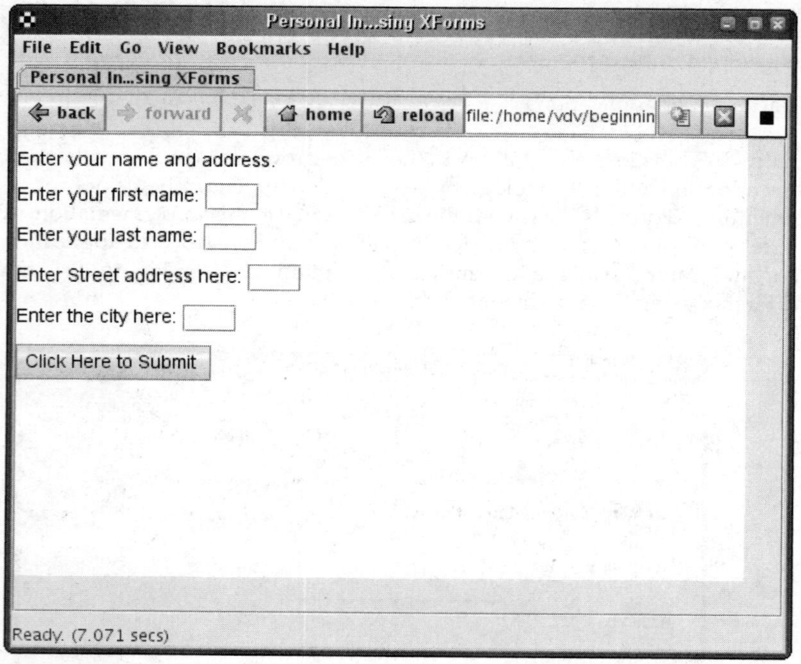

Figure 20-2

A feature of the X-Smiles browser enables you to supply an XML instance document, which includes an `xml-stylesheet` processing instruction, and the X-Smiles browser will generate the output format (for example, a multi-namespace XHTML and XForms document) on-the-fly.

The Firefox implementation should become a native part of the browser when it is stabilized. Microsoft is being quite reticent regarding XForms and there is no such plan for Internet Explorer. Several XForms processors are available, as final or prototype versions, for IE. The fairly widely used formsPlayer plug-in from x-port.net is a browser plug-in, which is described and available for download at a dedicated URL: `www.formsplayer.com/`.

An XForms document must have some way of signaling to IE that elements in the XForms namespace (`http://www.w3.org/2002/xforms`) are to be processed by an XForms processor. In the case of formsPlayer, this is achieved by embedding the following code in the head of an XHTML document:

```
<object id="FormsPlayer" classid="CLSID:4D0ABA11-C5F0-4478-991A-375C4B648F58"
width="0" height="0">
<b>FormsPlayer has failed to load! Please check your installation.</b>
  <br />
  <br />
</object>
<?import namespace="xforms" implementation="#FormsPlayer"?>
```

The `object` element enables the formsPlayer to be loaded. If loading fails, the markup content of the `object` element is displayed.

Notice the processing instruction (see Chapter 2 for more on processing instruction). The value of the `namespace` pseudo-attribute of the processing instruction must match the namespace prefix chosen in that document for the XForms namespace. In other words, to successfully use the `import` processing instruction as shown previously, you must have the following namespace declaration in scope:

```
xmlns:xforms="http://www.w3.org/2002/xforms
```

Typically, the namespace declaration is on the document element, as shown here in the `html` element for an XHTML document:

```
<html xmlns="http://www.w3.org/1999/xhtml"
  xmlns:xforms="http://www.w3.org/2002/xforms">
```

Used inside the XFormation Designer mentioned in the next section, the x-port.net formsPlayer is also used to display several of the examples in this chapter. Figure 20-3 shows a simple XForms document displayed in IE. The default behavior is to display an fP logo beside each XForms form control.

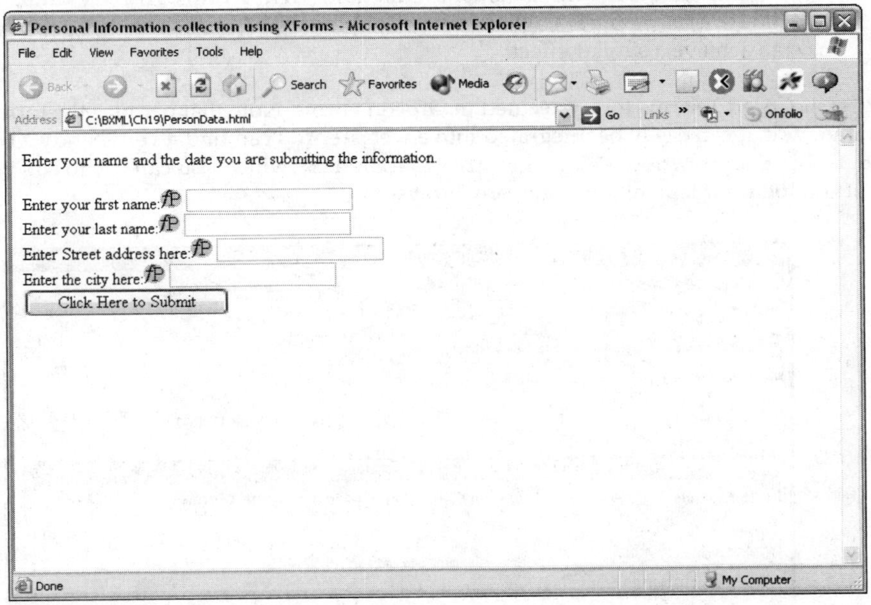

Figure 20-3

Both native and plug-in implementations depend on getting the right software installed on your user workstations; this is a very limiting factor for web applications. To work around this limitation, people have started developing implementations that enable you to use XForms with today's browsers. They fall into three different categories:

❑   Pure JavaScript implementations try to implement XForms with client-side JavaScript. XForms itself is a pretty complex piece of technology, and it relies on the W3C XML Schema, which is arguably still harder to implement. Although some of these projects have made good progress, their current versions are still not mature enough to be used in real-world implementations. They might represent good alternatives in the future, and if you want to try one, you can have a look at FormFaces (www.formfaces.com/).

❑ Pure server implementations have been developed as a temporary workaround to use XForms without needing browser support at all. They translate XForms into plain HTML forms and keep all the logic on the server side. Their main advantage is being relatively simple to implement, but their huge drawback is that each user's actions requires a full client/server interaction, which involves reloading the full HTML page. This makes them slow and not very responsive, so they tend to be replaced by client/server implementations.

❑ Client/server implementations can be seen as the next generation of pure server XForms implementations. XForms is translated into plain HTML forms, but user actions are trigger treatments that are spread between the client and the server using Ajax technologies. The most advanced of these implementations are so well integrated with Ajax that they can be seen as a unique way of modeling Web 2.0 applications with XForms. If you want to give one a try, take a look at Orbeon Forms (www.orbeon.com/forms/demos), which comes with a full XML web publishing framework to manipulate the XML documents edited through XForms. Also try Chiba (http://chiba.sourceforge.net/), which can be coupled with Cocoon (http://cocoon.apache.org/) to achieve a similar effect.

Figure 20-4 shows an XForms form executed in Orbeon Forms. Note that because the form is executed in a web framework, it can easily be integrated into a website. You can find a very handy XForms sandbox at www.orbeon.com/ops/goto-example/xforms-sandbox, which you can use to run your XForms documents on their implementation from any browser.

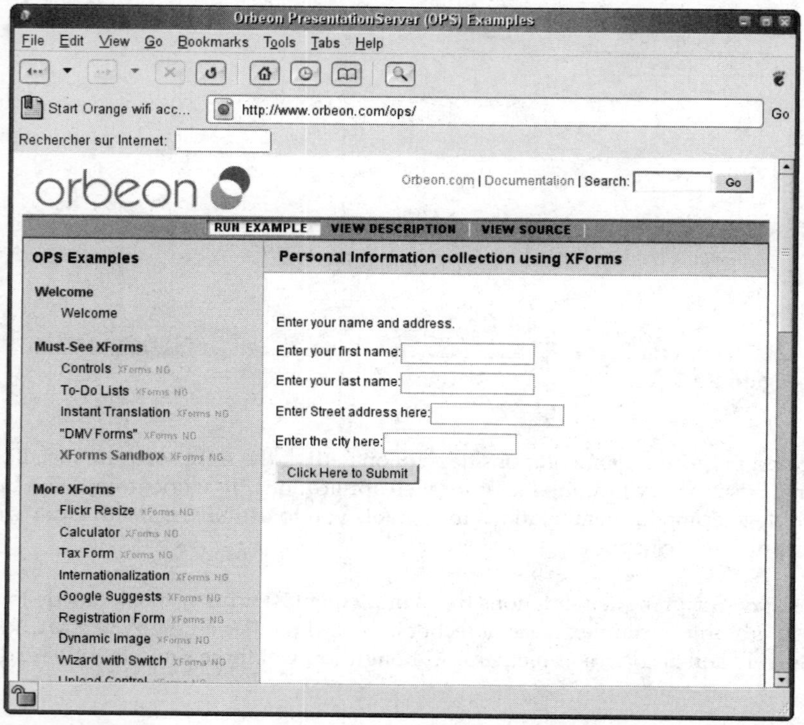

Figure 20-4

The last place where you can see XForms in action is within other applications. An interesting example is *Open Document Format (ODF)*, a standard XML vocabulary supported by OpenOffice, AbiWord, KWrite, and a number of other open-source tools, and Microsoft, has announced an import filter for Microsoft Office as well. ODF uses XForms to model its forms, and it includes both an XForms viewer and a user-friendly XForms, which is shown in Figure 20-5. Although OpenOffice makes no attempt to make these forms easy to import or export, it should be possible to do so using XSLT.

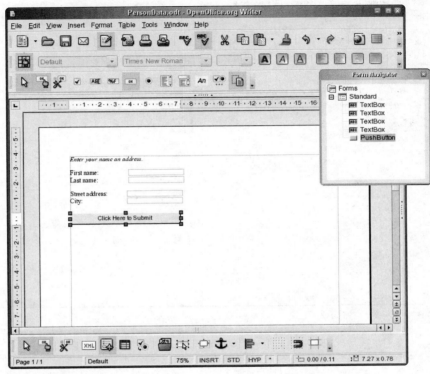

Figure 20-5

In addition to these XForms viewers, a few XForms designers are also available, such as AchieveForms (www.businesswebsoftware.com/Solutions/AchieveForms/) and XFormation (www.xformation.com). The goal of these tools is to provide user-friendly environments in which to edit and update XForms documents. Figure 20-6 shows a screenshot of XFormation during the design of an XForms document.

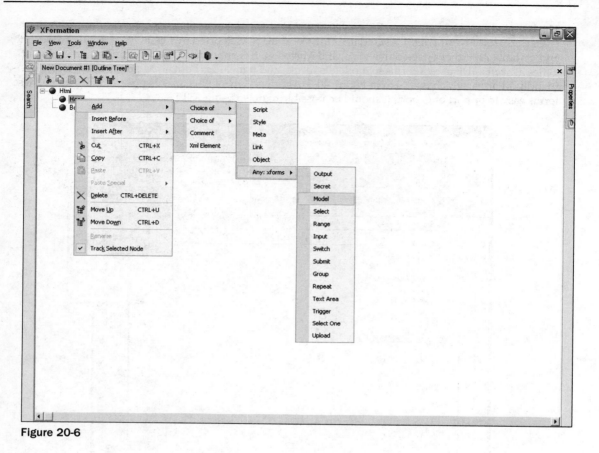

Figure 20-6

An Illustrative XForms Example

To create a working XForms document, several different parts need to be present and working together correctly. In order to focus on how XForms works, you will hand-code this example.

XForms documents are not intended to be free-standing. Instead, XForms markup is intended to be combined with markup in another XML namespace (for example, the XHTML namespace or SVG namespace, as appropriate) to produce XHTML or SVG documents that have XForms functionality.

> In all code in this chapter, the namespace prefix xforms is used when referring to elements in the XForms namespace (see www.w3.org/2002/xforms). In full code listings, an appropriate namespace declaration is provided. In code snippets, XForms elements are shown with the xforms namespace prefix, assuming that the corresponding namespace declaration is in scope for that element.

Try It Out   Creating an XForms Document

First, let's look at a simplified XForms document that demonstrates many of the fundamental techniques that you use regularly in XForms. In this example, the XForms markup is embedded inside an XHTML web page.

1. Create a file with the following XHTML and XForms code and save it as `PersonData.xhtml`:

```
<?xml version="1.0"?>

<html
 xmlns="http://www.w3.org/1999/xhtml"
 xmlns:xforms="http://www.w3.org/2002/xforms"
 xmlns:xmml="http://www.XMML.com/namespace" >
<head>
<title>Personal Information collection using XForms</title>
<xforms:model>
<xforms:instance  >
 <Person xmlns="http://www.XMML.com/namespace" >
  <FirstName></FirstName>
  <LastName></LastName>
  <Street></Street>
  <City></City>
 </Person>
</xforms:instance>
<xforms:submission id="PersonData" action="SavedPerson.xml" method="put" />
</xforms:model>
</head>
<body>
<p>Enter your name and address.</p>
<p>
 <xforms:input ref="xmml:FirstName">
  <xforms:label>Enter your first name:</xforms:label>
 </xforms:input>
</p>
<p>
 <xforms:input ref="xmml:LastName" >
  <xforms:label>Enter your last name:</xforms:label>
 </xforms:input>
</p>
<p>
 <xforms:input ref="xmml:Street" >
  <xforms:label>Enter Street address here:</xforms:label>
 </xforms:input>
</p>
<p>
 <xforms:input ref="xmml:City" >
  <xforms:label>Enter the city here:</xforms:label>
 </xforms:input>
</p>
<p>
 <xforms:submit submission="PersonData" replace="all" >
  <xforms:label>Click Here to Submit</xforms:label>
 </xforms:submit>
```

```
    </p>
  </body>
</html>
```

2. Open your browser and display the output from the file. The XHTML page produced by rendering this example in Firefox, X-Smiles, formsPlayer (after adding the object element and processing instruction mentioned in the section that introduced formsPlayer) and Orbeon Forms should resemble the screens in Figures 20-1, 20-2, 20-3, and 20-4, respectively. You will use this simple example to explore the fundamental building blocks of an XForms document.

How It Works

As with any XForms document, there are many aspects to how it works, as described in this section and the sections that follow. To begin, note the three namespace declarations in the start-tag of the `html` document element:

```
<html
xmlns="http://www.w3.org/1999/xhtml"
xmlns:xforms="http://www.w3.org/2002/xforms"
xmlns:xmml="http://www.XMML.com/namespace" >
```

The first namespace declaration signifies that elements in the XHTML namespace have no namespace prefix in this part of the document. Elements in the XForms namespace have the namespace prefix `xforms`, and elements in the XML document, which are submitted by the XForms processor, use the namespace prefix `xmml`, which is associated with a specified namespace Uniform Resource Identifier (URI). (Namespace issues are discussed in more detail later in this section.)

Apart from the page title, the main part of the content of the XHTML `head` element relates to the XForms model for the XForms document.

The XForms Model

Let's take a look at the XForms code contained in the `head` section of the XHTML document, which specifies the XForms model. After looking at the markup used in this example, you will also consider some other aspects of the `xforms:model` element:

```
<xforms:model >
 <xforms:instance >
  <Person xmlns="http://www.XMML.com/namespace" >
   <FirstName></FirstName>
   <LastName></LastName>
   <Street></Street>
   <City></City>
  </Person>
 </xforms:instance>
 <xforms:submission id="PersonData" action="SavedPerson.xml"  method="put" />
</xforms:model>
```

The XForms namespace is still in scope because the `xforms:model` element is a descendant of the XHTML `html` element where the XForms namespace was declared; therefore, no further namespace declaration is needed.

The xforms:model element has two child elements in this example: an xforms:instance element and an xforms:submission element. The other permitted child elements of xforms:model in the XForms namespace are xforms:bind and elements in the XForms Action module, each of which is discussed later in this chapter.

An xforms:model element may, optionally, have a functions attribute. The value of the functions attribute is a space-separated list of extension function names (which are QNames) needed by the XForms model. XForms uses the rather limited function library provided by XPath 1.0. Therefore, for example, for anything other than straightforward calculations, extension functions are likely needed, assuming that numeric processing is to be done client-side.

> *QNames (for Qualified Names) are the names with optional prefixes that are used by XML namespaces to identify elements and attributes such as* xforms:model, xforms:submission, *or* html. *Some XML vocabularies use such names in attributes or element contents, and the XML Schema* xs:QName *datatype was created to describe such values. Namespaces are described in Chapter 3, and the XML Schema is covered in Chapter 5.*

An XForms document may contain more than one xforms:model element. If, as in this initial example, there is only one xforms:model element, then there is no requirement that the xforms:model element have an id attribute. Any xforms:model element other than the default is identified by an id attribute. Some developers prefer that even the default xforms:model have an id attribute, often with a convenient value of default, to act as disambiguating identification. Some XForms processors or designers may also require that the default xforms:model element have an id attribute.

The xforms:instance Element

The xforms:instance element is a child element of the xforms:model element. The xforms:instance element is optional in any particular xforms:model element, but in cases where there is a single XForms model, it will include an xforms:instance element, as shown here:

```
<xforms:instance >
 <Person xmlns="http://www.XMML.com/namespace" >
  <FirstName></FirstName>
  <LastName></LastName>
  <Street></Street>
  <City></City>
 </Person>
</xforms:instance>
```

The preceding code shows one of the two permitted ways to define the initial structure of *instance data*, a term we return to in a moment. The other option is to have a src attribute on an empty xforms:instance element whose value is a URL from which a well-formed XML document can be retrieved:

```
<xforms:instance src="http://www.example.com/instancedata.xml" />
```

If retrieval of the XML document is unsuccessful, then an exception is raised.

The content of the xforms:instance element must itself be a well-formed XML document. If an XML document is accessed using a URL in the src attribute, then well-formedness is taken care of automatically, assuming retrieval is successful. If element content for the `xforms:instance` element is provided inline, then it is the developer's responsibility to ensure that the `xforms:instance` element has a single element child and satisfies the other well-formedness constraints.

Why the emphasis on the well-formedness of the descendant elements of `xforms:instance`? It is from these elements contained in the `xforms:instance` element that a separate XPath data model is constructed, which, as you will remember, can only be created from an XML document when it is well formed. The separate XPath data model is the *instance data* mentioned earlier.

It is this separate XPath data model to which XForms form controls are bound. If you change values in form controls and do a View Source on the XHTML page, you won't see the changes you made in the form controls reflected there. The changes in data are reflected in the separate XPath data model — the instance data.

The separate XPath data model for the instance data, of course, has its own root node. The `Person` element shown earlier is the document element for that separate copy. Suppose you wanted to bind a form control to the `FirstName` element. To access it, you could use the following XPath expression:

```
xmml:FirstName
```

If the meaning of that expression is unclear, refer to Chapter 7, "XPath." We return to the use of namespaces in XForms documents later in this section. Now that you know where the data from an XForms document is stored when the form is open, how do you specify what happens when you choose to submit the data?

The xforms:submission Element

An XForms document needs some way to specify how and where data is to be submitted. The `xforms:submission` element, an optional child element of the `xforms:model` element, specifies that information as follows:

```
<xforms:submission id="PersonData" action="SavedPerson.xml" method="put" />
```

The `action` attribute is required, and its value is a URI that specifies where the XForms instance data is to be sent after serialization. The previous example used the `file` protocol to save the data to a file on a hard disk. Of course, using the `file` protocol only works when you are running a form on a local file with a client implementation; it wouldn't work for a web application (including an Orbeon form) for obvious security reasons.

The `method` attribute is required, and its value is the method by which data is to be submitted. Permitted values include `post`, `get`, and `put`.

> Remember that XML is case sensitive. The values of the `method` attribute are always expressed entirely in lowercase characters.

The `xforms:submission` element must have an `id` attribute. The `id` attribute is used to bind an `xforms:submit` element (which you haven't learned about yet) in the visible part of the form to a particular `xforms:submission` element.

Following are several more attributes that can be used on the xforms:submission element:

❑ bind — An optional reference to an xforms:bind element

❑ cdata-section-elements — An optional attribute listing elements whose content is to be serialized using CDATA sections

❑ encoding — An optional attribute specifying the encoding of the serialized XML

❑ includenamespaceprefixes — An optional attribute that can be used to exclude (despite its name) some namespace prefixes from serialization by listing those which are to be serialized. The default is to serialize all.

❑ indent — An optional attribute indicating whether the serializer should add whitespace to the XML to aid readability

❑ mediatype — An optional attribute specifying the media type of the serialized XML

❑ omit-xml-declaration — An optional attribute indicating whether the XML declaration is to be omitted from the serialized XML

❑ ref — An optional binding expression to part of the instance data. This allows submission of only part of the instance data — the element node specified by the binding expression and all descendant elements. The default value for the ref attribute is /, indicating that all the instance data is to be submitted.

❑ replace — An optional attribute indicating how data returned after a submit is to be replaced

❑ standalone — An optional attribute specifying whether to include a standalone attribute in the XML declaration of the serialized XML

❑ version — An optional attribute that specifies the version of XML to be used when serializing the instance data prior to submission

The xforms:bind Element

The xforms:bind element is a child element of the xforms:model element but isn't used in the example. Using the xforms:bind element with *model item properties* is described later in this chapter.

XPath 1.0 in XForms

XForms form controls, such as xforms:input (described in detail later), must be associated with parts of the content of the xforms:instance element that is nested inside an xforms:model element. For simplicity in this initial description, it is assumed that the XForms document has a single xforms:model element that does not need an id attribute.

Somewhere inside the body of an XHTML document, you have an xforms:input element that has a ref attribute which might look like this:

```
<xforms:input ref="xmml:FirstName">
 <!- Content here. ->
</xforms:input>
```

If you are familiar with at least the basics of XPath, you will recognize that the value of the ref attribute on the xforms:input element is an XPath location path, assuming that the context node is the root element.

Which XML document is being referred to? The XPath data model created from the content of the `xforms:instance` element. Remember that the content of the `xforms:instance` element must be a well-formed XML document, as shown in the following:

```
<xforms:instance>
 <!- This content must have a single element which is a child
  of the xforms:instance element. In addition it must be well-formed on all
  other criteria. -->
</xforms:instance>
```

The XPath location path (the value of the `ref` attribute on the `xforms:input` element) looked like this:

```
xmml:FirstName
```

However, the content of the `xforms:instance` element showed the `FirstName` element:

```
<FirstName></FirstName>
```

To understand why this works, let's quickly review the use of XML namespaces in XForms documents.

XML Namespaces in XForms Documents

All XForms documents contain multiple namespaces. Typically, at least three namespaces are found in any one document: the XForms namespace itself, the namespace of the containing display format such as XHTML and SVG, and, very often, the namespace of the elements that make up the content of the `xforms:instance` element.

In this simple example, you had three namespace declarations on the document element, `html`:

```
<html
xmlns="http://www.w3.org/1999/xhtml" xmlns:xforms="http://www.w3.org/2002/xforms"
xmlns:xmml="http://www.XMML.com/namespace" >
```

Throughout the document, these namespace declarations apply except when there are other namespace declarations in descendant elements. The `Person` element, which is a child of the `xforms:instance` element, had the following namespace declaration:

```
<Person xmlns="http://www.XMML.com/namespace" >
```

Therefore, its child `FirstName` element is in the namespace `http://www.XMML.com/namespace` but is written simply as the following, because the namespace declaration on the `Person` element is in scope:

```
<FirstName></FirstName>
```

However, on the `xforms:input` element, which is in the body of the XHTML document, the namespace declaration in scope for that namespace is as follows:

```
xmlns:xmml="http://www.XMML.com/namespace"
```

Here, an element in the namespace `http://www.XMML.com/namespace` has the namespace prefix `xmml`. Therefore, to bind to a `FirstName` element in that namespace, you need to write the XPath expression like this:

```
<xforms:input ref="xmml:FirstName" >
```

That location path references the `FirstName` element in the instance data because both the location path and the element node in the instance data are associated with the namespace `http://www.XMML.com/namespace`.

> **The use of XML namespaces in XForms can seem quite confusing at first, but it is important to get a handle on this, because any errors in the handling of namespaces mean your XForms document won't work correctly (for example, data entered in a form control won't be captured in the corresponding part of the instance data) and, in all likelihood, the data will not be submitted.**

Having seen how the XForms `xforms:input` form control can be bound to instance data, let's take a closer look at the range of XForms form controls that are available in XForms 1.0.

XForms Form Controls

In principle, the XForms data model will work with a range of user interface technologies. As long as individual form controls can be bound to appropriate parts of the instance data, the data supplied by the end-user can be added to the instance data. In addition, as long as there is a binding from a submit form control to the `xforms:submission` element in the XForms model, the XML data can be submitted to an appropriate URL endpoint.

In practice, at the time of writing, the XForms form controls are the dominant set of form controls used with an XForms data model, although other sets of form controls may appear in time. This section briefly describes the XForms form controls and their characteristics.

The xforms:input Element

Specifying a textbox into which users can enter arbitrary text, the `xforms:input` element is bound to a node in the instance data using one of two techniques. First, as shown in the earlier example, a `ref` attribute can contain an XPath 1.0 location path, which specifies a node in the instance data. The alternative technique for binding is to use a `bind` attribute whose value is of type `xs:IDREF` and references an `xforms:bind` element. When only one XForms model is present in the document, it isn't necessary to specify the model to which the `ref` attribute is pointing. However, when there is more than one XForms model, the `model` attribute of the `xforms:input` element can be used to disambiguate the situation.

The `xforms:input` element, in common with many other XForms form controls, can optionally have an `appearance` attribute. An XForms processor must support the values `full`, `compact`, and `minimal`, but it may support other QNames, too.

An optional `navindex` attribute, whose value is an integer, can be used to specify the sequence in which form controls are navigated. Also option is the `accesskey` attribute, which defines a keyboard shortcut to access a particular form control.

The `incremental` attribute has `xs:boolean` value. The default value is `false`. When the value of the `incremental` attribute is set to `true`, then a change in the value contained in an `xforms:input` element causes the `xforms-value-changed` event to fire. This in turn enables the XForms developer to create an event handler that can provide additional functionality or information to the user, as appropriate to the situation.

If Cascading Style Sheets (CSS) styling is being used in an XForms document, then the `xforms:input` element will likely also have a `class` attribute.

The following elements are allowed in the content of the `xforms:input` element: `xforms:label`, `xforms:help`, `xforms:hint`, and `xforms:alert`. In addition, an element from the XForms Action Module (which is described later) is allowed.

You have already seen several examples of `xforms:input`:

```
<xforms:input ref="xmml:FirstName">
 <xforms:label>Enter your first name:</xforms:label>
</xforms:input>
```

The xforms:secret Element

The `xforms:secret` element has the same set of attributes and permitted element content as the `xforms:input` form control. The `xforms:secret` element is intended for use in entering passwords, and the character values entered by a user are echoed to the screen as some nonmeaningful characters. An example of `xforms:secret` would be as follows:

```
<xforms:secret ref="xmml:Password">
 <xforms:label>Enter your password:</xforms:label>
</xforms:secret>
```

The xforms:textarea Element

The `xforms:textarea` element has the same set of attributes and the same permitted element content as the `xforms:input` element. The `xforms:textarea` element allows multiline entry of character data. An example of `xforms:textarea` is as follows:

```
<xforms:textarea ref="xmml:Comments">
 <xforms:label>Enter comments here:</xforms:label>
</xforms:textarea>
```

The xforms:output Element

The `xforms:output` element differs in function from the XForms controls you have learned so far because it does not directly accept user input. It can be used, for example, to display a date value (perhaps the current date) to ensure that a correct date is submitted with a form. Another use is to display a calculated value—for example, the total cost of a number of items in an online purchase.

The xforms:output element may have a ref or bind attribute, but neither is required because the value need not be stored in the instance data. The xforms:output element has an appearance attribute with permitted values as described previously, but it doesn't have a navindex or accesskey attribute because data cannot be entered into an xforms:output form control.

The xforms:output element may have a value attribute whose value is an XPath 1.0 expression. This allows display in read-only mode of a specified part of the instance data, if the xforms:output is displaying part of the instance data: While the href attribute must refer to an actual node from an instance, the value attribute refers to the result of an XPath function or expression.

An xforms:output element may have an optional child xforms:label element, which is displayed before the output value, but no other child element content is allowed. An example of xforms:output is as follows:

```
<xforms:output model="myToppings" value="count(xmml:ToppingAvailable)" />
```

The xforms:upload Element

Often used to upload a file selected from the file system of the user's machine to a specified URL, the xforms:upload element uses either a ref attribute or a bind attribute to bind to an appropriate part of the instance data. The appearance, navindex, and accesskey attributes may be used as previously described.

The xforms:upload element may have the xforms:label, xforms:help, xforms:hint, and xforms:alert elements as child elements, as well as an element from the XForms Action Module. In addition, the xforms:upload element may optionally have xforms:filename and xforms:mediatype elements whose purpose is, respectively, to specify the filename for the uploaded file and its media type. An example of xforms:upload is as follows:

```
<xforms:upload ref="file">
  <xforms:label>Choose a file to upload:</xforms:label>
  <xforms:filename ref="@filename"/>
  <xforms:mediatype ref="@mediatype"/>
</xforms:upload>
```

The xforms:range Element

The XForms form control elements described so far are likely to remind you of HTML forms. The xforms:range element has no counterpart in HTML. The purpose of the xforms:range element is to specify, in a way visible to the user, a permitted range of values for the characteristic represented by the form control. It might be used to specify a minimum and maximum number of a particular item to be purchased, for example, when an item is in limited supply and a ceiling on purchases needs to be imposed. Another use is to specify an allowed range of numeric values when responding to a survey.

The xforms:range element may have a bind or ref attribute to specify the component of the instance data to which it is bound. It may also have appearance, navindex, and accesskey attributes.

The allowed values displayed by the xforms:range form control are specified by its start and end attributes. The intermediate values to be displayed are specified using the step and incremental attributes. These attributes must use numeric or date types.

The permitted content of the xforms:range form control are the xforms:label, xforms:hint, xforms:help, and xforms:alert elements as well as an element from the XForms Action Module. An example of xforms:upload is as follows:

```
<xforms:range ref="/config/speed" start="0" end="1" step=".1">
  <xforms:label>Speed:</xforms:label>
</xforms:range>
```

The xforms:trigger Element

The xforms:trigger element is broadly equivalent to the button element in HTML forms. The xforms:trigger element can be used to respond to user actions.

The xforms:trigger element may have a bind or ref attribute to specify the component of the instance data to which it is bound, but it does not need to be bound to any component of the instance data. It may also have appearance, navindex, and accesskey attributes.

The permitted content of the xforms:trigger form control are the xforms:label, xforms:hint, xforms:help, and xforms:alert elements as well as an element from the XForms Action Module. An example of xforms:trigger is as follows:

```
<xforms:trigger>
  <xforms:label>Say hello</xforms:label>
</xforms:trigger>
```

The xforms:submit Element

Used to submit instance data, the xforms:submit element has a mandatory submission attribute whose value is an IDREF to an xforms:submission element in an XForms model somewhere in the same document. Therefore, assuming the id attribute of the corresponding xforms:submission element has the value submitsurvey, you can write an xforms:submit element like this:

```
<xforms:submit submission="submitsurvey">
  <xforms:label>Click Here to Submit the Survey</xforms:label>
</xforms:submit>
```

The submission process depends on the xforms-submit event being raised on the xforms:submit element and being dispatched to the corresponding xforms:submission element.

A binding attribute, ref or bind, is not required because the xforms:submit element is not bound directly to instance data. However, the xforms:submit element may be affected by the model item properties (discussed later in this chapter) of a component of the instance data.

The xforms:submit element may have appearance, navindex, and accesskey attributes whose permitted values have been described previously.

The permitted content of the xforms:submit form control are the xforms:label, xforms:hint, xforms:help, and xforms:alert elements as well as an element from the XForms Action Module.

The xforms:select Element

The xforms:select element allows the user to make one or more selections from a set of options. The rough equivalent in an HTML form would be checkboxes that allow multiple choices to be made. To make a choice limited to a single option, the xforms:select1 element (described in the following section) is used. The xforms:select attribute is bound to a node in the instance data using either a ref attribute or a bind attribute.

The selection attribute of the xforms:select element defines whether values other than those supplied are permitted. The default value of the selection attribute is closed. To allow users to add additional values to the options available, the value of the selection attribute must be open.

The permitted content of the xforms:select element includes the following elements: xforms:label, xforms:choice, xforms:item, xforms:itemset, and an element from the XForms Action Module. For example, to allow a selection to be made among options for pizza toppings, the xforms:select element may be used like this:

```
<xforms:select ref="xmml:Toppings" >
 <xforms:label>Select the toppings for your pizza. You may select up to two
toppings.</xforms:label>
 <xforms:item>
  <xforms:label>Chocolate</xforms:label>
  <xforms:value>Choc</xforms:value>
 </xforms:item>
 <xforms:item>
  <xforms:label>Pepperoni</xforms:label>
  <xforms:value>Pepp</xforms:value>
 </xforms:item>
 <xforms:item>
  <xforms:label>Ham and Pineapple</xforms:label>
  <xforms:value>HamnPin</xforms:value>
 </xforms:item>
 <xforms:item>
  <xforms:label>Chilli Beef</xforms:label>
  <xforms:value>Chil</xforms:value>
 </xforms:item>
</xforms:select>
```

Because no value was expressed for the selection attribute in the previous code, users cannot add additional options to those offered by the developer.

> **Be careful when specifying values for the** xforms:value **element. The selections made are stored as a whitespace-separated list, so if the value for the Ham and Pineapple choice had been** Ham and Pineapple **in the** xforms:value **element, then this would be interpreted as a list of three options:** Ham, **and,** and Pineapple, **which is almost certainly not what you or the user intended.**

You can control the visual appearance of an `xforms:select` element using the `appearance` attribute. Navigation to an `xforms:select` element may be specified using the `navindex` attribute. Direct access to an `xforms:select` element can be provided using the `accesskey` attribute.

The `incremental` attribute of the `xforms:select` element defines whether `xforms-value-changed` events are raised after each value is selected. The default value of the `incremental` attribute is `true`.

As well as providing items for possible selection literally, as in the preceding code example, it is also possible to provide values for the `xforms:select` element by referencing the content of an `xforms:instance` element, whose content is not, typically, intended for submission. An example of this is shown in the `xforms:select1` section that follows.

The xforms:select1 Element

The `xforms:select1` element is intended to allow a single choice from a range of options. In HTML, forms would normally be created using a set of radio buttons. The `xforms:select1` element is bound to a node in the instance data using the `ref` or `bind` attribute. It has optional `appearance`, `navigationindex`, and `accesskey` attributes.

Like the `xforms:select` element, the `xforms:select1` element has optional `selection` and `incremental` attributes. The `selection` attribute specifies whether additional options, other than those provided by the form author, are allowed. The possible values are `open` and `closed`. The default value is `closed`. The `incremental` attribute specifies whether an `xforms-value-changed` event is raised each time the choice changes. The default value of the `incremental` attribute is `true`.

Try It Out   Using the xforms:select and xforms:select1 Elements

Let's take a look at how the selection elements can be used. The following example uses both the `xforms:select` and `xforms:select1` elements:

1.   Create the following XForms document and save it as `PizzaOrder.xhtml`:

```
<?xml version="1.0"?>

<html
 xmlns="http://www.w3.org/1999/xhtml"
 xmlns:xforms="http://www.w3.org/2002/xforms"
 xmlns:xmml="http://www.XMML.com/namespace" >
<head>
 <title>Using a schema and the &lt;xforms:itemset&gt; element.</title>

  <xforms:model id="default" schema="PizzaOrder.xsd">
     <xforms:instance >
   <xmml:Pizza >
    <xmml:Size>L</xmml:Size>
    <xmml:Toppings>Pepp</xmml:Toppings>
   </xmml:Pizza>
   </xforms:instance>
  <xforms:submission id="mySubmit" action="PizzaOrder.xml" method="put" />
 </xforms:model>

 <xforms:model id="myToppings">
```

```
   <xforms:instance id="myToppingsInstance">
    <xmml:ToppingsAvailable >
     <xmml:ToppingAvailable type="Choc">
      <xmml:Description>Chocolate</xmml:Description>
     </xmml:ToppingAvailable>
     <xmml:ToppingAvailable type="Pepp">
      <xmml:Description>Pepperoni</xmml:Description>
     </xmml:ToppingAvailable>
     <xmml:ToppingAvailable type="HamnPin">
      <xmml:Description>Ham and Pineapple</xmml:Description>
     </xmml:ToppingAvailable>
     <xmml:ToppingAvailable type="Chil">
      <xmml:Description>Chilli Beef</xmml:Description>
     </xmml:ToppingAvailable>
    </xmml:ToppingsAvailable>
   </xforms:instance>
  </xforms:model>

  <xforms:model id="mySizes">
   <xforms:instance>
    <xmml:SizesAvailable >
     <xmml:SizeAvailable type="S">
      <xmml:Description>Small</xmml:Description>
     </xmml:SizeAvailable>
     <xmml:SizeAvailable type="M">
      <xmml:Description>Medium</xmml:Description>
     </xmml:SizeAvailable>
     <xmml:SizeAvailable type="L">
      <xmml:Description>Large</xmml:Description>
     </xmml:SizeAvailable>
    </xmml:SizesAvailable>
   </xforms:instance>
  </xforms:model>

</head>
<body>
<p>Choose the size and toppings for your pizza.</p>
<p>
 <xforms:select1 model="default" ref="xmml:Size" >
  <xforms:label>Sizes offered.</xforms:label>
  <xforms:itemset model="mySizes" nodeset="xmml:SizeAvailable" >
   <xforms:label ref="xmml:Description" />
   <xforms:value ref="@type" />
  </xforms:itemset>
 </xforms:select1>
</p>
<p>Choose your toppings here. You may choose up to two toppings.</p>
<p>
 <xforms:select model="default" ref="xmml:Toppings" >
   <xforms:label>There are
     <xforms:output model="myToppings" value="count(xmml:ToppingAvailable)" />
     toppings to choose from.</xforms:label>
  <xforms:itemset model="myToppings" nodeset="xmml:ToppingAvailable" >
   <xforms:label ref="xmml:Description" />
   <xforms:value ref="@type" />
```

```
    </xforms:itemset>
   </xforms:select>
  </p>
  <p>
   <xforms:submit submission="mySubmit">
    <xforms:label>Click Here to submit your Order.</xforms:label>
   </xforms:submit>
  </p>
 </body>
</html>
```

2. Open this document in your favorite XForms processor.

How It Works.

This XForms document has three XForms models in it. The purpose of the first, the default, is to contain the instance data intended for submission by the user:

```
<xforms:model id="default" schema="PizzaOrder.xsd">
 <xforms:instance >
  <xmml:Pizza >
   <xmml:Size>L</xmml:Size>
   <xmml:Toppings>Pepp</xmml:Toppings>
  </xmml:Pizza>
 </xforms:instance>
 <xforms:submission id="mySubmit" action="PizzaOrder.xml" method="put" />
</xforms:model>
```

The document to be submitted is straightforward, having an xmml:Pizza element as its document element, and two child elements, xmml:Size and xmml:Toppings.

The xforms:submission element specifies that you will use the put method to save the instance data to an XML file at the relative URL PizzaOrder.xml. This is similar to what you've already seen but there are some differences:

❑ The schema PizzaOrder.xsd is attached to the model using a schema attribute. When specified, this W3C XML Schema document defines the permitted structure of the XML content of the xforms:instance element. When specified in the schema document, datatypes provide a hint to the XForms processor about how a particular component of the instance should be rendered. For example, the occurrence of an xs:date datatype typically results in a date form control being used. These datatypes are also used to validate the data entered by the user, and any submission is forbidden if the instance isn't valid per the schema.

❑ Instead of redefining the default namespace as shown in the previous example, a prefix is used to identify the namespace used by the instance. This prefix (xmml) is defined once in the root html element and can be used anywhere in the document.

❑ While the element values were empty in the first example, values are provided in this example: xmml:Size is set to L so that customers order a large pizza by default and xmml:Toppings is set to Pepp. Of course, users can select other values, but those are used as default values.

The next XForms model is shown in the following:

```
<xforms:model id="myToppings">
  <xforms:instance id="myToppingsInstance">
  <xmml:ToppingsAvailable >
   <xmml:ToppingAvailable type="Choc">
    <xmml:Description>Chocolate</xmml:Description>
   </xmml:ToppingAvailable>
   <xmml:ToppingAvailable type="Pepp">
    <xmml:Description>Pepperoni</xmml:Description>
   </xmml:ToppingAvailable>
   <xmml:ToppingAvailable type="HamnPin">
    <xmml:Description>Ham and Pineapple</xmml:Description>
   </xmml:ToppingAvailable>
   <xmml:ToppingAvailable type="Chil">
    <xmml:Description>Chilli Beef</xmml:Description>
   </xmml:ToppingAvailable>
  </xmml:ToppingsAvailable>
 </xforms:instance>
</xforms:model>
```

This model must have an `id` attribute because it is not the default XForms model. Later you will see how the value of that `id` attribute is used to retrieve the data contained inside it.

The `xforms:instance` element has as its content a well-formed XML document that provides basic information about a range of pizza toppings, which may or may not be to your taste. Here you have specified content literally. In a working environment it might be more appropriate to reference a separate XML file, using a `src` attribute on the `xforms:instance` element. By using that technique, available toppings for a range of XForms forms could then be modified when necessary in one place. Still more powerful, this `src` attribute can reference a RESTful web service, such as you've seen in Chapter 14, or even a query to an XML database using a REST interface as shown in Chapter 10. This could allow, for example, displaying only the toppings that the restaurant has in stock. The data in this XForms data model will be used to populate an `xforms:select` element.

The third XForms data model in the document (shown in the following code) is used to provide information about the range of pizza sizes available:

```
<xforms:model id="mySizes">
 <xforms:instance>
  <xmml:SizesAvailable >
   <xmml:SizeAvailable type="S">
    <xmml:Description>Small</xmml:Description>
   </xmml:SizeAvailable>
   <xmml:SizeAvailable type="M">
    <xmml:Description>Medium</xmml:Description>
   </xmml:SizeAvailable>
   <xmml:SizeAvailable type="L">
    <xmml:Description>Large</xmml:Description>
   </xmml:SizeAvailable>
  </xmml:SizesAvailable>
 </xforms:instance>
</xforms:model>
```

The instance data in the XPath model produced from the content of the xforms:instance element will be used to populate an xforms:select1 element. Here is the xforms:select1 element populated from the mySizes XForms model:

```
<xforms:select1 model="default" ref="xmml:Size" >
 <xforms:label>Sizes offered.</xforms:label>
 <xforms:itemset model="mySizes" nodeset="xmml:SizeAvailable" >
  <xforms:label ref="xmml:Description" />
  <xforms:value ref="@type" />
 </xforms:itemset>
</xforms:select1>
```

Notice on the xforms:select1 element that there is a model attribute, and its value is default, not mySizes, as you might have expected. The value of the model attribute refers to the XForms model in which the data is updated. That instance data is derived from the default XForms model. The value of the ref attribute references the node in the instance data to which the value of the xforms:select1 element is bound.

The content of the xforms:label element simply provides a label for the xforms:select1 element, as shown in Figure 20-7.

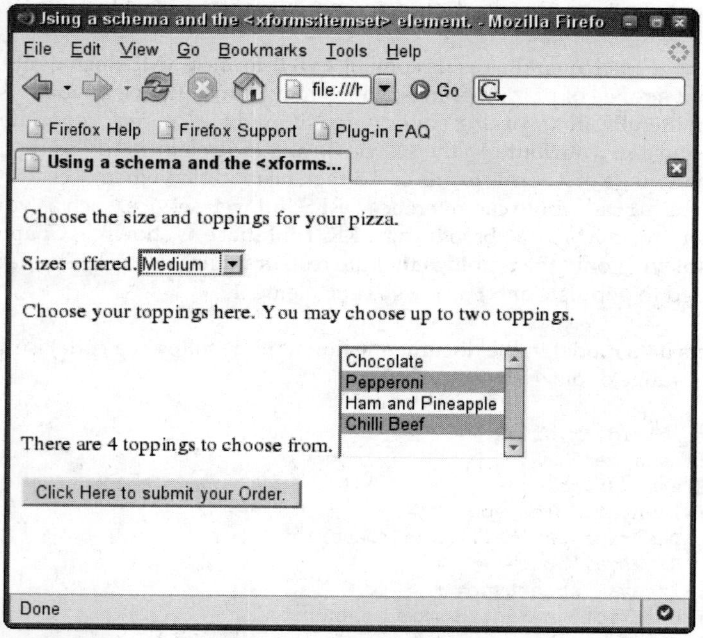

Figure 20-7

The other content of the xforms:select1 element is an xforms:itemset element:

```
<xforms:itemset model="mySizes" nodeset="xmml:SizeAvailable" >
 <xforms:label ref="xmml:Description" />
```

```
    <xforms:value ref="@type" />
  </xforms:itemset>
```

Notice that the `model` attribute of the `xforms:itemset` element references the `mySizes` XForms model. It is in that context that the value of the `nodeset` attribute is interpreted. The location path `xmml:SizeAvailable` in the `nodeset` attribute selects the three `xmml:SizeAvailable` elements in that XForms model.

The label to be displayed in the `xforms:select1` form control is defined using another XPath location path in the value of the `ref` attribute of the `xforms:label` element. Here, `xmml:Description` is used as the label. Finally, the value associated with the label is defined using a third XPath expression. In the example, that value is the `@type` attribute, which appears in the instance that is updated when the corresponding choice is selected, which in this case is the default instance.

The toppings for the chosen size of pizza are specified using the `xforms:select` element, and its content is shown here:

```
<xforms:select model="default" ref="xmml:Toppings" >
  <xforms:label>There are
    <xforms:output model="myToppings" value="count(xmml:ToppingAvailable)" />
    toppings to choose from.</xforms:label>
 <xforms:itemset model="myToppings" nodeset="xmml:ToppingAvailable" >
  <xforms:label ref="xmml:Description" />
  <xforms:value ref="@type" />
 </xforms:itemset>
</xforms:select>
```

Notice that on the `xforms:select` element the value of the model attribute is a reference to the `default` XForms model because it is that XForms model which specifies the instance data. The value of the `ref` attribute references the `xmml:Toppings` node.

Also notice how an `XForms:output` control is used in the `xforms:label` to display the number of `xmml:ToppingAvailable` elements, which determines the number of possible options. In this example, the available toppings are embedded in the model and the number of options could have been hard-coded, but remember that this XML instance could be the result of a call to a RESTful web service, in which case the number of options couldn't have been hard-coded.

The `xforms:itemset` element is used similarly to the provision of the sizes of pizza shown earlier. The value of the `model` attribute references the `myToppings` XForms model, so the location path specified in the value of the `nodeset` attribute is interpreted in that context.

The `xforms:label` and `xforms:value` elements are used, respectively, to specify the options to be displayed and the value to be submitted. Clicking the `xforms:submit` form control, because it is bound to the `mySubmit` `xforms:submission` element, causes the instance data, after serialization, to be saved to the file `PizzaOrder.xml`. The saved document from one use of the form is shown here:

```
<?xml version="1.0" encoding="UTF-8"?>
<xmml:Pizza xmlns="http://www.w3.org/1999/xhtml"
xmlns:xforms="http://www.w3.org/2002/xforms"
  xmlns:xmml="http://www.XMML.com/namespace">
  <xmml:Size>S</xmml:Size>
  <xmml:Toppings>Choc Chil</xmml:Toppings>
</xmml:Pizza>
```

Note how the value of the xmml:Toppings element is a whitespace-separated list of tokens. The two tokens specified here are Choc, which is the value attached to "Chocolate," and Chil, for "Chili Beef." Whether ordering a chili beef and chocolate pizza is a good idea is left to you to decide, but if you want to exclude such unexpected pairings, then you can do that by adding the following xforms:bind element to the default model:

```
<xforms:bind nodeset="xmml:Toppings"
         constraint="not(contains(., 'Choc') and contains(., 'Chil'))"/>
```

The constraint attribute enables you to define any constraint as an XPath expression and provides a very flexible way to define validation tests. This xforms:bind is one of the ways to define constraints on instance data. Now let's look deeper into how these constraints can be specified.

Constraining XForms Instances

XForms instances can be constrained using so called *XForms model item properties* that enable you to do things such as make a form control read-only or specify that its value is a calculated value. At the heart of how XForms model item properties work is the xforms:bind element.

The xforms:bind Element

The xforms:bind element is a child element of the xforms:model element. Depending on how many form controls you want to specify model item properties for, there can be multiple xforms:bind elements in any xforms:model element's content.

The nodeset attribute of the xforms:bind element specifies a node-set in the instance data for which an XForms model item property is to be specified.

A model item property is specified using an attribute, identically named to the property, on an xforms:bind element. For example, to specify that a Name is required, you would write something like the following (depending on the path to the node of interest in the instance data):

```
<xforms:bind required="true()" nodeset="/somePath/Name" />
```

More than one property can be specified on a single xforms:bind element.

The XForms model items properties are as follows:

- ❑ calculate – Specifies a calculation to be performed to provide a value for the component of the instance data

- ❑ constraint – Specifies a constraint on the value of the component of the data source, as shown for selecting pizza toppings

- ❑ p3ptype – Specifies a Platform for Privacy Preferences element to be associated with the component of the instance data

- ❑ readonly – Specifies whether a component of the instance data is read-only. Allowed values for the corresponding readonly attribute are true and false (the default).

❑ relevant—Specifies whether a component of the instance data is relevant in particular circumstances. For example, if an employee's gender is male, then maternity leave is unlikely to be relevant.

❑ required—Signifies whether a value is required for the bound component of the instance data

❑ type—Allows a W3C XML Schema datatype to be specified for a component of the instance data, in the absence of a W3C XML Schema document.

Try It Out Using Model Item Properties

This example uses several of the model item properties just covered. Here, you create a form that a company's human resources department might use to track maternity leave for its employees:

1. Type this XForms sample into a document named ModelItemPropertiesExample.xhtml:

```
<?xml version="1.0"?>
<html
 xmlns="http://www.w3.org/1999/xhtml"
 xmlns:xforms="http://www.w3.org/2002/xforms"
 xmlns:xmml="http://www.XMML.com/namespace"
 xmlns:xs="http://www.w3.org/2001/XMLSchema" >
<head>
 <title>Example using Model Item Properties.</title>

 <xforms:model id="default">
  <xforms:instance >
   <xmml:Employee >
    <xmml:Identity>
     <xmml:FirstName></xmml:FirstName>
     <xmml:LastName></xmml:LastName>
     <xmml:Gender></xmml:Gender>
    </xmml:Identity>
    <xmml:Employment>
     <xmml:StartDate></xmml:StartDate>
     <xmml:EndDate></xmml:EndDate>
     <xmml:MaternityLeave></xmml:MaternityLeave>
    </xmml:Employment>
    <xmml:Comments></xmml:Comments>
   </xmml:Employee>
  </xforms:instance>
  <xforms:submission id="mySubmit" action="EmployeeData.xml" method="put" />
  <xforms:bind nodeset="xmml:Identity/xmml:FirstName" required="true()" />
  <xforms:bind nodeset="xmml:Identity/xmml:LastName" required="true()" />
  <xforms:bind nodeset="xmml:Employment/xmml:StartDate" required="true()"
type="xs:date" />
  <xforms:bind nodeset="xmml:Employment/xmml:EndDate" type="xs:date"
required="false()"
                       constraint=". = '' or . >= ../xmml:StartDate"/>
  <xforms:bind nodeset="xmml:Employment/xmml:MaternityLeave"
              relevant="/xmml:Employee/xmml:Identity/xmml:Gender = 'Female'" />
 </xforms:model>

 <xforms:model id="myEmployeeInfo">
```

```
   <xforms:instance>
    <xmml:EmployeeChoices>
     <xmml:GenderChoices>
      <xmml:GenderChoice>Male</xmml:GenderChoice>
      <xmml:GenderChoice>Female</xmml:GenderChoice>
     </xmml:GenderChoices>
      <xmml:MaternityChoices >
      <xmml:MaternityChoice>Yes</xmml:MaternityChoice>
      <xmml:MaternityChoice>No</xmml:MaternityChoice>
     </xmml:MaternityChoices>
    </xmml:EmployeeChoices>
   </xforms:instance>
  </xforms:model>

</head>
<body>
<p>Enter employee information here.</p>
<p>
 <xforms:input model="default" ref="xmml:Identity/xmml:FirstName" >
  <xforms:label>First Name:</xforms:label>
</xforms:input>
</p>
 <p>
 <xforms:input model="default" ref="xmml:Identity/xmml:LastName" >
  <xforms:label>Last Name: </xforms:label>
 </xforms:input>
 </p>
<p>
 <xforms:select1 model="default" ref="xmml:Identity/xmml:Gender" >
  <xforms:label>Enter the employee's gender: </xforms:label>
  <xforms:itemset model="myEmployeeInfo"
          nodeset="xmml:GenderChoices/xmml:GenderChoice" >
   <xforms:label ref="." />
   <xforms:value ref="." />
  </xforms:itemset>
 </xforms:select1>
</p>
<p>Enter start and end dates of employment.</p>
<p>
 <xforms:input ref="xmml:Employment/xmml:StartDate">
  <xforms:label>Start Date:</xforms:label>
 </xforms:input>
</p>
<p>
 <xforms:input ref="xmml:Employment/xmml:EndDate">
  <xforms:label>End Date:   </xforms:label>
 </xforms:input>
</p>
<p>
 <xforms:select1 model="default" ref="xmml:Employment/xmml:MaternityLeave">
  <xforms:label>Has the employee had maternity leave?</xforms:label>
  <xforms:itemset model="myEmployeeInfo"
          nodeset="xmml:MaternityChoices/xmml:MaternityChoice" >
   <xforms:label ref="." />
   <xforms:value ref="." />
```

```
    </xforms:itemset>
  </xforms:select1>
</p>
<p>
 <xforms:textarea ref="xmml:Comments">
   <xforms:label>Enter comments here:</xforms:label>
 </xforms:textarea>
</p>
<p>
 <xforms:submit submission="mySubmit">
   <xforms:label>Click Here to submit your changes.</xforms:label>
 </xforms:submit>
</p>
</body>
</html>
```

2. Open the form in an XForms implementation. You should see something similar to Figure 20-8.

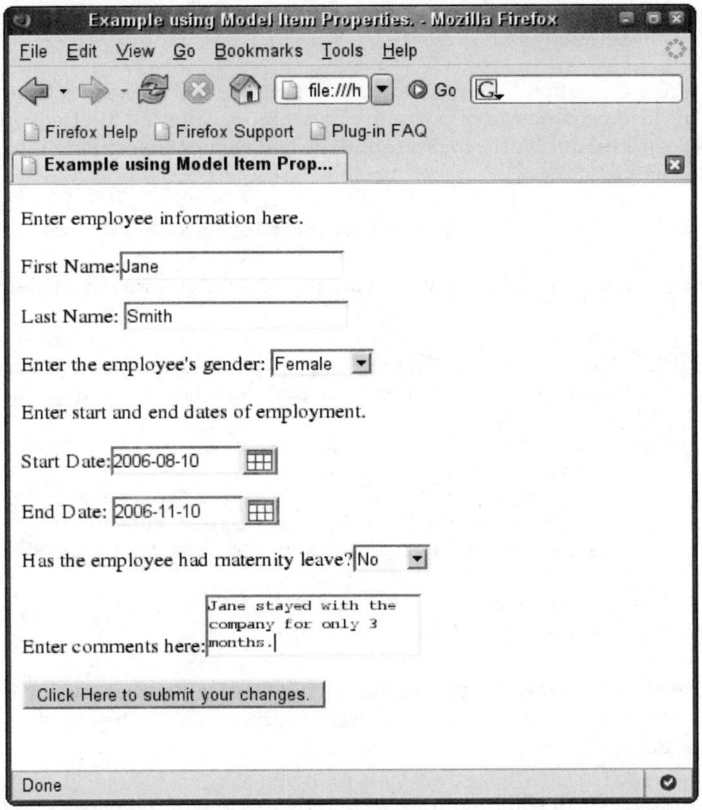

Figure 20-8

How It Works

In the default XForms model, the content of the `xforms:instance` element lists some basic data about an employee:

```
<xforms:instance >
 <xmml:Employee >
  <xmml:Identity>
   <xmml:FirstName></xmml:FirstName>
   <xmml:LastName></xmml:LastName>
   <xmml:Gender></xmml:Gender>
  </xmml:Identity>
  <xmml:Employment>
   <xmml:StartDate></xmml:StartDate>
   <xmml:EndDate></xmml:EndDate>
   <xmml:MaternityLeave></xmml:MaternityLeave>
  </xmml:Employment>
  <xmml:Comments></xmml:Comments>
 </xmml:Employee>
</xforms:instance>
```

This provides more information than the previous examples, and the values have been grouped into sub-elements. This also provides an opportunity to see more complex XPath expressions. The remainder of that default XForms model is an `xforms:submission` element specifying where the serialized instance data is to be saved:

```
<xforms:submission id="mySubmit" action="EmployeeData.xml" method="put" />
```

The most interesting part of the XForms model are the several `xforms:bind` elements shown here:

```
<xforms:bind nodeset="xmml:Identity/xmml:FirstName" required="true()" />
<xforms:bind nodeset="xmml:Identity/xmml:LastName" required="true()" />
<xforms:bind nodeset="xmml:Employment/xmml:StartDate" required="true()"
            type="xs:date" />
<xforms:bind nodeset="xmml:Employment/xmml:EndDate" type="xs:date"
            required="false()"
            constraint=". = '' or . >= ../xmml:StartDate"/>
<xforms:bind nodeset="xmml:Employment/xmml:MaternityLeave"
            relevant="/xmml:Employee/xmml:Identity/xmml:Gender = 'Female'" />
```

The first two `xforms:bind` elements use the required model item property simply to specify that both a first name and a last name are required for the employee.

The `xforms:bind` element, which relates to the start date, specifies that a value is required for start date and that the datatype is an `xs:date` value. As you can see, this also causes a date form control to be displayed for the start date.

Because some employees will still be employed and therefore won't have an end date, the `required` attribute on the `xforms:bind` element that binds to the end date is set to `false()`. Remember that to specify a Boolean value in XPath you must use the `true()` or `false()` functions, as `true` or `false` in a location path are interpreted as element type names. In addition, because an end date shouldn't be before the start date, this control has been added in a constraint attribute. The XPath expression that you see there just verifies that the end date is either empty or greater than or equal to the start date.

If an employee is male, then he isn't eligible for maternity leave. Therefore, if you set the value of gender to `Male`, you cannot set a value for maternity leave. The remainder of the form markup uses code techniques already shown, so it isn't explained further here.

The submitted data, `EmployeeData.xml`, is shown here:

```xml
<?xml version="1.0" encoding="UTF-8"?>
<xmml:Employee xmlns="http://www.w3.org/1999/xhtml"
xmlns:xforms="http://www.w3.org/2002/xforms"
  xmlns:xmml="http://www.XMML.com/namespace"
xmlns:xs="http://www.w3.org/2001/XMLSchema">
  <xmml:Identity>
    <xmml:FirstName>Jane</xmml:FirstName>
    <xmml:LastName>Smith</xmml:LastName>
    <xmml:Gender>Female</xmml:Gender>
  </xmml:Identity>
  <xmml:Employment>
    <xmml:StartDate>2006-08-10</xmml:StartDate>
    <xmml:EndDate>2006-11-10</xmml:EndDate>
    <xmml:MaternityLeave>No</xmml:MaternityLeave>
  </xmml:Employment>
  <xmml:Comments>Jane stayed with the company for only 3 months.</xmml:Comments>
</xmml:Employee>
```

Support of these features isn't flawless in current versions of XForms implementations, and you might have to remove some of these controls depending on the implementations you are using. For instance, with Firefox XForms 0.7, you need to remove the `constraint` attribute to get your form working.

W3C XML Schema in XForms

The data submitted from an XForms document is well-formed XML. An XForms processor has a W3C XML Schema processor built in so the option is available to validate data that a user enters against a specified schema.

Here is the schema document `PizzaOrder.xsd`, which defines the permitted structure of the content of the `xforms:instance` element of the pizza order example:

```xml
<?xml version="1.0" encoding="UTF-8"?>
<xs:schema xmlns:xs="http://www.w3.org/2001/XMLSchema"
  xmlns="http://www.XMML.com/namespace"
  targetNamespace="http://www.XMML.com/namespace"
  elementFormDefault="qualified">

<xs:element name="Pizza">
  <xs:complexType>
    <xs:sequence>
      <xs:element name="Size" type="xs:token"/>
      <xs:element name="Toppings">
        <xs:simpleType>
          <xs:restriction>
            <xs:simpleType>
              <xs:list itemType="xs:NMTOKEN"/>
            </xs:simpleType>
```

```
                    <xs:minLength value="1"/>
                    <xs:maxLength value="2"/>
                </xs:restriction>
              </xs:simpleType>
          </xs:element>
        </xs:sequence>
      </xs:complexType>
    </xs:element>

</xs:schema>
```

This schema defines a "Pizza" root element with two sub-elements. The Size element is declared as xs:token, meaning it can hold any value. The Toppings element is defined as a list of xs:NMTOKEN with a length between 1 and 2. The unit used to determine the length of W3C XML Schema list types is the number of tokens, so this confirms that the number of selected toppings is between 1 and 2. This means that this simple schema adds a constraint over the definitions defined in the form.

Schema or Bind Elements: Which One to Choose?

You've seen two different mechanisms to define constraints over instance documents:

❑　The xforms:bind element, with its set of attributes, which enables you to constrain sets of elements

❑　The schema attribute, which attaches a schema to an instance for validation purposes

These mechanisms are complementary: the xforms:bind element enables you to define constraints that can't be expressed with W3C XML Schema, such as when you've tested that an end date is greater than or equal to a start date. Its required attribute is also a simpler alternative to the equivalent expression with W3C XML Schema: To express that a date is optional with W3C XML Schema, you have to define a union type between xs:date and an empty xs:token. On the other hand, W3C XML Schema gives you a powerful means to validate an instance document as a whole.

There is still a fair amount of overlap between these mechanisms, and when you need to choose between one or the other, keep in mind that the xforms:bind element is usually more lightweight and often provides more user-friendly error messages, whereas a schema gives you the ability to validate the instance as a whole and can be reused out of the scope of your form.

XForms Events

XForms has a large number of events, which are described in more detail in the XForms specification at www.w3.org/TR/xforms/index-all.html#rpm-events.

XForms events are categorized into the following four groups:

❑　**Initialization events** — Fired when an XForms processor is starting up and loading an XForms document

❑　**Interaction events** — Fired in response to user actions

❑ **Notification events** — Indicate that something has happened in the form

❑ **Error events** — Indicate that something has gone wrong during form processing

Creating event handlers for XForms events enables you to add custom functionality to XForms documents that you create.

The XForms Action Module

The XForms Action Module specifies XForms elements that function as declarative event handlers. The events supported by XForms include the following:

❑ Initialization events that signal when the model is ready or destructed

❑ Interaction events triggered either by the user or by the XForms actions defined in XForms elements

❑ Notification events signaling that something has changed, either in an instance document or as a result of a user action

❑ Errors

XForms does not define any mechanism for scripted handling of events, leaving that to host languages, such as XHTML and SVG. On the other hand, this Action Module is so powerful and flexible that the need for scripting is almost eliminated.

It was mentioned earlier that an element from this module could be included in the content of several XForms form controls, so if you were to mimic the reset functionality available in HTML forms by using the xforms:trigger element, then you would use code like the following, assuming that the namespace for XML events was declared to be associated with the namespace prefix ev:

```
<xforms:trigger>
 <xforms:label>Reset the instance data.</xforms:label>
 <xforms:reset ev:event="DOMActivate" model="default" />
</xforms:trigger>
```

Describing the details of this module is beyond the scope of this introduction to XForms, and this section provides only a short description of its elements, which are described in more depth in the XForms recommendation (www.w3.org/TR/xforms/):

❑ xforms:action is used to group other elements from the XForms Action Module.

❑ xforms:dispatch dispatches an event.

❑ xforms:load causes an external resource to be loaded either to replace an existing instance or to serve as a new one.

❑ xforms:message specifies a message to be displayed to the user.

❑ xforms:rebuild rebuilds the internal data structures.

❑ xforms:recalculate forces a new evaluation of all the calculated fields.

❑ xforms:refresh refreshes the representation of the form.

- ❏ `xforms:reset` causes the `xforms-reset` event to be dispatched to a specified XForms model.
- ❏ `xforms:revalidate` forces a validation of an instance.
- ❏ `xforms:send` initiates the submission of instance data.
- ❏ `xforms:setfocus` sets the focus on an XForms control.
- ❏ `xforms:setvalue` sets the value of a specified node in the instance data.

All these action elements make extensive use of XPath to access nodes and calculate values, and they provide a very effective alternative to the scripting that is powering Ajax applications.

Developing and Debugging XForms

If you are new to both XForms and XML, creating even simple XForms documents can be difficult to get right at first, as there is such a large number of things that you can get wrong. It is recommended that you start with very simple forms until you are familiar with creating working XForms documents, assuming you are hand-coding. Be sure that you have mastered basic but essential techniques such as understanding XML namespaces, and be sure that you understand the section describing what instance data is and how XPath location paths are used to reference nodes inside the instance data.

You will save yourself a lot of grief by using an XML-aware editor to code. Examples of standalone XML editors include XMLwriter (`www.xmlwriter.net`), XMLSpy (`www.xmlspy.com`), and oXygen (`www.oxygenxml.com`), as well as the XML editors available with XFormation. An XML-aware editor will catch the simple well-formedness errors that can be very tough to spot by eye once a form moves beyond the trivial.

If form controls aren't working correctly (for example, an `xforms:input` element loses the value you entered when you tab away from the form control), it is likely that the binding to the instance data is faulty. That failure to bind can be due, for example, to omitting a `ref` attribute, to omitting a leading / character in the value of a `ref` attribute, or getting namespace declarations wrong. Another possible cause when you have multiple XForms models is not specifying a `model` attribute that has an `xs:IDREF` to the correct XForms model.

Alternatives to XForms

Many commercial software companies are developing tools in the XML forms arena, in response to the increased used of XML in enterprise applications. This section briefly introduces two tools in this space where XForms technology is not used.

Microsoft InfoPath

Microsoft InfoPath is a tool intended to be used to submit and retrieve XML from relational databases, such as Microsoft Access and SQL Server, to XML web services and Microsoft application servers, such as Microsoft Office SharePoint Server and BizTalk Server.

Microsoft InfoPath has a very nice visual designer, which enables users who are not familiar with XML to create InfoPath forms, which submit well-formed XML. For more advanced work, familiarity with XSLT, JScript, VBScript, or a .NET language is needed.

Figure 20-9 shows the InfoPath designer with a simple sample form open and the Controls task pane visible.

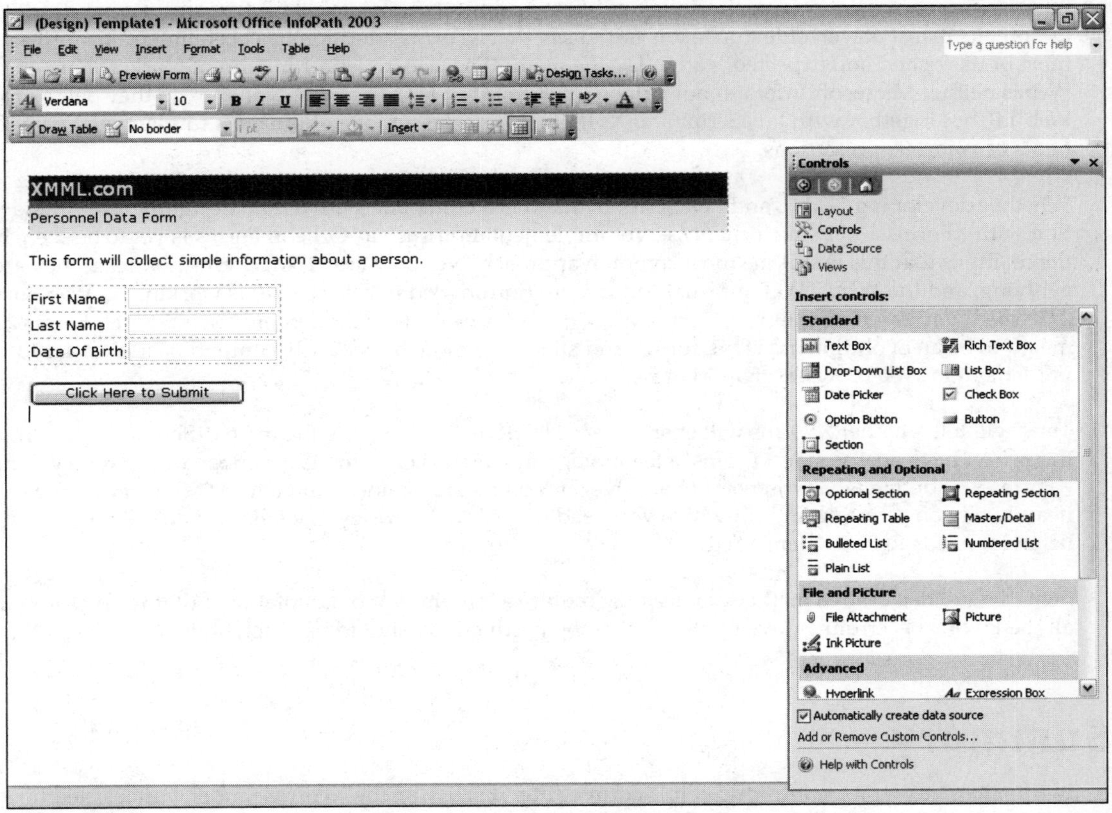

Figure 20-9

Further information about InfoPath is located at `http://office.microsoft.com/en-us/infopath/HA101656341033.aspx`.

Adobe LiveCycle

The Adobe LiveCycle product family uses Adobe Acrobat Reader to view and fill forms designed with Adobe LiveCycle Designer, server-side-powered by Adobe LiveCycle Designer, and managed by Adobe LiveCycle Designer. Like InfoPath, Adobe LiveCycle uses a proprietary file format that bundles several files necessary for the functioning of the Acrobat form. It resembles InfoPath in that respect because InfoPath uses a cabinet file with an `.xsn` extension to hold its XML files. Also like InfoPath, despite this use of a proprietary format for the forms themselves, Adobe LiveCycle can be used to edit XML documents that conform to arbitrary W3C XML Schema documents.

Like many other Adobe design tools, Adobe LiveCycle Designer is a very polished tool in many respects. You can find more information about this product family at `www.adobe.com/products/livecycle/`.

HTML Forms

You may be surprised to see HTML forms mentioned as an XForms alternative, but they deserve to be mentioned here for good reasons. First, you have to admit that plain old HTML forms are not dead. Despite its many powerful features, it is fair to say that XForms adoption has been much slower than most of us wished and expected, and today the main XForms competitor in term of market share on the Web is neither Microsoft InfoPath nor Adobe LiveCycle but HTML forms. Not only do they belong to Web 1.0, but together with JavaScript and XML, HTML forms are one of the most fundamental components of Web 2.0 applications.

Whether developing HTML and JavaScript by hand is a better alternative than designing user interaction with XForms and using a client/server implementation such as Orbeon Forms is yet to be seen, but the reality is that this is still the most common approach. Not only are HTML forms not dead, they are evolving, and the WHATWG informal consortium (introduced in Chapter 18) is working on Web Forms 2.0, which you can find at `http://whatwg.org/specs/web-forms/current-work/`. Web Forms 2.0 is meant to be an evolution of HTML forms, and should be more backwardly compatible and easier to implement in Web browsers than XForms.

Time will tell whether XForms will ever replace HTML forms, but note the main difference between them. You have on one side XForms, a technology in which everything is described declaratively — in XForms you define what you want to achieve; and on the other side, you have HTML forms, which heavily rely on scripting and for which you need to deal with low-level details and define how every behavior needs to be implemented.

Switching to declarative methodologies may require a fair amount of adaptation, but it relieves you from all the low-level scripting development, meaning productivity should be much higher.

Summary

In this chapter you were introduced to XForms. After discussing the XForms model, you learned how to create instance data and how to configure submission of a form. Then, you looked at XForms form controls, and finished up with XForms model item properties.

Exercise Questions

Suggested solutions to these questions can be found in Appendix A.

Question 1

Experiment with the code examples given in the chapter by changing the value of the `appearance` attribute on the `xforms:select` and `xforms:select1` elements. This, particularly, when viewed in more than one XForms viewer will give you an idea of the range of visual appearances available to an XForms developer.

Question 2

Describe the differences in purpose of the `xforms:submit` and `xforms:submission` elements.

Part VIII
Case Study

Chapter 21: Case Study: Payment Calculator

Case Study: Payment Calculator

Throughout this book, you have learned how XML can be used to construct and validate documents and for communications between systems, and you now know how to use several important XML display formats. Sometimes it can be difficult seeing how all of these fit together without a real-world business case. This case study demonstrates how you can build an online home loan calculator using a public web service, a .NET web application, JavaScript, and several of the XML technologies described in this book.

Specifically, this chapter describes how to do the following:

❑ Create a web page to enter loan information

❑ Call a web service to calculate the payments using SOAP

❑ Display the results using Ajax (Asynchronous JavaScript and XML) and SVG

Mortgage Calculations

Mortgages are commonly used throughout the world when purchasing a home or land. The word *mortgage* comes from French and literally means "death pledge." Before making such a pledge, consumers often want to see the proposed payments for the loan. These payments generally include interest and a principal reduction component, depending on various laws or religious guidelines.

In the most common mortgages, the schedule of payments (based on a repayment agreement, or note) must be determined before the annual percentage rate (APR) can be calculated. The amount of interest and principal paid in each payment is based on the loan terms selected and generally changes over the course of the loan. Depending on the kind of loan and the country from which it originates, these calculations can become extremely complex. In the United States, the complexity of the calculations is only the first hurdle. The calculations must adhere to a strict and evolving set of laws that can vary by the combination of jurisdictions in effect.

This case study uses a mortgage calculation web service from Compliance Studio (http://compli-ancestudio.com). The Compliance Studio engine is used by mortgage industry companies in the United States to handle complex lending compliance checks and simple mortgage estimates. Luckily, Compliance Studio offers a number of its programs free, which enables you to build a professional-grade application quickly. Because Compliance Studio is a U.S.-based company, the calculations may not be applicable for loans in other countries. Regardless, the examples in this case study can be applied to any number of alternative calculation engines.

What You'll Need

Before you get started, make sure you have everything you need. You will use Microsoft's Visual Studio .NET 2005 to create a local web service proxy. You will also be running an application on the built-in Windows web server Internet Information Server (IIS). An alternate version of this case study is available for download from the book's website at www.wrox.com. The alternate version uses Ruby on Rails instead of .NET, and the built-in Ruby on Rails web server instead of IIS.

For the examples in this chapter, you need the following:

- ❑ Microsoft Visual Studio .NET 2005 (or Microsoft Visual Web Designer)
- ❑ An SVG-enabled browser or an SVG plug-in for Internet Explorer

Microsoft's Visual Studio can be downloaded or purchased on its website. A free version of Visual Web Developer 2005 (Express Edition) is also available at http://msdn.microsoft.com/vstudio/express/vwd/. In general, these tools are very powerful, but they can take a considerable amount of time to download. Therefore, prepare well in advance. The examples in this book use the 2005 versions of these tools, but nothing in the examples requires .NET 2.0, so you can use earlier versions of Visual Studio or you can an alternate tool to create the proxy web service. Some of the samples in this chapter are long, so you can download all of the code for the examples on this book's website instead of typing them in yourself.

In addition to the web service, you can use Visual Studio or Visual Web Developer to design all of your web pages, stylesheets, and SVG documents. Of course, you will be looking at the code for each of these files instead of using the built-in designers, so you may also decide to use another text or XML editor to implement these samples.

A complete list of SVG-enabled browsers can be found in Chapter 19. If you plan to use Internet Explorer to test and debug your website, you currently need an SVG plug-in. The most popular plug-in is Adobe's SVG Viewer, available for download at www.adobe.com/svg.

Online Loan Calculator

As in the development of any web application, the easiest place to begin is the main web page. This page serves as the entry point into your complex server interactions. It needs to enable users to input various mortgage details, request a calculation, and see the resulting payment schedule. For starters, this page will be simple, containing some basic text, an entry form, and the payment schedule. You won't spend a lot of time on the design of the page, but you will make basic styling decisions using CSS.

In these examples, you host the page on your local web server. If you would like to use a public web server instead, replace the references to `http://localhost/` *with your own domain.*

Building the Loan Calculator Web Page

Begin by building the basic XHTML web page. In the next Try It Out, you will style this page using CSS and add a JavaScript library for the SOAP-based AJAX calls.

1.   Create the header of the HTML page. Open your text editor and copy the following. When you are finished, save the file as `loancalculator1.html`. If you are using Windows, you can save this file in the `C:\Inetpub\wwwroot\` folder.

```
<!DOCTYPE html PUBLIC "-//W3C//DTD XHTML 1.0 transitional//EN"
  "http://www.w3.org/TR/xhtml1/DTD/xhtml1-transitional.dtd">
<html xmlns="http://www.w3.org/1999/xhtml">
  <head>
    <title>Loan Calculator</title>
    <meta http-equiv="content-type" content="text/html; charset=iso-8859-1" />
  </head>
  <body>
```

The web page begins with a DOCTYPE declaration pointing to the transitional version of XHTML 1.0. Remember that this tells the web browser what specific version and flavor of XHTML you're using. Notice that you haven't included an `<?xml version="1.0"?>` declaration at the start of the page. Some web browsers will render the page in quirks mode if this included. *Quirks mode* is a rendering mode that doesn't always adhere to publishing web standards. This means can't be sure that your page will be rendered correctly in the user's browser. To avoid that, it is best to omit the declaration.

The namespace declaration `http://www.w3.org/1999/xhtml` is also included in the root element. This default namespace declaration indicates that all of the elements in this document belong to the XHTML namespace.

The `<head>` element also contains a `<title>` element. The `<title>` element is required for the web page to be valid. Also included is a `<meta>` element. This element isn't required; in fact, it is using a nonstandard media type as well. Regardless, this helps avoid other problems you might face when using different browsers.

2.   The main content of the loan calculator web page is fairly simple. It begins with some basic header text:

```
<div id="container">
  <div id="header">
    <div id="title">
      <h1><span>Loan Calculator</span></h1>
    </div>
  </div>
```

Notice that there are quite a few extra `<div>` elements, and inside the `<h1>` is an extra `<span>` element. All of this is unnecessary for the basic page rendering and validation, but it provides many more options when applying a Cascading Style Sheet to the page. If you are working with a professional designer for your website, he or she will appreciate the increased flexibility.

3. The most important part of this web page is the entry form, where users can input information about the loan:

```html
<div id="info">
  <h3><span>Tell us about the loan you would like</span></h3>
  <form id="loan" action="#">
    <div id="program_group">
      <label for="ProgramName">Choose the loan program</label>
      <select id="ProgramName">
        <option selected="selected" value="Fixed">Fixed</option>
        <option value="Hybrid">Fixed Hybrid</option>
        <option value="InterestOnlyOption">Interest Only Option</option>
      </select>
    </div>
    <div id="amounts_group">
      <label for="OriginalLoanAmount">Loan Amount</label>
      <input type="text" value="250000" id="OriginalLoanAmount" />
      <label for="DisclosedTotalSalesPriceAmount">Sales Price</label>
      <input type="text" value="0" id="DisclosedTotalSalesPriceAmount" />
      <label for="PropertyAppraisedValueAmount">Appraised Value</label>
      <input type="text" value="300000" id="PropertyAppraisedValueAmount" />
    </div>
    <div id="terms_fees_group">
      <label for="LoanOriginalMaturityTermMonths">Term</label>
      <input type="text" value="360" id="LoanOriginalMaturityTermMonths" />
      <label for="TotalAPRFeesAmount">Total Fees</label>
      <input type="text" value="3988" id="TotalAPRFeesAmount" />
    </div>
    <div id="rate_group">
      <label for="NoteRatePercent">Note Rate</label>
      <input type="text" value="0.08" id="NoteRatePercent" />
      <label for="IndexValue">Index Value</label>
      <input type="text" value="0.00" id="IndexValue" />
      <label for="MarginValue">Margin Value</label>
      <input type="text" value="0.00" id="MarginValue" />
    </div>
    <div id="buttons">
      <input id="calculate_button" type="submit" value="Calculate"
        onclick="return false;"/>
      <span id="working"><img src="indicator.gif" alt="Working..." /></span>
    </div>
  </form>
</div>
```

The `<form>` contains all of the `<input>` elements needed for the loan data. These elements are broken into logical groups based on the kind of data. Again, this will be useful when applying a stylesheet to the page. Also included are `<label>` elements to describe each of the inputs. Technically, you could use `<p>` elements for the descriptions, but the `<label>` element describes specifically what you are trying to accomplish.

In this example, loan information has been added to the `value` attributes. Normally, this data would be omitted, but it will be very useful when testing the application, so leave it in for now. Additional information on each of the mortgage concepts is available on the Compliance Studio website or at `http://en.wikipedia.org/wiki/Mortgage`.

The `action` attribute on the `<form>` element is `#`. In a more complete example, it would be better to have an actual URL here. Of course, as long as users have JavaScript enabled, they won't use the value of the `action` attribute at all. If JavaScript is not supported or is disabled, however, the application won't do anything. In public websites, providing fallback mechanisms for browsers that don't support JavaScript or CSS is important.

Note that the `onclick` attribute for the Submit button simply returns `false`. This means the `<form>` can never be submitted. You will modify this line a little later in the chapter.

You have included an `<img>` element that is used to indicate that something is happening when you make any Ajax calls. The image `indicator.gif` can be downloaded with the rest of the code at `www.wrox.com/`. The image was designed by Jakob Skjerning and is available at `http://mentalized.net/activity-indicators/`, along with several other public domain indicator graphics.

4. You need to include a placeholder for the payment information. Ultimately, the payments will appear in a `<table>`, but you use a `<div>` element as a container:

```
<div id="payments">
  <h3><span>Payments</span></h3>
  <div id="payments_table">
    Please submit a request and the payments will be displayed here.
  </div>
</div>
```

5. Finally, end the elements you started at the beginning of the page:

```
  </div>
 </body>
</html>
```

How It Works

This Try It Out built the main web page for the loan calculator. The page is fairly simple, and apart from some extra `<div>` elements, it is entirely content driven. Notice that you haven't included any extra information about the layout of the page. Separating the content of a web page from its presentation layer simplifies maintenance of the page in the future. Unfortunately, though, because you haven't yet created a stylesheet for the page, it isn't very pretty.

Figure 21-1 shows how the web page looks when rendered in Internet Explorer.

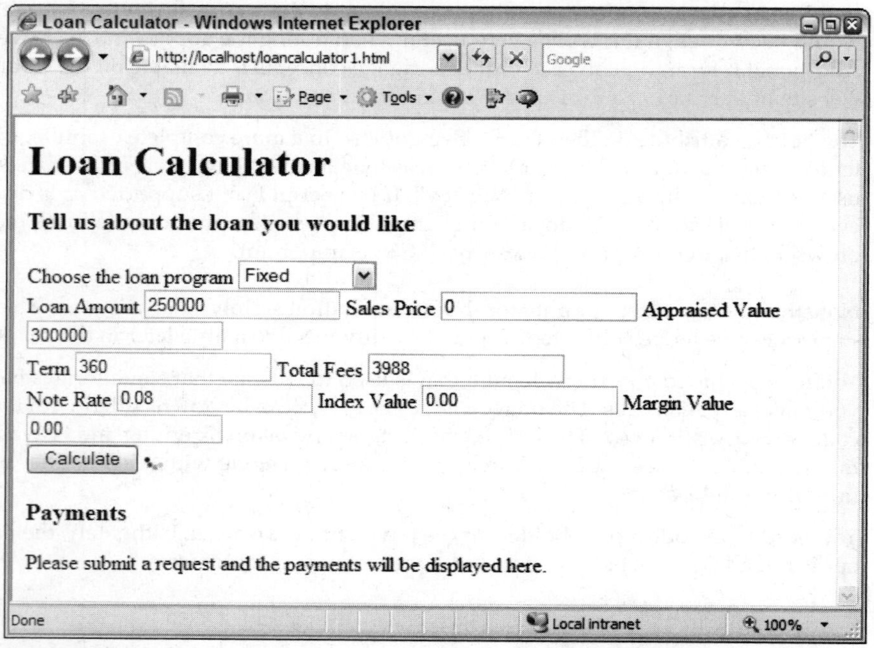

Figure 21-1

Before you add more functionality, you will add a basic stylesheet to the page.

Try It Out   **Improving the Look of the Loan Calculator**

For many professional sites, a design team is hired to create stunning graphics and page layouts. This case study focuses on the basics, building a CSS document that makes testing a little more enjoyable:

1. Open your text editor and create a new stylesheet document. The stylesheet begins with a default rule:

    ```
    * { margin: 0; padding: 0; }
    ```

    Even though you are building a basic stylesheet, it is good to follow best practice guidelines. Beginning a stylesheet by setting the margin and padding for all elements to 0 ensures that different browsers treat these properties the same. Tips like this are shared freely in online CSS communities such as `irc://irc.freenode.net/css`.

2. Define a template for the `<body>` tag:

    ```
    body {
      background-color:white;
      color:black;
      font-family:arial, sans-serif;
      margin-left:10px;
    }
    ```

Again, it isn't required to set default background and text colors, but it is good practice. In addition, choosing a font you like and providing a fallback font such as sans-serif guarantees that the page will remain fairly consistent across various platforms.

3. The biggest problem with the loan calculator is the layout of the `<input>` elements. Because you have grouped them in uniquely named `<div>` elements, you can be very precise with their position. You will use absolute positioning to define the layout of the various groups based on the `id` attribute of each `<div>` element:

```
#program_group {
    position:absolute;
    left:10px;
    top:70px;
}
#amounts_group {
    position:absolute;
    left:10px;
    top:120px;
}
#terms_fees_group {
    position:absolute;
    left:170px;
    top:120px;
}
#rate_group {
    position:absolute;
    left:330px;
    top:120px;
}
```

4. The `<label>` elements also need a template. Right now the labels appear next to the `<input>` controls. Instead, treat them as block-level elements so that there is a line break after each one:

```
label {
    display:block;
}
```

5. The `<img>` element for the spinning indicator shouldn't be visible unless the calculation is occurring. In the template, set the `display` to `none`:

```
#working {
    display:none;
}
```

6. Create a template for the `<form>` element. Because you used absolute positioning for the `<input>` groups, the `<form>` has no actual height, but you need to leave a space where the form contents should go. The `height` and `min-height` CSS properties are not implemented consistently in all browsers, so cheat and add padding to the top and bottom of the form instead:

```
form {
    padding-top:190px;
    padding-bottom:10px;
}
```

7. Even though you don't have any payments yet, add templates for the table, cells, and the `payments_table` container element:

```css
#payments_table {
  overflow:auto;
  margin:10px;
  padding:5px;
  width:488px;
  height:200px;
  border:1px solid black;
}
#payments_table td, #payments_table th{
  margin:0px;
  padding:10px;
}
.numeric_cell {
  text-align:right;
}
.even_row {
  color:black;
  background-color:#eee;
}
```

Notice that the overflow property of the `payments_table` template is set to `auto`. Each loan can have a lot of payments. Instead of allowing the page to become very long, the value `auto` ensures that the contents of the `payments_table` `<div>` element will scroll.

8. Finally, modify the web page to refer to the stylesheet. Add a `<link>` element into the `<head>` section of the document. Once completed, save the file as `loancalculator2.html`:

```html
<head>
  <title>Loan Calculator</title>
  <meta http-equiv="content-type" content="text/html; charset=iso-8859-1" />
  <link href="loancalculator1.css" rel="stylesheet" type="text/css" />
</head>
```

How It Works

In this Try It Out, you added a CSS stylesheet to the main web page for the loan calculator. The stylesheet may not win any design awards, but working with the input fields and visualizing the results is now much more pleasant. In the stylesheet, you followed best-practice guidelines and used a mix of CSS features. Some elements were styled using ID selectors, while others used element names. Using this stylesheet as a basis, you could alter the look of your page very quickly.

Figure 21-2 shows how the web page looks when rendered in Internet Explorer.

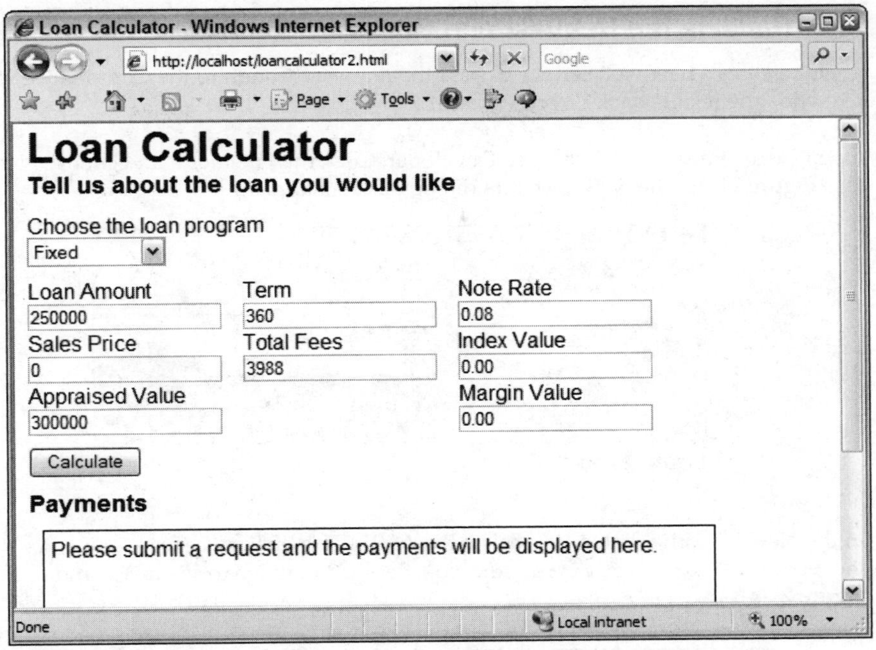

Figure 21-2

Integrating the Calculation Web Service

Now that you have your main loan calculator web page, all you have to do is connect it to the Compliance Studio web service and display the results. Unfortunately, the web page can't communicate directly with the Compliance Studio web service because the web page and the service are hosted in different domains. Currently, browsers don't permit web pages to make HTTP requests to URLs that have a different domain. These requests are commonly called *Cross-Domain XML HTTP Requests* or *Cross-Site Scripting (XSS)*. Cross Site Scripting is the source of many common security problems.

Luckily, you can call a web service that is hosted in the same domain. You need to create a second web service that you can call locally that will pass the request from the server to the Compliance Studio web service. This middle-man approach enables you to use the server as a proxy for the interaction.

Building a Proxy Web Service

To build the web service, you use Microsoft's Visual Studio 2005. Though you could build the code for the web service manually, using tools greatly simplifies the process and provides some additional benefits such as type-checking. The proxy web service has two web methods. The first simply passes through the request and the response. The second method uses the Compliance Studio XML Schema to enable you to construct the request using XML data-binding.

Try It Out   Building the Request and Response Service

This Try It Out creates a new web service to pass the request through to the Compliance Studio service. The service sends the results back directly as XML.

1. Open Visual Studio or Visual Web Developer. Click the File menu and choose New ⇨ Web Site (see Figure 21-3). The New Web Site dialog box will appear.

Figure 21-3

2. In the New Web Site dialog box, select the ASP.NET Web Service icon, and enter the name of the website, `ProxyCalculationService`. Set the language to Visual C# and click `OK` (see Figure 21-4).

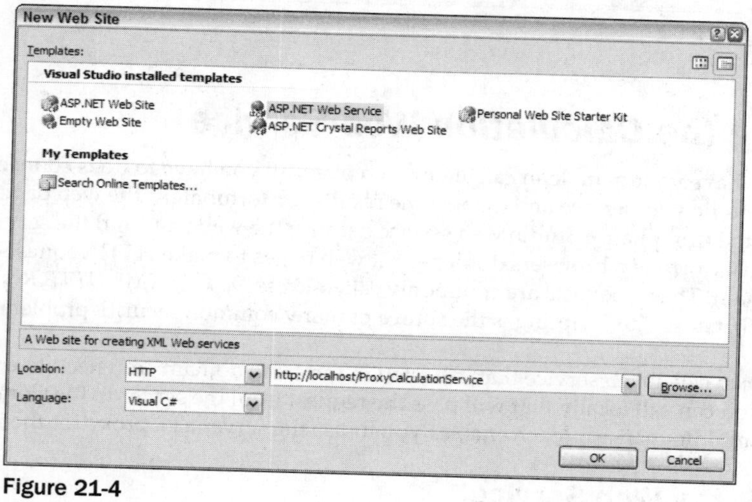

Figure 21-4

If you are having trouble creating the web service, refer to Chapter 14.

3. Because this web service will be calling the Compliance Studio service, add a web reference. Click the Website menu, and then select Add Web Reference. Type `http://compliancestudio .com/apr/1.0/` in the URL field and click the Go button. Once the service appears, click the Add Reference button (see Figure 21-5).

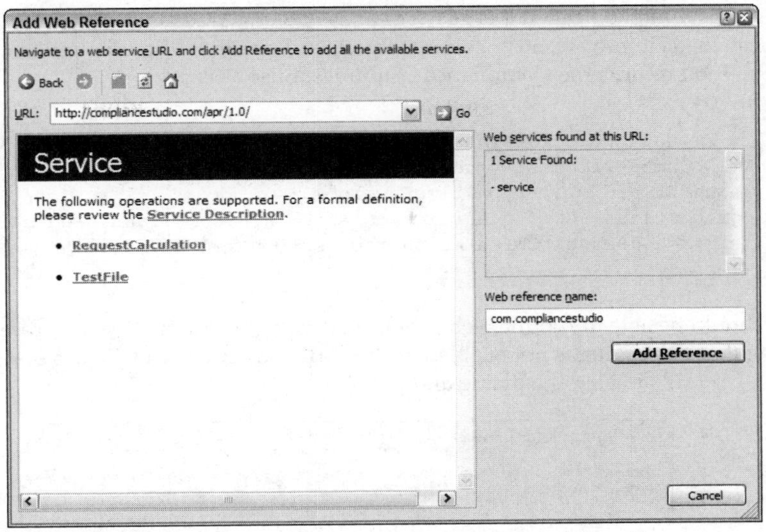

Figure 21-5

4. You need to add two `using` directives to the file `Service.cs`. The first enables you to work with the `System.Xml` package. The second enables you to use the classes that were automatically generated when you added the web reference:

```
using System;
using System.Web;
using System.Web.Services;
using System.Web.Services.Protocols;
using System.Xml;
using com.compliancestudio;
```

5. Modify the namespace that will identify the web service. By default, Visual Studio uses

```
[WebService(Namespace = "http://tempuri.org")]
```

but you can change this to something more meaningful:

```
[WebService(Namespace = "http://localhost/ProxyCalculationService")]
```

Of course, the namespace name doesn't have to be the same as the web service project name. Like all namespaces, it is just an identifier.

6. By default, Visual Studio has already created a web method called `HelloWorld`:

```
[WebMethod]
public string HelloWorld() {
    return "Hello World";
}
```

You don't need a `HelloWorld` method in the proxy web service so it can be deleted.

7. Insert a new method called `CalculatePassThrough`. This method captures the incoming request, loads it into an `XmlDocument` object, and passes it to the Compliance Studio service. The method returns the Compliance Studio response as is:

```
[WebMethod]
public XmlNode CalculatePassThrough(string TransactionEnvelope) {
    XmlDocument request = new XmlDocument();
    request.LoadXml(TransactionEnvelope);
    com.compliancestudio.Service cs = new com.compliancestudio.Service();
    return cs.RequestCalculation(request.DocumentElement);
}
```

8. You should be able to run the web service in debugging mode. You may receive a warning indicating that debugging is not enabled in the `Web.config` file (see Figure 21-6). Simply modify the `Web.config` using the dialog and press OK.

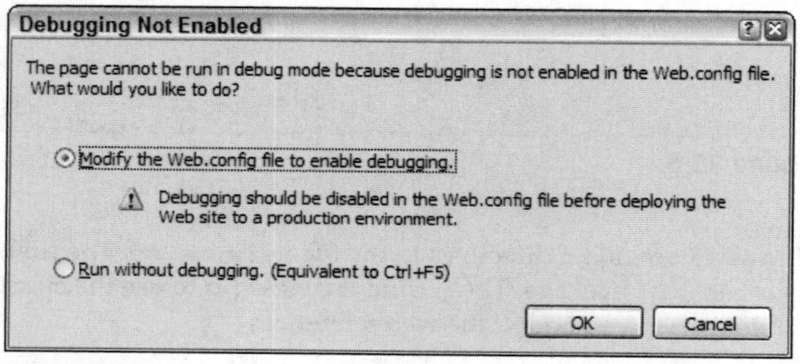

Figure 21-6

If you have trouble getting the web service to run on your local machine, it could be one of several common problems. Confirm that the World Wide Web Publishing service is running on your local machine. Sometimes, locally run programs such as Skype use port 80, which can conflict with the debugger. If you are deploying this application to an actual server, make sure you have created the application in the website configuration (click the folder in the Admin Console and choose Properties, and then click Create Application).

9. If the web service is working correctly, then you should be able to see the service description when you execute the `Service.asmx` page (see Figure 21-7).

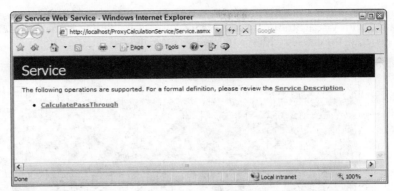

Figure 21-7

How It Works

This Try It Out built a proxy web service for the loan calculator. The service doesn't do very much; it passes any requests it receives to the Compliance Studio service and sends back the response. Visual Studio hid much of the complexity involved in building a web service. By pointing the Add Web Reference dialog box to the Compliance Studio website, you created a custom service wrapper inside the application. Visual Studio handled the WSDL (the Web Service Description Language file that describes the web service), the SOAP envelopes, and the HTTP traversal.

Modifying the Request and Response

Often, when building a proxy web service, you need to modify the request or the response before passing it on. A proxy web service is a good place to verify user credentials, add logs about the transaction, or supplement the request with additional data.

The next Try It Out makes a more advanced web method that does just that.

Try It Out   Using an XML Schema to Build the Request

Your current web service doesn't offer much assistance in constructing the requests that are sent to Compliance Studio. In fact, there isn't any type checking or data defaults. Compliance Studio provides an XML Schema for its request data. You can use this schema to generate .NET classes that can be used to check types and generate the request.

1. Download the Compliance Studio XML Schema and save it in your project folder. The current schema is `http://compliancestudio.com/apr/APRData-1-0.xsd`.

2. Open a command prompt (select Start ⇨ Run and type cmd) and change the current directory to the location of your project. By default, you could do this by entering the following command:

```
cd \Inetpub\wwwroot\ProxyCalculationService
```

From there, you can use the program `xsd.exe` to generate a set of .NET classes. `xsd.exe` is distributed with Visual Studio. If you have installed Visual Studio to the default location, then you can generate the classes with the following command (see Figure 21-8):

```
"c:\Progra~1\Microsoft Visual Studio 8\SDK\v2.0\Bin\xsd.exe" APRData-1-0.xsd /c
```

Figure 21-8

3. Now that you have generated the classes, you need to add them into the project. Click the Website menu, and then Add Existing Item. Browse for the new file, `APRData-1-0.cs`, in your project folder, select it, and click the Add button. Make sure the file is located in the `App_Code` folder of the website or you will get a build error when you try to execute the service.

4. Before you build the new web method, add two more `using` directives for `System.IO` and `System.Xml.Serialization` to the top of the `Service.cs` file:

```
using System;
using System.Web;
using System.Web.Services;
using System.Web.Services.Protocols;
using System.IO;
using System.Xml.Serialization;
using System.Xml;
using com.compliancestudio;
```

5. Create a custom enumeration for the various loan program types. This case study uses only three programs: `Fixed` for fixed rate loans, `Hybrid` for fixed-rate adjustable loans, and `InterestOnlyOption` for interest-only loans with various payment options. Insert the following code just after the `using` directives at the start of `Service.cs`:

```
public enum ProgramType
{
    Fixed,
    Hybrid,
    InterestOnlyOption
}
```

6. Now, within the `Service` class itself, you can add the second web method, called `Calculate`. Instead of receiving XML in the request, you include parameters for the various mortgage concepts you defined in the web page:

```
[WebMethod]
public XmlNode Calculate(PaymentStreamRequestType PaymentRequestType,
    ProgramType LoanProgram, double TotalAPRFeesAmount, double IndexValue,
    double MarginValue, double OriginalLoanAmount,
    double DisclosedTotalSalesPriceAmount, double PropertyAppraisedValueAmount,
    double NoteRatePercent, int LoanOriginalMaturityTermMonths,
    DateTime ApplicationSignedDate, DateTime LoanEstimatedClosingDate,
    DateTime ScheduledFirstPaymentDate, int EstimatedPrepaidDays)
{
    // Implementation
}
```

Recall that this case study doesn't define these mortgage concepts in detail; more information about each of these terms can be found on the Compliance Studio website or at `http://en.wikipedia.org/wiki/Mortgage`.

7. Within the function, create the request that will be sent to the Compliance Studio service. To do so, use the newly generated classes based on the XML Schema. You won't fill out all of the properties in the objects, just the information you are collecting in the XHTML page and default options. Start by creating the basic objects. Put the following code under the `// Implementation` comment from the previous step:

```
TRANSACTION aprTransaction = new TRANSACTION();
REQUEST aprRequest = new REQUEST();
REQUESTOPTIONS aprRequestOptions = new REQUESTOPTIONS();
DATA aprRequestOptionsData = new DATA();
APRREQUEST aprAprRequest = new APRREQUEST();
LOANDATA aprLoanData = new LOANDATA();
TERMS aprTerms = new TERMS();
```

8. Connect the various objects using the properties generated by `xsd.exe`:

```
aprTransaction.REQUEST = aprRequest;
aprTransaction.REQUEST.REQUESTOPTIONS = aprRequestOptions;
aprTransaction.REQUEST.REQUESTOPTIONS.DATA = aprRequestOptionsData;
aprTransaction.REQUEST.APRREQUEST = new APRREQUEST[1];
aprTransaction.REQUEST.APRREQUEST[0] = aprAprRequest;
aprTransaction.REQUEST.LOANDATA = aprLoanData;
aprTransaction.REQUEST.LOANDATA.TERMS = aprTerms;
```

9. Begin by assigning the request options. Again, these settings are applicable to United States mortgages. More information about these options can be found in the documentation on the Compliance Studio website:

```
aprRequestOptions.PaymentStreamAndApr = true;
aprRequestOptions.ReverseApr = false;
aprRequestOptions.ManualPaymentStream = false;
aprRequestOptions.AdditionalPrincipal = false;
aprRequestOptionsData.PaymentStreamRequestType = PaymentRequestType;
aprRequestOptionsData.AllowOddLastPayment = true;
```

855

```
aprRequestOptionsData.DaysPerYear = DaysPerYear.Item360;
aprRequestOptionsData.ConstructionTILType = ConstructionTILType.Seperate;
aprRequestOptionsData.AprIterations = 1;
aprRequestOptionsData.FeeIterations = 0;
```

10. Use the parameters that were passed in. Start by converting the `LoanProgram` value to actual program names based on the `ProgramType` enumeration. Use a static string `"Beginning XML Calculator"` as the Loan Origination System Identifier. This can be whatever you like. You also need to assign the rest of the loan details, including the fee total:

```
switch (LoanProgram)
{
    case ProgramType.Fixed:
        aprTerms.ProgramName = "FIXED 360/360";
        break;
    case ProgramType.Hybrid:
        aprTerms.ProgramName = "FIXED 50 30 10";
        break;
    case ProgramType.InterestOnlyOption:
        aprTerms.ProgramName = "GMAC IO Option Neg ARM";
        break;
}

aprTerms.LoanOriginationSystemLoanIdentifier = "Beginning XML Calculator";
aprTerms.OriginalLoanAmount = OriginalLoanAmount;
aprTerms.DisclosedTotalSalesPriceAmount = DisclosedTotalSalesPriceAmount;
aprTerms.PropertyAppraisedValueAmount = PropertyAppraisedValueAmount;
aprTerms.NoteRatePercent = NoteRatePercent;
aprTerms.InitialPaymentRatePercent = NoteRatePercent;
aprTerms.LoanOriginalMaturityTermMonths = LoanOriginalMaturityTermMonths;
aprTerms.ApplicationSignedDate = ApplicationSignedDate;
aprTerms.LoanEstimatedClosingDate = LoanEstimatedClosingDate;
aprTerms.ScheduledFirstPaymentDate = ScheduledFirstPaymentDate;
aprTerms.EstimatedPrepaidDays = EstimatedPrepaidDays;
aprAprRequest.TotalAPRFeesAmount = TotalAPRFeesAmount;
```

11. Because of the way `xsd.exe` has generated the classes, you need to do a little more work. Indicate to the `XmlSerializer` which properties you have modified (except for `string` properties) so that it knows which fields should be serialized to attributes and which fields should be skipped:

```
aprRequestOptions.PaymentStreamAndAprSpecified = true;
aprRequestOptions.ReverseAprSpecified = true;
aprRequestOptions.ManualPaymentStreamSpecified = true;
aprRequestOptions.AdditionalPrincipalSpecified = true;
aprRequestOptionsData.PaymentStreamRequestTypeSpecified = true;
aprRequestOptionsData.AllowOddLastPaymentSpecified = true;
aprRequestOptionsData.DaysPerYearSpecified = true;
aprRequestOptionsData.ConstructionTILTypeSpecified = true;
aprRequestOptionsData.AprIterationsSpecified = true;
aprRequestOptionsData.FeeIterationsSpecified = true;
aprAprRequest.TotalAPRFeesAmountSpecified = true;
aprTerms.OriginalLoanAmountSpecified = true;
aprTerms.DisclosedTotalSalesPriceAmountSpecified = true;
```

```
aprTerms.PropertyAppraisedValueAmountSpecified = true;
aprTerms.NoteRatePercentSpecified = true;
aprTerms.InitialPaymentRatePercentSpecified = true;
aprTerms.LoanOriginalMaturityTermMonthsSpecified = true;
aprTerms.ApplicationSignedDateSpecified = true;
aprTerms.LoanEstimatedClosingDateSpecified = true;
aprTerms.ScheduledFirstPaymentDateSpecified = true;
aprTerms.EstimatedPrepaidDaysSpecified = true;
```

12. You haven't assigned the index or margin values to your objects, because the index and margin may not be used (they are only applicable to the InterestOnlyOption loan program). You handle those only if the submitted values are not 0:

```
if (IndexValue != 0 && MarginValue != 0)
{
    INDEXVALUES aprIndexValues = new INDEXVALUES();
    MARGINVALUES aprMarginValues = new MARGINVALUES();

    aprTransaction.REQUEST.INDEXVALUES = new INDEXVALUES[1];
    aprTransaction.REQUEST.INDEXVALUES[0] = aprIndexValues;
    aprTransaction.REQUEST.MARGINVALUES = new MARGINVALUES[1];
    aprTransaction.REQUEST.MARGINVALUES[0] = aprMarginValues;

    aprIndexValues.IndexValue = IndexValue;
    aprMarginValues.MarginValue = MarginValue;
    aprIndexValues.IndexMonths = LoanOriginalMaturityTermMonths;
    aprMarginValues.MarginMonths = LoanOriginalMaturityTermMonths;

    aprIndexValues.IndexValueSpecified = true;
    aprIndexValues.IndexMonthsSpecified = true;
    aprMarginValues.MarginValueSpecified = true;
    aprMarginValues.MarginMonthsSpecified = true;
}
```

13. Finally, serialize the classes to a stream, load the stream into an XmlDocument, and pass the root element to the Compliance Studio service, as you did in the previous example. Again, return the Compliance Studio response as the web method's response:

```
MemoryStream ms = new MemoryStream();
XmlDocument request = new XmlDocument();
XmlSerializer serializer = new XmlSerializer(aprTransaction.GetType());
serializer.Serialize(ms, aprTransaction);
ms.Seek(0, SeekOrigin.Begin);
request.Load(ms);
com.compliancestudio.Service cs = new com.compliancestudio.Service();
XmlNode response = cs.RequestCalculation(request.DocumentElement);
return response;
```

This completes the implementation of the Calculate method.

How It Works

In this Try It Out you added a `Calculate` web method to the proxy web service for the loan calculator. Unlike the `CalculatePassThrough` function, the `Calculate` function handles many more details of constructing the Compliance Studio request. Though it makes the web service code more complex, it greatly reduces the amount of JavaScript needed in the web page.

In fact, you can communicate with the completed service in several ways. You could use local JavaScript to invoke the web service, or you could build additional communication layers as you have already done. Visual Studio has generated a WSDL and provides bindings for SOAP 1.1, SOAP 1.2, and simple HTTP. Viewing the `Service.asmx` file in a browser, you should see your two functions (see Figure 21-9).

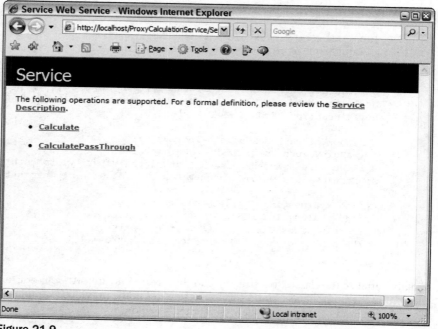

Figure 21-9

Communicating with the Proxy Web Service Using Ajax

Asynchronous JavaScript and XML, or *Ajax/AJAX*, has been growing in popularity over the past few years. In fact, Ajax has been possible in browsers for much longer than that. In the loan calculator, you use Ajax to call the proxy web service you built in the previous two examples. When the user clicks the calculate button, the application does the following:

1. Construct a SOAP message request and send it to the web service using `xmlhttp`.
2. Disable the `Calculate` button and show the progress indicator.
3. Display the results on the page by rewriting the `innerHTML` property of the table container.

Unfortunately, currently each of the major browsers provides different mechanisms for using XML over HTTP. To get around this, you need to use a custom library that hides the differences. Though many JavaScript libraries do this, the simplest is the `xmlhttp.js` library written by Jim Ley. The code for the `xmlhttp` library can be downloaded from www.wrox.com or from Jim's website at www.jibbering.com/2002/4/httprequest.html.

The full text of `xmlhttp.js` is provided here:

```
var xmlhttp=false;
/*@cc_on @*/
/*@if (@_jscript_version >= 5)
// JScript gives us Conditional compilation, we can cope with old IE versions.
// and security blocked creation of the objects.
 try {
  xmlhttp = new ActiveXObject("Msxml2.XMLHTTP");
 } catch (e) {
  try {
   xmlhttp = new ActiveXObject("Microsoft.XMLHTTP");
  } catch (E) {
   xmlhttp = false;
  }
 }
@end @*/
if (!xmlhttp && typeof XMLHttpRequest!='undefined') {
   try {
     xmlhttp = new XMLHttpRequest();
   } catch (e) {
     xmlhttp=false;
   }
}
if (!xmlhttp && window.createRequest) {
   try {
     xmlhttp = window.createRequest();
   } catch (e) {
     xmlhttp=false;
   }
}
```

Download the code (or type it into a file named `xmlhttp.js`) and save it in the same folder as `loan-calculator2.html`. The code uses advanced techniques to determine which `xmlhttp` object is supported by the current browser. Because there are many popular browsers, the code must support several different methods for constructing the object.

Try It Out   **The Loan Calculator JavaScript Layer**

This Try It Out builds the loan calculator JavaScript library. This file handles the SOAP request and response, displaying the results and indicating when the system is working on a request:

1. When working with asynchronous calls, it is best to provide some kind of visual feedback to show that the system is working, while enabling users to continue using the page. Of course, in this case you don't want over-anxious users to make multiple simultaneous requests. To prevent this, you will keep track of when you are submitting a request in a global variable. You also cre-

ate `showProgress` and `hideProgress` functions that reveal the indicator image and disable and enable the `Calculate` button:

```
var submitting = false;

function showProgress() {
  try {
    submitting = true;
    var working = document.getElementById("working");
    working.style.display = "inline";
    var calc = document.getElementById("calculate_button");
    calc.disabled = true;
  } catch(e) {
    // do nothing
  }
}

function hideProgress() {
  try {
    submitting = false;
    var working = document.getElementById("working");
    working.style.display = "none";
    var calc = document.getElementById("calculate_button");
    calc.disabled = false;
  } catch(e) {
    // do nothing
  }
}
```

These samples use some basic DOM functionality to control the document. The `getElementById` function enables you to look up the various elements in the document using the `id` attribute values specified in the XHTML. Once you have located the objects, you can modify the style definitions and the `disabled` property. These properties are part of the HTML Document Object Model.

You have also used a `try/catch` construction to handle any unexpected errors. In general, the error handling in this application is limited. In a public website, you may need to add additional error-checking.

2. Create a function to construct the SOAP request and submit it. You first need to verify that you are not already submitting a request and call the `showProgress` function:

```
function submitLoanInformation() {
  if (submitting) return;
  showProgress();
```

3. Check whether the `xmlhttp` object was correctly initialized. If so, you construct a request string:

```
  try {
    if (xmlhttp) {
      var request = ''+
'<soap:Envelope xmlns:soap="http://schemas.xmlsoap.org/soap/envelope/">'+
'<soap:Body>'+
'<Calculate xmlns="http://localhost/ProxyCalculationService">'+
'<PaymentRequestType>Long</PaymentRequestType>'+
```

```
'<LoanProgram>' + getSelectValue('ProgramName') + '</LoanProgram>'+
'<TotalAPRFeesAmount>' + getFloatValue('TotalAPRFeesAmount') +
'</TotalAPRFeesAmount>'+
'<IndexValue>' + getFloatValue('IndexValue') + '</IndexValue>'+
'<MarginValue>' + getFloatValue('MarginValue') + '</MarginValue>'+
'<OriginalLoanAmount>' + getFloatValue('OriginalLoanAmount') +
'</OriginalLoanAmount>'+
'<DisclosedTotalSalesPriceAmount>' +
  getFloatValue('DisclosedTotalSalesPriceAmount') +
'</DisclosedTotalSalesPriceAmount>'+
'<PropertyAppraisedValueAmount>' +
  getFloatValue('PropertyAppraisedValueAmount') +
'</PropertyAppraisedValueAmount>'+
'<NoteRatePercent>' +
  getFloatValue('NoteRatePercent') + '</NoteRatePercent>' +
'<LoanOriginalMaturityTermMonths>' +
  getFloatValue('LoanOriginalMaturityTermMonths') +
'</LoanOriginalMaturityTermMonths>'+
'<ApplicationSignedDate>' + getDateValue() + '</ApplicationSignedDate>'+
'<LoanEstimatedClosingDate>' + getDateValue() + '</LoanEstimatedClosingDate>'+
'<ScheduledFirstPaymentDate>' + getDateValue() + '</ScheduledFirstPaymentDate>'+
'<EstimatedPrepaidDays>' + getPrepaidDays() + '</EstimatedPrepaidDays>'+
'</Calculate>'+
'</soap:Body>'+
'</soap:Envelope>'+
'';
```

Here you have built a string that contains all of the XML. This is a little clumsy in JavaScript but it gets the job done. You insert all of the values from the `<form>` using `getSelectValue()`, `getFloatValue()`, `getDateValue()`, and `getPrepaidDays()`.

4. Set the options of the `xmlhttp` object. For starters, open a connection to the web service proxy URL, and then create a JavaScript closure that monitors the ready state of the object. If the ready state is 4 (complete), you call a function that can handle the response:

```
xmlhttp.open("POST", "/ProxyCalculationService/Service.asmx", true);
xmlhttp.onreadystatechange=function() {
  if (xmlhttp.readyState==4) {
    receiveLoanInformation(xmlhttp.responseXML);
  }
}
```

5. Configure the headers and send the request:

```
xmlhttp.setRequestHeader("SOAPAction",
  "http://localhost/ProxyCalculationService/Calculate");
xmlhttp.setRequestHeader("Content-Type", "text/xml");
xmlhttp.setRequestHeader("Content-Length", request.length);
xmlhttp.send(request);
```

6. Add the `catch` block for the try/catch construction:

```
    }
  } catch(ex) {
    hideProgress();
    alert(ex.toString());
  }
}
```

When using the `xmlhttp` *object, make sure you call the* `open` *method prior to setting the* `onreadystatechange` *event. This ensures that the* `xmlhttp` *object can be reused in Internet Explorer.*

7. The `getSelectValue()`, `getFloatValue()`, `getDateValue()`, and `getPrepaidDays()` functions don't exist yet. `getSelectValue()` and `getFloatValue()` look up a form field by `id` and get its current value. `getDateValue()` determines when the next 15th of the month is, and `getPrepaidDays()` determines the number of days between that date and the end of the month:

```
function getSelectValue(id) {
    var obj = document.getElementById(id);
    return (obj.selectedIndex > -1 ? obj.options[obj.selectedIndex].value : "");
}

function getFloatValue(id) {
    var obj = document.getElementById(id);
    return (obj ? parseFloat(obj.value) : 0);
}

function getDateValue() {
  var d = new Date();
  if (d.getDate() > 15)
    d.setMonth(d.getMonth()+1);
  return d.getFullYear() + "-" + (d.getMonth()+1) + "-15";
}

function getPrepaidDays() {
  var d = new Date();
  if (d.getDate() > 15)
    d.setMonth(d.getMonth()+1);
  d.setDate(0);
  return d.getDate()-15;
}
```

You have used a couple of tricks here to shortcut the calculations. Note that you increment the month values regardless of whether the current month is December. The JavaScript `Date` object handles this by incrementing the year and setting the month to January. Likewise, when you set the date to 0, the `Date` object decrements the month (and possibly year) and sets the day to the last day of the month.

8. The `receiveLoanInformation` function referred to in the `onreadystatechange` closure is passed the response XML document. After checking whether there is a root element using the `documentElement` property, you grab all of the contained `<PAYMENTSTREAM>` elements using the DOM method `getElementsByTagName`:

```
function receiveLoanInformation(responseXML) {
  try {
    if (responseXML.documentElement == null) return;
    var payments = response.getElementsByTagName("PAYMENTSTREAM");
```

9. Once you have a collection of `<PAYMENTSTREAM>` nodes, you can begin constructing the XHTML for the `<table>`. You grab the number of payments and loop through the collection, adding a `<tr>` element for each item. You use the CSS class `even_row` for all of the even numbered rows in the output, and `odd_row` for the odd ones. Each row contains the payment and balance from the current node:

```
var totalPayments = payments.length;
var payment = 0;
var balance = 0;
var tableHTML = "" +
  "<table border='0' cellpadding='0' cellspacing='0'>" +
  "  <tr>" +
  "    <th>Payment Date</th>" +
  "    <th>Payment Amount</th>" +
  "    <th>Remaining Balance</th>" +
  "  </tr>";
for (var i = 0; i < totalPayments; i++) {
  payment = parseFloat(payments[i].getAttribute("PmtTotal"));
  balance = parseFloat(payments[i].getAttribute("PmtEndingBalance"));
  tableHTML += ""+
    "<tr " + ((i % 2 == 0) ? "class='even_row'>" : "class='odd_row'>") +
    "<td>" + payments[i].getAttribute("PmtDate") + "</td>" +
    "<td class='numeric_cell'>" + formatDollar(payment) + "</td>" +
    "<td class='numeric_cell'>" + formatDollar(balance) + "</td>" +
    "</tr>";
}
tableHTML += "</table>";
```

10. Once the HTML is constructed, you can assign it to the `payments_table` container in the document using the `innerHTML` property:

```
var tableContainer = document.getElementById("payments_table");
tableContainer.innerHTML = tableHTML;
```

When inserting the payment table data, notice that you inserted the whole `<table>` into the `innerHTML` property of the container. Internet Explorer doesn't allow you to modify the `innerHTML` of a `<table>` element, so you have to use a container.

11. Call the `hideProgress` function to enable the `Calculate` button and hide the progress indicator:

```
  } finally {
    hideProgress();
  }
}
```

12. The only function left to create is `formatDollar`, which converts a floating-point number to a string with a leading "$". It also rounds the value to the nearest cent and prints trailing zeroes to two decimal places:

```
function formatDollar(value) {
  value *= 100;
  value = Math.round(value);
  value /= 100;
  var res = "$" + value;
  if (res.indexOf(".") == -1) {
    res += ".00";
  } else {
    while (res.indexOf(".") > res.length-2) res += "0";
  }
  return res;
}
```

13. Before the application will work, you need to modify `loancalulator2.html`. Open the file and save it as `loancalculator3.html` in the same folder. Modify the header to add references to the two script files:

```
<head>
  <title>Loan Calculator</title>
  <meta http-equiv="content-type" content="text/html; charset=iso-8859-1" />
  <link href="loancalculator1.css" rel="stylesheet" type="text/css" />
  <script type="text/javascript" src="xmlhttp.js"></script>
  <script type="text/javascript" src="loancalculator1.js"></script>
</head>
```

14. Modify the `onclick` attribute for the `Calculate` button so that it calls the `submitLoanInformation` function:

```
<div id="buttons">
  <input id="calculate_button" type="submit" value="Calculate"
         onclick="submitLoanInformation(); return false;"/>
  <span id="working"><img src="indicator.gif" alt="Working..." /></span>
</div>
```

How It Works

In this Try It Out, you completed the loan calculator by connecting the web page to the proxy web service using Ajax. Now when users click the Calculate button, the proposed payments are displayed on the page (see Figure 21-10); and while the request is being processed, a spinning indicator appears to let the user know that it is working.

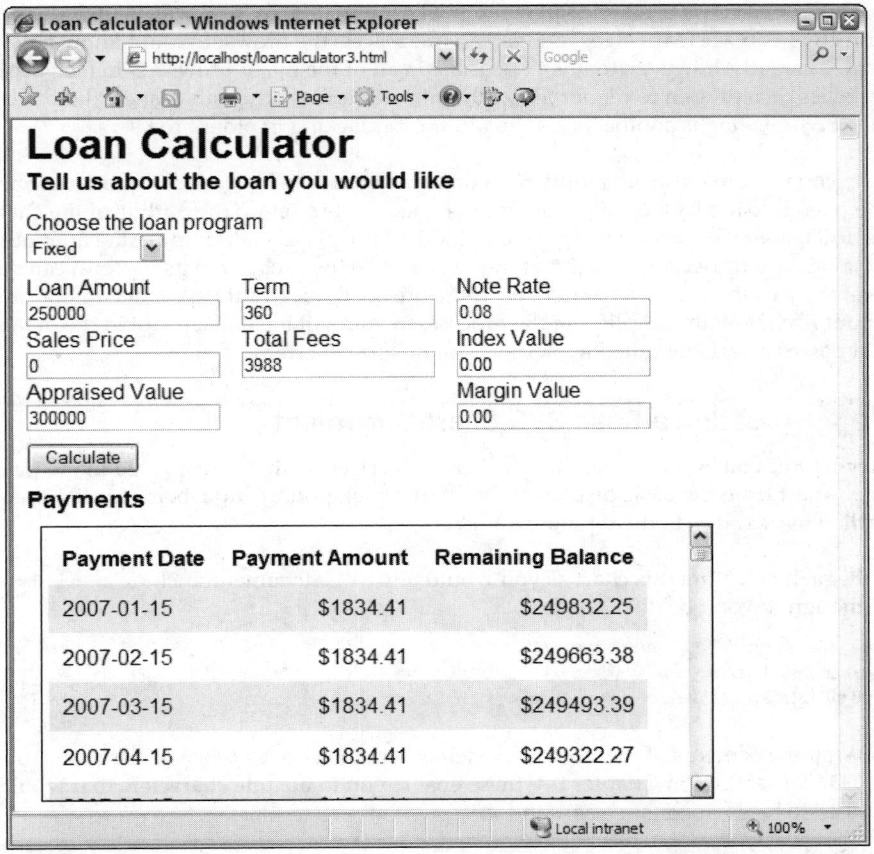

Figure 21-10

Enhancing the Display with SVG

Displaying the payments and ending balance in a table is very useful, but by using a chart of the balance over time, one could quickly compare the various loan programs visually. You can use Scalable Vector Graphics (SVG) to construct the chart and display it in the loan calculator web page. Again, in order for users to see the SVG graphic, they need to have a browser that supports SVG or an SVG plug-in.

Building the chart includes the following steps:

1. Create a base SVG document for the chart.
2. Display the SVG in an `<iframe>` element.
3. Use JavaScript to manipulate the SVG DOM and assign the chart data.

Note that an `<iframe>` is used to display the SVG content. Ideally, you would include the `<svg>` elements directly in an XHTML page; and using namespaces, the browser would know how to render the document. Currently, however, that isn't possible in all of the major browsers. In fact, because Internet Explorer relies on a plug-in to render SVG content, `<iframe>` is the only standard cross-browser solution. The `<object>` tag is another solution, but for it is lacking in older browsers.

Therefore, you need to create an empty SVG document that can be loaded into the `<iframe>` element when the page is loaded. Of course, you use the document to set up the outline of the chart and several other defaults, which makes drawing the chart in JavaScript easier. Manipulating an inner frame through JavaScript (especially when that frame has an ActiveX object in its content) can be cumbersome because of the varying security restrictions in the browser. Luckily, the SVG document can tell the parent frame about itself, greatly simplifying the process, so you will include a script in the default chart document that passes a variable called svgWindow to the topmost frame.

Try It Out   Creating a Base SVG Chart Document

In this Try It Out, you build the base for the loan balance chart that is displayed in the loan calculator web page. Apart from the basic display of the chart's background and labels, this file needs to pass a reference called svgWindow to the topmost frame:

1. Begin by creating this chart as you would any SVG document. Include a `<title>` element even though it won't be displayed:

```
<?xml version="1.0" encoding="UTF-8"?>
<svg xmlns="http://www.w3.org/2000/svg">
  <title>Loan Balance over Time</title>
```

2. Wrap the contents of the `<script>` element in a `<![CDATA[ ]]>` declaration. You learned about CDATA sections in Chapter 2 — these enable you to include characters that would normally need to be escaped (such as < and &):

```
<script type="text/javascript"><![CDATA[
  top.svgWindow = window;
// ]]></script>
```

The code does one thing: assigns the current `window` to a variable called `svgWindow` in the "top" frame. You can access the `svgWindow` variable directly from the main loan calculator page.

3. Include a grid for the data, using a simple rectangle and four lines. In a more complete application, you might enhance this with a decorative gradient or other design features:

```
<g id="grid">
  <rect x="10" y="10" width="500" height="200" fill="#f0f0f0"
    stroke="#000" stroke-width="2"/>
  <path d="M11,60 l 498,0 M11,110 l 498,0 M11,160 l 498,0 M11,210 l 498,0"
    stroke="#ddd"/>
</g>
```

4. Even though there is no data when the chart is loaded, it is helpful to insert a placeholder for the graph. Include a `<path>` that has only one command: a simple move command (`M0,0`):

```
<g id="data">
  <path id="balance" d="M0,0" fill="#77c" stroke="#aaf" fill-opacity="0.3"/>
</g>
```

5. The chart needs labels for the dates and balances. Create four basic balance labels and a container to insert the date labels:

```
<g id="balance_labels" font-size="8pt" font-weight="bold">
  <text id="balance100Percent" x="520" y="20">$0.00</text>
  <text id="balance75Percent" x="520" y="65">$0.00</text>
  <text id="balance50Percent" x="520" y="115">$0.00</text>
  <text id="balance25Percent" x="520" y="165">$0.00</text>
</g>
<g id="date_labels" font-size="6pt" font-weight="normal">
</g>
```

You have provided `id` attributes on all of the elements that you will want to modify later. Looking up elements by `id` is much easier than traversing the DOM using `firstChild` and `nextSibling` methods.

6. Finally, add the closing `<svg>` tag:

```
</svg>
```

7. Save the file as `chart.svg` in the same folder as `loancalculator3.html`.

How It Works

In this Try It Out you built a basic chart using SVG. You haven't added an `<iframe>` in the main page, but you can view the chart directly in a browser (see Figure 21-11).

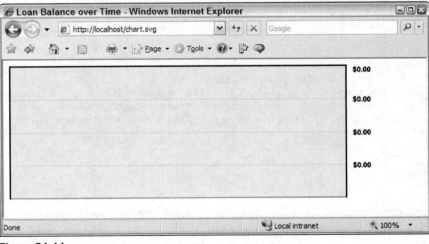

Figure 21-11

By default, the SVG should be viewable in your browser if you have the correct plug-in installed or you are using a browser that supports SVG natively. If the browser offers to let you download the file, then you may need to add an entry for the SVG MIME (`"image/svg+xml"`) type to your web server. For more information, see `http://wiki.svg.org/MIME_Type`*.*

Adding the Frame to the Main Page

Of course, a blank chart isn't very useful. Let's add the frame to the main loan calculator page and add some script to draw the data.

Try It Out   Integrating the SVG and the Loan Calculator

This Try It Out adds a frame to the main loan calculator page to display the SVG. It also modifies the JavaScript for the loan calculator so that it displays the results:

1. Open `loancalculator3.html` in your editor and make the following changes. Because you need to update the JavaScript for the loan calculator, you must update the reference in the header of the page:

```
<head>
  <title>Loan Calculator</title>
  <meta http-equiv="content-type" content="text/html; charset=iso-8859-1" />
  <link href="loancalculator1.css" rel="stylesheet" type="text/css" />
  <script type="text/javascript" src="xmlhttp.js"></script>
  <script type="text/javascript" src="loancalculator2.js"></script>
</head>
```

2. The `<iframe>` should refer to `chart.svg` and you need to set a default width and height. You also remove the frame border so that it looks consistent with the rest of the design:

```
    <div id="payments">
      <h3><span>Payments</span></h3>
      <div id="payments_table">
        Please submit a request and the payments will be displayed here.
      </div>
    </div>
    <div id="chart">
      <h3><span>Lending Balance</span></h3>
      <iframe src="chart.svg" width="650" height="260"
        frameborder="0" id="chart_frame" name="chart_frame">
        <p>It looks like your browser doesn't support frames</p>
      </iframe>
    </div>
  </div>
 </body>
</html>
```

This provides a fallback message for browsers that don't support frames. Once you are finished, save the file as `loancalculator4.html`.

3. To modify the JavaScript for the loan calculator, open `loancalculator1.js` in your editor and save it as `loancalculator2.js`. Modify the end of the `receiveLoanInformation` function so that it calls the new `drawChart` function and passes the `payments`:

```
tableHTML += "</table>";
var tableContainer = document.getElementById("payments_table");
tableContainer.innerHTML = tableHTML;
drawChart(payments);
} finally {
hideProgress();
}
```

4. Define the `drawChart` function at the end of the `loancalculator2.js` file. This function contains a lot of math and DOM manipulation, so you break it down into smaller parts. Declare the function and check whether the `svgWindow` variable that you created inside of `chart.svg` is available:

```
function drawChart(payments) {
  if (svgWindow == null) return;
```

5. Each payment is charted in the SVG. In order to calculate the points, you need to know the width and height as well as the offsets of the chart. You could figure this out programmatically, but because they won't be changing, just use constants:

```
var left = 10;
var top = 10;
var width = 500;
var height = 200;
```

6. In addition to the basic dimensions of the chart, you need to know the maximum balance. In some mortgages, the balance can exceed the original loan amount. Loop through all of the payments to determine the maximum balance at any given point in the loan:

```
var totalPayments = payments.length;
var maxBalance = -1;
var balance = 0;
for (var i = 0; i < totalPayments; i++) {
  balance = parseFloat(payments[i].getAttribute("PmtEndingBalance"));
  if (maxBalance == -1 || maxBalance < balance) maxBalance = balance;
}
```

7. You now have enough information to begin labeling the chart. Set up four labels for the balances: the maximum balance, 75% of the maximum, 50% of the maximum and 25% of the maximum. These labels give users some indication of the loan balance at any given point in the timeline:

```
var balance100Percent = svgWindow.document.getElementById("balance100Percent");
var balance75Percent = svgWindow.document.getElementById("balance75Percent");
var balance50Percent = svgWindow.document.getElementById("balance50Percent");
var balance25Percent = svgWindow.document.getElementById("balance25Percent");
balance100Percent.firstChild.nodeValue = formatDollar(maxBalance);
balance75Percent.firstChild.nodeValue = formatDollar(0.75 * maxBalance);
balance50Percent.firstChild.nodeValue = formatDollar(0.50 * maxBalance);
balance25Percent.firstChild.nodeValue = formatDollar(0.25 * maxBalance);
```

8. As shown elsewhere in this application, you look up the elements by their `id` attribute. To assign the value, you select the `firstChild` (in this case, the first text node in the element content) and set the `nodeValue` property to the amount.

9. Before you can build the data for the chart, you need to figure out the width each payment uses on the graph. Likewise, by dividing the height by the total balance, you can convert the balance amounts to percentages of the height:

```
var paymentWidth = (width / totalPayments);
var balanceHeight = (height / maxBalance);
```

10. Declare a variable `balancePath` for the path data that charts the balance, and initialize it with a move command (M) to the lower-left corner of the graph:

```
var balanceData = "M " + left + "," + (top+height);
```

11. Loop through the payments again, this time converting the payment number (i) to a horizontal position and the remaining balance to a vertical position. Use a `line` command (L) to move the pen to each point, appending the results to `balancePath` after each iteration:

```
for (var i = 0; i < totalPayments; i++) {
  balanceData += "L" + (left+(i*paymentWidth)) + "," + ((top+height) -
    (balanceHeight*parseFloat(payments[i].getAttribute("PmtEndingBalance"))));
}
```

12. Closing the path provides a complete polygon that can be filled in appropriately. Just draw a line to the bottom, right corner of the graph and close the path using the z command:

```
balanceData += " L" + (left+width) + "," + (top+height) + " z";
```

13. With the path data complete, you can look up the balance element in the chart and assign the data to the d attribute:

```
var balancePath = svgWindow.document.getElementById("balance");
balancePath.setAttribute("d", balanceData);
```

14. With the path data completed, add the date labels to the bottom of the chart. Before you do that, though, clear any existing elements in the `date_labels` container in the SVG. Use a `while` loop, which keeps deleting the `firstChild` as long as the element has children:

```
var labels = svgWindow.document.getElementById("date_labels");
while (labels.hasChildNodes()) {
  labels.removeChild(labels.firstChild);
}
```

15. Loop through the payments array one last time to add the date labels. Instead of adding a label for each payment, only add one label per year. Do this by checking whether the current iteration is evenly divisible by 12 (using the modulus operator %). If not, continue to the next iteration. Otherwise, create a `<text>` element in the SVG namespace:

```
for (var i = 1; i < totalPayments; i++) {
  if (i % 12 != 0) continue;
  var label =
    svgWindow.document.createElementNS("http://www.w3.org/2000/svg", "text");
```

16. The new element doesn't have any children by default, so you can't assign the content using the `firstChild.nodeValue`, as you did earlier. Instead, create a new text node with the content and immediately append it as a child of the `label`:

```
label.appendChild(svgWindow.document.createTextNode(
    payments[i].getAttribute("PmtDate")));
```

17. Positioning the dates is easier if they are right-justified. SVG controls the justification through the `text-anchor` property:

```
label.setAttribute("text-anchor", "end");
```

18. Rotate the text labels so that they don't overlap. Rotating them 45 degrees should be enough, but you also need to position them along the bottom of the graph. Use the `transform` attribute with a `translate(x,y)` command and a `rotate(degrees)` command:

```
label.setAttribute("transform",
    "translate(" + (20+(i*paymentWidth))+", "+(20+height)+"), rotate(-45)");
```

Each label is also offset by `20` on the left and the top. There is no significance to the value `20`, but it enables you to visually account for the rotation and the `text-anchor`.

19. Finally, append the new `label` to the `labels` group and add the closing braces for the loop and the `drawChart` function:

```
        labels.appendChild(label);
    }
}
```

How It Works

In this Try It Out, you completed the loan calculator by using the payment and balance information to build a chart showing how the balance is paid off over time. This kind of visualization greatly enhances the application. Moreover, because you used SVG, the data you are generating can be manipulated through JavaScript and the DOM. With the data returned from the Compliance Studio service, you could create dozens of charts in SVG. Figure 21-12 shows the completed chart for a fixed-loan program.

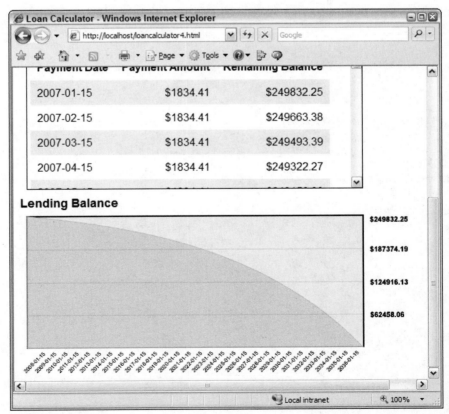

Figure 21-12

Even if you are using an SVG-capable browser, the browser may not realize that the material it's seeing is SVG. If you point your browser at one of your newly uploaded SVG masterpieces and all you see is XML code or a prompt to download the file, then review the steps in Chapter 19 on SVG in the section "SVG on Your Website."

Summary

This case study used a variety of XML technologies to build an advanced online loan calculator. By connecting to a freely available web service using a local proxy service, you were able to quickly execute advanced mortgage calculations and display the results to users. Though you may not be working in the mortgage industry, this pattern of connecting to a web service and displaying the results in your own page is used throughout the Web.

Of course, there is no reason to limit the loan calculator to a single web service. You could easily connect to other web services and combine the results on your page. A web page that uses disparate information sources is often called a *mashup*. Online applications frequently combine calculation engines, search engines, mapping engines, and even other mashups to build successful sites.

Exercise Solutions

This appendix contains some suggested solutions to the exercise questions posed at the end of most of the chapters throughout the book.

Chapter 1

This chapter gave an overview of XML and why it's so useful.

Question 1

Modify the <name> XML document you've been working with to include the person's title (Mr., Ms., Dr., and so on).

Solution

Because of the self-describing nature of XML, the only difficult part of adding a title to the <name> example is deciding what to call it. If you call it <title>, you can add it to your document as follows:

```
<name>
  <title>Mr.</title>
  <first>John</first>
  <middle>Fitzgerald Johansen</middle>
  <last>Doe</last>
</name>
```

Another possibility is to treat a title as a simple prefix to the name; this also allows you the flexibility of adding a suffix. This approach might look like the following:

```
<name>
  <prefix>Mr.</prefix>
  <first>John</first>
  <middle>Fitzgerald Johansen</middle>
  <last>Doe</last>
  <suffix>the 3rd</suffix>
</name>
```

In this case, instead of giving the data an explicit label, you're making it more generic and allowing some text to come before and after the name.

Question 2

The `<name>` example we've been using so far has been in English, but XML is language-agnostic, so you can create XML documents in any language you wish. Create a new French document type to represent a name. You can use the following table for the names of the XML elements:

English	French
name	identité
first	prénom
Last	nom
middle	deuxième-prénom

Solution

Although this might seem like a trick question, it's actually not. As shown in Chapter 2, XML allows the special French characters required here (as well as many thousands of other characters) in element names. That means creating the document in French is just as easy as creating it in English:

```
<identité>
  <prénom>John</prénom>
  <deuxiéme-prénom>Fitzgerald Johansen</deuxiéme-prénom>
  <nom>Doe</nom>
</identité>
```

If you enter this into Notepad, save it using the UTF-8 encoding, and view it in Internet Explorer, it will show up just as easily as the English version did, as shown in Figure A-1.

If you have trouble entering the "é" character, open the Character Map application and copy the character from there. You can then paste it into Notepad in the appropriate spots. On Windows XP, you can find Character Map in Start ➪ All Programs ➪ Accessories ➪ System Tools ➪ Character Map.

Figure A-1

When you save this document, however, be sure to specify to Notepad that you want to save the file using the UTF-8 encoding. If you use the default ANSI encoding, the document won't show up in the browser properly. Instead, you'll get an error message like the one shown in Figure A-2. In Chapter 2, you'll see why this encoding setting is so important.

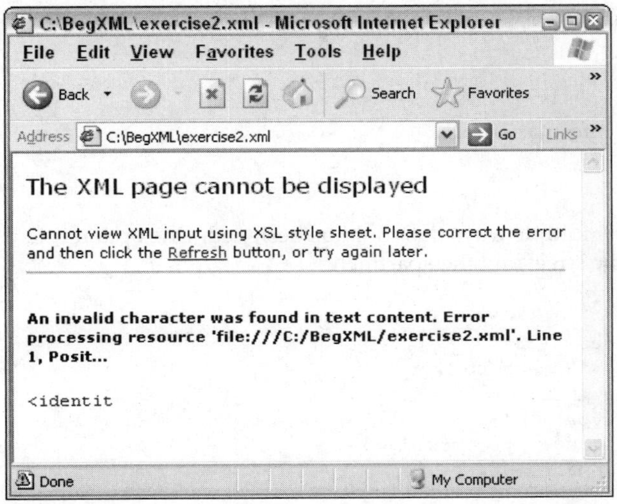

Figure A-2

Although XML is language-agnostic, allowing you to create markup in any language you want, remember that XML is not able to translate markup from one language to another. Therefore, if you write an application that handles names, and program that application to ask the XML parser for the information from the element called `last`, that's what the parser looks for. If you try to feed your French XML document to that application, the parser will find an element called `nom`, but it won't be able to find an element called `last`, which means the application won't be able to get the data it needs. There is no way for an XML parser to know that a `nom` element is equivalent to a `last` element; as far as the parser is concerned, you've created two completely different document types, even if they are equivalent to a human mind. This is an important concept to remember as you continue through the book.

Chapter 2

This chapter described the basic syntax for writing well-formed XML documents.

Question 1

For the addresses in our Order XML, we used a common format of "Address Line 1, Address Line 2, City, State, and Zip Code." Other applications need to be stricter with their addresses, and have separate elements for street number, street name, and so on. Rewrite the last version of the Order XML using the following information, instead of the Address Line 1/Address Line 2 format:

- ❑ Street number
- ❑ Street name
- ❑ Apt. number
- ❑ City
- ❑ State
- ❑ Zip code
- ❑ Additional information

Solution

As always, there are multiple ways this could be designed. One option is to use attributes, to break up information about the street and the apartment:

```
<Address>
  <Street number="123"
          name="Somewhere Ave." />
  <Apartment number=""
             type="" />
  <!--the apartment type would
      specify apartment, suite,
      room, etc. -->

  <City>Some Town</City>
  <State>TA</State>
  <Zip>000000000</Zip>
  <AdditionalInformation/>
</Address>
```

It's nice to have this flexibility, but for this example it would not be wise to design the address like that, because it isn't consistent with the rest of the document. Instead, to fit in with the naming convention used throughout the rest of the document, it's probably better to use child elements, as follows:

```
<Address>
  <StreetNumber>123</StreetNumber>
  <StreetName>Somewhere Ave.</StreetName>
  <ApartmentNumber/>
  <City>Some Town</City>
  <State>TA</State>
  <Zip>000000000</Zip>
  <AdditionalInformation/>
</Address>
```

That turns the overall document into this:

```
<?xml version="1.0"?>
<Orders Count="2">
  <Order ID="0000000001">
    <?SernaProcessor ManualIntervention reason:Insufficient Funds?>
    <Type>N</Type>
```

```
  <Date>Jan 1, 2004, 14:29</Date>
  <Customer>
    <SernaDirect>
      <SubscriptionType>B</SubscriptionType>
      <SubscriptionLength>12</SubscriptionLength>
    </SernaDirect>
    <Address>
      <StreetNumber>123</StreetNumber>
      <StreetName>Somewhere Ave.</StreetName>
      <ApartmentNumber/>
      <City>Some Town</City>
      <State>TA</State>
      <Zip>000000000</Zip>
      <AdditionalInformation/>
    </Address>
    <CreditCard>
      <Number>4111111111111111</Number>
      <CardHolderName>John Q Public</CardHolderName>
      <Expiry>11/09</Expiry>
    </CreditCard>
    <Phone>5555555555</Phone>
    <Name>John Public</Name>
    <Email>jpublic@someprovider.com</Email>
  </Customer>
  <Number>x582n9</Number>
  <Products Count="1">
    <Product>
      <Model>X9</Model>
      <Price>129.95</Price>
      <ID>x9000059</ID>
    </Product>
  </Products>
</Order>
<Order ID="0000000002">
  <Type>N</Type>
  <Date>Jan 1, 2004, 16:00</Date>
  <Customer>
    <SernaDirect>
      <SubscriptionType>D</SubscriptionType>
      <SubscriptionLength>12</SubscriptionLength>
    </SernaDirect>
    <Address>
      <StreetNumber>89</StreetNumber>
      <StreetName>Subscriber's Street</StreetName>
      <ApartmentNumber/>
      <City>Smallville</City>
      <State>XQ</State>
      <Zip>000000000</Zip>
      <AdditionalInformation>Box 882</AdditionalInformation>
    </Address>
    <CreditCard>
      <Number>4512451245124512</Number>
      <CardHolderName>Helen P Someperson</CardHolderName>
      <Expiry>01/08</Expiry>
```

```
        </CreditCard>
        <Phone>5554443333</Phone>
        <Name>Helen Someperson</Name>
        <Email>helens@isp.net</Email>
      </Customer>
      <Number>a98f78d</Number>
      <Products Count="1">
        <Product>
          <Model>Y9</Model>
          <Price>229.95</Price>
          <ID>y9000065</ID>
        </Product>
      </Products>
    </Order>
  </Orders>
```

This doesn't put to work all of the different things you learned in the chapter, but it is a better overall design, especially when the document as a whole is taken into consideration.

Question 2

Sometimes the syntax used by XML can be a little troublesome to figure out. The following XML document contains a few syntactical errors, preventing it from being well formed. Correct them so that the document can be read by IE.

Hint: When I'm trying to correct a file like this, I often open it in the browser and fix errors as the browser reports them to me. Be warned — some of the errors are a bit more difficult to figure out than others.

```
<?xml version="1"?>
<document>
  <--There are a couple of problems with this document.-->
  <Information>This document
  contains some < bold>information</bold>. Once
  it's corrected, it can be read by a parser.</Information>
</Document>
```

Solution

For this example, I purposely tried to pick some common errors that I find hard to spot when I'm working with XML. When you have an XML document that isn't well formed and you can't figure out why, your first step should always be to load the document into a parser that provides good error information. IE is an excellent example. When I load this document into a browser, the first thing that it complains about is the version number, as shown in Figure A-3.

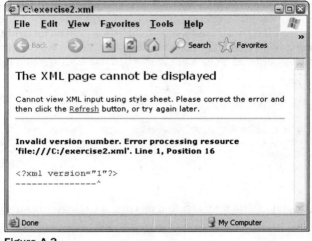

Figure A-3

XML parsers are very picky about the version number; it has to be exactly "1.0" — "1" isn't good enough. Correct the version number as follows:

```
<?xml version="1.0"?>
<document>
   <--There are a couple of problems with this document.-->
   <Information>This document
   contains some < bold>information</bold>. Once
   it's corrected, it can be read by a parser.</Information>
</Document>
```

Resave this and load it in the browser again. The file is still not correct, and the message shown in Figure A-4 appears.

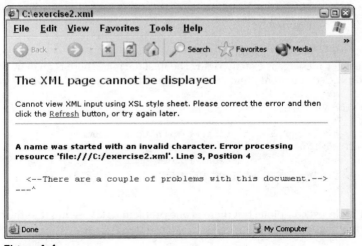

Figure A-4

This doesn't seem to make sense. Why is the XML parser trying to read what's in the comments? The answer is that there is no ! at the beginning of the comment, so the parser doesn't realize it's supposed to be a comment. As far as the parser is concerned, there is a < character, and there's no ! after it, so this should be the beginning of an element. Because a dash isn't a valid way to start an element name, the parser assumes it has encountered an element with a bad name. Correcting this problem is easy enough. Just add the !:

```
<?xml version="1.0"?>
<document>
  <!--There are a couple of problems with this document.-->
  <Information>This document
  contains some < bold>information</bold>. Once
  it's corrected, it can be read by a parser.</Information>
</Document>
```

The document is still not done, though. Loading this into the browser results in the error shown in Figure A-5.

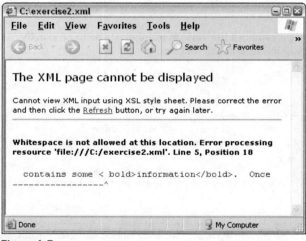

Figure A-5

In this case, the error message is exactly right. The mistake made here is an extra space added after the opening < of the <bold> element. Remove the space as follows:

```
<?xml version="1.0"?>
<document>
  <!--There are a couple of problems with this document.-->
  <Information>This document
  contains some <bold>information</bold>. Once
  it's corrected, it can be read by a parser.</Information>
</Document>
```

The document is almost complete, but there is one problem left. Viewing it in the browser now reveals the error shown in Figure A-6.

Figure A-6

Once again, the error message provided by IE is very descriptive. Although the start-tag is named docu-ment, with a lowercase "d," the end-tag is named Document, with the "D" in uppercase. Changing the end-tag to use a lowercase "d" fixes the document and results in the following XML:

```
<?xml version="1.0"?>
<document>
  <!--There are a couple of problems with this document.-->
  <Information>This document
  contains some <bold>information</bold>. Once
  it's corrected, it can be read by a parser.</Information>
</document>
```

Now the document finally loads properly in the browser, as shown in Figure A-7.

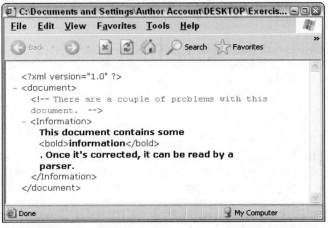

Figure A-7

Chapter 3

This chapter introduced the concept of namespaces, along with their implementation in XML.

Question 1

This chapter used the following XML document, in which you had to cancel the default namespace:

```
<employee>
   <name>Jane Doe</name>
    <notes>
        <p xmlns="http://www.w3.org/1999/xhtml">I've worked
        with <name xmlns="">Jane Doe</name> for over a <em>year</em>
        now.</p>
    </notes>
</employee>
```

Assuming that this document is for Wiley's HR department, create a namespace for employees, and use it in this document. Be sure to keep the XHTML elements in their namespace.

Solution

The URL we've been using for namespaces for Wiley has been `http://www.wiley.com`, followed by something to indicate the namespace being named. In this case, you're creating a namespace for employees, so `http://www.wiley.com/employee` makes sense.

Because you have a `<name>` element embedded inside an XHTML `<p>` element, it makes sense to use prefixes, rather than default namespaces, so the resulting document could look like this:

```
<emp:employee xmlns:emp="http://www.wiley.com/employee">
   <emp:name>Jane Doe</emp:name>
   <emp:notes>
     <p xmlns="http://www.w3.org/1999/xhtml">I've worked
     with <emp:name>Jane Doe</emp:name> for over a <em>year</em>
     now.</p>
   </emp:notes>
</emp:employee>
```

I decided to leave the XHTML elements in a default namespace, because I'm much more used to reading XHTML without all of the embedded namespace prefixes. Notice that I also removed the `xmlns=""` attribute, which was canceling the default namespace on the `<name>` element, but I then had to prefix the `<name>` element with the `emp` prefix.

Question 2

Imagine that Wiley has been going through their employee records and realize that they don't have a good, unique way to identify each employee. Create a global `id` attribute that can be attached to any XML element in the employee namespace you created earlier.

Put this attribute into effect by modifying the XML you created in Question 1, and mark the Jane Doe employee as employee number x125.

Solution

You already know the name of the attribute you want to create: The only question is what namespace you should put it in. You could put it in the `http://www.wiley.com/employee` namespace, if you think the attribute is about an employee, or you could use the `http://www.wiley.com/pers` namespace, if you think the attribute is about a person, or you could create a brand-new namespace, if you think it's distinct from both of these namespaces.

As is often the case, there is no right answer. More information is probably required to determine conceptually what namespace should be used. For the sake of discussion, assume that this attribute is used to identify not just employees of Wiley, but also customers, business contacts, and so on. In that case, it makes sense to include it in the `http://www.wiley.com/pers` namespace.

Therefore, you could modify the earlier document to create the following:

```
<emp:employee xmlns:emp="http://www.wiley.com/employee"
              xmlns:pers="http://www.wiley.com/pers"
              pers:id="x125">
  <emp:name>Jane Doe</emp:name>
  <emp:notes>
    <p xmlns="http://www.w3.org/1999/xhtml">I've worked
    with <emp:name pers:id="x125">Jane Doe</emp:name>
    for over a <em>year</em> now.</p>
  </emp:notes>
</emp:employee>
```

Notice that the attribute is also added to the `<name>` element in the Notes section. Depending on how the data will be used, this may or may not be necessary, but it couldn't hurt.

Question 3

Create a new XML file for an employee named Alfred Neuman, with employee number x393. In the notes for Alfred, mention that he has worked closely with Jane Doe, being sure to use the `<name>` element to refer to her.

Solution

Because there isn't really that much data in these files, Alfred's XML file will look very similar to Jane's. The only real data is the `<name>` element, as well as the `<notes>` field. The result should look similar to this:

```
<emp:employee xmlns:emp="http://www.wiley.com/employee"
              xmlns:pers="http://www.wiley.com/pers"
              pers:id="x393">
  <emp:name>Alfred Neuman</emp:name>
  <emp:notes>
    <p xmlns="http://www.w3.org/1999/xhtml">Alfred has worked
    with <emp:name pers:id="x125">Jane Doe</emp:name> in the
    past, and she has had nothing but good to say about him.</p>
  </emp:notes>
</emp:employee>
```

Chapter 4

This chapter showed how to utilize DTDs to easily validate your XML documents against a defined vocabulary of elements and attributes.

Question 1

Build a contact for yourself in the list based on the declarations in the contacts DTD. Once you have added the new contact, validate your document to ensure that it is correct.

Solution

Because I have already added a contact for myself in the chapter, here I add a new contact for "Weird Al" Yankovic, one of my favorite recording artists. Here is the contact information for "Weird Al":

```
<contact person="Weird_Al_Yankovic" tags="singer artist parody">
  <name>
    <first>Weird</first>
    <first>Al</first>
    <middle>Matthew</middle>
    <last>Yankovic</last>
  </name>
  <location>
    <address>Lynwood, CA, USA</address>
    <latitude>33.959878</latitude>
    <longitude>-118.210487</longitude>
  </location>
  <phone kind="Work">001-805-646-8433</phone>
  <knows contacts="Jeff_Rafter"/>
  <description>"Weird Al" is the most creative musical genius ever.
    Clearly chief among the White and Nerdy</description>
</contact>
```

Question 2

Add a `gender` attribute declaration for the `<contact>` elements. The attribute should allow two possible values: `male` and `female`. Make sure the attribute is required.

Solution

You first need to modify the DTD. Add the attribute declaration with an enumerated list as the data type. Also, make sure that you have included the #REQUIRED keyword:

```
<!ELEMENT contact (name, location, phone, knows, description)>
<!ATTLIST contact person ID #REQUIRED>
<!ATTLIST contact tags NMTOKENS #IMPLIED>
<!ATTLIST contact gender (male | female) #REQUIRED>
```

Of course, the new requirement means you need to change your XML instance document. Add a gender attribute to each of the contacts in your XML file, as shown in the following example:

```
<contact person="Jeff_Rafter" tags="author xml poetry" gender="male">
```

Question 3

Currently, each contact can have only one phone number. Modify the contact declaration so that each contact can have zero or more phone numbers. In addition, add declarations for website and email elements.

Solution

In order to allow for multiple <phone> elements as well as <website> and <email> elements, you needed to modify the declaration for the <contact> element:

```
<!ELEMENT contact (name, location, phone*, website*, email* knows, description)>
<!ATTLIST contact person ID #REQUIRED>
<!ATTLIST contact tags NMTOKENS #IMPLIED>
<!ATTLIST contact gender (male | female) #REQUIRED>
```

You also needed to add declarations for the new <website> and <email> elements:

```
<!ELEMENT website (#PCDATA)>
<!ELEMENT email (#PCDATA)>
```

Your existing contact list should still be valid. Of course, if you want to add more information to your contacts, you now can. For example, an updated contact may look like the following:

```
<contact person="Weird_Al_Yankovic" tags="singer artist parody">
  <name>
    <first>Weird</first>
    <first>Al</first>
    <middle>Matthew</middle>
    <last>Yankovic</last>
  </name>
  <location>
    <address>Lynwood, CA, USA</address>
    <latitude>33.959878</latitude>
    <longitude>-118.210487</longitude>
  </location>
  <phone kind="Work">001-805-646-8433</phone>
  <website>http://weirdal.com</website>
  <website>http://www.myspace.com/weirdal</website>
  <email>cpfoa@aol.com</email>
  <knows contacts="Jeff_Rafter"/>
  <description>"Weird Al" is the most creative musical genius ever.
    Clearly chief among the White and Nerdy.</description>
</contact>
```

Chapter 5

This chapter explained how to create XML Schemas that can be used to schema validate your XML documents.

Appendix A: Exercise Solutions

Question 1

Add a `gender` attribute declaration for the `<contact>` elements. The attribute should allow two possible values: `male` and `female`. Make sure the attribute is required.

Solution

Declare the new gender attribute within the `<complexType>` definition for the `<contact>` element. Within the attribute declaration, include an enumerated `<simpleType>` declaration that lists the values `male` and `female`:

```
<element name="contact" minOccurs="0" maxOccurs="unbounded">
    <complexType>
      <sequence>
        <element ref="name:name"/>
        <element name="location" type="contacts:LocationType"/>
        <element name="phone" type="contacts:PhoneType"/>
        <element name="knows" type="contacts:KnowsType"/>
        <element name="description" type="contacts:DescriptionType"/>
      </sequence>
      <attribute name="tags" type="token"/>
      <attribute name="person" type="ID"/>
      <attribute name="gender" required="true">
        <simpleType>
          <restriction base="string">
            <enumeration value="male"/>
            <enumeration value="female"/>
          </restriction>
        </simpleType>
      </attribute>
    </complexType>
</element>
```

Because the attribute is required, you must add these attributes to your current contacts listing.

Question 2

Currently, each contact can have only one phone number. Modify the contact declaration so that each contact can have zero or more phone numbers. In addition, add declarations for `website` and `email` elements.

Solution

Modify the `minOccurs` and `maxOccurs` of the `<phone>` element declaration within the `<complexType>` for the `<contact>` element. You can also add the new element declarations after the `<phone>` element declaration:

```
<element name="contact" minOccurs="0" maxOccurs="unbounded">
  <complexType>
    <sequence>
      <element ref="name:name"/>
      <element name="location" type="contacts:LocationType"/>
```

```
            <element name="phone" type="contacts:PhoneType"
              minOccurs="0" maxOccurs="unbounded"/>
            <element name="website" type="string"
              minOccurs="0" maxOccurs="unbounded"/>
            <element name="email" type="string"
              minOccurs="0" maxOccurs="unbounded"/>
            <element name="knows" type="contacts:KnowsType"/>
            <element name="description" type="contacts:DescriptionType"/>
          </sequence>
          <attribute name="tags" type="token"/>
          <attribute name="person" type="ID"/>
          <attribute name="gender" required="true">
            <simpleType>
              <restriction base="string">
                <enumeration value="male"/>
                <enumeration value="female"/>
              </restriction>
            </simpleType>
          </attribute>
        </complexType>
      </element>
```

Again, you can now add new content to each of your contacts, but your existing file should validate without any changes.

Question 3

Modify the `<description>` declaration to include an element wildcard. Within the wildcard, specify that the description element can accept any elements from the namespace http://www.w3.org/1999/xhtml. Set the processContents attribute to lax.

Solution

In this exercise, you want to modify the `<description>` element so that it can include any elements from the XHTML namespace. To do this, you need to replace the existing element declarations with an element wildcard declaration:

```
<complexType name="DescriptionType" mixed="true">
  <sequence>
    <any namespace="http://www.w3.org/1999/xhtml" processContents="lax"
      minOccurs="0" maxOccurs="unbounded"/>
  </sequence>
</complexType>
```

After you've completed the changes to the declaration, you need to update your XML document. Your document had the following:

```
Jeff is a developer &amp; author for Beginning XML <em>4th edition</em> &#169;
2006 Wiley Publishing.<br/>Jeff <strong>loves</strong> XML!
```

But you needed to modify this. In order for the content to be valid, you need to ensure that all of the elements used inside the description were from the XHTML namespace. To do this, you first add a namespace declaration to your root element. Then, you add the new prefix to all of your <br> and <em>, and <strong> elements:

```
Jeff is a developer &amp; author for Beginning XML <html:em>4th edition</html:em>
  &#169; 2006 Wiley Publishing.<html:br/>Jeff <html:strong>loves</html:strong> XML!
```

Don't forget to add the namespace declaration for the XHTML namespace to the header of the contacts listing:

```
<?xml version="1.0"?>
<contacts
  xmlns="http://www.example.com/contacts"
  xmlns:name="http://www.example.com/name"
  xmlns:html="http://www.w3.org/1999/xhtml"
  xmlns:xsi="http://www.w3.org/2001/XMLSchema-instance"
  xsi:schemaLocation="http://www.example.com/contacts contacts13_solution1.xsd"
  source="Beginning XML 4E"
  version="1.0">
```

Chapter 6

This chapter showed how to create RELAX NG compact schemas, which can be used to validate XML instance documents.

Question 1

Break the contacts19.rnc schema file into two schemas. In contacts-main.rnc, place the main schema elements. In contacts-names.rnc, place the name pattern definitions. At the top level, place an include directive in contacts-main.rnc to include contacts-names.rnc.

Solution 1

You first need to create contacts_names.rnc. You could do this by copying the name declarations from contacts15.rnc. The resulting file should look as follows:

```
name = element name { nameContents }
nameContents = (
  title?,
  first+,
  middle?,
  last
)
titles = ("Mr." | "Mrs." | "Ms." | "Miss" | "Sir" | "Rev" | "Dr.")
title = attribute title { titles }
first = element first { text }
middle = element middle { text }
last = element last { text }
```

You also need to create the document `contacts_main.rnc`. This file is the same as `contacts15.rnc` but the `name` declarations are removed and an `include` directive should be placed at the start of the document:

```
include "contacts_names.rnc"
start = contacts
contacts = element contacts { contactsContent }
contactsContent = (
  version,
  source?,
  contact*
)
version = attribute version { "1.0" }
source = attribute source { text }
contact = element contact { contactContents }
contactContents = (
  person?,
  tags?,
  name,
  location,
  phone,
  knows,
  description
)
person = attribute person { text }
tags = attribute tags { text }
location = element location { locationContents* }
locationContents = (
  address | ( latitude, longitude )
)
address = element address { text }
latitude = element latitude { text }
longitude = element longitude { text }

phone = element phone { phoneContents }
phoneContents = (
  kind?,
  text
)
kinds = ("Home" | "Work" | "Cell" | "Fax")
kind = attribute kind { kinds }

knows = element knows { knowsContents }
knowsContents = (
  attribute contacts { text },
  empty
)

description = element description {
  mixed { descriptionContents }*
}
descriptionContents = ( em | strong | br )
em = element em { text }
strong = element strong { text }
br = element br { empty }
```

Question 2

Add a wildcard extension to the descriptionContents pattern so that the users can extend the contacts schema by adding any elements they desire to the <description>.

Solution 2

The declaration for the description element referred to the descriptionContents pattern in the schema:

```
description = element description {
  mixed { descriptionContents }*
}
descriptionContents = ( em | strong | br )
em = element em { text }
strong = element strong { text }
br = element br { empty }
```

In the new schema, remove the declarations for the <em>, <strong>, and <br> elements and change the descriptionContents pattern as follows:

```
description = element description {
  mixed { descriptionContents }*
}
descriptionContents =
  element * { (attribute * {text})+ | descriptionContents | text }*
```

This declaration actually allows any attributes to be mixed in as well. To do this, you need to add one or more cardinality (+) indicators to the attribute declaration.

Chapter 7

This chapter covered XPath 1.0, and you learned about XPath axes and the functions in the XPath 1.0 function library.

Question 1

Name two XPath axes that, respectively, can be used to select element nodes and attribute nodes. If the context node is an element node, then provide the XPath location path, which selects the number attribute node of that element node. Show the answer in both abbreviated and unabbreviated syntax.

Solution

Element nodes are most commonly selected using the child axis. The descendant and descendant-or-self axes may also contain element nodes.

Attribute nodes are selected using the attribute axis.

Using abbreviated syntax, the location path @number selects the number attribute. Using unabbreviated syntax, the equivalent location path is written as attribute::number.

Question 2

XPath 1.0 allows wildcards to be used when selecting child nodes of the context node. What is the location path that selects all child nodes of the context node? Give the answer in both abbreviated and unabbreviated syntax.

Solution

Using abbreviated syntax, the asterisk (`*`) selects all child element nodes of the context node; in unabbreviated syntax, that is written as `child::*`.

Chapter 8

This chapter discussed how XML documents can be restructured for data interchange or transformed for presentation using XSLT.

Question 1

If you need to process a node in the source tree more than once but in different ways each time, what technique does XSLT provide to achieve this?

Solution

XSLT provides the use of modes to allow a node in the source tree to be processed multiple times. An `xsl:apply-templates` element can have a `mode` attribute. The same value as the value of the `mode` attribute of the `xsl:apply-templates` element will match, and therefore only that template rule will be processed.

Question 2

What are the two XSLT elements that provide conditional processing? Describe how the functionality provided by these two elements differs.

Solution

XSLT has the `xsl:if` and `xsl:choose` elements to provide conditional processing. The content of an `xsl:if` element is processed if a test is true and allows a single choice to be made. The `xsl:choose` element, together with its child elements, `xsl:when` and `xsl:otherwise`, allows multiple tests to be applied. No test is applied on the `xsl:choose` element or the `xsl:otherwise` element. Each `xsl:when` element has an associated test. Each test on the `xsl:when` elements is evaluated in turn. If a test returning `true` is found on an `xsl:when` element, then the content of that `xsl:when` element is processed and all subsequent `xsl:when` elements are ignored, as is the `xsl:otherwise` element. If no `xsl:when` element has a test that returns true, then the content of the `xsl:otherwise` element, if present, is processed.

Chapter 9

This chapter covered some foundational aspects of the upcoming XML Query Language, XQuery.

Question 1

What notation is used in an XQuery expression to indicate that its content is created dynamically?

Solution

Paired curly brackets, written as { and }, are used to indicate that their content is evaluated at runtime. Other parts of an XQuery expression — for example, start-tags and end-tags — of element constructors, are used literally in the output from a query.

Question 2

What are the component parts of a FLWOR expression and what does each do?

Solution

There are potentially five parts of a FLWOR expression: the for clause, the let clause, the where clause, the order by clause, and the return clause. In the for clause, a variable can be bound to multiple items in a sequence. In a let clause, a variable is bound to a single item. The where clause filters the results according to specified criteria. The order by clause specifies any ordering of the returned data. The return clause specifies the construct in the output for each variable, appropriately filtered and sorted.

Chapter 10

This chapter explored the increasing business need to store or expose data as XML through the use of a viable XML-enabled database.

Question 1

List some reasons why adding XML functionality to a relational database management system may be preferable to using a native XML database.

Solution

Be aware that this issue can generate discussions of religious intensity. The following offers a possible answer to the question: Most uses of XML are in a setting where relational database management systems are already in use. Using an RDBMS may be essentially free (for example, there would be no additional license costs), whereas acquiring a native XML database might have additional license or training costs. In addition, most commercial relational database management systems have good and well-tested security, reliability, and scalability. These considerations, which are important to enterprise use in a production setting, may not be as good in the early versions of native XML databases.

Question 2

What methods are available in SQL Server 2005 to manipulate data in a database column of type xml?

Solution

Five methods in SQL Server 2005 allow manipulation of type xml: query(), value(), exist(), modify(), and nodes().

query() is used to execute XQuery; value() to return a scalar value, rather than a node set. exist() tests for the existence of nodes and returns 1 if true, otherwise 0. modify() is Microsoft's extension to handle inserts, updates, and deletes; and nodes() is used when you need to transform XML into a traditional relational format, a process called *shredding*.

Question 3

Write a SQL query to get the ID and title of blog items from the XML category of the MySQL database. Would you expect this query to scale if your blog grows and includes many blog entries? What would you do to increase performance in that case?

Solution

The SQL query needs to use the function ExtractValue twice:

1. In the select clause, the title is extracted by the following function call: ExtractValue (content, '/item/title')

2. In the where clause, the category is extracted and tested using the following condition: ExtractValue(content, '/item[category]="XML"') != ''

The complete query is as follows:

```
select id, ExtractValue(content, '/item/title') as title
  FROM entries
  where ExtractValue(content, '/item[category]="XML"') != '';
```

Using this function as the only condition in the where clause means that the database engine needs to do a table scan and perform an XML parsing and an XPath query for each line in the table, which won't scale when your table grows.

To solve this performance issue, you would have to rely on the relational features of MySQL, rather than rely on XML and XPath. In that case, a solution would be to create a separate table to describe the relation between categories and blog entries, and perform a SQL join between this table and the table entries.

Chapter 11

This chapter introduced the XML Document Object Model (DOM), noting the differences between interfaces and nodes as well as describing several of the most common DOM interfaces and objects.

Question 1

Describe an important difference between the NamedNodeMap object and the NodeList object.

Solution

The `NamedNodeMap` object is unordered and is used to refer to attributes, because the attributes of an element are not ordered. A `NodeList` object is ordered, so it cannot be used to refer to attributes. A `NodeList` object often corresponds to the child nodes of a `Document` node or an `Element` node, because those child nodes are ordered.

Question 2

List the methods of the `Document` object that are used to add `Element` nodes — first, in no namespace and, second, in a namespace.

Solution

The `createElement()` method of the `Document` object is used to create new `Element` nodes where the element is not in a namespace. To add `Element` nodes where the element is in a namespace, use the `createElementNS()` method. Microsoft's offerings do not support `createElementNS`, but to make up for this, they do accept a namespace URI as an argument.

Chapter 12

This chapter covered the Simple API for XML (SAX).

Question 1

Calculate the weight, length, and total number of occupants on the entire train. Once the document has been parsed, print out the result of the calculations.

Solution

In general, this is a straightforward task; all you needed to do was record the values as you encountered them and add them to a total variable that could be printed out in the `endDocument` function. The first step was to rename the class to `TrainReader_Question1`. You also add declarations for your total variables and a `StringBuffer` to collect the element values:

```
import javax.xml.parsers.SAXParserFactory;
import javax.xml.parsers.SAXParser;
import org.xml.sax.*;
import org.xml.sax.helpers.*;

public class TrainReader_Question1 extends DefaultHandler

{
  private boolean isColor;
  private String trainCarType = "";
  private StringBuffer trainCarColor = new StringBuffer();
  private Locator trainLocator = null;

  private StringBuffer trainElementValue = new StringBuffer();
  private int totalWeight;
```

```
  private int totalLength;
  private int totalOccupants;
  public static void main (String[] args)
    throws Exception
  {
    System.out.println("Running train reader...");

    TrainReader_Question1 readerObj = new TrainReader_Question1();
    readerObj.read(args[0]);
  }
```

You then need to modify your startDocument and endDocument functions. Inside of startDocument, you reset your total values to 0. Within the endDocument function, you make sure to print out the results of the calculations:

```
public void startDocument()
  throws SAXException
{
  System.out.println("Start of the train");
  totalWeight = 0;
  totalLength = 0;
  totalOccupants = 0;
}

public void endDocument()
  throws SAXException
{
  System.out.println("End of the train");
  System.out.println("The train weighed " + totalWeight + " tons");
  System.out.println("The train was " + totalLength + " feet long");
  System.out.println("The train had " + totalOccupants + " occupants");
}
```

Next, inside of the startElement function, you reset the trainElementValue buffer if you are not working with a color:

```
public void startElement(String uri, String localName, String qName,  Attributes atts)
  throws SAXException
{
  if (localName.equals("car")) {
    if (atts != null) {
      trainCarType = atts.getValue("type");
    }
  }
  if (localName.equals("color"))
  {
    trainCarColor.setLength(0);
    isColor = true;
  }else {
    isColor = false;
    trainElementValue.setLength(0);
  }

}
```

As shown when collecting the value of the <color> elements, be sure to append any data you receive to a buffer. Although it is unlikely you would receive multiple calls to the characters function for a single value, it is possible, and you must be ready for it:

```java
public void characters(char[] ch, int start, int len)
  throws SAXException
{
  if (isColor)
  {
    trainCarColor.append(ch, start, len);
  }else {

    trainElementValue.append(ch, start, len);

  }
}
```

Finally, in the endElement function, you performed the calculations. You first copy the value of the buffer into the elementValue variable. This value could include "tons" or "feet," so you check whether there is a space and delete everything from the space until the end of the string. In a real application, you would need to do more error checking here to ensure that you don't receive a bad value. Once you obtain the right string, you parse it into a numeric value and add it to the correct total based on the localName:

```java
public void endElement(String uri, String localName, String qName)
  throws SAXException
{
  if (isColor)
  {
    System.out.println("The color of the " + trainCarType + " car is " +
      trainCarColor.toString());
    if ((trainCarType.equals("Caboose")) &&
      (!trainCarColor.toString().equals("Red")))
    {
      if (trainLocator != null)
       throw new SAXException("The caboose is not red at line " +
         trainLocator.getLineNumber() + ", column " +
         trainLocator.getColumnNumber() );
      else
        throw new SAXException("The caboose is not red!");
    }
  }else {

    String elementValue = trainElementValue.toString();
    if (elementValue.indexOf(" ") >= 0)
      elementValue = elementValue.substring(0, elementValue.indexOf(" "));
    int value = Integer.parseInt(elementValue);

    if ("weight".equals(localName)) {
      totalWeight += value;
    }else if ("length".equals(localName)) {
      totalLength += value;
    }else if ("occupants".equals(localName)) {
```

```
        totalOccupants += value;
    }
  }
  isColor = false;
}
```

In the end, you can quickly see how much the train weighed, how long it was, and how many occupants were on the train. If you ran the program against the `Train3.xml` sample document from Chapter 12, you would see the following results:

```
Running train reader...
Start of the train
The color of the Engine car is Black
The color of the Baggage car is Green
The color of the Passenger car is Green and Yellow
The color of the Caboose car is Red
End of the train
The train weighed 722 tons
The train was 190 feet long
The train had 30 occupants
```

Make sure you reset the caboose's color to Red if you receive an error.

Question 2

Print out a list of all elements declared in the DTD. To do this, descend the `TrainReader` class from `DefaultHandler2` instead of `DefaultHandler`. Register the `TrainReader` class with the parser so that you can receive `DeclHandler` events (hint: you need to use a property).

Solution

Although this exercise question may have seemed more difficult than the first, the code was actually shorter. You first need to import the helper class `DefaultHandler2`. Then, you modify your declaration to descend from `DefaultHandler2` (and change the name of this class for the example):

```
import javax.xml.parsers.SAXParserFactory;
import javax.xml.parsers.SAXParser;
import org.xml.sax.*;
import org.xml.sax.helpers.*;
import org.xml.sax.ext.DefaultHandler2;
public class TrainReader_Question2 extends DefaultHandler2
{

  private boolean isColor;
  private String trainCarType = "";
  private StringBuffer trainCarColor = new StringBuffer();
  private StringBuffer trainElementValue = new StringBuffer();
  private Locator trainLocator = null;
  private int totalWeight;
  private int totalLength;
  private int totalOccupants;

  public static void main (String[] args)
    throws Exception
```

```
    {
      System.out.println("Running train reader...");

      TrainReader_Question2 readerObj = new TrainReader_Question2();
      readerObj.read(args[0]);
    }
```

Before parsing the document, you need to register your class as a DeclHandler with the parser. Because the DeclHandler is an extension interface, the only way to register it is to set the property http://xml.org/sax/properties/declaration-handler:

```
public void read(String fileName)
  throws Exception
{
  XMLReader reader =
      XMLReaderFactory.createXMLReader("org.apache.xerces.parsers.SAXParser");
  reader.setContentHandler (this);
  reader.setErrorHandler (this);

  try
  {
    reader.setFeature("http://xml.org/sax/features/validation", true);
  }
  catch (SAXException e)
  {
    System.err.println("Cannot activate validation");
  }

  try
  {
    reader.setProperty("http://xml.org/sax/properties/declaration-handler",
      this);
  }
  catch (SAXException e)
  {
    System.err.println("Cannot set declaration handler");
  }
  try
  {
    reader.parse(fileName);
  }
  catch (SAXException e)
  {
    System.out.println("Parsing stopped : " + e.getMessage());
  }
}
```

Finally, you need to override the elementDecl function. Recall that in the DefaultHandler2 class this function does absolutely nothing. Inside the function, all you do is print out a message with the element name:

```
public void elementDecl(String name, String model)
  throws SAXException {
  System.out.println("Element declaration : " + name);
}
```

While the resulting output may not be very exciting, being able to access declaration events is. Many XML editors utilize this feature of SAX to generate lists of elements for tag completion. If you were to run the code on the `Train4.xml` sample documents from Chapter 12, you would see the following results:

```
Running train reader...
Start of the train
Element declaration : train
Element declaration : car
Element declaration : color
Element declaration : weight
Element declaration : length
Element declaration : occupants
The color of the Engine car is Black
The color of the Baggage car is Green
The color of the Passenger car is Green and Yellow
The color of the Caboose car is Red
End of the train
The train weighed 722 tons
The train was 190 feet long
The train had 30 occupants
```

If you receive an error, remember to change the `<conductors>` element back to `<occupants>` and correct any additional errors in the document.

Chapter 13

This chapter covered RSS and content syndication, introducing the fundamental concepts, some of the techniques that can be applied, and how XML is central to content syndication.

Question 1

At the end of the description of the simple Python aggregator, it was demonstrated how it is relatively simple to extend the range of the elements covered, by adding support for `dc:source`. Your first challenge is to extend the application so that it also displays the author of a feed entry, if that information is available.

You should check the specs and some real-world feeds yourself, but the elements used for identifying the author of an item are usually one of the following: `author`, `dc:creator`, `atom:name`, or `foaf:name`. The `author` element appears in the "simple" RSS versions (0.9x, 2.0) and has no namespace. However, there is a slight complication, as there is also an element in RSS 2.0 called `name`, which is used for the name of the text object in a text input area (the text input area elements are rarely encountered in practice, but it does make for a more interesting exercise). Therefore, part of this exercise is to ensure that this element won't be mistaken for the name of the author.

Solution

The core of the solution is just a matter of following what was done in the chapter for `dc:source` — that is, add an extra conditional to the `endElementNS` method in `feed_handler.py`. However, there is also the little matter of distinguishing between `atom:name`/`foaf:name` (author) and `name` (text area). The potential for naming clashes has been taken into account by using the SAX `endElementNS` method, rather than the marginally simpler `endElement`. Referring back to the `endElementNS` method in `feed_handler.py`, you see it begins like this:

```
def endElementNS(self, name, qname):
    "Collects element content, switches state as
                    appropriate (called by SAX parser)"
    (namespace, localname) = name
...
```

The `name` value passed to the method is actually a pair of individual values combined in a tuple. The `localname` part is what has been used in the conditionals so far, but the `namespace` string is also available. As a necessary step, check whether the unambiguous combination of `namespace` and `localname` is one that corresponds to the author. The extra conditional needed looks like this:

```
...
    if localname == "source": # dc:source
        self.current_item.source = '('+self.current_item.source+') '+ text
        return

    if (localname == "creator" or # dc:creator
        localname == "author" or # RSS 0.9x/2.0
        (localname == "name" and
         namespace == "http://purl.org/atom/ns#") or
        (localname == "name" and
         namespace == "http://xmlns.com/foaf/0.1/")):
        self.current_item.author = text
...
```

As you probably noticed by now, there was a little cheating in the text—a member variable `source` was included in the original code for the `Item` class (in `feed.py`), so when the `dc:source` extension was added, a destination for the value was already available. There isn't really any good place available for the value of author to go, but it's straightforward to create one—in other words, an `author` member variable in the `Item` class. Here's what the code looks like (in `feed.py`):

```
class Item:
    """ Simple model of a single item within a syndication feed """

    def __init__(self):
        """ Initialize properties to defaults """
        self.title = "
        self.content = "
        self.source = "
        self.date = time.time() - BAD_TIME_HANDICAP # seconds from the Epoch

        self.author = "
...
```

That's simply an additional member variable with its value initialized to an empty string, `class`, which provides a string representation of the class (like `toString()` in Java). Here is the code, again in `feed.py`:

```
def __str__(self):
    """ Custom 'toString()' method to pretty-print """
    return (self.source + ' : '
        + self.title +'\n'
        + self.content + '\n'
        + self.author + '\n'
        + self.get_formatted_date() + '\n')
```

The string that contains the name of the author is inserted, along with a newline character, into the string representation of Item objects, which is used by FeedReader to display them.

```
Binary Relations : WordPress
While WordPress gives you choices for translating the names of the
weekdays for use with the post calendar, ...
Morten Frederiksen Thu, 20 May 2004 16:16:38 +0200
```

As you can see, a name has been added:

```
<item rdf:about="http://purl.org/net/morten/...">
 ...
 <foaf:maker>
        <foaf:Person>
            <foaf:name>Morten Frederiksen</foaf:name>
            <foaf:nick>mortenf</foaf:nick>
 <foaf:mbox_sha1sum>65b983bb397fb71849da910996741752ace8369b</foaf:mbox_sha1sum>
            <foaf:weblog rdf:resource="http://purl.org/net/morten/blog"/>
        </foaf:Person>
 </foaf:maker>
 ...
</item>
```

It's worth mentioning again that the model used inside the demo application is specialized to particular kinds of feed data and is as simple as can be, and hence seriously limited. In feeds such as Morten's, a lot more information is potentially available structured in the RDF model (in RDF/XML syntax). The foaf:maker of the item is a foaf:Person with a foaf:name of Morten Frederiksen. This foaf:Person also has other properties, including a foaf:nick and a foaf:weblog. The foaf:mbox_sha1 property is a disguised reference to Morten's mailbox (e-mail address). This has a unique value, which makes it possible for RDF tools to tell that any other foaf:Person with the same foaf:mbox_sha1sum is the same person, enabling them to combine (merge or "smush") any properties associated with this foaf:Person and reason with the information as required. RDF code libraries are available for most languages, so if you're considering building a more sophisticated aggregator, it's relatively straightforward to use the richness available through RSS 1.0.

Question 2

You saw toward the end of the chapter how the most common syndication formats show themselves, and earlier in the chapter you saw how it was possible to run an XSLT stylesheet over RSS feeds to produce an XHTML rendering. The exercise here is to apply the second technique to the first task. Try to write an XSLT transformation that indicates the format of the feed, together with its title.

Appendix A: Exercise Solutions

Solution

The following (`version.xsl`) is one possible solution. The stylesheet starts with a list of namespace declarations that cover the kinds of data that might be encountered:

```
<xsl:stylesheet version="1.0"
    xmlns:xsl="http://www.w3.org/1999/XSL/Transform"
    xmlns:rdf="http://www.w3.org/1999/02/22-rdf-syntax-ns#"
    xmlns:rss="http://purl.org/rss/1.0/"
    xmlns:foaf="http://xmlns.com/foaf/0.1/"
    xmlns:atom="http://purl.org/atom/ns#">

<xsl:output method="text" indent="yes"/>
```

The output method here is set to `text`. To keep the listing short, this stylesheet only delivers plain text output.

To make the output more legible, it is preceded and followed by a new line, which is achieved by placing an escaped-text representation of the newline character (`&#xA;`) before and after the application of the detailed templates. The entry point into the stylesheet is through matching the root element, as shown here:

```
<xsl:template match="/">
    <xsl:text>&#xA;</xsl:text>
        <xsl:apply-templates />
    <xsl:text>&#xA;</xsl:text>
</xsl:template>
```

There now follows a series of templates that match according to simple rules intended to identify the feed format. First of all, here is a template to match RSS versions 0.9x and 2.0:

```
<xsl:template match="/rss">
    <xsl:text>RSS Version: </xsl:text>
    <xsl:value-of select="./@version" />
    <xsl:apply-templates select="channel/title" />
</xsl:template>
```

Text is output to state the name of the feed type (RSS), and then the value of the version attribute is extracted. An attempt is then made to match templates to anything with the path `/rss/channel/title`. The following template matches the root element of an Atom feed:

```
<xsl:template match="/atom:feed">
    <xsl:text>Atom Version: </xsl:text>
    <xsl:value-of select="./@version" />
    <xsl:apply-templates select="atom:title"/>
</xsl:template>
```

Again, the version is extracted, and then anything matching `/atom:feed/atom:title` is passed to other templates to deal with.

The next template matches RDF files:

```
<xsl:template match="/rdf:RDF">
(RDF)
   <xsl:apply-templates />
</xsl:template>
```

Note the requirement for RDF/XML files to have a root called `rdf:RDF`. This was removed from the latest specification, though the requirement is still in place for RSS 1.0.

If the feed is RSS 1.0, it has a `<channel>` element, which is picked up by the following template:

```
<xsl:template match="rss:channel">
    <xsl:text>RSS Version: 1.0</xsl:text>
    <xsl:apply-templates />
</xsl:template>
```

Next is a template that matches the feed title of the three feed formats:

```
<xsl:template match="rss:title | atom:title | title">
        <xsl:text>&#xA;Title: </xsl:text>
 <xsl:value-of select="text()" />
</xsl:template>
```

The FOAF document described in the text was a red herring, but for the sake of consistency here's a template that extracts the first named person in a FOAF profile:

```
<xsl:template match="//*[position() = 1]/foaf:Person/foaf:name">
    <xsl:text>FOAF Name: </xsl:text>
    <xsl:value-of select="text()" />
</xsl:template>
```

The stylesheet ends with a template that picks up loose ends that would otherwise go to the output:

```
<xsl:template match="rss:item | text()" />

</xsl:stylesheet>
```

Here are the results of running this transformation on the documents at the sample URIs, which were previously downloaded using `wget`:

`http://news.bbc.co.uk/rss/newsonline_world_edition/front_page/rss091.xml`:

```
D:\rss-samples>java -jar saxon7.jar rss091.xml version.xsl
RSS Version: 0.91
Title: BBC News | News Front Page | World Edition
```

`http://purl.org/net/morten/blog/feed/rdf/`:

```
D:\rss-samples>java -jar saxon7.jar index.html version.xsl

(RDF)
RSS Version: 1.0
Title: Binary Relations
```

`http://icite.net/blog/?flavor=atom&smm=y:`

```
D:\rss-samples>java -jar saxon7.jar index.html@flavor=atom version.xsl
Atom Version: 0.3
Title: the iCite net development blog
```

`http://blogs.it/0100198/rss.xml:`

```
D:\rss-samples>java -jar saxon7.jar rss.xml version.xsl
RSS Version: 2.0
Title: Marc's Voice
```

`http://swordfish.rdfweb.org/people/libby/rdfweb/webwho.xrdf:`

```
D:\rss-samples>java -jar saxon7.jar webwho.xrdf version.xsl

(RDF)
FOAF Name: Libby Miller
```

Chapter 14

This chapter looked at web services, a group of XML-based protocols for performing remote procedure calls.

Question 1

Imagine you are trying to contact an XML-RPC-based web service to submit a classified ad for a lost dog. The required information includes your name, phone number, and the body of the ad. What might the XML request look like?

Solution

There are two ways of doing this. The first example (shown next) is the simpler way, representing each of the parameters individually. It begins by including the name of the procedure to call (`classifieds.submit`) and then simply specifies each of the parameters, in order. (You could also add a `name` element that named each parameter, as shown in the second example.)

```
<methodCall>
  <methodName>classifieds.submit</methodName>
  <params>
    <param>
      <value><string>Nicholas Chase</string></value>
    </param>
    <param>
      <value><string>212-555-1234</string></value>
    </param>
    <param>
      <value><string>Lost: Large mixed-breed dog. Chunk out of one ear,
            missing an eye, limps on three legs. Answers to "Lucky".
            212-555-1234</string></value>
```

```
      </param>
    </params>
  </methodCall>
```

The second example adds the same information, but as part of a struct, with each member holding one parameter. Which technique you choose in the real world depends on the requirements of the procedure you're calling.

```
<methodCall>
  <methodName>classifieds.submit</methodName>
  <params>
    <param>
      <value>
        <struct>
          <member>
            <name>CustomerName</name>
            <value><string>Nicholas Chase</string></value>
          </member>
          <member>
            <name>CustomerPhone</name>
            <value><string>212-555-1234</string></value>
          </member>
          <member>
            <name>AdText</name>
            <value>
              <string> Lost: Large mixed-breed dog. Chunk out of one ear,
              missing an eye, limps on three legs. Answers to "Lucky".
              212-555-1234</string>
            </value>
          </member>
        </struct>
      </value>
    </param>
  </params>
</methodCall>
```

Question 2

You are trying to call a REST-based web service to check on the status of a service order. The service needs the following information:

```
cust_id: 3263827
order_id: THX1138
```

What might the request look like?

Solution

In a REST system, you add all of the information to the URL and then submit that URL as a GET request. In this case, you're adding two parameters, cust_id and order_id, separated by an ampersand (&):

```
http://www.example.com/checkServiceOrder?cust_id=3263827&order_id=THX1138
```

Chapter 15

This chapter covered SOAP, an XML-based protocol for performing remote procedure calls and passing information between computers. The chapter also looked at Web Services Definition Language (WSDL), which provides other developers with all the information they might need to access your service.

Question 1

Create a SOAP message that fulfills the following requirements:

1. It corresponds to an RPC called getRadioOperators().

2. It passes the following information:

   ❑ City and state or postal code

   ❑ Radius

   ❑ License class

3. The server must receive and verify a call sign from the sender.

Solution

In this case, you're creating a simple SOAP message, which includes the request as the contents of the Body element, as shown in the following code. You call the getRadioOperators() method, so that's the name of the root element for your payload, and each item is included in an element that corresponds to the name of the parameter you're passing. The sender's call sign is sent in the header, with the mustUnderstand attribute set to true. If the server doesn't understand how to handle this information before processing the message, then it must reject the message altogether.

```
<soap:Envelope xmlns:soap="http://www.w3.org/2003/05/soap-envelope">
  <soap:Header xmlns:s="http://www.example.com/radio/">
    <s:License mustUnderstand="true">
      WNEW
    </s:License>
  </soap:Header>
  <soap:Body xmlns:h="http://www.example.com/hams/">
    <h:getRadioOperators>
        <h:postalCode>02134</h:postalCode>
        <h:radius>5</h:radius>
        <h:licenseClass>General</h:licenseClass>
    </h:getRadioOperators>
  </soap:Body>
</soap:Envelope>
```

Question 2

Create a WSDL file that describes the document in Question 1.

Solution

Starting at the bottom, we've created a service that has an instance located at a particular URL, `http://localhost/hamsearch.asp`. That instance is "bound" to the `HamSearchBinding` binding, which specifies that the message is to be sent using the SOAP RPC style, and defines the encoding for the `input` and `output` messages, as well as their namespaces. The binding also specifies that it's using the `HamSearchPort` `portType`, or interface. This `portType` specifies the message types for the input and output messages, which refer back to element definitions in the schema at the top of the document, as shown in the following:

```
<?xml version="1.0"?>
<definitions name="HamSearch"
    targetNamespace="http://www.example.com/hamSearch"
    xmlns:typens=" http://www.example.com/hamSearch "
    xmlns:xsd="http://www.w3.org/2000/10/XMLSchema"
    xmlns:soap="http://schemas.xmlsoap.org/wsdl/soap/"
    xmlns:soapenc="http://schemas.xmlsoap.org/soap/encoding/"
    xmlns:wsdl="http://schemas.xmlsoap.org/wsdl/"
    xmlns="http://schemas.xmlsoap.org/wsdl/">
  <types>
    <xsd:schema xmlns=""
        xmlns:xsd="http://www.w3.org/2000/10/XMLSchema"
        targetNamespace="http://www.example.com/hamSearch">
        <xsd:complexType name="HamSearchType">

            <xsd:sequence>
                <xsd:choice>
                    <xsd:group>
                        <xsd:element name="City" type="xsd:string" />
                        <xsd:element name="State" type="xsd:string" />
                    </xsd:group>
                    <xsd:element name="Radius" type="xsd:number" />
                    <xsd:element name="LicenseClass" type="xsd:string" />
                </xsd:choice>
            </xsd:sequence>
        </xsd:complexType>
        <xsd:complexType name="HamSearchResponseType">
            <xsd:sequence>
                <xsd:element name="NumHamsFound" type="xsd:number"/>
            </xsd:sequence>
        </xsd:complexType>
    </xsd:schema>
  </types>

  <message name="HamSearchRequestMsg">
     <part name="HamSearchRequest" type="typens:HamSearchType"/>
  </message>
  <message name="HamSearchResponseMsg">
     <part name="HamSearchResponse" type="typens:HamSearchResponseType"/>
  </message>

  <portType name="HamSearchPort">
     <operation name="HamSearch">
        <input message="typens:HamSearchRequestMsg"/>
```

```
              <output message="typens:HamSearchResponseMsg"/>
         </operation>
     </portType>
     <binding name="HamSearchBinding" type="typens:HamSearchPort">
         <soap:binding style="rpc"
                 transport="http://schemas.xmlsoap.org/soap/http"/>
         <operation name="GetOperators">
             <soap:operation/>
             <input>
                 <soap:body use="encoded" namespace="http://www.example.com/
hamsearch" encodingStyle="http://schemas.xmlsoap.org/soap/encoding/"/>
             </input>
             <output>
                 <soap:body use="encoded" namespace="http://www.example.com/
hamsearch" encodingStyle="http://schemas.xmlsoap.org/soap/encoding/"/>
             </output>
         </operation>
     </binding>
     <service name="HamSearchService">
         <port name="HamSearchPort" binding="typens:HamSearchBinding">
             <soap:address location="http://localhost/hamsearch.asp"/>
         </port>
     </service>

</definitions>
```

Chapter 16

This chapter introduced Ajax (Asynchronous JavaScript and XML).

Question 1

Construct the equivalent JSON literal for the following XML:

```
<person>
  <forename>Joe</forename>
  <surname>Fawcett</surname>
  <profession>Developer</profession>
  <children>
    <child>
      <forename>Persephone</forename>
      <sex>female</sex>
    </child>
    <child>
      <forename>Xavier</forename>
      <sex>male</sex>
    </child>
  </children>
</person>
```

Solution

```
var person = "{forename: \"Joe\", surname: \"Fawcett\", profession: \"Developer\","
        + " children: [{forename: \"Persephone\", sex: \"female\"}, "
        + "           {forename: \"Xavier\", sex: \"male\"}]}";
```

Question 2

Why is it necessary to use a server-side proxy when calling a third-party web service?

Solution

The XMLHttpRequest object only allows calls to a service in the same domain as the page on which it resides. This is known as the *same origin policy*.

Question 3

What is the maximum number of simultaneous connections allowed by most browsers to a single URL?

Solution

Two.

Chapter 17

This chapter introduced Cascading Style Sheets (CSS) and how it can be used with XHTML.

Question 1

The exercises for this chapter focus on one example: a purchase order. You slowly build a more complex style sheet for the following XML file (ch17_ex01.xml):

```
<?xml version="1.0" encoding="UTF-8" ?>
<?xml-stylesheet type="text/css" href="ch17_ex01.css" ?>

<purchaseOrder orderID="x1129001">

<buyer>
  <companyName>Woodland Toys</companyName>
  <purchaserName>Tom Walter</purchaserName>
  <address>
    <address1>The Business Centre</address1>
    <address2>127 Main Road</address2>
    <town>Albury</town>
    <city>Seaforth</city>
    <state>BC</state>
    <zipCode>22001</zipCode>
  </address>
```

```
   </buyer>

   <orders>
      <item>
         <sku>126552</sku>
         <product>People Carrier</product>
         <description>Childs pedal operated car</description>
      </item>
      <item>
         <sku>122452</sku>
         <product>BubbleBaby</product>
         <description>Bean filled soft toy</description>
      </item>
      <item>
         <sku>129112</sku>
         <product>My First Drum Kit</product>
         <description>Childs plastic drum kit</description>
      </item>
   </orders>

   </purchaseOrder>
```

First, create a rule to put the purchase order in a box, with a 1-pixel black border, 20 pixels of padding inside, and a 20-pixel margin to separate the box from the browser window.

Solution

The `<purchaseOrder>` element is specified to be a block-level element. Use the `margin` and `padding` attributes to create some whitespace on either side of the 1-pixel black border:

```
purchaseOrder {
  display:block;

  margin:20px; padding:20px;
  border-style:solid; border-width:1px; border-color:#000000;}
```

Question 2

Create a rule that writes "Purchase Order Number" in a large, bold, Arial typeface as the heading (in case the user does not have Arial, add Verdana as a second option, and the default sans-serif font as the third option), and that collects the purchase order number from the `orderID` attribute.

Solution

To write out "Purchase Order Number" along with the value of the `orderID` attribute, first set the font you want. Then, use the `content` property to first write out "Purchase Order Number," and then use the special value of `attr(orderID)`:

```
purchaseOrder:before {
  font-family:arial, verdana, sans-serif;
  font-size:28px; font-weight:bold;
  content:"Purchase Order Number: " attr(orderID);}
```

This works in Firefox, Opera, and Safari, but not in Internet Explorer.

Question 3

Add the buyer's details to the purchase order, with the company name in bold and each part of the address on a new line in a smaller Arial font (and if the user does not have Arial, provide for Verdana or the default sans-serif font).

Solution

To add the buyer's details, you need to create styles for several elements. Rather than repeat the styles for each element, you can use the type selector, which separates element names with a comma:

```
buyer, companyName, purchaserName, address1, address2, town, city, state, zipcode {
    display:block;
    font-family:arial, verdana, sans-serif; font-size:14px;}
```

Then, you only need to write one rule for the element, whose content should be displayed in bold:

```
companyName {font-weight:bold;}
```

Question 4

Write out the items ordered in a table.

Solution

The writing out of the table is fairly straightforward using the special values for the display property designed for presenting tabular data. Remember to add some padding if you want to make your table more readable:

```
orders {display:table; padding-top:30px;}item {display:table-row;}sku, product,
description {display:table-cell; padding:10px;}
```

This works in Firefox, but unfortunately it doesn't work in Internet Explorer.

Chapter 18

This chapter discussed how HTML has been reformulated as an application of XML in XHTML 1.0. The exercises for Chapter 16 required you to turn a sample HTML 3.2 document first into a strict XHTML 1.0 document, and then into a transitional XHTML 1.0 document for use on legacy browsers.

Question 1

Take the following HTML 3.2 example and create a version in XHTML 1.1 without any stylistic markup:

```
<HTML>
<HEAD>
    <TITLE>Exercise One</TITLE>
</HEAD>
```

```
<BODY bgcolor=white>

<A NAME="top"></A>
<H1 align=center>XHTML</H1>

<FONT face=arial size=2>
  XHTML 1.0 is the reformulation of HTML in XHTML. There are three XHTML 1.0
  document types:

  <UL>
    <LI>Transitional
    <LI>Strict
    <LI>Frameset
  </UL>

  XHTML has also been split into <b>modules</b>, from which document types
  such as XHTML 1.1 and XHTML Basic have been formed.
</FONT>

<A href="#top">Back to top</a>
</BODY>
</HTML>
```

Solution

In order to turn this example of text into valid XHTML 1.1, you must make sure all element and attribute names are written in lowercase. XHTML (like all XML languages) is case sensitive, and all element and attribute names should be lowercase. Next, look at what goes before the root <html> element in a strict XHTML 1.0 document. You can start with the (optional) XML declaration (after all, this is an XML document). Many validators require that the character encoding of the document is specified, so you can use the encoding attribute on the XML declaration to indicate the character encoding used (you could also use the <meta> element to provide this information). After the XML declaration, add the DOCTYPE declaration, which indicates that the document is written according to the strict XHTML 1.0 document type:

```
<?xml version="1.0" encoding="UTF-8"?>
<!DOCTYPE html PUBLIC "-//W3C//DTD XHTML 1.1//EN"
    "http://www.w3.org/TR/xhtml11/DTD/xhtml11.dtd">
```

The root <html> element should feature the xmlns attribute, indicating that the markup in this document belongs to the XHTML namespace, as shown in the following:

```
<html xmlns="http://www.w3.org/1999/xhtml" lang="en">
```

You do not need to make any changes to the <head> element or its content (other than making sure the element names are lowercase):

```
<head>
    <title>Exercise One</title>
</head>
```

The `<body>` element is where you should start removing the styling markup. One of the aims of XHTML is to separate style from content, so remove the `bgcolor` attribute and its value; instead, use CSS to indicate the background color for the document. The opening `<body>` tag should now look like this:

```
<body>
```

The next task is to move the anchor element inside the heading, because the anchor element is an inline element and therefore should be inside a block-level element, such as a heading or paragraph (in the original version the anchor element was before the `h1` element). Remember also that in the strict XHTML 1.0 DTD, you should be using an `id` attribute for the fragment identifier instead of the `name` attribute. Finally, you need to remove the `align` attribute from the `h1` element:

```
<h1><a id="top">XHTML</a></h1>
```

Next, remove the font element. As the first line of text represents a paragraph, it should appear inside the opening `<p>` and closing `</p>` tags, as shown in the following:

```
<p>XHTML 1.0 is the reformulation of HTML in XHTML. There are three XHTML 1.0
document types:</p>
```

The HTML 3.2 specification actually says that "the end tag for LI elements can always be omitted." Of course, this is no longer the case with XHTML; you must include the closing `</li>` tags for each list item as follows:

```
<ul>
    <li>Transitional</li>
    <li>Strict</li>
    <li>Frameset</li>
</ul>
```

Following this list is another paragraph, which you put inside opening `<p>` and closing `</p>` tags. You could replace the `<b>` element with a `<strong>` element, indicating strong emphasis if you wanted to, but it is not necessary.

```
<p>XHTML has also been split into <b>modules</b>, from which document types  such
as XHTML 1.1 and XHTML Basic have been formed.</p>
```

As with the anchor element indicating the top of the document, the link that points to the top of the document should be contained within a block-level element, which in this case is a `<div>` element:

```
<div><a href="#top">Back to top</a></div>
```

Complete the document with the closing `<body>` and `<html>` tags:

```
</body>
</html>
```

Now you can run the document through a validator to ensure that it contains no errors.

Question 2

Using the same HTML 3.2 example, create a second version that uses transitional XHTML 1.0, can work in old browsers, and in which you could include legacy scripts and code. Once you have written your documents, validate them using the W3C validator at http://validator .w3.org.

Solution

The XHTML 1.1 document version won't work in very old browsers, so in this exercise you need to make a transitional version that works on legacy browsers. The first thing to avoid is the optional XML declaration, because older browsers do not understand it, and some of them will actually display it. You can start the exercise with a DOCTYPE declaration, as this won't cause a problem for older browsers:

```
<!DOCTYPE html PUBLIC "-//W3C//DTD XHTML 1.0 Transitional//EN"
    "http://www.w3.org/TR/xhtml1/DTD/xhtml1-transitional.dtd">
```

In the root element, it is best to avoid the namespace attribute. Although older browsers typically just ignore markup they do not understand, there is no point in putting it in here.

```
<html>
```

You can leave the <head> element and its content as it was in the original, but when it's time to validate, some validators complain if you have not indicated the character encoding, so you can use the meta element inside the head like so:

```
<head>
    <title>Excerise One</title>
    <meta http-equiv="Content-Type" content="text/html; charset=UTF-8" />
</head>
```

While the transitional DTD enables us to use deprecated stylistic markup, you should still avoid the use of the bgcolor attribute, as it is not essential to the meaning of the document. In fact, the default background of browsers is white, so the background will only be a different color for users who have specifically changed the default setting. Therefore, the opening <body> tag should now look like this:

```
<body>
```

With the transitional document, there is no need to move the anchor element inside the heading, as you had to in the strict XHTML 1.0 exercise. Older browsers do not recognize the id attribute as a destination anchor, so you shouldn't change the name attribute to an id attribute. You could leave the align attribute on the <h1> element, but it was removed here because that would be in the stylesheet if you had one. Therefore, leave the next two lines of the example as it was:

```
<a name="top"></a>
<h1 align="center">XHTML</h1>
```

You can leave in the <font> element if you wish. Recall, however, that there would be a CSS to replace styling rules, so you can remove them. It is good practice to put the sentence in a <p> element, so you could do that with the following:

```
<p>XHTML 1.0 is the reformulation of HTML in XHTML. There are three XHTML 1.0
    document types:</p>
```

When it comes to the unordered list, close the line item elements, with a closing `</li>` tag:

```
<ul>
  <li>Transitional</li>
  <li>Strict</li>
  <li>Frameset</li>
</ul>
```

Again, for good practice, put the sentence into a `<p>` element:

```
<p>XHTML has also been split into <b>modules</b>, from which document types
such as XHTML 1.1 and XHTML Basic have been formed.</p>
```

Finally, you have the link back to the top, which can be left on its own; you don't need to put it into a block-level element in the transitional DTD. Don't forget to finish the exercise with the closing `</body>` and `</html>` tags:

```
<a href="#top">Back to top</a>
</body>
</html>
```

Remember to validate your document to ensure that you have not made any mistakes.

Chapter 19

This chapter demonstrated how SVG is not only an extremely versatile drawing format, but also highly programmable, thanks to XML and scripting support.

Question 1

Figure 19-10 shows a picture of a stylized windmill. Write the SVG code needed to draw it. You can use the hint, but you if you like a challenge, try it before looking at the hint. Squared paper can help in working out the coordinates; don't forget that the y-axis starts with zero at the top.

Figure 19-10

*Hint: There are several different ways to do this with SVG, but here the body of the windmill was con-
structed from a (yellow) `<polygon>` element with a (yellow) `<circle>` element half-overlapping on
top. The four (blue) vanes are `<polygon>` elements with three points. The shape in the middle of the
vanes is a (blue) `<rect>` element, with a transform to rotate it 45 degrees. At the bottom of the windmill is a (green) `<line>` element.*

Solution

The windmill can be drawn using basic shapes as follows:

```
<?xml version="1.0"?>
<!DOCTYPE svg PUBLIC "-//W3C//DTD SVG 1.1//EN"
    "http://www.w3.org/Graphics/SVG/1.1/DTD/svg11.dtd">

<svg xmlns="http://www.w3.org/2000/svg" version="1.1">

<!-- windmill body -->
  <circle cx="250" cy="230" r="30" fill="yellow" />

  <polygon points="200,340 220,230 280,230 300,340"
           fill="yellow" />

<!-- vanes -->
  <polygon points="250,230 230,320 270,320"
           fill="red"
           transform="rotate(45, 250, 230)" />

  <polygon points="250,230 230,320 270,320"
           fill="red"
           transform="rotate(135, 250, 230)" />

  <polygon points="250,230 230,320 270,320"
           fill="red"
           transform="rotate(225, 250, 230)" />

  <polygon points="250,230 230,320 270,320"
           fill="red"
           transform="rotate(315, 250, 230)" />

<!-- centerpiece -->
  <rect x="240" y="220" width="20" height="20" fill="blue" />

<!-- bottom line -->
  <line x1="180" y1="340" x2="320" y2="340"
                stroke="green" stroke-width="6" />

</svg>
```

The different features of the windmill are drawn as eight different basic shapes. The `circle` and `poly-
gon` that make up the body of the windmill overlap and are the same color, giving the effect of a single
shape. Rather than figure out the coordinates of the four vanes separately, the coordinates of one vane
(as it would be positioned vertically) have been determined and the point values copied into the others,
with a `rotate` transform used to position them around a center point (250,230):

```
<?xml version="1.0"?>
<!DOCTYPE svg PUBLIC "-//W3C//DTD SVG 1.1//EN"
    "http://www.w3.org/Graphics/SVG/1.1/DTD/svg11.dtd">

<svg xmlns="http://www.w3.org/2000/svg"
    xmlns:xlink="http://www.w3.org/1999/xlink"
    version="1.1">

  <defs>
    <polygon id="vane" points="250,230 230,320 270,320"
          fill="red"/>
  </defs>

<! windmill body -->
  <path d="M 200,340 L 220,230 A 30,30 0 0 1 280,230 L 300,340 z"
  fill="yellow"/>
<!-- vanes -->

<use xlink:href="#vane" transform="rotate(45, 250, 230)" />

<use xlink:href="#vane" transform="rotate(135, 250, 230)" />

<use xlink:href="#vane" transform="rotate(225, 250, 230)" />

<use xlink:href="#vane" transform="rotate(315, 250, 230)" />

<!-- centerpiece -->
  <rect x="240" y="220" width="20" height="20" fill="blue" />

<!-- bottom line -->
  <line x1="180" y1="340" x2="320" y2="340"
                stroke="green" stroke-width="6" />

</svg>
```

The triangular vanes are all of the same shape and color, so these attributes are given in a defs element (see Section 5.3 of the SVG Specification). The shape defined here won't be drawn immediately, but it provides the description that is referred to by use elements (Section 5.6) further down the listing. Essentially, the use element is substituted with the linked definition, and any additional attributes that are provided locally are applied — here the rotate transform is defined for each vane. The reference is made through an element from the XLink namespace (xlink:href), so the namespace declaration at the beginning gives the namespace URI for the xlink prefix. In this version, the body of the windmill is defined using a path element (see Section 8 of the SVG Specification). It trades brevity of code for simplicity, something that generally has to be decided case by case. The path uses an absolute moveto to get to the starting point (M 200,340); the line of the left-hand side of the windmill body is then drawn (L 220,230). The curve at the top of the windmill is drawn using an elliptical arc (A 30,30 0 0 1 280,230), the last pair of figures being the right-hand side of the top (for details about arcs, see Section 8.3.8 of the specification). A line is drawn to form the right-hand side of the windmill body (L 300,340). Finally, the path is closed by drawing a line back to the starting point (z).

Question 2

Get a tangram puzzle application to start with the pieces organized into the stylized cat pictured in Figure 19-11. Everything else should stay the same — clicking Reset still places all the pieces into the square box.

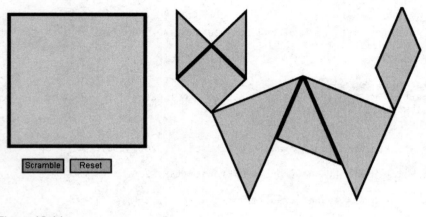

Figure 19-11

Solution

One solution starts with the puzzle pieces ready-transformed to their positions in the cat shape. The coordinates listed in the `points` attributes are exactly as in the original. The `transform` attribute contains an initial translation and rotation to place them as required. Pressing the Reset button still zeroes all these values, placing the pieces in the square box:

```
<polygon points="0,0 0,100 100,0"
    transform="translate(453.6,137.6) rotate(292.5,33.3,33.3)" />

<polygon points="100,0, 50,50 150,50 200,0"
    transform="translate(495,45) rotate(472.5,125,25)" />

<polygon points="50,50, 0,100 50,150 100,100"
    transform="translate(300,0) rotate(0,0,0)"/>

<polygon points="50,50, 100,100 150,50"
    transform="translate(285,-15) rotate(90,100,66.6)"/>

<polygon points="200,0, 100,100 200,200"
    transform="translate(245,76) rotate(22.5,166.6,100)"/>

<polygon points="0,100, 0,200 50,150"
    transform="translate(300,-100) rotate(0,0,0)"/>

<polygon points="0,200, 200,200 100,100"
    transform="translate(452,9.3) rotate(67.5,100,166.6)"/>
```

You might be wondering how those values were obtained. Using some cardboard, a ruler, and a protractor would be one approach. An easier way is to let the computer do the work. Because it's XML you're looking at, standard XML tools can be used. In the Tangram application, the pieces are moved by using code to dynamically manipulate the `transform` attributes of the `polygon` elements. These changes are made by modifying the DOM model in memory. It's not possible to view the contents of the DOM by saving the file from the viewer, but it is possible to expose it programmatically. It's simple to get the browser to display a piece of text using the built-in `alert('text')` function. This causes a small window to pop up displaying the text, and can be used to provide an inside view of the DOM part that contains the `transform` attributes of the `polygon` elements. In the original code, pressing any key causes a function to be called that rotates the currently selected shape. A minor modification can be made to the script (`tangram.es`) to recognize when the "x" key has been pressed.

```
var selectedPoly;
var track = false;
var svgDoc = null;
var polyGroup = null;

function init(evt){
  svgDoc = evt.target.ownerDocument;
  svgDoc.rootElement.addEventListener("keydown", rotatePolygon, false);
  polyGroup = svgDoc.getElementById("PolyGroup");
}
```

Modify the `rotatePolygon` event listener to print a message when the "x" key is pressed. That function is as follows:

```
function rotatePolygon(evt){
  if (evt.charCode)
    var charCode = evt.charCode;
  else
    var charCode = evt.keyCode;
  if(charCode == 88) {
    alert(getPolygonDetails(polyGroup));
    return;
  }
  if (selectedPoly == null)
    return;
  var rotation = getRotateAngle(selectedPoly);
  rotation = rotation + 22.5;
  var center = getCenter(selectedPoly);
  var transformString = getTransformBlock(selectedPoly, 0)
    + " rotate(" + rotation + "," + center.x + "," + center.y + ")";
  selectedPoly.setAttribute("transform", transformString);
}
```

The `charCode` property of the event object is obtained. Because key events are not specified in the SVG recommendation, they are implemented in different ways. To handle this, check for the `charCode` or `keyCode` property of the event. The code is then checked to determine whether it is an "x" by checking for the value 88. If it is, then the `polyGroup` object (the parent of the polygons, extracted previously) is passed to a function called `getPolygonDetails`. Whatever this returns appears as the text in a pop-up window. If the character isn't an "x," then the `rotatePolygon` function continues as in the original version. What's needed are the attributes of the individual `polygon` elements. These are all child nodes of the polygon group and are easy to get from the passed `polyGroup` element. Each of these is examined in turn to ensure it is actually an element node. If it is, then it has a `nodeType` value of 1. In that case, the attributes of that element can be obtained in turn, using the DOM `attributes.item(j)` method. The name of the node and its value are then added to a string. This accumulates all the attribute names and values in the elements as the loops step through them. After each line, a newline character (\n) is added for the sake of appearances:

```
var ELEMENT_NODE = 1;

function getPolygonDetails(group) {
  var string = "";
  var children = group.childNodes;
  var node;
  var attr;

  for (var i=0; i<children.length; i++){
    node = children.item(i);
    if (node.nodeType == ELEMENT_NODE){
      string += node.nodeName;
      for (var j = 0; j<node.attributes.length; j++){
        attr = node.attributes.item(j);
        string += " " + attr.nodeName + '="' + attr.nodeValue+ '"';
      }
      string += "\n";
    }
  }
  return string;
}
```

Once the string has been built, it is passed back to the preceding calling function (`rotatePolygon`), which uses it as the content of an `alert`. If the puzzle pieces are moved around and the "x" key pressed, then a window will appear, like the one shown in Figure A-8.

```
Alert                                                                                    [x]

 ⚠   polygon points="0,100, 0,200 50,150" transform="translate(300,-100) rotate(0,0,0)" fill="lightgreen"
     polygon points="50,50, 100,100 150,50" transform="translate(285,-15) rotate(90,100,66.6)"
     polygon points="200,0, 100,100 200,200" transform="translate(245,76) rotate(22.5,166.6,100)"
     polygon points="0,200, 200,200 100,100" transform="translate(452,9.3) rotate(67.5,100,166.6)"
     polygon points="0,0 0,100 100,0" transform="translate(453.6,137.6) rotate(292.5,33.3,33.3)"
     polygon points="100,0, 50,50 150,50 200,0" transform="translate(495,45) rotate(472.5,125,25)"
     polygon points="50,50, 0,100 50,150 100,100" transform="translate(300,0) rotate(0,0,0)" fill="orange"

                                    [    OK    ]
```

Figure A-8

Note that the order of the elements probably won't match that of the original, as selecting an element moves it to the last position in the list, so it shows up on top (following the painter's model).

Chapter 20

This chapter discussed the XForms model, including the creation of instance data, submission configuration of a form, XForms form controls, and XForms model item properties.

Question 1

Experiment with the code examples given in the chapter, changing the value of the `appearance` attribute on the `xforms:select` and `xforms:select1` elements. This, particularly when viewed in more than one XForms viewer, provides some idea of the range of visual appearances available to an XForms developer.

Solution

There is no "solution" to this one, but you're encouraged to explore this area further on your own.

Question 2

Describe the differences in purpose of the `xforms:submit` and `xforms:submission` elements.

Solution

The `xforms:submit` element controls a form control visible to users of the form to enable them to initiate submission of the form, typically by a mouse click. The `xforms:submission` element is part of an XForms model and is not directly visible to users. Attributes of the `xforms:submission` element control where the instance data is to be submitted and what method of submission should be used.

B

XPath Reference

XPath is a well-established W3C specification that describes a non-XML syntax for selecting a set of nodes from the in-memory model of an XML document. XPath version 1.0 reached W3C Recommendation status on November 16, 1999. The specification documents for XPath 2.0, which is a subset of XQuery 1.0, were in late Working Draft stage at the time of this writing. XPath, both 1.0 and 2.0, is an essential part of the corresponding XSLT specification. This appendix focuses on XPath 1.0.

An XPath location path contains one or more *location steps,* separated by forward slashes (/). Each location step has the following form:

```
axis-name::node-test[predicate]*
```

In plain English, this is an axis name, followed by two colons, a node test, and, finally, zero or more predicates each contained in square brackets. A predicate can contain literal values (for example, 4 or 'hello'), operators (+, −, =, and so on), and other XPath expressions. XPath also defines a set of functions that can be used in predicates.

An XPath axis defines how to select a part of the model of an XML document, from the perspective of a starting point called the *context node*. The context node serves as the starting point for selecting the result of an XPath expression. The node test makes a selection from the nodes on the specified axis. In other words, a node test filters the nodes in the specified axis. By adding predicates, it is possible to filter any nodes already selected by selecting a subset of the nodes selected by the axis, and node-test parts of the expression. If the expression in the predicate returns true, the node remains in the selected node set; otherwise, it is removed.

This reference lists the XPath axes, node tests, and functions. Each entry includes whether it is implemented in version 1.0 of the specification. At one time, there were significant variations among implementations, with, for example, the Microsoft XML Core Services lacking full XPath 1.0 compliance. The situation has now improved to the point that any XPath implementation is likely to be essentially fully XPath 1.0–compliant. Microsoft Core XML Services (MSXML) versions 3.0 and later have full XPath implementations. Versions of MSXML before version 3.0 are not suitable for XPath 1.0 processing.

Other implementations, such as Xalan and Saxon, essentially fully implement version XPath 1.0.

XPath 2.0 Is Emerging Slowly

The move from XPath 1.0 to XPath 2.0 is progressing slowly due to XPath's complicity with XQuery, XSLT, and other parsers. Any changes made to XPath have to be carefully planned and implemented. XPath 2.0 will use the same axes information as XPath 1.0, so there will be little change there. The major change from XPath 1.0 to XPath 2.0 is the basic concept of using sequences instead of node-sets. The XPath community found node-sets to be too limiting and complicated. The new sequences will allow more flexibility and power and are simpler to use. The move from node-sets to sequences also brings some new techniques and methods when manipulating data types and functions.

XPath 2.0 also embraces the use of XML schemas. To be good at XPath 2.0, you will have to hone those XML schema skills. XPath 2.0, like XML schemas, are all about datatypes. The bottom line is that XPath 2.0 supports all datatypes supported by XML schemas plus some new additions.

Changes to functions in XPath 2.0 are covered at the end of this appendix.

The New Sequencing

The new sequencing is conceptually different and can now be a singleton, empty, and/or contain duplicate entries. The flexibility here adds power when testing data results and using functions. A *sequence* is formally described as being an ordered collection of items (some of us would have called these *nodes* or simply a *result set*). The concept of ordered or unordered is also emphasized and can be taken advantage of by some of the new functions.

Datatyping Control

All existing datatypes from XML schemas are supported, plus any new derivations that can be constructed from simple primitive types. The following table shows a list of some of the basic datatypes. Note that the xs: prefix maps to the XML schema namespace.

xs:string	xs:boolean	xs:decimal
xs:float	xs:double	xs:duration
xs:dateTime	xs:time	xs:date
xs:gYearMonth	xs:gYear	xs:hexBinary
xs:anyURI	xs:QName	xs:NOTATION

Axes

This section lists each axis and includes a brief description of the nodes it selects. The principal node type of an axis indicates what type of nodes are selected by a literal node test or the * node test (look under the *literal name* node test for an example). For some axes, XPath defines an abbreviated syntax. This syntax's form and its primary node type are listed for every axis.

ancestor

Description:	Contains the context node's parent node, the parent node's parent node, and so on, all the way up to the document root. If the context node is the root node, the ancestor axis is empty
Principal node type:	Element
Abbreviated syntax:	No abbreviated syntax for this axis
Implemented:	W3C 1.0 specification (recommendation)

ancestor-or-self

Description:	Includes the context node itself and the nodes in the ancestor axis
Principal node type:	Element
Abbreviated syntax:	No abbreviated syntax for this axis
Implemented:	W3C 1.0 specification (recommendation)

attribute

Description:	Contains all attributes of the context node. The attribute axis will be empty unless the context node is an element node.
Principal node type:	Attribute
Abbreviated syntax:	@
Implemented:	W3C 1.0 specification (recommendation)

child

Description:	Contains all direct children of the context node (that is, the children, but not the children's children)
Principal node type:	Element
Abbreviated syntax:	The child axis is the default axis, so if no axis is expressed, it is assumed that a location path is using the child axis.
Implemented:	W3C 1.0 specification (recommendation)

descendant

Description:	All children of the context node, including all children's children recursively
Principal node type:	Element
Abbreviated syntax:	//
Implemented:	W3C 1.0 specification (recommendation)

descendant-or-self

Description:	Includes the context node itself plus the nodes in the descendant axis
Principal node type:	Element
Abbreviated syntax:	No abbreviated syntax for this axis
Implemented:	W3C 1.0 specification (recommendation)

following

Description:	Contains all nodes that come after the context node in document order. This means that for nodes in the following axis, the start-tag of the element to which the node corresponds must come after the context node's end-tag. Descendant nodes of the context node are not part of the following axis.
Principal node type:	Element
Abbreviated syntax:	No abbreviated syntax for this axis
Implemented:	W3C 1.0 specification (recommendation)

following-sibling

Description:	Contains all siblings (children of the same parent node) of the context node that come after the context node in document order
Principal node type:	Element
Abbreviated syntax:	No abbreviated syntax for this axis
Implemented:	W3C 1.0 specification (recommendation)

namespace

Description:	Contains all namespace nodes that are in scope on the context node. This includes the default namespace and the XML namespace (these are automatically declared in any document). The namespace axis is empty unless the context node is an element.
Principal node type:	Namespace
Abbreviated syntax:	No abbreviated syntax for this axis
Implemented:	W3C 1.0 specification (recommendation)

parent

Description:	Contains the direct parent node (and only the direct parent node) of the context node, if there is one. If the context node is the root node, the parent axis is empty.
Principal node type:	Element
Abbreviated syntax:	. .
Implemented:	W3C 1.0 specification (recommendation)

preceding

Description:	Contains all nodes that come before the context node in document order. This contains element nodes where the corresponding start-tag/end-tag pair are already closed (their end-tag comes before the context node's start-tag in the document). Ancestor nodes are not present in this axis because their end-tag is later in the document.
Principal node type:	Element
Abbreviated syntax:	No abbreviated syntax for this axis
Implemented:	W3C 1.0 specification (recommendation)

preceding-sibling

Description:	Contains all sibling nodes (children of the same parent node) of the context node that come before the context node in document order
Principal node type:	Element
Abbreviated syntax:	None
Implemented:	W3C 1.0 specification (recommendation)

self

Description:	Contains only the context node
Principal node type:	Element
Abbreviated syntax:	.
Implemented:	W3C 1.0 specification (recommendation)

Node Tests

A node test describes a test performed on each node in an axis to decide whether it should be included in the node-set. If the Boolean value true is returned by the node test, the node is included in the node-set. If false is returned, the node is not included in the node-set. Appending a predicate can further filter the node-set.

Examples using the meta character *:

child::* will select all element children of the context node.

attribute::* will select all attributes of the context node.

Description:	Returns true for all nodes of the principal node type for the axis
Implemented:	W3C 1.0 specification (recommendation)

Example using the comment() function:

child::comment() will select all comment node children of the context node.

comment( )

Description:	Returns true for all comment nodes
Implemented:	W3C 1.0 specification (recommendation)

node( )

Description:	Returns true for all nodes, except attributes and namespaces
Implemented:	W3C 1.0 specification (recommendation)

Example using the processing-instruction() function:

```
</xsl:template>
        <xsl:template match = "processing-instruction(''peanuts')" >
        </xsl:template>
```

processing-instruction(Literal)

Description:	The node test processing-instruction() is true for any processing instruction. The processing-instruction() test may have an argument that is Literal; in this case, it is true for any processing instruction that has a name equal to the value of the Literal.
Implemented:	W3C 1.0 specification (recommendation)

Examples using the text() function:

child::text() will select all text node children of the context node.

text( )

Description:	Returns true for all text nodes
Implemented:	W3C 1.0 specification (recommendation)

Functions

Functions in XPath 1.0 are limited to fairly simple manipulation of node-sets, numbers, strings, and Booleans. A common use of functions in XPath 1.0 is to filter a node-set that was selected using an axis and node test. To do that, an expression is written in square brackets, which can include literal values (numbers, strings, and so on), XPath location paths, and one or more functions defined by the XPath specification.

Each function in this section is described by a line of the following form:

```
return-type function-name (parameters)
```

For each parameter, you display the type (`object`, `string`, `number`, `node-set`) and, where necessary, a symbol indicating whether the parameter is optional (?) or can occur multiple times (+). The type `object` means that any type can be passed.

If an expression is passed as a parameter, it is first evaluated and (if necessary) converted to the expected type before passing it to the function.

---

boolean **boolean**(object)

Converts any object passed to it to a Boolean.
`boolean(attribute: name)` will return `true` if the context node has a `name` attribute.

Parameter:
object
  Numbers result in `true` if they are not zero or NaN.
  Strings result in `true` if their length is nonzero.
  Node-sets return `true` if they are non-empty.

Implemented: W3C 1.0 specification (recommendation)

---

number **ceiling**(number)
Rounds a passed number to the smallest integer that is not smaller than the passed number.

`ceiling(1.1)` returns 2

Parameter:
number
  The number that is to be rounded up to an integer

Implemented: W3C 1.0 specification (recommendation)

Table continued on following page

string **concat**(string1, string2+)

Concatenates all passed strings to one string.
`concat('con', 'c', 'a', 't')` returns `concat`

Parameters:
 string1
  The first string
 string2
  All following strings

Implemented: W3C 1.0 specification (recommendation)

boolean **contains**(string1, string2)

Returns `true` if string1 contains string2.
`contains('John Smith', 'John')` returns `true`

Parameters:
 string1
  The source string
 string2
  The string whose presence in the source string is to be tested

Implemented: W3C 1.0 specification (recommendation)

number **count**(node-set)

Returns the number of nodes in the passed node-set.
`count(child::*[@name])` returns the number of child elements of the context node that have a
`name` attribute.

Parameter:
 node-set
  The node-set that is to be counted

Implemented: W3C 1.0 specification (recommendation)

boolean **false**( )

Always returns `false`. This function is needed because an expression `False` tests whether the context node has child element nodes whose name is `False`.

Implemented: W3C 1.0 specification (recommendation)

number **floor**(number)

The `floor` function can be used to mathematically derive the number x (closest to positive infinity) either equal to but not greater than the number x in question expressed as an integer. Usually calculated in steps. Because infinity is not a number, it means that *x* becomes either larger and larger (for positive infinity) or smaller and smaller (for negative infinity). Rounds a passed number to the largest integer that is less than the passed number.

```
floor(2.9) returns 2
floor(-1.1) returns -2
```

Parameter:
number
   The number that must be rounded to an integer

Implemented: W3C 1.0 specification (recommendation)

node-set **id**(string)

Returns the element identified by the passed identifier. In a compliant XPath implementation, this will only work in validated documents, because for nonvalidated documents, the parser has no way of knowing which attributes represent ID values. The ID type is defined in a schema document.

Parameter:
string
   The ID value

Implemented: W3C 1.0 specification (recommendation)

boolean **lang**(string)

```
<?xml version="1.0"?>
<!-- This is LangTest.xsl -->
<xsl:stylesheet version="1.0"

xmlns:xsl="http://www.w3.org/1999/XSL/Transform">
<xsl:output method="xml" version="1.0" indent="yes"/>
<xsl:param name="LanguageSelected" select="'en'"/>
<xsl:variable name="phrases"
select="document('LanguageData.xml')/phrases"/>
```

Returns `true` if the language of the context node is the same as the passed language parameter. The language of the context node can be set using the `xml:lang` attribute on itself or any of its ancestors. `Lang('en')` returns `true` for English language nodes.

Parameter:
string
   Language identifier

Implemented: W3C 1.0 specification (recommendation)

Table continued on following page

number **last( )**

Returns the last node in a node-set. The node returned is, for forward axes,
the last node in document order. For reverse axes the opposite is true.
`child::*[last()-1]` selects the penultimate child element node of the context node.

Implemented: W3C 1.0 specification (recommendation)

String **local-name**(node-set?)

Returns the local part of the name of the first node in the passed node-set (the part of a namespace-
qualified name that occurs after the colon). For example, the local part of an `xsl:value-of` element is `value-of`.

Parameter:
Node-set
If no node-set is specified, the context node is used.

Implemented: W3C 1.0 specification (recommendation)

String **name**(node-set?)

Returns the name of the first node in a passed node-set. This is the fully qualified name, including
namespace prefix.

Parameter:
Node-set
If no node-set is specified, the context node is used.

Implemented: W3C 1.0 specification (recommendation)

string **namespace-uri**(node-set?)

Returns the URI of the namespace of the passed node

Parameter:
node-set
If no node-set is specified, the context node is used.

Implemented: W3C 1.0 specification (recommendation)

string **normalize-space**(string?)

Returns the whitespace-normalized version of the passed string. This means that leading and trailing whitespace is stripped and all sequences of whitespace characters are combined to one single-space character.
`normalize-space(' some text ')` would return `'some text'`.

Parameter:
string
If no string is passed, the value of the context node is converted to a string.

Implemented: W3C 1.0 specification (recommendation)

boolean **not**(boolean)

Returns the logical inverse of the passed value.
`not(@name)` returns `true` if there is no `name` attribute on the context node.

Parameter:
boolean
An expression that evaluates to a Boolean value

Implemented: W3C 1.0 specification (recommendation)

number **number**(object?)

Converts the parameter to a number.
`number('3.6')` returns the number `3.6` from the supplied string parameter.

Parameter:
object
If no parameter is specified, the context node is used.

Implemented: W3C 1.0 specification (recommendation)

number **position**( )

Returns the position of a node in a node-set.
`position()` returns `1` for the first node in a node-set.

Implemented: W3C 1.0 specification (recommendation)

Table continued on following page

number **round**(number)

Rounds a passed number to the nearest integer. If the value is exactly halfway between two integers, it is rounded to the integer nearer to positive infinity.
round(1.5) returns 2, round(-1.7) returns -2.

Parameter:
number
The number that is to be rounded [-1]

Implemented: W3C 1.0 specification (recommendation)

boolean **starts-with**(string1, string2)

Returns true if string1 starts with string2.
starts-with(@name, 'D') returns true if the value of the name attribute starts with an uppercase D.

Parameters:
string1
The string to be checked

Implemented: W3C 1.0 specification (recommendation)

string **string**(object?)

Converts the passed object to a string value

Parameter:
object
If no parameter is specified, the context node is evaluated.

Implemented: W3C 1.0 specification (recommendation)

number **string-length**(string?)

Returns the number of characters in the passed string.
string-length('Andrew Watt') returns 11.

Parameter:
string
If no parameter is specified, the context node is converted to a string.

Implemented: W3C 1.0 specification (recommendation)

string **substring**(string, number1, number2?)

Returns the substring from the passed string starting at the number1 character, with the length of number2. If no number2 parameter is passed, the substring runs to the end of the passed string. Characters are numbered from 1.
`substring('Andrew Watt', 8)` returns `'Watt'`.

Parameters:
string
The string that will be used as source for the substring extraction

Implemented: W3C 1.0 specification (recommendation)

string **substring-after**(string1, string2)

Returns the substring following the first occurrence of `string2` inside `string1`. For example, the return value of `substring-after('2004/3/22', '/')` would be `3/22`.

Parameters:
string1
The string to be searched for the specified substring
string2
The string that is searched in the source string

Implemented: W3C 1.0 specification (recommendation)

string **substring-before**(string1, string2)

Returns the string part preceding the first occurrence of `string2` inside `string1`. For example, the return value of `substring-before('2004/3/22', '/')` would be `2004`.

Parameters:
string1
The string to be searched for the specified substring
string2
The string that is searched in the source string

Implemented: W3C 1.0 specification (recommendation)

number **sum**(node-set)

Sums the values of all nodes in the set when converted to a number.
`sum(student/@age)` returns the sum of the values of all `age` attributes on the student elements in the `child` axis starting at the context node.

Parameter:
node-set
The node-set containing all values to be summed

Implemented: W3C 1.0 specification (recommendation)

Table continued on following page

string **translate** (string1, string2, string3)

Translates characters in `string1` to other characters. Translation pairs are specified by `string2` and `string3`. For example, `translate('A Space Odissei', 'i', 'y')` would result in `A Space Odyssey`, and `translate('abcdefg', 'aceg', 'ACE')` would result in `AbCdEf`. The characters a, c, and e are translated to the corresponding uppercase character, as specified in the `string3`. The final g is translated to nothing, because `string3` has no counterpart for that position in `string2`.

Parameter:
string1
   String is to be translated character by character

Implemented: W3C 1.0 specification (recommendation)

boolean **true**( )

Always returns `true`. This function is required in XPath because the expression `True` selects any child element nodes whose name is `True`.

Implemented: W3C 1.0 specification (recommendation)

XPath 2.0 Functions

Functions within XPath 2.0 are now quite naturally syntactically different and currently parallel development with XSLT 2.0. It would be no surprise if some XML editors currently were short some of these functions; perhaps this would be the reason why you would favor one tool over another at this time. We have listed some of the new functions in the following table. Note the `fn:` prefix to accommodate the XML schema style, and the reference to processing of sequences as opposed to node-sets. A complete list of XPath 2.0 and XSLT 2.0–compatible functions can be found on the W3C site. Keep in mind that the combination of function capability with XPath 2.0 and XQuery 1.0 and XSLT 1.0 are different at the time this book goes to press. As a practical note, the compatibility issues are born by the tool provider. It's up to you, the end user, to decide which tool is more useful or current.

fn:add-timezone-to-date(date $srcval) => date	fn:avg(atomic Value* $srcval) => numeric?	fn:base-uri(node $srcval) => anyURI?,returns String	fn:boolean(item* $srcval) => boolean	fn:ceiling(numeric? $srcval) => numeric?
fn:codepoints-to-string(integer* codes) => string	fn:collection (string $srcval) => node*	fn:compare(string? $comparand1, string? $comparand2) => integer?	fn:compare (string? $comparand1, string? $comparand2) => integer?	fn:concat(string $arg1, ...) => string
n:contains(string? $operand1, string? $operand2) => boolean?	fn:data(node $srcval) => atomic value*	n:deep-equal (node $parameter1, node $parameter2) => boolean	fn:distinct-values(item* $srcval) => item*	fn:distinct-values(item* $srcval, anyURI $collationLiteral) => item*
fn:error()	fn:escape-uri(string $uri-part, boolean $escape-reserved) => string	fn:index-of (item* $seqParam, item $srchParam) => unsignedInt*	fn:tokenize (string? $input, string? $pattern, string? $flags) => string*	fn:unordered (item* $sequence) => item*

C

XSLT Reference

This appendix provides a reference to the elements and functions that are part of XSLT 1.0. A reference to XPath 1.0 constructs, including functions that can also be used with XSLT, is in Appendix C.

The XSLT 1.0 specification became a W3C Recommendation on November 16, 1999. As this book goes to press, XSLT 2.0 has just been awarded W3C Recommendation status. XSLT 2.0 and XPath 2.0 go hand-in-hand, are inseparable, and have to be studied together. The development pace for both will be the same. In addition, be aware that XSLT, XPath, and XQuery are so dependent upon one another that you need to have all three skill sets or you will have serious problems. The good news is that they are becoming increasingly similar, meaning that once you master one you can master them all quickly.

XSLT 1.0 processors may or may not come with a description of the conformance to the XSLT 1.0 specification. However, most XSLT processors can be assumed to be close to 100 percent conformant to the W3C XSLT 1.0 specification. Some experimental XSLT processors, such as recent versions of Saxon, include a conformant XSLT 1.0 implementation, which was used in Chapter 8, and an experimental XSLT 2.0 processor. This new emerging XSLT 2.0 processor only works with XPath 2.0. You cannot mix XSLT 2.0 and XPath 1.0, nor the other way around. This is not to say that XSLT 1.0 features are obsolete, but that XSLT 2.0 will be different in philosophy, syntax, and construct.

Both the attributes on XSLT 1.0 elements and the parameters of XSLT 1.0 functions can be of several types. The end of this appendix contains a list of the types used in the elements and functions of XSLT.

> *For more information on the meaning of the element or function types, see the "Types" table at the end of this appendix.*

XSLT stands for XSL Transformations and plays a major role in XSL. XSLT can transform an XML document into another XML document type such as HTML and XHTML. Normally, XSLT does this by transforming each XML element into an (X)HTML element.

With XSLT you can add/remove elements and attributes to/from the output file. You can also rearrange and sort elements, perform tests, and make decisions about which elements to hide and display, and a lot more. Think of XSLT as a transformation tool that when paired with XPath functionality can be used to process information selectively and quickly.

In the transformation process, XSLT uses XPath to define parts of the source document that should match one or more predefined templates, such as attribute templates. Attribute templates can be predefined to standardize and simplify simple string substitutions used to process files known as *result documents*. When a match is found, XSLT will transform the matching part of the source document into the result document reformatted in the new syntax.

Elements

An XSLT stylesheet is itself an XML document, using elements in the XSLT namespace. The namespace URI is `http://www.w3.org/1999/XSL/Transform`. When XSLT is used, a namespace prefix is used in the element name as a proxy for the namespace URI. In this appendix we use the namespace prefix `xsl`.

For each XSLT 1.0 element we provide a short description of its use, describe the attributes that can or must be used on the element, and indicate where in the stylesheet the element can occur (as a child of which other elements).

xsl:apply-imports

Used to add additional information to an existing stylesheet that has implemented the `xsl:apply-templates` element using `xsl:apply-imports`. The information embedded using the `xsl:apply-imports` will be a subset of or considered a lower precedence to that brought forth using the `xsl:templates` element.

```
<?xml version="1.0"?>
<xsl:stylesheet xmlns:xsl="http://www.w3.org/1999/XSL/Transform"
    version="1.0">
 <xsl:import href="arith.xsl"/>
 <xsl:import href="str.xsl"/>
 <xsl:template match="op">
 <xsl:value-of select="operand[1]"/>
 <xsl:value-of select="@symbol"/>
 <xsl:value-of select="operand[2]"/>
 = <xsl:apply-imports/>
 <br/>
 </xsl:template>
</xsl:stylesheet>
```

Implemented:	W3C XSLT 1.0 specification
Can contain:	No other elements
Can be contained by:	`xsl:attribute`, `xsl:comment`, `xsl:copy`, `xsl:element`, `xsl:fallback` `xsl:for-each`, `xsl:if`, `xsl:message`, `xsl:otherwise`, `xsl:param` `xsl:processing-instruction`, `xsl:template`, `xsl:variable`, `xsl:when`

xsl:apply-templates

Used to select a set of nodes to be processed. The processor attempts to find templates that match the specified operator. Using curly braces, {}, around an expression in an attribute is known as an Attribute Value Template. You can use this technique on certain attributes to insert the result of an XPath expression where normally a fixed string would be expected.

Attributes:

select (optional)	Expression describing which nodes should be processed. Defaults to `child::*`	
	Type:	Location path
	Attribute Value Template:	No
mode (optional)	By adding a `mode` attribute, the processor will process nodes using only templates with a matching value for its `mode` attribute. This enables us to process a node in the source tree more than once.	
	Type:	QName
	Attribute Value Template:	No
Implemented:	W3C XSLT 1.0 specification	
Can contain:	`xsl:sort, xsl:with-param`	
Can be contained by:	`xsl:attribute, xsl:comment, xsl:copy, xsl:element, xsl:fallback, xsl:for-each, xsl:if, xsl:message, xsl:otherwise, xsl:param, xsl:processing-instruction, xsl:template, xsl:variable, xsl:when`	

xsl:attribute

Generates an attribute in the result document. It should be used in the context of an element (either `xsl:element` or a literal result element). It must occur before any text or element content is added to an element node.

Attributes:

name (required)	The name of the attribute	
	Type:	QName
	Attribute Value Template:	Yes
namespace (optional)	The namespace URI of the attribute node. By default, it uses the namespace of the element the attribute is placed on.	
	Type:	Uri-reference
	Attribute Value Template:	Yes
Implemented:	W3C XSLT 1.0 specification	

Table continued on following page

Can contain:	xsl:apply-imports, xsl:apply-templates, xsl:call-template, xsl:choose, xsl:copy, xsl:copy-of, xsl:fallback, xsl:for-each, xsl:if, xsl:message, xsl:number, xsl:text, xsl:value-of, xsl:variable
Can be contained by:	xsl:attribute-set, xsl:copy, xsl:element, xsl:fallback, xsl:for-each, xsl:if, xsl:message, xsl:otherwise, xsl:param, xsl:template, xsl:variable, xsl:when

xsl:attribute-set

Used to define a set of attributes that can then be added to an element as a group by specifying the xsl:attribute-set element's name attribute value in the use-attribute-sets attribute on the xsl:element element.

Attributes:		

name (required)	Name that can be used to refer to this set of attributes. Qualified names were introduced by [XML Namespaces]. They were defined for element and attribute *names* (only) and provide a mechanism for concisely identifying a {URI, local-name} pair. See, for example, the following document:
	
	`<?xml version='1.0'?>`
	`<doc xmlns:x="http://example.com/ns/foo">`
	`<x:p/>`
	`</doc>`	

	Type:	QName
	Attribute Value Template:	No
use-attribute-sets (optional)	For including one or more existing attribute sets in this attribute set	
	Type:	QNames
	Attribute Value Template:	No
Implemented:	W3C XSLT 1.0 specification	
Can contain:	xsl:attribute	
Can be contained by:	xsl:stylesheet, xsl:transform	

xsl:call-template

Used to call a template by name. This element causes no change of context node as `xsl:apply-templates` and `xsl:for-each` do. This element can be used to reuse the same functionality in several templates.

Attributes:		
name (required)	Name of the template you want to call	
	Type:	QName
	Attribute Value Template:	No
Implemented:	W3C XSLT 1.0 specification	
Can contain:	`xsl:with-param`	
Can be contained by:	`xsl:attribute, xsl:comment, xsl:copy xsl:element, xsl:fall back, xsl:for-each, xsl:if, xsl:message, xsl:otherwise, xsl:param, xsl:processing-instruction, xsl:template, xsl:variable, xsl:when`	

xsl:choose

Used for implementing the choose/when/otherwise construct. Compare to `Case/Select` in Visual Basic or `switch` in C and Java. The `xsl:choose` element has no attributes.

Implemented:	W3C XSLT 1.0 specification
Can contain:	`xsl:otherwise, xsl:when`. The `<xsl:when>` children of the `<xsl:choose>` element are tested, in order from top to bottom, until a test attribute on one of these elements accurately describes conditions in the source data, or until an `<xsl:otherwise>` element is reached. Once an `<xsl:when>` or `<xsl:otherwise>` element is chosen, the `<xsl:choose>` block is exited. No explicit break or exit statement is required. For simple conditional testing, use the `<xsl:if>` element.
Can be contained by:	`xsl:attribute, xsl:comment, xsl:copy, xsl:element, xsl:fallback, xsl:for-each, xsl:if, xsl:message, xsl:otherwise, xsl:param, xsl:processing-instruction, xsl:template, xsl:variable, xsl:when`

xsl:comment

Needed for generating a comment node in the result document. The `xsl:comment` element has no attributes.

Implemented:	W3C XSLT 1.0 specification
Can contain:	`xsl:apply-imports`, `xsl:apply-templates`, `xsl:call-template`, `xsl:choose`, `xsl:copy`, `xsl:copy-of`, `xsl:fallback`, `xsl:for-each`, `xsl:if`, `xsl:message`, `xsl:number`, `xsl:text`, `xsl:value-of`, `xsl:variable`
Can be contained by:	`xsl:copy`, `xsl:element`, `xsl:fallback`, `xsl:for-each`, `xsl:if`, `xsl:message`, `xsl:otherwise`, `xsl:param`, `xsl:template`, `xsl:variable`, `xsl:when`

xsl:copy

Generates a copy of the context node in the destination document. Does not copy any child nodes or attribute nodes.

Attributes:		
`use-attribute-sets` (optional)	For adding a set of attributes to the copied node, if it is an element node	
	Type:	QNames
	Attribute Value Template:	No
Implemented:	W3C XSLT 1.0 specification	
Can contain:	`xsl:apply-imports`, `xsl:apply-templates`, `xsl:attribute`, `xsl:call-template`, `xsl:choose`, `xsl:comment`, `xsl:copy-of`, `xsl:element`, `xsl:fallback`, `xsl:for-each`, `xsl:if`, `xsl:message`, `xsl:number`, `xsl:processing-instruction`, `xsl:text`, `xsl:value-of`, `xsl:variable`	
Can be contained by:	`xsl:attribute`, `xsl:comment`, `xsl:copy`, `xsl:element`, `xsl:fallback`, `xsl:for-each`, `xsl:if`, `xsl:message`, `xsl:otherwise`, `xsl:param`, `xsl:processing-instruction`, `xsl:template`, `xsl:variable`, `xsl:when`	

xsl:copy-of

Copies a node, together with any attribute nodes and child nodes, to the result tree. If multiple nodes are matched by the select attribute, all are copied. If you have an XML fragment stored in a variable, xsl:copy-of is a useful element for sending the variable's content to the result tree.

Attributes:		
select (required)	XPath expression that selects the nodes to be copied	
	Type:	Expression
	Attribute Value Template:	No
Implemented:	W3C XSLT 1.0 specification	
Can contain:	Cannot contain other elements	
Can be contained by:	xsl:attribute, xsl:comment, xsl:copy, , xsl:element, xsl:fallback, xsl:for-each, xsl:if, xsl:message, xsl:otherwise, xsl:param, xsl:processing-instruction, xsl:template, xsl:variable, xsl:when	

xsl:decimal-format

Declares a decimal format that controls the interpretation of a format pattern used by the format-number() function. Among the aspects of the format defined are the decimal separator and the thousands separator.

Attributes:		
name (optional)	The name of the defined format	
	Type:	QName
	Attribute Value Template:	No
decimal-separator (optional)	The character that will separate the integer part from the fraction part. The default is a dot (.)	
	Type:	Character
	Attribute Value Template:	No
grouping-separator (optional)	The character that will separate the grouped numbers in the integer part. The default is a comma (,)	
	Type:	Character
	Attribute Value Template:	No
infinity (optional)	The string that should appear if a number equals infinity. The default is the string Infinity.	
	Type:	String
	Attribute Value Template:	No

Table continued on following page

minus-sign (optional)	The character that will be used to indicate a negative number. The default is minus (-).	
	Type:	Character
	Attribute Value Template:	No
NaN (optional)	The string that should appear if a value is Not a Number. The default is the string NaN.	
	Type:	String
	Attribute Value Template:	No
percent (optional)	The character that will be used as the percent sign. The default is %.	
	Type:	Character
	Attribute Value Template:	No
per-mille (optional)	The character that will be used as the per-thousand sign. The default is the Unicode character #x2030, which looks like .	
	Type:	Character
	Attribute Value Template:	No

zero-digit (optional)	The character used as the digit zero. The default is 0 .
	
	``xml
	<?xml version="1.0"?>
	<xsl:stylesheet
	xmlns:xsl="http://www.w3.org/1999/XSL/Transform">
	
	<xsl:decimal-format zero-digit="0" />
	
	<xsl:template match="doc">
	 <out>
	 <xsl:value-of
	 select="format number(931.4857,'000.0000')"/>
	 </out>
	</xsl:template>
	
	</xsl:stylesheet>
	``	

	Type:	Character
	Attribute Value Template:	No
digit (optional)	The character used in a pattern to indicate the place where a leading zero is required. The default is 0.	
	Type:	Character
	Attribute Value Template:	No

pattern-separator (optional)	The character that is used to separate the negative and positive patterns (if they are different). The default is a semicolon (;). Being able to redefine the semicolon to an alternate character such as a colon enables the semicolon to be used inside the pattern(s) and resolves confusion regarding what is data and what is used as a delimeter between patterns.	
	Type:	Character
	Attribute Value Template:	No
Implemented:	W3C XSLT 1.0 specification	
Can contain:	Cannot contain other elements	
Can be contained by:	`xsl:stylesheet, xsl:transform`	

xsl:element

Generates an element with the specified name in the destination document		
Attributes:		
name (required)	Name of the element (this may include a namespace prefix bound to a namespace in the stylesheet)	
	Type:	QName
	Attribute Value Template:	Yes
namespace (optional)	Specifies the namespace URI of the element to be created	
	Type:	Uri-reference
	Attribute Value Template:	Yes
use-attribute-sets (optional)	Adds a predefined set of attributes to the element	
	Type:	QNames
	Attribute Value Template:	No
Implemented:	W3C XSLT 1.0 specification	
Can contain:	`xsl:apply-imports, xsl:apply-templates, xsl:attribute, xsl:call-template, xsl:choose, xsl:comment, xsl:copy, xsl:copy-of, xsl:element, xsl:fallback, xsl:for-each, xsl:if, xsl:message, xsl:number, xsl:processing-instruction, xsl:text, xsl:value-of, xsl:variable`	
Can be contained by:	`xsl:copy, xsl:element, xsl:fallback, xsl:for-each, xsl:if, xsl:otherwise, xsl:param, xsl:template, xsl:variable, xsl:when`	

xsl:fallback

Can be used to specify actions to be executed if its parent element is not supported by the processor. In this case, the fallback action will be executed instead.

```
<?xml version="1.0" encoding="ISO-8859-1"?>
<xsl:stylesheet version="1.0"
xmlns:xsl="http://www.w3.org/1999/XSL/Transform">
<xsl:template match="catalog/cd">
<xsl:loop select="title">
<xsl:fallback>
<xsl:for-each select="title">
<xsl:value-of select="."/>
</xsl:for-each>
</xsl:fallback>
</xsl:loop>
</xsl:template>
</xsl:stylesheet>
```

Implemented:	W3C XSLT 1.0 specification
Can contain:	xsl:apply-imports, xsl:apply-templates, xsl:attribute, xsl:call-template, xsl:choose, xsl:comment, xsl:copy, xsl:copy-of, xsl:element, xsl:for-each, xsl:if, xsl:message, xsl:number, xsl:processing-instruction, xsl:text, xsl:value-of, xsl:variable
Can be contained by:	xsl:attribute, xsl:comment, xsl:copy, xsl:element, xsl:for-each, xsl:if, xsl:message, xsl:otherwise, xsl:param, xsl:processing-instruction, xsl:template, xsl:variable, xsl:when

xsl:for-each

Used for looping through the node-set selected by the XPath expression in the select attribute. The context is shifted to the current node in the loop.

Attributes:		
select (required)	Expression that selects the node-set to loop through	
	Type:	Node-set-expression
	Attribute Value Template:	No
Implemented:	W3C XSLT 1.0 specification	
Can contain:	xsl:apply-imports, xsl:apply-templates, xsl:attribute, xsl:call-template, xsl:choose, xsl:comment, xsl:copy, xsl:copy-of, xsl:element, xsl:fallback, xsl:for-each, xsl:if, xsl:message, xsl:number, xsl:processing-instruction, xsl:sort, xsl:text, xsl:value-of, xsl:variable	

Can be contained by:	xsl:attribute, xsl:comment, xsl:copy, xsl:element, xsl:fallback, xsl:for-each, xsl:if, xsl:message, xsl:otherwise, xsl:param, xsl:processing-instruction, xsl:template, xsl:variable, xsl:when

xsl:if

The contained instructions are instantiated only if the test expression returns true.

Attributes:		
test (required)	The expression that is tested. If it returns true the instructions contained in the xsl:if element are executed.	
	Type	Boolean-expression
	Attribute Value Template:	No
Implemented:	W3C XSLT 1.0 specification	
Can contain:	xsl:apply-imports, xsl:apply-templates, xsl:attribute, xsl:call-template, xsl:choose, xsl:comment, xsl:copy, xsl:copy-of, xsl:element, xsl:fallback, xsl:for-each, xsl:if, xsl:message, xsl:number, xsl:processing-instruction, xsl:text, xsl:value-of, xsl:variable	
Can be contained by:	xsl:attribute, xsl:comment, xsl:copy, xsl:element, xsl:fallback, xsl:for-each, xsl:if, xsl:message, xsl:otherwise, xsl:param, xsl:processing-instruction, xsl:template, xsl:variable, xsl:when	

xsl:import

Imports the templates from an external stylesheet document into the current document. The priority of these imported templates is lower than the priority of templates in the importing stylesheet, so if a template in the importing document is implemented for the same pattern, it will always be instantiated, rather than a similar template in the imported template being instantiated. An imported template can be called from the overriding template using xsl:apply-imports.

Attributes:		
href (required)	Reference to the stylesheet to be imported	
	Type:	Uri-reference
	Attribute Value Template:	No
Implemented:	W3C XSLT 1.0 specification	
Can contain:	Cannot contain other elements	
Can be contained by:	xsl:stylesheet, xsl:transform	

xsl:include

Includes templates from an external document as if they were part of the stylesheet document that contains the xsl:include element. This means that templates from the included stylesheet have the same priority as they would have had if they were part of the including stylesheet. An error occurs if a template with the same match and priority attributes exists in both the including and included stylesheets.

Attributes:		
href (required)	Reference to the stylesheet to be imported	
	Type:	Uri-reference
	Attribute Value Template:	No
Implemented:	W3C XSLT 1.0 specification	
Can contain:	Cannot contain other elements	
Can be contained by:	xsl:stylesheet, xsl:transform	

xsl:key

Used to create indexlike structures that can be queried from the key() function. It is basically a way to describe name/value pairs inside the source document (such as a Dictionary object in VB, a hash table in Java, or an associative array in Perl). However, in XSLT, more than one value can be found for one key and the same value can be accessed by multiple keys.

Attributes:		
name (required)	The name that can be used to refer to this key	
	Type:	QName
	Attribute Value Template:	No
match (required)	Contains a pattern that defines the nodes in the source document that can be accessed using this key. In the name/value pair analogy, this would be the definition of the value.	
	Type:	Pattern
	Attribute Value Template:	No
use (required)	This expression defines what the key for accessing each value would be. For example, if an element PERSON is matched by the match attribute and the use attribute equals " @name", the key() function can be used to find this specific PERSON element by passing the value of its name attribute.	
	Type:	Expression
	Attribute Value Template:	No
Implemented:	W3C XSLT 1.0 specification	
Can contain:	Cannot contain other elements	
Can be contained by:	xsl:stylesheet, xsl:transform	

xsl:message

Used to issue error messages or warnings. The content of the element is the message. What the XSLT processor does with the message is left to the implementation. It could be displayed in a message box or logged to an error log.

Attributes:

terminate (optional)	If terminate is set to yes, the execution of the transformation is stopped after issuing the message.	
	Type:	Yes/no
	Attribute Value Template:	No
Implemented:	W3C 1.0 XSLT specification	
Can contain:	xsl:apply-imports, xsl:apply-templates, xsl:attribute, xsl:call-template, xsl:choose, xsl:comment, xsl:copy, xsl:copy-of, xsl:element, xsl:fallback, xsl:for-each, xsl:if, xsl:message, xsl:number, xsl:processing-instruction, xsl:text, xsl:value-of, xsl:variable, xsl:attribute, xsl:comment	
Can be contained by:	xsl:copy, xsl:element, xsl:fallback, xsl:for-each, xsl:if, xsl:message, xsl:otherwise, xsl:param, xsl:processing-instruction, xsl:template, xsl:variable, xsl:when	

xsl:namespace-alias

Used to make a certain namespace appear in the result document without using the desired namespace prefix for that namespace in the stylesheet. The main use of this element is in generating new XSLT stylesheets.

The `<xsl:namespace-alias>` element replaces the prefix associated with a given namespace with another prefix. A simple substitution.

`<xsl:namespace-alias stylesheet-prefix = NCName result-prefix = NCName/>`

Attributes:

stylesheet-prefix (required)	The prefix for the namespace used in the stylesheet	
	Type:	Prefix/#default
	Attribute Value Template:	No
result-prefix (required)	The prefix for the namespace that must replace the aliased namespace in the destination document	
	Type:	Prefix/#default
	Attribute Value Template:	No

Table continued on following page

Implemented:	W3C XSLT 1.0 specification
Can contain:	Cannot contain other elements
Can be contained by:	`xsl:stylesheet, xsl:transform`

xsl:number

Needed for outputting the number of a paragraph or chapter in a specified format. It has flexible features to allow for different numbering rules.

Attributes:		
`level` (optional)	The value `single` counts the location of the nearest node matched by the `count` attribute (along the ancestor axis) relative to its preceding siblings of the same name. Typical output: chapter number.	
	The value `multiple` counts the location of all nodes matched by the `count` attribute (along the ancestor axis) relative to their preceding siblings of the same name. Typical output: paragraph number of form 4.5.3.	
	The value `any` counts the location of the nearest node matched by the `count` attribute (along the ancestor axis) relative to its preceding nodes (not only siblings) of the same name. Typical output: bookmark number.	
	Type:	Single/multiple/any
	Attribute Value Template:	No
`count` (optional)	Specifies the node-set that is to be counted	
	Type:	Pattern
	Attribute Value Template:	No
`from` (optional)	Specifies the starting point for counting	
	Type:	Pattern
	Attribute Value Template:	No
`value` (optional)	Used to specify the numeric value directly instead of using `'level'`, `'count'` and `'from'`	
	Type:	Number-expression
	Attribute Value Template:	No
`format` (optional)	How to format the numeric value to a string (1 indicates 1, 2, 3, a indicates a, b, c,)	
	Type:	String
	Attribute Value Template:	Yes

lang (optional)	Language used for alphabetic numbering	
	Type:	Token
	Attribute Value Template:	Yes
letter-value (optional)	Some languages have traditional orders of letters specifically for numbering. These orders are often different from the alphabetic order.	
	Type:	Alphabetic/traditional
	Attribute Value Template:	Yes
grouping-separator (optional)	Character to be used for group separation	
	Type:	Character
	Attribute Value Template:	Yes
grouping-size (optional)	Number of digits to be separated. grouping-separator=";" and grouping-size="3" causes: 1;000;000	
	Type:	Number
	Attribute Value Template:	Yes
Implemented:	W3C XSLT 1.0 specification	
Can contain:	Cannot contain other elements	
Can be contained by:	xsl:attribute, xsl:comment, xsl:copy, xsl:element, xsl:fallback, xsl:for-each, xsl:if, xsl:message, xsl:otherwise, xsl:param, xsl:processing-instruction, xsl:template, xsl:variable, xsl:when	

xsl:otherwise

Content is executed if none of the xsl:when elements in an xsl:choose is matched.	
Implemented:	W3C 1.0 specification (recommendation)
Can contain:	xsl:apply-imports, xsl:apply-templates, xsl:attribute, xsl:call-template, xsl:choose, xsl:comment, xsl:copy, xsl:copy-of, xsl:element, xsl:fallback, xsl:for-each, xsl:if, xsl:message, xsl:number, xsl:processing-instruction, xsl:text, xsl:value-of, xsl:variable
Can be contained by:	xsl:choose

xsl:output

Top-level element for setting properties regarding the output characteristics of the result document. The xsl:output element describes how serialization from a created tree of nodes to a string happens.

Attributes:		
method (optional)	xml is the default	
	html creates empty elements such as BR (with no end-tag) and uses HTML entities such as .	
	text causes no output escaping to happen at all (no entity references in output)	
	Type:	xml/html/text/qname-but-not-ncname
		To simplify a little, an NCName is any name that begins with a letter or underscore and has no space or colon in it ("NC" = "No Colon"). It can't contain a colon because a namespace prefix may be added to its beginning, and namespace prefixes themselves are also defined as NCNames. Because the prefix and the part after it are connected by a colon, a colon within these names would confuse a processor trying to figure out where the prefix ended and the other part began, so they both must be "No Colon" names. Further, QName is "Qualified Name" and includes an optional namespace prefix and colon before a required "local part," which is an NCName. For example, the value of an xsl:template element's name attribute is a QName. It can be a simple name like "indexTemplate" or it can include a namespace prefix and colon, as with "foo:indexTemplate."
	Attribute Value Template:	No
version (optional)	The version number that will appear in the XML declaration of the output document	
	Type:	Token
	Attribute Value Template:	No
encoding (optional)	The encoding of the output document	
	Type:	String
	Attribute Value Template:	No

omit-xml-declaration (optional)	Specifies whether the resulting document should contain an XML declaration (`<?xml version="1.0"?>`)	
	Type:	Yes/no
	Attribute Value Template:	No
standalone (optional)	Specifies whether the XSLT processor should output a stand-alone document declaration	
	Type:	Yes/no
	Attribute Value Template:	No
doctype-public (optional)	Specifies the public identifier to be used in the DOCTYPE declaration	
	Type:	String
	Attribute Value Template:	No
doctype-system (optional)	Specifies the system identifier to be used in the DOCTYPE declaration	
	Type:	String
	Attribute Value Template:	No
cdata-section-elements (optional)	Specifies a list of elements that should have their content escaped by using a CDATA section instead of entities	
	Type:	QNames
	Attribute Value Template:	No
indent (optional)	Specifies the addition of extra whitespace for readability	
	Type:	Yes/no
	Attribute Value Template:	No
media-type (optional)	Specifies a particular MIME type while writing out content	
	Type:	String
	Attribute Value Template:	No
Implemented:	W3C XSLT 1.0 specification	
Can contain:	Cannot contain other elements	
Can be contained by:	xsl:stylesheet, xsl:transform	

xsl:param

Defines a parameter in an `xsl:template` or `xsl:stylesheet`

Attributes:		
`name` (required)	Name of the parameter	
	Type:	QName
	Attribute Value Template:	No
`select` (optional)	Specifies the default value for the `xsl:param` to declare a local or global parameter and to give that parameter a name and a default value. The default value is used only if no other value is provided when the template is called.	
	Type:	Expression
	Attribute Value Template:	No
Implemented:	W3C XSLT 1.0 specification	
Can contain:	`xsl:apply-imports, xsl:apply-templates, xsl:attribute, xsl:call-template, xsl:choose, xsl:comment, xsl:copy, xsl:copy-of, xsl:element, xsl:fallback, xsl:for-each, xsl:if, xsl:message, xsl:number, xsl:processing-instruction, xsl:text, xsl:value-of, xsl:variable`	
Can be contained by:	`xsl:stylesheet, xsl:transform`	

xsl:preserve-space

Enables you to define which elements in the source document should have their whitespace preserved. See also `xsl:strip-space`.

Attributes:		
`elements` (required)	In this attribute you can list the elements (separated by whitespace) for which you want to preserve the whitespace content.	
	Type:	Tokens
	Attribute Value Template:	No
Implemented:	W3C XSLT 1.0 specification	
Can contain:	Cannot contain other elements	
Can be contained by:	`xsl:stylesheet, xsl:transform`	

xsl:processing-instruction

Generates a processing instruction in the destination document	
Attributes:	
name (required)	The name of the processing instruction (the part between the first question mark and the first whitespace of the processing instruction)
	Type:	Ncname
	Attribute Value Template:	Yes
Implemented:	W3C 1.0 specification
Can contain:	xsl:apply-imports, xsl:apply-templates, xsl:call-template, xsl:choose, xsl:copy, xsl:copy-of, xsl:fallback, xsl:for-each, xsl:if, xsl:message, xsl:number, xsl:text, xsl:value-of, xsl:variable
Can be contained by:	xsl:copy, xsl:element, xsl:fallback, xsl:for-each, xsl:if, xsl:message, xsl:otherwise, xsl:param, xsl:template, xsl:variable, xsl:when

xsl:sort

Enables you to specify a sort order for xsl:apply-templates and xsl:for-each elements. Multiple xsl:sort elements can be specified to provide primary, secondary, and other sorting keys.		
Attributes:		
select (optional)	Expression that indicates the criterion that should be used for the ordering	
	Type:	String-expression
	Attribute Value Template:	No
lang (optional)	Sets the language used while ordering. (In different languages the rules for alphabetic ordering can be different.)	
	Type:	Token
	Attribute Value Template:	Yes
data-type (optional)	Specifies alphabetic or numeric ordering	
ncname	Type:	Text/number/qname-but-not-
	Attribute Value Template:	Yes
order (optional)	Specifies ascending or descending ordering	
	Type:	Ascending/descending
	Attribute Value Template:	Yes

Table continued on following page

case-order (optional)	Specifies whether uppercase characters should come before or after lowercase characters. Note that case-insensitive sorting is not supported.	
	Type:	Upper-first/lower-first
	Attribute Value Template:	Yes
Implemented:	W3C XSLT 1.0 specification	
Can contain:	Cannot contain other elements	
Can be contained by:	xsl:apply-templates, xsl:for-each	

xsl:strip-space

Enables you to define which elements in the source document should have their whitespace content stripped. See also xsl:preserve-space.

Attributes:		
elements (required)	Specifies the elements whose whitespace should be stripped	
	Type:	Tokens
	Attribute Value Template:	No
Implemented:	W3C 1.0 specification	
Can contain:	Cannot contain other elements	
Can be contained by:	xsl:stylesheet, xsl:transform	

xsl:stylesheet

The root element for a stylesheet. Synonym to xsl:transform.

Attributes:		
id (optional)	A reference for the stylesheet	
	Type:	ID
	Attribute Value Template:	No
extension-element-prefixes (optional)	Enables you to specify which namespace prefixes are XSLT extension namespaces	
	Type:	Tokens
	Attribute Value Template:	No
exclude-result-prefixes (optional)	Namespaces that are only relevant in the stylesheet or in the source document, but not in the result document, can be removed from the output by specifying them here.	
	Type:	Tokens
	Attribute Value Template:	No

version (required)	Version number	
	Type:	Number
	Attribute Value Template:	No
Implemented:	W3C XSLT 1.0 specification	
Can contain:	xsl:attribute-set, xsl:decimal-format, xsl:import, xsl:include, xsl:key, xsl:namespace-alias, xsl:output, xsl:param, xsl:preserve-space, xsl:strip-space, xsl:template, xsl:variable	
Can be contained by:	No other elements	

xsl:template

Defines a transformation rule. Some templates are built in and don't have to be defined. Refer to Chapter 8 for more information about writing templates.

Attributes:		
match (optional)	Defines the set of nodes on which the template can be applied	
	Type:	Pattern
	Attribute Value Template:	No
name (optional)	Name to identify the template when calling it using xsl:call-template	
	Type:	QName
	Attribute Value Template:	No
priority (optional)	If several templates can be applied (through matches on their match attributes) on a node, the priority attribute can be used to determine which template is instantiated.	
	Type:	Number
	Attribute Value Template:	No
mode (optional)	If a mode attribute is present on a template, the template will be instantiated only if there is a matching mode attribute on an xsl:apply-templates element whose select attribute's value matches the value of the template's match attribute.	
	Type:	QName
	Attribute Value Template:	No
Implemented:	W3C XSLT 1.0 specification	
Can contain:	xsl:apply-imports, xsl:apply-templates, xsl:attribute, xsl:call-template, xsl:choose, xsl:comment, xsl:copy, xsl:copy-of, xsl:element, xsl:fallback, xsl:for-each, xsl:if, xsl:message, xsl:number, xsl:processing-instruction, xsl:text, xsl:value-of, xsl:variable	
Can be contained by:	xsl:stylesheet, xsl:transform	

xsl:text

Generates a text string from its content. Whitespace is never stripped from the content of an `xsl:text` element.

Attributes:		
`disable-output-escaping` (optional)	If set to `yes`, the output will not be escaped: this means that a string " `&lt;`" will be written to the output as " `<`" instead of " `&lt;`". This means that the result document will not be a well-formed XML document	
	Type:	Yes/no
	Attribute Value Template:	No
Implemented:	W3C XSLT 1.0 specification	
Can contain:	Cannot contain other elements	
Can be contained by:	`xsl:attribute`, `xsl:comment`, `xsl:copy`, `xsl:element`, `xsl:fallback`, `xsl:for-each`, `xsl:if`, `xsl:message`, `xsl:otherwise`, `xsl:param`, `xsl:processing-instruction`, `xsl:template`, `xsl:variable`, `xsl:when`	

xsl:transform

Identical to `xsl:stylesheet`.		
Attributes:		
`id` (optional)	A unique reference for the stylesheet	
	Type:	ID
	Attribute Value Template:	No
`extension-element-prefixes` (optional)	Enables you to specify which namespace prefixes are XSLT extension namespaces	
	Type:	Tokens
	Attribute Value Template:	No
`exclude-result-prefixes` (optional)	Namespaces that are only relevant in the stylesheet or in the source document, but not in the result document, can be removed from the result document by specifying them here.	
	Type:	Tokens
	Attribute Value Template:	No
`version` (required)	The version of XSLT being used	
	Type:	Number
	Attribute Value Template:	No
Implemented:	W3C XSLT 1.0 specification	

Can contain:	xsl:attribute-set, xsl:decimal-format, xsl:import, xsl:include, xsl:key, xsl:namespace-alias, xsl:output, xsl:param, xsl:preserve-space, xsl:strip-space, xsl:template, xsl:variable
Can be contained by:	No other elements. It is the document element.

xsl:value-of

Generates a text string from the value of the expression in its `select` attribute.

Attributes:		
select (required)	Expression that selects the node-set that will be converted to a string	
	Type:	Expression
	Attribute Value Template:	No
disable-output-escaping (optional)	You can use this to output < instead of < to the destination document. Note that this will cause the result document to be not well-formed XML. Normally used when generating HTML or text files.	
	Type:	Yes/no
	Attribute Value Template:	No
Implemented:	W3C XSLT 1.0 specification	
Can contain:	Cannot contain other elements	
Can be contained by:	xsl:attribute, xsl:comment, xsl:copy, xsl:element, xsl:fallback, xsl:for-each, xsl:if, xsl:message, xsl:otherwise, xsl:param, xsl:processing-instruction, xsl:template, xsl:variable, xsl:when	

xsl:variable

Defines a variable with a value. Note that in XSLT, the value of a variable cannot change — you can bind a variable using `xsl:variable` but it cannot be changed afterward. The XSLT variable resembles a constant in some other programming languages.

Attributes:		
name (required)	Name of the variable	
	Type:	QName
	Attribute Value Template:	No

Table continued on following page

961

select (optional)	Value of the variable (if the select attribute is omitted, the content of the xsl:variable element is the value)	
	Type:	Expression
	Attribute Value Template:	No
Implemented:	W3C XSLT 1.0 specification	
Can contain:	xsl:apply-imports, xsl:apply-templates, xsl:attribute, xsl:call-template, xsl:choose, xsl:comment, xsl:copy, xsl:copy-of, xsl:element, xsl:fallback, xsl:for-each, xsl:if, xsl:message, xsl:number, xsl:processing-instruction, xsl:text, xsl:value-of, xsl:variable	
Can be contained by:	xsl:attribute, xsl:comment, xsl:copy, xsl:element, xsl:fallback, xsl:for-each, xsl:if, xsl:message, xsl:otherwise, xsl:param, xsl:processing-instruction, xsl:stylesheet, xsl:template, xsl:transform, xsl:variable, xsl:when	

xsl:when

Represents an option for execution in a xsl:choose block		
Attributes:		
test (required)	Expression to be tested	
	Type:	Boolean-expression
	Attribute Value Template:	No
Implemented:	W3C XSLT 1.0 specification	
Can contain:	xsl:apply-imports, xsl:apply-templates, xsl:attribute, xsl:call-template, xsl:choose, xsl:comment, xsl:copy, xsl:copy-of, xsl:element, xsl:fallback, xsl:for-each, xsl:if, xsl:message, xsl:number, xsl:processing-instruction, xsl:text, xsl:value-of, xsl:variable	
Can be contained by:	xsl:choose	

xsl:with-param

Used to pass a parameter to a template using xsl:apply-templates or xsl:call-template. The template called must have a parameter of the same name defined using xsl:param.		
Attributes:		
name (required)	Name of the parameter	
	Type:	QName
	Attribute Value Template:	No

select (optional)	XPath expression selecting the passed value	
	Type:	Expression
	Attribute Value Template:	No
Implemented:	W3C XSLT 1.0 specification	
Can contain:	Cannot contain other elements	
Can be contained by:	`xsl:apply-templates, xsl:call-template`	

Functions

Within expressions in an XSLT stylesheet, you can use the XPath functions in Appendix C and a number of XSLT functions. These XSLT functions are described in this section.

Each function is described by a line of the following form:

```
return-type function-name (parameters)
```

For each parameter, we display the type (`object`, `string`, `number`, `node-set`), and, where necessary, a symbol indicating whether the parameter is optional (?) or can occur multiple times (+). The type `object` means that any type can be passed.

If an expression is passed as a parameter, then it is first evaluated and (if necessary) converted to the expected type before passing it to the function.

`node-set current ( )`
Returns the current context node-set, outside the current expression

Implemented: W3C 1.0 XSLT specification

`node-set document ( object, node-set? )`
Used to get a reference to an external source document

Parameters:
`object`
If of type `String`, then this is the URL of the document to be retrieved. If a node-set, all nodes are converted to strings and all these URLs are retrieved in a node-set.

`node-set`
Represents the base URL from where relative URLs are resolved.

Implemented: W3C 1.0 XSLT specification

Table continued on following page

```
boolean element-available( string )
```
Determines availability of a specified extension element

Parameters:
```
string
```
Name of the extension element

Implemented: W3C XSLT 1.0 specification

```
string format-number( number, string1, string2? )
```
Formats a numeric value into a formatted and localized string

Parameters:
```
number
```
The numeric value to be represented

```
string1
```
The format string that should be used for the formatting

```
<td>
<xsl:value-of select="format-number(number(@TimeRate),'000.00')" />
</td>
<td>
<xsl:value-of select="format-number(number(@TimeRate),'$#00%')" />
</td>
<td>
<xsl:value-of select="format-number(number(@TimeRate),'###0.00')" />
</td>
<td>
<xsl:value-of select="format-number(number(@TimeRate),'#,00;(#,00)')" />
</td>
```

```
string2
```
Reference to an `xsl:decimal-format` element to indicate localization parameters

Implemented: W3C XSLT 1.0 specification

```
boolean function-available( string )
```
Determines availability of a specified extension function

Parameter:
```
string
```
Name of the extension function

Implemented: W3C XSLT 1.0 specification

```
string generate-id( node-set? )
```
Generates a unique identifier for the specified node. Each node will be given a different ID, but the same node will always generate the same ID. You cannot be sure that the IDs generated for a document during multiple transformations will remain identical.

Parameter:
```
node-set
```
The first node of the passed node-set is used. If no node-set is passed, the context node is used.

Implemented: W3C XSLT 1.0 specification

```
node-set key( string, object )
```
Used to get a reference to a node using the specified `xsl:key`. The `key()` function returns a node-set from the document, using the index specified by an `<xsl:key>` element. Once defined, a match element can be used to evaluate the resulting expressions efficiently, similarly to any key used in a data(base) environment.

Parameters:
```
string
```
The name of the referenced `xsl:key`

```
object
```
If of type `String`, this is the index string for the key. If of type `node-set`, all nodes are converted to strings and are used to get nodes back from the key.

Implemented: W3C XSLT 1.0 specification

```
object system-property( string )
```
Used to get certain system properties from the processor

Parameter:
```
string
```
The name of a system property. Properties that are always available in a conformant XSLT processor are `xsl:version`, `xsl:vendor`, and `xsl:vendor-url`

Implemented: W3C XSLT 1.0 specification

```
string unparsed-entity-uri ( string )
```
Returns the URI of the unparsed entity with the passed name

Parameter:
```
string
```
Name of the unparsed entity

Implemented: W3C XSLT 1.0 specification

Available XPath Functions

See Appendix C for information on the XPath functions. They can all be used in XSLT.

XPath 1.0 and XSLT 1.0 are natural pairs, and XPath 2.0 and XSLT 2.0 are natural pairs. The development efforts are working in parallel and are most compatible when used appropriately. In both cases there has been a combination of additional features and functionality, along with deprecated features. The current transition of moving both specifications from 1.0 to 2.0 is under development. A detailed list of changes is a matter of record at the W3C website. A complete list of compatibility issues is also documented along with the changes and improvements.

`boolean()`	`not()`
`ceiling()`	`number()`
`concat()`	`position()`
`contains()`	`round()`
`count()`	`starts-with()`
`false()`	`string()`
`floor()`	`string-length()`
`id()`	`substring()`
`lang()`	`substring-after()`
`last()`	`substring-before()`
`local-name()`	`sum()`
`name()`	`translate()`
`namespace-uri()`	`true()`
`normalize-space()`	

Types

The following types are used to specify the types of the attributes for the XSLT elements provided in the previous tables.

`boolean`	Can have values `true` and `false`
`character`	A single character
`expression`	A string value containing an XPath expression
`id`	A string value. Must be an XML name. The string value can be used only once as an id in any document.
`language-name`	A string containing one of the defined language identifiers. American English = en-us

name	A string value that conforms to the naming conventions of XML. That means no whitespace, and it should start with either a letter or an underscore (_).
names	Multiple name values separated by whitespace
namespace-prefix	Any string that is defined as a prefix for a namespace
ncname	A name value that does not contain a colon
node	A node in an XPath tree. It can be of several types, including element, attribute, comment, processing instruction, text node, etc.
node-set	A set of nodes of any length
node-set-expression	A string value containing an XPath expression that returns nodes
number	A numeric value that can be either floating point or integer
object	Anything: a string, a node, a node-set or a Boolean
qname	Qualified name; the full name of a node. It is made up of two parts: the local name and the namespace identifier.
qnames	A set of QName values separated by whitespace
string	A string value
token	A string value that contains no whitespace
tokens	Multiple token values separated by whitespace
uri-reference	Any string that conforms to the URI specification

New in XSLT 2.0

A new version of XSLT is on the horizon but is taking its time. Moving ever so slowly along with XPath 2.0, it uses only those basic XSLT 1.0 features that are somewhat generic and do not require modification for use with the new regime. Since November 16, 1999, when XSLT 1.0 became a *recommendation*, it has become quite apparent that many changes need to be made to satisfy the ever-growing sophistication of XML parsing and processing. XSLT 2.0 has been totally rethought, with many added features and enhanced capability.

More Powerful Expressions

The following table provides a comparison of XSLT 1.0 and XSLT 2.0. Note the use of parentheses in XSLT 2.0—bear in mind that the use of parentheses was forbidden in XSLT 1.0. The power to use this new syntax will save many lines of code and make the code much more readable.

XSLT 1.0	XSLT 2.0
```<xsl:for-each select = "//name" > <xsl:sort /> <xsl:value-of select = "." /> <xsl:text > </xsl:text> </xsl:for-each>```	```<xsl:for-each select="(@name[.='Position'] | @name[.='AccountsType'])">```

Muenchian's Everywhere

Grouping resulting processed data in XSLT has always been an interesting problem — not an easy one, but an interesting one. A gentleman called Steve Muench worked diligently at solving this problem and thus won notoriety for his solution, known as the Muenchian Method of grouping for XSLT processors. A typical problem was trying to maintain information retrieved from either a database or other XML query process in an orderly fashion during further processing by XSLT so that it would not lose its structure or relationships. In addition, he sought to do this with a minimal amount of code.

The basic premise of the method involves the use of keys that XPath can use to efficiently access node data that has been grouped. This, of course, means that the Muenchian Method can only be used with XSLT processors that implement support for keys and the necessary features and functions for XPath to use the keys. We shall see which XSLT processors will support the XSLT key( ) functions. For example, consider the following example of defining a key and then using the key.

First define an XSLT key:

```
<xsl:for-each select="country
[generate-id(.)=generate-id
(key('country',zipcode))]">
```

Then use the key:

```
<xsl:for-each select ="key('country', zipcode)">
```

Planning on Using XSLT 2.0

The processors are starting to emerge. There are also many recommendations, tips, and tricks emerging to help you move slowly from 1.0 stylesheets to 2.0 stylesheets. Whether you choose to perform a total rewrite on your documents or just gradually transition is up to you, but be aware that not all processors allow backward compatibility. Some processors allow you to combine 1.0 and 2.0 code via the xsl:stylesheet element using an attribute of version=1.0 or version=2.0. (I need not lecture you on how together your head has to be to take this on.) Alternately, just open your XSLT 1.0 code inside a XSLT 2.0 processor and debug from there. It's your choice.

Most but not all of the XSLT processors and tools offer a backward compatibility mode that enables you to blend XSLT 1.0 and XSLT 2.0 features, but you need to do some research before choosing the tools to use.

New Functions

The list of new functions available with XSLT 2.0 is breathtaking. A complete list of XSLT 2.0 features is available in the XSL Transformations (XSLT) Version 2.0 W3C Working Draft at `http://www.w3 .org/TR/xslt20/#major-features`. In addition, of course, they will be implemented inside all the XSLT 2.0 proclaimed editors and processors available.

A Quick Note on XSLT 2.0 and XQuery 1.0

No doubt there is a lot of overlap here. Both XSLT 2.0 and XQuery 1.0 are used to manipulate the data but have different features. XQuery 1.0 was strongly typed to compensate for the lack of datatype functionality inside XPath 1.0, but now XPath 2.0 has improved greatly in this respect and now supports XSLT 2.0. They may emerge as equivalent for some uses, but where XQuery shines is in its ability to extract data with a minimal amount of code.

Index

Index

Perl language

Perl language

Perl language